# MARKETING

## Fourth Canadian Edition

**DHRUV GREWAL, PH.D.**
Babson College

**MICHAEL LEVY, PH.D.**
Babson College

**SHIRLEY LICHTI, B.A., M.A.**
Wilfrid Laurier University

McGraw Hill Education

**MARKETING**
FOURTH CANADIAN EDITION

The Internet addresses listed in the text were accurate at the time of publication. The inclusion of a website does not indicate an endorsement by the authors or McGraw-Hill Ryerson, and McGraw-Hill Ryerson does not guarantee the accuracy of the information presented at these sites.

ISBN-13: 978-1-25-926876-2
ISBN-10: 1-25-926876-4

1 2 3 4 5 6 7 8 9 10 TCP 22 21 20 19 18

Printed and bound in Canada.

Care has been taken to trace ownership of copyright material contained in this text; however, the publisher will welcome any information that enables them to rectify any reference or credit for subsequent editions.

Portfolio Director, Business & Economics, International: *Nicole Meehan*
Portfolio Manager: *Sara Braithwaite*
Director, Portfolio Marketing: *Joy Armitage Taylor*
Content Developer: *Amy Rydzanicz*
Senior Portfolio Associate: *Marina Seguin*
Supervising Editor: *Jeanette McCurdy*
Photo/Permissions Editor: *Derek Capitaine*
Copy Editor: *Laurel Sparrow*
Plant Production Coordinator: *Sarah Strynatka*
Manufacturing Production Coordinator: *Sheryl MacAdam*
Cover Design: *Dave Murphy*
Cover Image: *Courtesy of Dave Dunford / © McGraw-Hill Education*
Interior Design: *First Image Graphic Design*
Page Layout: *MPS Limited*
Printer: *Transcontinental Printing Group*

Authors Michael Levy (left) and Dhruv Grewal (right).

**Dhruv Grewal, Ph.D.** (Virginia Tech), is the Toyota Chair in Commerce and Electronic Business and a Professor of Marketing at Babson College. He was awarded the 2010 AMS Cutco/Vector Distinguished Educator Award, the 2010 Lifetime Achievement Award in Retailing (AMA Retailing SIG), and in 2005 the Lifetime Achievement in Behavioral Pricing Award (Fordham University, November 2005). He is a Distinguished Fellow of the Academy of Marketing Science. He was ranked first in the marketing field in terms of publications in the top-six marketing journals during the 1991–1998 period and again for the 2000–2007 period. He has served as VP Research and Conferences, American Marketing Association Academic Council (1999–2001), and as VP Development for the Academy of Marketing Science (2000–2002). He was co-editor of *Journal of Retailing* from 2001 to 2007. He co-chaired the 1993 Academy of Marketing Science Conference, the 1998 Winter American Marketing Association Conference, the 2001 American Marketing Association Doctoral Consortium, and the American Marketing Association 2006 Summer Educators Conference.

He has published more than 95 articles in journals such as the *Journal of Retailing, Journal of Marketing, Journal of Consumer Research, Journal of Marketing Research*, and *Journal of the Academy of Marketing Science*, as well as other journals. He currently serves on numerous editorial review boards, such as the *Journal of Retailing, Journal of Marketing, Journal of the Academy of Marketing Science, Journal of Interactive Marketing, Journal of Business Research*, and *Journal of Public Policy & Marketing*.

He has won a number of awards for his teaching: 2005 Sherwin-Williams Distinguished Teaching Award, Society for Marketing Advances, 2003 American Marketing Association, Award for Innovative Excellence in Marketing Education, 1999 Academy of Marketing Science Great Teachers in Marketing Award, Executive MBA

Teaching Excellence Award (1998), School of Business Teaching Excellence Awards (1993, 1999), and Virginia Tech Certificate of Recognition for Outstanding Teaching (1989).

He has taught executive seminars/courses and/or worked on research projects with numerous firms, such as IRI, TJX, RadioShack, Telcordia, Khimetriks, Profit-Logic, Monsanto, McKinsey, Ericsson, Council of Insurance Agents & Brokers (CIAB), Met-Life, AT&T, Motorola, Nextel, FP&L, Lucent, Sabre, Goodyear Tire & Rubber Company, Sherwin Williams, Esso International, Asahi, and numerous law firms. He has taught seminars in the United States, Europe, and Asia.

**Michael Levy, Ph.D.** (Ohio State University), is the Charles Clarke Reynolds Professor of Marketing and Director of the Retail Supply Chain Institute at Babson College. He received his Ph.D. in business administration from The Ohio State University and his undergraduate and M.S. degrees in business administration from the University of Colorado at Boulder. He taught at Southern Methodist University before joining the faculty as professor and chair of the marketing department at the University of Miami.

Professor Levy received the 2009 Lifetime Achievement Award from the American Marketing Association Retailing Special Interest Group. He was rated one of the Best Researchers in Marketing in a survey published in *Marketing Educator* in the summer of 1997. He has developed a strong stream of research in retailing, business logistics, financial retailing strategy, pricing, and sales management. He has published more than 50 articles in leading marketing and logistics journals, including the *Journal of Retailing, Journal of Marketing, Journal of the Academy of Marketing Science*, and *Journal of Marketing Research*. He currently serves on the editorial review board of the *Journal of Retailing, International Journal of Logistics Management, International Journal of Logistics and Materials Management*, and *European Business Review*. He is co-author of *Retailing Management*, eighth edition (2012), the bestselling college-level retailing text in the world. Professor Levy was co-editor of the *Journal of Retailing* from 2001 to 2007. He co-chaired the 1993 Academy of Marketing Science conference and the 2006 Summer American Marketing Association conference.

Professor Levy has worked in retailing and related disciplines throughout his professional life. Prior to his academic career, he worked for several retailers and a housewares distributor in Colorado. He has performed research projects with many retailers and retail technology firms, including Accenture, Federated Department Stores, Khimetrics (SAP), Mervyn's, Neiman Marcus, ProfitLogic (Oracle), Zale Corporation, and numerous law firms.

Photo by Ken Jantzi. Courtesy of Shirley Lichti.

**Shirley Lichti, B.A., M.A.,** has taught in the School of Business and Economics (SBE) at Wilfrid Laurier University since 1993 as a part-time and full-time instructor. She has taught a range of undergraduate and graduate courses, including Introductory Marketing; Building and Managing Products, Services, and Brands; Integrated Marketing Communications; and Consumer Behaviour. Shirley has an extensive background in marketing, advertising, promotion, and training, which was developed during a 14-year career with IBM. She has worked in Canada, the Caribbean, and Japan.

A dedicated educator, Shirley was recognized with the 2002 SBE Outstanding Teacher Award. She was honoured to be included as one of Laurier's "Most Popular Professors" in the *Maclean's Guide to Canadian Universities* in 2003, 2004, 2005, and 2006. In 2007, Shirley was recognized by the Ontario Ministry of Training, Colleges and Universities with The LIFT Award for Teaching Excellence. The Zonta Club of Kitchener-Waterloo presented her with its Women of Achievement Award in 2015.

She also runs Marketing Magic, a Waterloo-based marketing communication consulting and training company. She has been a featured keynote speaker at conferences and has developed and delivered marketing seminars and workshops for many organizations. Her clients include companies of all sizes, ranging from the Stratford Festival to Fortune 500 companies such as Manulife Financial, Scotiabank, and Lexus Canada.

For more than 10 years, Shirley wrote a regular marketing column for *The Record*. She has been an active board member and volunteer in many organizations, including Communitech, the Business Success for Women Conference, K-W Business Women's Association, and the Sexual Assault Support Centre of Waterloo Region.

# brief contents

# table of contents

**SECTION FIVE**  Transacting Value  322

## SECTION SEVEN    Value Communication   420

### 14  Integrated Marketing Communications   420

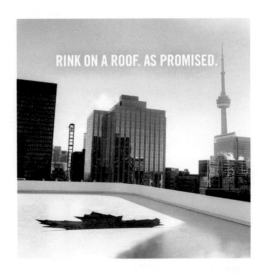

## SECTION EIGHT   Marketing in the Global Environment   516

**18  Ethics and Socially Responsible Marketing   550**

# what is marketing?

## THE FUNCTION OF MARKETING IS MULTI-FACETED, BUT ITS FUNDAMENTAL PURPOSE IS TO CREATE VALUE. CONSIDER THESE EXAMPLES:

**Why do people spend $5.49 for a latte at Starbucks when they could buy one from Tim Hortons® for $3.49?** The answer lies in marketing brand value: Starbucks has created a prestige image for its coffee, food, and other products using grassroots advertising and innovative marketing tactics such as mobile apps and rewards programs. When trendsetters embraced the brand, it didn't take long for others to follow.

**Similarly, why would people pay for bottled water when they could get it for free from a tap?** Companies such as Aberfoyle Springs, Clearly Canadian, Canadian Springs, and Montclair have created bottled water products that offer customers the convenience of an easy-to-carry format. But after years of explosive growth, the industry faced challenges. Environmental concerns have led to unprecedented criticism related to the sea of plastic bottles hitting landfill and recycling sites. Many municipalities have banned bottled water outright. How can the industry continue to flourish while being mindful of such concerns?

**Regardless of your age, your gender, or the city in which you live, you already know something about marketing.** You have been an involved consumer in the marketing process since childhood when, for example, you accompanied your mother or father to the grocery store and asked to buy a particular brand of cereal because you saw a friend eating it or heard about it on television. The prize inside the box of cereal was of value to you as a child; the nutritional information offered on the box panel was of value to your mother or father. Once you begin to explore the many ways in which companies and brands create value for their customers through marketing, you will also begin to appreciate the complex set of decisions and activities that are necessary to provide you with the products and services you use every day.

# changes to the fourth canadian edition

The central theme in this book is **Marketing Adds Value**. Beyond teaching students the principles of marketing, we need to impress upon them why marketing in and of itself is valuable, regardless of a chosen career direction. Marketing creates enduring and mutually valuable relationships. It identifies what customers value locally and globally. Without marketing, it would be difficult for anyone to learn about new products or services. A solid understanding of marketing can help job-seeking students demonstrate their value to market themselves on graduation. It can help them to embrace the power of small businesses and entrepreneurship in the Canadian economy. *Marketing*, Fourth Canadian Edition, is all about the core concepts and tools that marketers use to create value for customers. Throughout this book you will find many examples that define how companies create value through branding, packaging, pricing, retailing, service, and advertising. The concept of value is introduced in Chapter 1 and carried through the entire text.

## SECTION ONE    Assessing the Marketplace

**Assessing the Marketplace** is the central theme of Section One, which contains three chapters. Following an introduction to marketing in Chapter 1, "Overview of Marketing," Chapter 2 ("Developing Marketing Strategies and a Marketing Plan") focuses on how a firm creates a marketing plan. A central theme of the chapter is how firms can effectively create, capture, deliver, and communicate value to their customers. Finally, Chapter 3, "Analyzing the Marketing Environment," focuses on how marketers can systematically uncover and evaluate opportunities.

Changes to Section One include:

- New Chapter Vignettes in Chapters 2 and 3 and a revised Chapter Vignette for Chapter 1.
- More emphasis on the role of social media in marketing and the importance of sustainable marketing in Chapter 1 with new Social and Mobile Marketing boxes.
- New Sustainable Marketing boxes in all three chapters.

- New Entrepreneurial Marketing box in Chapter 1.
- Easy-to-understand coverage of marketing orientations in Chapter 1 to help students appreciate the different ways marketing is practised. To lay the foundation for following chapters, we have included a short discussion and an example showing how the four Ps need to be integrated and coordinated into a seamless whole rather than treated as individual components of the marketing mix.
- Continued focus on ethics with new Ethical Dilemma boxes in Chapters 1, 2, and 3.
- Revised material on marketing strategies to make it simpler to follow.
- Appendix 2A, which walks students through the process of writing a marketing plan, and presents a plan's components.
- Expanded emphasis on sustainability in the "Social and Natural Trends" section in Chapter 3.

## SECTION TWO    Understanding the Marketplace

**Understanding the Marketplace** is the focus of Section Two, which is composed of two chapters. Chapter 4, "Consumer Behaviour," discusses why consumers purchase products and services, and highlights the consumer decision process. Chapter 5, "Business-to-Business Marketing," looks at why and how business-to-business buying takes place.

Changes to Section Two include:

- New Chapter Vignettes in Chapters 4 and 5.
- New Social and Mobile Marketing boxes in Chapters 4 and 5.

- New Ethical Dilemma boxes in Chapters 4 and 5.
- New Sustainable Marketing boxes in Chapters 4 and 5.
- New Entrepreneurial Marketing box in Chapter 5.
- New Chapter Case Studies in Chapters 4 and 5.
- A discussion in Chapter 4 about how marketers can mitigate the various risks associated with the consumer buying decision.
- An expanded focus on smaller companies in Chapter 5, reflecting the importance of entrepreneurship along with the challenges in serving B2B customers.

## SECTION THREE — Targeting the Marketplace

**Targeting the Marketplace** is the subject of the third section of the book. Chapter 6, "Segmentation, Targeting, and Positioning," focuses on how firms segment the marketplace, pick a target market, and then position their good/service in line with their customers' needs and wants. Chapter 7, "Marketing Research," identifies the various tools and techniques that marketers use to uncover these needs and ensure that they create goods and services that provide value to their target markets.

### Changes to Section Three include:

- New Chapter Vignettes for Chapters 6 and 7.
- New Social and Mobile Marketing boxes in Chapters 6 and 7.
- New Ethical Dilemma boxes in Chapters 6 and 7.
- New Sustainable Marketing boxes in Chapters 6 and 7.
- New Chapter Case Studies in Chapters 6 and 7.
- Simplified discussion of segmentation in Chapter 6, including new exhibits and a segmentation grid tied back to the Chapter Vignette to help students more easily grasp the theory.
- Reorganized Chapter 7 to present the marketing research process first, followed by a more in-depth discussion explaining how marketers use research, including examples of the types of objectives set and how the research might be conducted.
- Appendix 7A, "Using Secondary Data to Assess Customer Lifetime Value (CLV)," demonstrates the expected financial contribution from a customer to a company's overall profitability over the course of the relationship.

## SECTION FOUR — Value Creation

**Value Creation** is the topic of discussion in Section Four's three chapters. The first two—Chapter 8, "Developing New Products," and Chapter 9, "Product, Branding, and Packaging Decisions"—cover the development and management of products and brands. While many of the concepts involved in developing and managing services are similar to those of physical brands, Chapter 10, "Services: The Intangible Product," addresses the unique challenges of the marketing of services.

### Changes to Section Four include:

- Revised Chapter Vignettes in Chapters 8, 9, and 10.
- New Sustainable Marketing boxes in Chapters 8, 9, and 10.
- New Social and Mobile Marketing boxes in Chapters 8, 9, and 10.
- New Ethical Dilemma boxes in Chapters 9 and 10.
- New Entrepreneurial Marketing boxes in Chapters 8 and 10.
- New Real Marketer profiles in Chapters 8 and 9.
- New Chapter Case Studies in Chapters 8 and 9, and a revised Chapter Case Study in Chapter 10.
- A discussion of metrics in Chapter 10 in a section titled "Evaluating Service Quality by Using Well Established Marketing Metrics."

## SECTION FIVE — Transacting Value

**Transacting Value** is accomplished within a firm by pricing products and services to bring in money and affect revenues. Chapter 11, "Pricing Concepts and Strategies: Establishing Value," examines the importance of setting the right price, the relationship between price and quantity sold, break-even analysis, the impact of price wars, and how the Internet has changed the way people shop.

### Changes to Section Five include:

- A new Chapter Vignette.
- The following new boxed features: Entrepreneurial Marketing, Social and Mobile Marketing, Sustainable Marketing, Ethical Dilemma.
- A new Chapter Case Study.
- A discussion of competition including four levels: oligopolistic competition, monopolistic competition, pure competition, and monopoly.
- A clear delineation between pricing methods, pricing strategies, and pricing tactics.
- A discussion of the impact of currency exchange fluctuations on pricing decisions.

## SECTION SIX — Value Delivery: Designing the Distribution Channel and Supply Chain

**Value Delivery** is one of the major reasons why Amazon and Walmart have become the world's largest retailers. Walmart delivers merchandise to stores just in time to meet customer demand. Amazon can deliver products to customers within hours of the order being placed. To achieve this, both have initiated innovative programs with vendors and developed sophisticated transportation and warehousing systems. *Marketing*, Fourth Canadian Edition, devotes two chapters to value delivery. Chapter 12, "Distribution Channels," takes a look at marketing channels, distribution strategy, and the supply chain, while Chapter 13, "Retailing and Omnichannel Marketing," concentrates on retailing.

### Changes to Section Six include:

- New Chapter Vignettes in Chapters 12 and 13.
- New Ethical Dilemma boxes in Chapters 12 and 13.

- New Entrepreneurial Marketing box in Chapter 13.
- New Sustainable Marketing boxes in Chapters 12 and 13.
- New Social and Mobile Marketing box in Chapter 13 and a revised box for Chapter 12.
- New Chapter Case Study in Chapter 13 and a revised Chapter Case Study for Chapter 12.
- The discussion on retailing in Chapter 13 has been updated to reflect the rapidly changing Canadian market, with an applied discussion on creating a retail strategy, and exploring omnichannel strategies. The last section has been updated to reflect the shift from a multi-channel to an omnichannel retail world.

## SECTION SEVEN — Value Communications

**Value Communication** today is complex because of new technologies that add email, blogs, the Internet, and social media to an advertising mix that once utilized only radio and television to relay messages to consumers. *Marketing*, Fourth Canadian Edition, devotes three chapters to value communication: Chapter 14, "Integrated Marketing Communications," Chapter 15, "Advertising, Sales Promotions, and Personal Selling," and Chapter 16, "Social and Mobile Marketing."

### Changes to Section Seven include:

- New Chapter Vignettes for Chapters 14, 15, and 16.
- New Social and Mobile Marketing and Ethical Dilemma boxes in all three chapters.

- New Sustainable Marketing boxes in Chapters 14 and 15.
- New Entrepreneurial Marketing boxes in Chapters 14 and 15.
- Revised "Digital Media" section in Chapter 14 focuses on websites, blogs, social media, and mobile apps. This discussion is expanded further in Chapter 16.
- New Chapter Case Studies in Chapter 14 and Chapter 16 and revised Chapter Case Study in Chapter 15.
- New Real Marketer Profiles in Chapter 14 and Chapter 16.
- A discussion of personal branding in Chapter 16 shows students how to apply marketing principles to themselves.

## SECTION EIGHT — Marketing in the Global Environment

**Marketing in the Global Environment** is done by most firms at some level. It took less than 10 years for Lululemon to transform into a global company and a great Canadian success story in the athletic and sportswear industry. But even small entrepreneurial firms are affected because they get their materials, products, or services from firms located in other countries. Chapter 17, "Global Marketing," focuses on marketing in today's connected world. Chapter 18, "Ethics and Socially Responsible Marketing," provides rich illustrations of corporate responsibility and introduces an ethical decision-making framework that is useful

for assessing potentially ethically troubling situations that are presented throughout the rest of the book. It can be used to set the tone for ethical material throughout the textbook as desired.

### Changes to Section Eight include:

- New Chapter Vignettes for Chapters 17 and 18.
- New Chapter Case Studies for Chapters 17 and 18.
- The following new boxed features: Ethical Dilemma, Sustainable Marketing, and Social and Mobile Marketing.
- New Entrepreneurial Marketing box for Chapter 17.

# features inside *marketing,* fourth canadian edition

In addition to our emphasis on value in *Marketing*, Fourth Canadian Edition, you will also find integrated and highlighted coverage of ethics, sustainability, entrepreneurship, services, social and mobile marketing, and globalization within the framework of the marketing discipline:

Chapters 1 to 18 contain an **Ethical Dilemma** box with a compelling ethical discussion and end-of-chapter discussion questions that force students to consider and evaluate each situation. The Fourth Canadian Edition contains 17 new Ethical Dilemma boxes.

 **Ethical Dilemma 10.1**

### Fake Reviews[37]

Yelp, TripAdvisor, and Amazon have all made user ratings and reviews a familiar—and even essential—part of the online toolbox for shoppers and other consumers. From the con- authors looking to increase book sales 100 book reviews for $2,200; it was one of over 1,000 alleged fake review sites targeted in lawsuits filed by Amazon. Yelp has also clamped down on businesses with suspicious reviews by posting consumer alerts. Among others, it flagged a

**Sustainable Marketing** boxes encourage students to consider the environmental concerns that marketers face in bringing new products and services to the market. Many companies have faced increased scrutiny and criticism over the use of plastic packaging and recycling issues. The boxes will help students see how consumers are driving smart marketers to more fully embrace sustainable practices for the good of their companies as well as for consumers.

For example, in Chapter 13 we discuss how the goal to leave the world a better place than they found it, set by the founders of Mountain Equipment Co-Op, means no decisions are made in the company before considering society and the environment.

 **Sustainable Marketing 12.1**

### Ethics and Sustainability Key to Doing Business

After two years working in the world of finance, Pascal Benaksas-Couture spent six months providing humanitarian aid in Costa Rica. When he returned to Montreal, he wanted to pursue a career that aligned with his values.[11]In looking around Quebec, he found a sector that was underserved—that of ethical clothing. His goal was to produce clothing with positive messages, not insignificant sayings or clothing with logos. In 2005, he and his business partner, Pascale Cloutier, launched OÖM Ethikwear. Its first collection of ethically made clothing was produced entirely in Quebec.

You may be surprised to learn that three decades ago.

OÖM Ethikwear produces clothing in Quebec using

**Entrepreneurship**. An entrepreneurial spirit pervades most marketing innovations and is necessary to keep firms growing and healthy. *Marketing*, Fourth Canadian Edition, nurtures students' entrepreneurial spirit by providing examples of young entrepreneurial firms and successful entrepreneurs such as Aeryon Labs, AWAKE Chocolate, Amazeballs, velofix, and more.

Each chapter contains an **Entrepreneurial Marketing** box that depicts recognizable and interesting young entrepreneurial firms. There are nine new Entrepreneurial Marketing boxes in the Fourth Canadian Edition.

 **Entrepreneurial Marketing 3.1**

### Turning Trash Into Cash[56]

Lisa von Sturmer is a compost crusader who sees dollar signs in dirt. During a weeklong vacation with friends on Savary Island in British Columbia, where composting is mandatory, she was shocked to see how little waste the group generated. When she returned to work she was dismayed at how much organic material was thrown in organics for other c largest recycling co

Having started from the Canadiar needed money to *Dragons' Den*, she for a 25 percent sha ons that she'd had their help to do th

Lisa von Sturmer turns trash into cash with her Growing City office compost bins.

**Social and Mobile Marketing** boxes further explore the explosive growth of tools such as Facebook, YouTube, Instagram, and Snapchat, which help marketers communicate with their target markets and promote products or services to them.

For example, Chapter 4 discusses how Sephora uses its mobile app, Sephora to Go, to allow consumers to engage in any activities they would pursue in stores.

**Real Marketer Profile** boxes appear in seven chapters. They focus on the transition students make from attending post-secondary education to applying their marketing skills in the "real" world. While some of the profiles feature relatively new graduates who are still with their first employer, others show the career paths that grads and seasoned veterans have taken within a company or in a new role at a different organization.

For example, in Chapter 14 we discuss Debra Goldblatt-Sadowski's phenomenal success story from being a creative writing grad to starting rock-it promotions, a PR agency that works with Adidas, Toronto Fashion Week, and a host of well known stars such as Emily Blunt, Anthony Hopkins, and Morgan Freeman.

# REINFORCING LEARNING

## LEARNING OBJECTIVES

Listed at the beginning of each chapter, **Learning Objectives** show students the chapter's main concepts. These Learning Objectives are then presented in the margins throughout the chapter when the concepts are introduced. At the end of each chapter, the Learning Objectives are revisited and reviewed, reinforcing for students the key sections in the chapter and allowing them to follow their own progress to know where they need help.

## CHAPTER VIGNETTE

Each chapter begins with a Chapter Vignette that helps to introduce and illustrate some of the main content that follows. These vignettes have been carefully selected to pique student interest and are designed to provide real-world examples of how the theory has been applied by a variety of companies. There are 13 new Chapter Vignettes in the Fourth Canadian Edition.

# Overview of Marketing

It's nearing the end of the spring semester, and it's a hot day. Leaving the sweltering classroom to go study, you and your friends decide to grab a drink. Someone suggests iced coffee. There are several options on campus. Now the negotiations begin: a Tim Hortons® Iced Capp® or a Starbucks Mocha Frappuccino? Someone wants a soy-based beverage instead of a milk-based drink. Another friend insists that it's time for everyone to check out the new McCafé for an Iced Latte. Although McDonald's does not have a location on campus, your friend argues that the McCafé latte is cheaper and has fewer calories. Each of these drinks represents a cool treat, and various companies provide multiple options. So what's the difference among them, and what makes customers loyal to one choice over another?

Let's think about the options available for any caffeine indulgence: hot, cold, or frozen; dark, medium, or light roast; and plain, flavoured, or blended drinks. You can also choose from reduced-fat,

## UNIQUE END-OF-CHAPTER APPLICATIONS AND EXERCISES

- **Marketing Applications.** Student-tested at Wilfrid Laurier University and the University of Ottawa, these questions encourage students to become more critical in their thinking of how marketing theory relates to practice. At least one of the Marketing Applications in each chapter poses an ethical dilemma based on material covered in the chapter.
- **Net Savvy.** Each chapter contains two exercises that drive students to the Internet to apply material covered in the text. For example, in Chapter 15, we direct students to the Canadian Children's Food & Beverage Advertising Initiative website (http://www.adstandards.com/en/childrensinitiative/default.htm); this organization is one of the industry's self-regulatory bodies for children's advertising. We ask students to choose one of the news releases and discuss what the main issue was in the case.
- **Chapter Case Study.** Each chapter ends with a case covering a current marketing idea, concept, or company. The Fourth Canadian Edition includes 17 new cases.

# superior learning solutions and support

The McGraw-Hill Education team is ready to help instructors assess and integrate any of our products, technology, and services into your course for optimal teaching and learning performance. Whether it's helping your students improve their grades, or putting your entire course online, the McGraw-Hill Education team is here to help you do it. Contact your Learning Solutions Consultant today to learn how to maximize all of McGraw-Hill Education's resources.

For more information, please visit us online: http://www.mheducation.ca/he/solutions

# acknowledgments

I could not have completed this text without the help of others. In particular, I would like to thank Luiza Pirvu, who diligently worked with me throughout the project as an invaluable research assistant and sounding board. Thanks also to Erin Schnore for her research, and numerous Wilfrid Laurier University students and professors who provided feedback on the chapter content, cases, and exercises.

A special thanks to the many talented staff and freelance members at McGraw-Hill Education—Sara Braithwaite, Amy Rydzanicz, Derek Capitaine, Jeanette McCurdy, Laurel Sparrow, and Joy Armitage Taylor. You made my job so much easier. It was a pleasure working with you.

I gratefully acknowledge feedback and constructive criticism from marketing colleagues across Canada.

| | |
|---|---|
| Jane-Michele Clark | York University |
| Jennifer Ford | Vancouver Island University |
| Irene Lu | Carleton University |
| Michael Rod | Carleton University |
| Robert Saks | Concordia University |
| Peter Sianchuk | Mount Allison University |
| Anne Marie Webb-Hughes | British Columbia Institute of Technology |

*Shirley Lichti*

# The Complete Course Solution

**We listened to educators from around the world, learned about their challenges, and created a whole new way to deliver a course.**

Connect2 is a collaborative teaching and learning platform that includes an instructionally designed complete course framework of learning materials that is flexible and open for instructors to easily personalize, add their own content, or integrate with other tools and platforms.

- Save time and resources building and managing a course.
- Gain confidence knowing that each course framework is pedagogically sound.
- Help students master course content.
- Make smarter decisions by using real-time data to guide course design, content changes, and remediation.

## MANAGE — Dynamic Curriculum Builder

Quickly and easily launch a complete course framework developed by instructional design experts. Each Connect2 course is a flexible foundation for instructors to build upon by adding their own content or drawing upon the wide repository of additional resources.

- Easily customize Connect2 by personalizing the course scope and sequence.
- Get access to a wide range of McGraw-Hill Education content within one powerful teaching and learning platform.
- Receive expert support and guidance on how best to utilize content to achieve a variety of teaching goals.

## MASTER — Student Experience

Improve student performance with instructional alignment and leverage Connect2's carefully curated learning resources. Deliver required reading through Connect2's award-winning adaptive learning system.

- Teach at a higher level in class by helping students retain core concepts.
- Tailor in-class instruction based on student progress and engagement.
- Help focus students on the content they don't know so they can prioritize their study time.

## MEASURE — Advanced Analytics

Collect, analyze and act upon class and individual student performance data. Make real-time course updates and teaching decisions backed by data.

- Visually explore class and student performance data.
- Easily identify key relationships between assignments and student performance.
- Maximize in-class time by using data to focus on areas where students need the most help.

### Course Map

The flexible and customizable course map provides instructors full control over the pre-designed courses within Connect2. Instructors can easily add, delete, or rearrange content to adjust the course scope and sequence to their personal preferences.

### Implementation Guide

Each Connect2 course includes a detailed implementation guide that provides guidance on what the course can do and how best to utilize course content based on individual teaching approaches.

### Instructor Resources

A comprehensive collection of instructor resources are available within Connect2. Instructor Support and Seminar Materials provide additional exercises and activities to use for in-class discussion and teamwork.

For more information, please visit www.mheconnect2.com

# CHAPTER 1

## LEARNING OBJECTIVES

**After studying this chapter you should be able to**

**LO1** Define the role of marketing and explain its core concepts

**LO2** Describe how marketers create value for a product or service

**LO3** Summarize the four orientations of marketing

**LO4** Understand the importance of marketing both within and outside the firm

All Tim Hortons® trademarks referenced herein are owned by Tim Hortons®. Used with permission.

# Overview of Marketing

It's nearing the end of the spring semester, and it's a hot day. Leaving the sweltering classroom to go study, you and your friends decide to grab a drink. Someone suggests iced coffee. There are several options on campus. Now the negotiations begin: a Tim Hortons® Iced Capp® or a Starbucks Mocha Frappuccino? Someone wants a soy-based beverage instead of a milk-based drink. Another friend insists that it's time for everyone to check out the new McCafé for an Iced Latte. Although McDonald's does not have a location on campus, your friend argues that the McCafé latte is cheaper and has fewer calories. Each of these drinks represents a cool treat, and various companies provide multiple options. So what's the difference among them, and what makes customers loyal to one choice over another?

Let's think about the options available for any caffeine indulgence: hot, cold, or frozen; dark, medium, or light roast; and plain, flavoured, or blended drinks. You can also choose from reduced-fat, soy, organic, or fair trade, or add whipped cream, cinnamon, or chocolate sprinkles. In the grocery store, while brands such as Nabob, Maxwell House, and Nescafé dominate the coffee aisle, you can also find products from Tim Hortons® and Starbucks on the shelves. McDonald's now sells bagged coffee in its Canadian restaurants and has entered the grocery channel as well.

To build and maintain a loyal customer base, each company must distinguish itself from its competitors by offering products, services, and a strong brand that appeal to customers. Although its focus is on coffee, when Tim Hortons® noticed industry sales of non-caffeinated beverages were increasing, it launched Creamy Chocolate Chill®. The frozen drink is decadent and caffeine-free. Not only did it boost cold beverage sales, but it outsold McDonald's shakes, and earned a 46 percent share of the market, without cannibalizing sales of its Iced Capp® product.[1] Customers described Creamy Chocolate Chill® as a heavenly treat.

Ranked second in the Reputation Institute's survey of Canada's top brands and offering over 3,665 restaurants, Tim Hortons® is a brand many consumers gravitate toward.[2] Having convenient locations (one for every 9,000 people[3]) and a variety of product offerings has helped it win 41 percent of the quick-service restaurant traffic in Canada.[4] The company differentiates itself through its community involvement as a sponsor of Timbits® minor sports. Tim Horton Children's Foundation serves youth from low-income families. As part of the company's community initiatives, restaurant owners hold an annual Camp Day®, donating coffee sales and collecting public donations to help send children from economically disadvantaged families to camp. The Tim Hortons® Coffee Partnership has been working for almost a decade to improve the lives of Central and South American coffee farmers.[5] The company publicly reports on sustainability and responsibility efforts, and, as part of a new pilot project, allows owners of electric vehicles to charge their cars at no cost.[6]

To ensure that consumers keep coming back, Tim Hortons® runs promotions such as RRRoll Up the Rim to Win®, which has been an annual event for over 30 years. It connects with consumers on social media through Facebook and Twitter, and has rolled out TimmyMe™, a mobile app designed to simplify mobile payments that includes additional features including Restaurant Locator, TimCard® Reload, and Nutritional Information. The company even rolled out its own in-restaurant channel, TimsTV®, streaming news, weather, and sports content as well as highlighting its community initiatives, such as free skates and Timbits® Minor Sports."[7] And it continually improves its product offering, recently introducing premium espresso coffees made with freshly ground beans and steamed milk.[8]

As this example demonstrates, companies constantly protect their brand in the market. Businesses must grow and change their product offerings and corporate citizenry to keep pace with customer needs and tastes. Its emphasis on freshness and variety helps Tim Hortons® succeed in providing good value to its customers. ■

## WHAT IS MARKETING?

Unlike other subjects you may have studied, marketing is already very familiar to you. You start your day by agreeing to do the dishes in exchange for a freshly made cup of coffee. Then you fill up your car with gas. You attend a class that you have chosen and paid for. After class, you pick up lunch (and maybe an iced coffee!), which you consume while checking Facebook messages on your iPad. Then you get your hair cut and check out a movie. During your bus ride to the movie theatre, you listen to new songs on iTunes and maybe even buy some. In each case, you have acted as the buyer and made a decision about whether you should part with your time and/or money to receive a particular service or type of merchandise. If, after you return home from the movie, you decide to auction your old smartphone on eBay, you have become a seller. In each of these transactions, you were engaged in marketing.

This chapter will look at the definition of marketing and at how marketing is used to create value in products or in services. We will examine the interrelated marketing mix, and see how the four Ps create, transact, communicate, and deliver value. We will look at where marketing happens and how it has evolved over the years into today's concept of value-based marketing. Lastly, we will discuss why marketing is an important function for any successful firm.

The Canadian Marketing Association states that "**Marketing** is a set of business practices designed to plan for and present an organization's products or services in ways that build effective customer relationships."[9] What does this definition really mean? Good marketing is not a random activity; it requires thoughtful planning with an emphasis on the ethical implications of any of those decisions on consumers and society in general. Firms develop a **marketing plan** (see Chapter 2) that specifies their marketing activities for a specific period of time. The marketing plan is broken down into various components—how the product or service will be conceived or designed, how much it should cost, where and how it will be promoted, and how it will get to the consumer. In any exchange, the buyer and the seller should be satisfied with the value they obtained from a transaction. In our earlier example, you should be satisfied or even delighted with the song you downloaded on iTunes, and Apple should be satisfied with the amount of money it received from you. The core aspects of marketing are shown in Exhibit 1.1. Let's see how they look in practice.

## Marketing Is About Satisfying Customer Needs and Wants

Understanding the marketplace—and especially consumer needs and wants—is fundamental to marketing success. A **need** is one of the basic necessities of life, such as food, clothing, shelter, or safety. A **want** is the particular way in which the person chooses to

**marketing**
A set of business practices designed to plan for and present an organization's products or services in ways that build effective customer relationships.

**marketing plan**
A written document composed of an analysis of the current marketing situation, opportunities and threats for the firm, marketing objectives and strategy specified in terms of the four Ps, action programs, and projected or pro forma income (and other financial) statements.

**LO1**

**need**
A basic necessity, such as food, clothing, shelter, and safety.

**want**
The particular way in which a person chooses to satisfy a need, which is shaped by a person's knowledge, culture, and personality.

**EXHIBIT 1.1** Core Aspects of Marketing

Marketing

- Marketing helps create value.
- Marketing is about satisfying customer needs and wants.
- Marketing entails an exchange.
- Marketing requires product, price, place, and promotion decisions.
- Marketing can be performed by both individuals and organizations.
- Marketing occurs in many settings.

fulfill his or her need, which is shaped by a person's knowledge, culture, and personality. For example, when we are hungry, we need something to eat. Some people want a submarine sandwich to satisfy that hunger, whereas others want a salad and some soup instead. Of course, needs and wants must be backed by demand, in order for marketing to be effective. There are many things you may want, and even need. Demand is demonstrated by your ability and willingness to act on those needs and wants. The topic of understanding customer needs is described in detail in Chapter 4, which deals with consumer behaviour.

To understand customer needs and wants, the company must first identify the customers or **market** for its product or service. In the broadest terms, the market refers to the world of trade. More narrowly, however, the market can be segmented or divided into groups of people who are pertinent to an organization for particular reasons. For example, the marketplace for soft drinks may include most people in the world, but as Pepsi and Coke battle each other worldwide, they divide the global population into a host of categories: men versus women, calorie-conscious or not, people who prefer carbonated versus noncarbonated drinks, and multiple categories of flavour preferences, among others.[10] If you manufacture a beverage with zero calories, you want to know for which market segments your product is most relevant, then make sure that you build a marketing strategy that targets those groups. Certain diet- and health-conscious customers may prefer Diet Coke or Diet Pepsi; others may opt for bottled water products like Dasani or Aquafina.

Although marketers would prefer to sell their products and services to everyone, it is not practical to do so. Because marketing costs money, good marketers carefully seek out potential customers who have both an interest in the product and an ability to buy it. For example, most people need some form of transportation, and many people probably would like to own the new hybrid from Lexus. Starting at more than $120,000, the Lexus LS 600h L is one of the most sophisticated hybrid cars on the market. But Lexus is not actually interested in everyone who wants an LS 600h L, because not everyone can afford to spend that much on a car. Instead, Lexus defines its viable **target market** as those consumers who want and can afford such a product.[11] Although not all companies focus on such a specific and wealthy target, all marketers are interested in finding the buyers who are most likely to be interested in their offerings.

The process of how companies segment the market for their products and services and then choose which segment to target and how best to reach that segment is described in Chapter 6. The process of identifying customer segments the company wants to target with its products and services requires market research. The types of market research that help marketers make good decisions about various aspects of the marketing mix are discussed in Chapter 7.

**market**
The groups of people who need or want a company's products or services and have the ability and willingness to buy them.

**target market**
The customer segment or group to whom the firm is interested in selling its products and services.

**exchange**
The trade of things of value between the buyer and the seller so that each is better off as a result.

## Marketing Entails an Exchange

Marketing is about an **exchange**—the trade of things of value between the buyer and the seller so that each is better off as a result. As depicted in Exhibit 1.2, sellers provide goods or services, then communicate and facilitate the delivery of their offering to consumers. Buyers complete the exchange by giving money and information to the seller. Suppose you learn about a new Katy Perry album by hearing one of her songs on Sirius XM Satellite radio, The same day, a friend tweets on

**CREATING AMAZING***

*MOT

LS 600h

What type of customer would buy a $120,000 hybrid car?

Coke and Pepsi are constantly battling to be number one.

(left): © TaurusPhotography/Alamy Stock Photo; (right): PRNewsFoto/PR Newswire/PepsiCo via AP Photo

Twitter that she loves the new album, and so you visit the Katy Perry Facebook fan page, which offers several recommendations. From there, you visit iTunes, where you can purchase the song you heard, multiple songs, or the entire album. You begin with the song you heard, which you love even more after hearing it several times. So you go back to iTunes and take advantage of its offer to complete the album by downloading the rest of the songs to your iTunes library. Your billing information is already in the company's system, saving you from having to enter your credit card number or other information. Furthermore, iTunes creates a record of your purchase, which it uses, together with your other purchase trends, to create personalized recommendations of other albums or songs that you might like. This example shows how Apple uses the valuable information you provide to facilitate future exchanges and solidify its relationship with you.

**EXHIBIT 1.2**    Exchange: The Underpinning of Seller–Buyer Relationships

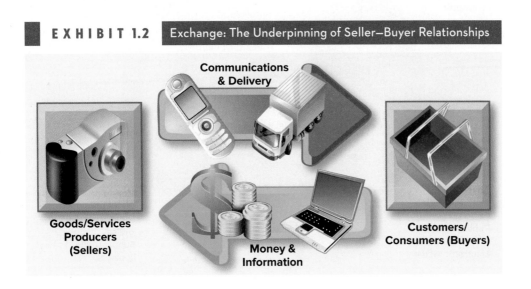

**LO2**

## Marketing Requires Marketing Mix Decisions

Marketing traditionally has been divided into a set of four interrelated decisions known as the **marketing mix**, or **four Ps**: product, price, place, and promotion, as shown in Exhibit 1.3.[12] Together, the four Ps compose the marketing mix, which is the controllable set of activities that the firm uses to respond to the wants of its target markets. But what does each of these elements in the marketing mix entail?

**Product: Creating Value**  The fundamental purpose of marketing is to create value by developing a variety of offerings—including goods, services, and ideas—to satisfy customer needs. As an example of the first P, *product*, consider water. Not too long ago, consumers perceived this basic commodity as simply water. It came out of a faucet and was consumed for drinking and washing. But, taking a cue from European firms such as Perrier (France) and San Pellegrino (Italy), several Canadian-based firms, such as Canadian Springs and Montclair, have created a product with benefits that consumers find valuable. The same is true of coffee. At one time, people simply made it at home. Today, Tim Hortons®, McDonald's, and Starbucks realize that customers have needs beyond caffeine and offer

You can exchange your money on the iTunes store for the latest Katy Perry album.

© Christie Goodwin/Getty Images/Entertainment/Getty Images

**marketing mix (four Ps)** Product, price, place, and promotion—the controllable set of activities that a firm uses to respond to the wants of its target markets.

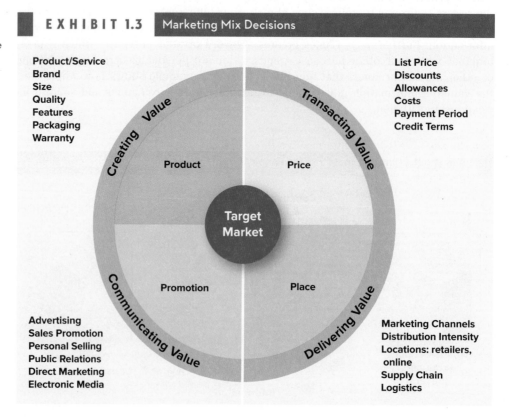

**EXHIBIT 1.3**   Marketing Mix Decisions

Product/Service
Brand
Size
Quality
Features
Packaging
Warranty

List Price
Discounts
Allowances
Costs
Payment Period
Credit Terms

Creating Value — Product

Transacting Value — Price

Target Market

Communicating Value — Promotion

Delivering Value — Place

Advertising
Sales Promotion
Personal Selling
Public Relations
Direct Marketing
Electronic Media

Marketing Channels
Distribution Intensity
Locations: retailers, online
Supply Chain
Logistics

a variety of options. This variety includes lattes, cappuccinos, macchiatos, Frappuccino, hot chocolate, smoothies, teas, bottled juices, Refreshers, and regular brewed coffee, providing customers with interesting choices for which they are willing to pay a premium. The chapter end case looks at Starbucks' marketing mix in more detail.

**Goods** are items that you can physically touch. Roots clothing, Nike shoes, Molson Canadian beer, Kraft Dinner, and countless other products are examples of goods. As we describe in Chapter 2, Nike primarily makes shoes but also adds value to its products. For example, it offers custom designs under its Nike ID brand that increase their fashionable appeal, and enlists popular celebrities such as Rafael Nadal to add their names to the designs.

Unlike goods, **services** are intangible customer benefits that are produced by people or machines and cannot be separated from the producer. When people buy tickets—whether for air travel, a sporting event, or a movie—they are paying not for the physical ticket stub but for the experience. Hotels, insurance agencies, and spas all provide services. Getting money from your bank by using an ATM or teller is another example of using a service. In this case, cash machines usually add value to your banking experience by being conveniently located, fast, and easy to use.

Many offerings represent a combination of goods and services. When you go to Hakim Optical, for example, you can have your eyes examined (service) and purchase new contact lenses (good). If you attend a Drake concert, you can be enthralled by the world-class performance. At the event, you might buy a shirt or a souvenir. With these tangible goods, you can relive and remember the enjoyment of the experience over and over again.

**Ideas** include thoughts, opinions, philosophies, and intellectual concepts that also can be marketed. Groups promoting bicycle safety go to schools, give talks, and sponsor bike helmet poster contests for the members of their primary target market: children. Then, their secondary target market segment—parents and siblings—gets involved through interactions with the young contest participants. The exchange of value occurs when the children listen to the sponsor's presentation and wear their helmets while bicycling, which means they have adopted—or become "purchasers" of—the safety idea that the group marketed. In Chapters 8, 9, and 10 of this book, you will learn much more about the decisions, theories, applications, and strategies of product and services marketing.

**goods**
Items that can be physically touched.

**services**
Intangible customer benefits that are produced by people or machines and cannot be separated from the producer.

Montclair has created a product with benefits that consumers find valuable.

Used by permission of Nestlé Waters Canada. Montclair is a registered trademark of Société des Produits Nestlé S.A., Vevey, Switzerland.

Rafael Nadal adds value to the Nike brand.

pdrocha/Shutterstock.com

**ideas**
Thoughts, opinions, philosophies, and intellectual concepts.

**Price: Transacting Value** Everything has a price, though it doesn't always have to be monetary. **Price**, the second P, is everything the buyer gives up—money, time, energy—in exchange for the product. Marketers must determine the price of a product carefully on the basis of the potential buyer's belief about its value. For example, Air Canada can take you from Toronto to Vancouver or New York. The price you pay depends on how far in advance you book the ticket, the time of year, whether you want to fly economy or business class, and, more recently, whether or not you have luggage to check. Passengers are charged a fee if they have more than one piece of checked luggage. If you value the convenience of buying your ticket at the last minute for a

**price**
The overall sacrifice a consumer is willing to make—money, time, energy—to acquire a specific product or service.

When you attend a Drake concert, you are paying for a service.
RMV/REX/Shutterstock/The Canadian Press

ski trip between Christmas and New Year's Day and you want to fly business class, you can expect to pay four or five times as much as you would for the cheapest available ticket. That is, you have traded a lower price for convenience. For marketers, the key to determining prices is figuring out how much customers are willing to pay so that they are satisfied with the purchase and the seller achieves a reasonable profit. In Chapter 11, you will learn much more about pricing concepts, decisions, and strategies.

**Place: Delivering Value**   The third P, *place*, describes all the activities necessary to get the product from the manufacturer or producer to the right customer when that customer wants it. For Starbucks, that means expanding its storefronts constantly and proactively, so that it is easy for caffeine junkies to find their fix. Creative locations, such as kiosks at the baggage claim in airports or small booths in grocery stores, represent the chain's effort to improve its offering on this dimension of the marketing mix. Place deals specifically with retailing and distribution management. This is also known as supply chain management, which is the set of approaches and techniques that firms employ to efficiently and effectively integrate their suppliers, manufacturers, warehouses, stores, and other firms involved in the transaction (e.g., transportation companies) into a seamless value chain in which merchandise is produced and distributed in the right quantities, to the right locations, and at the right time, while minimizing systemwide costs and satisfying the service levels required by the customers.

Many marketing students initially overlook the importance of distribution management because a lot of these activities occur behind the scenes. But without a strong and

Parasuco is known for its provocative advertising, which appears on billboards and uses celebrities to market its denim lines.

Stringer/Getty Images

efficient distribution system, merchandise isn't available when or where customers want it. Then customers are disappointed, and sales and profits suffer. Place or distribution activities and decisions are discussed in detail in Chapters 12 and 13.

Promotion: Communicating Value   Even the best products and services will go unsold if marketers cannot communicate their value to customers. The fourth P, *promotion*, is communication by a marketer that informs, persuades, and reminds potential buyers about a product or service to influence their opinions or elicit a response. Promotion generally can enhance a product or service's value, as happened for Parasuco jeans. The company's provocative advertising has helped create an image that says more than "Use this product and you will look good." Rather, the promotion sells youth, style, and sex appeal. Such collaborative promotions can be especially effective tactics for marketers, particularly if they can team up with a popular sport, as Social and Mobile Marketing 1.1 details.

The four Ps work together. Although marketers deliver value through each of the 4Ps individually, far greater value is delivered to consumers by treating the 4Ps as a whole. That is, the product or service offered must satisfy the target customers' specific needs and wants, be priced appropriately, be available at locations where customers want it, and be promoted in a manner and through media that are consistent with the target consumers. For instance, luxury or high-fashion items from retailers such as Coach, Louis Vuitton, and Swarovski are well made, priced at a premium, available at exclusive locations, and promoted only in certain media where the advertisements emphasize style, fashion, sex appeal, and so on.

## Marketing Can Be Performed by Both Individuals and Organizations

Imagine how complicated the world would be if you had to buy everything you consumed directly from producers or manufacturers. You would have to go from farm to farm buying your food and then from manufacturer to manufacturer to purchase the table, plates, and utensils you need to eat that food. Fortunately, marketing intermediaries, such as retailers, accumulate merchandise from producers in large amounts and then sell it to you in smaller amounts. The process in which businesses sell to consumers is known as **B2C (business-to-consumer)** marketing, whereas the process of selling merchandise or services from one business to another is called **B2B (business-to-business)** marketing. Some companies, such as General Electric (GE), are engaged in both B2B and B2C marketing at the same time. However, with the advent of various auction sites (such as eBay and Kijiji) and payment sites (such as PayPal), consumers have started marketing their products and services to other consumers, which requires a third category in which consumers sell to other consumers, or **C2C (consumer-to-consumer)** marketing. Individuals can also undertake activities to market themselves. When you apply for a job, for instance, the research you do about the firm, the resumé and cover letter you submit with your application, and the way you dress for an interview and conduct yourself during it are all forms of marketing activities. Accountants, lawyers, financial planners, physicians, and other professional service providers also market their services.

Regardless of whether organizations or individuals are engaged in B2B, B2C, or C2C marketing, one thing seems to be clear: **social media** has become an integral part of their marketing and communications strategies. Social media is widely used in federal elections in Canada, as politicians try to win the hearts and minds of Canadians. Even more dramatically, social media played a major role in the crises observed in several Middle East and European countries. Social media was used to organize protesters and to report news of events in these countries to the rest of the world as the events unfolded in real time. Social media will be explored further in Chapter 16.

**B2C (business-to-consumer)**
The process in which businesses sell to consumers.

**B2B (business-to-business)**
The process of selling merchandise or services from one business to another.

**C2C (consumer-to-consumer)**
The process in which consumers sell to other consumers.

**social media**
The use of digital tools to easily and quickly create and share content to foster dialogue, social relationships, and personal identities.

## Social and Mobile Marketing 1.1

### Snacks and Soccer Star Promotions[13]

Sponsorships of sports teams are nothing new. Firms have been naming stadiums, providing gear, and calling themselves "the official product of" popular sporting events and teams for years. But such promotions can take on new life and new facets when they bring the power of social media marketing to bear on their campaigns.

In Canada, Mondelēz launched its "Pass the Love" campaign in support of youth soccer. Desiree Scott, from the Canadian national women's soccer team, challenged fans to submit a video showing how many Keep Ups they could do. Teams could earn points based on their Keep Up totals and number of times the videos were shared on social media.

The company's product assortment is quite strongly geared toward children and families. It offers such well known brands as Chips Ahoy! and Oreo cookies, Wheat Thins and Ritz crackers, Cadbury candies, and Sour Patch Kids Stride gum.

Recent trends suggest that more children today play soccer (17.1 percent of them play at least once a year) than other sports such as baseball (13.4 percent), football (4.5 percent), or hockey (1.1 percent). In the United States, Mondelēz was quick to make the connection and entered into a sponsorship agreement that made it the official snack brand of the U.S. men's and women's national soccer teams. Furthermore, it signed individual sponsorship deals with some stars of the sport, such as Alex Morgan, Omar Gonzalez, and Clint Dempsey.

Despite this popularity among children and their infamous soccer moms, soccer still struggles in television ratings compared with other sports. Accordingly, the promotional campaigns associated with the sponsorship have very little to do with television. Instead, the focus is on in-store and social media efforts.

In conjunction with its soccer sponsorship, Mondelēz has entered into a partnership with Twitter to increase its advertising spending at the site. In return, Twitter will share its real-time marketing expertise, offer customized marketing research findings, and host various training programs for the packaged-goods company.

This effort represents a continuation of Mondelēz's already strong social media presence. By linking a snack that appeals to children with a sport they love, Mondelēz vastly increases the chances that moms will bring the tasty cookies for a postgame celebration with the little league team.

Mondelēz is the official snack brand for the U.S. men's and women's national soccer teams. To appeal to its young target market, it uses social media instead of television. Pictured here, wearing a Sour Patch Kids T-shirt, is U.S. soccer star Alex Morgan giving a "high five."

© Stephen Brashear/AP Images for Mondelēz International

## Marketing Impacts Many Stakeholders

Most people think of marketing as a way for firms to make profits, but marketing works equally well in the nonprofit sector. Think about what influenced your selection of your college or university, other than family, friends, and convenience. It's likely that your college or university has a sophisticated marketing program to attract and retain students. Marketing also affects stakeholders, for example, supply chain partners such as wholesalers, retailers, or intermediaries such as transportation or warehousing companies. All of these entities market to one another. Manufacturers sell merchandise to retailers, but the retailers often have to convince manufacturers to sell to them. As Sustainable Marketing 1.1 shows, some marketers are greening their marketing practices to communicate that they are socially responsible in their business practices.

## Sustainable Marketing 1.1

### Tim Hortons® Commits to Green Living[14]

The idea of sustainable development, or sustainability, has become popular with environmentalists, non-profit organizations, politicians, business executives, the media, andconsumers. But what exactly does *sustainability* mean? Is the adoption of sustainable development practices and policies in the business world truly widespread? And what are the benefits to companies that embrace sustainability?

You might be surprised to learn that sustainability means different things to different people. A global survey of 1,749 business executives by McKinsey & Company reported that 55 percent consider sustainability to be about managing environmental issues such as greenhouse-gas emissions, energy efficiency, waste management, green-product development, and water conservation. Further, 48 percent say that sustainability is about governance issues such as complying with regulations, maintaining ethical practices, and meeting accepted industry standards; and 41 percent say that it includes the management of social issues such as working conditions and labour standards. No matter how you define it, organizations that practise sustainability must strive to conduct their business in such a way as to minimize harm to the environment, follow good governance practices, and comply with social standards.

For Tim Hortons®, sustainability is about managing "the personal impact we have in all we do." It's a three-tiered approach that focuses on individuals, communities, and the planet. From reducing sodium content in muffins to raising money to send children to camp, whether implementing energy saving measures in over 200 restaurants or diverting waste from landfill, the company is committed to making a true difference. The Tim Hortons® coffee partnership helps improve lives by providing technical training to small-scale farmers to increase crop yields and manage the land in an environmentally responsible way. Over 20,000 people in Brazil, Colombia, Guatemala, and Honduras have benefited from this partnership.

As consumers have become more aware of the environmental impact of products or services they use, many companies have started to use green marketing claims as evidence of their commitment to sustainable development. Many consumers buy products labelled as "eco-friendly," "biodegradable," or "green" without giving much thought to what the terms mean. Some consumers wonder if they are being "greenwashed." Their skepticism may be warranted, as there are no laws in Canada specifically governing green claims.

To counter such skepticism, Tim Hortons® produces an annual Sustainability and Responsibility Report to publicly demonstrate its commitment to sustainability. Throughout this book, we will present various examples of sustainable marketing efforts undertaken by Canadian companies.

Marketing can also benefit society at large. The dairy industry used a very successful, award-winning campaign with its slogan "Got Milk?" aimed at different target segments. This campaign not only created high levels of awareness about the benefits of drinking milk, but also increased milk consumption in various target segments,[15] possibly in response to the use of celebrities, from Dwayne "The Rock" Johnson and Victor Cruz to Miranda Lambert and Nina Dobrev. Although hugely successful, "Got Milk" ran its course. It has been replaced with "Milk Life"—which focuses on milk as a source of protein. The new campaign continues to benefit the entire dairy industry and promote the benefits of drinking milk to society at large.

Now that we've examined what marketing is and how it creates value, let's consider how it fits into the world of commerce, as well as into society in general.

## The Four Orientations of Marketing          **L03**

Marketing didn't get to its current prominence among individuals, corporations, and society at large overnight. Over the last 100 years, marketing has evolved from an activity

"Milk Life" replaced the well known "Got Milk?" campaign, but the ads still create a high level of awareness for the milk industry.

Courtesy of Lowe Campbell Ewald and MilkPEP

designed simply to produce and sell products to an integral business function aimed at creating value for consumers and the company's shareholders. As we have examined marketing practices over the years, we have observed four different marketing orientations or philosophies: product orientation, sales orientation, market orientation, and value-based orientation (see Exhibit 1.4).

**Product Orientation**  Product-oriented companies focus on developing and distributing innovative products with little concern about whether the products best satisfy customers' needs. This philosophy is best illustrated by a famous quote made around the turn of the 20th century by Henry Ford, the founder of Ford Motor Company, who remarked, "Customers can have any colour they want so long as it's black." Manufacturers believed that a good product would sell itself, and retail stores typically were considered places to hold the merchandise until a consumer wanted it. Companies with a product orientation generally start out by thinking about the product they want to build; they try selling the product after it is developed rather than starting with an understanding of the customers' needs and then developing a product to satisfy those needs.

**Sales Orientation**  Companies that have a sales orientation basically view marketing as a selling function where companies try to sell as many of their products as possible rather than focus on making products consumers really want. These firms typically depend on heavy doses of personal selling and advertising to attract new customers. Companies with a selling orientation tend to focus on making a sale or on each transaction rather than building long-term customer relationships. They generally believe that if consumers try their products, they will like them. The focus of these companies tends to be on the products or services they have to offer, more than on consumer needs and wants.

**EXHIBIT 1.4**  Marketing Evolution: Product, Sales, Market, and Value-Based

(a): © Ryan McVay/Getty Images RF; (b): © CMCD/Getty Images RF; (c): Ted Dayton Photography/Beateworks/Corbis; (d): © Ryan McVay/Getty Images RF; (e): Courtesy of Apple

Profits come from sales volume rather than from repeat business from satisfied customers.

### Market Orientation
Market-oriented companies start out by focusing on what consumers want and need before they design, make, or attempt to sell their products and services. They believe that customers have choice and make purchase decisions based on several factors, including quality, convenience, and price. Basically, "the customer is king," and the market is a buyer's market since consumers wield tremendous power. In this orientation, marketers' role is to understand and respond to the needs of consumers and to do everything possible to satisfy them. There is a focus on making marketing an integrated process throughout the entire company rather than just in one department. Satisfied customers become long-term loyal customers, contributing to bottom-line profitability.

### Value-Based Orientation
Most successful firms today are market oriented.[16] That means they have gone beyond a product or sales orientation and have attempted to discover and satisfy their customers' needs and wants. Some marketing firms recognized that there was more to good marketing. To compete successfully, they would have to focus on the triple bottom line: people (consumer needs and wants), profits (long-term profitable relationships with customers and suppliers), and planet (do all this in a way that is socially and environmentally responsible). Value-based companies provide their customers with greater value than their competitors.

**Value** reflects the relationship of benefits to costs, or what you *get* for what you *give*.[17] In a marketing context, customers seek a fair return in goods and/or services for their hard-earned money and scarce time. They want products or services that meet their specific needs or wants and are offered at a price that they believe provides good value. A creative way to provide value to customers is to engage in *value cocreation*.[18] In this case, customers can act as collaborators to create the product or service. When clients work with their investment advisors, they cocreate their investment portfolios; when Nike allows customers to custom design their sneakers, they are cocreating.

**value**
Reflects the relationship of benefits to costs, or what the consumer gets for what he or she gives.

Every value-based marketing firm must implement its strategy according to what its customers value. Depending on the specific product or service for sale, these valuable benefits could include speed, convenience, size, accuracy, price, cost savings, or user-friendliness. Sometimes providing greater value means providing a lot of merchandise for relatively little money, such as Subway's foot-long subs for $5 or a diamond for 40 percent off the suggested retail price at Costco. But value is in the eye of the beholder and doesn't always come inexpensively. Satisfied Louis Vuitton customers probably believe the Vuitton clothing, bags, or shoes they buy are good value because they have received many benefits for a reasonable price. Similarly, teenagers may be willing to pay a premium for Apple's iPhone because of its extraordinary design and packaging, even though cheaper substitutes are available. This is the power of marketing in general and branding in particular. Value-based marketing is examined in greater detail in the following section.

## HOW DO FIRMS BECOME MORE VALUE DRIVEN?

Firms become value driven by focusing on four activities. First, they share information about their customers and competitors across their own organization and with other firms that might be involved in getting the product or service to the marketplace,

Fashion designers for Zara, the Spain-based fashion retailer, collect purchase information and research customer trends to determine what their customers will want to wear in the next few weeks. They share this information with other departments to forecast sales and coordinate deliveries.

© Steve White

**relational orientation**
A method of building a relationship with customers based on the philosophy that buyers and sellers should develop a long-term relationship.

such as manufacturers and transportation companies. Second, they strive to balance their customers' benefits and costs. Third, they concentrate on building relationships with customers. Fourth, they take advantage of new technologies and connect with their customers using social and mobile media.

## Sharing Information

In a value-based, market-oriented firm, marketers share information about customers and competitors that has been collected through customer relationship management, and integrate it across the firm's various departments. The fashion designers for Zara, the Spain-based fashion retailer, for instance, collect purchase information and research customer trends to determine what their customers will want to wear in the next few weeks; simultaneously, the logisticians—those persons in charge of getting the merchandise to the stores—use the same purchase history to forecast sales and allocate appropriate merchandise to individual stores. Sharing and coordinating such information represents a critical success factor for any firm. Imagine what might happen if Zara's advertising department were to plan a special promotion but not share its sales projections with those people in charge of creating the merchandise or getting it to stores.

## Balancing Benefits With Costs

Value-oriented marketers constantly measure the benefits that customers perceive against the cost of their offering. They use available customer data to find opportunities to better satisfy their customers' needs and in turn develop long-term loyalties. Such a value-based orientation has helped Canadian Tire and Walmart outperform other department stores, and WestJet Airlines and Southwest Airlines outperform mainstream carriers. IKEA does not have highly paid salespeople to sell its furniture. Its simple designs mean customers can easily choose a product and assemble it themselves.

Furniture retailer IKEA focuses on what its customers value—low prices and great design.

Michael Gordon/Shutterstock.com

## Building Relationships With Customers

During the past decade or so, marketers have begun to develop a **relational orientation** as they have become aware of the need to think about customers in terms of relationships rather than transactions.[19] To build relationships, firms focus on the lifetime value of the relationship, not how much money is made during each transaction. Apple ensures that its new innovations are compatible with existing products so that consumers will maintain a long-term relationship with the company across all their electronic needs.

This relationship approach uses a process known as **customer relationship management (CRM)**, a business philosophy and set of strategies, programs, and systems that focus on identifying and building loyalty among the firm's most valued customers.[20] Firms that employ CRM systematically collect information about their customers' needs and then use that information to target their best customers with the products, services, and special promotions that appear most important to them.

**customer relationship management (CRM)**
A business philosophy and set of strategies, programs, and systems that focus on identifying and building loyalty among the firm's most valued customers.

## Connecting With Customers Using Social and Mobile Media

Marketers are steadily embracing new technologies, such as social and mobile media, to allow them to connect better with their customers and thereby serve their needs more effectively. Businesses take social and mobile media seriously, including these advanced tools in the development of their marketing strategies. In turn, 93 percent of marketers say that they use social media tools for their businesses[21] and 52 percent of Internet users in North America access social media using a mobile device.[22]

Yet even with this astounding penetration, only 16 percent of the world's population uses Facebook. North America and the United Kingdom may be approaching saturation, but there is still huge growth potential for social networks. Before users can sign up for Facebook, however, they need access to high-speed Internet. Other countries continue to experience higher Facebook growth rates as they gain greater Internet access and as Facebook becomes available in more languages (around 70 currently). The global average Internet penetration rate hovers below 40 percent, with massive populations in Africa and Asia still limited in their access.[23]

Beyond social media sites, online travel agencies such as Expedia, Travelocity, and Priceline have become the first place that users go to book travel arrangements. In addition to asking friends and relying on their own experience, 10 percent of travellers turned to destination websites, 9 percent relied on websites run by specific providers, another 5 percent used social networking, and 4 percent depended on their mobile devices to plan their trips.[24]

Customers who book hotels using travel agencies become loyal to the agency that gives them the lowest prices, rather than to any particular hotel brand. So hotels are using social media and mobile applications to lure customers back to their specific brands by engaging in conversations with them and allowing fans of the page to book their hotel reservations through Facebook. Some hotel chains have mobile applications that allow customers to make changes to their reservations, shift check-in and checkout times, and add amenities or services to their stays. The hotels know a lot about their customers, because they collect information about their previous visits, including the type of room they stayed in, their preferences (from pillows to drinks consumed from the minibar), and the type of room service they prefer.

Several restaurant chains are exploiting location-based social media applications, such as Foursquare, Urbanspoon, Foodspotting, and Facebook Places. These customers tend to be more loyal and can help spread the word to others about the restaurant.[25] By using location-based apps on mobile phones, customers can find restaurants that cater to their specific dietary requirements or find restaurants highly rated by Yelp users nearby. The result is that users are driving the way in which brands and stores are interacting with social media. Location-based services are appealing, though they also may create some concerns, as Ethical Dilemma 1.1 describes.

Marketers connect with customers by using social and mobile media.

Copyright © Intelity, LLC Inc. A Self-Service Software Solutions Company—IntegrityCorp .com.

## Ethical Dilemma 1.1

### Beckoning Consumers With the iBeacon[26]

When iPad and iPhone owners first updated their systems to iOS 7, they also transformed their devices into a new type ofcommunication channel, whether they realized it or not. Specifically, that operating system update installed iBeacon software onto their mobile devices.

The iBeacon software works as a location service, such that transmitters can send messages to any user with an iPhone or iPad running on iOS 7 or higher. Apple soon announced that it already had installed transmitters in its stores. When Apple fans visit the stores, the iBeacon location service will push notifications to them based on their specific location. A shopper who pauses by the updated MacBook Air might receive a message on her phone about its battery life or compatibility with her phone. Another consumer who breezes past the phones could receive a reminder that he is eligible for an upgrade.

This application is notable; it indicates that Apple has jumped ahead of its competitors in devising and implementing hypertargeted, micro-location-based marketing. For its retail stores, the software reveals not just whether a potential customer is in the same town or near the parking lot, but also whether a shopper is literally standing near the accessory display.

This rollout in the Apple stores appears to be just the tip of the iceberg. Recent model iPhones and iPads not only receive messages using the iBeacon software but also are easily configured to serve as a transmitter of iBeacon messages. This means that virtually every retailer that invests in an iPad can use the software like Apple uses it: pushing notifications to shoppers who are already in the store, locating them precisely, and learning exactly how they move through the store. One estimate suggests that there are approximately 200 million potential iBeacon transmitters already in circulation—even before the functionality has gained widespread acclaim.

For Apple, the competitive advantage appears nearly insurmountable because when users update, they also opt in to the iBeacon application, agreeing to accept the micro-location-based push notifications. Other stores will need to get consumers to agree to receive similar messages. For big retailers such as Walmart, it might not be hard; they can simply include the software in their regular apps that consumers already may have downloaded.

Furthermore, Apple has essentially blazed the trail for this latest innovation for retail. Combining its dominance in the tablet market, popularity in the mobile phone market, and first-mover advantages in the location service market, it appears that the iBeacon is set to become the standard.

But even if Apple has thought ahead about how to make sure users adopt the iBeacon, it might not have considered all the implications for users' privacy. Are companies responsible for making sure their customers know that their identity and location are being revealed to marketers all the time? Or are customers the ones responsible for opting out of such location-based services?

This Estimote Beacon lets Apple users opt in to receive micro-location-based messages in physical locations, helping them find products, deals, and more information about their surroundings.
Courtesy of Estimote, Inc.

## L04  WHY IS MARKETING IMPORTANT?

Marketing was once only an afterthought to production. Early marketing philosophy went something like this: "We've made it; now how do we get rid of it?" However, marketing has not only shifted its focus dramatically, but also evolved into a major business function that crosses all areas of a firm or organization, as illustrated in Exhibit 1.5. Marketing advises production about how much of the company's product to make and then tells logistics when to ship it. It creates mutually valuable relationships between the company and the firms from which it buys. It identifies those elements that local customers value and makes it possible for the firm to expand globally. Marketing has had a significant impact on consumers as well. Without marketing, it would be difficult for any of us to learn about new products and services. Understanding marketing can even help you find a job after you graduate.

## Marketing Expands Firms' Global Presence

A generation ago, Coca-Cola was available in many nations, but Levi's and most other American and Canadian brands were not. Today, most jeans, including those by Levi Strauss & Co. and Parasuco, are made in places other than Canada and the United States and are available nearly everywhere. Thanks to MTV and other global entertainment venues, cheap foreign travel, and the Internet, you share many of your

**EXHIBIT 1.5**    Importance of Marketing

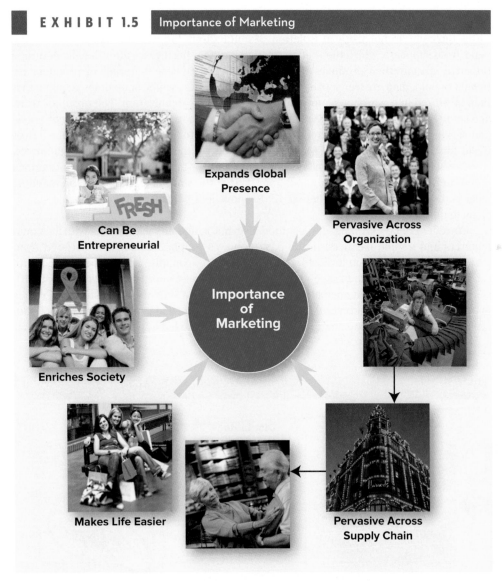

(global): Jason Reed/Getty Images RF; (organization): © Digital Vision/PunchStock; (tailor): Royalty-Free/CORBIS; (supply chain): Andrew Ward/Life File/Getty Images; (elderly couple): Purestock/SuperStock; (life easier): © Brand X Pictures/PunchStock; (society): BananaStock/JupiterImages; (entrepreneurial): Caia Image/Glow Images

consumption behaviours with college and university students in countries all over the globe. The best fashions, music, and even food trends disseminate rapidly around the world.

Take a look at your next shopping bag. Whether it contains groceries or apparel, you will find goods from many countries: produce from Mexico, jeans from Italy, and T-shirts from China. Global manufacturers and retailers continue to make inroads into the Canadian market. Companies such as Honda, Sony, and Heineken sell as well in Canada as they do in their home countries. Sweden's fashion retailer H&M operates in 38 countries, including Canada.[27] Its upscale competitor, Spain's Zara, operates in more than 80 countries, including Canada.[28] Starbucks even adjusted its menu to meet customer wants in the Japanese market more effectively. How does marketing contribute to a company's successful global expansion? Understanding customers is critical. Without the knowledge that can be gained by analyzing new customers' needs and wants on a segment-by-segment, region-by-region basis—one of marketing's main tasks—it would be difficult for a firm to expand globally.

## Marketing Is Pervasive Across Marketing Channel Members

Firms typically do not work in isolation. Manufacturers buy raw materials and components from suppliers, which they sell to retailers or other businesses after they have turned the materials into their products (see Exhibit 1.6). Every time materials or products are bought or sold, they are transported to a different location, which sometimes requires that they be stored in a warehouse operated by yet another organization. The group of firms and set of techniques and approaches firms use to make and deliver a given set of goods and services is commonly referred to as a **supply chain**. Excellent supply chains effectively and efficiently integrate their supply chain partners—suppliers, manufacturers, warehouses, stores, and transportation intermediaries—to produce and distribute goods in the right quantities, to the right locations, and at the right time. Supply chain management is discussed in detail in Chapter 12; for now, let's consider the value of the supply chain in marketing.

Consider Loblaw, Canada's largest food distributor, and its relationships with its manufacturers and trading partners. In the past, Loblaw's supply chain system suffered from inefficiencies that drove up its costs substantially.[29] For example, inaccurate demand forecasts led trading partners to stock huge inventory to meet unpredictable demand. Inefficient use of customer data meant that stock replenishment was made by estimation rather than by knowing true customer data. Disconnected supply chain systems, limited collaboration, reduced information sharing, and supply variability led to poor quality information

**supply chain**
The group of firms and set of techniques and approaches firms use to make and deliver a given set of goods and services.

## EXHIBIT 1.6    Supply Chain

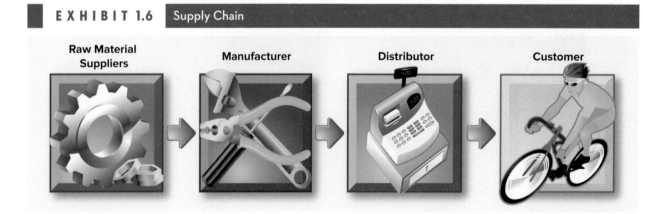

Raw Material Suppliers → Manufacturer → Distributor → Customer

on which to base sales forecasts, production plans, and replenishment schemes. The company has since made many changes to improve the efficiency of its supply chain. Loblaw's participation in a radio frequency identification (RFID) pilot project for the grocery industry conducted by the Canadian RFID Centre has helped it improve its operations. Preliminary results seem to indicate that Loblaw has improved its inventory management and use of promotions.

## Marketing Enriches Society

Should marketing focus on factors other than financial profitability, such as good corporate citizenry? Many of Canada's best-known corporations seem to think so, because they encourage their employees to participate in activities that benefit their communities and invest heavily in socially responsible actions and charities. When World Wildlife Fund (WWF) launched its "Spring Things" campaign to promote workplace giving toward environmental conservation, HP Canada was one of 40 organizations that championed the cause. The campaign resulted in employee engagement and raised almost $400,000 in the first year.[30]

Canadian companies recognize that a strong social orientation is in both their and their customers' best interests. It shows the consumer that the firm can be trusted with their business. Also, investors view firms that operate with high levels of corporate responsibility and ethics as safe investments. Similarly, firms have come to realize that good corporate citizenship through socially responsible actions should be a priority because it will help their bottom line in the long run.[31] In a world in which consumers constantly hear about negative examples of ethics, the need for companies to live up to their ethical promises becomes even more important.

Ron Joyce cofounded the Tim Hortons® doughnut chain and was the first franchisee.

Scott Gardner/Hamilton Spectator

## Marketing Can Be Entrepreneurial

Marketing plays a major role in the success of large corporations, and it is also at the centre of the successes of numerous new ventures initiated by entrepreneurs, or people who organize, operate, and assume the risk of a business venture.[32] Key to the success of many such entrepreneurs is that they launch ventures that aim to satisfy unfilled needs. Some examples of successful ventures (and their founders) that understood their customers and added value include:

- Tim Hortons® (Ron Joyce)
- Lululemon (Chip Wilson)

Ron Joyce is best known for partnering with hockey legend Tim Horton to cofound the Canadian coffee chain Tim Hortons®. Joyce met Horton while walking the beat as an officer with the Hamilton Police Force. The first shop opened in 1964 and served only coffee and doughnuts.[33] From humble beginnings, that first store in Hamilton became the launch pad for future growth. As the first franchisee, Joyce quickly set up three locations. By 1974, the chain had grown to 40 stores. When Tim Horton was killed in a car accident, Joyce bought his shares. He has won numerous awards and honorary degrees, and in 1999 was inducted into the Canadian Business Hall of Fame and named Entrepreneur of the Year for Ontario and Canada.[34]

When you think of Lululemon, you probably think of Chip (Dennis) Wilson, who founded the athletic apparel retailer.

Ian Lindsay/Vancouver Sun

Another extraordinary entrepreneur and marketer is Chip (Dennis) Wilson. A self-made billionaire, Wilson got his start in the surf, skate, and snowboard industry. After trying his first yoga class, his discontent with the cotton clothing available provided him with the opportunity to indulge his passion in athletic fabrics. He opened his first Lululemon store in Kitsilano, British Columbia, in 2000 and took the company public in 2007.[35] Today, the company has a market capitalization of $9.4 billion[36] and has stores or showrooms in Canada, the United States, the United Kingdom, Australia, China, Germany, Holland, New Zealand, and Singapore.[37]

Great and distinguished entrepreneurs have a vision of how certain combinations of products and services can satisfy unfilled needs. They find and understand a marketing opportunity (i.e., the unfilled need), conduct a thorough examination of the marketplace, and develop and communicate the value of their products and services to potential consumers. An example of this is found in Entrepreneurial Marketing 1.1.

## Entrepreneurial Marketing 1.1

## Mosquito Preventer Trap[38]

Public health officials concerned over the rise of the Zika virus in Central and South America are interested in Kacee Vasudeva's mosquito trap. Founder and president of Maxtech Mosquito Control in Waterloo, Ontario, Vasudeva is a veteran entrepreneur. He started his first company in his garage and later founded Maxtech Manufacturing, a group of six auto parts manufacturing plants with peak annual sales of $100 million. Another venture, Maxtech Consumer Products, designs and manufactures hand tools and power tool accessories.

The automotive industry was hit hard by the recession of 2008–2010, forcing the auto parts business into receivership but not affecting the consumer products company. The loss didn't dampen Vasudeva's entrepreneurial zeal. Instead, he turned his focus to public health initiatives. He began by tackling bed bug infestations crippling many hotels and public places. His company, Beapco, created products that help detect bed bugs in a non-toxic way, including a power bar that doubles as a bed bug trap. He then aimed to reduce the spread of mosquito-borne diseases such as Zika, West Nile virus, malaria, dengue fever, yellow fever, and others. Under the brand name

Kacee Vasudeva's GreenStrike Mosquito Preventer drastically reduces the population of disease-carrying mosquitoes.

Used with permission of Maxtech Mosquito Control Inc.

GreenStrike, he has launched a variety of products to help eliminate mosquitoes. The GreenStrike Mosquito Preventer is the largest. It looks simple—a barrel that holds six litres of water to which an all-natural product is added to attract female mosquitoes. While females only live for six weeks, they lay up to 30,000 eggs. With GreenStrike, the eggs never hatch because water flushed though a filter traps the eggs, and they dry out.

Introduced in 2014, the products are sold through Home Hardware, Canadian Tire, Amazon, and Shopify at prices ranging from $79 to $349. Vasudeva is currently pursuing global opportunities, mostrecently in China and India. The company has adapted its product's marketing mix for the needs and wants of the developing world by offering a lower priced unit that can be manually operated.

As this example illustrates, the entrepreneurial path sometimes leads in many different directions. Although the domestic auto parts business failed due to the recession, it was eventually sold off, opening the door for a new venture that is leading to global opportunities. Innovation in Canada is driven by entrepreneurs like Kacee Vasudeva. You'll see many more examples like this in the coming chapters.

# LEARNING OBJECTIVES REVIEW

**LO1** **Define the role of marketing and explain its core concepts**

In definition form, "marketing is a set of business practices designed to plan for and present an organization's products or services in ways that build effective customer relationships." Marketing strives to *create value* in many ways. If marketers are to succeed, their customers must believe that the firm's products and services are valuable; that is, the products and services are worth more to the customers than they cost.

Marketers also enhance the value of products and services through various forms of *communication*, such as advertising and personal selling. Through communications, marketers educate and inform customers about the benefits of their products and services and thereby increase their perceived value.

Marketers facilitate the *delivery of value* by ensuring the right products and services are available when, where, and in the quantities their customers want. Better marketers are not concerned about just one transaction with their customers; they recognize the value of loyal customers and strive to develop *long-term relationships* with them.

**LO2** **Describe how marketers create value for a product or service**

Value represents the relationship of benefits to costs. Firms can improve their value by increasing benefits, reducing costs, or both. The best firms integrate a value orientation into everything they do. If a move doesn't increase benefits or reduce costs, it probably shouldn't occur.

Firms become value driven by finding out as much as they can about their customers and those customers' needs and wants. They share this information with their partners, both up and down the supply chain, so the entire chain collectively can focus on the customer. The key to true value-based marketing is the ability to design products and services that achieve the right balance between benefits and costs—not too little, not too much.

Value-based marketers aren't necessarily worried about how much money they will make on the next sale. Instead, they are concerned with developing a lasting relationship with their customers so those customers return again and again.

**LO3** **Summarize the four orientations of marketing**

Firms with a *product orientation* tend to believe that a good product will sell itself. Manufacturers are concerned with product innovation, not with satisfying the needs of individual consumers, and keep producing with the assumption that people will buy it. Marketing with this orientation is simply about informing the customer that a product exists, whether it is used at all.

Firms with a *sales orientation* rely on a sales team to sell. Production is maximized and then heavy doses of personal selling and advertising help distribute and sell the product. The role of marketing is focused only on the sale of products.

If a firm has a *market orientation*, it celebrates the customer. Here the customer can decide what is best for him or her, based on the attributes of a product or service. Rather than simply producing and selling, manufacturers with this orientation seek to learn customer needs and wants, and design products to fit the customers. Marketing plays an important role by communicating the different attributes, or value, created by each product.

Most successful firms today have transcended other views and instead support a *value-based orientation*. In addition to discovering needs and wants, it is critical to deliver more value to customers than competitors do. Value reflects the relationship of benefits to costs, or what you get for what you give. Marketing plays an integral role not only in creating and delivering that valuable product, but also in communicating the value, especially in relation to other products available, and transacting the value through to customers.

**LO4** **Understand the importance of marketing both within and outside the firm**

Successful firms integrate marketing throughout their organizations so that marketing activities coordinate with other functional areas, such as product design, production, logistics, and human resources, enabling them to get the right product to the right customers at the right time. Marketing helps facilitate the smooth flow of goods through the supply chain, all the way from raw materials to the consumer. From a personal perspective, the marketing function facilitates your buying process, and can support your career goals.

Marketing also can be important for society through its embrace of solid, ethical business practices. Firms "do the right thing" when they sponsor charitable events, seek to reduce environmental impacts, and avoid unethical practices. Such efforts endear the firm to customers. Finally, marketing is a cornerstone of entrepreneurialism. Many great companies have been founded by outstanding marketers, and an entrepreneurial spirit pervades the marketing decisions of firms of all sizes.

# KEY TERMS

- B2B (business-to-business)
- B2C (business-to-consumer)
- C2C (consumer-to-consumer)
- customer relationship management (CRM)
- exchange
- goods
- ideas
- market
- marketing
- marketing mix (four Ps)
- marketing plan
- need
- price
- relational orientation
- services
- social media
- supply chain
- target market
- value
- want

# CONCEPT REVIEW

1. What is marketing and why is it important?

2. Is the marketing mix (the four Ps) enough to guarantee successful marketing? Explain.

3. Explain how a strike at one of a company's supplier firms or a new technology would influence the company's marketing efforts.

4. Discuss the main elements of value-based marketing. List four ways in which marketing helps to create value.

5. Explain the relationship between customer value and customer satisfaction.

6. Generally, all companies are in business to generate profits and increase shareholder value. Yet, the Canadian Marketing Association's definition of marketing does not explicitly mention profits or shareholder value. Why do you think these are not included in the definition? Should they be included?

7. Today, many marketers are not interested in selling their products and services to everyone who wants them; instead, they want to sell them only to selected target markets. What do you think the main reasons are for targeting specific market segments?

8. Give reasons why understanding customer needs and wants is fundamental to marketing success. How can marketers go about understanding customer needs and wants?

9. Which marketing orientation would most likely help a company build strong customer relationships that are profitable? Why?

10. Explain how customer value is created or increased when the company's marketing department works closely with other departments within the firm as well as with the firm's suppliers and customers.

# MARKETING APPLICATIONS

1. When apparel manufacturers develop their marketing strategies, do they concentrate on satisfying their customers' needs or wants? What about a utility company? A cellphone company?

2. Choose a product that you use every day. Describe its four Ps.

3. One of your friends was recently watching TV and saw an advertisement that she liked. She said, "Wow, that was great marketing!" Was the ad in fact marketing? Why?

4. Mercedes-Benz manufactures the Smart Car, which sells for around $16,000, and the SL65 AMG 2-door Roadster for over $200,000. Is Mercedes providing the target markets for these cars with a good value? Explain why.

5. Assume you have been hired by the marketing department of a major consumer products manufacturer such as Colgate-Palmolive. You are having lunch with some new colleagues in the finance, manufacturing, and logistics departments. They are arguing that the company could save millions of dollars if it just got rid of the marketing department. Develop an argument that would persuade them otherwise.

6. Why do marketers find it important to embrace societal needs and ethical business practices? Provide an example of a societal need or ethical business practice being addressed by a specific marketer.

7. Visit the website of Rogers Communications (www.rogers.com) and compare the four Ps marketing mix for the BlackBerry PRIV and the Apple iPhone 7 Plus. What factors might explain the differences you observe?

8. For many consumers, the difference between Dasani water made by Coca-Cola (www.dasani.com) and Aquafina

water made by Pepsi (www.aquafina.com) is hardly noticeable. However, both companies and their loyal customers would argue that there are many differences between these two brands of water. What is your view? Explain how customer perceptions and emotions may influence the way they value a company's product.

9. As described in this chapter, customer relationship management is a very important aspect of value-based marketing. Pick any one of Canada's major retailers—for example, The Bay (www.hbc.com), Loblaw (www.loblaws .ca), or Shoppers Drug Mart (www.shoppersdrugmart .ca)—and explain how it goes about building strong relationships with its customers.

10. Using the four Ps, discuss how the Apple iBeacon will create value for customers.

## NET SAVVY

1. Happy Planet (www.happyplanet.com), a Vancouver-based organic juice producer, is an emerging player in the organic beverage market. It supplies all of Canada and some of the United States with organic juice. Visit its website and describe how the company delivers value above and beyond that provided by traditional grocery retailers. Describe the ways in which the company communicates this value through its website.

2. Montréal Biodôme (http://www2.ville.montreal.qc.ca /biodome) has developed an excellent reputation in international scientific and cultural circles for the diversity of its collection. Visit its website and describe the ways in which it creates value for patrons. What else could Montréal Biodôme do to offer even more value to its patrons?

## CHAPTER CASE STUDY

### A STARBUCKS JUGGERNAUT[39]

As this chapter has sought to demonstrate, good marketing requires practitioners to understand customer needs, wants, and demands. Marketing requires concentration and creativity, close attention and open-mindedness, as well as careful analysis and the courage to take risks. Howard Schultz, CEO of Starbucks, once said, "We cannot be content with the status quo. Any business today that embraces the status quo as an operating principle is going to be on a death march."[40]

Starbucks' march is clearly going in the opposite direction. It recently reported its highest shareholder return in 10 years, and reported record revenues of $19.2 billion. Indeed, it is working to achieve its mission: "To inspire and nurture the human spirit—one person, one cup and one neighbourhood at a time."[41]

### International Expansion

Part of the reason for these increased sales has been Starbucks' continued pursuit of growth and expansion. Along with finding new locations in its home market, recent international expansions have spread the brand to Colombia, Turkey, India, and Norway. Accordingly, the number of stores worldwide has grown to more than 22,519[42] in 68 countries, demonstrating its commitment to getting better, rather than resting on its laurels (or tea leaves).

Such expansion requires flexibility to make sure the marketing plan matches the market. Generally, Starbucks actively avoids any franchise agreements. It wants to own all its stores to ensure consistency and quality. But that strict preference has not worked well in Europe, where it discovered it needed some help to access smaller markets. Although it no longer offers franchises in the United Kingdom, at last count nine franchisees in the United Kingdom owned 45 Starbucks stores.[43] In nations with strict laws regarding foreign ownership of business, such as India and China, Starbucks enters into joint venture partnerships, to make sure it can access these massive and growing markets.

Yet Starbucks is well aware of the damage done in the mid-2000s, when it expanded so rapidly and indiscriminately that customers started rejecting the chain as too ubiquitous—too much, everywhere they turned. The company slumped during that period, suffering from a weakened reputation, negative press, and consumer complaints about quality.

Let's look at how Starbucks is managing its marketing mix, or the 4Ps, as it moves forward.

Starbucks has quickly spread across the globe, including to this location in China.

© Jing wei-Imaginechina/AP Images

## Product Innovation

Growth for the corporation also comes about through introducing new product lines. For Starbucks, the purchase of Teavana should do for tea what has already been done for coffee—turn it into a pleasurable, happy experience that people can treat themselves to on a daily basis. Teavana stores offer more than 100 flavours, including non-traditional names such as Slimful Chocolate Decadence Oolong, Cococaramel Sea Salt, Yunnan Golden Pu-Erh, and Spice of Life.[44] Tea sales grew by 17 percent last year. Starbucks plans to expand the Teavana brand in Europe, as well as in China and other Asia-Pacific countries. And in 2016, Starbucks rolled out an Evenings Menu at three Toronto locations that allows consumers to purchase alcoholic beverages such as wine, beer, and cider.[45]

Of course, this is not to suggest that Starbucks has never erred in its marketing decisions. Even the best marketers are prone to stumbling sometimes. When Starbucks sought to expand its line of breakfast foods, consumers found the offerings bland and unappealing. The food often took too long to prepare, especially for busy baristas during the morning rush.

But part of the success of the chain is its ability to learn from its mistakes. When Starbucks purchased La Boulange Café and Bakery for $100 million, it tasked the chain's founder, Pascal Rigo, with laying out a specific plan for adding to the pastries in its display cases. Rigo had multiple tasks to complete before his croissants and muffins would make it into Starbucks. He had to find a way to fit freezers into every single Starbucks store (not an easy task in tiny shops, where space is at a premium). He had to define a training plan to help baristas learn how and when to suggest and sell the pastries. And he needed to identify or create local bakeries that could be trusted to make the products consistently and on time and supply them to each store.[46]

These tasks were part of the marketing plan; without establishing a good supply, Starbucks would not allow the foods into its well designed, appealing stores. But by paying attention to the detail and thinking creatively, Rigo and Starbucks found a way to make La Boulange pastries an appealing addition to Starbucks stores.

## Promotion Innovations

Starbucks is leveraging the promotion P as well by developing thoughtful campaigns that reflect currency and the image and corporate personality that it wishes to portray. It often promotes new products with "buy one, get one free" offers. Its rewards program, although dramatically revised in the spring of 2016, continues to bring loyal customers back to its stores. The rewards program allows Starbucks to track customer purchases, capturing buying history and preferences. It also allows the company to create personalized offers and make unique recommendations for customers. Promotions are also tied into the use of the Starbucks app to make payment fast and easy, or the Mobile Order & Pay app, which lets customers order ahead and bypass the line on arrival.

## Pricing

From its inception, Starbucks has charged premium prices. With relatively few specialty coffeehouses at the time, it stood out as being unique in many markets. Most North Americans had never tasted freshly ground espresso, let alone cappuccinos or lattes. They certainly hadn't experienced the warm, inviting, and relaxing atmosphere in which they could sit and visit with friends or do some reading or work. The personalized exchange customers had with a barista was also unusual.

Even after it experienced intense competition from McDonald's, Tim Hortons®, and independent coffeehouses; rapid expansion both domestically and internationally; and a back-to-its-roots change of strategy that reflects quality products and superior service, it still commands a premium price. Moving into the future, Starbucks is counting on the increased use of payment via smartphone apps, prepaid cards, and credit cards to take away some of the sting of its relatively high prices.

## Improvements to the Supply Chain

As the La Boulange example shows, Starbucks has learned the importance of a consistent supply of products, part of the place P. The supply chain is critical to any good marketing effort, another lesson that Starbucks seemingly has learned the hard way. When it first chose to distribute ground coffee and beans through grocery stores, it turned to an existing consumer packaged-goods company, Kraft, for help. The partnership was not successful and ultimately fell apart.

In particular, Starbucks alleged that Kraft was not doing enough to market and promote its branded goods. In demonstrating its ability to pay attention to changes in its situation, Starbucks also contended that the partnership was limiting its marketing capacities. For example, the agreement required that it produce only single-serve coffee pods that fit Kraft's Tassimo system. This left Starbucks unable to compete for the segment of consumers who had purchased other systems. The company now has a partnership with Keurig Green Mountain to supply Starbucks K-cup pods.

By securing greater control over its distribution, Starbucks also can more rapidly and effectively implement new strategies for its consumer packaged-goods business. This sector is a strong focus for Starbucks, which hopes to sell more packaged goods through additional channels, such as hotels and restaurants, as well as grocery stores.

## Commitment to Sustainability

Like Tim Hortons®, Starbucks is also committed to sustainability. It launched the Sustainable Coffee Challenge along with Conservation International and other organizations to work toward making coffee a sustainable agricultural product. Its "One Tree for Every Bag" program demonstrates a commitment to ethical sourcing. Through this program, Starbucks can scale support to farmers in need. For example, this year it will donate 20 million rust-resistant coffee tree seedlings.

These aspects of Starbucks' strategy highlight how marketing can lead to success. But they also demonstrate that the coffee chain's success was not predestined or guaranteed. In its past marketing efforts, Starbucks has made plenty of missteps, and likely will do so again. The goal, for Starbucks and for any great marketer, is to make sure that the value for customers is sufficient to overcome any stumbles, and then to work harder to avoid them.

### Questions

1. Visit the Starbucks website and list ways, beyond those mentioned in the case, in which it creates and provides value for customers.

2. What sorts of expansions seem most likely to benefit Starbucks in the future? Which seem riskiest?

3. How can Starbucks ensure that it continues to meet customers' expectations and needs? List some specific ways.

4. Visit the Starbucks website and identify its latest promotion. How does this promotion help create value for the customer and, ultimately, Starbucks?

5. Why can Starbucks charge so much for a latte when they are much less expensive at chains like Tim Hortons®?

# CHAPTER 2

**LEARNING OBJECTIVES**

After studying this chapter you should be able to

**LO1** Define a marketing strategy

**LO2** Describe the elements of a marketing plan

**LO3** Analyze a marketing situation using a SWOT analysis

**LO4** Explain how a firm chooses what consumer group(s) to pursue with its marketing efforts

**LO5** Outline the implementation of the marketing mix as a means to increase customer value

**LO6** Describe how firms grow their businesses

© Jing wei-Imaginechina/AP Images

# Developing Marketing Strategies and a Marketing Plan

For world-class athletes, the drive to improve is never-ending: They constantly train to run faster, hit harder, or complete more flips in the air. Victory is hard won but gratifying, and remaining at the top demands constant vigilance.

And so it is for Nike, a company dedicated to providing both top athletes and their casual counterparts with all the tools they need to compete at their highest levels. Nike's marketing strategy rests on several key points and concepts that spread throughout the company and influence everything it does. In particular, it constantly seeks to improve its own performance through innovation and in-depth analyses of its competitors. Sounds a little like the Olympics, doesn't it?

Created by runners in Oregon, Nike began in the early 1970s as an American company, focused mainly on the American market. Its first running shoes featured a then-innovative design with a waffle-patterned sole. The customers were mainly elite runners, determined to find the lightest shoe they could. But, as *Forrest Gump* demonstrated, running was also gaining popularity among casual athletes, and just like Forrest, many members of this community sported Nikes on their feet.

By 1984, the company had gone public, and it had found Michael Jordan. The entire market—and the very concept of sponsorship—changed forever. The Air Jordan line of basketball shoes turned Nike into a massive success, with broad appeal to sports fans of virtually all ages and profiles. Nike continues to affiliate with high-profile, elite basketball players, including NBA All-Stars such as Dwyane Wade and LeBron James.

Waffle-soled shoes and athletic partnerships sparked the notion of innovative ideas as the keys to victory. The company persists in introducing new and exciting concepts, at a rapid pace rarely matched by other firms. For example, Nike's partnership with Apple allows runners with the Nike+ Sensor inserted in their shoes to program their iPhones or iPods to play a collection of songs that matches their distance or time goals. The sensor also keeps track of their speed and distance, and Nike saves the data and provides platforms for social interactions among runners in the same area.

Going a step farther down the tech road, Nike also introduced the FuelBand, a flexible wrist monitor that keeps track of how much a person moves during the day. Even the most chair-bound office worker could determine if she had reached her goal of 10,000 steps per day by taking the stairs to go to lunch. The simple interface turned red if movement was insufficient and green when the goal was in reach. Nike also provided a means for users to share the Nike Fuel points they earned throughout the day online. Yet, in spite of reviews noting, "Nike has transformed itself into a digital force,"[1] the company abandoned the FuelBand when the Apple Watch was introduced.

Nike demonstrates innovation in another modern realm: creative sustainability. By paying attention to its broader environment, Nike recognized that it needed to be more environmentally conscious, for three main reasons. First, when resources become scarcer, competition for them increases, which means higher costs. Second, rising energy costs mean Nike's production costs would rise even further. Third, if it could divorce its own growth from reliance on such scarce resources, Nike realized that it would not be limited in its expansion.[2]

For example, it has changed the production process for its clothing lines to make it more environmentally efficient. Traditional fabric dyeing processes would use around 150 litres of water to process 1 kilogram of fabric. With its new ColorDry system, Nike not only eliminates water completely from the dyeing process but also reduces the chemicals needed and minimizes the amount of dye that gets wasted. Nike estimates that it reduces energy consumption by 63 percent.[3]

It has also completely revamped its shoe manufacturing process. To create the Flyknit Racer, Nike came up with not just a new shoe but an entirely new production method. Rather than stitching together pieces of prefabricated material to make the shoe's upper, the Flyknit process knits together polyester yarn. Each shoe uses only as much material as is required, can be adjusted regularly

The Nike FuelBand allowed athletes to track their workouts seamlessly.

© Bebeto Matthews/AP Images

(i.e., micro engineered) to improve fit or durability, and weighs in at nearly an ounce lighter than competitive running shoes.

These strategies clearly have been working. Nike's annual revenues have seen double-digit increases, with a five-year compounded growth rate of 11 percent.[4] Revenues rose to $32.4 billion in 2016, largely due to the company's strategic focus on innovation. Furthermore, its market share continues to increase, outpacing both the average growth of the market and its competitors' rates of growth.[5]

The significance of such stellar performance is not lost on some of the brand's most famous customers. Serena Williams—who has worn the company's products for years but who is also a clothing entrepreneur in her own right—notes that observing Nike has helped her realize "I'm not disrupting my brand enough. I need to do it more. Nike always tries to improve. They never say, 'I'm Number 1, and I'm happy.' They always say, 'How can we get better?' Beyond a company, beyond entrepreneurship, you can really take that attitude in your life, like, I want to be a great mother, or a great student, or a great doctor. What can I do to be better?"[6] ∎

In this chapter, we start by discussing marketing strategy, which outlines the specific actions a firm intends to implement to appeal to potential customers. Then we discuss how to create a marketing plan, which provides a blueprint for implementing the strategy. The chapter concludes with a discussion of strategies firms use to grow. Appendix 2A explains how to write a marketing plan and provides an annotated example.

## **LO1**  WHAT IS A MARKETING STRATEGY?

**marketing strategy**
Identifies a firm's target market(s), a related marketing mix—the four Ps, and the bases upon which the firm plans to build a sustainable competitive advantage.

**sustainable competitive advantage**
Something the firm can persistently do better than its competitors that is not easily copied and thus can be maintained over a long period of time.

A **marketing strategy** identifies (1) a firm's target market(s), (2) a related marketing mix—the four Ps, and (3) the bases upon which the firm plans to build a sustainable competitive advantage. A **sustainable competitive advantage** is an advantage over the competition that is not easily copied and thus can be maintained over a long period of time. A competitive advantage acts like a wall, or barrier, that the firm has built around its position in a market. This wall makes it hard for competitors to contact customers inside. Of course, if the marketer has built a wall around an attractive target market, competitors will attempt to break it down.

Nike's best competitive advantage is the result of its solid foundation of innovation, which has produced a strong brand and a loyal customer base. Customers know the Nike swoosh well and consider the brand as a first option when they need running, basketball, or even just casual athletic shoes. This appeal reflects Nike's careful targeting and marketing mix implementation. In terms of the four Ps, Nike is constantly trying to come up with new versions of its relatively basic products, namely, shoes and related apparel. To sell these varied products, it relies on multiple channels: online, in dedicated Nike stores and superstores, and through independent retailers such as Foot Locker. Its pricing spans a broad range, from lower end, simpler options for casual shoes to the most expensive, technically sophisticated, highly reputed lines associated with big-name athletes. And these popular athletes are central to its promotion efforts. Nike remains dominant in most athletic fields, and it feels confident about expanding further.

Likewise, Starbucks and Tim Hortons® have built solid foundations that appeal to different target markets. And so they implement their marketing mixes—the four Ps—in different ways, with very different marketing strategies. Although both stores' customers seek a good cup of coffee and a tasty pastry, Starbucks attempts to reach customers who want a coffee-drinking experience that includes a warm, social atmosphere and personable baristas to make their esoteric drinks. And people are willing to pay relatively high prices for this. Tim Hortons® customers, on the other hand, aren't particularly interested in having an experience. They just want a good-tasting cup of coffee at a fair price, and to get in and out of the store quickly.

There are four overarching strategies that focus on aspects of the marketing mix to create and deliver value and to develop sustainable competitive advantages, as we depict in Exhibit 2.1:[7]

- **Customer excellence:** Focuses on retaining loyal customers and excellent customer service.
- **Operational excellence:** Achieved through efficient operations and excellent supply chain and human resource management.
- **Product excellence:** Having products with high perceived value and effective branding and positioning.
- **Locational excellence:** Having a good physical location and Internet presence.

Foot Locker is one of many independent retailers that carry Nike shoes.
© Patrick T. Fallon/Bloomberg via Getty Images

**customer excellence**
Involves a focus on retaining loyal customers and excellent customer service.

**operational excellence**
Involves a focus on efficient operations and excellent supply chain management.

**product excellence**
Involves a focus on achieving high-quality products and effective branding and positioning.

**locational excellence**
Involves a focus on a good physical location and Internet presence.

## Customer Excellence

Customer excellence is achieved when a firm develops value-based strategies for retaining loyal customers and provides outstanding customer service.

**EXHIBIT 2.1**  Macro Strategies for Developing Customer Value

Customer Value

Customer Excellence

Operational Excellence

Locational Excellence

Product Excellence

### Retaining Loyal Customers

Sometimes, the methods a firm uses to maintain a sustainable competitive advantage help attract and maintain loyal customers. For instance, having a strong brand, unique merchandise, and superior customer service all help solidify a loyal customer base. However, having loyal customers is, in and of itself, an important method of sustaining an advantage over competitors.

Loyalty is more than simply preferring to purchase from one firm instead of another;[8] it means that customers are reluctant to patronize competitive firms. Loyal customers buy Nike apparel for all their sporting and casual needs, even if Adidas goes on sale or opens a new store right around the corner from their home.

More and more firms realize the value of achieving customer excellence through focusing their strategy on retaining their loyal customers. Nike doesn't think in terms of selling a single pair of fashionable shoes for $100; instead, it focuses on satisfying the customer who buys track shoes for herself, Cole-Haan dress shoes for her spouse, soccer shoes for her daughter, and basketball shoes for her son. Conservatively, she might buy five pairs of shoes every year for 20 years. She is not a $100 customer; combining all purchases for her family over the years, she is at least a $10,000 shoe customer—and that doesn't even count the shorts, shirts, and socks she adds on to her purchases. Viewing customers with a lifetime value perspective, rather than on a transaction-by-transaction basis, is key to modern customer retention programs.[9] We will examine how the lifetime value of a customer is calculated in Appendix 7A.

Marketers use several methods to build customer loyalty. With its long history in the sport, Adidas is clearly positioned as a provider of soccer cleats, far more so than Nike. That positioning helps explain why Nike might have bought Umbro. But Nike also left the Umbro brand name alone, so that it could continue to appeal to players of one of the fastest-growing sports in the world.

Another method of achieving customer loyalty is to create an emotional attachment through loyalty programs. Loyalty programs, which constitute part of an overall customer relationship management (CRM) program, prevail in many industries, from airlines to hotels to movie theatres to retail stores. The majority of Canadians belong to at least one loyalty program.[10] Although the benefits to consumers of loyalty programs are limited since only a small percentage of customers save enough points to claim their rewards, loyalty programs are a boon to marketers. With such programs, companies can combine membership data with customer purchase data to develop a deeper understanding of the customer. Companies often use this data to tailor their offerings to better meet the needs of their loyal customers. For instance, by analyzing their databases, financial institutions, such as Bank of Montreal, develop profiles of customers who have defected in the past and use that information to identify customers who may defect in the future. Once it identifies these customers, the firm can implement special retention programs to keep them.

### Providing Outstanding Customer Service

Marketers may also build sustainable competitive advantage by offering excellent customer service,[11] though consistently offering excellent service can prove difficult. Customer service is provided by employees, and invariably, humans are less consistent than machines. On every visit, for example, Starbucks must attempt to ensure that every single barista greets customers in a friendly way and makes drinks consistently. Firms that offer good customer service must instill its importance in their employees over a long period of time so that it becomes part of the organizational culture. Although it may take considerable time and effort to build a reputation for customer service, once a marketer has earned a good service reputation, it can sustain this advantage for a long time because a competitor is hard pressed to develop a comparable reputation.

Disney offers excellent examples of both of these types of customer excellence. First, Disney's "My Magic" system enables visitors to swipe their Magic Band wristbands to make purchases, open their hotel room door, get dinner reservations, or check in for rides, throughout the park and its grounds. The system also enables Disney to collect a remarkable amount of information about what each guest is doing, at virtually every moment of his or her visit to its theme parks.[12]

Second, its customer service is virtually unparalleled. Visitors to Disney parks are greeted by friendly staff who have been extensively trained to find ways to provide better service. The training includes information about how to recognize the signs that a visitor is lost, so the Disney employee can offer help locating a destination. It also highlights the need to communicate frequently and collaboratively about every aspect of the park, so a custodian at one end of the Magic Kingdom likely knows what time a restaurant on the other side opens.[13]

Disney's employees and cast members provide the highest level of customer service.

© Tao Images/age fotostock

## Operational Excellence

Firms achieve *operational excellence*, the second way to achieve a sustainable competitive advantage, through their efficient operations, excellent supply chain management, and strong relationships with their suppliers.

All marketers strive for efficient operations to get their customers the merchandise they want, when they want it, in the required quantities, and at a lower delivered cost than that of their competitors. By so doing, they ensure good value to their customers, earn profitability for themselves, and satisfy their customers' needs. In addition, efficient operations enable firms to provide their consumers with lower-priced merchandise. Even if their prices are not lower than those of the competition, they may use the additional margin they earn to attract customers away from competitors by offering even better service, merchandise assortments, or visual presentations.

Firms achieve efficiencies by developing sophisticated distribution and information systems as well as strong relationships with vendors. Like customer relationships, vendor relations must be developed over the long term and generally cannot be easily undermined by a competitor.[14] Furthermore, firms with strong relationships may gain exclusive rights to:

Amazon's Prime service offers two-day shipping so customers can get their order quickly.

Jonathan Weiss/Shutterstock.com

● sell merchandise in a particular region

● obtain special terms of purchase that are not available to competitors

● receive popular merchandise that may be in short supply

The supply chain for Amazon is innovative. Through its high-tech distribution centres, it can get products to customers quickly. Perhaps you have taken advantage of Amazon's Prime shipping program, offering free two-day shipping on all orders for $99 a year. You may even have paid for overnight delivery with Amazon, or if you live in one of the cities that offer it, you may have paid for same-day shipping. Attractive shipping options like these make it tough for other online retailers to compete.

## Product Excellence

Product excellence, the third way to achieve a sustainable competitive advantage, occurs by having products with high perceived value and effective branding and positioning. Some firms have difficulty developing a competitive advantage through their merchandise and service offerings, especially if competitors can deliver similar products or services easily. However, others have been able to maintain their sustainable competitive advantage by investing in their brand itself; positioning their product or service by using a clear, distinctive brand image; and constantly reinforcing that image through their merchandise, service, and promotion. For instance, RBC Financial Group, Shoppers Drug Mart, Bell, Tim Hortons®, Molson, and Loblaw are all leaders in their respective industries, at least in part because they have strong brands and a clear position in the marketplace.[15]

One of the world's leading consumer electronics brands, Apple overtook the mobile music market and displaced established market leaders, such as Sony, with its iPod and iTunes combination. Although critics claimed that there was nothing revolutionary about the iPod technology, the fact remains that Apple not only redesigned the mobile music device to make it an accessory that consumers felt proud to carry and display, but also revolutionized how music is purchased and consumed with its iTunes store. The iPhone and iPad have further consolidated Apple's brand image as a world-class innovative technology company with an enviable reputation for building high quality, well designed, and fashionable products. How did Apple come from behind to dislodge established market leaders and create such buzz around its technology? According to various reports, Apple's former CEO, Steve Jobs, saw Apple as a marketing company first. Understanding customer needs and satisfying those needs is what it does best. Technology comes second.

## Locational Excellence

Location is particularly important for retailers and service providers. Many say that the three most important things in retailing are location, location, location. Most people will not walk or drive very far when looking to buy a cup of coffee. A competitive advantage based on location is sustainable because it is not easily duplicated.

Tim Hortons® and Starbucks have developed a strong competitive advantage with their location selection. They have such a high density of stores in some markets that it is very difficult for a competitor to enter the market and find good locations. Of course, when McDonald's entered the fancy coffee drink battle, it did not need to worry too much about finding new locations; its stores already appeared nearly everywhere!

## Multiple Sources of Advantage

In most cases, however, a single strategy, such as low prices or excellent service, is not sufficient to build a sustainable competitive advantage. Firms require multiple approaches to build a wall around their position that stands as high as possible. For example, WestJet has achieved success by providing customers with good value that meets their expectations, offering good customer service, maintaining good customer relations, and offering great prices. The company has consistently positioned itself as a carrier that provides good service at a good value—customers get to their destination on time for a reasonable price. At the same time, its customers don't have extraordinary expectations and don't expect food service, seat assignments, or flights out of certain airports.[16] By fulfilling all of these strategies, WestJet has developed a huge cadre of loyal customers and has built a very formidable barrier around its position as the value player in the Canadian airline industry.

WestJet Airlines provides good service at a good price—a good value—and has fun doing it!

Richard Lam/The Canadian Press

# THE MARKETING PLAN

**LO2**

Effective marketing doesn't just happen. Firms such as Tim Hortons®, The Bay, and Nike carefully plan their marketing strategies to react to changes in the environment, the competition, and their customers by creating a marketing plan. A marketing plan is a written document composed of an analysis of the current marketing situation, opportunities and threats for the firm, marketing objectives and strategy specified in terms of the four Ps, action programs, and projected or pro forma income (and other financial) statements.[17] The three major phases of the marketing plan are planning, implementation, and control.[18]

Although most people do not have a written plan that outlines what they are planning to accomplish in the next year, and how they expect to do it, firms do need such a document. It is important that everyone involved in implementing the plan knows what the overall objectives for the firm are and how they will be met. Other stakeholders, such as investors and potential investors, also want to know what the firm plans to do. A written marketing plan also provides a reference point for evaluating whether or not the firm met its objectives.

A marketing plan entails five steps, depicted in Exhibit 2.2. The first two steps are in the **planning phase.** In Step 1, marketing executives and other top managers define the mission and objectives of the business. In Step 2, they evaluate the situation by assessing how various players, both inside and outside the organization, affect the firm's potential for success. There are two steps in the **implementation phase.** In Step 3, marketing managers identify and evaluate different opportunities by engaging in a process known as segmentation, targeting, and positioning (STP). Then, in Step 4, they implement the marketing mix by using the four Ps. Finally, Step 5, the **control phase,** entails evaluating the performance of the marketing strategy by using marketing metrics and taking any necessary corrective actions.

As indicated in Exhibit 2.2, it is not always necessary to go through the entire process for every evaluation (Step 5). For instance, a firm could evaluate its performance in Step 5, and then go directly to Step 2 to conduct a situation analysis without redefining its overall mission.

We will first discuss each step involved in developing a marketing plan. Then we consider ways of analyzing a marketing situation, as well as identifying and evaluating marketing opportunities. We also examine some specific strategies marketers use to grow a business. Finally, we consider how the implementation of the marketing mix increases customer value. A sample marketing plan outline and a marketing plan are provided in Appendix 2A, following this chapter.

**planning phase**
Where marketing executives and other top managers define the mission and objectives of the business, and evaluate the situation by assessing how various players, both inside and outside the organization, affect the firm's potential for success.

**implementation phase**
Where marketing managers identify and evaluate different opportunities by engaging in a process known as segmentation, targeting, and positioning. They then develop and implement the marketing mix by using the four Ps.

**control phase**
The part of the strategic marketing planning process when managers evaluate the performance of the marketing strategy and take any necessary corrective actions.

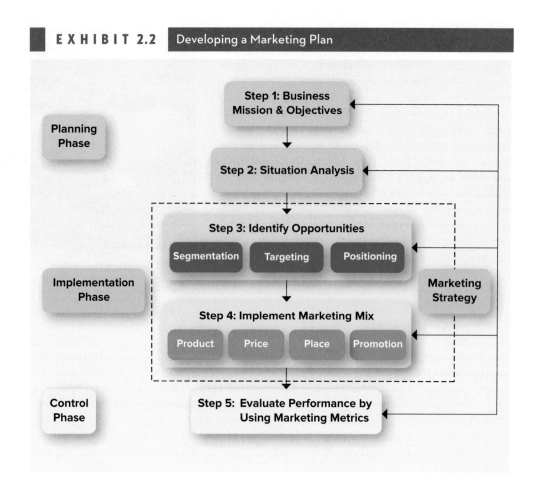

**EXHIBIT 2.2** | Developing a Marketing Plan

## Step 1: Define the Business Mission and Objectives

**mission statement**
A broad description of a firm's objectives and the scope of activities it plans to undertake; attempts to answer two main questions: What type of business is it? and What does it need to do to accomplish its goals and objectives?

The **mission statement,** a broad description of a firm's objectives and the scope of activities it plans to undertake,[19] attempts to answer two main questions: What type of business are we? and What do we need to do to accomplish our goals and objectives? These fundamental business issues must be answered at the highest corporate levels before marketing executives can get involved. Most firms want to maximize shareholders' wealth by increasing the value of the firm's stock and paying dividends.[20] However, owners of small, privately held firms frequently have other objectives, such as achieving a specific level of income and avoiding risks, while not-for-profit organizations set non-monetary objectives. (See Exhibit 2.3 for several mission statement examples.)

Non-profit organizations, such as the Heart and Stroke Foundation, specify non-monetary objectives such as improving the health of Canadians through research, health promotion, and advocacy. The Tim Hortons® mission is very focused: delivering superior quality products and services to customers and being the quality leader in what it does.[21] Nike's and Adidas's mission statements are sufficiently broad to encompass the diversity and global nature of their businesses. For all these organizations, marketing holds the primary responsibility of enhancing the value of the company's products for its customers and other constituents, whether or not the company pursues profit. Another key goal or objective often embedded in a mission statement is how the firm is building a sustainable competitive advantage.

**EXHIBIT 2.3**    Mission Statements

**Nike**'s mission is "to bring inspiration and innovation to every athlete* in the world." (With its asterisk, it defines an athlete by quoting one of its founders: "If you have a body, you are an athlete.")

**Adidas**'s mission states that "The adidas group strives to be the global leader in the sporting goods industry with brands built on a passion for sport and a sporting lifestyle."

**The Heart and Stroke Foundation** mission is to improve the health of Canadians by preventing and reducing disability and death from heart disease and stroke through research, health promotion, and advocacy.

**Tim Hortons**® states, "Our guiding mission is to deliver superior quality products and services for our customers and communities through leadership, innovation and partnerships. Our vision is to be the quality leader in everything we do."

*Sources:* "Nike's Mission Statement," http://help-en-us.nike.com/app/answers/detail/a_id/113/p/3897; "Adidas Group Annual Report," http://careers.adidas-group.com/mission-and-values.aspx; "About Us," www.heartandstrokefoundation.ca; "Company Facts," www.timhortons.com/ca/en/about/2908.html.

## Step 2: Conduct a Situation Analysis

**L03**

After developing its mission, a firm next must perform a **situation analysis,** using a **SWOT** analysis that assesses both the internal environment with regard to its **s**trengths and **w**eaknesses (internal analysis) and the external environment in terms of its **o**pportunities and **t**hreats (external analysis). Situation analysis also includes an examination of market trends, customer analysis, and competitive analysis. Additionally, the firms should assess the opportunities and uncertainties of the marketplace due to changes in **c**ultural, **d**emographic, **s**ocial, **t**echnological, **e**conomic, and **p**olitical forces (CDSTEP). These factors are discussed in Chapter 3. With this information, firms can anticipate and interpret change, and then allocate appropriate resources.

A SWOT analysis is designed to help the firm determine areas in which it is strong and can compete effectively, and areas where it is weak and vulnerable to competitive attacks. It also enables the firm to understand where it has sustainable competitive advantage or unique advantages that cannot be easily copied by competitors and how it can

**situation analysis (SWOT)**
The second step in a marketing plan; uses a SWOT analysis that assesses both the internal environment with regard to its **s**trengths and **w**eaknesses and the external environment in terms of its **o**pportunities and **t**hreats.

Both Nike's and Adidas's ads reflect their mission statements. Nike's ads (left) consistently inspire athletes to excel; Adidas's ads (right) emphasize passion for sports.

(left): © Matthew Chattle/Alamy Stock Photos; (right): © Stephen Shaver/Bloomberg via Getty Images

leverage those advantages in response to new opportunities arising from changes in its external environment. By understanding its competitive strengths and weaknesses, the firm will be better positioned to address weaknesses and deal with threats arising from its external business environment. A SWOT analysis requires the firm to undertake a critical assessment of its resources, capabilities, organization, strategies, and performance in relation to competitors. Similarly, the firm must conduct a careful analysis of changes in the environment and understand how they affect its business, whether they represent threats or opportunities. Strengths and weaknesses are within the control of the firm, and it can take actions to alleviate weaknesses and consolidate its strengths. Opportunities and threats are outside the control of the firm; therefore, the firm can decide only how it wants to respond.

Exhibit 2.4 lists several general elements that are usually examined when conducting a SWOT analysis. The relevance of specific elements will depend on the nature of the firm. This list is for illustration purposes and is by no means exhaustive.

Consider how Nike might conduct a SWOT analysis as outlined in Exhibit 2.5. We focus on Nike here, but we also recognize that its marketing managers might find it helpful to perform parallel analyses for competitors, such as Adidas. Because a company's strengths (Exhibit 2.5, upper left) refer to the positive internal attributes of the firm, in this example we might include Nike's great brand recognition and the visibility of the celebrities who wear its products. Furthermore, its  Nike+ iPod, FuelBand and Flyknit were the first of their kind, continuing the innovative tradition that has marked Nike since it first came up with waffle-soled running shoes. Its name recognition makes consumers more likely to try out these innovations when they appear on the market—especially when they see their favourite athlete wearing similar apparel on the court or on the field.

Yet every firm has its weaknesses, and Nike is no exception. Weaknesses (Exhibit 2.5, upper right) are negative attributes of the firm. Nike relies heavily—perhaps even too heavily—on its athletic shoe lines, especially for running and basketball.

---

**EXHIBIT 2.4**   Examples of Elements Considered in a SWOT Analysis

| Environment | Evaluation | |
|---|---|---|
| | **Positive** | **Negative** |
| **Internal** | **Strengths** | **Weaknesses** |
| | • Superior resources and capabilities | • Little or no brand recognition |
| | • Superior management, marketing, technical talent | • Lack of financial resources |
| | • Strong brand | • Lack of other resources and capabilities |
| | • Superior product offerings | • Lack of marketing, management, and technical talent |
| | • Extensive marketing reach | • Limited market reach or distribution network |
| | • Wide distribution networks (national/global) | • No proprietary technology |
| | • Strong financial resources | • Poor location |
| | • Excellent geographic location | • Limited customer base or loyalty |
| | • Proprietary technologies/intellectual property | • Lack of credibility |
| | • Strong base of loyal customers | |
| **External** | **Opportunities** | **Threats** |
| | • CDSTEP changes that offer opportunities for the firm to serve new markets with existing products and/or pursue completely new market opportunities | • Political or regulatory changes (e.g., new laws affecting business or products) |
| | • Existing firms exit the market because of financial or other difficulties (i.e., reduced competition) | • New entrants into the industry or market |
| | • Acquiring another firm and gaining market access, new customers, new technology and expertise, and financial resources | • New technology that could render existing technology or business practices obsolete |
| | | • Natural or human-made disasters |
| | | • Recession or economic downturn that affects consumers' purchasing power and confidence |
| | | • Changes in sociocultural or demographic trends |

| | Environment | Evaluation | |
|---|---|---|---|
| | | **Positive** | **Negative** |
| **Nike** | **Internal** | **Strengths**<br>• Strong brand<br>• Strong celebrity endorsers<br>• Innovative products | **Weakness**<br>• Overreliance on footwear |
| | **External** | **Opportunities**<br>• Emerging countries<br>• Other fashion segments | **Threats**<br>• Cheaper imports<br>• Imitation products<br>• Retail becoming price competitive |
| **Adidas** | **Internal** | **Strengths**<br>• Strong brand<br>• Portfolio of brands<br>• Strong global presence | **Weakness**<br>• Management of numerous brands |
| | **External** | **Opportunity**<br>• Emerging countries | **Threats**<br>• Cheaper imports<br>• Imitation products<br>• Recessionary forces |

**EXHIBIT 2.5** SWOT Analysis for Nike Versus Adidas

It also aligns itself closely with the athletes who serve as its brand ambassadors, highlighting them as "heroes." But on multiple occasions these athletes have become embroiled in scandals that were embarrassing and potentially damaging to the brand. Furthermore, in response to the popular emergence of other options, such as "toning" and "barefoot" models, Nike has largely suggested they are fads that will not last, stressing instead its traditional athletic shoe models and innovating new forms.[22]

Opportunities (Exhibit 2.5, lower left) pertain to positive aspects of the external environment. Among Nike's opportunities, it appears determined to pursue dominance in other, sometime niche, sports markets. For the Olympic Games, it introduced footwear for less familiar sports, including fencing, wrestling, and equestrian events.[23] This goal also aligns with another notable opportunity for Nike, that is, growth in global markets. It sells products in 170 countries worldwide, through independent distributors, Nike stores, the website, and licences.[24] It aims to expand further, and it has devoted significant resources to improving its prominence among European football players and fans.[25]

Finally, threats (Exhibit 2.5, lower right) represent the negative aspects of the company's external environment. For example, its widespread market dominance makes Nike the primary target for all its competitors,[26] from Adidas to New Balance to Li Ning, China's largest shoe maker. All of these firms want to take market share from Nike, which means the company must constantly be a little bit on the defensive. Furthermore, as Nike itself acknowledges: "The intense competition and the rapid changes in technology and consumer preferences in the

Nike's strengths include its innovative product tradition. It introduced the Nike+ iPod sensor that, when inserted into shoes, gives the runner instant feedback about running time, distance, pace, and calories burned.

© Bongarts/Getty Images Publicity/Getty Images for Nike

markets for athletic and leisure footwear and apparel, and athletic equipment, constitute significant risk factors in our operations."[27]

## Step 3: Identify and Evaluate Opportunities by Using STP (Segmentation, Targeting, and Positioning)

After completing the situation analysis, the next step is to identify and evaluate opportunities for increasing sales and profits by using **STP** (segmentation, targeting, and positioning). With STP, the firm must first understand customer needs and wants through market research, then divide the market or customers into distinct subgroups or segments, determine which of those segments it should pursue or target, and finally decide how it should position its products and services to best meet the needs of those chosen targets. The criteria to evaluate target segments are discussed in detail in Chapter 6.

**Segmentation**   Many types of customers appear in any market, and most firms cannot satisfy everyone's needs. For instance, among Internet users, some users do research online, some shop, some look for entertainment, and many do all three. Each of these groups might be a **market segment** consisting of consumers who respond similarly to a firm's marketing efforts. The process of dividing the market into distinct groups of customers where each individual group has similar needs, wants, or characteristics—who therefore might appreciate products or services geared especially for them in similar ways—is called **market segmentation.** Let's look at Hertz, the car rental company. The example in Exhibit 2.6 reveals that one of the Hertz segments is the Adrenaline Collection, which includes the Corvette ZHZ and Chevrolet Camaro, targeting single people wanting to have a bit of fun. Its Prestige Collection, featuring the Cadillac Escalade and Infiniti QX56, targets business customers and families who prefer a luxurious ride. With its Green Collection of cars such as the Toyota Prius and Ford Fusion, Hertz appeals to environmentally conscious customers. It also offers commercial vans for service customers.[28] Note that Hertz uses a variety of demographic factors—gender, age, income, interests—to identify customers who might want the Adrenaline, Prestige, and Green Collections. But it also applies psychographic or behavioural factors, such as a need to move possessions across town, to identify likely consumers of its commercial vans. Firms may also segment consumers based on benefits sought or geographic factors, which will be discussed in Chapter 6.

Going back to our Nike example, we can see that it segments customers based on gender and how the products are used. Nike focuses on the following segments: men's training, women's training, running, basketball, football (soccer), action sports, sportswear, and golf.

**STP**
The processes of segmentation, targeting, and positioning that firms use to identify and evaluate opportunities for increasing sales and profits.

**market segment**
A group of consumers who respond similarly to a firm's marketing efforts.

**market segmentation**
The process of dividing the market into distinct groups of customers—where each individual group has similar needs, wants, or characteristics—who therefore might appreciate products or services geared especially for them in similar ways.

**EXHIBIT 2.6**     **Hertz Market Segmentation**

|  | Segment 1 | Segment 2 | Segment 3 | Segment 4 | Segment 5 |
|---|---|---|---|---|---|
| **Segments** | Single thrill seekers and gear heads on vacation | Business customers and families who prefer a luxurious ride | Environmentally conscious customers | Families | Commercial customers |
|  | Adrenaline Collection | Prestige Collection | Green Collection | SUV/ crossover/4 × 4 | Commercial van/ truck |
| **Cars Offered** | Corvette ZHZ | Infiniti QX56 | Toyota Prius | Toyota Rav 4 | Ford cargo van |
|  | Chevrolet Camaro | Cadillac Escalade | Ford Fusion | Ford Explorer |  |

Hertz targets several markets. Its "Green Collection" (left) appeals to environmentally conscious consumers; its "SUV Collection" (right) appeals to families

(left): Teddy Leung/Shutterstock.com; (right): Teddy Leung/Shutterstock.com

**Targeting**    After a firm has identified the various market segments it might pursue, it evaluates each segment's attractiveness and decides which to pursue by using a process known as **target marketing** or **targeting.** For example, Hertz realizes that its primary appeal for the SUV Collection centres on young families, so the bulk of its marketing efforts for this business are directed toward that group. Similarly, soft drink manufacturers also divide their markets into submarkets or segments. Coca-Cola, for instance, makes several different types of Coke, including regular, Coke II, and Cherry Coke. Among its diet colas, it targets Coke Zero to men and Diet Coke to women because men prefer not to be associated with diets. It also markets Sprite to those who don't like dark colas, Fruitopia and Minute Maid to more health-conscious consumers, and Dasani bottled water to purists.

**target marketing/ targeting**
The process of evaluating the attractiveness of various segments and then deciding which to pursue as a market.

**Positioning**    Finally, when the firm decides which segments to pursue, it must determine how it wants to be positioned within those segments. **Market positioning** involves the process of defining the marketing mix variables so that target customers have a clear, distinct, desirable understanding of what the product does or represents in comparison with competing products. Hertz positions itself as a quality car (and truck) rental company that is the first choice for each of its target segments. In its marketing communications, it stresses that customers will get peace of mind when they rent from Hertz, the market leader in the car rental business, and will be able to enjoy their journey (e.g., leisure consumers) and reduce travel time (e.g., business consumers).

**market positioning**
Involves the process of defining the marketing mix variables so that target customers have a clear, distinct, desirable understanding of what the product does or represents in comparison with competing products.

To segment the coffee drinker market, Starbucks uses a variety of methods, including geography (e.g., college campuses versus shopping/business districts) and benefits (e.g., drinkers of caffeinated versus decaffeinated products). After determining which of those segments represent effective targets, Starbucks positions itself as a firm that develops a variety of products that match the wants and needs of the different market segments—espresso drinks, coffees, teas, bottled drinks, pastries, and cooler foods.

After identifying its target segments, a firm must evaluate each of its strategic opportunities. A method of examining which segments to pursue is described in the Growth Strategies section later in the chapter. Firms are typically most successful when they focus on opportunities that build on their strengths relative to those of their competition. In Step 4 of the marketing plan, the firm implements its marketing mix and allocates resources to different products and services.

## Step 4: Implement Marketing Mix and Allocate Resources    **L05**

When the firm has identified and evaluated different growth opportunities by performing an STP analysis, the real action begins. The company has decided what to do, how to do it, and how many resources the firm should allocate to it. In the fourth step of

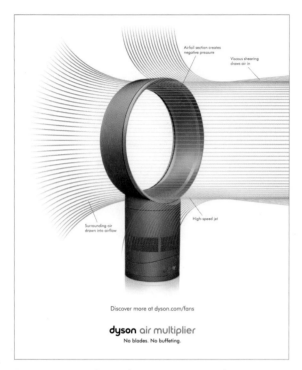

Discover more at dyson.com/fans

**dyson** air multiplier
No blades. No buffeting.

Dyson creates value with its innovative products.

Used with permission of Dyson, Inc.

the planning process, marketers implement the marketing mix—product, price, promotion, and place—for each product and service on the basis of what the company believes its target markets will value (Exhibit 2.7). At the same time, it makes important decisions about how it will allocate its scarce resources to its various products and services. Each element of the four Ps must be fully integrated to achieve a coherent strategy.

**Product and Value Creation**    Products, which include services, constitute the first of the four Ps. Because the key to the success of any marketing program is the creation of value, firms attempt to develop products and services that customers perceive as valuable enough to buy. Dyson fans and space heaters draw in and redirect surrounding air without potentially dangerous or fast spinning blades or visible heating elements. Although more expensive than conventional fans and space heaters, these sculpturally beautiful appliances are perceived by consumers to be a valuable alternative to products that haven't significantly changed since the early 1900s. You'll learn more about product and branding decisions in Chapters 8 and 9.

**Price and Value for Money**    The second element of the marketing mix is price. As part of the exchange process, a firm provides a product or a service, or some combination thereof, and in return it receives money. Value-based marketing requires that firms charge a price that customers perceive as giving them good value for the products and services they receive. It is important for a firm to have a clear focus in terms of what products to sell, where to buy them, and what methods to use in selling them. Pricing is the only activity that actually brings in money by generating revenues. If a price is set too high, it will not generate much volume. If a price is set too low, it may result in lower-than-necessary margins and profits. Therefore, marketers should base price on the value that the customer perceives. Dyson fans retail for $150 or more while conventional fans retail for around $25. Customers thus can decide just what they want from their fan and choose the one at the price they prefer. Pricing decisions and strategies are discussed in detail in Chapter 11.

**EXHIBIT 2.7**    Developing the Marketing Mix

**Place and Value Delivery**    For the third P, place, the firm must be able to make the product or service readily accessible when and where the customer wants it. Consider Lee Valley Tools, a small Ottawa-based company and one of the world's leading Internet and retail suppliers of innovative woodworking and gardening tools. The company was founded more than 40 years ago as a catalogue mail-order supplier of woodworking and gardening tools by entrepreneur Leonard Lee. Over the years, Lee has opened 19 stores across Canada and launched a fully functional ecommerce website, www.leevalley.com. To make its products and services accessible to all of its customers, Lee Valley has integrated its stores and catalogue operations with its online presence and used place to create value in its delivery process. Through its website, Lee Valley is able to reach a wider market segment more efficiently and cost-effectively. Thus, Lee Valley turned the integration of its different channels into a seamless customer experience, a key value driver for the company.[29] Chapters 12 and 13 deal with in-depth place, or distribution, decisions. Although many companies have developed sophisticated website and online marketing strategies to deliver place value for their customers, the same cannot be said for non-profit organizations.

**Promotion and Value Communication**   The fourth P of the marketing mix is promotion. Marketers communicate the value of their offering, or the value proposition, to their customers through a variety of media, including TV, radio, magazines, buses, trains, blimps, sales promotion, publicity, the sales force, and the Internet. It is now possible for firms in out-of-the-way locations to expand their market area to the whole world. For example, Canadians living in such places as Africa, Australia, and New Zealand can order their favourite sporting good products through the Mountain Equipment Co-Op website, www.mec.ca. Daily deal websites such as Groupon or LivingSocial offer another way to get the word out. Many smaller companies find that these sites give them greater name recognition than they ever could have achieved on their own. Retailers add value to their offerings through their efficient and effective communications strategies, which will be discussed in more detail in Chapters 14, 15, and 16.

Marketers must consider the most efficient and effective methods to communicate with their customers. This goes back to understanding customers, the value created, and the message being communicated. An increasing number of companies are using the Internet and their own websites to advertise and communicate with their customers and build closer relationships. For example, apart from enabling customers to order tools through its website, Lee Valley uses it to tell customers of upcoming training seminars that are held in its physical stores. These seminars teach customers about the use and care of the tools and demonstrate new, innovative tools being developed. The website also contains a variety of technical articles on woodworking and gardening that help customers learn more and enjoy their favourite activities. The regular enewsletter, which customers sign up for, provides technical information, trade-show dates, company news, special event dates, and other topics of interest to woodworkers and gardeners. Customers can even send letters about their experiences with specific tools, which are posted publicly on the company's website. Lee Valley is building loyal customer relationships one customer at a time.

In addition to developing the four Ps and allocating resources, marketing managers must develop schedules—timelines for each activity and the personnel responsible for the respective activity—to avoid bottlenecks and ensure smooth and timely implementation of the marketing mix activities. Also, marketers must determine who will be responsible for putting the plan into action. In most established companies, the marketing organization already exists and marketing managers must simply assign responsibilities to various employees within the marketing department. The marketing organization is usually responsible for the day-to-day operational decisions involved in executing the plan.

## Step 5: Evaluate Performance by Using Marketing Metrics

The final step in the planning process includes evaluating the results of the strategy and implementation program by using marketing metrics. A metric

Customers purchase Lee Valley woodworking and gardening tools by catalogue, by phone, online, or in store.

Used with permission of Lee Valley Tools Ltd.

The Salvation Army is one of a few not-for-profit organizations that leverage the Internet effectively.

Mark Abraham/The Canadian Press

is a measuring system that quantifies a trend, dynamic, or characteristic. Metrics are used to explain why things happened and to project the future. They make it possible to compare results across regions, business units, product lines, and time periods. The firm can determine why it achieved or did not achieve its performance goals with the help of these metrics. Understanding the causes of the performance—regardless of whether that performance exceeded, met, or fell below the firm's goals—enables firms to make appropriate adjustments.

Typically, managers begin by reviewing the implementation programs, and their analysis may indicate that the strategy (or even the mission statement) needs to be reconsidered. Problems can arise both when firms successfully implement poor strategies and when they poorly implement good strategies.

### Who Is Accountable for Performance?

At each level of an organization, the business unit and its manager should be held accountable only for the revenues, expenses, and profits that they can control. Expenses that affect several levels of the organization, such as the labour and capital expenses associated with operating a corporate headquarters, shouldn't be arbitrarily assigned to lower levels. In the case of a store, for example, it may be appropriate to evaluate performance objectives based on sales, sales associate productivity, and energy costs. If the corporate office lowers prices to get rid of merchandise and therefore profits suffer, then it's not fair to assess a store manager's performance based on the resulting decline in store profit.

Performance evaluations are used to pinpoint problem areas. Reasons that performance may be above or below planned levels must be examined. If a manager's performance is below planned levels, was it because the sales force didn't do an adequate job, because the economy took a downward turn, because competition successfully implemented a new strategy, or because the managers involved in setting the objectives aren't very good at making estimates? The manager should be held accountable only in the case of the inadequate sales force job or setting inappropriate forecasts.

When it appears that actual performance is going to be below the plan because of circumstances beyond the manager's control, the firm can still take action to minimize the harm. For example, the cereal industry has been beset by a wealth of setbacks due to trends in the wider consumer environment. People seek to cut carbohydrates out of their diets, but cereal is mostly carbs. Many consumers are recognizing their allergies to gluten, but many cereals include wheat as a main ingredient. In response, the largest cereal maker, General Mills (GM), has called on its competitors to step up their marketing efforts to save the industry. Leading the way, it increased its advertising budget by 7 percent and initiated promotional discounts on some of its most popular cereal brands, including Cheerios.[30]

In cases like this, marketing managers must ask themselves several relevant questions: How quickly were plans adjusted? How rapidly and appropriately were pricing and promotional policies modified? In short, did the manager react to salvage an adverse situation, or did those reactions worsen the situation?

### Performance Objectives and Metrics

Many factors contribute to a firm's overall performance, which makes it hard to find a single metric to evaluate performance. One approach is to compare a firm's performance over time or to competing firms, using common financial metrics such as sales and profits. Another method of assessing performance is to view the firm's products or services as a portfolio. Depending on the firm's relative performance, the profits from some products or services are used to fuel growth for others.

With its extensive data, Google claims that it can use a combination of metrics to predict the performance of a major motion picture, up to a month prior to the date it opens in theatres. Using search volume for the movie title in combination with several other metrics, such as the season and whether the movie is a sequel, Google promises a 94 percent accurate prediction of box office performance. Other proprietary metrics include the volume of clicks on search ads. If, for example, one movie prompted 20,000 more paid clicks than another film, it is expected to bring in approximately $7.5 million more in revenues during its opening weekend.

Beyond the implications for opening weekend, Google asserts that weekday searches in the weeks leading up to the release offer better predictors of continued revenues. That is, if a film fan searches for a movie title on a Tuesday, she or he is more likely to hold off on seeing the movie, rather than rushing out during opening weekend.[31]

**Financial Performance Metrics**   Some commonly used metrics to assess performance include revenues, or sales, and profits. For instance, sales are a global measure of a firm's activity level. A manager could easily increase sales by lowering prices, but the profit realized on that merchandise (gross margin) would suffer as a result. Clearly, an attempt to maximize one metric may lower another. Managers must therefore understand how their actions affect multiple performance metrics. It's usually unwise to use only one metric because it rarely tells the whole story. As Ethical Dilemma 2.1 details, focusing too much on financial metrics could be deadly, especially if it means ignoring measures reflecting labour safety.

In addition to assessing the absolute level of sales and profits, a firm may wish to measure the relative level of sales and profits. For example, a relative metric of sales or

## Ethical Dilemma 2.1

# The High Cost of Lowering Costs[32]

When observers assess flexible, global, rapid supply chains, they tend to rely on financial metrics and focus on the benefits: Effective supply chains help multinational retailers get the merchandise that customers want on the shelves when they want it, usually at much lower production costs. In turn, they lower prices for customers. As a result, the firm enjoys higher profits by selling more of a product that cost it less to produce. Such supply chains also encourage the sort of innovation that induces the fast-changing fashion industry or makes the average life cycle of consumer electronics products run less than eight months, which can be good for economies overall, as people buy more stuff more frequently.

But flexible, global, rapid supply chains also require suppliers to find ways to work faster and more efficiently, even if that sometimes means putting workers' health, safety, and even lives at risk. In April 2013 the Rana Plaza in Bangladesh collapsed, killing more than 1,100 garment workers—the deadliest disaster in the history of an industry that has never been known for great working conditions.

It might be easy to assume that the terrible events are simply evidence of poor oversight in Bangladesh, where a fire in November 2012 also killed more than 100 factory workers. But some of the companies that had outsourced their manufacturing to Rana Plaza had corporate codes in place, mandating safe working conditions. They also checked some of the factories for their compliance with the codes. The remarkable news is that at least two of the factories that were located in Rana Plaza had passed recent safety audits—when they clearly were unsafe.

For international firms, this situation is unsettling. If they implement corporate codes of conduct for their suppliers, then use predetermined metrics to monitor those suppliers, yet still face controversy, what further

steps can they take to protect the people who make the products they sell? One option is to work more closely with suppliers, rather than just auditing them. Big multinationals also could simply pay for safety improvements in their factories all over the world.

Another argument suggests that changing safety standards ultimately will require government intervention, because an efficient supply chain will never prioritize costly preventative moves to increase worker safety. Performance metrics almost automatically prioritize the financial side. To shift the focus to worker safety in Bangladesh, for example, the central government announced a cooperative effort with the International Labour Organization to enforce labour standards.

Ultimately, the responsibility may be the consumers'. As long as buyers demand low-priced products rather than responsible supply chains, that's what they will get.

The garment factory collapse in Bangladesh was a great tragedy that forced international firms to improve working conditions.
© Abir Abdullah/EPA/Newscom

| EXHIBIT 2.8 | Performance Metrics: Nike Versus Adidas | | | |
|---|---|---|---|---|
| | | **2014** | **2015** | **%Change** |
| **Nike** | Net Sales | $27.8B | $30.6B | 10% |
| | Net Profit | $2.7B | $3.3B | 22% |
| | Net Profit/Net Sales | 10% | 10.8% | |
| **Adidas** | Net Sales | €2.14B | €2.4B | 12% |
| | Net Profit | €0.18B | €0.64B | 256% |
| | Net Profit/Net Sales | 8.4% | 2.7% | |

profits is its increase or decrease over the prior year. Additionally, a firm may compare its growth in sales or profits relative to other benchmark companies (e.g., Nike may compare itself to Adidas).

The metrics used to evaluate a firm vary depending on (1) the level of the organization at which the decision is made and (2) the resources the manager controls. For example, while the top executives of a firm have control over all of the firm's resources and resulting expenses, a regional sales manager has control over only the sales and expenses generated by his or her salespeople.

Let's look at Nike's sales revenue and profits (after taxes) and compare them with those of Adidas (Exhibit 2.8).

As corporate consciousness of the importance of social responsibility grows, firms are starting to report corporate social responsibility metrics in major areas, such as their impact on the environment, their ability to diversify their workforce, their energy conservation initiatives, and their policies on protecting the human rights of their employees and the employees of their suppliers.

**Social Responsibility Performance Metrics** As Canadian companies become more convinced of the importance of social responsibility, we will likely see an increasing number of companies reporting corporate social responsibility metrics, such as their impact on the environment, their ability to diversify their workforce, their energy conservation initiatives, and their policies on protecting the human rights of their employees and the employees of their suppliers. Sustainable Marketing 2.1 presents an example that illustrates the importance of having such performance metrics.

## Strategic Planning Is Not Sequential

The planning process in Exhibit 2.2 suggests that managers follow a set sequence when they make strategic decisions. Namely, after they've defined the business mission, they perform the situation analysis; identify opportunities; evaluate alternatives; set objectives; allocate resources; develop the implementation plan; and, finally, evaluate their performance and make adjustments. But actual planning processes can move back and forth among these steps. For example, a situation analysis may uncover a logical alternative, even though this alternative might not be included in the mission statement, which would mean that the mission statement would need to be revised. Or, the development of the implementation plan might reveal that insufficient resources have been allocated to a particular product for it to achieve its objective. In that case, the firm would need to either change the objective or increase the resources; alternatively, the marketer might consider not investing in the product at all.

Now that we have gone through the steps of the strategic marketing planning process, let's look at some strategies that have been responsible for making many marketing firms successful. First we look at portfolio analysis, and then some product-market growth strategies.

## Sustainable Marketing 2.1

### Reputation Management— Organizing for Sustainability[33]

Many executives today see sustainability as an integral part of their marketing strategy. At the same time, sustainability presents its share of challenges. Companies that make sustainability programs a priority must ensure that these initiatives are aligned with their mission and business goals. And they have to address accountability by putting the appropriate measures and staff in place. Many companies still struggle with program execution.

A truly comprehensive and proactive approach to sustainability requires businesses to develop practices and policies around three perspectives: environmental, governance, and social. This means that sustainability practices and policies must be embedded in all facets of the organization, from human resource management to manufacturing, marketing, production, planning, investments, and corporate strategy. Also, sustainability must involve all employees, from the CEO to the employee on the shop floor. Implementing a comprehensive sustainability program is quite expensive and therefore many businesses tend to do the bare minimum or implement low-cost programs. In fact, according to a McKinsey

Global Survey, 36 percent of executives believe that the main benefit of sustainability is that it improves corporate and brand reputation, while less than 20 percent believe that it improves operational efficiency, lowers costs, presents growth opportunities (new markets and products), or strengthens competitive position.

Reputation management as an outcome of sustainability programs is seen as representing higher value-creation potential to companies than reducing energy use or reducing waste. However, while reputation management is seen as important, it can be difficult to define. Companies are beginning to incorporate activities into key organizational processes. Some of these activities include external reporting to stakeholders and consumers, policy implementation around ethical issues, participation in sustainability-focused organizations, and making investments in communities where they operate.

Sustainability leaders foster an organizational culture that sets a direction for their programs. They also set clear strategies and measurable targets. As sustainability continues to grow in importance, more companies will focus on performance management, with metrics to measure results, ensuring that their reputation does not suffer.

---

**Portfolio Analysis**   In portfolio analysis, for example, management evaluates the firm's various products and businesses—its "portfolio"—and allocates resources according to which products are expected to be the most profitable for the firm in the future. Portfolio analysis is typically performed at the **strategic business unit (SBU)** or **product line** level of the firm, though managers can also use it to analyze brands or even individual items. A strategic business unit is a division of the company that can be managed somewhat independently from other divisions since it markets a specific set of products to a clearly defined group of customers. For example, Loblaw Companies Limited consists of its general merchandise, drugstores, President's Choice brand, and financial products and services operations.[34] Each of these is an SBU. A product line, in contrast, is a group of products that consumers may use together or perceive as similar in some way. There are several product lines within Loblaw's PC Financial SBU: PC banking, PC MasterCard, mortgages, and insurance.

**strategic business unit (SBU)**
A division of the company that can be managed somewhat independently from other divisions since it markets a specific set of products to a clearly defined group of customers.

**product line**
A group of products that consumers may use together or perceive as similar in some way.

| Loblaw Companies Limited | | | |
| --- | --- | --- | --- |
| Loblaws | Valu-Mart | Joe Fresh | Maxi |
| Real Canadian Superstore | Fortinos | Bloorstreet Market | Extra Foods |
| Zehrs Markets | Provigo | Save Easy | Joe Fresh |
| No Frills | Dominion | Wholesale Club | PC Financial |

The table above shows some of the business lines of Loblaw Companies Limited.

## BOSTON CONSULTING GROUP'S PORTFOLIO ANALYSIS

One of the most popular portfolio analysis methods, developed by the Boston Consulting Group (BCG), requires that firms classify all their products into a two-by-two matrix, as depicted in Exhibit 2.9.[35] The circles represent brands, and their sizes are in direct proportion to the brands' annual sales—that is, larger circles correspond to higher levels of sales, and smaller circles indicate lower levels of sales. The horizontal axis represents the **relative market share.** In general, market share is the percentage of a market accounted for by a specific entity,[36] and it is used to establish the product's strength in a particular market. It is usually discussed in units, revenue, or sales. A special type of market share metric, relative market share, is used in this application because it provides managers with a product's relative strength, compared to that of the largest firm in the industry.[37] The vertical axis is the **market growth rate,** or the annual rate of growth of the specific market in which the product competes. Market growth rate thus measures how attractive a particular market is. Each quadrant has been named on the basis of the amount of resources it generates for and requires from the firm.

**Stars.** Stars (upper left quadrant) occur in high-growth markets and are high-market-share products. That is, stars often require a heavy resource investment in things such as promotions and new production facilities to fuel their rapid growth. As their market growth slows, stars will migrate from heavy users of resources to heavy generators of resources and become cash cows.

**Cash cows.** Cash cows (lower left quadrant) are in low-growth markets but are high-market-share products. Because these products have already received heavy investments to develop their high market share, they have excess resources that can be spun off to those products that need it. For example, in Exhibit 2.9, Brand C can use its excess resources to fund products in the question mark quadrant.

**relative market share**
A measure of the product's strength in a particular market, defined as the sales of the focal product divided by the sales achieved by the largest firm in the industry.

**market growth rate**
The annual rate of growth of the specific market in which the product competes.

**EXHIBIT 2.9**     Boston Consulting Group Product Portfolio Analysis

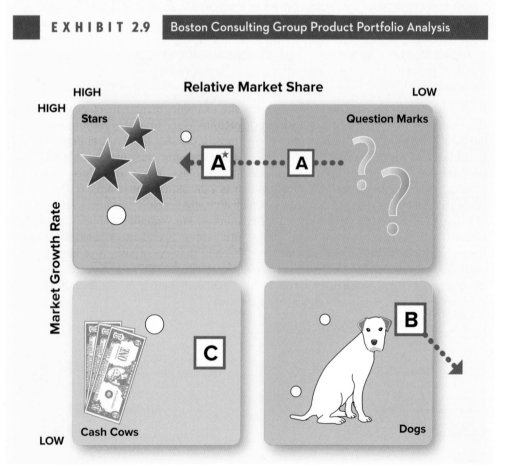

**Question marks.** Question marks (upper right quadrant) appear in high-growth markets but have relatively low market shares; thus, they are often the most managerially intensive products in that they require significant resources to maintain and potentially increase their market share. Managers must decide whether to infuse question marks with resources generated by the cash cows, so that they can become stars, or withdraw resources and eventually phase out the products. Brand A, for instance, is currently a question mark, but by infusing it with resources, the firm hopes to turn it into a star.

**Dogs.** Dogs (lower right quadrant) are in low-growth markets and have relatively low market shares. Although they may generate enough resources to sustain themselves, dogs are not destined for stardom and should be phased out unless they are needed to complement or boost the sales of another product or for competitive purposes. In this case, the company has decided to stop making Brand B.

Now let's look at Apple and some of its products. The four that we will focus our attention on are:

- iPhone
- iPod
- iMac Desktop
- iPad

Let's consider each of these products and place them into the BCG matrix based on these data. While Android sales caused sales to slow, the iPhone was still a star with a high growth rate. By the end of 2015, Apple had sold 78 million units in its fourth quarter alone, representing the most profitable quarter ever recorded by any public company.[38] However even stars can fade and the iPhone may be losing its lustre. When Apple reported its second-quarter earnings for 2016, the company disclosed that iPhone sales had fallen by 16 percent over the past year, below 51.2 million units.[39] Even after announcing the iPhone 7 and 7 Plus in the fall, Apple reported that its annual revenues declined for the first time in 15 years.[40] Some analysts are expressing concern that Apple has "hit a wall." Where would you place the iPhone in light of this news? Is it still a star?

Apple's iPod is a different story. With a staggering absolute market share consistently above 75 percent, its relative market share is also 100 percent. More than 300 million iPods were sold in a little over 10 years. However, the company lumped iPod sales in the "other" category in its 2015 earnings report. It was the first time in 13 years that exact numbers sold and revenues earned were not reported.[41] While the iPod has been an important product for Apple, the MP3 market is contracting. Given its lack of growth and large relative market share, the iPod has been a cash cow for Apple. Where do you think it is headed?

Although popular with graphic designers, the growth rate of the Mac Desktop has also declined. Given that it also has a small relative market share in the desktop market, the iMac can be tentatively classified as a dog. Should Apple get rid of the iMac? For at least two

In which Boston Consulting Group quadrant do these products fit?

Courtesy of Apple

reasons, this is probably a bad idea. First, it risks alienating graphic designers and other Apple loyalists who depend on the iMac. Since these customers may also enjoy other Apple products, their dissatisfaction might adversely affect sales of these other products. Second, discontinuing the iMac would leave a gaping hole in its portfolio, and would therefore hurt its brand image as a computer company.

Then we have the iPad with an incredible sales growth rate from 2011 to 2012 of 61.6 percent, and sales of approximately 16.1 million units in the first quarter of 2016.[42][43] In 2011, its absolute market share was 59 percent, making it the market leader with a relative market share of 100 percent.[44] Looking at 2012 as a whole, the iPad captured 57 percent of the tablet market (more than 1 out of every 2 tablets sold was an iPad). But by the end of 2012 its absolute market share had dropped to 51 percent.[45] More recently, growth has slowed to a mere 3 percent.[46] Where on the BCG matrix would you classify the iPad? Would its market share place it in the star category? Or is the erosion in growth enough to make it a question mark?

Like the Dalai Lama, Apple approaches the world by thinking differently.
© Gilles Mingasson/Liaison/Hulton Archive/Getty Imagesle

Although quite useful for conceptualizing the resource allocation task, the BCG approach, and others like it, are often difficult to implement in practice. In particular, it is difficult to accurately measure both relative market share and industry growth. Furthermore, other measures could easily serve as substitutes to represent a product's competitive position and the market's relative attractiveness. Another issue for marketers is the potential self-fulfilling prophecy of placing a product into a quadrant. As we have shown in our Apple iPad example, whether it is classified as a star or a question mark has profound implications on how it is treated and supported within the firm. Question marks require more marketing and production support.

Because of these limitations, many firms have tempered their use of matrix approaches to achieve a more balanced way of allocating their resources. Instead of assigning allocation decisions to the top levels of the organization, many firms start at lower management levels and employ checks and balances to force managers at each level of the organizational hierarchy to negotiate with those above and below them to reach their final decisions.

# GROWTH STRATEGIES

**L06**

Firms consider pursuing various market segments as part of their overall growth strategies, which may include the four major strategies shown in Exhibit 2.10.[47] The rows distinguish those opportunities a firm possesses in its current markets from those it has in new markets, whereas the columns distinguish between the firm's current marketing offering and that of a new opportunity. Let's consider each of them in detail.

## Market Penetration

A **market penetration strategy** employs the existing marketing mix and focuses the firm's efforts on existing customers. Such a growth strategy might be achieved by encouraging current customers to patronize the firm more often or buy more merchandise on each visit or by attracting new consumers from within the firm's existing target market. A market penetration strategy generally requires greater marketing efforts, such as increased advertising, additional sales and promotions, or intensified distribution efforts in geographic areas in which the product or service is already sold.

To penetrate its target market, TV network MTV found that it needed new ways to engage its viewers. The young audience to which MTV traditionally appeals consists of text-messaging, video-gaming multi-taskers who no longer accept plain video programming on their televisions. The network is working hard to develop additional strategies and outlets to retain viewers, as well as to encourage them to spend more time interacting with its content. MTV discovered that interactions with the audience through alternative channels increase ratings for its shows. In addition to producing and airing reality shows such as *America's Best Dance Crew* and *Jersey Shore*, MTV has partnered with video game producer Yoostar to offer "Yoostar on MTV" for Xbox 360. The game provides a massive library of constantly updated shows, music videos, and recordings of live events. Using the green-screen technology contained in the game, fans of these shows can insert themselves into scenes in which they've already seen their more famous teen peers. Of course, the game also allows them to upload their

**market penetration strategy** A growth strategy that employs the existing marketing mix and focuses the firm's efforts on existing customers.

**EXHIBIT 2.10**  Market/Product and Services Strategies

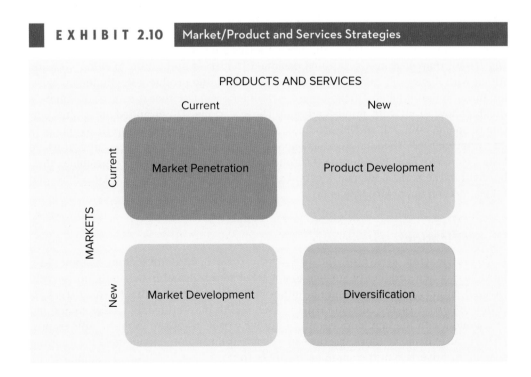

PRODUCTS AND SERVICES

| | Current | New |
|---|---|---|
| **Current** | Market Penetration | Product Development |
| **New** | Market Development | Diversification |

MARKETS

completed performance to Facebook, Twitter, or a Yoostar-dedicated website.[48] On MTV's website, dedicated forums, blogs, and activities for each show also encourage viewers to connect with characters in their shows. Viewers can not only talk about the characters as if they were friends, but also buy the products they wear and download the music played during the show.[49]

## Market Development

A **market development strategy** employs the existing marketing offering to reach new market segments, whether domestic or international. Domestically, MTV pursues a market development strategy by targeting older customers who were MTV viewers in their youth, but are now attracted to Much Television shows reminiscent of their teen years. International expansion is generally riskier than domestic expansion because firms must deal with differences in government regulations, cultural traditions, supply chain considerations, and language.

However, many firms, including MTV, enjoy a competitive advantage in global markets—such as Mexico, Latin America, Europe, China, and Japan—because, especially among young people, North American culture is widely emulated for consumer products.

For example, because of rising prosperity worldwide and rapidly increasing access to cable television, fashion trends from North America have spread to young people in emerging countries. Since its founding in 1981, MTV has expanded, with niche sites in nearly 50 countries including the United Kingdom, Japan, Brazil, Pakistan, and Slovakia. It is available in 562 million households in 161 countries and 33 languages.[50] The global MTV generation prefers soft drinks to tea, athletic shoes to sandals, french fries to rice, and credit cards to cash. To achieve such growth, MTV leveraged its existing media content but also delivers culturally relevant content using local DJs and show formats.

## Product Development

The third growth strategy option, a **product development strategy,** offers a new product or service to a firm's current target market. Consider MTV's dynamic lineup: The network constantly develops new pilots and show concepts to increase the amount of time viewers can spend watching MTV. For example, each version of *The Real World* reality series—and newer series such as *Generation Cryo* and *Faking It*—all represent new programs designed to attract and retain existing viewers. Along with its new TV series, MTV develops new online products to engage consumers through more than 25 niche blogs, as well as a website that it uses to dominate a greater share of viewers' minds and time. These various MTV-branded niche sites pertain to social, political, and environmental issues that appeal to different segments in its target market. The sites further encourage viewers to get involved in real-world issues (not *The Real World* issues) through mobile technologies. MTV promises that, by visiting the sites, consumers can share mobile content, educate themselves, and take action on important issues.[51]

## Diversification

A **diversification strategy**, the last of the growth strategies from Exhibit 2.10, introduces a new product or service to a market segment that is currently not served. Diversification opportunities may be either related or unrelated. In a *related diversification opportunity*, the current target market and/or marketing mix shares something in common with the new opportunity. In other words, the firm might be able to purchase from existing vendors, use the same distribution and/or management information system, or advertise in the same newspapers to target markets that are similar to its current consumers. MTV has pursued related diversification by introducing TV series that focus on more positive social messages, instead of on wealth, celebrities, and excessive youth culture (e.g., *The Hills, My Super Sweet 16*). In series such as *I Used to Be Fat* and *Made*, recognizable and seemingly similar teens still appeal to viewers and provide a healthy dose of drama. However, the plotlines of these shows focus on how people overcome adversity or struggle with everyday challenges to attain some level of happiness.[52]

In contrast, in an *unrelated diversification*, the new business lacks any common elements with the present business. Unrelated diversifications do not capitalize on core strengths associated with markets or with products. Thus, they would be viewed as very risky. In the technology innovation company 3M, however, we find an excellent and successful example of unrelated diversification strategies: What began as a sandpaper products company now markets its products in six major business segments, from consumer office supplies to orthodontic technologies.[53]

While all four growth strategies present unique challenges for marketers, a market penetration strategy is the easiest to implement since it focuses on promoting existing products to existing customers. In this case, marketers know both their products and markets. With market development or product development, marketers have experience with one element and must learn the other element. Diversification requires marketers to go outside both their current products and markets, and the risks of making mistakes are substantially greater with this strategy. The particular growth strategy a company chooses depends on its goals and capabilities, among other things. Also, marketers tend to pursue multiple growth strategies simultaneously.

Marketers may also develop strategies for **downsizing** their business operations by either exiting markets or reducing their product portfolios. They may exit markets or abandon products for many reasons; for example, because they have entered new markets where they have little or no experience; diversified into markets or products that do not quite fit with current products, markets, or capabilities; developed products that offer very little value for customers; or encountered declining demand for some products.

**downsizing**
Exiting markets, reducing product portfolios, or closing certain businesses or store or plant locations.

# LEARNING OBJECTIVES REVIEW

### LO1 Define a marketing strategy

A marketing strategy identifies (1) a firm's target markets(s), (2) a related marketing mix (four Ps), and (3) the bases on which the firm plans to build a sustainable competitive advantage. Firms use four macro strategies to build their sustainable competitive advantage. Customer excellence focuses on retaining loyal customers and excellent customer service. Operational excellence is achieved through efficient operations and excellent supply chain and human resource management. Product excellence entails having products with high perceived value and effective branding and positioning. Finally, locational excellence entails having a good physical location and Internet presence.

### LO2 Describe the elements of a marketing plan

A marketing plan is composed of an analysis of the current marketing situation, its objectives, the strategy for the four Ps, and appropriate financial statements. A marketing plan represents the output of a three-phase process: planning, implementation, and control. The planning phase requires that managers first define the firm's mission and vision, which helps to answer the questions "What business are we in now?" and "What do we intend to be in the future?" In the first phase, planning, managers conduct a situation analysis to evaluate how various players, both inside and outside the organization, affect the firm's potential for success. In the second phase, implementation, the firm identifies and evaluates different opportunities through a process known as segmentation, targeting, and positioning, and develops the marketing mix, the four Ps. Specifically, managers focus on implementing the marketing mix, allocating resources, designing the marketing organization, and developing schedules and action plans. Finally, in the third phase, control, the firm evaluates its performance to determine what worked, what didn't, and how performance can be improved in the future.

**L03** **Analyze a marketing situation using a SWOT analysis**

SWOT stands for *strengths, weaknesses, opportunities, and threats*. A SWOT analysis occurs during the second step in the strategic planning process, the situation analysis. By analyzing what the firm is good at (its strengths), where it could improve (its weaknesses), where in the marketplace it might excel (its opportunities), and what is happening in the marketplace that could harm the firm (its threats), managers can assess their firm's situation accurately and plan its strategy accordingly.

**L04** **Explain how a firm chooses what consumer group(s) to pursue with its marketing efforts**

Once a firm identifies different marketing opportunities, it must determine which are the best to pursue. To accomplish this task, marketers go through a segmentation, targeting, and positioning (STP) process. Firms segment various markets by dividing the total market into those groups of customers with different needs, wants, or characteristics who therefore might appreciate products or services geared especially toward them. After identifying the different segments, the firm goes after, or targets, certain groups on the basis of the firm's perceived ability to satisfy the needs of those groups better and more profitably than competitors. To complete the STP process, firms position their products or services according to the marketing mix variables so that target customers have a clear, distinctive, and desirable understanding of what the product or service does or represents relative to competing products or services.

**L05** **Outline the implementation of the marketing mix as a means to increase customer value**

The marketing mix consists of the four Ps—product, price, promotion, and place—and each P contributes to customer value. To provide value, the firm must offer a mix of products and services at prices its target markets will view as indicating good value. Thus, firms make trade-offs between the first two Ps, product and price, to give customers the best value. The third P, promotion, informs customers and helps them form a positive image about the firm and its products and services. The last P, place, adds value by getting the appropriate products and services to customers when they want them and in the quantities they need.

**L06** **Describe how firms grow their businesses**

Firms use four basic growth strategies: market penetration, market development, product development, and diversification. A market penetration strategy directs the firm's efforts toward existing customers and uses the present marketing mix. In other words, it attempts to get current customers to buy more. In a market development strategy, the firm uses its current marketing mix to appeal to new market segments, as might occur in international expansion. A product development growth strategy involves offering a new product or service to the firm's current target market. Finally, a diversification strategy takes place when a firm introduces a new product or service to a new customer segment. Sometimes a diversification strategy relates to the firm's current business, such as when a women's clothing manufacturer starts making and selling men's clothes, but a more risky strategy is when a firm diversifies into a completely unrelated business.

# KEY TERMS

- control phase
- customer excellence
- diversification strategy
- downsizing
- implementation phase
- locational excellence
- market development strategy
- market growth rate
- market penetration strategy
- market positioning
- market segment
- market segmentation
- marketing strategy
- mission statement
- operational excellence
- planning phase
- product development strategy
- product excellence
- product line
- relative market share
- situation analysis (SWOT)
- STP
- strategic business unit (SBU)
- sustainable competitive advantage
- target marketing/targeting

## CONCEPT REVIEW

1. Briefly describe the activities involved at each of the three phases of the marketing planning process: (1) planning, (2) implementation, and (3) control.

2. What is meant by a mission or vision statement? What purpose does a mission statement serve, and how does it influence marketing planning?

3. What does SWOT mean? List two benefits of SWOT analyses. What do you think the differences are between a SWOT analysis for the entire firm and a SWOT analysis for a product?

4. What type of information is required to conduct a SWOT analysis, and where do marketers typically look for this information?

5. Why are segmentation, targeting, and positioning (STP) crucial for identifying and evaluating market opportunities? How does STP influence the development of the marketing mix—the four Ps?

6. Describe the four growth strategies that firms typically pursue. Use a fast-food restaurant or a grocery chain in Canada (e.g., Loblaw, Safeway, or Food Basics) to illustrate each of the four growth strategies.

7. Of the four growth strategies described in the chapter, which is the most risky? Which is the easiest to implement? Why?

8. Identify and describe the four strategies that firms could use to grow their business. What other strategies could companies use to compete in the market?

9. What are the four components of the BCG matrix? When would stars be preferred over cash cows?

10. Explain why in the BCG matrix all products start out as question marks and end up as either stars, cash cows, or dogs.

## MARKETING APPLICATIONS

1. How has WestJet created a sustainable competitive advantage?

2. Perform a SWOT analysis for your college or university.

3. Describe the primary target markets for the Toronto Blue Jays, Victoria's Secret, and Gatorade. How do these three firms position their products and services so that they appeal to their respective target markets?

4. Pick your favourite product, service provider, or retailer. How do marketers add value to it through the implementation of the four Ps?

5. Choose three retailers. You believe the first builds customer value through product excellence, the second through operational excellence, and the third through customer excellence. Justify your answer.

6. Visit the website of your bank and try to identify how it uses STP to develop various types of bank accounts (products) and charge different fees (prices) for different types of accounts.

7. Select a company with which you are familiar or search online to find a company that has pursued a diversification strategy as one of its growth strategies. How successful was the company's diversification strategy? What factors do you think account for its success or failure?

8. Imagine that you have just developed and launched a new sports bike for cycling enthusiasts and your business has become an instant success. You would like to capitalize on this success and fame to grow your business. Explain how you would go about expanding your business over the next three years.

9. Using the sports bike scenario from the previous question, describe what kinds of analysis you might conduct before deciding which growth strategies to implement.

10. You and a few of your classmates are planning to open a new spa facility near the campus of your university. Explain how you would segment the market for your services, which segment you would target, and how you would position your spa to the chosen target market.

## NET SAVVY

**1.** Petro-Canada is considered a progressive company in terms of its values and the mission statement that drives its business. Visit its website (www.petro-canada.ca) and review the portion that discusses the company, its mission, and its values. Discuss aspects of its mission and values that might be considered progressive. Do you believe its progressive attitude creates a special position in the market that contributes to a sustainable competitive advantage?

**2.** More and more firms seem to be entering the dating service industry. Visit eHarmony (www.eharmony.com) and tour its website to find the types of activities and methods such companies use to help match compatible couples. Analyze the environment that might affect Internet dating services by using a SWOT analysis.

## CHAPTER CASE STUDY

### THE GREAT FROZEN YOGURT BATTLE

Let's think about the options available for your frozen dessert indulgence: ice cream, frozen custard, gelato, frozen yogurt, sherbet, sorbet, single-serving desserts such as Popsicles, milkshakes, and blended treats that combine frozen dairy products with bits of cookies or candies. In addition to their wide variety of flavours, they also come in reduced-fat, soy, organic, fair-trade, probiotic, nutrition-enhanced, and gluten-free versions. Faced with all these choices and options, how is a brand to make its mark?

This case focuses on sales of frozen yogurt—a relatively small, but growing, part of the $25 billion frozen dessert market. Its growth trends have spawned intense competition among existing frozen yogurt shops, as well as inspired new brands to set up shop. There are about 1,500 shops owned by 268 different companies doing business in the U.S. market with projected revenues of $800 million.[54]

At Yogurty's® customers can choose from a variety of flavours and toppings to create personalized snacks.

Used with permission of Yogurty's Yogurt Inc. Froyo® is a registered trademark owned by International Franchise Inc. in Canada. Yogen Früz®, Yogurty's® and Pinkberry® are all registered trademarks and are the sole property of their respective owners.

By 2011, the popularity of frozen yogurt had reached a fever pitch in the frozen Canadian north. Crossing the border to join Canadian firms such as Yogen Früz® and Yogurty's® were American brands Menchie's and Pinkberry®. To build and maintain a loyal customer base, each frozen yogurt brand is seeking to distinguish itself from its competitors by offering products, services, and ambiance so appealing that customers shun competitors. For example, Yogurty's® offers more than 85 different flavours of frozen yogurt. Customers can select low-fat, no-fat, gluten-free or kosher products and then choose from dozens of toppings to complete their treat.[55] Pinkberry® has attracted loyal fans devoted to its tart-flavoured yogurt, which contains probiotics and promises to aid digestion. Stores offer a limited number of exotic flavours, many of which are seasonal, and a wide array of high-end toppings.[56] Menchie's offers its own custom blend of flavours, using natural flavours and the highest quality ingredients. All products are certified kosher, perhaps part of its vision "to make the Menchie's experience available to every guest all over the world as a legacy for generations to come." Its mission statement—"We make you smile"—conveys the fun side of the brand.[57] The more traditional dessert idea offered by TCBY allows consumers to help themselves to yogurt flavours like cake batter, red velvet cake, and peanut butter, and then pile on candy, cookies, fruit, sauces, and sprinkles.[58] All these stores calculate the costs of each dessert by weight rather than by serving size, so customers feel free to create towering frozen creations that they might have felt awkward ordering. It also results in a higher per-serving cost.

These chains and their smaller competitors are adding new product lines to leverage the exploding popularity of Greek-style yogurt. Adding desserts based on the newly introduced style has expanded the market dramatically. Yet analysts argue that there is still plenty of room for growth. Canadians eat far less yogurt per capita than most European nations, for example. In contrast, other observers caution that frozen yogurt is just one more dessert fad, rather like cupcake shops, that will reach a peak and then fade away relatively soon.

The Canadian Dairy Information Centre reports that the frozen yogurt segment is growing.[59] Indeed, Pinkberry® exceeded its forecasts by almost 20 percent in its first year of operation.[60] In spite of this, industry experts predict the frozen yogurt trend will cool. Newcomers will need to find a unique foothold in the market. Already established businesses must grow and change their product offerings and corporate citizenry to keep pace with customer needs and tastes.

### Questions

1. Perform a SWOT analysis for Yogurty's and Menchie's. How are the results similar? How do they differ?

2. Which growth strategies seem most likely for the two companies mentioned above? Why?

# Writing a Marketing Plan

Have a plan. Follow the plan, and you'll be surprised how successful you can be. Most people don't have a plan. That's why it's easy to beat most folks.

—Paul "Bear" Bryant, football coach, University of Alabama

## WHY WRITE A MARKETING PLAN?[1]

As a student, you likely plan out much in your life—where to meet for dinner, how much time to spend studying for exams, which courses to take next semester, how to get home for winter break, and so on. Plans enable us to figure out where we want to go and how we might get there.

For a firm, the goal is not much different. Any company that wants to succeed (which means any firm whatsoever) needs to plan for a variety of contingencies, and marketing represents one of the most significant. A marketing plan—which we defined in Chapter 2 as a written document composed of an analysis of the current marketing situation, opportunities and threats for the firm, marketing objectives and strategy specified in terms of the four Ps, action programs, and projected or pro forma income (and other financial) statements—enables marketing personnel and the firm as a whole to understand their own actions, the market in which they operate, their future direction, and the means to obtain support for new initiatives.[2]

Because these elements—internal activities, external environments, goals, and forms of support—differ for every firm, the marketing plan is different for each firm as well. However, several guidelines apply to marketing plans in general; this appendix summarizes those points and offers an annotated example. ■

## MARKETING PLAN VERSUS BUSINESS PLAN

Of course, firms consider more than marketing when they make plans and therefore commonly develop business plans as well. Yet, as this book highlights, marketing constitutes such an important element of business that business plans and marketing plans coincide in many ways.[3] Both marketing and business plans generally encompass the following:

1. Executive summary
2. Company overview

3.  Objectives/goals, usually according to strategic plan and focus
4.  Situation analysis
5.  STP analysis (market/product/customer analysis)
6.  Marketing strategy
7.  Financial projections
8.  Implementation plan
9.  Evaluation and control metrics

However, a business plan also includes details about R&D and operations, and both documents may feature details about other key topics, depending on the focus of the company and the plan.

# STRUCTURE OF A MARKETING PLAN

This section briefly describes each of the elements of a marketing plan.[4]

## Executive Summary

The executive summary essentially tells the reader why he or she is reading this marketing plan—what changes require consideration, what new products need discussion, and so forth—and suggests possible actions to take in response to the information the plan contains.

## Company Overview

In this section, the plan provides a brief description of the company, including perhaps its mission statement, background, and competitive advantages.

## Objectives/Goals

This section offers more specifics about why readers are reading the marketing plan. What does the company want to achieve, both overall and with this particular marketing plan?

## Situation Analysis

Recall from Chapter 2 that a situation analysis generally relies on SWOT considerations; therefore, this section describes the strengths, weaknesses, opportunities, and threats facing the company.

## STP Analysis

The analysis proceeds by assessing the market in which the company functions, the products it currently offers or plans to offer in the future, and the characteristics of current or potential customers.

## Marketing Strategy

The marketing strategy may be very specific, especially if the plan pertains to, for example, a stable product in a familiar market, or it may be somewhat open to varied possibilities, such as when the firm plans to enter a new market with an innovative product.

### Financial Projections

On the basis of the knowledge already obtained, the marketing plan should provide possible developments and returns on the marketing investments outlined in the marketing strategy.

### Implementation Plan

This portion of the marketing plan includes the timing of promotional activities, when monitoring will take place, and how expansions likely will proceed.

### Evaluation and Control Metrics

The firm must have a means of assessing the marketing plan's recommendations; the marketing plan therefore must indicate the methods for undertaking this assessment, whether quantitatively or qualitatively.

### Appendix

The final section(s) offer(s) additional information that might be of benefit, such as a list of key personnel, data limitations that may influence the findings, and suggestions of the plan, relevant legislation, and so forth.

## INFORMATION SOURCES[5]

When writing a marketing plan, you likely can turn to a variety of your firm's in-house information sources, including annual reports, previous marketing plans, published mission statements, and so on. In addition, various sources offer suggestions and examples that may provide you with direction and ideas. Exhibits 7.5 and 7.6 also list many sources that you may find very helpful.

- Knowthis.com—"a knowledge source for marketing" (www.knowthis.com /principles-of-marketing-tutorials/how-to-write-a-marketing-plan)
- Encyclopedia of American Industries—introduces industry structure; arranged by SIC and NAICS codes
- Standard & Poor's NetAdvantage—surveys of more than 50 different industries, with financial data about companies in each industry
- Investext Plus—brokerage house reports
- IBISWorld—market research on thousands of industries; classified by NAICS code
- Statistics Canada surveys on virtually all aspects of business, the economy, social statistics, and population data—a vast variety of statistics on a range of topics
- Statistics Canada Census—detailed statistical data gathered every 10 years on all aspects of the Canadian population
- LifeStyle Market Analyst—lifestyle information about geographic areas, lifestyle interest groups, and age and income groups
- Mediamark Reporter—information about demographics, lifestyles, product and brand usage, and advertising media preferences
- Arbitron/Scarborough—local market consumer information for various media in 75 local markets for consumer retail shopping behaviour, product consumption, media usage, lifestyle behaviour, and demographics
- Simmons Study of Media and Markets—products and consumer characteristics; various media audiences and their characteristics

- Rand McNally Commercial Atlas and Marketing Guide—maps and tables showing demographic, industrial, transportation, railroad, airline, and hospital data
- Annual & 10-K reports from Thomson ONE Banker, Edgar, and LexisNexis— business descriptions, product listings, distribution channels, possible impact of regulations and lawsuits, and discussions of strategic issues
- MarketResearch.com Academic—market research reports on a variety of consumer products
- Mintel Reports Database—market research reports focusing on consumer products, lifestyles, retailing, and international travel industry

## LINGUISTIC AND VISUAL SUGGESTIONS

Again, recall that all marketing plans differ, because all firms differ. However, just as rules exist that dictate what makes for good writing, some rules or guidelines apply to all well written marketing plans.

- Maintain a professional attitude in the writing and presentation.
- Keep descriptions and summaries concise. Get to the point.
- Use standard, edited English.
- Proofread the entire plan multiple times to catch grammatical, spelling, or other such errors that could dampen the professionalism of the writing.
- Adopt a businesslike tone; avoid flowery or jargon-filled writing.
- Employ direct (rather than passive) and present (rather than past) tense whenever possible (e.g., "We plan to achieve 30 percent growth in two years" rather than "The plan was that 30 percent growth would be achieved by the firm within two years").
- Be positive.
- Avoid meaningless superlatives (e.g., "Our goal is tremendous growth").
- Be specific; use quantitative information whenever possible.
- Insert graphics to convey important concepts succinctly, including photos, graphs, illustrations, and charts.
- However, avoid using so many visual elements that they clutter the plan.
- Lay out the plan clearly and logically.
- Organize sections logically, using multiple levels of headings, distinguished clearly by font differences (e.g., bold for first-level heads, italics for second-level heads).
- Consider the use of bullet points or numbered lists to emphasize important points.
- Exploit modern technology (e.g., graphics software, page-layout software, laser printers) to ensure that the plan looks professional.
- Adopt an appropriate font to make the text easy to read and visually appealing— avoid using anything smaller than 10-point font at a minimum.
- Avoid unusual or decorative fonts; stick with a common serif type to make the text easy to read.
- Consider binding the report with a clear cover and an attractive title page.
- Generally aim for a plan that consists of 15–30 pages.

# PeopleAhead MARKETING PLAN ILLUSTRATION[6]

**PeopleAhead Marketing Plan: Condensed**

## 1. Executive Summary[A-1]

PeopleAhead focuses on career advancement done right. Instead of making job search a one-time event, PeopleAhead provides a platform for people to find, advance, and develop their careers by sharing career goals, discussing professional development plans, and socializing with other professionals.[A-2]

PeopleAhead culminates the career advancement experience with its proprietary True-Match® technology, which identifies synergies between the companies hiring talent (employers) and PeopleAhead members (job candidates) who wish to be hired. By anonymously presenting only prequalified career opportunities to members, who confirm their interest and recommend others, PeopleAhead transforms the ineffective online hiring process into a highly efficient career-matching system. PeopleAhead was founded by Carlos Larracilla and Tom Chevalier to improve people's lives by helping them achieve their career aspirations. The vision for PeopleAhead was conceived in January 2006, with a notion that personality alignment is critical to matching the right people with the right career opportunities. Since then, the idea has grown and morphed into a company that matches the right person with the right career opportunity by aligning personality, competencies, experience, and interests.

Tom and Carlos[A-3] combine human resources, system development, and sales experience to deliver a groundbreaking, TrueMatch®-branded talent matching network that makes it easier for people to achieve their career aspirations and improves the way companies identify individuals who will be able to contribute to their long-term success. The organizational chart of PeopleAhead is available in Appendix A.

## 2. Strategic Objectives

### 2.1. Mission

PeopleAhead's mission is to help individuals with career advancement and improve the human capital in companies. The site will act as a networking platform for professionals and career matching as opposed to job and resumé-posting searches.[A-4]

---

**A-1**
Instead of using separate "Executive Summary" and "Company Overview" sections, this marketing plan begins with a general overview that includes both aspects and answers the key questions: "What type of business are we?" and "What do we need to do to accomplish our objectives?" (see Chapter 2).

**A-2**
As this plan does, a marketing plan should start with a positive, upbeat assessment of what the company does and what it hopes to continue doing.

**A-3**
Note the personalization of the company founders, which may help readers feel connected to the company.

**A-4**
The paragraph provides a general outline of the firm's objectives; the bulleted list offers more specific goals, and the subsequent sections go into more detail about the various factors that may influence these objectives.

## 2.2. Goals

- Use brand-matching technology: TrueMatch®
- Build critical mass of users.
- Drive traffic to the website through marketing blitzes.
- Utilize word-of-mouth advertising from satisfied users.

## 2.3. Business Summary

- *Business Customers:* This group provides PeopleAhead's revenues. Customers purchase contact information about the Top Ten PROfiles gleaned from the individual member base that have been sorted and ranked by the TrueMatch® technology. PeopleAhead will focus on small and medium businesses (see Market Segmentation section[A-5]), because these entities are underserved by large competitors in the online recruitment market, and because research shows that this demographic has a less efficient recruitment process that would benefit most readily from PeopleAhead's services. Within this segment, customers include HR managers who are responsible for the sourcing of candidates, functional area managers who require new talent for their team, and executives whose business objectives rely on human capital and efficiency of operations.

- *Individual Members:* This group does not pay for services but is the main source of data points for PeopleAhead's TrueMatch® system. PeopleAhead will focus on building a base of individual members who range from recent graduates to individuals with 5–7 years of continuous employment. Ideal members are those who are currently employed or will be graduating within nine months and are "poised" to make a career change. These individuals can utilize the services to the fullest extent and are valuable candidates for business customers.[A-6]

## 2.4. Competitive Advantage

- *TrueMatch® offers a branded technology*, marketed to both business customers and individual candidates for its "black box" value proposition, which establishes PeopleAhead as the category leader for recruitment-matching software. This technology provides a point of differentiation from competitors, which may have technically similar matching software but constantly need to reinforce their marketing messages with explanations of their value proposition.

- *For individual candidates*, PeopleAhead will be the favoured career advancement platform online, where individuals enthusiastically create a history and have connections (invited friends, co-workers, and mentors[A-7]) in place that will make PeopleAhead a staple among their favourite websites. PeopleAhead delivers TrueMatch® career opportunities, professional development plans that let people establish a professional record, and valuable career advancement tools, including automatic position feedback, "recommend-a-friend," and team-based career networking.

- *For business customers*, PeopleAhead makes online sourcing and qualification of candidates quick and efficient by prequalifying potential candidates, seeking recommendations for hard-to-find individuals, and delivering only the Top 10 most highly qualified candidates who have preconfirmed interest in the available position. PeopleAhead will be the most effective candidate–company matching platform available in the market, delivering prequalified, preconfirmed candidates.[A-8]

## 3. Situation Analysis—Online Recruitment

Online recruitment is the system whereby companies use the web to locate and qualify prospective candidates for available positions. The methods employed by online recruitment service providers to serve this market range from resumé aggregation to assessment test application to linking strategies. However, the common underlying objective is to locate candidates who would not be found by traditional recruitment methods and use computing power to qualify candidates quickly and with more accuracy than would be possible manually.

## 3.1. Industry Analysis

Large online recruitment websites make this a tedious process by requiring companies to search through many resumés manually to find the "right" candidate. Other sites solicit recommendations for positions. However, resumés are often "enhanced," such that almost all candidates appear qualified, and information found in the resumé or provided through a recommendation is

**A-5**
By referring to another section, the plan makes clear where it is heading and enables readers to cross-reference the information.

**A-6**
The plan acknowledges both a general, potential target market and the ideal targets.

**A-7**
As Chapter 2 suggests, the plan notes PeopleAhead's sustainable competitive advantage as part of its overall mission statement.

**A-8**
In discussing both the external market and the internal advantages of PeopleAhead, the plan carefully distinguishes between individual job candidates and businesses, thus differentiating the focus and objectives according to this segmentation.

simply insufficient to make an educated hiring decision. Companies need more information and intelligent tools that make this screening process more accurate.

### 3.1.1. Market Size

The market size for both member segments in 2005 was as follows:[A-9]

A-9
Figures provide a visually attractive break in the text and summarize a lot of information in an easy-to-read format.

**Individual Members Segments**

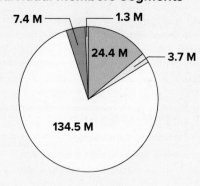

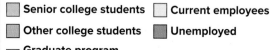

**Company Members Segments**

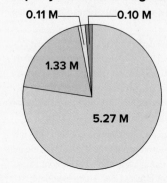

The most critical issue in examining market size is the relationship between the number of companies and the number of workers employed, because sales are based on the number of positions (profiles purchased), not the number of companies that use the service.

The following figure shows the number of people employed by each enterprise market segment as of January 2006, according to the U.S. Department of Labor. This segment information will be useful in defining PeopleAhead's target market.

**Employment by Enterprise Type**

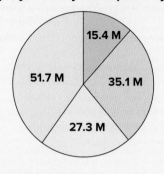

- Very small enterprises
- Small enterprises
- Medium enterprises
- Large enterprises

*3.1.2. Market Growth*

PeopleAhead will operate in the online recruitment market. The growth of this industry is subject to two primary constraints: U.S. economic health and online recruitment advertisement adoption rates. Understanding these constraints will help to identify PeopleAhead's opportunity. General indicators suggest the U.S. economy (GDP) will grow at an average annual rate of 4 percent for the next decade.[7] Online recruitment advertising is expected to grow by 35 percent per year to reach $7.6 billion by 2010.[8] Not only is the market expanding, but it is exhibiting rapid adoption by new entities, as the following graph shows.[A-10 9]

**A-10**

Another visually attractive graph summarizes complicated information easily. The use of high-quality colour can add a professional feel to a marketing plan.

**Recruitment Advertisement Industry Growth**

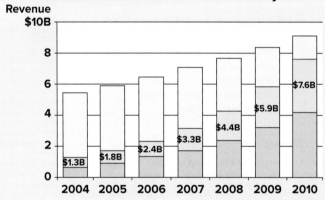

- Total recruitment advertisement
- Total online recruitment market
- Main competitors: Monster, CareerBuilder, and Yahoo/HotJobs

*3.1.3. Market Needs*

- **The right person for the right position:** The right employee for one company or position is not the same for all others. Companies must locate intelligent individuals with relevant experience, and prefer people who are aligned with the position requirements in terms of personality, competencies, and fit with the company culture.
- **Prescreening qualification tools:** Increasing the number of candidates through online recruitment can be advantageous, but it can also be a hindrance. When sourcing candidates, recruiters need tools that help them qualify applicants.
- **Time savings:** Companies need to complete the online sourcing and qualification of candidates quickly. Leaving positions unfilled can cause critical performance gaps to emerge within the company.

### 3.1.4. Market Trends[A-11]

The methods by which online recruitment service providers deliver candidates has been undergoing a migration from resumé aggregation and search services such as Monster and CareerBuilder to new Web 2.0 methodologies that include passive recruitment, "meta tagging," and social networking.

The underlying objective of these Web 2.0 services is to allow individuals to remain on a few trusted websites while enabling companies to access those individuals for financial purposes. In parallel, the focus is moving from aggregation of unique visitors toward engaging existing users more intensively. Internet users are growing familiar with sites that encourage socializing, collaborating, and distributing private information online to help to improve network benefits, and need to be engaged to maintain contact.

### 3.2. SWOT Analysis

|  | Positive | Negative |
|---|---|---|
| **Internal** | **Strengths**<br>• Industry best practices: The networking model used by PeopleAhead draws on the industry accepted "best practices" contact protocols drawn from multiple industries, including online feedback, recruitment, and social networking and offline professional networking. TrueMatch® software aligns business objectives with appropriate candidates.<br>• Team expertise: The combined talents of the founders include human resources, system development, sales, and marketing.<br>• Web development expertise: PeopleAhead has partnered with an award-winning European software development provider. This company provides quality usually reserved for high-budget projects, at terms that are favourable for a start-up company. | **Weaknesses**<br>• Absence of industry "influentials": As a start-up, PeopleAhead does not currently have resources to attract influential industry managers.<br>• Inability to guarantee critical mass: As is true of many Internet companies, the business must solve the "chicken and egg" puzzle to build critical mass.<br>• Verifying efficiency of matching capabilities: In theory, the system has an absolute guarantee of effectiveness; computations make decisions rather than humans. However, the matching capabilities must be verified as accurate to gain widespread acceptance.<br>• Broad target market: Because PeopleAhead is targeting a wide range of businesses, the product being developed has not been "customized" ideally for each segment. |
| **External** | **Opportunities**<br>• Service gap: Recruiters are not pleased with current online recruitment vendors.<br>• Industry gap: Job turnover is every 3.5 years per person.<br>• Demand for productive candidates.<br>• Online recruitment advertising: Growing by 35% per year, to reach $7.6 billion by 2010.[A-12 10]<br>• Fragmented business models: Online recruitment is fragmented by recruitment methodology: active (people who need jobs), passive (people who are not looking but would move if enticed), poised (people unsatisfied with jobs they have), and network (finding people of interest based on who or what they know). | **Threats**<br>• Convergence: existing competitors may form strategic alliances and establish powerful positions before PeopleAhead can establish itself.<br>• Inability to protect model: Very little intellectual property created by online websites is protected by law. Although PeopleAhead will pursue aggressive IP protection strategies, the model could be copied or mimicked by competitors.<br>• Inadequate differentiation: Inability to explain our differentiation would relegate PeopleAhead to (unfair) comparisons with competitors. Without differentiation, PeopleAhead will not be able to create scale through network effects. |

**A-11**
Before engaging in a firm-specific SWOT analysis (see Chapter 2), this marketing plan assesses the external market environment further and thus establishes a basis for the subsequent SWOT analysis.

**A-12**
Note that the analysis uses outside sources to support its claims.

### 3.3. Competition

Most online recruitment websites compete in the active recruitment market, including Monster, CareerBuilder, and Yahoo/HotJobs. The pervasive segment includes job seekers who actively look for jobs, post their resumés, and search for jobs on company websites. Most active recruiters offer free services to users and charge companies on a fee basis. Companies can post jobs and search for candidate resumés in the database (average fee for local searches is $500 and nationwide is $1000). In this first-generation online recruitment business model, competitors face the challenge to make the process more user-friendly and reduce the effort required to make these sites deliver results.[A-13]

- **Monster:** Monster.com is the sixteenth most visited website in the United States, with more than 43 million professionals in its viewer base. Monster earns revenue from job postings, access to its resumé database, and advertisements on websites of partner companies.[A-14]

- **Careerbuilder:** Careerbuilder.com has experienced 75 percent growth for the past five years. This job post/resumé search company uses its media ownership to attract "passive" candidates from partner websites. It achieves growth through affiliate partnerships that host job searches on affiliated web pages, such as Google, MSN, AOL, USA Today, Earthlink, BellSouth, and CNN. Job posting is the primary activity, sold together with or separately from resumé searches.

- **Passive Recruitment:** The second generation of online recruitment locates candidates who are not necessarily looking for jobs but who could be convinced to move to a new position if the right opportunity was presented. The most recognized competitors in this category include Jobster, LinkedIn, and H3 (Appendix B).[A-15]

### 3.4. Company Analysis[A-16]

PeopleAhead's mission is simple: improve people's lives through career advancement. PeopleAhead recognizes that career advancement means many things to many people and provides a fresh perspective on career networking that is flexible yet powerful:

- **Users are not alone:** Finding a job is not easy. Why search solo? PeopleAhead unites groups of friends, co-workers, and mentors to create natural, team-based career discovery.

- **Job posting is not natural:** People spend countless hours searching job listings and posting resumés, only to be overlooked because their writing style or resumé format does not match an overburdened recruiter's preference. Good people make great companies, not resumés. PeopleAhead's TrueMatch® technology matches the right people with the right position. No posting, no applying—just good, quality matches.

- Professionals being professionals: There is a place online for social networking, pet networking, and music networking. So why is there no outlet for career networking online—the activity that consumes the majority of our professional lives? PeopleAhead is a place where professionals share their experiences, achievements, and objectives with other professionals that care and can be found by employers who value their professionalism.

### 3.5. Customer Analysis[A-17]

PeopleAhead's R&D efforts show that the impetus to improve recruitment effectivity is pervasive and that unmet needs revolve around a few core issues: the ability to find qualified talent, establishing a fit between the candidate and the company culture, verifying the candidate's career progression, and working quickly and cost-effectively. The following customer characteristics represent ideal attributes that align with PeopleAhead's service offering. This information might be used in conjunction with the Marketing Strategy.

#### 3.5.1. Business Customer

- **Industry:** Because companies that value human capital are more likely to take a chance on a startup that promotes professional development, the broadly defined professional services industry, including insurance, banking, and consulting, is the primary focus.

- **Functional area:** PeopleAhead's system identifies "people" people, so positions that require human interaction are more aligned with system capabilities than those with stringent skill requirements, sets such as programming or accounting.

- **Size:** Large businesses (>1000 employees) have high-volume requirements and demand vendors with proven track records; small businesses (<25 employees) hire fewer people and may not justify acquisition costs. PeopleAhead aligns best with medium-sized customers.

**A-13**
If PeopleAhead chooses to adopt a competitor-based pricing strategy (see Chapter 11), detailed information about how other recruitment firms work will be mandatory.

**A-14**
Information about competitors' revenues, customers, growth, and so forth often is available publicly through a variety of sources.

**A-15**
For information that may not belong in the main text, an appendix offers an effective means to provide detail without distracting readers.

**A-16**
This section offers the "product" component of the market/product/customer analysis. Because PeopleAhead's product is mostly a service (see Chapter 10), it focuses on some intangible features of its offering.

**A-17**
The last—and some would say most important—piece of the analysis puzzle: customers.

- **Hiring need:** PeopleAhead serves two types of searches very well: those with too many applicants and those with too few applicants. By drawing applicants that most systems overlook and delivering only the most qualified applicants, the system assures the right candidate is identified quickly.[A-18]

### 3.5.2. Individual Member

- **Background:** People who value professional development and are familiar with computer networking technologies; most are likely college educated, motivated by career success, and aware of their professional competencies/deficiencies.
- **Situation:** Members should have a professional development plan to share with others who can help them achieve their objectives—likely people who are inquisitive about their professional future and not content with their current situation. The common industry terminology for this group of people is "poised candidates."[A-19]
- **Outlook:** Proactive people who research, plan, self-educate, and talk about their career. Probably the clearest example of proactivity is a student who devotes time, effort, and financial resources toward career advancement.

## 4. Marketing Strategy[A-20]

### 4.1. Market Segmentation

#### 4.1.1. Business Customers

- Small enterprises. Businesses with 10–99 employees. Companies with fewer than 10 employees are categorized as "Very Small Enterprises" and will not be a primary target market.
- Medium enterprises. Businesses with 100–1000 employees.

#### 4.1.2. Individual Members

- Senior college students. Students in the process of searching for a first career.
- Graduate program students. Mid-career candidates searching for new career opportunities, such as internships, part-time during enrollment, or full-time after graduation.
- Current employees. Persons who are currently employed but are poised to locate better career opportunities.
- Unemployed. Persons searching for a job not included in previous segments.

### 4.2. Target Market[A-21]

PeopleAhead plans to focus resources on small to medium enterprises (SMEs) in the New England Metro market, including Boston, Providence, Hartford, Stamford, Norwalk, Worcester, and Springfield. Online recruitment companies compete for national recruitment spending, but most job seekers are locally based, so market penetration is possible by covering a single geographical location. By maintaining this focus, PeopleAhead will be better equipped to build a critical mass of users that represent the job-seeking population and thus improve both users' and customers' experience, customer service, and the use of financial resources.

### 4.3. User Positioning[A-22]

To the proactive professional, PeopleAhead is career advancement done right—providing a platform to discover, plan, and advance careers by uniting friends, co-workers, and mentors with companies searching for the right talent.[A-23]

**A-18**
Although the introduction to this appendix and the plan's organization suggest that analyses of competitors, products, and customers are separate, as this plan shows, a firm usually cannot address one without considering the other. Here, in the Business Customer section, the plan notes what PeopleAhead's competitors fail to do and therefore why it offers a more valuable service.

**A-19**
Understanding a target customer is not just about numbers. PeopleAhead tries to consider what customers think and feel when searching for jobs too.

**A-20**
The plan continues with the same segmentation throughout. Here the plan discusses targeting and what makes each segment attractive.

**A-21**
By already identifying key markets in the previous section, the plan provides a foundation for a more specific targeting statement in this section.

**A-22**
The final step in the STP process: positioning for the segmented, targeted market.

**A-23**
PeopleAhead's mission

5. **Marketing Mix**[A-24]

## 5.1. Products/Services Offered[A-25]

The first planned offering is group profiling; users self-associate with groups to share development plans. Access to groupings is permission based and similar to social networking. Members will be able to share professional experiences with people they know. Group profiling may prompt "voyeur" networking, such that members join to view the profiles of the people they know.[A-26] PeopleAhead will then open group profiling to business customers, who will be granted access to groups of members to target people they want to hire.

The next added feature will be user feedback on professional development plans. PeopleAhead will track data from successful member profile matches to provide feedback for members who have not been matched successfully.

## 5.2. Price

In addition to a basic pricing schedule, PeopleAhead will offer bulk pricing and contract pricing to business customers to satisfy unique customer needs. The pricing model is expected to remain constant, but customer feedback will be analyzed to ensure alignment with their requirements.

Continuing the new customer acquisition plan, PeopleAhead will encourage new trials by offering promotional pricing to new customers.

## 5.3. Distribution[A-27]

- PeopleAhead Challenge: The PeopleAhead Challenge will act as a primary user acquisition strategy. Selection will be focused on successful target segments demanded by customers.
- Direct Sales: Direct customer contact is the preferred method of communication during the first six months. Telesales is the anticipated eventual sales model, due to reduced costs and quicker customer sales cycle, but it limits intimacy between the customer and PeopleAhead. During the initial stages, intimacy and excellent customer service are more highly desired than reduced cost, and direct sales achieve that objective.
- Industry Events: Attendance at HR industry and recruitment events will supplement direct sales efforts.
- Challenge Groups: Word-of-mouth distribution by PeopleAhead members.

## 5.4. Promotion

- Public Profiling: When the product is ready, with proper precautions for protecting competitive advantages, PeopleAhead can increase its web presence. Strategies include contributing articles to recruitment publishers, writing op/ed pieces, public profiling of the founders on websites such as LinkedIn, Ziggs, and ZoomInfo, and blogging.
- Blogger Community Testimonials: Influential users of blogs will be invited to try the system and be granted "exclusive" access to the inner workings of the site. A subsequent linking blitz will put opinion pieces in front of recruiters, job seekers, and the investment community.
- Strategic Alliances: PeopleAhead offers a product that complements the services offered by many large organizations. Partner opportunities exist with
    a. universities, colleges, academic institutions
    b. professional associations, clubs, industry affiliation groups
    c. online associations, groups, blogs
    d. professional services firms, outplacement firms, and executive search firms

Strategic alliances serve multiple purposes: They can help PeopleAhead increase public exposure, increase the user base, expand product offerings, and increase revenue opportunities. These benefits will be considered and partnerships proposed prior to the official launch. For strategic purposes, PeopleAhead prefers to focus on product development in the near term (three months) and then reassess potential alliances after system efficacy has been proven.[A-28]

**A-24**
Given its own section in this plan, a discussion of the marketing mix constitutes a key element of the strategic planning process (see Chapter 2).

**A-25**
According to well known marketing concepts, the marketing mix consists of the four Ps: product (service here), price, place (distribution here), and promotion.

**A-26**
The product (service) offering must establish the value for consumers: Why should they expend effort or resources to obtain the offering?

**A-27**
Making the product (service) available where and when consumers want it may seem somewhat easier for PeopleAhead because of the vast development of the Internet; however, the firm still needs to consider how it can ensure people know where and how to access its offering.

**A-28**
The plan offers a specific time frame, which recognizes the potential need to make changes in the future, as the market dictates.

### 6. Financials

Start-up costs consist primarily of website design and development, legal representation (business formation, contract negotiation, and intellectual property protection), and general overhead. PeopleAhead projects start-up expenditures of $70,000 during inception, of which $30,000 has been funded by the founding team.[A-29]

After the website launches, the cost structure will consist of sales agent salaries, general and administrative operating costs, and marketing. In the first year, marketing expenses are projected to be $6250 per month. Monthly overhead likely will reach $24,750 and remain constant.[A-30]

#### A. Projected Income Statement

**Pro Forma Income Statement**[A-31]

|  | Year 1 | Year 2 | Year 3 | Year 4 | Year 5 |
|---|---|---|---|---|---|
| **Sales** | $56,453 | $2,683,665 | $8,170,655 | $16,312,843 | $30,921,013 |
| **Gross Margin** | $54,194 | $2,316,318 | $7,383,829 | $14,780,329 | $28,244,172 |
| **Gross Margin %** | 96.00% | 86.31% | 90.37% | 90.61% | 91.34% |
| **Net Profit** | $(156,906) | $717,403 | $3,356,768 | $7,035,155 | $14,180,041 |

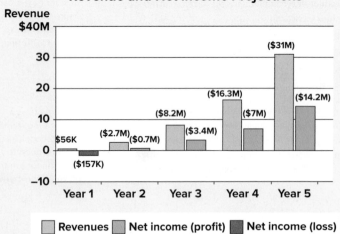

### Revenue and Net Income Projections

**A-29**
The marketing plan needs to identify not only costs, but also potential revenues to cover those costs.

**A-30**
Certain assumptions or marketing research form the basis for its estimation of start-up costs.

**A-31**
This section contains a lot of numbers in a small space; the graphs and tables help to depict those numbers clearly and visually.

7. **Implementation Plan**

The launch of PeopleAhead will use a phased approach, beginning with building brand awareness. Brand awareness should be developed through the founders' visible presence at professional events, online searches, membership in professional associations, networking, and strategic alliances. This visibility will help to gain investment capital.

### 7.1. Objective—Growth[A-32]

- During the first six months of commercial availability, the primary objective is to expand both the user and customer base to maintain a 100:1 user to customer ratio.
  - **Business Customers:** Sign 24 regular customers and 72 occasional customers. Execute 117 position matches.
  - **Individual Members:** Convert 10,000 people to PeopleAhead members.

### 7.2. Marketing Objectives—Growth

- **PeopleAhead Challenge:** Pursue groups that were effective during Beta trial and represent a cohesive set of profiles. Expand and refine the Challenge to reflect lessons learned.
- **Increase member networking activity:** Increase user numbers through networking initiated by existing members. Improve user experience to promote networking.
- **Increase profile completeness:** Increase user engagement with platform.
- **Generate traffic.**
- **Public relations campaign (PR):** Increase awareness of PeopleAhead brand through concentrated PR efforts directed at the target market of customers and users.

### 7.3. Financial Objectives

- **Efficient marketing expenditures:** 9,000 target users (10,000 year-end total −1000 during beta) × $5.00 target acquisition cost = $45,000 budget.
- **Revenue:** $482.50 per position × 117 positions = $56,452.50 revenue.[A-33]

### 7.4. Key Success Factors

- **Economical marketing to relevant constituents:** PeopleAhead needs to establish communication (distribution) channels that pinpoint relevant constituents in a manner consistent with mission values. Limited by resources, chosen channels must aggregate many relevant eyes with free, minimal, or deferred costs involved.
- **Crafting of brand identity:** The contrast between PeopleAhead and competitors lies not only in product differentiation, but also in the company's mission statement and delivery. One-time job search is available from thousands of online recruitment sources. Social networking has been covered from diverse angles, attracting many different audiences. The challenge is to associate www.PeopleAhead.com and TrueMatch® technology with "career advancement done right." The goal is to become the only company that a person thinks of for long-term career discovery, advancement, and development.
- **Efficient value delivery:** The base of customers (both individual and business) needs to receive the proposed value in a timely manner, with consideration given to quality versus quantity of results, alignment with existing objectives, and overall experience with the PeopleAhead brand.
- **Critical mass of business customers and individual users:** The matching process requires that both customers and users exist in the system from the outset of commercialization. This need brings to the forefront the "chicken and egg" scenario; establishing either customers or users requires the other constituent to exist already. The exact number that constitutes "critical mass" ranges from 100 users per position to 10 users per position, depending on compatibility between constituencies.
- **System effectivity:** The ability of PeopleAhead's TrueMatch® software to provide relevant candidate recommendations is critical. The effectiveness of the software depends on the algorithms that match users with positions and the networking protocol that initiates recommendations between users and the people they know. Proposing an inappropriate match could jeopardize the credibility of the system.

**A-32**
This plan divides the objectives into three categories: overall objective, marketing, and financial. Although this is a marketing plan, it must also include other aspects that influence marketing, such as financial status.

**A-33**
By offering quantitative, direct goals, PeopleAhead ensures that it can measure its progress toward those goals.

- **Intellectual property (IP) strategy:** PeopleAhead is engaged in two primary segments of online enterprise: online recruitment and social networking. Existing competitors have made many efforts to protect their methodologies through U.S. patents. However, precedent has not been established for the legal assertions made by these companies. As a result, PeopleAhead will assume an offensive IP strategy, consisting of diligent IP infringement review, patent application where appropriate, and aggressive trade secret protection of best practices.

- **Financial support:** The founders' investment is sufficient to form the business core and take delivery of PeopleAhead's website and software. Financial support will be required to fund operations, execute the IP strategy, and secure customers and users to meet financial targets. Without funding, PeopleAhead will not be able to proceed beyond the product development stage.

- **Sales process:** PeopleAhead's business model requires the acquisition of both business customers who have available positions and users who will be matched with those positions. These two constituents may be reached through different sales processes without overlap.

## 8.   Evaluation and Control

PeopleAhead will evaluate user profiles to identify sets of profiles that are valuable to new business customers, which will aid in the selection of subsequent target market customers.

### 8.1. Business Customer[A-34]

Face-to-face meetings, phone conversations, and email survey contacts with people from a range of industries, company sizes, and functional areas provide a means to (1) build relationships with prospective customers, (2) understand customer needs, and (3) ensure alignment between PeopleAhead's product and customers' recruitment preferences. A summary of the key findings is listed here:

- **Employee fit:** Will the applicant fit our corporate culture? Will the applicant fit with the team we're considering? Will the applicants' competencies fit with the position requirements?

- **Pay for performance:** Objections to recruitment services focus not on price (though it is a consideration) but rather on lack of performance.

- **Unqualified applicants:** Many people who want a job apply, whether they are qualified or not. Recruiters then must scan resumés and weed out unqualified applicants instead of getting to know the qualified applicants.

- **Hard costs vs. soft costs:** Most companies track the recruitment costs of hiring providers, but few measure the time costs of hiring, opportunity costs of hiring the wrong employee, or productivity costs of leaving a position unfilled. Recruitment performance must be easy to measure. Value selling is difficult in human resources departments.

- **Valuable recommendations:** Most recruiters use online recruitment as a necessary but ineffective means of candidate sourcing, secondary to recommendations. Recommendations include the recommender's judgment of the candidate's fit with the available position.

### 8.2. Individual Members

Periodic surveys of various prospective users of online recruitment services indicate (1) current services, (2) methods that work well, and (3) biggest problems with online recruitment providers. The following is a qualitative summary of the key findings:

- **Willingness to try:** Careers are important to people; they are averse to spending time uploading resumé information to online recruitment websites only because of the lack of perceived value. They will spend time when the career opportunities are perceived as valuable.

- **Frustration:** Job seekers are frustrated with available online recruitment providers. Networking is the favoured method for career advancement.

- **Lack of differentiation:** Regardless of the qualifications a job seeker possesses, it is difficult to make them evident in a traditional resumé.

- **Motivation shift over time:** Early professionals are motivated by financial rewards. Mid-career professionals recommend people because it helps the people they know. Late-career professionals hope to improve their own job search opportunities.

## Appendix A. Organizational Chart of PeopleAhead[A-35]

## Appendix B. Competition: Passive Recruiters

A-34
The evaluation section retains the segmentation scheme established previously between business customers and individual members.

A-35
Additional useful information that might clutter the plan should appear in an appendix. The appendices are not included in this illustration.

© Wavebreakmedia Ltd | Dreamstime.com

# Analyzing the Marketing Environment

As we learned in Chapter 2, it is important for firms to perform a SWOT analysis to continuously monitor their internal and external environments to identify new opportunities for or threats to their business. Such analyses help firms identify areas where they are vulnerable to competition and areas where they are dominant. They also need to do a broader analysis that considers other factors such as the economy, political or legal issues, demographics, and concern for the environment. Over time, such factors change in importance for companies and their consumers. Smart marketers continually monitor the marketing environment to develop new strategies or action plans to attack the competition or defend their market position.

For example, it seems that today just about everyone has gone green. Yet companies such as Loblaw first introduced earth-friendly products more than 30 years ago. Not all consumers were ready to pay higher prices for the sake of the environment at that time. However, in 2007, Loblaw scanned the consumer and competitive landscape and sensed that the market was changing. Consumers were ready to accept greater responsibility for the planet. The company launched reusable shopping bags made from 85 percent recycled material that sold for 99 cents. Clearly Loblaw had read the market correctly. The first shipment of bags sold out in only three weeks.

How did Loblaw and other retailers who followed suit make the decision to move away from single-use plastic bags? Cloth and reusable bags had been available for decades. They were not a new concept. However, Al Gore's documentary, *An Inconvenient Truth*, had a tremendous impact on consumer attitudes. Younger consumers had been raised to embrace the green movement. Older demographic cohorts were also learning the importance of protecting the environment. Consumers responded by recycling, replacing incandescent light bulbs, and toting reusable bags when shopping. They also purchased environmentally friendly cleaning products and laundry detergents and reusable water bottles from companies such as Seventh Generation, a company you will learn more about in the Chapter Case Study.

As a result of its environmental scan, Loblaw learned that other countries had already initiated changes involving plastic bags. For example, Ireland had passed a bag tax in 2002 and South Africa banned plastic bags in 2003. In 2007, San Francisco became the first city in North America to ban plastic grocery bags in grocery stores and pharmacies. There were no laws in place that forced Loblaw or other retailers to stop using plastic bags. In fact, the small town of Leaf Rapids, in Northern Manitoba, became the first municipality in Canada to ban plastic shopping bags.

Yet, in 2012, the City of Toronto failed in its efforts to impose a complete ban on plastic bags. In spite of this, the City of Montreal plans to ban thin plastic bags by January 2018.[1] If the ban goes ahead, Montreal will become the first major Canadian city to address the environmental and economic impact of using plastic bags. Vancouver and Victoria are also considering banning plastic bags.

When Loblaw first launched its reusable bags, it incented consumers with 50 PC points for every bag used when they paid with a PC Financial MasterCard or bank card. That incentive is still in place a decade later. Other retailers are also working to encourage consumers to shun plastic bags. For example, Mountain Equipment Co-Op donates 5 cents to an environmental charity when customers use their own bags.

As the above examples demonstrate, commitment to environmental issues can be driven by a number of factors. One thing that does not change is that, as consumers search for green options, marketers need to rethink the way they sell products and services. ∎

# A MARKETING ENVIRONMENT ANALYSIS FRAMEWORK

As the chapter vignette suggests, marketers who understand and manage the changes in their marketing environments are able to adapt their product and service offerings to meet new challenges and opportunities. Loblaw, for example, introduced Click and Collect, a convenient way for time-starved consumers to order and pick up groceries, based on its understanding of the marketplace. Many marketers get their ideas for new products or services from monitoring and studying the marketing environment, as demonstrated in the case of Seventh Generation at the end of this chapter. Analyzing the marketing environment also helps marketers assess their continued strengths and the value of their products and services, and any weaknesses resulting from changes in the marketing environment.

**EXHIBIT 3.1**   Understanding the Marketing Environment

Companies analyze their marketing environment using a framework. At the heart of the analysis is, as always, the consumer. Consumers may be influenced directly by the firm's microenvironment, including the immediate actions of the focal company, the company's competition, and the corporate partners that work with the firm to make and supply products and services to consumers. The firm is—and therefore consumers indirectly are—influenced by the macroenvironment, which includes influences such as culture and demographics, as well as social, technological, economic, and political/legal factors. We'll discuss each of these components in detail in this chapter and suggest how they interrelate. Exhibit 3.1 also illustrates these ideas.

Because the consumer is the centre of all marketing efforts, value-based marketing aims to provide greater value to consumers than competitors offer. The marketing firm must consider the entire business process from a consumer's point of view.[2] Consumers' needs and wants, as well as their ability to purchase, are affected by a host of factors that change and evolve over time. Firms use a variety of tools to keep track of their competitors' activities and communicate with their corporate partners. Furthermore, they monitor their macroenvironment to determine how such factors influence consumers and how they should respond to them. Sometimes, firms can even anticipate trends. For example, pharmaceutical companies have done an excellent job of monitoring market trends and consumers, and responding to consumers' needs. Based on observing and monitoring the aging baby boomer generation of consumers, they have made and marketed drugs to lower cholesterol, improve sexual performance, slow aging, and stem hair loss.

## MICROENVIRONMENTAL FACTORS                    LO1

Exhibit 3.2 illustrates the factors affecting consumers' microenvironment: the company (i.e., its capabilities), its competition, and its corporate partners.

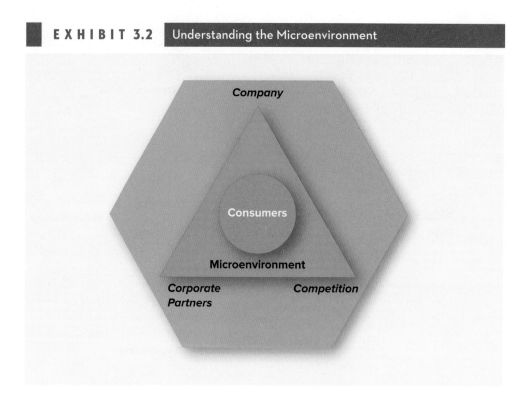

**EXHIBIT 3.2**    Understanding the Microenvironment

## Company Capabilities

In the firm's microenvironment, the first factor that affects the consumer is the firm itself. Successful marketing firms focus their efforts on satisfying customer needs that match their core competencies. The primary strength of Apple, for instance, originally rested in the design, manufacture, distribution, and promotion of Macintosh computers. But Apple has successfully leveraged its core competency in the digital audio player arena with its iPod, iPhone, and iPad. It recognized a trend among consumers for sleek but functional portable devices, which can become one of their personal accessories. Marketers can use an analysis of the external environment, like the SWOT analysis described in Chapter 2, to categorize an opportunity as either attractive or unattractive and, if it appears attractive, to assess it relative to the firm's existing competencies.

## Competition

Competition also significantly affects consumers in the microenvironment. Greater competition may mean more choices for consumers, which influences their buying decisions. It is critical that marketers understand their firm's competitors, including their strengths, weaknesses, and likely reactions to the marketing activities their own firm undertakes. Such questions can become very complicated when one parent company, such as Luxottica, owns several competing brands, such as Pearle Vision, LensCrafters, and Sunglass Hut. When Luxottica devotes more of its marketing budget to one "child," the others suffer. In one year in which advertising for LensCrafters reached $48.5 million but the budget for Pearle Vision was only $14 million, sales for the former jumped 8 percent but those of the latter fell by 3.3 percent.[3] At the same time, Luxottica must consider the moves of true competitors, especially as discount retailers such as Walmart expand their optical services offerings.

Watching competitors is a constant effort—and often a serious battle—in many consumer goods categories. No one would want to get caught in the war between the two razor giants, Gillette and Schick, as each manufacturer works to add ever more blades to its disposable razors.[4] Gillette accused Schick of engaging in false and misleading advertising when ads claimed that its *Hydro* razor would hydrate skin. Schick's parent company countered with the complaint that Gillette's *Fusion ProGlide Razor* ads attempt to deceive when they assert that the blades are "Gillette's thinnest blades ever." All these efforts represent the companies' recognition of what their closest competitor is doing, as well as their attempts to halt tactics they consider damaging. But at the same time, each razor company touts its benefits over its competitors, because the ultimate goal, of course, is to appeal to consumers.

Gillette and Schick are actively engaged in fierce competition for the razor market.

(left): PRNewsFoto/PR NEWSWIRE/Energizer Personal Care via AP Images; (right): © Handout/MCT/Newscom

Firms use **competitive intelligence (CI)** to collect and synthesize information about their position with respect to their rivals. In this way, CI enables companies to anticipate changes in the marketplace rather than merely react to them.[5] In Canada, an Ipsos-Reid study conducted on behalf of the Marketing Research and Intelligence Association reports that, while overall awareness of various business intelligence components ranges from medium to high among CI decision makers and business executives, existing CI activities are fairly limited in practice, and require more resources and attention in the future. The study found that less than half of decision makers say that their company is involved in various CI initiatives.[6]

**competitive intelligence (CI)**
Used by firms to collect and synthesize information about their position with respect to their rivals; enables companies to anticipate changes in the marketplace rather than merely react to them.

The strategies to gather CI can range from simply sending a retail employee to a competitive store to check merchandise, prices, and foot traffic to more involved methods, such as:

- reviewing public materials, including websites, press releases, industry journals, annual reports, subscription databases, permit applications, patent applications, and trade shows
- interviewing customers, suppliers, partners, or former employees
- analyzing a rival's marketing tactics, distribution practices, pricing, and hiring needs

These more sophisticated CI strategies are implicitly obvious in the modern smartphone market. Even though the first cellphone was invented in 1973, it wasn't until the mid-1990s that the introduction of features like text messaging and PDA functions catalyzed an industry metamorphosis that continues to this day. Amid the frenzy of continuously evolving technologies and increasing market competition to serve ever-changing consumer preferences, Apple Inc. has established itself as a front-runner in the smartphone industry. With the introduction of its first generation iPhone, one of the first phones to use a multitouch interface, Apple secured itself a strong position in the market and in the hearts and minds of consumers. As of July 2016, Apple had sold more than 1 billion iPhones.[7] Even so, after facing very strong competition from Samsung's Galaxy line of products, Apple has been

Who copied whom? Apple and Samsung engaged in a patent infringement lawsuit.

© mackney/Alamy Stock Photo

dethroned. And so began a battle for the title of the "King of Smartphones" and global market share. This has entailed the release of subsequent versions of the Galaxy and the iPhone 7, creative marketing campaigns with Samsung branding the Galaxy as the "anti-iPhone," and costly promotional strategies to ensure consumer loyalty and retention. It also resulted in a very high profile lawsuit against Samsung for patent infringement. In situations such as this, it becomes critical for firms to keep close tabs on each other's activities by using CI techniques. If Samsung hadn't paid attention to the market's response to Apple's innovation in design and interface technology, it might never have introduced the Galaxy.

Although CI is widely regarded as a necessary function in today's world, certain uses of this information have come under ethical and legal scrutiny. Take, for example, Apple's case against Samsung. In April 2011, Apple launched a lawsuit against Samsung, claiming deliberate patent infringement on four design patents. These alleged patent infringements in question pertained to features such as the tap-to-zoom, pinch-to-zoom, and bounce-back scrolling.[8] Apple supported these allegations by illustrating the evolution of the design of Samsung phones prior to and after the release of the iPhone in 2007. Apple also presented evidence citing that prior to the launch of the Galaxy Tab, Google and other third parties had warned Samsung that the product too closely resembled the iPad. Google reportedly even asked Samsung to revise the product for a more "distinguishable design." In light of these allegations, Samsung countersued Apple for the alleged infringement of five of its patents. To support this stance, Samsung cited that, in 2006 and prior to the conception of the iPhone, an article dwelling on the design of Samsung devices was circulated to Apple executives. Immediately following the review of this article, Apple's designers were instructed to conceive a "Samsung-like" design for an Apple phone.[9] In the end, the jury ruled in favour of Apple, finding that Samsung had in fact deliberately violated a series of Apple patents whereas Apple did not violate any of Samsung's patents. Samsung was then instructed to pay Apple $1 billion in damages.[10] While some believe that this decision could potentially limit market competition and consumer choice, others argue that it forces companies to innovate rather than imitate. This lawsuit is just one in a series of many dealing with patent infringement in the smartphone industry. One year later, the U.S. International Trade Commission ruled that some iPhone products did in fact violate a Samsung patent and overturned the case.[11]

## Corporate Partners

Few firms operate in isolation. For example, automobile manufacturers collaborate with suppliers of sheet metal, tire manufacturers, component part makers, unions, transport companies, and dealerships to produce and market their automobiles successfully. Even firms such as Dell, which makes its own computers and sells them to customers, must purchase components, consulting services, advertising, and transportation from others. Parties that work with the focal firm are its corporate partners. Consider an example that demonstrates the role these partners play and how they work with the firm to create a single, efficient manufacturing system. Unlike most outdoor clothing manufacturers that use synthetic nonrenewable materials, Nau makes outdoor and ski clothing from renewable sources such as corn and recycled plastic bottles. The company was founded by a team of entrepreneurs who left companies such as Nike and Patagonia. To develop rugged and beautiful clothing from sustainable materials, these founders turned to manufacturing partners around the world to develop new fabrics, such as PLA (polylactic acid), a fast-wicking biopolymer made from corn. To complement the new fabrics, the company uses only organic cotton and wool from "happy sheep," provided by partners in the ranching industry that embrace animal-friendly practices. Thus, Nau not only represents the cutting edge of sustainability and green business, but also clearly demonstrates how "going green" can prompt companies to work more closely with their partners to innovate.[12]

Nau works with its corporate partners to develop socially responsible outdoor (left) and urban (right) apparel.

Courtesy of Nau International, Inc.

# MACROENVIRONMENTAL FACTORS

**L02**

In addition to understanding the company itself, its competition, and its corporate partners, marketers must also understand the **macroenvironmental factors** that operate in the external environment, namely, the culture, demographics, social/natural trends, technological advances, economic situation, and political/legal environment, or CDSTEP, as shown in Exhibit 3.3.

**macroenvironmental factors**
Aspects of the external environment—culture, demographics, social trends, technological advances, economic situation, and political/legal environment (CDSTEP)—that affect companies.

## Culture

We broadly define **culture** as the shared meanings, beliefs, morals, values, and customs of a group of people.[13] Transmitted by words, literature, and institutions, culture is passed down from generation to generation and learned over time. You participate in many cultures. For example, based on your family's cultural heritage, perhaps your mealtime traditions include eating rugelach (a traditional Jewish pastry), or sharing corned beef and cabbage to celebrate your Irish ancestry on St. Patrick's Day. Your school or workplace also shares its own common culture. In a broader sense, you also participate in the cultural aspects of the town and country in which you live. The challenge for marketers is to have products or services identifiable by and relevant to a particular group of people. Our various cultures influence what, why, how, where, and when we buy. Two dimensions of culture that marketers must take into account as they develop their marketing strategies are the culture of the country and that of a region within a country.

**culture**
The shared meanings, beliefs, morals, values, and customs of a group of people.

**Country Culture**   The visible nuances of **country culture**—such as artifacts, behaviour, dress, symbols, physical settings, ceremonies, language differences, colours and tastes, and food preferences—are easy to spot. But the subtle aspects of culture generally are trickier to identify and navigate. BMW's Mini and other global automobile manufacturers have successfully bridged the cultural gap by producing advertising that appeals to the same target market across countries. The pictures and copy are the same. The only thing that changes is the language.

**country culture**
Easy-to-spot visible nuances that are particular to a country, such as dress, symbols, ceremonies, language, colours, and food preferences, and more subtle aspects, which are trickier to identify.

**EXHIBIT 3.3**   The Macroenvironment

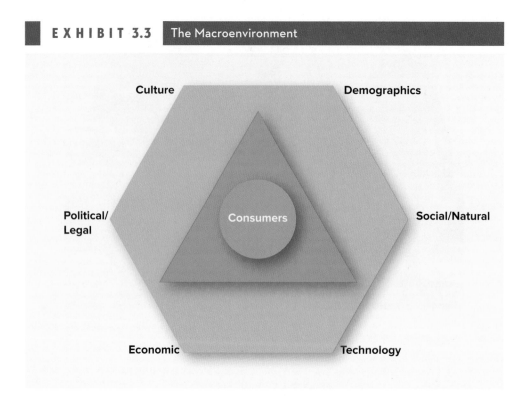

**Regional Subcultures**   The region in which people live in a particular country affects the way they react to different cultural rituals, or even how they refer to a particular product category. A resident of Quebec is 25 percent less likely to buy a hot prepared

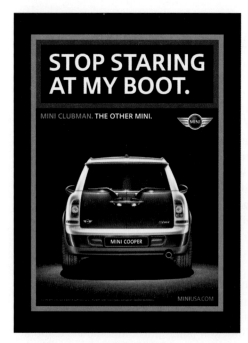

Some firms, such as BMW's Mini, have successfully bridged the cultural gap by producing advertising that appeals to the same target market across countries.

Courtesy MINI USA

meal or reheatable meal than a resident of Ontario. This difference is attributed to Quebec women's desire to cook as a way to be more involved in their family's lives. As well, Quebec consumers are less price sensitive when grocery shopping than residents of Ontario. In Quebec, the most popular stores are IGA and Metro, as compared with No Frills and Food Basics in Ontario.[14] These kinds of differences can be the insight that helps a marketer make a strong connection with a consumer, rather than communicating the same way to all Canadians.

Another example of a regional subcultural difference is how we refer to our beverages. For instance, 37 percent of Canadians refer to carbonated beverages as *soda*, whereas another 40 percent call it *pop*, and an additional 17 percent call any such beverage a "Coke," even when the drink is a Pepsi. Eat lunch in British Columbia, and you'll have the best luck ordering a pop, but if you head to Quebec for dinner, you'd better order a *soft drink*. Imagine the difficulty these firms have in developing promotional materials that transcend regional boundaries.[15]

## Demographics

**Demographics** indicate the characteristics of human populations and segments, especially those used to identify consumer markets. Typical demographics such as age (which includes generational cohorts), gender, income, race, and ethnicity are readily available from market research firms such as Nielsen, Ipsos-Reid, Leger Marketing, and Statistics Canada. For instance, Nielsen collects information about TV viewership and sells it to networks and potential advertisers. The networks then use this information to set their advertising fees, whereas advertisers use it to choose the best shows on which to advertise. For a show popular among the desirable 18- to 35-year-old viewing segment, a network can charge the highest fees. But advertisers also might want to know whether a show is more popular with women than men or with urban or rural viewers. Demographics thus provide an easily understood "snapshot" of the typical consumer in a specific target market.

In the next few sections, we examine how firms use such demographics to assess their customers' needs and position themselves to deliver better value for those customers.

**demographics**
Characteristics of human populations and segments, especially those used to identify consumer markets, such as age, gender, income, race, ethnicity, and education.

**generational cohort**
A group of people of the same generation who typically have similar purchase behaviours because they have shared experiences and are in the same stage of life.

### Generational Cohorts    A group of people of the same generation, a **generational cohort** has similar purchase behaviours because they have shared experiences and are in the same stage of life. Applying age as a basis to identify consumers is quite useful to marketers, as long as it is used in conjunction with other consumer characteristics. For instance, baby boomers (people born between 1946 and 1965) and Generation X (people born between 1966 and 1971) both gravitate toward products and services that foster a casual lifestyle; however, they tend to do so for different reasons.[16] The aging baby boomers, who grew up with jeans and khakis and brought casual dressing into the business arena, are often trying to maintain their youth. Gen Xers, in contrast, typically wear jeans and khakis because they are less impressed with the symbols of conspicuous consumption that their parents seem to have embraced. Age groups can help to identify appropriate media in which firms should advertise, as discussed in Social and Mobile Marketing 3.1. Although there are many ways to cut the generational pie, we discuss four major groups: Generation Z, Generation Y, Generation X, and baby boomers.

Marketers position their products and services differently depending on which generational cohort they are targeting.

Jack Hollingsworth/Getty Images

## Social and Mobile Marketing 3.1

### Understanding Millennial Media Habits[17]

For marketing executives, choices about where and how much to spend to appeal to consumers should depend mainly on a careful analysis of where those consumers are exposed to marketing messages. But when a generation gap appears between these two groups, advertising choices may reflect marketers' preferences more than consumers'.

A clear manifestation comes from advertising for beauty products. Previous generations of consumers often relied on insights and advice from big, glossy fashion magazines. Lush, expensive, two-page spreads, with glamorous shots of beauty products in use, seemed effective and appropriate. But millennials who still read such magazines likely access them online and skip quickly over such long and intrusive ads, with little appreciation for the quality of the shot. Furthermore, recent research shows that such high-quality visual tactics used in print advertisements do not translate particularly well to online product sites. On retail websites, the pretty pictures are largely ineffective because shoppers seek concrete information about their purchase decisions.

According to Forrester Research, 91 percent of millennials are active Internet users. To reach the web, 59 percent of them use smartphones, 35 percent rely on tablets, and 70 percent employ their laptops. This young generation of consumers spends an average of 25 hours online every week.

Their electronic media usage is not the only impressive number describing these consumers: The millennial market encompasses over 9 million consumers, with more spending power than their parents. Yet even when they recognize and appreciate the market size and opportunity that these consumers represent, many marketers—especially those who have reached executive positions after long careers—continue to devote the bulk of their media spending to traditional media channels that millennials don't use much, such as magazines and television.

The main reason for this error might be a somewhat clichéd image of baby boomers, confused and overwhelmed by the new options created through technological advances. Faced with a wealth of choices, such as small independent blogs, content-generating sites, and aggregators, these marketing executives retreat to familiar ground. If they aren't sure what each type of site does, they can't determine the best option.

Even marketers who embrace technology channels for advertising exhibit a tendency to prefer well established, widely known options, such as Facebook or Google. For young consumers who seek exciting, interactive media content, such options have little chances of success.

---

**Generation Z/ digital natives** Generational cohort of people born after 1993.

**Generation Y/ millennials** Generational cohort of people born between 1972 and 1992; the biggest cohort since the original postwar baby boom.

*Generation Z.*    Members of **Generation Z (Gen Z)** are also known as **digital natives**. Born after 1993, people in this group were born into a world that already was full of electronic gadgets and digital technologies such as the Internet and social networks. These technologies are being developed and adopted at an unprecedented rate. Whereas it took 38 years for the radio to be adopted by 50 million people and 13 years for television, it only took 2 years for the same number of consumers to sign up for Facebook.

*Generation Y.*    Generation Y, also called **millennials** or the "echo boom" generation, represent just over 9 million Canadians, or about 27 percent of the population.[18] Born between 1972 and 1992, this group varies the most in age, ranging from people in their 20s to people in their 40s who have started their own families.[19] Generation Y grew up in a more media-intensive and brand-conscious era than their parents. Thus, they are more skeptical about what they hear in the media, which makes marketing to this group even more challenging. If Gen Y members believe the sell is "too hard," they won't buy. Regardless of where they live, they watch an hour less TV than an average household, use the Internet at work for personal reasons, and expect a healthy option at fast-food restaurants.[20] Gen Yers are Internet and technology savvy and love digital electronics such as cellphones, digital music players, digital cameras, and video games. Members of Gen Y often look the same across countries. MTV and CNN are available in most developed countries and so these consumers have similar lifestyles, as well as music and entertainment tastes. Even their "uniforms" of jeans, running shoes, and T-shirts are similar.

Many Gen Yers are starting families and will be prime targets for homes and durable household products such as appliances, furniture, and gardening equipment and tools. In addition, now that Gen Y is established in the workplace, it is becoming apparent that its members have different expectations and requirements than those of other cohorts. Gen Y puts a strong emphasis on balancing work and life; these young adults want a good job, but they also want to live in a location that supports their lifestyle.

Multitasking is no big deal for Gen Y.

© Chuck Savage/Corbis

***Generation X.*** The next group, **Generation X**, includes people born between 1966 and 1971. This group represents more than 2.8 million Canadians, or about 8 percent of the Canadian population.[21] Unlike their baby boomer parents, Gen X is the first generation of latchkey kids (those who grew up in homes in which both parents worked), and 50 percent of them have divorced parents. These young adults, having grown up in times of economic recession, are more likely than previous generations to be unemployed, carry higher debt loads, travel the world, and move far away from their parents; they are also more likely to live longer with their parents, compared with baby boomers, who, at their age, couldn't wait to move away from home.[22]

**Generation X**
Generational cohort of people born between 1966 and 1971.

Gen Xers possesses considerable spending power because they tend to wait to get married and buy houses later in life. However, they are unlikely to enjoy greater prosperity than their parents. They're much less interested in shopping than their parents and are far more cynical, which tends to make them astute consumers. They demand convenience and tend to be less likely to believe advertising claims or what salespeople tell them. Marketing to Gen X is difficult, but word-of-mouth advertising from people they know and trust can give marketers the credibility needed to market to this cohort. Because of their experience as children of working parents who had little time to shop, Gen X were shopping savvy at an early age and knew how to make shopping decisions by the time they were teenagers. As a result, they grew more knowledgeable about products and more risk averse than other generational cohorts. Finally, Gen X is much less interested in status

No matter how old they get, baby boomers will always love rock 'n' roll.

REUTERS/Alamy Stock Photo

products than older generations, not because they can't afford luxury brands but because they just don't see the point. Many companies—such as Harley-Davidson and the Starwood Hotels and Resorts chain—have developed products targeted specifically to Gen X.

**baby boomers**
Generational cohort of people born after World War II until 1965.

*Baby Boomers.*     After World War II, the birth rate in Canada rose sharply, resulting in a group known as the **baby boomers**, who were born between 1946 and 1964. Once the largest cohort of Canadians, they now represent 24 percent of the population , surpassed in size by Gen Y. Although the baby boomer generation spans 18 years, experts agree that its members share several traits that set them apart from those born before World War II. First, they are individualistic. Second, leisure time is a high priority for them. Third, they believe that they will always be able to take care of themselves, partly driven by their feeling of economic security, even though they are a little careless about the way they spend their money. Fourth, they have an obsession with maintaining their youth. Fifth and finally, they will always love rock 'n' roll.

The oldest baby boomers have passed age 65 and many have retired. The baby boomers' quest for youth, in both attitude and appearance, provides a massive market for anti-aging products, cosmetics, pharmaceuticals, and biotechnology. It is estimated that this pursuit of youth will push the global market for anti-aging products to more than $191.7 billion by 2019.[23] Salon services used to be a purely feminine domain, but with boomers rapidly aging, providers are recognizing the potential of positioning themselves as being in the rejuvenation business. In ways that previous generations would have considered unthinkable, men have begun pampering themselves with salon services such as manicures, facials, and pedicures. Indeed, many boomers, including older baby boomers, are driving sports cars and going on adventure-based vacations.

Food companies have also targeted baby boomers with healthier options for cereals, frozen entrees, and snacks that have low fat, and no cholesterol or sugar. General Mills has introduced new products to appeal to boomer preferences including Yoplait Plenti Oatmeal Meets Greek Yogurt and Nature Valley Cereal. Recognizing the aging population's desire for portion control and healthy snacks, Mondelēz launched Wheat Thins Even Thinner. Kellogg added to its line of ready-to-eat cereals with products such as Kashi Heart to Heart Chia and Raisin Bran Omega-3.[24]

Retailers also recognize the immense buying power of the aging baby boomers, so they cater directly to them with larger fonts in signage, staff available to read the small print on product packaging, and seating options in stores. They note that their older customers, even those with moderate incomes, are more focused on quality than price and retailers make decisions accordingly on what merchandise to carry.

Income    The median income of Canadian families in 2015 was $70,336.[25] Canadians may be classified into distinct groups based on their income and other factors such as background, education, and occupation: upper class, middle class, working class (or low-income earners), and underclass (at or below poverty). *Upper-class* consumers are very affluent, and their spending patterns are not influenced by economic conditions. They have high discretionary incomes and tend to purchase luxury items. The top 10 percent of Canadians have family income in excess of $226,000. They are more likely to be highly educated and work in managerial and executive roles. About 48 percent of Canadian households are in the upper class.[26] *Middle-class* families earn between $41,707 and $100,260,[27] with the majority tending toward the higher end of this scale. They can afford a good life most of the time. They tend to be careful about their spending and are often value conscious. Approximately 38 percent of Canadian households fall into the middle class. *Working-class* (or low-income) families represent 14.2 percent of the population and earn between $17,267 and $41,707, barely sufficient income to cover their basic needs. According to a report by Statistics Canada, the richest 20 percent of Canadians spend five or six times more in every shopping category than the poorest 20 percent of Canadians.[28] Family income distribution in Canada varies by province, education level, gender, and profession. This broad range in incomes creates marketing opportunities at both the high and low ends of the market.

Although some marketers choose to target only affluent population segments, others have had great success delivering value to middle- and low-income earners. Consider, for example, the toys presented by the specialty retailer Hammacher Schlemmer versus the mass appeal of Walmart's toy sections. Toy buyers at Walmart are looking for inexpensive products; those at Hammacher Schlemmer go to great lengths to find unusual toys such as the Giant Gumball Machine pictured.[29]

Another aspect of the income demographic relates to the concept of value. Why are customers searching for this value more today than in recent decades? During the first three decades after World War II, most families experienced real income growth but, after 1980, that growth began to idle. Family incomes have stayed slightly ahead of inflation (the general rate of price increases), but their health care costs, property taxes, and tuition bills have risen much faster than inflation.

Education   Studies show that higher levels of education lead to better jobs and higher incomes. Moreover, average annual earnings are higher for those with degrees than for those without. For example, the median earnings for the top 10 percent of Canadians with a bachelor's degree were $105,800.[30] Those with a college diploma earned on average $38,000, and those with less than a high school education earned considerably less at $30,900.[31] The median income for immigrants with a university degree was $36,451, and without a university degree $27,698.[32]

For some products, marketers can combine education level with other data such as occupation and income to obtain quite accurate predictions of purchase behaviour. For instance, a full-time college or university student with a part-time job may have relatively little personal income but will spend his or her disposable dollars differently than would a high school graduate who works in a factory and earns a similar income. College and university students tend to be engaged in playing sports and going to nightclubs, whereas the high school graduate more likely watches sports and goes to bars. Marketers are therefore quite cognizant of the interaction among education, income, and occupation.

Hammacher Schlemmer's Giant Gumball Machine targets an affluent population segment.

© Splash News/Hammacher Schlemmer/ Newscom

Gender   Years ago, gender roles appeared clear, but those male/female roles have been blurred. This shift in attitude and behaviour affects the way many firms design and promote their products and services. For example, more firms are careful about gender neutrality in positioning their products and, furthermore, attempt to transcend gender boundaries whenever they can.

From cars to copiers, sweaters to sweeteners, women make the majority of purchasing decisions and then influence most of the remainder. For instance, despite the

Since women are such an important segment of their customers, Rona, the giant home-improvement chain, has designed its stores with women in mind.

Don Denton/The Canadian Press

Women are no longer the only family member doing the grocery shopping.

Jochen Sand/Digital Vision/Getty Images

traditional view that hardware stores appeal mostly to men, women shoppers are so important to Rona, the home improvement chain, that the stores have been designed with women in mind.[33] Furthermore, women now head more than 20 percent of Canadian households.[34] Clearly, the working women's segment is a large, complex, and lucrative market.

But that doesn't mean marketers have forgotten about men. The days of commercials that show Mom alone with the kids are over. To reflect changing family roles, commercials for most children's gear now include Dad interacting with the kids and being involved in purchase decisions. Although the gap has narrowed, men still earn more money than women. Of 34 industrialized countries, Canada has the eighth highest gap between the incomes of men versus women. In 2015, women working full time earned 73.5 cents for every dollar earned by men. This gap was noted across all education levels and industry sectors; women with university degrees earned 10–30 percent less than men. The difference was even larger for Aboriginal and immigrant women.[35]

**Ethnicity**  Statistics Canada data shows that the ethnic composition of Canada has changed over the last two decades and will continue to change in the next decade. Current research shows that one out of every five Canadians was not born here, accounting for nearly 70 percent of Canada's population growth. If this trend continues, Canada's population growth will be attributed almost exclusively to immigration by 2030.[36] The two fastest-growing groups are the Chinese (from Hong Kong, mainland China, and Taiwan) and South Asians (from India, Pakistan, Sri Lanka, and Bangladesh). It is estimated that by 2031, ethnic groups or visible minorities will include 14.4 million people, almost 42 percent of Canada's population, because of immigration and increasing birth rates among various ethnic groups.[37] Many new immigrants choose to settle in Montreal, Toronto, or Vancouver; however, areas such as Calgary, Edmonton, Winnipeg, and London are growing in popularity. These groups of South Asians and Chinese are typically young, educated, and wealthy. Currently, more than a quarter of all visible minorities in Canada are under 14 years of age; thus, they are likely to have considerable influence over the economy in the future. South Asians are the largest ethnic group in Ontario.[38] Aboriginal people represent another key to Canada's diverse ethnicities, representing 4.3 percent of the total population. Unlike immigrant groups who live primarily in Canada's most urban areas, Aboriginal people live mostly in the territories, western provinces, and Ontario. This population has been growing at a fast pace; from 2006 to 2011, it grew by 20.1 percent to 1.5 million people. By 2036, it is estimated the population will reach 2.6 million.[39] Will a growing population present new opportunities for businesses to market to Aboriginal people?

What does this ethnic demographic shift mean for marketers? Simply put, the growing number of ethnic groups or visible minorities represents both a challenge and a marketing opportunity. The challenge is for marketers to understand the culture, value, and spending patterns of the various groups and determine the best way to communicate and serve them. For example, Nissan started to aim advertising campaigns at South Asians and focused messages around in-vehicle technology since research has shown that South Asians like technology.[40]

In terms of marketing opportunity, it is estimated that ethnic groups spend more than $42 billion on retail goods and services, and the average Chinese household spends

Sobeys' Chalo! FreshCo. store was designed to appeal to the needs of South Asian consumers.

(both): Used with permission of Sobeys Capital Incorporated

$63,500 per year, compared with the Canadian average of $58,500. In general, ethnic Canadians spend more than their white counterparts on big-ticket items such as cars, clothing, and home furnishings. Many also have an affinity for brand-name products because they equate them with quality.[41]

Recognizing this huge opportunity and believing that much of their future growth will come from ethnic markets, Canadian grocers have been adapting existing stores and launching new stores. Loblaws acquired T&T Supermarket in 2009 to reach the Asian market. More recently, it bought Arz Fine Foods in an effort to attract Middle Eastern consumers. The director of ethnic merchandising for Save-On-Foods in Surrey, British Columbia, convinced the produce manager to stock 50 pound bags of onions to meet the needs of large South Asian families. While much smaller bags had not been selling, the first shipment of larger bags sold out in seven days. The experiment proved the demand for competitively priced large bags of other high quality products, including flour, lentils, and spices.[42] Heavyweight Sobeys developed a new store concept, FreshCo, to target the unique needs of the ethnic consumer. After converting existing Price Chopper stores in particularly diverse Brampton and Mississauga markets, it went on to launch over 88 stores across Ontario.[43] The concept is a value-driven store with low prices like No Frills or Food Basics but with a focus on fresh produce, halal meats, and freshly baked breads (unlike most discount banners) to meet the demands of ethnic clientele. As well, the layout of the store is different. After the store's layout guides consumers through the fresh produce, bakery, and meat departments, as in a typical retail grocery store, the natural flow of the store takes shoppers through the extended international foods aisle, which highlights Asian, West Indian, Middle Eastern, and Eastern European food products, before the customers reach the centre grocery aisles.[44] Further adapting the FreshCo store format to match the demographics of the surrounding neighbourhood, it launched Chalo! FreshCo in Brampton in late 2015. It offers the largest assortment of produce of any FreshCo store. That's because 30 percent of its South Asian consumers are vegetarian. Other products designed to meet its shoppers' unique needs include separate meat counters for halal and non-halal products, more than 100 varieties of rice, and even rice cookers and pressure cookers imported from India.[45]

Other grocery stores are responding to remain competitive. Some of the tactics retailers are using to accommodate the ethnic consumer include adapting signs and flyers to feature different languages; choosing ethnic-targeted media to advertise; and offering ethnic merchandise for sale and ensuring it is merchandised correctly. Even smaller retailers such as M&M Food Market celebrate important ethnic holidays such as Chinese New Year, Ramadan, Eid, and Hanukkah with events, promotions, and seasonal products.

## Technological Advances

**technological advances**
Technological changes
that have contributed to
the improvement of the
value of both products
and services in the past
few decades.

**Technological advances** have accelerated greatly during the past few decades, improving the value of both products and services. Consumers have constant access to the Internet everywhere they go via Wi-Fi, mobile hotspots, 4G, and LTE. Smartphones using the iOS and Android operating systems allow for greater computing, data storage, and communication. Tablet computers have extended mobile computing even further by offering a larger mobile interface in environments that traditionally limited access. Flat-screen and high-definition televisions, as well as video on demand, have changed the way we view TV, and their impact is expected only to increase in the next few years.

These examples of advanced technology make consumers increasingly dependent on the help they can provide, especially in terms of making decisions and communicating with others. Netflix suggests which movies we should watch, Spotify outlines the music we should listen to, and Amazon tells us what we should read. Nearfield communication technology takes payments, coupons, and loyalty card data from customers as they walk by the scanner. The next wave of mobile applications is likely to expand the use of wireless payments through mobile wallet applications from Canadian banks or wireless carriers such as Rogers, which offers Suretap Wallet.

Firms use radio frequency identification (RFID) technology to track an item from the moment it is manufactured, through the distribution system, to the retail store, and into the hands of the final consumer. Because they are able to determine exactly how much of each product is at a given point in the supply chain, retailers can also communicate with their suppliers and collaboratively plan to meet their inventory needs.

Mobile devices enhance the customer's experience by making it easier to interact with the manufacturer or retailer or other customers, and they add a new channel of access, which makes customers more loyal and more likely to spend more with a particular retailer. Shoppers Drug Mart's applications allow customers to access new flyer offers, load personalized coupons, add items to a shopping list, order prescription refills, and set up reminder refills. Steve Madden, the footwear retailer, attracts more than 10 percent of its web traffic from mobile devices—which earns it more than $1 million in mobile sales annually. Furthermore, these shoppers spend an average of seven minutes on Steve Madden's mobile site.[46] Whereas customers view an average of seven web pages during online visits, they browse only four or five pages in a mobile setting.

Mobile applications are not just about shopping with a phone. People access the web more often through smartphones than through laptops and desktops combined. But mobile experiences cannot be identical to web experiences, because the interface is different, and thus the way users employ the sites differs. In particular, the smaller screen on mobile devices means that less information must convey the same brand image.

Different technology adoption levels also matter to marketers when communicating about a new product or using a new media type. As noted so far and as described throughout this book in the Social and Mobile Marketing boxes, not only are marketers trying to make social media an integral part of their marketing strategy, but consumers are also using social media to share information and their experiences and frustrations with products, services, and marketers. The relative ease with which consumers can use social media has dramatically increased the power of consumers to affect a firm's marketing strategy. Some firms have embraced social media as a way to get excellent feedback from consumers, which is then used to design new or redesign existing products, services, and marketing campaigns and strategies. Moreover, even traditional media such as TV networks are encouraging consumers to share their experiences, gripes, and frustrations through their websites; these consumer accounts are then aired. For example, the CBC show *The National* has a Go Public link on its website, which encourages consumers to share their stories; one story is reported on every night that the show airs.[47] One story concerned Sears' Kenmore stoves, which consumers said would turn on by themselves, creating a very dangerous situation. And, because they were dissatisfied with the response from Sears, the consumers went public with their story. Needless to say, this story generated a lot of negative publicity for Sears.

## Economic Situation

Marketers monitor the general **economic situation**, both in their home country and abroad, because it affects the way consumers buy merchandise and spend money. Some major factors that influence the state of an economy include the rate of inflation, foreign currency exchange rates, interest rates, and recession.

**Inflation** refers to the persistent increase in the prices of goods and services.[48] Increasing prices cause the purchasing power of the dollar to decline; in other words, a dollar buys less than it used to.

In a similar fashion, **foreign currency fluctuations** can influence consumer spending. For instance, on January 21, 2007, C$1.00 was worth US$0.6179, the lowest exchange rate ever between these two currencies. In less than four months, the value of the Canadian dollar relative to the U.S. dollar increased to $0.9071[49]—a 32 percent increase—and by September the Canadian dollar increased to $1.10. After hovering at parity for two years, the Canadian dollar dropped to $0.90 and has continued to fall since then. Rapid increases in the exchange rate between the currencies of Canada and the United States, our largest trading partner, have both negative and positive consequences for Canadian marketers, depending on whether they are exporters or importers and whether they report their earnings in Canadian or U.S. dollars. The exchange rate changes also have serious implications for consumers. As the value of the Canadian dollar increases compared with the U.S. dollar, merchandise made in Canada and exported to the United States becomes more costly to Americans, and Canadian exporting companies suddenly lose a good chunk of their cost advantage. However, imports of products made in the United States cost less for both Canadian importers and consumers.

Another perhaps unexpected result of the strength of the Canadian dollar compared with the U.S. dollar is that imports of raw material from the United States are cheaper. During such inflationary times, "made in America" claims become more important, which means that Canadian manufacturers and U.S. retailers that specialize in Canadian merchandise must decide whether they should attempt to maintain their profit margins or accept a lower price to keep their customer base. It is not always easy for marketers to respond quickly to rapid increases; however, marketers who monitor the economic environment have the advantage, as they will be able to adjust their strategies if they foresee the increase.

**Interest rates** represent the cost of borrowing money. For example, when customers borrow money from a bank, they agree to pay back the loan, plus the interest that accrues. The interest, in effect, is the cost to the customers or the fee the bank charges those customers for borrowing the money. Likewise, if a customer opens a savings account at a bank, he or she will earn interest on the amount saved, which means the interest becomes the fee the consumer gets for "loaning" the money to the bank. If the interest rate goes up, consumers have an incentive to save more, because they earn more for loaning the bank their money; when interest rates go down, however, consumers generally borrow more.

For instance, when the Bank of Canada cut its overnight lending rate (the rate at which it lends to banks) by 4.25 percent to 0.25 percent in April 2009, record numbers of Canadians took advantage of the historic low interest rates and took out mortgages. The 0.25 percent interest rate broke the previous record low of 1.12 percent, which had been set in 1958, 50 years earlier. The cut was considered absolutely necessary to deal with the worsening global economic and financial crisis. The overnight lending rate has been at 0.5 percent since July 2015,[50] and cheap credit has led to a situation in Canada where the average Canadian income-to-debt ratio is 167.3—that is, for every $1 earned, Canadians owe $1.67. If this situation continues, it could impose negative consequences on the economy and ultimately on consumers and marketers.[51]

Finally, **recession** is a period of economic downturn when the economic growth of the country is negative for at least two consecutive quarters. We last experienced this in 2008–2009. In a recession, the stock market declines sharply, unemployment increases,

**economic situation**
Economic changes that affect the way consumers buy merchandise and spend money; see inflation, foreign currency fluctuations, interest rates, and recession.

**inflation**
Refers to the persistent increase in the prices of goods and services.

**foreign currency fluctuations**
Changes in the value of a country's currency relative to the currency of another country; can influence consumer spending.

**interest rates**
Represent the cost of borrowing money.

**recession**
A period of economic downturn when the economic growth of the country is negative for at least two consecutive quarters.

Tourists from many other countries flock to the United States to shop because the value of the dollar is low compared with their own currency.

Caz Shiba/Digital Vision/Getty Images

business and consumer confidence falls, and spending by both businesses and consumers is severely reduced.

In recessionary times, consumers alter their spending patterns by postponing big-ticket or discretionary items and look for the best deals for items they need. Marketers must adjust their marketing strategies accordingly. Most marketers try to cut costs, lower prices to keep their existing customers and to attract new customers, and may even introduce slightly lower quality goods or reduce the level of services offered in order to manage costs. In a recession, some industries do well and others struggle. Marketers must be vigilant in monitoring the environment and understanding the impact that an economic downturn has on their business.

How do these four important economic factors—inflation, foreign currency fluctuations, interest rates, and recession—affect a firm's ability to market goods and services? Shifts in the four economic factors make marketing easier for some and harder for others. For instance, when inflation increases, consumers probably don't buy less food, but they may shift their expenditures from expensive steaks to less-expensive hamburgers. Grocery stores and inexpensive restaurants win, but expensive restaurants lose. Consumers also buy less discretionary merchandise. For instance, the sale of expensive jewellery, fancy cars, and extravagant vacations will decrease but, curiously, the sale of low-cost luxuries, such as personal care products and home entertainment, tends to increase. It appears that, instead of rewarding themselves with a new Lexus or a health spa vacation, consumers buy a few cosmetics and stream a movie. As noted above, lower interest rates encourage more consumers to borrow to finance purchases, especially of big-ticket or discretionary items such as cars, houses, furniture, and home entertainment systems. Not surprisingly, the building industry and housing market did extremely well in the period leading up to the recent recession. As consumers switched from more- to less-expensive goods and services and demanded greater value, marketers who were able to adjust their offering did much better than those that did not change their value offering.

## Political/Legal Environment

The **political/legal environment** comprises political parties, government organizations, and legislation and laws that promote or inhibit trade and marketing activities. Organizations must fully understand and comply with any legislation regarding fair competition, consumer protection, or industry-specific regulation. Since the turn of the century, the government has enacted laws that promote both fair trade and competition by prohibiting the formation of monopolies or alliances that would damage a competitive marketplace, fostering fair pricing practices for all suppliers and consumers, and promoting free trade agreements among foreign nations.

Legislation also has been enacted to protect consumers in a variety of ways. First, regulations require manufacturers to abstain from false or misleading advertising practices that might mislead consumers, such as claims that a medication can cure a disease when in fact it causes other health risks. Second, manufacturers are required to identify and remove any harmful or hazardous materials (e.g., asbestos) that might place a consumer at risk. As a result, the Alberta Energy Regulator ordered Nexen to shut down 95 pipelines after a rupture at the Long Lake oilsands project leaked 5 million litres of bitumen, sand, and water in the area. The spill was one of the biggest in Alberta's history.[52] Third, organizations must adhere to fair and reasonable business practices when they communicate with consumers. For example, Montreal, Maine, and Atlantic Railway

(MMA) seems to have ignored its own safety procedures regarding the use of hand brakes, which resulted in the fourth deadliest rail accident in Canadian history, killing 42 people and devastating the core of Lac Megantic.

Last but not least, the government enacts laws focused on specific industries and on consumers. These laws may be geared toward increasing competition, such as the deregulation of the telephone and energy industries. Or they may be in response to current events or to achieve specific objectives, such as when the governments of Ontario and British Columbia introduced the harmonized sales tax (HST) to improve the competitiveness of Canadian businesses, or when the federal government introduced the one-year home renovation tax credit to encourage consumers to spend during the recession. Similarly, the government has developed laws to regulate consumer behaviour, such as banning smoking in some areas, mandating child car seats, and requiring drivers to use only hands-free cellphones.

Generally, government regulations may have a negative or positive impact on marketers. On the positive side, certain laws create an opportunity for marketers to sell more of their products, as was the case with Bluetooth devices or car seats. Also, regulation may help to create a level playing field for competition and set standards for marketers to follow. In other cases, regulation tends to increase the cost of compliance; compliance usually requires more paperwork, time, effort, and money, and may cause delays when government approval is needed. Some of the most significant legislation affecting marketing interests appears in Exhibits 3.4 and 3.5.

## Social and Natural Trends

**L03**

Social and natural trends shape consumer values in Canada and the United States, and around the world. These trends tend to change over time in their popularity and importance, and savvy marketers work hard to identify emerging trends to understand whether they present an opportunity or pose a threat to their business. Here, we discuss a few current social and natural trends of key importance today. This list is by no means exhaustive but includes greener consumers, marketing to children, privacy concerns, the time-poor society, and health and wellness concerns.

**Greener Consumers**[53]  **Green marketing** involves a strategic effort by firms to supply customers with environmentally friendly merchandise. Although this "green" trend

**green marketing**
Involves a strategic effort by firms to supply customers with environmentally friendly merchandise.

| **EXHIBIT 3.4** | Major Federal Legislation to Protect Competition and Consumers |
|---|---|

| | |
|---|---|
| Access to Information Act | Income Tax Act |
| Bankruptcy Act | Interest Act |
| Bills of Exchange Act | Investment Canada Act |
| Broadcasting Act | Lobbyist Registration Act |
| Canada Agricultural Product Standards Act | Official Languages Act |
| | Patent Act |
| Canada Corporations Act | Personal Information Protection and Electronic Documents Act (PIPEDA) |
| Canada Dairy Products Act | |
| Canada Human Rights Act | Privacy Act |
| Canada Small Business Financing Act | Small Loans Act |
| Competition Act | Standards Council of Canada Act |
| Consumer Packaging and Labelling Act | Textile Labelling Act |
| Copyright Act | Trade-Marks Act |
| Criminal Code | True Labelling Act |
| Electricity and Gas Inspection Act | Weight and Measures Act |
| Food and Drugs Act | Winding-up Act |

| EXHIBIT 3.5 | Marketing Practices Covered by the Competition Act |

| Law | Description |
| --- | --- |
| **Price** | |
| Price fixing | Sellers conspire to set the price of a product, usually higher than it would be in a free market |
| Price discrimination | Charging different prices to different (competing) buyers for goods of the same quality and of the same quantity |
| Predatory pricing | Pricing that is intended to drive competitors out of the market or keep competitors from entering the market—usually low prices |
| Resale price maintenance | Manufacturers or channel members try to influence the price at which the product is sold to subsequent purchasers |
| Bid rigging | Sellers collude to set prices in response to bids or quotations for products |
| **External** | |
| Misleading advertising | All types of advertising about a product or service that are false or misleading |
| Bait-and-switch | Sellers try to attract customers to their stores by offering a low price on a product (bait); but, once the customers are in the store, sellers try to persuade them to buy a higher-priced item (switch) |
| Referral selling | Incentives offered to consumers to provide the names of other potential consumers |
| **Distribution (Place)** | |
| Refusal to deal | A seller refuses to sell products or services to legitimate buyers |
| Exclusive dealing | A seller refuses to sell to other channel members unless that member agrees to buy exclusively from that particular seller |
| Pyramid selling | Schemes where salespersons are paid to recruit other salespeople, and each new salesperson pays for the right to recruit other salespeople, with some of that money going to earlier recruiters. Participants are often asked to buy a specific quantity of goods or are knowingly sold unreasonable quantities of goods and are not allowed to return the goods on commercially reasonable terms. |

is not new, it is growing. Many consumers, concerned about everything from the purity of air and water to the safety of beef and salmon, believe that each person can make a difference in the environment. A study found that more than 90 percent of Canadians feel that individuals can take action to reduce air pollution. More than half of Canadian households now recycle their soft-drink bottles, cardboard boxes, and newspapers. European consumers are even more green. Germans are required by law to recycle bottles, and the European Union does not allow beef raised on artificial growth hormones to be imported. Ethical Dilemma 3.1 examines some of the challenges companies face in the ethical sourcing of products.

In many cities across Canada, the use of pesticides on lawns is banned and many consumers are trying alternative, environmentally friendly lawn care treatment. Many cities across Canada have introduced the "green bin" program that encourages consumers to recycle their food and yard waste to make compost for gardening. Initial results suggest that this program is hugely successful everywhere it has been introduced. Composting has also spawned business opportunities, as seen in Entrepreneurial Marketing 3.1. The trend for green marketing is likely to persist as we still have a long way to go. According to a Conference Board of Canada report, Canadians produce more garbage than any other country in the developed world and use almost double the amount of fresh water of other countries.[55]

## Ethical Dilemma 3.1

### Consumers Demand Ethical Sourcing[54]

At times it may seem that massive conglomerates are slow to change, but some companies are clearly learning some lessons when it comes to responsible sourcing. A few years ago, Nestlé suffered terrible consumer backlash when it agreed to purchase a small amount of palm oil (used in its chocolate candies) from a company that cleared rainforests to access the palms.

Wary of such reactions, General Mills (GM) quickly promised that all the palm oil used in any of its products and packaging would come from responsible, sustainable sources by 2015. Recent estimates suggest that such moves have achieved some success. The rate of Amazonian deforestation in 2012 was lower than at any other point since the Brazilian government started tracking this statistic in 1988. Today the rate remains well below historical levels.

General Mills is close to meeting its commitment to sustainably source 100 percent of priority ingredients. Determined not to limit itself to palm oil, GM also committed to improving the trade conditions for vanilla farmers that supply the raw material for the traditional, favourite flavour of its Häagen-Dazs ice cream. With a two-year investment of $125 million in Madagascar, GM plans to train small vanilla farmers in sustainable methods that also increase crop quality, such as yield improvements and curing techniques. Ideally, these tactics also will enhance the earnings of local farmers and their communities.

The company has released Global Responsibility Reports annually for more than 46 years to update stakeholders on its sustainability mission and efforts. It also touts its efforts widely through its blog, press releases, and other communications. In this sense, GM runs the risk that skeptical consumers will come to believe it publicizes its good works to cover up bad behaviour. But as the CEO of General Mills has readily acknowledged, "We're finding opportunities to collaborate with business, government and non-governmental organizations on important systemic solutions. While we're proud of our progress, we also know there is still much more to be done. We are committed to continued progress in these areas. Our business requires it and future generations depend on it."

The demand for palm oil can often lead to rainforests, such as this one, being clear cut.

© Warwick Lister-Kaye/Getty Images RF

The demand for green-oriented products has been a boon to the firms that supply them. Marketers encourage consumers to replace their older versions of washing machines and dishwashers with water- and energy-saving models and to invest in phosphate-free laundry detergent and mercury-free, rechargeable batteries. Canada's love affair with recycling also has created markets for recycled building products, packaging, paper goods, and sweaters. Similarly, this higher energy consciousness has spurred the growth of more-efficient appliances, lighting, and heating and cooling systems in homes and offices. Health-conscious consumers continue to fuel the markets for organic foods, natural cleaning and personal care products, air- and water-filtration devices, bottled water, and organic fertilizers. As discussed in Sustainable Marketing 3.1, sneakers made from ocean waste help educate consumers about plastic pollution.

For companies selling environmentally friendly products, the green marketing trend represents a great opportunity. Firms that sell products considered harmful to the environment may find this trend a threat to their business and must innovate to stay in business. However, some green options are more expensive than traditional products and initiatives. Are consumers willing to pay higher prices for green products? Are firms really interested in improving the environment? Or are they disingenuously marketing

## Entrepreneurial Marketing 3.1

# Turning Trash Into Cash[56]

Lisa von Sturmer is a compost crusader who sees dollar signs in dirt. During a weeklong vacation with friends on Savary Island in British Columbia, where composting is mandatory, she was shocked to see how little waste the group generated. When she returned to work she was dismayed at how much organic material was thrown in the garbage, especially since her recent experience had shown just how much of it could diverted. That insight was the impetus to launch Growing City, a service to pick up food scraps from offices in the Vancouver area.

According to von Sturmer, 67 percent of Canadian waste today comes from the office and industrial sector. And that's a growing problem. In 2015 organic materials were banned from landfill sites in Vancouver. Other municipalities and provinces across Canada will also implement bans in the coming years. And that is putting pressure on companies to change the way they deal with organic waste. The solution? Growing City will place stainless steel compost bins in your office kitchens. Employees simply put their food scraps in the bins and Growing City staff does the rest: picks them up, empties and cleans them, and takes the organic material away to an industrial composting facility in Delta, B.C.

Growing City was founded in late 2010. In only two years, it diverted 130 tonnes of waste from landfills. Plus, the company made money doing it: $100,000 in sales the first year. Referrals and word-of-mouth helped the business grow to $212,000 in the second year, leaving enough profits to pay von Sturmer a salary of $55,000. Despite having no business background, von Sturmer has won numerous awards, including the 2010 Small Business B.C.'s Best Business Concept award,[57] and 2012 Canadian Youth Business Foundation's National Best Green Business award,[58] as well as Notable.ca's Best in Social Entrepreneurship award in 2015. By the third year, the company had contracts with 82 offices in Vancouver, Richmond, and Burnaby and was expanding to Surrey. It has also been subcontracted to handle

organics for other companies, including one of Canada's largest recycling companies.

Having started Growing City with a $15,000 loan from the Canadian Business Foundation, von Sturmer needed money to grow. When she pitched on CBC's *Dragons' Den*, she asked for an investment of $100,000 for a 25 percent share of her company, telling the Dragons that she'd had requests for franchises and needed their help to do this. Her compelling presentation led three Dragons to express interest. In the end, she took an offer from Jim Treliving, who could both provide a cash infusion and help with franchising. She had no idea that her appearance on the show would generate so much exposure. Over 1,200 people applied to open franchises, with half of the applicants coming from global markets.

In 2013, the Vancouver market produced 270,000 tonnes of organic waste. By 2015, it had to deal with 540,000 tonnes, representing almost $200 million in revenue. Three months before the ban came into effect, Growing City added hundreds of new locations. One client alone had 110 buildings that the company quickly brought on board. The Convention Centre was a big win that let the company scale up but without the same complexity of servicing numerous smaller locations. Revenue growth in 2015 surpassed 87 percent. The company was on track for another 50 percent growth in sales in 2016.

Growing City competes with billion dollar waste management companies, so von Sturmer leverages technology to sell her services since she can't compete on price. QR codes are used at pick-up locations that show building managers when a truck was on site, the weight of materials picked up, and how much waste was diverted from landfill. This data is used in the company's asset management database and used to generate client reports. Good customer service, the use of metrics, and technology to generate reports is putting Growing City on track to turn even more trash into cash.

Lisa von Sturmer turns trash into cash with her Growing City office compost bins.

Used with permission of Growing City

products or services as environmentally friendly, with the goal of gaining public approval and sales rather than actually improving the environment?

Companies also need to rise above suspicions of "greenwashing." Consumers often question whether a firm is spending significantly more money and time advertising being

## Sustainable Marketing 3.1

# Sneakers From Ocean Plastic Trash[59]

The Adidas Group is always looking to make better products and use innovative manufacturing techniques. To show just how much of an impact companies can make, Adidas and Parley for the Oceans have launched a new sneaker design made with plastic trash reclaimed from the ocean. The recycling project helps the Adidas Group meet its ongoing sustainability goals. More importantly, it helps to educate consumers and raise awareness of what can be done to stop ocean plastic pollution.

Concerned that the oceans are being destroyed by plastic, Adidas joined with Parley for the Oceans to show that ocean waste can be turned into something cool. Eric Liedtke, the executive board member for global brands with the Adidas Group, said that the company would produce 1 million pairs of shoes in 2017 using Parley Ocean Plastic. He noted, "This partnership allows us to tap into new areas and create innovative materials and products for our athletes. We invite everyone to join us on this journey to clean up the oceans."

The new sneaker is designed with an upper part from ocean plastic content and a 3D printed midsole that uses recycled polyamid and gill net content. Introduced at the Sustainable Innovation Forum in Paris in December 2015, the timing coincided with the addition of the ocean movement cause to COP21's agenda. According to a recent sustainability report, Adidas says the sneaker is not a standalone project. It intends to integrate ocean waste into future products.

Adidas and Parley for the Oceans use waste pulled from the ocean to create sustainable sneakers.

Krisztian Bocsi/Bloomberg via Getty Images

Although the recycled shoe project is intended to kickstart change in ocean health, the Adidas Group has long been committed to sustainability initiatives. For example, it ended the use of plastic microbeads in its products as of December 2015 and completed the phasing out of plastic bags in its retail stores in March 2016. Its DryDye project reduces the amount of water needed to manufacture its products. Between 2011 and 2015, a virtualization project allowed the company to produce 2.4 million fewer samples.

green and operating with consideration for the environment than actually spending these resources on environmentally sound practices. To show it is a responsible retailer, Rona has adopted a strict scientific method that monitors a product over all stages of its life cycle: acquisition of materials, manufacturing, packaging and transportation, and finally, use and end of life.[60] The Sustainable Marketing boxes throughout this book provide many more examples of how individual Canadians and businesses are taking actions to reduce the harmful effects of their consumption and production decisions.

**Privacy Concerns**   More and more consumers worldwide sense a loss of privacy. At the same time that the Internet has created an erupting volcano of accessibility to consumer information, improvements in computer storage facilities and the manipulation of information have led to more and better credit-check services. In addition, consumers are constantly reminded that their identity may not be their own, as in the humorous series of Citibank commercials that depict unsuspecting credit card users who have had their identities stolen. In one, a sweet-looking older woman describes her new pickup truck in a deep, masculine voiceover. Although these commercials promote a new credit card with identity theft protection, most consumers have no such protection. In July 2015, the Ashley Madison website was hacked. The Toronto-based company offered a service to 32 million members looking for extramarital affairs. These members assumed their email addresses and other contact information was secure. The breach, which made global news, caused outraged members to launch a class-action lawsuit. Canada's

Time-poor consumers multitask to cope with their lack of leisure time.

© Monkeybusinessimages/Dreamstime.com/GetStock.com

privacy commissioner probed the issue and a criminal investigation was launched. The company suffered huge revenue losses and Ashley Madison's founder, Noel Bidermann, stepped down as CEO.[61] Given recent security breaches at retailers such as Winners, Home Depot, and Staples, it is hardly surprising that more than three-quarters of Canadians are concerned about the security and privacy of the information they provide over the Internet.[62]

**The Time-Poor Society**    Reaching a target market has always been a major challenge, but it is made even more complicated by several trends that increase the difficulty of grabbing those markets' attention. First, in the majority of families, both parents work, and the kids are busier than ever. For example, on average, Canadians worked 8.9 hours during a typical workday, but 25 percent said they devote more than 10 hours a day to their work. That means Canadians have less time for leisure and to spend with family. Canadian workers spend about 200 hours less with family per year than they did two decades ago.[63]

Second, consumers today have hundreds of shows and programs available to them through TV, radio, DVDs, smartphones, personal computers, and the Internet. With many shows and programs available on the Internet, consumers can choose when, where, and what shows they want to watch or listen to at their convenience. By fast-forwarding through the commercials, they can catch an entire one-hour show in approximately 47 minutes, which means they miss all the messages marketers are attempting to send them.

Third, many consumers attempt to cope with their lack of leisure time by multi-tasking: watching TV or listening to music while talking on the telephone or doing homework. Their divided attention means they simply cannot focus as well on the advertisements that appear in those media.

Marketers are thus faced with the challenge of finding more creative ways to get their marketing messages out to consumers under these ever-changing media consumption trends. Some marketers have responded to the challenge of getting consumers' attention by, for example, moving some of their advertising expenditures from traditional venues such as TV and print media to instant messaging, Internet-based reviews and ads, social media ads, movie screens, fortune cookies, baggage claim conveyor belts, billboards, and ads in airports and on taxis, buses, and mass transport vehicles.[64] Retailers are doing their part by making their products available to customers whenever and wherever they want. For instance, retailers such as Sears Canada and The Bay are becoming full-fledged multi-channel retailers that offer stores, catalogues, and Internet shopping options. Others, such as Metro, Shoppers Drug Mart, and Walmart, have extended their hours of operation so that their customers can shop during hours that they aren't working. In addition, automated processes such as self-checkout lanes and electronic kiosks speed the shopping process and provide customers with product and ordering information.

To find and develop methods to make life easier for many diverse consumers in a time-poor society, marketers often rely on technology, another macroenvironmental factor we discussed earlier in this section.

Self-checkout lanes speed the shopping process, but do they improve customer service?

Mira/Alamy Stock Photo

**Health and Wellness Concerns** Health concerns, especially those pertaining to children, are prevalent, critical, and widespread. In Canada, 60.1 percent of adult men and 44.2 percent of adult women are categorized as obese or overweight.[65] In the past 20 years, child obesity has doubled and teenage obesity tripled in North America, leading to sky-rocketing rates of high blood pressure, high cholesterol, early signs of heart disease, and Type 2 diabetes among children. In response, the Center for Science and the Public Interest (CSPI) has proposed *Guidelines for Responsible Food Marketing to Children*, which outlines a variety of changes to advertising directed at children. The CSPI notes that children are highly impressionable, and most food advertising to these young consumers touts high-calorie, low-nutrition products, associated in advertising with various toys, cartoons, and celebrities. The new guidelines require advertisers to market food in reasonably proportioned sizes. The advertised food items also must provide basic nutrients, have less than 30 percent of their total calories from fat, and include no added sweeteners. The advertising also cannot be aired during children's programming, and companies cannot link unhealthy foods with cartoon and celebrity figures. For example, Burger King no longer uses SpongeBob SquarePants to promote burgers and fries. Other organizations such as the Chronic Disease Prevention Alliance of Canada (CDPAC) and health and citizens' groups are also working to ensure proper advertising to children.[66]

Consumers' interest in improving their health has opened up several new markets and niches focused on healthy living. For example, consumer spending on yoga classes, mats, and clothing has increased consistently, leading to an 87 percent increase in yoga product spending in the last five years.[67] Yoga studios actually combine multiple modern trends: As the economy sours, people face increasing stress, which they hope to reduce through yoga. In addition, yoga studios are relatively inexpensive to open and operate, so entrepreneurs and consumers appreciate the value for the money they offer. And of course, North Americans are always on the lookout for exercise methods that can help them shed pounds and match media images of athletic prowess. As a result, competition is growing in this industry and some studios are starting to combine yoga classes with additional offers to attract clients, such as smoothie bars, acupuncture, and massages.

# LEARNING OBJECTIVES REVIEW

**LO1** **Outline how the factors in a firm's microenvironment influence its marketing strategy**

The three factors in a firm's microenvironment are its capabilities, corporate partners, and competition. Everything a firm does should utilize its strengths and revolve around the customer; without the customer, nothing gets sold. Firms must discover their customers' wants and needs and then be able to provide a valuable product or service that will satisfy those needs. If there were only one firm and many customers, a marketer's life would be simple. But because this set-up rarely occurs, firms must monitor their competitors to discover how they might be appealing to their customers. Without competitive intelligence, a firm's customers might soon belong to its competitors. Though life would certainly be easier without competitors, it would be difficult, if not impossible, without corporate partners. Good marketing firms work closely with their suppliers, marketing research firms, consultants, and transportation firms to coordinate the extensive process of discovering what customers want and getting it to them when and where they want it. Each of these activities—identifying corporate strengths, discovering customer needs, and working with corporate partners—is central to the firm's marketing strategy and helps add value to firms' products and services.

**LO2** **Identify the factors in a firm's macroenvironment and explain how they influence its overall marketing strategy**

The factors in the firm's external environment are culture, demographics, social and natural trends, technological advances, economic situation, and political/legal environment (CDSTEP). A clear understanding of these factors enables marketers to understand whether they pose threats or present new opportunities.

What are the chances that a fast-food hamburger restaurant would be successful in a predominantly Hindu neighbourhood? Not very good. Marketers must be sensitive to such cultural issues to be successful, and then they must also consider competitors as well as customer demographics—age, gender, income, race, ethnicity, and education—to identify specific customer groups. In any society, major social and natural trends influence the way people live. Understanding these trends can help marketers serve their customers better. At no other time in history has technology moved so rapidly and had such a pervasive influence on the way we live. Not only do marketers help to develop technologies for practical, everyday uses, but technological advances also help marketers provide consumers with more products and services more quickly and efficiently. The general state of the economy influences how people spend their disposable income. When the economy is healthy, marketing success comes relatively easily. But when the economy gets bumpy, only well honed marketing skill can yield long-term successes. Naturally, all firms must abide by the law, but many legal issues also affect marketing directly. These laws can be broken into those that pertain to competitive practices, such as antitrust legislation, and those designed to protect consumers from unfair or dangerous practices, such as warning labels on cigarette packages.

**LO3    Identify important social and natural trends that impact marketing decisions**

In any society, major social and natural trends influence the way people live. Social trends have a tremendous impact on what consumers purchase and consume. Understanding these trends—such as price sensitivity, health and wellness, green marketing, privacy issues, and the time-poor society—can help marketers serve their customers better by offering them products and services that closely match their needs and wants.

## KEY TERMS

- baby boomers
- competitive intelligence (CI)
- country culture
- culture
- demographics
- economic situation
- foreign currency fluctuations
- Generation X
- Generation Y/millennials
- Generation Z/digital natives
- generational cohort
- green marketing
- inflation
- interest rates
- macroenvironmental factors
- political/legal environment
- recession
- technological advances

## CONCEPT REVIEW

1. List the three elements a firm must assess before looking externally (i.e., microenvironmental factors).

2. List and describe the elements of a firm's macroenvironment. Select a Canadian company that you think has done a great job at managing the macroenvironmental factors and discuss what it has done.

3. List five ways in which baby boomers, Generation X, and Generation Y are different.

4. If a store permanently offers extended shopping hours, what macroenvironmental factor(s) is it appealing to?

5. List some of the important social and natural trends affecting the Canadian market.

6. Besides language, explain why using the same advertisement for Ontario and for Quebec wouldn't be equally successful.

7. Why should marketers care about engaging tweens quickly and sincerely?

8. How do changes in the value of the Canadian dollar in relation to the U.S. dollar affect Canadian companies that sell to American consumers?

9. Why is understanding cultures and subcultures so important in marketing?

10. The Chinese and South Asian consumer segment is rapidly growing in Canada. What opportunities and challenges does this trend pose for food and grocery retailers? What strategies could they use to market effectively to this segment of consumers?

## MARKETING APPLICATIONS

1. Assume you are going to open a new store selling fitness products. Describe it. Who are your competitors? What would you do to monitor your competitors' actions? Who are your customers? What are you going to do to appeal to them?

2. How do you approach buying a computer differently than your parents would? What about buying an outfit to wear to a party? How can firms use their knowledge of different age or generational cohorts to market their products and services better?

3. How can firms use customer demographics such as income, education, and ethnicity to market to their customers better?

4. Identify some of the changes in the gender landscape. Describe how they might affect the marketing practices of (a) men's apparel retailers, (b) do-it-yourself home improvement retailers, and (c) upscale salon services.

5. Identify some recent technological innovations in the marketplace and describe how they have affected consumers' everyday activities.

6. Do you feel that firms are invading or could invade your privacy? Why or why not?

7. Why should Canadian companies selling goods in the United States care about the value of the U.S. dollar?

8. Time-poor consumers have adopted various approaches to "buy" themselves more time, such as (a) voluntarily simplifying their complex lives, (b) using new technologies for greater empowerment and control, (c) using their time productively when travelling or commuting, and (d) multi-tasking. Identify and describe some products and services that consumers use to implement each of these strategies.

9. Identify a company that you believe does a particularly good job of marketing to different cultural groups. Justify your answer.

10. You have recently been hired by a major department store in its marketing department. Your boss informs you that you will supervise a field research study. You arrive at your assigned store and find that the study consists of shadowing customers. The store has set up a "private" shopping event for store credit card holders. All who attend must swipe their cards to receive the special discount coupon book. The shadow shoppers (who the store manager hired) are given hand-held devices loaded with a specific customer's information and past purchase behaviour. Thus, each shadow shopper knows the name, address, income, family size, and spending patterns for the customer she or he is observing. You begin to feel uncomfortable about this study since the consumers have no idea they are being tracked, nor do they know the level of confidential information about them that a stranger can access. You are also concerned that the shadow customers are not regular employees or employees of an established marketing research provider. What, if anything, would or should you do about your concerns?

## NET SAVVY

1. Seventh Generation is the leading brand of nontoxic, environmentally safe household products in Canada (products are sold at Home Depot). Visit Seventh Generation's website (http://www.seventhgeneration.com) and review the philosophy behind the business. Next, review the site to identify the products that the company offers. Briefly summarize some of the consumer trends you note, and describe the ways in which the company's products address the wants and needs of its customers.

2. Visit the Cool Hunter (http://www.thecoolhunter.net) and identify examples that would provide marketers with insights regarding social trends.

## CHAPTER CASE STUDY

### A NEXT-GENERATION CLEANER

Taking an Iroquois directive—"In our every deliberation, we must consider the impact of our decisions on the next seven generations"—the consumer product company Seventh Generation has applied a distinctly modern sensibility to derive a long-term approach to the marketing environment. Although its mission statement might be focused on future generations, its efforts to appeal to current consumers are always responsive to their immediate demands.

Seventh Generation dominates the environmentally friendly cleaning products market.
© HO Marketwire/Newscom

From its start in 1988, Seventh Generation has grown to become a national brand with over $200 million in revenues.[68] Its growth has been sparked largely by consumer desires to buy more sustainable, environmentally safe green products. Approximately 71 percent of consumers in a recent survey indicated that they thought it was important to buy green offerings, and consumer demand for products in a wide range of categories continues to grow.[69]

But even as more categories appear to offer promising green opportunities for marketers, the primary purchase area continues to be groceries and household products—exactly the space that Seventh Generation dominates. As it has gained brand recognition and trust, it also has proactively altered its market. That is, Seventh Generation does not simply wait for customers to request options; it creates entirely new categories.

With a new line of detergents, Seventh Generation began promoting the idea that perhaps chemical brighteners—common to virtually all commercially available detergents, even those that avoid dyes or fragrances—are not necessary. The company took care not to suggest that these chemicals were dangerous. It just says they're unnecessary, and for consumers interested in environmental concerns, that may be enough.

Previously, household magazines such as *Good Housekeeping* or *Real Simple* might have ranked the best detergent, the best dishwashing soap, and the best surface cleaner. But the entry of companies such as Seventh Generation has created new categories: best green detergent, best green dishwashing soap, and best green cleaner. Seventh Generation products consistently emerge victorious in these new category contests.[70]

In addition, to maintain its brand recognition, it uses extensive multimedia marketing initiatives. In print ads, it highlights the environmentally friendly contents of its laundry detergent. It provides free samples to active bloggers, along with blacklights so these consumers can test their own clothes to see the residues left by other detergents. Dozens have posted the results of their own in-home experiments.[71]

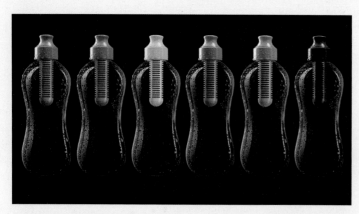

To appeal to its environmentally conscious customers, Seventh Generation is incorporating reusable, self-filtering water bottles into its products.

© PRNewsFoto/PR NEWSWIRE/bobble via AP Images

Yet its products also cost more, which offers a significant challenge in the very price-competitive cleaning products market. Even as many consumer product companies increasingly tout their down-market brands, Seventh Generation introduced a 4× concentrated laundry detergent that costs significantly more. The new derivation avoids all volatile organic compounds and relies on enzymes to get clothes clean.[72] It also introduced a new line of dishwasher detergent. Both product lines are formulated to work in either hot or cold water with low energy settings.

In 2013, Seventh Generation spent a significant sum to acquire Bobble, a company that produces reusable, self-filtering water bottles. Because many consumers worry about their environmentally unfriendly consumption of plastic water bottles, but also are not willing to trust unfiltered tap water, the new product provides an effective solution.

More recently it introduced Presse by Bobble, a way for consumers to brew one cup of coffee at a time that avoids the waste that results from most single serve pod systems.[73]

With these moves, Seventh Generation appears poised to "extend our influence and spread our practices more broadly by acquiring innovative brands in the sustainability space," in the words of the company CEO.[74] It's not surprising that "The Better World Shopping Guide" ranked the company as the best company on the planet five consecutive times.[75]

### Questions

1. What macroenvironmental factors and consumer trends does Seventh Generation respond to most effectively?

2. If it were to perform an environmental scan now, could you identify any factors or consumer trends it should consider?

# CHAPTER 4

## LEARNING OBJECTIVES

**After studying this chapter you should be able to**

**LO1** Describe the steps in the consumer buying decision process

**LO2** Identify what determines how much time consumers will spend searching for information before buying a product or service

**LO3** Summarize how psychological, social, and situational factors influence consumers' buying behaviour

**LO4** Explain how involvement influences the consumer buying decision process

Newzulu/Alamy Stock Photo

# Consumer Behaviour

Consumers should be at the heart of all marketing decisions and strategies. This point has been emphasized in every chapter so far. Marketers who develop a deep understanding of consumer needs and wants are able to act even before customers articulate those needs. Such insights help companies gain strategic competitive advantage over competitors. In trying to satisfy consumer needs, one particularly difficult challenge for marketers is to understand consumers' behaviour—why they prefer one brand, store, or service provider over another. And how do the factors that influence their purchase behaviour change over time or with the types of purchases? In some cases, consumer behaviour must change for products to be successful. The introduction of electric vehicles is a case in point.

Toyota was arguably the first car manufacturer to recognize that consumer concerns about the harmful effects of their carbon footprint would lead to a market for more fuel-efficient cars. It recognized this consumer need a decade before its competition when it launched the Prius, a hybrid gas–electric car, in 1997. Prior to the car's launch, skeptics and critics questioned its appeal and consumer acceptance. Unfamiliar with battery powered vehicles, consumers were reluctant to pay a premium for the car at the outset. Changing consumer habits is hard but not impossible. Today, Prius global sales have grown and are projected to reach 300,000–350,000 cars annually.[1]

While consumers gradually embraced the Prius, convincing them to move to fully electric vehicles will require even more attitude, learning, and motivational changes. For example, people who buy conventional vehicles don't need to be educated on where or how to buy gas. With electric vehicles, the buying process is very different since consumers need to understand how far they can drive on a charge, how long it takes to recharge, where charging stations are located, the life of a battery, and much more.

Tesla's goal for its battery powered vehicles is to turn the world "energy positive." From the outset, Tesla's mission has been "to accelerate the advent of sustainable transport by bringing compelling mass market electric cars to market as soon as possible."[2] Its strategy has been to offer high-end vehicles to consumers willing to pay a premium, then drive down the price point with each new model introduced. For example, the base price of the initial model, the Roadster, was over $109,000. While it only sold about 2,500 cars worldwide, it led the way to the Model S, with a much lower base price of $69,000.[3] Most recently, plans were announced for the Model 3, priced at only $35,000. In a testament to just how much consumer behaviour has changed, in Montreal, hundreds of people lined up in the rain for a chance to put their names on the pre-order list. No details about the design of the car were published. And in spite of the $1,000 deposit for a car that would not be available until late 2017 at best, almost 400,000 pre-orders were received.[4] What motivates such behaviour?

Although "green" is becoming a determinant attribute in some consumers' buying decisions, the decision to buy an electric car is complex, involving such variables as personal style, vehicle appearance, price, reliability, and safety. Tesla's goal to sell 500,000 cars annually by 2020 is a big leap from the 50,000 cars it currently sells each year. Consumer attitudes toward electric cars must continue to change for the company to achieve this ambitious goal and make inroads into the mass market. ∎

We begin this chapter by exploring the process that consumers go through when buying products and services. Then we discuss the psychological, social, and situational factors that influence this consumer decision process. We end the chapter with a discussion of how the level of consumer involvement influences the buying decision process. Throughout the chapter, we illustrate what firms can do to influence consumers to purchase their products and services.

# THE CONSUMER DECISION PROCESS

LO1

The consumer decision process model represents the steps that consumers go through before, during, and after making purchases. Because marketers often find it difficult to determine how consumers make purchasing decisions, it is useful for us to break the process into a series of steps and to examine each step individually,[5] as in Exhibit 4.1.

## Step 1: Need Recognition

The consumer decision process begins when consumers recognize they have an unsatisfied need and want to go from their needy state to a different, desired state. The greater the discrepancy between these two states, the greater the **need recognition**

**need recognition**
The beginning of the consumer decision process; occurs when consumers recognize they have an unsatisfied need and want to go from their needy state to a different, desired state.

**EXHIBIT 4.1**  The Consumer Decision Process

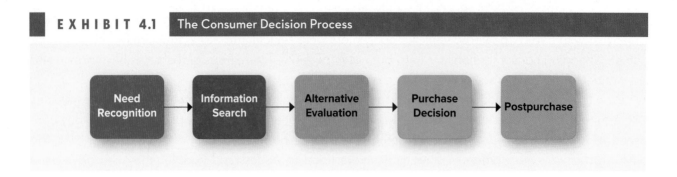

Need Recognition → Information Search → Alternative Evaluation → Purchase Decision → Postpurchase

will be. For example, your stomach tells you that you are hungry, and you would rather not have that particular feeling. If you are only a little hungry, you may ignore the feeling and decide to eat later. But if your stomach is growling and you cannot concentrate, the need—the difference between your actual (hungry) state and your desired (not hungry) state—is greater, and you'll want to eat immediately to get to your desired state. Consumer needs like these can be classified as functional, psychological, or both.[6]

**functional needs**
Pertain to the performance of a product or service.

**psychological needs**
Pertain to the personal gratification consumers associate with a product or service.

Functional Needs    **Functional needs** pertain to the performance of a product or service. For years, BMW has made functionally superior motorcycles. BMW's K1600 model has an inline six-cylinder motor, something previously available only in BMW automobiles, combined with a stiff aluminum frame. Thus it offers remarkable power on a lightweight bike, enabling it to outperform both the best luxury touring bikes in terms of comfort and serious sporty motorcycles in terms of speed.

Psychological Needs    **Psychological needs** pertain to the personal gratification consumers associate with a product and/or service. Purses, for instance, provide a functional need: to transport wallets and other personal items and keep them organized and safe. So why would anyone pay more than $5,000 for a purse that does not perform these tasks any better than a $100 purse? Because they seek to satisfy psychological needs. Each year, Lana Marks produces a single Cleopatra clutch purse valued at $250,000. The purse might be embellished, such as one version that featured more than 1,500 black and white diamonds, 18-carat gold, and alligator skin. The company permits one star each year to bring its purse to the Oscars; recent winners of this informal contest were Charlize Theron and Helen Mirren.[7] Even though these bags are not known for being particularly practical, strong demand for Lana Marks bags persists among women who love exciting (and expensive) purses.

These examples highlight that most goods and services seek to satisfy both functional and psychological needs, albeit to different degrees. Whereas the functional characteristics of a BMW K1600 are its main selling point, it also maintains a fashionable appeal for bikers and comes in several colours to match buyers' aesthetic preferences. Lana Marks purses satisfy psychological needs that overshadow the functional needs, though they still ultimately serve the function of carrying personal items. You can get a $15 haircut at First Choice Haircutters or spend $80 or more to get basically the same thing at an upscale salon. Are the two haircuts objectively different? The

Do Lana Marks bags, like this one carried by Bingbing Li, satisfy psychological or functional needs?
© Ethan Miller/Staff/Getty Images

answer might vary depending on which you believe represents a good haircut and good value. One person might value getting a really good deal; another might enjoy the extra attention and amenities associated with a fancy salon.

Successful marketing requires determining the correct balance of functional and psychological needs that best appeals to the firm's target markets. Harley-Davidson, for instance, produces motorcycles that do much more than get their riders to the mall and back. Harleys are a way of life for motorcycle enthusiasts who want to ride and have fun. Even though other manufacturers—such as Yamaha, Honda, Suzuki, and Kawasaki—offer functional, dependable, and fast motorcycles, they cannot compete with the Harley mystique.

So, what can marketers do at the need recognition stage to influence consumer purchase decisions? Marketers use numerous tactics to either remind customers of a need or create new needs. Researching and understanding what products and services customers need or want and why—these are the first steps in developing appropriate tactics. Common tactics marketers employ include using reminder advertising for their products, creating awareness about a new product and its capabilities, showing how a product could enhance consumers' image, and even altering the physical layout of a store or where products are placed in stores. For example, placing products near checkout lanes or placing products that customers buy together (e.g., eggs and bread) near each other means that when customers come to buy one item (eggs), they are reminded of the other item (bread).

What needs does a BMW K1600 satisfy?
© ZUMA Press, Inc./Alamy Stock Photo

## Step 2: Information Search

**L02**

The second step, after a consumer recognizes a need, is to search for information about the various options that exist to satisfy that need. The length and intensity of the search are based on several factors, including the degree of perceived risk associated with purchasing the product or service and the importance of the product to the consumer. If the way your hair is cut is important to your appearance and self-image, you may engage in an involved search for the right salon and stylist. Alternatively, an athlete looking for a buzz cut might go to the closest, most convenient, and cheapest barber shop. Regardless of the required search level, there are two key types of information: internal and external.

**Internal Search for Information**    In an **internal search for information**, the buyer examines his or her own memory and knowledge about the product or service, gathered through past experiences. For example, every time Katie wants to eat salad for lunch, she and her friends go to Cultures. But if she's craving dessert, she heads straight to Cold Stone Creamery. In making these choices, she relies on her memory of past experiences when she has eaten at these restaurants.

**External Search for Information**    In an **external search for information**, the buyer seeks information outside his or her personal knowledge base to help make the buying decision. Consumers might fill in their personal knowledge gaps by talking with friends, family, or a salesperson. They can also scour commercial media for unsponsored and (it is hoped) unbiased information, such as that available through *Consumer Reports*, or peruse sponsored media such as magazines, TV, or radio. With the explosive growth of smartphones, consumers can turn to the Internet to search for information in real time simply because they have their phones with them all the time. Perhaps the most common sources of external information these days are online search engines, such as Google and Bing. But to be effective, those search engines also must ensure that consumers' searches lead them to the most informative or helpful sites, as Ethical Dilemma 4.1 notes.

**internal search for information**
Occurs when the buyer examines his or her own memory and knowledge about the product or service, gathered through past experiences.

**external search for information**
Occurs when the buyer seeks information outside his or her personal knowledge base to help make the buying decision.

## Ethical Dilemma 4.1

## Penalizing Negative SEO[8]

Companies that seek to get their websites featured prominently on search engines such as Google and Bing turn to well known search engine optimization (SEO) techniques. The techniques vary in their cost, effectiveness, and ethicality. It's one thing to pay a fee to Google to achieve a top-five ranking in the search results. It's another thing completely to try to game the system or, even worse, create fake, poor-quality links to competitors, such that their sites fall in the rankings.

Such negative SEO seems to be on the rise, in two main forms. First, some companies work to increase the number of links their websites show by setting up "dummy" sites that link only to their main website. These links are often spurious. For example, a consumer searching for information about a particular city might find an apparent informational page. However, every time that page mentions the word hotel, it leads to a single company's hotel booking page. Second, competitors might build poor-quality links. Although the increase in the number of links would increase search visibility, the resulting connections would be bloated, unhelpful, and uninformative. Consumers quickly would learn to avoid the site.

In response to these concerns, Google has cracked down, punishing sites that feature any of these questionable tactics. Expedia recently saw a massive drop of approximately 25 percent in its web visibility after Google imposed penalties on it, causing its stock value to drop by 4.3 percent in a single day. The source of the poor links on Expedia's site is unclear—whether its marketing department got careless or competitors sought to damage it. But for Google, the source does not matter much.

Nor is Expedia the only example. A lyric site, Rap-Genius, acknowledged that it had engaged in some questionable tactics too, though it alleged essentially that everyone else was doing it already. Halifax Bank, owned by the renowned Lloyd's of London, also suffered penalties and a substantial drop in its search engine visibility.

The increasing prevalence and notoriety of these punishments create significant questions for consumers. Can they really trust the results they uncover when they type a search term into a search engine? Are the first few entries really the best links? Because consumers overwhelmingly choose from among the results that appear in the first page of a search engine query, companies continue to seek ways to improve their rankings. But if Google, Bing, or any other search engine wants to keep customers coming back, it needs to prevent any tactics that ultimately leave the customer unsatisfied and uninformed.

Expedia.com's SEO visibility dropped significantly when Google imposed a penalty for poor links on its site.

Searchmetrics, Inc.

The Internet provides information in various ways. For example, while watching a rerun of *Glee*, Katie saw the character Marley wearing a fantastic outfit that included a flare dress and silver pendant. She pulled her laptop over, went to WornOnTv.net, and found the focal episode, which in turn told her where to purchase the items she loved. The pendant was designed by Baroni and available for $119, and the dress cost $48. But Katie is also a savvy shopper, so when she searched for "Baroni Expressive Pendant" on Bing, she found that she could get it at a lower price from another retailer. Satisfied with that purchase, she began flipping through a magazine and saw Reese Witherspoon wearing a pair of adorable jeans. This time she navigated directly to TrueFit.com, which featured those very jeans, designed by 7 for All Mankind, on its home page. Katie entered her measurements and style preferences, and the website returned recommendations of jeans that would be a good fit for her.

All these examples are external searches for information. Katie used the television show's dedicated site to find a style she liked; she referred to a magazine for additional style tips; and she found jeans that would be a perfect fit for her using the web. All these events took place without Katie ever leaving her home to go to the store or try on dozens of pairs of pants.

Katie liked the picture of Reese Witherspoon in jeans that she found in a magazine so much that she navigated to TrueFit.com and purchased them.

JB Lacroix/WireImage/Getty Images

## Factors Affecting Consumers' Search Processes

It is important for marketers to understand the many factors that affect consumers' search processes. Among them are the following:

- *The perceived benefits versus perceived costs of search.*   Is it worth the time and effort to search for information about a product or service? For instance, most families spend a lot of time researching the automobile market before they make a purchase because cars are a relatively expensive and important purchase with significant safety implications, whereas families likely spend little time researching which inexpensive plastic toy car to buy for the youngest member of the family.

- *The locus of control.*   People who have an **internal locus of control** believe they have some control over the outcomes of their actions, in which case they generally engage in more search activities. With an **external locus of control**, consumers believe that fate or other external factors control all outcomes. In that case, they believe it doesn't matter how much information they gather; if they make a wise decision, it isn't to their credit, and if they make a poor one, it isn't their fault. For example, if Brad believes he can get a better deal when buying his first car, he will conduct an extensive search for information and try to use the information when negotiating his purchase. However, if Brad feels that regardless of what information he has, he can do little to influence the outcome of the deal, he will not engage in an extensive search.

- *Actual or perceived risk.*   Five types of risk associated with purchase decisions can delay or discourage a purchase: performance, financial, social, physiological, and psychological. The higher the risk, the more likely the consumer is to engage in an extended search.

**internal locus of control**
Refers to when consumers believe they have some control over the outcomes of their actions, in which case they generally engage in more search activities.

**external locus of control**
Refers to when consumers believe that fate or other external factors control all outcomes.

**performance risk**
Involves the perceived danger inherent in a poorly performing product or service.

**financial risk**
Risk associated with a monetary outlay; includes the initial cost of the purchase, as well as the costs of using the item or service.

**social risk**
Involves the fears that consumers suffer when they worry that others might not regard their purchases positively.

**physiological risk**
Risk associated with the fear of an actual harm should the product not perform properly.

**psychological risk**
Associated with the way people will feel if the product or service does not convey the right image.

**Performance risk** involves the perceived danger inherent in a poorly performing product or service. Examples of performance risk might be the possibility that the Tesla Model 3 battery takes longer to charge than expected or that Brad's sports car does not start on the day he is supposed to take his girlfriend out for a drive.

**Financial risk** is risk associated with a monetary outlay and includes the initial cost of the purchase, as well as the costs of using the item or service. Car manufacturers, for instance, recognize that extended warranties help alleviate financial risk because consumers fear extensive postpurchase repair costs. For example, Brad bought two additional years of warranty over the manufacturer's standard "three-year, 60,000 kilometre" coverage for his sports car to reduce his financial risk within the first five years of buying the car.

**Social risk** involves the fears that consumers suffer when they worry that others might not regard their purchases positively. When buying a dress, consumers like Katie, Brad's girlfriend, consider what her friends would think. Alternatively, since a job interview is so important, Katie might make a conscious effort to assert a distinctive identity or make a statement by buying a unique, more stylish, and possibly more expensive dress than her friends would typically buy.

**Physiological risk** could also be called safety risk. Whereas performance risk involves what might happen if a product does not perform as expected, physiological (or safety) risk refers to the fear of actual harm should the product not perform properly. Although physiological risk is typically not an issue with apparel, it can be an important issue when buying other products, such as a car. External agencies and government bodies publish safety ratings for cars to help assuage this risk. Consumers compare the safety records of their various choices because they recognize the real danger to their well-being if the automobile they purchase fails to perform a basic task, such as stopping when the driver steps on the brakes. An example of this is the safety recalls by Honda, Toyota, and Nissan that recalled over 200,000 cars in Canada due to issues with faulty airbags that sent pieces of plastic flying when the inflator burst.

Finally, a **psychological risk** is associated with the way people will feel if the product or service does not convey the right image. For example, Brad looked up reviews of the various sports cars and asked his friends their opinions because he wanted people to perceive his choice as a really good one.

Knowing that consumers go through various levels of information search, marketers must try to understand the sources customers use to search for information and the importance of each source. With this knowledge, marketers could implement various tactics, including providing information about their products or even educating customers about their product in general or a product category as a way to build trust and credibility (e.g., teaching consumers about digital cameras or photography while promoting their own brand of camera). Additionally, marketers must ensure they communicate tactics aimed at reducing risks to customers. For example, marketers can provide guarantees through which defective products can be returned for a full refund or replaced at the company's expense, or that allow consumers to return products if they are not completely satisfied with them. Marketers also sometimes reduce the perception of risk by showing consumers that others have purchased the product and are proud owners or users.

## Step 3: Alternative Evaluation

Once consumers have recognized a problem and explored the possible options, they must sift through the choices available and evaluate the alternatives. Alternative evaluation often occurs while consumers are engaged in the process of information search. For example, a vegetarian consumer might learn about a new brand of yogurt that he or she can immediately rule out as a viable alternative because it contains unsuitable animal

Ann Taylor is part of the retrieval set of stores available to women for business apparel, but Banana Republic is in the evoked set for young women looking for business apparel.

(left): Anonymous/AP Images; (right): Sang Tan/AP Images

by-products. Consumers forgo alternative evaluations altogether when buying habitual (convenience) products; you'll rarely catch a loyal skim milk drinker buying a carton of full fat milk.

**Attribute Sets**   Research has shown that a consumer's mind organizes and categorizes alternatives to aid his or her decision process. **Universal sets** include all possible choices for a product category, but because it would be unwieldy for a person to recall all possible alternatives for every purchase decision, marketers tend to focus on only a subset of choices. One important subset is **retrieval sets**, which are those brands or stores that can be readily brought forth from memory. Another is a consumer's **evoked set**, which comprises the alternative brands or stores that the consumer states he or she would consider when making a purchase decision. If a firm can get its brand or store into a consumer's evoked set, it has increased the likelihood of purchase and therefore reduced search time because the consumer will think specifically of that brand when considering choices.

Katie Smith knows that there are a lot of apparel stores (universal set). However, only some have the style that she is looking for, such as Le Château, Ann Taylor, The Gap, and Banana Republic (retrieval set). She recalls that Ann Taylor is where her mother shops and The Gap is a favourite of her younger sister. But she is sure that Le Château and Banana Republic carry business attire she would like, so only those stores are in her evoked set.

When consumers begin to evaluate different alternatives, they often base their evaluations on a set of important attributes or evaluative criteria. **Evaluative criteria** consist of a set of salient, or important, attributes about a particular product that are used to compare alternative products. For example, when Katie is looking for her outfit, she might consider things like the selling price, fit, materials and construction quality, reputation of the brand, and service support that the retailer offers. At times, however, it becomes difficult to evaluate different brands or stores because there are so many choices, especially when those choices involve aspects of the garment that are difficult to evaluate, such as materials and construction quality.

To simplify the potentially complicated decision process, consumers use shortcuts such as determinant attributes and consumer decision rules. **Determinant attributes** are product or service features that are *important* to the buyer and on which competing brands or stores are perceived to *differ*.[9] Because many important and desirable attributes are equal among the various choices, consumers look for something special—a determinant attribute—to differentiate one brand or store from another and

**universal sets**
Consist of all possible choices for a product category.

**retrieval sets**
Consist of those brands or stores that can be readily brought forth from memory.

**evoked set**
Comprises the alternative brands or stores that the consumer states would be considered when making a purchase decision.

**evaluative criteria**
Consist of a set of salient, or important, attributes about a particular product that are used to compare alternative products.

**determinant attributes**
Product or service features that are important to the buyer and on which competing brands or stores are perceived to differ.

| EXHIBIT 4.2 | Compensatory Versus Noncompensatory Choices for Buying a Car | | | | |
|---|---|---|---|---|---|
| | **Mileage** | **Style** | **Price** | **Accessories** | **Overall Score** |
| **Importance Weight** | 0.4 | 0.1 | 0.3 | 0.2 | |
| **Toyota** | 10 | 8 | 6 | 8 | 8.2 |
| **Honda** | 8 | 9 | 8 | 3 | 7.1 |
| **Nissan** | 6 | 8 | 10 | 5 | 7.2 |

Evaluations are based on a 1 (very poor) to 10 (very good) scale.
Based on the noncompensatory decision rule (based on price), Nissan is the best candidate for purchase.

on which to base their choice. Determinant attributes may appear perfectly rational, such as health and nutrition claims offered by certain foods and beverages, or they may be more subtle and psychologically based, such as the red soles on a pair of Christian Louboutin heels.

**consumer decision rules**
The set of criteria consumers use consciously or subconsciously to quickly and efficiently select from among several alternatives.

**Consumer decision rules** are the set of criteria that consumers use consciously or subconsciously to quickly and efficiently select from among several alternatives. These rules take several different forms: compensatory, noncompensatory, or decision heuristics.

**compensatory decision rule**
Is at work when the consumer is evaluating alternatives and trades off one characteristic against another, such that good characteristics compensate for bad ones.

Compensatory    A **compensatory decision rule** assumes that the consumer, when evaluating alternatives, trades off one characteristic against another, such that good characteristics compensate for bad characteristics.[10] For instance, when Brad was looking to buy a new car he considered several factors, such as mileage, style, price, and accessories. Even if the car's price is a little more than Brad was planning to spend, the superb mileage offsets, or *compensates* for, the higher price.

Although Brad probably would not go through the formal process of making the purchasing decision based on the model described in Exhibit 4.2, it illustrates how a compensatory model would work. Brad assigns weights to each factor depending on their importance to him. These weights must add up to 1.0. So, for instance, mileage is the most important with a weight of 0.4, and style is least important with a weight of 0.1. Then Brad assigns weights to how well each of the cars might perform, with 1 being very poor, and 10 being very good. For instance, he thinks Toyota has the best mileage, so he assigns it a 10. Brad multiplies each performance rating by its importance rating to get an overall score for each car. The rating for Toyota in this example is the highest of the three cars ($[0.4 \times 10] + [0.1 \times 8] + [0.3 \times 6] + [0.2 \times 8] = 8.2$).

**noncompensatory decision rule**
Is at work when consumers choose a product or service on the basis of a subset of its characteristics, regardless of the values of its other attributes.

Noncompensatory    Sometimes, however, consumers use a **noncompensatory decision rule**, in which they choose a product or service on the basis of a subset of its characteristics, regardless of the values of its other attributes.[11] Thus, Brad might find a car with a lot of accessories and great mileage that costs considerably more than he is willing to spend, but might reject the car simply on the basis of price. Because the Nissan offers a better price (he rated the price of a Toyota as 6 and a Nissan as 10 on the 10-point scale), he decides that the strength of the good points of the Toyota does not compensate for its biggest weakness—a high ticket price. Thus, based on compensatory decision rules, Brad should choose the Toyota car; but, using a noncompensatory decision rule, the prices of the cars, Brad chose the Nissan.

Once consumers have considered the possible alternatives and weighed the pros and cons, they can move toward a purchase decision.

**decision heuristics**
Mental shortcuts that help consumers narrow down choices; examples include price, brand, and product presentation.

Decision Heuristics    Not everyone uses compensatory or noncompensatory decision rules. Some people use **decision heuristics**, which are mental shortcuts that help them narrow down their choices. Some examples of these heuristics follow:

- *Price.* Consumers can choose the more expensive option, thinking they are getting better quality along with the higher price ("You get what you pay for"), or they might buy the product priced in the middle of the alternatives, neither the most expensive nor the cheapest, thinking that it is a good compromise between the two extremes.[12]

- *Brand.* Always buying brand-name goods allows some consumers to feel safe with their choices. Purchasing a national brand, even if it is more expensive, gives many consumers the sense that they are buying a higher quality item.[13] For example, many consumers buy more expensive Tylenol or Advil pain relief tablets over Shoppers Drug Mart's Life brand pain tablets because they believe the former are higher quality products, despite identical ingredients in the generic brand.

The distinctive style of these Lululemon yoga pants is a determinant attribute that distinguishes the product from other brands.

Xaume Olleros/Bloomberg via Getty Images

- *Product presentation.* Many times, the manner in which a product is presented can influence the decision process. For example, two similar homes that are comparably priced will be perceived quite differently if one is presented in a perfectly clean and uncluttered condition, with fresh flowers and the smell of chocolate chip cookies wafting through it, whereas the other appears messy, has too much furniture for the rooms, and emits an unappealing smell. Consumers want to see that some effort has been put into the selling process, and just the way the product is presented can make or break a sale.[14]

Generally, the extent of alternative evaluation depends on several factors, such as the types of products or services (specialty, shopping, or convenience), the importance of the purchase, the perceived risks, and the expressive value of the purchase (i.e., to what extent the customers feel the product reflects an aspect of their personality). Shopping products tend to involve greater evaluation than convenience products. The purchase of highly expressive products that carry greater risks and that are more important to consumers involves more evaluation than the purchase of products that are less expressive or that have lower perceived risks.

Marketers can assist consumers in their evaluation process not only by educating them about the company's products, but also by providing detailed comparison information on price, technical specifications, unique features and benefits, and so on. Marketers may even provide free samples or trials of their products, which may enable consumers to compare the actual products.

## Step 4: Purchase Decision

After evaluating the alternatives, customers are ready to buy. However, they don't always patronize the store or purchase the brand or item on which they had originally decided. It may not be available at the retail store or there may be some other stumbling block. Retailers therefore turn to the conversion rate to measure how well they have converted purchase intentions into purchases. One method of measuring the conversion rate is the number of real or virtual abandoned carts in the retailer's store or on its website.

Gilt.com encourages customers to buy now by offering a limited number of items for a short time period.

Courtesy of Gilt

Retailers use various tactics to increase the chances that customers will convert their positive evaluations into purchases. They can reduce the number of abandoned carts by making it easier to purchase merchandise. Most importantly, they should have plenty of stock on hand of the merchandise that customers want. Retailers can also reduce the actual wait time to buy merchandise by opening more checkout lanes and placing them conveniently inside the store. To reduce perceived wait times, they might install digital displays to entertain customers waiting in line.[15]

Conversion rates tend to be lower for consumers using an Internet channel because they are able to examine and store products in their online shopping cart and still delay their purchase decision. To encourage customers to make purchase decisions, Zappos.com and Overstock.com create urgency by alerting customers when an item in their shopping cart is almost sold out. Other online retailers, such as Gilt, offer items for a specified 36-hour period or until they run out, and Neiman Marcus runs two-hour, online-only sales. Many retailers send reminder emails to visitors about items in carts they have abandoned.[16]

After consumers purchase the product or service, they usually consume it, or "put it to the test." A special type of consumption is called **ritual consumption**, which refers to a pattern of behaviours tied to life events that affect what and how we consume. These behaviours tend to have symbolic meanings and vary greatly by culture. They might take the form of everyday rituals, such as Brad going to Tim Hortons® for his daily morning coffee or you brushing your teeth, or they can be reserved for special occasions, such as rites of passage or holiday rituals. Many firms try to tie their products and services to ritual consumption; just imagine, where would Hallmark be without holidays?

Situational factors can help facilitate purchases: having the merchandise in stock, offering multiple payment options (e.g., cash, cheque, credit card, debit card, interest-free loans, no down payment), having many checkout lanes open and placing the checkouts conveniently in the store, installing digital displays to entertain customers waiting in line,[17] and offering tactics such as delivery, price-match guarantee, a warranty, or a simple return policy. Additional factors that affect whether the purchase decision is made immediately or later—such as store atmospherics, shopping situation, and temporal states—are discussed later in this chapter.

**ritual consumption**
Refers to a pattern of behaviours tied to life events that affect what and how people consume.

## Step 5: Postpurchase

The final step of the consumer decision process is postpurchase behaviour. Marketers are particularly interested in postpurchase behaviour because it entails actual, rather than potential, customers. Marketers hope to create satisfied customers who become loyal, purchase again, and spread positive word-of-mouth. However, dissatisfied customers are not likely to patronize the store again and will spread negative word-of-mouth.

There are three possible postpurchase outcomes, as illustrated in Exhibit 4.3: customer satisfaction, postpurchase cognitive dissonance (buyer's remorse), and customer loyalty (or disloyalty).

**Customer Satisfaction**   Setting unrealistically high consumer expectations of the product through advertising, personal selling, or other types of promotion may lead to higher initial sales, but eventually it will result in dissatisfaction when the product fails

**EXHIBIT 4.3**   Postpurchase Outcomes

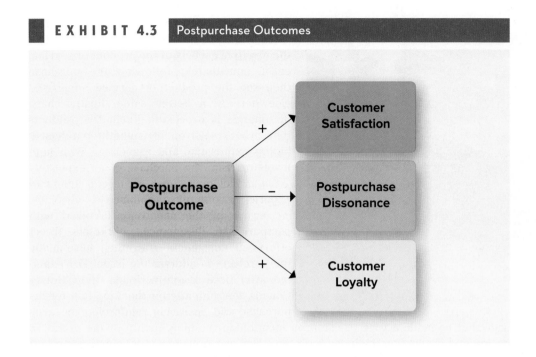

to achieve these high performance expectations. This failure can lead to dissatisfied customers and the potential for negative word-of-mouth. (For a related discussion about communication gaps, see Chapter 10.)

Setting customer expectations too low is an equally dangerous strategy. Many retailers don't "put their best foot forward"; no matter how good their merchandise and service may be, if their store is not clean and appealing, customers are not likely to enter.

Marketers can take the following steps to ensure postpurchase satisfaction:

- Build realistic expectations—not too high and not too low—and deliver on those expectations.
- Demonstrate correct product use; improper usage can cause dissatisfaction.
- Stand behind the product or service by providing money-back guarantees and warranties.
- Encourage customer feedback, which cuts down on negative word-of-mouth and helps marketers adjust their offerings.
- Periodically make contact with customers and thank them for their support. This contact reminds customers the marketer cares about their business and wants them to be satisfied. It also provides an opportunity to correct any problems. Customers appreciate human contact, though it is more expensive for marketers than email or postal mail contacts.

**Postpurchase Cognitive Dissonance**   **Postpurchase dissonance** (or buyer's remorse) is an internal conflict that arises from an inconsistency between two beliefs, or between beliefs and behaviour. For example, you might have buyer's remorse after purchasing an expensive TV because you question whether a high-priced TV has appreciably better quality than a similar-size TV at a lower price. Thus, postpurchase cognitive dissonance is a feeling of regret, guilt, or grave uneasiness, which generally occurs when a consumer questions the appropriateness of a purchase after his or her decision has been made. This usually occurs when consumers feel, for example, that they made the purchase without all the information they needed, they were persuaded

**postpurchase dissonance**
An internal conflict that arises from an inconsistency between two beliefs, or between beliefs and behaviour; buyer's remorse.

Consumers often feel dissonance when purchasing products or services.

Andrei Tudoran/Shutterstock.com

by a salesperson, or they liked the good features of the product or service but do not like the negative aspects of the product or service, or if immediately following the purchase they see the product or service advertised elsewhere at a better value. Postpurchase dissonance is especially likely for products that are expensive, infrequently purchased, highly expressive, and associated with high levels of risk. The purchase of an expensive Tesla model may cause some consumers to experience cognitive dissonance.

Aware of the negativity involved with postpurchase dissonance, marketers direct efforts at consumers after they have made the purchase to address the issue. For example, after Brad bought a Honda Civic, Honda Canada sent him a letter thanking him for his purchase and positively reinforcing the message that he made a wise decision by mentioning the high quality of the product's design and production. Included with the letter was a customer satisfaction survey) that asked about Brad's satisfaction with the dealership, the salesperson, and other aspects of his purchase experience. Brad also received additional information about Honda services available to Honda Civic owners. To reduce the dissonance, Brad can take several actions:

● Pay attention to positive information about the Honda Civic, such as looking up reviews by owners and car buffs on the Internet.

● Get positive feedback from friends about his new sports car.

● Seek negative information about sports cars he did not buy. Reading these reviews makes him feel more comfortable with his purchase decision.

### Customer Loyalty

Customer loyalty develops over time with multiple repeat purchases of the product or brand from the same marketer. In the postpurchase stage of the decision-making process, marketers attempt to build and nurture a loyal relationship with their customers from the very first purchase and with each subsequent purchase. They want customers to be satisfied with their purchase every time and buy from the same company again. Loyal customers will buy only certain brands and shop at certain stores, and they do not consider other brands or firms in their decision. As we explained in Chapter 2, such customers are therefore very valuable to firms, and marketers have designed customer relationship management (CRM) programs specifically to retain them.

### Undesirable Consumer Behaviour

Although firms want satisfied, loyal customers, sometimes they fail to obtain them. Passive consumers are those who don't repeat purchase or who fail to recommend the product to others. More serious and potentially damaging, however, is negative consumer behaviour, such as negative word-of-mouth and rumours.

**negative word-of-mouth**
Occurs when consumers spread negative information about a product, service, or store to others.

**Negative word-of-mouth** occurs when consumers spread negative information about a product, service, or store to others. When customers' expectations are met or even exceeded, they often don't tell anyone about it. But when consumers believe that they have been treated unfairly in some way, they usually want to complain, often to many people. The Internet has provided an effective means of spreading negative word-of-mouth to millions of people instantaneously through personal blogs, Twitter, and corporate websites. To lessen the impact of negative word-of-mouth, firms provide customer service representatives—whether online, on the phone, or in stores—to handle and respond to complaints.

Some companies allow customers to post comments and complaints on their social media sites. For example, Whirlpool set up Facebook pages for its appliance brands, Maytag, KitchenAid, and Whirlpool. Customers can share their thoughts on these sites without fear of their negative feedback being deleted. Whirlpool believes it should "keep the bad" to open up discussions and emphasize the proactive measures the company is taking to remedy service or product failures. If a customer believes that positive action will be taken as a result of the complaint, he or she is less likely to complain to family and friends or through the Internet. (A detailed example of word-of-mouth appears in Chapter 10.)

# FACTORS INFLUENCING CONSUMER BUYING DECISIONS

**L03**

The consumer decision process can be influenced by several factors, as illustrated in Exhibit 4.4. First are psychological factors, which are influences internal to the customer, such as motives, attitudes, perceptions, learning, and lifestyles. Second, social factors, such as family, reference groups, and culture, also influence the decision process. Third, situational factors, such as the specific purchase situation, a particular shopping situation, and temporal states (the time of day), affect the decision process.

Every decision people make as consumers will take them through some form of the consumer decision process. But, like life itself, this process does not exist in a vacuum.

**EXHIBIT 4.4** | Factors Affecting the Consumer Decision Process

Motives
Attitudes
Perceptions
Learning
Lifestyle

Psychological Factors

Consumer Decision Process

Social Factors

Family
Reference Groups
Culture

Situational Factors

Purchase Situation
Shopping Situation
Temporal State

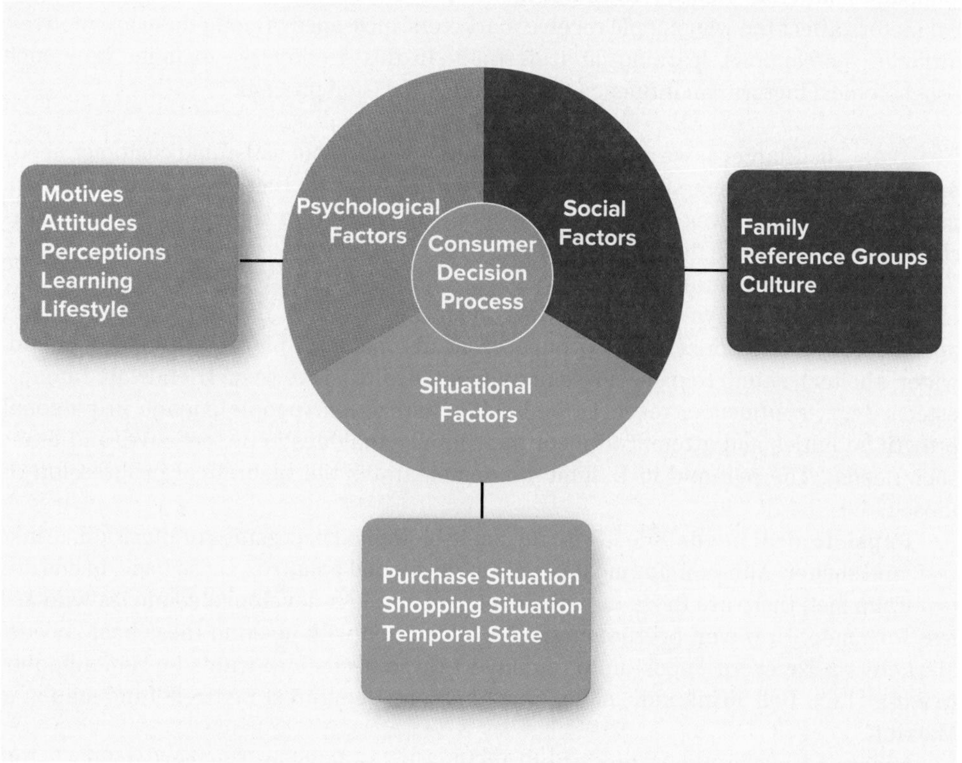

**EXHIBIT 4.5** | Maslow's Hierarchy of Needs

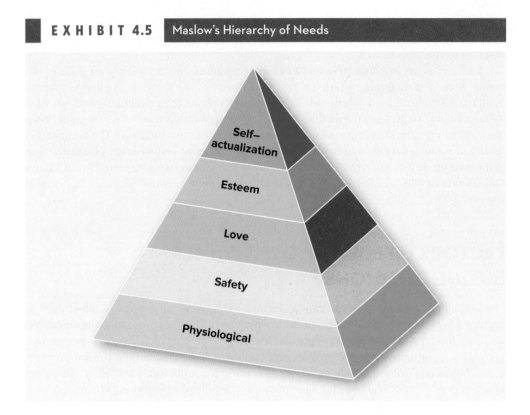

## Psychological Factors

Although marketers themselves can influence purchase decisions, a host of psychological factors affect the way people receive marketers' messages. Among them are motives, attitudes, perceptions, learning, and lifestyles. In this section, we examine how such psychological factors can influence the consumer decision process.

Motives    In Chapter 1, we argued that marketing is all about satisfying customer needs and wants. When a need (such as thirst) or a want (such as a Diet Coke) is not satisfied, it motivates us (or drives us) to get satisfaction. So, a **motive** is a need or want that is strong enough to cause the person to seek satisfaction.

People have several types of motives. One of the best-known paradigms for explaining these motive types was developed by Abraham Maslow nearly 50 years ago.[18] Maslow categorized five groups of needs, namely, physiological (e.g., food, water, shelter), safety (e.g., secure employment, health), love (e.g., friendship, family), esteem (e.g., confidence, respect), and self-actualization (people engage in personal growth activities and attempt to meet their intellectual, aesthetic, creative, and other such needs). The pyramid in Exhibit 4.5 demonstrates the theoretical progression of those needs.

**Physiological needs**    deal with the basic biological necessities of life: food, drink, rest, and shelter. Although for most people in developed countries these basic needs are generally met, there are those in both developed and less-developed countries who are less fortunate. However, everyone remains concerned with meeting these basic needs. Marketers seize every opportunity to convert these needs into wants by reminding us to eat at Taco Bell, drink milk, sleep on a Simmons Beautyrest mattress, and stay at a Marriott.

**Safety needs** pertain to protection and physical well-being. The marketplace is full of products and services that are designed to make you safer, such as airbags in cars and

**motive**
A need or want that is strong enough to cause the person to seek satisfaction.

**physiological needs**
Relate to the basic biological necessities of life: food, drink, rest, and shelter.

**safety needs**
Pertain to protection and physical well-being.

**love (social) needs**
Relate to our interactions with others.

**esteem needs**
Allow people to satisfy their inner desires.

burglar alarms in homes, or healthier, such as vitamins and organic meats and vegetables.

**Love (social) needs** relate to our interactions with others. Haircuts and makeup make you look more attractive, and deodorants prevent odour. Greeting cards help you express your feelings toward others.

**Esteem needs** allow people to satisfy their inner desires. Yoga, meditation, health clubs, and many books appeal to people's desires to grow or maintain a happy, satisfied outlook on life.

Finally, **self-actualization** occurs when you feel completely satisfied with your life and how you live. You don't care what others think. You drive a Prius because it suits the person you are, not because some celebrity endorses it or because you want others to think better of you.

Which of these needs applies when a consumer purchases a magazine? Magazines such as *Men's Health*, for instance, help satisfy *physiological* needs, such as how to eat healthy and exercise, but also *esteem* needs, such as how to be happy with life. Magazines such as *Family Circle*, on the other hand, provide tips on how to make the home a *safer* place to live. Finally, magazines such as *Weddings* help satisfy *love and belonging* needs, because they provide instructions on such topics as how to prepare gracious invitations for friends and family. Many of these magazines can fulfill several of these needs simultaneously. Good marketers add value to their products or services by nudging people up the needs hierarchy and offering information on as many of the pyramid needs as they can.

Yoga satisfies self-esteem needs by helping people satisfy their inner desires.
Ryan McVay/Getty Images

**Attitude**   We have attitudes about almost everything. For instance, we don't like this class, but we do like the instructor. We like where we live, but we don't like the weather. An **attitude** is a person's enduring evaluation of his or her feelings about and behavioural tendencies toward an object or idea. Attitudes are learned and long lasting, and they might develop over a long period of time, though they can also abruptly change. For instance, you might like your instructor for much of the semester—until she returns your first exam. One thing we all have in common is that our attitudes have the ability to influence our decisions and actions.

**self-actualization**
Occurs when you feel completely satisfied with your life and how you live.

**attitude**
A person's enduring evaluation of his or her feelings about and behavioural tendencies toward an object or idea; consists of three components: cognitive, affective, and behavioural.

An attitude consists of three components. The **cognitive component** reflects what we *believe* to be true, the **affective component** involves what we *feel* about the issue at hand—our like or dislike of something—and the **behavioural component** comprises the *action(s)* we take based on what we know and feel. For example, Ed and Tracy Lee see an ad for a Volvo that shows a family of five driving down the road, with the kids strapped into their car seats and mom and dad talking in the front. An announcer lists the features included with each model, as well as government safety ratings that indicate Volvo is the safest brand on the road in its class. On the basis of this advertisement, Ed and Tracy believe that the government statistics must be true and that the car is therefore safe (cognitive component). Watching the happy family looking comfortable while driving this safe car allows Ed and Tracy to feel that they would like to have this car for their family (affective). Thus encouraged, they go to the Volvo dealership closest to them to make a purchase (behavioural).

Ideally, agreement exists among these components. When there is incongruence among the three, however, cognitive dissonance might occur. Suppose, for instance, that though Ed and Tracy believe the Volvo is safe and they like the car, they buy another brand because it is cheaper. It is likely that they will experience the discomfort of buyers' remorse, or cognitive dissonance.

Although attitudes are pervasive and usually slow to change, the important fact from a marketer's point of view is that they can be influenced and

Which hierarchy of needs does this magazine fulfill?
The McGraw-Hill Companies, Inc./Andrew Resek, photographer

People buy Volvos because they believe they are safe (cognitive component of an attitude), because they like them (affective), and because they have many convenient dealerships to visit (behavioural).

Ekasit Wangprasert/Alamy Stock Photo

**cognitive component**
A component of attitude that reflects what a person believes to be true.

**affective component**
A component of attitude that reflects what a person feels about the issue at hand—his or her like or dislike of something.

**behavioural component**
A component of attitude that comprises the actions a person takes with regard to the issue at hand.

**perception**
The process by which people select, organize, and interpret information to form a meaningful picture of the world.

**learning**
Refers to a change in a person's thought process or behaviour that arises from experience and takes place throughout the consumer decision process.

perhaps changed through persuasive communications and personal experience. Marketing communication—through salespeople, advertisements, free samples, or other such methods—can attempt to change what people believe to be true about a product or service (cognitive) or how they feel toward it (affective). If the marketer is successful, the cognitive and affective components work in concert to affect behaviour. Continuing with our example, suppose that prior to viewing the ad, Ed and Tracy thought that a Toyota Camry was the safest car on the road, but they liked the looks of the Volvo. The ad positively influenced the cognitive component of their attitude toward Volvo, making it consistent with the affective component.

Perception   Another psychological factor, **perception**, is the process by which we select, organize, and interpret information to form a meaningful picture of the world. Perception influences our acquisition and consumption of goods and services through our tendency to assign meaning to things such as colour, symbols, taste, and packaging. Culture, tradition, and our overall upbringing determine our perceptual view of the world. For instance, Tracy has always wanted a Volvo because her best friend in university had one, and they had a great time driving across the country together one summer. However, based on his past experiences, Ed has a different perception. Ed thinks Volvos are slow, stodgy, unfashionable, and meant to be driven by little old ladies with grey hair—though they are safe! Volvo has worked hard in recent years to overcome this long-standing, negative perceptual bias that Ed and many others hold by creating faster cars with more stylish designs and by using promotion to reposition the brand to portray a more positive image.

In trying to influence perceptions, marketers must understand and focus on the four components of perception: *selective exposure, selective attention, selective comprehension*, and *selective retention*. People who look at the news and sports channels only, but not the comedy or women's TV network channels, are engaged in selective exposure because they are excluding other programs or channels. Similarly, consumers who listen only to messages that are consistent with their beliefs, and not others, are practising selective attention. For instance, although someone may look at the sports channel, he or she may watch hockey, soccer, or baseball but not boxing or wrestling because these may be too violent for his or her taste. Selective comprehension occurs when consumers interpret a marketing message in a way that is different from what the marketer intends. For example, a Dolce & Gabbana ad was intended to be edgy and sexual but consumers felt that it reinforced stereotypes about rape and degraded women. Knowing this, marketers can target their communications in those media that maximize exposure to their target market and create messages that are consistent with their beliefs and attitudes so that they will pay attention to the messages and interpret them in the intended way. Finally, selective retention describes the situation where consumers do not remember all the information they see, read, or hear. Marketers can provide the information in various other forms such as print, online, and other displays to reinforce their message.

Learning   **Learning** refers to a change in a person's thought process or behaviour that arises from experience and takes place throughout the consumer decision process.

For instance, after Brad recognized that he wanted a sports car, he started looking for ads and searching for reviews and articles on the Internet. He learned from each new piece of information, so that his thoughts about sports cars were different from what they had been before he had read anything. In addition, Brad liked the salesperson at the dealership who served him. Brad learned from this experience, and it became part of his memory to be used in the future, possibly so he would recommend the dealership or salesperson to his friends.

Learning affects both attitudes and perceptions. Throughout the buying process, Brad's attitudes shifted. The cognitive component changed for him when he learned that the dealership offers various additional services at low costs to Honda Civic owners. Once he started getting the additional services (e.g., free car washes, special rates for car detailing), he realized how much he liked the service, which indicates the affective component, and he then subscribed to it—the behavioural component. Each time Brad was exposed to information about the service, he learned something different that affected his perception of the dealership. Before he tried it, Brad hadn't realized how friendly and helpful the people at the dealership were; thus, his perception of the dealership service changed through learning.

Lifestyle  **Lifestyle** refers to the way consumers spend their time and money to live. For many consumers, the question of whether the product or service fits with their actual lifestyle, which may be fairly sedentary, or their perceived lifestyle, which might be outdoorsy, is an important one. Some of the many consumers sporting North Face jackets certainly need the high-tech, cold-weather gear because they are planning their next hike up Mount Robson and want to be sure they have sufficient protection against the elements. Others, however, simply like the image that the jacket conveys—the image that they might be leaving for their own mountain-climbing expedition any day now—even if the closest they have come to this trip has been shovelling their driveway. Similarly, people buy the Cadillac Escalade luxury four-wheel-drive SUV so that they can get over almost any off-road obstacle, but they also like the leather seats with lumbar support, six-speaker audio system preloaded with XM satellite radio, remote keyless entry system, and the fact that they can whiz over speed bumps at the local grocery store. And as seen in Entrepreneurial Marketing 4.1, even wearing fun and trendy socks can be an expression of lifestyle.

> **lifestyle**
> Refers to the way consumers spend their time and money.

A person's perceptions and ability to learn are affected by their social experiences, which we discuss next. Furthermore, Sustainable Marketing 4.1 shows how consumers' changing attitudes and lifestyles are influencing their decision to support companies that produce sustainable products.

## Social Factors

Exhibit 4.4 illustrates that the consumer decision process is also influenced by the external, social environment, which consists of the customer's family, reference groups, and culture.[23]

Family  Many purchase decisions are made about products or services that the entire family will consume or use. Thus, firms must consider how families make purchase decisions and understand how various family members might influence these decisions.

When families make purchase decisions, they often consider the needs of all the family members. In choosing a restaurant, for example, all the family members may participate in the decision making. In other situations, however, different members of the family may take on different roles. For example, Brad recalled that when he was a kid, his dad and two older brothers were the ones who looked through car magazines and *Consumer Reports* to search for information about a new car. But once the family

## Entrepreneurial Marketing 4.1

# Socks That Start Businesses

Many of us have heard the saying "sharing is caring." Today's entrepreneurs are taking this concept to a completely new level unimaginable just a few years ago. The concept of One for One has developed into an emerging business trend with companies like TOMS Shoes donating one pair of shoes for each pair sold. Diana and Jeff House wanted to take this concept farther, giving it a life of its own, one that would take it into the future and make it sustainable. They founded Cole + Parker, named for jazz greats John Coltrane and Charlie Parker,[19] with a One for Many business model.

Based in London, Ontario, Cole + Parker sells socks: bold, colourful, creative, premium-quality socks. Working with a world-class designer, Diana and Jeff came up with socks that make a statement, let you stand out in a crowd, and, well, jazz up your life. The socks sell for around $24 a pair. Cole + Parker's tagline is "Socks That Start Businesses" because 1 percent of all sales revenue is used to help entrepreneurs in developing countries.

To implement the One for Many concept, the couple works with non-profit partner Kiva, the largest microfinance organization in the world. Kiva has a proven track record, having facilitated more than $550 million in loans, with a 99 percent repayment rate.[20] Entrepreneurs receive loans and the opportunity to start businesses. Every dollar of sock revenue generated goes directly to entrepreneurs as Kiva does not charge any administrative fees. Cole + Parker has contributed to over 415 loans so far.

Consider why people would pay $20 to $28 for socks. While the socks have that cool factor, people who buy them like the fact that their purchases help others. To illustrate, let's revisit some of the factors that affect consumer buying decisions. Psychological factors such as motives, attitudes, and lifestyle likely play a role. Purchasers may be motivated by esteem or self-actualization needs as shown in Exhibit 4.5 (Maslow's Hierarchy of Needs). Their attitude may be shaped by an affective component that makes them feel good about the socks, which prompts the behavioural component, resulting in taking action to buy the socks. Lifestyle can also play a part because the socks are fun and trendy. For consumers who are looking for a way to differentiate themselves, buying Cole + Parker socks lets them express their personality.

To raise money and visibility for their fledgling company, Diana and Jeff pitched their idea on CBC's *Dragons'*

Used with permission of Cole + Parker

*Den.* At that time, they had been in business for only two weeks. Still, they had generated $32,000 worth of socks selling online only. They found a champion in David Chilton. Since then, distribution has expanded dramatically. The socks are now sold in over 140 retail outlets in Canada and the United States. Diana says their goal is to have 1,000 retailers, primarily smaller, privately owned, upscale men's stores[21] whose clients are looking for a little socks appeal.

## Consumers Support Companies With Sustainable Business Practices[22]

Research studies show that consumers overwhelmingly state their support for companies with sustainable business practices. Motivated to reduce their environmental impact, consumers are buying and using less. Millennials, in particular, believe that companies need to change for the better. Learning plays a big role in changing consumer habits. Millennials have been taught about protecting the environment from an early age, leading to the formation of strong attitudes. For habits to change, attitudes need to be backed by action, and millennial buying behaviour demonstrates that they are embracing sustainable products.

However, 75 percent of them want these products to perform just as well as competitive ones and 70 percent are willing to make the switch only if the products don't cost more. For example, school and office supplies contribute about 10 percent of waste sent to landfill sites. In the U.S., more than 1.6 billion disposable pens are thrown away every year. That's a lot of pens!

Based in Lachine, Quebec, Onyx+Green has found ways to address sustainability issues around school and office supplies. Rather than using new materials in the manufacturing process, it uses waste and recycled materials. It also incorporates materials that are natural and biodegradable. For example, bamboo, recycled aluminum, and PET plastic are used to manufacture pens and mechanical pencils. Scissors are biodegradable, made with corn-based plastic handles. Pencil cases use natural and biodegradable fabrics such as ramie leaf and jute plant. Notepads are made using no trees. Unbelievable as it may sound, Onyx+Green's notepads are made from crushed stone which is transformed into smooth, white "paper." The company's goal is to create beautiful products and sell them at reasonable prices. It aims to help students and their parents become more aware of the need to protect the environment.

Consumers rely on several indicators when building trust in products. Marketers can use different tactics to encourage consumers not only to trust the brand and the label, but also to trust partners, such as producers. While Onyx+Green's products are manufactured

Onyx+Green uses recycled and biodegradable materials in its school supplies to help educate students and parents about the environment.

(both): Used with permission of Onyx+Blue

in China, they are designed in Canada by a company whose headquarters are in Quebec. That allows them to provide affordable products while supporting Canadian jobs and profits.

Most consumers want to learn about the source of sustainable products and their production practices. Consumers' trust of points of sale may be an important factor in deciding where they buy sustainable products. Consumer knowledge and awareness are also important since they affect people's perception and attitudes, and, ultimately, buying decisions.

Family members often influence buying decisions.

ThinkStock/JupiterImages

arrived at the dealership, his dad, not his brothers, decided which model and colour to buy, and his mom negotiated the final deal.

Despite that example, children and adolescents play an increasingly important role in family buying decisions. For instance, the tween segment alone in Canada is estimated to spend $2.9 billion per year on personal items such as snacks, soft drinks, electronics, and apparel. Tweens in Canada also indirectly influence family purchases in excess of $20 billion on big-ticket items such as recreation, vacations, technology, and the family car.[24]

Influencing a group that holds this much spending power is vitally important. Traditional food retailers are already caught in a squeeze between Walmart, which lures low-end customers, and specialty retailers, such as Whole Foods, which target the high end. Knowing how children influence food-buying decisions is a strategic opportunity for traditional supermarkets and their suppliers to exploit. Getting this group to prefer one store, chain, or product over another can make a difference in the bottom line, as well as in the chances for survival in a difficult marketplace.[25]

**reference group**

One or more persons an individual uses as a basis for comparison regarding beliefs, feelings, and behaviours.

Reference Groups   A **reference group** is one or more persons an individual uses as a basis for comparison regarding beliefs, feelings, and behaviours. A consumer might have various reference groups, including family, friends, co-workers, or famous people the consumer would like to emulate. These reference groups affect buying decisions by (1) offering information, (2) providing rewards for specific purchasing behaviours, and (3) enhancing a consumer's self-image.

Reference groups provide information to consumers directly through conversation or indirectly through observation. For example, when Emily, a second-year business student at the University of British Columbia, saw that almost all her colleagues had an activity tracker (Fitbit, Jawbone, or Garmin), she quickly decided it was time for her to purchase a smartphone in order to fit in with her peers.

Some reference groups also influence behaviours by rewarding behaviour that meets with their approval or chastising those who engage in behaviour that doesn't. For example, smokers are often criticized by their friends and made to smoke outside or in restricted areas. Research suggests that consumers who feel ostracized tend to make riskier purchase decisions,[26] so ostracizing smokers may make them smoke more or engage in even riskier behaviours.

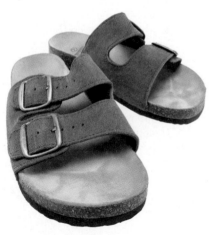

What reference group is evoked by these Birkenstock sandals?

Stockdisc/Getty Images RF

Consumers can identify and affiliate with reference groups to create, enhance, or maintain their self-image. Customers who want to be seen as "earthy" might buy Birkenstock sandals, whereas those wanting to be seen as "high fashion" might buy Lana Marks bags, as we discussed earlier in this chapter. If they purchase a gift for someone else and that gift conflicts with their self-image, they also seek to reestablish their preferred affiliation quickly by purchasing something more in line with their identity.

With the increasing popularity of blogs, more and more people are getting recommendations for products from their favorite bloggers. When you follow a blog about kittens, you might notice that the author posts a scathing review of a particular cat tree or strongly recommends a product that encourages kittens to use their litter boxes. Because this blogger offers insights you appreciate, you go out to buy the litter box product but avoid adding that cat tree to your shopping cart. In realizing the vast influence of this reference group, companies today offer prominent bloggers free products and sometimes even pay them to write positive reviews.[27]

## Culture

We defined *culture* in Chapter 3 as the shared meanings, beliefs, morals, values, and customs of a group of people. Your cultural group might be as small as your reference group at school or as large as the country in which you live or the religion in which you participate. For instance, the culture at Brad's university evokes a "high-achiever" attitude. This reputation influences, to some extent, the way he spends his leisure time, the types of people he hangs out with, and the kinds of products he buys. Culture is one of the most pervasive factors influencing consumer behaviour. Therefore, marketers must work hard to understand how it is different not only in Canada but also in those countries to which they plan to market their products. Marketing strategies that may work in Canada or North America may not work well in Japan or India because consumers in those countries are culturally different, as discussed in Chapter 17. Additionally, even within Canada, there are cultural differences between various subgroups or subcultures. A *subculture* is a group of people whose beliefs and values are different from the rest of the larger society in which they live. Examples of subcultures in Canada include French-Canadian subculture, Chinese-Canadian subculture, South-Asian subculture, and Acadian subculture. Research has shown that Chinese- and Asian-Canadians prefer to do business with marketers who truly understand their culture and needs

Bloggers can influence their readers to buy or not buy certain products or services.

Courtesy of geekgirlreviewsblog.com

Marketers work to understand consumer culture and respond with products such as halal meats to meet specific needs.

Colin Mcconnell/ZUMAPRESS/Newscom

rather than those who have very superficial ways of acknowledging their community, which a lot of people in the community find irritating.[28]

Marketers are working hard to understand how culture affects consumer behaviour in Canada. For example, Clorox commissioned research on South Asians and Chinese, the country's two largest ethnic groups, that showed their tastes and preferences in a variety of categories. The findings led the company to launch a limited edition Year of the Dragon red Brita water filter to celebrate Chinese New Year. It quickly became one of Clorox's fastest selling products, growing sales by 25 percent in January and February that year.[29] More recently, Lego launched a specially designed Creator set to celebrate the Year of the Monkey. Grocers have responded to Canada's changing cultural makeup by carrying a much wider selection of ethnic foods on store shelves. These days it's hard to find a grocery store that doesn't carry fresh sushi. The Sobeys store in Thornhill employs multiple rabbis to oversee the kosher food section to ensure that meat preparation follows strict Jewish dietary rules and that baked goods are milk-free. Its Brampton store carries a large selection of East Indian foods and halal meat is available for Muslim families in the Malton store.

## Situational Factors

**situational factors**
Factors affecting the consumer decision process; those that are specific to the purchase and shopping situation and temporal state that may override, or at least influence, psychological and social issues.

Psychological and social factors typically influence the consumer decision process the same way each time. For example, your motivation to quench your thirst usually drives you to drink a Pepsi, and your reference group at the workplace coerces you to wear appropriate attire. But sometimes, **situational factors**, or factors specific to the situation, override (or at least influence) psychological and social issues. These situational factors are related to the purchase and shopping situation, as well as to the temporal state, as illustrated in Exhibit 4.4.

### Purchase Situation
Customers may be predisposed to purchase certain products or services because of some underlying psychological trait or social factor, but these factors may change in certain purchase situations. For instance, Priya Persaud, a Vancouverite, considers herself a thrifty, cautious shopper—someone who likes to get a good deal. But her best friend is getting married, and she wants to buy the couple a silver tray. If the tray were for herself, she would probably go to Stokes, HomeSense, or possibly even Walmart. But since it is for her best friend, she went to Birks. Why? To purchase something fitting for the special occasion of a wedding.

### Shopping Situation
Consumers might be ready to purchase a product or service but, for a variety of reasons, be completely derailed once they arrive in the store. Marketers use several techniques to influence consumers at this choice stage of the decision process. Consider the following techniques:

- *Store atmosphere.* Some retailers and service providers have developed unique images that are based at least in part on their internal environment, also known as their atmospherics.[30] Research has shown that, if used in concert with other aspects of a retailer's strategy, music, scent, lighting, and even colour can positively influence the decision process.[31] Some Whole Foods stores have built bars and restaurants inside their stores, where customers can stop and relax, have a glass of wine or a bite to eat, but still get their shopping done for the week. Whole Foods has cutting-edge culinary centres that offer cooking classes in several of its stores. Other grocery store chains are following suit; some have a band play in the store on Friday nights, or offer flat-screen televisions, comfortable chairs, free Wi-Fi hotspots, in-store cooking classes, or wine-tasting events to create interactive atmospheres that will appeal to customers.[32]

- *Salespeople.* Well trained sales personnel can influence the sale at the point of purchase by pointing out the advantages of one item over another and by encouraging multiple purchases. The salesperson at Birks, for instance, explained to Priya why one platter was better than the next and suggested some serving pieces to go with it. Each Apple store features a simple layout that enables shoppers to play with the latest gadgets, though the real key to success is the salespeople. Apple keeps its product lines relatively minimal so salespeople can become familiar with every product in the store. For more technical questions, Apple Geniuses are available and consultations can be scheduled. A training manual recently leaked online shows that the company takes nothing for granted when training its employees, such that it uses role-playing scenarios, lists banned words, and specifies exactly how to communicate with agitated customers. Although technical expertise is a must, Apple also looks for salespeople with "magnetic personalities" and trains them in a five-point selling technique based on the acronym APPLE: **a**pproach customers warmly, **p**robe politely to assess their needs, **p**resent solutions the customer can do today, **l**isten and resolve worries the customer may still have, **e**nd by giving the customer a warm goodbye and invite them back.[33]

Abercrombie & Fitch stores blast loud dance music through powerful speakers and pump the company's signature cologne, Fierce, into the air.

AP Photo/Rick Bowmer/The Canadian Press

- *Crowding.* Customers can feel crowded because there are too many people, too much merchandise, or lines that are too long. If there are too many people in a store, some people become distracted and may even leave.[34] Others have difficulty purchasing if the merchandise is packed too closely together. This issue is a particular problem for shoppers with mobility challenges.

- *In-store demonstrations.* The taste and smell of new food items may attract people to try something they normally wouldn't. Similarly, some fashion retailers offer "trunk shows," during which their vendors show their whole line on a certain day. During these well advertised events, customers are often enticed to purchase that day because they get special assistance from the salespeople and can order merchandise that the retailer otherwise does not carry.

- *Promotions.* Retailers employ various promotional vehicles to influence customers once they have arrived in the store. For instance, an unadvertised price promotion can alter a person's preconceived buying plan. Multi-item discounts, such as "buy one, get one free" sales, are popular means to get people to buy more than they normally would. Because many people regard clipping coupons from the newspaper as too much trouble, some stores make coupons available in the store, on the Internet, or on mobile devices. Another form of promotion is offering a "free" gift with the purchase of a good or service. This type of promotion is particularly popular with cosmetics. Sephora has worked hard to integrate various elements of its shopping situation to encourage purchase, as Social & Mobile Marketing 4.1 shows.

In-store demonstrations entice people to buy.

Tyler Olson/Shutterstock

● *Packaging.* It is difficult to make a product stand out in the crowd when it competes for shelf space with several other brands. Customers spend just a few seconds standing in front of products as they decide whether to buy them. This problem is particularly difficult for consumer packaged goods, such as groceries and health and beauty products. Marketers therefore spend millions of dollars designing and updating their packages to be more appealing and eye catching. This is why Pringles keeps packaging its chips in tubes that look very different from competitors' formless bags.

**Temporal State**  Our state of mind at any particular time can alter our preconceived notions of what we are going to purchase. For instance, some people are "morning people," whereas others function better at night. In turn, a purchase situation may have

## Social and Mobile Marketing 4.1

### Mobile Dominance Through In-Store Promotions[35]

Some consumers rely on websites to reach their favourite retailers. Others like to head to the stores themselves to check out the options. Still others want a mobile app that enables them to shop quickly and on the go. And increasingly, today's customers demand that retailers offer them all of these options, consistently and constantly, so that they can pick and choose the channel they want to use at any specific time.

This demand is the impetus for the latest developments in the marketing strategy of Sephora, the specialized beauty product retailer. Although it has long maintained a good reputation for its interactive website, the company remains in constant pursuit of a strategy that enables it to reach all its customers through the most channels at the most frequent times. It integrates these efforts with its constantly evolving loyalty program, in an effort to become nearly irresistible to beauty product consumers.

Users of the most recent version of its mobile app, Sephora to Go, can engage in any activities they would pursue in stores. The close alignment across these channels provides a seamless experience. The app offers a barcode scan feature that customers can use in stores to access product ratings, reviews, photos, and videos. The Visual Artist feature turns the phone's camera on to let consumers try out different lip colours and other products at home. And a Pinterest-inspired Beauty Board filters results based on eyeshadow colour, skin tone, and hair colour, making it easy to shop for different looks.

The app encourages customers to sign up for the loyalty program and create a Beauty Insider account. Once they have done so, they can access a mobile version of

their loyalty card, letting them check or redeem loyalty points any time they wish. Sephora's in-store signage also encourages shoppers to sign up for the loyalty program and create a Beauty Insider account. That is, both channels issue similar calls to action. Moreover, the in-store signs encourage brick-and-mortar shoppers to take advantage of the benefits they can gain from interacting with the retailer, either online or through mobile apps.

The app provides an alternative method to buy Sephora products, leveraging the mobile platform in thoughtful ways that encourage customers to use it at home and in stores. The company recognizes that "the majority of Sephora's clients are cross-channel shoppers," so it wants consumers to go ahead and use their phones while in the stores. In return, Sephora has enjoyed a 150 percent increase in the amount of mobile shopping its customers undertake.

Sephora engages its customers in the store with its mobile app, Sephora to Go.

Victor J. Blue/Bloomberg via Getty Images

different appeal levels depending on the time of day and the type of person the consumer is. Mood swings can also alter consumer behaviour. Suppose Priya received a parking ticket just prior to shopping at Birks. It is likely that she would be less receptive to the salesperson's influence than if she came into the store in a good mood. Her bad mood may even cause her to have a less positive postpurchase feeling about the store. Unfortunately, such temporal factors are usually beyond the control of even the most creative marketer.

As we've seen, people's lives are lived in different contexts and consumer decisions are made in unique contexts. Marketers who understand this fact are better positioned to serve their target consumers. All the factors that affect the consumer decision process that we have discussed—psychological factors, social factors, and situational factors—are impacted by the level of consumer involvement, the subject of the next section.

# INVOLVEMENT AND CONSUMER BUYING DECISIONS   L04

Consumers engage in two types of buying process/decisions depending on their level of involvement: extended problem solving for high-priced, risky, infrequent, or highly expressive purchases; and limited problem solving, which includes impulse buying and habitual purchases/decision making. **Involvement** is the consumer's degree of interest in or concern about the product or service.[36] Consumers may have different levels of involvement for the same type of product. One consumer behaviour theory, the elaboration likelihood model illustrated in Exhibit 4.6, proposes that high- and low-involvement consumers process different aspects of a marketing message or advertisement.

**involvement**
The consumer's degree of interest in or concern about the product or service.

If both types of consumers viewed ads for hybrids produced by Toyota and Ford, the high-involvement consumer (e.g., Katie who is researching hybrids) will scrutinize all

**EXHIBIT 4.6**   Elaboration Likelihood Model

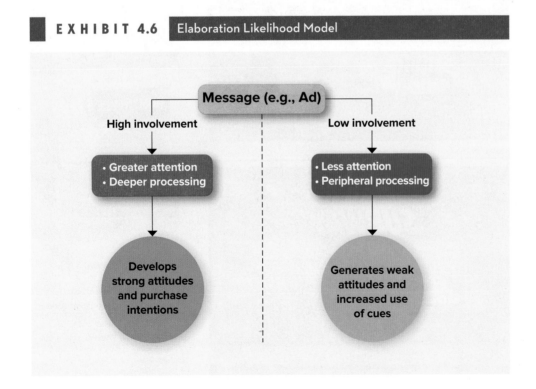

Message (e.g., Ad)

High involvement — Low involvement

- Greater attention
- Deeper processing

- Less attention
- Peripheral processing

Develops strong attitudes and purchase intentions

Generates weak attitudes and increased use of cues

the information provided (e.g., gas savings, eco-friendly) and process the key elements of the message deeply. As a consequence, Katie, an involved consumer, is likely to either (1) judge the ad to be truthful and form a favourable impression of the product, or (2) view the message as superficial and develop negative product impressions (i.e., her research suggests that the product is not as good as is being portrayed).

In contrast, a low-involvement consumer will likely process the same advertisement in a less thorough manner. Such a consumer might pay less attention to the key elements of the message (e.g., gas savings, eco-friendly) and focus on heuristic elements such as brand name (Toyota), price, and the presence of a celebrity endorser. The impressions of the low-involvement consumer are likely to be more superficial.

## Extended Problem Solving

**extended problem solving**
A purchase decision process during which the consumer devotes considerable time and effort to analyzing alternatives; often occurs when the consumer perceives that the purchase decision entails a great deal of risk.

As we noted at the beginning of this chapter, the buying process begins when consumers recognize that they have an unsatisfied need. Katie recognized her need to have access to transportation when she went away to college. She sought information by asking for advice from her friends, by reading consumer reports, and by researching online. Once she decided that a car and not a bike or the bus was her best option, she visited several car dealerships to test drive the models she was interested in and to find out which dealer offered the best price. Finally, after considerable time and effort spent analyzing her alternatives, Katie purchased a Toyota Prius. This process is an example of **extended problem solving**, which is common when the customer perceives that the purchase decision entails a great deal of risk. The potential risks associated with Katie's decision to buy her car include financial (Did I pay too much?), physiological (Will it keep me safe in an accident?), social (Will my friends think I look cool?), performance (Will the car perform

What types of buying decisions does each of these products represent?

(vehicle): © Digital Vision; (restaurant): © The McGraw-Hill Companies, Inc./ Andrew Resek, photographer; (juice): © David Tietz, Editorial Image, LLC

as expected?), and psychological (Will the car convey the right image of me?) risks. To reduce her perceived risk, Katie spent a lot of effort searching for information about cars before she actually made her purchase.

## Limited Problem Solving

**Limited problem solving** occurs during a purchase decision that calls for, at most, a moderate amount of effort and time. Customers engage in this type of buying process when they have had some prior experience with the product or service and the perceived risk is moderate. Limited problem solving usually relies on past experience more than on external information. For some people even a car purchase could require limited effort.

A common type of limited problem solving is **impulse buying**, a buying decision made by customers on the spot when they see the merchandise.[37] When Katie went to the grocery store to do her weekly shopping, she saw a display case of popcorn and Dr Pepper near the checkout counter. Knowing that some of her friends were coming to her place to watch a movie later, she stocked up. The popcorn and pop were an impulse purchase. Katie didn't go through the entire decision process; instead, she recognized her need and jumped directly to the purchase stage without spending any time searching for additional information or evaluating alternatives. The grocery store facilitated this impulse purchase by providing easily accessible cues (i.e., by offering the popcorn and soft drinks in a prominent display, at an accessible location in the store, and at a reasonable price).

Some purchases require even less thought. **Habitual decision making** describes a purchase decision process in which consumers engage with little conscious effort. On her way home from the grocery store, for example, Katie drove past a Tim Hortons® and swung into the drive-through for a maple pecan danish and an Iced Capp. She did not ponder the potential benefits of going to Second Cup or Starbucks; rather, she simply reacted to the cue provided by the sign and engaged in habitual decision making. Marketers strive to attract and maintain habitual purchasers by creating strong brands and store loyalty (see Chapter 9) because these customers don't even consider alternative brands or stores. Marketers who are trying to get consumers to switch to their brands often use marketing tactics that require greater involvement in the purchase decisions. For instance, toothpaste is a habitual or routine purchase; however, in attempts to lure customers away from each other's products, both Crest and Colgate have developed toothpaste with a variety of ingredients and benefits designed to get customers to stop and think that all toothpastes are not created equal and that toothpaste is not just toothpaste—it offers various health benefits. The same thing can be said of bread and a host of other consumer packaged goods.

**limited problem solving**
Occurs during a purchase decision that calls for, at most, a moderate amount of effort and time.

**impulse buying**
A buying decision made by customers on the spot when they see the merchandise.

**habitual decision making**
A purchase decision process in which consumers engage with little conscious effort.

## LEARNING OBJECTIVES REVIEW

**LO1**  **Describe the steps in the consumer buying decision process**

The consumer buying process consists of five main steps: First, during need recognition, consumers simply realize they have an unsatisfied need or want that they hope to address. Sometimes the needs are simple: I need food because I am hungry. Often, however, they become more complex: I want to buy my girlfriend an engagement ring.

Second, they begin to search for information to determine how to satisfy that need. Generally, the more important the purchase, the more time and effort the consumer will spend on the search process. Firms facilitate this search by providing promotional materials and personal selling. Third, during the alternative evaluation stage, they assess the various options available to them to determine which is the best for their purposes. Fourth, the purchase stage involves obtaining and using the product. Fifth and finally, consumers enter the postpurchase stage, during which they determine whether they are satisfied or dissatisfied with their choice, or if they experience postpurchase dissonance. Every marketer wants satisfied customers, but when instead they are confronted with dissatisfied customers who are in some way unsure about their purchase, marketers must proactively turn the situation around. If they don't, the customer may be gone for good.

**LO2**  **Identify what determines how much time consumers will spend searching for information before buying a product or service**

A variety of factors affect consumers' searches for information about a potential purchase. First, they consider the time and effort associated with searching versus the benefits derived from the search. Second, people who have an internal locus of control—those who believe they have control over the outcomes of their actions—are more likely to spend time searching for information than those with an external locus of control. Third, consumers who perceive a high performance, financial, social, physiological, or psychological risk associated with the purchase will spend relatively more time searching for information than those who do not.

**LO3**  **Summarize how psychological, social, and situational factors influence consumers' buying behaviour**

First and foremost, firms must design their products and services to meet their customers' wants and needs, but understanding certain aspects of consumer behaviour can help as well. For instance, it is important to understand people's motives (i.e., what drives them to buy), their attitudes (i.e., how they feel about a product or service), and their perceptions (i.e., how information about that product or service fits into their worldview). Knowledge about these psychological characteristics helps firms design and provide products and services that their customers want and need.

In addition, people don't live in a vacuum. Consumers are influenced by their family, their reference groups, and their culture. Understanding these social groups and people's roles within them provides important insights into consumers' buying behaviour. Finally, although consumers already carry a host of psychological and social factors along with them on a shopping expedition, certain other factors can influence a purchase at the point of sale. For instance, customers might change their buying behaviour because the purchase situation is different from the one they are used to. Also, things can happen to customers, both positive and negative, once they are in a store that might alter their preconceived notion of what they plan to purchase. Finally, people can be just plain finicky, and being in an unusually good or extremely bad mood can also alter a purchase decision. The more firms understand these psychological, social, and situational factors, the more likely they will be to influence purchase decisions.

**LO4**  **Explain how involvement influences the consumer buying decision process**

More involved consumers, who are more interested or invested in the product or service they are considering, tend to engage in extended problem solving. They gather lots of information, scrutinize it carefully, and then make their decisions with caution, to minimize any risk they may confront. In contrast, less involved consumers often engage in limited problem solving, undertake impulse purchases, or rely on habit to make their purchase decisions. Some purchasing decisions require limited problem solving because the perceived risk of the purchase is low or the consumer has previous experience purchasing the product or service. Impulse and habitual purchases fall into this category.

# KEY TERMS

- affective component
- attitude
- behavioural component
- cognitive component
- compensatory decision rule
- consumer decision rules
- decision heuristics
- determinant attributes
- esteem needs
- evaluative criteria
- evoked set
- extended problem solving
- external locus of control
- external search for information
- financial risk
- functional needs
- habitual decision making
- impulse buying
- internal locus of control
- internal search for information
- involvement
- learning
- lifestyle
- limited problem solving
- love (social) needs
- motive
- need recognition
- negative word-of-mouth
- noncompensatory decision rule
- perception
- performance risk
- physiological needs
- physiological risk
- postpurchase dissonance
- psychological needs
- psychological risk
- reference group
- retrieval sets
- ritual consumption
- safety needs
- self-actualization
- situational factors
- social risk
- specialty goods/services
- universal sets

## CONCEPT REVIEW

1. Give three reasons why it is important for marketers to understand the factors that influence consumers' purchasing decisions.

2. List the five steps of the consumer buying decision process. What should be the primary focus of marketing strategy at the alternative evaluation stage? The purchase stage?

3. What are the primary factors that affect consumers' search processes? What marketing strategies can marketers employ to ensure that customers get the information they need in order to make their shopping decisions?

4. Briefly explain how the extent of problem solving influences consumers' buying behaviour, and describe four strategies marketers could use to facilitate consumer purchasing in each case. Give examples of products you would classify as high-involvement purchases.

5. Identify and briefly explain the five psychological factors that influence consumer buying decisions.

6. What marketing tactics could be used to break through customers' selective perception (i.e., selective exposure, selective attention, selective comprehension, and selective retention)?

7. How can marketers use Maslow's hierarchy of needs model to develop successful marketing programs for their target market?

8. Briefly explain how social and situational considerations influence customer buying decisions.

9. Perceived risks are a key determinant of consumer buying decisions. Explain what is meant by perceived risks and identify tactics marketers could use to mitigate these risks.

10. Culture is one of the most important but least understood influences on consumer buying decisions. Explain how marketers can ensure that their marketing efforts are suited to their culturally diverse target market. What are the challenges involved in developing such efforts?

## MARKETING APPLICATIONS

1. Does buying Kashi cereal satisfy a consumer's functional or psychological need? How might this information help a Kashi brand manager better promote the product?

2. When consumers buy a new notebook computer, what sort of information search (internal versus external) would they conduct? If you were a marketing manager for Sony, how would you use this information?

3. Explain the factors that affect the amount of time and effort a consumer might expend when choosing an oral surgeon to get his or her wisdom teeth removed. How would your answer change if the consumer were looking for a dentist to get a cleaning? How should the office manager for a dental practice use this information?

4. Explain how a consumer would use decision heuristics to narrow down the choice of restaurants when evaluating different alternatives for a Saturday night outing at a fine restaurant. Give examples of heuristics such as price, brand, and presentation in your answer.

5. What can retailers do to make sure that they have satisfied customers after the sale is complete?

6. Tazo blends exotic green teas, spearmint, and rare herbs to create a tea called Zen. Using Maslow's hierarchy of needs, explain which need(s) are being fulfilled by this tea.

7. You recently were invited to a formal event at the home of the president of your university. You decide such an event warrants a completely new outfit. Describe three social factors that might influence your purchase decision.

8. Trek has designed a new off-road bicycle designed to stand up to the rugged conditions of trail riding. Develop a theme for an advertising strategy that covers all three components of attitude.

9. What can a marketer do to positively influence a situation in which a consumer is ready to buy but has not yet done so?

10. You were recently hired by a retail and catalogue company that promotes itself as a Canadian firm selling only Canadian-made goods. The products featured in advertising and in the catalogues tell the stories of the firms that produced the goods in Canada. The sales response to the firm's Made in Canada position has been incredible and growth has been impressive. One day while speaking to a vendor, you learn that a shipment of merchandise will be delayed since the product is coming from overseas and is late. A few days later you hear a similar story. As it turns out, the firm just barely earns the Made in Canada label. Although technically the products meet the standard to be classified as Canadian-made, you worry that the firm is not being truthful to its customers. You decide to write a letter to the vice-president of marketing detailing your concerns. What would you put in the letter?

## NET SAVVY

1. Visit the Harley-Davidson website (http://www.harley-davidson.com) and review the information provided about its Harley Owners Group (HOG). Describe the efforts the company makes to maintain customer loyalty through its programs. What are the benefits to HOG members? Discuss how these measures might be effective in creating value for members.

2. Customers use a variety of methods to provide feedback to companies about their experiences. Planetfeedback.com was developed as one such venue. Visit its website (http://www.planetfeedback.com) and identify the types of feedback that customers can provide. Look over the feedback about Ford, and summarize some of the most recent comments. What is the ratio of positive to negative comments about Ford during the last year or so? Describe the effect these comments might have on customer perceptions of Ford.

## CHAPTER CASE STUDY

### THE SHARING ECONOMY

Think back to the first time you learned about Uber. Did you hear about it from a friend who raved about the ability of users to track their rides on the Uber app? Maybe you read about it on a tech blog and learned about the driver and rider rating system that helps filter out poor drivers and disrespectful users. Or perhaps a family member offered to pay for a ride and you got to see Uber in action. After learning that Uber provides the same type of service as a taxi, whenever you need a ride, you must decide between ordering an Uber and calling a cab. How do you make that decision and what factors influence it?

Uber is part of a movement called the sharing economy. The premise of the sharing economy is the ability of users to rent or borrow goods rather than buy and own them. It allows individuals who share their belongings to make money from assets that are not being fully utilized, while providing users with less expensive alternatives to the conventional means. Globally, PricewaterhouseCoopers estimated that sharing economy revenues will grow to $335 billion in 2025, up from $15 billion in 2015.[38] Statistics Canada reported that 10 percent of Canadian adults have used ride sharing or room sharing services in the past year.[39]

The sharing economy has flourished thanks to millennials. Lower employment levels, smaller incomes, and student debt have left younger millennials with less money than previous generations.[40] Many millennials have watched their parents struggle through the recession and they themselves are having a difficult time finding stable jobs in a post-recession economy.[41] As a result, they have learned to maximize their dollars spent by avoiding large purchases, and taking advantage of the smaller incremental costs by using the sharing economy where it makes sense.

Furthermore, the millennial mindset is shifting in terms of where they place value. They are starting to value experiences over owning things that have historically been measures of wealth, like owning property or vehicles. In a survey of 1,500 Canadians by Vision Critical commissioned by Capital One Canada, 32 percent of millennials surveyed said they would rather spend money on five years of "amazing experiences" than owning a house. Millennials are also three times more likely than those over 55 to try out a new service just so they can tell friends about it.[42] They don't see ownership as empowerment; they see it as a burden. Not only do they not want ownership, but they don't want the responsibility that comes with ownership.[43]

### Why does a consumer choose to ride in an Uber vehicle as opposed to a taxi?

Some consumers may choose Uber simply because it costs less than a taxi and price is the key determinant attribute for the buyer. Other consumers may be influenced by other features that Uber offers. For example, many consumers value the enhanced convenience associated with the ability to order a ride with a few taps of a screen—there is no need to wait to speak to a human operator. Others may value the increased certainty and reliability from the real-time ride-tracking feature that allows users to feel in control and decreases the unpleasant feeling of waiting for a ride. Still others may prefer the accountability that comes with Uber.

Drivers are motivated to provide excellent service because users will be prompted to rate them after every ride—if users have a bad experience, they know that their opinion will have the effect of ultimately improving the experience for themselves and everyone else because the driver can be put on probation or even banned from operating as an Uber driver. Customer service and customer feedback are not well tracked by regular taxi companies, and customers may feel frustrated at the lack of action taken on the part of taxi companies after a bad experience.[44]

### Consumers are beginning to see ride-sharing as an alternative to owning a car.

With the ease of car-sharing services like Zipcar and car2go, more consumers are seeing sharing cars as an alternative to purchasing or leasing one of their own. According to data from *Consumer Reports*, the median car costs more than $9,100 a year to own over the first five years.[45] Alternatively, Zipcar charges $8–$10 per hour plus a $7 monthly membership, while car2go charges $0.41 per minute to use its cars.[46] If, by participating in the sharing economy, consumers can get access to a car on demand at a reasonable price, then purchasing a car that wouldn't be used at capacity will start to become less attractive. For drivers who bike or walk to work and need a car occasionally, they may consider using these services instead of investing in a car. Before making a decision, these consumers will likely check in with their groups of friends or family members who have raved about how easy, convenient, or cost effective it was. When making this decision, these consumers will consider the trade-off they would need to make between convenience and cost.

Many consumers choose Uber because it is cheaper than a taxi.

McGraw-Hill Education. Mark Dierker, photographer

Will their cost-savings compensate for the fact that they won't have their car with them everywhere they go? Alternatively, they may consider the benefit of the peace of mind they will get from not having to worry about car maintenance costs, oil changes, and monthly insurance bills.

### Why does a consumer choose to stay in an Airbnb as opposed to a hotel?

Increasingly there is growing traveller demand for experiences that are not like the typical tourist experiences but that reflect what it's like to live in local places. Travellers don't want to feel like a tourist—they want to experience travel through the eyes of a local. In fact, according to data from Airbnb, 86 percent of its users pick the platform because they want to live more like a local. A large part of this group is made up of millennials. People under 30 are 2.6 times more likely than the average Canadian to use Airbnb.[47]

Airbnb connects homeowners with travellers looking for a place to stay for a night to a few weeks. Homeowners are able to put a bed, a room, or a full apartment up for rent on their site. Because Airbnb connects strangers, the company has implemented several practices to reduce decision risk and help users feel safe. For example, many listings require guests to contact the host before booking so they can ask questions and determine whether guests and host are a good match. Prior to booking, users can also see reviews written by people who have stayed with that host at that location in the past, giving users insight into what others thought. Although staying at an Airbnb will require consumers to dedicate more time to finding and booking a perfect place compared to a hotel, many users prefer the authenticity of the stay, the lower price, and the additional perks that come with it. Oftentimes, the best part about chatting with Airbnb hosts is all the local tips they give about coffee joints, restaurants, and favourite stores, which help make a guest's stay a more individualized and interesting experience.

### Questions

1. How might you go through the steps in the consumer decision process if you were thinking of buying a car?

2. How would your consumer decision process differ if you were deciding to use Uber?

3. How have sharing economy companies created value for consumers?

4. Which factors examined in the chapter do you think would have the most impact on consumers when looking for an Airbnb location for an upcoming holiday?

# CHAPTER 5

## LEARNING OBJECTIVES

**After studying this chapter you should be able to**

**LO1** Describe the nature and composition of B2B markets

**LO2** Explain the key differences between B2B buying and B2C buying

**LO3** Describe the ways B2B firms classify and segment their markets

**LO4** List the steps in the B2B buying process

**LO5** Identify the roles within the buying centre

**LO6** Detail different buying situations

Image of Rosa Scribe (Cree, Norway House) holding a pair of Storyboot Mukluks she produced for Manitobah Mukluks. Photograph by Vincent Tsang. Used with permission of Manitobah Mukluks.

# Business-to-Business Marketing

The first store that Ottawa-based Shopify built was its own. Founder Tobias Luke wanted to sell snowboards online. When he couldn't find an ecommerce solution that suited his needs, the self-professed computer nerd built one. Little did he know that he would later abandon his snowboard business and sell his merchant system to retailers. Today, Shopify has become the leading cloud-based platform for merchants to set up and manage their stores. The company has over 377,500 active stores and $29 billion worth of sales[1] with a mission to make commerce better for everyone.[2]

Don't be surprised if you've never heard of Shopify. As a B2B brand, the company is well known to merchants, but not consumers. While Shopify's initial goal was to help retailers set up ecommerce sites, the system has evolved to merge digital and physical retail, working across multiple channels: brick-and-mortar, pop-up stores, web, mobile, and social media.[3]

Although the Shopify platform is suitable for merchants of all sizes, the company's focus is on small to medium sized businesses. Given that, the system needed to be very user friendly. Even the smallest merchants can quickly and easily create landing pages to start their stores. One such example is Manitobah Mukluks. Sean McMormick, a self-made Métis entrepreneur from Winnipeg, launched the company with Josh Fine in 2008 on a very limited marketing budget.[4]

While the pair could have used other commerce platforms, they needed one that let them tell their brand story. Customers paying upwards of $1,000 for Mukluk boots wanted to learn about Sean's ancestry and commitment to giving back to the Aboriginal community. Other platforms would have helped them sell their goods but were too expensive and not well suited for storytelling. The decision to go with Shopify helped propel Manitobah Mukluks from a small business to the fastest growing brand of footwear in Canada, ranking among the top 300 fastest growing companies on the Profit 500 list,[5] and competing with large companies such as Uggs in the global market.[6]

Shopify's theme-based system is ideal for businesses entering the world of ecommerce. Professionally designed online templates make it easy for even the smallest company to create an appealing retail presence. Most companies start with ready-to-go bundled themes. Merchants can also purchase custom designed themes or have their developers design their own. The system is subscription based, usually on a one-month term. That necessitates excellent customer service since there is no guarantee retailers will continue to use the system. Shopify invests heavily in training its support team and customers praise the company for its ability to quickly answer their questions.[7]

Innovative marketing programs such as the Build a Business competition attract clients. Tens of thousands of new businesses entered the eight-month competition, selling more than $250 million worth of products using the Shopify platform.[8] To increase its own bottom line, Shopify realizes it must help merchants achieve higher sales. Retail tour roadshows, a blog, and Shopify Guru are initiatives geared at educating merchants and propelling them to higher success. The Shopify Blog has become a top ecommerce and entrepreneurial blog with over 20 million page views in 2015.[9]

COO Harvey Finkelstein is quoted as saying, "In the future, consumers will dictate to the retailer how they want to purchase."[10] The insight that retail is increasingly becoming digital led the company to develop partnerships with social media platforms such as Pinterest and Facebook. Integrating its platform with Facebook Messenger gives merchants the ability to provide live customer support, as well as automatically send order confirmations and shipping updates. Shopify is also building bots for Messenger so merchants can better engage with their customers.[11] To serve customers at brick-and-mortar locations, Shopify offers a point-of-sale system and allows merchants to accept mobile payments[12] at smaller venues such as farmers' markets. To further help its clients grow, the company introduced Shopify Capital, a fast and easy way for merchants to secure financing and grow their businesses.[13]

Such marketing initiatives helped Shopify grow its employee base threefold from December 2013 to over 1,900 four years later,[14] and record 95 percent revenue growth only one year after going public. It has been able to attract clients such as Tesla, Red Bull, Jones Soda, the Golf Channel, and Ellen DeGeneres. Even Kanye West uses the platform, selling his clothing line and music through Universal Music Group on Shopify.[15] ∎

**business-to-business (B2B) marketing**
The process of buying and selling goods or services to be used in the production of other goods and services, for consumption by the buying organization, or for resale by wholesalers and retailers.

**Business-to-business (B2B) marketing** refers to the process of buying and selling goods or services to be used in the production of other goods and services, for consumption by the buying organization, or for resale by wholesalers and retailers. Therefore, B2B marketing involves manufacturers, (e.g., Levi's, IBM, Ford) selling to wholesalers that, in turn, sell products to retailers. B2B transactions can also involve service firms (e.g., Shopify, UPS, Accenture) that market their services to other businesses but not to the ultimate consumer. The distinction between a B2B and a B2C transaction is not the product or service itself; rather, it is the ultimate purchaser and *user of* that product or service. Had your jeans been sold to an industrial supply firm, which then sold them to a custodial firm whose employees would wear them on the job, the transaction would still be a B2B transaction because the jeans are being purchased and used by a business rather than by an individual household consumer. You will read more about B2B transactions involving jeans in the Chapter Case Study on Levi Strauss.

In this chapter, we will look at the different types of B2B markets and examine the B2B buying process with an eye toward how it differs from the B2C buying process, which we discussed in Chapter 4. Several factors influence the B2B buying process, and we discuss these as well. Finally, the chapter concludes with a discussion about the role of the Internet and its influence on the way B2B marketing is conducted.

## LO1  B2B MARKETS

Just like organizations that sell directly to final consumers in B2C transactions, B2B firms focus their efforts on serving specific types of customer markets to create value for those customers. For instance, Shopify helps small and medium sized companies establish online stores and reach their ultimate target markets.

Many firms find it more productive to focus their efforts on key industries or market segments rather than on ultimate consumers. Cossette Communication Group and BBDO Canada, two of Canada's largest advertising agencies, provide advertising, public relations, and other marketing communications services to large and small business clients across Canada. Similarly, Canada's Magna International designs, develops, and manufactures automotive systems, assemblies, modules, and components primarily for sale to original equipment manufacturers (OEMs) of cars and light trucks in North America, Europe, Asia, South America, and Africa.[16]

In the chapter opening vignette, we saw how both small and large merchants sell their products using Shopify's commerce platform. Basically, manufacturers, resellers, institutions, and governments are all involved in B2B transactions (see Exhibit 5.1). In the next sections, we describe each of these B2B organizations.

### Manufacturers or Producers

Manufacturers buy raw materials, components, and parts that allow them to manufacture their own goods. For example, the German-based Volkswagen Group, the largest auto manufacturer in Europe, owns and distributes the Audi, Bentley, Bugatti, Lamborghini, Seat, Skoda, Scania VW, and VW Commercial Vehicles brands.[17] Whereas purchasing agents formerly spent 70 percent of their time searching for, analyzing, validating, and forwarding information about parts and components, today they can use VWSupplyGroup .com to communicate with suppliers for all transactions, from procurement to logistics.

The VW Group is used by 45,600 suppliers engaged in transactions worth nearly C\$3 billion.[18] Purchasing agents receive product descriptions directly from suppliers online, which means search processes that used to take two hours now require about nine minutes. Users of the system receive alerts of potential parts shortages before they occur and thus can focus on efficiencies instead of redundant paperwork.

**EXHIBIT 5.1** B2B Markets

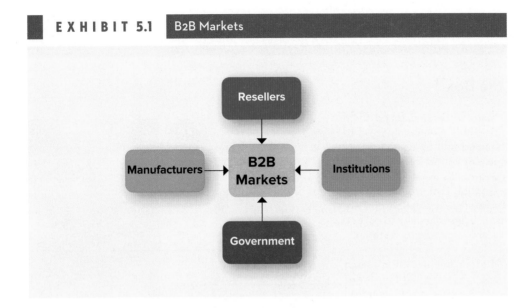

IBM provided the consulting services necessary to design the Volkswagen Group's system. IBM, which was once a major manufacturer of computers and related products, now generates over 90 percent of its profits from its software, consulting, and financing businesses—all of which are considered services. Like Volkswagen Group, it requires a host of B2B products and services to support these businesses. For instance, the airlines that IBM consultants and service providers rely on to shuttle them around the globe also utilize a mix of products like airplanes and fuel, as well as consulting, legal, and other services.

Today, many B2B companies are demanding, as a condition for doing business, that suppliers demonstrate social responsibility by instituting policies and practices to reduce their carbon footprint. Sustainable Marketing 5.1 explains how a small company provides packing solutions for its customers in a cost effective and environmentally friendly manner.

**resellers**
Marketing intermediaries that resell manufactured products without significantly altering their form.

## Resellers

**Resellers** are marketing intermediaries that resell manufactured products without significantly altering their form. For instance, wholesalers and distributors buy jeans from Levi Strauss and sell them to retailers (a B2B transaction), and retailers in turn resell those same jeans to the ultimate consumer (a B2C transaction). Wholesalers, distributors, and retailers are all resellers. The Retail Council of Canada estimates that there are more than 215,000 retail establishments in Canada, which employ 2.2 million Canadians and generate sales of $500 billion, making the retail industry the country's largest employer.[21] Similarly, the wholesale sector consists of more than 170,000 firms, generating sales of $661 billion in 2016.[22] The role of wholesalers, retailers, and other intermediaries involved in the distribution of goods is discussed in greater detail in Chapters 12 and 13.

German-based Volkswagen Group, the largest auto manufacturer in Europe, owns and distributes numerous brands.

Oliver Hardt/AFP/Getty Images

## Sustainable Marketing 5.1

# Thinking Out of the Box[19]

You've probably opened many boxes and found them packed with Styrofoam "peanuts." Commonly used to protect products being shipped and fill up the empty space in boxes, the peanuts are lightweight, work well, and are relatively inexpensive. It's what happens to them after they've done their job that creates a problem. According to the Packaging Association of Canada, it costs an estimated $12 billion annually to collect, recover, and dispose of discarded packaging material in North America.[20]

Scott MacRae travelled to Finland in 2011 in search of a better solution. He found a machine that transforms enormous rolls of 100 percent recycled Kraft paper into twisted peanut-like shapes. The end result is cheaper and more environmentally friendly than traditional Styrofoam, plastic, or cornstarch fillers. Plus, the "papernuts" interlock, ensuring that the contents of the box won't migrate during shipping. MacRae secured a Canada-wide licence from the Finnish engineer who came up with the technology to sell the papernuts and the equipment that manufactures it.

Together with business partner Joanne Secord, he launched PaperNuts in St. Catharines, Ontario. The challenge was to identify the target market. Originally their plan was to make the product, bag it, and sell it to companies for use in their shipping departments. Later on they hoped to rent machines as a Factory-in-a-Box, allowing companies to produce unlimited papernuts on site. PaperNuts estimated they could make $1 million in the first year by selling paper to companies. After appearing on CBC's *Dragons' Den* to pitch their idea, they got calls from all over the world and learned that many companies wanted to own—not rent—the machines. Other companies requested licences to resell the equipment.

Thinking out of the box, MacRae changed the plan, and secured the global rights to PaperNuts. They embarked on a geographical approach to segmenting the market. Other factors used to define their target market included the industry, population (number of companies in a geographic area), and the number of exports (countries that ship high volumes such as China and Korea). Exclusive licences were set up with distributors to resell the equipment in

The PaperNuts Factory-in-a-Box produces environmentally friendly packing material that is easily recycled.

geographic territories covering the Ottawa area and the province of Alberta. More opportunities were explored across Ontario as well as in Russia. Under the new arrangement, companies could buy rolls of paper from PaperNuts or source it themselves. MacRae and Secord earned a royalty on every papernut produced and the satisfaction of knowing that their solution can be easily recycled.

The business strategy changed again when the company went public in 2015, part of a reverse merger with Axiom Corp. With expertise in the global packaging industry, PaperNuts' new CEO, Tyler Pearson, shifted the focus to selling paper. With increased demand for sustainable products in the North American and European markets, the company focused on the global market. Company size and volume of product shipped were key considerations when segmenting the market. Today, large ecommerce companies, increasingly concerned about reducing their environmental impact, are attractive target markets and a steady source of recurring revenue.

## Institutions

Institutions—such as hospitals, educational organizations, prisons, religious organizations, and other non-profit organizations—also purchase all kinds of goods and services for the people they serve. For instance, there are over 170,000 non-profit organizations in Canada, employing about 2 million people and generating revenues in excess of

$110 billion annually.[23] Public institutions engage in B2B relationships to fulfill their needs for capital construction, equipment, supplies, food, and janitorial services. A public school board with a $40 million annual budget for textbooks has significant buying power, enabling it to take advantage of bulk discounts that would not be available to individual schools.

## Government

In most countries, the central government tends to be one of the largest purchasers of goods and services. For example, the Canadian federal government spends about $240 billion annually on procuring goods and services. If you add in the amounts spent by provincial and municipal governments, as well as the academic, social, and health sectors, this amount increases to more than $550 billion annually. The bulk of the federal government's buying of goods and services is done centrally by Public Works and Government Services Canada on behalf of more than 85 departments, agencies, Crown corporations, and Special Operating Agencies.[24] Information about government buying can be obtained from Business Access Canada or from MERX.[25] MERX is the most complete source of Canadian public tenders, private tenders, U.S. tenders, and private-sector construction news available in Canada. MERX makes it possible for businesses of any size to have easy and affordable access to billions of dollars in contracting opportunities with the government of Canada, participating provincial and municipal governments, the U.S. government, state and local governments, and the private sector.[26]

## Key Challenges of Reaching B2B Clients

For marketers to be effective and successful at B2B marketing, they must master three key challenges for each business customer they want to serve. First, marketers must identify the right persons or decision makers within the organizations who can authorize or influence purchases. Second, they must understand the buying process of each potential client. Third, they need to identify the factors that influence the buying process of potential clients. B2B markets differ in varying degrees on these three dimensions; hence, marketers must invest the time and resources to understand these challenges. For example, institutional buyers, such as nursing homes and universities, tend to have relatively small budgets and therefore seek the best value when buying products and services for their organizations. That is, if two suppliers are offering roughly similar products, they may opt for the supplier with the lower price. Governments, on the other hand, make much larger purchases, but their buying processes must not only satisfy strict policy guidelines and directives set by the government, but also meet international trade rules set by the World Trade Organization (WTO) or the North American Free Trade Agreement (NAFTA). Additionally, government purchases are subject to public scrutiny and can be legally challenged or be cancelled or modified. Governments consider a wide range of factors in their purchases and may not always

MERX is the most complete source of public tenders, private tenders, U.S. tenders, and private-sector construction news available in Canada
Reprinted with permission from MERX

buy from the vendor with the lowest price. Institutional organizations are not under such public scrutiny and rarely disclose their purchase decisions and practices, although they may try to make their buying processes transparent. Finally, private-sector companies such as manufacturers, producers, and resellers rarely, if ever, disclose their buying criteria or buying process. They are likely to engage in reciprocal buying, a situation where two companies agree to buy each other's products as appropriate.

To address the complexity of B2B markets, many companies have salespeople or a sales team dedicated to specific clients. For instance, many companies wishing to sell to the government (e.g., IBM, Microsoft) have business–government relations experts or departments. Some companies rely on business from governments and institutions, as seen in Entrepreneurial Marketing 5.1.

Let us now explore in a little more detail some of the unique characteristics of B2B markets that distinguish them from B2C markets. Exhibit 5.2 lists the key characteristics of B2B and B2C buying behaviour.

## Entrepreneurial Marketing 5.1

# Fighting Fires With Drones[27]

Drones have been used for applications from military and police surveillance, to search and rescue missions, to helping victims of natural disasters. You may be familiar with drones because of Amazon, which hopes to use them to deliver goods to customers through its Prime Air service. A growing market—global sales for unmanned aerial vehicles (UAVs) or drones—is estimated at more than US$127 billion.

Waterloo-based Aeryon Labs has been developing drones since 2007. Founder Dave Kroetsch has always liked to tinker with electronics and participated in the International Aerial Robotics Competition while he was still in high school. After studying engineering at the University of Waterloo, he started a robotics business in a garage with two friends. They knew that drones had many uses but weren't sure what the best fit would be. Cold calls identified land surveyors, power line inspectors, and farmers as potential customers. But early drones were hard to manoeuvre. After getting feedback from RCMP drug enforcement officers, Aeryon Labs refined its design to use Google Maps and point and click technology, making the drones simple for anyone to fly.

Kroetsch became the company's CEO by default. Neither of his partners wanted the job. Together they secured angel funding and got government grants allowing them to launch the Aeryon Scout. Their first customer was the Canadian Military with a million dollar contract for drones to help rebels fight Gadhafi forces in Libya. Soon after, the Ontario Provincial Police started using Scouts for search and rescue missions as well as highway accident forensics.

Business exploded and the company grew from three partners to 125 employees. Its newest drone, the SkyRanger, sells for $65,000–$200,000 and is being

Aeryon Labs drones were used to assess wildfire damage in Fort McMurray in 2016.

Jonathan Hayward/The Canadian Press

used to inspect power lines in northern Ontario. SkyRangers' infrared cameras can identify hot spots before problems occur and power line connections fail. Transport Canada recently granted special permission for SkyRangers to fly to assess wildfire damage in Fort McMurray, Alberta. Equipped with high resolution geolocated imagery and thermal infrared sensors, drones were able to measure the heat of the fire in Fort McMurray and surrounding area.

About half of the company's business still comes from government clients for military applications, with sales increasing by 100 percent per year. However, Kroetsch says private sector growth is promising. Engineers use drones to inspect bridges and farmers rely on them to fertilize crops, deal with pests, and identify fields that need irrigation. As aviation authorities continue to adapt regulations to accommodate drone flights, Aeryon Labs' sky high growth is likely to continue.

**EXHIBIT 5.2**  Characteristics of B2B Buying as Compared With B2C Buying

**Market Characteristics**
- Demand for business products is derived, fluctuates more, and more frequently
- Fewer customers, more geographically concentrated, and orders are larger
- Demand is more inelastic

**Product Characteristics**
- Products are technical in nature and purchased based on specifications
- Mainly raw and semifinished goods are purchased
- Heavy emphasis is placed on delivery time, technical assistance, after-sale service, and financing assistance

**Buying Process Characteristics**
- Buying decision is more complex
- Buying may involve competitive bidding, negotiated pricing, and complex financial arrangements
- Buying involves qualified, professional buyers who follow a more formalized buying process
- Buying criteria and objective are specified, as are procedures for evaluating and selecting vendors and products
- Multiple people with varied interests participate in purchase decisions
- Reciprocal arrangements exist, and negotiations between buyers and sellers are common
- Buyers and sellers usually work closely to build close long-term relationships
- Online buying over the Internet is common

**Marketing Mix Characteristics**
- Direct selling is the primary form of selling and physical distribution is often essential
- Advertising is technical in nature, and promotions emphasize personal selling
- Price is often negotiated, inelastic, frequently affected by trade and quantity discounts; price usually includes a service or maintenance component

## Differences Between B2B and B2C Markets

**L02**

Market Characteristics   In B2C markets, consumers buy goods to satisfy their own individual or household needs and are heavily influenced by price, personal tastes, brand reputation, and personal recommendations of friends and family. In B2B markets, demand for goods and services is often derived from B2C sales in the same supply chain. More specifically, **derived demand** is the linkage between consumers' demand for a company's output and its purchase of necessary inputs to manufacture or assemble that particular output. For instance, the demand for raw denim used to make Levi's jeans is derived from the sale of the jeans to consumers. Thus, demand for raw material and semifinished goods purchased by business firms tends to fluctuate more, and more frequently. In addition, demand in many business markets is inelastic—that is, the total demand for goods is not affected much by price changes in the short run. For instance, a small increase in the price for raw denim will not cause a huge drop in the demand for denim in the apparel industry in the short run. Another characteristic of B2B markets is that the number of business buyers is substantially fewer than in B2C markets, and the business buyers are more concentrated in big cities, towns, and industrial areas. Also, the sizes of the orders are substantially larger than consumer purchases. For example, Bombardier announced that Delta Air Lines signed an order valued at US$5.6 billion for 75 CS100 airplanes, with options for 50 more.[28]

Product Characteristics   In B2B markets, the products ordered are primarily raw materials and semifinished goods that are processed or assembled into finished goods for the ultimate consumers. For example, Dell orders all the computer components from different suppliers and then assembles the computers before shipping to the final consumer. In certain B2B markets (e.g., aerospace, medical, pharmaceutical, shipping, defence), the products are very technical and sophisticated in nature and must conform to technical standards specified

**derived demand**
The linkage between consumers' demand for a company's output and its purchase of necessary inputs to manufacture or assemble that particular output.

by the buyer. Thus, the raw materials, components, and semifinished goods undergo rigorous testing before shipping. Also, orders must be delivered on the dates agreed to by both buyers and sellers. Technical services and financing assistance are important aspects of B2B buying behaviour. Companies such as Bombardier often provide vendor financing—a practice where a company provides its customer with a loan that is used to buy goods from the company.[29] In B2C markets, consumers buy finished goods for their own personal consumption.

**Buying Process Characteristics**    Generally, for routine purchases or small-dollar-value purchases, only one or a few individuals within a department or the company may be responsible for the buying decision. However, for purchases of highly technical or complex products involving thousands or millions of dollars, the buying effort is much more structured, formalized, and professional. More people are usually involved in complex buying decisions. They are usually technically trained and qualified professionals, and they represent different interests (e.g., managerial, technical, and departmental) within the organization. The group of people involved in the buying decision is often referred to as the buying centre, which is described in detail below. Most companies have formal policies and procedures to guide buying decisions that must be closely followed by the people involved in the buying decisions. Examples of such procedures include rules governing competitive bidding, negotiated pricing, complex financial arrangements, buying criteria, and objectives, as well as procedures for evaluating competitive bids.

Another major difference between B2B and B2C buying lies in the nature of the relationship between the firm and its suppliers. Generally, the buying decision is based on negotiations, which for complex purchases could be quite extended. The negotiated contract normally covers a range of concerns, including price, delivery, warranty, technical specifications, and claim policies. In B2B markets, buyers and sellers strive to develop close relationships with each other and so will often provide help or advice to ensure a win–win situation for both parties. For example, Shepherd Thermoforming and Packaging—a leading Canadian manufacturer of plastic products ranging from your hot tub to your chocolate tray, Tylenol package, smoke detector cover, or other plastic item in your home or car—noted that its B2B customers often chose to come in and work with its engineering staff to create the desired look and product functionality that they needed.[30]

In addition, some firms may engage in reciprocal buying arrangements—a practice where two firms agree to buy each other's products and services. Clearly, reciprocal buying has both negative and positive consequences for both the buying and selling firms involved, as well as for other suppliers. Two such consequences are that it excludes other vendors from participating in the buying process and may limit the firms to each other's products, which may not be the best thing.

**Marketing Mix Characteristics**    Another major difference between the typical B2B and B2C transaction is the role of the salesperson. On the one hand, while salespeople are an important component of the communications mix for B2C transactions such as sales of real estate, insurance, jewellery, consumer electronics, and high-end apparel, most fast-moving consumer goods (FMCG) found in grocery and discount stores are not sold with the aid of salespeople. On the other hand, in most B2B sales, the salesperson is an integral component of the transaction. Pharmaceutical manufacturers rely primarily on sales representatives to promote their drugs to doctors. Also, many manufacturers provide trade and quantity discounts to resellers for carrying their products.

**North American Industry Classification System (NAICS ) codes**
A classification scheme that categorizes all firms into a hierarchical set of six-digit codes.

**L03**    ## B2B Classification System and Segmentation

Statistics Canada collects data about business activity in Canada through its classification scheme, which categorizes all firms into a hierarchical set of six-digit **North American Industry Classification System (NAICS) codes**.[31] The NAICS was developed jointly by Canada, the United States, and Mexico to provide comparable statistics about business activity in all of North America. The NAICS codes

| EXHIBIT 5.3 | Telecommunications NAICS Codes |
| --- | --- |
| **NAICS Code** | **Level** |
| 51 | Information |
| 515 | Broadcasting except Internet |
| 5151 | Radio and Television Broadcasting |
| 51511 | Radio Broadcasting |
| 515111 | Radio Networks |

*Source:* Industry Canada. "Information and Cultural Industries (NAICS 51): Definition" https://www.ic.gc.ca/app/scr/sbms/sbb/cis/definition.html?code=51&lang=eng (accessed January 2, 2017)

The NAICS classification system could help a high-tech telecommunications components manufacturer identify groups of customers to pursue.

Marmaduke St. John/Alamy Stock Photo

replaced the Standard Industrial Classification (SIC) system that had been in use since the 1930s. The NAICS groups economic activity into 20 sectors and 928 Canadian industries. The NAICS six-digit numerical system works as shown in Exhibit 5.3. The first two digits represent the sector in the economy (e.g., 51 is the information sector); the third digit represents the subsector (e.g., 515 is "Broadcasting except Internet"); the fourth digit represents the industry group; the fifth digit represents a specific subgroup within the industry; and the full six digits refer to the country-level or national industry. The NAICS system is revised periodically to add new industries or to consolidate or delete others.

The NAICS classification system can be quite useful to B2B marketers for segmenting and targeting markets. Suppose, for instance, that a high-tech telecommunications components manufacturer has developed a new product that will significantly speed data transmission. Which of the types of firms listed under NAICS classification 515111 (radio networks) would be the most worthwhile to pursue as customers? To answer this question, the components manufacturer would first do research, probably by having company sales representatives conduct interviews, to determine which types of firms would find the new component most useful for their products. Then, using the NAICS data collected by Statistics Canada or the U.S. Census Bureau, the manufacturer could assess the number, size, and geographical dispersion of firms within each type, which might indicate both the product's potential and the types of firms that constitute the target market.

In addition to NAICS, marketers may segment B2B markets in several other ways, including geographic location (e.g., by country, provinces, region, cities), firm size (e.g., by the number of employees in the firm or by sales volume), account size (by small, medium, and large accounts or purchase size), and types of products purchased. Refer back to Sustainable Marketing 5.1 to see an example of how PaperNuts used geographic location, industry, company size, and number of exports in segmenting its markets.

## THE B2B BUYING PROCESS      `LO4`

The B2B buying process (Exhibit 5.4) parallels the B2C process, though it differs in many ways. Both start with need recognition, but the information search and alternative evaluation stages are more formal and structured in the B2B process. Typically, B2B buyers specify their needs in writing and ask potential suppliers to submit formal proposals, whereas B2C buying decisions are usually made by individuals or families

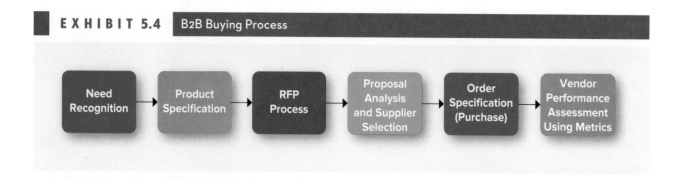

**EXHIBIT 5.4**  B2B Buying Process

Need Recognition → Product Specification → RFP Process → Proposal Analysis and Supplier Selection → Order Specification (Purchase) → Vendor Performance Assessment Using Metrics

and sometimes are unplanned or impulsive. For an individual to buy a tablet computer, all that is required is a trip to the store or a few minutes online and perhaps some preliminary research about iPads versus competitors. For a university to buy 1,000 tablet computers, however, it must complete requisition forms, accept bids from manufacturers, and obtain approval for the expenditure. The final decision rests with a committee, as is the case for most B2B buying decisions, which often demand a great deal of consideration. Finally, in B2C buying situations, customers evaluate their purchase decision and sometimes experience postpurchase dissonance. However, formal performance evaluations of the vendor and the products sold generally do not occur, as they do in the B2B setting. Let's examine all six stages in the context of a hypothetical university buying tablets for students as a resource.

## Stage 1: Need Recognition

In the first stage of the B2B buying process, the buying organization recognizes, through either internal or external sources, that it has an unfilled need. Our hypothetical university wants to ensure its students are well educated and able to participate in a technologically connected workforce. It seeks to grant them affordable access to required educational resources, from textbooks to library access to administrative tasks. The administration of the university reviewed research suggesting that portable devices, including tablet computers, can enhance students' in-class learning because they can directly interact with the materials rather than only hearing information or seeing it on a whiteboard. The tablets support innovative learning methodologies, such as the uses of interactive clickers in lecture-based courses. Using this information, the university determined it will issue a tablet to each of the students entering as its next graduating class.

**request for proposals (RFP)**
A process through which buying organizations invite alternative suppliers to bid on supplying their required components.

## Stage 2: Product Specification

After recognizing the need and considering alternative solutions, including laptop and desktop computers, the university wrote a list of potential specifications that vendors might use to develop their proposals. The school's specifications include screen size, battery life, processor speed, how the device connects to the Internet, and delivery date.

In addition, the board of directors requested that a bundle of educational apps be preloaded on the tablets, that all other apps be removed, and that each tablet come equipped with a screen protector, power cord, cover, stand, keyboard, and headphones. The school requested a three-year service contract that includes replacement within 24 hours for any tablets that are returned to the vendor for servicing.

The first step in the B2B decision process is to recognize that the schools need to purchase 1000 tablets.

Courtesy of Apple

## Stage 3: RFP Process

The **request for proposals (RFP)** is a common process through which buying organizations invite alternative suppliers to bid on supplying their required components or specifications. The purchasing company may simply post its RFP needs on its website, work through various B2B web portals, or contact potential suppliers directly. Firms may narrow the process to a few suppliers, often those with which they have existing relationships. In a recent case, the Royal Ontario Museum in Toronto issued a complicated RFP with an unprecedented request for caterers who responded to pay an annual fee of $10,000 for up to 10 years to earn points in the assessment process. While the fee might secure a place on the preferred vendor list, it is not a guarantee of winning any catering business.[32]

If the school does not have a preferred vendor, it issues an RFP and invites various tablet suppliers, technology companies, and other interested parties to bid on the contract. Smaller companies may lack the ability to attract broad attention to their requests, so they might turn to a web portal, an Internet site whose purpose is to be a major starting point for users when they connect to the web. Although there are general portals such as Yahoo or MSN, B2B partners connect to specialized or niche portals to participate in online information exchanges and transactions. These exchanges help streamline procurement or distribution processes. Portals can provide tremendous cost savings because they eliminate periodic negotiations and routine paperwork, and they offer the means to form a supply chain that can respond quickly to the buyer's needs.

## Stage 4: Proposal Analysis and Supplier Selection

The buying organization, in conjunction with its critical decision makers, evaluates all the proposals it receives in response to its RFP. At this stage, the school reviews all proposals received together with faculty and student government members. Many firms narrow the process to a few suppliers, often those with which they have existing relationships, and discuss key terms of the sale, such as price, quality, delivery, and financing. The university likely considers the bid by the company that installed computers in its library, assuming that provider performed well. Some firms have a policy that requires them to negotiate with several suppliers, particularly if the product or service represents a critical component or aspect of the business. This policy keeps suppliers on their toes; they know that the buying firm can always shift a greater portion of its business to an alternative supplier if it offers better terms.

The school evaluates proposals on the basis of the amount of experience the vendor has with tablet computers and similar technology products, because it wants to make sure that its investment is reliable in the short term and flexible enough to accommodate new apps or updates. In addition, it wants to be sure the technology will remain relevant in the longer term and not become obsolete. The vendor's ability to meet its specifications also is important, because if the processor is too slow, students are unlikely to make use of the devices. The vendor's financial position also provides an important indication of whether the vendor will be able to stay in business.

## Stage 5: Order Specification (Purchase)

In the fifth stage, the firm places its order with its preferred supplier (or suppliers). The order will include a detailed description of the goods, prices, delivery dates, and, in some cases, penalties if the order is not filled on time. The supplier then sends an acknowledgment that it has received the order and will fill it by the specified date. In the case of the school's tablets, the terms are clearly laid out regarding when and how the vendor is expected to perform any preventive maintenance, who the contact person is for any problems with delivery or the tablets themselves, and under what circumstances the vendor will be expected to provide a replacement for a malfunctioning tablet. Issues like maintenance and replacement are important to the school, because it is not planning to keep an inventory of extra tablets on hand.

| EXHIBIT 5.5 | Evaluating a Vendor's Performance | | |
|---|---|---|---|
| (1) Key Issues | (2) Importance Score | (3) Vendor's Performance | (4) Importance × Performance [(2) × (3)] |
| Customer Service | 0.4 | 5 | 2.0 |
| Issue Resolution | 0.2 | 4 | 0.8 |
| Delivery | 0.1 | 5 | 0.5 |
| Quality | 0.3 | 3 | 0.9 |
| Total | 1.0 | | 4.2 |

## Stage 6: Vendor Performance Assessment Using Metrics

Just as in the consumer buying process, firms analyze their vendors' performance so they can make decisions about their future purchases. The difference is that, in a B2B setting, this analysis is typically more formal and objective. Let's consider how the school might evaluate the tablet vendor's performance, as in Exhibit 5.5, using the following metrics: delivery (based on promised delivery date), quality, customer service, and issue resolution.

1. The buying team develops a list of issues that it believes are important to consider in the vendor evaluation.

2. To determine the importance of each issue (column 1), the buying team assigns an importance score to each (column 2). The more important the issue, the higher its score, but the importance scores must add up to 1. In this case, the buying team believes that customer service and quality are most important, whereas the issue resolution and delivery are comparatively less important.

3. In the third column, the buying team assigns numbers that reflect its judgments about how well the vendor performs. Using a five-point scale, where 1 equals "poor performance" and 5 equals "excellent performance," the school district decides that the tablet vendor performs quite well on all issues except product quality.

4. To calculate an overall performance score in the fourth column, the team combines the importance of each issue and the vendor's performance scores by multiplying them. Because the tablet vendor performed well on the most important issues, when we add the importance/performance scores in column 4, we find that the overall evaluation is pretty good—4.2 on a five-point scale.

Although most B2B organizations utilize the buying process described above as a way to ensure they get the best value for their money, some organizations simply operate based on a sole source or on longer-term business relationships.

## L05    THE BUYING CENTRE

**buying centre**
The group of people typically responsible for the buying decisions in large organizations.

The six-stage B2B buying process may be influenced by three factors within the purchasing organization: the buying centre, the buying organization's philosophy or corporate culture, and the buying situation. In most large organizations, several people typically are responsible for the buying decisions. These **buying centre** participants can range from employees who have a formal role in purchasing decisions (e.g., the purchasing or procurement department), to members of the design team that is specifying the particular equipment or raw material needed, to employees who will be using a new machine that is

**EXHIBIT 5.6** | The Buying Centre Roles

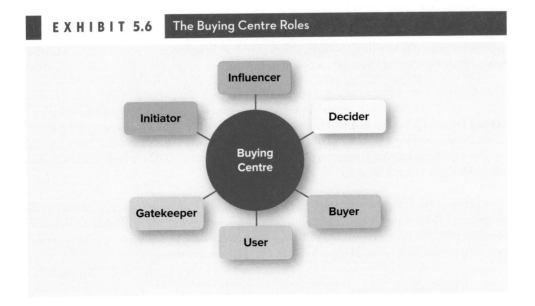

being ordered. All these employees are likely to play different roles in the buying process, which vendors must understand and adapt to in their marketing and sales efforts.

We can categorize six different buying roles within a typical buying centre (see Exhibit 5.6). One or more people may take on a certain role, or one person may take on more than one of the following roles: "(1) **initiator**, the person who first suggests buying the particular product or service; (2) **influencer**, the person whose views influence other members of the buying centre in making the final decision; (3) **decider**, the person who ultimately determines any part of or the entire buying decision—whether to buy, what to buy, how to buy, or where to buy; (4) **buyer**, the person who handles the paperwork of the actual purchase; (5) **user**, the person(s) who consumes or uses the product or service; and (6) **gatekeeper**, the person(s) who controls information or access, or both, to decision makers and influencers."[33]

To illustrate how a buying centre operates, consider purchases made by a hospital. Where do hospitals obtain their X-ray machines, syringes, or bedpans? Why are some medical procedures covered in whole or in part by insurance, whereas others are not? Why might your doctor recommend one type of allergy medication instead of another?

### The Initiator—Your Doctor

When you seek treatment from your physician, he or she *initiates* the buying process by determining the products and services that will best address and treat your illness or injury. For example, say that you fell backward on your snowboard and, in trying to catch yourself, shattered your elbow. You require surgery to mend the affected area, which includes the insertion of several screws to hold the bones in place. Your doctor promptly notifies the hospital to schedule a time for the procedure and specifies the brand of screws she wants for your surgery.

### The Influencer—The Medical Device Supplier, the Pharmacy

For years, your doctor has been using ElbowMed screws, a slightly higher-priced screw. Her first introduction to ElbowMed screws came from the company's sales representative, who visited her office to demonstrate how ElbowMed's screws were far superior to those of its competition. Your doctor recognized ElbowMed as good value. Armed with empirical data and case studies, ElbowMed's sales rep effectively *influenced* your doctor's decision to use that screw.

### The Decider—The Hospital

Even though your doctor requested ElbowMed screws, the hospital ultimately is responsible for *deciding* whether to buy ElbowMed

**initiator**
The buying centre participant who first suggests buying the particular product or service.

**influencer**
The buying centre participant whose views influence other members of the buying centre in making the final decision.

**decider**
The buying centre participant who ultimately determines any part of or the entire buying decision—whether to buy, what to buy, how to buy, or where to buy.

**buyer**
The buying centre participant who handles the paperwork of the actual purchase.

**user**
The person who consumes or uses the product or service purchased by the buying centre.

**gatekeeper**
The buying centre participant who controls information or access to decision makers and influencers.

screws. The hospital supplies the operating room, instrumentation, and surgical supplies, and therefore, the hospital administrators must weigh a variety of factors to determine not only whether the ElbowMed screw is best for patients, but also whether using ElbowMed screws involves a cost that is justified.

**The Buyer—The Hospital's Materials Manager**    The actual *buyer* of the screw will likely be the hospital's materials manager, who is charged with buying and maintaining inventory for the hospital in the most cost-effective manner. Whereas ElbowMed screws are specific to your type of procedure, other items, such as gauze and sutures, may be purchased through a group purchasing organization (GPO), which obtains better prices through volume buying.

**The User—The Patient**    Ultimately though, the buying process for this procedure will be greatly affected by the *user*, namely, you and your broken elbow. If you are uncomfortable with the procedure or have read about alternative procedures that you prefer, you may decide that ElbowMed screws are not the best treatment.

**The Gatekeeper—The Purchasing Department**    The hospital's purchasing department may believe that ElbowMed screws are too expensive and that other screws deliver equally effective results. Therefore, it might ask the hospital to reconsider the purchase of the screws.

In the end, the final purchase decision must take into consideration every single buying centre participant. Ethical Dilemma 5.1 examines the unethical, illegal, but also international practice of influencing the influencers through expensive gifts and payments.

## Organizational Culture

**organizational culture**
Reflects the set of values, traditions, and customs that guides a firm's employees' behaviour.

**autocratic buying centre**
A buying centre in which one person makes the decision alone, though there may be multiple participants.

**democratic buying centre**
A buying centre in which the majority rules in making decisions.

**consultative buying centre**
A buying centre in which one person makes the decision, but he or she solicits input from others before doing so.

**consensus buying centre**
A buying centre in which all members of the team must reach a collective agreement that they can support a particular purchase.

A firm's **organizational culture** reflects the set of values, traditions, and customs that guides its managers' and employees' behaviour. The firm's culture often comprises a set of unspoken guidelines that employees share with one another through various work situations. For example, Walmart buyers are not allowed to accept even the smallest gift from a vendor, not even a cup of coffee. This rule highlights the company's overall corporate culture: It is a low-cost operator whose buyers must base their decisions only on the products' and vendors' merits.

At GE, the culture aims to ensure that members and partners regard B2B as a source of innovation, not a "boring-to-boring" proposition. Rather than lament the relatively less glamorous B2B processes, GE has "decided we are geeky and we are proud of it."[35] To promote its offerings, the company thus focuses on how it innovates in B2B settings, and it brings this attitude into its purchasing decisions.

As these examples show, organizational culture can have a profound influence on purchasing decisions, and corporate buying centre cultures might be divided into four general types: autocratic, democratic, consultative, and consensus, as illustrated in Exhibit 5.7. Knowing which buying centre culture is prevalent in a given organization helps the seller decide how to approach that particular client, how and to whom to deliver pertinent information, and to whom to make the sales presentations.

In an **autocratic buying centre**, though there may be multiple participants, one person makes the decision alone, whereas the majority rules in a **democratic buying centre**. A **consultative buying centre** uses one person to make a decision, but he or she solicits input from others before doing so. Finally, in a **consensus buying centre**, all members of the team must reach a collective agreement that they can support a particular purchase.[36]

Cultures act like living, breathing entities that change and grow, just as organizations do. Even within some companies, culture may vary by geography, division, or functional department. Whether you are a member of the buying centre or a supplier trying to sell

## Ethical Dilemma 5.1

### Is It Business or Bribery?[34]

In some parts of the world, accepting money, offering expensive gifts, or distributing payments to government and business officials to influence business decisions is considered an acceptable business practice. In other nations, these practices are unethical and illegal. As the world moves to a more global economy, pressure is mounting to level the playing field by eliminating bribery. Yet companies that have traditionally relied on business bribery argue that criminalizing this activity will negatively affect their ability to compete. How do executives doing business on an international scale respond when a behaviour that could earn them a lucrative contract in one country could earn them jail time in another?

Whenever businesses cooperate with one another or companies intersect with governments, the opportunity exists for bribery. An extravagant gift or economic incentive may mean one contractor lands a lucrative contract. A private exchange of money between an executive and a public official may result in the official driving a new car while the executive's company bypasses a restriction that could hinder its growth. These types of interactions occur behind closed doors and between two people, yet they can have significant repercussions, including unsafe infrastructure, bridges, and buildings, if they occur in the context of large business transactions. Increasingly, players in the world's economies thus are pushing for an end to foreign bribery.

One tactic they are using is a public report by Transparency International that compares corruption rates of countries and industries. This investigation reveals unexpected trends, such as evidence that bribes passing from one business to another are almost as common as bribes slipped to public officials. By highlighting those business sectors or countries perceived as the worst offenders, the Bribery Index also aims to bring about change, whether through embarrassment or through economic repercussions that result when companies refuse to do business in corrupt economies. Finally, this report highlights suggestions for reducing corruption and incentives for improvement.

Although in some parts of the world bribes are part of doing business, in Canada and the United States they are unethical and illegal.

James Lauritz/Getty Images

The Transparency International Bribery Index reveals that all the world's 28 largest economies engage in bribery; China and Russia emerged as those most likely to be using money and gifts to influence decisions. Both countries have recently begun enforcing legal repercussions for companies and individuals that engage in international business bribery. For example, when reports surfaced that representatives of GlaxoSmithKline (GSK) had bribed doctors, medical practices, and hospitals to prescribe only GSK drugs, China's news media and central government reacted with anger. Chinese authorities encouraged consumers to boycott its products. As a result, GSK's business revenues fell by two-thirds in China.

The Transparency International report also highlights positive results of reduced corruption: A business survey conducted in Europe found that two-thirds of respondents believe that a company with a reputation for ethical behaviour enjoys a commercial advantage. Findings such as these—along with improved transparency added to business practices, international anticorruption standards, monitoring and enforcement of anticorruption business policies and laws, and empowerment of whistle-blowers—may also help reduce international bribery rates.

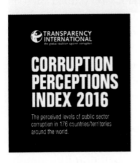

The Corruption Perceptions Index illustrates countries that experience high levels of public sector corruption.

Source: "Corruption Perceptions Index: Global 2016" © 2016 by Transparency International. Licensed under CC-BY-ND 4.0

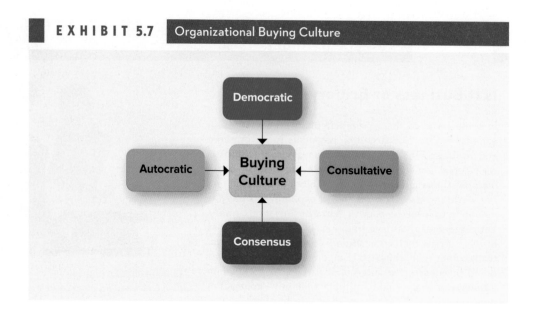

**EXHIBIT 5.7**     Organizational Buying Culture

to it, it is extremely important to understand its culture and the roles of the key players in the buying process. Not knowing the roles of the key players in that case could waste a lot of time—both yours and the buying centre's—and could even alienate the real decision maker.

## Building B2B Relationships

In B2B contexts, there are a vast variety of ways to enhance relationships, and these methods seem to be advancing and evolving by the minute. For example, blogs and social media can build awareness, provide search engine results, educate potential and existing clients about products or services, and warm up a seemingly cold corporate culture.[37] An expert who offers advice and knowledge about products increases brand awareness, and a blog is a great medium for this information. Web analytics, such as traffic on the website and the number of comments, can offer tangible evaluations, but a better measure is how often the blog gets mentioned elsewhere, the media attention it receives, and the interaction, involvement, intimacy, and influence that it promotes.

The LinkedIn social network is mainly used for professional networking in the B2B marketplace. Twitter, the microblogging site, is also valuable for B2B marketers, because they can communicate with other businesses as often as they want. Companies such as HootSuite and TweetDeck make it easier for companies using Twitter to manage their followers, update their posts, track analytics, and even schedule tweets, just as they would to manage a traditional marketing campaign.[38]

The majority of B2B marketers use white papers for their marketing efforts, and the majority of B2B buyers regularly read them prior to making a purchase.[39] When executives confront an unfulfilled business need, they normally turn to white papers. Their B2B partner may have a technologically advanced solution, but buyers have to understand the solution before they can consider a purchase. A good white paper provides information about the industry and its challenges in an educational context, rather than a promotional sense, to avoid seeming like simply propaganda. That is, the goal of white papers is to provide valuable information that a businessperson can easily understand and that will help the company address its problems with new solutions.

# BUYING SITUATIONS

**L06**

The type of buying situation also affects the B2B decision process. Most B2B buying situations can be categorized into three types: new buys, modified rebuys, and straight rebuys (see Exhibit 5.8). To illustrate the nuances between these three buying situations, consider how colleges and universities develop relationships with some of their suppliers.

Most universities negotiate with sports apparel manufacturers, such as Nike, Reebok, and New Balance, to establish purchasing agreements for their sports teams. Those with successful sports teams have been very successful in managing these relationships, to the benefit of both the team and the company. Large universities that win national championships can solicit sponsorships in exchange for free athletic equipment, whereas less popular teams or smaller schools typically must accept an upfront sponsorship and then agree to buy from that vendor for a specified period of time. In exchange for this sponsorship, the vendors gain the right to sell apparel with the university logo and require the school's team to purchase only their equipment. Many apparel companies make a significant portion of their revenue through sponsorship deals that grant them the right to sell apparel with popular university logos.

Social and Mobile Marketing 5.1 highlights how HubSpot helps buyers become more informed about products before engaging in the B2B buying process.

In a **new buy** situation, a customer purchases a good or service for the first time,[41] which means the buying decision is likely to be quite involved because the buyer or the buying organization does not have any experience with the item. In the B2B context, the buying centre is likely to proceed through all six steps in the buying process and involve many people in the buying decision. Typical new buys might range from capital equipment to components that the firm previously made itself but now has decided to purchase instead. For example, a small university might need to decide which apparel company to approach for a sponsorship. For smaller universities, finding a company that will sponsor multiple sports teams—such as women's soccer as well as men's basketball—is a priority, though it also must balance other considerations, such as the length of the contract. Some vendors offer perks to attract new buyers; New Balance offers teams that sign up for long-term contracts custom fittings for their players' shoes. Each season, a sales team from New Balance visits the school and custom fits each player to achieve the best fit possible.

Another example of a new buy occurs in the fashion industry, where runway shows offer wholesale buyers an opportunity to inspect new lines of clothing and place orders. Designer sales often occur during private meetings with buyers, both before and after

**new buy**
In a B2B setting, a purchase of a good or service for the first time; the buying decision is likely to be quite involved because the buyer or the buying organization does not have any experience with the item.

**EXHIBIT 5.8** Buying Situations

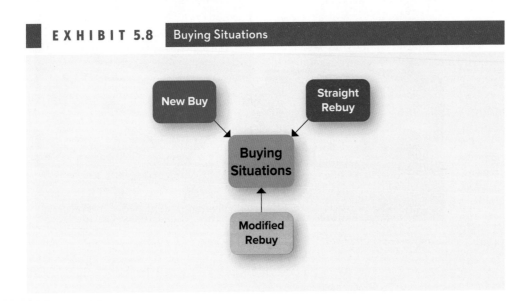

# Social and Mobile Marketing 5.1

## Social Media and Search Habits Lead to Inbound Marketing Software[40]

Search engines, company web pages, social media sites, and the blogosphere have transformed the way businesses learn about and shop for products and services. Unlike a decade ago, when a prospective customer had little knowledge of a vendor's products at first contact, today's customers have searched the Internet using relevant keywords and reviewed company websites by the time they speak with a vendor. As a result, they are well informed and seriously interested in a purchase, adding new efficiency to B2B transactions. But this development works only if companies have the marketing savvy to use today's technology to their advantage.

Two entrepreneurs noticed that small companies and start-ups without the skills to use these tools effectively get lost in the noise, even if prospective customers are searching for vendors in their niche. Furthermore, companies that enlist marketing firms are disadvantaged if those firms rely solely on traditional best practices, such as print advertising, telemarketing, and trade shows. To help these businesses, the two launched a software marketing program, HubSpot, designed to help companies transform their marketing approach. The idea was to abandon intrusive outbound marketing, which people are increasingly able to screen out, and replace it with inbound marketing. Inbound marketing, defined as any marketing tactic that relies on earning customer interest rather than buying it, is built on the understanding that Facebook, Twitter, online user reviews, smartphones, blogs, and websites are the true force behind the way consumers in today's marketplace actually learn and shop.

HubSpot's software contains easy-to-use tools that help companies get noticed, convert website visitors to customers, and analyze the effectiveness of marketing efforts across channels. Among the tools in the first category, for example, is a keyword grader that helps companies create content and a list of relevant keywords to improve search engine odds and ranking. Using the lead conversion tools, marketers without technical skills can create landing pages with customizable lead capture forms, auto-response emails, and thank-you pages. These tools can also be used to send customized emails to new leads on a self-selected schedule. The marketing analytics tools allow HubSpot's customers to track competitors, evaluate the impact of a blog, and compare the effectiveness of all marketing channels to provide important insight into the behaviours of customers and the value of each channel to the bottom line.

HubSpot's approach has been successful for both the founders and their customers. The company, launched in June 2006, reached 3,500 customers in four years and is the second-fastest-growing software-as-a-service (SAAS) company in history.

One customer, Shopify, switched from using multiple tools from other vendors to HubSpot's CRM. The old tools were hard to use and time consuming, which made it difficult for sales reps to enter new leads, let alone retrieve the information when needed. The new system provided immediate benefits. Sales reps could easily track opened emails and links clicked,and set schedules to follow up with prospective clients. They were also able to create email templates to respond to routine inquiries instead of starting fresh each time.

Companies such as HubSpot are taking advantage of changes that have already occurred in the marketplace to reduce costs and improve the effectiveness of marketing. As technology evolves and more business and individual shoppers use online information to make their purchasing decisions, businesses will have to adapt their marketing strategies to encompass new technologies and new shopping behaviours.

HubSpot helps its customers get noticed on the Internet.

Images/hubspot

runway shows. Buyers meet with the designers, discuss the line, and observe a model wearing the clothing. The buyer's challenge then is to determine which items will sell best in the retail stores he or she represents while trying to imagine what the item will look like in regular (as opposed to model) sizes. Buyers must also negotiate purchases for orders that may not be delivered for as much as six months. Buyers can suggest modifications to make the clothing more or less expensive or more comfortable for their customers. Buyers and designers recognize the significant value of this relationship, which occasionally prompts buyers to purchase a few items from a designer, even if those items do not exactly fit the store's core customers' tastes. Doing so ensures that the buyer will have access to the designer's collection for the next season.[42]

In a **modified rebuy**, the buyer has purchased a similar product in the past but has decided to change some specifications, such as the desired price, quality level, customer service level, and options. Current vendors are likely to have an advantage in acquiring the sale in a modified rebuy situation, as long as the reason for the modification is not dissatisfaction with the vendor or its products. For example, a university's sports department might ask Adidas to modify the specifications for its basketball shoes after noticing some improvements made to the Adidas shoes used by a winning university team.

A **straight rebuy** occurs when the buyer or buying organization simply buys additional units of products that had previously been purchased. A tremendous amount of B2B purchases are likely to fall into the straight rebuy category. For example, sports teams need to repurchase a tremendous amount of equipment that is not covered by apparel sponsorships, such as tape for athletes' ankles or weights for the weight room. The purchase of bottled water also typically involves a straight rebuy from an existing supplier.

These varied types of buying situations call for very different marketing and selling strategies. The most complex and difficult is the new buy because it requires the buying organization to make changes in its current practices and purchases. As a result, several members of the buying centre will likely become involved, and the level of their involvement will be more intense than in the case of modified and straight rebuys. In new buying situations, buying centre members also typically spend more time at each stage of the B2B buying process, similar to the extended decision-making process that consumers use in the B2C process. In comparison, in modified rebuys, the buyers spend less time at each stage of the B2B buying process, similar to limited decision making in the B2C process (see Chapter 4).

In straight rebuys, however, the buyer is often the only member of the buying centre involved in the process. Similar to a consumer's habitual purchase, straight rebuys often enable the buyer to recognize the firm's need and go directly to the fifth step in the B2B buying process, skipping the product specification, RFP process, and proposal analysis and supplier selection steps.

Over the course of a B2B relationship, the type of buying process also can change. The buying process for restaurants appears poised to undergo a significant transformation, because of the potential merger between Sysco and GFS Canada, two of the country's largest food distributors. Restaurants that once considered their purchases of hamburger meat a straight rebuy might find that they need to reconsider the process. Because the merger would create a single, dominant food supplier, the new company will gain much more power over pricing. In turn, restaurants might need to enter into a modified rebuy (e.g., purchase lower quality hamburger to cut costs).

In various ways, B2B marketing both differs from and mirrors the consumer behaviour (B2C) process we detailed in Chapter 4. The differences in the six stages of the buying process make sense in view of the many unique factors that come into play. The constitution of the buying centre (initiator, influencer, decider, buyer, user, and gatekeeper), the culture of the purchasing firm (autocratic, democratic, consultative, or consensus), and the context of the buying situation (new buy, modified rebuy, straight rebuy) all influence the B2B buying process in various ways, which means that sellers must be constantly aware of these factors if they want to be successful in their sales attempts. Finally, just as it has done seemingly everywhere we look, the Internet has radically changed some elements of the B2B world, increasing the frequency of both private electronic exchanges and auctions.

**modified rebuy**
Refers to when the buyer has purchased a similar product in the past but has decided to change some specifications, such as the desired price, quality level, customer service level, and options.

**straight rebuy**
Refers to when the buyer or buying organization simply buys additional units of products that had previously been purchased.

# LEARNING OBJECTIVES REVIEW

**LO1** Describe the nature and composition of B2B markets

The B2B market comprises four groups of organizations: manufacturers/producers, resellers, governments, and institutions. Manufacturers such as HP and Dell spend huge amounts to buy raw materials and parts for the computers, printers, and other products they produce. Similarly, producers such as farmers spend a great deal of money to buy fertilizers, seeds, and other agricultural products for their crops. Resellers are mainly wholesalers, distributors, and retailers who distribute the goods of manufacturers. In Canada, wholesale and retail trades are among the largest sectors of the economy. The government sector—federal, provincial, and municipal—in Canada and in most other countries is the largest buyer in a country. Institutions such as non-profit organizations, universities, and prisons also spend millions of dollars buying finished products for their organizations and clients. The B2B market is substantially larger than the B2C market in terms of both volume and value of their purchases.

**LO2** Explain the key differences between B2B buying and B2C buying

B2B markets are different from B2C markets in terms of (1) the characteristics of market demand; (2) the types, value, and volume of products bought; (3) the nature of the buying process, which is more formalized and professional, and involves more people; and (4) the nature of the marketing mix—personal and online selling is more prevalent and prices are negotiated and inelastic in the short run. At first glance, the B2B buying process looks similar to the consumer process described in Chapter 4. It starts with need recognition and ends with an evaluation of the product's or service's performance. But it is really quite different, primarily because of its formality. For instance, in the second stage, product specification, the buying group spells out very specific requirements for the products or services it wants to purchase. Then, in the RFP process of the third stage, the buying firm announces its need for a product or service and solicits formal proposals. In the fourth stage, buyers analyze the various proposals and select a supplier. Unlike the consumer process, the fifth stage, in which the B2B firm places the order, is very formal and spells out every detail of the sales contract.

**LO3** Describe the ways B2B firms classify and segment their markets

The basic principles behind market segmentation remain the same for both B2B and consumer markets. Specifically, B2B firms want to divide the market into groups of customers with different needs, wants, or characteristics and that therefore might appreciate products or services geared especially toward them. On a broad level, B2B firms divide the market into four types: manufacturers or producers, resellers, institutions, and government. Each of these types is described in more detail in the summary for Learning Objective 1. To assist in their market segmentation, B2B businesses can use the NAICS, developed by Canada, the United States, and Mexico, to identify potential customers by type and then develop marketing strategies to reach them. Businesses may also segment B2B markets by account size and types of products purchased.

**LO4** List the steps in the B2B buying process

Similar to the B2C buying process, the B2B process consists of several stages: need recognition, product specification, the RFP process, proposal analysis and supplier selection, order specification (purchase), and vendor performance assessment using metrics. The B2B process tends to be more formalized and structured than the B2C buying process. Also, suppliers and customers tend to be more involved in the B2B buying process, which is dependent to a large extent on the close relationships between the company and its suppliers and customers.

**LO5** Identify the roles within the buying centre

The initiator first suggests the purchase. The influencer affects important people's perceptions and final decisions. The decider ultimately determines at least some of the buying decision—whether, what, how, or where to buy. The buyer handles the details of the actual purchase. The user consumes or employs the product or service. The gatekeeper controls information and access to decision makers and influencers.

In B2B situations, it is likely that several people, organized into a buying centre, will be involved in making the purchase decision. The vendor must understand the relationships among the participants of the buying centre to be effective. A firm's organizational culture can also influence the decision process. For instance, if a firm is trying to sell to a young, high-tech computer component manufacturer, it might be advised to send salespeople who are fluent in technology-speak and can easily relate to the customer. Firm culture consists of unspoken guidelines that employees share through various work situations. Cultures generally can be classified as autocratic, such that one person makes most decisions; democratic, where the majority rules; consultative, in which one person makes decisions based on the input of others; or consensus, which requires all members of the team to reach collective agreement.

**LO6** Detail different buying situations

The buying process depends to a great extent on the situation. If a firm is purchasing a product or service for the first time (i.e., new buy), the process is much more involved than if it is engaging in a straight rebuy of the same item again. A modified rebuy falls somewhere in the middle, such that the buyer wants essentially the same thing but with slightly different terms or features.

## KEY TERMS

- autocratic buying centre
- business-to-business (B2B) marketing
- buyer
- buying centre
- consensus buying centre
- consultative buying centre
- decider

- democratic buying centre
- derived demand
- gatekeeper
- influencer
- initiator
- modified rebuy
- new buy

- North American Industry Classification System (NAICS) codes
- organizational culture
- request for proposals (RFP)
- resellers
- straight rebuy
- user

## CONCEPT REVIEW

1. Explain how marketers may use NAICS codes to segment B2B markets. List two other ways marketers may segment B2B markets. Support your answer with appropriate examples.

2. List and discuss the unique characteristics of B2B markets relative to B2C markets.

3. What are the major differences between the consumer buying process discussed in Chapter 4 and the B2B buying process discussed in this chapter?

4. Explain why all B2B purchases may not go through all the stages of the B2B buying decision process and why some may go through the process in a more systematic and rigorous manner. Give examples of buying situations to support your answer.

5. What are the key bases for distinguishing between new buys, modified buys, and straight rebuys? Support your answer with three clear examples.

6. List five specific ways in which the Internet has enhanced B2B buying and decision making.

7. Explain the concept of the buying centre. What factors may influence the behaviour of the buying centre? What is the role of gatekeepers in buying centres, and how do they influence the buying decision?

8. Explain how understanding the role, structure, and behaviour of a buying centre may help a marketer sell to B2B buyers.

9. This book claims that the six-step B2B buying process is similar to the five-step B2C buying process. How would you go about mapping the B2B process to fit the B2C process?

10. How does understanding the organizational culture and buying centre's culture of a potential B2B customer help a salesperson who is targeting that organization?

## MARKETING APPLICATIONS

1. Provide an example of each of the four key types of B2B organizations.

2. Mazda is trying to assess the performance of two manufacturers that could supply music systems for its vehicles. Using the information in the table below, determine which manufacturer Mazda should use.

**Table for Marketing Application 2**

| Performance Evaluation of Brands | | | |
|---|---|---|---|
| Issues | Importance Weights | Manufacturer A's Performance | Manufacturer B's Performance |
| Sound | 0.4 | 5 | 3 |
| Cost | 0.3 | 2 | 4 |
| Delivery time | 0.1 | 2 | 2 |
| Brand cachet | 0.2 | 5 | 1 |
| **Total** | 1 | | 4.2 |

Notes: Performance is rated on a 5-point scale, where 1 is "Poor" and 5 is "Excellent."

3. Imagine you have written this book and are going to attempt to sell it to your school. Identify the six members of the buying centre. What role would each play in the decision process? Rank them in terms of how much influence they would have on the decision, with 1 being most influential and 6 being least influential. Will this ranking be different in other situations?

4. Provide an example of the three types of buying situations that the bookstore at your school might face when buying textbooks.

5. Describe the organizational culture at your school or job. How is it different from the one at the last school you attended or the last job you had?

6. Nike manufactures shoes and sportswear. How has the Internet changed the way this company communicates with its suppliers and retail customers?

7. What are the major differences between the consumer buying process (discussed in Chapter 4) and the B2B buying process discussed in this chapter? Use buying iPads for personal use versus buying more than 100 iPads for a firm to illustrate the key points.

8. You have recently been hired by Cognos as a salesperson for its suite of business intelligence applications, Pick one prospective company you plan to sell to and explain how you would go about identifying the persons in the different roles in the buying centre for the chosen company. How would you try to target the needs of the different members in the buying centre?

9. Cognos has developed a new business intelligence application that it would like to sell to some of its existing customers. You are part of the sales team. How would your approach to selling to an existing customer be different from selling to a new customer?

10. You have just started to work in the purchasing office of a major pharmaceutical firm. The purchasing manager has asked you to assist in writing an RFP for a major purchase. The manager gives you a sheet detailing the specifications for the RFP. While reading the specifications, you realize that they have been written to be extremely favourable to one bidder. How should you handle this situation?

## NET SAVVY

1. Browse the Public Services and Procurement Canada website (http://www.tpsgc-pwgsc.gc.ca) to learn more about how you may sell goods and services to the federal government. Using the information on the website, describe the buying process used by the federal government and explain how the electronic tendering system supports buying and selling between Canadian companies and the government of Canada.

2. Mark's, a Canadian company that currently operates mainly in the B2C market, has hired you as its government–business relations officer with the primary task of helping the company move into the B2B marketplace, selling its merchandise primarily to government departments. Explain how you would go about getting Mark's ready to do business with the Canadian government. *Hint:* You will find helpful information on the following websites: Public Services and Procurement Canada (http://www.tpsgc-pwgsc.gc.ca), Public Works and Government Services Canada (https://buyandsell.gc.ca), and Innovation, Science and Economic Development Canada (http://www.ic.gc.ca).

## CHAPTER CASE STUDY

### LEVI STRAUSS, COTTON FARMERS, AND INTERNATIONAL PRODUCTION

Most people have multiple pairs of jeans, relying on them as a staple of their wardrobes. But few consumers really consider what has gone into each pair as they get dressed in the morning. Questions such as where they were made, how much material they contain, or the impact they have on the environment are insignificant for most consumers. But for businesses such as Levi Strauss & Co., they are critical to the company's long-term survival and success.

Levi's is a major consumer of cotton: A single pair of its 501 jeans uses nearly two pounds of cotton, and the vast majority of all Levi's products are made with cotton. Cotton needs water to grow, and jeans continue to require water throughout their life cycle, whether as part of the stone-wash softening process or in the laundry. By the time a pair of jeans bought today has reached the end of its life cycle, it will have used more than 900 gallons of water.[43]

A decade ago, this water consumption was of less concern. But changes in rainfall patterns caused by global climate change are directly tying Levi's future to water: Less water means less moisture for cotton crops, and less cotton means Levi's will have to either incorporate more synthetics into its clothing—a significant change to its brand—or pay more for scarce raw materials. If the company pays more, the increased prices may be passed along to customers, possibly resulting in Levi's loyalists moving to other brands. A third alternative, reducing the cost of other garment materials such as buttons and zippers, affects both the brand and quality standards, though it can help control the end cost charged to consumers.

To address these challenges, Levi's is working with suppliers to implement more sustainable water use and other environmental practices as well as more responsible practices with regard to workers throughout its supply chain. These partnerships are challenging to instigate and oversee because cot-

Levi's works with its suppliers to implement sustainable water use in the production of its jeans.

Jim Wilson/The New York Times/Redux Pictures

ton is raised in more than 100 countries and grown primarily on small, family-owned farms.[44] Levi's began focusing on being more environmentally conscious more than 20 years ago by creating a Terms of Engagement code of conduct that spells out what the company requires from its business partners in terms of social, ethical, legal, and environmental practices and employment standards. The agreement covers such issues as working ages, health and safety, and child labour, as well as wages, benefits, and disciplinary practices.[45]

The company has also partnered with other large consumers of cotton, including H&M, IKEA, Marks & Spencer, and Adidas; environmental organizations such as the World Wildlife Federation; and the Better Cotton Initiative, a cotton industry association, to study growing practices that reduce water and pesticide use.[46] In one such study, conducted on a farm in India, cotton plants using a new drip irrigation system were taller and bore more flowers than those using traditional methods. The drip system reduced water use by about 70 percent and shortened the duration of electricity use for the system from three days to three hours. It also distributed fertilizer more evenly. Levi Strauss, IKEA, and Adidas thus agreed to set aggressive goals for increasing the amount of this better cotton in their products. Innovative finishing techniques were introduced, called Water<Less, saving more than 1 billion litres of water since 2011. This technology and other water saving tools are now being made available to other companies to use in their production processes.[47]

Another initiative aims to reorient the goals of the entire supply chain to produce more durable clothing options, rather than fast fashion. With input from Bangladeshi factory owners and cotton farmers from Pakistan, Levi Strauss has developed a Wellthread line of clothing that promises to last far longer than most other apparel items. By addressing the needs of its B2B partners, Levi Strauss hopes "to weave responsibility into every stage of design, manufacturing and usage, from the cotton fields to the factories to the market and beyond."[48]

Levi Strauss conducted a study, "The Lifecycle of a Jean," to determine the environmental and human impact of its products.[49] These efforts go beyond water use to include every step of the garment's life cycle—from cradle to grave, or from raw material production to disposal. The findings showed that cotton cultivation and consumer use have the greatest impact on water and energy usage. For example, North Americans typically wash their jeans after wearing them only twice, so the company encourages consumers to wear them at least 10 times, which reduces the environmental impact by 77 percent. In a LinkedIn article called "The Dirty Jeans Manifesto," Levi Strauss CEO Chip Bergh said he spot washes his jeans.[50] It saves water and helps jeans last longer by not washing them so often. And when the life cycle of your jeans comes to an end, drop them off at Levi Strauss stores for recycling. Your reward? The company will give you a voucher for 20 percent off your next purchase.[51]

## Questions

1. In pursuing more sustainable production, what steps of the B2B buying process will Levi Strauss need to revisit? Which are likely to become less important? More important?

2. For this pursuit to be successful, what type of organizational culture should Levi's foster?

## SECTION THREE
### TARGETING THE MARKETPLACE

CHAPTER 6  Segmentation, Targeting, and Positioning
CHAPTER 7  Marketing Research
APPENDIX 7A  Using Secondary Data to Assess Customer Lifetime Value (CLV)

# CHAPTER 6

## LEARNING OBJECTIVES

**After studying this chapter you should be able to**

**LO1** Describe the bases marketers use to segment a market

**LO2** Identify the criteria for determining the attractiveness of a segment and whether it is worth pursuing (targeting)

**LO3** Explain the differences among targeting strategies: undifferentiated, differentiated, concentrated, or micromarketing

**LO4** Define positioning and describe how firms do it

Used with permission of SoCIAL LITE Vodka

# Segmentation, Targeting, and Positioning

Segmentation is key to identifying the right target markets. As a start-up company, SoCIAL LITE Vodka knew it had to be extremely focused on segmentation. Its alcoholic beverages were made with 100 percent natural flavours, were unsweetened, and had only 80 calories. Two great flavours were available: Lemon Cucumber Mint and Lime Ginger. SoCIAL LITE co-founder Neetu Godara said they had to very quickly identify who would fall in love with the products.[1]

You might think it would be easy to determine the target market for a new alcoholic drink. In this day and age of heightened health-consciousness, SoCIAL LITE Vodka is the type of product that could appeal to a wide variety of consumers. So it would seem like an obvious choice to use a psychographic approach to segment the market, based on health and wellness. Sugar is in the news every day and it's not hard to find groups of people who read labels when shopping for new products.

Although the product appeals primarily to women, SoCIAL LITE Vodka was started in Toronto by two men—Dan Beach and Kevin Folk—in their kitchen as they were mixing drinks. They wanted to be able to enjoy a drink that wouldn't impact their ability to go for a long run the following day. Given their Ontario roots, you might wonder why the entrepreneurs decided to launch their product in Alberta. After all, other geographical regions in the country offer much higher population density. Godara says Alberta was chosen because liquor stores there are privately owned, not government-owned, which makes it easier to get products listed. Still, there were challenges. With 1,400 independently owned locations, it took a lot of phone calls to convince store managers to carry the products.

Logistically it would have been far easier to sell into the Ontario market via government-owned Liquor Control Board of Ontario (LCBO) stores. And the Ontario geography was on their radar from day one. But convincing the LCBO was a slow process. In the meantime, the Alberta launch allowed SoCIAL LITE to get its products into affluent urban centres such as Calgary and Edmonton. Success in Alberta paved the way to move farther west into British Columbia, where the liquor market is half publicly and half privately owned. Three years later, after seeing sales results that proved the market for the products in Western Canada, the LCBO agreed to list SoCIAL LITE Vodka.

For SoCIAL LITE, segmentation bases such as psychographics or geographics were an important part of identifying and describing potential target markets. But marketers need to consider more than just one segmentation base to find the right target markets. Godara notes that, demographically, you can target whomever you like. For example, an ideal target market might include older women in their mid-thirties to late fifties. But you also need to consider if their psychographic profile indicates that they seek out healthy products and carefully watch what they eat.

When segmenting the overall market, Godara says you also need to consider the retail environment in which your product will sell. The reality is that the ready-to-drink category skews heavily to a younger crowd. If you stop to think about store placement, ready-to-drink products are found in the cooler aisle. And the vast majority of traffic in that aisle is under the age of 25. While older women matched the demographic profile for the products, behaviourally, it was going to be harder to attract them in-store. Age became an important demographic variable, together with a focus on psychographics in SoCIAL LITE's segmentation analysis. Multiple target markets were identified, with "Socialite Andy" being primary. You will read more about other segments later in the chapter.

Having identified appropriate target markets, the company turned its marketing efforts to positioning its products in the minds of target consumers. SoCIAL LITE Vodka focuses on functional benefits and taste, as a way to socialize without regret—have fun without having to worry about calories, sugar, artificial ingredients, or gluten. With benefits like these, Godara says SoCIAL LITE will soon be on everyone's lips. ∎

In Chapter 1, we learned that marketing is about satisfying consumers' wants and needs. A company could make one type of beverage and hope that every customer would buy it, but that's the kind of mistake that causes companies to go out of business. Beverage manufacturers could analyze the market to determine the different types of drinks people want and then make several varieties that cater to specific groups. It is not enough just to make the product, however. Drink manufacturers, such as SoCIAL LITE, must position their products in the minds of their target market so those consumers understand why a particular drink meets their needs better than competitive brands do. Chapter 3 noted how companies analyze their markets and the environment around them to determine the different kinds of products and services people want. This process requires a plan, as we discussed in Chapter 2. As you might recall, the third step of this plan is identifying and evaluating opportunities by performing a segmentation, targeting, and positioning (STP) analysis. This chapter now expands on that very analysis.

In the chapter vignette, SoCIAL LITE identified the various groups, or market segments, of people who would respond similarly to the firm's marketing efforts. Those who like low calorie drinks are one market segment; people who prefer drinks with higher alcohol content constitute a different segment. After evaluating the attractiveness of different market segments, SoCIAL LITE decided to concentrate its new product line on one group of consumers—its target market—because it believed it could satisfy this group's needs better than its competitors could.

Once the target market was identified, SoCIAL LITE had to convince members of the targeted group that, when trying a new drink, their choice should be SoCIAL LITE Vodka. It achieved this task by defining the marketing mix variables so that the target customers had a clear, distinctive, desirable understanding of what the product or services do or represent, relative to competing products. To achieve its market positioning, SoCIAL LITE designed messaging that has positioned its vodka drinks as low-calorie, healthy, and sin-free. Packaging was prominently used in all advertising efforts so customers would be able to recall SoCIAL LITE Vodka at the need recognition stage of the consumer buying process described in Chapter 4. The company has also made sure that the drinks are available most places its customers would want to buy them.

# THE SEGMENTATION-TARGETING-POSITIONING PROCESS

In this chapter, we discuss how a firm conducts a market segmentation or STP analysis. We start by discussing market segmentation, or how a segmentation strategy fits into a firm's overall strategy and objectives and which segments are worth pursuing. Then we consider how to choose a target market or markets by evaluating each segment's attractiveness and, on the basis of this evaluation, choosing which segment or segments to pursue. Finally, we describe how a firm develops its positioning strategy. The segmentation, targeting, and positioning process is shown in Exhibit 6.1.

## Step 1: Establish Overall Strategy or Objectives

As discussed in Chapter 2, the first step in the planning process is to articulate the mission and the objectives of the company's marketing strategy clearly. The segmentation strategy must then be consistent with and derived from the firm's mission and objectives, as well as its current situation—its strengths, weaknesses, opportunities, and threats (SWOT). SoCIAL LITE's objective, for instance, is to gain trial in a very competitive market. The company recognized that its strengths were its health and wellness functional attributes and its ability to place new products on retailers' shelves. Its primary weaknesses were that it was not a recognized brand and the company had a limited promotional budget. Attracting a share of new customers in this large and profitable market segment before mainstream competitors followed suit offered a great opportunity, though following through on that opportunity could lead to the threat of competitive retaliation. To make use of its strengths, SoCIAL LITE decided to look at segments that would benefit from its health and wellness attributes, which is clearly consistent with its overall strategy and objectives.

Now let's take a look at the methods, or bases, that can be used to segment the market.

**geographic segmentation**
The grouping of consumers on the basis of where they live.

## Step 2: Segmentation Bases

The second step in the segmentation process is to use a formal approach to segment the market. This step develops descriptions of the different target market segments—and their needs, wants, and characteristics—using a variety of segmentation bases. This helps firms better understand the profile of the customers in each segment. With this information, they can distinguish the customer similarities within a segment and dissimilarities across segments. Beverage marketers, for instance, have broken up the carbonated-beverage landscape into caffeinated or decaffeinated, regular or diet, and with or without alcohol. This segmentation method is based on the benefits that consumers derive from the products.

Marketers use various segmentation bases, including geographic, demographic, psychographic, and behavioural, or a combination of these segmentation approaches when defining consumer target markets. (see Exhibit 6.2). Refer back to Chapter 5 for examples of how businesses segment their markets. Chapter 17 will address how marketers approach segmentation in global markets.

**Geographic Segmentation** **Geographic segmentation** organizes customers into groups on the basis of *where they live*. Thus, a market could be grouped by country (Canada, Germany, China), by region (Atlantic Canada, Western Canada), by areas within a region (province, city, neighbourhoods, area codes), or by climate and topography (warm, cold and snowy, mountainous). For example, SoCIAL LITE launched its products in Western Canada first and then moved to Ontario. Not surprisingly, geographic segmentation is most useful for companies whose products satisfy needs that vary by region. As discussed in Sustainable Marketing 6.1, Frogbox examined population density when deciding to expand to new cities.

Firms can provide the same basic goods or services to all segments even if they market globally or nationally, but better marketers make

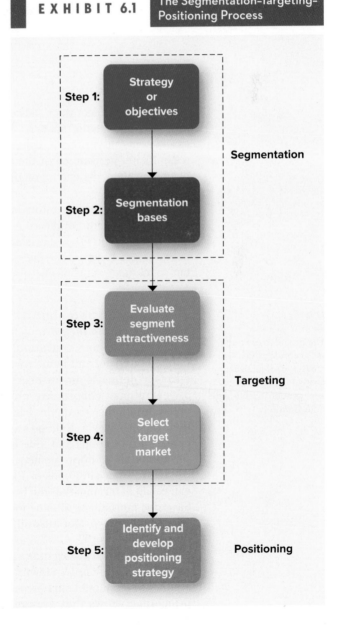

**EXHIBIT 6.1** The Segmentation-Targeting-Positioning Process

Step 1: Strategy or objectives
Step 2: Segmentation bases
— Segmentation

Step 3: Evaluate segment attractiveness
Step 4: Select target market
— Targeting

Step 5: Identify and develop positioning strategy
— Positioning

| ■ E X H I B I T   6.2 | Bases for Segmenting Markets |
|---|---|
| **Segmentation Base** | **Sample Segments** |
| Geographic | Continent (North America, Asia, Europe, Africa), country, region (West Coast, Prairies, Central, Maritimes), province, city, urban, suburban, rural, climate |
| Demographic | Age, gender, income, education, occupation, race, marital status, family size, family life cycle, religion, ethnic background (white, black, Asian, Indian, German, Irish, Arab), generational cohort (baby boomer, Generation X, Generation Y), home ownership |
| Psychographic | Lifestyle (Innovators, Thinkers, Achievers, Experiencers, Believers, Strivers, Makers, Survivors), personality/self-concept (conservative, liberal, adventuresome, outgoing, health- and fitness-conscious), social class (upper class, middle class, working class) |
| Behavioural | Benefits sought (convenience, economy, prestige, quality, speed, service, environmental impact), usage (heavy, moderate, light, non-user, ex-user, potential user, first-time user), loyalty (not loyal, somewhat loyal, completely loyal) |

adjustments to meet the needs of smaller geographic groups. For instance, a national grocery store chain, such as Sobeys or Loblaws, runs similar stores with similar assortments in various locations across Canada. Within those similar stores, though, a significant percentage of the assortment of goods will vary by region, city, or even neighbourhood, depending on the different needs of the customers who surround each location.

Consider a new superstore in Surrey, British Columbia, designed to cater specifically to the surrounding Southeast Asian (Punjabi) neighbourhood. In the produce section, piles of shiny, green pasilla chiles sit beside paddle-shaped cactus leaves and bumpy, brown yucca roots. At the meat counter, a customer greets a clerk in Punjabi and asks him to marinate some meat.

**demographic segmentation**
The grouping of consumers according to easily measured, objective characteristics such as age, gender, income, and education.

Demographic Segmentation   **Demographic segmentation** groups consumers according to *who they are* using easily measured, objective characteristics such as age, gender, income, education, race, occupation, religion, marital status, family size, family life cycle, and home ownership. These variables represent the most common means to define segments because they are easy to identify. As discussed in Chapter 3, generational cohorts are often used by marketers and millennials are often targeted. In another example, car makers often consider market segments defined by their income levels. Kellogg's uses age to define segments for its line of breakfast cereals. Froot Loops and Rice Krispies are for kids, while Special K and All-Bran are for adults. In addition, demographically segmented markets are easy to reach. For instance, if McCain Foods or Pizza Hut wants to advertise its newest pizza to kids, it can easily determine that the best time for TV ads would be during cartoons shown on Saturday morning or after school on weekdays. By considering the viewer profiles of various TV shows, McCain and Pizza Hut can find those that fit their target market's demographic profile.

Gender plays a very important role in how most firms market products and services. For instance, TV viewing habits vary significantly between men and women. Men tend to channel surf—switching quickly from channel to channel—and watch prime-time shows that are action oriented and feature physically attractive cast members. Women, in contrast, tend to view shows to which they can personally

## Sustainable Marketing 6.1

### Frogbox Makes Moving Green[2]

Moving is stressful! Before you can even start packing you have to go to local stores to snag boxes. If they don't have enough, you have to buy some. Having to buy, build, and dispose of all those boxes is a needless hassle and expense. And, worst of all, those cardboard boxes may contain dirt, bacteria, and other things you really don't want all over your stuff.

Now there's a better, more sustainable solution. Founded in 2008 in Vancouver by Doug Burgoyne, Frogbox will rent you reusable plastic boxes, an eco-friendly alternative to traditional cardboard moving boxes. Burgyone estimates that Greater Vancouver uses about 450,000 cardboard moving boxes every month and Seattle uses about 1 million. The company identified two possible customer markets: residential and business. The residential market includes three segments: people who didn't buy boxes but sourced them for free from retail stores, do-it-yourself movers who bought boxes and moved themselves, and affluent consumers who hired professionals to pack and move them. The business market included moving companies who wanted to offer customers a sustainable solution.

Unlike cardboard boxes, the Frogbox solution has a low impact on the environment, as its boxes can be reused hundreds of times. The boxes are 2.4 cubic feet (70 litres). To put this in perspective, approximately 25 boxes would be needed to move the contents of a one-bedroom apartment.

Frogbox will rent you as many boxes as you need for a week or longer, and it can deliver them and pick them up when you've finished with your move. The boxes stack neatly inside each other and don't require any assembly, eliminating the need to spend hours building and taping cardboard boxes.

The Frogbox name is fitting because both the company and frogs have a connection to the sustainable environment. The company donates 1 percent of gross revenues to frog habitation restoration.[3] But its sustainability efforts are hopping in other areas, too. For example, the company uses solar energy to power its website and waste-generated biodiesel to fuel its fleet vehicles.

The company has big goals. Since launching in Vancouver, it has opened locations in the Okanagan, across the prairie provinces and southern Ontario, in Halifax, and in St. John's. It also has two locations in the United States: Seattle, Washington, and Boise, Idaho. It's on its way to expanding into the top 30 cities in North America. In 2015, the company hit 1 million uses of its reusable boxes,[4] redefining how people move, making it easier on you, easier on your wallet, and, best of all, easier on the planet.

Frogbox offers an eco-friendly alternative to traditional cardboard moving boxes.

Used with permission of Frogbox

relate through the situational plot or characters and those recommended by friends. Print media are similar: A company such as Proactiv, which seeks to appeal to both men and women worried about the condition of their skin, therefore carefully considers the gender-based appeal of different magazines when it purchases advertising space.

However, demographics may not be useful for defining the target segments for other companies. For example, demographics are poor predictors of the users of activewear, such as yoga pants or athletic shoes. At one time, firms such as Nike assumed that activewear would be purchased exclusively by young, active people, but the health and fitness trend has led people of all ages to buy such merchandise. Even relatively inactive consumers of all ages, incomes, and education levels find activewear more comfortable than traditional street clothes.

Because it is relatively easy to gather information, demographic variables are often used for segmenting markets. Depending on the nature of the product and market, however, marketers may find it more advantageous to combine demographic segmentation

Proctor & Gamble uses an important demographic factor, gender, to sell different types of razors to men (Fusion ad on the left) and women (Venus ad on the right).

Courtesy The Gillette Company

with other segmentation bases, described below, to derive a richer understanding of their potential customers. Rethinking some stereotypical ideas about who is buying thus has become a relatively common trend among firms that once thought their target market was well defined. As seen in Social and Mobile Marketing 6.1, even some of the most well known companies in the world must continually reconsider the true identity of their prime targets.

### Psychographic Segmentation

Of the various methods for segmenting, or breaking down the market, **psychographics** is the one that delves into how consumers actually describe themselves, or *how they live*. As you read in the opening vignette, SoCIAL LITE Vodka targets people whose psychographic profile indicates that they are health conscious and carefully choose what they eat and drink. Usually marketers determine (through demographics, buying patterns, or usage) into which segment an individual consumer falls. Psychographics studies how people self-select, as it were, based on characteristics that help them choose how they occupy their time and what underlying psychological reasons determine those choices.[6] For example, a person might have a strong need for inclusion or belonging, which motivates him or her to seek out activities and interests that involve others, which then influences the products he or she buys to fit in with the group. If a consumer becomes attached to a group that enjoys literary discussions, he or she is motivated to buy the latest books and spend time in stores such as Indigo. Such self-segmentation by the consumer could be very valuable knowledge for bookstore managers trying to find new ways of attracting customers. As you will read in the chapter case study, when determining what ads customers see on its site, Netflix focuses on what they like and then shows options that match those interests. Determining psychographics involves knowing and understanding three components: self-values, self-concept, and lifestyles.

**Self-values** are life goals, not just the goals one wants to accomplish in a day. They are the overriding desires that drive how a person lives his or her life. Examples of

---

**psychographics**
This segmentation base delves into how consumers describe themselves; allows people to describe themselves by using those characteristics that help them choose how they occupy their time (behaviour) and what underlying psychological reasons determine those choices.

**self-values**
Goals for life, not just the goals one wants to accomplish in a day; a component of psychographics that refers to overriding desires that drive how a person lives his or her life.

## Social and Mobile Marketing 6.1

# Is Facebook Over?[5]

According to a recent study funded by the European Union, the terms that United Kingdom teens (16–18 years of age) use to describe Facebook include *embarrassing, old,* and *dead and buried.* These are not exactly the sorts of images that a company that revolutionized social media prefers to embrace. So what has led Facebook, once the social media home base of teens, to become the last place they want to be seen?

Most analysis suggests that the main problem was its growing popularity—and more specifically, its growing popularity among their parents' generation. As moms, dads, aunts, uncles, and even grandparents joined the network, teens quickly became less willing to share quite so much. Humour sites collect various awkward moments when a teenager railed against an unfair parent on Facebook, only to have that parent respond with deeply embarrassing accounts of the teen's behaviour or the imposition of a new punishment.

Beyond these direct contacts, teens tend to assume that anything their parents like cannot be cool for them as well. If their grandmother posts pictures of her vacation to Facebook, seemingly by definition the site cannot be cool anymore.

As challenging as these trends are for Facebook, it could always rebrand itself as the social media location for middle-aged users who want to share their thoughts about their children or grandchildren. The larger question is where teens will go next to get their social media fix. The growing popularity of Snapchat implies that teens might begin preferring temporary, ephemeral sharing, possibly in reaction to the lessons learned when Facebook posts remain accessible to employers and school administrators. Moreover, teens seemingly use various sites for different purposes: Snapchat for more personal sharing, Instagram for visual sharing, and WhatsApp for more personal interactions.

The variety suggests a gap in the market, waiting for some innovative entrepreneur to devise the next big thing: a site that teens consider cool and compelling—until their parents find it and ruin it, too, of course.

Teens embrace Snapchat for sharing messages and photos in a place their parents and grandparents don't go.
dennizn/Shutterstock.com

Marketers such as Mountain Equipment Co-Op want their ads to appeal to one's self-concept. "I'm like them, so I should buy their products."
Photo by Felix Rioux and Mountain Equipment Co-Op (MEC)

self-value goals might include self-respect, self-fulfillment, or a sense of belonging. This motivation causes people to develop self-images of how they want to be and then determine a way of life that will help them arrive at these ultimate goals. From a marketing point of view, self-values help determine the benefits the target market may be looking for from a product. Lexus uses the tagline "Amazing in Motion" and BMW uses "'Designed for Driving Pleasure" and "The Ultimate Driving Machine" to target these values. In this sense, the underlying, fundamental, personal need that pushes a person to seek out certain products or brands stems from his or her desire to fulfill a self-value, or goal.[7]

**self-concept**

The image a person has of himself or herself; a component of psychographics.

People's self-image, or **self-concept**, is the image people have of themselves.[7] A person who has a goal to belong may see, or want to see, himself or herself as a fun-loving, gregarious type whom people wish to be around. Marketers can make use of this image through communications that show their products being used by groups of laughing people who are having a good time. The connection emerges between the group fun and the product being shown and connotes a certain lifestyle that many consumers seek. TV commercials for dating services such as eHarmony use this technique to sell their services. L'Oréal uses the tagline, "Because I'm Worth It," for its hair colour products.

Such tactics need to balance the ideal with the realistic. Advertisements for men's underwear tend to feature salacious shots of incredibly cut men, usually with shaved chests. But in making this appeal to women who might purchase briefs, boxers, and T-shirts for their husbands or partners, underwear marketers forgot about men as their underlying target market. And these male shoppers have long felt uncomfortable in stores, reaching for a box featuring a nearly naked man. Rather than being aspirational, the models had become so outside the norm that they seemed like a cruel taunt. Thus a recent advertising campaign by the men's underwear brand 2(x)ist features a handsome but not "perfect" model, wearing a robe that covers most of his body. The Mack Weldon brand offers up another handsome but slightly goofy model, who trips while trying to take off his pants to reveal his underwear.[8]

**lifestyles**

Lifestyles are how we live our lives to achieve goals.

**Lifestyles**, the third component of people's psychographic makeup, are the ways we live.[9] If values provide an end goal and self-concept is the way one sees oneself in the context of that goal, lifestyles are how we live our lives to achieve goals. Someone with a strong sense of belonging who sees himself as a "people person" will probably live in a well populated area that allows for many activities. He likely will join clubs or partake in activities that attract like-minded people. This gives marketers a built-in target group with similar interests and buying desires. Lululemon quickly built a global empire of sportswear clothing and accessories based not on demographics but on the philosophy of a healthy, balanced, fun-filled lifestyle.

One of the most storied lifestyles in North American legend is the Harley way of life. The open road, wind in your hair, rebelling against convention—the image nearly always depicted decades ago by actor Dennis Hopper in the movie *Easy Rider*. But the notions of freedom, rebellion, and standing out from a crowd vastly appeal to all sorts of people. In response, Harley-Davidson has shifted its STP methods to define four main target markets: core (men older

Using lifestyle segmentation, Harley-Davidson has four main target markets, including white women older than 35 years.

Jeffry Phelps/AP Images for Harley-Davidson

than 35 years), young adults (both genders, 18–34 years), women (older than 35 years), and diverse (men and women, African American and Hispanic, older than 35 years).[10]

The most widely used tool to support such psychographic segmentation efforts is the Values and Lifestyle Survey (**VALS™**), owned and operated by Strategic Business Insights (SBI).[11] Adults aged 18 and older are classified into one of eight segments based on their answers to the questionnaire (find out what VALS type you are at http://www .strategicbusinessinsights.com/vals/presurvey.shtml). The vertical dimension of the VALS™ framework indicates level of resources, including income, education, curiosity, energy level, and degree of innovativeness. The upper segments (Innovators, Thinkers, Achievers, Experiencers) have more resources and are more innovative than those on the bottom (Believers, Makers, Strivers, Survivors).

The horizontal dimension shows the segment's primary psychological motivation. Consumers buy products and services because of their primary motivations—that is, how they see themselves in the world and how that self-image governs their activities. The three universal primary motivations are ideals, achievement, and self-expression. People who are motivated by ideals (e.g., Thinkers, Believers) are guided by knowledge and principles, whereas those who are motivated by achievement (e.g., Achievers, Strivers) look for products and services that demonstrate success to their peers. Exhibit 6.3 provides a description of the VALS™ types. You can view a visual comparison of these types on the SBI website (http://www.strategicbusinessinsights.com/vals/demobehav. shtml).

VALS™ explores the intersection of psychology, demographics, and lifestyle. It enables firms to identify target segments on the basis of their underlying motivations.

**VALS**

A psychological tool developed by Strategic Business Insights that classifies consumers into eight segments: Innovators, Thinkers, Believers, Achievers, Strivers, Experiencers, Makers, or Survivors.

---

**EXHIBIT 6.3** | Description of VALS™ Categories

| Innovators | Thinkers | Believers | Achievers |
|---|---|---|---|
| • Successful, sophisticated, take-charge people<br>• High-esteem<br>• Change leaders, open to new ideas and technology<br>• Actively seek new information<br>• Experiment with confidence, future oriented<br>• Problem-solvers<br>• Active consumers, cultivated tastes | • Old guard, respect authority<br>• Well-educated<br>• Mature, satisfied, comfortable<br>• Carefully research and plan before taking action<br>• Appreciate historical perspective<br>• Act in accordance with what's right<br>• Not influenced by latest trends | • Hold conservative belief systems, deep-rooted moral codes<br>• Value family, religion, community<br>• Value stability<br>• Dislike ambiguity<br>• Not looking to change society<br>• Predictable, loyal consumers<br>• Choose familiar products, established brands | • Goal-oriented professionals<br>• View money as source of authority<br>• Deep commitment to career, family<br>• Respect authority and the status quo<br>• Active consumers<br>• Favour prestige products, conscious of peers<br>• Embrace technology with productivity benefits |

| Strivers | Experiencers | Makers | Survivors |
|---|---|---|---|
| • Live in the moment<br>• Trendy, fun-loving<br>• Money defines success<br>• Favour stylish products<br>• Revolving rates of temporary unemployment<br>• Looking for a better life, not easily achieved<br>• Active yet impulsive consumers | • Seek variety, excitement<br>• Enthusiastic, impulsive consumers<br>• Want it all mentality<br>• Active in sports and social activities<br>• Heightened sense of visual stimulation<br>• Keep up with latest fashions<br>• Want to look good, have cool stuff | • Practical people with constructive skills<br>• Strong mechanical and automotive inerests<br>• Traditional views of family, work, gender roles<br>• Protect what they see as theirs<br>• Value self-sufficiency<br>• Suspicious of new ideas<br>• Unimpressed with material possessions | • Oldest consumers<br>• Cautious, risk averse, feel world is changing too fast<br>• Concern for safety, security<br>• Comfortable with routine and the familiar<br>• Loyal to favourite brands<br>• Laggards in technology<br>• Focus on needs vs. wants |

*Source:* Strategic Business Insights (SBI), *The VALS™ Types.* http://www.strategicbusinessinsights.com/vals/ustypes.shtml

It is just as easy to identify Thinkers (left) as it is Makers (right). A person is given the VALS questionnaire, and the VALS program at SRIC-BI runs the answers through the computer for scoring to determine the VALS type.

(left): Sam Edwards/Getty Images RF; (right): Huntstock/Getty Images RF

For instance, a European auto manufacturer used VALS™ to identify online, mobile applications that would appeal to affluent, early-adopter consumers within the next five years. The VALS™ analysis enabled the company to prioritize the most promising applications to develop. In another case, VALS was used to help a medical centre identify those customers most interested in and able to afford cosmetic surgery. Based on the underlying motivations of its target customers, the centre's ad agency developed a campaign that was so successful it had to be pulled early to avoid overbooking at the surgical centre.

Firms are finding that psychographic segmentation systems like VALS are a very good complement to demographics to produce an in-depth profile and predict consumer behaviour. For instance, first-year college students and some day labourers may share similar demographics such as their age, education, and income, but they spend their income quite differently because of their very different mindsets. Likewise, Harpreet and Javinder are both 30 years old, married, and college graduates. From a demographic standpoint they are the same, yet Harpreet is risk averse while Javinder is a risk taker. Harpreet is socially conscious. Javinder is focused on himself. Lumping these two men in the same target market does not make sense because they think and act very differently.

There are limitations to using psychographic segmentation, however. Psychographics are more expensive as a way to identify potential customers. With demographics, for example, a firm such as Nike can easily identify its customers as men or women and then direct its marketing strategies to each group differently. The problem is that not all men are alike, as we saw with Harpreet and Javinder. Women are not all alike either! Since it can be expensive to identify and target "Thinkers" versus "Makers," psychographic segmentation is often used in conjunction with other segmentation methods.[12]

**behavioural segmentation**
Groups consumers based on the benefits they derive from products or services, their usage rate, their loyalty, and the occasion.

Behavioural Segmentation **Behavioural segmentation** groups consumers on the basis of *why they buy*, *how often*, and *how they plan to use the products or services*. Each segmentation base addresses specific aspects related to consumers. How geographic segmentation differs from demographic is perhaps more obvious than how psychographic versus behavioural segmentation is applied. To make it easier to remember how each base is used, refer to Exhibit 6.4.

As mentioned above, behavioural segmentation looks at the benefits consumers are looking for in a product or service, their usage rates (in other words, how often they buy or use the product or service,) how loyal they are to it, and the occasion for which the product or service is used. Some universities consider interest in sustainability initiatives as a way to segment and target both students and their parents. Because marketing is about satisfying consumers' needs and wants, dividing the market into segments whose needs and wants are best satisfied by the product benefits can be very powerful. It is also relatively easy to portray a product's or service's benefits in the firm's communication strategies: usage rates of products or services, user status, and loyalty. Some companies track consumer behaviour and use it for better customer experiences or interactions with the firm. For example, Amazon makes recommendations to customers while they are browsing its site by matching their profiles to those of other customers.

| EXHIBIT 6.4 | Segmentation Bases Simplified |
| --- | --- |
| **Segmentation Base** | **Simplification** |
| Geographic | Where do they live? |
| Demographic | Who are they? |
| Psychographic | How do they live? What is their lifestyle? |
| Behavioural | Why do they buy? How often? How do they plan to use the products? |

Behavioural segmentation based on when a product or service is purchased or consumed is called **occasion segmentation**. Moores Clothing for Men uses this type of segmentation to develop its merchandise selection and its promotions. Sometimes men need a suit for their everyday work, but other suits are expressly for special occasions, like a prom or a wedding. Snack food companies like Frito-Lay also make and promote snacks for various occasions—individual servings of potato chips for a snack on the run, but 255 gram bags for parties.

**occasion segmentation**
Groups consumers based on when they purchase or consume a product or service.

As mentioned previously, **benefit segmentation** considers the benefits customers are looking for from products or services. Because marketing is all about satisfying needs and wants, dividing the market into segments according to which consumers' needs and wants your offerings can best satisfy makes a lot of sense. An excellent illustration of benefit segmentation can be found in the Royal Bank of Canada. Although it considers that its customers may be defined in a number of ways, its primary categorization centres on the benefits that customers seek from a bank. RBC divides personal (i.e., nonbusiness) customers into five primary benefit groups: Youth, Nexus, Borrowers/Builders, Wealth Accumulators, and Wealth Preservers.[13] As the names of these segments suggest, RBC approaches them according to the benefits they want their banks to provide, such as the accumulation or the preservation of their wealth.

**benefit segmentation**
Groups consumers based on the benefits they derive from products or services.

Hollywood is a constant and effective practitioner of benefit segmentation. Although all movies may seem to provide the same service—entertainment for a few hours—film producers know that people visit the theatre or stream films to get a variety of benefits and so they market them accordingly. Need a laugh? Try the latest comedy. Want to cry and then feel warm and fuzzy? Take in a romance. By the time you leave the theatre, you will feel heartwarmingly happy because the lead characters are sure to have overcome their differences to find love.

Firms have long known that it pays to retain loyal customers. Loyal customers are those who feel so strongly that the firm can meet their relevant needs best that any competitors are virtually excluded from their consideration—that is, these customers buy almost exclusively from the firm. These loyal customers are the most profitable in the long term.[14] In light of the high cost of finding new customers and the profitability of loyal customers, today's companies are using **loyalty segmentation** and investing in retention and loyalty initiatives to retain their most profitable customers. Canadians are

**loyalty segmentation**
Strategy of investing in retention and loyalty initiatives to retain the firm's most profitable customers.

crazy about loyalty cards, with nearly 9 in 10 adults (87 percent) actively participating in at least one loyalty program, whether it's retail or air travel. Loyalty card participation cuts across all demographics; for instance, 96 percent of affluent consumers actively participate in a loyalty program, 78 percent of young adults (18 to 25 years old), 90 percent of seniors (60 years or older), and 95 percent of women (25 to 49) do as well. Grocery stores have embraced this concept, too. For example, Loblaw rolled out a digital loyalty program. PC Plus, that lets it target and reward customers with offers tied to their specific needs.

Spotify customers can be very loyal to their favourite genre of music. With over 1,300 genres available, you might be surprised to learn that metal inspires the highest level of loyalty. Pop trails far behind in second place and folk is a distant third. Although many people view metal listeners as dangerous and destructive, a personality study conducted by the Harriet Watt University in Scotland showed that they are open minded, curious, risk takers, and skeptical of authority, and have far more emotional stability than pop fans. Imagine how useful these insights are to Spotify when analyzing its members' preferences.[15]

**usage rate**
How often a person uses the product or service: occasional, light, regular, or heavy users.

**Usage rate** (heavy users, regular users, light users, occasional users) can also act as a segmentation variable. For example, fast-food restaurants often use promotional coupons to target occasional visitors to their restaurant or to entice people who have never visited their restaurant to come in and try their food and services. Of course, they hope those same people will return and become regular customers.

And airlines definitely pamper their frequent flyers. At Air Canada, the customers who have flown the most miles with the company, the "Super Elite," receive a distinctive card, personalized Air Canada Super Elite luggage tags, special access to Aeroplan Reward seats, priority reservation waitlist, preferred seat selection, Air Canada concierge service, priority airport check-in, extra checked-baggage allowance, priority boarding, guaranteed reservations for full-fare tickets, and priority baggage handling, among other benefits.[16] None of these special services are available to the occasional flyer.

### Using Multiple Segmentation Methods

Although all segmentation methods are useful, each has its unique advantages and disadvantages. For example, segmenting by demographics and geography is easy because information about who the customers are and where they are located is readily available, but these characteristics don't help marketers determine their customer needs. Because "birds of a feather flock together," companies use a combination of geographic, demographic, and lifestyle characteristics, called **geodemographic segmentation**, to classify consumers. Consumers in the same neighbourhoods tend to buy the same types of cars, appliances, and apparel; shop at the same types of retailers; and respond similarly to media and promotions. One tool used by Canada Post for geodemographic segmentation in Canada is PSYTE cluster profiles. The PSYTE system groups all neighbourhoods in Canada into 60 different lifestyles clusters with specific locations. The information in Exhibit 6.5 describes three **PSYTE clusters**.[17] PRIZM CE, a tool developed by Environics Research, groups Canadians into one of 66 lifestyle types—with names such as Cosmopolitan Elite, Electric Avenues, Les Chics, and Lunch at Tim's—and is also widely used in Canada. The system provides a Canadian segmentation model that has linked geodemographics to psychographics, incorporating "Social Values" data from Environics Research with demographics and product preferences to explain consumer behaviour.[18]

**geodemographic segmentation**
The grouping of consumers on the basis of a combination of geographic, demographic, and lifestyle characteristics.

**PSYTE clusters**
The grouping of all neighbourhoods in Canada into 60 different lifestyles clusters.

Geodemographic segmentation can be particularly useful for retailers because customers typically patronize stores close to their neighbourhood. Thus, retailers can use geodemographic segmentation to tailor each store's assortment to the preferences of the local community. If a toy chain discovers that one of its stores is surrounded by a less affluent segment, "Big Sky Families," it can adjust its offerings

**EXHIBIT 6.5** | PSYTE Cluster

| Cluster Name | Urban Lower Middle (U4): Urban Bohemia | Suburban Affluent (S1): Suburban Affluence | Suburban Affluent (S1): Asian Heights |
|---|---|---|---|
| Description | From body piercing to tattoos, Urban Bohemia includes a diverse population by design. A neighbourhood with a youthful skew, this cluster occupies itself in a variety of artistic, retail, and generally creative employment. Men and women employed in cultural, artistic, and entertainment-related jobs abound. Household maintainers under age 25, many with college degrees, are also found in this cluster. | This cluster with a flair for fine living represents both old and new wealth. Because wealth accumulates throughout life stages, this cluster exhibits an older skew with many empty nests. Suburban Affluence indexes high on managerial and technical employment and are married with children. | Asian ancestries combined with hard work and growing wealth create and mould these upscale neighbourhoods. Asian Heights represents the affirmation of dreams cultivated through generations of immigrants and often through hardship. These families boost local economies as well as family prospects. Asian Heights indexes high on Chinese, Korean, and Japanese immigration as well as households of six or more persons. |
| Average Household Income | $46,000 | $166,000 | $96,000 |

*Source:* Used by permission of Pitney Bowes Software.

(left): Stockbyte/PunchStock Images; (middle): Jack Hollingsworth/Getty Images; (right): Ryan McVay/Getty Images

to include less expensive merchandise. This kind of segmentation is also useful for finding new locations; retailers identify their "best" locations and determine what type of people live in the area surrounding those stores, according to the geodemographic clusters. They can then find other potential locations where similar segments reside. Geodemographic systems, such as PSYTE and PRIZM CE, can also help marketers track and compare sales performance among various clusters in different locations.

Knowing what benefits customers are seeking or how the product or service fits a particular lifestyle is important for designing an overall marketing strategy, but such segmentation schemes present a problem for marketers attempting to identify specifically which customers are seeking these benefits. Thus, firms often employ a combination of segmentation methods, using demographics and geography, as discussed above, to identify and target marketing communications to their customers, and then using benefits or lifestyles to design the product or service and the substance of the marketing message.

Segmentation grids can be a useful tool when trying to identify possible target markets, describe them using segmentation bases, and determine the most attractive segments to pursue. Refer to Exhibit 6.6 for an example of a segmentation grid for SoCIAL LITE Vodka.

| EXHIBIT 6.6 | Segmentation Grid for SoCIAL LITE Vodka | | |
|---|---|---|---|
| | **Segment 1 (Primary)** | **Segment 2 (Secondary)** | **Segment 3 (Tertiary)** |
| **Segmentation Base** | **Socialite Andy** | **Looking for LITE Liz** | **Fitness and Diet Seekers** |
| **Geographic** <br> *Where do they live?* | Urbanite, Campus | Urban/suburban areas in Ontario, Alberta, and British Columbia | Urban/suburban areas in Ontario, Alberta, and British Columbia |
| **Demographic** <br> *Who are they?* | Women <br> Ages 19–34 <br> Income <$50K | Women <br> Ages 25–55 <br> Professionals Income >$60K | Men and women <br> Ages 25+ |
| **Psychographic** <br> *How do they live?* <br> *What is their lifestyle?* | Fun loving party type, into yoga, running. Always on top of trends. Enjoys fashion, pop culture, weekends with friends at barbecues, concerts, and parties. | Mindful shopper of what she eats and drinks. Reads labels and avoids negative ingredients. Tries to cook fresh and local. Active, works out, successful but doesn't take herself too seriously. | Proactively seek out "better for you" products that fit their active and clean lifestyle. Active on social media posting everything from gym selfies to new gluten-free recipes and latest protein powder find. Still encourage things that support a balanced lifestyle. |
| **Behavioural** <br> *Why do they buy?* <br> *How often?* <br> *How do they plan to use the products/services?* | Very loyal to products she likes, e.g., low calorie, all natural, no added sugar. Influencer, likes introducing her network to new products and trends. <br> Always searching for new taste sensations. | Wants to have a good time and drink with friends but without the high calorie and sugar content of other drinks. Wants single serve refreshments. | Super loyal to new finds that fit lifestyle. Brand advocates for products they love online. Niche segments include: <br> - Fitness buffs looking for healthy options <br> - Sugar-free dieters (paleo) who avoid sugary drinks <br> - Gluten-free community to deal with health concerns |

## L02  Step 3: Evaluate Segment Attractiveness

The third step in the segmentation process involves evaluating the attractiveness of the various target market segments. To undertake this evaluation, marketers first must determine whether the target market is worth pursuing by using several descriptive criteria: Is the segment identifiable, reachable, responsive, and substantial and profitable? (See Exhibit 6.7.)

Identifiable  Firms must determine who is within their market to be able to design products or services to meet their needs. It is equally important to ensure that the segments are distinct from one another because too much overlap between segments means that distinct marketing strategies aren't necessary to meet segment members' needs.

The Gap has identified several distinct segments to pursue. Recognizing that many of its core customers had families, The Gap opened GapKids and babyGap. Its research also indicated an opportunity to compete with Victoria's Secret in the women's intimate apparel market, so it opened GapBody. Finally, though The Gap is largely successful with middle-of-the-road customers, it was too expensive for some customers and not

**EXHIBIT 6.7**  Evaluation of Segment Attractiveness

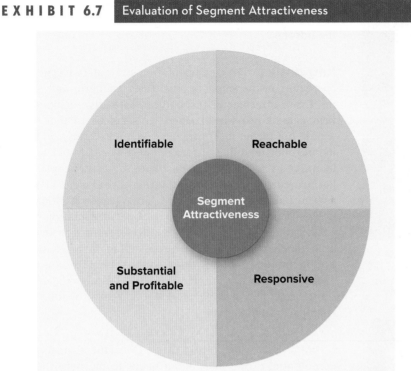

fashion-forward enough for others. Its Old Navy and Banana Republic stores appeal better to these markets.

**Reachable**  The best product or service cannot have any impact if that market cannot be reached (or accessed) through persuasive communications and product distribution. Consumers must know the product or service exists, understand what it can do for them, and recognize how to buy it.

La Senza is one of Canada's leading specialty retailers of women's lingerie and apparel. It is composed of La Senza Lingerie, La Senza Express, La Senza Spirit, and lasenza.com, and it sells through stores and the Internet. The company simply uses its website to attract its targeted customers to explore its merchandise and fashions so that they can be comfortable and knowledgeable when they visit the physical stores to shop. Advertisements appear in media that are consistent with the lifestyle La Senza is trying to portray: lively, attractive, stylish, fun, and cool.

Firms trying to reach university students have a much more difficult time because students' media habits are quite diverse, and generally they are cynical about firms that try too hard to sell to them. High-end fashion jeans companies, for instance, often underpromote their lines or promote them very subtly through traditional media because if their customers start to believe the brand is too mainstream, they won't buy it. Other hard-to-reach segments are composed of people with

La Senza must ensure that any new segment it considers is identifiable, reachable, responsive, substantial, and profitable.

Chris Rout/Alamy Stock Photo

The Gap has identified several distinct segments to pursue. Two of its brands: Gap (top) and Gap Kids (bottom) appeal to different target markets.

(top): The McGraw-Hill Companies, Inc./Andrew Resek, photographer; (bottom): Andrew Walters/ Alamy Stock Photo

disabilities or those whose religious beliefs restrict their media choices. For example, Amish Mennonites eschew TV, radio, and the Internet.

Responsive   For a segmentation strategy to be successful, the customers in the segment must react similarly and positively to the firm's offering. If, through its distinctive competencies, the firm cannot provide products or services to that segment, it should not target it. For instance, suppose La Senza is considering introducing a line of formal dress wear for its large and very lucrative 18- to 35-year-old customer segment. People in this market are currently purchasing formal dress wear at stores such as The Bay, Holt Renfrew, and Les Ailes de la Mode (Wings of Fashion). In contrast, La Senza has built a reputation for carrying a full range of intimate, stylish, and sexy daywear and sleepwear bras, panties, camisoles, pyjamas, and nightshirts and competes best in this apparel line. Although the formal dress wear segment meets all the other criteria for a successful segment, La Senza should not pursue it because the market probably will not be responsive to it.

Substantial and Profitable   Once the firm has identified its potential target markets, it needs to measure their size and growth potential. If a market is too small or its buying power is insignificant, it won't generate sufficient profits or be able to support the marketing mix activities. As China's economy started growing, there were not enough middle-class car buyers to push foreign automakers to design an entry-level vehicle. It was only after that group reached substantial numbers that it became worthwhile for foreign producers to market to these identified consumers.

Marketers must also focus their assessments on the potential profitability of each segment, both current and future. Some key factors to keep in mind in this analysis include market growth (current size and expected growth rate), market competitiveness (number of competitors, entry barriers, product substitutes), and market access (ease of developing or accessing distribution channels and brand familiarity). Some straightforward calculations can help illustrate the profitability of a segment:[19]

Segment profitability = (Segment size × Segment adoption percentage × Purchase behaviour × Profit margin percentage) − Fixed costs

where

Segment size = Number of people in the segment

Segment adoption percentage = Percentage of customers in the segment who are likely to adopt the product/service

Purchase behaviour = Purchase price × Number of times the customer would buy the product or service during a given time period

Profit margin percentage = (Selling price − Variable costs) ÷ Selling price

Fixed costs = Advertising expenditure, rent, utilities, insurance, administration, salaries

To illustrate how a business might determine a segment's profitability, consider Camillo's start-up lawn service. He is trying to determine whether to target homeowners

Which segment will be more profitable to Mark's: its traditional market for rugged work clothes (left), or the fashion-forward segment (right)?

(both): Trademarks of Canadian Tire Corporation, Limited used under licence.

or businesses in a small prairie town. Exhibit 6.8 estimates the profitability of the two target markets. The homeowner segment is much larger than the business segment, but there are already several lawn services with established customers. There is much less competition in the business segment. So, the segment adoption rate for the homeowner segment is only 1 percent, compared with 20 percent for the business segment. Camillo can charge a much higher price to businesses, and they utilize lawn services more frequently. The profit margin for the business segment is higher as well because Camillo can use large equipment to cut the grass and therefore save on variable labour costs. However, the fixed costs for purchasing and maintaining the large equipment are much higher for the business segment. Furthermore, he needs to spend more money obtaining and maintaining the business customers, whereas he would use less expensive door-to-door flyers to reach household customers. On the basis of these informed predictions, Camillo decides the business segment is more profitable for his lawn service.

Using this formula, several segments could appear to be equally profitable. In some cases, it is more accurate to evaluate the profitability of a segment over the lifetime of one of its typical customers—that is, through customer lifetime value (CLV), the total value of purchases of the customer over a lifetime of patronage. For example, Ken Danns has been a loyal Costco customer for the last five years, spending about $300 per week at Costco. He plans to continue patronizing Costco for at least another five years. To Costco, Ken Danns is not a $300 customer but a $156,000 customer if he patronizes Costco

| **EXHIBIT 6.8** | Profitability of Two Market Segments for Camillo's Lawn Service | |
|---|---|---|
| | **Homeowners** | **Businesses** |
| Segment size | 75,000 | 1,000 |
| Segment adoption percentage | 1% | 20% |
| Purchase behaviour<br>Purchase price<br>Frequency of purchase | $100<br>12 times | $500<br>20 times |
| Profit margin percentage | 60% | 80% |
| Fixed costs | $400,000 | $1,000,000 |
| Segment profit | $140,000 | $600,000 |

for 10 years ($300 × 52 weeks × 10 years). To address the issue of CLV, marketers consider factors such as how long the customer will remain loyal to the firm, the defection rate (percentage of customers who switch on a yearly basis), the costs of replacing lost customers (advertising, promotion), whether customers will buy more or more-expensive merchandise in the future, and other such factors. They would also consider the time value of money. See Appendix 7A for more details on determining the lifetime value of customers.

Now that we've evaluated each segment's attractiveness (Step 3), we can select the target markets to pursue (Step 4).

### L03  Step 4: Select Target Market

The fourth step in the STP process is selecting a target market. The key factor likely to affect this decision is the marketer's ability to pursue such an opportunity or target segment. Thus, as we mentioned in Chapter 2, a firm is likely to assess both the attractiveness of the opportunity (opportunities and threats based on the SWOT analysis—i.e., profitability of the segment) and its own competencies (strengths and weaknesses based on SWOT analysis) very carefully.

Determining how to select target markets is not always straightforward. Exhibit 6.9 illustrates several targeting strategies, which are now discussed in more detail.

**EXHIBIT 6.9**   Targeting Strategies

Mass or Undifferentiated

Differentiated

Concentrated

Micromarketing
One-to-One

(top left): © Digital Vision; (top right): © BananaStock/PunchStock; (bottom left): © Jose Luis Pelaez Inc/Blend Images LLC; (bottom right): © Digital Vision.

**Undifferentiated Targeting Strategy, or Mass Marketing** When everyone might be considered a potential user of its product, a firm uses an **undifferentiated targeting strategy (mass marketing)** (see Exhibit 6.9). If the product or service is perceived to provide the same benefits to everyone, there simply is no need to develop separate strategies for different groups. Although not a common strategy in today's complex marketplace, an undifferentiated strategy can be effective for very basic items, such as salt, sugar, or greeting cards. However, even those firms that offer salt, sugar, or greeting cards now are trying to differentiate their products.

An undifferentiated strategy also is common among smaller firms that offer products or services that consumers perceive to be indistinguishable, such as a neighbourhood bakery. But again, more marketing-savvy entrepreneurs typically try to differentiate themselves in the marketplace. The corner bakery thus becomes "Kettleman's Bagel" or "The Great Canadian Bagel." By making their commodity-like products appear special, these companies add value for the customer and differentiate themselves from their competition.

What about gasoline? Everyone with a car needs it. Yet gasoline companies have vigorously moved from an undifferentiated strategy to a differentiated one by segmenting their market into low-, medium-, and high-octane gasoline users. Esso even uses its Speedpass to differentiate its quick service to consumers: With just a swipe at the pump with Speedpass, you are ready to pump gas—no need to swipe cards, enter personal information, or sign receipts. Plus customers earn Esso Extra points or Aeroplan Miles on every eligible purchase made at Esso. Points can be redeemed for gas, car washes, snacks, and travel rewards.

**Differentiated Targeting Strategy** Firms using a **differentiated targeting strategy** target several market segments with a different offering for each (see Exhibit 6.9). La Senza, for instance, employs three store formats—La Senza, La Senza Spirit, and La Senza Express—to appeal to three different segments respectively: (1) confident, fashion-forward 18- to 35-year-old women; (2) women looking for activewear and yoga and workout gear; and (3) women looking for the ultimate destination for bras and panties for everyday and trend-forward styles.[20] In a similar fashion, Adidas Group appeals to various segments through its various companies, including Adidas Reebok (athletic shoes), Rockport (comfortable walking shoes), and TaylorMade–Adidas Golf lines of clothing and footwear.

Firms embrace differentiated segmentation because it helps them obtain a bigger share of the market and increase the market for their products overall. The more retail formats La Senza develops to reach different market segments, the more apparel and accessories it can and will sell. Offering several different lingerie lines enables La Senza to appeal to more customer segments than if it had just one line. Furthermore, providing products or services that appeal to multiple segments helps diversify the business, thereby lowering the company's overall risk. For example, if a line directed toward one segment is performing poorly, the impact on the firm's profitability can be offset by revenue from another line that is doing well. But a differentiated strategy can be expensive. Consider La Senza's investment in accessories alone. The firm must develop, manufacture, transport, store, and promote the accessories separately for each of its store concepts.

Condé Nast has more than 20 niche magazines focused on different aspects of life—from *Vogue* for fashionistas to *Bon Appetit* for foodies to GQ for fashion-conscious men to *The New Yorker* for literature lovers to *Golf Digest* for those who walk the links. Firms embrace differentiated targeting because it helps them obtain a bigger share of the market and increase the market for their products overall. Readers of *Golf Digest* probably are unlike readers of *Architectural Digest* in their interests, or demographically, such as regarding gender, age, and income. Providing products or services that appeal to multiple segments helps diversify the business and therefore lowers the company's overall risk. Even if one magazine suffers a circulation decline, the impact on the firm's profitability can be offset by revenue from another publication that continues to do well.

**Concentrated (Niche) Targeting Strategy** When an organization selects a single, primary target market and focuses all its energies on providing a product to fit

**undifferentiated targeting strategy (mass marketing)** A marketing strategy a firm can use if the product or service is perceived to provide the same benefits to everyone, with no need to develop separate strategies for different groups.

**differentiated targeting strategy** A strategy through which a firm targets several market segments with a different offering for each.

**concentrated (or niche) targeting strategy**
A marketing strategy of selecting a single, primary target market and focusing all energies on providing a product to fit that market's needs.

that market's needs, it is using a **concentrated (or niche) targeting strategy** (see Exhibit 6.9). Entrepreneurial start-up ventures often benefit from using a concentrated strategy, which allows them to employ their limited resources more efficiently. The story of Cora's restaurants in Entrepreneurial Marketing 6.1 is an example of a niche strategy since it focuses on serving breakfast and lunch only; restaurants are open only until 3 p.m.

Newton Running has concentrated its targeting strategy on runners—but not all runners. It focuses only on those who prefer to land on their forefeet while running, a style that recently has been suggested to be more natural, efficient, and less injury-prone than the style encouraged by more traditional running shoes with their heel-first construction and substantial cushioning. In comparison, though it also is known for its running shoes, Nike uses a differentiated targeting strategy (recall the opening vignette about Nike in Chapter 2). It makes shoes for segments that include basketball and football players and skateboarders as well as fashion-conscious white-collar workers with its subsidiary brand Cole Haan.

## Entrepreneurial Marketing 6.1

### Chez Cora: The Business of Breakfast

When Cora Tsouflidou became a single mother to three teenage children, she bought a small eatery, worked hard, tripled its value, and sold it. From there she worked her way up from a hostess to the general manager in a well known Montreal restaurant, mastering her food service industry knowledge along the way.[21]

These skills served her well when she bought a defunct 29-seat snack bar in Montreal's Ville St-Laurent in 1987 and launched the first Chez Cora restaurant. Plates garnished with a variety of artistically presented fresh fruits made Cora's dishes both unique and popular. Her homey, healthy food was a hit, which led to franchising Chez Cora in Quebec, followed by franchising Cora Breakfast and Lunch across the rest of the country. Today, there are more than 130 Cora restaurants across Canada, all of which have traditional family-style breakfast and lunch menus featuring new dishes created and tested by Cora herself.

When deciding to open a new franchise, the company starts with a demographic analysis to determine whether there are enough people in an area to feed a Cora restaurant.[22] Psychographics and behavioural segmentation are also important to identify and attract customers who are interested in healthy eating and want the benefit of nutritious meals.

A unique strategy attracts franchisees based on their desired lifestyle. Restaurants serve only breakfast and lunch and thus are open between 6 a.m. and 3 p.m., an approach born out of necessity from Cora's early days as a single mom. These hours are considerably shorter than most restaurant operations and thus appeal to franchisees, allowing them to spend more time with their families.

It's not surprising that Cora's image is used in advertising campaigns. She looks like a mom who really cares about family, which resonates with both customers and

Cora Breakfast and Lunch serves up nutritious meals featuring a variety of colourful fruits.

Used with permission of Cora Franchise Group Inc.

franchisees. Behind that colourful image is a self-made businesswoman who has won the Governor General's Award and the Ernst & Young Entrepreneur of the Year Award.[23] In 2013, she received Queen Elizabeth II's Diamond Jubilee Medal and the Life Achievement Award from the Canadian Franchise Association. She has been inducted into the Quebec franchise industry association's Hall of Fame and received international recognition when she was named Veuve Clicquot Business Woman of the Year.[24] Her unique business plan has made Cora Breakfast and Lunch one of the fastest-growing restaurant chains in Canada.

**Micromarketing**[25]   Take a look at your collection of belts. Have you ever had a belt made to match your exact specifications? When a firm tailors a product or service to suit an individual customer's wants or needs, it is undertaking an extreme form of segmentation called **micromarketing (one-to-one)** (see Exhibit 6.9). Small producers and service providers generally can tailor their offering to individual customers more easily, whereas it is far more difficult for larger companies to achieve this degree of segmentation. Nonetheless, companies such as Dell and Lands' End have capitalized on Internet technologies to offer custom products. Lands' End used to let customers choose from a variety of options in the fabric, type of collar, sleeve, and shape, and based on the customer's specific measurements—but it halted this service when it could not manage to achieve profitable sales. Dell allowed customers to choose the size, colour, and speed of their laptops, though it has backed off its promotions and limits the choice of software included.

Firms that interact on a one-to-one basis with many people to create custom-made products or services (such as Build-a-Bear Workshop), are engaged in **mass customization**, providing one-to-one marketing to the masses. Sport Chek offers several options to consumers who want custom products. A Reebok "build-your-own" sneaker kiosk lets consumers create their own designs, which are shipped to them four to six weeks later. Sports fans can create a custom Toronto Maple Leafs, Toronto Blue Jays, or Team Canada jersey that includes the name and number of their favourite player.[26]

Which segment is being targeted?

Courtesy of Newton Running

**micromarketing (one-to-one)**
An extreme form of segmentation that tailors a product or service to suit an individual customer's wants or needs.

**mass customization**
The practice of interacting on a one-to-one basis with many people to create custom-made products or services; providing one-to-one marketing to the masses.

Build-a-Bear lets customers design their own stuffed furry friend with unique clothes, accessories, sounds, and the name printed on its birth certificate.

Courtesy of Build-a-Bear Workshop, Inc.

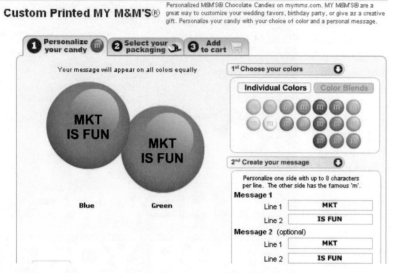

Mars' M&M's site allows customers to customize their candy.

Courtesy of Mars, Inc.

The Internet facilitates such a targeting strategy. Companies can cater to very small segments, sometimes as small as one customer at a time, relatively efficiently and inexpensively (e.g., mortgage and insurance sites provide personalized quotes). An Internet-based company can offer one-to-one service more inexpensively than can other venues, such as retail stores or telephone-based businesses. For example, frequent fliers of Air Canada can check prices and choose special services online at a fraction of the cost that the company would incur for a phone consultation with a ticket agent.

The Internet also simplifies customer identification. Cookies, or small text files a website stores in a visitor's browser, provide a unique identification of each potential customer who visits and details how the customer has searched the site. Marketers also can ask visitors to fill out an online registration form. Using such information, the company can make a variety of recommendations to customers. Amazon.ca is renowned for the algorithms it uses to provide recommendations for related products to customers as they browse the site, which match customer profiles to those of other customers. The marketing strategy is customized in real time, using known and accurate data about the customer. Customers can even do the work themselves, both to create items for themselves and to find the perfect gifts for others.[27] Mars' M&M's site (http://www.mymms.com) lets customers customize their own M&M's with personalized greetings, including messages for birthday parties, sporting events, graduations, and weddings—even wedding proposals!

The degree to which firms should target their markets—from no segmentation to one segment to multiple segments to one-to-one segments—depends on the balance the firm wants to achieve between the added perceived customer value that segmentation can offer and its cost.

## **L04** Step 5: Identify and Develop Positioning Strategy

**positioning**
The mental picture that people have about a company and its products or services relative to competitors.

The last step in developing a market segmentation strategy is **positioning**. Positioning is the mental picture or perception—the thoughts, feelings, and impressions—that people have about a company and its products and brands relative to competing products, brands, or companies. This mental picture is formed from multiple sources such as friends, family, relatives, and reference groups; published articles in magazines and newspapers; reports and stories from radio, TV, and the Internet; as well as the customer's own experience. Regardless of whether companies want them to or not, consumers form their own ideas and feelings about a product or brand, and it is those very ideas and emotions that drive them toward or away from a brand or company. The positioning strategy can help communicate the firm's or the product's **value proposition**, which communicates the customer benefits to be received from a product or service and thereby provides reasons for wanting to purchase it. For example, SoCIAL LITE Vodka offers consumers a way to socialize without regret. Positioning is one of the most important but difficult and least understood aspects of marketing strategy development. Why?

**value proposition**
Communicates the customer benefits to be received from a product or service and the reason(s) for wanting to buy it.

It is not easy to shape consumers' perceptions in the way marketers may want. It is also difficult because, while marketers must keep their positioning fresh to keep abreast of the ever-changing marketplace, consumers' perceptions are enduring and do not change easily. Positioning is very risky for marketers because if it is not done correctly, the brand may not succeed in the marketplace. Effective positioning requires that marketers not only shape their customers' thinking and feelings, but also evolve these feelings as they reposition their products and brands to keep up with the dynamic marketplace. For example, Old Spice successfully repositioned itself from "your father's after-shave" to a fresh new product sought by younger consumers. It is now a leading brand offering soap, body wash, body spray, shave, gel, deodorant, and antiperspirant products.

Market positioning involves a process of defining the marketing mix variables so that target customers have a clear, distinctive, desirable understanding of what the product does or represents in comparison with competing products. Effective positioning is about letting consumers know what the company's unique value proposition is and for whom it is intended. Clarity of this message is crucial for successful positioning. For example, Abercrombie & Fitch offers casual luxury to young, sexy, athletic- and cheerleading-type university students. Its advertising messages, models, store design, and merchandise all reinforce this message.

A firm's positioning strategies must focus on the value a product or service offers the target consumer, or how it is better than competitors' products and services. When positioning against competitors, the objective is to play up how the brand being marketed provides the desired benefits better than those of competitors. Positioning strategies are realized by communicating particular messages (i.e., the **positioning statement**) in persuasive communications through different media.

**positioning statement**
Expresses how a company wants to be perceived by consumers.

In Exhibit 6.10, we illustrate some elements of a positioning statement as follows:

1. target market
2. offering name or brand
3. product/service category or concept
4. unique point of difference/benefits

Let's focus on a couple of well known products—Gatorade and 7-Up—and their potential value propositions (brackets added to separate the components):

- **Gatorade:**[28] For [athletes around the world] [Gatorade] is the [sports drink] that [represents the heart and soul of athleticism. Unlike water, it gives the fuel for working muscles, fluid for hydration, and electrolytes to help replace what is lost in sweat before, during, and after activity to get the most out of your body].

- **7-Up:**[29] For [noncola consumers] [7-Up] is a [noncaffeinated soft drink] that [is light, refreshing, lemon-lime flavoured. Unlike colas, it has a crisp, bubbly, and clean taste].

**EXHIBIT 6.10** | Positioning Statement Elements

|  | Gatorade | 7-Up |
|---|---|---|
| Target market | For athletes around the world | For noncola consumers |
| Offering name or brand | Gatorade | 7-Up |
| Product/service category or concept: | is the sports drink | is a noncaffeinated soft drink |
| Unique point of difference/ benefits | representing the heart and soul of athleticism. Unlike water, it gives the fuel for working muscles, fluid for hydration, and electrolytes to help replace what is lost in sweat before, during, and after activity to get the most out of your body. | that is light, refreshing, lemon-lime flavoured. Unlike colas it has a crisp, bubbly, and clean taste. |

## Positioning Methods

Usually, firms position their products and services based on different methods such as value, product attributes, benefits and symbolism, and competition. Let's explore each of these in a bit more detail.

**Value**   Value is a popular positioning method because the relationship of price to quality is among the most important considerations for consumers when they make a purchase decision. Remember that value does not necessarily mean low priced. For example, in the kids' toy market, Mega Bloks uses a low-price, value-based strategy, whereas its competitor, Lego, relies on a high-price positioning strategy. Watchmaker Patek Philippe uses the advertising tagline, "You never actually own a Patek Philippe. You merely take care of it for the next generation," to encourage buyers to consider its arm candy an investment.[30] Other brands that rely on a similar idea of luxury value include Hermès, Chanel, and Mercedes-Benz.

Some companies claim that they are offering the same value for much less money. This type of positioning is common among wireless service providers (e.g., Rogers, Bell, TELUS), cable/satellite TV and radio providers (Sirius, Rogers), electronics retailers (Future Shop), and department stores (Target). Companies such as Internet Superstore, Buy.com, and TigerDirect emphasize that consumers are getting the best computer deals anywhere and at much lower prices. Finally, companies may use value positioning to let consumers know that while they are getting much less, they are also paying much less. WestJet, dollar stores (e.g., Buck or Two, Dollar Store), and countless retailers targeting cost-conscious consumers commonly use this strategy.

**Product Attributes**   Another common positioning strategy focuses on those attributes that are most important to the target market. Car company Volvo traditionally positioned itself for the safety-conscious driver but now wants to stretch its safety image to one focused on driving performance and excitement. The company expects the positioning adjustment to be difficult but achievable, because so many of Volvo's boxier vehicles remain on the road today, which reinforces its more conservative image. Volvo's goal is not to abandon the safety perception associated with

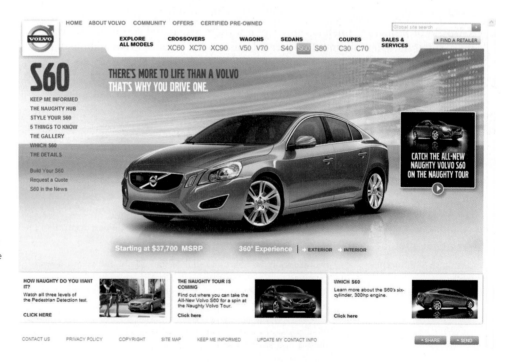

Can Volvo reposition its cars to be more exciting with higher performance without losing its traditional position that appeals to safety-conscious drivers?

Courtesy of Volvo of North America

the brand but rather to expand its image to compete with other top luxury brands.[31] Positioning strategies that are based on product attributes tend to focus on product leadership, emphasizing dimensions such as innovation, quality, performance, design, and reliability. 3M and HP focus on their innovations, while Rockport focuses on comfort and a wide selection of shoes for all occasions. Cora's, a product-attributes success story, is able to compete in the highly competitive restaurant market by attracting a target market that wants a healthy and homey breakfast or lunch (see Entrepreneurial Marketing 6.1).

### Benefits and Symbolism

This type of positioning emphasizes the benefits of the brand as well as the psychological meaning of the brand to consumers. For example, SoCIAL LITE Vodka is positioned on its functional benefits. It tastes great, has only 80 calories and no sugar, and is 100 percent natural. Lolë is about technical but versatile clothing in a casual, modern style, and strikes a balance between active life and social life, nature and urban lifestyle, well-being and energy. La Senza Express is the ultimate destination dedicated to bras and panties. The meanings created by these brands are often the reasons consumers buy them rather than lesser-known brands that sometimes offer similar benefits or quality. For established companies, a well known symbol can also be used as a positioning tool, especially to appeal to loyal customers. What comes to mind when you think of Colonel Sanders, the Jolly Green Giant, the Gerber Baby, or Tony the Tiger? Or consider the Nike swoosh or the Ralph Lauren polo player. These symbols are so strong and well known that they create a position for the brand that distinguishes it from its competition.

### Competition

Firms can choose to position their products or services *head-to-head* against a specific competitor or an entire product/service classification on similar attributes within the target market. Using head-to-head positioning, Avis positioned itself alongside Hertz with its message "We try harder." Ranked second in the rental car market, Avis used this approach for more than 50 years. Head-to-head positioning can lead to price wars such as the "cola wars" and "cellphone wars," which are good for consumers but bad for businesses. Marketers must be careful that they don't position their product too closely to their competition because they risk confusing customers or facing legal challenges. If, for instance, their package or logo looks too much like a competitor's, they might be opening themselves up to a trademark infringement lawsuit. Numerous store brands have been challenged for having packaging confusingly similar to that of national brands. McDonald's, for example, sues anyone who uses the *Mc* prefix. It sued Quality Inns International when it named its no-frills chain McSleep Inns.[32] However, courts have allowed parody jeans for full-figured women to be sold under the Lardashe label, despite the objections of Jordache jeans.

Firms can also choose a *differentiation* strategy by going after a less competitive, smaller market niche.[33] For instance, Goodrich tires were promoted as "The Other Guys," or the ones without the blimp, to set them apart from Goodyear tires. McDonald's, which has long been  known as the world's number-one beef burger joint, has responded to industry critics and health-conscious consumers by improving the "health of its menu" with more healthy choices such as salads and chicken sandwiches. In doing so, it tried to avoid competition with archrivals Wendy's and Burger King while minimizing the impact of cannibalization of its existing menu items.

As Ethical Dilemma 6.1 notes, Walmart positions itself as the low-cost leader, even when selling typically premium priced organic products.

### Market Leadership

Instead of positioning head-to-head, companies, especially market leaders, may emphasize their leadership position within their industry. Canadian companies such as RBC Royal Bank, Loblaw, and Canadian Tire, and global companies

## Ethical Dilemma 6.1

### Walmart's Low-Priced Organic Foods[34]

One word can strike fear into the heart of any small retailer: Walmart! Because it enjoys massive economies of scale, Walmart's entry into a market can cause tremors for even other large retailers, because somehow it always manages to underprice everyone else. Over the years, Walmart has gone from being a consumer-goods giant to becoming a large grocer as well.

Walmart's target markets are generally price conscious and it positions itself as the low-cost leader. To attract even more customers to its stores, the company is looking to gain a substantial share of the lucrative organic food market. Organic products are typically sold at a premium, but Walmart says its customers "will be able to purchase organic at non-organic prices." In-house research indicated that consumers would overwhelmingly purchase organic products if they cost less, so Walmart responded.

But how can Walmart afford to offer organic products at nonorganic prices? The plan is to collaborate with WildOats to deliver organic items through an atypical "bigger is better" mentality. Organic foods typically come from small farms, which send their products out to be processed at facilities that simultaneously process conventional foods. The switches from organic to conventional processing and back again require a great deal of labour, which increases costs and thus prices. By switching to a large industrial model, Walmart can achieve economies of scale. Working with larger farms and processing plants that cater only to organic food production can save time, labour, and money—by a margin of as much as 20–30 percent.

To attract new customers, Walmart is offering organic products at non-organic prices.

© McGraw-Hill Education

As promising as this sounds, some consumers question if Walmart's foray into organics will hurt small farmers and cheapen the concept. Since the premise requires high-quality organic products at nonorganic prices, to ensure that they can stock shelves to meet demand, company executives will have to lock suppliers into long-term agreements. Others worry that, in addition to purchasing from huge industrial farms, Walmart may try to influence regulators to water down standards or focus on cheap imports. All of this is at odds with the values and ethics of many small organic farmers.

such as Amazon, Intel, HP, Google, and eBay, play up their status as market leaders in their respective industry. All of these companies are the leader in their industry and so consumers often perceive them as setting the standards of their industry.

### Positioning by Using Perceptual Mapping

**perceptual map**
Displays, in two or more dimensions, the position of products or brands in the consumer's mind.

**ideal point**
The position at which a particular market segment's ideal product would lie on a perceptual map.

Now that we've identified the various methods firms use to position their products and services, let's look at the steps they go through to establish that position. When developing a positioning strategy, firms go through six important steps. Before you read about these steps though, take a look at Exhibit 6.11 (Charts A–D), a hypothetical perceptual map of the soft-drink industry. A **perceptual map** displays, in two or more dimensions, the position of products or brands in the consumer's mind. We have chosen two dimensions for illustrative purposes: sweet versus light taste (vertical) and less natural versus healthy (horizontal). Although this industry is quite complex, we have simplified the diagram to include only a few players in the market. The position of each brand is denoted by a small circle, and the numbered circles denote a consumer's **ideal point**—where a particular market segment's ideal product would lie on the map. The larger the numbered circle, the larger the market size.

To derive a perceptual map such as this, marketers follow steps.

1. *Determine consumers' perceptions and evaluations of the firm's product or service in relation to competitors.* Marketers determine their brand's position by asking consumers a series of questions about their and competitors' products. For instance, they might ask how the consumer uses the existing product or services, what items the consumer regards as alternative sources to satisfy his or her needs, what the person likes or dislikes about the brand in relation to competitors, and what might make that person choose one brand over another. Exhibit 6.11A depicts the six products using two dimensions (light taste–sweet taste; and less natural–healthy).

2. *Identify the market's ideal points and size.* On a perceptual map, marketers can represent the size of current and potential markets. For example, Exhibit 6.11B uses different sized ovals that correspond to the market size. Ideal point 1 represents the largest market, so if the firm does not already have a product positioned close to this point, it should consider an introduction. Point 3 is the smallest market, so there are relatively few customers who want a healthy, light-tasting drink. This is not to suggest that this market should be ignored; however, the company might want to consider a niche- rather than mass-market strategy for this group of consumers.

Goodrich positions its tires as the ones without the blimp to set them apart from Goodyear.

**EXHIBIT 6.11A** Perceptual Maps

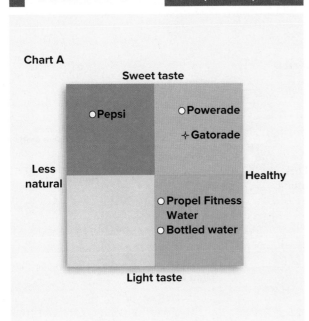

**EXHIBIT 6.11B** Perceptual Maps

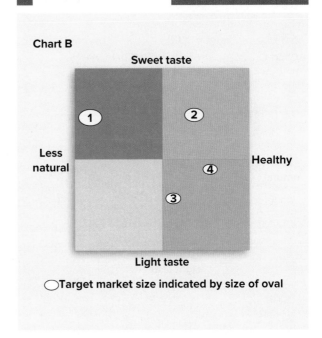

3. *Identify competitors' positions.* When the firm understands how its customers view its brand relative to competitors', it must study how those same competitors position themselves. For instance, Powerade positions itself closely to Gatorade, which means they appear next to each other on the perceptual map and appeal to target market 2. (See Exhibit 6.11C.) They are also often found next to each other on store shelves, are similarly priced, and are viewed by customers as sports drinks. Gatorade knows that its sports drink is perceived to be more like Powerade than like its own Propel Fitness Water (located near target market 3), or Coke (target market 1).

4. *Determine consumer preferences.* The firm knows what the consumer thinks of the products or services in the marketplace and their positions relative to one another. Now it must find out what the consumer really wants—that is, determine the "ideal" product or service that appeals to each market. For example, a huge market exists for traditional Gatorade, and that market is shared by Powerade. Gatorade also recognizes a market, depicted as the ideal product for segment 4 on the perceptual map, of consumers who would prefer a less sweet, less calorie-laden drink that offers the same rejuvenating properties as Gatorade. Currently, no product is adequately serving market 4.

5. *Select the position.* Continuing with the Gatorade example, the company has three choices to appeal to the "less sweet sports drink" target market 4. It could develop a new product to meet the needs of market 4. (See Exhibit 6.11D.) Alternatively, it could adjust or reposition its marketing approach—its product and promotion—to sell original Gatorade to market 4. Finally, it could ignore what target market 4 really wants and hope that consumers will be attracted to the original Gatorade because it is closer to their ideal product than anything else on the market.

6. *Monitor the positioning strategy.* Markets are not stagnant. Consumers' tastes shift, and competitors react to those shifts. Attempting to maintain the same position year after year can spell disaster for any company. Thus, firms must always view the first three steps of the positioning process as ongoing, with adjustments made in step 4 as necessary.

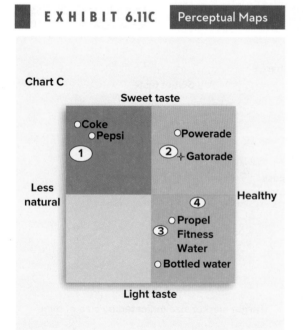

**EXHIBIT 6.11C** Perceptual Maps

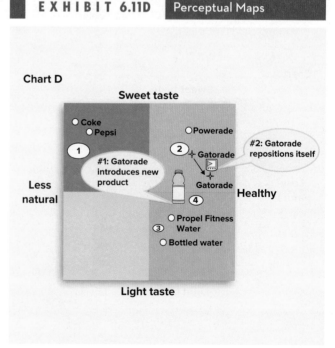

**EXHIBIT 6.11D** Perceptual Maps

## Repositioning

Sometimes firms try to change their positioning. In its earliest days, Skechers was mostly a lifestyle brand, with hip styles and vibrant designs that appealed to young trendsetters and hipsters, both men and women. When it realized that older consumers wanted hip lifestyle shoes too, it introduced its Shape-Up line and repositioned its image accordingly. Electronics retailer The Source wanted to convince consumers that it was more than just a place to buy batteries or accessories. It shifted its positioning to "On the Go" to promote stores as a destination for top tier electronic products.[35] Tiffany & Co. has long been known for luxury jewellery that is most often purchased by wealthy individuals. In the 1990s, the company, following a trend of "affordable luxury," tried to reposition by expanding its product assortment to appeal more to the middle class. Tiffany introduced a silver charm bracelet priced at $110 that became very popular with teenagers and resulted in explosive sales growth for the company. Although it was a financial success, at least in the short term, the image of inexpensive silver jewellery alienated older, more affluent customers who now viewed Tiffany as a common brand. In response, the company increased prices on its silver products by 30 percent in an attempt to reclaim its position as a luxury jeweller.

Good marketers constantly reevaluate their brand's position to determine when to reposition it. Companies should reposition their brands to keep up with changes in the marketplace or to put a fresh spin on their stale and stodgy brand. Many companies that operate on the idea "If it ain't broke, then don't fix it" often find out too late that their brand needs a serious makeover. The result is that their positioning is so badly damaged that it takes years and huge budgets to rebuild. Proactive companies change or tinker with their positioning to keep up with market dynamics. For example, for most of General Electric Company's history, its positioning was based on product—"We Bring Good Things to Life"—which served GE very well. More recently, GE replaced that positioning with one that focuses on its rich history of innovation: "Imagination at Work."

**Brand repositioning (rebranding)** refers to a strategy in which marketers change a brand's focus to target new markets or realign the brand's core emphasis with changing market preferences.[36] Although repositioning can improve the brand's fit with its target segment or boost the vitality of old brands, it is not without costs and risks. Firms often need to spend tremendous amounts of money to make tangible changes to the product and packages, as well as intangible changes to the brand's image through various forms of promotion. These costs may not be recovered if the repositioned brand and messages are not credible to the consumer or if the firm has mistaken a fad for a long-term market trend.

Repositioning can change the quality image of the brand, as noted earlier in the Tiffany example. However, WestJet successfully repositioned itself from a no-frills low-cost leader to a considerably higher quality airline by adding luxuries such as leather seats and seat-back LCD TV screens. Repositioning can breathe life into old brands.

**brand repositioning (rebranding)**
A strategy in which marketers change a brand's focus to target new markets or realign the brand's core emphasis with changing market preferences.

Gatorade with football player Jason Taylor (left) and Powerade with soccer player David Beckham (right) are positioned to compete for target market 3 in Exhibit 6.11.

(left): Doug Benc/Getty Images; (right): Ezra Shaw/Getty Images

# LEARNING OBJECTIVES REVIEW

**LO1** **Describe the bases marketers use to segment a market**

There is really no one "best" method to segment a market. Firms choose from various segmentation bases depending on the type of product/service they offer and their goals for the segmentation strategy. For instance, if the firm wants to identify its customers easily, geographic or demographic segmentation likely will work best. But if the firm is trying to dig deeper into why customers might buy its offering, then lifestyle, benefits, and loyalty segmentation work best. Geodemographic segmentation provides a nice blend of geographic, demographic, and psychographic approaches. Typically, a combination of several segmentation methods is most effective.

**LO2** **Identify the criteria for determining the attractiveness of a segment and whether it is worth pursuing (targeting)**

Marketers use several criteria to assess a segment's attractiveness. First, the customer should be *identifiable*—companies must know what types of people are in the market so they can direct their efforts appropriately. Second, the market must be *reachable*—the firm must be able to reach the segment through effective communications and distribution. Third, the firm must be *responsive* to the needs of customers in a segment. It must be able to deliver a product or service that the segment will embrace. Finally, the market must be *substantial* enough to be worth pursuing. If relatively few people appear in a segment, it is probably not cost-effective to direct special marketing mix efforts toward them. Additionally, the segment must be *profitable*, both in the near term and over the lifetime of the customer.

**LO3** **Explain the differences among targeting strategies: undifferentiated, differentiated, concentrated, or micromarketing**

Firms use a targeting strategy after they have identified the segments. An *undifferentiated strategy* is really no segmentation at all and works for only products or services that most consumers consider to be commodities. The difference between a *differentiated* and a *concentrated strategy* is that the differentiated approach targets multiple segments, whereas the concentrated approach targets only one. Larger firms with multiple product/service offerings generally use a differentiated strategy; smaller firms or those with a limited product/service offering often use a concentrated strategy. Firms that employ a *micromarketing* or *one-to-one marketing strategy* tailor their product/service offering to each customer—that is, it is custom-made. In the past, micromarketing was reserved primarily for artisans, tailors, or other craftspeople who would make items exactly as the customer wanted. Recently, however, larger manufacturers and retailers have begun experimenting with custom-made merchandise as well. Service providers, in contrast, are largely familiar with customizing their offering. Hair salons could not flourish if every customer got the same cut.

**LO4** **Define positioning and describe how firms do it**

Positioning is the "P" in the STP (segmentation, targeting, and positioning) process. It refers to how customers think about a product, service, or brand in the market relative to competitors' offerings. Firms position their products and services according to several criteria. Some focus on their offering's *value*—customers get a lot for what the product or service costs. Others determine the most *important product attributes* for customers and position their offering on the basis of those attributes. *Benefits* and *symbols* can also be used for positioning, though few products or services are associated with symbols that are compelling enough to drive people to buy. Companies may also use their dominant position in their market—*market leadership*—to position their products or services. Finally, *competition* is one of the most common positioning methods and relies on the favourable comparison of the firm's offering with the products or services marketed by competitors (head-to-head). Companies may also choose to compete by differentiating their value proposition.

# KEY TERMS

- behavioural segmentation
- benefit segmentation
- brand repositioning (rebranding)
- concentrated (or niche) targeting strategy
- demographic segmentation
- differentiated targeting strategy
- geodemographic segmentation
- geographic segmentation
- ideal point
- lifestyles
- loyalty segmentation
- mass customization
- micromarketing (one-to-one)
- occasion segmentation
- perceptual map
- positioning
- positioning statement
- psychographics
- PSYTE clusters
- self-concept
- self-values
- undifferentiated targeting strategy (mass marketing)
- VALS™
- value proposition

## CONCEPT REVIEW

1. How do segmentation, targeting, and positioning add value to a company's value proposition?

2. Outline the steps in the STP process. What are some of the key decisions marketers have to make at each step?

3. List the bases that can be used to segment a market for a product or service. Which of these bases is considered to be the most difficult to use and which is the easiest? Why?

4. Describe the segmentation bases you think Coca-Cola used to develop its target segment. What kinds of products do you think this segment was buying before Coca-Cola introduced its Coke Zero brand? Thinking back to the consumer buying decision process, what kinds of strategies do you think were necessary to get this segment to switch to Coke Zero?

5. List the four types of targeting strategies companies can use to serve selected market segments. What are the main points to consider before selecting one or more of these strategies? What are the advantages and disadvantages of each strategy, and how can competitors influence the strategy a company chooses?

6. Explain the difference between positioning and a positioning statement. Why do you think marketers find market positioning one of the most difficult aspects of the STP process? How can marketers try to influence the positioning of their products or services in the marketplace?

7. List four types of strategies companies could use to position their products or services in the marketplace. When Home Depot says, "You Can Do It, We Can Help," for what type of positioning is it striving?

8. What is a perceptual map? How is it used in developing positioning strategies or identifying market opportunities?

9. Why should marketers consider repositioning their brand? Explain what is meant by *repositioning* and the major challenges and risks inherent in repositioning.

10. An online news article suggests that Sony is thinking of repositioning its PlayStation 4 game console as a computer. Do you think that Sony can do this successfully? Give reasons. Do you think consumers will ever see the PlayStation as a computer? Why or why not?

## MARKETING APPLICATIONS

1. What segmentation methods would you suggest for a small entrepreneur starting her own business selling gourmet chocolates? Justify why you would recommend those methods.

2. You have been asked to identify various segments in the market and then a potential targeting strategy. Describe the segments for a pet supply store. Justify the best targeting strategy to use.

3. What types of products would you use demographic segmentation for? How about psychographic segmentation? Explain how these products differ.

4. How and why would a retailer use micromarketing?

5. You have been asked to evaluate the attractiveness of several potential market segments. What criteria should you use to evaluate those segments? Why are these appropriate criteria?

6. A small-business owner is trying to evaluate the profitability of different segments. What are the key factors he or she must consider? For how long should the business owner conduct the evaluation?

7. Think about the various soft drink brands that you know (e.g., Coke, Pepsi, 7-Up, Gatorade, Powerade). How do those brands position themselves in the market?

8. Put yourself in the position of an entrepreneur who is developing a new product to introduce into the market. Briefly describe the product. Then, develop the segmentation, targeting, and positioning strategy for marketing the new product. Be sure to discuss (a) the overall strategy, (b) characteristics of the target market, (c) why that target market is attractive, and (d) the positioning strategy. Provide justifications for your decisions.

9. Think of a specific company or organization that uses various types of promotional material to market its offerings. (The Internet, magazine ads, newspaper ads, catalogues, newspaper inserts, direct mail pieces, and flyers might all be sources of promotional materials.) Locate two or three promotional pieces for the company and use them as a basis to analyze the segment(s) being targeted. Describe the basic segmentation strategy reflected in these materials, and describe characteristics of the target market according to the materials. Be sure to include a copy of all the materials used in the analysis.

10. You have been hired recently by a large bank in its credit card marketing division. The bank has relationships with a large number of colleges and universities and prints a wide variety of credit cards featuring college and university logos, images, and the like. You have been asked to oversee the implementation of a new program targeting

first-year students at the schools with which the bank has a relationship. The bank has already purchased the names and home addresses of the incoming students. You have been told that no credit checks will be required for these cards as long as the student is older than 18 years of age.

The bank plans a first-day-of-school marketing blitz that includes free hats, T-shirts, and book promotions, as well as free pizza, if the students simply fill out an application. Do you think it is a good idea to offer this program to these new students?

## NET SAVVY

1. Go to the L'Oréal Canada website (http://www.lorealparis.ca) and try to describe the segmentation approach it uses to group customers. Apply the vocabulary presented in this chapter to describe its segmentation strategy. Then click on "Haircare," and look for "Everfresh Shampoo." Who do you think is the target market for this product? How would you describe L'Oréal's product positioning in Canada?

2. Go to the VALS website (http://www.strategicbusiness insights.com/vals/presurvey.shtml), and click on the link to complete the VALS survey. After you submit your responses, a screen will display your primary and secondary VALS types. Click on the coloured names of each segment to get additional information about them, and print out your results. Assess the extent to which these results reflect your lifestyle, and identify which characteristics accurately reflect your interests and activities and which do not.

## CHAPTER CASE STUDY

### NETFLIX: POSITIONED FOR SUCCESS AS A GLOBAL CONTENT PROVIDER

Imagine that you had access to 30 million pieces of daily information about how viewers pause, rewind, or fast-forward the shows they watch. Next imagine that you attracted around 4 million customer ratings each day. What if you could also glean information about when, where, and how viewers conducted their approximately 3 million daily searches for entertainment?

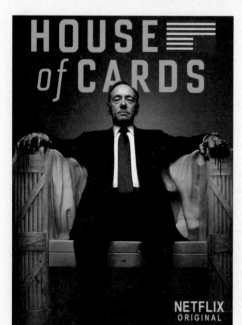

In spite of a male dominant target market, *House of Cards* has widespread appeal.

AF Archive/Alamy Stock Photo

For one, you might be exhausted: That's a lot of data. But for another, you would know precisely who was watching what, when, and through what channels, which would give you a great deal of information about what else those audiences would want to watch.[37]

You would also be Netflix, the movie rental company that has quickly and readily become one of the most popular and successful streaming content providers. Founded in 1997, Netflix revolutionized the movie rental industry, attracting 81 million subscribers in over 190 countries today.[38] [39] Through careful analysis of its viewers and how they watched shows, it realized that they liked the actor Kevin Spacey, the director David Fincher, and a British political thriller called *House of Cards*. Putting those three elements together meant that Netflix could produce a show that would appeal to a wide range of viewers.

The target market that watches *House of Cards* is male dominant, with most of the show's rating coming from men aged 18–29, followed by those in the 30–44 age bracket.[40] And men talk about the show more online than women do, accounting for 63 percent of social commenting. Still, the show has widespread appeal. Recognizing this, Netflix made sure to target advertisements for it to each specific segment. That is, Spacey's fans, viewing *The Usual Suspects* one more time on Netflix, saw advertisements for *House of Cards* that featured his powerful character. Female subscribers who had given top ratings to movies starring strong female leads instead got a preview of Robin Wright and her powerful lead role. For serious cinemaphiles, the marketing centred on Fincher's risk-taking and daring oeuvre.

As a global company, you might expect Netflix to target anime fans in Japan. But a mere 10 percent of Japanese consumers stream anime. Most of the people who watch anime live all around the world. Whatever shows your neighbours have been binge watching may have no correlation whatsoever to your own interests. That means when segmenting markets, geography is not that important to Netflix. Based on its global algorithm, the "titles you're shown when you sign onto Netflix are just as likely to be influenced by someone from Abu Dhabi as Des Moines."[41] And so, Netflix's algorithms ignore things like geography, gender, and age. Instead, it focuses on what its consumers like, segments these interests into clusters, and shows people 40 to 50 options that match those interests.

Part of the reason Netflix has been able to establish clear appeals for different segments of customers stemmed from the categorization it already had in place. To help recommend movies to its customers, Netflix has created approximately 79,000 categories of movie types—not just "New Releases" but also "Witty Romantic Independent Comedies," "Dark Thrillers Based on Books," or "Understated Movies. But just because you once watched a romantic comedy doesn't mean you will forever be shown "Rom-Com" options.

The results of Netflix's careful data analysis and precise targeting are impressive—especially for a company that just a few short years ago seemed to be offering things customers most certainly did not want. For example, its efforts to separate its DVD-by-mail service from its streaming videos in the United States prompted customers to complain bitterly. The company's CEO, Reed Hastings, ultimately admitted fault and begged forgiveness, but it was a notable stumble, and one he vowed not to make again.

Through remarkably precise and careful assessments, Netflix is the source for 37 percent of the streaming done by North American households during peak hours.[42] That is, of everyone in North America streaming content of any kind, more than one in every three is watching something on Netflix. But the company knows that customers can be fickle. When faced with something they don't like, adults just switch to another entertainment offering. Children, in contrast, have fewer options and less room to switch. As a result, Netflix's original content features an offering developed in cooperation with DreamWorks Animation to target youthful audiences explicitly.

The *Turbo: F.A.S.T.* television series was launched in December 2013, following the release of an animated film about the same character (a snail who gains super speed after being in a freak accident). Season 2 followed in July 2015 and the third season premiered the following year. The deal came after another agreement between DreamWorks and Netflix, in which Netflix purchased the rights to show some of DreamWorks' most well known titles. Around the same time, it also inked an agreement with Disney to access its library—including its recently acquired set of LucasFilm movies.[43]

By appealing to children and their families, Netflix believes it can achieve new levels of customer loyalty. The children themselves are unlikely to switch because Netflix offers them easy access through their parents' iPads or their Wii consoles. Furthermore, few parents are willing to incur their children's wrath by cancelling their Netflix subscription, when Netflix offers those children some of their favourite shows and movies.

Although the company got its start in the mail order video rental business, and took 10 years to stream its first video, today Netflix positions itself on market leadership as the first truly global content network.[44]

## Questions

1. Based on your experience, would Netflix be able to use "the birds of a feather" approach to segmenting markets of young students? Why or why not?

2. Describe the type of segmentation strategy Netflix uses. Provide support for your answer.

3. Why doesn't a conventional segmentation approach based on demographics and geographic bases work well for Netflix?

4. What targeting strategy should Netflix use when it launches in new countries (e.g., differentiated, undifferentiated, etc.)?

5. How could Netflix adapt its advertising to reflect different cultures when targeting Canada's growing ethnic population?

# CHAPTER 7

## LEARNING OBJECTIVES

**After studying this chapter you should be able to**

**LO1** Identify the five steps in the marketing research process

**LO2** Describe the various secondary data sources

**LO3** Describe primary data collection techniques and summarize the differences between secondary data and primary data

**LO4** Outline ethical issues firms encounter when conducting marketing research

# Marketing Research

When used in games and movies, virtual reality allows people to participate in scenarios they might never encounter in daily life. Special 3D glasses and realistically rendered images create the sensation of "being there"—whether "there" is participating in a military operation, climbing Mt. Everest, or playing a challenging game of tennis. When applied to marketing research, this same technology provides manufacturers with valuable information about how consumers are likely to respond to new products and product displays. Used properly, virtual shopping tools provide more accurate information about customer behaviours than traditional research methods and are more efficient than field testing.[1]

Virtual store testing is not especially new. Companies such as Procter & Gamble (P&G) have been using these tools to conduct market research for more than a decade.[2] But as the technology has evolved, P&G's reliance on it to create, test, and improve package designs, shelf displays, and store layouts has increased.[3] Today, more than three-quarters of global manufacturers' business initiatives rely on virtual solution tools.

For P&G, virtual reality centres on life-sized, 3D images of new products as they might appear on a retailer's shelves, which helps create a fully interactive world. As consumers peruse the shelves, sophisticated software analyzes their reactions, providing insight into common responses to packaging and messaging. Product development teams use this information to make improvements early in the design process, which in turn increases the speed to market, reduces the number of costly physical prototypes, and maximizes the chances of success when the product actually goes live.

The technology also allows P&G to create virtual store environments for analyzing product placement strategies. Marketing researchers supply retailers with information and customer feedback from these tests to help them improve customer satisfaction and build sales. The approach can be used for a single product, such as a new type of fabric refresher aimed at sports enthusiasts. Or it can be used to research an entire line of new products in a private environment, which enables an innovating firm to protect its strategic marketing decisions from snooping competitors.[4]

Today's refinements in virtual reality for marketing research are making the software easier to use for both business decision makers and communicators. The technology has also evolved to provide remarkably realistic graphics and interactivity, which improve insights into consumer responses.[5] Such advanced forms of market research are helping firms like Procter & Gamble understand how to serve their customers and business partners better. And better service means better profits. ∎

---

As the P&G example shows, **marketing research** is a key prerequisite to successful decision making; it consists of a set of techniques and principles for systematically collecting, recording, analyzing, and interpreting data that can aid decision makers involved in marketing goods, services, or ideas.[6] When marketing managers attempt to develop their strategies, marketing research can provide valuable information that will help them make segmentation, positioning, product, place, price, and promotion decisions. Marketing research is also key to understanding topics such as competitive intelligence (Chapter 3); consumer and B2B buying behaviour (Chapters 4 and 5); global marketing and cultural differences (Chapter 17); and new product development, branding, and customer service (Chapters 8, 9, and 10). It is also important for assessing the effectiveness of pricing, promotions, and product and service delivery strategies (Chapters 11, 12, 13, 14, and 15).

This chapter discusses the five steps in the marketing research process. Then, we evaluate the various types of data used in marketing research, and data collection methods. We will also examine the circumstances under which it is ethical to collect and use customer information in marketing research.

In Chapter 3, we discussed why firms need **competitive intelligence**. Firms invest millions of dollars in marketing research every year, and Canada's market research industry is valued at just under a half-billion dollars. Some of the major players in Canada's multi-million dollar market research and polling industry include the Angus Reid Institute, COMPAS, Harris/Decima, EKOS Research Associates, Ipsos-Reid, Léger Marketing, Pollara Strategic Insights, and the Strategic Counsel. In addition, there are foreign-owned firms with offices in Canada, such as Nielsen Canada and Forrester Research. Why do marketers find this research valuable? First, it helps reduce some of the uncertainty under which they currently operate. Successful managers know when research might help their decision making and take appropriate steps to acquire the information they need. Second, marketing research provides a crucial link between firms and their environments, which enables firms to be customer oriented because they build their strategies by using customer input and continual feedback. Third, by constantly monitoring their competitors, firms can anticipate and respond quickly to

**marketing research**
A set of techniques and principles for systematically collecting, recording, analyzing, and interpreting data that can aid decision makers involved in marketing goods, services, or ideas.

**competitive intelligence (CI)**
Used by firms to collect and synthesize information about their position with respect to their rivals; enables companies to anticipate changes in the marketplace rather than merely react to them.

Politicians and non-profit organizations do research to understand their constituencies.

Chris Batson/Alamy Stock Photo

**customer lifetime value (CLV)**
The expected financial contribution from a particular customer to the firm's profits over the course of their relationship.

competitive moves. Fourth, ongoing marketing research can identify emerging opportunities and new and improved ways of satisfying consumer needs and wants from changes in the external environment.

If you think market research is applicable only to corporate or retailing ventures, think again. Non-profit organizations and governments also use research to serve their constituencies better. Political parties have been slicing and dicing the voting public for decades to determine relevant messages for different demographics. Politicians desperately want to understand who makes up the voting public to determine how to reach them. They want to know not only your political views but also your media habits, such as what magazines you subscribe to, so they can target you more effectively. To do so, they rely on the five-step marketing research process we describe in this chapter. We also discuss some of the ethical implications of collecting and using information. In Appendix 7A, we detail the concept of **customer lifetime value (CLV)**, a popular metric to determine a customer's value to a firm.

## L01    THE MARKETING RESEARCH PROCESS

Managers consider several factors before embarking on a marketing research project. First, will the research be useful and provide insights beyond what the managers already know and reduce uncertainty associated with the project? Second, is top management committed to the project and willing to abide by the results of the research? Related to both of these questions is the value of the research. Marketing research can be very expensive, and if the results won't be useful or management does not abide by the findings, it represents a waste of money. Third, should the marketing research project be small or large? A project might involve a simple analysis of data that the firm already has, or it could be an in-depth assessment that costs hundreds of thousands of dollars and takes months to complete.

The marketing research process itself consists of five steps, as shown in Exhibit 7.1. Although the stages of the marketing research process are shown as a step-by-step progression, of course, research doesn't always happen this way. Sometimes, researchers

**EXHIBIT 7.1    The Marketing Research Process**

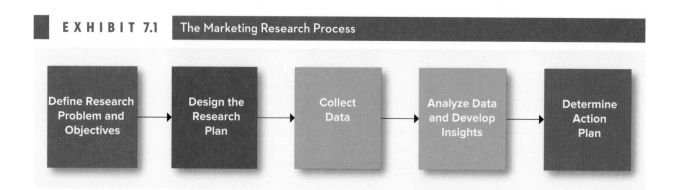

go back and forth from one step to another as the need arises. For example, marketers may establish a specific research objective, which they follow with data collection and preliminary analysis. If they uncover new information during the data collection step or if the findings of the analysis spotlight new research needs, they might redefine their objectives and begin again from a new starting point. A major automobile manufacturer once set out to identify consumer responses to its new company logo, only to discover in preliminary focus groups that some of the respondents thought the company had gone out of business! Clearly, those researchers had to regroup and set out in a different direction with an entirely different objective.

Before embarking on a research project, it is important to plan the entire project in advance. When setting up a questionnaire, marketers should consider the data collection process and anticipate the types of analyses that might produce meaningful results for decision makers. For example, open-ended questions on a questionnaire can slow down the coding process and make it difficult to run some sophisticated statistical analyses. If the decision makers want a sophisticated analysis fast, a questionnaire filled with open-ended questions may not be the best choice. By planning the entire research process well in advance of starting the project, researchers can avoid unnecessary alterations to the research plan as they move through the process. Now let's examine each step of the research process in more detail.

## Step 1: Define the Research Problem and Objectives

Because research is both expensive and time consuming, it is important to establish in advance exactly what problem needs to be solved. Correctly defining the problem is one of the most important elements of the marketing research process. To underscore the importance of this first step, some marketing researchers claim that this aspect is the most difficult of the marketing research process. Why? It's like the "iceberg principle." While the tip may look obvious, much of the iceberg (or the cause of the problem) may not be easily visible. If you define the problem incorrectly, you will more than likely end up with the wrong solution even though the rest of the process is done perfectly. On the contrary, if you define the problem correctly but fail to carry out the rest of the process correctly, you may end up with misleading or even useless results.

Once the research problem is defined, marketers must specify the research objectives or questions to be answered. Marketing research efforts and resources can be wasted if the research objectives are poorly defined.[7] Poor design arises from three major sources: basing research on irrelevant research questions, focusing on research questions that marketing research cannot answer, or addressing research questions to which the answers are already known.

Consider the following scenario: McDonald's wants a better understanding of its customers' experience. It also needs to understand how customers view the experience at Wendy's, a main competitor. McDonald's hopes to gain some insight into how it should set a price for and market its latest combo meal of a hamburger, fries, and drink. Finally, McDonald's is considering ways to address concerns that its breakfast service ends before noon. Any one of these questions could initiate a research project. The complexity of the project that the company eventually undertakes depends on how much time and resources it has available, as well as the amount of in-depth knowledge it needs. Research objectives are driven by business issues that companies want to examine, and a wide variety of testing methods and inputs can be used, as shown in Exhibit 7.2.

When conducting research, it's also important to separate the symptoms of a problem from the actual problem. For example, Pria, the owner of a small clothing store in downtown Ottawa that caters to girls between the ages of 10 and 16, thought that the declining sales she was observing in her store were due to inadequate or poor advertising. She increased her advertising and promotions to boost sales and regain her lost customers. Unfortunately, this effort provided only temporary benefits, and the declining

| EXHIBIT 7.2 | Research Objectives | | |
|---|---|---|---|
| **Business Issue** | **Research Objectives** | **Testing Method** | **Inputs Needed** |
| Evaluate new launch idea | Gain consumer feedback on new product ideas Can also be used to evaluate changes to an existing product | Concept testing | Product concepts including image and description, group of qualified consumers |
| Evaluate new flavour of cereal against other flavours | Measure consumer purchase intent for new launch with actual live product in a central, controlled environment | Central location test (CLT) | Product concepts including image and description, control product samples, new product samples, group of qualified consumers |
| Test new flavour of cookies or a new formulation of laundry detergent | Measure consumer purchase intent for new launch with actual live product in their typical daily life | Home usage test (HUT) | Product concepts including image and description, actual product samples, group of qualified consumers |
| Measure the effect of a major product change, like branding or significant downsizing | Quantitatively measure product appeal before and after the change May also include qualitative feedback on specific areas | Restager research | Product concepts for current and new product, including image and description, group of qualified consumers |
| Predict success of new packaging design | Measure consumer purchase intent for and appeal of packaging redesign | Packaging testing | Product packaging including current and new designs, group of qualified consumers |
| Assess consumer attitudes and behaviours on a particular category such as snack foods | Understand consumer opinions and self-reported behaviours on a category of products: what they choose and avoid, why, when, where, and how it is consumed | Usage and attitude study | Formal questionnaire, group of qualified consumers |
| Map out how a consumer shops the dairy aisle in a grocery store | Collect real-time observations of an individual in your specific target market performing a specific task | Live consumer immersion | Discussion guide, moderator, consumer (one at a time) |
| Evaluate new idea for communications campaign | Gain qualitative feedback on a small number of topics; for example, determine preference between Campaign A and B A moderator will guide the discussion but the participants are free to give any feedback they'd like | Focus group | Discussion guide, advertising samples, moderator, focus group participants (4–10 at a time) |

sales continued after the promotions ended. After hiring a marketing researcher, Pria realized that the declining sales were just a symptom of the real problem: outdated merchandise. She learned that the current target market of 10- to 16-year-olds is quite different from their predecessors, the girls who were this age when Pria first opened her store.

## Step 2: Design the Research Plan

After researchers have defined the problem to be addressed, the second step is to design the market research plan. In this step, researchers identify the type of data needed and determine the type of research necessary to collect it. Recall that the objectives of the project drive the type of data needed, as outlined in Step 1. Let's look at how this second step works using the McDonald's customer experience. McDonald's needs to ask its customers about their McDonald's experience. However, because people don't always tell the whole truth in surveys, the company also may want to observe customers to see how they actually enter the stores, interact with employees, and consume the product.

The project's design might begin with available data, such as information that shows how many customers arrive at 10:45 a.m. asking for breakfast items, or that people with children often come into the restaurants at lunchtime and order Happy Meals. Then McDonald's market researchers can start to ask customers specific questions about their McDonald's experience.

## Step 3: Collect Data

Data collection begins only after the research design process. Based on the design of the project, data can be collected from secondary or primary data sources. **Secondary data** are pieces of information that have been collected prior to the start of the focal research project. Secondary data include both external and internal data sources. **Primary data**, in contrast, are those data collected to address specific research needs. Some common primary data collection methods include focus groups, in-depth interviews, and surveys. More discussion on secondary and primary data follows later in the chapter.

For our hypothetical fast-food scenario, McDonald's may decide to get relevant secondary data from external providers such as National Purchase Diary Panel and Nielsen. The data might include the prices of different ingredients, sales figures, growth or decline in the category, and advertising and promotional spending. McDonald's is likely to gather pertinent data about sales from its franchisees. However, it also wants competitor data, overall food consumption data, and other information about the quick service restaurant category, which it likely obtains from appropriate syndicated data providers. Based on the data, it might decide to follow up with some primary data using a survey.

McDonald's assesses its customers' market experience by examining available data, and then asks customers about their experience with products like Happy Meals.

Michael Neelon(misc)/Alamy Stock Photo

No company can ask every customer their opinions or observe every customer, so researchers must choose a group of customers who represent the customers of interest, or a sample, and then generalize their opinions to describe all customers with the same characteristics. They may choose the sample participants at random to represent the entire customer market. Or they may choose to select the sample on the basis of some characteristic, such as whether they have children, so they can research the experience associated with buying a Happy Meal.

Marketing researchers use various methods of asking questions to measure the issues they are tackling. Different types of scales are used to measure certain concepts such as attitudes, perceived quality, perceived value, loyalty, and convenience. In our hypothetical McDonald's scenario, assume the research team has developed a questionnaire (see Exhibit 7.3), using a few different types of questions. Section A measures the customer's experience in McDonald's, Section B measures the customer's experience in Wendy's, Section C measures the customer's habits at McDonald's, and Section D measures customer demographics.[8]

Furthermore, suppose the research team administered the survey to 1000 customers. The results of the first question, "McDonald's food tastes good," were as follows:

**secondary data**
Pieces of information that have been collected prior to the start of the focal project.

**primary data**
Data collected to address the specific research needs/questions currently under investigation. Some primary data collection methods include focus groups, in-depth interviews, and surveys.

| 1 | 2 | 3 | 4 | 5 |
|---|---|---|---|---|
| **Strongly Disagree** | **Disagree** | **Neither Agree nor Disagree** | **Agree** | **Strongly Agree** |
| N = 50 | N = 50 | N = 100 | N = 300 | N = 500 |

Their responses are indicated by "N = ." Marketers could report several metrics, but two common metrics would be that 80 percent [(300 + 500)/1,000] of respondents had high satisfaction since they responded to "Agree" or "Strongly Agree." It could also be reported that satisfaction was high because the mean was 4.15 [(50 × 1 + 50 × 2 + 100 × 3 + 300 × 4 + 500 × 5)/1,000] on the 5-point scale.

**EXHIBIT 7.3**    A Hypothetical Fast-Food Survey

Please take a few minutes to tell us about your experience at McDonald's and Wendy's. For each question, please respond by checking the box that applies or writing your response in the space provided.

## Please Evaluate Your Experience

### A. McDonald's

| | Strongly Disagree 1 | Disagree 2 | Neither Agree nor Disagree 3 | Agree 4 | Strongly Agree 5 |
|---|---|---|---|---|---|
| McDonald's food tastes good | ☐ | ☐ | ☐ | ☑ | ☐ |
| McDonald's is clean | ☐ | ☐ | ☐ | ☑ | ☐ |
| McDonald's has low prices | ☐ | ☐ | ☐ | ☑ | ☐ |

### B. Wendy's

| | Strongly Disagree 1 | Disagree 2 | Neither Agree nor Disagree 3 | Agree 4 | Strongly Agree 5 |
|---|---|---|---|---|---|
| Wendy's food tastes good | ☐ | ☐ | ☐ | ☑ | ☐ |
| Wendy's is clean | ☐ | ☐ | ☐ | ☑ | ☐ |
| Wendy's has low prices | ☐ | ☐ | ☐ | ☑ | ☐ |

### C. McDonald's

| | Never | 1–2 times | 3–4 times | More than 5 times |
|---|---|---|---|---|
| In the last month, how many times have you been to McDonald's? How often did you order breakfast items? | ☐ | ☐ | ☐ | ☑ |

If McDonald's offered breakfast items all the time, how often would you order them outside of normal breakfast times in a typical month?    ☐

On average, how much do you spend during each visit to McDonald's?    $ _____

What is your favourite item at McDonald's?    _____

## D. Please Tell Us About Yourself

| | under 16 | 17–24 | 25–35 | 36+ |
|---|---|---|---|---|
| What is your age? | ☐ | ☐ | ☐ | ☐ |

| | Male | Female | | |
|---|---|---|---|---|
| What is your gender? | ☐ | ☐ | | |

## Step 4: Analyze Data and Develop Insights

The next step in the marketing research process—analyzing and interpreting the data—should be both thorough and methodical. To generate meaningful information, researchers analyze and make use of the collected data. In this context, **data** can be defined as raw numbers or other pieces of factual information that, on their own, have limited value to marketers. However, when the data are interpreted, they become **information**, which results from organizing, analyzing, and interpreting the data, and putting it into a form that is useful to marketing decision makers. For example, a checkout scanner in a grocery store collects sales data about individual consumer purchases. Not until those data are categorized and examined do they provide information about which products and services were purchased together or how an in-store promotional activity translated into sales.

For example, a cologne producer learns from secondary data sources that its product is priced lower than its competition, it spends more money on traditional advertising in fashion magazines, and it is slowly losing market share to a new upstart competitor. Putting these disparate data points together provides information that indicates the need to find out what is so good about the competitor's new cologne. The firm commissions a series of focus groups, which is useful in developing a survey of users of its cologne and of its competitor. The survey provides conclusive information that the firm uses to change its strategy. In particular, it found that its product's scent was a little too strong and wasn't as appealing to its younger target market. It also discovered that peers have a tremendous influence on scent preferences. So the company decided to tone down the scent and reapportion its promotional budget to include more innovative social media initiatives through Facebook, Snapchat, and YouTube. Data analysis might be as simple as calculating the average purchases of different customer segments or as complex as forecasting sales by market segment by using elaborate statistical techniques.

For the McDonald's example, we can summarize the results of the survey (from Exhibit 7.3) in Exhibit 7.4. McDonald's and Wendy's scored approximately the same on the cleanliness of the restaurant, but McDonald's had lower prices, while Wendy's food tasted better. McDonald's may want to improve the taste of its food to better compete with Wendy's.

The purpose of converting data to information is to describe, explain, predict, and/or evaluate a particular situation and then use it to develop insights. For example, Pria, the downtown Ottawa-based retailer of tween clothing, learned that her core customers live in various suburbs around downtown. This piece of data takes on new meaning when she learns that none of these customers were drawn to her store by a clever and expensive direct mail campaign. By analyzing data she collected through a survey,

**data**
Raw numbers or other factual information of limited value.

**information**
Data that has been organized, analyzed, interpreted, and converted into a useful form for decision makers.

**EXHIBIT 7.4**  Survey Results for McDonald's and Wendy's

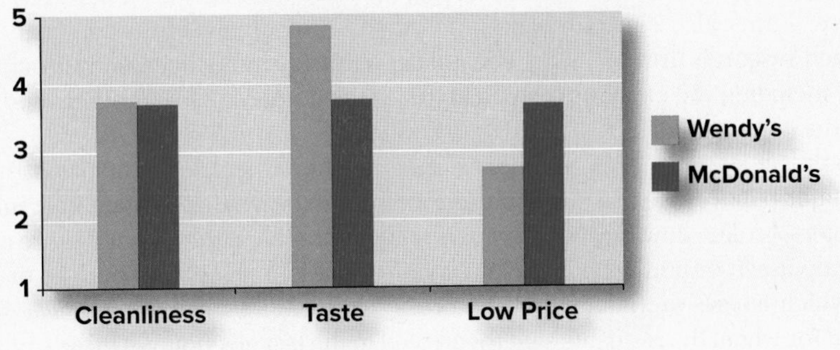

she discovered that her core customers are working professionals who are drawn to the store when they walk by it on their way to and from work, not people from the upscale apartments in the downtown region whom she targeted with her direct mail advertisements.

It is important for market researchers to analyze and interpret the data in an objective manner. They should not try to hide or sugar-coat findings that are different from what they had hoped for. Misinterpreting the findings or manipulating the statistics to suit the researcher's hunch or prediction could lead to the wrong decision, which could have serious consequences for marketers. The temptation to lie with statistics is something market researchers must always be aware of and try to avoid.

## Step 5: Determine the Action Plan

In the final phase of the marketing research process, the analyst prepares the results and presents them to decision makers, who undertake appropriate marketing actions and strategies. A typical marketing research presentation includes an executive summary, the body of the report (which discusses the research objectives, methodology used, and detailed findings), the conclusions, the limitations, and appropriate supplemental tables, figures, and appendices. To be effective, written reports must be short, interesting, methodical, precise, lucid, and free of errors.[9] Furthermore, the reports should use a style appropriate to the audience, be devoid of technical jargon, and include recommendations that managers can actually implement.

Let's go back to the hypothetical McDonald's scenario. According to the research findings, the company is doing fine in terms of cleanliness (as are its competitors), it is perceived to have lower prices, and the taste of its food could be improved. It also found that of those customers who purchased breakfast items relatively frequently (at least three times per month), 35 percent would go for breakfast outside the normal breakfast times frequently. Also, of those who never ordered breakfast items, 25 percent would order breakfast items outside the normal breakfast times occasionally (at least once a month). Using this analysis and insights gained, McDonald's might consider hiring gourmet chefs as consultants to improve the menu and offer breakfast items 24/7 on a trial basis. It could highlight its efforts to improve the taste of the food and add desired offerings (e.g., breakfast items) in its marketing communications and promotions. McDonald's should also consider performing additional pricing research to determine whether its lower prices are positively impacting sales and profits, or whether it should price more competitively with Wendy's. Now let's take a closer look at sources of secondary and primary data.

## L02   SECONDARY DATA

A marketing research project often begins with a review of the relevant secondary data. Secondary data might come from free or very inexpensive external sources such as census data, information from trade associations, books, journal articles, and reports published in magazines and newspapers. Although readily accessible, these inexpensive sources may not be specific or timely enough to solve the marketer's research needs and objectives. Firms also can purchase more specific or applicable secondary data from specialized research firms. Finally, secondary sources can be accessed through internal sources, including the company's sales invoices, customer lists, and other reports generated by the company itself.

In political settings, such secondary data can be critical for candidates running for office. Major political parties develop proprietary databases that contain vast information about voters, broken down by demographic and geographic information. Before a local politician, canvasser, or poll taker even knocks on doors in a neighbourhood, he or she likely knows which houses are inhabited by retirees, who has a subscription to *The Globe and Mail*, and for whom the residents said they voted in the last election. All these traits can give hints about the voters' likely concerns, which a good politician can address immediately upon knocking on the door. Information gleaned can be documented in a database so lists can be generated later. For example, households may be noted as friendly but not supporting the party in an upcoming election because they don't like its record on the environment. If the party makes announcements regarding the environment, it can reach out to people in its database to ensure they are informed. Such research also can dictate tactics for designing broader campaign materials, or zero in on very specific issues. Social media campaigns are a growing mechanism used to interact with potential voters in a more timely manner than more traditional methods. Monitoring tweets after a major address by a candidate, for instance, would provide instant feedback and direction for future communications.

**Internal Secondary Data**   One of the most valuable resources firms have at their disposal is their rich cache of customer information and purchase history. However, it can be difficult to make sense of the millions or even billions of pieces of individual data, which are stored in large computer files called data warehouses. For this reason, firms find it necessary to use data-mining techniques to extract valuable information from their databases.

**Data mining** uses a variety of statistical analysis tools to uncover previously unknown patterns in the data or relationships among variables. Some retailers try to customize their product and service offerings to match the needs of their customers. For instance, the U.K. grocer Tesco uses its loyalty card to collect massive amounts of information about its individual customers. Every time a loyalty card member buys something, the card is scanned, and the store captures key purchase data specific to that member. But these specific data are basically useless until Tesco mines and analyzes them to identify three income groups: upscale, middle income, and less affluent. With this mined information, Tesco has been able to create appealing private-label product offerings for each group, according to their preferences, and began targeting promotions to each customer according to his or her income classification.

Marketers use data-mining techniques to determine what items people buy at the same time so they can be promoted and displayed together.

B2M Productions/Photographer's Choice/Getty Images RF

**data mining**
The use of statistical analysis tools to search for patterns in data or relationships among variables.

If you watch content on Netflix, your viewing habits become valuable data that are added to a global database and mined for insights. The algorithm at the core of the Netflix software records every action subscribers take, allowing the company to analyze what content you watch, at what time of day, and how much you watch at a given time. Correlations can then be established (for example, between actors and movies, movie genres, or actors themselves) and used to make recommendations to subscribers. The software also identifies what scenes in an episode or movie are watched the most, and if scenes get skipped, which can then be compared to user reviews and ratings. Although collecting data from one person would not prove very helpful, a wealth of data can be mined from 81 million subscribers.

Data mining can also enable a home improvement retailer such as Lowe's to learn that, 25 percent of the time, customers buying a garden hose also purchase a sprinkler. With such information, the retailer may decide to put the garden hoses next to the sprinklers in the store. Outside the retail realm, an investment firm might use statistical techniques to group clients according to their income, age, types of securities purchased, and prior investment experience. This categorization identifies different segments to which the firm can offer valuable packages that meet their specific needs. The firm also can tailor separate marketing programs to each of these segments. Data mining thus can be useful for a broad range of situations and organizations. By analyzing the enormous amount of information that they possess about their customers, companies have developed statistical models that help identify when a customer is dissatisfied with his or her service. Once the company identifies an unhappy customer, it can follow up and proactively address that customer's issues. By mining customer data and information, the company also reduces its churn levels. *Churn* is the number of participants who discontinue use of a service, divided by the average number of total participants.

Overall, firms hope to use data mining to generate customer-based analytics that they can apply to their strategic decision making, and thereby make good customers better, and make better customers their best. Firms can also use secondary data to assess the profitability of their customers by determining the customer lifetime value (CLV). We offer more details about calculating CLV in Appendix 7A.

**big data**

Refers to extremely large quantities of data that companies have access to but are unable to handle using conventional data management and data mining software.

**Big Data** The field of marketing research has seen enormous changes in the last few years because of (1) the increase in the amounts of data to which retailers, service providers, and manufacturers have access; (2) their ability to collect these data from transactions, customer relationship management (CRM) systems, websites, and social media platforms that firms increasingly use to engage with their customers;[10] (3) the ease of collecting and storing these data; (4) the computing ability readily available to manipulate data in real time; and (5) access to in-house or available software to convert the data into valuable decision-making insights using analytic dashboards.

To specify this explosion of data, which firms have access to but cannot handle using conventional data management and data mining software, the term **big data** has arisen in the popular media. Leading firms such as Amazon, Netflix, Google, Nordstrom, Tesco, American Express, and Walmart are already converting their big data into customer insights, and this list keeps growing.[11]

Amazon may be the poster child for big data. Any Amazon shopper is familiar with its recommendation engine, which notes what the consumer is purchasing, analyzes purchase patterns by similar customers, and suggests other items the customer might enjoy, as well as what other people who bought the focal item also added to their shopping carts.[12] With more than 200 million active customers and billions of pieces of shopping data,[13] Amazon certainly qualifies as a big data user; its item-to-item collaborative filtering helps it determine which relevant products to suggest, generating almost one-third of its sales.[14]

To enable these efforts, firms such as SAP, Splunk, and GoodData offer a host of software solutions to help firms better integrate their data, visualize them, and then move from data to real-time insights.[15] The suite of options previously were available only to the largest firms, but with costs falling they are now more accessible to smaller firms.

The big data explosion also stems from the growth of online and social media. In response, Google, Facebook, and Twitter all provide analytic dashboards designed to help their customers understand their own web traffic. In particular, Google has developed tremendous marketing analytical capabilities that it makes available to partner firms. Google helps firms attract customer traffic to their sites through the use of more relevant keywords, the purchase of Google AdWords, and better conversion methods.[16] Using Google Analytics, Puma has gained insights into which online content and products most engaged its web visitors, while also defining where these visitors lived. With these visitor behavioural data in hand, Puma has revised its website to be more dynamic (http://www.puma.com) and has created unique identifiers for its various product categories (e.g., PUMA Golf), targeting them in accordance with the home region of the visitor.[17]

### External Secondary Data

Some sources of external secondary data can be accessed quickly and at relatively low cost. For example, Statistics Canada data on retail trade provides information about sales of different types of retail establishments either free or inexpensively. These patterns may be the only accurate sources available to a new small business that wants to determine the size of its potential market. For such a firm, gathering accurate and comprehensive data on its own would be quite difficult. Researchers must ensure that the secondary data they use, especially from external sources, are

**EXHIBIT 7.5**  Sample List of Sources for Secondary Data[18]

**Guides, Indexes, and Directories**
*Business Periodicals Index*
*Canadian Almanac and Directory*
*Canadian News Index*
*Canadian Periodical Index*
*Canadian Small Business Index and Directory*
*Canadian Trade Index*
*Directory of Canadian Associations*
*Fraser's Canadian Trade Directory*
*Predicasts F&S Index*
*Scott's Directories*
*Standard Periodical Directory*

**Periodicals and Newspapers**
*Advertising Age*
*Adweek*
*American Demographics*
*Business Horizons*
*Canadian Business*
*Canadian Consumer*
*Canadian Grocer*
*Financial Post*
*Financial Post Magazine*
*Forbes*
*Fortune*
*The Globe and Mail*
*Harvard Business Review*
*Journal of Advertising*
*Journal of Marketing Management*
*Journal of Personal Selling and Sales Management*
*Journal of Small Business Management*
*Marketing Magazine*
*Marketing & Media Decisions*
*Marketing News*
*Sales and Marketing Management*
*The Wall Street Journal*

**Databases**
CANSIM (Statistics Canada)
CompuServe
Dialog
Dow Jones
Factiva
FPinfomart
Infoglobe
LexisNexis
SEDAR
SymphonyIRI Group

**Statistics Canada and Other Government Publications**
*Annual Retail Trade*
*Canadian Economic Observer*
*Canada Yearbook*
*Family Expenditure Guide*
*Market Research Handbook*
*Statistics Canada Catalogue*
Western Economic Diversification Canada
Ontario Ministry for Economic Development and Trade
Department of Foreign Affairs and Trade
U.S. Census
Stat-USA

**Trade Sources**
Aberdeen Research
Nielsen
Conference Board of Canada
Dun & Bradstreet Canada
Financial Post Publishing
Find/SVP
Gale Research
Interactive Advertising Bureau
Jupiter Research
Forrester Research
MacLean Hunter Research Bureau
MapInfo Canada
Predicasts International

**Online Sources**
Websites of competitors
White papers from industry associations
Search engines
Industry publication websites
Competitive annual reports
Business and strategy sites
(e.g., http://www.canadianbusiness.com)
News alerts and online news searches
(e.g., Google Alerts)
Finance sites for publicly traded companies
(e.g., Yahoo! Finance)
Wikipedia (Always validate data from here!)
The Free Library (http://www.thefreelibrary.com)

current and relevant, and can shed light on the research problem or objectives. More examples of external secondary data are listed in Exhibits 7.5 and 7.6.

Sometimes, however, secondary data are not adequate to meet researchers' needs. Because the data initially were acquired for some purpose other than the research question at hand, they may not be completely relevant. For instance, Statistics Canada's Census is a great source for demographic data about a particular market area, and it can be easily accessed at a low cost. However, the data are collected only every 10 years, so they quickly become outdated. For example, if a firm were interested in opening a retail

| EXHIBIT 7.6 | Syndicated Data Providers in Canada and the United States and Their Services |
| --- | --- |
| Bureau of Broadcasting Measurement (http://bbm.ca) | Provides broadcast measurement and consumer behaviour data, as well as intelligence to broadcasters, advertisers, and agencies on audience behaviours during and after broadcasts. |
| GfK Mediamark Research Inc. (http://www.gfkmri.com) | Supplies multimedia audience research pertaining to media and marketing planning for advertised brands. |
| GfK NOP (http://www.gfknop.com) | The mKids US research study tracks mobile telephone ownership and usage, brand affinities, and entertainment habits of American youth between 12 and 19 years of age. |
| Ipsos Canada, Harris/Decima, Léger Marketing, Angus Reid, SES Research, EKOS Research Associates, The Strategic Counsel, Pollara, and COMPAS | Provides polling services and marketing research on all aspects of marketing, including loyalty, branding, media analysis, pricing, position, image enhancement, customer satisfaction, focus groups, online panels, and surveys across many industries. |
| J.D. Power and Associates (http://www.jdpower.com) | Widely known for its automotive ratings, the company produces quality and customer satisfaction research for a variety of industries. |
| National Purchase Diary Group (http://www.npd.com) | Tracking services provide information about product movement and consumer behaviour in a variety of industries. |
| Nielsen (http://www.nielsen.com) | With its market measurement services, the company tracks data on the sales of consumer packaged goods, gathered at the point of sale in retail stores of all types and sizes. |
| Print Measurement Bureau (http://www.pmb.ca) | Provides single-source data on print readership, non-print media exposure, product usage, and lifestyles of Canadians. It uses an annual sample of 24,000 to measure the readership of more than 115 publications and consumer usage of more than 2,500 products and brands. |
| Research and Markets (http://www.researchandmarkets.com) | Promotes itself as a "one-stop shop" for market research and data from most leading publishers, consultants, and analysts. |
| Roper Centre for Public Opinion Research (http://www.ropercenter.uconn.edu) | The General Social Survey is one of the United States' longest-running surveys of social, cultural, and political indicators. |
| Simmons Market Research Bureau (http://www.smrb.com) | Reports on the products American consumers buy, the brands they prefer, and their lifestyles, attitudes, and media preferences. |
| Yankelovich (http://www.yankelovich.com) | The MONITOR tracks the consumer attitudes, values, and lifestyles shaping the American marketplace. |

flooring store in 2018, it would have to rely on Statistics Canada Census data collected in 2011, which would be seven years old. If it hoped to locate in an area where housing starts are projected to grow rapidly in the next three to four years, these data would not include any of these new housing developments and thus would not provide much in the way of insights.

Although the secondary data described above is either free or inexpensive and can be quickly accessed, it may not always be adequate to answer the research objective. Under these circumstances, marketers may find it useful to purchase external secondary data called **syndicated data**, which are data available for a fee from commercial research firms such as SymphonyIRI Group, National Purchase Diary Panel, Nielsen, and Léger Marketing. Exhibit 7.6 contains information about various firms that provide syndicated data. For our hypothetical cologne example, the pertinent data available from these sources might include the prices of various colognes, sales figures, growth or decline in the category, and advertising and promotional spending. Consumer packaged-goods

**syndicated data**

Data available for a fee from commercial research firms such as Symphony IRI Group, National Diary Panel, Nielsen, and Léger Marketing.

firms that sell to wholesalers often lack the means to gather pertinent data directly from the retailers that sell their products to consumers, which makes syndicated data a valuable resource for them. Some syndicated data providers also offer information about shifting brand preferences and product usage in households, which they gather from consumer panels.

**Scanner data** are obtained from scanner readings of UPC codes at checkout counters and used in quantitative research. Whenever you go into your local grocery store, your purchases are rung up by using scanner systems. The data from these purchases are likely to be acquired by leading marketing research firms, such as SymphonyIRI Group or Nielsen. They use this information to help leading consumer packaged-goods firms (e.g., Kellogg's, Pepsi, and Kraft) assess what is happening in the marketplace. For example, a firm can determine what happened to sales when it reduced its price by 10 percent in a given month. Did sales increase, decrease, or stay the same?

**Panel data** is information collected from a group of consumers (the panel) over time. The data collected from the panelists often include records of what they have purchased (i.e., secondary data), as well as their responses to survey questions that the client gives to the panel to ask the panelists (i.e., primary data). Secondary panel data thus might show that when Diet Pepsi is offered at a deep discount, 80 percent of usual Diet Coke consumers switch to Diet Pepsi. Primary panel data could give insights into what they think of each option.

Léger Marketing, one of the largest Canadian-owned independent marketing research and polling firms, has an online panel of 350,000 people that represents various consumer segments of the Canadian population. This impressive panel makes it possible for Léger Marketing to complete surveys among the general public and more specific consumer segments. It is therefore hardly surprising that Léger Marketing can offer marketers 48-hour service—a solution for businesses and decision makers who wish to receive reliable information quickly from a large representative sample of consumers regarding their marketing campaigns, products, and brands. Léger Marketing offers its clients strategic advice in a wide array of areas, including media and advertising analysis, marketing planning, market research, product launch, segmentation analysis, positioning, customer satisfaction and loyalty strategies, pricing and packaging strategies, mystery shoppers, and image assessment. It also offers website analytics, which marketers can use to evaluate and improve the performance of their websites.[19]

**scanner data**
A type of quantitative research that uses data obtained from scanner readings of UPC codes at checkout counters.

**panel data**
A type of quantitative research that involves collecting information from a group of consumers (the panel) over time; data collected may be from a survey or a record of purchases.

Syndicated external secondary data are scanner readings of UPC codes at checkout counters (left) and panel data collected from consumers in electronically recording their purchases (right).

(left): Sozaijiten/Datacraft/ Getty Images; (right): Courtesy The Neilsen Co.

Overall though, both panel and scanner data provide firms with a comprehensive picture of what consumers are buying or not buying. The key difference between scanner research and panel research is how the data get aggregated. Scanner research typically focuses on weekly consumption of a particular product at a given unit of analysis (e.g., individual store, chain, region); panel research focuses on the total weekly consumption by a particular person or household. We discuss how marketing researchers use panel data to answer specific research questions further in the primary data section.

Remember, when it comes to secondary data, marketers must pay careful attention to how the secondary data were collected. Despite the great deal of data available on the Internet and elsewhere, easy access does not ensure that the data are trustworthy. Without knowing the research design—for instance, information pertaining to the purpose of the research, sample size, respondents, response rate, questions asked, and so on—researchers could make wrong or misleading inferences or conclusions. The Internet is a huge repository of all sorts of information about consumers, including shopping behaviours, attitudes, perceptions, and even emotions. Marketers are increasingly relying on technologies to mine this data to help them learn more about customers so they can serve them better. In Appendix 7A, we explain how secondary data can be used to assess **customer lifetime value (CLV)**, a popular marketing metric to determine a customer's value to a firm.

**customer lifetime value (CLV)**
The expected financial contribution from a particular customer to the firm's profits over the course of their relationship.

## L03 PRIMARY DATA COLLECTION TECHNIQUES

In many cases, the information researchers need is available only through primary data, or data collected to address the specific research needs/questions currently under investigation. Marketers collect primary data by using a variety of means, such as observing consumer behaviour, conducting focus groups, or surveying customers by using the mail, the telephone, in-person interviews, or the Internet. Primary data collection can help eliminate some of the problems inherent to secondary data. Depending on the nature of the research problem, the primary data collection can use a qualitative or a quantitative approach.

A major advantage of primary research is that it can be tailored to fit the research questions; however, it also has its own set of disadvantages. For one thing, it is usually more costly to collect primary than secondary data, and the collection typically takes longer. Furthermore, marketers often require extensive training and experience to design and collect primary data that are unbiased, valid, and reliable. For a summary of the advantages and disadvantages of each type of research, see Exhibit 7.7. Biased data results when, for example, the sample does not represent the entire population, researchers inject their own biases by the way they ask questions or try to get respondents to answer in specific ways,

**EXHIBIT 7.7** Advantages and Disadvantages of Secondary and Primary Research

| Type | Examples | Advantages | Disadvantages |
|---|---|---|---|
| **Secondary Research** | • Census data<br>• Sales invoices<br>• Internet information<br>• Books<br>• Journal articles<br>• Syndicated data | • Saves time in collecting data because they are readily available<br>• Reduces data collection costs | • Information may not be precisely relevant to information needs<br>• Information may not be as timely as needed<br>• Sources may not be original; therefore, usefulness is an issue<br>• Methodologies for collecting data may not be relevant or may contain bias in the subject matter |
| **Primary Research** | • Observed consumer behaviour<br>• Focus groups<br>• In-depth interviews<br>• Surveys<br>• Experiments | • Is specific to the immediate data needs and topic at hand<br>• Offers behavioural insights generally not available from secondary research | • Information is usually more costly to collect<br>• Data typically takes longer to collect<br>• It often requires more sophisticated training and experience to design and collect unbiased, valid, and reliable data |

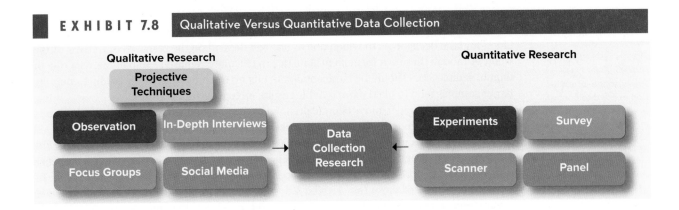

**EXHIBIT 7.8**     Qualitative Versus Quantitative Data Collection

or the respondents may be the wrong people or provide answers they think researchers want to hear.

Exploratory in nature, **qualitative research** attempts to begin to understand the phenomenon of interest; it also provides initial information that helps the researcher more clearly formulate the research problem or objectives. Qualitative research is more informal than quantitative research methods and includes observation, following social media sites, in-depth interviews, focus groups, and projective techniques (see Exhibit 7.8).

Data collection through primary research requires that the researcher make several important decisions, including which methods to use (see Exhibit 7.8 for a list of methods), what types of sampling plans are best in light of the research objective, what types of research instruments (e.g., questionnaire, observation) to use, how the research instrument should be designed (described below), and how best to contact potential respondents (telephone, online, in person, or by mail). Improper execution of any of these important aspects of primary data collection could seriously reduce the reliability and validity of the research study.

Simply put, **reliability** is the extent to which you will get the same result if the study is repeated in identical situations.[20] For example, on a Saturday in August, you randomly stop shoppers in a mall and ask them to fill out a short questionnaire about why they shop at that particular mall. Let's say your data analysis shows that they shop at that mall because they get very good deals. Now, if you were to repeat the study in the same mall, using the same questionnaire, on another Saturday, and randomly ask shoppers to fill out the questionnaire, you should find the same result: people shop at the mall because they get good deals. If you found otherwise, then the reliability of your study is called into question. **Validity** is the extent to which the study actually measures what it is supposed to measure.[21] For example, suppose you want to measure consumers' trust in online retailers by using a questionnaire. Validity seeks to determine whether the questions you asked on the questionnaire actually measure online trust or if they measure some other construct. It is important to note that a market research study must be both reliable and valid for it to be useful.

One very important aspect of market research that can affect the reliability and validity of a study is the sampling plan. Often it is too difficult, impractical, or costly to study the entire group of consumers, so marketers usually select a **sample**, a segment or subset of the population that adequately represents the entire population of interest. For example, if you are interested in studying the loyalty of Canadian teenage boys to brand-name clothing, then your population is all Canadian teenage boys and your sample is the small subset of boys selected for your study. How you select the sample is also very important. Three important questions that must be answered are (1) who should be surveyed, (2) how big should the sample be, and (3) what types of sampling procedures should be used; for example, simple random sampling (uses a subset of a statistical population with each person having the equal probability to be selected), convenience sampling (subjects are selected on the basis of accessibility and proximity to the researcher), stratified sampling (the population is divided

**qualitative research**
Attempts to begin to understand the phenomenon of interest; also provides initial information when the problem lacks any clear definition.

**reliability**
The extent to which the same result is achieved when a study is repeated in identical situations.

**validity**
The extent to which a study measures what it is supposed to measure.

**sample**
A segment or subset of the population that adequately represents the entire population of interest.

into smaller groups, or strata), or cluster sampling (the population is formed into separate groups, or clusters). Each of these sampling procedures has its advantages and disadvantages, and the decision as to which one to use will depend on the research objectives of the study. Although there is a formula in statistics to calculate required sample size, as a rule of thumb, sample sizes should be large enough to ensure the reliability of the study. Generally, larger samples tend to yield more reliable results up to a certain point.

If the firm is ready to move beyond preliminary insights gained from qualitative research, it is likely ready to engage in **quantitative research**, which provides the information needed to confirm those insights that managers can use to pursue appropriate courses of action. For marketing researchers, quantitative research offers a means to confirm implicit hunches through surveys, formal studies such as specific experiments, scanner and panel data, or some combination of these (see Exhibit 7.8, right side). Quantitative research also enables researchers to test their prediction or **hypothesis**, which is a statement or proposition predicting a particular relationship among multiple variables. The following is an example of a hypothesis: customer satisfaction leads to or is positively related to customer loyalty.

We now examine each of these primary data collection techniques, starting with the qualitative and ending with the quantitative. Many research projects use qualitative research as the first phase of the research process and then follow it up with quantitative research.

## Qualitative Research Methods

Observation    The **observation** research method entails examining purchase and consumption behaviours through personal means or the use of technology, such as a video camera or other tracking devices. For example, researchers might observe customers while they shop or when they go about their daily lives, during which processes they use a variety of products. Observation can last for a very brief period of time (e.g., two hours watching teenagers shop for clothing in the mall), or it may take days or weeks (e.g., researchers live with families to observe their use of products). When consumers are unable to articulate their experiences, observation research becomes particularly useful. How else could researchers determine which educational toys babies choose to play with or confirm purchase details that consumers might not be able to recall accurately?

**Ethnography** is an observational method that studies people in their daily lives and activities in their homes, work, and communities. It is often used to determine how consumers might use a product, and yields insights and intimate details that respondents may not be able to articulate or otherwise share. It is increasingly being used by companies (e.g., Unilever, P&G, Miller Brewing Co.). Ethnographic studies require highly trained researchers who often use video cameras, audio recording devices, and diaries to keep detailed records of their observations. Analysis of ethnographic data requires very experienced and knowledgeable market researchers to make sense of hours of video or audio recordings, or a volume of notes from the researcher's diary.

Although traditionally firms might videotape customers' movements, Microsoft's Kinect sensors are providing a less intrusive option. Discreetly embedded in aisles of retail stores, the sensors provide three-dimensional spatial recognition. Retailers and their suppliers can unobtrusively track the amount of time people spend in front of a shelf, which products they touch or pick up, the products they return to shelves, and finally what they add to their carts for purchase.[22] The data gathered can be used to improve store layouts because they can identify causes of slow-selling merchandise, such as poor shelf placement. By studying customers' movements, marketers can also learn where customers pause or move quickly or where there is congestion. This information can help them decide if the layout and merchandise placement is operating as expected, such as whether new or promoted merchandise is getting the attention it deserves.

Observation may be the best—and is sometimes the only—way to determine how consumers might use a product, and therefore is useful for designing and marketing it. By watching women wash their hair in a rural town in China, Procter & Gamble recognized the

---

**quantitative research**
Provides the information needed to confirm preliminary insights, which managers can use to pursue appropriate courses of action.

**hypothesis**
A statement or proposition predicting a particular relationship among multiple variables that can be tested through research.

**observation**
A qualitative research method that entails examining purchase and consumption behaviours through personal or video camera scrutiny.

**ethnography**
An observational method that studies people in their daily lives and activities in their homes, work, and communities.

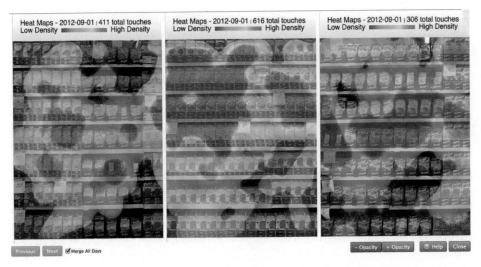

Using Microsoft Kinect sensors, firms like Shopperception create heat maps of shopper interactions with the products (touches, pick-ups, and returns). The red represents the hot zones where shoppers touch the most, yellow less, and blue not at all.

© Shopperception

fallacy of its assumption that the poorest consumers were only interested in functionality of a product—how to get hair clean. One woman struggled to find ways to wash her long hair effectively, even in the face of severe water shortages, rather than cut off what she considered the source of her beauty. Based on its research, P&G has added value by selling Rejoice shampoo inexpensively ($1.50) to a market that was using alternative options such as laundry detergent. Other observations pushed P&G to develop a more skin-sensitive laundry detergent after noting how many people in developing markets wash their clothes by hand.[23] These insights can be helpful, both for the company that gathers them and for consumers who ultimately benefit from better products.

**Social Media**   Social media sites are a booming source of data for marketers. Marketers have realized that social media can provide valuable information that could aid their marketing research and strategy endeavours. In particular, contributors to social media sites rarely are shy about providing their opinions about the firm's own products or its competitors' offerings. If companies can monitor, gather, and mine these vast social media data, they can learn a lot about their customers' likes, dislikes, and preferences. They then might cross-reference such social media commentary with consumers' past purchases to derive a better sense of what they want. Customers also appear keen to submit their opinions about their friends' purchases, interests, polls, and blogs.

Blogs in particular represent valuable sources of marketing research insights. Marketers are paying attention to online reviews about everything from restaurants to running shoes to recycling. The Truth About Cars blog is known for its unflinchingly objective reviews of various makes and models, as well as discussions about the industry as a whole, marketing tactics, and global competition, among other topics.[24] Analyzing the content of this blog, and others like it, provides an excellent source of ideas and information for auto industry executives.

By watching women in rural China wash their hair, Procter & Gamble learned that even their poorest customers wanted beautiful hair, but products have to be packaged affordably.

Benjamin Lowy/Getty Images

When Kraft considered the launch of its South Beach product line, it created a virtual community of women who wanted to lose weight and "health and wellness" opinion leaders.

© Mike Hruby.

Facebook polls can be used to collect a wealth of data ranging from single-question polls to customer satisfaction surveys. The polls are easy for even the smallest company to use and very affordable at between $96 and $336 per year depending on the plan chosen.[25] Twitter recently introduced a new research initiative to allow advertisers to recruit respondents and design and collect research insights from its Twitter Insiders program. Both qualitative and quantitative options are available, from forum-like environments to surveys. The research can also be linked to participants' behaviour, such as what they tweet, whom they follow, and what tweets they like.[26]

Another creative use of social media for market research involves building online communities for companies. When it considered the launch of its South Beach product line, Kraft hired Communispace to create a virtual community of target consumers: 150 women who wanted to lose weight and 150 "health and wellness" opinion leaders. The participants openly shared their frustrations and difficulties managing their weight, because the community environment prompted them to sense that everyone else on the site struggled with similar issues and concerns. By monitoring the community, Kraft learned that it would need to educate consumers about the South Beach Diet and would need to offer products that could address cravings throughout the day, not just at meal-times. Six months after the line's introduction, Kraft had earned profits of $100 million.[27]

Noting these various opportunities and market research sources online, many companies—including Ford Motor Co., PepsiCo, Coca-Cola, and WestJet Airlines—have added "heads of social media" to their management teams. These managers take responsibility for scanning the web for blogs, postings, tweets, or Facebook posts in which customers mention their experience with a brand. By staying abreast of this continuous stream of information, companies can gather the most up-to-date news about their company, products, and services, as well as their competitors'. These social media searches allow companies to learn about customers' perceptions and resolve customer complaints they may never have heard about through other channels.[28] Social media has its pros and cons, as seen in Exhibit 7.9, and is best used in combination with other research techniques.

## EXHIBIT 7.9 Pros and Cons of Using Social Media in Research[29]

| Pros | Result | Cons | Result |
|------|--------|------|--------|
| Large accessible sample | Greater objectivity | Not a statistically representative sample | Could skew findings |
| People of all ages use social media | Wider sample, greater representation | Feedback may not be well thought out | Not useful to research problem |
| Large amount of information posted on social media sites | Easier to find data related to your brand | Anonymity | Could encourage extreme opinions and comments |
| Very current feedback | High relevance | No depth of information about consumer | Cannot distinguish differences among consumersv |
| Consumers freely offer opinions and insights | No interviewer bias | Conversations are observed only | No opportunity to probe for more detail |
| Can search for and filter data | More timely | No consent to study data | Potential ethical issues |

The data gathered through the searches also undergo careful analyses: Are customer sentiments generally positive, negative, or neutral? What sort of intensity or interest levels do they imply? How many customers are talking about the firm's products, and how many focus instead on competitors'? This data analysis is understandably challenging, considering the amount of data available online. However, monitoring consumer sentiments has grown easier with the development of social media monitoring platforms.

Sysomos is steadily becoming one of the most sought-after firms for monitoring customers using sentiment mining. Using social media sites like Facebook, Twitter, and online blogs, Sysomos and other firms collect consumer comments about companies and their products. The data are then analyzed to distill customer attitudes toward and preferences for products and advertising campaigns. Scouring millions of sites by combining automated online search tools with text analysis techniques, sentiment mining yields qualitative data that provide new insight into what consumers really think. Companies plugged into this real-time information can become more nimble, allowing for quick changes in a product roll-out or a new advertising campaign. Some companies take it a step further, by joining the online conversation with customers, a process called *social engagement*.[30] As seen in Social and Mobile Marketing 7.1, Starbucks actively seeks out ideas from consumers.

## Social and Mobile Marketing 7.1

### Your Ideas in Action at Starbucks

Consumers use the Internet and social media as a part of their daily lives to share information, discuss interests, and air grievances. Starbucks recognized that its loyal consumers wanted to share ideas for new products, and launched a website, My Starbucks Idea (http://mystarbucksidea.force.com/), supported by a Twitter page (@MyStarbucksIdea) to make it easy for them to do so. Since its customers know better than anyone how and what they want the company to serve them, Starbucks is encouraging customers to submit their ideas, revolutionary or otherwise.

This example of corporate democracy in action allows anyone who signs up for an account to make suggestions. Over 56,000 Twitter followers[31] and others can discuss and vote on the ideas in an online forum while Starbucks watches to see which ideas are the most popular. All "Ideas in Action" have icons beside them to note whether they are under review, reviewed, in the works, or launched.

Involving consumers in this way is a gold mine for Starbucks because it provides a way to invite customers into the research lab, so to speak. Integrating customer views into a company's new product development process can provide an untapped source of new ideas, refinements to existing products, and access to a knowledgeable test market—all

at little or no cost. In its first five years, consumers cast over 2 million votes and submitted more than 150,000 ideas, resulting in 277 innovations that the company has implemented.[32]

One example of a new product introduction that resulted from consumer feedback was the addition of soy-based beverages to cater to lactose-intolerant customers. Starbucks later added coconut milk, which is certified vegan, gluten-free, and non-GMO,[33] as an alternative to milk and soy. However, a suggestion to add ice cubes made from coffee to iced coffee drinks so the beverage would not get diluted could not be implemented because the majority of Starbucks locations did not have freezers. Although the website is a great place for Starbucks to get feedback on new products customers want, ideas are not restricted to that category. Feedback is also welcome in other categories, including "experience ideas" (ordering, payment, pick-up, atmosphere, locations) and "involvement ideas" (building communities, social responsibility).

Some of the posted ideas include:[34]

- Create a splash stick to prevent spills from drink lid.
- Don't throw out used Starbucks cards; instead, give people a 25 cent credit for reloading them.
- Offer gluten-free food.
- Reward customers based on the value of their purchases, not just one star per visit.

Changes were made to the Rewards program so that customers now receive two stars for every $1 spent.

Nor Gal/Shutterstock.com

A consumer is being interviewed.

The McGraw-Hill Companies, Inc./John Flournoy, photographer

**in-depth interview**

A research technique in which trained researchers ask questions, listen to and record the answers, and then pose additional questions to clarify or expand on a particular issue.

**focus group**

A research technique in which a small group of persons (usually 8 to 12) comes together for an in-depth discussion about a particular topic, with the conversation guided by a trained moderator using an unstructured method of inquiry.

**In-Depth Interviews** In an **in-depth interview**, trained researchers ask questions, listen to and record the answers, and then pose additional questions to clarify or expand on a particular issue. For instance, in addition to simply watching teenagers shop for apparel, interviewers might stop them one at a time in the mall to ask them a few questions, such as "We noticed that you went into and came out of Aritzia very quickly, and without buying anything. Why was that?" If the subject responds that no one had bothered to wait on her, the interviewer might ask a follow-up question, such as "Oh? Has that happened to you before?" or "Do you expect sales assistance in that store?" The results often provide insights that help managers better understand the nature of their industry, as well as important trends and consumer preferences, which can be invaluable for developing marketing strategies.

In-depth interviews can provide a historical context for the phenomenon of interest, particularly when they include industry experts or experienced consumers. They also can communicate how people really feel about a product or service at the individual level, a level that rarely emerges from other methods that use group discussions. Finally, marketers can use the results of in-depth interviews to develop surveys. In-depth interviews are relatively expensive and time consuming, however; one interview may cost $200 or more, depending on its length and the characteristics of the people used in the sample. For instance, if the sample requires medical doctors, the costs of getting interviews will be higher than they would be for intercepting teenagers at a mall.

**Focus Group Interviews** In a **focus group**, a small group of persons (usually 8 to 12) comes together for an in-depth discussion about a particular topic. Using an unstructured method of inquiry, a trained moderator guides the conversation on the basis of a predetermined general outline of the topics of interest. Researchers usually make video or audio recordings of the interactions so that they can carefully comb through the interviews later to catch any patterns of verbal or nonverbal responses.

In particular, focus groups gather qualitative data about initial reactions to a new or existing product or service, opinions about different competitive offerings, or reactions to marketing stimuli, like a new ad campaign or point-of-purchase display materials.

To obtain new information to help it continue its innovative success derived from its introduction of low-sodium choices, Campbell's Soup conducted extensive focus groups with female shoppers who indicated they would buy ready-to-eat soups. The groups clearly revealed the women's top priorities: a nutritious soup that contained the ingredients they would use if they made soup. They wanted, for example, white-meat chicken, fresh vegetables, and sea salt. In addition, focus group participants were equally clear about what they did not want, like high fructose corn syrup, MSG, and other ingredients whose names they could not even pronounce.[35] The resulting Select Harvest product line showcases the 100 percent natural, flavourful, and healthful ingredients, including vegetables and whole grains. The packaging also reflects the focus groups' preferences, using a simple, clean design that highlights the short list of ingredients. In its first year on the market, the line generated $202 million in sales.[36]

The growth of online technology, as well as computer and video capabilities, has provided tremendous benefits for focus group research, which now often takes place online. For example, eFocusGroups offers a secure site as a platform for companies to listen in on focus groups and even interact with consumers, without anyone having to travel. The client company not only saves costs but also gains access to a broader range of potential customers who live in various neighbourhoods, provinces, or even countries. Because eFocusGroups automatically records all the online interactions, the company also has a detailed, verbatim transcript of consumers' comments and responses.[37] However, these online focus groups rarely include video feeds, so companies lose some important information that can be gleaned from body language.

Virtual focus groups have started to make inroads into the market researchers' toolkit. Lego, for instance, invited more than 10,000 kids to participate in a virtual focus group to get ideas for new products.[38] The participants saw short lists of proposed toys and clicked on the ones they liked. They ranked their choices and even suggested new ideas. These ideas were fed, in turn, to other potential customers and were rated against the ideas from Lego's own toy creators. The new suggestions, in turn, got creative juices flowing among still other potential customers. The resulting product, the Star Wars Imperial Star Destroyer, was different from anything else in Lego's 73-year history—it was Lego's largest and most expensive set ever, at 3,100 parts and with a $300 price tag. Its first production run sold out in less than five weeks.

**Projective Technique**   A **projective technique** is a type of qualitative research in which subjects are provided with a scenario and asked to express their thoughts and feelings about it. For example, consumers may be shown a cartoon that has a consumer looking at a shelf display in a supermarket with a text box above the consumer. The respondent would write his or her thoughts on the issue in the text box. Thus, the cartoon allows respondents to visualize the situation and project their thoughts or feelings by filling in the text box.

You might be wondering which of these primary qualitative data collection techniques are used most frequently. Generally, focus groups and in-depth interviews are used more frequently than personal observations, especially ethnography. Deciding which technique to use depends on several important considerations, such as the objective of the research, the cost to undertake the research, the time required to undertake the research, how soon the results are needed, and whether the marketer has the research expertise in-house or has to hire a market research firm to do the research, especially with methods such as ethnography and projective techniques. Normally, marketers have to make a trade-off between these considerations to get the results in a timely and cost-effective manner. Often a company may use several methods together to get actionable results.

> **projective technique**
> A type of qualitative research in which subjects are provided with a scenario and asked to express their thoughts and feelings about it.

## Quantitative Research Methods

Quantitative research is intended to verify insights and to aid decision makers in selecting a specific course of action.[39] Quantitative research can be descriptive in nature, such as when it profiles a typical user or non-user of a particular brand according to a survey. It can also be experimental, such as when a soft-drink producer conducts a taste test to determine which formulation of a green, high-caffeine drink is preferred by customers. Quantitative research can also be collected from the merchandise that is scanned at a store, or from a group of customers, known as a panel, who record all of their purchases. In this section, we will discuss the following quantitative research techniques: survey, panel, and experimental.

**Survey Research**   Arguably a survey is the most popular type of quantitative, primary data collection method used in marketing research. It is widely used to study consumers' attitudes, preferences, behaviours, and knowledge about products and brands. It is generally more cost-effective than other methods for reaching a large sample of consumers. Hockey Canada and Bauer Hockey wanted to understand why more children were not playing hockey. Surveys of 875 families in Ontario and Nova Scotia revealed some interesting findings: the game was viewed as not fun, too time consuming, not affordable, and having safety concerns.[40] Pilot programs to "Grow the Game" have since been launched to change attitudes and attract new players.

Survey questionnaires usually yield quantitative data that can be easily analyzed by using sophisticated statistical methods to examine the relationships among variables. However, surveys suffer from a few shortcomings. Consumers may be unable to answer some of the questions on the questionnaire, may not be able to recall the information, or may even interpret the questions differently than the researchers intended. Some may

## Sustainable Marketing 7.1

### The Automotive Future Looks Green, or Does It?

A new study conducted by Kanetix, a company that sells online auto insurance, found that many Canadians are thinking green for their next vehicle purchase. Of nearly 3,800 people surveyed, almost half of them, 48.7 percent, said they would consider buying an electric or hybrid car. Some of this interest may be a direct result of Tesla's Model 3 announcement. With a low entry price of $35,000, the electric car generated a lot of interest. Almost 400,000 pre-orders were received.

For some consumers, provincial rebates and other incentives are a motivating factor to go green. The survey found that residents of British Columbia are most likely to consider an electric vehicle, at 54.9 percent of everyone polled. The province offers a rebate of up to $6,000. In Ontario and Quebec, where cash-back rebates are available, 45 percent of consumers said they would lean green. And, in spite of no provincial incentives, the highest level of interest comes from Nova Scotia at 64.5 percent. Gas- and oil-rich Albertans are the least likely consumers to consider an electric or hybrid vehicle.[41]

Based on these results, the future looks green. However, auto makers are unlikely to ramp up their manufacturing capacity on the strength of just one survey. The auto market is complex and consumers don't always follow through on their stated intentions.

For example, a survey conducted by Ipsos-Reid and Offsetters, a Canadian provider of sustainability and carbon-management solutions, reported that 64 percent of consumers polled are ready to drive a hydrogen fuel cell vehicle (FCV).[42] However, although the majority of people want a car that is not fueled by gasoline, they are not quite ready to embrace traditional battery electric vehicles. While the appetite for new technology is strong, consumers want more government support before they dive in. Marketers

Consumers say they want one but are confused about the different options for plug-in electric vehicles.

lmfoto/Shutterstock.com

need to carefully evaluate research data to determine what people say as opposed to what they actually do.

One last study conducted by Simon Fraser University in Vancouver drives this point home. Researchers there discovered that many consumers don't really understand all the green options available. When it comes to plug-in cars, there are two main types: plug-in hybrid electric vehicles (PHEV) and battery electric vehicles (BEV). Few consumers were able to correctly identify the differences between fueling the Toyota Prius, Chevrolet Volt, and Nissan Leaf. The study showed that, in spite of stated intentions reported in other surveys, consumption of plug-in cars in Canada makes up only 0.27 percent of all new vehicle sales. Compared to Norway, where 14 percent of all new cars sold are plug-in electric,[43] Canada lags far behind.

While at least one research study shows conclusive evidence that Canadians want more environmentally friendly options for their next vehicle, marketers should carefully interpret all the data before declaring that the future is green.

---

**survey**

A systematic means of collecting information from people using a questionnaire.

**questionnaire**

A form that features a set of questions designed to gather information from respondents and thereby accomplish the researchers' objectives; questions can be either unstructured or structured.

even try to answer the questions according to what they think the researchers want. Another big problem, especially in the data analysis phase, is when respondents answer some but not all of the questions on the questionnaire. Incomplete data makes the analysis and interpretation of the data more complicated and tricky. Sustainable Marketing 7.1 demonstrates how difficult it can sometimes be to interpret results from multiple surveys when making decisions.

A **survey** is a systematic means of collecting information from people that generally uses a questionnaire. A **questionnaire** is a form that features a set of questions designed to gather information from respondents and thereby accomplish the researchers' objectives. Survey questionnaires can take different forms: done by phone, mail, or fax; delivered via the Internet; or even conducted in person, for example, mall intercepts. Individual questions on a questionnaire can be either unstructured or

**EXHIBIT 7.10** Structured Versus Unstructured Response

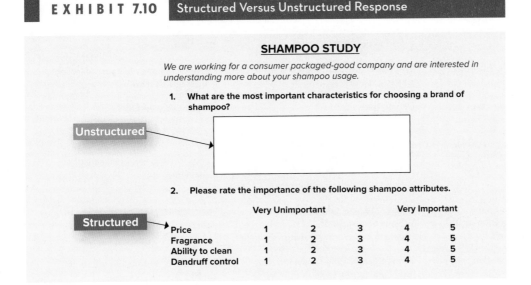

**SHAMPOO STUDY**

*We are working for a consumer packaged-good company and are interested in understanding more about your shampoo usage.*

1. **What are the most important characteristics for choosing a brand of shampoo?**

Unstructured

2. **Please rate the importance of the following shampoo attributes.**

| | Very Unimportant | | | Very Important | |
|---|---|---|---|---|---|
| Price | 1 | 2 | 3 | 4 | 5 |
| Fragrance | 1 | 2 | 3 | 4 | 5 |
| Ability to clean | 1 | 2 | 3 | 4 | 5 |
| Dandruff control | 1 | 2 | 3 | 4 | 5 |

Structured

structured. **Unstructured questions** are open-ended and allow respondents to answer in their own words. An unstructured question like "What are the most important characteristics for choosing a brand of shampoo?" yields an unstructured response. However, the same question could be posed to respondents in a structured format by providing a fixed set of response categories (such as price, fragrance, ability to clean, and dandruff control) and then asking respondents to rate the importance of each. **Structured questions** thus are closed-ended questions for which a discrete set of response alternatives, or specific answers, is provided for respondents to evaluate (see Exhibit 7.10).

Developing a questionnaire is part art and part science. The questions must be carefully designed to address the specific set of research questions. Moreover, for a questionnaire to produce meaningful results, its questions cannot be misleading in any fashion (e.g., open to multiple interpretations), and they must address only one issue at a time. Furthermore, they must be worded in vocabulary that will be familiar and comfortable to those being surveyed. More specifically, the questions should be sequenced appropriately: general questions first, more specific questions next, and demographic questions at the end. Finally, the layout and appearance of the questionnaire must be professional and easy to follow, with appropriate instructions in suitable places. For some tips on what *not* to do when designing a questionnaire, see Exhibit 7.11.

Similar to focus groups, marketing surveys can be conducted either online or offline, but online marketing surveys offer researchers the chance to develop a database quickly with many responses, whereas offline marketing surveys provide a more direct approach that includes interactions with the target market.

Web surveys have steadily grown as a percentage of all quantitative surveys. Many online survey tools let researchers quickly design a survey, launch it, download the data, and analyze the data even as the survey is progressing, as well as at the end of the data collection. SurveyMonkey and Qualtrics are two popular online survey tools with vastly different capabilities, services, and pricing models. Online surveys have a lot to offer marketers with tight deadlines and small budgets.[45] Response rates

**unstructured questions** Open-ended questions that allow respondents to answer in their own words.

**structured questions** Closed-ended questions for which a discrete set of response alternatives, or specific answers, is provided for respondents to evaluate.

Online marketing surveys enable researchers to develop a database quickly with many responses at a relatively low cost.

The McGraw-Hill Companies, Inc./John Flournoy, photographer

**EXHIBIT 7.11**     **What Not to Do When Designing a Questionnaire[44]**

| Issue | Good Question | Bad Question |
|---|---|---|
| Avoid questions the respondent cannot easily or accurately answer. | When was the last time you went to the grocery store? | How much money did you spend on groceries last month? |
| Avoid sensitive questions unless they are absolutely necessary. | Do you take vitamins? | Do you dye your hair? |
| Avoid double-barrelled questions, which refer to more than one issue with only one set of responses. | 1. Do you think Justin Trudeau would make a good prime minister?<br>2. Do you think Elizabeth May would make a good prime minister? | Do you think that Elizabeth May or Justin Trudeau would make a good prime minister? |
| Avoid leading questions, which steer respondents to a particular response, irrespective of their true beliefs. | Please rate how safe you believe a Volvo is on a scale of 1 to 10, with 1 being not safe and 10 being very safe. | Volvo is the safest car on the road, right? |
| Avoid one-sided questions that present only one side of the issue. | To what extent do you feel that fast food contributes to adult obesity? 1: Does not contribute, 5: Main cause | Fast food is responsible for adult obesity: Agree/Disagree |
| Avoid questions with implicit assumptions, which presume the same point of reference for all respondents. | Should children be allowed to drink Coca-Cola in school? | Since caffeine is a stimulant, should children be allowed to drink Coca-Cola in school? |
| Avoid complex questions and those that may seem unfamiliar to respondents. | What brand of wristwatch do you typically wear? | Do you believe that mechanical watches are better than quartz watches? |

are relatively high. Typical response rates run from 1 to 2 percent for mail and 10 to 15 percent for phone surveys. For online surveys, in contrast, the response rate can reach 30 to 35 percent, or even higher in B2B research. It is inexpensive. An average 20-minute phone interview can cost $30 to $40, compared with $7 to $10 for an online interview. Costs likely will continue to fall more as users become more familiar with the online survey process. Results are processed and received quickly. Reports and summaries can be developed in real time and delivered directly to managers in simple, easy-to-digest reports, complete with colour, graphics, and charts. Traditional phone or mail surveys require laborious data collection, tabulation, summary, and distribution before anyone can grasp their results.

The Internet can also be used to collect data other than that available from quantitative surveys. If consumers give a firm permission to market to them, the firm can collect data about their usage of its website and other Internet applications. In addition, open-ended questionnaires can be used to collect more in-depth qualitative data. Diverse online survey software—such as Qualtrics, SurveyMonkey, and Zoomerang—makes it very easy to draft an online survey using questions from existing survey libraries. A survey link can be sent easily in an email to potential respondents or panelists as well as posted on specific sites that are likely to attract the target audience or people who are willing to perform online work (e.g., Amazon's Mechanical Turk Site).

**Panel Research**   As previously discussed, panel research can be either secondary or primary. In this section, we consider the use of a panel to collect primary data. Shaw Media wanted to collect insights for three of its channels: Global Television, HGTV, and Food Network Canada. To do this, it needed to understand attitudes and purchase intention toward brands featured in the programming and advertising. Online panels of 5,000

**EXHIBIT 7.12**    Hypothetical Pricing Experiment for McDonald's

| | 1 | 2 | 3 | 4 | 5 |
| --- | --- | --- | --- | --- | --- |
| Market | Unit Price | Market Demand at Price (in Units) | Total Revenue (Col. 1 × Col. 2) | Total Cost of Units Sold ($300,000 Fixed Cost; $2.00/ Unit Variable Cost) | Total Profits (Col. 3 – Col. 4) |
| 1 | $4 | 200,000 | $800,000 | $700,000 | $100,000 |
| 2 | 5 | 150,000 | 750,000 | 600,000 | 150,000 |
| 3 | 6 | 100,000 | 600,000 | 500,000 | 100,000 |
| 4 | 7 | 50,000 | 350,000 | 400,000 | (50,000) |

people for each channel[46] now help collect feedback used to enhance Shaw's offerings. Walmart's Asda subsidiary in the United Kingdom uses an 18,000-customer panel it calls "Pulse of the Nation" to help it determine which products to carry. Asda sends emails to each participant with product images and descriptions of potential new products. The customers' responses indicate whether they think the product should be carried in the stores. As a thank-you for participating, those customers who respond are automatically entered in a draw for free prizes.[47]

**Experimental Research**    **Experimental research** is a type of quantitative research that systematically manipulates one or more variables to determine which variable(s) have a causal effect on another variable. In the hypothetical McDonald's example, the research team was trying to determine the most profitable price for a new combo item (a hamburger, fries, and a drink or all day breakfast items). Assume that the fixed cost of developing the item is $300,000, and the variable cost, which is primarily composed of the cost of the food itself, is $2.00. McDonald's puts the item on the menu at four different prices in four different markets (see Exhibit 7.12). In general, the more expensive the item, the less it will sell. But, by running this experiment, the restaurant chain determines that the most profitable item is the second least expensive item ($5.00). These findings suggest that some people may have believed the most expensive item ($7.00) was too expensive, so they refused to buy it. The least expensive item ($4.00) sold fairly well, but McDonald's did not make as much money on each item sold. In this experiment, the changes in price likely caused the changes in quantities sold and therefore affected the restaurant's profitability.

Firms are also actively using experimental techniques on Facebook. Once a firm has created its Facebook page, it can devise advertisements and rely on Facebook's targeting options to deliver those ads to the most appropriate customer segments. To make sure the communication is just right, companies can experiment with alternative versions and identify which advertisement is most effective. State Bicycle Co., a manufacturer in Arizona, needed to determine what other interests its customers had, as well as who its main competitors were. Therefore, it tested a range of ads, targeting customers who searched for different bands (e.g., did more Arcade Fire or Passion Pit fans click their link?) and other bicycle manufacturers. With this information, it devised new contests and offerings on its own homepage to attract more of the visitors who were likely to buy.[48] Facebook tries to help its corporate clients enhance their own

**experimental research** A type of quantitative research that systematically manipulates one or more variables to determine which variable has a causal effect on another variable.

McDonald's could experiment with different price points in different markets to test the optimal price for its all day breakfast combos.

Geoffrey Robinson/Alamy Stock Photo

customers' engagement and influence through a variety of options: check-ins, asking for customer comments, sharing information with friends, and so on.[49] It measures all these forms of data, contributing even further to the information businesses have about their page visitors.

Now that we have discussed the various secondary and primary data collection methods, we can see that both primary data and secondary data have certain inherent advantages and disadvantages. Regardless of how marketers collect data, research can be an expensive process for entrepreneurs working on a limited budget. Entrepreneurial Marketing 7.1 suggests a host of avenues entrepreneurs might pursue.

## LO4 THE ETHICS OF USING CUSTOMER INFORMATION

As we will note in Chapter 18, upholding strong business ethics requires more than a token nod to ethics in the mission statement. A strong ethical orientation must be an integral part of a firm's marketing strategy and decision making. In Chapter 18, we will discuss how marketers have a duty to understand and address the concerns of the various stakeholders in the firm. From charitable giving to medical records to Internet tracking, consumers are more anxious than ever about preserving their fundamental right to privacy.

Many firms voluntarily notify their customers that any information provided to them will be kept confidential and not given or sold to any other firm. As more firms adopt advanced marketing research technology, such as neuromarketing and facial recognition software, they also are working to ensure they receive permission from consumers. For example, Coca-Cola's neuromarketing experiments will record participants' faces as they watch advertisements or prototypes, then assess how their eyes moved, when they smiled or frowned, and so on—but only after those participants have agreed to be recorded.[50]

As technology continues to advance, the potential threats to consumers' personal information grow in number and intensity. Ethical Dilemma 7.1 discusses an interesting example of how retailers are using mannequins with hidden cameras to monitor shoppers. Marketing researchers must be careful to avoid abusing their access to these data. Unauthorized sharing of customer data with third parties or for purposes other than legitimate company business is a serious breach of customer trust. Also, marketers must take every step possible to protect customer data from security breaches from hackers and other unauthorized individuals. In the event of a security breach, the company must quickly notify its affected customers and state clearly what steps it is taking to protect their data and privacy.

More and more, consumers want to be assured that they have control over the information that has been collected about them through various means, such as a website or product registration or rebate form. Consumers' anxiety has become so intense that the Canadian government has implemented various regulations, such as the Privacy Act, that govern the collection, use, disclosure, and retention of personal information by federal government institutions, and the Personal Information Protection and Electronic Documents Act (PIPEDA), which governs the collection, use, disclosure, and retention of personal information by certain parts of the private sector.[52] When conducting marketing research, researchers must assure respondents that the information they provide will be treated as confidential and used solely for the purpose of research. Without such assurances, consumers will be reluctant to provide honest responses to marketing research inquiries or even agree to participate in the first place.

It is extremely important to adhere to ethical practices when conducting marketing research. The Canadian Marketing Association, for example, provides three guidelines for conducting marketing research: (1) it prohibits selling or fundraising under the guise of conducting research, (2) it supports maintaining research integrity by avoiding misrepresentation or the omission of pertinent research data, and (3) it encourages the fair treatment of clients and suppliers. Numerous codes of conduct written by various

## Entrepreneurial Marketing 7.1

# Marketing Research on a Shoestring Budget

Imagine your company needs some research to be conducted but has a relatively small budget. Fortunately, marketing research does not have to have a high price tag, though it always takes drive and knowledge. Here are some ways to uncover the information you and your company might need without breaking the bank.

**Objective:** What is it that you need to know?

- *Network.* Use the directory on your cellphone to call friends and professional colleagues. In most cases, researchers probably already know people in the industry who will be able to share their knowledge. They can help marketers determine what their objectives should be in upcoming research projects.

**Customer Analysis:** Who are your customers, and what do they want?

- *Customers.* Talk with current and prospective customers. Ask them the right questions, and they will provide the necessary answers. This approach is remarkably cheap because it needs only the researcher's labour, though it will require a large time commitment. Marketers need to take care how they ask the questions; people tend to provide answers that they think the questioner wants to hear or that seem socially acceptable.

- *Online.* Use a search engine such as Google by typing in some appropriate keywords.

- *Statistics Canada.* Statistics Canada is an important source of information. At http://www.statcan.gc.ca, industry, demographic, and economic reports are accessible for free. Although not known for its ease of use, the website offers a wealth of information.

**Competitive Analysis:** What are your competitors doing?

**Secondary Sources:** Many are listed in Exhibit 7.5 in this chapter.

- *Websites.* Visit competitors' websites, if they have them. Learn about their products and services, pricing, management teams, and philosophies. Read their press releases. You can even infer what parts of the businesses are thriving by reading their career pages.

- *SEC Filings.* If competitors are public companies in the United States, they are required to file 10K forms annually with the U.S. Securities and Exchange Commission (SEC). Search for SEC filings by using http://finance.yahoo.com or http://money.msn.com,

both of which provide sales and expense numbers, in addition to other important information in the footnotes. In Canada, most public companies file securities documents and information on the System for Electronic Document Analysis and Retrieval (SEDAR) (http://www.sedar.com).

- *University Libraries Electronic Databases.* Most Canadian universities subscribe to several electronic business databases that provide information on Canadian companies. These databases are usually accessible remotely by students, staff, and alumni at no cost to users. A sample of these databases includes Canadian Business Resource, Canadian Business & Current Affairs Database, Factiva, *Financial Post* databases, MarketResearch.com, Mergent Online, Mergent WebReports, ProQuest Asian Business and Reference, and ProQuest European Business. Many of these databases provide company profiles, financial data, contact information, and short stories or case studies on company successes, failures, and innovations.

- *Personal Visits.* If competitors are smaller mom-and-pop stores, visit them. Hang out in front of the store armed with a pad and paper and count the number of people who walk in. Then calculate the percentage of people who walk out having purchased something. Use logic and judgment. Have the customers purchased items that appear to have high profit margins? Find out where and what competitors are advertising.

**Focus Groups, Surveys, and Analyst Reports:** What detailed information can you gather?

- Be specific. Determine precisely what information is required; it is very costly to pay for research that does not assist in a decision or provide strategic direction.

- *Surveys.* Determine what form will provide the most value. Phone surveys cost about $40 per interview, mailings average from $5,000 to $15,000 for 200 responses, and email and Internet-based surveys are usually much cheaper.

- *Focus Groups.* Although focus groups can be more expensive, there are ways to cut corners. Develop the questions in-house, and don't outsource the moderator or facility. It is important, however, to find the right participants.

- *Analyst Reports.* Prewritten reports, covering a broad price range and a wide variety of questions, are available for purchase from the hundreds of companies that write and sell reports. Two of the best known are http://www.forrester.com and http://www.hoovers.com.

## Ethical Dilemma 7.1

# Oh, Say, Can You See? The Implications of Mannequins That Capture Shoppers' Demographic[51]

The basic elements of a new data gathering tool development for retailers are not in any real contention. By spending about $5,000 to purchase an EyeSee mannequin from a provider called Almax, retailers gain not only a place to display clothing but also a discreet recording tool that indicates the genders, ages, and ethnicities of the customers who walk by the display.

Rather more controversial are the discussions about the implications of this innovation. On one side, consumer privacy advocates complain that the mannequins obtain information about shoppers without their permission. Although Almax asserts that the technology embedded in the displays does not actually record the information, these commentators worry that the mannequins could be used to survey shoppers solely for the benefit of the retailer. Because the mannequins do not look different from regular mannequins, shoppers have no way of knowing whether someone (or something) is watching them as they walk through the store. Furthermore, consumers have no control over what retailers do with the aggregated data.

On the other side, retailers note that because the mannequins do not record, their use is no different from that of a closed-circuit system.

EyeSee mannequins do not record, or store, any image, so the privacy of the customer is protected.
Almax S.p.A.

Furthermore, some commentators argue that consumers should have no expectation of privacy in public spaces. Certainly, a staffer could similarly mark down people's ages, races, and genders as they walk through the shop doors. The electronic form simply does this work better and more accurately.

In implementing the new technology, one retailer recognized the predominance of Asian shoppers after about 4:00 p.m., so it hired more Chinese-speaking staffers to put on the floor to assist them. Another retailer realized that a lot of children were walking through its stores, so it added an entirely new children's clothing line to its offerings. Buoyed by its early successes, Almax also plans to add a function that would capture shoppers' conversations as they pass by the mannequins.

Current legislation allows retailers to maintain cameras and record customers for security purposes as long as they post warnings that customers might be recorded. However, the use of the mannequins is clearly for marketing purposes, not security. And most retailers seem to prefer to keep their usage of the new technology under wraps. Almax has not officially released the names of any of its clients—perhaps somewhat ironically, citing their need for privacy.

From your perspective as a consumer, do you believe that mannequins that record your movements, image, and possibly conversations in a store invade your privacy? If so, would you avoid stores that use this technology?

marketing research societies all reinforce the duty of researchers to respect the rights of the subjects in the course of their research. The bottom line: Marketing research should be used only to produce unbiased, factual information.

Laws have yet to catch up with advances in other areas, including social media, neuromarketing, and facial recognition software. As we noted previously in this chapter, social media have grown into an important resource for marketing researchers because consumers are so willing and likely to share their attitudes and opinions there. In this case, protecting consumers' privacy is mainly up to the consumer.

In contrast, consumers have little control over facial recognition software that allows companies to detect demographic information based on their appearances. For example, digital billboards embedded with such software can identify passersby and then display ads targeted to them, based on their age, gender, and attention level.[53] The

## REAL MARKETER PROFILE

# Tim Penner
# (P&G Canada)

Used with permission of Tim Penner

When I think about consumer research, I'm reminded of a presentation I heard at P&G over 30 years ago, when I was just starting my career. The presenter showed a video of a consumer named "Ina," who was going through her household chores, doing the laundry and cleaning her house. Ina did some things that seemed a bit silly. She didn't follow the usage instructions very closely and she had a number of quirky habits. I remember my peers and I chuckling as we watched the video of Ina's cleaning regimen.

The presenter later informed us that Ina was an actress, but everything she did in her cleaning regimen had come from in-depth research of what real consumers do. He showed us the video to impress upon us a very important message, and we should remember the message by remembering Ina. INA stands for "I'm Not Average." One of the most important things that marketers need to learn is that they need to suppress their personal experiences and their personal habits, because those experiences are not average. Instead of relying on their personal experiences, marketers need to listen very carefully to what real consumers say and do. The insights that a marketer discovers by watching and listening to real consumers can lead to innovative new products and marketing campaigns that really connect with real consumers.

One of the areas where this message proved to be particularly relevant was in-store. As a marketer, I would often look at packaging or in-store materials in a conference room and think the work was quite brilliant. But when I researched these in-store materials with consumers, by putting them in a simulated store environment and asking consumers to shop the section, I often learned that consumers hadn't even noticed the in-store materials that I thought were so clever. Even a video screen in the aisle would often go completely unseen by consumers intent on finding a brand. You see, when consumers shop, they are bombarded by so many messages and symbols that their brain has to select a few things to look for. Their brain deselects a lot of extraneous information. The clever words on the label and the images on in-store signage can go completely unnoticed. Once again, it's not the opinion of the marketer that matters. It is only by exposing real consumers to the work, in a representative situation, that you can really understand the merits of an idea.

Never forget Ina!

resulting communication is precisely targeted, which should make the advertisement more interesting to the consumer walking by—though it also could lead to embarrassing encounters. Imagine, for example, a teenager with skin problems having a billboard loudly broadcast an acne product ad as he walks by!

On Facebook, facial detection software applied to photographs eliminates the need for users to continue to tag the same people multiple times. It also stores all users' biometric data. Biometric data include one or more physical traits such as facial characteristics, iris scans, or fingerprints. Facebookers can turn off the facial detection function, but their biometric data is still collected. In Germany, with its strict privacy laws, regulators have demanded that Facebook stop collecting any biometric data.

Going even deeper than using biometric data, neuromarketing claims the ability to read consumers' minds, using wireless electroencephalogram (EEG) scanners that measure the involuntary brainwaves that occur when they view a product, advertisement, or brand images. Such insights would be invaluable for marketers to discover what truly appeals to consumers. For example, based on results of a series of neuromarketing studies, Campbell's has recently changed its soup labels by shrinking the logo and emphasizing the soup to increase customers' emotional responses to the cans.[54] But as anyone who has ever seen a science fiction movie can imagine, the potential for abuses of such tools is immense. And a key question remains: Do any consumers want marketers reading their brain waves and marketing goods and services to them in a manner that bypasses their conscious thoughts? One firm, NeuroFocus, used neuromarketing techniques with several global firms to garner customer information that would be difficult, if not impossible, to obtain using more traditional research methods.

# LEARNING OBJECTIVES REVIEW

## LO1 Identify the five steps in the marketing research process

There are five steps in the marketing research process. Step 1 is to define the research problem and objectives, which sounds so simple that managers often gloss over it. However, this step is crucial to the success of any research project because, quite simply, the research must answer those questions that are important for making decisions. In Step 2, designing the research plan, researchers identify the types of data that are needed, whether primary or secondary, on the basis of the objectives of the project from Step 1, and then determine the type of research that enables them to collect those data. Step 3 involves deciding on the data collection process and collecting the data. Depending on the research objectives and the findings from the secondary data search, researchers will choose either qualitative or quantitative research. Qualitative research usually involves observation, in-depth interviews, or projective techniques, whereas if the project calls for conclusive research, the researchers may perform a survey or an experiment, or use panel data. Step 4 is to analyze and interpret the data, and Step 5 is to present an action plan. Although these steps appear to progress in a linear fashion, researchers often work backward through the process as they learn at each step.

## LO2 Describe the various secondary data sources

Secondary data are pieces of information that have been collected from other sources, such as the Census, internal company sources, the Internet, books, articles, trade associations, or syndicated data services. Research projects typically start with secondary research, which provides a background for what information is already known and what research has been done previously. External secondary data are pieces of information that have been collected from other sources, such as Statistics Canada, the Internet, books, articles, magazines, newspapers, trade associations, scanner data, panel data, or syndicated data services. Internal secondary data are derived from internal company records such as sales, customer lists, and other company reports.

## LO3 Describe primary data collection techniques and summarize the differences between secondary data and primary data

Primary data are collected to address specific research needs. Techniques used for primary qualitative research include observation, social media, in-depth interviews, focus groups and projective techniques. Quantitative research is used to verify the insights gained from exploratory qualitative research and to aid in choosing a course of action. Techniques used for primary quantitative research include surveys (both offline and online), panel data, and experiments. With both types of research, the specific methods managers choose depends foremost on the marketing research objectives, which must be balanced by other considerations such as costs, timeliness, and usefulness of the results.

Compared with primary research, secondary research is quicker, easier, and generally less expensive. The ability to use secondary data also requires less methodological expertise. However, because secondary research is collected for reasons other than those pertaining to the specific problem at hand, the information may be dated, biased, or simply not specific enough to answer the research questions. Primary research, in contrast, can be designed to answer very specific questions, but it also tends to be more expensive and time consuming.

## LO4 Outline ethical issues firms encounter when conducting marketing research

Marketing researchers have obligations to their subjects and to society to behave in an ethical manner. Marketing researchers should gain permission to collect information on consumers, and it should be for the sole purpose of conducting marketing research endeavours. Information should not be collected under the guise of marketing research when the intent is to sell products or to fundraise. In addition, marketers must take responsibility for protecting any information they collect.

# KEY TERMS

- big data
- data
- data mining
- ethnography
- experimental research
- focus group
- hypothesis
- in-depth interview
- information

- marketing research
- observation
- panel data
- primary data
- projective technique
- qualitative research
- quantitative research
- questionnaire
- reliability

- sample
- scanner data
- secondary data
- structured questions
- survey
- syndicated data
- unstructured questions
- validity

# CONCEPT REVIEW

1. Is marketing research really necessary? Defend your answer.

2. Briefly describe the steps in the marketing research process. Explain why it is important to clearly define the research problem and objectives from the very outset of the process.

3. What is the difference between secondary and primary data? What are some of the advantages of each type of data? When should each type of data be used?

4. In data collection methods, researchers may choose between qualitative research methods and quantitative research methods, or use both methods. What considerations guide their choice of data collection methods?

5. Today, information and communications technologies (ICT), including the Internet, are changing not only the way marketing is practised, but also how market research is conducted. In response, many companies are using a wide variety of observational methods (e.g., GPS, RFID, video cameras, audio devices, ethnography) to gather customer data. Discuss the ethical issues underlying the increasing use of observational research methods that use technology.

6. Marketing research is designed to help marketers make better decisions on various aspects of their businesses.

The quality of research findings is as good as the quality of the data on which they are based. What are some things marketers could do to ensure that they obtain the best quality data?

7. Explain the main advantages and disadvantages of using the Internet for marketing research versus conventional offline methods.

8. Identify and explain the ways in which the design of a market research study could reduce the reliability and validity of the study. Can a market research study that has high reliability lack validity? Can a study that has high validity lack reliability? Explain your answers.

9. What do you think are some of the differences between qualitative data collection methods, which are mainly exploratory, and quantitative research methods, which are more conclusive in nature? Which type of method should a researcher prefer and why?

10. Explain some of the problems and challenges market researchers face in the data analysis and interpretation stage of the marketing research process. Should they report these problems when presenting their action plan? Why or why not?

# MARKETING APPLICATIONS

1. A large department store collects data about what its customers buy and stores these data in a data warehouse. If you were the store's buyer for children's clothing, what would you want to know from the data warehouse that would help you be a more successful buyer?

2. A consumer packaged-goods company (e.g., Pepsi) has just developed a new beverage. The company needs to estimate the demand for such a new product. What sources of syndicated data could it explore?

3. Marketing researchers do not always go through the steps in the marketing research process in sequential order. Provide an example of a research project that might not follow this sequence.

4. A new men's clothing store is trying to determine whether there is a significant market for its type of merchandise in a specific location where it is considering putting a store. Would it be most likely to use primary or secondary data, or a combination of the two, to answer this question?

5. A high-tech firm has just developed a new technology to correct bad vision without surgery or contact lenses. The company needs to estimate the demand for such a service. Would it use primary or secondary data, or a combination of the two?

6. A bank manager notices that by the time customers get to the teller, they seem irritated and impatient. She wants to investigate the problem further, so she hires you to design a research project to figure out what is bothering the customers. The bank wants two studies: (a) several focus groups of its customers, and (b) an online survey of 500 customers. Which study is qualitative and which is quantitative?

7. PomWonderful has developed a coffee-flavoured pomegranate beverage, and it wants to determine whether it should begin to market it throughout Canada. The company used two separate studies to help develop the advertising campaign:

   - a focus group to identify the appropriate advertising message for the new beverage

   - a survey to assess the effectiveness of the advertising campaign for the new PomWonderful beverage

   Which study was qualitative and which was quantitative?

8. What other studies would you recommend that PomWonderful undertake?

9. Suppose your university wants to modify its course scheduling procedures to better serve students. What

are some secondary sources of information that might be used to conduct research into this topic? Describe how these sources might be used. Describe a method you could use to gather primary research data about the topic. Would you recommend a specific order in obtaining each of these types of data? Explain your answer.

**10.** Tony is planning to launch a new shampoo and is trying to decide what features and price would interest consumers. He sends a Request for Proposal (RFP) to four marketing research vendors, and three respond, as described in the table below. Which vendor should Tony use? Explain your rationale for picking this vendor over the others.

**Table for Marketing Application 10**

| Vendor A | Vendor B | Vendor C |
|---|---|---|
| The vendor that Tony has used in the past, it estimates it can get the job done for $200,000 in two months. The vendor plans to do a telephone-based survey analysis and use secondary data. | Tony's key competitor has used this vendor, which claims that it can get the job done for $150,000 in one month. This vendor plans to do a telephone-based survey analysis and use secondary data. During a discussion pertaining to its price and time estimates, the vendor indicates it will draw on insights it has learned from a recent report prepared for one of Tony's competitors. | This well known vendor has recently started to focus on consumer packaged-goods clients. It quotes a price of $180,000 and a time of one month. The vendor plans to conduct an Internet-based survey analysis and use secondary data. |

## NET SAVVY

**1.** Go to the website of either Harris/Decima (http://www.decima.com) or Ipsos Canada (http://www.ipsos.ca), which administer public opinion polls. Search the site for results from any recent survey that are available for free. Print out the results. Identify the objective(s) of the survey. Discuss one of the major findings, and provide an interpretation of the data.

**2.** Select two online survey tools (e.g., SurveyMonkey, Qualtrics, Zoomerang, Survey Solutions) and compare and contrast them in terms of their features, capabilities, ease of use, support service, pricing models, clientele, and any other characteristics you think would be useful for a market researcher to know.

## CHAPTER CASE STUDY

### AUTOTRADER.COM: HOW RESEARCH SEPARATES FACT FROM FICTION

Imagine you are responsible for making next year's media buys for a large automobile dealership. You have your choice among traditional media, like television and newspaper advertising, and Internet-based channels, like social networking sites and automotive sites. How do you decide which types of advertising are most likely to build sales? How can you determine if an approach that works for a dealership in one city will work in another?

The online automobile dealer AutoTrader.com recognizes that convincing car dealers, associations, and manufacturers to advertise on its site requires proof that their media dollars will be well spent. To provide that proof, it offers the numbers that it collects from its website, which show that it hosts more than 4 million vehicle listings from 20,000 dealers and 85,000 private owners and more than 18 million unique website visitors each month.[55] But these basic quantitative details cannot prove that advertising on the site actually leads to sales. To accomplish that goal, AutoTrader.com also conducts market research to help dealers understand how people shop for cars and how the site can deliver those customers as an integral part of the car-shopping process.[56]

Many media buyers assume that the most accurate measure of the success of an online advertisement is click-through rates, that is, the number of clicks on an ad, divided by the number of times the ad gets shown. Although this measure indicates how many times an advertisement is viewed, it does not provide a reliable metric for the ad's impact on customer behaviour, especially when it comes to making the final purchase decision. Car dealers also hold their own beliefs about their customers' behaviour, which may be inaccurate but still determine their advertising choices. Therefore, to attract advertising dollars, AutoTrader.com needed to provide hard data, coming directly from the source—that is, the dealers and customers themselves.

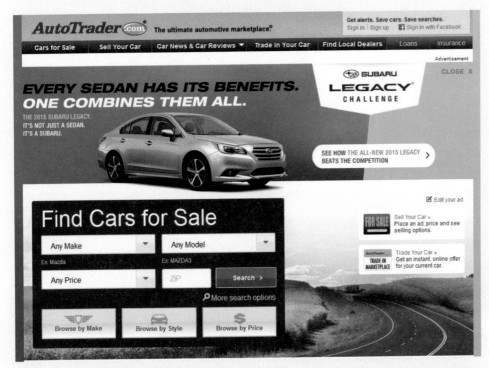

Buying or selling a car? Check out AutoTrader.com.

Courtesy of Autotrader.com

The marketing research performed by AutoTrader.com mainly serves to demonstrate the value of the Internet for selling vehicles.[57] In a survey of recent car buyers, the company found that 71 percent of respondents consulted the Internet to facilitate their new or used car purchase. Most of these buyers reported that the Internet was the single most influential source behind their ultimate purchase choice, that it was the most helpful source of information, and that social media sites played only a small role in their final decision. The importance of the Internet was reinforced by an online survey conducted by J.D. Power. It found that 63 percent of Canadians looking for a new car were more likely to schedule test drives with automakers whose websites provided a positive experience. Key elements a website had to deliver on included being easy to use, being fast, and providing a lot of useful content.[58]

The AutoTrader study also helped quantify other metrics surrounding car shopping behaviour, such as the average length of time consumers spend shopping for a car and how much of that time involves Internet browsing versus visiting dealerships. The result—that buyers spend more than half their shopping time online—helped substantiate the value of advertising on AutoTrader.com. This finding was strengthened by further data showing that independent sites like AutoTrader were used more frequently than dealer or manufacturer sites.

Going even a step further, AutoTrader.com sought to connect advertising on its site to dealership visits, which represent the main goal of advertising on AutoTrader.com by car dealers. Marketing researchers first determined what dealers believed about their customers' behaviour, using surveys. Then they gathered information from customers as they left dealerships, to find out the truth. To ensure accuracy and applicability, these researchers solicited customers of dealerships located in diverse markets, selling a variety of brands, and operating both as franchises and independently. The results debunked a lot of conventional wisdom (see Exhibit 7.13). For example, newspaper advertising was less effective than dealers had imagined, but Internet advertising played a more significant role in driving walk-in traffic.

■ **EXHIBIT 7.13** Reality Versus Dealer's Perception

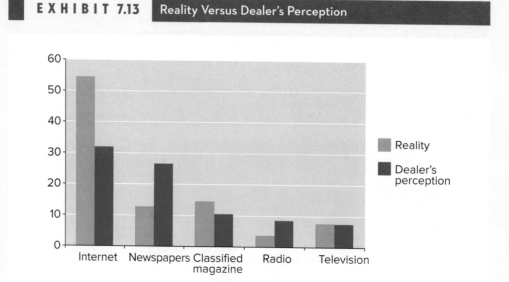

*Sources:* Adapted from Joe Richard, "How AutoTrader.com Uses Primary Research to Clarify the Car-Shopping Process," Quirk's Marketing Research Review, July 2011, p. 36, http://www.quirks.com/articles/2011/20110704.aspx.

While this information might be true based on an average across national dealerships, some dealers believed it was not the case at their particular business. To help convince these skeptics, AutoTrader.com launched hundreds of mini-research studies, including phone interviews with car buyers from individual stores. The results that emerged were remarkably similar to the national study, though some differences reflected geographic locations of the dealership.

Armed with this research, you are now confident that you understand the behaviour of car buyers well enough to make your media buy. But can you be completely sure that marketing research accurately predicts customer behaviour? Probably not, because human behaviour depends on a vast array of factors, many of which cannot be measured. But marketing research can help you ensure that your advertising dollars are spent wisely and in ways that seem most likely to increase sales.

### Questions

1. What are the objectives of AutoTrader.com's marketing research? How have its research projects contributed to the firm's ability to meet these objectives?

2. What methods has AutoTrader.com used to collect data about the effectiveness of dealer advertisements displayed on its site?

# Using Secondary Data to Assess Customer Lifetime Value (CLV)

This appendix examines how secondary data from customer transactions can help determine the value of a customer over time. Specifically, **customer lifetime value (CLV)** refers to the expected financial contribution from a particular customer to the firm's profits over the course of their relationship.[1]

**customer lifetime value (CLV)** The expected financial contribution from a particular customer to the firm's profits over the course of their relationship.

To estimate CLV, firms use past behaviours to forecast future purchases, the gross margin from these purchases, and the costs associated with servicing the customers. Some costs associated with maintaining customer relationships include communicating with customers through advertising, personal selling, or other promotional vehicles to acquire their business initially and then retain it over time.

Measures of CLV typically apply to a group or segment of customers and use available secondary data. A basic formula for CLV,[2] with the assumption that revenues and profits arrive at the start of the year, is as follows:

$$CLV = \frac{\sum_{t=1}^{T}\left[\text{Profit at t} \times \text{Retention rate}^{t-1}\right]}{(1 + i)^{t-1}} - \text{Acquisition costs}$$

To implement this CLV formula, we must answer the following questions:

1. How many years (t) can we expect to do business with a customer? The total number of years is denoted by T.

2. What can we expect the annual profits to be from an individual customer or an average customer? These profits are based on sales minus the costs of merchandise and the costs of serving and retaining the customer.

3. What is the retention rate, that is, the average percentage of customers who continue to purchase from the firm from one time period to another? A 90 percent retention rate means that if we have 100 customers in the first year, we will have 90 of those at the beginning of the second year.

4. What is the discount rate (i)? The discount rate is based on the idea that a dollar is worth less in the future than it is today, so the company can use it to adjust future profits and determine a customer's value today for the customer's purchases in the future. For example, if the discount rate is 10 percent, $100 in profits at the beginning of year 2 are worth only $90.91 (= 100/(1 + 0.1)) at the beginning of year 1.

Consider Gregory Missoni, a fairly new client of Very Clean Cleaners who switched from his other dry cleaner because Very Clean sent him $100 worth of coupons in a direct mailing. ∎

Greg just picked up his $200 shirt from Very Clean and found that the dry cleaner had broken a brown button and replaced it with a white button. When he complained, the clerk acted as if it was no big deal. Greg explained to the clerk that it was a very expensive shirt that deserved more careful handling and then asked to speak with the manager. At this point, how important is it that the manager makes sure Greg is satisfied, so that he will continue to bring his dry cleaning to Very Clean Cleaners? To answer this question, the manager uses the following information:

● It cost Very Clean $100 to acquire Greg as a customer. Thus, the acquisition cost is $100.

● Very Clean expects Greg to remain a client for 5 years (time horizon T = 5 years).

● Very Clean expects to make a $1,000 profit each year from Greg's dry cleaning.

● On average, 10 percent of customers defect to another cleaner each year. Therefore, the expected retention rate is 90 percent.

● The discount rate is 10 percent per year (i in this illustration). For simplicity, Very Clean assumes all profits are accrued at the beginning of the year.

Applying the formula, such that CLV equals the profits from years 1 to 5, less the acquisition costs, we obtain the following:

$$\text{CLV} = \underbrace{\frac{\$1,000 \times (0.90)^0}{(1 + 0.1)^0}}_{\textbf{Year 1}} + \underbrace{\frac{\$1,000 \times (0.90)^1}{(1 + 0.1)^1}}_{\textbf{Year 2}} + \underbrace{\frac{\$1,000 \times (0.90)^2}{(1 + 0.1)^2}}_{\textbf{Year 3}}$$

$$+ \underbrace{\frac{\$1,000 \times (0.90)^3}{(1 + 0.1)^3}}_{\textbf{Year 4}} + \underbrace{\frac{\$1,000 \times (0.90)^4}{(1 + 0.1)^4}}_{\textbf{Year 5}} - \$100$$

Or

$$\text{CLV} = \$1,000 + \$818.2 + \$669.4 + \$547.7 + \$448.1 - \$100 = \$3,383.40$$

Let's see how the formula works. The expected profit from Greg is $1,000 per year. Very Clean assumes profits accrue at the beginning of the year, so the profits for the first year equal $1,000; they are not affected by the retention rate or the discount rate.

However, the retention and discount rates have effects on the profits for the subsequent time periods. In the second year, the retention rate, which Very Clean determined was 90 percent (i.e., 90 percent of customers continue to do business with it) modifies profits, such that expected profits in the second year equal $1,000 × 90% = $900. Moreover, the discount rate is applied such that the profits received in the second year are worth less than if they had been received in the first year. Therefore, the $900 received at the beginning of the second year must be divided by 1.1, which is equivalent to $818.20.

Using similar calculations for the third year, the expected profits adjusted for retention are $1,000 × 0.9 × 0.9 = $810. The discount rate then reduces the profit to $810 ÷ 1.12 = $669.40 in today's dollars. (Note that the discount rate is squared because it refers to two years in the future.) After calculating the adjusted and discounted profits for the fourth and fifth years in similar fashion, we realize that the sum of estimated discounted profits for five years is $3,483.40. However, we still must subtract the $100 spent to acquire Greg, which provides a CLV of $3,383.40.

According to this analysis, it would be a good idea for the manager to take a long-term perspective when evaluating how to respond to Greg's complaint about his button. Greg cannot be viewed as a $2.50 customer, as he would be if Very Clean determined his value based on the cost of laundering his shirt, nor should he be viewed as a $200 customer, based on the cost of the shirt. He actually is worth a lot more than that.

For illustrative purposes, we have simplified the CLV calculations in this example. We assumed that the average profits remain constant at $1,000. But firms usually expect profits to grow over time, or else grow, level off, and then perhaps decline. Retention costs, such as special promotions used to keep Greg coming back, also do not appear in our illustration, though such additional costs would reduce annual profits and CLV. Finally, we assume a five-year time horizon; the CLV obviously would differ for longer or shorter periods. For an infinite time horizon, with first period payments upfront, the formula becomes fairly simple:[3]

$$\text{CLV} = \text{Profits} \times \left[ 1 + \frac{\text{Retention rate}}{(\$1 + \text{Discount rate} + \text{Retention rate})} \right] - \text{Acquisition cost}$$

$$= \$1,000 \left[ \frac{1 + 0.9}{(1 + 0.1 - 0.9)} \right] - \$100$$

$$= \$1,000 \times (1 + 4.5) - \$100$$

$$= \$5,500 - \$100 = \$5,400$$

This illustration thus explains how firms can use secondary data to calculate CLV; it further demonstrates the importance of knowing a customer's lifetime value when executing marketing tactics and strategies.

# SECTION FOUR
## VALUE CREATION

**CHAPTER 8**  Developing New Products
**CHAPTER 9**  Product, Branding, and Packaging Decisions
**CHAPTER 10**  Services: The Intangible Product

# CHAPTER 8

## LEARNING OBJECTIVES

**After studying this chapter you should be able to**

**LO1** Identify the reasons firms create new products

**LO2** Describe the diffusion of innovatio theory and how managers can use to make product line decisions

**LO3** List the stages involved in developir new products and services

**LO4** Describe the product life cycle an summarize how it is used to make product line decisions

dpa picture alliance/Alamy Stock Photo

# Developing New Products

When Lego first arrived in North America in the early 1960s, the company had devised a set of principles for the design of the moulded stud-and-tube bricks.[1] The toys had to offer unlimited play potential, be suitable for girls and for boys, and be fun for all ages. Lego wanted its products to provide long hours of healthy, quiet play, year-round, in a way that would stimulate development, imagination, and creativity. Quality would be built into every detail and extra sets would be available.

Over time, the Danish firm grew to become one of the top toy manufacturers in the world, introducing new sets and variations on its basic theme, including an extensive line of Star Wars models (as well as lines related to other popular movie franchises), basic robot technology, and superhero-themed collections. Perhaps unintentionally, it appeared that Lego had come to violate one of its basic principles, in that its toys appealed widely to boys but not specifically to girls.

Faced with declining profits in early 2000, Lego had determined that the popularity of video and automated games meant it needed to refocus on these areas. It developed Lego-branded video games to match its Star Wars line of building sets. It pushed its website and interactive opportunities. The "My Lego Network" social media site encouraged children to build their own web pages, personalized with pictures of their Lego creations, music, and sticker compositions.[2]

But these changes caused some members of the Lego team to worry about the effects on its long-standing traditions. Perhaps the predesigned sets were hindering creativity, rather than encouraging it. Maybe telling kids to go online was not really healthy for long-lasting play. And perhaps product lines focused on pirates, science fiction, and robots were not appealing enough to girls and the ways they like to play.

In market research involving in-depth observations of children playing—on their own and as they wished, without any direction or guidance from outside—Lego gained some notable insights.[3] For example, rather than appealing to children by simplifying its toys, Lego had made its sets too easy to construct, without room for careful thought or creativity. The observational research showed that children wanted a sense of mastery and accomplishment, not just instant gratification. In addition, its research with girls revealed that they were not uninterested in building. They just wanted to tell stories to go along with their construction—an effort that was undermined by the preset stories in Lego video games. As a Lego vice-president summarized, "We heard very clear requests from moms and girls for more details and interior building, a brighter colour palette, a more realistic figure, role-play opportunities and a story line that they would find interesting."[4]

And so, the company introduced Lego Friends, mini-doll figures whose names, back stories, and adventures are up to girls to develop and include in their own narratives.[5] The friends—Mia, Emma, Stephanie, Olivia, and Andrea—live in tree houses, drive convertibles, run a beauty parlour and a bakery, and play with their dogs. The colour schemes for all the sets are heavy in pink and purple. Furthermore, the doll figures are slimmer and curvier than the traditional, blocky Lego figures. Some parents found the products problematic because Lego Friends do not require children to complete the assembly to begin playing, which seemingly could diminish girls' sense of accomplishment. Others felt that beauty parlour and café sets reinforce gender stereotypes. Nevertheless, Lego Friends exceeded sales expectations, doubling the initial sales forecast in the first year.[6]

The company is always innovating. New products were launched as a result of Future Lab research that showed children don't differentiate between the physical and digital worlds.[7] It's all just play to them. One product, Lego Fusion, let children build a model, take a photo of it, and then bring the creation to life in a virtual world via an app on a tablet. Another product, Portal Racers, is a digital game that works with a 3D laptop camera to track body movements. In the future, children may be able to build a hovercraft out of Lego bricks and upload an image to the game. One reason to continually develop new products is because not all of them will succeed. While Portal Racers is still available, Lego Fusion has been retired. Still, Lego tripled its profits by focusing on sets. Its last annual report noted that revenues increased by 26 percent, with net profits of $1.4 billion, making it the most profitable toy company in the world.[8] With an estimated 100 million children having had a Lego experience, the company is likely to inspire and develop children through play well into the future. ■

Few three-letter words are more exciting than "new." It brings forth an image of freshness, adventure, and excitement. Yet "new" also is a complex term when it comes to market offerings, because it might mean adding something new to an existing product, introducing a flavour never offered before, or relying on different packaging that provides added value. But the most exhilarating type of new product is something never seen before. Thousands of patent applications pursue this elusive prize: a successful and truly innovative new product.

Imagine living 200 years ago. You cook your meals on a stove fuelled by coal or wood. As a student, you do your homework by hand, illuminated only by candlelight. You get to school on foot, by horseback, or in a horse-drawn carriage, if you're really fortunate. Your classroom is small and basic, and you have very few classmates. The professor simply lectures and writes on a chalkboard.

Today you finish your homework on a laptop with word-processing software that appears to have a mind of its own and corrects your spelling automatically. Your climate-controlled room has ample electric lighting. While you work on your laptop, you can also talk with a friend by using the hands-free headset of your phone. On your way to school, in your car, you pick up fast food from a convenient drive-through window while browsing or listening to your personal selection of songs playing through your car speakers, connected by Bluetooth to your smartphone. Your friend calls to discuss a slight change to an assignment, so you pull over to grab your iPhone, make the necessary changes, and email the assignment from your smartphone to your professor. When you arrive at university, you sit in a 200-person classroom where you plug in your laptop, take notes on it, and use it to digitally record the lecture. The professor adds notes on the day's PowerPoint presentations by using her tablet computer. You have already downloaded the PowerPoint presentations and add similar notes through your own laptop. After class, to complete your planning for a last-minute party, you send out a Facebook invitation to your friends and ask for responses to get a head count. Then you text your roommate, telling her to get food and drinks for the right number of people, which she orders through an online grocer that will deliver later in the day.

Our lives are defined by the many new products and services developed through scientific and technological advances and by the added features included in products we have always used.

This chapter deals with the first P in the marketing mix: product, specifically new products. As a key element of a firm's marketing mix (four Ps) strategies, product strategies are central to the creation of value for the consumer. A **product** is anything that is of value to a consumer and can be offered through a marketing exchange. In addition to goods (such as toothpaste) or services (such as a haircut), products might also be places (e.g., Whistler, British Columbia), ideas (e.g., "stop smoking"), organizations (e.g., Canadian Blood Services), people (e.g., Taylor Swift), or communities (e.g., Facebook) that create value for consumers in their respective competitive marketing arenas.

**product**
Anything that is of value to a consumer and can be offered through a marketing exchange.

Product branding and packaging will be examined in Chapter 9. Now we explore how companies add value to firms' product and service offerings through innovation. We also look at the process firms go through to develop new products and services. We conclude the chapter with an examination of how new products and services are adopted by the market and how firms change their marketing mix as the product or service moves through its life cycle.

## LO1   WHY DO FIRMS CREATE NEW PRODUCTS?

New market offerings provide value to both firms and customers. But the degree to which they do so depends on how new they really are. When we say a "new product," we don't necessarily mean that the product has never existed before—kids have played with LEGO for a long time, but Lego Portal Racers are new for them. Completely new-to-the-market products represent less than 10 percent of all new product introductions each year. (Refer to Sustainable Marketing 8.1 for an example of a "new product" that improves on an existing concept.) It is more useful to think of the degree of newness of a product on a continuum from "new-to-the-world"—as Wi-Fi was a few years ago—to "slightly repositioned," such as the repositioning of Kraft's Capri Sun brand of ready-to-drink beverages, which was repackaged in a bigger pouch to appeal more to teens. Regardless of where on the continuum a new product fits, firms have to innovate.

**Innovation** is the process by which ideas are transformed into new products and services that will help firms grow. Without innovation and its resulting new products and services, firms would have only two choices: continue to market current products to current customers, or take the same product to another market with similar customers.

Kraft's Capri Sun was repackaged to appeal to teens.
© McGraw-Hill Education

**Innovation**
The process by which ideas are transformed into new products and services that will help firms grow.

## Sustainable Marketing 8.1

### P&G Makes the World Cleaner and Greener

Large consumer packaged goods companies are sometimes viewed as contributing to the amount of waste consumers generate. In stark contrast, P&G's vision is that, one day, there will be no waste going to a landfill.[9] The company wants consumers who choose its products to understand its commitment to sustainability, a commitment that starts with product formulation, through the manufacturing process, package design, and distribution to stores. P&G not only wants to reduce its own waste but is working toward zero consumer waste going to landfill, too.

According to its Sustainability Report, nearly half of P&G's global manufacturing sites have already achieved zero manufacturing waste to landfill (ZMWTL).[10] In addition to initiatives involving waste, the company has stated its goal to reduce greenhouse gas (GHG) emissions from its operations by 30 percent by 2020. To do this, it is moving to more renewable fuel sources and increasing the use of renewable materials. For example, in partnership with EDF Renewable Energy, P&G is developing a wind farm in Texas. The farm will provide 100 megawatts of renewable power and eliminate 200,000 tonnes of GHG emissions annually. That's enough power to make all fabric and home care products—such as Tide, Downy, Febreze, and Cascade—in all of North America.

Product and packaging innovations are part and parcel of the company's efforts to help consumers reduce their own greenhouse gas emissions. You can get a sense of the difference the company's sustainability efforts make by examining just one P&G brand, Tide. For example, since 2008, product design improvements have resulted in using 40 percent less water and 40 percent less plastic. Tide packaging uses 25 percent recycled content. By consolidating distribution centres, trucks are driven 3 million fewer miles on the road each year. An industry first product improvement was achieved for Tide Coldwater. Discarded corn leaves and waste are now used in its production, resulting in 7,000 tonnes of agricultural waste being repurposed annually.[11]

New product development also takes sustainability into consideration. P&G's research showed that while consumers want bio-friendly products, those products still need to perform in a superior way. Tide Purclean is a breakthrough product. Manufactured with 65 percent renewable ingredients, it has been certified by the USDA BioPreferred program.[12] The new bio-based detergent offers the same cleaning power as Tide, in hot or cold water. It is made using wind power electricity in a plant that has zero manufacturing waste to landfill impact.[13] And, demonstrating commitment to making a difference at every step of the product life cycle, P&G's Tide Purclean bottle is 100 percent recyclable.

# A warning about wheels.

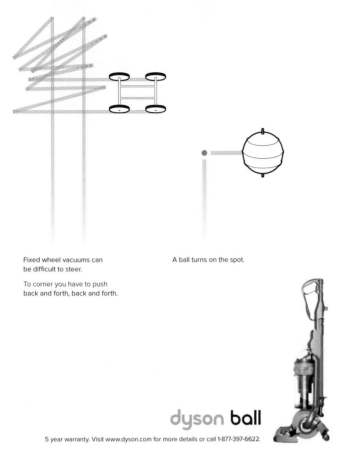

Fixed wheel vacuums can be difficult to steer.

To corner you have to push back and forth, back and forth.

A ball turns on the spot.

dyson **ball**

5 year warranty. Visit www.dyson.com for more details or call 1-877-397-6622.

Dyson added value by taking a well known product, the vacuum cleaner, and redesigning it so that it won't lose suction.

Used with permission of Dyson, Inc.

Although innovation strategies may not work in the short run—some estimates indicate that only about 3 percent of new products actually succeed—overriding long-term reasons compel firms to introduce new products and services. Firms innovate for a number of reasons, as we discuss next.

## Changing Customer Needs

When they add new products to their offerings, firms can create and deliver value more effectively by satisfying the changing needs of their current and new customers, or simply by keeping customers from getting bored with the current product or service offering. For example, Unilever's Dove Beauty Bar product line successfully extended the brand into hair, face, and skin-care lines, all under the Dove umbrella. Today, Dove loyalists can enjoy not only bar soap, but also antiperspirants and deodorants, moisturizing lotions, cleansers, toners, shampoo, conditioner, and much more.[14] Sometimes, companies can identify problems and develop products that customers never knew they needed. For example, a car wash offers a basic wash; a wash and polish; or a wash, polish, and undercarriage wash. Customers may never have thought about washing the undercarriage of their car prior to their exposure to the new service offering. In other cases, the firms take a well known offering and innovate to make it more interesting, as Dyson has done for the vacuum cleaner. According to the company's mythology, James Dyson caught sight of a local sawmill that used a cyclone to collect sawdust from the air, and then decided to apply the concept to a vacuum cleaner so he could create a vacuum that won't lose suction. The experience he had developing and protecting his innovative technology also formed the company's present innovation process, which relies heavily on secrecy, protection of ideas, and risk taking.

## Market Saturation

The longer a product exists in the marketplace, the more likely it is that the market will become saturated. Without new products or services, the value of the firm will ultimately decline. Imagine, for example, if car companies simply expected that people would keep their cars until they stopped running.[15] If that were the case, there would be no need to come up with new and innovative models; companies could just stick with the models that sell well. But few consumers actually keep the same car that long. Even those who want to stay with the same make and model often want something new, just to add some variety to their lives. So car companies revamp their models every year, whether by including new features, such as an automatic parking system or a more powerful engine, or by redesigning the entire look of the vehicle. The firms sustain their growth by getting consumers excited by the new looks and new features, prompting many car buyers to exchange their old vehicle years before its functional life is over.

Saturated markets can also offer opportunities for a company that is willing to adopt a new process or mentality. At one point in time, mass marketers would not even consider entering a market that they believed would not earn at least $50 million. But General Mills is looking to niche markets for its future growth. Whereas only 1 percent of the North American population suffers from celiac disease—a condition that damages the digestive system when sufferers ingest gluten—a much higher percentage of consumers say they want to reduce or eliminate gluten, a wheat protein, from their diet. As awareness increases, those percentages are growing, such that the North American market could be worth up to $10 billion.[16] General Mills has created more than 300 gluten-free products, including both variations on its regular offerings, like Chex cereals, and brand new concepts, such as gluten-free desserts and pancake mixes.[17]

## Managing Risk Through Diversity

Through innovation, firms often create a broader portfolio of products, which helps them diversify their risk and enhance firm value better than a single product can.[18] If some products in a portfolio are doing poorly, others may be doing well. Tapping innovative ideas allows companies to create new products to add to their existing portfolio. Firms with multiple products are better able to withstand external shocks, including changes in consumer preferences or intensive competitive activity. For this reason, firms such as 3M demand that a specific percentage of their sales each year must come from new products introduced within the previous few years. And, in the cereal aisle, Kellogg's offers many variations of its long-standing basic Special K product, including cereal bars and protein shakes. This diversification enables the company to achieve better results than it would with just one kind of Special K cereal.

General Mills provides a number of gluten-free options at http://www.chex.com/Recipes/GlutenFree.aspx.

Used with permission of General Mills Marketing Inc. (GMMI)

## Fashion Cycles

In industries that rely on fashion trends and experience short product life cycles—including apparel, arts, books, and software—most sales come from new products. For example, a motion picture generates most of its theatre, DVD, and cable TV revenues within a year of its release. If the same selection of books were always available for sale, with no new titles, there would be no reason to buy more. Consumers of computer

The Kellogg's Special K line's risk is lessened by offering many variations of its basic cereal product.

© Mike Hruby

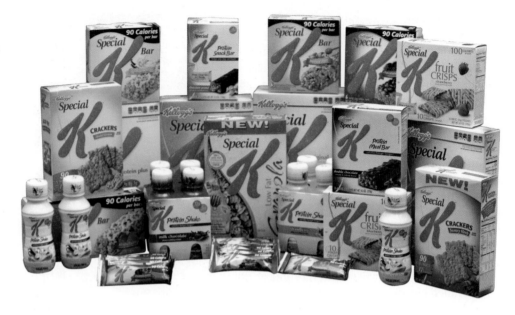

software and video games demand new products because once they have "beaten" the game, they want to be challenged by another game or experience the most recent version, as the remarkable sales of successive versions of the Call of Duty game exemplify.[19] In the case of apparel, fashion designers typically produce entirely new product selections a few times per year.

To generate sales, apparel fashion designers produce entirely new product selections a few times a year.

Zou Zheng Xinhua News Agency/Newscom

Video games like Call of Duty Infinite Warfare are "fashionable" because consumers demand new versions. Once they "beat" the game, they want to be challenged with a new experience.

mjmediabox/Alamy Stock Photo

## Improving Business Relationships

New products do not always target end consumers; sometimes they function to improve relationships with suppliers. For example, Kraft, the maker of Capri Sun, found that its lemonade flavour was selling poorly. Through a little market research, it realized that the reason was the placement of the packages in pallets. Because it was placed at the bottom of the stack in pallets, lemonade was the last flavour retailers would sell. By changing and innovating its pallet, Kraft offered chimney stacks for each flavour, enabling the retail stockers to reach whichever flavour they needed easily. Sales of Capri Sun's lemonade improved by 162 percent.[20]

# ADOPTION OF INNOVATION

**L02**

The process by which the use of an innovation—whether a product or a service—spreads throughout a market group, over time and over various categories of adopters, is referred to as **diffusion of innovation**[21] or adoption of innovation. The theory surrounding diffusion or adoption of innovation helps marketers understand the rate at which consumers are likely to adopt a new product or service. It also gives them a means to identify potential markets for their new products or services and predict their potential sales, even before they introduce the innovations.

Truly new product introductions, that is, new-to-the-world products that create new markets, can add tremendous value to firms. These new products, services, or processes are called **pioneers**, or breakthroughs, because they establish a completely new market or radically change both the rules of competition and consumer preferences in a market.[22] The Apple iPod was a pioneer product. Not only did it change the way people listen to music, but it also created an entirely new industry devoted to accessories, such as cases, ear buds, docking stations, and speakers. Although Apple offers many of these accessories itself, other companies have jumped on the bandwagon, ensuring that you can strap your iPod to your arm while on the move or insert it into the base of a desk lamp equipped with speakers to get music and light from your desk. And don't forget: The iPod also launched perhaps the most notable other recent pioneer, the iPhone, along with the iTunes service, the iPod Touch, and even the iPad.[23] **Disruptive innovations**, while new, are generally simpler, are less sophisticated, and may be less expensive than existing products or services. As an example, Netflix's introduction of streaming video disrupted the movie rental industry. The company gained share at the expense of entrenched competitors such as Blockbuster which eventually closed all its Canadian locations.

Pioneers have the advantage of being **first movers**; as the first to create the market or product category, they become readily recognizable to consumers and often establish a commanding and early market share lead. Studies have found that market pioneers can command a greater market share over a longer time period than later entrants can.[24] Yet not all pioneers succeed. In many cases, imitators capitalize on the weaknesses of pioneers and subsequently gain advantage in the market. Because pioneering products and brands face the uphill task of establishing the market alone, they pave the way for followers, which can spend less marketing effort creating demand for the product category and instead focus directly on creating demand for their specific brand. Also, because the pioneer is the first product in the market, it often has a less sophisticated design and may be priced relatively higher, leaving room for better and lower-priced competitive products.

An important question to ask is, why is the failure rate of new products so high? One of the main reasons is the failure to assess the market properly by neglecting to do appropriate product testing, targeting the wrong segment, and/or poor positioning. As many as 95 percent of all consumer goods fail. Why? There are many reasons. Most commonly they offer consumers too few benefits, are too complex, or require substantial learning and effort. Sometimes bad timing is responsible—that is, new products or services are

**diffusion of innovation**
The process by which the use of an innovation, whether a product or a service, spreads throughout a market group over time and over various categories of adopters.

**pioneers**
New product introductions that establish a completely new market or radically change both the rules of competition and consumer preferences in a market; also called breakthroughs.

**disruptive innovations**
New product introductions that are simpler, less sophisticated, and usually less expensive than existing products or services.

**first movers**
Product pioneers that are the first to create a market or product category, making them readily recognizable to consumers and thus establishing a commanding and early market share lead.

| EXHIBIT 8.1 | Illustrative Product Failures |
|---|---|

| Product | Concept | Why It Failed |
|---|---|---|
| New Coke | In response to growing market pressure, Coca-Cola launched a reformulated version of its classic cola in 1985 that was so hated it was pulled from shelves three months later. | Coke underestimated consumers' affinity to the original formulation and their unwillingness to change. |
| Sony Betamax | In 1975, Sony bet big on the Betamax, one of the first ever mass-produced home video recording systems. | Unfortunately, the next year, JVC launched the VHS player, leading to a format war similar to the Blu-ray and HD-DVD format wars of 2006. |
| Harley-Davidson Perfume | After being successful with lighters and T-shirts bearing the Harley logo, Harley-Davidson branched out into its own line of perfumes "associated" with the motorcycle lifestyle. | Although lighters and T-shirts may resonate with the Harley image, customers were not as attracted to smelling like a motorcycle. |
| Bic Underwear | Bic is well known for its disposable products: pens, lighters, and razors. Capitalizing on its ability to cross product categories, Bic began producing underwear. | The concept of buying underwear from a company well known for disposable pens was confusing and off-putting to consumers. |
| Frito-Lay Lemonade | To Frito-Lay, lemonade seemed like a reasonable enough brand extension. After all, the high salt content of corn chips often leads consumers to search out something to quench their thirst. | Associating a salty snack with a supposed "thirst quencher" did not go over well. |
| Colgate Kitchen Entrees | Colgate launched a line of frozen dinners. Apparently the idea was that consumers would enjoy eating a Colgate meal and then using Colgate on their toothbrush afterward. | The association of toothpaste with a chicken stir fry was something customers did not find appetizing. |

Source: DailyFinance.com, "Top 25 Biggest Product Flops of All Time," http://www.dailyfinance.com/photos/top-25-biggest-product-flops-of-all-time/3662621.

introduced at a time when consumers are not ready for them. Firms may also overextend their abilities or competencies by venturing into products or services that are inconsistent with their brand image and/or value proposition. We discuss some infamous product failures in Exhibit 8.1.

Even if they succeed, new-to-the-world products are not adopted by everyone at the same time. Rather, they diffuse or spread through a population in a process known as diffusion or adoption of innovation.

As the consumer adoption cycle in Exhibit 8.2 shows, the number of users of an innovative product or service spreads through the population over time and generally follows a bell-shaped curve. A few people buy the product or service at first, then increasingly more buy, and finally fewer people buy as the degree of the diffusion slows. For example, it took close to 20 years to get about 90 percent of Canadians to use automated teller machines (ATMs), but within five years more than 60 percent of Canadians adopted the Internet. Comparing the iPod and Sony Walkman, Merrill Lynch analyst Steve Milunovich observes that after only 2.5 years, iPod shipments were approximately 1 million units ahead of the Walkman's pace after being on the market for the same period of time in the 1980s when the Walkman was first released.[25] Apple's iPad reached 1 million units in its first 28 days—less than half the 74 days it took for the iPhone to reach the same milestone.[26]

Purchasers can be divided into five groups—innovators, early adopters, early majority, late majority, and laggards—according to how soon they buy the product after it has been introduced.

**EXHIBIT 8.2**    Consumer Adoption Cycle

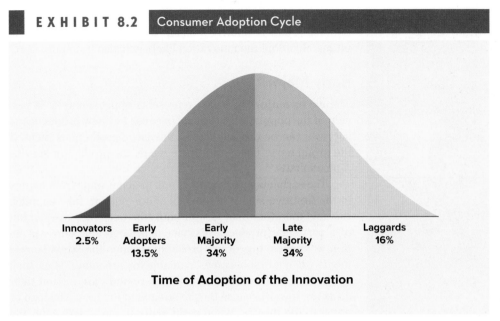

*Source:* Adapted from Everett M. Rodgers, *Diffusion of Innovation* (New York: The Free Press, 1983).

## Innovators

**Innovators** are those buyers who want to be the first on the block to have the new product or service. These buyers enjoy taking risks, are regarded as highly knowledgeable, and are not price sensitive. You probably know someone who is an innovator—or perhaps you are one for a particular product or service category. For example, the person who stood in line for days to be sure to get a ticket for the very first showing of the latest superhero movie is an innovator in that context. Consumers who already have 3D printers in their homes are likely innovators. Firms that invest in the latest technology, either to use in their products or services or to make the firm more efficient, also are considered innovators. Typically, innovators keep themselves very well informed about the product category by subscribing to trade and specialty magazines, talking to other "experts," searching the Internet, and attending product-related forums, seminars, and special events. Typically, innovators represent only about 2.5 percent of the total market for any new product or service.

These innovators are crucial to the success of any new product or service because they help the product gain market acceptance. Through talking and spreading positive word-of-mouth about the new product, they prove instrumental in bringing in the next adopter category, known as early adopters.

**innovators**
Those buyers who want to be the first to have the new product or service.

## Early Adopters

The second subgroup that begins to use a product or service innovation is the **early adopters**. They generally don't like to take as much risk as innovators but instead wait and purchase the product after careful review. Early adopters tend to enjoy novelty and often are regarded as the opinion leaders for particular product categories. This market waits for the first reviews of the latest movie before purchasing a ticket, though they likely still go a week or two after it opens. They don't stand in line to grab the first Samsung 4K televisions; only after reading the innovators' complaints and praises do they decide whether it is worth the cost. But most of them go ahead and purchase products because early adopters tend to enjoy novelty and are often regarded as opinion leaders for particular product categories.

This group, which represents about 13.5 percent of all buyers in the market, acts as opinion leaders and spreads the word. As a result, early adopters are crucial for bringing

**early adopters**
The second group of consumers in the diffusion of innovation model, after innovators, to use a product or service innovation; generally don't like to take as much risk as innovators.

Early majority members would probably wait to see the latest Guardians of the Galaxy movie. They may assess movie reviews and the cost to stream it will be lower than seeing it at the theatre.

ZCHE/Supplied by WENN/Newscom

**early majority**
A group of consumers in the diffusion of innovation model that represents approximately 34 percent of the population; members don't like to take much risk and therefore tend to wait until bugs are worked out.

**late majority**
The last group of buyers to enter a new product market.

**laggards**
Consumers who like to avoid change and rely on traditional products until they are no longer available.

the other three buyer categories to the market. If the early adopter group is relatively small, the number of people who ultimately adopt the innovation likely will also be small.

## Early Majority

The **early majority**, which represents approximately 34 percent of the population, is crucial because few new products and services can be profitable until this large group buys them. If the group never becomes large enough, the product or service typically fails.

The early majority group differs in many ways from buyers in the first two stages. Its members don't like to take as much risk and therefore tend to wait until "the bugs" are worked out of a particular product or service. If we continue our application to movies, this group probably streams the latest Marvel movie when it first becomes available for streaming. Thus, they experience little risk, because all the reviews are in, and their costs are lower because they're streaming the movie instead of going to the theatre. When early majority customers enter the market, the number of competitors in the marketplace usually also has reached its peak, so these buyers have many different price and quality choices.

## Late Majority

At 34 percent of the market, the **late majority** is the last group of buyers to enter a new product market; when they do, the product has achieved its full market potential. Perhaps these movie watchers wait until the latest movie is easy to find at a rental outlet or when it finally comes to cable television. Either way, they watch the movie long after the other consumers interested in it have already seen it. By the time the late majority enters the market, sales tend to level off or may be in decline.

## Laggards

**Laggards** make up roughly 16 percent of the market. These consumers like to avoid change and rely on traditional products until they are no longer available.[27] In some cases, laggards may never adopt a certain product or service. When the final *Hunger Games* movie eventually shows up on regular TV networks, they are likely to go ahead and watch it. Other examples of laggards are households that still use flip phones versus smartphones or listen to music on audiocassettes because they do not own an MP3 player.

## Using the Adoption Cycle

Using the diffusion of innovation theory or adoption cycle, firms can predict which types of customers will buy their new product or service immediately after its introduction, as well as later as the product gets more and more accepted by the market. With this knowledge, the firm can develop effective promotion, pricing, and other marketing strategies to push acceptance within each customer group.

Although they are not as flashy as wearable tech or the latest iPhone, everyone uses cleaning supplies. Oftentimes the innovators who adopt new cleaning products are the ones who are the most fanatical about cleaning. Firms conduct in-depth research into how people clean their homes to identify such segments. This research finds that some people are so obsessive about cleaning that they spend nearly 20 hours every week doing it, while others are so reluctant that they avoid cleaning as much as they can; their average weekly cleaning time is about 2.5 hours.[28] Their options with regard to the products to purchase to assist them in their cleaning tasks are vast, from scrubbers to sprays to vacuums to dusters. Thus, in the vacuum cleaner market, manufacturers recognize that the segment of consumers who will spend substantial amounts for the most technologically advanced, powerful, easy-to-maneuver machines, such as the latest Dyson model, are likely to be the segment of consumers that is most fixated on cleaning.[29] But another segment just wants some basic suction to get the grit out of their rugs.

However, because different products are adopted at different rates, marketers must understand what the diffusion curve for the new product looks like, as well as the characteristics of the target customers in each stage of the diffusion. For example, the marketing decisions for ereaders are notably different from the parallel decisions for electronic books. When the ereaders first emerged on the market, the price of ebooks was a fraction of the price of hardcover versions—a policy that made sense to consumers. But as ereaders have grown increasingly popular and widespread, the price of ebooks has become comparable to, and in some cases higher than, the price of the hardcover versions.[30] The speed with which products are adopted depends on several product characteristics, illustrated in Exhibit 8.3.

**Relative Advantage**  If a product is perceived to be better than substitutes, then the diffusion will be relatively quick. As advertising for Swiffer products emphasizes, its mops and dusters promise to make cleaning faster, easier, and more efficient. In featuring real families, it seeks to highlight the relative advantage for all types of cleaners. Older people who might once have gotten on their hands and knees to scrub the floor can now rely on the design of the cleaning pads on the end of the mop to get the job done. Their children, who have never been very good at cleaning, can swipe a few surfaces and get the house looking clean before their parents visit. And a man who has lost an arm to cancer can still help his family keep the house clean, because the duster does not require him to use a spray or climb a ladder to dust the ceiling fan.[31]

**Compatibility**  A diffusion process may be faster or slower, depending on various consumer features, including international cultural differences. Electrolux's latest bagless vacuums offer a key innovation: They solve the age-old problem of how to empty the chamber without having a cloud of particles fly out by compacting the dirt into a "pellet."

---

**EXHIBIT 8.3**  Factors Affecting Product Diffusion Speed

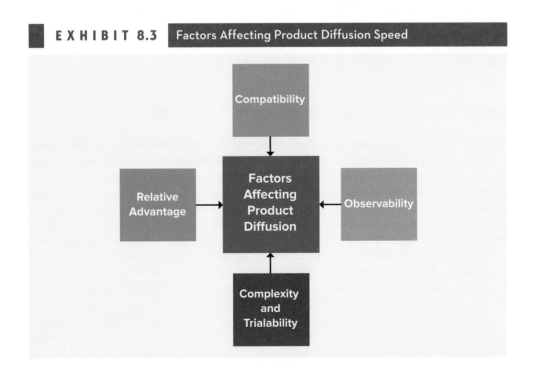

Electrolux revolutionized
the vacuum market
with a bagless vacuum
cleaner.

Electrolux

To make the product more compatible with the needs of people in different cultures, it is made in various sizes. The North American version offers a carpet nozzle with a motor, to deal with the dirt accumulated in larger, often carpeted homes. Because in many Asian "megacities" consumers live in tiny apartments, Electrolux has introduced a smaller version that is also very quiet.[32] Similarly, the ritual of "having a coffee" is well ingrained in many cultures, including Canadian culture. "Having a coffee" is consistent with people's past behaviour, their needs, and their values. Since people are accustomed to drinking coffee, it has been relatively easy for Starbucks to acquire customers in Canada. The diffusion has been much slower in countries such as China and Japan, where tea has been the traditional drink.

Observability   When products are easily observed, their benefits or uses are easily communicated to others, which enhances the diffusion process. To demonstrate to consumers why they should spend $400 on a blender, Blendtec launched an extensive YouTube campaign titled "Will It Blend?" to demonstrate the effectiveness of the blender. In each video, a spokesperson in a white lab coat blends a different product in the Blendtec—from iPads to baseballs to Justin Bieber's autobiography—and gives visible proof to consumers of the quality of the product. The humour and innovativeness of this product demonstration has caused these videos to go viral, with over 230 million views and 910,000 subscribers.[33] Yet some cleaning products face a serious challenge in making their innovations widely observable because few consumers spend a lot of time talking about the products that are of a more personal nature, such as what they use to clean their toilets. Even a great product might diffuse more slowly if people feel uncomfortable talking about what they perceive to be involved in their personal care.

Complexity and Trialability   Products that are relatively less complex are also relatively easy to try. These products will generally diffuse more quickly than those that are not.  In the cleaning products range, it is far easier to pick up a new spray cleaner at the grocery store to try at home than it is to assess and test a new vacuum. In response, manufacturers seek ways to help people conduct trials. For example, Dyson's displays in national retailers such as Bed, Bath, & Beyond often include floor space that allows shoppers to run the machine, to see how well the roller ball works or watch it pick up dirt.

The diffusion of innovation theory thus comes into play in the immediate and long-term aftermath of a new product or service introduction. But before the introduction, firms must actually develop those new offerings. Therefore, in the next section, we detail the process by which most firms develop new products and services and how they initially introduce them into the market.

## LO3    HOW FIRMS DEVELOP NEW PRODUCTS

The new product development process begins with the generation of new product ideas and culminates in the launch of the new product and the evaluation of its success. The stages of the new product development process, along with the important objectives of each stage, are summarized in Exhibit 8.4. Although this exhibit depicts linear and sequential stages, in reality, the process is iterative, consisting of a number of feedback loops at various stages. Generally the process is a team effort with the new product team composed of members from various functions: marketing, design, engineering, manufacturing, procurement, and finance, all of which play different roles at different stages of the process. Marketing plays a crucial role in the new product development process by communicating customer needs and wants and marketplace preferences and attitudes to the research and development (R&D) and engineering group.

Bear in mind that it's not always necessary to take a new product through each stage in the process. Substantially new products will likely follow the process fairly closely, while products imitating a successful product from a competitor, having a low development

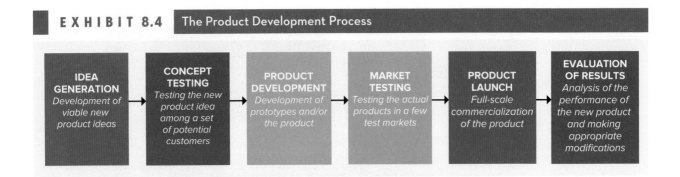

**EXHIBIT 8.4**  The Product Development Process

| IDEA GENERATION | CONCEPT TESTING | PRODUCT DEVELOPMENT | MARKET TESTING | PRODUCT LAUNCH | EVALUATION OF RESULTS |
|---|---|---|---|---|---|
| *Development of viable new product ideas* | *Testing the new product idea among a set of potential customers* | *Development of prototypes and/or the product* | *Testing the actual products in a few test markets* | *Full-scale commercialization of the product* | *Analysis of the performance of the new product and making appropriate modifications* |

cost, or involving incremental changes (such as line extensions) may skip one or more steps. For example, P&G launched its Folgers brand of decaffeinated crystal coffee without market testing. Although skipping stages in the new product development process is very risky, companies often do it to reduce costs or launch new products quickly.

## Idea Generation

To generate ideas for new products, a firm can use its own internal R&D efforts, collaborate with other firms and institutions, license technology from research-intensive firms, brainstorm, research competitors' products and services, and/or conduct consumer research. Sometimes new product ideas come from employees, customers, suppliers, and partners or are generated by attending trade shows and conferences. Companies also generate ideas by using reverse engineering or, in more extreme cases, even by digging through a competitor's garbage. Firms that want to be pioneers rely more extensively on R&D efforts, whereas those that tend to adopt a follower strategy are more likely to scan the market for ideas. Let's look at each of these idea sources.

**Internal Research and Development**  Many firms have their own R&D departments, in which scientists work to solve complex problems and develop new ideas.[34] Historically, firms such as IBM in the computer industry, Black and Decker in the consumer goods industry, 3M in the industrial goods industry, and Merck and Pfizer in the pharmaceuticals industry have relied on R&D efforts for their new products. In other industries—such as software, music, and motion pictures—product development efforts also tend to come from internal ideas and investments. 3M is known for innovation and has product offerings spanning an incredible range of categories from health care to highway safety, and from office and pet care products to fly fishing equipment and solar film. Because the company is committed to providing useful, new products to customers, 3M reinvests a significant percentage of its revenues in research.[35] It allows its researchers to spend time pursuing their own interests so when industrial architects asked 3M for some ideas for lighting their studios, it put one of its creative designers on the project. The result, the nine-foot Hoop Light, won 3M design awards at interior design international competitions.[36]

The product development costs for firms are quite high, but the resulting new product or service has a good chance of being a technological or market breakthrough. Firms expect such products to generate enough revenue and profits to make the costs of R&D worthwhile; however, R&D investments generally are considered continuous investments, so firms may lose money on a few new products. In the long run though, these firms are betting that a few extremely successful new products, often known as blockbusters, can generate enough revenues and profits to cover the losses from other introductions that might not fare so well.

Some global firms also are taking an approach called "reverse innovation." They turn to subsidiaries in less developed markets for new product ideas. From its Shanghai research centre, Coca-Cola developed Minute Maid Pulpy, a new juice drink that the

Where do you think the idea for a waterproof tablet from Fujitsu came from? Internal R&D, licensing, brainstorming, outsourcing, competitors' products, customer input, or a combination?
Odd Andersen/AFP/Getty Images

corporation has moved into 19 countries and is now worth more than $1 billion. Levi's Denizen brand got its start in India and China, where the company worked on ideas for producing more affordable jeans. In the U.S. market, Denizen jeans sell for about half the cost of a pair of regular Levi's.[37]

Licensing   For many new scientific and technological products, firms buy the rights to use the technology or ideas from other research-intensive firms through a licensing agreement. This approach saves the high costs of in-house R&D, but it means that the firm is banking on a solution that already exists but has not been marketed. Some of the largest recent licensing deals in the pharmaceutical industry are for potential weight-loss solutions. In separate deals, one worth $1.4 billion and another worth $1.1 billion, two big pharmaceutical firms licensed the marketing rights for new products developed by small biotechnology firms to combat obesity.[38]

Brainstorming   Firms often engage in brainstorming sessions during which a group works together to generate ideas. One of the key characteristics of a brainstorming session is that no idea can be immediately accepted or rejected. The moderator of the session may channel participants' attention to specific product features and attributes, performance expectations, or packaging. Only at the end of the session do the members vote on the best ideas or combinations of ideas. Those ideas that receive the most votes are carried forward to the next stage of the product development process.

Outsourcing   In some cases, companies have trouble moving through these steps alone, which prompts them to turn to outside firms such as IDEO, a design firm based in Palo Alto, California. IDEO offers not new products but rather a stellar service that helps clients generate new product and service ideas in industries such as health care, toys, and computers. IDEO employs anthropologists, graphic designers, engineers, and psychologists whose special skills help foster creativity and innovation. As exercise is becoming more and more popular, companies are looking for ways to capitalize on the beginners market. Balanced Body is a company that makes and sells reformers to be used with Pilates. A reformer is a device that helps Pilates participants develop good alignment, core strength, and flexibility. When Balanced Body did research and found that people starting Pilates found the reformers that were currently on the market to be too intimidating, it partnered with IDEO to develop a reformer that had better user experience while maintaining the high level of functionality its products engender. In an eight-week period, IDEO created a redesigned model with fewer wheels while improving functionality and adjustability of the product and reducing the cost of the machine.

Balanced Body partnered with IDEO to develop a less intimidating, more user-friendly reformer to be used with Pilates.

Courtesy of Balanced Body, Inc.

**Competitors' Products** A new product entry by a competitor may trigger a market opportunity for a firm, which can use reverse engineering to understand the competitor's product and then bring an improved version to market. **Reverse engineering** involves taking apart a competitor's product, analyzing it, and creating an improved product that does not infringe on the competitor's patents, if any exist. This copycat approach to new product development is widespread and practised by even the most research-intensive firms. Copycat consumer goods show up in grocery and drugstore products, as well as in technologically more complex products such as automobiles and computers, as noted in Social and Mobile Marketing 8.1.

**reverse engineering** Involves taking apart a competitor's product, analyzing it, and creating an improved product that does not infringe on the competitor's patents, if any exist.

**Customer Input** Listening to the customer is essential for successful idea generation.[40] Prior studies have found that as much as 85 percent of all new business-to-business (B2B) product ideas come from customers.[41] Because customers for B2B products are relatively few in number, firms can follow their use of products closely and survey them often for suggestions and ideas to improve those products. The firm's design and development team then works on these suggestions, sometimes in consultation with the customer. This joint effort between the selling firm and the customer significantly increases the probability that the customer eventually will buy the new product.

Customer input in B2C markets comes from a variety of sources, though increasingly through social media. By monitoring online feedback, whether requested by the firm or provided voluntarily in customer reviews, companies can get better ideas about new products or necessary changes to existing ones. The recent introduction of Green Giant snack chips provides a good example of using inputs from various types of partners. General Mills (which owns the Green Giant brand) heard a pitch for a new vegetable-based snack chip from its supplier Shearer's Chips. The chip manufacturer developed 10 options for its business customer, General Mills. Then General Mills solicited input from its end consumers to find out which flavours they might like best. Online reviews suggested the need for a much zestier version of the roasted vegetable tortilla chips, which ultimately appeared on store shelves.[42]

In some cases, consumers may not expressly demand a new product, though their behaviour demonstrates their desire for it. For example, Home Depot conducted some in-home research with consumers to see where they might have unexpressed needs. Although women never mentioned their need, the researchers realized that women engaged in heavy-duty gardening tasks wound up struggling with the bulky, heavy buckets they were using to transport dirt and fertilizer to different

In response to consumers' input, the Big Gripper bucket was designed to make it easier to handle.

Courtesy of Leaktite Corporation

## Social and Mobile Marketing 8.1

### When Microsoft Plays Catch-Up[39]

Microsoft is one of the most innovative companies of all time. After revolutionizing the home computer industry, it set out to be a leader in the information technology home entertainment fields. It seems like not a year ever goes by without something new from the brainchild of Bill Gates.

But one area in which Microsoft has been behind the curve is the search engine market. Google, with nearly 70 percent global market share and massive name recognition, does not appear to be in any real danger from competitors, including Microsoft's Bing.com. But Bing already has outpaced Yahoo.com for the remainder of the market, and its market share has been growing, slowly but surely. Perhaps most importantly, it is distinguishing itself by providing more frequent updates and feature additions than other search engines. Consumers benefit overall because Bing is forcing competitors to improve their offering to keep pace with Microsoft or prevent it from stealing market share from them.

Its efforts have paid off somewhat: Bing now attracts an approximately 21 percent market share among North American users, whereas Yahoo! accounts for only about 12 percent. Google maintains a remarkably high share, though that level has decreased in recent years. Despite these seeming successes, the costs of its copycat efforts have meant that the division responsible for Bing lost $2.56 billion in one recent fiscal year.

Microsoft's Bing competes with Google in the search engine market.

M4OS Photos/Alamy Stock Photo

To differentiate itself better, Bing is being promoted as a decision engine rather than a search engine. It integrates Foursquare, a location-based phone application, into Bing Maps results. Users can focus on a particular area, such as West Vancouver, which means Bing can act like an integrative day planner and list the best things to do in that area. It is working on developing a desktop application, and Bing links seamlessly with Facebook to show users which search outcome their friends like best. Despite Microsoft's problems developing search engines, Bing suggests it intends to stay aggressive in this market.

---

**lead users**
Innovative product users who modify existing products according to their own ideas to suit their specific needs.

Innovative customers called lead users are especially influential in the fashion industry because designers frequently change their designs based on trends they see on the street.

Big Cheese Photo/SuperStock RF

areas of the yard. In partnership with a design firm, it thus developed the Big Gripper bucket with a more ergonomic handle, a secondary grip on the side (to make it easier to tip the bucket), and another grip on the bottom. In this case, Home Depot has improved on a product that has not changed notably in decades, by observing how people use it.[43]

Another particularly successful customer input approach is to analyze **lead users**, those innovative product users who modify existing products according to their own ideas to suit their specific needs.[44] If lead users customize the firm's products, other customers might wish to do so as well. Studying lead users helps the firm understand general market trends that might be just on the horizon. Manufacturers and retailers of fashion products often spot new trends by noticing how trendsetters have altered their clothing and shoes. Designers of high-fashion jeans distress their products in different ways depending on signals they pick up "on the street." One season, jeans appear with whiskers; the next, holes; the next, paint spots.

At the end of the idea-generation stage, the firm should have several ideas that it can take forward to the next stage: concept testing.

## Concept Testing

Ideas with potential are developed further into **concepts**, which in this context refers to brief written descriptions of the product; its technology, working principles, and forms; and what customer needs it would satisfy.[45] A concept might also include visual images of what the product would look like.

**Concept testing** refers to the process in which a concept statement is presented to potential buyers representative of the target market or users to obtain their reactions. These reactions enable the developer to estimate the sales value of the product or service concept, possibly make changes to enhance its sales value, and determine whether the idea is worth further development.[46] If the concept fails to meet customers' expectations, it is doubtful it would succeed if it were to be produced and marketed. Because concept testing occurs very early in the new product introduction process, even before a real product has been made, it helps the firm avoid the costs of unnecessary product development.

The concept for an electric scooter might be written as follows:

> The product is a lightweight electric scooter that can be easily folded and taken with you inside a building or on public transportation. The scooter weighs 25 pounds [11 kg]. It travels at speeds of up to 15 miles [24 km] per hour and can go about 12 miles [19 km] on a single charge. The scooter can be recharged in about two hours from a standard electric outlet. The scooter is easy to ride and has simple controls—just an accelerator button and a brake. It sells for $299.[47]

Concept testing progresses along the research techniques described in Chapter 7. The firm likely starts with qualitative research, such as in-depth interviews or focus groups, to test the concept, after which it can undertake quantitative research through Internet or mall-intercept surveys. Video clips on the Internet might show a virtual prototype and the way the product or service works so that potential customers can evaluate it.[48] In a mall-intercept survey, an interviewer would provide a description of the concept to the respondent and then ask several questions to obtain his or her feedback.

The most important question pertains to the respondent's purchase intentions if the product or service were to be made available. Marketers also should ask whether the product would satisfy a need that other products currently are not meeting. Depending on the type of product or service, researchers might also ask about the expected frequency of purchase, how much customers would buy, whether they would buy it for themselves or as a gift, when they would buy, and whether the price information (if provided) indicates a good value. In addition, marketers usually collect some demographic information so they can analyze which consumer segments are likely to be most interested in the product.

Some concepts never make it past this stage, particularly if respondents seem uninterested. Those that do receive high evaluations from potential consumers, however, move on to the next step, product development.

## Product Development

**Product development** or product design entails a process of balancing various engineering, manufacturing, marketing, and economic considerations to develop a product's form and features or a service's features. An engineering team develops a product prototype that is based on research findings from the previous concept testing step, as well as their own knowledge about materials and technology. A **prototype** is the first physical form or service description of a new product, still in rough or tentative form, that has the same properties as a new product but is produced through different manufacturing processes, sometimes even crafted individually.[49] As discussed in Entrepreneurial Marketing 8.1, sometimes many iterations are needed to come up with a design that works.

**concepts**
Brief written descriptions of a product or service; its technology, working principles, and forms; and what customer needs it would satisfy.

**concept testing**
The process in which a concept statement that describes a product or a service is presented to potential buyers or users to obtain their reactions.

**product development**
Entails a process of balancing various engineering, manufacturing, marketing, and economic considerations to develop a product.

**prototype**
The first physical form or service description of a new product, still in rough or tentative form, that has the same properties as a new product but is produced through different manufacturing processes, sometimes even crafted individually.

## Entrepreneurial Marketing 8.1

### Bartesian—Premium Cocktails on Demand[50]

Sometimes the quest for a new venture leads in strange directions. For Bryan Fedorak, the path moved from educational toys for children to cocktails. Fedorak graduated from mechanical engineering and later went on to do an MBA. With the help of Velocity Garage, a unique program for start-up businesses offered through the University of Waterloo, he was able to launch Bartesian with a partner.

Margarita    Sex on the Beach    Cosmopolitan    Zest Martini    Bartesian Breeze    Uptown Rocks

Bartesian lets consumers make their own cocktails as easily as making a cup of coffee. Six different cocktails are available currently.

Used with permission of Bartesian, www.bartesian.com

Their idea was a Keurig-like machine that would make cocktails instead of coffee. Coming up with the idea was easy. Testing the concept and creating a prototype proved to be a lot harder. The original prototype, P1, was really just a retrofitted coffee machine—a very minimalistic device. The basic idea for the product didn't change much over time, however, the design and target market did. Fedorak and his partner originally thought that the target market would be female college and university students. Research through customer discovery sessions showed that their market was indeed female, albeit older and more affluent—essentially the "hostess with the mostest."

A trade show allowed them to collect more feedback and reactions from potential customers as well as get more input on how people might use the unit. From there they came up with a second prototype, P2, which was the first working functional model. Fedorak says it was really ugly, and made from scrap plywood, but it was sufficient to prove the concept. Having passed that hurdle, the team faced design challenges and so applied to take part in HAX, a hardware accelerator program in Shenzhen, China. It allowed them to build more prototypes much faster than was possible in Canada. Over a four-month period in Shenzhen, Fedorak, his co-founder, and a co-op student worked on P3, which was still pretty ugly but proved the mechanical concept. That was followed by P4, a foam core model. Until this point, the cost to develop prototypes was very low. That was about to change.

The key to prototyping was to always be testing. Along the way they discovered that users didn't always know what type of glass to use for certain drinks (e.g., a tall glass is needed for a highball, otherwise the glass will overflow). And so the Bartesian unit was designed to tell customers the best glass to use for the drink they select. The P5 prototype cost $2,000 and helped advance the design, but the team still wasn't happy with the way it looked. Realizing they were not industrial designers, they hired Swedish designers who came up with a great concept, P6. Another $5,000 was invested. However, it eventually led to the final prototype, P7. The $5,000 spent on this iteration included touch screen controls to avoid potential problems with sticky buttons that could stop working. That might seem like a lot of prototypes and a lot of expense, but given the high fixed costs to begin production, Fedorak absolutely had to be certain the design was perfected before starting the manufacturing process.

All the while the hardware prototype was being developed, Fedorak's team was also working with a mixologist to create special drink pods for the machine. The taste had to be authentic, which meant using real ingredients, not drink crystals. The key was to come up with pods (just like a Keurig machine) that provided the drink flavour. Oh, and the pods had to be recyclable. Since selling alcohol would create regulatory challenges, Bartesian was designed to let consumers use their own gin, vodka, rum, or tequila in the built-in reservoirs. Each drink pod has a barcode which tells the machine what drink is being made. Bartesian automatically measures the right amount of alcohol, although consumers can tell the system to make a drink stronger if desired. Six cocktails are being launched including three classics (Margarita, Cosmopolitan, Sex on the Beach) and three unique flavours (Zest Martini, Bartesian Breeze, and Uptown Rocks).

The product will test launch in multiple distribution channels: retail and business-to-business. The team secured purchase orders from several large retailers, including Amazon, Bloomingdale's, Hudson's Bay Company, and Canadian Tire. Partnering with large retailers is an attractive option, but means giving up a lot of margin and having to support the launch with a heavy marketing budget. The B2B channel, with corporate chains such as Delta Hotels, avoids those issues and is less risky, but is a much slower process for getting to market. And the cherry in the whisky sour? The partners secured a deal with Beam Suntory after appearing on *Dragons' Den*. The company invested in their product and also signed a multi-million dollar licensing contract.

Many prototypes were developed before Bartesian was finalized. P1, P2, P4, and P5 protoypes are shown here.
Used with permission of Bartesian, www.bartesian.com

Product prototypes are usually tested through alpha and beta testing. In **alpha testing**, the firm attempts to determine whether the product will perform according to its design and whether it satisfies the need for which it was intended.[51] Rather than using potential consumers, alpha tests usually take place in the firm's R&D department. For instance, Ben & Jerry's alpha tests all its proposed new ice cream flavours on its own employees at its corporate headquarters in Vermont.

In contrast, **beta testing** uses potential consumers, who examine the product prototype in a "real use" setting to determine its functionality, performance, potential problems, and other issues specific to its use. The firm might develop several prototype products that it gives to users, and then survey those users to determine whether the product worked as intended and to identify any issues that need resolution. Application developers can easily conduct beta testing via sites such as Beta Family to get feedback on the user experience from potential users.

The Internet has made recruiting beta testers easier than ever. Through sites such as OnlineBeta (http://www.onlinebeta.com), everyday people can sign up to become beta testers for products from companies such as Dell, Kodak, and TomTom. To further automate the beta testing process, YouEye is developing eye tracking technology that works with an individual's webcam. Instead of needing to spend thousands of dollars on eye tracking equipment and having customers come into labs, firms will be able to utilize everyday webcams to track not only what a person attends to on a computer screen, but also his or her emotional reactions to these products.[52]

**alpha testing**

An attempt by the firm to determine whether a product will perform according to its design and whether it satisfies the need for which it was intended; occurs in the firm's R&D department.

**beta testing**

Having potential consumers examine a product prototype in a real-use setting to determine its functionality, performance, potential problems, and other issues specific to its use.

## Market Testing

The firm has developed its new product or service and tested the prototypes. Now it must test the market for the new product with a trial batch of products although, as mentioned earlier, companies sometimes skip this step because of competitive, timing, or cost pressures. These tests can take two forms: premarket testing or test marketing.

Ben & Jerry's uses alpha testing with its own employees to make sure its products have the right taste and feel.
AP Photo/Nick Wass

**premarket tests**
Conducted before a product or service is brought to market to determine how many customers will try and then continue to use it.

**Premarket Tests**  Firms conduct **premarket tests** before they actually bring a product or service to market to determine how many customers will try and then continue to use the product or service according to a small group of potential consumers. One popular proprietary premarket test version is called Nielsen BASES. During the test, potential customers are exposed to the marketing mix variables, such as the advertising, and then surveyed and given a sample of the product to try.[53] After some period of time, during which the potential customers try the product, they are surveyed about whether they would buy/use the product again. This second survey indicates an estimation of the probability of a consumer's repeat purchase. From these data, the firm generates a sales estimate for the new product that enables it to decide whether to introduce the product, abandon it, redesign it before introduction, or revise the marketing plan. An early evaluation of this sort—that is, before the product is introduced to the whole market—saves marketers the costs of a nationwide launch if the product fails.

Sometimes firms simulate a product or service introduction,[54] in which case potential customers view the advertising of various currently available products or services along with advertising for the new product or service. They receive money to buy the product or service from a simulated environment, such as a mock web page or store, and respond to a survey after they make their purchases. This test thus can determine the effectiveness of a firm's advertising as well as the expected trial rates for the new product.

**test marketing**
Introduces a new product or service to a limited geographical area (usually a few cities) prior to a national launch.

**Test Marketing**  A method of determining the success potential of a new product, **test marketing** introduces the offering to a limited geographical area (usually a few cities) prior to a national launch. A test marketing effort uses all the elements of the marketing mix. It includes promotions such as advertising and coupons, just as if the product were being introduced nationally, and the product appears in targeted retail outlets, with appropriate pricing. On the basis of the results of the test marketing, the firm can estimate demand for the entire market. McDonald's tested its McCafé concept—cappuccinos, lattes, European-style pastries—in 70 Atlantic Canada locations before deciding to roll them out across the country.[55] In 2016, all day breakfast was tested at the Union Station McCafé in Toronto, before being rolled out across the country.

Test marketing costs more and takes longer than premarket tests, which may provide an advantage to competitors that could get a similar or better product to market first. For this reason, some firms might launch new products without extensive consumer testing and rely instead on intuition, instincts, and guts.[56] However, test marketing offers a key advantage: The firm can study actual consumer behaviour, which is more reliable than a simulated test. Beer makers and other product companies like testing in Calgary. As a test market, Calgary offers an attractive demographic in terms of income levels, lifestyle, and a relatively youthful population.

Other cities often used for test markets include London, Ontario, because its population is reflective of a "typical" Canadian city. That might be why Tim Hortons® tested a dark roast coffee in London as well as in Columbus, Ohio.[57] Winnipeg is a good location to test shampoos and skin lotions for dry skin because of its long, cold winters. Recognizing that health food is no longer a niche segment, Loblaw tested a small, health-focused retail store concept in Toronto called Nutshell Live Life Well. The pilot store on King Street in Toronto was designed to attract the urban shoppers who flock to upscale grocers such as Whole Foods. The store sold a variety of prepared, fresh, and packaged foods, as well as health and beauty products, vitamins and supplements, and prescription drugs from an in-store pharmacy.[58] Loblaw cancelled the pilot after buying Shoppers Drug Mart. In the restaurant industry, "fast-casual" chains have experienced the fastest growth. As a result,

KFC tested a new concept with a location called "KFCeleven." The name was a nod to the 11 herbs and spices used by Colonel Sanders in the original recipe. The venue featured boneless pieces of chicken, fresh salads, flatbread sandwiches, rice bowls, garlic mashed potatoes, and waffle fries aimed at winning back consumers in their twenties and thirties who moved to chains perceived as offering better food for only marginally higher prices.[59] Not all test marketing yields a positive outcome—KFCeleven was abruptly closed at the end of the test period.

## Product Launch

If the market testing returns with positive results, the firm is ready to introduce the product to the entire market. This is the most critical step in the new product introduction and requires tremendous financial resources and extensive coordination of all aspects of the marketing mix. If the new product launch is a failure, it may be difficult for the product—and perhaps the firm—to recover. For example, though the number of 3D movie theatres continues to grow, ticket sales for these offerings first leveled off and now have started to decline. The introduction of the new technology was popular enough that sellers invested heavily in building more than 15,000 3D screens, and Hollywood promised a wider range of 3D film options. But if—as appears to be the case—moviegoers have decided that the realistic, three-dimensional images are not worth the higher ticket price, such investments might be painful for both movie studios and movie theatres.[60] In the food and beverage industry, where new product failure rates are as high as 78 percent, Kraft minimizes its risk through a new product development process that includes consumer research. Some products show great promise after launch though, as Exhibit 8.5 describes.

So what does a product launch involve? First, the firm confirms its target market(s) and decides how the product will be positioned. This is done using research it has gathered on consumer perceptions and tests it has conducted, as well as any competitive considerations. Then the firm finalizes the remaining marketing mix variables for the new product, including the marketing budget for the first year.[62]

Is the 3D experience worth the price?

Jasper White CM/Image Source RF

**EXHIBIT 8.5** Best New Products[61]

Below is a sampling of winners as voted by Canadians in the Product of the Year Awards.

| Product | Company | Category |
| --- | --- | --- |
| Hemp Heart Bar | Manitoba Harvest Hemp Foods | Granola Bar |
| Dual Breakfast Sandwich Maker | Hamilton Beach | Small Kitchen Appliances |
| Vim Cream Eucalyptus Scent | Unilever | Household Products |
| Stacy's Fire Roasted Jalepeño Pita Chips | PepsiCo Foods Canada | Snack Food |

Used by permission of Product of the Year Management. http://productoftheyear.ca/winners/winning-products/winning-products-2016/ (accessed February 7, 2017).

**Promotion**   The test results help the firm determine an appropriate integrated marketing communications strategy.[63] Promotion for new products is required at each link in the supply chain. If the products are not sold and stocked by retailers, no amount of promotion to consumers will sell the products. Trade promotions, which are promotions to wholesalers or retailers to get them to purchase the new products, often combine introductory price promotions, special events, and personal selling. Introductory price promotions are limited-duration, lower-than-normal prices designed to provide retailers with an incentive to try the products.

Manufacturers also use promotion to generate demand for new products with consumers. If a manufacturer can create demand for the product among consumers, they will go to retailers asking for it (pull demand; see Chapter 12), further inducing retailers to carry the product. These promotions are often coupled with short-term price reductions, coupons, or rebates. Sometimes manufacturers promote new products in advance of the product launch to create excitement with potential customers as well as to measure the likely demand so they have appropriate supply available. Automobile and motorcycle manufacturers, for instance, advertise their new products months before they are available on the dealers' floors.

For products that are somewhat complex or conceptually new, marketers may need to provide for more consumer education about the product's benefits than they would for simpler and more familiar products. For example, the quantum dot technology that is being developed to improve the LCD screens on televisions, computers, and mobile phones is not something that most consumers understand. But marketers can encourage quantum dot adoption by highlighting the clearly evident appeal of energy efficiency, longer battery life, and more vibrant colour offered by the innovative technology.[64] In addition, technical support staff, like Apple's Geniuses, often must be trained to answer customer questions that may arise immediately after the launch of a new technical innovation.

**Place**   The manufacturer coordinates the delivery and storage of the new products with its retailers to ensure that a product is available for sale when the customer wants it, at the stores the customer is expecting to find it, and in sufficient quantities to meet demand. The firm must have an adequate quantity of products available for shipment and to keep in stock at relevant stores. The product offering should also be as complete as possible.

For example, a firm launching a new printer should ensure it has an adequate supply of the related cartridges or toners. Interested consumers can purchase an iPhone from any Bell, Rogers, or TELUS wireless product location. This accessibility not only provides the new product in a convenient location, but also allows the opportunity for tailored customer service and subscription to appropriate service plans.

Price   Like the promotion of new products, setting prices is a supply chain–wide decision. Manufacturers must decide at what price they would like products to sell to consumers on the basis of the factors discussed in Chapter 11. They often encourage retailers to sell at a specified price known as the manufacturer's suggested retail price (MSRP). Although retailers often don't abide by the MSRP, manufacturers can withhold benefits such as paying for all or part of a promotion or even refusing to deliver merchandise to noncomplying retailers. The firm needs to ensure that it gets the price right. It is sometimes easier to start with a higher price and offer promotions (e.g., coupons, rebates) and then over time to lower the price than it is to introduce the new product at a low price and then try to raise it.

Timing   The timing of the launch may be important, depending on the product.[65] Hollywood studios typically release movies targeted toward general audiences (i.e., those rated G or PG) during the summer when children are out of school. New automobile models traditionally are released for sale during September, and fashion products are launched just before the season of the year for which they are intended.

## Evaluation of Results

After the product has been launched, marketers must undertake a critical postlaunch review to determine whether the product and its launch were a success or a failure and what additional resources or changes to the marketing mix are needed, if any. Some products never make it out of the introduction stage and are almost laughable in retrospect. Bic underwear?[66] Harley-Davidson perfume? Bottled water for pets? Firms measure the success of a new product by three interrelated factors: (1) its satisfaction of technical requirements, such as performance; (2) customer acceptance; and (3) its satisfaction of the firm's financial requirements, such as sales and profits.[67] If the product is not performing sufficiently well, poor customer acceptance will result, which in turn leads to poor financial performance. McDonald's introduced salads to compete against Wendy's. However, McDonald's CEO Donald Thompson later stated that salads were a failed strategy, and represented only 1 to 2 percent of total sales.[68] The new product development process, when followed rationally and sequentially, helps avoid such domino-type failures. Coca-Cola learned from past mistakes when launching Coke Freestyle. And, as discussed in Ethical Dilemma 8.1, Earls Restaurants learned just how much its customers cared about the source of the beef it serves. The product life cycle, discussed in the next section, helps marketers manage their product's marketing mix during and after its introduction.

# THE PRODUCT LIFE CYCLE

The **product life cycle** (PLC) defines the stages that new products move through as they enter, get established in, and ultimately leave the marketplace and thereby offers marketers a starting point for their strategy planning. Exhibit 8.6A illustrates a typical product life cycle, including the industry sales and profits over time. In their life cycles, products pass through four stages: introduction, growth, maturity, and decline. When innovators start buying the product, the product enters the **introduction stage** of its life cycle. In the **growth stage**, the product gains acceptance, demand and sales increase, and competitors emerge in the product category. In the **maturity stage**, industry sales

**L04**

**product life cycle**
Defines the stages that new products move through as they enter, get established in, and ultimately leave the marketplace and thereby offers marketers a starting point for their strategy planning.

**introduction stage**
Stage of the product life cycle when innovators start buying the product.

**growth stage**
Stage of the product life cycle when the product gains acceptance, demand and sales increase, and competitors emerge in the product category.

**maturity stage**
Stage of the product life cycle when industry sales reach their peak, so firms try to rejuvenate their products by adding new features or repositioning them.

## Ethical Dilemma 8.1

### Where's the Beef? Ethical Meat Standards Cause Backlash

Earls Kitchen + Bar opened its first restaurant in Edmonton in 1982. Its success was based on product innovation using the best ingredients for burgers, real Parmesan cheese, homemade tomato sauce, and freshly baked bread.[69] Over the years, the family-owned business grew. Today there are 67 locations: 59 in Canada and 8 in the United States with more planned in both countries. The menu also expanded, and with it, a desire to serve the very best beef. In 2016, Earls made the decision to commit to conscious sourcing to align with the values of its guests. This meant serving only beef that is raised without antibiotics, added hormones, or steroids. In its quest for ethical sourcing, Earls decided that its beef would only come from Certified Humane farms,[70] meaning that it was third-party audited for animal welfare.

You might think this decision would have been a win for Alberta beef ranchers, however, it left many of them with a beef. While some raised cattle without the use of antibiotics, added hormones, drugs, or animal by-products, it wasn't enough to come close to the supply that Earls needed for its 67 restaurants. No Canadian rancher had the Certified Humane designation at that time. There wasn't a comparable certification in Canada.

Alberta beef is touted as being the best in the world, so it was no surprise that Earls, the Canadian-based restaurant company, received consumer backlash when it began sourcing Certified Humane beef from the United States. The decision to go south of the border was due to the need to receive a consistent supply of ethically raised beef. However, critics raised concerns that it implied that beef from Canada was not treated humanely and not good enough. Consumers quickly took to social media and called for others to boycott Earls restaurants.[71]

As a result of the outcry, Earls reversed its decision and apologized to consumers, ranchers, and the Canadian beef industry—after all, the company has deep roots in Alberta. It is now working with multiple Canadian ranchers to source Canadian beef that meets

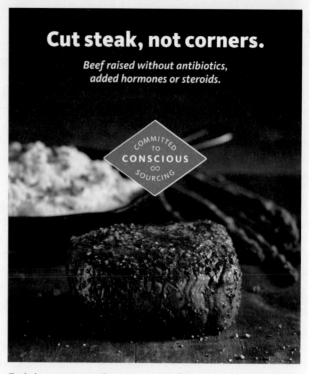

### Cut steak, not corners.

*Beef raised without antibiotics, added hormones or steroids.*

COMMITTED TO CONSCIOUS SOURCING

Earls has committed to serving beef that is raised without antibiotics, added hormones, or steroids.

Used with permission of Earls

its standards, rather than working with only one supplier. And it is accepting any third-party auditing for animal welfare rather than just the Certified Humane designation.

The lessons learned were that "Made in Canada" was valued as much as or more than ethical sourcing for consumers in Alberta (not as much so in the rest of Canada), and that Earls needed to work not only with its supplier of beef but also with the industry and local ranchers. Today, Earls is an active member in the Canadian beef industry, including the Canadian Roundtable for Sustainable Beef, and is working closely with ranchers and farmers.

---

reach their peak, so firms try to rejuvenate their products by adding new features or repositioning them. If these efforts succeed, the product achieves new life.[72] If not, it goes into the **decline stage** and eventually exits the market.

**decline stage**
Stage of the product life cycle when sales decline and the product eventually exits the market.

Not every product follows the same life cycle curve. Many products, such as home appliances, stay in the maturity period for a very long time. Manufacturers may add features to dishwashing machines, but the mature product category remains essentially the same. It seems unlikely to enter the decline stage unless some innovative, superior solution comes along to replace it.

**EXHIBIT 8.6A**  Product Life Cycle

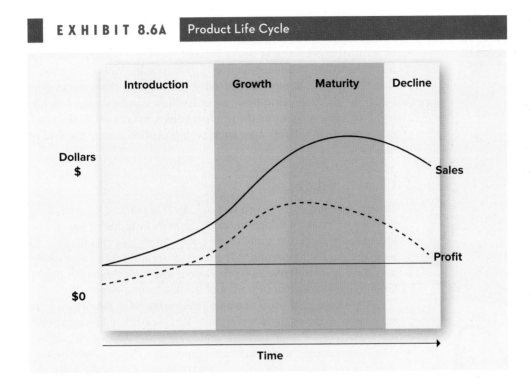

The product life cycle also offers a useful tool for managers to analyze the types of strategies that may be required over the life of their products. Even the strategic emphasis of a firm and its marketing mix (four Ps) strategies can be adapted from insights about the characteristics of each stage of the cycle, as we summarize in Exhibit 8.6B.

Let's look at each of these stages in depth.

## Introduction Stage

The introduction stage for a new, innovative product or service usually starts with a single firm, and innovators are the ones to try the new offering. Some new-to-the-world products and services that defined their own product category and industry include the telephone (invented by Alexander Graham Bell in 1876), the transistor semiconductor (Bell Laboratories in 1947), the Walkman portable cassette player (Sony in 1979), the Internet browser (Netscape in 1994), iTunes (Apple in 2001), BlackBerry (RIM in 2003), Blu-ray (Sony in 2006), iPad (Apple in 2010), and smart watch (Pebble in 2013). Sensing

**EXHIBIT 8.6B**  Characteristics of Different Stages of the Product Life Cycle

|  | Introduction | Growth | Maturity | Decline |
|---|---|---|---|---|
| **Sales** | Low | Rising | Peak | Declining |
| **Profits** | Negative or low | Rapidly rising | Peak to declining | Declining |
| **Typical consumers** | Innovators | Early adopters and early majority | Late majority | Laggards |
| **Competitors (number of firms and products)** | One or few | Few but increasing | High number of competitors and competitive products | Low number of competitors and products |

These new-to-the-world products defined their own product category and industry. The telephone (top) was invented in 1876, and the Sony Walkman (bottom) came out in 1979.

(top): © Kasiden/Dreamstime.com/GetStock.com; (bottom): Comstock Images/Alamy

the viability and commercialization possibilities of this market-creating new product, other firms soon enter the market with similar or improved products at lower prices. The same pattern holds for less innovative products such as apparel, some music, or even a new soft-drink flavour. The introduction stage is characterized by initial losses to the firm because of its high start-up costs and low levels of sales revenue as the product begins to take off. If the product is successful, firms may start seeing profits toward the end of this stage.

## Growth Stage

The growth stage of the product life cycle is marked by a growing number of product adopters, rapid growth in industry sales, and increases in both the number of competitors and the number of available product versions.[73] The market becomes more segmented and consumer preferences more varied, which increases the potential for new markets or new uses of the product or service.[74]

Also during the growth stage, firms attempt to reach new consumers by studying their preferences and producing different product variations—varied colours, styles, or features—which enables them to segment the market more precisely. The goal of this segmentation is to ride the rising sales trend and firmly establish the firm's brand, so as not to be outdone by competitors. In recognizing the growing demand for and appeal of organic products, many food manufacturers are working hard to become the first brand that consumers think of when they consider organic products. Del Monte was the first of the major canned vegetable sellers to go organic, releasing organic versions of its tomatoes, green beans, corn, and sweet peas, along with an organic chicken broth product under its College Inn line. The cans feature bold "organic" banners across the front and promise that no pesticides were used to produce the food items. Even though Del Monte products have been around for more than 100 years, in this growth category, the company must work to establish its distinctive appeal in the organic market in particular.[75]

As firms ride the crest of increasing industry sales, profits in the growth stage also rise because of the economies of scale associated with manufacturing and marketing costs, especially promotion and advertising. At the same time, firms that have not yet established a stronghold in the market, even in narrow segments, may decide to exit in what is referred to as an "industry shakeout."

## Maturity Stage

The maturity stage of the product life cycle is characterized by the adoption of the product by the late majority and intense competition for market share among firms. Marketing costs (e.g., promotion, distribution) increase as these firms vigorously defend their market share against competitors. At the same time, they face intense competition on price as the average price of the product falls substantially compared with the shifts during the previous two stages of the life cycle. Lower prices and increased marketing costs begin to erode the profit margins for many firms. In the later phases of the maturity stage, the market has become quite saturated, and practically all potential customers for the product have already adopted the product.

Such saturated markets are prevalent in developed countries; in Canada, most consumer packaged goods found in grocery and discount stores are already in the maturity stage. For example, in the well established hair care product market, consumer goods companies constantly search for innovations to set themselves apart and extend the time in which they maintain their position in the maturity stage. Observing the popularity of new skin care products, hair care manufacturers have integrated similar product benefits to their products. These companies have introduced anti-aging shampoos and conditioners, prewash hair masks, serums, and multiple-step solutions that go beyond the old mantra of wash, rinse, and repeat.

Firms may pursue several strategies during this stage to increase their customer base and/or defend their market share, such as entering into new markets and market segments and developing new products or promotions. See Exhibit 8.7 for additional strategies for extending the maturity stage of the product life cycle.

### Entry Into New Markets or Market Segments
Because the market is saturated at this point, firms may attempt to enter new geographical markets, including international markets (as we will discuss in Chapter 17), that may be less saturated. For example, Whirlpool has started manufacturing washing machines for Brazil, China, and India that it prices lower than those it sells in North America to attract the large consumer base of lower-income consumers in these countries.[76] In many developing economies, the large and growing proportion of middle-class households is just beginning to buy the home, kitchen, and entertainment appliances that have been fairly standard in Canadian households for several decades.

Recognizing that shampoo is a mature product category, Alterna and other manufacturers have introduced anti-aging hair products.

Alterna Haircare

### EXHIBIT 8.7  Strategies for Extending the Product Life Cycle

| Strategy | Example |
| --- | --- |
| Develop new uses for products | • Baking soda is now promoted for deodorizing refrigerators, as an environmentally friendly cleaning product, and much more. |
| Modify the product:<br>• Change quality<br>• Boost performance<br>• Alter appearance | • Add graphite to tennis racquets and golf clubs.<br>• Enhance computer chip speed.<br>• Modify packaging; change colours, or introduce a new scent. |
| Increase frequency of use | • Dentyne gum is promoted as a way to help clean your teeth when you can't brush after a meal. |
| Increase the number of users | • Tums have always contained calcium, but when this fact was promoted, people concerned about bone density began to purchase the product. |
| Find new users | • Club Med introduced vacations geared to baby boomers, seniors, golfers, and those looking for cruises after some of their original target market of swinging singles got married and had children. |
| Reposition product | • Suntan lotion has evolved to become sunscreen protection.<br>• Vitamin D is sold as a cancer deterrent. |
| Tweak marketing strategy | • Greeting cards are sold in supermarkets.<br>• Upscale cosmetics are sold in drug stores. |

Just a few years ago, baby wipes accounted for most of the sales of personal wipes. Firms have seen the opportunity to enter new markets, so products have proliferated.
© Mike Hruby

However, even in mature markets, firms may be able to find new market segments. Laundry may be a mundane chore that most people dislike, but it is also a huge marketing opportunity. New product development tends to focus on the detergent delivery methods. In North America, laundry tablets have never been very popular (consumers prefer to pour their liquid detergent and thus control the amount they add to the wash basket). In spite of this, P&G successfully introduced Tide Pods, boosting sales and making Tide the company's first billion-dollar brand.[77]

New market opportunities also may emerge through simple product design changes, such as in the market for "wipes." Just a few years ago, baby wipes accounted for most of the sales of personal wipes, but P&G's Oil of Olay Facial Cleansing Cloths and Unilever's Ponds Age-Defying wipes have gained significant market share.[78] In the household sector, products such as P&G's Swiffer, the electrostatic wipe for mopping floors, expanded the market greatly. Clorox has added premoistened Armor All wipes to its do-it-yourself car cleaning line[79] and the Clorox® ToiletWand™ for consumers who don't enjoy unsightly and unsanitary toilet brushes hanging around in their bathrooms.[80] Although the household cleaning and cosmetic markets are both well established and mature, marketers working in these product categories saw trends early and moved to create new products that offer value for consumers.

**Development of New Products**  Despite market saturation, firms continually introduce new products with improved features or find new uses for existing products because they need constant innovation and product proliferation to defend market share during intense competition. Firms such as 3M, P&G, and HP, for instance, continuously introduce new products. Innovations by such firms ensure that they are able to retain or grow their respective market shares. Hallmark, which has been the hallmark name for greeting cards for a long time, is trying a variety of innovations. They include customizable greeting cards, plates, and interactive storybooks that can be personalized for various recipients, as well as greeting applications that are available for both iPod and iPad users.[81]

## Decline Stage

Firms with products in the decline stage either position themselves for a niche segment of diehard consumers or those with special needs, or they completely exit the market.

The few laggards who have not yet tried the product or service enter the market at this stage. Take vinyl long-playing records (LPs) for example. In an age of CDs and Internet-downloaded music in MP3 and other formats, it may seem surprising that vinyl records are still made and sold. Although the sales of vinyl LPs had been declining in the past 15 years, about 2 million are sold in the United States each year. In Canada, vinyl sales declined from $913,000 in 2000 to $608,000 three years later.[82] Since then, however, vinyl records have been on the rebound. According to Nielsen Music, 517,400 vinyl records were sold in Canada in 2015, 30 percent higher than the year before, while 2016 sales were the highest to date.[83]

In spite of some die-hard music lovers who prefer vinyl, long-playing records have experienced years of falling sales and are in the decline stage.

© Bellafotosolo/Dreamstime.com/GetStock.com.

Diehard music lovers prefer the unique sound of a vinyl record to the digital sound of CDs and music in other formats. Because the grooves in vinyl records create sound waves that are similar to those of a live performance, and therefore provide a more authentic sound, nightclub DJs, discerning music listeners, and collectors prefer them. Even some younger listeners have been buying vinyl records, influenced perhaps by their parents' collections, the sound, or simply the uniqueness of an LP. In Edmonton, independent and high-profile bands alike are competing for limited record-pressing resources, a sign that vinyl is in vogue again.[84]

The nostalgia factor associated with the old albums has given new life to the older medium that has caused a problem and created an opportunity. No one had made new record-pressing machines since vinyl first went out of favour, forcing long waits for those who wanted to create vinyl records. Toronto-based Viryl Technologies has since seized the opportunity by designing a fully modernized, automated press to satisfy pent up demand.[85]

## The Shape of the Product Life Cycle Curve

In theory, the product life cycle curve is assumed to be bell-shaped with regard to sales and profits. In reality, however, each product or service has its own individual shape; some move more rapidly through their product life cycles than others, depending on how different the product or service is from products currently in the market and how valuable it is to the consumer. New products and services that consumers accept very quickly have higher consumer adoption rates very early in their product life cycles and move faster across the various stages.

For example, Blu-ray players and Blu-ray discs moved much faster than DVDs across the life cycle curve and have already reached the maturity stage, likely because consumers who already owned DVDs were accustomed to recording TV shows and playing prerecorded movies and programs. It also was easy to switch DVD customers to Blu-ray technology because Blu-rays played on Blu-ray players, and Blu-rays had better video and audio quality than DVDs. With the advent of 4K televisions that offer resolutions four times higher than current 1080p HD TVs, it is likely we may see another fast adoption of a new video format, such as 4K Blu-ray.

Lastly, as shown in Exhibit 8.8, the type of product affects variations in the shape of the product life cycle curve. When first introduced, microwave ovens were considered

**EXHIBIT 8.8** Variations on the Product Life Cycle Curve

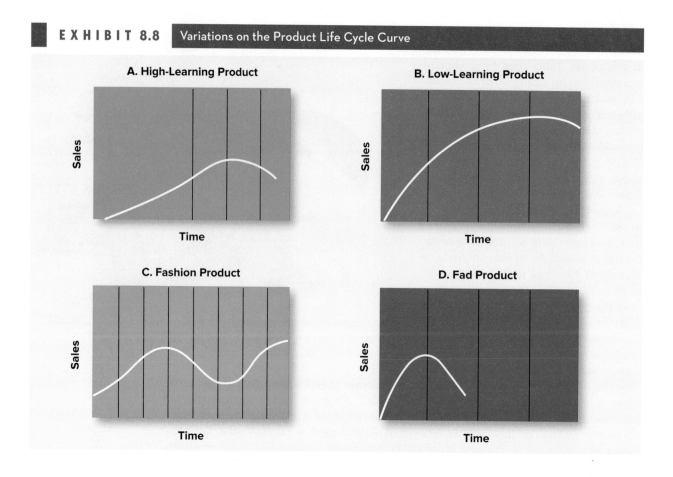

high-learning products and spent much longer in the introduction stage than subsequent low-learning products such as microwave popcorn. Fads move through the stages very quickly, while fashion products tend to be cyclical in nature. For example, wide ties for men and suit lapels may be out of style today but may well become fashionable again in the future.

## Strategies Based on Product Life Cycle: Some Caveats

Although the product life cycle concept provides a starting point for managers to think about the strategy they want to implement during each stage of the life cycle of a product, this tool must be used with care. The most challenging part of applying the product life cycle concept is that managers do not know exactly what shape each product's life cycle will take, so there is no way to know precisely what stage a product is in. If, for example, a product experiences several seasons of declining sales, a manager may decide that it has moved from the growth stage to the decline stage and stop promoting the product. As a result, of course, sales decline further. The manager then believes he or she made the right decision because the product continues to follow a predetermined life cycle. But what if the original sales decline was due to a poor strategy or increased competition—issues that could have been addressed with positive marketing support? In this case, the product life cycle decision became a self-fulfilling prophecy, and a growth product was doomed to an unnecessary decline.[86] Fortunately, new research, based on the history of dozens of consumer products, suggests that the product life cycle concept is indeed a valid idea, and new analytical tools now provide rules for detecting the key turning points in the cycle.

## REAL MARKETER PROFILE

# Greg Taylor and Cam Heaps (Steam Whistle Brewing)

An independent craft brewery located in a historic railway roundhouse in the heart of Toronto, Steam Whistle is known for "Doing One Thing Really, Really Well." That thing is making a single style of beer ... a Canadian craft Pilsner. The premise is that by forsaking variety, Steam Whistle can focus on quality. That singular focus has separated Steam Whistle from the pack among a sea of competitors with broad portfolios who are constantly launching new products.

The brewery's co-founders, Greg Taylor and Cam Heaps, give all employees a clear goal when they come to work: make Steam Whistle pilsner, better and better each day. Greg studied economics at the University of Toronto and worked in a number of sales, media, and high-tech jobs and several of his own start-ups before getting into the beer business in 1989. Here Greg met Cam, a Wilfrid Laurier philosophy graduate, also a budding entrepreneur. They learned about brewery operations, sales and marketing, and the importance of a strong workplace culture.

Launched in 1998, Steam Whistle revolves around creativity and innovation. Co-founders Cam and Greg encourage employee engagement through open communication, inviting ideas and celebrating employee contributions. To retain relevancy with today's beer consumer and stand out on store shelves full of new brands, Steam Whistle innovates the brand regularly with new package offerings and seasonal gift packs.

**Identifying an opportunity:** Steam Whistle pilsner is packaged in an old-fashioned bottle with a crimp-style bottle cap. While not as convenient as twist-off beer caps, the crimp bottle cap provides a superior seal, protecting beer from damaging air pick-up, helping to keep it tasting as fresh as the day it left the brewery. Steam Whistle created a promotion to kick off the summer of 2005 offering a free bottle opener in beer cases. The free gift could be put to use during the "drinking ritual," provided an opportunity to communicate the reason behind this old-fashioned quality

Photo by Mike Palmer. Used with permission of Steam Whistle Brewing.

bottle, and gave loyal and new customers alike an incentive to pick up a case of Steam Whistle pilsner at the start of the warm-weather beer drinking season.

**The results:** Beer drinkers loved not only the innovative promotion but the quality of the prize itself, reflective of the Steam Whistle brand in its material construction, design aesthetic, and story-telling. The promotion was so successful in driving beer sales that Steam Whistle now releases an original bottle opener free in cases annually on the May 24 weekend, complete with the opener story on a hang-tag and a dedicated web page (www.steamwhistle.ca/opener), all supported through in-store signage, a social media strategy, and an advertising campaign. The annual openers have become quite collectible. A Facebook fan page is dedicated to buying, selling, and trading Steam Whistle merchandise (www.facebook.com/SteamWhistleRetroOpeners). Some of the rare openers now fetch hundreds of dollars on eBay.

Innovation is definitely part of a successful growth strategy at Steam Whistle Brewing, but the company is disciplined in the way it applies innovation to its business. Greg, Cam, and the marketing team make sure that the hunt for "novelty and new" doesn't lead them too far from Steam Whistle's steadfast brand identity that customers have grown to love.

## LEARNING OBJECTIVES REVIEW

**LO1** Identify the reasons firms create new products

Firms need to innovate to respond to changing customer needs, prevent decline in sales, avoid market saturation, diversify their risk, and respond to short product life cycles. This is especially true in industries such as fashion, apparel, arts, books, and software markets, where most sales come from new products. New products and services keep current customers coming back for more and induce new customers into the market. Risky, new-to-the-world products have tremendous potential because they are the first in the market to offer something that has never before been available.

**LO2**  **Describe the diffusion of innovation theory and how managers can use it to make product line decisions**

The diffusion of innovation theory helps firms predict which types of customers will buy their products or services immediately upon introduction, and as they gain more acceptance in the market. Innovators are those buyers who want to be the first to have the new product or service. Early adopters do not take as much risk as innovators but instead wait and purchase the product after careful review. The members of the early majority really don't like to take risks and therefore tend to wait until "the bugs" have been worked out of a particular product or service. The late majority are buyers who purchase the product after it has achieved its full market potential. Finally, laggards like to avoid change and rely on traditional products until they are no longer available. Laggards may never adopt a certain product or service.

**LO3**  **List the stages involved in developing new products and services**

When firms develop new products, they go through several steps. First, they generate ideas for the product or service by using several alternative techniques, such as internal research and development, licensing, brainstorming, tracking competitors' products or services, and working with customers. Second, firms test their concepts by either describing the idea of the new product or service to potential customers or showing them images of what the product would look like. Third, the design process entails determining what the product or service will actually include and provide. Fourth, firms test-market their designs. Fifth, if everything goes well in the test market, the product is launched. Sixth, firms must evaluate the new product or service to determine its success.

**LO4**  **Describe the product life cycle and summarize how it is used to make product line decisions**

The product life cycle helps firms make marketing mix decisions on the basis of the product's stage in its life cycle. In the introduction stage, companies attempt to gain a strong foothold in the market quickly by appealing to innovators. During the growth stage, the objective is to establish the brand firmly. When the product reaches the maturity stage, firms compete intensely for market share, and many potential customers already own the product or use the service. Eventually, most products enter the decline phase, during which firms withdraw marketing support and eventually phase out the product. Knowing where a product or service is in its life cycle helps managers determine its specific strategy at any given point in time.

## KEY TERMS

- alpha testing
- beta testing
- concepts
- concept testing
- decline stage
- diffusion of innovation
- early adopters
- early majority
- first movers

- growth stage
- innovation
- innovators
- introduction stage
- laggards
- late majority
- lead users
- maturity stage
- pioneers

- premarket test
- product
- product development (product design)
- product life cycle
- prototype
- reverse engineering
- test marketing

## CONCEPT REVIEW

1. Explain how new product or service innovations add value to the firm.

2. Sketch and describe the diffusion of innovation curve. How can marketers use the information provided by this curve to make marketing strategies and decisions?

3. Identify and discuss the factors that influence the adoption of new products.

4. List the steps in the new product development process. Describe some of the sources companies use to generate ideas for new products at the beginning of this process.

5. Why might a company need to exercise caution during the test marketing stage of the new development process?

6. What other factors besides the product itself does a company need to finalize during the product launch stage?

7. Do all products go through each and every stage of this process? Explain your answer.

8. What is the product life cycle (PLC)? Describe the characteristics of each stage of the PLC in terms of sales, profits, typical consumers, competition, and four Ps strategies.

9. Describe some of the strategies companies can use to extend the life of a mature product.

10. Explain why the product life cycle is not a fail-proof tool in managing products.

# MARKETING APPLICATIONS

1. Some people think that a product should be considered "new" only if it is completely new to the market and has never existed before. Describe or give examples of other types of new products.

2. Panasonic's new 3D HD personal camcorder allows users to record live events in three dimensions, instead of two. How quickly do you think this product will diffuse among the Canadian population? Describe the types of people whom you expect to be in each of the diffusion of innovation stages.

3. Are there any advantages for companies that are the first to introduce products that create new markets? Justify your answer. If you see advantages, explain why some new products fail.

4. Identify and describe the ways that companies generate new product ideas. Which of these ways involve the customer? How can firms assess the value of the ideas that customers generate?

5. Describe an example of a new product or service that is targeted at the student market. Using the concept testing discussion in this chapter, describe how you would conduct a concept test for this product or service.

6. How does the Internet help companies gain customer input on their existing and new products?

7. Nature's Path is about to introduce a type of granola and is in the market testing phase of the new product development process. Describe two ways that Nature's Path might conduct initial market testing prior to launching this new product.

8. What shampoo do you use? What stage of the product life cycle is it in? Is the shampoo manufacturer's marketing strategy—its four Ps—consistent with the product's stage in its life cycle? Explain.

9. Android Wear is a new category of wearable computing devices that link to android smartphones. How quickly do you think this product will diffuse among the Canadian population? Describe the types of people that you expect will be in each of the diffusion of innovation stages.

10. You have recently been hired by a cosmetics company for its product development group. The firm's brand is a top-selling, high-end line of cosmetics. The head of the development team has just presented research that shows that tween girls, aged 9 to 12, are very interested in cosmetics and have money to spend on them. The decision is made to create a line of tween cosmetics based on the existing adult line. As the product moves through development, you begin to notice that the team seems to lean toward a very edgy and sexual theme for the line, including naming the various lines "Envy," "Desire," "Prowl," and "Fatal Attraction." You begin to wonder if this concept is too much for girls in the targeted age group. Explain your thoughts.

# NET SAVVY

1. Go to the *Canadian Living* Best New Products Awards website (http://www.canadianliving.com/life/best_new _product_awards) and search for an interesting new product. Is this an innovative, new-to-the-world product? Discuss the extent to which the new product has the properties that would be important for new product design and development.

2. The automotive industry is constantly adding new and different products to cars and trucks. Conduct an Internet or library database search for innovative new automotive technologies. Choose products that fit each stage of the product life cycle, and justify your choices.

# CHAPTER CASE STUDY

## THE GLASS IS HALF EMPTY—THE FAILURE OF GOOGLE GLASS

From its very start, Google has embraced the idea of innovation actively. The founders began their company with—at the time—a totally innovative concept of an online search engine. Then they instituted the "20 percent" rule, according to which all employees had to spend at least one workday per week on creative, off-the-wall project ideas. With such a foundation, Google's record of innovation is naturally impressive, from Google Maps to Street View to driverless cars, from the

Google Glass was one of many Google innovations.

Michal Karkowiak/spooh/iStock.com

Android operating system to Chromebooks. One innovation that generated a lot of attention was Google Glass.

Even before the device was introduced, it seemed as if everyone knew what Google Glass was—and had an opinion about its efficacy, appeal, and look. The wearable product allowed users to surf the Internet and gather information simply by looking up and to the right. They could swipe their finger over a sensor behind their ears to pull up a Google map and navigate, take pictures, or initiate the embedded Bluetooth technology to make a call.[87]

The initial rollout of Google Glass was limited, purposefully, by a couple of factors. First, Google set the price very high, at around US$1,500. That meant that only early adopters, the most dedicated tech geeks, and those with plenty of disposable income would be sporting the headband-like devices. Second, Google required people to register for the chance to receive a set.[88] Even if thousands wanted to spend the money, Google allowed only a select few to receive them at any one time.

This slow, measured rollout provided several benefits for Google. Because it sought to minimize the supply available, Google created a perception that Glass was extremely popular and stirred up excitement in potential customers. The press buzz and word of mouth spread remarkably far and quickly. Furthermore, it identified a ready-made segment of beta testers. By making sure that those who used the early versions of Google Glass were really interested in it, Google knew that the feedback they provided was more likely to be insightful and related to the underlying technology. Thus it did not initially have to filter out complaints about it being too hard to use from people without much technological savvy, or other reviews that seemed less important to the developers.

But as Google quickly learned, anytime you give people access to a new device, their feedback is going to include some unexpected elements. Google assumed most comments would be about technology improvements. Instead, much of the information it gleaned involved the look of the device and the alternative uses it could support. For example, although there was never any danger that Google Glass would become a high-fashion option, people sought to make them at least a little more attractive. The solution was an easy one: offer Google Glass in several colours, so that fashionable folks could coordinate with their phones, purses, or favourite hues.

In terms of the functions for which people actually use Google Glass, the innovator's predictions again were inaccurate. Google anticipated that Glass would resonate most with busy business professionals who found the act of taking their smartphones out of their pockets too inefficient. But it learned quickly that even these professional segments used Glass in far more casual ways. In one example, a pet lover explained that it was far easier to record funny cat videos when both hands were free to tempt the feline with a toy.[89]

Along with this feedback, Google noted some surprise at the diversity of people interested in Glass. As Leila Takayama, a researcher with Google, explained, "We were expecting the people to be extremely tech savvy—to kind of look like us Googlers. But what we actually saw were people who were much more diverse. They were people who were just sort of curious."[90] The company felt this surprising finding would bode very well for Google Glass, because the next step for Google would seemingly be to expand the target market beyond the early adopter segment.

One means to do this was by adding more functions. Google entered into an agreement with a nationwide vision care insurer covering people who need corrective lenses, and allowed them to add those lenses to the Google Glass device at a subsidized price.[91] That expanded the market to a health care setting, in which Glass was not just a fun technology tool but a means for people to see better while also gaining access to the search benefits inherent to the innovation. Google actively encouraged app developers to expand their related offerings, to make sure Glass users would have access to a vast range of relevant games, tools, and uses. Music capability was added so that users could tell Google Glass to play music they have loaded into their Google Play accounts.[92]

The Internet was abuzz with predictions of how far the price of Google Glass would drop. One analyst predicted a price cut to $600, followed by a further reduction.[93] Most estimates suggested that ultimately it would settle in the range of $300.[94] Noting that approximately 10,000 users had been willing to pay $1,500 for the devices, these price predictions argued that at $350, Google might have nearly 70,000 adopters within just a few years.

But in spite of optimists who saw the glass as half full, today Google Glass is seen as a failed experiment. Casual users found it ugly and awkward; high-tech early adopters complained about its short battery life and expressed their disgust with the "terrible product" online, noting that it was plagued by defects, bugs, and poor performance. The company stopped short of saying it had abandoned the product. The Google Glass homepage currently greets visitors with the message, "Thanks for exploring with us. The journey doesn't end here."[95]

Google Glass faced a number of problems in the effort to diffuse its wearable technology globally. The product was innovative and held appeal for early adopters. Ralph Waldo Emerson once said, "If you build a better mousetrap the world will beat a path to your door." However, one question all new product developers should ask themselves is whether people need or want a better mousetrap. Many consumers viewed Google Glass as cool, but they weren't sure why they needed one. Google failed to make it clear to consumers what problem the product would solve.[96]

Critics said Google Glass was not aesthetically pleasing and looked awkward and uncomfortable to wear.

lferrantraite/iStock.com

Critics said the product was not aesthetically pleasing and looked awkward and uncomfortable to wear, as if it was still in the prototype stage. People expressed safety concerns, questioning how safe it was to wear a device on their head that emitted harmful radiation. Two years after it was released, the product saw very little progress beyond the beta stage.[97] Google Glass was never sold in retail outlets but was only available to early adopters, sometimes called "Glass Explorers" who paid handsomely for the privilege of being able to say they were among the first users. Media skeptics coined the term "glassholes" to describe these early adopters. The term quickly went mainstream.[98]

Privacy concerns were raised. Without any legal framework in place, Glass wearers conceivably could record others without their permission or add face recognition software that identifies passersby. Several casinos banned the devices, and privacy experts worried about the potential abuses in private-seeming locations in public places, such as restrooms and changing rooms.[99] Considering such technology "creepy," some consumers rejected the innovations out of hand. It was enough of a problem that Google released an official guide on how not to be rude or creepy. Its suggestions included making sure that users asked for permission before recording anyone and took the device off before entering restrooms. Google also takes the time to explain that "Standing alone in the corner of a room staring at people while recording them through Glass is not going to win you any friends."[100]

The Google Glass journey may not be over yet. Although it stopped selling the product and cancelled the beta tests, it has stopped short of cancelling the entire project. It's possible the company will take another crack at it. For Google, the glass may yet be half full.

## Questions

1. What was the go-to-market strategy for Google Glass? Why did it fail?

2. How did the product diffuse? What was its stage in the adoption curve when Google stopped beta testing? Explain your answer.

3. What can later entrants into the wearable technology market learn from Google's new product introduction?

# CHAPTER 9

## LEARNING OBJECTIVES

After studying this chapter you should be able to

**LO1** Describe the components of a product

**LO2** Identify the types of consumer products

**LO3** Explain the difference between a product mix's breadth and a product line's depth

**LO4** Identify the advantages that brands provide firms and consumers

**LO5** Summarize the components of brand equity

**LO6** Describe the types of branding strategies used by firms

**LO7** State how a product's packaging an label contribute to a firm's overall strategy

Aaron Vincent Elkaim/The Canadian Press

# Product, Branding, and Packaging Decisions

Look around. You see them everywhere: in remote communities, in heavily populated business districts, on university campuses, even on Justin Trudeau's family holiday card. From humble roots as a product designed to protect people who worked in extreme cold conditions, Canada Goose parkas have now also become a fashion statement for the urban chic. Fusing function with fashion while staying true to its heritage, Canada Goose offers the highest quality outerwear in the world.

The brand has undergone a lot of change since 1957 when Sam Tick started Metro Sportswear Ltd. in Toronto, making clothing and outerwear for automotive and industrial companies. In 1970, the company moved into down-filled manufacturing and began producing a wide range of down-filled jackets for private-label brands such as Eddie Bauer, L.L. Bean, and others. The company went on to make its own down-filled parkas, known at first as Snow Goose[1] and then as Canada Goose—all made entirely in Canada.

In 1997, Tick's grandson, Dani Reiss, joined the company to earn money to travel. He stayed on after listening to consumers tell him how much they loved the made-in-Canada coats. Filled with goose and duck down and trimmed with coyote fur, the coats are designed with the company's mission in mind: to free people from the cold, no matter where they live, and empower them to experience more from life. The coats have become so popular that a holographic badge has been added to prevent counterfeiting.

Consumers seek products with authentic stories and love the mythology of Canada, the Arctic, wide-open spaces, and the polar bear.[2] Reiss says that "Made in Canada" is a brand differentiator. Visit the Canada Goose website and you'll see stories of Yukon Quest dogsledders, world-class mountaineers, and adventure athletes who swear by the brand. In the early days, Reiss spread word of mouth by giving jackets to bouncers who stood outside in the cold for long periods. Canada Goose has also been used in the film industry, outfitting film crews on movie sets where it is cold. The parkas have been featured in movies such as *Man of Steel, World War Z,* and *National Treasure.*[3] A partnership with Fairmont Hotels has outfitted all doormen and bellmen with a Canada Goose jacket, making the brand very visible. A Sports *Illustrated* Swimsuit Edition cover featuring supermodel Kate Upton photographed in Antarctica wearing a Canada Goose parka and skimpy bikini bottom created a social media storm. Consumers love to share their own stories on platforms like Facebook and Twitter, helping to make Canada Goose a Canadian success story. A five-minute film about the company, featuring real adventurers wearing the iconic parkas, won a Gold Lion in Design at Cannes 2016, further fuelling global publicity for the brand.[4]

In the past decade, sales have grown more than 4,000 percent with no signs of slowing. Sales projections this year have soared past $300 million, representing an annual compound growth rate of nearly 50 percent.[5] Canada Goose has not only created a valued product, but also built strong brand equity, high customer awareness, and intense loyalty. Such popularity has created competition. In 2008, Montreal-based Moose Knuckles started making parkas that are modern, warm, stylish, and well made. Its down-filled parkas feature fox fur hoods and sell in the same price range as Canada Goose products. The company name builds on two very Canadian icons: the moose and hockey fights. Recently Moose Knuckles expanded to the U.S. market and sells at Saks Fifth Avenue, Nordstrom, and Bloomingdale's. However, claims that the parkas are Canadian-made were challenged and, after an investigation by the Competition Bureau, the company admitted that most of its coats are made in Vietnam.[6]

Consumers value the "Made in Canada" label and Canada Goose's longstanding commitment not to manufacture outside of the country. That should help as the company expands beyond cold weather gear. A three-minute video featuring ultra-marathon runner Ray Zahab[7] was used to help launch its new line of ultra-lightweight jackets. Reiss says that Canada Goose has built its brand on proprietary fabrics and performance and that the new line is a sign of things to come. He plans to launch even morewindwear, rainwear, and ultra-lightweight items in the future, as well as other products suited for urban environments.[8] Fans will be able to check out these products and more in standalone Canada Goose stores in Yorkdale Shopping Centre in Toronto and in New York's SoHo area. Products resulting from collaboration with Drake's OVO brand, Levi's, and Wings + Horns will extend the company's own seasonal collections.[9]

In 2017, it extended its brand beyond clothing to adventure tours in partnership with travel company Butterfield & Robinson. The first three tours to Iceland, Newfoundland and Labrador, and British Columbia[10] featured activities and environments for which Canada Goose products were a good fit. ■

This chapter is the second that deals with the first P in the marketing mix: product. In the last chapter, you learned that developing new products is key to a firm's marketing mix and central to the creation of value for consumers. Continuing our discussion, we now explore how companies add value to their offerings by developing an assortment of products and product lines and by creating strong brands.

This chapter begins with a discussion of the complexity and types of products. Next we examine how firms adjust their product lines to meet and respond to changing market conditions. Then we turn our attention to branding: Why are brands valuable to the firm, and what are the different branding strategies firms use? We also never want to underestimate the value of a product's packaging and labelling in product strategies and promotion. Packaging and labelling must send out a strong message from the shelf: Buy me! The final section of this chapter examines packaging and labelling issues.

## L01 COMPLEXITY OF PRODUCTS AND TYPES OF PRODUCTS

### Complexity of Products

**core customer value**

The basic problem-solving benefits that consumers are seeking.

There is more to a product than its physical characteristics or its basic service function. Marketers involved with the development, design, and sale of products think of them in an interrelated fashion, as depicted in Exhibit 9.1. At the centre is the **core customer value**, which defines the basic problem-solving benefits that consumers are seeking. When Canada Goose makes coats, when Mars manufactures M&M's, and when Trek designs its bicycles, this is their core question: "What are customers looking for?" Do people buy Canada Goose jackets for extreme cold weather defence or because they want to make a fashion statement? With Mars, is it a sweet, great-tasting snack, or is it an energy boost? With Trek, is the bike being used for basic green transportation (a cruiser), or is it for speed and excitement (a road, hybrid, or mountain bike)?

Marketers convert core customer value into an *actual product*. Attributes such as the brand name, features/design, quality level, and packaging are considered, though

**EXHIBIT 9.1**  Product Complexity

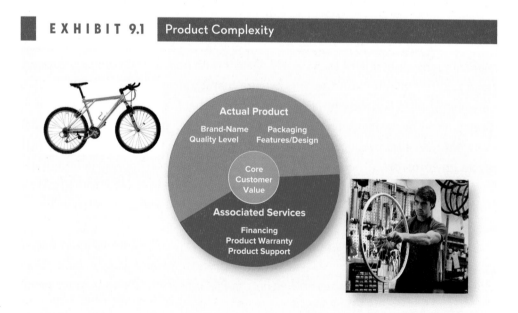

Actual Product

Brand-Name
Quality Level

Packaging
Features/Design

Core Customer Value

Associated Services

Financing
Product Warranty
Product Support

(left): Photodisc/Getty Images RF; (right): Michael Blann/Digital Vision/Getty Images

the importance of these attributes varies depending on the product. The Trek Madone 9 Series features a carbon frame that is light, stiff, and comfortable; an advanced shifting system; and other high-tech features. Not only is it beautiful to look at, but customers also can choose from three different fits: pro, performance, and touring. Canada Goose coats are made with goose down, coyote fur, and premium materials to offer superior warmth.

The **associated services** in Exhibit 9.1, also referred to as the **augmented product**, include the nonphysical aspects of the product, such as product warranties, financing, product support, and after-sale service. For example, Canada Goose coats come with a lifetime warranty for defects in materials or workmanship. The amount of associated services varies depending on the product. The associated services for a package of M&M's may include only a customer complaint line, which means they are relatively less important than the associated services for a Trek bicycle. The frame of the Madone 9 Series bicycle is guaranteed for the lifetime of the original owner. Trek sells its bikes only to shops that have the expertise to properly service them. Every possible consumer question is answered on Trek's comprehensive website. Trek even has a financing program that allows customers to purchase a new bike on credit.

When developing or changing a product, marketers start with the core customer value to determine what their potential customers are seeking. Then they make the actual physical product and add associated services to round out the offering.

## Types of Products

**L04**

Marketers consider the types of products they are designing and selling because that impacts how they promote, price, and distribute their products. There are two primary categories of products and services based on who is buying them: consumers or businesses (Chapter 5 discusses products for businesses).

**Consumer products** are products and services used by people for their personal use. Marketers further classify these products by the way they are used and purchased.

### Specialty Products/Services

**Specialty goods/services** are products or services toward which customers show such a strong preference that they will expend considerable effort to search for the best suppliers. Road bike enthusiasts, like those interested in the Trek Madone 9 Series, will devote lots of time and effort to selecting just the right bike. Other examples might include luxury cars, legal or medical professionals, or designer apparel. Canada Goose can be considered a specialty product. The extensive process used to approve authorized retailers helps maintain a premium image.[11]

### Shopping Products/Services

**Shopping goods/services** are products or services—such as furniture, apparel, fragrances, appliances, and travel alternatives—for which consumers will spend a fair amount of time comparing alternatives. When people need new sneakers, for instance, they will go from store to store shopping—trying shoes on, comparing alternatives, and chatting with salespeople. Canada Goose jackets may become a shopping product as more authorized retailers and freestanding stores are added.

### Convenience Products/Services

**Convenience goods/services** are those products or services for which the consumer is not willing to spend any effort to evaluate prior to purchase. They are frequently purchased commodity items, usually bought with very little thought, such as common beverages, bread, or soap.

---

**associated services (or augmented product)** The nonphysical attributes of the product, including product warranties, financing, product support, and after-sale service.

**consumer products** Products and services used by people for their personal use.

**specialty goods/services** Products or services toward which the customer shows a strong preference and for which he or she will expend considerable effort to search for the best suppliers.

**shopping goods/services** Products or services—such as apparel, fragrances, and appliances—for which consumers will spend time comparing alternatives.

**convenience goods/services** Products or services for which the consumer is not willing to spend any effort to evaluate prior to purchase.

A medical professional is a specialty service. Apparel is a shopping product. Soft drinks are a convenience product. Insurance is an unsought service.

(top left): Comstock Images/SuperStock RF; (top right): Big Cheese Photo/SuperStock RF; (bottom left): © McGraw-Hill Education/Jill Braaten, photographer; (bottom right): numbeos/E+/Getty Images RF

**product mix**
The complete set of all products offered by a firm.

**product lines**
Groups of associated items, such as those that consumers use together or think of as part of a group of similar products.

**Unsought Products/Services**   Unsought products/services are products consumers either do not normally think of buying (e.g., funeral services, fire extinguishers) or do not know about. Because of their very nature, these products require lots of marketing effort and various forms of promotion. When new-to-the-world products, such as GPS systems, are first introduced, they often represent unsought products. Do you have cold hands and don't know what to do about it? You must not yet have heard of HeatMax HotHands Hand Warmers, air-activated packets that provide warmth for up to 10 hours.

## L03   PRODUCT MIX AND PRODUCT LINE DECISIONS

The complete set of all products offered by a firm is called its **product mix**. Colgate-Palmolive's product mix is shown in Exhibit 9.2. The product mix typically consists of various **product lines**, which are groups of associated items, such as items that consumers use together or think of as part of a group of similar products. Colgate-Palmolive's product lines include oral care, personal care, household care, fabric care, and pet nutrition. While the main focus for Canada Goose is jackets, its product lines also include snow pants, hats, and gloves.

**product category**
An assortment of items that the customer sees as reasonable substitutes for one another.

**brands**
The names, terms, designs, symbols, or any other features that identify one seller's good or service as distinct from those of other sellers.

Within each product line, there are often multiple product categories. A **product category** is an assortment of items that the customer sees as reasonable substitutes for one another. For example, in the oral care product line, Colgate-Palmolive offers several categories with a variety of offerings to choose from in each: toothpaste, whitening products, toothbrushes, kids' oral-care products, floss, and oral first aid. Each category within a product line may use the same or different **brands**. For instance, Colgate-Palmolive offers several brands of toothbrushes (e.g., 360°, Motion Whitening, Massager, Navigator).

| **EXHIBIT 9.2** | Colgate-Palmolive Product Mix |

| | **Product Lines** Product line breadth | | | |
| | **Oral Care** | **Personal Care** | **Home Care** | **Pet Nutrition** |
| **Product Categories** Product line depth | *Toothpaste* (Colgate Total) *Toothbrush* (Colgate Plus) *Kids' products* (Colgate Barbie Bubble Fruit toothpaste) *Whitening products* (Colgate Simply White) *Floss* (Colgate Total Dental Floss) *Oral first aid* (Colgate Orabase) | *Deodorants* (Speed Stick) *Bar soap* (Irish Spring) *Body wash* (Soft Soap) *Hand wash* (Soft Soap) *Men's toiletries* (Skin Bracer Aftershave) | *Dishwashing liquid* (Palmolive) *Automatic dishwashing liquid* (Palmolive) *Household cleaners* (Ajax) *Dish wipes* (Palmolive) *Soap* (Murphy Oil) *Fabric softener* (Fleecy) | Hill's Pet Nutrition, Inc.—subsidiary *Dog and cat food* (Science Diet) *Dog and cat food* (Ideal Balance) *Dog and cat food* (Prescription) *Dog and cat food* (Healthy Advantage) |

*Source:* Colgate-Palmolive Company, www.colgate.ca/app/Colgate/CA/EN/CompanyHomePage.cvsp

The product mix reflects the breadth and depth of a company's product lines. A firm's **product mix breadth** (sometimes also referred to as variety) represents the number of product lines offered by the firm; Colgate-Palmolive has four, as indicated by the four columns in Exhibit 9.2. **Product line depth**, in contrast, is the number of product categories within a product line. Within Colgate-Palmolive's oral-care line, for example, it offers toothpaste, toothbrushes, kids' products, and so forth. Its pet nutrition product line, however, comprises fewer offerings and therefore has less depth. In our Canada Goose example, Arctic program jackets, parkas, vests, mountaineer jackets, bomber jackets, hoodies, trench coats, and technical shells show product line depth for jackets.

Within each product category are a number of individual items called **stock keeping units (SKUs)**, which are the smallest unit available for inventory control. For instance, within the toothpaste category, Colgate-Palmolive offers 49 Colgate SKUs that represent various sizes, flavours, and configurations of Colgate Total, Colgate Optic White, Colgate Enamel Health, and Colgate Sensitive Pro Relief.[12] Each individual product is a unique SKU. The 100 millilitre size of Colgate Total Clean Mint is one SKU, while the 100 millilitre package of Colgate 2 in 1 Whitening is a second SKU. The same size package of Colgate Sensitive Whitening represents a third SKU. The category depth is the number of SKUs within a category. Each SKU has its own unique universal product code (UPC) as well.

However, adding unlimited numbers of new products can have adverse consequences. Too much variety in the product mix is often too costly to maintain, and too many brands may dilute the overall reputation. In the past several years, for example, Revlon undertook a significant restructuring. It introduced a new line, Vital Radiance, aimed at women over the age of 45 years. But this line cut into the sales of its other brands and harmed its reputation among younger consumers, so Revlon eliminated the Vital Radiance line, to refocus on those products and markets that were doing well.[13]

So why do firms change their product mix's breadth or depth?

**product mix breadth**
The number of product lines, or variety, offered by the firm.

**product line depth**
The number of products within a product line.

**stock keeping units (SKUs)**
Individual items within each product category; the smallest unit available for inventory control.

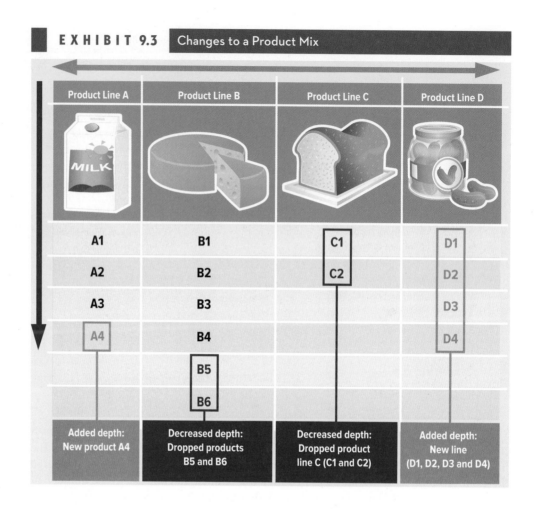

**EXHIBIT 9.3** Changes to a Product Mix

| Product Line A | Product Line B | Product Line C | Product Line D |
| --- | --- | --- | --- |
| A1 | B1 | C1 | D1 |
| A2 | B2 | C2 | D2 |
| A3 | B3 | | D3 |
| A4 | B4 | | D4 |
| | B5 | | |
| | B6 | | |
| **Added depth: New product A4** | **Decreased depth: Dropped products B5 and B6** | **Decreased depth: Dropped product line C (C1 and C2)** | **Added depth: New line (D1, D2, D3 and D4)** |

## Change Product Mix Breadth and Depth

Exhibit 9.3 offers a hypothetical example of a company with four product lines in its product mix. Firms may change their product mix breadth by either adding to or deleting from product lines or by increasing or decreasing product line depth.

Increase Breadth   Firms often add new product lines to capture new or evolving markets, increase sales, and compete in new venues (e.g., addition of Product Line D in Exhibit 9.3). With the introduction of VIA Ready Brew, Starbucks changed the way people thought about instant coffee. The new line is expected to produce more than a billion dollars in sales.[14] And when the company learned that more than 60 percent of its consumers enjoyed flavoured coffee, it introduced Natural Fusions, a line of premium coffee available for sale in grocery stores in vanilla, cinnamon, and caramel flavours. As part of Starbucks' business strategy, it was a natural way to grow its consumer products business.[15]

Decrease Breadth   Sometimes it is necessary to delete entire product lines to address changing market conditions or meet internal strategic priorities (e.g., deletion of Product Line C in Exhibit 9.3). For example, SC Johnson sold off many products in its skin care line, including its successful Aveeno brand, to Johnson & Johnson.[16] The firm no longer competes in the skin care business but it remains a strong competitor in its original product lines, such as home cleaning (Pledge, Windex), air care (Glade), and home storage (Saran, Ziploc).[17]

**Increase Depth**    Firms may add new products within a line to address changing consumer preferences or preempt competitors while boosting sales (e.g., addition of A4 in Exhibit 9.3). At Taco Bell, the addition of new varieties of its Doritos Locos Tacos enable it to appeal better to consumers who enjoy spicy foods or love Cool Ranch flavour. The tacos still contain the same ingredients, but the availability of 123 different Doritos flavours significantly increases the product line's depth.[18]

**Decrease Depth**    From time to time, it is necessary to delete product categories to realign resources (e.g., deletion of B5 and B6 in Exhibit 9.3). The decision to delete products is never taken lightly. Generally, substantial investments have been made to develop the brand and manufacture the products. Yet firms often make pruning decisions regularly to eliminate unprofitable items and refocus their marketing efforts on more profitable items. Procter & Gamble (P&G) introduced Tide Basic as an extension of its Tide line—probably the best-known detergent brand and a product that enjoys a reputation as an innovative, high-end brand. Tide Basic was priced 20 percent cheaper than regular Tide, but P&G deleted the extension less than a year after introducing it, worried that an inexpensive, less effective version undermined its brand.[19]

# BRANDING

A company lives or dies based on brand awareness. Consumers can't buy products that they don't know exist. Even if the overall brand name is familiar, it won't help sales of individual products unless consumers know what products are available under that name. Sports fans have long been familiar with the rallying cry for Under Armour and its line of athletic gear: "Protect This House." But when the company chose to refresh its tagline, it undertook a massive ad campaign to introduce a new slogan, "I Will." In addition to extensive online and outdoor advertising, Under Armour intensified its branding efforts during the NBA All-Star Weekend, when television ads flooded the airwaves, promising new technology introductions and working to expand its appeal to both male and female sportswear consumers.[20]

Branding provides a way for a firm to differentiate its product offerings from those of its competitors. Both Snapple and Tropicana make and sell fruit drinks; yet a consumer may choose one over the other because of the associations that the brands evoke. Brand names, logos, symbols, characters, slogans, jingles, and even distinctive packages constitute the various brand elements firms use,[21] which they usually choose to be easy for consumers to recognize and remember. For example, most consumers are aware of the Nike swoosh logo and would recognize it even if the word *Nike* did not appear on the product or in an advertisement. Exhibit 9.4 summarizes these brand elements.

Using its slogan, "I Will," Under Armour featured Canelo Alvarez, boxing's welterweight World Champion, wearing its digital performance monitoring system.

PRNewsFoto/Under Armour/AP Images

| | EXHIBIT 9.4 | What Makes a Brand? |
| --- | --- | --- |

| Brand Element | Description |
| --- | --- |
| Brand name | The spoken component of branding, it can either describe the product or service/product characteristics and/or be composed of words invented or derived from colloquial or contemporary language. Examples include Comfort Inn (suggests product characteristics), Apple (no association with the product), or Accenture (invented term). |
| URLs (uniform resource locators) or domain names | The location of pages on the Internet, which often substitutes for the firm's name, such as Toyota (www.toyota.ca) or Ben & Jerry's (www.benandjerrys.ca). |
| Logos and symbols | Logos are visual branding elements that stand for corporate names or trademarks. Symbols are logos without words. Examples include the Nike swoosh and the Mercedes star. |
| Characters | Brand symbols that could be human, animal, or animated. Examples include the Pillsbury Doughboy and Rice Krispies' Snap, Crackle, and Pop. |
| Slogans | Short phrases used to describe the brand or persuade consumers about some characteristics of the brand. Examples include State Farm's "Like A Good Neighbour" and Tim Hortons®' "Always Fresh." |
| Jingles | Audio messages about the brand that are composed of words or distinctive music. Examples are Intel's four-note sound signature that accompanies the "Intel Inside" slogan. |

*Source:* Adapted from Kevin Lane Keller, *Strategic Brand Management*, 4th ed. (Upper Saddle River, NJ: Prentice Hall, 2012).

## LO4  Value of Branding

Brands add value to merchandise and services beyond physical and functional characteristics or the pure act of performing the service.[22] Let's examine some ways in which brands add value for both customers and the firm (see Exhibit 9.5).

| | EXHIBIT 9.5 | Value of Branding |
| --- | --- | --- |

**Brands Facilitate Purchasing**  Brands are often easily recognized by consumers and, because they signify a certain quality level and contain familiar attributes, brands help consumers make quick decisions.[23] Imagine how much time it would take to buy groceries if the brands on the shelves were unfamiliar! The cola market is a particularly strong example of this benefit. Some people think cola is cola, such that one brand is not too different from another. But branding has made it easy for Pepsi drinkers to find the familiar logo on the store shelf and more likely that they simply buy one of Pepsi's other products, should they decide to switch to a diet soda or a flavoured version. From promotions, past purchases, or information from friends and family, they recognize the offering before they even read any text on the label, and they likely possess a perception of the brand's level of quality, how it tastes, whether it is a good value, and, most importantly, whether they like it and want to buy it.

**Brands Establish Loyalty** Over time and with continued use, consumers learn to trust certain brands. They know, for instance, that Band-Aid® bandages always perform in the exact same way. Many customers become loyal to certain brands and wouldn't consider switching brands. In some cases, they may feel a strong affinity to certain brands. For instance, Coca-Cola drinkers don't drink Pepsi, and wouldn't touch a Dr Pepper. Other consumers are loyal to Canada Goose and feel as though they are part of a club.[24] And loyal fans help build buzz, as Social and Mobile Marketing 9.1 notes. As a result of this loyalty, these companies can maintain great depth in their product lines since their customers will buy other brands within their product mix.

**Brands Protect From Competition and Price Competition** Strong brands are somewhat protected from competition and price competition. Because such brands are more established in the market and have a more loyal customer base, neither competitive pressures on price nor retail-level competition is as threatening to the firm. Lacoste is known for its golf shirts. Although many similar brands are available and some retailers offer their own brands, Lacoste is perceived to be of superior quality and garners a certain status among its users, and, therefore, can command a premium price. Likewise, consumers willingly pay a premium for Canada Goose jackets, which are recognized as a best-of-breed brand.

*Sensational offer! Large, colorful nursery-rhyme pictures by Vernon Grant, artist who created the characters "Snap!" "Crackle!" and "Pop!" See back of Rice Krispies package.*

Characters like Rice Krispies' Snap, Crackle, and Pop help build a brand.

Kellogg's Rice Krispies, Snap Crackle Pop, and all related characters are trademarks of Kellogg North America Company, used with permission.

**Brands Reduce Marketing Costs** Firms with well known brands can spend relatively less on marketing costs than firms with little known brands because the brand sells itself. People have become familiar with Lululemon's white, stylized "A" logo, so its advertisements don't need to explain what the company is or what it does. People just know. The popularity of Canada Goose, spread by word-of-mouth and supported by partnerships and sponsorships, reduces the need to invest in a lot of print advertising.[26]

Tiffany & Co. works hard to protect its brand, including its famous blue box.

© Simon Lord/Alamy Stock Photo

The fact that consumers are familiar with Lululemon as a brand helps the company reduce marketing costs.

Richard Lam/The Canadian Press

## Social and Mobile Marketing 9.1[25]

### Ben & Jerry's Engages Loyal Fans via Social Media

When it comes to restaurant chains and social media, Ben & Jerry's has the best presence, according to a report by NetBase. It tracks social media analytics for considerably larger restaurant brands such as McDonald's, Subway, Chipotle, and Denny's. NetBase judged 100 different restaurant chains on elements such as reach, number of mentions, positive versus negative sentiments, and the passion behind the comments. While Ben & Jerry's didn't

have as many mentions as larger brands, it earned top marks for the volume of conversation compared to the volume of sales—5,627 mentions for every dollar in sales. That was 39 percent higher than Chipotle and almost double that of Starbucks.

So how does such a small company generate results like these? Ben & Jerry's identifies brand advocates, listens to them, engages with them, and responds fast. Promotions such as #FreeConeDay encourage social media activity and create buzz. It also works with other organizations to promote and discuss social and political issues. For example, Ben & Jerry's partnered with *The Guardian* to launch "Too Hot to Handle," a multimedia campaign using humour to get people talking about climate change.

The company has a small in-house team that lives and breathes social media and understands the need to treat each platform separately. All platforms have different strengths and are used accordingly. For example, Facebook is best for reach and engagement. When it comes to activism or engaging with NGO partners and fans, Twitter is better. Instagram is great at generating fan interaction and community engagement. In its #CaptureEuphoria campaign, Ben & Jerry's asked fans to post photos on Instagram that captured moments of euphoria. The campaign wasn't about selling ice cream. In fact, almost none of the winning images the company used in billboards and ads showed ice cream. Instead, a shout out to the Instagrammer was featured, as a way to celebrate community.

Ben & Jerry's may be a small player as a restaurant brand but, as Paige Leidig, chief marketing officer at Net-Base, noted, "Size doesn't necessarily matter. It's about really knowing your audience and using why they think you're different and incorporating that into your engagement with them."

Ben & Jerry's uses social media to get people talking about issues such as climate change.

Rob Crandall/Shutterstock.com

| Ben & Jerry's Social Media Presence | |
| --- | --- |
| **Platform** | **Number of Followers** |
| Snapchat | 14,000 |
| Instagram | 648,000 |
| Facebook | 8.3 million |
| Twitter | 306,000 |

**Brands Are Assets** Brands are also assets that can be legally protected through trademarks and copyrights and thus constitute a unique ownership for the firm. Firms sometimes have to fight to keep their brands "pure." Rolex and

Canada Goose are ever watchful to ensure that the value of their brands is not diluted with counterfeit merchandise or sales through unauthorized dealers. Likewise, Tiffany & Co.'s iconic blue box is instantly recognizable and associated with high-quality items.

**Brands Impact Market Value**  Having well known brands can have a direct impact on the company's bottom line. The value of a company is its overall monetary worth, comprising a vast number of assets. When the brand loses value, it also threatens other assets. For RadioShack, once the first destination for consumers seeking a Walkman or boom box, the loss of brand value as it has struggled to maintain relevance as a provider of modern, cutting-edge technology has pushed it to close approximately 500 stores and pursue an aggressive strategy to rebrand and gain back some of the value.[27]

The value of a brand can be calculated by assessing the earning potential of the brand over the next 12 months;[28] see examples of Canada's most valuable brands in Exhibit 9.6.

**EXHIBIT 9.6**  Canada's 10 Most Valuable Brands[29]

| Rank | Brand | Sector | 2017 Brand Value (C$ Million) |
|---|---|---|---|
| 1 | Royal Bank of Canada | Financial Services | 16.6 |
| 2 | TD Bank | Financial Services | 16.5 |
| 3 | Bell | Telecom | 12.7 |
| 4 | Scotiabank | Financial Services | 11.3 |
| 5 | Bank of Montreal | Financial Services | 10.2 |
| 6 | Tim Hortons® | Food | 10.1 |
| 7 | Rogers | Telecom | 9.05 |
| 8 | Telus | Telecom | 8.6 |
| 9 | CIBC | Financial Services | 8.2 |
| 10 | Brookfield | Financial Services | 6.9 |

*Source:* Brand Finance®, "Canada 100: The Annual Report on the World' Most Valuable Canadian Brands," February 2017.

## Brand Equity

**L05**

To understand branding, we look at three areas: brand equity (which consists of brand awareness, perceived value, brand associations, and brand loyalty); brand ownership; and brand names, as illustrated in Exhibit 9.7. The value of a brand translates into **brand equity**, or the set of assets and liabilities linked to a brand that add to or subtract from the value provided by the product or service.[30] Brand health must be actively managed to maintain a positive image. A recall of Lululemon yoga pants, for example, could hurt brand equity in the absence of corrective action. Apple ranks number one on the Best Global Brands list with a value of $170.3 billion; Coca-Cola is third with $78.4 billion. McDonald's is ninth, with a value of just under $40 billion.[31] Like the physical possessions of a firm, brands are assets the firm can build, manage, and harness over time to increase its revenue, profitability, and overall value. Firms spend millions of dollars on promotion, advertising, and other marketing efforts throughout a brand's life cycle. This can sometimes cause regulators to react if spending comes close to crossing ethical lines, as

**brand equity**
The set of assets and liabilities linked to a brand that add to or subtract from the value provided by the product or service.

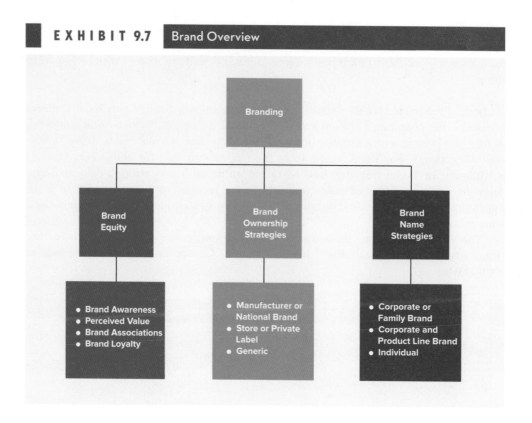

**EXHIBIT 9.7** | Brand Overview

described in Ethical Dilemma 9.1. Marketing expenditures allocated carefully can result in greater brand recognition, awareness, and consumer loyalty for the brand, enhancing overall brand equity.

How do we know how "good" a brand is, or how much equity it has? Experts look at four aspects of a brand to determine its equity: brand awareness, perceived value, brand associations, and brand loyalty.

**Brand Awareness**   **Brand awareness** measures how many consumers in a market are familiar with the brand and what it stands for, and have an opinion about that brand. The more customers are aware of or familiar with a brand, the easier their decision-making process will be. Familiarity matters most for products that are bought without much thought, such as soap or chewing gum. However, brand awareness is also important for infrequently purchased items or items the consumer has never purchased before. If the consumer recognizes the brand, it probably has attributes that make it valuable.[33] For those who have never purchased a Toyota, for instance, just being aware of the brand can help facilitate a purchase. Certain brands gain such predominance in a particular product market over time that they become synonymous with the product itself; that is, the brand name starts being used as the generic product category. Examples include Kleenex tissue, Clorox bleach, Band-Aid bandages, and the Google search engine. Companies must be vigilant in protecting their brand names, because if they are used so generically, over

**brand awareness** Measures how many consumers in a market are familiar with the brand and what it stands for; created through repeated exposures of the various brand elements (brand name, logo, symbol, character, packaging, or slogan) in the firm's communications to consumers.

These brands are so strong that they have become synonymous with the product itself.

© McGraw-Hill Education

## Ethical Dilemma 9.1

### Does Taxing Sugary Drinks Reduce Obesity?[32]

Obesity rates are often highest in the nations and regions that drink the most soda. The sugary, high-calorie versions of popular carbonated beverage brands in turn have been widely blamed for the growing rates of obesity, especially among children. Those complaints also are growing as brands expand outside the United States and potentially threaten the long-term health of children across the globe.

Should Coca-Cola and other consumer packaged goods companies be allowed to advertise to children?

GL Archive/Alamy Stock Photo

To fight obesity, Denmark planned to introduce a tax on sugary drinks. However, when its tax on fatty foods was rescinded less than a year after being passed, the proposed sugar tax was abandoned. Mexico added a 10 percent tax on sugary drinks in 2014. The U.K. government also proceeded with its tax on sweetened drinks and Philadelphia became the first major U.S. city to impose a tax on soft drinks, in 2016. Senators filed a report on obesity in Canada the same year that recommended similar taxes. Diabetes Canada has also called for higher taxes on sugary beverages. According to a Mintel survey, 69 percent of Canadians are concerned about the impact of sugar on their overall health.

Although it strongly maintains that sodas are not the main culprit in rising obesity rates, Coca-Cola has acknowledged its own limited responsibility and therefore vowed not to advertise in settings in which children make up more than 35 percent of the anticipated audience (previously, it set this standard at 50 percent). Coke ads have disappeared from cartoon networks and youth-oriented shows, children's magazines, and so forth.

In addition to its commitment not to advertise directly to children younger than 12 years of age, Coke has invested in initiatives to promote more physical activity and to encourage consumers to consider lower calorie alternatives, whether Diet Coke or Minute Maid juices (which Coca-Cola also owns). Beyond advertising, Coke's new product development efforts are largely focused on identifying and integrating natural low-calorie sweeteners. In some countries, its packaging also will feature more prominent information about calorie contents. The soft drink industry prefers these types of actions over additional taxes.

Does taxing sugary drinks work? Over 30 states and cities tried this approach and most found taxing did not yield the desired effect. Sales of soft drinks fell for two years after the tax was introduced in Mexico but have rebounded since then. With such mixed results, should Canada consider imposing a sugar tax?

time, the brand itself can lose its trademark status. Thermos, trampoline, linoleum, and yo-yo are all examples of brands that lost their trademark status. Aspirin has become a generic brand in the United States; however, it remains a registered trademark in Canada.[34]

Marketers create brand awareness through repeated exposures of the various brand elements (brand name, logo, symbol, character, packaging, or slogan) in the firm's communications to consumers. Such communication media include advertising and promotions, personal selling, sponsorship and event marketing, publicity, public relations, and social media (see Chapters 14, 15, and 16). Because consumer awareness is one of the most important elements in creating a strong brand, firms are willing to spend tremendous amounts of money advertising the brand, including more than $5 million for just one 30-second spot on TV during the Super Bowl.

**Perceived Value**  Brand awareness alone does not ensure a strong brand. Consumers could be aware of a brand but have a negative opinion of its value or the firm's reputation. **Perceived value** is the relationship between a product or service's benefits and its cost. Customers usually determine the offering's value in relationship to that of its close competitors. If they feel an inexpensive brand is about the same quality as a premium brand, the perceived value of the cheaper choice is high.

Many private-label brands are less expensive than brands developed by manufacturers. These brands, commonly found in supermarkets or drugstores, have seen a rise in popularity in recent years because of their high perceived value.

Retailers such as Joe Fresh and Giant Tiger specialize in providing great value. Certainly, merchandise at these stores is not always of the highest possible quality, and the apparel is not the most fashion-forward. But customers don't necessarily want to buy a wastebasket that will last for 50 years and be suitable for display in a living room, nor do they need to show up at school looking like they came from a fashion-show runway. Instead, they want products to do what they were designed to do and be available at a reasonable price. First Choice Haircutters, a national haircutting chain, provides "Affordable, Professional Haircare"—usually at one-half to one-third salon prices. Its customers perceive the chain to be a great value because the haircut is better than good and the price is more than reasonable.

**Brand Associations**  **Brand associations** reflect the mental links that consumers make between a brand and its key product attributes, such as a logo, slogan, or famous personality. These brand associations often result from a firm's advertising and promotion efforts. Toyota's hybrid car, the Prius, is known for being economical, stylish, and good for the environment. Associations with specific attributes help create differentiation between the brand and its competitors; for example, Volvo stresses that its cars are made with consumer safety in mind. Firms also attempt to create specific associations for their brands with positive consumer emotions, such as fun, friendship, good feelings, family gatherings, and parties. Until recently, State Farm Insurance used the slogan "Like a good neighbour, State Farm is there." Hallmark Cards associates its brand with helping people show they care about quality: "When you care enough to send the very best."

Because of her vast viral popularity, Grumpy Cat (real name: Tardar Sauce) has been approached by several brands that seek to be associated with her, to benefit from her entertaining, satirical, and hip image. The feline's naturally unhappy looking mouth now appears across Friskies' product line. Mashable featured Grumpy Cat in its tent at South by Southwest, and a bidding process led to the promise of an upcoming Grumpy Cat movie.[35]

**perceived value**
The relationship between a product or service's benefits and its cost.

First Choice Haircutters, a national haircutting chain, provides its customers with great value because the haircut is better than good and the price is more than reasonable.

Mary Altaffer/AP Photo/The Canadian Press

**brand associations**
The mental links that consumers make between a brand and its key product attributes; can involve a logo, slogan, or famous personality.

**brand personality**
Refers to a set of human characteristics associated with a brand, which has symbolic or self-expressive meanings for consumers.

Friskies cat food is associated with its famous "spokesperson," Grumpy Cat.

lNestle Purina PetCare/AP Images

Firms sometimes even develop a personality for their brands, as if the brand were human. **Brand personality** refers to a set of human characteristics associated with a brand[36] that has symbolic or self-expressive meanings for consumers.[37] Brand personality elements include male, female, young, old, fun loving, and conservative, as well as qualities such as fresh, smooth, round, clean, or floral. McDonald's has created a fun-loving, youth-oriented brand personality with its golden arches, brightly lit and coloured restaurants, exciting and youthful packaging and advertising, and spokesperson and mascot Ronald McDonald, the clown.

Brand Loyalty    **Brand loyalty** occurs when a consumer buys the same brand's product or service again and again over time. As a result, brand-loyal customers are an important source of value for firms. First, such consumers are often less sensitive to price. In return, firms sometimes reward loyal consumers with loyalty or customer relationship management (CRM) programs, such as points that customers can redeem for extra discounts or free services, advance notice of sale items, and invitations to special events sponsored by the company. Second, the marketing costs of reaching loyal consumers are much lower because the firm does not have to spend money on advertising and promotion campaigns to attract these customers. Loyal consumers simply do not need persuasion or an extra push to buy the firm's brands. Third, loyal customers tend to praise the virtues of their favourite products, retailers, or services. This positive word-of-mouth reaches potential customers and reinforces the perceived value at no cost to the firm. Fourth, a high level of brand loyalty insulates the firm from competition because, as we noted in Chapter 2, brand-loyal customers do not switch to competitors' brands, even when provided with a variety of incentives.

Brand loyalty is not always easy to achieve, though. In most cases, it requires substantially better quality or a distinctive promise. For example, lifetime satisfaction guarantees are expensive to maintain. They mean that any customer, at any time, can come back to the company to complain about some feature they find unappealing, even if the item was purchased decades before. They are accordingly quite rare. But, for the companies that offer them—such as The North Face, Craftsman, and Darn Tough socks—unconditional guarantees evoke tremendous loyalty. Even if customers never need to replace one of these products, knowing that the company is willing to offer the guarantee makes them more likely to purchase a related item from the same brand.[38]

Dove rewarded consumers for their loyalty with double Optimum points at Shoppers Drug Mart.

DOVE is a trademark owned or used under licence by Unilever Canada, Toronto, Ontario M4W 3R2

**brand loyalty**
Occurs when a consumer buys the same brand's product or service repeatedly over time rather than buying from multiple suppliers within the same category.

# BRANDING STRATEGIES

Firms institute a variety of brand-related strategies to create and manage key brand assets, such as deciding to own the brands, establishing a branding policy, extending the brand name to other products and markets, cooperatively using the brand name with that of another firm, and licensing the brand to other firms.

## Brand Ownership

**L06**

Brands can be owned by any firm in the supply chain, whether manufacturers, wholesalers, or retailers. There are three basic brand ownership strategies: manufacturer brands, private-label or store brands, and generic brands (see Exhibit 9.8). **Manufacturer brands** are owned and managed by the manufacturer, and include Nike, Mountain Dew, KitchenAid, and Marriott. With these brands, the manufacturer develops the merchandise, produces it to ensure consistent quality, and invests in a

**manufacturer brands**
Brands owned and managed by the manufacturer.

**EXHIBIT 9.8**     Brand Ownership Strategies

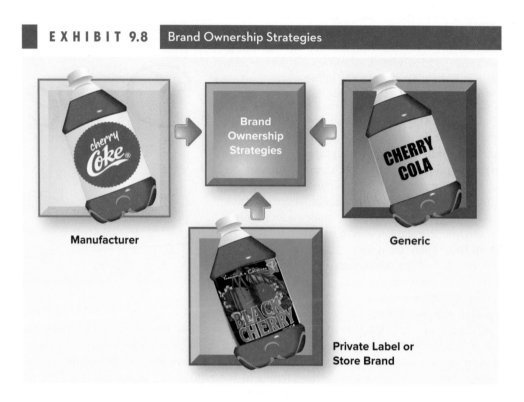

Manufacturer

Generic

Private Label or
Store Brand

marketing program to establish an appealing brand image. The majority of the brands marketed in Canada are manufacturer brands. Manufacturing firms spend millions of dollars each year to promote their brands. By owning their brands, manufacturers retain more control over their marketing strategy, are able to choose the appropriate market segments and positioning for the brand, and can build the brand and thereby create their own brand equity.

**private-label brands (store brands)**
Brands developed and marketed by a retailer and available only from that retailer.

Brands that are owned and managed by retailers, in contrast, are called **private-label brands (store brands)**. Some manufacturers prefer to make only private-label merchandise because the costs of branding and marketing their own products are prohibitive, whereas other firms manufacture both their own brand and merchandise for other brands or retailers. For instance, Whirlpool sells appliances under its own name and also makes them for Sears under the Kenmore brand. President's Choice, a private label developed and marketed by Canada's largest food distributor, offers high-quality products at moderate prices and is becoming a lifestyle brand.[39] In the past, sales of private-label brands were limited. But more recently, more retailers have developed their own store brands and use them to establish a distinctive identity. Private-label brands are particularly common in supermarkets, discount stores, and drugstores. Their popularity among consumers depends on several factors, including consumer preferences for a lower-cost brand and the trust consumers have in the store and its brand. Such private-label brands, especially those marketed by large chains such as Walmart and Costco, are fast gaining in popularity and consumer loyalty. After 28 years, President's Choice Decadent Chocolate Chip Cookies are still Loblaw's best-selling cookies.[40] Private-label brands have also gained popularity in apparel and other categories found in department and specialty stores. The Bay, for instance, provides several store brands, including Beaumark, Mantles, Truly, and Togo.

**generic**
A product sold without a brand name, typically in commodities markets.

**Generic** products are those sold without brand names, typically in commodities markets. For instance, shoppers can purchase unbranded salt, grains, produce, meat, or nuts in grocery stores. Hardware stores often sell unbranded screws, nuts, and lumber. However, even in these markets, the popularity and acceptance of generic products has declined. Consumers question the quality and origin of the products, and retailers have found better profit potential and the ability to build brand equity with manufacturer and store brands. For example, many fruits and vegetables sold through supermarket chains now carry either the manufacturer's brand name (e.g., Dole bananas) or the store's. No-Name was launched as a generic brand by Loblaw in 1978. Over the years it has expanded from 16 products to over 2600,[41] leaving some people questioning if No-Name products have evolved out of the generic category.

## Naming Brands and Product Lines

Although there is no simple way to decide how to name a brand or a product line, the more the products vary in their usage or performance, the more likely it is that the firm should use individual brands. For example, General Motors utilizes several different individual brands (Cadillac, Chevrolet, GMC), each catering to very different target markets and meeting different needs.

**EXHIBIT 9.9** | Brand Name Strategies

Individual brand

Family brand

Hyundai, on the other hand, utilizes only one brand since usage and level of performance are relatively homogeneous. Firms use several very different strategies to name their brands and product lines (see Exhibit 9.9).

**Family Brands**   A firm also can use its corporate name to brand similar product lines and products. For example, Kellogg's incorporates its company name into the brand name for its cereal brands (e.g., Kellogg's Corn Flakes, Kellogg's Froot Loops, Kellogg's Rice Krispies), helping to maintain its powerhouse status on grocery store shelves. When all products in a line are sold under one **family brand**, individual brands benefit from the overall awareness associated with the family name.

**Individual Brands**   A firm can use **individual brand** names for each of its products. For example, in its house and home products line, P&G markets various detergent products (Tide, Gain, Cheer, Downy, Febreze), paper products (Bounty, Charmin), household cleaners (Mr. Clean, Swiffer), and dishwashing products (Cascade, Dawn, Joy). Furthermore, it markets brands in various other product lines, such as personal and beauty products (Olay, Old Spice, Secret, CoverGirl), health and wellness products (Pepto-Bismol, Oral-B, Puffs), and baby products (Pampers, Huggies).[42] Similarly, Loblaw operates across Canada under the following brands: Atlantic Super-store, Dominion, Extra Foods, Fortinos, Loblaws, Maxi, No Frills, Provigo, Your Independent Grocer, and Zehrs. Sobeys operates under the following retail banners: Sobeys, IGA Extra, IGA, Foodland, and Price Chopper. Individual brands allow a company to compete within one category, for example, laundry detergent, offering a variety of products to different

**family brand**
The use of a combination of the company brand name and individual brand name to distinguish a firm's products.

**individual brand**
The use of individual brand names for each of a firm's products.

Kellogg's uses a family branding strategy in which several product lines are sold under one name.

© Mike Hruby

target markets. And if one brand experiences problems, other products with unique brand names are protected from any negative association with the failed brand.

Choosing a Name    What's in a name? When it comes to naming new products, companies should consider the following desirable qualities: (1) The brand name should be descriptive and suggestive of benefits and qualities associated with the product. For example, the name *Sunkist* evokes images of oranges ripening on the trees kissed by the sun. (2) The brand name should be easy to pronounce, recognize, and remember, such as Tide, Crest, or Kodak. (3) The company should be able to register the brand name as a trademark and legally protect it. (4) For companies looking to global markets, the brand name should be easy to translate into other languages. Starbucks invited Canadians to submit names for a new Blonde Roast coffee. The winning name was True North Blend, reflecting the stunning geography, vast landscape, and spirit of Canada.

Sometimes a change of name is in order. Vancouver's Backwoods Brewery had been selling its beer to restaurants and bars for nearly a decade when it decided to rebrand as Dead Frog. Competing against wacky wine names such as Fat Bastard and Cat's Pee on a Gooseberry Bush, beer marketing had been pretty conservative. The company wanted a memorable but irreverent name that would appeal to a younger audience.[43] And chances are that a band called Rainbow Butt Monkeys never would have become a hit sensation. While it may have been memorable, band members received a better reception after they changed their name to Finger Eleven.

## Brand Extension

A **brand extension** refers to the use of the same brand name for new products being introduced to the same or new markets.[44] The dental hygiene market, for instance, is full of brand extensions; Colgate, Crest, and Butler all sell toothpaste, toothbrushes, and other dental hygiene products. Roots has extended its brand from athletic clothing to leather bags, yoga wear and accessories, and even a line of baby clothes. Brand extensions are also common in global expansions. For example, Coca-Cola, Nike, Starbucks, and Levi's are sold the world over under the same name.

There are several advantages to using the same brand name for new products. First, because the brand name is already well established, such as the Canada Goose example discussed in the chapter vignette, the firm can spend less in developing consumer brand awareness and brand associations for the new product.[45] The Braun brand started selling kitchen appliances (coffeemakers, toasters, food processors, blenders, juicers), and then extended into various other product categories, including shaving (dry razors, beard care), beauty care (cordless hair stylers), oral care (power toothbrushes), and steam irons.[46]

Second, if the brand is known for its high quality, that perception will carry over to the new product. Consumers who had not used the Neutrogena brand before trying the brand extension, Neutrogena Wave power cleanser, might be encouraged to try Neutrogena's core product line of cleansers and moisturizing lotions, especially if their experience with Wave has been positive.[47]

Brand extensions are often used for complementary products such as chips and dips.
© Mike Hruby

Third, when brand extensions are used for complementary products, a synergy exists between the two products that can increase overall sales. For example, Frito-Lay markets both chips and dips under its Frito-Lay and Doritos brand names.[48] When people buy the chips, they tend to buy the dips as well.

Not all brand extensions are successful, however. Some can dilute brand equity.[49] **Brand dilution** occurs when the brand extension adversely affects consumer perceptions about the attributes the core brand is believed to hold.[50] For example, Bic thought that since people wanted its disposable lighters and razors, they would also want disposable underwear; Bic was wrong. While Life Savers soft drinks did well in prelaunch taste tests, they didn't do well in subsequent sales.

To prevent the potentially negative consequences of brand extensions, firms must consider the following caveats:

- Marketers should carefully evaluate the fit between the product class of the core brand and that of the extension.[51] If the fit between the product categories is high, consumers will consider the extension credible, and the brand association will be stronger for the extension. When Starbucks introduced VIA, its line of instant coffee, it made sense to consumers.

- Firms should carefully evaluate consumer perceptions of the attributes of the core brand and seek out similar attributes for the extension, because brand-specific associations are very important for extensions.[52] For example, if HP printers were associated with reliability, performance, and value, consumers would expect the same brand-specific attributes in other products that carried the HP brand name.

Life Savers unsuccessfully attempted a brand extension strategy with its line of soft drinks.
© GK Custom Research, LLC

- Firms should refrain from extending the brand name to too many products and product categories to avoid diluting the brand and damaging brand equity. While Donald Trump had been successful lending his name to real estate properties and TV shows, he was unsuccessful in extending his name to branding steaks.

- Firms should consider whether the brand extension will be distanced from the core brand, especially if the firm wants to use some but not all of the existing brand associations. Marriott has budget, mid-tier, and luxury hotels. Its luxury hotels, including the Ritz-Carlton, Edition, and Renaissance, do not use the name Marriott at all.[53]

## Cobranding

**Cobranding** is the practice of marketing two or more brands together, on the same package or promotion. Primarily because of credit card companies, such as Visa and MasterCard, the practice has greatly increased in the past decade. Airlines were among the first to cobrand with credit card companies (such as the CIBC Aeroplan Visa Card); recently, firms in other industries (such as banking, retail, and restaurants) have begun forming similar alliances, resulting in cards such as BMO Mosaic MasterCard, TD Gold Visa, and President's Choice MasterCard, to name a few.

Cobranding enhances consumers' perceptions of product quality by signalling otherwise unobservable product quality through links between the firm's brand and a well known quality brand. For example, Yum Brands frequently combines two or more of its restaurant chains—including A&W, KFC, Long John Silver's, Pizza Hut, and Taco Bell—into one store space. This cobranding strategy is designed to appeal to diverse market segments and extend the hours in which each restaurant attracts customers. Loblaw partnered with Mattel in a cobranding agreement for its affordable fashion line, Joe Fresh, to create a limited-edition collection of Barbie-branded sleepwear and underwear.[54] Tim Hortons® found that its customers responded enthusiastically to its efforts to cobrand with Cold Stone Creamery ice cream in the United States. It tested and then launched the concept in its Canadian stores, however later discontinued the brand in Canada.[55]

However, there are some risks to cobranding, especially when customers for each of the brands are vastly different. For example, the Burger King and Häagen-Dazs cobranding strategy failed because the customer profiles for the brands were too different.[56] Cobranding may also fail when there are financial disputes or conflicts of interest.

## Brand Licensing

**Brand licensing** is a contractual arrangement between firms, whereby one firm allows another to use its brand name, logo, symbols, and/or characters in exchange for a negotiated fee.[57] Brand licensing is common for toys, apparel, accessories, and entertainment products, such as video games. The firm that provides the right to use its brand (licensor) obtains revenues through royalty payments from the firm that has obtained the right to use the brand (licensee). These royalty payments sometimes take the form of an upfront, lump-sum licensing fee or may be based on the dollar value of sales of the licensed merchandise.

Several aspects of a brand can be licensed. Popular apparel designers, such as Ralph Lauren, Calvin Klein, and Eddie Bauer, and luxury goods manufacturers often license the right to use their brand name on a variety of products. The Porsche name is used by Grundig radios and also appears on watches, luggage sets, and tennis racquets. The computer world has even capitalized on the Porsche brand name with the game *Need for Speed: Porsche Unleashed.* Canadian Tire built on the growing popularity of NASCAR racing to become the official automotive retailer of NASCAR in Canada, only recently ending the decade-long partnership.[58] One very popular form of licensing is the use of characters created in books and other media. Such entertainment licensing has generated tremendous revenues for movie studios such as Disney and Lucas Films (think of the *Star Wars* memorabilia), as well as for comic book publishers such as Marvel Entertainment (*Spider-Man*). A long-standing staple of licensing has been major league sports teams that play in the NBA, NFL, or NHL.

Licensing is an effective form of attracting visibility for the brand and thereby building brand equity while also generating additional revenue. There are, however, some risks associated with it. For the licensor, the major risk is the dilution of its brand equity through overexposure of the brand, especially if the brand name and characters are used inappropriately.[59]

## L07 PACKAGING

Packaging is an important brand element with more tangible or physical benefits than the other brand elements because packages come in different types and offer a variety of benefits to consumers, manufacturers, and retailers. Packaging attracts the consumer's attention, enables products to stand out from their competitors, and offers a promotional tool (e.g., "NEW" and "IMPROVED" promises on labels). It also allows the same product to appeal to different markets with different sizes, such that convenience stores stock little packages that travellers can buy at the last minute, whereas Costco sells extra-large versions of products. As discussed in Entrepreneurial Marketing 9.1, packaging plays a key role in launching a new product.

But packaging also serves to protect products. Wrappers and exterior cartons protect eggs from being broken and help prevent tampering with products such as toothpaste. Packaging provides the UPC label used by retail scanners as well as contents, directions, and other additional product information. The package can also be an important marketing tool for the manufacturer if it is used to convey the brand's positioning. Cosmetics giant Estée Lauder considers packaging to be key to brand image—if its packaging is beautiful and perfectly executed, consumers have more confidence in the products inside.[61] Packaging is considered by many marketers to be the last frontier in advertising because of its role in promoting products to consumers on the floor of the store at the point of purchase. Packaging may also affect consumers' emotions and drive impulse buying. The shapes of fragrance, perfume, and deodorant bottles and containers are good

## Entrepreneurial Marketing 9.1

## Three Farmers[60]

Camelina sativa? Perhaps the biggest hurdle in launching Three Farmers, after getting novel foods approval from Health Canada, was educating consumers about the ancient grain used to produce camelina oil. Sisters Natasha and Elysia Vandenhurk explained on CBC's *Dragons' Den* that camelina originated in Northern Europe and had historically been used as cooking oil until it fell out of favour in the 16th century. A nutritionally dense seed, camelina is rich in Omega 3 and Vitamin E, which can be difficult to incorporate in your diet if you don't like fish. It can be used at high temperatures (up to 475°F) and won't break down. Plus it has a 24-month shelf life without refrigeration, highly unusual for omega oils.

Although the grain had never been grown in Saskatchewan, it was drought resistant and cold tolerant, making it a perfect crop. The sisters joined their father and two neighbouring farmers to form Three Farmers, to grow camelina and produce cold-pressed oil. Each sister brings unique skills to the partnership: Natasha is a business graduate from the University of Saskatchewan, and Elysia is a Red Seal chef who has worked with celebrity chef Susur Lee.

The oil market is extremely competitive. It's incredibly difficult to convince someone who has been using olive oil for years to switch to something new. To do this meant offering a unique, high quality product with a great brand story and attractive packaging. Chef Elysia says camelina oil has a great taste profile—light flavour, earthy fragrance, and slightly nutty taste. That unique

Three Farmers Camelina Oil is a unique and versatile product that is healthy and tastes great.

Used with permission of Three Farmers

edge helped the sisters convince retailers that their product wasn't just cooking oil.

Packaging played a key role. Elysia says they chose tinted glass bottles because they look classier than tins and protect the cold-pressed oil which is very sensitive to light. Round bottles provide production efficiencies when wrapping labels around them. The sisters wanted a heritage authentic story to match the product and even the website is designed with that in mind, featuring stories about the three farmers who grow the camelina. Consumer feedback has been useful, too, and led to a change from a twist cap to a spout like a wine bottle to pour better.

The brand is packaged in two sizes and has already had line extensions with new flavours (roasted garlic and chili infused, and roasted onion and basil). It sells at independent stores across Canada for about $15 for a 500 mL bottle. Distribution has exploded from 150 retailers to over 900. Restaurants are also using camelina oil due to its high smoke point. Roasted chickpeas made with camelina oil were introduced in five different flavours and won the SABEX 2016 New Product of the Year Award.

Consumers love the brand's story—a Canadian product from a family business based on sustainable practices. Each bottle offers traceability back to the farmer who grew the camelina and even to the field in which it was grown simply by scanning the QR code on the package or entering the code on the web. Such transparency is unique, says Elysia. Very few products offer traceability, something she feels is an important trend in the food industry.

examples of marketers extending the use of packaging beyond a distribution function to encourage purchase and differentiation. Many children also pressure their parents to buy products, like breakfast cereal, more because of the packaging than for the product. In these instances, packaging acts as a point of differentiation and makes consumers feel proud to own the brand.

Some packaging changes are designed to make the product more ecological, such as PepsiCo's response to concerns about the waste associated with bottled water. To reduce the amount of plastic it uses, PepsiCo has decreased the weight of its water

## Sustainable Marketing 9.1

## Unilever Wants Consumers to Rinse, Recycle, Reimagine[63]

As a company, Unilever has been very vocal about its efforts to reduce the company's environmental impact. Over the past decade, it produced fewer emissions by 37 percent and decreased waste going to landfills by 85 percent. That's impressive for any company, but as the third largest consumer packaged goods company in the world, these initiatives make a big impact.

Its research showed that 54 percent of consumers wanted to buy more sustainably. So, in addition to addressing the manufacturing process, Unilever has been working hard to decrease waste created after its products are used. As a result of its efforts, consumer generated waste decreased by 29 percent from 2010 to 2015. A special sustainability campaign was launched in advance of Earth Day to encourage consumers to rethink recycling. The company's research showed that while the majority of people were recycling kitchen bottles and containers, only 14 percent of them were diligent when it came to empty bottles that came out of bathrooms. The campaign was used to make

To make consumers aware of gaps in recycling habits for empty bottles used in bathrooms, Unilever launched a #RethinkRecycling campaign.

monticello/Shutterstock.com

consumers aware of the gap in recycling habits and asked them to rinse, recycle, and reimagine to give plastics new life.

In 2010, Unilever created a Sustainable Living Plan as a blueprint for achieving business growth while decreasing its environmental footprint and increasing its positive social impact. The plan identified specific products (Knorr, Dove, Dirt Is Good, Lipton, and Hellmann's) as Sustainable Living Brands that integrate sustainability into both purpose and product. On the packaging front, a new improved squeeze bottle was created for Hellmann's that allowed consumers to get more mayonnaise out with less waste. The Dove body wash bottle was redesigned to reduce its weight by 15 percent. And Lipton Tea packaging removed individual envelopes and reduced the size of cartons and cases, which reduced waste by 7–12 percent.

Five years later, the Sustainable Living Brands had grown 30 percent faster than other products, accounting for almost half of Unilever's business. Putting sustainable living at the heart of the company is inspiring customers and growing sales, showing that sustainability is no longer a niche issue.

bottles by 20 percent, which means less plastic in landfills. More companies are moving toward sustainable packaging, as noted in Sustainable Marketing 9.1. Leaders in this area include Coca-Cola, Microsoft, Waste Management, Aveda, and Zappos. These firms host a sustainable packaging conference that brings together more than 250 firms to discuss new methods to produce environmentally responsible packaging that is also cost effective. Ideas from this conference include returnable packaging, use of 3D printing, and flexible packaging. They have also set up a website with information on future conferences, and information for the industry at http://www.sustainability-in-packaging.com.[62]

Sometimes packaging changes can backfire, though, such as when Tropicana changed its packaging to feature a picture of a glass of juice, rather than the familiar straw in an orange. Customers balked, and said the new image was reminiscent of a generic bargain brand. The company poorly misjudged its customers' loyalty to its existing brand position, as exemplified by its packaging. Frito-Lay's efforts to launch compostable SunChips packaging resulted in many consumers complaining that the bags were too noisy.

Many consumers experience "wrap rage"—a great frustration with packaging that makes it seemingly impossible to get at the actual products. So companies are moving away from traditional clamshells, which are the curved plastic packages around many electronics goods, because they are so difficult to open. Costco has replaced the clamshells with packaging made of coated paperboard; it still requires scissors to be opened but is flat and therefore can be opened easily.

In addition, items may often be packed into larger cartons, pallets, or containers to facilitate shipment and storage from the manufacturer to the retailer. These shipping packages benefit the manufacturer and the retailer in that they protect the shipment during transit; aid in loading, unloading, and storage; and allow cost efficiencies because of the larger order and shipment sizes.

Packaging can also be used in other subtler ways to help suppliers save costs. When the costs of producing a product rise significantly, manufacturers are faced with either raising prices (something customers don't usually like) or reducing the amount of product sold in a package. Chobani reduced the size of its Greek yogurt containers from 6 ounces to 5.3 ounces without changing the price. Although there was a time when customers might not have noticed this 12 percent decrease, today consumers are very aware that everything from cleansing tissues to ice cream containers is shrinking. Today's customers are more empowered as well, as the Chobani example shows. As soon as these newer, smaller packages hit store shelves, customers took to Twitter and Facebook and immediately began complaining about the change, further raising awareness of the packaging change.[64]

Because packaging is critical to the firm's brand positioning and shelf appeal, many innovations in design and materials have occurred in the past few decades. Some examples include reclosable zipper pouches, childproof packages, senior-friendly designs that are easy to open, Tetra Pak aseptic packaging, green and biodegradable packaging, and transparent packaging that allows consumers to see what they are buying.

The packaging and label for Astro® Zero® highlights the fact that the yogurt does not contain artificial sweeteners.

## LABELLING

Labels on products and packages provide information the consumer needs for his or her purchase decision and consumption of the product. In that they identify the product and brand, labels are also an important element of branding and can be used for promotion. The information required on them must comply with general and industry-specific laws and regulations, including the constituents or ingredients contained in the product, where the product was made, directions for use, and/or safety precautions.

Many labelling requirements stem from various laws, including the Competition Act, the Consumer Packaging and Labelling Act and Regulations, the Food and Drugs Act, and the Hazardous Materials Act. Several federal agencies, industry groups, and consumer watchdogs carefully monitor product labels. The Food and Drugs Act regulates the information on food, drugs, and cosmetics package labels. Quaker Canada had to wait for Health Canada approval before it could state on its labels that oat fibre helps reduce cholesterol. The Consumer Packaging and Labelling Act covers food products and ensures that the claims made by the manufacturer are true and that labels accurately reflect ingredients and quantities. All this has to be done in both of Canada's official languages, French and English.

A product label is much more than just a sticker on the package; it is a communication tool. Many of the elements on the label are required by laws and regulations (i.e., ingredients, fat content, sodium content, serving size, calories), but other elements of the label remain within the control of the manufacturer. How manufacturers use labels

# REAL MARKETER PROFILE

## Diane Laberge (Unilever)

Used with permission of Diane Laberge

During my career in brand management, I have had the privilege to work with many talented teams and build one of the most iconic brands in the world. Dove is a brand with purpose that has inspired confidence in millions of women and girls and is proof that relevant and authentic campaigns can make a positive impact.

At Unilever, as a director of marketing, I have had the opportunity to coach, mentor, and train dozens of marketing professionals. Reflecting on my experience, I have learned that a career is a journey and that everyone's path is unique, but what is constant is that diverse experiences early in your marketing career will prove beneficial in the long run.

I began my career at an industrial food company where I spent a year in a B2B marketing and sales role developing a rebranding strategy, doing experiential event planning, and working with R&D on product development and trends. In this role, I was able to lead key strategic projects but I knew that I wanted to follow my passion for consumer marketing and work at a traditional consumer packaged goods company.

Subsequently, I decided to pursue a trade marketing role at Maple Leaf Foods Inc. working on Michelina's frozen entrees. Some of my responsibilities included reporting on sales, developing trade promotion strategies, doing trade spend analysis, creating product launch presentations, and working closely with both sales and marketing to execute launch plans with key retailers. This customer development role provided incredibly vital experience because I gained a strong understanding of the consumer but more importantly of the retail customer, their needs, and how to develop a category growth strategy. This is a critical skill for any successful product marketer.

Next I joined Unilever as an assistant brand manager; over a period of 10 years, I undertook more challenging and progressive marketing roles on its personal care business.

My most recent role as director of marketing for Dove Masterbrand and the Skin portfolio includes brands such as Dove Men+Care, Vaseline, and St. Ives. What I love most about brand management is that it is the perfect combination of strategic and creative thinking and every day is completely different due to the variety of work.

As business owners, brand marketers are ultimately responsible for the delivery of all financial and market share results. Daily activities can range from AC Nielsen market analysis to budget management, ROI evaluations, working closely with trade and sales teams to optimize pricing and promotion strategies, closing distribution gaps or bringing new opportunities such as innovations or shopper marketing programs to retailers. Data analytics and consumer research is important and it is up to managers to derive insights and create clear action plans to deliver profitable growth opportunities for the brand.

Building a brand with purpose such as Dove that inspires confidence in women and girls has been rewarding but it also requires strong creative and communications. Developing Dove campaigns and executing product launch plans entails working closely with creative agency partners to develop communication plans that connect with consumers in a meaningful way. Briefing agencies, evaluating creative ideas, media and PR strategies as well as providing feedback on communication such as TV commercials, video content, social posts, and ecommerce messaging is all in a day's work! What is most exciting is that the way we connect with consumers is ever changing in the fast paced omnichannel world, so staying on top of trends and different technologies is critical to success.

Brand management challenges you to develop a broad business understanding and strong interpersonal skills to lead cross-functional teams. The more diverse experiences you attain early on will allow for a holistic understanding of business and therefore you will be a better marketer over the long term!

to communicate the benefits of their products to consumers varies by the product. For example, the label for Astro® Zero® highlights the fact that the yogurt does not contain artificial sweeteners. Many other products highlight other specific ingredients, vitamin content, or nutrient content. This focus signals to consumers that the product offers these benefits. Although often overlooked, the importance of the label as a communication tool should not be underestimated.

## LEARNING OBJECTIVES REVIEW

**LO1**  **Describe the components of a product**

The product itself is important but so are its associated services, such as support or financing. Other elements combine to produce the core customer value of a product: the brand name, quality level, packaging, and additional features.

**LO2**  **Identify the types of consumer products**

These products tend to be classified into four groups: specialty, shopping, convenience, and unsought products. Each classification involves a different purchase situation and consumer goal.

**LO3**  **Explain the difference between a product mix's breadth and a product line's depth**

Breadth, or variety, entails the number of product lines that a company offers. Depth involves the number of categories in one specific product line. Firms grow their product lines by adding either new product categories or new SKUs within a product category. The decision to add products should be made carefully. Excessive product line expansions can confuse consumers and dilute the appeal of the brand's core products. Sometimes products or product lines become unprofitable, the firm's priorities change, or consumer preferences shift. When this happens, firms must prune their product lines by deleting items or possibly even entire product categories.

**LO4**  **Identify the advantages that brands provide firms and consumers**

Brands facilitate the consumer search process. Some customers are loyal to certain brands, which essentially protects those brands from competition. In addition, brands are valuable in a legal sense, in that trademarks and copyrights protect firms from counterfeiters and knock-off artists. Firms with well known brands can spend relatively less on marketing because the brand and its associations help sell the product. Finally, brands have real market value as a company asset.

**LO5**  **Summarize the components of brand equity**

Brand equity summarizes the value that a brand adds to—or subtracts from—the offering's value. It comprises brand awareness, or how many consumers in the market are familiar with the brand; brand associations, which are the links consumers make between the brand and its image; and brand loyalty, which occurs when a consumer will buy only that brand's offer. Brand equity also encompasses the concept of perceived value, which is a subjective measure that consumers develop to assess the costs of obtaining the brand.

**LO6**  **Describe the types of branding strategies used by firms**

Firms use a variety of strategies to manage their brands. First, they must decide whether to offer national, private-label, or generic brands. Second, they have a choice of using an overall corporate brand or a collection of product line or individual brands. Third, to reach new markets or extend their current market, they can extend their current brands to new products. Fourth, firms can cobrand with another brand to create sales and profit synergies for both. Fifth, firms with strong brands have the opportunity to license their brands to other firms.

**LO7**  **State how a product's packaging and label contribute to a firm's overall strategy**

Like brands, packaging and labels help sell the product and facilitate its use. The package holds the product, and its label provides product information. The package also provides additional consumer information on its label and facilitates transportation and storage for both retailers and their customers. Labels have become increasingly important to consumers because they supply important safety, nutritional, and product usage information.

## KEY TERMS

- associated services (or augmented product)
- brand associations
- brand awareness
- brand dilution
- brand equity
- brand extension
- brand licensing
- brand loyalty
- brand personality

- brands
- cobranding
- consumer products
- convenience goods/services
- core customer value
- family brand
- generic
- individual brand
- manufacturer brands
- perceived value

- private-label brands (store brands)
- product category
- product line depth
- product lines
- product mix
- product mix breadth
- shopping goods/services
- specialty goods/services
- stock keeping units (SKUs)

# CONCEPT REVIEW

1. Explain the differences between product mix breadth and product line depth. Why is understanding this difference important?

2. Explain why branding is important to marketers. What value do customers derive from purchasing and using brand name products?

3. What is brand equity? Describe the strategies marketers could employ to increase the value of their brand equity.

4. Differentiate between a manufacturer's brand, generic brand, and store brand. Should retailers carry all three types of brands? Why?

5. Describe the desirable qualities companies should consider when choosing product names.

6. What are the advantages of using the same brand name and extending it to new products?

7. Explain how brand licensing differs from cobranding.

8. What is cobranding? When does it make sense for a company to use a cobranding strategy?

9. Explain how marketers increase the value of their product offering through packaging. Discuss the ethical issues surrounding product packaging and labelling. How might some of these issues be resolved?

10. Explain how labelling could be used as a marketing weapon rather than just to provide legally required information.

# MARKETING APPLICATIONS

1. Prepared foods at Whole Foods Market, the world's largest retailer of organic foods, are very profitable. To make them even more profitable, suggest two strategies that would alter the product mix breadth and depth.

2. Visit a grocery store and look for Colgate Total toothpaste on the shelves. How many different SKUs (including all sizes and flavour variations) are sold at the store? What are the advantages and disadvantages of having so many different variations?

3. Suppose you have just been hired by a jewellery manufacturer as a marketing consultant. The manufacturer has been making private-label jewellery for 75 years but is thinking about developing its own brand of jewellery. Discuss the advantages and disadvantages of such a strategy.

4. Identify a specific brand that has developed a high level of brand equity. What specific aspects of that brand establish its brand equity?

5. Are you loyal to any brands? If so, pick one and explain why you believe you are loyal, beyond that you simply like the brand. If not, pick a brand that you like and explain how you would feel and act differently toward the brand if you were loyal to it.

6. Ford Motor Company owns several brands: Ford, Lincoln, Mercury, Mazda, and Aston Martin. Within each brand are many models, each of which has a unique identifying name. Wouldn't it be easier to just identify them all as Fords? Justify your answer.

7. Unlike Ford Motor Company, BMW has only one brand and gives each car it makes a number instead of a name, for example, the BMW Series 3, Series 5, or Series 7. What are the advantages to BMW of this approach?

8. Identify a specific company that has recently introduced a new brand extension to the marketplace. Discuss whether you believe the brand extension example you provided will benefit or harm the firm.

9. Do you think all food sold in a grocery store should have an ingredient and nutrition label? Consider the perspectives of consumers, the manufacturer, and the store.

10. You are hired by a small bakery interested in distributing its product through supermarkets. The market for the bakery's products has been steadily growing and it is time to expand distribution now that the bakery has expanded its production capacity. You have an appointment with the manager of a local grocery chain. The manager is familiar with the bakery's products and is excited about the possibility of having them in the store. He has asked you to come up with a plan to package your products in a way that makes them attractive to shoppers, keeps baked goods fresh, and uses the least amount of packaging possible to satisfy even the most stringent environmentalist. You've never had to deal with this issue before. At the bakery, goods are packed in paper bags after being selected from protective glass displays. Come up with a package that works for the retailer and is affordable for the bakery.

## NET SAVVY

1. Visit the P&G website (http://www.pg.ca). Identify and briefly describe its different *product lines*. Now identify one of its *product categories*, and discuss the *depth* of that particular category.

2. Interbrand Corporation is a leading brand consultancy firm headquartered in New York that conducts research on the monetary value of different brands. Visit the company's website (http://www.interbrand.com) and access the most recent "Best Global Brands" survey. Identify the top five brands, their brand values, and their countries of origin. Describe changes in the rankings of these firms from the previous year. Why do you think the rankings changed? Identify the brands with the greatest increase and the greatest decrease in terms of percentage change in brand value from the previous year.

## CHAPTER CASE STUDY

### OPRAH WINFREY, A BRAND UNTO HERSELF

A cultural icon who rose from poverty to become one of the world's most influential entrepreneurs, Oprah Winfrey is many things to many people. Certainly she is an entertainer who comes across as women's most intimate friend and advocate. Winfrey also has inspired and coached an audience of millions on how to "live your best life." But perhaps most of all, Oprah Winfrey is a marketer and the savvy leader of a media empire that has extended her brand worldwide.

Starting with her immensely successful TV program, *The Oprah Winfrey Show*, Winfrey expanded her personal brand through a range of other vehicles, which in any other context would be known as product lines. These lines include her production companies, Harpo Films, Harpo Radio, Harpo Print, and Harpo Studios; *O, The Oprah Magazine*; Oprah.com, her website, which profiles all her ventures; Oprah's Book Club, which some have credited with saving the publishing industry; multiple TV and radio spin-offs; and OWN, the Oprah Winfrey Network, also called her "next chapter."[65] Each element functions as a division of Harpo Productions, her multimedia entertainment company.

When you think of Oprah Winfrey, think big: Harpo Productions, Inc.; *O, The Oprah Magazine*; *O at Home Magazine*; Harpo Films; and the Oxygen television network; not to mention her philanthropic work with the Oprah Winfrey Foundation.

Frederick M. Brown/Stringer/Getty Images

Building on Oprah's own compelling story of personal triumph, the Winfrey brand offers multitudes of fans not only an example of self-improvement but also authentic proof, from Winfrey's own life, that anyone can control his or her own destiny. Over the years, Winfrey has chronicled her childhood of poverty and sexual abuse, struggles to control her weight, and the difficulties of being a powerful woman in a highly competitive industry. The revealing details have only strengthened the connection with her viewers, who adore her. The message is compelling and authentic: If I can do it, you can, too.

Viewers believe her. That trust gives Winfrey tremendous influence, and it also translates into a flair for helping other brands connect with her audience. An inveterate shopper, she likes to showcase the products she loves. Her endorsements, offered without compensation, can make little-known products into superstars overnight. The month following her episode featuring aromatherapy slippers called Foot Cozys, manufacturer DreamTimes sold 20,000 pairs, up from its usual monthly volume of 3,000. Marketing experts say the Oprah brand, built on the credo of self-improvement and living well, now ranks with the towering brands of Coca-Cola and the Marlboro Man, leaving one observer to admit, "I'm hard-pressed to think of a stronger brand than Oprah."[66] That means that the Oprah brand has been enormously profitable, making Winfrey the second wealthiest of America's 400 richest self-made women, with a combined worth of $3.1 billion.[67]

Winfrey began building her public persona long before she gained any national recognition, starting as a local news anchor in Nashville and then a talk-show host in Baltimore. With her move to Chicago in 1984, Winfrey gained increasing attention when her morning program, *AM Chicago*, surpassed the ratings achieved by the then–talk show king Phil Donahue. By 1986, her program was rebranded as *The Oprah Winfrey Show*, and its host was gaining a reputation for offering confessional, straight talk, like a "group therapy session."[68]

Her daily program reigned supreme among talk shows for 25 years, drawing 12 million U.S. viewers at its peak, with more than 4,500 episodes and 30,000 guests. The messages of confronting life's difficult realities and taking time for self-care remained central in brand extensions, including syndicated spin-offs such as *Dr. Phil* and *Rachael Ray*. Newer shows, usually featuring Winfrey's favoured celebrity life coaches, have also increased her brand recognition. On his shows, Dr. Mehmet Oz provides insights into living a "longer, more vibrant life." *In the Bedroom With Dr. Laura Berman* counsels women about how to juggle the pressures of home and work and still feel sexy.[69]

Other extensions focus on different areas. Winfrey has continued to promote her brand and ethos of personal growth in her monthly magazine *O, The Oprah Magazine*, which features Winfrey on every cover and has a circulation of about 2.4 million, making it the 18th largest in terms of circulation in the United States.[70] Movies produced by Harpo Films also have brought some of the country's most respected actors together with scripts arising from acclaimed books, such as *Tuesdays With Morrie*, featuring Jack Lemmon and based on the best-selling novel by Detroit sportswriter Mitch Albom; *Their Eyes Were Watching God*, based on the Zora Neale Hurston novel and starring Halle Berry; *Beloved*, a film based on Toni Morrison's Pulitzer Prize-winning novel, directed by Jonathan Demme and co-starring Winfrey and Danny Glover; and *The Great Debaters*, which received a Golden Globe nomination and co-starred Denzel Washington and Forest Whitaker. Winfrey also provided backing for the release of *Precious*, an Oscar-winning film based on a novel by Sapphire. Each new introduction celebrated the preservation of human dignity against terrible odds—disabling disease, crippling poverty and abuse, or racism.

The latest venture—launching her own cable television network—took Winfrey into new territory, with lots of challenges, though still aligned with her brand's promise of controlling one's own destiny. It's not her first risky move: Buoyed by the terrific success of *The Oprah Winfrey Show*, in the late 1980s, Winfrey bolted from both King World Productions, which syndicated the show, and ABC, which produced it. Taking total control through Harpo Productions gave her complete ownership of the brand and syndication fees, estimated at $100 million. That move established the cornerstone of her empire.

But the initial launch of OWN was rocky, and for its first two years the network struggled to earn profits. Early reviews criticized Winfrey for taking the fun out of her programming.[71] *Oprah's Lifeclass*, the flagship show and latest incarnation of Winfrey's personal brand, came off like a series of lectures, preaching that "you are responsible for changing your life and making it better."[72] More recently, the network has sought to balance such uplifting but boring messages with viewers' appetite for gossip. Its reality series *Lindsay* documents the efforts of the young actor and frequent news item Lindsay Lohan to get her life in order.[73]

Just a few months after the launch of OWN, Winfrey shuffled her leadership structure and took the top post herself. As always, she was determined to take control of her brand and her company. She would do what she had always exhorted others to do: Live her best life through her own brand.

### Questions

1. Visit the company website (http://www.oprah.com) and identify and describe the different product lines that it markets.

2. How would you describe its product line breadth?

3. Review the different product categories in each of the company's product lines. Which has the greatest depth? Which has the least?

4. How has the company positioned its brand? How does it go about communicating its position?

# CHAPTER 10

## LEARNING OBJECTIVES

After studying this chapter you should be able to

**LO1** Describe how marketing a service differs from marketing a product by applying the principles of intangibility, inseparability, inconsistency, and inventory

**LO2** Outline the four gaps in the Gaps model used to understand and manage customer expectations

**LO3** Describe strategies that firms can use to help employees provide better service

**LO4** Identify three service recovery strategies

(both): Used with permission of GoTire

# Services: The Intangible Product

"Who has time to be without the car for a whole day?" When Heather Murphy and Craig Howes ran custom window franchises, having their vehicles serviced was a big frustration. It took too much time to have the tires changed and cost them $6,000 a day in lost revenue. The most expensive part of changing tires was vehicle downtime. And so they launched GoTire, Canada's first mobile tire service business.[1] Offering an entire shop in a van, their motto is "We bring the shop to you."

The intangible nature of services means consumers can't always see what they are getting before they buy it. Murphy and Howes developed their business with a view to franchising and knew they would have to focus on tangibility. One way GoTire achieves this is with professional-looking trucks emblazoned with the company logo. The trucks not only add tangibility to the service but also serve as mobile billboards. They invested in a high quality video before their *Dragons' Den* appearance which impressed the Dragons and has since been repurposed to attract franchisees. Videos are created of all new franchisees so prospective customers can see who will be delivering the service, making customers more comfortable trying the service.

Another challenge for GoTire is the seasonal nature of tire changes. It's busy in the spring and fall but what happens in the shoulder season? You can't hold services in inventory like you can with products. To spread demand throughout the year, franchises offer glass and car detailing services. The mobile windshield service is convenient for consumers. Along with interior and exterior auto detailing, wiper blades plus headlight and taillight care are offered. Other optional services—such as emergency unlock, battery sales, battery service, and headlight restoration—help increase demand.

A "Tire Hotel" is used to house tires in the off-season. It's a great feature for people who live in apartments or don't want to use space in their garage. Murphy says it's also a customer retention system because once someone leaves their tires with you, you know the person will be coming back. GoTire contacts all customers who use the Tire Hotel to book tire changes in advance of the first snowfall, to further even out demand.

Guarantees are used to de-risk the service and deal with inseparability. While all tire manufacturers offer warranties, Murphy says they aren't always very good. GoTire offers low-cost insurance that provides a tire repair guarantee. A warranty is offered on windshield repairs. If the windshield breaks within six months of being repaired, customers can apply the cost of the repair to a new windshield.

Extensive training helps overcome inconsistency and ensures franchisees are ready to launch their business. Training lasts for three weeks and addresses technical skills, product knowledge, sales, and marketing, as well as how to set up an office and warehouse. Each franchisee receives social media training on Facebook and Twitter and learns GoTire's proprietary customer relationship management (CRM) system. Because brand consistency is key, franchisees receive a brand standards guide complete with templates for brochures, invoices, and promotional materials.

Addressing the unique characteristics of services paid dividends. GoTire broke even in its first year, has over 30 franchises coast to coast, and is Canada's fastest-growing mobile tire franchise,[2] and is now looking into expansion into the U.S. market.[3] ∎

---

In this chapter, we examine the unique characteristics of services that differentiate them from products. Then we discuss how companies can provide great service and use elements in the Gaps model to help them meet customer expectations. Lastly, we look at how companies can recover from inevitable service failures.

Whereas a **service** is any intangible offering that involves an act, performance, or effort that cannot be physically possessed, **customer service** specifically refers to human or mechanical activities firms undertake to help satisfy their customers' needs and wants. By providing good customer service, firms add value to their products.

Exhibit 10.1 illustrates the continuum from a pure service to a pure product. For example, some businesses install tires (pure service) while others only sell them (pure product). And some companies, like GoTire, lie somewhere in the middle and include some service and some product. Still other firms sell products with an "embedded" service element (e.g., restaurants). Some pure service companies operate in the online or mobile world, for example, dating app firms such as Tinder. As we noted in Chapter 2, even firms engaged primarily in selling a product, such as apparel stores, typically view service as a means to maintain a sustainable competitive advantage. This chapter takes an inclusive view of services as anything from pure service businesses to a business that uses service as a differentiating tool to help it sell physical products.

**service**
Any intangible offering that cannot be physically possessed.

**customer service**
Specifically refers to human or mechanical activities firms undertake to help satisfy their customers' needs and wants.

**EXHIBIT 10.1** | The Service-Product Continuum

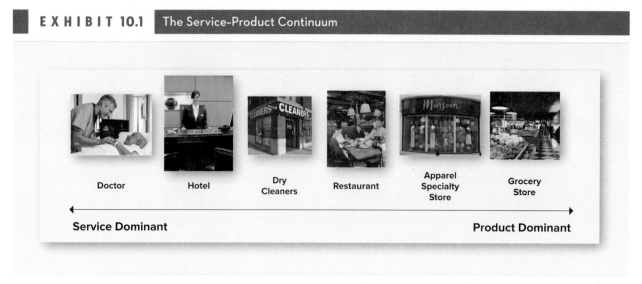

Doctor    Hotel    Dry Cleaners    Restaurant    Apparel Specialty Store    Grocery Store

Service Dominant ⟷ Product Dominant

(doctor): Ariel Skelley/Getty Images; (hotel): Onoky/SuperStock; (dry cleaners): The McGraw-Hill Companies, Inc./Andrew Resek, photographer; (restaurant): John A. Rizzo/Getty Images; (apparel store): © Charles Bowman/Alamy; (grocery store): Photodisc; Brand X Pictures/Getty Images.

Economies of developed countries such as Canada have become increasingly dependent on services. For example, the service sector fuels the Canadian economy, accounting for the lion's share of jobs (more than 80 percent of the population works in services[4]), and is growing far faster than goods-producing industries. This dependence and the growth of service-oriented economies in developed countries have emerged for several reasons.

First, it is generally less expensive for firms to manufacture their products in less-developed countries. Even if the goods are finished in Canada, some of their components likely were produced elsewhere. In turn, the proportion of service production to goods production in Canada, and other similar economies, has steadily increased over time.

Specialized services like personal training are thriving.

Chris Clinton/Getty Images

## Sustainable Marketing 10.1

## Scooping Poop for Profit[5]

No one likes to pick up poop. As people who own pets get busier and busier, this is one task that many are more than happy to pay others to do on their behalf. Recognizing that time is a precious commodity, pet poop services have sprung up across the country. In Coal Harbour, Halifax, enterprising teenager Justin Sheppard and his friend Jared Williams launched their Pooper Scooper service. He was already offering snow shovelling and lawn care services and "sniffed out" a new opportunity when snow started to melt.

But these days it's not enough to simply remove pet waste. You have to consider the environment as well. In Montreal, Scoopy Doo trains all its franchisees to scoop and then thoroughly clean the yard and/or litter boxes using special cleaners to destroy potentially dangerous bacteria. They also use certified compostable bags to ensure customers that pet waste won't languish in landfill sites.

Poop Patrol started in one small Toronto neighbourhood and has since expanded to other areas of the city. Like Scoopy Doo, it has put measures in place to inform customers of its sustainable practices. All tools are carefully cleaned with hospital-approved solutions to avoid the risk of cross-contamination from yard to yard. Poop Patrol uses only oxo-biodegradable, not plastic, bags for pet waste. These bags break down in months and cause no harm to the environment. In addition to services for four-legged friends, Poop Patrol also offers services to remove goose poop and deter geese from depositing more. The company offers a money back satisfaction guarantee as a way of showing

Poop and scoop services have popped up across the country.

Used with permission of Scoopy Doo Pet Services

clients its commitment to providing high-quality and customer-focused service. Guarantees are an invaluable way for companies to de-risk the decision to try a new service.

In Western Canada, the Calgary Poop Troop stresses the convenience and low cost of its service, as well as the fact that pet owners no longer have to deal with pet waste odour or contamination in their garbage cans. Like other services, it also offers a guarantee and the peace of mind that pets can safely be left in the yard since all employees are trained to double-check that gates are closed on arrival and departure.

Intangibility is a challenge for any service company, especially for poop services businesses. When the businesses do their jobs properly, pet owners have nothing to see except a clean lawn. So some companies add tangibility by selling pet related products such as biodegradable bags and odour eliminator treatments. Poop Patrol also sells outdoor pet sheds that look like children's play houses, and dog rocks which reduce nitrate levels to avoid urine burn marks in grass.

Companies with catchy names such as Doggy Doo and Scooby's offer convenient pick-up and disposal of pet waste in the Vancouver area. Doggie Detail ensures pet owners understand the need for proper disposal since waste left on lawns can lead to contaminated water. Protecting the environment and reducing pet owners' ecological footprint helps differentiate its service from competitors'. So does having a sense of humour; Angela Bartnik, owner of Turd Wranglers, calls herself the CEO, or chief excrement officer.

Second, people place a high value on convenience and leisure. Most households have little time for the household maintenance tasks, and many are willing to pay others to do their chores, as discussed in Sustainable Marketing 10.1.

Third, as the world has become more complicated, people are demanding more specialized services—everything from plumbers to personal trainers, from massage therapists to tax preparation specialists, from lawyers to travel and leisure specialists and even to health care providers. The aging population in particular has increased the need for health care specialists, including doctors, nurses, and caregivers in assisted living facilities and nursing homes, and many of those consumers want their specialists to provide personalized, dedicated services.

**LOI** # SERVICES MARKETING DIFFERS FROM PRODUCT MARKETING

The marketing of services differs from product marketing because of four fundamental differences unique to services: they are intangible, inseparable, variable, and perishable.[6] To help remember these differences, think of them as the four Is of services in that they are Intangible, Inseparable from their providers, Inconsistent (variable), and cannot be held in Inventory (perishable). (See Exhibit 10.2.) These differences make marketing services considerably more challenging than marketing products. This section examines these four differences and discusses how they affect marketing strategies.

## Intangible

As the title of this chapter implies, the most fundamental difference between products and services is that services are **intangible**; they cannot be touched, tasted, or seen like a pure product can. When you get a physical examination, you see and hear the doctor, but the service itself is intangible. This intangibility can prove highly challenging to marketers. For instance, it makes it difficult to convey the benefits of services. Try describing whether the experience of visiting your dentist was good or bad and why. Service providers (e.g., physicians, dentists) offer cues to help their customers experience and perceive their service more positively, such as a waiting room stocked with TV sets, computer games, and toys for children; upscale beverages; and comfortable chairs to create an atmosphere that appeals to the target market.

Similarly, Starbucks has always enhanced its service offering by providing a comfortable and cozy atmosphere for drinking coffee, working, reading, or chatting with friends. It adds tangibility to its service by creating a warm and inviting environment and

**intangible**
A characteristic of a service; it cannot be touched, tasted, or seen like a pure product can.

**EXHIBIT 10.2**   Core Differences Between Services and Goods

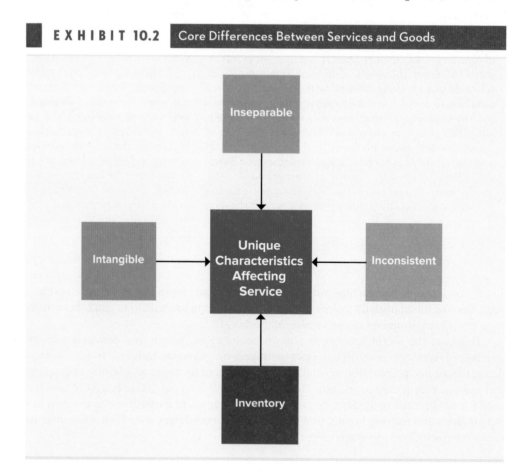

offering free Wi-Fi to customers nationwide. RBC Royal Bank offers clients *my*Finance-Tracker, an online financial management tool that tracks expenses, categorizes transactions, and provides advanced budgeting capabilities for personal banking and credit card accounts.[7] The tool improves RBC's service offering and adds tangibility to the banking experience by helping clients save time and money.

A service that can't be shown directly to potential customers is difficult to promote. Marketers must therefore creatively employ symbols and images to promote and sell services, as Walt Disney World does in using its advertising to evoke images of happy families and nostalgic memories of

At Starbucks, customers can have a drink, pick up iTunes Pick of the Week cards, and surf the Internet by using the stores' free Wi-Fi access.
RosalreneBetancourt 3/Alamy Stock Photo

Mickey Mouse and previous visits to the theme park. Likewise, Cirque du Soleil, considered Canada's top cultural export, adds tangibility to its performances with mesmerizing staged acrobatics, which are backed by a live orchestra playing an original score. The entire circus experience is carefully coordinated to create memorable impressions—the portable toilets on its big-top sites even have running water.[8] Fans can also buy a wide variety of Cirque du Soleil branded merchandise (e.g., music, videos, books, clothing, and accessories) to extend their positive memories of the performances. In another example, professional medical services provide appropriate images of personnel doing their jobs in white coats surrounded by high-tech equipment. Dentists provide patients with tangible evidence of their visits in the form of free toothbrushes. Educational institutions promote the quality of their services by touting their famous faculty and alumni, as well as their accreditations. They also often use images of happy students sitting spellbound in front of a fascinating professor or going on to lucrative careers of their own.

Because of the intangibility of services, the images marketers use reinforce the benefit or value that a service provides. Professional service providers—such as doctors, lawyers, accountants, and consultants—depend heavily on consumers' perceptions of their integrity and trustworthiness. Yet the promotional campaigns some of these professionals use have been criticized by their peers and consumer welfare groups. Tension is created when service providers such as personal injury lawyers use aggressive marketing tactics to attract clients to their service but still attempt to maintain a perception of integrity and trustworthiness, or when invasion of privacy becomes an issue.

## Inseparable Production and Consumption

Unlike a pair of jeans that may have been made months before their purchase, services are produced and consumed at the same time—that is, service and consumption are **inseparable**. When getting a haircut, the customer not only is present but may also participate in the service process. Furthermore, the interaction with the service provider may have an important impact on the customer's perception of the service outcome. If the hairstylist appears to be having fun while cutting hair, it may affect the experience positively. Because service production can't be separated from consumption, astute service marketers provide opportunities for their customers to get directly involved in the service. Health care providers have found, for instance, that the more control they allow their patients in determining their course of treatment, the more satisfied those patients are.

Because the service is inseparable from its consumption, customers rarely have the opportunity to try the service before they purchase it. And after the service has

**inseparable**
A characteristic of a service: it is produced and consumed at the same time—that is, service and consumption are inseparable.

Enterprise Rent-a-Car reduces its service inconsistency through training and standardization. You get the same great service everywhere you go.

© James A. Finley/AP Photo/ The Canadian Press

**inconsistent**
A characteristic of a service: its quality may vary because it is provided by humans.

Service offerings from Planet Fitness are customized to customers' needs.

PRNewsFoto/Planet Fitness/ AP Images

been performed, it can't be returned. Imagine telling your dentist that you want a "test" cavity filled before he or she starts drilling a real one, or asking to try out a new look before your stylist lops several inches off your hair. Because the purchase risk in these scenarios can be relatively high, services sometimes provide extended warranties and 100 percent satisfaction guarantees, such as First Choice Haircutters, which promotes "Affordable, Professional Haircare. Guaranteed." The Choice Hotels chain states: "When you choose to stay at a Comfort Inn, Comfort Suites, Quality, Clarion, or Sleep Inn hotel, we are committed to making you feel understood, welcome, and important."[9]

## Inconsistent

The more humans that are needed to provide a service, the more likely that the service's quality will be **inconsistent** or variable. A hair stylist may give bad haircuts in the morning because he or she went out the night before; yet, that stylist may still offer a better service than the undertrained stylist working at the next station. A restaurant, which offers a mixture of services and products, generally can control its food quality but not the variability in food preparation or delivery. If a consumer has a problem with a product, it can be replaced, remade, destroyed, or, if it is already in the supply chain, recalled. In many cases, the problem can even be fixed before the product gets into consumers' hands. But an inferior service can't be recalled; by the time the firm recognizes a problem, the damage has been done.

**Training and Standardization**   Some marketers of services strive to reduce service inconsistency through training and standardization. Enterprise Rent-a-Car, for instance, has worked to standardize its service delivery across North America and, to that end, provides extensive training to its associates. Go to any Enterprise outlet at any airport and chances are you will be greeted in the same personalized way. The airport shuttle drivers will load and unload your bags. When you get off the shuttle, you will be greeted by name, and your car will be ready to go in minutes. This smooth and pleasant service transaction is the result of the company's very specific service standards and excellent training program.

Marketers also can use the inconsistent nature of services to their advantage. A micromarketing segmentation strategy can customize a service to meet customers' needs exactly (see Chapter 6). Exercise facilities might generally provide the same weights, machines, and mats, but at Planet Fitness, customers know that the gym explicitly seeks to offer a laid back, less intense setting. Planet Fitness actively avoids targeting hardcore gym rats with its service offering. Instead, local storefronts offer pizza nights and bowls of free Tootsie Rolls, varying the details to match the needs and preferences of their local members. Thus each gym seeks to live up to the chain's overall promise to make going to exercise a pleasant experience, rather than an intimidation festival.[10]

**Replace People With Machines**   In an alternative approach, some service providers tackle the inconsistency issue by replacing people with machines. For simple transactions such as getting cash, using an automated teller machine (ATM) is usually quicker and more convenient—and less variable—than waiting in line for a bank teller. Self-checkout machines are multiplying in grocery and discount stores at blistering speed. Even libraries are installing self-checkout machines for books. Canadians are accustomed to serving themselves and quickly adopt new technology. An Ipsos-Reid/NCR study showed that 56 percent of Canadians are more likely to shop at stores with self-service than those without.[11] Yet not everyone embraces the idea of replacing a human with a machine. Sometimes the technology does not perform adequately, resulting in customer dissatisfaction and queuing problems.

Self-checkouts can be successful and increase customer loyalty, because they appeal to shoppers who want to move quickly and believe they can zip through checkouts faster by using the machines. Although expensive, the machines reduce labour costs; one cashier can oversee the operation of four to eight self-checkouts. And the machines don't have to be trained—nor do they ever come to work late or with a bad attitude, thereby reducing service inconsistency. Airlines routinely encourage self check-in. Even McDonald's offers self-ordering systems in some locations. In an early experiment, it found that customers spent 30 percent more when using the self-serve kiosks, making the systems a good investment.[12]

**Internet-Enabled Kiosks** Many retailers have installed Internet-enabled kiosks. In addition to offering customers the opportunity to order merchandise not available in the store, kiosks can provide routine customer service, freeing employees to deal with more demanding customer requests and problems and reducing service variability. For example, customers can use kiosks to locate merchandise in the store and determine whether specific products, brands, and sizes are available. Kiosks can also be used to automate existing store services, such as gift registry management, rain checks, film dropoff, credit applications, and preordering service for bakeries and delicatessens.

Do self-checkout machines increase or reduce consumers' perception of service?

© Caro/Alamy Stock Photo

The Internet has reduced service inconsistency in several areas. Customers can purchase travel items (e.g., airline tickets, hotel rooms, rental cars), concert and movie tickets, insurance, mortgages, and merchandise directly via the Internet or by cellphone. Cineplex launched mobile applications to allow customers to buy movie tickets faster. The apps not only reduce inconsistency for moviegoers, but also reduce costs for theatres. And if the customer wants more information than is available online, websites provide ways to contact customer service personnel by email, telephone, or live chat. The app has been downloaded 14.6 million times, with over 780 million app sessions.[13]

Beyond online benefits, the Internet has also reduced service inconsistency. Many Canadian YMCA locations use FitLinxx, a computerized system, to track their clients' workout performance. At the YMCA of Simcoe/Muskoka in Barrie, members establish goals, workouts, and schedules, and receive detailed workout programs (e.g., at least 14 abdominal muscle workouts pop up when users select "abs"). FitLinxx learns users' programs, coaches them individually throughout workouts, and tracks progress over time. The system not only has health benefits for users, who always get a consistent workout, but also has boosted customer retention, and users typically exercise more often than average.[14]

### Inventory

Services are perishable because they cannot be held in **inventory** or stored for use in the future. You can't stockpile a yoga class like you could a six-pack of beer, for

**inventory**
A characteristic of a service: it is perishable and cannot be stored in inventory for future use.

instance. The perishability of services provides both challenges and opportunities to marketers in terms of the critical task of matching demand and supply. As long as the demand for and the supply of the service match closely, there is no problem; but, unfortunately, this perfect matching rarely occurs. A ski area, for instance, can be open as long as there is snow, even at night, but demand peaks on weekends and holidays, so ski areas often offer less expensive tickets during off-peak periods to stimulate demand. Airlines, cruise ships, movie theatres, and restaurants confront similar challenges and attack them in similar ways. Airlines offer promotional pricing to encourage people to book flights during the off-season, and movie theatres routinely discount matinee showings when demand is typically lower. Looking to increase facility usage and reach new audiences, Cineplex Galaxy started broadcasting NHL games live in Canadian cities. For some hockey fans, it's the next best thing to being there, and with tickets priced at $10.95, fans paid only a fraction of the cost of watching, for example, the Toronto Maple Leafs at the Air Canada Centre, which costs between $80 and $381 a ticket.[15] Cineplex followed with livestreaming of concerts such as Mötley Crüe, Metropolitan Opera performances, WWE events, and other shows. Gaming fans can rent theatre space for private gaming sessions to indulge in two hours of playing *Halo*, *Assassin's Creed* or other Xbox games.

Balancing the ups and downs of demand and capacity is challenging. As noted earlier, unlike products, services can't be stockpiled in inventory. For services companies, excess demand results in having to turn customers away in peak periods, while excess capacity may mean less desirable expense to revenue ratios. For example, dental hygienists, rent, and other expenses still need to be paid even if customers forget their appointments, so dental offices maximize capacity by making advance reminder calls to patients or by charging cancellation fees to clients who do not show up for their appointments without adequate notice. Hotel reservation systems offer guaranteed late arrivals, ensuring that revenue is not forfeited by holding rooms until very late in the day. Dealing with the ups and downs of weather can also pose a challenge to some businesses, for example ski resorts or outdoor water parks. As discussed in Entrepreneurial Marketing 10.1, velofix uses cloud-based software for scheduling and route optimization to ensure its mobile bicycle repair service operates at capacity.

Since services are perishable, service providers such as ski areas offer less expensive tickets at night to stimulate demand.

© Buddy Mays/CORBIS

## Entrepreneurial Marketing 10.1

### velofix Keeps Cyclists Riding[16]

Avid cyclists, whether they use their bikes for commuting or for pleasure, know that like cars, bikes need to be tuned up from time to time. But getting your bike serviced can take one to two weeks, plus you have to get your bike to and from the shop. That frustration led three Vancouver friends and avid cyclists to launch velofix. Chris Guillemet, Davide Xausa, and Boris Martin came up with the idea of a mobile repair service that would go to the customer's location based on their own cycling challenges.

velofix lets avid cyclists save time and ride more.

Used with permission of velofix

They started with a full service shop housed in a van with all the tools, bike parts, and technical expertise to service just about any kind of bike. Given that a bike can have as many as 500 parts, a van could carry $25,000 to $35,000 worth of inventory. Cyclists can book appointments online or via a 1-800 number to suit their schedules. Depending on the work that needs to be done, an appointment can take one to two hours.

The mobile service concept took off. Sales in the first year exceeded expectations by 120 percent and led the partners to consider franchising to quickly grow the business. Fourteen franchises were sold the very first year. Only two years later, velofix has grown to over 50 franchises across Canada and the United States.

As a service based business, velofix must deal with the four Is every day. To address intangibility, it allows customers to stay in the van while the repairs are being performed. That way, the client can see exactly what the mechanic is doing and even learn a little about bike repair. Each van is equipped with an espresso machine, free Wi-Fi, and a flat screen TV for customer comfort and convenience. Customers are encouraged to take a test ride when the mechanic is finished so they can be comfortable that their bike works well. To further deal with inseparability, a 100 percent guarantee for service ensures they will be satisfied and helps to de-risk the decision to try the service. A comprehensive training program for franchisees is in place to ensure consistency of service, whether it is related to online booking, the repair work, or payment processing. All lead mechanics are professionally certified and must maintain minimum certification levels.

A proprietary cloud-based scheduling system handles online booking and route optimization. This lets mechanics deal with perishability. The more efficient their route is, the more bikes they can service. The system also lets them know what types of bikes need to be repaired, enabling them to have the right parts in the van. The system was designed for efficiency and to save time for the mobile service. But the velofix tagline, "Save time. Ride more," is not just about fixing bikes, it's also an attitude that allows people to spend more time enjoying a healthy, environmentally friendly way of life.

## PROVIDING GREAT SERVICE: THE GAPS MODEL

**L02**

Certainly, providing great service is not easy, and it requires a diligent effort to analyze service processes step by step in order to improve them. We now examine what is known as the Gaps model, which is designed to highlight those areas where customers believe they are getting fewer or poorer services than they expect (the gaps) and how these gaps can be closed.

Customers have certain expectations about how a service should be delivered. When the delivery of that service fails to meet those expectations, a **service gap** results. The Gaps model (Exhibit 10.3) is designed to encourage the systematic examination of all aspects of the service delivery process and prescribe the steps needed to develop an optimal service strategy.[17]

As Exhibit 10.3 shows, there are four service gaps:

1. The **knowledge gap** reflects the difference between customers' expectations and the firm's perception of those customer expectations. Firms can close this gap by matching customer expectations with actual service through research.

**service gap**
Results when a service fails to meet the expectations that customers have about how it should be delivered.

**knowledge gap**
Reflects the difference between customers' expectations and the firm's perception of those expectations.

2. The **standards gap** pertains to the difference between the firm's perceptions of customers' expectations and the service standards it sets. Firms can narrow this gap by setting appropriate service standards and measuring service performance.

3. The **delivery gap** is the difference between the firm's service standards and the actual service it provides to customers. This gap can be closed by getting employees to meet or exceed service standards.

4. The **communication gap** refers to the difference between the actual service provided to customers and the service that the firm's promotion program promises. Generally firms can close this gap if they are more realistic about the services they can provide and manage customer expectations effectively.

**EXHIBIT 10.3**   Gaps Model for Improving Service

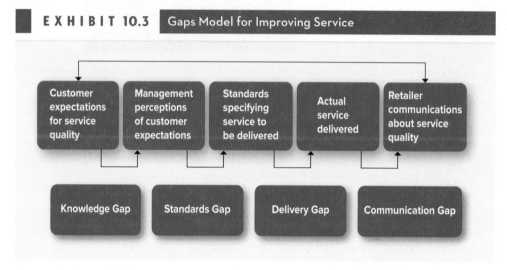

Source: Michael Levy and Barton Weitz, *Retailing Management*, 6th ed. (Burr Ridge, IL: McGraw-Hill, 2007). Adapted from Valerie Zeithaml, A. Parasuraman, and Leonard Berry, *Delivering Quality Customer Service* (New York: The Free Press, 1990) and Valerie Zeithaml, Leonard Berry, and A. Parasuraman, "Communication and Control Processes in the Delivery of Service Quality," *Journal of Marketing* 52, no. 2 (April 1988), pp. 35–48.

As we discuss the four gaps, we will apply them to the experience that Marcia Kessler had with a motel in Muskoka, Ontario. She saw an ad for a weekend package that quoted a very reasonable daily rate and listed the amenities available at Paradise Motel: free babysitting services, a piano bar with a nightly singer, a free continental breakfast, a heated swimming pool, and newly decorated rooms. When she booked the room, Marcia discovered that the price advertised was not available during the weekend, and a three-day minimum stay was required. After checking in with a very unpleasant person at the front desk, Marcia and her husband found that their room appeared to have last been updated in 1950 and had not been cleaned. When she complained, all she got was attitude from the assistant manager. Resigned to the fact that they were slated to spend the weekend, she decided to go for a swim. Unfortunately, the water was "heated" by Georgian Bay and hovered at around 10 degrees. No one was using the babysitting services because there were few young children at the resort. It turns out that the piano bar singer was the second cousin of the owner, and he couldn't carry a tune, let alone play the piano very well. The continental breakfast must have come all the way from another continent, because everything was stale and tasteless. Marcia couldn't wait to get home.

What service gaps did Marcia experience while on vacation at the Paradise Motel in Muskoka?

National Geographic Creative/ Alamy Stock Photo

## The Knowledge Gap: Knowing What Customers Want

An important early step in providing good service is knowing what the customer wants. It doesn't pay to invest in services that don't improve customer satisfaction. To reduce the knowledge gap, firms must understand the customers' expectations. To understand these expectations, firms undertake customer research and increase the interaction and communication between managers and employees.

**Understanding Customer Expectations**  Customers' expectations are based on their knowledge and experiences.[18] Marcia's expectations were that her room would be ready and clean when she got there, the swimming pool would be heated, the singer would be able to sing, and the breakfast would be fresh. That is not a lot to expect, but in this extreme example, the Paradise Motel was suffering a severe knowledge gap, perhaps based on its assumption that being on a lake in Muskoka was enough. If the resort never understood her expectations, it is unlikely it would ever be able to meet them.

Expectations vary according to the type of service. Marcia's expectations might have been higher, for instance, if she were staying at a Fairmont rather than the Paradise Motel. At a Fairmont, she might expect employees to know her by name, be aware of her dietary preferences, and have placed fresh fruit of her choice and fresh-cut flowers in her room before she arrived. At the Paradise Motel, she expected easy check-in/checkout, easy access to a major highway, a clean room with a comfortable bed, and a TV, at a bare minimum.

People's expectations also vary depending on the situation. Marcia may be satisfied with both of the preceding hotel properties, depending on the circumstances. If she were travelling on business, the Paradise Motel might be fine (had the room been clean and modern), but if she were celebrating her wedding anniversary, she probably would prefer the Fairmont. Regardless of these choices, however, the service provider needs to know and understand the expectations of the customers in its target market.

**Evaluating Service Quality by Using Well Established Marketing Metrics**
To meet or exceed customers' expectations, marketers must determine what those expectations are. Yet because of their intangibility, the **service quality**, or customers' perceptions of how well a service meets or exceeds their expectations, often is difficult for customers to evaluate.[19]

**service quality**
Customers' perceptions of how well a service meets or exceeds their expectations.

Customers generally use five distinct service dimensions to determine overall service quality: reliability, responsiveness, assurance, empathy, and tangibles (Exhibit 10.4).

If you were to apply the five service dimensions to your own decision-making process when you selected a university—which provides the service of education—you might find results like those in Exhibit 10.5.

If your expectations include an individualized experience at a state-of-the-art institution, perhaps University B is a better alternative for you. But if you are relying heavily on academic performance and career placement from your university experience, then University A might be a better choice. If a strong culture and tradition are important to you, University A offers this type of environment. What were your expectations, and how did your university choices fall within these service dimensions?

Marketing research (see Chapter 7) provides a means to better understand consumers' service expectations and their perceptions of service quality. This research can be extensive and expensive, or it can be integrated into a firm's everyday interactions with customers. Today, most service firms have developed voice-of-customer programs and employ ongoing marketing research to assess how well they are meeting their customers' expectations.

A systematic **voice-of-customer (VOC) program** collects customer insights and intelligence to influence and drive business decisions. For instance, Aeroplan uses online surveys and conducts in-person "kitchen table" meetings with selected members, asking them everything from what their redemption experience is like to what new services and

**voice-of-customer (VOC) program**
An ongoing marketing research system that collects customer insights and intelligence to influence and drive business decisions.

**zone of tolerance**
The area between customers' expectations regarding their desired service and the minimum level of acceptable service—that is, the difference between what the customer really wants and what he or she will accept before going elsewhere.

improvements they'd like to see.[20] Apple CEO Tim Cook reads up to 100 customer emails a day, demonstrating the importance of listening to the voice of the customer.[21]

An important marketing metric to evaluate how well firms perform on the five service quality dimensions (Exhibit 10.4), the concept of the **zone of tolerance** refers to the

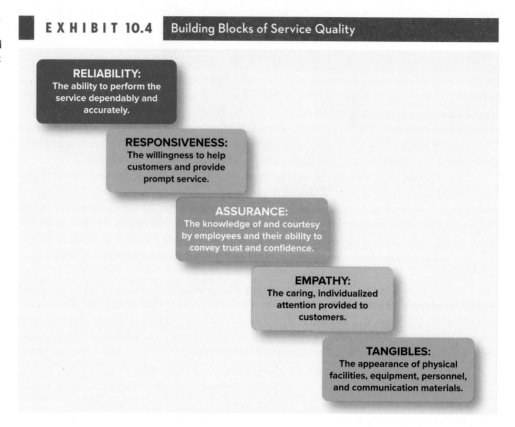

**EXHIBIT 10.4** Building Blocks of Service Quality

**RELIABILITY:**
The ability to perform the service dependably and accurately.

**RESPONSIVENESS:**
The willingness to help customers and provide prompt service.

**ASSURANCE:**
The knowledge of and courtesy by employees and their ability to convey trust and confidence.

**EMPATHY:**
The caring, individualized attention provided to customers.

**TANGIBLES:**
The appearance of physical facilities, equipment, personnel, and communication materials.

**EXHIBIT 10.5** Collegiate Service Dimensions

|  | University A | University B |
|---|---|---|
| Reliability | Offers sound curriculum with extensive placement services and internships. | Curriculum covers all the basics but important courses are not always available. Career placement is haphazard at best. |
| Responsiveness | Slow to respond to application. Very structured visitation policy. Rather inflexible with regard to personal inquiries or additional meetings. | Quick response during application process. Open visitation policy. Offers variety of campus resources to help with decision making. |
| Assurance | Staff seems very confident in reputation and services. | Informal staff conveys enthusiasm for institution. |
| Empathy | Seems to process student body as a whole rather than according to individual needs or concerns. | Very interested in providing a unique experience for each student. |
| Tangibles | Very traditional campus with old-world look and feel. Facilities are manicured. Dorm rooms are large, but bathrooms are a little old. | New campus with modern architecture. Campus is less manicured. Dorm rooms are spacious with newer bathrooms. |

area between customers' expectations regarding their desired service and the minimum level of acceptable service—that is, the difference between what the customer really wants and what he or she will accept before going elsewhere. To define the zone of tolerance, firms ask a series of questions about each service quality dimension that relate to:

- the desired and expected level of service for each dimension, from low to high
- customers' perceptions of how well the focal service performs and how well a competitive service performs, from low to high
- the importance of each service quality dimension.

Exhibit 10.6 illustrates the results of such an analysis for Lou's Local Diner, a family-owned restaurant. The rankings on the left are based on a 9-point scale, on which 1 is low and 9 is high. The length of each box illustrates the zone of tolerance for each service quality dimension. For instance, according to the length of the reliability box, customers expect a fairly high level of reliability (top of the box) and will also accept only a fairly high level of reliability (bottom of the box). On the other end of the scale, customers expect a high level of assurance (top of the box) but will accept a fairly low level (bottom of the box). This difference is to be expected, because the customers also were asked to assign an importance score to the five service quality dimensions so that the total equals 100 percent (see bottom of Exhibit 10.6). Looking at the average importance score, we conclude that reliability is relatively important to these customers, but assurance is not. So customers have a fairly narrow zone of tolerance for service dimensions that are fairly important to them and a wider range of tolerance for those service dimensions that are less important. Also note that Lou's Local Diner always rates higher than its primary competitor, Well-Known National Chain, on each dimension.

Further note that Well-Known National Chain scores below the zone of tolerance on the tangibles dimension, meaning that customers are not willing to accept the way the restaurant looks and smells. Lou's Local Diner, in contrast, performs above the zone of tolerance on the responsiveness dimension—maybe even too well. Lou's may wish to conduct further research to verify which responsiveness aspects it is performing so well, and

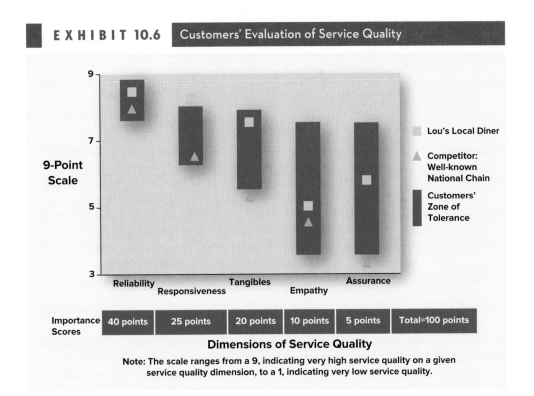

**EXHIBIT 10.6**  Customers' Evaluation of Service Quality

Note: The scale ranges from a 9, indicating very high service quality on a given service quality dimension, to a 1, indicating very low service quality.

Lou's Local Diner always rates higher than its primary competitor, Well-Known National Chain, on each service quality dimension.

© McGraw-Hill Education/ Gideon Kindall

then consider toning those aspects down. For example, being responsive to customers' desires to have a diner that serves breakfast 24 hours a day can be expensive and may not add any further value to Lou's Local Diner, because customers would accept more limited times.

A very straightforward and inexpensive method of collecting consumers' perceptions of service quality is to gather them at the time of the sale. Service providers can ask customers how they liked the service—though customers often are hesitant to provide negative feedback directly to the person who provided the service—or distribute a simple questionnaire. Starbucks customers can rate their experience by visiting the web survey whose Internet address is at the bottom of their receipt. Using this method, a customer does not have to make the complaint directly to the barista who may have caused the problem, but Starbucks still gets almost instantaneous feedback. The company must take care not to lose much of this information, which can happen if there is no effective mechanism for filtering it up to the key decision makers. Furthermore, in some cases, customers cannot effectively evaluate the service until several days or weeks later. Automobile dealers, for instance, often call their customers a week after they perform a service like an oil change to assess their service quality.

Another excellent method for assessing customers' expectations is making effective use of customer-complaint behaviour. Even if complaints are handled effectively to solve customers' problems, the essence of the complaint is too often lost on managers. For instance, an airline established a policy that customer service reps could not discuss any issues involving fees to travel agents with customers. So when a customer calls to complain about these fees, the representative just changes the subject, and management therefore never finds out about the complaint.[22]

Even firms with the best formal research mechanisms in place must put managers on the front lines occasionally to interact directly with the customers. The late Sam Walton, founder of Walmart, participated in and advocated this strategy, which is known as "management by walking around." Unless the managers who make the service quality decisions know what their service providers are facing every day, and unless they can talk directly to the customers with whom those service providers interact, any customer service program they create will not be as good as it could be.

## L03 The Standards Gap: Setting Service Standards

Suppose that, because of a number of complaints or because business was falling off, the Paradise Motel in Muskoka set out to determine its customers' service expectations and gained a pretty good idea of them. Its work is still far from over; the next step is to set its service standards and develop systems to ensure high-quality service. How can it make sure that every room is cleaned by an optimum time of day in the eyes of the customers? Or that food is checked for freshness and quality every day? Firms need to set high service standards, enforce these standards, and train employees on how to perform their tasks to these standards. Managers must lead by example and demonstrate high service standards, which will permeate throughout the organization.

**Achieving Service Goals Through Training**   To consistently deliver service that meets customers' expectations, firms must set specific, measurable goals. For instance, the Paradise Motel may find it most efficient to start cleaning rooms at 8:00 a.m. and finish by 5:00 p.m. But many guests want to sleep late and new arrivals want to get into their room as soon as they arrive, often before 5:00. A customer-oriented standard would mandate that the rooms get cleaned between 10:00 a.m. and 2:00 p.m.

Service providers generally want to do a good job, as long as they know what is expected of them. Motel employees should be shown, for instance, exactly how managers expect them to clean a room and what specific tasks they are responsible for performing.

The employees must be thoroughly trained not only to complete their specific tasks but also to know how to treat guests, and the manager needs to set an example of high service standards, which will permeate throughout the organization. The kind of attitude Marcia got, for instance, when she registered a complaint with the assistant manager at the Paradise Motel is not a recipe for generating repeat customers and should not be tolerated. For frontline service employees under stress, however, pleasant interactions with customers do not always come naturally. Although people can be taught specific tasks related to their jobs, this is not easily extended to interpersonal relations. It is simply not enough to tell employees to "be nice" or "do what customers want." A quality goal should be specific: "Greet every customer you encounter with 'Good morning/afternoon/evening, sir or ma'am.' Try to greet customers by name."

In extreme cases, such training becomes even more crucial. From long ticket lines to cancelled flights to lost baggage, customer service incidents are on the rise in the airline industry. Faced with mounting complaints, airlines are responding with better employee training geared toward identifying and defusing potentially explosive situations. For example, Delta Airlines has implemented a "Customer First" training program for its ground operations, customer service agents, flight attendants, and pilots that mandates specific performance measures and standardized practices throughout Delta's service areas. Policies for service during delays, such as providing snacks on board or trucking food out to waiting planes and offering status updates every 15 minutes, have given employees the tools and guidelines they need to better service their customers. Delta also added diversity training to reduce tensions between passengers and crew members.[23]

Service providers, like this room service delivery person at a hotel, generally want to do a good job, but they need to be trained to know exactly what a good job entails.

Chris Ryan/OJO Images/Getty Images

**Commitment to Service Quality**   Service providers take their cues from management. If managers strive for excellent service, treat their customers well, and demand the same attitudes from everyone in the organization, it is likely employees will do the same. Take, for example, WestJet president and CEO Gregg Saretsky. Named one of Canada's most respected CEOs in the tenth annual Canada's Most Respected Corporations Survey, Saretsky is perfectly happy to clean cabins and lend a hand on flights when he is a passenger.[24] WestJet's legendary reputation for customer service has resulted in revenues of nearly $4 billion and years of record-breaking net earnings.[25] This commitment to service quality has been modelled by company executives from the start. When WestJet launched in 1996, executive vice-president Don Bell spent a lot of time in the airline's call centre fielding questions and booking flights for customers.[26]

Employees who understand that operating on time is a critical component to service quality and guest experience work hard to improve on-time performance. In 2016, 82.7 percent of WestJet flights arrived within 15 minutes of their scheduled time.[27] WestJet sales agents also strive to provide the highest standard of customer service. Their efforts were recognized when Skytrax named WestJet the second best low-cost airline in North America.[28] An employee profit-sharing plan provides rewards beyond public recognition. The vast majority of employees belong to the WestJet Employee Share Purchase Plan, making them owners of the company and giving them all the more reason to ensure high levels of service quality. This has resulted in WestJet's being named as one of Canada's Best Employers and in its induction into Canada's Most Admired Corporate Cultures Hall of Fame.

## The Delivery Gap: Delivering Service Quality

The delivery gap is where "the rubber meets the road," where the customer directly interacts with the service provider. Even if there are no other gaps, a delivery gap always results in a service failure. Marcia experienced several delivery gaps at the Paradise Motel. It could have been that the unclean room, the assistant manager's attitude, the unheated swimming pool, the poor piano bar singer, and the stale food resulted from unforeseen or unusual circumstances. Although some of these issues (such as an unclean room or the attitude Marcia encountered) should have been avoided, it is possible that the motel had a power outage resulting in the unheated swimming pool, the regular piano bar singer was ill, and the breakfast was stale because of a missed delivery. The maid could not vacuum the room because of the lack of power, and the assistant manager felt beset on all sides by these problems. But the result was a lost customer. Even if there are no other gaps, a delivery gap always results in a service failure.

Delivery gaps can be reduced when employees are empowered to spontaneously act in the customers' and the firm's best interests when problems or crises are experienced. Such empowerment might have saved the day for Marcia and the Paradise Motel. Empowerment means employees are supported in their efforts so they can do their jobs effectively.[29] Technology can also be employed to reduce delivery gaps (see Exhibit 10.7).

**empowerment**
In the context of service delivery, means allowing employees to make decisions about how service is provided to customers.

**Empowering Service Providers**   In this context, **empowerment** means allowing employees to make decisions about how service is provided to customers. When front line employees are authorized to make decisions to help their customers, service quality generally improves. Best Buy, for instance, has re-engineered its organizational structure to empower employees to be more involved in the day-to-day running of the business and to make adjustments as necessary. The new employee-centric culture has helped Best Buy significantly lower its employee turnover rate. Happy employees make for happy customers.[30]

However, empowering service providers can be difficult and costly. In cases in which the service is very repetitive and routine, such as at a fast-food restaurant, it might be more efficient and easier for service providers to follow a few simple rules. For instance, if a customer doesn't like his hamburger, ask him what he would like instead or offer him a refund. If an exceptional circumstance that does not fit the rules arises, then a manager should handle the issue.

Empowerment becomes more important when price points edge higher and services are more individualized. The Keg Steakhouse & Bar hires the best staff and empowers them through superlative training programs. Staff members are professional—their friendliness, warmth, personality, and enthusiasm are all part of the Keg dining

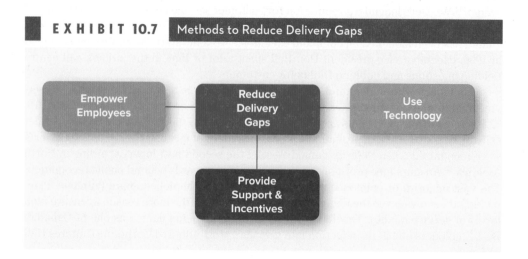

**EXHIBIT 10.7**   Methods to Reduce Delivery Gaps

experience. It is because of this that The Keg has been consistently recognized as one of the 50 Best Employers in Canada.[31]

**Providing Support and Incentives**  A service provider's job can often be difficult, especially when customers are unpleasant or less than reasonable. This is basic. But the service provider cannot be rude or offensive just because the customer is. The old cliché "service with a smile" remains the best approach, but for this to work, employees must feel supported. To ensure that service is delivered properly, management needs to support service providers and give them incentives.

First, managers and co-workers should provide emotional support to service providers by demonstrating a concern for their well-being and by standing behind their decisions. Because it can be very disconcerting when a waiter is abused by a customer who believes her food was improperly prepared, for instance, restaurant managers must be supportive and understanding and work to help employees get through their often emotional reaction to the beration they experienced. Such support can extend to empowering the server to rectify the situation by giving the customer new food and a free dessert, in which case the manager must stand behind the waiter's decision, not punish her for giving away too much.

Second, service providers require instrumental support—the systems and equipment to deliver the service properly. Many retailers provide state-of-the-art instrumental support for their service providers. In-store kiosks help sales associates provide more detailed and complete product information and enable them to make sales of merchandise that is either not carried in the store or temporarily out of stock.

Third, the support that managers provide must be consistent throughout the organization. Patients expect physicians to provide great patient care by using state-of-the-art procedures and medications; yet many doctors must squeeze more people into their office hours. These conflicting goals can be so frustrating and emotionally draining on physicians and other health care providers that some have found work outside medicine.

Finally, a key part of any customer service program is providing rewards to employees for excellent service. Numerous firms have developed a service reputation by ensuring that their employees are themselves recognized for recognizing the value the firm places on customer service. Travelocity, for example, features employees who champion the customer service experience in a weekly email. Believing that engaged employees are the key to customer satisfaction, it works to create an atmosphere that reinforces the commitment to customers by encouraging employees to nominate colleagues who exemplify its commitment to customers. Through constant feedback about who is serving the customer best, as well as smaller events such as monthly lunches with the CEO for selected employees, Travelocity creates a business environment that recognizes and rewards customer service with a Customer First Guarantee.[32] The results for Travelocity have been a wealth of awards, such as a top ranking for overall satisfaction in J.D. Power's Online Travel Agency Satisfaction Report.[33]

**Using Technology**    Technology has become an increasingly important means of facilitating the delivery of services. In the past decade, firms have invested heavily in technologies that have enabled customers to buy more quickly, more easily, and with more information than in the past. Electronic kiosks, for instance, have found their way into many service venues. Ticketing kiosks at airports allow customers to get boarding passes and seat assignments, often in less than a minute. As previously noted, electronic kiosks and other technologies can reduce the inconsistency of providing a service. Kiosks and self-checkout machines can also help close the delivery gap.

Web-enabled services have also changed the way firms do business. Marsha Vanwynsberghe found the Waterloo, Ontario, region too small a market for her life adversity coaching service for parents of drug-addicted children. Offering one-on-one or group sessions online allowed her to reach a much broader audience in a timely, convenient manner. It also provided a level of anonymity to parents who wanted to avoid being shamed by friends and relatives when dealing with the issue. The need for convenience has driven some fitness companies and personal trainers to offer online classes and services. In Bolton, Ontario, Lee-Anne Simpson teaches a variety of classes via Skype through her company, Revive Fitness Training and Wellness Centre. And in Steinbach, Manitoba, Tami Tyson holds live online bootcamps that have been a hit with new mothers who can't get away from the house for conventional gym workouts.[34]

Using technology to facilitate service delivery can provide many benefits, such as access to a wider variety of services, a greater degree of control by the customer over the services, and the ability to obtain information. Management also benefits from the increased efficiency in service processes through reduced servicing costs and, in some cases, can develop a competitive advantage over less service-oriented competitors. Social and Mobile Marketing 10.1 highlights how technology can be used to reach and engage customers.

Technological advances that help close the delivery gap are expanding. Salons and cosmetics counters use kiosks to show customers how they would look with different beauty products and various hair colours. Stores enable customers to scan price tags and then have a kiosk recommend complementary items. Touchscreen order kiosks have been installed at some McDonald's locations.[36] The technological delivery of services can cause problems, though. Some customers have problems using the technology. Supermarket self-checkout devices are too challenging for some customers. In other cases, the technology may not perform adequately, such as when ATMs run out of money or are out of order.

## The Communication Gap: Communicating the Service Promise

Poor communication between marketers and their customers can result in a mismatch between an ad campaign's or a salesperson's promises and the service the firm can actually offer. Although firms have difficulty controlling service quality because it can vary

## Social and Mobile Marketing 10.1

### Google Analytics Helps Theatres Predict Attendance, Dealing With Perishability[35]

When a lot of movie watchers search for the trailer for a film in the month before the movie opens, it foreshadows a bigger opening weekend. Such a claim might seem somewhat self-evident, but Google has announced that it has the means to quantify this effect and thereby help movie studios predict their profits, up to a month prior to the opening day. Information like that can help theatres determine how many screens they should devote to the movie and helps them to balance demand against capacity.

Google asserts that search volume for the movie title (combined with a few other metrics, such as the season and whether the movie is a franchise) offers a 94 percent accurate prediction of box office performance. Other proprietary information that Google can use to predict success includes the volume of clicks on search ads. If, for example, one movie prompted 20,000 more paid clicks than another film, it will bring in approximately $7.5 million more

Google analytics are used to predict the success of movies, helping theatres deal with the perishability aspect of their service.

Frazer Harrison/Getty Images

in revenues during its opening weekend. Furthermore, the search effects are not limited to Google; social media sites and YouTube searches reveal similar predictive information. From its analysis, Google recommends that studios need to go beyond just a one-week window, because studying the search and click trends for a month increases the accuracy and power of its predictions significantly.

Moving beyond the implications for opening weekend, Google claims that weekday searches in the weeks leading up to the release offer better predictors of continued revenues. That is, if a film fan searches for a movie title on a Tuesday, she or he is more likely to hold off on seeing the movie, rather than rushing out during opening weekend. Google also notes that nearly half of all moviegoers choose the film they will see that night on the same day. Thus, studios need to maintain a marketing presence far past opening day, to be sure to catch the laggard customers' attention. That helps theatres deal with the perishability of their service, since they can increase the number of showtimes accordingly to ensure that capacity crowds can be accommodated.

from day to day and from provider to provider, they have nearly constant control over how they communicate their service package to their customers. This control involves a significant responsibility, as Ethical Dilemma 10.1 notes.

If a firm promises more than it can deliver, customers' expectations won't be met. An advertisement may lure a customer into a service situation once but, if the service doesn't deliver on the promise, the customer may never return. Dissatisfied customers also are likely to tell others about the underperforming service, using word-of-mouth or, increasingly, the Internet, which has become an important channel for dissatisfied customers to vent their frustrations.

The communication gap can be reduced by managing customer expectations. Suppose you need an operation, and the surgeon explains, "You'll be out of the hospital in five days and back to your normal routine in a month." You have the surgery and feel well enough to leave the hospital three days later. Two weeks after that, you're playing tennis again. Clearly, you will tend to think your surgeon is a genius. However, regardless of the operation's success, if you had to stay in the hospital for 10 days and it took you two months to recover, you would undoubtedly be upset.

A relatively easy way to manage customer expectations considers both the time the expectation is created and the time the service is provided. Expectations typically are created through promotions, whether in advertising or personal selling. For instance, if a

## Ethical Dilemma 10.1

### Fake Reviews[37]

Yelp, TripAdvisor, and Amazon have all made user ratings and reviews a familiar—and even essential—part of the online toolbox for shoppers and other consumers. From the consumer's perspective, what better preparation could there be for a major purchase than to see what other, objective customers have to say about the product or service under consideration? For retailers and service professionals, online reviews offer a huge benefit too. A Harvard Business School study found that even a one-star increase in restaurant ratings resulted in a 5–9 percent increase in sales.

For some companies, especially small service providers that cannot afford much marketing, online reviews function as a low-cost form of advertising. A business seeking to meet or exceed customer expectations receives valuable, candid feedback from customers, which it can use to measure how well it is meeting customer expectations. Some firms even use this feedback in their formal voice-of-customer programs to improve company operations.

But who benefits from fake consumer reviews? Seemingly the company might, assuming it does not get caught. However, recent events suggest that companies that fake their reviews often do get caught. Amazon and Yelp are taking action to ensure that deceptive advertising does not pay. For example, PaidBookReviews.org offered

authors looking to increase book sales 100 book reviews for $2,200; it was one of over 1,000 alleged fake review sites targeted in lawsuits filed by Amazon. Yelp has also clamped down on businesses with suspicious reviews by posting consumer alerts. Among others, it flagged a weight loss clinic that gave customers discounts in return for a five-star review and a moving company that paid $20 for positive reviews.

A fake restaurant review is one thing. Accurate, truthful information takes on paramount importance for a service like plastic surgery. But Lifestyle Lift seemed to disregard customers' expectations that they could receive truthful information. When unhappy customers started posting too many negative comments on its website, the company launched a cover-up, rather than investigating the complaints to help its physicians and staff address the problems. On bogus websites, fictitious posters gave high praise to the company, while also asserting that previously posted complaints had been phony.

Crowd-sourced online opinions of consumers have become a major source of information about products and services (recall our discussion of crowd-sourcing in Chapter 9). When that information is authentic, it serves consumers and companies both. But when companies manipulate online reviews, it seems as if all of society is harmed. What—if anything—should be done about it?

---

salesperson promises a client that work can be performed in one day, and it actually takes a week, the client will be disappointed. However, if the salesperson coordinates the work with those responsible for the service delivery, the client's expectations likely will be met.

Customer expectations can also be managed when the service is delivered. Recorded messages can tell customers who have telephoned a company how many minutes they will have to wait before the next operator is available. Sellers automatically inform online customers of any items that are out of stock. Whether online or in a store, retailers can warn their customers to shop early during a sale because supplies of the sale item are limited. People are generally reasonable when they are warned that some aspect of the service may be below their expectations. They just don't like surprises!

The Amazon Prime $99/year delivery service helps create customer loyalty and satisfaction.

Web Pix/Alamy Stock Photo

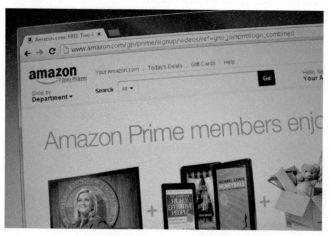

## Service Quality and Customer Satisfaction and Loyalty

Good service quality leads to satisfied and loyal customers. As we discussed in Chapter 4, customers inevitably wind up their purchase decision process by undertaking a postpurchase evaluation. This evaluation after the purchase may produce three outcomes: customer satisfaction, postpurchase dissonance, and customer loyalty (see again Exhibit 4.3 in Chapter 4). Dissonance may just be a passing emotion that is overcome; we will discuss recovery from an actual service failure in the next section. Satisfaction, on the other hand, often leads to loyalty.

Assuming that customers do not experience the service gaps that we have discussed, they should be more or less satisfied. A service provider that does a good job one year is likely to keep customers satisfied the next year too. Some of the best service providers year after year include Amazon, Zappos, L.L. Bean, and Nordstrom. If a firm not only minimizes but eliminates any service gaps, customers are likely to exhibit significant loyalty to that firm. Customers want to continue receiving such superior service and have no desire to go elsewhere for the offerings it provides them.

# SERVICE RECOVERY

Despite a firm's best efforts, sometimes service providers fail to meet customer expectations. When this happens, the best course of action is to attempt to make amends with the customer and learn from the experience. Of course, it is best to avoid a service failure altogether, but when it does occur, the firm has a unique opportunity to demonstrate its customer commitment. Effective service recovery efforts can significantly increase customer satisfaction, purchase intentions, and positive word-of-mouth, though customers' postrecovery satisfaction levels are usually lower than their satisfaction level prior to the service failure.

Remember the Paradise Motel in Muskoka? It could have made amends with Marcia Kessler after its service failures if it had taken some relatively simple, immediate steps: the assistant manager could have apologized for his bad behaviour and quickly upgraded her to a suite and/or given her a free night's lodging for a future stay. The motel could also have given her a free lunch or dinner to make up for the bad breakfast. None of these actions would have cost the motel much money. Had it used the customer lifetime value approach we described in Chapter 6, the motel would have realized that by not taking action, it lost Marcia as a customer forever. Over the next few years, she could have been responsible for several thousand dollars in sales. Instead, Marcia is likely to spread negative word-of-mouth about the motel to her friends and family and through social media like Yelp.com, because of its failure to recover. Quite simply, effective service recovery entails (1) listening to the customer, (2) providing a fair solution, and (3) resolving the problem quickly.[38]

## Listening to the Customer

Firms often don't find out about service failures until a customer complains. Whether the firm has a formal complaint department or the complaint is offered directly to the service provider, the customer must have the opportunity to air the complaint completely, and the firm must listen carefully to what he or she is saying.

Customers can become very emotional about a service failure, whether the failure is serious (a botched surgical operation) or minor (the wrong change at a restaurant). In many cases, the customer may just want to be heard, and the service provider should give the customer all the time he or she needs to "get it out." The very process of describing a perceived wrong to a sympathetic listener is therapeutic in and of itself. Service providers therefore should welcome the opportunity to be that sympathetic ear, listen carefully, and appear anxious to rectify the situation to ensure it doesn't happen again.[39]

When the company and the customer work together, the outcome is often better than either could achieve alone. This co-creation logic applies especially well to service recovery. A service failure is a negative experience, but when customers participate in its resolution, it results in a more positive outcome than simply listening to their complaint and providing a preapproved set of potential solutions that may satisfy them.

Suppose, for instance, that when you arrived at the airport in Vancouver, your flight had been overbooked and you were bumped. Of course, good customer service required the ticket agent to listen to your frustration and help provide a fair solution. But the

When a service failure occurs, such as receiving a poor meal at a restaurant, goodwill can be recovered by giving the customer a free dessert.

Dmytro Zinkevych/Shutterstock

most obvious potential solution from the airline's perspective might not have been the best solution for you. It might have been inclined to put you on the next available flight, which would be a red-eye that left at midnight and got you to Montreal at 6:30 a.m. But if you don't sleep well on planes and you have an important business meeting the next afternoon, the best solution from your perspective would be to have the airline put you up in an airport hotel so you can get a good night's sleep and then put you on an early morning flight that would get you to Montreal in time for your meeting, well rested and ready to go. Thus, by working closely with you to understand your needs, the ticket agent would be able to co-create a great solution to the service failure.

## Finding a Fair Solution

Most people realize that mistakes happen. But when they happen, customers want to be treated fairly. Their perception of what *fair* means is based on their previous experience with other firms, how they have seen other customers treated, material they have read, and stories recounted by their friends.

Fairness relates to a customer's perception of the benefits he or she received compared with the costs (inconvenience or loss). Customers want to be compensated a fair amount for a perceived loss that resulted from a service failure. If, for instance, a person arrives at the airport gate and finds her flight is overbooked, she may believe that taking the next flight that day and receiving a travel voucher is adequate compensation for the inconvenience. But if no flights are available until the next day, the traveller may require additional compensation, such as overnight accommodations, meals, and a round-trip ticket to be used at a later date.

The key to fairness, of course, is listening carefully to the customer. One customer, travelling on vacation, may be satisfied with a travel voucher, whereas another may need to get to the destination on time because of a business appointment. Regardless of how the problem is solved, customers typically want tangible restitution—in this case, to get to their destination—not just an apology. If providing a tangible restitution isn't possible, the next best thing is to assure the customer that steps are being taken to prevent the failure from recurring.

With regard to complaints, customers care about the fairness of the process used to resolve them. Customers want efficient complaint procedures over whose outcomes they have some influence. They tend to believe they have been treated fairly if the service providers follow specific company guidelines. A rigid adherence to rules can have damaging effects. Have you ever returned an item to a store, even a very inexpensive item, and been told that the return needed a manager's approval? The process likely took several minutes and irritated everyone in the checkout line. As we noted previously, service providers should be empowered with some procedural flexibility to solve customer complaints.

When handling returns or other services issues, it is important to use procedures that are perceived to be fair by the customers.

allesalltag/Alamy Stock Photo

## Resolving Problems Quickly

The longer it takes to resolve a service failure, the more irritated the customer will become and the more people he or she is likely to tell about the problem. To resolve service failures quickly, firms need clear policies, adequate training for their employees, and empowered employees. Extended health care insurance companies, for instance, have made a concerted effort in recent years to avoid service failures that occur because customers' insurance claims have not been handled quickly or to the customers' satisfaction.

Companies should welcome complaints, make it easy for customers to provide feedback, and listen carefully to what customers have to say. Although customers may be

## REAL MARKETER PROFILE

# Marc-Olivier Vachon (Kangaride)

The idea behind Kangaride struck like lightning: Why not enable people to share something they don't often think of as a resource, like seats in their car? Long-distance ridesharing on an occasional basis (for example, between Toronto and Montreal or Edmonton and Calgary) is a concept with a clear selling proposition: Passengers travel for less and drivers get help paying for gas. From the eager perspective of a budding entrepreneur in Montreal, this seemed like one of those ideas that would spread like wildfire. Marketing the idea would be a piece of cake, right? However, gaining traction proved to be quite the challenge. Ridesharing sounds good on paper, but we really didn't know how many people would actually use it, no matter how brilliantly we built our service and website. Two major hurdles needed to be overcome.

RichLegg/iStock/Getty Images Plus

### Hurdle 1: Perception about safety and reliability
When we asked people about ridesharing, we almost invariably heard concerns about safety or reliability: "I can't see myself travelling with people I don't even know!" And "How can I be sure my driver/passenger is going to show up?" Both are concerns I had when hitchhiking around the country, and later when trying to hook up with passengers through classified ad websites.

This is why we built both the service and our communication strategy around these simple words: "We care." First and foremost, Kangaride needed to be a team of dedicated individuals providing a very high level of professional monitoring while maintaining constant communication with customers.

In the very beginning, it seemed a little crazy to validate all of our drivers' licences. It seemed even crazier to build a customer service centre that would take calls seven days a week, 365 days a year. These things represented a sizeable investment for a start-up with no proof of concept, but not doing them was not an option. Our marketing strategy depended on it. And contrary to most services you will find on the web, we clearly advertised our phone number on every page. Why? Because we actually wanted people to give us a call! If we were to make ridesharing an option as safe and reliable as a bus service, collaboration with our customers was paramount.

### Hurdle 2: This is no splash
Your idea may be excellent, even revolutionary, but not all people will share your visionary outlook on the world.

In other words, it probably won't make the big splash you have in mind. When launching Kangaride, we were a little disappointed with the pace at which the idea was adopted. Still caught in the preconceived notion that success would translate in supersonic adoption, we tried to make a splash in the public eye (marketing, press relations, stunts), but to no avail. Our participation on CBC's *Dragons' Den* was probably our very last attempt and brought to light something that we had all taken for granted: The most powerful form of marketing is customer service. Period.

When our pitch aired on CBC, coast to coast, a thousand new people subscribed to Kangaride in the next few days. This represents the average number of people who join the service on a weekly basis without any publicity on our part. And the secret behind that is no secret at all. World-class execution and truly caring about your customers is what gets people talking about you. The word-of-mouth we created was far from instantaneous, but it had grown appreciably over time—very slowly at first, but very steadily, one phone call at a time, one reliable ride at a time, just like a trickling brook turns into a quiet but very powerful river.

This is the ultimate form of marketing. It's what we do best and, for us, is the easiest thing in the world. Kangaride does not get its 15 minutes of fame every week on TV, but from a consistent focus on customer service. Between making a splash or feeding a river, we choose the river. Every day.

complaining, they are nevertheless exhibiting a degree of loyalty and a genuine desire to get their problem fixed. Of customers who do complain, 56–70 percent will do business with the company again if the complaint is resolved. That goes up to 96 percent if the complaint is resolved quickly! The speed of social media connections puts increasing pressure on providers to resolve any failures as fast as possible.

It may seem overly simple, but to recover effectively from service failures, firms must not only listen to the customers' complaints but also act on them. It is the implementation of this simple rule that offers firms such challenges.

# LEARNING OBJECTIVES REVIEW

**LO1** **Describe how marketing a service differs from marketing a product by applying the principles of intangibility, inseparability, inconsistency, and inventory**

First and foremost, services are intangible—they can't be seen or touched—which makes it difficult to describe a service's benefits or promote it to others. Service providers attempt to reduce the impact of the service's intangibility by enhancing its delivery with more tangible attributes, such as a nice atmosphere or price benefits. Second, services are produced and consumed at the same time. Third, services are more inconsistent than products, though service providers attempt to reduce this variability through standardization, training, service bundling, and technology. Fourth, because services can't be stockpiled, marketers provide incentives to stagger demand over time.

**LO2** **Outline the four gaps in the Gaps model used to understand and manage customer expectations**

A knowledge gap occurs when marketers don't understand what their customers want. They may not be providing customers enough or the right service, in which case customers will be disappointed. To understand customer expectations, marketers analyze service quality through comprehensive studies and by interacting with customers. The standards gap is the difference between the firm's perceptions of customers' expectations and the service standards it sets. The delivery gap is the difference between the firm's service standards and the actual service it provides to customers.

The communication gap refers to the difference between the actual service provided to customers and the service that the firm's promotion program promises.

**LO3** **Describe strategies that firms can use to help employees provide better service**

First, appropriate service standards and measurements of service performance help close the standards gap. Firms need to demonstrate a strong commitment to service by setting high standards and enforcing these standards, and to lead by example. Next they should provide training to employees regarding how to do their job and interact with customers to address the delivery gap. Then, they can empower service providers to solve service issues and problems and provide employees with both emotional support and the tools they need to do a good job. The service program should be consistent throughout the organization. Service providers need incentives that encourage them to do a good job. Lastly, firms close the communications gap by managing customer expectations and promising only what they can deliver.

**LO4** **Identify three service recovery strategies**

In the best-case scenario, the service does not fail in the first place. But failures are inevitable. When they do happen, the firm must make amends to the customer by (1) listening and involving the customer in the service recovery, (2) finding a fair solution to the problem that compensates the customer for the failure and follows procedures that the customer believes are fair, and (3) resolving the problem quickly.

# KEY TERMS

- communication gap
- customer service
- delivery gap
- empowerment
- inconsistent

- inseparable
- intangible
- inventory
- knowledge gap
- service

- service gap
- service quality
- standards gap
- voice-of-customer (VOC) program
- zone of tolerance

# CONCEPT REVIEW

1. Describe the four dimensions in which services marketing is different from product marketing.

2. Why is intangibility described as the most fundamental difference between products and services?

3. Discuss the actions companies can implement to minimize the potential negative impact of service inconsistency on the delivery of customer service.

4. How can companies deal with the perishability of their services?

5. Identify the components of the Gaps model. Describe each component and explain the strategies companies can implement to reduce the gaps in service delivery.

6. Describe the five dimensions of service quality that consumers often use to judge the quality of a service experience.

7. Explain how the use of technology can help companies deliver higher quality service.

8. Discuss why underpromising and overdelivering is an important way to control the communication gap.

9. What is meant by service recovery? How can companies use service recovery to ensure that a service failure does not lead to a lost customer?

10. Explain the differences between distributive and procedural fairness in the context of service recovery.

# MARKETING APPLICATIONS

1. Those companies from which you purchase products and services are not pure sellers of services, nor are they pure sellers of products. What services does a department store provide? What goods does a dentist provide?

2. You have been sitting in the waiting room of your doctor's office for an hour. With the knowledge that products are different from services, develop a list of the things the office manager could do to improve the overall service delivery. Consider how the office might overcome problems of intangibility, inseparability, inconsistency, and inventory issues associated with services.

3. You have conducted a zone of tolerance analysis for a local dry cleaner. You find that the lengths of the reliability and responsiveness boxes are much greater than those of the other three service quality dimensions. You also find that the dry cleaner is positioned above the zone box on reliability but below the box on responsiveness. What should you tell the manager of the dry cleaner to do?

4. Assume you were hired by the Paradise Motel to help assess its service quality. How would you go about undertaking this project?

5. What should a restaurant server do who is faced with an irate customer who has received undercooked food after a long wait? How can the server avoid a service failure by being empowered? What should the server do?

6. Describe a specific situation in which a service provider could have avoided a service failure if he or she had been empowered by an employer to do so. What should the service provider have done?

7. What types of support and incentives could your university provide advisers to help make them more attentive to students' needs?

8. What mobile apps do you use that help facilitate your transactions with a specific retailer or service provider? Would you rather use the apps or engage in a face-to-face relationship with a person? How, if at all, would your parents' answers to these two questions differ from yours?

9. A local health club is running a promotional campaign that promises you can lose an inch a month off your waist if you join the club and follow its program. How might this claim cause a communication gap? What should the club do to avoid a service failure?

10. You are hired by a career consulting firm that promises to market new graduates to high-paying employers. The firm provides potential clients with an impressive client list. It charges the clients a fee, and then a separate finder's fee if the client gets a position. The firm aggressively markets its services and has a large client base. You learn that the firm simply takes any submitted resumés and posts them to a variety of online job search engines. The firm never actually contacts any companies on its clients' behalf. The CEO, himself a recent university grad, tells you that the firm never promises to contact potential employees, only that the firm has access to employers and will distribute clients' resumés. What do you think of the career consulting firm's practices?

# NET SAVVY

1. What services does WestJet offer (http://www.westjet.com)? Compare its services to those offered by Air Canada (http://www.aircanada.ca) by using the five service quality dimensions (tangibility, responsiveness, reliability, assurance, and empathy).

2. Evaluate the ease with which you can make hotel reservations when using Fairmont's online reservation system (http://www.fairmont.com). Check out the hotel's privacy policy. Are you comfortable with its use of cookies to identify visitors when they return to the site?

## ZIPCAR: DELIVERING ONLY AS MUCH DRIVING AS YOU WANT

Canadians have enjoyed a long love affair with their cars. The growth of the auto industry led to the expectation that your car would be waiting for you at the curb every morning. But that expectation is now changing for many city dwellers, frustrated by the soaring costs and parking pressures that confront modern drivers. For them, Zipcar, the world's leading car-sharing company and the largest provider of car-sharing services in Canada,[40] offers the pleasure of driving without the hassles of ownership.

The Boston, Massachusetts–based company offers self-service vehicles by the hour or day to urban residents who prefer to pay for only the minimal amount of driving they absolutely need, unlike rental cars. Car sharing eliminates issues related to parking shortages; overnight parking restrictions; or soaring gas, insurance, and tax bills. That promise resonates well with consumer expectations on many fronts, especially among Zipcar's primary urban customers, suburbanites who just work in the city, and the large segments of college or university students who also enjoy the service. Zipcar access provides a convenient solution to students, faculty, and staff who live on or near campus and helps college or university administrators reduce demand for the limited parking available.[41]

Still, Zipcar president Tracey Zhen realizes that the company's biggest growth obstacle is consumers' attachment to owning personal cars.[42] To push an attitude shift, Zipcar makes the car-sharing experience as easy as possible, with just four simple steps:

1. Join the network online.
2. Reserve your car online or from your smartphone.
3. Unlock the car with your Zipcard.
4. Drive away.

Today the car-sharing network has more than a million members and 12,000 vehicles in 31 major metropolitan areas and on 600 campuses and 50 airports throughout the United States, Canada, Great Britain, France, Austria, Germany, Turkey, Belgium, and Spain.[43] As the company continues to grow, it expects to bring convenient car-sharing services to an even larger market; it envisions a future where car-sharing members outnumber car owners in major cities across the globe. Most residents of these cities will live within a five-to-ten-minute walk of a self-service Zipcar.[44]

Zipcar is banking on more than shifting attitudes. Emerging trends due to changing buying habits have helped spur growth. On average, automobiles consume 19 percent of household incomes,[45] yet many cars stand idle for 90 percent of each day. Drivers seeking a less expensive and less wasteful alternative might save up to 70 percent on their transportation costs. There is a one-time fee of $25 for an individual to join Zipcar with hourly rates starting at $7.50 an hour and $69 per day, including the cost of gas, maintenance, and insurance. On average, members report savings of $600 per month versus owning a car.[46]

Zipcar's service model fits in with the emergence of on-demand, pay-per-use options, such as Netflix for movies, iTunes for music, and ereaders for books. Moreover, the popularity of mobile shopping and the growing expectation that they can order anything, anywhere, anytime from their smartphones have made urban young adults and college students two of Zipcar's most fervent member groups. For these "Zipsters," ordering up a set of wheels on the go is far more appealing than being saddled with car payments.

A strong urban public transportation system also helps make car sharing more attractive. That's why Zipcar started off in high-density urban areas such as Boston, New York, Toronto, and Vancouver, with their great public transportation systems already in place. Wherever subways and buses work, car sharing can extend the transit system's reach. By using cars located near transit route endpoints, travellers gain an easy extension

Zipcars are for people who don't need a car all the time, like urbanites and university students.

Used with permission of Zipcar

on subway or bus schedules to their final destinations. Zipcar even offers members an overnight option, for grabbing a car in the evening and returning it the next morning.

Finally, the logic of car sharing works well in settings marked by increased urbanization. According to the United Nations, cities will contain 59 percent of the world's population by 2030.[47] Many of these areas already face congestion, space demands, and environmental threats from crowding too many gas-driven vehicles into a small, population-dense space. Zhen estimates that for every car Zipcar puts on the road, up to 13 personal cars are taken off.[48] Thus some cities work with the company to identify and secure parking spaces close to subway stops and rail stations. Zipcar also provides special programs for businesses big and small, and fleet management services for local, municipal, and federal agencies.

Navigant Research says that car sharing revenue could reach $6.5 billion globally by 2024.[49] Cities in Europe and Asia are well primed for car sharing, by virtue of their strong rail systems, heavy reliance on public transit, and widespread adoption of mobile and wireless technologies. A deal with the United Kingdom's largest car-sharing company, Streetcar Limited, was a first venture in Zipcar's global expansion.[50]

Such growth requires strong logistics, and Zipcar is backed by a corps of fleet managers and vehicle coordinators who track, schedule, and oversee vehicle maintenance; proprietary hardware and software technology that helps it communicate with drivers and track vehicles; and a large fleet that includes more than 60 makes and models from hybrid vehicles for fuel efficiency to minivans that appeal to families who want to take a trip to the beach.[51]

These behind-the-scenes moves aim to make Zipcar's service simple, convenient, and reliable. But with a community of members who share common goods, there are occasional bumps in the road, as one customer's experience showed. The customer went to pick up his designated vehicle at the time and place reserved for him, but he discovered no car there. The Zipcar representative told him that it might be out, being serviced or cleaned, or it could have been delayed by another driver running late. But such explanations did little to alleviate the frustration of being stuck with no transportation. Learning of his predicament, Zipcar tried but was unable to find another car in close proximity. Therefore, it quickly authorized the customer to take a taxi and promised to reimburse him up to $100. Although the "free ride" did not altogether mitigate the stress and inconvenience of the service failure, Zipcar's response showed him that the company was committed to doing right by him, even if that meant sending business to a competitor, the taxi company.

The considerable dimensions of a global car-sharing market are already emerging. Zipcar's experience and first-mover status in the market positions it well to compete. But the race to dominate is sure to intensify, especially as traditional car rental companies with great name recognition, such as Hertz and Enterprise, move into the marketplace.[52] Perhaps it is no surprise that Avis purchased Zipcar in early 2013, enabling Zipcar to scale its service even further.[53] It didn't take long for the company to make the cars available at Pearson International Airport in Toronto, the Macdonald–Cartier International Airport in Ottawa, and the Vancouver International Airport.[54] How well Zipcar performs in the future depends mostly on its ability to meet its own standards for customer service—simplicity, convenience, and reliability—consistently and effectively.

## Questions

1. Using the building blocks (five dimensions) of service quality (see Exhibit 10.4), evaluate Zipcar.

2. Compare Zipcar's service quality performance with that of the most recent car rental service (e.g., Hertz, Enterprise) that you have used.

3. How well has Zipcar handled service failure situations? What could it do to improve recovery efforts?

# CHAPTER 11

© McGraw-Hill Education

## LEARNING OBJECTIVES

After studying this chapter you should be able to

**LO1** Explain what price is and its importance in establishing value in marketing

**LO2** Illustrate how the five Cs—company objectives, customers, costs, competition, and channel members—influence pricing decisions

**LO3** Understand the considerations for setting prices; three pricing methods (e.g., cost-based methods, competitor-based methods, and value-based methods); and various strategies (e.g., EDLP, high/low, and new product pricing) used in marketing

**LO4** Identify pricing tactics targeted to channel members and consumers

**LO5** Summarize the legal and ethical issues involved in pricing

# Pricing Concepts and Strategies: Establishing Value

Pricing is a key part of the value proposition for any purchase. After all, among the other definitions we have used in this book, value reflects the relationship between benefits and costs. When the economy sours, and consumer income drops, no sticker prices can escape sharp scrutiny, especially in the supermarket. For example, shoppers on tight budgets still need to buy cleaning supplies, but when they do so, they tend to be much more sensitive to the prices for the various detergents their household needs.

In such price sensitive and highly competitive markets, companies must be creative in finding ways to balance profits and consumers. Procter & Gamble (P&G) had long floated high above its competitors in the sea of laundry detergents, with its Tide brand enjoying a 38 percent share of the laundry soap market in North America.[1] However, a wave of lower-priced competitors crashed onto P&G when consumers began looking more actively for better deals. Thrifty shoppers began turning from their trusty Tide brand to cheaper alternatives, such as Arm & Hammer detergent, made by Church & Dwight, Co.

Not a company to rest on its laurels, P&G pursued several strategic responses to the challenge. For consumers interested in convenience, it introduced, developed, and expanded on the concept of laundry detergent pods—single-use packs that eliminate the mess and the need for measuring associated with liquids or powders. Although this option has expanded the breadth of Tide's product lines, and established an approximately $1 billion market for P&G, the pods create higher per-wash costs for consumers.[2]

So, for budget conscious consumers, it introduced Tide Simply Clean & Fresh, a liquid detergent that retails for about 35 percent less than the $12 price of a 100-ounce bottle of regular Tide.[3] It is advertised as a laundry detergent that is "tough on odors and easy on your wallet."[4] It's not the first time the company has launched cheaper versions of its products. For example, it introduced Bounty Basic and Charmin Basic at a 25 percent discount from regular Bounty paper towels and Charmin toilet paper. The new products now represent 15 percent of overall sales and offer higher profit margins for P&G.[5]

In an effort to reduce the risk of sales cannibalization of its premium, higher-priced products, P&G makes sure that Simply Clean never appears for sale alongside other Tide brands, nor does it sport the easily recognizable orange Tide-branded container. In stores, Simply Clean is placed alongside its competitor brand on store shelves, despite having a higher price point. The primary target markets are consumers from hardworking households, many of whom work in tough, odour-generating jobs and environments. With this approach, P&G can ensure that it never turns its back on its flagship brand.

However, to offset the lower profit margins earned on Tide Simply Clean, P&G needed to increase margins on premium Tide detergents, including Tide Plus, which contain extra ingredients (e.g., colour-safe bleach). In the consumer-goods industry a popular pricing method allows brands to raise their prices in a way that remains largely hidden to consumers, unless they do a lot of extra research. Specifically, the brand increases wholesale prices while also reducing the size of the containers; what was formerly a 2.95 litre bottle of detergent becomes a 2.72 litre bottle, and the previously 1.48 litre bottle contains only 1.36 litres. The retail price remains the same; the package looks practically identical. Few consumers check the actual volume of such commonly purchased products, so they likely never realize that their detergent costs more per litre.

Although P&G's product portfolio is broad, including other detergent brands such as Gain and Ivory Snow, it has chosen to focus where consumers are most invested, namely, in its Tide products. In trying to ensure Tide's market share advantage, P&G has shown its willingness to adjust its regular pricing strategies, develop new products with varying profit margins, and reduce bottle sizes while maintaining the same retail price. In essence, Procter & Gamble is keeping an eye on the way the tides are turning in the laundry detergent market. ∎

LO1 # THE IMPORTANCE OF PRICING

Although knowing how consumers arrive at their perceptions of value is critical to developing successful pricing strategies, sellers also must consider other factors—which is why developing a good pricing strategy is such a formidable challenge to all firms. Do it right and the rewards to the firm will be substantial. Do it wrong and failure will be swift and severe. But even if a pricing strategy is implemented well, consumers, economic conditions, markets, competitors, government regulations, and even a firm's own products change constantly—and that means that a good pricing strategy today may not remain an effective pricing strategy tomorrow.

So much rides on marketers setting the right price, so it's important to understand the role price plays in the marketing mix. We start by explaining what "price" is as a marketing concept, why it is important, how marketers set pricing objectives, and how various factors influence price setting. Then, we extend this foundation by focusing on specific pricing strategies as well as the psychological aspects of pricing. Lastly, we describe various B2B and consumer pricing tactics and some important legal and ethical issues associated with pricing.

Imagine that a consumer realizes that to save money on a particular item, she will have to drive an additional 20 kilometres. She may judge that her time and travel costs are not worth the savings, so even though the price tag is higher at a nearby store, she judges the overall cost of buying the product there to be lower. To include aspects of price such as this, we define price as the overall sacrifice a consumer is willing to make to acquire a specific product or service. This sacrifice usually includes the money that must be paid to the seller to acquire the item but it also may involve other sacrifices, whether nonmonetary (such as the value of the time necessary to acquire the product or service) or monetary (such as travel costs, taxes, and shipping costs), all of which the buyer must give up to take possession of the product.[6] It's useful to think of overall price like this to see how the narrower sense of purchase price fits in.

Consumers judge the benefits a product delivers against the sacrifice necessary to obtain it, and then make a purchase decision based on this overall judgment of value. Thus, a great but overpriced product can be judged as low in value and may not sell as well as an inferior but well priced item. In turn, we cannot define price without referring to the product or service associated with it. The key to successful pricing is to match the product or service with the consumer's value perceptions.

Coming up with the "right" price is never easy. If firms can price their products or services too high, can they price them too low as well? Quite simply, yes. A price set too low may signal low quality, poor performance, or other negative attributes about the product or service. Consumers don't necessarily want a low price all the time or for all products. Rather, they want high value, which may come with a relatively high or low price, depending on the bundle of benefits the product or service delivers. Deeply discounted pricing may bring in new customers, but it can cause retailers and manufacturers to lose money. And it may also negatively impact perceived positioning of the product or service.

Price is the only element of the marketing mix that generates revenue. Every other element in the marketing mix may be perfect but, with the wrong price, sales simply will not occur. Research has consistently shown that consumers usually rank price as one of the most important factors in their purchase decisions.[7]

Knowing that price is so critical to success, why don't managers put greater emphasis on it as a strategic decision variable? Price is the most challenging of the four Ps to manage, partly because it is often the least understood. Historically, managers have treated price as an afterthought to their marketing strategy, setting prices according to what competitors were charging or, worse yet, by adding up their costs and tacking on a desired profit to set the sales price. Prices rarely changed except in response to radical shifts in market conditions. Even today, pricing decisions often fail to reflect our current understanding of the role of price in the marketing mix.

Moreover, managers have held an overly simplistic view of the role of price, considering it simply the amount of money a consumer must part with to acquire a product or service. We now know that price is not only a sacrifice but also an information cue as well. That is, consumers use the price of a product or service to judge its quality,[8] particularly when they are less knowledgeable about the product category. For example, most college and university students know little about fine wine, so if a student found herself in the Vintages section of the liquor store and had to make a decision about which bottle to purchase, she might judge the quality of the various options according to their prices and assume that a higher price means higher quality.

When shopping for wine, most of us infer that a higher price means higher quality.

Jasminko Ibrakovic/Shutterstock

In summary, marketers should view pricing decisions as a strategic opportunity to create value rather than as an afterthought to the rest of the marketing mix. Price communicates more than how much a product or service costs; it can signal quality, or lack thereof. Let's now turn to the five basic components of pricing strategies.

# THE FIVE CS OF PRICING

**L02**

Successful pricing strategies are built through the five critical components: company objectives, customers, costs, competition, and channel members (see Exhibit 11.1). We examine these components in some detail because each makes a significant contribution to formulating good pricing decisions.[9] To start, the first step is to develop the company's pricing objectives.

**EXHIBIT 11.1** Five Cs of Pricing

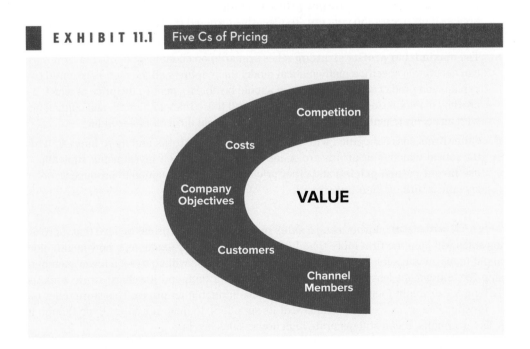

| EXHIBIT 11.2 | Company Objectives and Pricing Strategy Implications |
|---|---|

| Company Objective | Examples of Pricing Strategy Implications |
|---|---|
| Profit oriented | Institute a companywide policy that all products must provide for at least an 18 percent profit margin to reach a particular profit goal for the firm. |
| Sales oriented | Set prices very low to generate new sales and take sales away from competitors, even if profits suffer. |
| Competitor oriented | Set prices very low to discourage more competitors from entering the market. |
| | Set prices higher than competitors to signal higher quality or market leadership. |
| | Match competitor prices to show similar value. |
| Customer oriented | Target a market segment of consumers who highly value a particular product benefit and set prices relatively high (referred to as premium pricing). |

**profit orientation**
A company objective that can be implemented by focusing on target profit pricing, maximizing profits, or target return pricing.

**target profit pricing**
A pricing strategy implemented by firms when they have a particular profit goal as their overriding concern; uses price to stimulate a certain level of sales at a certain profit per unit.

**maximizing profits strategy**
A mathematical model that captures all the factors required to explain and predict sales and profits, which should be able to identify the price at which its profits are maximized.

**target return pricing**
A pricing strategy implemented by firms less concerned with the absolute level of profits and more interested in the rate at which their profits are generated relative to their investments; designed to produce a specific return on investment, usually expressed as a percentage of sales.

**sales orientation**
A company objective based on the belief that increasing sales will help the firm more than will increasing profits.

## Company Objectives

By now, you know that different firms embrace different goals. Walmart, for example, wants to be seen as a value-based company and so uses **everyday low pricing** (EDLP), whereas Holt Renfrew's high prices reflect its high-fashion image.

Each firm embraces an objective that fits with where management thinks the firm needs to go to be successful, in whatever way they define success. These specific objectives usually reflect how the firm intends to grow. Do managers want it to grow by increasing profits, increasing sales, decreasing competition, or building customer satisfaction?

Company objectives are not as simple as they might first appear; they often can be expressed in slightly different forms that mean very different things. Exhibit 11.2 introduces some common company objectives and examples of their implications for pricing strategies. These objectives are not always mutually exclusive, because a firm may embrace two or more noncompeting objectives.

### Profit Orientation
Even though all company objectives may ultimately be oriented toward making a profit, firms implement a **profit orientation** by focusing on target profit pricing, maximizing profits, or target return pricing.

- Firms usually implement **target profit pricing** when they have a particular profit goal as their overriding concern. To meet this targeted profit objective, firms use price to stimulate a certain level of sales at a certain profit per unit.

- The **maximizing profits strategy** relies primarily on economic theory. If a firm can accurately specify a mathematical model that captures all the factors required to explain and predict sales and profits, it should be able to identify the price at which its profits are maximized. Gathering the data on all these relevant factors and coming up with an accurate mathematical model is an extremely difficult undertaking.

- Other firms, less concerned with the absolute level of profits and more interested in the rate at which their profits are generated relative to their investments, typically use **target return pricing** and other pricing strategies designed to produce a specific return on their investment.

### Sales Orientation
Firms using a **sales orientation** to set prices believe that increasing sales will help the firm more than increasing profits. For example, a new health club might focus on unit sales or market share and therefore be willing to set a lower membership fee and accept less profit at first. In contrast, a high-end jewellery store, such as Tiffany & Co., might focus on dollar sales and maintain higher prices. This store relies on its prestige image, as well as the image of its suppliers, to generate sales. Even though it sells fewer units, it can still generate high dollar sales levels.

Some firms may be more concerned about their overall market share than about dollar sales per se because they believe that market share better reflects their success relative to the market conditions than do sales alone. A firm may set low prices to discourage new firms from entering the market, encourage current firms to leave the market, take market share away from competitors—all to gain overall market share. For example, though Apple has sold more than 10 billion songs since the introduction of its iTunes service, it wants to keep increasing its market share, especially as competitors make inroads. So, instead of the previous fixed priced structure of 99 cents per song, Apple offers three price tiers (69 cents, 99 cents, and $1.29) based on popularity and recency of the songs. The most popular songs cost the most, but by charging less for others, Apple aims to increase its sales per customer.[10] Its streaming music service launched at $10/month with a free three-month trial to compete with Spotify and Rdio. Based on Apple's lower cost for adding multiple users, Spotify adjusted its prices to match Apple Music.[11] While Spotify has a free version of its service, Apple only offers a paid version to fans after their initial three-month trial is up.[12]

Tiffany & Co. keeps its prices high even during a recession to protect its prestigious image, symbolized by its famous blue box.

Felix Choo/Alamy Stock Photo

Adopting a market share objective does not always imply setting low prices. Rarely is the lowest-price offering the dominant brand in a given market. Heinz ketchup, Philadelphia cream cheese, Crest toothpaste, and Nike athletic shoes have all dominated their markets, yet all are premium-priced brands. Thus, companies can gain market share simply by offering a high-quality product at a fair price, as long as they generate high-value perceptions among consumers. Although the concept of value is not overtly expressed in sales-oriented strategies, it is at least implicit because for sales to increase, consumers must see greater value.

**Competitor Orientation**    When firms undertake a **competitor orientation**, they strategize according to the premise that they should measure themselves primarily against their competition. Some firms focus on **competitive parity**, which means they set prices that are similar to those of their major competitors. Value is only implicitly considered in competitor-oriented strategies, in the sense that competitors may be using value as part of their pricing strategies, so copying their strategy might provide value.

**Customer Orientation**    A **customer orientation** explicitly invokes the concept of value. Sometimes a firm may attempt to increase value by focusing on customer satisfaction and setting prices to match consumer expectations. Or a firm can use a "no-haggle" price structure to make the purchase process simpler and easier for consumers, thereby lowering the overall price and ultimately increasing value. Some car companies have embraced the "no-haggle" price policy to do just that. Other companies make it easy for consumers to pay by offering a variety of payment methods including mobile wallet apps.

Firms also may offer very high-priced, "state-of-the-art" products or services in full anticipation of limited sales. These offerings are designed to enhance the company's reputation and image and thereby increase the company's value in the minds of consumers. For example, Paradigm, a Canadian speaker manufacturer in Mississauga, Ontario, produces what many audiophiles consider a high-value product, offering speakers priced as low as $320 per pair. However, Paradigm also offers a high-end pair of speakers for $8,500. Although few people will spend $8,500 on a pair of speakers, this "statement" speaker communicates what the company is capable of and can increase the image of the firm and the rest of its products—even that $320 pair of speakers. For an unprecedented 22 years

**competitor orientation**
A company objective based on the premise that the firm should measure itself primarily against its competition.

**competitive parity**
A firm's strategy of setting prices that are similar to those of major competitors.

**customer orientation**
Pricing orientation that explicitly invokes the concept of customer value and setting prices to match consumer expectations.

Can you tell the difference between the $8,500 and the $320 Paradigm speaker?

Courtesy Paradigm Electronics, Inc.

in a row, Paradigm has been rated number one best price/value by *Inside Track*.[13] Setting prices with a close eye to how consumers develop their perceptions of value can often be the most effective pricing strategy, especially if it is supported by consistent advertising and distribution strategies.

After a company has a good grasp on its overall objectives, it must implement pricing strategies that enable it to achieve those objectives. As the second step in this process, the firm should look toward consumer demand to lay the foundation for its pricing strategy.

## Customers

The second C of the five Cs of pricing is the most important because it is about understanding consumers' reactions to different prices. Consumers want value and, as you may recall, price is half of the value equation. Look at how two young women with vision set pricing for a new construction app in Entrepreneurial Marketing 11.1.

 ### Entrepreneurial Marketing 11.1

## "Blink Test" Paves the Way for Setting App Price

Sometimes the most important part of setting a price for your product or service is learning to read prospective customers' reactions. Lauren Lake and Mallorie Brodie decided they wanted to be entrepreneurs while they were finishing their studies at the University of Western Ontario in London. Equipped with degrees in structural engineering and business, the two partners founded Bridgit in December 2012 to improve communication on construction sites.

Their market research was unusual but effective. While at university they used to go "crane hunting" early in the mornings to locate job sites. Once there, they spent a lot of time talking to contractors and learned that to-do lists were often tracked using sticky notes, plans scribbled on walls, Excel spreadsheets, and emails.[14] The partners came up with an idea to create a mobile app to automate the communication process. They developed an early prototype which they tested on site, tweaked, and re-tested until it met the needs of the users.

One contractor could end up managing thousands of tasks and 30 to 50 subcontractors. For example, in a new condo, windows, appliances, and crown moulding need to be installed. It's inevitable that some things will need to be fixed, requiring an updated installation schedule and lots of communication with subcontractors. Bridgit's mobile app automates all this. On site, a project manager can simply take a photo of the task that requires attention and note the location and responsible stakeholder,

Mallorie Brodie and Lauren Lake used the "blink test" to set prices when they first started to sell their construction app to companies.

Used with permission of Bridgit, www.gobridgit.com

and the app automatically sends the information out to all of the subcontractors involved.[15]

After thorough field testing, the challenge was to convince contractors to buy the app. How do you put a price on better work flow, improved communication, and not having tasks fall through the cracks? Lauren set up a sales call with a contractor hoping he could be convinced to pay $10/month for the app. In reality, she was prepared to let him have it at no cost since he would be a beta customer. When she presented the price, she carefully watched for the "blink test." In other words, would the contractor balk at the price? He did. But he quickly followed with a loud guffaw, and agreed to the price. That same customer is now generating revenues of $60,000 a year.[16]

Since then, Bridgit's developers have learned a lot about pricing. They now use a model that ranges from $900 to $4,000 per month based on project size. Support packages are priced separately, generating more revenue for the company.

In a few short years, Bridgit has won numerous awards. It was named to Canadian Innovation Exchange's top 20 list of Canada's most innovative companies working in digital media and information and communication technology, and won big at Google's very first Entrepreneurs Demo Day Women's Edition. With over 450 competitors, Bridgit was the lone Canadian company, yet landed one of 11 spots in the finals.[17] In the spring of 2016, the company raised $2.2 million in seed funding which will be used to expand operations, especially in the United States. Since the company was launched, over 100 contractors in Canada and the United States have signed up for the app.[18]

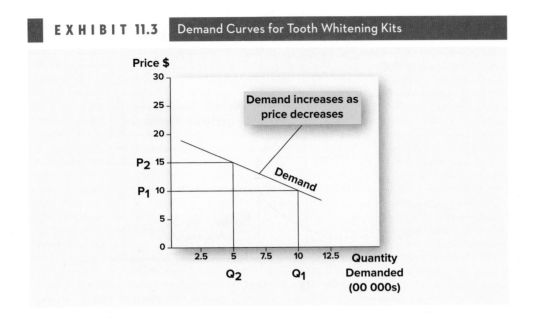

**EXHIBIT 11.3**   Demand Curves for Tooth Whitening Kits

To determine how firms account for consumers' preferences when they develop pricing strategies, we must first lay a foundation of traditional economic theory that helps explain how prices are related to demand (consumers' desire for products) and how managers can incorporate this knowledge into their pricing strategies.

**Demand Curves and Pricing**   A **demand curve** shows how many units of a product or service consumers will demand during a specific period of time at different prices. Although we call them "curves," demand curves can be either straight or curved, as Exhibit 11.3 shows. Of course, any static demand curve assumes that everything else remains unchanged. For example, marketers creating a demand curve must assume that the firm will not increase its expenditures on advertising and that the economy will not change in any significant way.

Exhibit 11.3 illustrates the common downward-sloping demand curve in which, as price increases, demand for the product or service decreases. In this case, consumers will buy more tooth whitening kits as the price decreases. We can expect to uncover a demand curve similar to this one for many, if not most, products and services.

The horizontal axis measures the quantity demanded for the kits in units and plots it against the various price possibilities indicated on the vertical axis. Each point on the demand curve then represents the quantity demanded at a specific price. So, in this instance, if the price of a kit is $10 per unit ($P_1$), the demand is 1,000,000 units ($Q_1$), but if the price were set at $15 ($P_2$), the demand would be only 500,000 units ($Q_2$). The firm will sell far more kits at $10 each than at $15 each. Why? Because of the greater value this price point offers.

Knowing the demand curve for a product or service enables a firm to examine different prices in terms of the resulting demand and relative to its overall objective. In our preceding example, the tooth whitening kit distributor will generate a total of $10,000,000 in sales at the $10 price ($10 × 1,000,000 units) and $7,500,000 in sales at the $15 price ($15 × 500,000 units). In this case, given only the two choices of $10 or $15, the $10 price is preferable as long as the firm wants to maximize its sales in terms of dollars and units. But what about a firm that is more interested in profit? To calculate profit, it must consider its costs, which we cover in the next section.

Interestingly enough, not all products or services follow the downward-sloping demand curve for all levels of price depicted in Exhibit 11.3. Consider **prestige products or services**, which consumers purchase for their status rather than their

**demand curve**
Shows how many units of a product or service consumers will demand during a specific period at different prices.

**prestige products or services**
Those that consumers purchase for status rather than functionality.

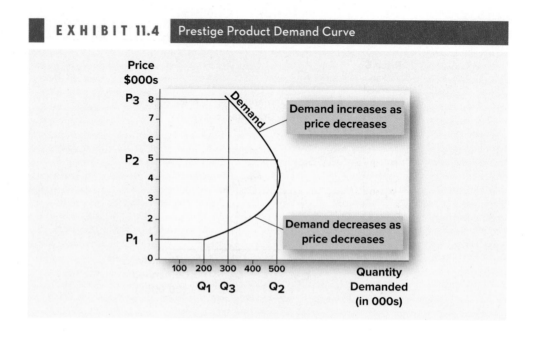

**EXHIBIT 11.4** Prestige Product Demand Curve

functionality. The higher the price, the greater the status associated with it and the greater the exclusivity, because fewer people can afford to purchase it. Most important, in this case, a higher price also leads to a greater quantity sold—up to a certain point. When customers value the increase in prestige more than the price differential between the prestige product and other products, the prestige product attains the greater value overall.

Exhibit 11.4 illustrates a demand curve for a hypothetical prestige service, such as a Caribbean cruise. As the graph indicates, when the price increases from $1,000 ($P_1$) to $5,000 ($P_2$), the quantity demanded actually increases from 200,000 ($Q_1$) to 500,000 ($Q_2$) units. However, when the price increases to $8,000 ($P_3$), the demand then decreases to 300,000 ($Q_3$) units, after peaking at about 500,000.

Although the firm likely will earn more profit selling 300,000 cruises at $8,000 each than 500,000 cruises at $5,000 each, we do not know for sure until we consider costs. However, we do know that more consumers are willing to book the cruise as the price increases initially from $1,000 to $5,000 and that most consumers will choose an alternative vacation as the price increases further from $5,000 to $8,000.

### Price Elasticity of Demand

Although we now know something about how consumers react to different price levels, we still need to determine how consumers respond to actual changes in price. Consumers are generally less sensitive to price increases for necessary items, such as milk, because they have to purchase these items even if the price climbs. When the price of milk goes up, demand does not fall significantly. However, if the price of steak rises beyond a certain point, people will buy less because there are many substitutes. Marketers need to know how consumers will respond to a price increase (or decrease) for a specific product or brand so they can determine whether it makes sense for them to raise or lower prices.

**Price elasticity of demand** measures how changes in a price affect the quantity of the product demanded. We can calculate it with the following formula:

**price elasticity of demand**

Measures how changes in a price affect the quantity of the product demanded; specifically, the ratio of the percentage change in quantity demanded to the percentage change in price.

$$\text{Price elasticity of demand} = \frac{\%\,\text{change in quantity demanded}}{\%\,\text{change in price}}$$

Consumers are less sensitive to the price of milk (left) than to steak (right). When the price of milk goes up, demand does not fall significantly because people still need to buy milk. However, if the price of steak rises beyond a certain point, people will buy less because they can turn to the many substitutes for steak.

(left): Alessandra Tarantino/AP Photo/The Canadian Press; (right): Tom Hanson/The Canadian Press

In general, the market for a product or service is price sensitive (or **elastic**) when the price elasticity is less than –1: that is, when a 1 percent decrease in price produces more than a 1 percent increase in the quantity sold. In an elastic scenario, relatively small changes in price will generate fairly large changes in the quantity demanded, so if a firm is trying to increase its sales, it can do so by lowering prices.

The market for a product is generally viewed as price insensitive (or **inelastic**) when its price elasticity is greater than –1: that is, when a 1 percent decrease in price results in less than a 1 percent increase in quantity sold. Generally, if a firm must raise prices, it is helpful to do so with inelastic products or services because in such a market, fewer customers will stop buying or reduce their purchases—customers just don't notice or care about the lower price.

Consumers are generally more sensitive to price increases than to price decreases.[19] Also, the price elasticity of demand usually changes at different points in the demand curve unless the curve is actually a straight line, as in Exhibit 11.3. For instance, a prestige product or service, such as our Caribbean cruise example in Exhibit 11.4, enjoys a highly inelastic demand curve up to a certain point, so price increases do not affect sales significantly. But when the price reaches that certain point, consumers start turning to other alternatives because the value of the cruise has finally been reduced by the extremely high price.

The Canadian economy has experienced the full force of this elasticity phenomenon. Over the past decade, the Canadian dollar has fluctuated against the U.S. dollar. For example, in 2011 the exchange rate hovered near parity before falling to $0.90 in 2014. By mid-2017 the exchange rate was $0.75. An American family planning a two-week vacation to Canada in 2011 on a US$5,000 budget would have enjoyed a nice trip. However, six years later, the same family would need to spend less because of currency fluctuations. Not surprisingly, the low dollar encourages American travel and is a boon to tourism. The TD Bank projected an increase in travel related spending as a result of the exchange rate, reaching $4 billion–$5 billion for 2015–2016.[20]

**Factors Influencing Price Elasticity of Demand** We have illustrated how price elasticity of demand varies across different products and at different points along a demand curve, as well as how it can change over time. What causes these differences in the price elasticity of demand? We discuss a few of the more important factors next.

***Income Effect.*** Generally, as people's income increases, their spending behaviour changes: They tend to shift their demand from lower-priced products to higher-priced

**elastic**
Refers to a market for a product or service that is price sensitive; that is, relatively small changes in price will generate fairly large changes in the quantity demanded.

**inelastic**
Refers to a market for a product or service that is price insensitive; that is, relatively small changes in price will not generate large changes in the quantity demanded.

Travelling to Canada on vacation is much less expensive for Americans today than it was a decade ago because of currency fluctuations.

Andrew Vaughan/The Canadian Press

**income effect**
Refers to the change in the quantity of a product demanded by consumers because of a change in their income.

**substitution effect**
Refers to consumers' ability to substitute other products for the focal brand, thus increasing the price elasticity of demand for the focal brand.

**cross-price elasticity**
The percentage change in demand for Product A that occurs in response to a percentage change in price of Product B.

**complementary products**
Products whose demand curves are positively related, such that they rise or fall together; a percentage increase in demand for one results in a percentage increase in demand for the other.

alternatives. That is, consumers may buy steak instead of ground beef and splurge on a movie a week instead of one per month. In turn, when the economy is good and consumers' incomes are rising overall, the price elasticity of steak or movies may actually drop, even though the price remains constant. Conversely, when incomes drop, consumers turn to less expensive alternatives or purchase less. This **income effect** refers to the change in the quantity of a product demanded by consumers because of a change in their income.

*Substitution Effect.*   The **substitution effect** refers to consumers' ability to substitute other products for the focal brand. The greater the availability of substitute products, the higher the price elasticity of demand for any given product will be. For example, there are many close substitutes for the various brands of peanut butter. If Kraft raises its prices, many consumers will turn to Jif, President's Choice, or another brand because they can easily find lower-priced substitutes. Extremely brand-loyal consumers, however, are willing to pay a higher price because in their minds, Kraft still offers better value than the competing brands.

Keep in mind that marketing plays a critical role in making consumers brand loyal, making the price elasticity of demand for some brands very low. For example, Polo Ralph Lauren sells millions of its classic polo shirts at $85, while shirts of equal quality but without the polo player logo sell for much less. Getting consumers to believe that a particular brand is unique or extraordinary in some way makes other brands seem less substitutable.

*Price Elasticity.*   **Cross-price elasticity** is the percentage change in the quantity of Product A demanded compared with the percentage change in price in Product B. For example, when the price of coffee pods dropped rapidly, the demand for single-serve coffee machines, such as Keurig and Nespresso, also increased rapidly. Products such as coffee pods and single-serve coffee machines are **complementary products**, which are products whose demands are positively related, such that they rise or fall together. In other words, a percentage increase in the quantity demanded for Product A results in a percentage increase in the quantity demanded for Product B.[21] However, when the price for regular coffee makers dropped, the demand for Keurig machines went down, so

If there are many close substitutes for a product, customers will be sensitive to small price changes, and the product will be highly price elastic. If, for instance, Kraft raises its price, many customers will switch to another brand.

Felix Choo/Alamy Stock Photo

regular coffee makers and Keurig or Nespresso machines are **substitute products** because changes in their demand are negatively related. Today, shopping bots like PriceGrabber.com and Bizrate.com have made it much easier for people to shop for substitutable products like consumer electronics, which has affected the price elasticity of demand.

Clearly, knowing how prices affect sales is important, but it cannot give us the whole picture. To know how profitable a pricing strategy will be, we must also consider the third C, costs.

## Costs

To make effective pricing decisions, firms must understand their cost structures so they can determine the degree to which their products or services will be profitable at different prices. In general, prices should not be based on costs because consumers make purchase decisions based on their perceived value; they care little about the firm's costs to produce and sell a product or deliver a service. Consumers use just the price they must pay and the benefits they may receive to judge value; they will not pay a higher price for an inferior product simply because the firm cannot be as cost-efficient as its competitors.

If, for instance, a CD were available at both HMV and Walmart, most consumers would buy it at Walmart, where it likely will be priced lower. But many consumers see additional benefits to shopping at HMV because it also offers a good selection of movies and they can find their choice more easily. If consumers did not value these benefits, HMV would not survive.

Although companies incur many different types of costs as a natural part of doing business, there are two primary cost categories: variable and fixed.

### Variable Costs

**Variable costs** are those costs, primarily labour and materials, that vary with production volume. As a firm produces more or less of a good or service, the total variable costs increase or decrease at the same time. Because each unit of the product produced incurs the same cost, marketers generally express variable costs on a per-unit basis. Continuing with our CD example, the variable costs include the labour needed to burn each CD; the costs of the blank CDs, jewel cases, and labels; and royalties paid to the artist. Each of these costs is incurred each time the producer makes a new CD.

In the service industry, variable costs are far more complex. As noted in Social and Mobile Marketing 11.1, banks must pay a fee for each mobile wallet transaction, adding more cost as increasing numbers of consumers choose to pay using their phones. Likewise, a hotel incurs certain variable costs each time it rents a room, including the costs associated with the labour and supplies necessary to clean and restock the room. Note that the hotel does not incur these costs if the room is not booked. Suppose that a particular hotel calculates its total variable costs to be $20 per room; each time it rents a room, it incurs $20 in variable costs. If the hotel rents out 100 rooms on a given night, the total variable cost is $2,000 (= $20/room × 100 rooms).

Variable costs tend to change depending on the quantity produced. If a record producer creates five CDs, it must pay a set amount for each one. If it makes 500, though, it can probably get the discs at a lower price by buying in bulk. Though it's not always the case, variable costs per unit may go up or down (for all units) with significant changes in volume.

### Fixed Costs

**Fixed costs** are those costs that remain essentially at the same level, regardless of any changes in the volume of production. Typically, these costs include items such as rent, utilities, insurance, administrative salaries (for executives and higher-level managers), and the depreciation of the physical plant and equipment. Across reasonable fluctuations in production volume, these costs remain stable; whether the producer makes five or 500 CDs, the rent it pays for the building in which it burns the CDs remains unchanged.

**substitute products** Products for which changes in demand are negatively related—that is, a percentage increase in the quantity demanded for Product A results in a percentage decrease in the quantity demanded for Product B.

**variable costs** Those costs, primarily labour and materials, that vary with production volume.

**fixed costs** Those costs that remain essentially at the same level, regardless of any changes in the volume of production.

## Social and Mobile Marketing 11.1

### Apple Pay Adds Costs for Banks

While American Express credit card holders had been able to purchase in stores using Apple Pay since it was launched in Canada in the fall of 2015, everyone else had to wait almost a year for the biggest banks to roll out the same convenience. Why did it take so long? Resistance came partly because the banks had all developed their own digital wallet applications. However, consumers did not embrace the apps as fast as banks hoped. People had to have the right phone and retailers had to have the correct merchant terminals.

The delay was also because the banks had to negotiate payment terms with Apple. With more than $450 billion in credit card transactions and $200 billion in debit transactions,[22] it is clear why banks would want to "own" these profitable transactions. They generate a steady stream of revenue as opposed to incurring cost, since a fee must be paid to companies that handle transactions. The deal struck with Apple will cost Canada's banks 15 cents for each $100 credit card transaction or 4 cents on debit card transactions.[23] That could add up fast.

For now, the extra variable costs to banks should be low. Only 38 percent of smartphones in Canada are iPhones, many of which are too old to use Apple Pay. The payment app requires an iPhone 6, iPhone 6 Plus, iPhone 6S,

Apple Pay adds convenience for consumers but cost for the banks.

ZUMA Press Inc/Alamy Stock Photo

iPhone 6S Plus, or iPhone SE, or an Apple Watch paired with an iPhone 5 or later for in-store payment.[24] People who don't have an Apple Pay–ready phone can still conveniently pay for their purchases, however. Any credit card or debit card that is near field communication-enabled can already do everything that an iPhone with Apple Pay can.

**total cost**
The sum of the variable and fixed costs.

**Total Cost**  Finally, the **total cost** is simply the sum of the variable and fixed costs. For example, in one year, our hypothetical hotel incurred $100,000 in fixed costs. We also know that because the hotel booked 10,000 room nights, its total variable cost is $200,000 (= 10,000 room nights × $20/room). Thus, its total cost is $300,000.

Next, we illustrate how to use these costs in simple analyses that can inform managerial decision making about setting prices.

**Break-Even Analysis and Decision Making**  A useful technique that enables managers to examine the relationships among cost, price, revenue, and profit over different levels of production and sales is called *break-even analysis*. Central to this analysis is the determination of the **break-even point**, or the point at which the number of units sold generates just enough revenue to equal the total costs. At this point, profits are zero. Profit represents the difference between the total cost and the total revenue (Total revenue or sales = Selling price of each unit sold × Number of units sold). Although profit can indicate how much money the firm is making or losing at a single period of time, it cannot tell managers how many units a firm must produce and sell before it stops losing money and at least breaks even.

**break-even point**
The point at which the number of units sold generates just enough revenue to equal the total costs; at this point, profits are zero.

How do we determine the break-even point? Let's use the hotel example to illustrate the break-even analysis. Exhibit 11.5 presents the various cost and revenue information we have discussed in a graphic format.

Recall that the fixed costs are $100,000 and the variable costs are $20/room rented. If the rooms rent for $100 per night, how many rooms must the hotel rent over the course of a year to break even? If we study the graph, we find the break-even point at 1,250, which means that the hotel must rent 1,250 rooms before its revenues equal its costs. If it rents fewer rooms, it loses money; if it rents more, it makes a profit. To determine the

**EXHIBIT 11.5**   Break-Even Analysis

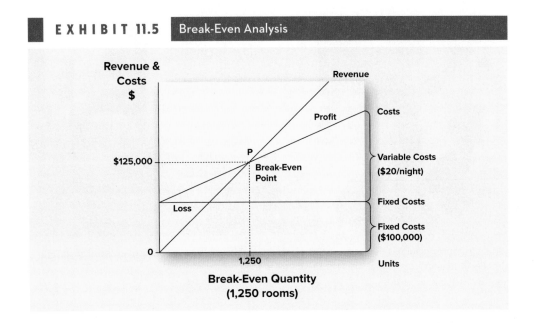

**Break-Even Quantity
(1,250 rooms)**

break-even point in units mathematically, we must consider fixed costs and the **contribution per unit**, which is the price less the variable cost per unit. We use the following formula to calculate the break-even point in units:

$$\text{Break-even point (units)} = \frac{\text{Fixed costs}}{\text{Contribution per unit}}$$

In this case,

$$\text{Break-even point (units)} = \frac{\$100,000}{\$100 - \$20 = \$80} = 1{,}250 \text{ room nights}$$

When the hotel has crossed that break-even point of 1,250 rooms, it will then start earning profit at the same rate of the contribution per unit. So if the hotel rents 2,500 rooms—which is 1,250 rooms more than the break-even point—its profit will be $100,000 (= 1,250 rooms × $80 contribution per unit). Bear in mind that hotels are limited by the number of rooms they have to offer and the number of days in a year. So if this hotel had 50 rooms, it would need a full house 25 days of the year.

Although a break-even analysis cannot actually help managers set prices, it does help them assess their pricing strategies because it clarifies the conditions in which different prices may make a product or service profitable. It becomes an even more powerful tool when performed on a range of possible prices for comparative purposes. For example, the hotel management could analyze various prices, not just $100, to determine how many hotel rooms it would have to rent at what price to make a $200,000 profit.

Naturally, however, a break-even analysis has limitations. First, it is unlikely that a hotel has one specific price that it charges for each and every room, so the price it would use in its break-even analysis probably represents an average price that attempts to account for these variances.

Second, prices often get reduced as quantity increases because the costs decrease, so firms must perform several break-even analyses at different quantities.

Third, a break-even analysis cannot indicate for sure how many rooms will be rented or, in the case of products, how many units will sell at a given price. It tells the firm only what its costs, revenues, and profitability will be given a set price and an assumed quantity. To determine how many units the firm actually will sell, it must bring in the demand estimates we discussed previously.

**contribution per unit**
Equals the price less the variable cost per unit; variable used to determine the break-even point in units.

In a hotel, the cost of the physical structure, including the lobby, is fixed—it is incurred even if no rooms are rented. The costs to clean towels and sheets are variable—the more rooms that are rented, the more the costs.

The Canadian Press/Adrian Wyld; Inti St. Clair/PhotoDisc Red/Getty Images

## Competition

Because the fourth C, competition, has a profound impact on pricing strategies, we use this section to focus on its effect, as well as on how competitors react to certain pricing strategies. There are four levels of competition—monopoly, oligopoly, monopolistic competition, and pure competition—and each has its own set of pricing challenges and opportunities (see Exhibit 11.6).

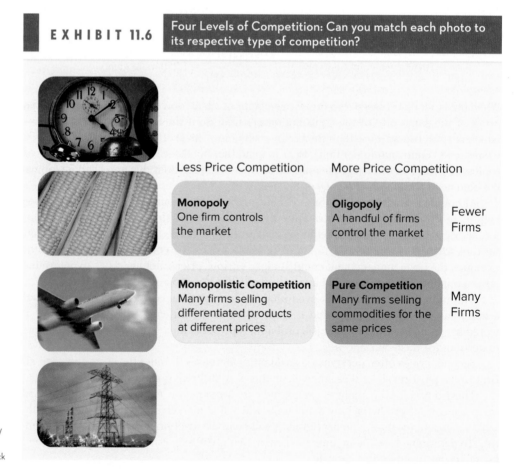

**EXHIBIT 11.6**    Four Levels of Competition: Can you match each photo to its respective type of competition?

Less Price Competition    More Price Competition

**Monopoly**
One firm controls
the market

**Oligopoly**
A handful of firms
control the market

Fewer
Firms

**Monopolistic Competition**
Many firms selling
differentiated products
at different prices

**Pure Competition**
Many firms selling
commodities for the
same prices

Many
Firms

(clocks): milos luzanin/Alamy Stock Photo; (corn): Corbis RF; (plane): Ingram Publishing/SuperStock; (power pylon): © Brand X Pictures/PunchStock

In a **monopoly**, only one firm provides the product or service in a particular industry, and as such results in less price competition. For example, in the utilities industry, there is only one provider of power in each region of the country—for example, Hydro One in most of Ontario and SaskPower in Saskatchewan. Power companies operate more efficiently when there is one service provider, so the government regulates the pricing of utility monopolies to prevent them from raising prices uncontrollably. Monopolies have had a long history in the United States, starting with Standard Oil, which the government broke up in 1911. A monopoly that restricts competition by controlling an industry can be deemed illegal and broken apart by the government.

When a market is an **oligopoly**, only a few firms dominate. Firms typically change their prices in reaction to competition to avoid upsetting an otherwise stable competitive environment. Often-cited examples of oligopolistic markets include the banking industry, the retail gasoline industry, and commercial airline travel.

Sometimes reactions to prices in oligopolistic markets can result in a **price war**, which occurs when two or more firms compete primarily by lowering their prices. Price wars often appear in the airline industry when a low-cost provider enters a market in which established carriers already exist. But what motivates firms to enter price wars?[25] In the airline example, the new entrants might want to gain market share, whereas the established airlines drop their prices to preserve their market share. Other reasons include avoiding the appearance of being insensitive to consumers and simply overreacting to a price decrease offered by competitors. In many cases, companies do not need to respond to price cuts with price cuts of their own[26] because consumers do not buy solely on the basis of price. Better service, higher quality, and brand loyalty might be used as competitive strategies instead.

**Monopolistic competition** occurs when many firms are competing for customers in a given market but their products are differentiated. When so many firms compete, product differentiation rather than a strict pricing competition tends to appeal to consumers. This form of competition is the most common. Hundreds of firms make wristwatches, and the market is highly differentiated. For example, Timex is known for durability, Swatch for style, Armani for fashion, and Rolex for prestige.

With **pure competition**, consumers perceive a large number of sellers of standardized products or commodities as substitutable, such as grains, spices, gold, or minerals. In such markets, price usually is set according to the laws of supply and demand. For example, wheat is wheat, so it does not matter to a commercial bakery whose wheat it buys. However, the secret to pricing success in a pure competition market is not necessarily to offer the lowest price because doing so might create a price war and erode profits. Instead, some firms have brilliantly decommoditized their products. For example, coffee beans used to be regarded as all the same, and then Juan Valdez and the Colombian Coffee Growers Federation made their "100% Colombian Coffee" special, ensuring that coffee drinkers now know the difference between those beans and everything else.

When a commodity can be differentiated somehow, even if simply by a sticker or logo, there is an opportunity for consumers to identify it as distinct from the rest, and in this case, firms can at least partially extricate their product from a pure-competitive market.

**monopoly**
Occurs when only one firm provides the product or service in a particular industry.

**oligopoly**
Occurs when only a few firms dominate a market.

**price war**
Occurs when two or more firms compete primarily by lowering their prices.

**monopolistic competition**
Occurs when many firms sell closely related but not homogeneous products; these products may be viewed as substitutes but are not perfect substitutes.

**pure competition**
Occurs when different companies sell commodity products that consumers perceive as substitutable; price usually is set according to the laws of supply and demand.

## Channel Members

Channel members—manufacturers, wholesalers, and retailers—can have different perspectives when it comes to pricing strategies. Consider a manufacturer that is focused on increasing the image and reputation of its brand but working with a retailer that is primarily concerned with increasing its sales. The manufacturer may desire to keep prices higher to convey a better image, whereas the retailer wants lower prices and will accept lower profits to move the product, regardless of consumers' impressions of the brand. Unless channel members carefully communicate their pricing goals and select channel partners that agree with them, conflict will surely arise.

TV sets and other consumer electronics are commonly sold in the grey market.

Vladislav Kochelaevskiy/Shutterstock

**grey market**
Employs irregular but not necessarily illegal methods; generally, it legally circumvents authorized channels of distribution to sell goods at prices lower than those intended by the manufacturer.

Channels can be very difficult to manage, and distribution outside normal channels does occur. A **grey market**, for example, employs irregular but not necessarily illegal methods; generally, it legally circumvents authorized channels of distribution to sell goods at prices lower than those intended by the manufacturer.[27] Many manufacturers of consumer electronics therefore require retailers to sign an agreement that demands certain activities (and prohibits others) before they may become authorized dealers. But if a retailer has too many high-definition TVs in stock, it may sell them at just above its own cost to an unauthorized discount dealer. This move places the merchandise on the street at prices far below what authorized dealers can charge, and in the long term, it may tarnish the image of the manufacturer if the discount dealer fails to provide sufficient return policies, support, service, and so forth.

To discourage this type of grey market distribution, some manufacturers have resorted to large disclaimers on their websites, packaging, and other communications to warn consumers that the manufacturer's product warranty becomes null and void unless the item has been purchased from an authorized dealer.

## L02  CONSIDERATIONS FOR SETTING PRICES

Coming up with the "right" price is never easy. If the Apple Watch had been priced at a low point initially, how might it have affected future sales? Firms embrace different objectives, face different market conditions, and operate in different ways; thus, they employ unique pricing strategies that seem best for the particular set of circumstances in which they find themselves. Even a single firm needs different strategies across its products and services and over time as market conditions change. The choice of a pricing strategy is specific to the product/service and target market. Although firms tend to rely on similar strategies when they can, each product or service requires its own specific strategy because no two are ever exactly the same in terms of the marketing mix. In this section, we discuss three different approaches to developing pricing strategies: cost-based methods, competitor-based methods, and value-based methods.

## PRICING METHODS

### Cost-Based Methods

**cost-based pricing method**
Determines the final price to charge by starting with the cost, without recognizing the role that consumers or competitors' prices play in the marketplace.

As its name implies, a **cost-based pricing method** determines the final price to charge by starting with the cost. Cost-based methods do not recognize the role that consumers or competitors' prices play in the marketplace. Although relatively simple compared with other methods used to set prices, cost-based pricing requires that all costs can be identified and calculated on a per-unit basis. Moreover, the process assumes that these costs will not vary much for different levels of production. If they do, the price might need to be raised or lowered according to the production level. Thus, with cost-based pricing, prices are usually set on the basis of estimates of average costs.

## Competitor-Based Methods

Most firms know that consumers compare the prices of their products with the different product/price combinations competitors offer. Thus, using a **competitor-based pricing method**, they may set their prices to reflect the way they want consumers to interpret their own prices relative to the competitors' offerings. Setting prices at the same level as or very close to a competitor's price signals to consumers that the product is similar, whereas setting prices much higher signals greater features, better quality, or some other valued benefit. When McDonald's offers free coffee promotions, it forces rivals such as Tim Hortons® to reduce prices and accept lower profits. This was a strategic price promotion for McDonald's, since it helped double its market share to 11.5 percent of the out-of-home coffee market.[28] In a bid to win customers and return to profit, Sears announced it would match competitors' lowest prices on appliances and mattresses. This means changing prices in its stores on a daily basis.[29]

> **competitor-based pricing method**
> An approach that attempts to reflect how the firm wants consumers to interpret its products relative to the competitors' offerings.

## Value-Based Methods

A **value-based pricing method** is an approach to setting prices that focuses on the overall value of the product offering as perceived by the consumer. Consumers determine value by comparing the benefits they expect the product to deliver with the sacrifice they will need to make to acquire the product. Of course, different consumers perceive value differently. When Vancouver band Wintermitts went on tour, it offered CDs for sale at $10. In an attempt to encourage fans to access the band's music digitally, download cards were priced at $5. To band members' surprise, they sold out of CDs and sold only half as many download cards as expected.[30] As noted in Sustainable Marketing 11.1, Walmart is known for low prices and is now aiming to be seen as a sustainability leader as well. So how does a manager use value-based pricing methods? We consider two key approaches.

> **value-based pricing method**
> Focuses on the overall value of the product offering as perceived by consumers, who determine value by comparing the benefits they expect the product to deliver with the sacrifice they will need to make to acquire the product.

### Sustainable Marketing 11.1

### It Isn't Easy to Sell to Walmart[31]

Walmart is known for its low prices and for driving its vendors nearly to tears to get them. Now it is pressuring its vendors to supply it with environmentally friendly merchandise with labels to prove it. In the future, merchandise sold at Walmart will have the environmental equivalent of nutrition labels, providing information on the product's carbon footprint, the amount of water used and air pollution produced to make it, and other environmental issues. To measure how a vendor's products are doing, it has developed a sustainability index that simultaneously takes several issues into consideration. From this index it developed scorecards to help its buyers further evaluate products.

Walmart required its top 200 factories to become 20 percent more energy efficient by 2012—a feat that many experts believed impossible, even with Walmart's help. Initial results proved promising. For example, Jiangsu Redbud Dyeing Technology in China cut coal consumption by one-tenth and is attempting to cut its toxic emissions to zero. Waste was reduced by 82 percent by the end of 2015 as part of its Zero Waste initiative.[32]

Walmart hasn't always been touted as a good corporate citizen. In the 1990s, it came to light that workers at some factories producing clothing for Walmart were subjected to inhumane conditions. More recently, two governmental organizations accused Walmart of buying from 15 factories that engage in abuse and labour violations, including child labour, 19-hour shifts, and below-subsistence wages.[33]

Some wonder why Walmart is attempting to position itself as the retail industry's sustainability leader. Certainly, initiatives that show it to be a good corporate citizen enhance its image. But it expects this to be good for business as well. Its customers, especially those born after 1980, are increasingly concerned about how the products they use impact the environment and the people who produce them. Also, Walmart believes that many of these initiatives will help streamline supply chain processes and therefore provide additional financial benefits to its suppliers and customers.

Is the improvement value of compact fluorescent lightbulbs sufficiently greater than other types so that a higher price can be charged for them?

© Ozmedia | Dreamstime.com

**improvement value**
Represents an estimate of how much more (or less) consumers are willing to pay for a product relative to other comparable products.

**cost of ownership method**
A value-based method for setting prices that determines the total cost of owning the product over its useful life.

**Improvement Value Method**   With this method, the manager must estimate the improvement value of a new product or service. This **improvement value** represents an estimate of how much more (or less) consumers are willing to pay for a product relative to other comparable products. For example, suppose a major telecommunications company has developed a new cellphone. Using any of a host of research methods, such as consumer surveys, the manager could get customers to assess the new product relative to an existing product and provide an estimate of how much better it is, or its improvement value. Cinemas understand that moviegoers will pay more for improved viewing experiences: about $3 more for 3D and a $7 premium for IMAX. Premium tickets account for 46 percent of box office sales for Cineplex.[34]

**Cost of Ownership Method**   Another value-based method for setting prices determines the total cost of owning the product over its useful life. Using the **cost of ownership method**, consumers may be willing to pay more for a particular product because, over its entire lifetime, it will eventually cost less to own than a cheaper alternative.[35]

Consider, for example, that an energy-efficient fluorescent light bulb costs $3 and is expected to last 6,000 hours. Alternatively, a conventional light bulb costs $1 but its average life is only 1,500 hours. Even though the fluorescent bulb is expected to last four times longer than a conventional bulb, it costs only three times as much. Using the cost of ownership method, and considering the cost per hour, the fluorescent bulb manufacturer could charge $4 for each bulb to give it an equivalent cost to a conventional bulb. However, given its research indicated that many consumers would be reluctant to spend $4 for a bulb, the manufacturer chose to charge only $3, thereby offering customers greater value.

Although value-based pricing strategies can be quite effective, they also necessitate a great deal of consumer research to be implemented successfully. Sellers must know how consumers in different market segments will attach value to the benefits delivered by their products. They also must account for changes in consumer attitudes because the way customers perceive value today may not be the way they perceive it tomorrow.

## PRICING STRATEGIES

Understanding the psychology underlying the way consumers arrive at their perceptions, make judgments, and finally invoke a choice is critical to effective pricing strategies, so marketers must examine some of the more important psychological processes that influence consumers' reactions to and use of price. When consumers see a price, they place it in a category, such as "expensive," "a deal," "cheap," "overpriced," or "fair."

In this section we discuss a number of commonly used pricing strategies—including everyday low pricing (EDLP), high/low pricing, and new product pricing—and also discuss how consumers use reference pricing when making purchase decisions.

### Everyday Low Pricing (EDLP)

**everyday low pricing (EDLP)**
A strategy companies use to emphasize the continuity of their retail prices at a level somewhere between the regular, nonsale price and the deep-discount sale prices their competitors may offer.

With an **everyday low pricing (EDLP)** strategy, companies stress the continuity of their retail prices at a level somewhere between the regular, nonsale price and the deep-discount sale prices their competitors may offer.[36] By reducing consumers' search costs, EDLP adds value; consumers can spend less of their valuable time comparing prices, including sale prices, at different stores. For example, Walmart relies on EDLP to communicate to consumers that, for any given group of frequently purchased items, its prices are lower than those of any other company in that market. This claim does not necessarily mean that every item that consumers may purchase will be priced lower at Walmart than anywhere else—in fact, some competitive retailers will offer lower prices on some items. However, on average, Walmart's prices tend to be lower.

But even this categorization gets more complicated, in that it needs to include quality perceptions as well. Some consumers perceive that stores that use EDLP carry lower quality goods, whereas high/low pricing stores tend to carry better quality items. In part, this perception forms because consumers view the initial price at a high/low store as the reference price. In the end, however, the consumer's decision, once again and as always, comes down to value.

## High/Low Pricing

Alternatively, some retailers prefer a **high/low pricing** strategy, which relies on the promotion of sales, during which prices are temporarily reduced to encourage purchases. In the end, which consumers prefer which strategy depends on how those consumers evaluate prices and quality. Some prefer not to expend the time to find the lowest price and favour EDLP as an efficient way to get low prices. Alternatively, other consumers may relish the challenge of getting the lowest price or be so price sensitive that they are willing to expend the time and effort to seek out the lowest price every time.

**high/low pricing**
A pricing strategy that relies on the promotion of sales, during which prices are temporarily reduced to encourage purchases.

## New Product Pricing

Developing pricing strategies for new products is one of the most challenging tasks a manager can undertake. When the new product is just another "me-too" product, similar to what already appears on the market, this job is somewhat easier because the product's approximate value has already been established. But when the product is truly innovative, or what we call "new to the world," determining consumers' perceptions of its value and pricing it accordingly becomes far more difficult. Let's turn our attention to two distinct pricing strategies for new products: price skimming and market penetration pricing.

**Price Skimming**  In many markets, and particularly for new and innovative products or services, innovators and early adopters (see Chapter 8) are willing to pay a higher price to obtain the new product or service. This strategy, known as **price skimming**, appeals

**price skimming**
A strategy of selling a new product or service at a high price that innovators and early adopters are willing to pay to obtain it; after the high-price market segment becomes saturated and sales begin to slow down, the firm generally lowers the price to capture (or skim) the next most price-sensitive segment.

Price skimming is often used for high demand video games like *Call of Duty* because fans will pay a higher price to be one of the first to own the newest version.

PA Images/Alamy Stock Photo

to these segments of consumers who are willing to pay the premium price to have the innovation first. This tactic is particularly common in technology markets, where sellers know that *Call of Duty* fans will wait in line for hours, desperate to be among the first to own the newest version. These innovators are willing to pay top dollar to get the new product and its exciting enhancements. After this high-price market segment becomes saturated and sales begin to slow down, companies generally lower the price to capture (or skim) the next most price-sensitive market segment, which is willing to pay a somewhat lower price. This process can continue until the demand for the product has been satisfied, even at the lowest price points. Luxury products are often an exception. For example, Louis Vuitton does not lower the price of its bags, but rather keeps prices high to support its prestige image.

For price skimming to work, the product or service must be perceived as breaking new ground in some way, offering consumers new benefits currently unavailable in alternative products. Firms use skimming strategies for a variety of reasons. Some may start by pricing relatively high to signal high quality to the market. Others may decide to price high at first to limit demand, which gives them time to build their production capacities. Similarly, some firms employ a skimming strategy to try to quickly earn back some of the high R&D investments they made for the new product. Finally, firms employ skimming strategies to test consumers' price sensitivity. A firm that prices too high can always lower the price; but, if the price is initially set too low, it is almost impossible to raise it without significant consumer resistance.

For a skimming pricing strategy to be successful, competitors cannot be able to enter the market easily; otherwise, price competition will likely force lower prices and undermine the whole strategy. Competitors might be prevented from entering the market through patent protections, their inability to copy the innovation (because it is complex to manufacture, its raw materials are hard to get, or the product relies on proprietary technology), or the high costs of entry.

Skimming strategies also face a significant potential drawback in the relatively high unit costs often associated with producing small volumes of products. Therefore, firms must consider the trade-off between earning a higher price and suffering higher production costs. Price skimming also can cause discontent for consumers. Those who pay a higher price to purchase the latest iPhone early may feel cheated if the prices drop quickly.

## Market Penetration Pricing

Instead of setting the price high, firms using **market penetration pricing** set the initial price low for the introduction of the new product or service. Their objective is to build sales, market share, and profits quickly. The low market penetration price encourages consumers to purchase the product immediately. With price skimming, profits are generated through margin, whereas with penetration pricing, profits flow through volume. Although it is not always the case, many firms expect the unit cost to drop significantly as the accumulated volume sold increases, an effect known as the **experience curve effect**. With this effect, as sales continue to grow, the costs continue to drop, allowing even further reductions in the price.

In addition to offering the potential to build sales, market share, and profits, penetration pricing discourages competitors from entering the market because the profit margin is relatively low. Furthermore, if the costs to produce the product drop because of the accumulated volume, competitors that enter the market later will face higher unit costs, at least until their volume catches up with the early entrant.

A penetration strategy also has its drawbacks. First, the firm must have the capacity to satisfy a rapid rise in demand—or at least be able to add that capacity quickly. Second, low price does not signal high quality. Of course, a price below their expectations decreases the risk for consumers to purchase the product and test its quality for themselves. Third, firms should avoid a penetration pricing strategy if some segments of the market are willing to pay more for the product; otherwise, the firm is just "leaving money on the table."

**market penetration pricing**
A pricing strategy of setting the initial price low for the introduction of the new product or service, with the objective of building sales, market share, and profits quickly.

**experience curve effect**
Refers to the drop in unit cost as the accumulated volume sold increases; as sales continue to grow, the costs continue to drop, allowing even further reductions in the price.

## Consumers' Use of Reference Pricing

A **reference price** is the price against which buyers compare the actual selling price of the product and that facilitates their evaluation process. The seller labels the reference price as the "regular price" or an "original price." When consumers view the "sale price" and compare it with the provided external reference price, their perceptions of the value of the deal will likely increase.[37] Winners provides external reference prices, in smaller print to reflect how much consumers would have to pay for a comparable product elsewhere. The price of $100.00 is contrasted against the Winners price of only $49.99. Thus, the external reference price suggests to consumers that they are getting a good deal and will save money.

Consumers may also rely on reference prices stored in their memory—perhaps the last price they paid or what they expect to pay. For instance, a consumer seated in a restaurant viewing the price of a large pepperoni pizza as $12 may recall that the price she usually pays for a large pepperoni pizza at another restaurant is only $10 and may judge the menu price as high.

**reference price**
The price against which buyers compare the actual selling price of the product and that facilitates their evaluation process.

Winners shows its price and then compares it to how much the product would cost elsewhere to set a reference price in consumers' minds.
© AKD Photography

# PRICING TACTICS

**L04**

It is important to distinguish clearly between *pricing strategies* and pricing tactics. A pricing strategy is a long-term approach to setting prices broadly in an integrative effort (across all the firm's products) based on the five Cs (company objectives, customers, costs, competition, and channel members) of pricing. **Pricing tactics**, in contrast, offer short-term methods to focus on select components of the five Cs. Generally, a pricing tactic represents either a short-term response to a competitive threat (e.g., lowering price temporarily to meet a competitor's price reduction) or a broadly accepted method of calculating a final price for the customer that is short-term in nature. We separate our discussion of pricing tactics into those aimed at end consumers and those directed at intermediaries in a business-to-business (B2B) setting.

**pricing tactics**
Short-term methods, in contrast to long-term pricing strategies, used to focus on company objectives, customers, costs, competition, or channel members; can be responses to competitive threats (e.g., lowering price temporarily to meet a competitor's price reduction) or broadly accepted methods of calculating a final price for the customer that is short-term in nature.

## Consumer Pricing Tactics

When firms sell their products and services directly to consumers, rather than to other businesses, the pricing tactics they use naturally differ. In this section, we analyze some tactics for products and services aimed directly at consumers: price lining, price bundling, and leader pricing (see Exhibit 11.7).

| **EXHIBIT 11.7** | Pricing Tactics Aimed at Consumers |
| --- | --- |
| **Tactic** | |
| **Price lining** | Establishing a price floor and a price ceiling for an entire line of similar products and then setting price points in between to represent distinct differences in quality. |
| **Price bundling** | Pricing of more than one product for a single, lower price. |
| **Leader pricing** | Building store traffic by aggressively pricing and advertising a regularly purchased item, often priced at or just above the store's cost. |

### Price Lining

**Price Lining**   When marketers establish a price floor and a price ceiling for an entire line of similar products and then set a few other price points in between to represent distinct differences in quality, the tactic is called **price lining**.

Consider the specific price lines used by Moores Clothing for Men. The firm prices its sports jackets at different price points. For example, its house brand, Joseph & Feiss, sells for around $119. Move up to a middle-range price point and you can buy an Alfred Sung jacket for between $159 and $199. At the top end of the line, you can find a pure wool Pronto Uomo sports jacket for $229.

While it may be difficult to determine which is the better jacket, having options at different price points means Moores can satisfy a range of tastes and budgets.

**price lining**
Consumer market pricing tactic of establishing a price floor and a price ceiling for an entire line of similar products and then setting a few other price points in between to represent distinct differences in quality.

### Price Bundling

**Price Bundling**   When you signed up for your high-speed Internet connection, did you also get cable TV and telephone? If so, you probably pay less than if you were to get the three services separately. This practice of selling more than one product for a single, lower price is called **price bundling**. Firms bundle products together to encourage customers to stock up so they won't purchase competing brands, to encourage trial of a new product, or to provide an incentive to purchase a less desirable product or service to obtain a more desirable one in the same bundle.

We present a price bundling example in Exhibit 11.8. Imagine we have four different offerings for sale: home phone line, Internet, satellite TV services, and cellphone. Customers use combinations of these products and services differently, and each customer has unique needs. Subscribing to each service separately is the most expensive option, as shown in the first line. However, if customers bundle together three or more services, they can take advantage of lower prices.

Let's look at how Bell uses price bundling to add value for its customers. For example, a student away at university on a tight budget may elect to subscribe to only the essentials: Internet and a cellphone. Regular price for these items would be $121.95/month. Through its bundled service offering, Bell can entice the student to also sign up for cable TV by reducing the price of the Internet service when the cable TV service is added. The

**price bundling**
Consumer pricing tactic of selling more than one product for a single, lower price than the items would cost sold separately; can be used to sell slow-moving items, to encourage customers to stock up so they won't purchase competing brands, to encourage trial of a new product, or to provide an incentive to purchase a less desirable product or service to obtain a more desirable one in the same bundle.

**EXHIBIT 11.8**   An Illustration of Price Bundling

| | Home Phone Basic | Bell Fibe Internet 25/10 | Bell Fibe TV Good Package | Bell Mobility Voice & Data Plus 60 | Total | Annual Savings |
|---|---|---|---|---|---|---|
| **Regular price** | $42.94 | $69.95 | $53.95 | $70.00 | | |
| **Bundled price** | $38.94 | $65.95 | $46.95 | $67.00 | | |
| **Student example: Internet and cellphone** | | | | | | |
| **Full-price services** | | $69.95 | | $70.00 | $139.95 | |
| **Full price with added service** | | $69.95 | $53.95 | $70.00 | $193.90 | |
| **Bundled services** | | $65.95 | $46.95 | $67.00 | $179.90 | $168.00 |
| **Family example: Home phone, Internet, cable TV, and cellphone** | | | | | | |
| **Full-price services** | $42.94 | $69.95 | | $70.00 | $182.89 | |
| **Full price with added service** | $42.94 | $69.95 | $53.95 | $70.00 | $236.84 | |
| **Bundled services** | $38.94 | $65.95 | $46.95 | $67.00 | $218.84 | $216.00 |

*Sources:* Prices from "Bundle and Save," http://www.bell.ca/Bell-bundles (accessed July 5, 2016).

company benefits from enhancing the relationship with the customer and by collecting additional revenue. While the student's monthly bill will rise slightly to $168.71, he will save $192.00/year from the unbundled service prices and should now be able to enjoy playoff hockey matches while at home!

Similarly, a family could be currently subscribing to home phone, cellphone, and Internet service through Bell for $163.89/month, while obtaining its cable TV service from another provider. Again, by bundling the services, Bell can entice the family to switch its cable TV service to Bell by reducing the price of the other services. Adding the new service increases the monthly fee to $190.65, but the family saves $240.00/year compared to the regular-priced services and will also enjoy the convenience of receiving a single bill each month.

**Leader Pricing**    **Leader pricing** is a tactic that attempts to build store traffic by aggressively pricing and advertising a regularly purchased item, often priced at or just above the store's cost. The rationale behind this tactic is that, while in the store to get the great deal on, say, milk, the consumer will also probably pick up other items he or she needs. The store has priced these items at higher profit margins, so their purchase will more than cover the lower markup on the milk. Imagine the marketing potential of various combinations of products; the store uses leader pricing on cocktail sauce, which gives employees the perfect opportunity to ask, "How about a pound of fresh shrimp to go with the cocktail sauce you're purchasing?"

**leader pricing**
Consumer pricing tactic that attempts to build store traffic by aggressively pricing and advertising a regularly purchased item, often priced at or just above the store's cost.

## Consumer Price Reductions

The final price a customer pays for a product or service often has been adjusted from the original price because marketers have used various techniques designed to enhance value. Some of these techniques include markdowns, quantity discounts, coupons, and rebates.

**Markdowns**    **Markdowns** are the reductions retailers take on the initial selling price of the product or service.[38] An integral component of the high/low pricing strategy we described previously, markdowns enable retailers to get rid of slow-moving or obsolete merchandise, sell seasonal items after the appropriate season, and match competitors' prices on specific merchandise. Retailers must get rid of merchandise that isn't selling because holding on to such items hurts the retailer's image and ties up money in inventory that could be used more productively elsewhere.

Retailers also use markdowns to promote merchandise and increase sales. Particularly when used in conjunction with promotions, markdowns can increase traffic into the store, which many retailers view as half the battle. Once customers are in the store, retailers always hope they will purchase other products at regular prices.

**markdowns**
Reductions retailers take on the initial selling price of the product or service.

**size discount**
The most common implementation of a quantity discount at the consumer level; the larger the quantity bought, the less the cost per unit (e.g., per gram).

**Quantity Discounts for Consumers**    We have already discussed how firms use quantity discounts in the B2B marketplace, but the most common implementation of a quantity discount at the consumer level is the **size discount**. For example, there are three sizes of General Mills' popular cereal Cheerios: 425 gram, 575 gram, and 1.5 kilogram boxes, priced at approximately $4.19, $4.49, and $6.89, respectively. The larger the quantity, the lower the cost per gram, which means the manufacturer is providing a quantity discount. Most grocery stores now post the price per 100 grams on the shelves so consumers can easily compare value for money. The goal of this

Customers get a size discount for buying larger sizes. With Cheerios, the larger the box, the less it costs per gram.
© Mike Hruby

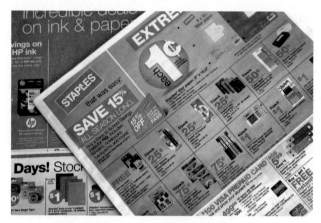

Coupons offer a discount on the price of specific items when they're purchased.

© Mike Hruby

**coupon**

Provides a stated discount to consumers on the final selling price of a specific item; the retailer handles the discount.

**rebate**

A consumer discount in which a portion of the purchase price is returned to the buyer in cash; the manufacturer, not the retailer, issues the refund.

tactic is to encourage consumers to purchase larger quantities each time they buy. In turn, these consumers are less likely to switch brands and often tend to consume more of the product, depending on the product usage characteristics. Typically, buying a larger package of toilet tissue does not mean consumers will use it faster, but buying a larger box of cereal may encourage them to eat more of it or to eat it more often.[39]

**Coupons and Rebates**    Coupons and rebates both provide discounts to consumers on the final selling price. However, for the **coupon**, the retailer handles the discount, whereas the manufacturer issues the refund in the case of the **rebate**, which is defined as a portion of the purchase price returned to the buyer in the form of cash.

The goal of coupons is to prompt consumers to try a product, reward loyal customers, or encourage repurchases. By saving the consumer money, firms add value to their products. Whereas a coupon provides instant savings when presented, a rebate promises savings, usually mailed to the consumer at some later date. The "hassle factor" for rebates is higher than for coupons; the consumer must first buy the item during a specified time period, then mail in the required documentation—which usually includes the original sales receipt—and finally wait four to six weeks (or more!) for a cheque to arrive. Although consumers may believe this process adds value when the potential rebate is $50, they might question whether a rebate for a couple of dollars is worth their time and effort. From the marketer's viewpoint, however, rebates offer greater control than coupons and provide valuable customer information. Coupons and rebates are considered to be sales promotion tools as well as pricing tactics, so you'll read more about them in Chapter 15.

## Business-to-Business Pricing Tactics

The pricing tactics employed in B2B settings differ significantly from those used in consumer markets. Among the most prominent are seasonal and cash discounts, allowances, quantity discounts, and uniform delivered versus geographic pricing (see Exhibit 11.9).

**EXHIBIT 11.9**  |  **B2B Pricing Tactics**

| Tactic | |
|---|---|
| **Seasonal discounts** | An additional reduction offered as an incentive to retailers to order merchandise in advance of the normal buying season. |
| **Cash discounts** | An additional reduction that reduces the invoice cost if the buyer pays the invoice prior to the end of the discount period. |
| **Allowances** | Advertising or listing allowances (additional price reductions) offered in return for specific behaviours. *Advertising allowances* are offered to retailers if they agree to feature the manufacturer's product in their advertising and promotional efforts. *Listing allowances* are offered to get new products into stores or to gain more or better shelf space. |
| **Quantity discounts** | Providing a reduced price according to the amount purchased. |
| **Uniform delivered versus geographic pricing** | With *uniform delivered* pricing, the shipper charges one rate, no matter where the buyer is located. With *geographic pricing*, different prices are charged depending on the geographical delivery area. |

Seasonal Discounts    A **seasonal discount** is an additional reduction offered as an incentive to retailers to order merchandise in advance of the normal buying season. For instance, Lennox may offer its air conditioning dealers an additional seasonal discount if they place their orders and receive delivery before April 1, prior to the warm months when air conditioner sales are highest. If it can ship earlier in the season, Lennox can plan its production schedules more easily and lessen its finished goods inventory. Its dealers, however, must weigh the benefits of a larger profit because of the discount versus the extra cost of carrying the inventory for a longer period of time.

Cash Discounts    A **cash discount** reduces the invoice cost if the buyer pays the invoice prior to the end of the discount period. Typically, it is expressed in the form of a percentage, such as "3/10, n/30," or "3 percent, 10 days, net 30," all of which means the buyer can take a 3 percent discount on the total amount of the invoice if the bill is paid within 10 days of the invoice date; otherwise, the full, or net, amount is due within 30 days. Why do B2B sellers offer cash discounts to customers? By encouraging early payment, they benefit from the time value of money. Getting money earlier rather than later enables the firm to either invest the money to earn a return on it or to avoid borrowing money and paying interest on it. In both instances, the firm is better off financially.

Allowances    Another pricing tactic that lowers the final cost to channel members is allowances, such as advertising or listing allowances, offered in return for specific behaviours. An **advertising allowance** offers a price reduction to channel members if they agree to feature the manufacturer's product in their advertising and promotional efforts. **Listing allowances** are fees paid to retailers simply to get new products into stores or to gain more or better shelf space for their products. Some argue that listing allowances are unethical because they put small manufacturers that cannot readily afford allowances at a competitive disadvantage. Demanding large listing allowances could be considered a form of bribery—that is, paying off the retailer to get preferential treatment.

Quantity Discounts    A **quantity discount** provides a reduced price according to the amount purchased. The more the buyer purchases, the higher the discount and, of course, the greater the value.

A **cumulative quantity discount** uses the amount purchased over a specified time period and usually involves several transactions. This type of discount encourages resellers to maintain their current supplier because the cost to switch must include the loss of the discount. For example, automobile dealers often attempt to meet a quota or a sales goal for a specific period, such as a quarter or a year. If they meet their quotas, they earn discounts on all the cars they purchased from the manufacturer during that period in the form of a rebate cheque. For this very reason, you will often find good deals on cars at the end of a quarter or fiscal year. If the dealership can just sell a few more cars to meet its quota, the rebate earned can be substantial, so taking a few hundred dollars less on those last few cars is well worth the opportunity to receive a rebate worth many times the amount of the losses.

A **noncumulative quantity discount**, though still a quantity discount, is based only on the amount purchased in a single order. Therefore, it provides the buyer with an incentive to purchase more merchandise immediately. Such larger, less frequent orders can save manufacturers order processing, sales, and transportation expenses. For example, a jeans store might get a 40 percent discount off the manufacturer's suggested retail price for placing a $500 order; a 50 percent discount for an order of $501 to $4,999; and a 60 percent discount for an order greater than $5,000.

Uniform Delivered Versus Geographic Pricing    These pricing tactics are specific to shipping, which represents a major cost for many manufacturers. With a **uniform delivered pricing** tactic, the shipper charges one rate, no matter where the buyer is

**seasonal discount**
Pricing tactic of offering an additional reduction as an incentive to retailers to order merchandise in advance of the normal buying season.

**cash discount**
Tactic of offering a reduction in the invoice cost if the buyer pays the invoice prior to the end of the discount period.

**advertising allowance**
Tactic of offering a price reduction to channel members if they agree to feature the manufacturer's product in their advertising and promotional efforts.

**listing allowances**
Fees paid to retailers simply to get new products into stores or to gain more or better shelf space for their products.

**quantity discount**
Pricing tactic of offering a reduced price according to the amount purchased; the more the buyer purchases, the higher the discount and, of course, the greater the value.

**cumulative quantity discount**
Pricing tactic that offers a discount based on the amount purchased over a specified period and usually involves several transactions.

**noncumulative quantity discount**
Pricing tactic that offers a discount based on only the amount purchased in a single order.

**uniform delivered pricing**
The shipper charges one rate, no matter where the buyer is located.

geographic pricing
The setting of different prices depending on a geographical division of the delivery areas.

located, which makes things very simple for both the seller and the buyer. **Geographic pricing**, however, sets different prices depending on a geographical division of the delivery areas. For example, a manufacturer based in Montreal might divide Canada into five different zones and use different shipping rates for each zone to reflect the average shipping cost for customers located therein. This way, each customer in a zone is charged the same cost for shipping. Geographic pricing can be advantageous to the shipper because it reflects the actual shipping charges more closely than uniform delivered pricing can.

With so many different pricing strategies and tactics, it is no wonder that unscrupulous firms find ample opportunity to engage in pricing practices that can hurt consumers. We now take a look at some of the legal and ethical implications of pricing.

## L05 LEGAL AND ETHICAL ASPECTS OF PRICING

Prices tend to fluctuate naturally and respond to varying market conditions. Though we rarely see firms attempting to control the market in terms of product quality or advertising, they often engage in pricing practices that can unfairly reduce competition or harm consumers directly through fraud and deception. A host of laws and regulations at the federal, provincial, and municipal levels attempt to prevent unfair pricing practices, but some are poorly enforced, and others are difficult to prove.

### Deceptive or Illegal Price Advertising

Although it is always illegal and unethical to lie in advertising, a certain amount of "puffery" is typically allowed (see Chapter 15). But price advertisements should never deceive consumers to the point of causing harm. For example, a local car dealer's advertising that it had the "best deals in town" would likely be considered puffery. In contrast, advertising "the lowest prices, guaranteed" makes a very specific claim and, if not true, can be considered deceptive.

**Deceptive Reference Prices** Previously, we introduced reference prices, which create reference points for the buyer against which to compare the selling price. If the reference price is bona fide, the advertisement is informative. If the reference price has been inflated or is just plain fictitious, however, the advertisement is deceptive and may cause harm to consumers. The Competition Bureau is investigating Sears and Hudson's Bay Company regarding deceptive mattress pricing. Both stores advertised certain mattresses and sets as being on sale. Yet, since they were never offered at a higher "regular" price for any length of time, consumers are not getting a genuine discount.[40] But it is not easy to determine whether a reference price is bona fide. If an advertisement specifies a "regular price," what qualifies as regular? How many units must the store sell at this price for it to be a bona fide regular price? Finally, what if the store offers the item for sale at the regular price but customers do not buy any? Can it still be considered a regular price? The Competition Bureau determines the regular price by using one of two tests: a volume test, which demonstrated that a substantial quantity of products were sold at the price noted or higher; and a time test, which necessitates products being sold at the regular price for a substantial period of time.[41] The Better Business Bureau suggests that if a seller is going to label a price as a regular price, at least 50 percent of the sales have occurred at that price.

Is this a legitimate sale or is the retailer using deceptive reference prices?

© Tom Prettyman/PhotoEdit

**Loss Leader Pricing** As we discussed previously, leader pricing is a legitimate attempt to build store traffic by pricing a regularly purchased item aggressively but still above the store's cost. **Loss leader pricing** takes this tactic one step further by lowering the price below the store's cost. No doubt you have seen "buy one, get one free" offers at grocery and discount stores. Unless the markup for the item is 100 percent of the cost, these sales obviously do not generate enough revenue from the sale of one unit to cover the store's cost, which means it has essentially priced the total for both items below cost.

**loss leader pricing**
Loss leader pricing takes the tactic of leader pricing one step further by lowering the price below the store's cost.

Bait and Switch    Another form of deceptive price advertising occurs when sellers advertise items for a very low price without the intent to really sell any. This **bait and switch** tactic is a deceptive practice because the store lures customers in with a very low price on an item (the bait), only to aggressively pressure these customers into purchasing a higher-priced item (the switch) by disparaging the low-priced item, comparing it unfavourably with the higher-priced model, or professing an inadequate supply of the lower-priced item. Again, the laws against bait and switch practices are difficult to enforce because salespeople, simply as a function of their jobs, are always trying to get customers to trade up to a higher-priced model without necessarily deliberately baiting them. The key to proving deception centres on the intent of the seller, which is also difficult to prove.

**bait and switch**
A deceptive practice of luring customers into the store with a very low advertised price on an item (the bait), only to aggressively pressure them into purchasing a higher-priced item (the switch) by disparaging the low-priced item, comparing it unfavourably with the higher-priced model, or professing an inadequate supply of the lower-priced item.

## Predatory Pricing

When a firm sets a very low price for one or more of its products with the intent to drive its competition out of business, it is using **predatory pricing**. Predatory pricing is illegal under the Competition Act because it constrains free trade and represents a form of unfair competition. It also tends to promote a concentrated market with a few dominant firms (an oligopoly). But again, predation is difficult to prove. First, one must demonstrate intent—that is, that the firm intended to drive out its competition or prevent competitors from entering the market. Second, the complainant must prove that the firm charged prices lower than its average cost, an equally difficult task.

**predatory pricing**
A firm's practice of setting a very low price for one or more of its products with the intent of driving its competition out of business; illegal under the Competition Act.

The issue of predatory pricing has arisen because of Google's dominance in the search engine market. Advertisers on Google bid on specific keywords; if they win the auction, their product appears first in the paid results section on the search engine. However, Google also includes a "quality handicap" and charges poor quality advertisers more. It claims this tactic ensures that users are more likely to find high-quality results from their searches. The algorithm it uses to define quality is confidential, but some experts allege that Google has manipulated the paid search results in such a way that it undermines competitors' offerings while promoting its own. It appears these claims may be true; in 2012 the Federal Trade Commission (FTC) found enough evidence for search results manipulation that it recommended the government sue Google, and in 2013 a European Commission came to similar conclusions.[42] In 2015, Google formally rejected all charges and even argued that its search engine practices facilitate competition.[43] The Commission is still investigating whether Google's dominance in the search engine market, with its resulting ability to control prices, and its practice of charging more for its "quality handicap" should be deemed predatory.

## Price Discrimination

There are many forms of price discrimination, but only some of them are considered illegal under the Competition Act. When firms sell the same product to different resellers (wholesalers, distributors, or retailers) at different prices, it can be considered **price discrimination**; usually, larger firms receive lower prices.

We have already discussed the use of quantity discounts, which is a legitimate method of charging different prices to different customers on the basis of the quantity they purchase. The legality of this tactic stems from the assumption that it costs less to sell and service 1,000 units to one customer than 100 units to 10 customers. But

**price discrimination**
The practice of selling the same product to different resellers (wholesalers, distributors, or retailers) or to the ultimate consumer at different prices; some, but not all, forms of price discrimination are illegal.

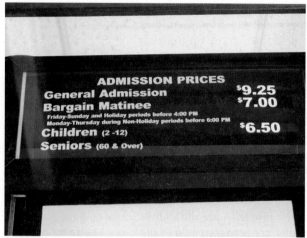

ADMISSION PRICES
General Admission                          $9.25
Bargain Matinee                            $7.00
Friday-Sunday and Holiday periods before 4:00 PM
Monday-Thursday during Non-Holiday periods before 6:00 PM
Children (2 -12)                           $6.50
Seniors (60 & Over)

Is this price discrimination illegal?

© Tom Prettyman/PhotoEdit

**price fixing**

The practice of colluding with other firms to control prices.

**horizontal price fixing**

Occurs when competitors that produce and sell competing products collude, or work together, to control prices, effectively taking price out of the decision process for consumers.

**vertical price fixing**

Occurs when parties at different levels of the same marketing channel (e.g., manufacturers and retailers) collude to control the prices passed on to consumers.

**manufacturer's suggested retail price (MSRP)**

Manufacturers encourage retailers to sell their merchandise at a specific price.

quantity discounts must be available to all customers and not be structured in such a way that they consistently and obviously favour one or a few buyers over others. Still, some marketers have found ways to get around these rules, for example, by offering "preferred member" pricing. The Competition Act requires companies to demonstrate only that their price discounts do not restrict competition. While quantity discounts may be a grey area, it is perfectly legitimate to charge a different price to a reseller if the firm is attempting to meet a specific competitor's price. In addition, a barter agreement, in which buyers and sellers negotiate a mutually agreed upon price, is commonplace and absolutely legal in retail settings such as car sales and collectibles markets.

## Price Fixing

**Price fixing** is the practice of colluding with other firms to control prices. Tate & Lyle, which makes Splenda, a low-calorie sweetener, agreed to pay $650,000 to settle a lawsuit in British Columbia that accused sugar substitute companies of conspiring to fix prices in the 1980s and 1990s.[44] More recently, the former head of Nestlé Canada and two other executives were criminally charged with price fixing after a six-year investigation by the Competition Bureau. Charges were also laid against Cadbury Adams Canada, Mars Canada, and Hershey Canada for colluding with Nestlé to raise prices of chocolate products. You will read more about this in Ethical Dilemma 11.1. Penalties for price fixing include fines of up to $10 million and up to five years in prison.[45] The four companies denied the allegations yet agreed to pay $23.2 million to settle the lawsuit.[46]

This particular case of price fixing is especially interesting because it includes both horizontal and vertical price fixing. **Horizontal price fixing** occurs when competitors that produce and sell competing products collude, or work together, to control prices, effectively taking price out of the decision process for consumers. This practice clearly reduces competition and is illegal. The major tobacco companies also have been accused of colluding to fix the prices of cigarettes worldwide.[47] As a general rule of thumb, competing firms should refrain from discussing prices or terms and conditions of sale with competitors. If firms want to know competitors' prices, they can look at a competitor's advertisements, its websites, or its stores.

**Vertical price fixing** occurs when parties at different levels of the same marketing channel (e.g., manufacturers and retailers) collude to control the prices passed on to consumers. Manufacturers often encourage retailers to sell their merchandise at a specific price, known as the **manufacturer's suggested retail price (MSRP)**. Manufacturers set MSRPs to reduce retail price competition among retailers, stimulate retailers to provide complementary services, and support the manufacturer's merchandise. Manufacturers enforce MSRPs by withholding benefits such as cooperative advertising or even refusing to deliver merchandise to noncomplying retailers.

As mentioned earlier, and as you will read in Ethical Dilemma 11.1, Canada's Competition Bureau charged several well known candy producers for engaging in both types of price fixing.

As these legal issues clearly demonstrate, pricing decisions involve many ethical considerations. In determining both their pricing strategies and their pricing tactics, marketers must always balance their goal of inducing customers (through price) to find value, and their need to deal honestly and fairly with those same customers. Whether another business or an individual consumer, buyers can be influenced by a variety of pricing methods; it is up to marketers to determine which of these methods works best for the seller, the buyer, and the community.

## Ethical Dilemma 11.1

### Getting Your Chocolate Fix Might Get More Expensive

Mars, maker of Snickers, and its competitor, Nestlé, have been accused of collaborating with independent wholesalers to bump up the prices of their chocolates to a fixed level.

© McGraw-Hill/Mark Dierker

According to Canada's official Competition Bureau, long-time rivals Mars (maker of such candies as M&M's, Snickers, and the Dove line of chocolates) and Nestlé (which produces Butterfinger and Crunch candies, among others) have collaborated with various independent wholesalers to bump up the prices of their chocolates to a fixed level.

In addition to the corporations themselves, the executives in charge of Nestlé Canada, Mars Canada, and ITWAL (a wholesale distributor) have been named individually in the prosecution. All of the firms denied the allegations yet agreed to pay $23.2 million to avoid "the expense,

inconvenience and distraction" of ongoing litigation.[48]

Although Hershey's Canadian arm was initially included as another co-conspirator in the scheme, its cooperation with authorities has allowed it to avoid direct prosecution. Even as it admits engaging in price fixing, Hershey's claims that the events in question occurred under previous management, and that all such ethical issues have since been resolved. John Pacman, Canada's interim commissioner of competition, appeared confident in the case, noting that "Price-fixing is a serious criminal offence and today's charges demonstrate the Competition Bureau's resolve to stop cartel activity in Canada."

Two years later, the Crown stayed the charges, abandoning the case because it believed there was no reasonable prospect of conviction.[49]

## LEARNING OBJECTIVES REVIEW

 **Explain what price is and its importance in establishing value in marketing**

Price is the only element of the marketing mix that generates revenues. It is also half the value equation. Although costs and other factors should be taken into consideration when setting prices, the most important factor is how the customer views the price in relationship to what he or she receives.

 **Illustrate how the five Cs—company objectives, customers, costs, competition, and channel members—influence pricing decisions**

Successful pricing strategies are built on the five Cs— company objectives, customers, costs, competition, and channel members. (1) Company goals and objectives set the framework for pricing strategies. Companies focusing on image set high prices, while those that focus on value tend to use everyday low prices. (2) Understanding customers' reactions to different prices helps marketers set prices that are consistent with their customers' attitudes and preferences. The demand curve and price elasticity of demand are two related tools that marketers use to gauge customers' sensitivity to price changes. Customers' income and the availability of

substitute products also influence customers' reaction to price changes. (3) Costs are a major determinant of pricing. Cost of producing a good helps marketers determine the possible prices they can charge and the levels of profitability they can expect. Break-even analysis is a helpful tool that is used to help marketers determine the price level at which the number of units sold exactly covers the cost of producing the good. (4) Competition influences pricing because a firm usually pays close attention and reacts to a competitor's moves. Intense competition may produce price wars. The level of competition is usually determined by the market structure of the industry; that is, whether the industry structure features a monopoly, an oligopoly, monopolistic competition, or pure competition. (5) Channel members—manufacturers, wholesalers, and retailers—influence prices because they play a key role in getting the product to the final consumer, and they are independent and usually have their own objectives and competitive situation to deal with. The company may want to set a certain price level for its products in order to reflect quality and value, but retailers may decide they want to move more volume and so reduce the price, hence the possibility for conflict. Also, manufacturers may give discounts to channel members, which may influence the price the ultimate consumer pays.

**LO3** Understand the considerations for setting prices; three pricing methods (e.g., cost-based methods, competitor-based methods, and value-based methods); and various strategies (e.g., EDLP, high/low, and new product pricing) used in marketing

The various methods of setting prices have their own sets of advantages and disadvantages. The fixed percentage and markup approaches are quick and easy but fail to reflect the competitive environment or consumer demand. Although it is always advisable to be aware of what competitors are doing, using competitor-based pricing should not occur in isolation without considering consumers' reactions. Taking a value-based approach to pricing, whether the improvement value or the total cost of ownership, in conjunction with these other methods provides a nicely balanced method of setting prices.

Companies tend to use different pricing strategies for different products or different markets. Pricing strategies are a long-term approach to pricing products. The various pricing methods can be grouped into three broad categories: cost-based, competitor-based, and value-based. Cost-based methods are based on the firm ascertaining the cost of producing and marketing the product, and then adding some markup for profit. Competitor-based pricing is based on a firm understanding what competitors are doing and reacting accordingly. Firms may choose to set prices below, at, or above competitors' prices. Value-based pricing is based on a firm understanding consumers' perceptions of value as reflected in the price of the product (e.g., cheap, expensive, bargain). Consumers' assessments of value may be influenced by their reference prices of similar products or may use marketers' prices to infer a price–quality relationship. Marketers often use price skimming or penetration pricing when they introduce new products in the marketplace based on the nature of the product and their marketing goals; for example, whether they want to gain market share, show price leadership, or signal innovation.

**LO4** Identify pricing tactics targeted to channel members and consumers

Pricing tactics focus more on the short-term aspects of the five Cs of pricing. Companies may use a wide variety of pricing tactics from two categories: (1) pricing tactics aimed at consumers, and (2) business-to-business pricing tactics and discounts. Pricing tactics aimed at consumers include price lining, price bundling, leader pricing, markdowns, quantity discounts, and coupons and rebates. B2B pricing tactics and discounts usually include seasonal discounts, cash discounts, allowances, quantity discounts, and uniform delivered or geographic pricing.

**LO5** Summarize the legal and ethical issues involved in pricing

There are almost as many ways to get into trouble by setting or changing a price as there are pricing strategies and tactics. Three of the most common legal issues pertain to advertising deceptive prices. (1) Deceptive reference prices: If a firm compares a reduced price with a "regular" or reference price, it must actually have sold that product or service at the regular price. (2) Loss leader pricing: Advertising the sale of products priced below the retailer's cost constitutes an unfair competitive practice. (3) Bait and switch advertising constitutes an unfair competitive practice. Predatory pricing, or setting a very low price in order to drive the competition out of business, is illegal. Charging different prices to different customers is sometimes, but not always, illegal, whereas any collusion among firms to fix prices is always illegal.

## KEY TERMS

- advertising allowance
- bait and switch
- break-even point
- cash discount
- competitive parity
- competitor-based pricing method
- competitor orientation
- complementary products
- contribution per unit
- cost-based pricing method
- cost of ownership method
- coupon
- cross-price elasticity
- cumulative quantity discount
- customer orientation
- demand curve

- elastic
- everyday low pricing (EDLP)
- experience curve effect
- fixed costs
- geographic pricing
- grey market
- high/low pricing
- horizontal price fixing
- improvement value
- income effect
- inelastic
- leader pricing
- listing allowances
- loss leader pricing
- manufacturer's suggested retail price (MSRP)

- markdowns
- market penetration pricing
- maximizing profits strategy
- monopolistic competition
- monopoly
- noncumulative quantity discount
- oligopoly
- predatory pricing
- prestige products or services
- price bundling
- price discrimination
- price elasticity of demand
- price fixing
- price lining
- price skimming
- price war

- pricing tactics
- profit orientation
- pure competition
- quantity discount
- rebate
- reference price

- sales orientation
- seasonal discount
- size discount
- substitute products
- substitution effect
- target profit pricing

- target return pricing
- total cost
- uniform delivered pricing
- value-based pricing method
- variable costs
- vertical price fixing

## CONCEPT REVIEW

1. Explain the importance of pricing in the marketing mix from the perspective of the firm and the consumer.

2. List the five Cs of pricing. Which one do you consider to be the most important and why?

3. Explain how companies try to determine consumers' sensitivity to price changes. What factors influence their price sensitivity?

4. Why is it important for firms to determine costs when setting prices?

5. Why does a company need to understand a product's break-even point?

6. How has the Internet changed the way some people use price to make purchasing decisions?

7. What is the major difference between pricing strategies and pricing tactics? Give three examples of each.

8. Explain how psychological factors may influence a firm's pricing strategy.

9. In what conditions should a price skimming strategy be used? When is it appropriate to use a market penetration strategy?

10. Explain the four types of illegal or unethical pricing practices.

## MARKETING APPLICATIONS

1. You and your two roommates are starting a pet grooming service to help put yourself through university. There are two other well established pet services in your area. Should you set your price higher or lower than that of the competition? Justify your answer.

2. One roommate believes the most important objective in setting prices for the new pet grooming business is to generate a large profit, while keeping an eye on your competitors' prices; the other roommate believes it is important to maximize sales and set prices according to what your customers expect to pay. Who is right and why?

3. Assume you have decided to buy an advertisement in the local newspaper to publicize your new pet grooming service. The cost of the ad is $1000. You have decided to charge $40 for a dog grooming, and you want to make $20 on each dog. How many dogs do you have to groom to break even on the cost of the ad? What is your break-even point if you charge $50 per dog?

4. On your weekly grocery shopping trip, you notice that the price of ground beef has gone up 50 cents a kilogram. How will this price increase affect the demand for ground beef, ground turkey, and hamburger buns? Explain your answer in terms of the price elasticity of demand.

5. Zinc Energy Resources Co., a new division of a major battery manufacturing company, recently patented a new battery that uses zinc-air technology. The unit costs for the zinc-air battery are as follows: battery housing, $8; materials $6; and direct labour, $6 per unit. Retooling the existing factory facilities to manufacture the zinc-air batteries amounts to an additional $1 million in equipment costs. Annual fixed costs include sales, marketing, and advertising expenses of $1 million; general and administrative expenses of $1 million; and other fixed costs totalling $2 million.

    a. What is the total per-unit variable cost associated with the new battery?

    b. What are the total fixed costs for the new battery?

    c. If the price for the new battery was set at $35, what would the break-even point be?

6. How do pricing strategies vary across markets that are characterized by monopoly, oligopoly, monopolistic competition, and pure competition?

7. Many firms operating over the Internet have been experimenting with charging different consumers different prices for the same product or service; this practice is legal. Since stores in different parts of the country might have different prices, some websites require postal code information before providing prices. Why would retailers charge different prices in different markets or postal codes? Is it ethical for retailers to do so? Is it a good business practice?

8. As the product manager for Whirlpool's line of washing machines, you are in charge of pricing new products. Your product team has developed a revolutionary new washing machine that relies on radically new technology and requires very little water to get clothes clean. This technology will likely be difficult for your competition to copy. Should you adopt a skimming or a penetration pricing strategy? Justify your answer.

9. Coupons and rebates benefit different channel members. Which would you prefer if you were a manufacturer, a retailer, or a consumer? Why?

10. Imagine that you are the newly hired brand manager for a restaurant that is about to open. Both the local newspaper and a gourmet food magazine recently ran articles about your new head chef, calling her one of the best young chefs in the country. In response to these positive reviews, the company wants to position its brand as a premium, gourmet restaurant. Your boss asks what price you should charge for the chef's signature filet mignon dish. Other restaurants in the area charge around $40 for their own filet offerings. What steps might you take to determine what the new price should be?

## NET SAVVY

1. Several different pricing models can be found on the Internet. Each model appeals to different customer groups. Go to http://www.ebay.com and try to buy this book. What pricing options and prices are available? Do you believe that everyone will choose the least expensive option? Why or why not? Now go to http://www.amazon.ca. Is there more than one price available for this book? If so, what are those prices? If you had to buy another copy of this book, where would you buy it, and why would you buy it there?

2. Prices can vary depending on the market being served. Because Dell sells its computers directly to consumers all around the world, the Dell website makes it easy to compare prices for various markets. Go to http://www.dell.com. Begin on the Dell Canada site and determine the price of an All-in-One 3000 series desktop computer. Next go to the Dell U.K. website and another country of your choice to find the price of the same computer. (If you need to convert currency, go to http://www.xe.com.) How does the price of the desktop computer vary? What would account for these differences in price?

## CHAPTER CASE STUDY

### PLANET FITNESS PRICING FOR SUCCESS[50]

How does going completely against the grain of a typical fitness club strategy lead to success? That's the question that Planet Fitness appears uniquely positioned to answer. Most health clubs provide members with vast and seemingly valuable extra amenities, such as child care, juice bars and protein supplements, on-staff professional trainers, and a broad range of fitness classes.[51] But many customers find the prices too high because they see little value in some of these amenities. Further reducing the value of traditional gym memberships, many consumers regard the social aspects unpleasant and off-putting—whether that means observing others with nearly perfect bodies posturing in the mirror or listening to grunting exercisers huff with every lift.

While its competitors target upscale fitness buffs working on their six-pack abs, Planet Fitness successfully pursues an entirely different market: those who do not really enjoy going to the gym but know they need to do so to stay healthy. These exercisers are unlikely to hit the gym five or six times a week, making conventional gym memberships, which demand yearly contracts and fees of $49 to $95 per month, appear more expensive on a per-visit basis. Planet Fitness's formula is different: At $10 a month, the membership offers good value, even if customers get to the club only a couple of times each week.[52]

In combination with its low price point, Planet Fitness promises a clean, friendly, laid-back workout environment featuring brand-name cardiovascular and strength equipment. Although it does not have the high-end amenities its competitors promise (e.g., pools, juice bars), the club maintains the key elements its members want: brand-name equipment, unlimited fitness training, flat-screen televisions, and large locker rooms. Its customers know from its advertising that they can expect a non-intimidating workout environment, or as Planet Fitness promises, "No gymtimidation. No lunks. Just $10 a month."[53] With its foundation in the idea that simple is better,[54] Planet Fitness has become the fastest-growing full-sized fitness club in the United States.

For those who want a little more, Planet Fitness also offers a premium PF BlackCard membership for $19.99 a month, which promises access to nearly all the clubs in the Planet Fitness chain, unlimited guest privileges, use of tanning and massage chairs, and half-priced drinks.[55]

In addition to these in-club benefits, Planet Fitness's growth has been reinforced by its effective location strategy and marketing efforts that focus on attracting new customers. The low-cost monthly membership makes it easy to draw new members. Because most members come in only a couple of times each week, Planet Fitness also enjoys operating efficiencies and economies of scale, achieved by welcoming a high volume of members on any one day.[56]

Planet Fitness treats customers like real people. What kind of fitness club offers members pizza on the first Monday of every month, bagels on the first Tuesday, and Tootsie Rolls on a regular basis?[57] The kind of gym that had over 1,050 locations in 2015,[58] with an eventual goal of more than 2,000, and that attracts more than 5 million members and has systemwide sales approaching $700 million.[59]

## Questions

1. What benefits do customers receive in return for the sacrifice they make when buying a membership at Planet Fitness?

2. How does this benefit–sacrifice ratio give Planet Fitness a competitive advantage in its industry?

3. Given its price strategy, why is it essential for Planet Fitness to continually attract new members? Do its high-end pricing competitors face the same need? Why or why not?

# CHAPTER 12

Bloomberg/Getty Images

## LEARNING OBJECTIVES

**After studying this chapter you should be able to**

**LO1** Explain the importance of distributi[on] and the interrelationships among distribution channels, supply cha[in] management, and logistics management

**LO2** Identify how distribution channels add value to businesses and consumers

**LO3** Describe distribution channel desi[gn] and management decisions and strategies

**LO4** Explain how logistics managemen[t] affects distribution strategy

# Distribution Channels

Already well established as an efficient shipper of orders, Amazon continues to seek to do even better. Currently, Amazon receives an order, labels and packages it, loads it onto a delivery truck (run by UPS or the U.S. Postal Service, depending on the day and delivery details), and waits for confirmation that this third-party logistics provider has delivered the product directly to the customer's door. In this traditional process, the online retail giant seeks to improve by adding more warehouses that can provide more customers with overnight or same-day delivery.

But more innovations aim to reinvent the supply chain completely, to benefit both customers and itself. Using a variety of distribution, fulfillment, and sortation centres helps Amazon get merchandise to consumers quickly. The company also introduced Amazon Prime Now Hubs that stock fast moving products such as bestselling books. Recently Amazon applied for and received a patent for its "anticipatory shipping" system, which starts readying packages for delivery before the customer even adds the item to his or her virtual cart.[1] With anticipatory shipping, Amazon boxes and ships out products that it expects customers will want, according to their previous purchases, in the belief that they are likely to order them soon. To determine what to ship, Amazon uses information from customers' previous orders, product searches, shopping cart contents, and previous returns.

This innovation promises to be particularly beneficial for popular books, movies, and games, for which people clearly announce their desire to have the item in hand the very day it is released. If Amazon can get it to their homes on that same day, it might discourage customers from visiting physical retail locations, because their wait times would be even lower than brick-and-mortar stores can offer. In this sense, Amazon is using Big Data to predict demand and thus edge out its rivals. However, critics caution that when Amazon's algorithms are incorrect, the necessary returns could grow rapidly to become quite costly. In response, Amazon has suggested that it might simply convert any unwanted deliveries into gifts, thus building goodwill among customers who receive a desirable new order for no cost.

However, Amazon has not limited its streamlining efforts to the retailer–customer link. Instead, it has created its Vendor Flex program, which seeks to lower overall transportation costs. Among the first partners in Amazon's Vendor Flex program is Procter & Gamble (P&G), which agreed to allow Amazon to build fulfillment centres within P&G's own warehouses. The cost savings accrue because the new system eliminates the costs of transporting P&G's products to Amazon's fulfillment centres.

Not everyone is excited about this innovative new partnership, though. Companies such as Target, which have enjoyed long-term relationships with P&G, are taking notice and taking action. After learning of the Vendor Flex program between Amazon and P&G, Target reacted by moving all P&G products from prominent end-cap positions in its stores to less prestigious and less visible locations. Target also stopped using P&G as its primary source of advice for planning merchandising strategies within each category. ■

In this chapter, we discuss the third P, place, which includes all activities required to get the right product to the right customer when that customer wants it. Students of marketing often overlook or underestimate the importance of place in the marketing mix simply because it happens behind the scenes. Yet distribution channels, or place, add value for customers because they get products to customers efficiently: quickly and at low cost.

We begin by understanding the importance of distribution, how distribution channels are designed, how they are structured, and how they are managed. Then we move to a discussion of the supply chain and the critical role it plays in distribution strategy. We end the chapter by examining how logistics management integrates activities from the efficient flow of raw materials through to the delivery of finished goods.

## THE IMPORTANCE OF DISTRIBUTION                    LO1

So far in this book, we've examined how companies conduct in-depth market research, gain insights into consumer and business behaviour, carefully segment markets and select the best target markets, develop new products and services, and set prices that signal good value. However, even if they execute these activities flawlessly, if they are unable to secure placement of their products in appropriate outlets, in sufficient quantities exactly when customers want them, they are likely to fail.

Convincing wholesalers and retailers to carry new products can prove to be more difficult than you might think. For example, a typical grocery store may carry between 30,000 and 40,000 different items. But a good number of these would have to be cleared off the shelves to make room for all the new foods, beverages, household goods, pet products, and other miscellaneous items launched each year. With dozens of new products being introduced each day, the fight for shelf space is fierce. For many companies, distribution is not only difficult but also expensive, and involves paying listing fees to get shelf space, as we discuss later in the chapter.

All goods and services organizations need a well thought-out distribution strategy to convince retailers to carry their products. PenAgain, a small manufacturer of ergonomic pens and other writing instruments, wanted to put its offerings in Walmart stores, but first it had to convince Walmart to buy what it was selling.[2] After tough negotiations, Walmart agreed to give PenAgain a one-month trial in 500 stores, but only if it lowered its costs. PenAgain moved production overseas to meet this requirement. Walmart provided no marketing support and since PenAgain was too small to afford traditional print or television advertising, it developed a viral marketing program and produced displays to use in the stores. To keep track of sales, it relied on Walmart's Internet-based Retail Link system, and hired a firm that sends representatives into stores to check out display placement and customer traffic. Finally, PenAgain also agreed to adhere to strict packaging, labelling, and shipping requirements. And remember, for all this effort, its entry in stores was only a test, and a very expensive gamble! But it led to success in Walmart stores, helping PenAgain on its way to prosperity.

As seen in Entrepreneurial Marketing 12.1, a good distribution strategy that is integrated with other marketing mix elements is key to the successful launch of a new product.

## Distribution Channels, Supply Chain, and Logistics

People often talk about distribution channel management, supply chain management, and logistics management as if they were the same thing. A **distribution channel** transfers the ownership of goods and moves them from the point of production to the point of consumption, most often to retailers. As such, it consists of all the institutions and marketing activities in the marketing process.[4] *Distribution channels* are a part of the overall *supply chain*. As indicated in Exhibit 12.1, distribution channels make products available to consumers, whether they are individuals or businesses. In some cases, companies use direct market channels to deliver their goods to consumers; in other instances, distribution is accomplished indirectly through the use of intermediaries.

As we noted in Chapter 1, **supply chain management** refers to a set of approaches and techniques firms employ to efficiently and effectively integrate their suppliers, manufacturers, warehouses, stores, and transportation intermediaries into a seamless value chain in which merchandise is produced and distributed in the right quantities, to the right locations, and at the right time, as well as to minimize systemwide costs while satisfying the service levels their customers require.

Supply chain management takes a systemwide approach to coordinating the flow of merchandise and includes both distribution management and logistics management. Zara, a well known global specialty apparel chain, has a completely integrated supply chain because the company owns or at least has considerable control over each phase. It not only owns most of its stores, but also produces the majority of its clothes and makes more than 40 percent of its fabric. As a result, it is able to conceive of, design, manufacture, transport, and ultimately sell high-fashion apparel much more quickly and efficiently than any of its major competitors.

A simplified supply chain would be one in which manufacturers make products and sell them to intermediaries such as retailers or wholesalers. This chain becomes much

**distribution channel**
The institutions that transfer the ownership of goods and move goods from the point of production to the point of consumption.

**supply chain management**
Refers to a set of approaches and techniques firms employ to efficiently and effectively integrate their suppliers, manufacturers, warehouses, stores, and transportation intermediaries into a seamless value chain in which merchandise is produced and distributed in the right quantities, to the right locations, and at the right time.

## Entrepreneurial Marketing 12.1

### Chocolate With a Purpose[3]

Reading this chapter and struggling to stay awake? The founders of AWAKE Chocolate hope that their caffeinated chocolate bar will become your new study buddy. Think Kit Kat meets Red Bull, or, as cofounder Matt Schnarr says, "chocolate with a purpose." Schnarr and two friends, Dan Tzotzis and Adam Deremo, had worked together at Pepsi. With backgrounds in consumer packaged goods (CPG), they followed macro trends to see what was driving sales of food products. Companies took existing products and shook them up by adding new ingredients such as probiotics in yogurt, vitamins in water, or caffeine in energy drinks. Although the energy drink category was exploding and was very profitable, the three partners noted that most drinks were expensive and didn't taste very good. A caffeinated chocolate bar could compete in the energy drink space and at a lower cost.

When Schnarr, Tzotzis, and Deremo launched AWAKE Chocolate in 2012, they knew they needed to do things right to get shelf space for their new product. Packaging and pricing quickly became two key elements in their distribution strategy. So they abandoned their first package design and hired Seattle-based ad agency Tether. Its chief creative officer, Stanley Hainsworth, who had worked with Lego, Starbucks, and Nike, was tasked with designing an eye-catching package for AWAKE. The chocolate bar category is crowded so the package had to jump off the shelf and grab the attention of consumers. The new design featuring mascot Nevill the Owl was used to introduce the product to the brand's primary

AWAKE Chocolate cofounders knew their packaging had to stand out in order to get shelf space.

Used with permission of AWAKE Chocolate

target market of 18- to 25-year-olds in a back-to-school sampling campaign on university campuses.

Pricing was another element AWAKE founders knew would impact distribution. Since most energy drinks were sold through gas stations and convenience stores, these outlets became key distribution channels. A decision was made to price the caffeinated chocolate bars at a premium, still lower than energy drinks but higher than regular chocolate bars. The rationale to sell at $2.49 was to "margin up" the category, since vendors would be more likely to carry the product knowing they could make more margin on AWAKE than on a regular chocolate bar.

They pitched their concept on CBC's *Dragons' Den* only four weeks after they first started shipping products and signed a deal with David Chilton. They already had distribution in gas bars (Husky, Shell) and drug stores (Shoppers Drug Mart, Rexall). Two days after they taped the show, they got a listing at Loblaws. This was followed with a host of other gas stations, convenience and grocery stores, and university campus stores. Not only did AWAKE get distribution in Canada, but it was also able to get shelf space in the United States in similar outlets.

Less than a year later, the company had booked $1 million in total sales and increased distribution to 10,000 locations including Walmart, drugstores, and online at Amazon. A new, smaller format was introduced (one-third the size and with half the amount of caffeine of the original product) in an effort to make consumption more of an everyday ritual. With a product that tastes like a chocolate bar but performs like coffee, and good distribution, the company will keep consumers awake.

more complicated if we include suppliers of materials to manufacturers and all of the manufacturers, wholesalers, and stores in a typical supply chain. **Wholesalers** buy products from manufacturers and resell them to **retailers**, who sell products directly to consumers. Manufacturers ship to a wholesaler, or, in the case of many multi-store retailers, to the retailer's distribution centre or directly to stores. The more intermediaries that are involved in the supply chain, the greater the complexity and number of transactions involved for a company to reach consumers.

Although the above discussion reflects the typical flow of manufactured goods, many variations to this supply chain exist. Some retail chains, such as Home Depot and Costco, function as both retailers and wholesalers; they act as retailers when they sell to consumers directly and as wholesalers when they sell to other businesses, such as

**wholesalers**
Those firms engaged in buying, taking title to, often storing, and physically handling goods in large quantities, and then reselling the goods (usually in smaller quantities) to retailers or industrial or business users.

**retailers**
Sell products directly to consumers.

**EXHIBIT 12.1**    Supply Chain Management

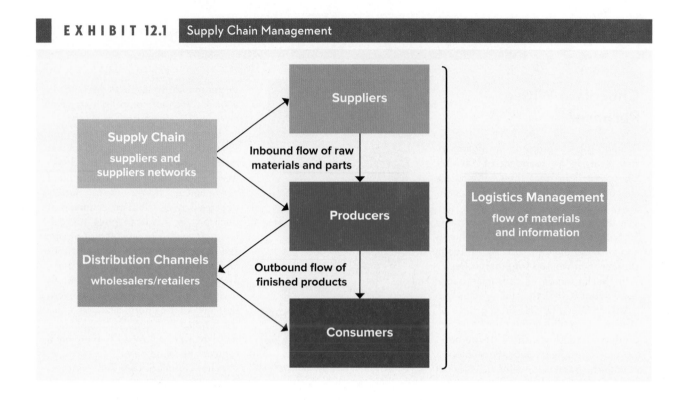

building contractors or restaurant owners. When manufacturers such as Dell or Avon sell directly to consumers, they are performing both production and retailing activities. Amazon has added its own private label brand for electronics, food, detergent, and diapers, performing both production and retailing roles. When Dell sells directly to a university or business, it becomes a business-to-business (B2B) transaction, but when it sells to the students or employees individually, it is a business-to-consumer (B2C) operation.

Supply chain management focuses on the relationships among members of the supply chain and distribution channel and the need to coordinate efforts to provide customers with the best value.

**logistics management**
The integration of two or more activities for the purpose of planning, implementing, and controlling the efficient flow of raw materials, in-process inventory, and finished goods from the point of origin to the point of consumption.

**Logistics management** describes the integration of two or more activities to plan, implement, and control the efficient flow of raw materials, in-process inventory, and finished goods from the point of origin to the point of consumption. These activities may include, but are not limited to, customer service, demand forecasting, distribution communications, inventory control, materials handling, order processing, parts and service support, plant and warehouse site selection, procurement, packaging, return goods handling, salvage and scrap disposal, traffic and transportation, and warehousing and storage.[5]

Distribution channel management, supply chain management, and logistics management are related but have been handled differently in the past. The management of distribution channels has traditionally been the responsibility of marketing departments, under the direction of a marketing vice-president. Someone with responsibility for distribution channels in a consumer packaged goods company would manage the relationship with retailers such as Loblaw or Shoppers Drug Mart. Logistics was traditionally the responsibility of operations, under a vice-president of operations. Although their goals were similar, these departments often saw solutions differently, and sometimes worked at cross-purposes. For instance, the marketing department's goal might have been to make sales, whereas logistics wanted to keep costs low. Firms have come to realize that there is tremendous opportunity in coordinating marketing and logistics activities not only within a firm, but also throughout the supply chain.

## DISTRIBUTION CHANNELS ADD VALUE

**L02**

Why would a manufacturer want to use a wholesaler or a retailer? Don't these supply chain members just cut into their profits? Wouldn't it be cheaper for consumers to buy directly from manufacturers? In a simple agrarian economy, the best supply chain may in fact follow a direct route from manufacturer to consumer: the consumer goes to the farm and buys food directly from the farmer. But how will the food get cooked? The consumer doesn't know how to make a stove, nor does she have the materials to do so. The stove maker who has the necessary knowledge must buy raw materials and components from various suppliers, make the stove, and then make it available to the consumer. If the stove maker isn't located near the consumer, the stove must be transported to where the consumer has access to it. To make matters even more complicated, the consumer may want to view a choice of stoves, hear about all their features, and have the stove delivered and installed.

How many companies are involved in making and getting a stove to your kitchen?
© ThinkStock/Alamy Stock Photo/Getty Images

Each participant in the supply chain adds value. The components manufacturer helps the stove manufacturer by supplying parts and materials. The stove maker then turns the components into the stove. The transportation company gets the stove to the retailer. The retailer stores the stove until the customer wants it, educates the customer about product features, and delivers and installs the stove. At each step, the stove becomes more costly but also more valuable to the consumer.

Exhibits 12.2A and 12.2B show how using supply chain partners can provide value overall. Exhibit 12.2A shows three manufacturers, each of which sells directly to three consumers in a system that requires nine transactions. Each transaction costs money—for example, the manufacturer must fill the order, package it, write up the paperwork, and ship it—and each cost is passed on to the customer. Exhibit 12.2B shows the same three manufacturers and consumers; but, this time they go through a single retailer. The number of transactions falls to six, and as transactions are eliminated, the supply chain becomes more efficient, which adds value for customers by making it more convenient and less expensive to purchase merchandise.

**EXHIBIT 12.2A**    Direct Supply Chain With No Retailer

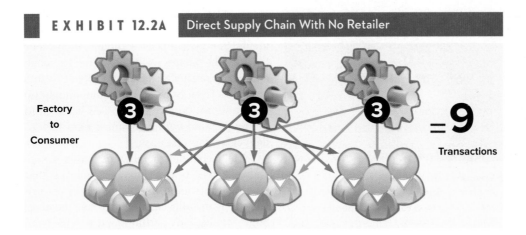

Factory to Consumer

= **9** Transactions

**EXHIBIT 12.2B**  Indirect Supply Chain With Retailer

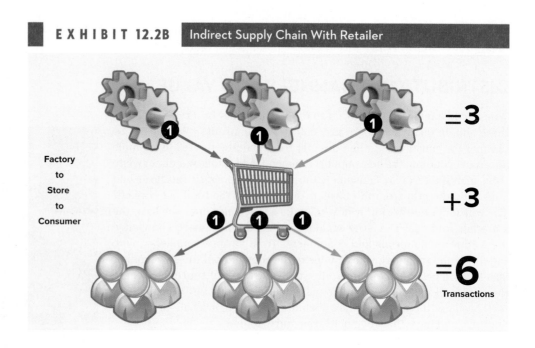

Factory to Store to Consumer

=3

+3

=6 Transactions

When products are designed and manufactured, how and when the critical components reach the factory must be coordinated with production. The sales department must coordinate its delivery promises with the factory or distribution centres. A **distribution centre**—a facility for the receipt, storage, and redistribution of goods to company stores or customers—may be operated by retailers, manufacturers, or distribution specialists.[6] Amazon operates a number of fulfillment and distribution centres as well as sortation centres that can speed up delivery of products even further. Advertising and promotion must be coordinated with all departments that control inventory and transportation. There is no faster way to lose credibility with customers than to promise deliveries or run a promotion and then not have the merchandise when the customer expects it.

**distribution centre**
A facility for the receipt, storage, and redistribution of goods to company stores or customers; may be operated by retailers, manufacturers, or distribution specialists.

Home Depot and Stanley Tool Company have a mutually beneficial partnership. Home Depot buys tools from Stanley because its customers find value in Stanley products. Stanley sells tools to Home Depot because it has established an excellent market for its products.

REUTERS/Alamy Stock Photo

Distribution channels are composed of various entities that are buying, such as retailers or wholesalers; selling, such as manufacturers or wholesalers; or helping facilitate the exchange, such as transportation companies. Like interactions between people, these relationships can range from close working partnerships to one-time arrangements. In almost all cases, though, they occur because the parties want something from one another. For instance, Home Depot wants hammers from Stanley Tool Company; Stanley wants an opportunity to sell its tools to the public; and both companies want UPS to deliver the merchandise.

Each channel member performs a specialized role. If one member believes that another isn't doing its job correctly or efficiently, it usually can replace that member. So, if Stanley isn't getting good service from UPS, it can switch to FedEx. Likewise, if

Home Depot believes its customers don't perceive Stanley tools to be a good value, it may buy from another tool company such as Hitachi, Skil, or others. Home Depot could even decide to make its own tools or use its own trucks to pick up tools from Stanley. However, even if a channel member is replaced, the function it performed remains, so someone needs to complete it.

As the Chapter Case Study notes, Zara gains its competitive advantage by bringing fashions to the store and its customers much faster than other clothing retailers. It holds minimal inventory, produces new fashions quickly, and rarely gets stuck with old inventory. Deliveries are made to stores once a week, and the clothes rarely remain on shelves for more than a week. But this speedy system is not limited to the retail side; Zara also takes only four to five weeks to design a new collection and then about a week to manufacture it, so it continually cycles through its inventory of fabric and materials needed to make its clothing. Its competitors, in comparison, need an average of six months to design a new collection and another three weeks to manufacture it.

Distribution channels perform a variety of transactional, logistical, and facilitating functions, as noted in Exhibit 12.3. One important role played by intermediaries is to reduce the number of marketplace contacts, resulting in more efficient systems. Intermediaries also match the requirements of individual consumers to the goods that manufacturers produce; handle physical distribution and storage of goods, making them available for customers to purchase; facilitate searches by both buyers and sellers; and standardize exchange transactions. While channel functions may shift from one intermediary or channel member to another, it's important to recognize that they cannot be eliminated. As noted in the Home Depot example above, these functions must be completed by some organization to get the right products to the right customers when they want them.

## Managing Distribution Channels

Like any large, complicated system, a distribution channel is difficult to manage. Whether the balance of power rests with large retailers like Walmart or with large manufacturers like Procter & Gamble, channel members benefit by working together to develop and implement their channel strategy. If a distribution channel is to run efficiently, the participating members must cooperate. Oftentimes, however, channel members have conflicting goals. For instance, Stanley wants Home Depot to carry all its tools but not those of its

| **EXHIBIT 12.3** | Functions Performed by Intermediaries |
|---|---|
| **Transactional Function** | |
| **Buying** | Purchase goods for resale to other intermediaries or consumers |
| **Risk taking** | Own inventory that can become outdated |
| **Promotion** | Promote products to attract consumers |
| **Selling** | Transact with potential customers |
| **Logistical Function** | |
| **Physical distribution** | Transport goods to point of purchase |
| **Risk taking** | Maintain inventory and protect goods |
| **Facilitating Function** | |
| **Gathering information** | Share competitive intelligence about customers or other channel members |
| **Financing** | Extend credit and other financial services to consumers |

Amazon and Procter & Gamble recognize that it is in their common interest to remain profitable business partners.

Daniel Mihailescu/AFP/Getty Images

**channel conflict**
Results when supply chain members are not in agreement about their goals, roles, or rewards.

competitors so that Stanley can maximize its sales. But Home Depot carries a mix of tool brands so it can maximize the sales in its tool category. When channel members are not in agreement about their goals, roles, or rewards, **channel conflict** results.

Avoiding vertical channel conflicts demands open, honest communication. Buyers and vendors all must understand what drives the other party's business, their roles in the relationship, each firm's strategies, and any problems that might arise over the course of the relationship. Target experiences a conflict with Amazon because of its Vendor Flex program with Procter & Gamble (P&G). Amazon benefits from the program, which lowers its transportation costs, but Target believes that it gives its competitor an unfair advantage. Amazon and Procter & Gamble (P&G) recognize that it is in their common interest to remain profitable business partners. Amazon's customers demand and expect to find P&G products on its website; P&G needs the sales generated through Amazon. Amazon cannot demand prices so low that P&G cannot make money, and P&G must be flexible enough to accommodate the needs of this important customer. With a common goal, both firms then have the incentive to cooperate, because they know that by doing so, each will boost its sales.

**Managing Channels Through Vertical Marketing Systems**    Although conflict is likely to occur in any distribution channel, it is generally more pronounced when the channel members are independent entities. Distribution channels that are more closely aligned, whether by contract or by ownership, share common goals and therefore are less prone to conflict.

In an independent distribution channel (the left panel of Exhibit 12.4), the several independent members—a manufacturer, a wholesaler, and a retailer—each attempt to satisfy their own objectives and maximize their own profits, often at the expense of the other members. None of the participants has any control over the others. Using our previous example, the first time Walmart purchases pens from PenAgain, both parties likely

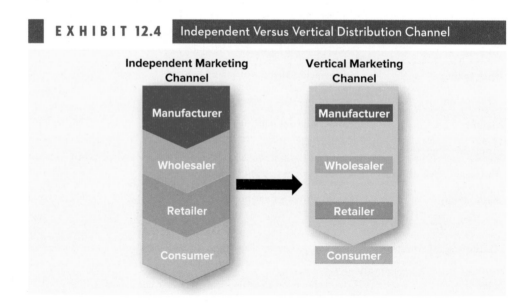

**EXHIBIT 12.4**    Independent Versus Vertical Distribution Channel

**Independent Marketing Channel**

Manufacturer
Wholesaler
Retailer
Consumer

**Vertical Marketing Channel**

Manufacturer
Wholesaler
Retailer
Consumer

try to extract as much profit from the deal as possible. After the deal is consummated, neither party feels any responsibility to the other.

Over time, though, Walmart and PenAgain might develop a relationship marked by routinized, automatic transactions, such that Walmart's customers come to expect PenAgain products in stores, and PenAgain depends on Walmart to buy a good portion of its output. This scenario represents the first phase of a **vertical marketing system** (the right panel of Exhibit 12.4) in which the members act as a unified system because they realize that each party can maximize its individual benefits by working together to make the distribution system more efficient rather than working individually or at cross-purposes. Three types of vertical marketing systems—administered, contractual, and corporate—reflect increasing phases of formalization and control. The more formal the vertical marketing system, the less likely conflict is to ensue.

*Administered Vertical Marketing System.* The Walmart–PenAgain marketing channel relationship offers an example of an **administered vertical marketing system**. There is no common ownership or contractual relationship, but the dominant channel member controls or holds the balance of power. Because of its size and relative power, Walmart imposes controls on PenAgain. Power in a marketing channel exists when one firm has the means or ability to dictate the actions of another member at a different level of distribution. A retailer like Walmart exercises its power over suppliers in several ways. With its reward power, Walmart offers rewards (often a monetary incentive) if PenAgain will do what Walmart wants it to do. Coercive power arises when Walmart threatens to punish or punishes the other channel member for not undertaking certain tasks, such as if it were to delay payment to PenAgain for a late delivery. Walmart may also have referent power over PenAgain if the supplier desperately wants to be associated with Walmart, because being known as an important Walmart supplier enables PenAgain to attract other retailers' business. As Walmart deals with PenAgain and its other suppliers, it likely exerts multiple types of power to influence their behaviours. If either party dislikes the way the relationship is going, though, it can simply walk away.

*Contractual Vertical Marketing System.* Over time, Walmart and PenAgain may formalize their relationship by entering into contracts that dictate various terms, such as how much Walmart will buy each month and at what price, as well as the penalties for late deliveries. In a **contractual vertical marketing system** like this, independent firms at different levels of the supply chain join together through contracts to obtain economies of scale and coordination and to reduce conflict.[7]

Franchising is the most common type of contractual vertical marketing system; franchising companies and their franchisees account for $68 billion in Canadian retail sales and employ more than 1 million people.[8] **Franchising** is a contractual agreement between a franchisor and a franchisee that allows the franchisee to operate a retail outlet, using a name and format developed and supported by the franchisor. Exhibit 12.5 lists some of Canada's favourite franchises.

In a franchise contract, the franchisee pays a lump sum plus a royalty on all sales in return for the right to operate a business in a specific location. The franchisee also agrees to operate the outlet in accordance with the procedures prescribed by the franchisor. The franchisor typically provides assistance in locating and building the business, developing the products or services sold, training the managers, and advertising. To maintain the franchisee's reputation, the franchisor also makes sure that all outlets provide the same quality of services and products. M&M Food Market opened its first franchise nine months after the first store was launched; today, it has 342 locations across Canada.[9] Some franchisees invest their life savings (a typical store costs around $325,000) and the company wants them to be successful. So it does careful screening to ensure that the right people are invited to join the team. And while entrepreneurial skills are an asset, M&M Food Market also needs franchisees who will adhere to the corporate formula instead of doing things their own way.

**vertical marketing system**
A supply chain in which the members act as a unified system; there are three types: administrated, contractual, and corporate.

**administered vertical marketing system**
A supply chain system in which there is no common ownership and no contractual relationship, but the dominant channel member controls the channel relationship.

**contractual vertical marketing system**
A system in which independent firms at different levels of the supply chain join together through contracts to obtain economies of scale and coordination and to reduce conflict.

**franchising**
A contractual agreement between a franchisor and a franchisee that allows the franchisee to operate a retail outlet, using a name and format developed and supported by the franchisor.

**EXHIBIT 12.5**    The 10 Largest Franchises in Canada

| Rank | Franchise | Type | Number of Outlets |
|------|-----------|------|-------------------|
| 1 | Tim Hortons® | Coffee, doughnuts, sandwiches | 3,500 |
| 2 | Subway | Submarine sandwiches, salads | 3,032 |
| 3 | McDonald's | Hamburgers, chicken, salads | 1,400 |
| 4 | Jan-Pro Cleaning Systems | Commercial janitorial services | 1,281 |
| 5 | A&W Food Services | Hamburgers, onion rings, root beer | 803 |
| 6 | Remax | Real estate | 785 |
| 7 | Pizza Pizza | Pizza, wings, fries | 724 |
| 8 | KFC | Fried chicken | 650 |
| 9 | Dairy Queen Canada | Ice cream, desserts | 602 |
| 10 | Country Style Foods | Coffee, doughnuts, bakery items | 600 |

*Source:* "Canada's Top 100 Franchises," http://www.betheboss.ca/top-100-franchises

A franchise system combines the entrepreneurial advantages of owning a business with the efficiencies of vertical marketing systems that function under single ownership (a corporate system, as we discuss next). Franchisees are motivated to make their stores successful because they receive the profits, after they pay the royalty to the franchisor. The franchisor is motivated to develop new products, services, and systems and to promote the franchise because it receives royalties on all sales. Advertising, product development, and system development are all done efficiently by the franchisor, with costs shared by all franchisees.

**corporate vertical marketing system**
A system in which the parent company has complete control and can dictate the priorities and objectives of the supply chain; it may own facilities such as manufacturing plants, warehouse facilities, retail outlets, and design studios.

***Corporate Vertical Marketing System.*** In a **corporate vertical marketing system**, the parent company has complete control and can dictate the priorities and objectives of the marketing channel because it owns multiple segments of the channel, such as manufacturing plants, warehouse facilities, and retail outlets. By virtue of its ownership and resulting control, potential conflict among segments of the channel is lessened.

# WARBY PARKER

Warby Parker represents a corporate vertical marketing system because it designs its own glasses and operates its retail stores.

Used with permission of Warby Parker

Warby Parker, an eyeglass retailer based in New York, represents a corporate vertical marketing system because it designs its own glasses in-house rather than having contractual relationships with other firms, and it operates its own retail and online stores selling its products.[10] With this corporate ownership structure, it is able to achieve critical cost savings needed to sell its products at low prices.

## Managing Supply Chains Through Strategic Relationships

There is more to managing supply chains than simply exercising power over other members in an administered system or establishing a contractual or corporate vertical marketing system. There is also a human side. As shown in Sustainable Marketing 12.1, some companies make their supply chain decisions based on their concern for the environment.

### Sustainable Marketing 12.1

## Ethics and Sustainability Key to Doing Business

After two years working in the world of finance, Pascal Benaksas-Couture spent six months providing humanitarian aid in Costa Rica. When he returned to Montreal, he wanted to pursue a career that aligned with his values.[11] In looking around Quebec, he found a sector that was underserved—that of ethical clothing. His goal was to produce clothing with positive messages, not insignificant sayings or clothing with logos. In 2005, he and his business partner, Pascale Cloutier, launched OÖM Ethikwear. Its first collection of ethically made clothing was produced entirely in Quebec.

You may be surprised to learn that three decades ago, 70 percent of clothing worn in Canada was made in Canada. Today that has dropped to less than 5 percent.[12] Most clothing sold in Canada is manufactured in other countries. Local production is expensive compared to labour costs in Bangladesh, for example. Even after factoring in shipping, duty, and taxes, producing offshore (with its low costs) allows companies to make healthy profits on the items they sell.

It didn't take long for OÖM's founders to apply their ethical philosophy beyond just local manufacturing. Sustainable materials such as organic cotton, lyocell, hemp, and flax are used in the company's eco-responsible clothing. In order to recycle cotton remnants generated by the manufacturing process, it launched Bébé OÖM,[13] although this division has since been closed. Rêv-Évolution was introduced as a line of promotional clothing when OÖM recognized the growing desire of businesses to purchase ethical products for printing made by Quebecois designers.[14] Later, polar fleece clothing was added, made with 100 percent PET plastic bottles.

OÖM Ethikwear produces clothing in Quebec using sustainable materials such as organic cotton, hemp, flax, and polar fleece made from recycled plastic bottles.

Used with permission of OÖM Ethikwear

After recycling and washing, the bottles are shredded, melted, and turned into pellets before being transformed into fibre.[15] OÖM was sold in 2015 to Message Factory, another sustainable Quebec brand that shares the same values. Pascal Benaksas-Couture continues to work with new owner Julie Rochefort to grow the brand.

In keeping with the ethical values of its founders, OÖM works with manufacturers committed to helping people who are less fortunate. OÖM's clothing is all locally made in Quebec, primarily by socially responsible companies. This not only creates jobs, but also reduces the company's carbon footprint by avoiding shipping from other countries. And because the founders believe in giving back, 1 percent of profits are donated to organizations working to improve society and the environment.[16] It's all part of their philosophy—the world would be a better place if all businesses played their part.

In a conventional distribution channel, relationships between members often are based on the argument over the split of the profit pie: if one party gets ahead, the other party falls behind. Sometimes this type of transactional approach is acceptable if the parties have no interest in a long-term relationship. For example, if Walmart believes that PenAgain's ergonomic pens are just a short-term fad, it may only be interested in purchasing once. In that case, it might seek to get the best one-time price it can, even if doing so means that PenAgain will make very little money and therefore might not want to sell to Walmart again. On the other hand, if Harry Rosen sees a trend for very narrow white belts, it would be interested in purchasing from a vendor with whom an ongoing relationship would be built. Harry Rosen would not purchase from a vendor on a one-time basis just to get a one-time good price, because long-term relationship building is important to the company's business practices.

**strategic relationship (partnering relationship)** A supply chain relationship that the members are committed to maintaining long-term, investing in opportunities that are mutually beneficial; requires mutual trust, open communication, common goals, and credible commitments.

Frequently, firms seek a **strategic relationship (partnering relationship)**, in which the supply chain members are committed to maintaining the relationship over the long term and investing in opportunities that are mutually beneficial. In a conventional or administered supply chain, there are significant incentives to establish a strategic relationship, even without contracts or ownership relationships. Both parties benefit because the size of the profit pie has increased, so both the buyer and the seller increase their sales and profits. These strategic relationships are created explicitly to uncover and exploit joint opportunities, so members depend on and trust each other heavily; share goals and agree on how to accomplish those goals; and are willing to take risks, share confidential information, and make significant investments for the sake of the relationship. Successful strategic relationships require mutual trust, open communication, common goals, and credible commitments.

**Mutual Trust** Mutual trust holds a strategic relationship together. Trust is the belief that a partner is honest (i.e., is reliable, stands by its word, is sincere, fulfills obligations) and is benevolent (i.e., is concerned about the other party's welfare). When vendors and buyers trust each other, they're more willing to share relevant ideas, clarify goals and problems, and communicate efficiently. Information shared between the parties thus becomes increasingly comprehensive, accurate, and timely. With trust, there's also less need for the supply chain members to constantly monitor and check up on each other's actions, because each believes the other won't take advantage, even given the opportunity. RFID systems that enable sealed cartons to be checked into a distribution centre without being opened would be impossible without mutual trust. Although it is important in all relationships, monitoring supply chain members becomes particularly pertinent when suppliers are located in less-developed countries, where issues such as the use of child labour, poor working conditions, and below-subsistence wages have become a shared responsibility.

Five interrelated activities emerge in supply chain management: designing distribution channels (discussed earlier in this chapter), making information flow, managing the relationships among supply chain partners, making merchandise flow, and managing inventory. In the next few sections, we examine these remaining activities.

**Open Communication** To share information, develop sales forecasts together, and coordinate deliveries, Harry Rosen and its suppliers maintain open and honest communication. This maintenance may sound easy in principle, but most businesses don't tend to share information with their business partners. But open, honest communication is key to developing successful relationships because supply chain members need to understand what is driving each other's business, their roles in the relationship, each firm's strategies, and any problems that arise over the course of the relationship.

**Common Goals** Supply chain members must have common goals for a successful relationship to develop. Shared goals give both members of the relationship an incentive

Harry Rosen grew from a single 46-square-metre Toronto tailor shop to a national upscale menswear chain. It works hard to develop strategic partnerships with its suppliers based on mutual trust, open communications, common goals, and credible commitments.

Used with permission of Harry Rosen Inc.

to pool their strengths and abilities and exploit potential opportunities together. For example, Harry Rosen and its local suppliers recognize that it is in their common interest to be strategic partners. Harry Rosen needs the quick response local manufacturers afford, and those manufacturers recognize that if they can keep Harry Rosen happy, they will have more than enough business for years to come. So if Harry Rosen needs a special production run to make an emergency shipment, suppliers will work to meet the challenge. If one of Harry Rosen's suppliers has difficulty getting a particular fabric or financing its inventory, it is in Harry Rosen's best interest to help it because they are committed to the same goals in the long run.

**Credible Commitments** Successful relationships develop because both parties make credible commitments to, or tangible investments in, the relationship. These commitments involve spending money to improve the products or services provided to the customer.[17] For example, if Harry Rosen makes a financial commitment to its suppliers to help them develop state-of-the-art manufacturing facilities and computer systems for improved communication, it is making a credible commitment—putting its money where its mouth is. As our chapter opener described, Amazon and P&G have worked closely to set up their Vendor Flex program, enabling Amazon to operate fulfillment centres within P&G's own warehouses and thereby lower transportation expenses.

Similar to many other elements of marketing, managing the supply chain can seem like an easy task at first glance: Put the merchandise in the right place at the right time. But the various elements and actors involved in a supply chain create unique and compelling complexities and require that firms work carefully to ensure that they are achieving the most efficient and effective chain possible. Ethical Dilemma 12.1 highlights the importance of having credible supply chain partners to ensure food safety.

## Ethical Dilemma 12.1

# Supply Chain Critical to Food Safety

For many years, there were certain words that came to mind when you thought of Chipotle: *fresh, tasty,* and *wholesome* being a few of them. Chipotle, despite originally accepting start-up capital from McDonald's, is the antithesis of the golden arches. It is a new kind of fast dining that was introduced in 1993 in Denver, Colorado, by founder and current CEO Steve Ells.[18] From the beginning, Chipotle knew what it stood for: "Food with integrity." This became a pillar of the chain's marketing, and despite pressures from McDonald's executives, Ells never once compromised the integrity of Chipotle's supply chain by cutting corners.[19] Chipotle appealed to a younger market looking for freshness and tasty food prepared by a socially responsible company.[20]

Forgoing drive-through options and maintaining a simple menu, Chipotle's brand stood on its own in a market saturated with McDonald's, Taco Bell, Wendy's, and other burger joints. With minimal marketing efforts, Chipotle's growth was astounding. Within the first month, it was selling more than 1,000 burritos a day, and was profitable within months.[21] Now, Chipotle has almost 2,000 restaurants in the United States and 11 restaurants in Canada.[22] Chipotle's entire brand is propped up by the idea that it's fast, while still being made with fresh, high quality ingredients. However, with quality being the foundation of the business, it's important that Chipotle maintain its reputation.

In 2015, Chipotle was involved in numerous high profile food poisoning incidents. Chipotle was associated with six outbreaks at its locations involving norovirus, salmonella, and *E. coli* in its food.[23] These cases involved restaurants in 13 states, and sickened more than 500 people, with more than 20 needing to be hospitalized.[24] Investigations by the Centers for Disease Control into these concentrated incidents revealed concerns about Chipotle's supply chain, and raised questions about whether sourcing from smaller local grocers compromises food safety. The blame does not fall entirely on its suppliers. Chipotle was also directly involved after one of its restaurants was shut down due to mishandling cooked meat, while two norovirus incidents were caused by sick employees who weren't sent home.

Chipotle had previously built a brand synonymous with healthy, sustainable "food with integrity" by focusing on using local and organic ingredients that were free of antibiotics and genetically modified foods.[25] However, the pervasive food scandals have undermined these core values, making Chipotle's target consumers wary of eating unprocessed ingredients and distrustful of Chipotle's ability to guarantee food safety and provide high quality food. Chipotle is facing at least nine lawsuits, and financial performance has fallen significantly. Same-store sales in January 2016 showed a 36 percent

Chipotle requires supply chain partners to meet elevated standards in a bid to improve food safety.

Ken Wolter/Shutterstock.com

decrease from 2015.[26] As a result, stock prices decreased by more than 30 percent from October 2015 to around $458 in May 2016.

As a result of these recurring incidents, Chipotle has taken aggressive actions to implement food safety and food handling practices in all of its restaurants and throughout its supply chain. The company hired IEH Laboratories and Consulting Group to design a more robust food safety program to improve the company's practices. Chipotle has elevated requirements for all of its produce suppliers (chiefly in the area of testing of ingredients). It faced a significant challenge ensuring its local suppliers have the ability to meet those elevated protocols.

Among the changes made, Chipotle initiated the following:[27]

- Using DNA-based tests on small batches of ingredients before they are shipped to stores

- Testing ingredient samples to ensure that quality is maintained throughout the shelf life of an ingredient

- Using data from test results to enhance Chipotle's ability to measure the performance of its vendors and suppliers

- Enhancing internal training to ensure that all employees thoroughly understand the company's high standards for food safety and food handling

To get customers back into its stores, Chipotle launched Chiptopia, a summer rewards program running from July through September of 2016. The program was designed to entice customers who used to be the most frequent to return to Chipotle stores by rewarding them with a fifth burrito for every four they buy.[28]

Although Chipotle has made significant changes to its supply chain and launched initiatives to reconnect with its lost customers, the company has a long way to go to rebuild trust in the brand.

# DESIGNING DISTRIBUTION CHANNELS

**L03**

## Channel Structure

When a firm is just starting out or entering a new market, it doesn't typically have the option of designing the "best" distribution channel structure—that is, choosing from whom it buys or to whom it sells. A new sporting goods retailer may not have the option of carrying all the manufacturer lines it wants, because other competing retailers in its market might carry the same products. Some manufacturers won't want to sell to this new retailer initially because its credit isn't established. On the other hand, a small specialty sporting goods manufacturer may not be able to get shelf space in major stores like Sport Chek because its line is unproven and the products might duplicate lines that the retailer already carries. Chapter 13 discusses how manufacturers choose their retail partners in more depth.

Every company must develop a distribution strategy for how it will sell goods to consumers. The distribution system may take the form of direct distribution, indirect distribution, and multi-channel distribution, or some combination of these forms.

Direct Distribution     As shown in Exhibit 12.6, there are no intermediaries between the buyer and the seller in direct distribution channels. Typically, the seller is a manufacturer, such as when a carpentry business sells bookcases through its own store and online to individual consumers. The seller also can be an individual, such as when a knitter sells blankets and scarves at craft fairs, on Etsy, and through eBay. Other companies—such as TigerDirect.com, Avon, and Tupperware—use a direct-only model. Some companies choose direct distribution to avoid the high cost of using retailers. For example, retail outlets such as Canadian Tire, the Hudson's Bay Company, or Crate and Barrel command a 50 percent margin on products like the Bartesian cocktail machine (see Entrepreneurial Marketing 8.1) which would dramatically lower profits.

Social and Mobile Marketing 12.1 discusses how Clearly (formerly Clearly Contacts) uses a direct model to sell glasses and contact lenses. When the buyer is another business, such as when Boeing sells planes to Air Canada, the marketing channel still is direct, but in this case, the transaction is a business-to-business one. Lastly, some companies may be forced to distribute their goods directly because they are unable to secure shelf space in retail outlets or are unable to pay the high listing fees demanded by retailers for the shelf space.

**EXHIBIT 12.6**    Direct and Indirect Distribution

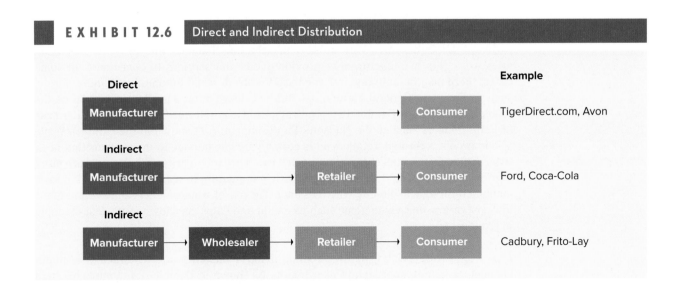

## Social and Mobile Marketing 12.1

### Clearly a Winning Strategy

Would you buy glasses or contact lenses over the Internet or because of a post on a friend's Facebook page? You might, for the right price. Roger Hardy and his sister Michaela Tokarski founded Clearly Contacts in 2000 in a Vancouver basement office that had a computer, a phone, and a Ping-Pong table. In a few short years, it has become the world's fastest growing online retailer of eyeglasses and contact lenses. While working for a contact lens manufacturer, Hardy realized that the margins were extremely high. He knew there had to be a better, cheaper way for consumers to buy eye-care products and so he set out to change that, defining his mission as "Saving the World From Overpriced Eyeglasses."[29] The company has come a long way since then, changing its name to Clearly in May 2015 to reflect its plan to become a design powerhouse.[30]

In the past, the prescription glasses market was dominated by opticians. The Clearly business model eliminated the middleman, automated the order process, and shipped direct to consumers for 50–70 percent less than traditional eye-care retailers. Prices range from $38 to $198, which is a great value for designer brands such as Prada, Dior, Armani, and Fendi.[31] Still, Hardy discovered that although consumers were willing to purchase books or clothes over the Internet, they had reservations about buying eyeglasses online. Curtis Petersen, director of acquisition and retention for Clearly, noted that it was a more complex purchase. You had to convince consumers to change their behaviour and do something a little different to complete the purchase.[32] A Virtual Mirror application let customers see how some of the 500 designs would look on their faces. In fact, more than 10 percent of purchases were made after someone used this application.[33] Free shipping and liberal payment terms helped minimize the risk of the purchase.

To persuade Vancouverites to try the products, the company gave 3,000 pairs of designer glasses away for free in June 2010. Consumers signed up online to get a coupon code for the glasses. Clearly's strategy was to get the high-quality glasses into the hands of consumers to dispel concerns about buying them on the Internet. The company ran a similar promotion in Toronto the year before with a one-day offer of free prescription eyeglasses. It was so successful that it brought the company's website down for more than two hours. In spite of the crash, it managed to give away 1,000 pairs of designer glasses by 1:00 p.m.[34] and generated positive word-of-mouth advertising.

Its Facebook page has over 534,000 Likes,[35] offering tremendous reach at a low cost. Most of Clearly's advertising budget is spent online on banner ads and search engine optimization, very appropriate for an online retailer. The company owned "contact lens" as a keyword, which meant that anyone who did a search would see Clearly's banner ads. It helped to boost sales and propel the company to become the world's largest online eyeglass retailer in the $112 billion global market.[36]

Today it has operations in North America, Europe, and Asia, more than 2 million customers, and cumulative revenues surpassing $1 billion.[37] The company opened its first brick-and-mortar store in Vancouver[38] to help it expand its direct-to-consumer distribution strategy. The strategy worked and Clearly has opened another store in Toronto and a second location in Vancouver. Given projections that nearly 5 billion people will need glasses by 2050,[39] Clearly is on track to fulfill its vision.

**Indirect Distribution**   With indirect distribution channels, one or more intermediaries work with manufacturers to provide goods and services to consumers. In some cases, there may be only one intermediary involved. Many automotive manufacturers, such as Ford and General Motors, use indirect distribution with dealers acting as the retailer, as shown in Exhibit 12.6. Typically only one intermediary is used in the case of large retailers such as the Hudson's Bay Company (not shown in the exhibit). While selling products through retailers adds costs to a company due to the margins that need to be paid to them, retail outlets can reach a much broader market. Wholesalers are often used when a company does not buy in sufficient quantity to make it cost-effective for a manufacturer to deal directly with a retailer. The use of wholesalers is quite common for low-cost or low-unit value items such as candy and chips, as shown in the last example in Exhibit 12.6.

**Multi-Channel Distribution**   Today, many companies are embracing a multi-channel, or hybrid, approach to distribution. As shown in Exhibit 12.7, companies such

**EXHIBIT 12.7** | Multi-Channel Distribution

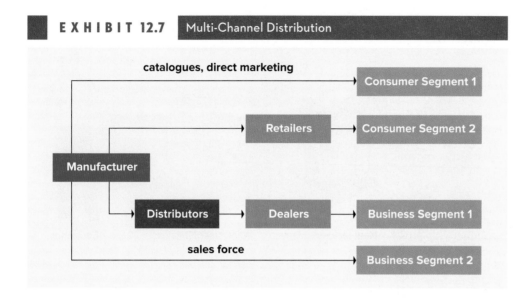

as Sony are better able to reach both consumers and business customers by using a combination of both direct and indirect distribution channels. In very large cities, Sony may sell directly via its own branded stores, while in other areas it may sell indirectly through retailers such as Best Buy. Some companies engage a sales force to deliver products to customers, while others pursue a direct marketing approach through the use of catalogues. Sears Canada sells directly at its retail stores as well as online and through the use of catalogues.

## Push Versus Pull Distribution Strategies

When developing its distribution strategy, a company may choose to use a **push marketing strategy** or a **pull marketing strategy** as illustrated in Exhibit 12.8. With a push strategy, a manufacturer focuses its promotional efforts—for example, personal selling or sales promotion—on channel members to convince them to carry its product. This strategy literally pushes the product through distribution channels to end consumers. As mentioned earlier, companies often need to pay listing fees to get shelf space.

Manufacturers can pay thousands of dollars in listing fees to have their products stocked. Many large grocery store chains charge listing fees that cover their costs in rearranging the store shelves and the warehouse, plus the administration costs associated with adding a new product. Listing fees can determine whether an item gets placed at eye level or down on a bottom shelf where it's harder to find. In Canada, listing fees can range from a few hundred dollars, to $25,000 per item per store, to $1 million per item per grocery chain.[40] The fee depends on many variables, including potential sales volume, trade allowances, product promotion

**push marketing strategy**
Designed to increase demand by focusing on wholesalers, distributors, or salespeople, who push the product to consumers via distribution channels.

**pull marketing strategy**
Designed to get consumers to pull the product into the supply chain by demanding that retailers carry it.

Martin's used a sampling campaign as part of a pull strategy to launch Apple Chips to consumers.

Used by permission of Martin's Family Fruit Farm

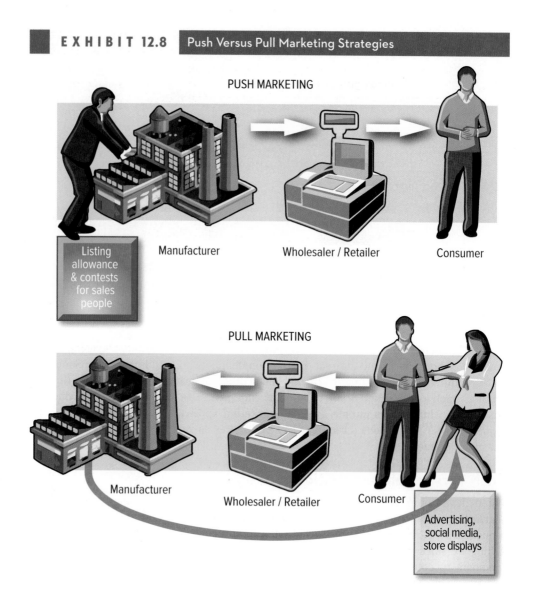

**EXHIBIT 12.8**  Push Versus Pull Marketing Strategies

offered (e.g., samples, in-store demos, promotional pricing, co-op advertising), product category, and company size. Grocery retailers know that large companies such as Kraft or Colgate-Palmolive can afford listing fees. However, some category leaders don't have to pay them because retailers know they simply must stock popular products such as Coke and Tide. To get shelf space, companies need to get retailers onside and show them how their product can help them grow a category, bring new consumers to the category, or add to their profit.

Sometimes, if channel members are reluctant to stock new products, manufacturers may use a pull strategy. In this case, promotional efforts are directed at consumers to build demand for products that, in turn, may convince retailers to carry them. Consumers who see TV commercials or print advertisements or who receive direct mail information or coupons regarding new products may approach local retailers and request that they stock these products, thus pulling them through the distribution channels.

One of Canada's leading growers and packers, Martin's Family Fruit Farm in Elmira, Ontario, produces and distributes apples and apple cider. The company decided to diversify and access new markets and suppliers. It came up with a concept that lets it use imperfect apples to produce dried apple "chips" made from apples sliced into circles and then dehydrated. The chips are all-natural, fat free, gluten free, wheat free, dairy free, and vegan. They contain no preservatives, artificial colouring, or sugar, and have only 100 calories for 25 grams. To be accepted on grocery store shelves, the company had to prove that consumer demand for healthier snacks would translate to sales of its Apple Chips. Working with Vancouver advertising agency BrandFX, the company launched a sampling campaign targeting 45,000 GoodLife Fitness members and also sent the product home with 35,000 children in Ontario daycare centres.[41] This pull strategy reached the target market of nutrition-conscious moms and helped pave the way for a distribution agreement with Loblaws, which agreed to carry Apple Chips at 37 Real Canadian Superstores.[42] Since then, distribution has expanded and consumers can buy the product at Starbucks and Costco in Canada and Sam's Club in the United States.[43]

## Distribution Intensity

When setting up distribution for the first time or introducing new products, firms decide the appropriate level of **distribution intensity**—the number of channel members to use at each level of the supply chain. Distribution intensity commonly is divided into three levels: intensive, selective, and exclusive (see Exhibit 12.9). Although increased sales and access to more consumers is often desirable, that's not always the case. Over the years, companies such as Walmart and Esso have asked to carry M&M Food Market products. These retailers would have dramatically expanded the company's distribution intensity; however, the company decided against such deals, sensing the move would ultimately hurt the brand. M&M Food Market prides itself on offering high quality, whereas retailers such as Walmart focus on low price.

**distribution intensity** The number of channel members to use at each level of the supply chain.

### Intensive Distribution

An **intensive distribution** strategy is designed to get products into as many outlets as possible. Most consumer packaged-goods companies—such as PepsiCo, P&G, Kraft, and most other nationally branded products found in grocery and discount stores—strive for and often achieve intensive distribution. PepsiCo, for instance, wants its product available everywhere: grocery stores, convenience stores, restaurants, and vending machines. Timex watches, starting at around $60, can also be found in many locations. The more exposure these products get, the more they sell.

**intensive distribution** A strategy designed to get products into as many outlets as possible.

### Exclusive Distribution

Manufacturers also might use an **exclusive distribution** policy by granting exclusive geographic territories to one or very few retail customers so

**exclusive distribution** Strategy of granting exclusive rights to sell to one or very few retail customers so no other customers can sell a particular brand.

---

**■ EXHIBIT 12.9** | Distribution Intensity

Intensive

Selective

Exclusive

(Walmart): DayOwl/Shutterstock.com; (Loblaws) T Boris Spremo/The Canadian Press; (Shoppers): Lester Balajadia/Shutterstock.com (Hudson's Bay): Douglas Carr/Alamy Stock Photo; (Sears): Carolyn Chappo/AP Photo//The Canadian Press; (Tiffany): Christian Mueller/ Shutterstock.com; (Cartier): Stephanie Paschal/Rex Features/The Canadian Press

Most consumer packaged-goods companies, such as PepsiCo (top), strive for intensive distribution—they want to be everywhere. But cosmetics firms such as Estée Lauder (bottom) use an exclusive distribution strategy by limiting distribution to a few select, higher-end retailers in each region.

(top): © Jeff Greenberg/PhotoEdit; (bottom): © Susan Van Etten/PhotoEdit

**selective distribution**
Lies between the intensive and exclusive distribution strategies; uses a few selected customers in a territory.

no other customers in the territory can sell a particular brand. Exclusive distribution can benefit manufacturers by assuring them that the most appropriate customers represent their products. Cosmetics firms such as Estée Lauder, for instance, limit their distribution to a few select, higher-end retailers in each region. They believe that selling their products to drugstores, discount stores, and grocery stores would weaken their image. Likewise, Rolex watches are sold only by high-end jewellers and a few retail outlets in keeping with their prestigious brand image. In some cases, limiting distribution can limit sales. Nespresso invented the single-serve capsule coffee machine and sells the pods only in a direct-to-consumer model through its own physical and online stores. In spite of competition from new entrants such as Kraft (Tassimo), Green Mountain (Keurig K-Cup), and Starbucks (Verismo), Nespresso refuses to sell in grocery stores and mass merchants. This notable absence on retail shelves has led other brands to introduce pods that fit Nespresso machines,[44] thus impacting sales potential.

In cases of limited supply or when a firm is just starting out, providing an exclusive territory to one customer helps ensure enough inventory to offer the customer an adequate selection. For instance, Cervélo is a Canadian bicycle manufacturer that makes lightweight racing bikes. It selects its authorized dealers carefully. By controlling sales territories, it guarantees dealers adequate supply, which gives them a strong incentive to push Cervélo's products. Dealers know there will be no competing retailers to cut prices, so their profit margins are protected, which also gives them an incentive to carry more inventory and use extra advertising, personal selling, and sales promotions.

**Selective Distribution**  Between the intensive and exclusive distribution strategies lies **selective distribution**, which uses a few selected customers in a territory. Similar to exclusive distribution, selective distribution helps a seller maintain a particular image and control the flow of merchandise into an area, so many shopping goods manufacturers use it. Recall that shopping goods are those products for which consumers are willing to spend time comparing alternatives, such as most apparel items; home items such as branded pots and pans, sheets, and towels; branded hardware and tools; and consumer electronics. Seiko uses a selective distribution strategy for its watches to match its more upscale image and pricing. Retailers still have a strong incentive to sell the products but not to the same extent as if they had an exclusive territory.

Five interrelated activities emerge in supply chain management: designing distribution channels, making information flow, managing the relationships among supply chain partners, making merchandise flow, and managing inventory. In the next few sections, we examine these remaining activities.

## LO4  LOGISTICS MANAGEMENT: MAKING INFORMATION FLOW

Information flows from the customer to stores, to and from distribution centres, possibly to and from wholesalers, to and from product manufacturers, and then on to the producers of any components and the suppliers of raw materials. To simplify our discussion and because information flows are similar in other supply chain links and B2B

**E X H I B I T  12.10**　│　Information Flows

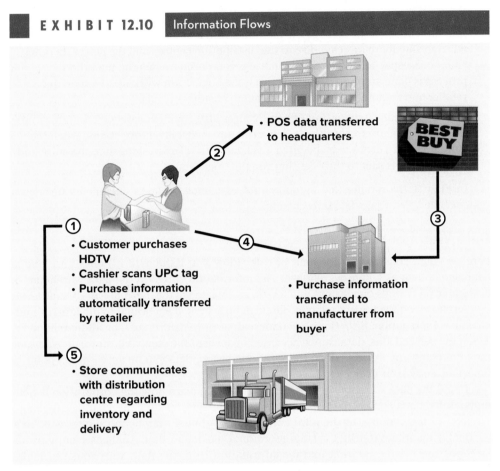

• **POS data transferred to headquarters**

BEST BUY

① • **Customer purchases HDTV**
• **Cashier scans UPC tag**
• **Purchase information automatically transferred by retailer**

④

③

• **Purchase information transferred to manufacturer from buyer**

⑤ • **Store communicates with distribution centre regarding inventory and delivery**

© Ken Wolter | Dreamstime.com

channels, we shorten the supply chain in this section to exclude wholesalers, as well as the link from suppliers to manufacturers. Exhibit 12.10 illustrates the flow of information that starts when a customer buys a Sony HDTV at Best Buy. The flow follows these steps:

- *Flow 1 (Customer to Store).* The sales associate at Best Buy scans the **universal product code (UPC)** tag (the black and white bar code found on most merchandise) on the HDTV packaging, and the customer receives a receipt. The UPC tag contains a 13-digit code that includes the manufacturer of an item and information about special packaging and special promotions. In the future, RFID tags (discussed later in this chapter) may replace UPC codes.

- *Flow 2 (Store to Buyer).* The point-of-sale (POS) terminal records the purchase information and electronically sends it to the buyer at Best Buy's corporate office. The sales information is incorporated into an inventory management system and used to monitor and analyze sales and to decide to reorder more HDTVs, change a price, or plan a promotion. Buyers also send information to stores on overall sales for the chain, how to display merchandise, upcoming promotions, and so on.

- *Flow 3 (Buyer to Manufacturer).* The purchase information from each Best Buy store is typically aggregated by the retailer as a whole, which creates an order for new merchandise and sends it to Sony. The buyer at Best Buy may also communicate directly with Sony to get information and negotiate prices, shipping dates, promotional events, or other merchandise-related issues.

**universal product code (UPC)**
The black and white bar code found on most merchandise.

- *Flow 4 (Store to Manufacturer).* In some situations, the sales transaction data are sent directly from the store to the manufacturer, and the manufacturer decides when to ship more merchandise to the distribution centres and the stores. In other situations, especially when merchandise is reordered frequently, the ordering process is done automatically, bypassing the buyers. By working together, the retailer and manufacturer can better satisfy customer needs.

- *Flow 5 (Store to Distribution Centre).* Stores also communicate with the Best Buy distribution centre to coordinate deliveries and check inventory status. When the store inventory drops to a specified level, more HDTVs are shipped to the store and the shipment is sent to the Best Buy computer system.

In Flow 3, the retailer and manufacturer exchange business documents through a system called electronic data interchange.

## Data Warehouse

Purchase data collected at the point of sale (Flow 2 in Exhibit 12.10) goes into a huge database known as a data warehouse. The information stored in the data warehouse is accessible on various dimensions and levels, as depicted in the data cube in Exhibit 12.11.

As shown on the horizontal axis, data can be accessed according to the level of merchandise aggregation: SKU (item), vendor, category (e.g., dresses), or all merchandise. Along the vertical axis, data can be accessed by level of the company: store, divisions, or the total company. Finally, along the third dimension, data can be accessed by point in time: day, season, or year.

Using the data warehouse, the CEO can not only learn how the corporation is generally doing but also look at the data aggregated by quarter for a merchandise division, a region of the country, or the total corporation. A buyer may be more interested in a particular manufacturer in a certain store on a particular day. Analysts from various levels of the retail operation extract information from the data warehouse to make a plethora of marketing decisions about developing and replenishing merchandise assortments.

**EXHIBIT 12.11**    Retail Data Warehouse

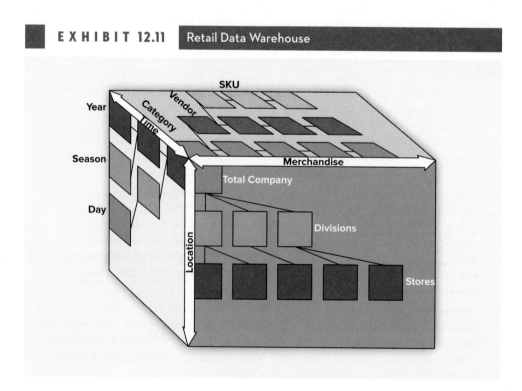

In some cases, manufacturers also have access to this data warehouse. They communicate with retailers by using electronic data interchange and use supply chain systems known as vendor-managed inventory.

## Electronic Data Interchange

**Electronic data interchange (EDI)** is the computer-to-computer exchange of business documents from a retailer to a vendor and back. In addition to sales data, purchase orders, invoices, and data about returned merchandise can be transmitted back and forth. With EDI, vendors can transmit information about on-hand inventory status, vendor promotions, and cost changes to the retailer, as well as information about purchase order changes, order status, retail prices, and transportation routings. Thus EDI enables channel members to communicate more quickly and with fewer errors than in the past, ensuring that merchandise moves from vendors to retailers more quickly.

Many retailers now require vendors to provide them with notification of deliveries before they take place by using an **advanced shipping notice**, an electronic document that the supplier sends the retailer in advance of a shipment to tell the retailer exactly what to expect in the shipment. If the advanced shipping notice is accurate, the retailer can dispense with opening all the received cartons and checking in merchandise. With EDI, vendors can transmit information about on-hand inventory status, vendor promotions, and cost changes to the retailer, as well as information about purchase order changes, order status, retail prices, and transportation routings.

Using EDI, suppliers can describe and show pictures of their products, and buyers can issue requests for proposals. The two parties can then electronically negotiate prices and specify how the product will be made and how it should look. This enables channel members to communicate more quickly and with fewer errors than in the past, ensuring that merchandise moves from vendors to retailers more quickly.

The use of EDI provides three main benefits to supply chain members. First, EDI reduces the cycle time, or the time between the decision to place an order and the receipt of merchandise. When EDI is used, information flows more quickly, which means that inventory turnover is higher. Second, EDI improves the overall quality of communications through better record keeping; fewer errors in inputting and receiving an order; and less human error in the interpretation of data. Third, the data transmitted by EDI are in a computer-readable format that can be easily analyzed and used for a variety of tasks, ranging from evaluating vendor delivery performance to automating reorder processes.

Because of these benefits, many retailers are asking their suppliers to interface with them by using EDI. However, small to medium-sized suppliers and retailers face significant barriers, specifically cost and the lack of information technology (IT) expertise, to becoming EDI-enabled. However, EDI remains an important component of any vendor-managed inventory system.

## Vendor-Managed Inventory

**Vendor-managed inventory (VMI)** is an approach for improving marketing channel efficiency in which the manufacturer is responsible for maintaining the retailer's inventory levels in each of its stores. By sharing the data in the retailer's data warehouse and communicating that information via EDI, the manufacturer automatically sends merchandise to the retailer's store or distribution or fulfillment centre when the inventory at the store reaches a pre-specified level.[45]

In ideal conditions, the manufacturer replenishes inventories in quantities that meet the retailer's immediate demand, reducing stockouts with minimal inventory. In addition to providing a better match between retail demand and supply, VMI can reduce the vendor's and the retailer's costs. Manufacturers' salespeople no longer need to spend time generating orders on items that are already in the stores, and their role shifts to selling new items and maintaining relationships. Retail buyers and planners no longer need to monitor inventory levels and place orders.

**electronic data interchange (EDI)** The computer-to-computer exchange of business documents from a retailer to a vendor and back.

**advanced shipping notice** An electronic document that the supplier sends the retailer in advance of a shipment to tell the retailer exactly what to expect in the shipment.

**vendor-managed inventory (VMI)** An approach in which the manufacturer is responsible for replenishing inventory to meet retailers' needs.

# LOGISTICS MANAGEMENT: MAKING MERCHANDISE FLOW

To explore the different types of merchandise flows, consider the following scenario.[46] Merchandise is shipped from Sony to Best Buy's distribution centres or from Sony directly to stores. If the merchandise goes through distribution centres, it is then shipped to stores and then to the customer.

## Distribution Centres Versus Direct Store Delivery

Manufacturers can ship merchandise directly to a retailer's stores—direct store delivery—or to its distribution centres. Although manufacturers and retailers may collaborate, the ultimate decision is usually up to the retailer and depends on the characteristics of the merchandise and the nature of demand. To determine which distribution system—distribution centres or direct store delivery—is better, retailers consider the total cost associated with each alternative and the customer service criterion of having the right merchandise at the store when the customer wants to buy it.

## The Distribution (or Fulfillment) Centre

The distribution centre performs the following activities: management of inbound transportation; receiving and checking; storing and cross-docking; getting merchandise floor-ready; ticketing and marking; preparing to ship merchandise to stores; and shipping merchandise to stores. Fulfillment centres perform the same functions, but because they deliver directly to customers, rather than to stores, they do not have to get merchandise floor ready.

**dispatcher**
The person who coordinates deliveries to distribution centres.

**Inbound Transportation**     Because its distribution centres typically are quite busy, a **dispatcher**—the person who coordinates deliveries to Best Buy's distribution centres—assigns a time slot for each shipment of HDTVs to arrive. If the truck misses the time slot, it is fined. Although many manufacturers pay transportation expenses, some retailers negotiate with their vendors to absorb this expense. These retailers believe they can lower net merchandise cost and control their merchandise flow better if they negotiate directly with truck companies and consolidate shipments from many vendors.

**Receiving and Checking Using UPC or RFID**     Receiving refers to the process of recording the receipt of merchandise as it arrives at a distribution centre or store. Checking is the process of going through the goods upon receipt to ensure that they arrived undamaged and that the merchandise ordered was the merchandise received.

Today, many distribution systems use EDI designed to minimize, if not eliminate, these processes. The advance shipping notice tells the distribution centre what should be in each box. The recipient scans the UPC label on the shipping carton or the radio frequency identification tag, which identifies the carton's contents, and those contents then are automatically counted as being received and checked. **Radio frequency identification (RFID) tags** are tiny computer chips that automatically transmit to a special scanner all the information about a container's contents or individual products. A key advantage of RFID is that it eliminates the need to handle items individually by enabling distribution centres and stores to receive whole truckloads of merchandise without having to check each carton in. The tags also act as passive tracking devices, signalling their presence over a radio frequency when they pass within a few metres of a special scanner. The tags have long been used in high-cost applications, such as automated highway toll systems and security identification badges. As the cost of the tags and implementation technology has decreased, their uses have become more prevalent in retail supply chain applications and even as a research tool.

**radio frequency identification (RFID) tags**
Tiny computer chips that automatically transmit to a special scanner all the information about a container's contents or individual products.

**Storing and Cross-Docking**     After the merchandise is received and checked, it is either stored or cross-docked. A traditional distribution centre is a warehouse in which merchandise is unloaded from trucks and placed on racks or shelves for storage. When the merchandise is needed in the stores, a worker goes to the rack, picks up a carton, and places it on a conveyor system that routes the carton merchandise to the loading dock of a truck going to the store.

Using a cross-docking distribution centre, cartons are prepackaged for a specific store. The merchandise already contains price and theft detection tags. Because the merchandise is ready for sale, it is placed on a conveyor system that routes it from the unloading dock at which it was received to the loading dock for the truck going to the specific store—hence the term *cross-docked*. The cartons are routed on the conveyor system automatically by sensors that read the UPC or RFID label on the cartons. Cross-docked merchandise is in the distribution centre only for a few hours before it is shipped to the stores.

Merchandise sales rate and degree of perishability or fashionability typically determine whether cartons are cross-docked or stored. Most modern distribution centres combine the two previous approaches. It is difficult for a firm to operate without some storage facilities, even if merchandise is stored for only a few days. For instance, some merchandise, such as tent stakes at Mountain Equipment Co-Op, has relatively slow sales but must be carried because it rounds out an assortment. These items are good candidates for storage in a distribution centre, even if the rest of the merchandise is cross-docked. Also, no matter how good a sales forecasting system may be, sometimes the merchandise arrives before it is needed in the stores. In these cases, the retailer must have a system to store the merchandise temporarily.

**Getting Merchandise Floor-Ready** Floor-ready merchandise is merchandise that's ready to be placed on the selling floor immediately. Getting merchandise floor-ready entails ticketing, marking, and, in the case of apparel, placing garments on hangers. *Ticketing and marking* refers to creating price and identification labels and placing them on the merchandise. It is more efficient for a retailer to perform these activities at a distribution centre than in its stores because the work is time consuming and messy. Some retailers require their suppliers to ship merchandise floor-ready, thus totally eliminating this expensive, time-consuming process for themselves.

**Shipping Merchandise to Stores** Shipping merchandise to stores is quite complex for multistore chains. A Best Buy distribution centre will run approximately 100 trucks to its stores per day. To handle such complex transportation problems, distribution centres use a sophisticated routing and scheduling computer system that considers the rate of sales in the store, road conditions, and transportation operating constraints to develop the most efficient routes possible. As a result, stores receive an accurate estimated time of arrival, and the supply chain maximizes vehicle use. In Canada, different shipping methods are chosen depending on the nature of the goods, costs, location of customers relative to manufacturers, and needs of the customers. These methods include air (e.g., Air Canada), rail (e.g., Canadian Pacific Railway), land (e.g., Challenger Motor Freight), and sea (e.g., SEA-CAN).

## Inventory Management Through Just-in-Time Systems

Customers demand specific SKUs, and they want to be able to buy them when needed. At the same time, firms can't afford to carry more than they really need of an SKU, because to do so is very

In a cross-docking distribution centre, merchandise moves from vendors' trucks to the retailer's delivery trucks in a matter of hours.

## REAL MARKETER PROFILE

# David Chilton
# (*The Wealthy Barber*)

Armed with a degree in economics and an award for achieving the highest mark in the country on the Canadian Securities Course, David Chilton started his career as a stockbroker. Working with clients led him to the realization that while there were a lot of books about personal finances, there weren't many that made the topic easy to understand. He soon changed that, publishing *The Wealthy Barber* when he was only 27 years old. The book introduced Canadians to Roy, a barber who imparted sound financial advice while cutting his customers' hair. Based on common sense and an uncommon sense of humour, the book quickly became a bestseller with over 2 million copies sold. It is still the best-selling book of all time in Canada.

Photograph by Mike Rao.

The success of the book led to a career on the speaking circuit. His talks include topics such as "Success Strategies From the Wealthy Barber" and revolve around lessons from his business and personal experience. He claims his recipe for success is "a clear vision, hard work, and some clever marketing."[7] In truth, Chilton has experienced both success and failure, and says that "if you're not failing a lot, you're probably not trying enough."[8]

His publishing success brought sisters Janet and Greta Podleski to his door with a plea to help them get distribution for their *Looney Spoons* cookbook. Chilton famously says he can't cook. Fortunately his mother does. She tested the recipes and was so impressed she told him he had to back the venture. It was sound advice. The book spent 85 consecutive weeks on the bestseller list. He joined the Podleski sisters in Granet Publishing to produce two more best-selling cookbooks: *Crazy Plates* and *Eat, Shrink & Be Merry!*

Chilton also worked with the sisters to bring a frozen entrée, Crazy Plates, to Loblaws grocery stores. While it is normally very difficult to secure distribution, Chilton said that "having a great brand and sales of over 1.3 million cookbooks"[9] helped open doors. However, initial sales of the frozen food line did not meet expectations. While consumers loved the concept, the packaging and large size didn't work. The trio revitalized their marketing efforts with new package designs and a smaller size. While the product sold well after these changes, it has since been withdrawn from the market.

Although he swore he'd never write another book, 22 years later Chilton published *The Wealthy Barber Returns*. Unlike the first book, which focuses on saving more, the second book offers advice on spending less. It advises readers to track their spending and to live within their means. For anyone who knows Chilton, this is not surprising. He has a very modest lifestyle and isn't much of a shopper, in stark contrast to many people whose lives revolve around buying "stuff."

Chilton also spent time as a Dragon on CBC's popular *Dragons' Den*. It was gruelling work with long days spent listening to business pitches while taping shows. The "aw shucks, down-to-earth" personality you saw on the show reflects Chilton's true character. He's a genuinely nice guy who often stays in touch with companies even when deals collapsed after taping a show. With a sincere interest in people and their businesses, he likes to help if he can.

**just-in-time (JIT) inventory systems**
Inventory management systems designed to deliver less merchandise on a more frequent basis than traditional inventory systems; the firm gets the merchandise "just in time" for it to be used in the manufacture of another product; also known as quick-response (QR) systems in retailing.

expensive. Suppose, for instance, that a shoe store carries $1 million worth of inventory at its own expense. Experts estimate that it would cost 20–40 percent of the value of the inventory, or $200,000 to $400,000 per year, to hold that inventory! So firms must balance having enough inventory to satisfy customer demands with not having more than they need.

To help reconcile these seemingly conflicting goals, many firms have adopted just-in-time inventory systems. **Just-in-time (JIT) inventory systems**, also known as **quick-response (QR)** systems in retailing, are inventory management systems designed to deliver less merchandise on a more frequent basis than traditional inventory systems. The firm gets the merchandise "just in time" for it to be used in the manufacture of another product (in the case of parts or components) or for sale when the customer wants it (in the case of consumer goods). The benefits of a JIT system include reduced

**lead time** (by eliminating the need for paper transactions by mail and overnight deliveries), increased product availability, and lower inventory investment. JIT systems lower inventory investments, but product availability actually increases.

Although firms achieve great benefits from a JIT system, it is not without its costs. The distribution function becomes much more complicated with more frequent deliveries. With greater order frequency also come smaller orders, which are more expensive to transport and more difficult to coordinate. Therefore, JIT systems require a strong commitment by the firm and its vendors to cooperate, share data, and develop systems.

For more on JIT inventory systems, see the Chapter Case Study, "Zara Delivers Fast Fashion."

**quick-response (QR)**
An inventory management system used in retailing; merchandise is received just in time for sale when the customer wants it.

**lead time**
The amount of time between the recognition that an order needs to be placed and the arrival of the needed merchandise at the seller's store, ready for sale.

## LEARNING OBJECTIVES REVIEW

**LO1** Explain the importance of distribution and the interrelationships among distribution channels, supply chain management, and logistics management

Companies cannot take the distribution of products for granted. Appropriate distribution channels must be identified and channel members need to be convinced to carry these new products, both of which are integral to a successful distribution strategy. A distribution channel is the set of institutions and marketing activities that transfer the ownership of goods and move goods from the manufacturer or producer to the consumer. Supply chain management refers to the effort to coordinate suppliers, manufacturers, warehouses, stores, and transportation intermediaries so that the merchandise the customer wants is produced in the right quantities and sent to the right locations at the time the customer wants it. In this sense, the supply chain is considered to be longer and covers more aspects of the distribution strategy since it extends backward to include suppliers. Logistics concentrates on the physical movement and control of the products, whereas supply chain management includes the managerial aspects of the process as well.

**LO2** Identify how distribution channels add value to businesses and consumers

Without distribution channels, consumers would be forced to find raw materials, manufacture products, and somehow get them to where they could be used, all on their own. Each channel member adds value to the product by performing one of these functions. Supply chain management creates value for each firm in the chain and helps bind together many company functions, including manufacturing, inventory management, transportation, advertising, and marketing.

**LO3** Describe distribution channel design and management decisions and strategies

Sometimes, particularly when firms are starting out, companies cannot choose their ideal partners but instead take any partners they can get to obtain the materials or customers they need. In general, the larger and more sophisticated the company, the more likely it is to perform some supply chain activities itself rather than use third-party intermediaries. When deciding on the distribution channel structure, firms can choose from direct, indirect, and multi-channel distribution. Firms that want as much market exposure as possible use intensive distribution, whereas firms that either want to maintain an exclusive image or are not large enough to sell to everyone tend to use an exclusive distribution strategy. Somewhere in the middle lies a selective distribution strategy.

**LO4** Explain how logistics management affects distribution strategy

For a supply chain to operate properly, the flow of information and merchandise must be coordinated, and supply chain members must work together to their mutual benefit. In more sophisticated supply chains, information flows seamlessly between supply chain members through EDI. Many of the best supply chains use a JIT or QR inventory management system, which provides the right amount of inventory just when it is needed. The JIT systems thus improve product availability and reduce inventory investments. The increasing use of RFID technology is expected to have a revolutionary impact on distribution channels, supply chain management, and logistics management in the future. The expectation is that the overall system of producing and delivering will become much more sophisticated and efficient.

The more closely aligned the supply chain members are with each other, the less likely it is that there will be significant conflict. An administered supply chain occurs when a dominant and powerful supply chain member has control over the other members. In a contractual supply chain (e.g., franchising), coordination and control are dictated by contractual relationships between members. Corporate supply chains can operate relatively smoothly because one firm owns the various levels of the chains. Supply chains also can be effectively managed through strong relationships developed with supply chain partners. To create such relationships, the partners must trust each other, communicate openly, have compatible goals, and be willing to invest in each other's success.

## KEY TERMS

- administered vertical marketing system
- advanced shipping notice
- channel conflict
- contractual vertical marketing system
- corporate vertical marketing system
- dispatcher
- distribution centre
- distribution channel
- distribution intensity

- electronic data interchange (EDI)
- exclusive distribution
- franchising
- intensive distribution
- just-in-time (JIT) inventory systems
- lead time
- logistics management
- pull marketing strategy
- push marketing strategy
- quick-response (QR)

- radio frequency identification (RFID) tags
- retailers
- selective distribution
- strategic relationship (partnering relationship)
- supply chain management
- universal product code (UPC)
- vendor-managed inventory (VMI)
- vertical marketing system
- wholesalers

## CONCEPT REVIEW

1. Explain why having a well thought out distribution strategy is important to a company's success.

2. Explain the factors that must be considered when designing a distribution strategy.

3. Explain the differences between direct, indirect, and multi-channel distribution systems. What role do technologies and consumer behaviour play in the rise of multi-channel distribution?

4. Describe the functions performed by intermediaries. Why would companies choose to have intermediaries fulfill these functions rather than perform them themselves?

5. Explain how customer expectations and channel member characteristics impact a company's distribution strategy.

6. Explain intensive, selective, and exclusive distribution intensity. Under what circumstances would it be best to use each of these strategies?

7. Describe how companies manage distribution channels by using vertical marketing systems.

8. Explain how supply chain management and logistics management add value to a company's consumer offerings.

9. Explain how supply chain management improves marketing activities.

10. What are the major elements of a logistics management system? Explain the benefits of a well run just-in-time inventory management system.

## MARKETING APPLICATIONS

1. Explain distribution strategy and identify the major activities that distribution channels, supply chain, and logistics management involve. Identify several ways that supply chain management adds value to a company's offerings, with regard to both consumers and business partners.

2. You are hired by a small bakery that is interested in distributing its product through supermarkets. The market for the bakery's products has been steadily growing and it is time to expand distribution now that the bakery has expanded its production capacity. You have an appointment with the manager of a local grocery chain. The manager is familiar with the bakery's products and is excited about the possibility of having them in the store. He presents the contract and you notice a $10,000 fee for stocking the product. When you ask about the fee, you are told it is simply the cost of doing business and that the bigger bakeries are not in favour of adding your product line to the chain. You know that the bakery cannot afford to pay the fee. What should you do now?

3. Discuss the advantages and disadvantages of Dell's decision to change from using a direct distribution strategy to a multi-channel approach to distribution.

4. Research the "100-mile diet" trend and discuss how growing consumer awareness of shipping costs and environmental concerns has led to a push for more locally produced foods.

5. Give an example of a retailer that participates in an independent (conventional) supply chain and one involved in a vertical marketing system. Discuss the advantages and disadvantages of each.

**6.** In what ways can the flow of information be managed in the supply chain? How can the ready flow of information increase a firm's operating efficiencies?

**7.** Describe how B2B transactions might employ EDI to process purchase information. Considering the information discussed in Chapter 5 about B2B buying situations, determine which buying situation (new task, modified re-buy, or straight rebuy) would most likely align with the use of EDI technology. Justify your answer.

**8.** Discuss the advantages to a retailer such as Sport Chek of expending the time and effort to get merchandise floor-ready at either the point of manufacture or in the distribution centre rather than having retail store staff members do it in the stores. Provide the logic behind your answer.

**9.** Why would a large company such as Nike want to develop strategic partnerships with locally owned running stores? Describe what Nike would have to do to maintain such relationships.

**10.** You are hired as an assistant brand manager for a popular consumer product. One day in an emergency meeting, the brand manager informs the group that there is a problem with one of the suppliers and that she has decided to send you over to the manufacturing facilities to investigate the problem. When you arrive at the plant, you learn that a key supplier has become increasingly unreliable in terms of quality and delivery. You ask the plant manager why he doesn't switch suppliers since this is becoming a major problem for your brand. He informs you that the troubled supplier is his cousin, whose wife has been very ill, and he just can't switch right now. What course of action should you take?

## NET SAVVY

**1.** Dell is considered exemplary in its ability to manage its supply chain efficiently. Go to the company's website (http://www.dell.com) and go through the process of configuring a computer to purchase. Print a summary of the computer system you have designed, making note of the delivery date and price. Describe how Dell has revolutionized computer sales and delivery. Is there any indication that Dell has partnered with other companies to sell peripheral equipment such as printers or scanners? How would this partnership add value to customers?

**2.** The Chapter Case Study examines how Zara, a division of Inditex, successfully manages its supply chain. Visit Inditex's website (http://www.inditex.com) and review the company's commitment to social responsibility, particularly the section that pertains to its code of conduct. Considering the discussion in this chapter about strategic relationships, how does Inditex address the factors necessary for mutually beneficial partnerships according to its code of conduct?

## CHAPTER CASE STUDY

### ZARA DELIVERS FAST FASHION[50]

In the fast fashion retail business strategy, supply chain management processes serve to introduce fashionable merchandise rapidly, such that stores can respond immediately to customer demand for merchandise. This was pioneered by Zara, a global specialty apparel chain located in La Coruna, Spain. It has also been adopted by other retailers, including American Apparel, H&M (headquartered in Sweden), TopShop (United Kingdom) and Forever 21 (United States).

The approach is particularly effective for specialty apparel retailers that target fashion-conscious consumers who simply must have the latest looks—but they want to do so on a very limited budget. These shoppers load up on new fast fashions every few weeks, instead of purchasing a few higher-priced basics every few months.

To fit with such short cycles and meet customers' demands, the fast fashion process starts with the receipt of timely information from store managers. At Zara, store managers always have their reporting devices literally in hand. These handheld devices, which are linked directly to the company's corporate office in Spain, enable daily reports on what customers are buying (or not) and what they are asking for but not finding.

For example, customers might want a purple version of a pink shirt that they see on the shop floor. Managers immediately pass the information on to the designers in Spain. Those designers

Zara's competitive advantage in specialty apparel retailing is based on its efficient supply chain that delivers fashionable merchandise to its stores frequently.

Denis Doyle/AP Photo

then communicate electronically with the factory that produces fabric for shirts. This factory starts up its automated equipment, which is run by assemblers who live in close proximity to the factory. (The undyed fabric comes from Asia, where Zara finds inexpensive sources, and then bulk ships fabric to Spain and Portugal to be manufactured into apparel.) The robots in the company's 23 highly automated factories start cutting out shirts and mixing purple dye. For final construction, a network of 300 or so small assemblers, located near the factories in Galicia, Spain, and northern Portugal, take responsibility for making the final product. Finally, to ensure timely delivery, the shirts get shipped by truck to stores in Europe and by air express to stores in the rest of the world.

## The Benefits of Fast Fashion for Zara

Zara's main advantage over its competitors, such as The Gap and H&M, has resulted from its highly responsive and tightly organized supply chain. Unlike these competitors, Zara selects factory locations that are in close geographic proximity to the company's headquarters in Spain. Although this approach increases labour costs, compared with outsourced production in lower-cost countries in Asia, it also improves communication, reduces shipping costs and time, and reduces the time before new fashions appear in stores. It also gives Zara the flexibility to modify its operations in one supply chain function to expedite processes in another, such as pricing or tagging. It might hang merchandise on racks in the warehouse so that store employees can move apparel directly from delivery to the sales floor. And it can do all this because it maintains complete control over the entire process.

Furthermore, instead of shipping new products a few times a season, as many of its competitors do, Zara makes deliveries to every one of its stores every few days. The purple shirts would be in stores in two weeks—compared with the several months it would take most department stores and other specialty apparel stores to accomplish the same feat. Because its fast fashion system also ensures shorter lead times, it's less likely that any Zara store will be out of stock before the next sweater shipment arrives. Limiting the stock in stores even can create a sense of scarcity among its customers. If they don't buy now, the item might not be available next time they visit the store. By producing and shipping in these small quantities, Zara can quickly recover from its (rare) fashion faux pas.

Finally, the efficiency of its supply chain means Zara rarely has to discount merchandise that is not selling. At Zara, the number of items that end up marked down is about half the industry average. Even with these results, Zara still manages to introduce around 10,000 new designs and 40,000 new SKUs each year.

## Moving Too Fast? The Negative Effects of Fast Fashion

Despite some strong signals of success—including annual growth rates of approximately 20 percent in terms of sales and number of stores—Zara started to outgrow its own strategy. By their very nature, fashion trends change rapidly and constantly, and so must the merchandise on Zara's shop floors. Faced with disappointed customers, some sales managers ordered extra quantities of hot items, to avoid stockouts. Even with this attempt to circumvent the replenishment system, some stores still suffered from stockouts, because they received fewer units than they had ordered when overall demand exceeded inventory levels. For some items, Zara even confronted perhaps the most frustrating scenario in a supply chain: inventory sat unused, eating up storage costs, at one location, even as another store desperately pleaded for the same inventory to meet its customers' demand.

As noted above, the company launches as many as 10,000 new styles annually, with a range of colours and sizes, resulting in hundreds of thousands of SKUs in the system. Counting replenishment orders, which are received twice weekly, Zara's average shipping total reached nearly 2.5 million items per week, all coming from the company's distribution centre. Its legendary supply chain efficiency thus was in danger of a clogged artery.

In response, Zara has adopted some new mathematical processes that turn human experience and mountains of data into actionable information. These models factor in store managers' unique requests for merchandise replenishments, together with historical trends in the sales of the same item. Merchandise display practices have been altered, such as removing all sizes of a garment from the sales floor if a popular size is not available. This practice helps reduce customer frustration, in that they never see an item that might not be available in their size. It also diminishes shipping; if the medium size is unavailable, the small and large sizes do not get shipped either. Instead, these remaining sizes head toward the stores that still have all sizes in stock, so they can be available to customers there.

Growth, costs, market demand, and technology advances all can push retail executives to rethink their business processes. But truly savvy managers search for ways to optimize operations, even when business is running smoothly. As Zara learned, current approaches will not necessarily work tomorrow. As the founder of Zara's corporate owner Inditex told the company's first deputy chair and CEO, "Once a month, come here thinking that we are near bankruptcy. You will find a lot of things to change."[51]

## Questions

1. How does an individual firm like Zara manage a supply chain? How does it get new products from design to store so quickly?

2. What are some of the ways that Zara's supply chain management system has helped create value for its customers? Provide specific examples.

3. What challenges did Zara's focus on supply chain efficiency create? Are all such systems destined to suffer such "growing pains"?

# CHAPTER 13

## LEARNING OBJECTIVES

After studying this chapter you should be able to

**LO1** Outline the considerations associated with choosing retail partners

**LO2** Identify what types of retailers are available to distribute products

**LO3** Describe the components of a retail strategy building on the four Ps to create value for consumers

**LO4** Identify the benefits and challenges of omnichannel retailing

Trademarks of Canadian Tire Corporation, Limited used under licence.

# Retailing and Omnichannel Marketing

Canadian Tire Corporation (CTC) has been providing customers with everything they need for the jobs and joys in life in Canada since 1922. The company started with a single store called Hamilton Tire and Garage Limited in Toronto, which was purchased by brothers A.J. and J.W. Billes in 1922. They renamed the company Canadian Tire Corporation in 1927 and grew it into a powerhouse.

Almost a century later, Canadian Tire Corporation has become a family of companies that includes Canadian Tire Retail, Canadian Tire Financial Services, FGL Sports (Sport Chek, Hockey Experts, Sports Experts, National Sports, Intersport, Pro Hockey Life and Atmosphere), Mark's, Canadian Tire Gas+, PartSource, CT Real Estate Investment Trust, and Canadian Tire Jumpstart Charities.

- Canadian Tire has a network of approximately 500 retail stores across Canada that offer everything from automotive parts and services to sports, leisure, home products, and a strong network of private label brands.[1]

- Canadian Tire Financial Services, through its Canadian Tire Options® MasterCard®, has nearly 2.4 million card members. The credit card is accepted at more than 24 million locations worldwide and offers customers the ability to collect e-Canadian Tire 'Money'™.

- FGL Sports is the largest and only national sporting goods retailer in Canada, with over 430 locations across multiple banners. The company sells a vast assortment of sports-related products, from athletic footwear to athletic/leisure apparel, and to the equipment required for performing a favourite sport.

- Mark's, known as L'Équipeur in Quebec, is one of Canada's leading apparel retailers. Since it was founded in 1977, Mark's has evolved from one small store in Calgary to over 380 stores across Canada.

- Canadian Tire Gas+ is one of Canada's largest independent gasoline retailers, pumping more than 1.8 billion litres of gasoline each year at approximately 296 outlets nationwide.

- PartSource, launched in 1999, is an automotive parts specialty chain with over 90 corporate specialty stores staffed by experts to meet the needs of professional automotive installers and serious "do-it-yourselfers."

- CT Real Estate Investment Trust is an unincorporated, closed end real estate investment trust formed to own income producing commercial properties primarily located in Canada.

- Canadian Tire Jumpstart Charities is a national charitable program that helps financially disadvantaged kids participate in organized sport and recreation. Since 2005, Jumpstart has helped give more than 1,000,000 Canadian kids aged 4–18 the chance to play.

Canadian Tire Corporation, through its various businesses, employs more than 85,000 people and earned revenues of $12.68 billion in 2016.[2] It is one of the most trusted brands in Canada, and its CEO, Stephen Wetmore, was named Retailer of the Year by the Retail Council of Canada in 2013. The company has been called one of the best brands and most successful companies in Canada, earning a spot on Canada's Top 10 Most Reputable Brands every year for well over a decade.[3] It has a unique assortment of products and services, a modern store network, and global sourcing capabilities. The company does an excellent job of leveraging its trusted brand across its multiple businesses. Because of Canadian Tire's level of success over the years, one wonders about its secret for success and whether it has always been smooth sailing for the company.

Canadian Tire has received lumps, bumps, and bruises on several occasions. For example, in 1982, Canadian Tire debuted in the United States, but the venture failed miserably and by 1985 the company was forced to withdraw.[4] In 1992, the company decided to take another stab at the U.S. market under the name Auto Source. It again failed and bailed out in 1995, after three years and huge losses.[5] Despite these and other challenges, Canadian Tire has emerged as a successful and well managed business, part of Canadian culture and found in virtually every community across the country. Its success has been attributed to CTC's strong brand, vision, good strategic planning, and excellent execution of its marketing strategies.

When global giants Walmart, Home Depot, and Lowes entered the already crowded Canadian market, many industry analysts feared that their deep pockets and aggressive business strategies would spell the end of Canadian Tire Corporation. However, it not only has held its own against these global behemoths, but has steadily grown. The company has responded to advancing technology by integrating its website into its physical store operations and upgrading its information technology and communication infrastructure. It has adopted a wide range of environmental initiatives aimed at reducing its carbon footprint. Its acquisition in 2001 of Mark's Work Wearhouse (now called simply Mark's) allowed it to pursue a broader target market, including women. Expansion continued in 2011 with the purchase of FGL Sports, including store banners such as Sport Chek, Atmosphere, National Sports, and Hockey Experts among others.

The company implemented a wide range of strategies aimed at improving cost efficiencies and productivity, enhancing customer service, bolstering its brands, growing its businesses, strengthening its loyalty program, and renewing its store concepts. The company launched its Winnipeg Data Centre in 2013, to better identify how customers want to shop—from home and in-store—and turned pain points into retail opportunities. It also launched an innovation lab in the Communitech Hub in Kitchener, Ontario, in 2013, followed by opening a Digital Garage in the same location two years later to further its digital innovation strategy.

Its wide variety of products had resulted in cluttered stores that were hard to navigate. In 2015, it launched a new showcase store in Edmonton, featuring varied shelf sizes, better sight lines, more natural light, and a cleaner overall look. Over 100 digital screens facilitate locating items and let customers watch tutorial videos to identify the right tools and products needed for projects. Virtual reality simulators allow shoppers to see how furniture would look in a backyard setting. A car simulator lets them test tires in different weather conditions.[6] The effort paid off when the Edmonton store won the Best In-Store Experience and Design Award at the Retail Council of Canada's Excellence in Retailing Awards.[7]

To reach consumers in a competitive retail environment, the company has invested heavily in the digital realm. After years of not producing a catalogue, it reintroduced one—*The WOW Guide*—with a digital twist, combining print and online features. Consumers could access online information from the hard copy catalogue using a mobile app. The new catalogue had an immediate impact on the company's ecommerce business, doubling its weekly online sales in the company's first quarter of 2016.[8] Facebook and Google now represent the company's top advertising channels. When Canadian Tire learned that Facebook users spent only seven seconds watching videos and the majority did so without sound, it created seven-second silent ads. The new format worked, increasing sell-through rate by 50 percent in comparison to previous ads.[9] After monitoring popular search terms on the Sport Chek website, merchandisers noted that FlipBelts (used by runners for storing keys and cash) were a top phrase and quickly added them to its product offerings.

Canadian Tire's retail innovations have created sustainable competitive advantage. Now, can it stay relevant for the next 100 years? ∎

Retailing sits at the end of the supply chain, where marketing meets the consumer. But there is far more to retailing than just manufacturing a product and making it available to customers. This chapter extends the discussion of supply chain management from Chapter 12 by examining why and how manufacturers use retailers. We explain how manufacturers choose retailers to carry their products and we discuss the types of retailers currently operating in Canada. Then we examine how retailers create value by implementing marketing mix strategies. We follow this with a discussion of how omnichannel options are changing the face of retailing and the ongoing evolution toward omnichannel marketing.

**Retailing** is defined as the set of business activities that add value to products and services sold to consumers for their personal or family use. Our definition of retailing includes products bought at stores, through catalogues, and over the Internet, as well as services such as fast-food restaurants, airlines, and hotels. Some retailers claim they sell at "wholesale" prices, but if they sell to customers for their personal use, they are still retailers, regardless of their prices. Wholesalers (see Chapter 12) buy products from manufacturers and resell them to retailers or industrial or business users.

Retailing today is changing, both in Canada and around the world. No longer do manufacturers rule many marketing channels, as they once did. Retailers such as Walmart, Costco, Carrefour (a French hypermarket), Home Depot, Loblaws, and Metro (a German retail conglomerate)[10]—the largest retailers in the world—dictate to their suppliers what should be made, how it should be configured, when it should be delivered, and, to some extent, what it should cost. These retailers are clearly in the driver's seat.

Retailing in the aggregate is a big business. Virtually every penny you personally spend, except for taxes, goes to retailers. Food, rent, clothing, tuition, insurance, and haircuts are all either retail services or goods provided by retailers. Even non-profit organizations such as The Salvation Army, Goodwill Industries, and the Ontario Science Centre have retail operations. Canadian retail sales in 2016 were $533 billion,[11] representing more than 227,000 retail establishments. Retailing is Canada's third largest industry by size, employing approximately 2 million people.[12]

This chapter examines how and why manufacturers use retailers. The manufacturer's strategy depends on its overall market power and on how consistent a new product or product line is with its current offerings.

Even non-profit organizations such as The Salvation Army have retail operations.

Martin Good/Shutterstock.com

Exhibit 13.1 illustrates four factors manufacturers consider when developing strategies for working with retailers.[13] In choosing retail partners, the first factor, manufacturers assess how likely it is for certain retailers to carry their products. Manufacturers also consider where their target customers expect to find the products, because those are exactly the stores in which they want to place their products.

**retailing**
The set of business activities that add value to products and services sold to consumers for their personal or family use; includes products bought at stores, through catalogues, and over the Internet, as well as services such as fast-food restaurants, airlines, and hotels.

**EXHIBIT 13.1**    Factors for Establishing a Relationship With Retailers

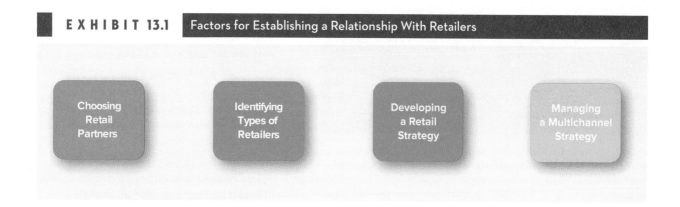

Choosing Retail Partners

Identifying Types of Retailers

Developing a Retail Strategy

Managing a Multichannel Strategy

The overall size and level of sophistication of the manufacturer will determine how many of the supply chain functions it performs and how many it will hand off to other channel members such as wholesalers (see Chapter 12). Finally, the type and availability of the product and the image the manufacturer wishes to portray will determine how many retailers within a geographic region will carry the products.

For the second factor, manufacturers identify the types of retailers that would be appropriate to carry their products. Although the choice is often obvious—such as a supermarket for fresh produce—manufacturers may have a choice of retailer types for some products.

As we discussed in Chapter 12, a hallmark of a strong distribution channel is that manufacturers and retailers coordinate their efforts. In the third factor, manufacturers and retailers therefore develop their strategy by implementing the four Ps.

**omnichannel strategy**
Selling in more than one channel (e.g., store, catalogue, kiosk, and Internet).

Finally, many retailers and some manufacturers are exploring an **omnichannel strategy** in which they sell in more than one channel (e.g., store, catalogue, kiosk, and Internet). The fourth factor therefore consists of examining the circumstances in which sellers may prefer to adopt a particular strategy. Although these factors are listed consecutively, manufacturers may consider them all simultaneously or in a different order.

## LO1    CHOOSING RETAIL PARTNERS

Imagine trying to buy a suit for a job interview without being able to visit a retailer. You would have to figure out exactly what size, colour, and style of suit you wanted. Then you'd have to contact various manufacturers, whether in person, by phone, or over the Internet, and order the suit. Assuming it fit you reasonably well, you might still need to take it to a tailor to have the sleeves shortened. Then you'd have to go through the same process for a shirt or blouse, accessories, and shoes. It would not be very convenient.

Retailers such as Moores Clothing for Men create value by pulling it all together for you. The store offers a broad selection of suits, shirts, ties, and other accessories that it has carefully chosen in advance. You can see, touch, and try on each item while in the store. You can buy one suit or shirt at a time or buy several shirts to go with your new suit. Finally, the store provides a salesperson to help you coordinate your outfit and a tailor to make the whole thing fit perfectly.

When choosing retail partners, manufacturers consider the basic channel structure, where their target customers expect to find the products, and channel member characteristics. A manufacturer's strategy depends on its overall market power, and how consistent a new product or line is with current offerings. As discussed in Chapter 12, distribution intensity is also a factor to be considered. Think about the following scenarios:

Moores Clothing for Men creates value by helping men put it all together. Its wardrobe consultants provide fashion advice, and their tailors make sure everything fits properly.

© Lars A. Niki

- **Scenario 1**: Cosmetics conglomerate Estée Lauder's subsidiary brand MAC is introducing a new line of mascara.

- **Scenario 2**: Coach, well known for its women's handbags, is introducing a line of men's leather goods, apparel, shoes, and accessories—products not previously in its assortment.

- **Scenario 3**: Britt, a young entrepreneur, is launching a new line of environmentally friendly (green) hair care products.

Each of these scenarios is different and requires the manufacturer to consider different alternatives for reaching its target markets through retailers.

## Channel Structure

The level of difficulty a manufacturer has in getting retailers to purchase its products is determined by the degree to which the channel is vertically integrated, as described in Chapter 12; the degree to which the manufacturer has a strong brand or is otherwise desirable in the market; and the relative power of the manufacturer and retailer.

Scenario 1 represents a corporate vertical marketing system. Because MAC is made by Estée Lauder and operates its own stores, when the new mascara line is introduced, the stores will simply receive the new line automatically. They have no choice.

When an established firm such as Coach enters a new market with men's leather goods, apparel, shoes, and accessories, as is the case in Scenario 2, it cannot just place the products with any retailer. It must determine where its customers would expect to find higher-end scarves, leather goods, and accessories, and then use its established relationships with women's handbag buyers, the power of its brand, and its overall reputation to leverage its position in this new product area.

In Scenario 3, our young entrepreneur Britt would have an even more difficult time getting a retailer to buy and sell her green hair care line, because she lacks power in the marketplace—she is small, and her brand is unknown. It would be difficult to get buyers to see her, let alone consider her line. She might face relatively high listing fees (see Chapter 12) just to get space on retailers' shelves. But like Coach in Scenario 2, when choosing retailers to which to sell, Britt should consider where the end customer expects to find her products, as well as some important retailer characteristics.

## Customer Expectations

From a retailer's perspective, it is important to know from which manufacturers its customers want to buy. Manufacturers, in contrast, need to know where their target market customers expect to find their products and those of their competitors. Customers generally expect to find certain products at some stores but not at others. For example, Estée Lauder and Coach would not choose to sell to Giant Tiger because their customers would not expect to shop at this store for high-end cosmetics or leather goods. Instead, such stores might carry less expensive cosmetic brands, such as Revlon and Maybelline, or even discontinued lines. But Coach customers would definitely expect to find the brand's clothing offerings at major department stores and at Coach stores.

Companies need to stay abreast of changes in where customers buy products and what products they request, and then change their distribution strategies accordingly. As an example, Fitbit is both an electronic device and a fitness tool. Due to the nature of its product, the company distributes through electronics stores (Best Buy and The Source), sporting goods stores (Atmosphere and Sport Chek) and even Chapters, which has increased its electronics offerings.

## Channel Member Characteristics

Several factors pertaining to the channel members themselves will help determine the channel structure. Generally, the larger and more sophisticated the channel member, the less likely it is to use supply chain intermediaries. Britt will probably use a group of independent salespeople to help sell her green hair care line, whereas a large manufacturer such as Estée Lauder will use its own sales force that already has existing relationships in the industry. In the same way, an independent grocery store might buy merchandise from a wholesaler; but Walmart, the world's largest grocer, buys only directly from the manufacturer. Larger firms often find that by performing the channel functions themselves, they can gain more control, be more efficient, and save money.

As we noted in Chapter 12, like any large, complicated system, a distribution channel is difficult to manage. Whether the balance of power rests with large retailers like

Walmart or with large manufacturers like P&G, channel members benefit by working together to develop and implement their channel strategy. In the next section, we explore the different types of retailers with an eye toward which would be most appropriate for each of our scenarios: MAC Cosmetics, Coach's products for men, and Britt's new line of environmentally friendly hair care products.

## L02  IDENTIFYING TYPES OF RETAILERS

Although it may seem clear which type of retailer Coach and Britt may wish to pursue when attempting to place their new lines, the choice is not always straightforward. Manufacturers need to understand the general characteristics of different types of retailers so they can determine the best channels for their product. For instance, the characteristics of a retailer that are important to a food manufacturer may be quite different from those of a cosmetics manufacturer. In the next few sections, we examine the various types of retailers, identify some major players, and discuss some of the issues facing each type.

### Food Retailers

The food retailing landscape is changing dramatically. Not too long ago, people shopped for food primarily at traditional grocery stores. Today, however, you can buy food at drugstores, discount stores, warehouse clubs, and convenience stores. Pharmacy chains such as Shoppers Drug Mart offer milk, bread, and even fresh fruit in some locations. Walmart and the Real Canadian Superstore both provide supercentres whose product mix contains 30–40 percent food items. Even Amazon is getting into the grocery business. To stay competitive, Loblaw has tested ecommerce sales and launched its "Click & Collect" program to allow customers to order online and pick the order up at their convenience. Walmart, which wants to become the leading grocery store in Canada, quickly followed suit, launching a similar pick-up service.

Food sales represent about 50 percent of the total sales in warehouse clubs such as Costco. Convenience stores now offer more than a slushie and gasoline; for example, Petro-Canada Neighbours stores provide upscale sandwiches and salads. And retailers such as Walmart and IKEA have in-store restaurants, making it easy for customers to shop longer. And, of course, restaurants also compete for consumers' food dollars. The characteristics of the three major categories of food retailers—the **conventional supermarket**, the **big-box food retailer**, and the convenience store—are summarized in Exhibit 13.2.

**conventional supermarket**
Offers groceries, meat, and produce with limited sales of nonfood items, such as health and beauty aids and general merchandise, in a self-service format.

**big-box food retailer**
Comes in three types: supercentre, hypermarket, and warehouse club; larger than a conventional supermarket; carries both food and nonfood items.

| **EXHIBIT 13.2** | Food Retailer Characteristics | |
|---|---|---|
| **Category** | **Description** | **Examples** |
| Conventional supermarket | Offers groceries, meat, and produce with limited sales of nonfood items, such as health and beauty aids and general merchandise, in a self-service format. | Safeway is a popular supermarket in Western Canada; Sobeys is common in Central Canada and on the East Coast. |
| Big-box food retailer | Comes in three types: supercentres, hypermarkets, and warehouse clubs. Larger than conventional supermarkets, they carry both food and nonfood items. | Supercentres and warehouse clubs are popular in Canada, whereas hypermarkets tend to flourish in Europe and South America. Hypermarkets (Carrefour) and warehouse clubs (Costco) generally carry a greater percentage of food. |
| Convenience store | Provides a limited number of items at convenient locations in small stores with speedy checkout. | Stores such as 7-Eleven generally charge higher prices than most other types of food stores. Most convenience stores also sell gasoline, which accounts for more than 55 percent of their annual sales. |

All this competition can mean trouble for traditional grocery stores. Yet some continue to thrive because they offer their target customers great value—they are conveniently located, make shopping easy, have fair prices, and find special products and services that are important to their customers. Pete's Fine Foods, a Halifax-based grocery store, effectively competes on selection and service. Knowledgeable staff members offer information about the selection of produce, storage, and cooking tips, and an in-house registered dietitian helps shoppers understand which foods can re-energize their health.[14]

## General Merchandise Retailers

The main types of **general merchandise retailers** are discount stores, specialty stores, category specialists, department stores, drugstores, off-price retailers, and extreme-value retailers. Many of these general merchandise retailers sell through multiple channels, such as the Internet and catalogues, as discussed later in this chapter.

### Discount Stores

A **discount store** offers a broad variety of merchandise, limited service, and low prices. Walmart and Giant Tiger dominate the discount store industry in Canada and vie for similar target markets. But because their competencies are slightly distinct, they both can survive. Walmart pioneered the everyday low-price concept, and its efficient operations have allowed it to offer the lowest-priced basket of merchandise in every market in which it competes—which doesn't necessarily mean that Walmart has the lowest price on every item in every market. But it does try to be the lowest across a wide variety. Giant Tiger sells a large volume of merchandise at everyday low prices. It aims to offer everything a customer could want, all under one roof, including a large assortment of casual clothing and footwear, groceries, cleaning supplies, housewares, toys, and health and beauty products.

People love to shop at Giant Tiger stores because their merchandise is inexpensive, the stores are conveniently located and easy to shop in, and treasures are found every day among the basics.

Used with permission of Giant Tiger Stores Limited

### Specialty Stores

**Specialty stores** concentrate on a limited number of complementary merchandise categories in relatively small stores. These stores tailor their retail strategy toward very specific market segments by offering deep but narrow assortments and sales associate expertise. For example, Payless ShoeSource is the largest specialty family footwear retailer in the western hemisphere. Payless stores feature fashionable, quality footwear and accessories for women, men, and children at affordable prices in a self-selection format.

Estée Lauder's MAC line of cosmetics sells in the company's own retail specialty stores, as well as in some department stores. Specialty stores would be excellent outlets for the new lines by Estée Lauder and Britt. Customers likely expect to find Coach's line of men's leather goods and accessories in men's apparel, gift, or leather stores. Britt's line of green hair care products would fit nicely in a specialty store such as Sephora.

Sephora, France's leading perfume and cosmetic chain—a division of the luxury goods conglomerate LVMH (Louis Vuitton–Moët Hennessy)—is an example of an innovative specialty store concept. In Canada, prestigious cosmetics are typically sold in department stores. Each brand has a separate counter and a commissioned salesperson is stationed behind the counter to help customers. Sephora is a cosmetic and perfume specialty store offering a deep assortment in a self-service, 550- to 840-square-metre format. Its stores provide more than 15 000 SKUs and more than 200 brands, including its

**general merchandise retailers**
May be discount stores, specialty stores, category specialists, department stores, drugstores, off-price retailers, or extreme-value retailers; may sell through multiple channels, such as the Internet and catalogues.

**discount store**
Offers a broad variety of merchandise, limited service, and low prices.

**specialty stores**
Concentrate on a limited number of complementary merchandise categories in a relatively small store.

own, private-label brand. Merchandise is grouped by product category, with the brands displayed alphabetically so customers can locate them easily. Customers are free to shop and experiment on their own. Product testing is encouraged. The knowledgeable salespeople, always available to assist customers, are paid a salary by Sephora, unlike department store cosmetic salespeople, who are compensated in part by incentives provided by the vendors. The low-key, open-sell environment results in customers spending more time shopping.

**category specialist**
Offers a narrow variety but a deep assortment of merchandise.

**category killer**
Offers an extensive assortment in a particular category, so overwhelming the category that other retailers have difficulty competing.

Category Specialists  A **category specialist** offers a narrow variety but a deep assortment of merchandise. Some are like large specialty stores, such as Paderno (home and kitchen tools) or Chapters Indigo (books); others resemble discount stores in appearance and have similar low prices but offer a more concentrated assortment of goods, such as Best Buy (consumer electronics) or Rona (home improvement). Most category specialists use a self-service approach, but some, such as Home Depot, provide extensive customer service. Because category specialists offer such an extensive assortment in a particular category, they can so overwhelm the category that other retailers have difficulty competing; in these cases, the specialist is frequently called a **category killer**. Using their category dominance, these retailers are able to exploit their buying power to negotiate low prices.

Department Stores  Department stores are retailers that carry many different types of merchandise (broad variety) and lots of items within each type (deep assortment), offer some customer services, and are organized into separate departments to display their merchandise. Department stores often resemble a collection of specialty shops, including women's, men's, and children's clothing and accessories; home furnishings and furniture; and kitchenwares and small appliances.

Stores such as Home Depot are known as category specialists because they offer a narrow variety but a deep assortment of merchandise.

AP Photo/Virginia Hart, File/The Canadian Press

With the demise of Eaton's and Sears, the largest remaining department store chain in Canada is the Hudson's Bay Company. Other store chains are very diverse. Some, such as Saks OFF Fifth, carry less expensive products and compete more closely with discount stores, whereas others, such as Holt Renfrew, sell expensive, exclusive merchandise and compete with high-end specialty store chains. Founded in 1840, higher end fashion retailer Simons has been rapidly expanding outside of its home province of Quebec with new stores in Ontario, Alberta, and British Columbia.

Department stores have lost market share to specialty stores, discount stores, and category specialists in recent years. They seem to have gotten stuck in the middle, between those retailers that provide a better value at lower prices and those that offer more complete and fashionable assortments and better customer service, according to consumer perceptions. But they are fighting back with a vengeance. Hudson's Bay has begun placing a greater emphasis on high-fashion, private-label merchandise than it did in the past. Facing a flood of American rivals (including Nordstrom, Nordstrom Rack, Bloomingdales, and J. Crew) that have opened Canadian locations, both Holt Renfrew and Hudson's Bay leapt into the discount category. Holt's launched hr2 stores in Brossard, Quebec, and Vaughan, Ontario, offering leading brands at discount prices, however, closed both in mid-2017.[15] Hudson's Bay unveiled its first outlet store outside Toronto featuring "mid-tier" brands such as Calvin Klein, Guess, and DKNY, followed by a second store in Montreal. However, one year later, both outlets were closed.[16]

Drugstores   A **drugstore** is a specialty store that concentrates on health and personal grooming merchandise, though pharmaceuticals often represent more than 60 percent of its sales. The largest drugstore chains in Canada—Shoppers Drug Mart (Pharmaprix in Quebec), Jean Coutu, PharmaSave, and London Drugs—face a major challenge because of the low margins they earn on prescription drugs; health insurance companies and government programs pay most of the cost of many prescriptions, and the health insurance companies negotiate substantially lower prices with drugstores. These drugstores therefore are attempting to make up for their lost profits on prescriptions by concentrating their efforts on nonpharmaceutical products. Shoppers Drug Mart has redesigned its cosmetic counters as Beauty Boutiques to capitalize on attractive profit margins from cosmetic products. General merchandise has long been a staple in drugstores, but food, particularly fresh food such as milk and fruit, has become a relatively new addition to their assortment.

**drugstore**
A specialty store that concentrates on health and personal grooming merchandise, though pharmaceuticals may represent more than 60 percent of its sales.

Off-Price Retailers   An **off-price retailer**—such as Winners, Designer Depot, Marshalls, and HomeSense—offers an inconsistent assortment of merchandise at relatively low prices. They typically buy from manufacturers or other retailers with excess inventory or at the end of a season for one-quarter to one-fifth the original wholesale price. Because of the way these retailers buy, customers can never be confident that the same type of merchandise will be in stock each time they visit the store. Different bargains also will be available on each visit. To improve their offerings' consistency, some off-price retailers complement their opportunistically bought merchandise with merchandise purchased at regular wholesale prices. In addition to their low prices, the key to off-price retailers' success is the treasure hunt environment they create. Customers often make purchase decisions based on price tags that are compared to "regular" retail prices. However, as noted in Ethical Dilemma 13.1, these comparisons can sometimes be misleading.

**off-price retailer**
A type of retailer that offers an inconsistent assortment of merchandise at relatively low prices.

Extreme-value retailers, such as Dollarama, are a subset of off-price retailers and one of the fastest growing retailing segments. An **extreme-value retailer** is a general merchandise discount store found in a lower-income urban or rural area. They are much smaller than traditional discount stores, usually less than 840 square metres.

**extreme-value retailer**
A general merchandise discount store found in lower-income urban or rural areas.

Shoppers Drug Mart has opened numerous Beauty Boutiques to capitalize on attractive profit margins from cosmetics.

Deborah Baic/The Globe and Mail/The Canadian Press

## Ethical Dilemma 13.1

### When Is a Bargain Not a Bargain?

Consumers who shop at discount stores like Winners generally feel they are getting a good deal. The "compare at" information on price tags shows the manufacturer's suggested retail price alongside the price being charged. This information facilitates purchase decisions by suggesting that consumers will in fact pay less than they would at other stores.

However, when CBC's *Marketplace* made a trip to Winners and purchased products such as perfume, clothing, and toys, it was largely unable to find those items elsewhere at the "compare at" price.[17] In his book, *Bargain Fever: How To Shop in a Discounted World,* author Mark Ellwood says that when consumers see two numbers on a tag, they instantly take note. Such anchor pricing makes a Risk board game, sold at $49.99 at Winners, look cheap against the comparison price of $100. However, *Marketplace* researchers discovered that the Risk game was available at the regular price of $74.99 from toy retailer F.G. Bradley. Similarly, *Marketplace* found that Nine West shoes they purchased for $69.99, and which had a comparison price of $130, could be purchased for $99.99 at Nine West's Shoe Studio.[18]

As a discount retailer, Winners sells brand name products at prices it says are 20–60 percent less than regular prices at other stores. The company notes that "compare at" prices are set by buyers who are knowledgeable about regular retail selling prices.[19] When contacted by *Marketplace*, Winners stated, "Our 'compare at' price reflects our buyer's assessment of the regular, retail selling price of a comparable item in traditional department

Shoppers at Winners have been surprised to find that the "compare at" price on tags does not always match actual retail prices elsewhere.

Radharc Images/Alamy Stock Photo

or specialty stores."[20] While it claimed the prices were accurate and fair, the company changed prices on some items soon after being contacted by researchers.

Winners is not alone in being scrutinized. Its parent company, TJX, is facing a class action lawsuit over misleading prices based on "compare at" pricing on merchandise at its TJMaxx stores.[21]

So how can consumers protect themselves? Retail experts suggest shoppers should use their smartphones to check prices and not rush into purchase decisions. That great deal might be more expensive than they think.

---

**services retailers**

Firms that primarily sell services rather than merchandise.

**Services Retailers**   The retail firms discussed in the previous sections sell products to consumers. However, **services retailers**, or firms that primarily sell services rather than merchandise, are a large and growing part of the retail industry. Consider a typical Saturday: After a bagel and cup of coffee at a nearby Great Canadian Bagel, you go to the laundromat to wash and dry your clothes, drop a suit off at a dry cleaner, have a prescription filled at a Rexall drugstore, and make your way to Jiffy Lube to have your car's oil changed. In a hurry, you drive through a Burger King so you can eat lunch quickly and be on time for your haircut at Supercuts. By mid-afternoon, you're ready for a workout at the YMCA. After stopping at home for a change of clothes, you're off to dinner, a movie, and dancing with a friend. Finally, to end your day, you buy a caffè latte at Starbucks, having interacted with 10 different services retailers during the day.

There are a wide variety of services retailers, along with some national companies, that provide these services. These companies are retailers because they sell goods and services to consumers. However, some are not just retailers. For example, airlines, banks, hotels, and insurance and express mail companies sell their services to businesses as well as consumers.

Organizations such as banks, hospitals, health spas, legal clinics, entertainment firms, and universities that offer services to consumers traditionally have not considered themselves retailers. Yet due to increased competition, these organizations are adopting retailing principles to attract customers and satisfy their needs.

Several trends suggest considerable future growth in services retailing. For example, the aging population will increase demand for health care services. Younger people are also spending more time and money on health and fitness. Busy parents in two-income families are willing to pay to have their homes cleaned, lawns maintained, clothes washed and pressed, and meals prepared so they can spend more time with their families.

# DEVELOPING A RETAIL STRATEGY

**LO3**

In a time when more and more Canadian consumers are value conscious, retailers need strategies that deliver. Today's consumers shop at any retailer or through any retailing channel they feel provides the best value for their money. And the lines between the different types of retailers are increasingly becoming blurred as retailers expand the range of their merchandise and services. For example, Walmart (and, to a lesser extent, Shoppers Drug Mart) has moved into the grocery business. Thus, it is extremely important for retailers to develop effective retailing strategies and market positioning in order to differentiate themselves in the increasingly competitive landscape and give customers a compelling reason to shop at their stores.

In developing an effective retailing strategy, many of the principles we discussed in Chapter 6 on segmentation, targeting, and positioning can be very helpful. Retailers must first obtain a deep understanding of the consumers in their markets—their attitudes, behaviours, and preferences. Then they must use this knowledge of their consumers to develop market segments and select those segments they want to serve. Retailers that try to be all things to all people often end up not being able to serve any particular segment appropriately and soon find themselves in serious trouble. Once the target market is selected, retailers must develop the **retail mix**: product (merchandise assortment), pricing, promotion, place, personnel, and presentation (store design and display) strategies to reach and serve these consumers. These elements must be closely coordinated so that they portray a consistent and clear positioning such that consumers know what type of customers the retailer is targeting and how it wants to serve them. For example, a retailer such as Harry Rosen, which wants to be perceived as a high-end clothing retailer, carries high-quality clothing, offers personalized services, and charges premium prices for its merchandise. Harry Rosen's store image and atmospherics (presentation) also portray an image of affluence and professionalism—an image that is consistent with its customers' perceptions of themselves.

**retail mix**
Product (merchandise assortment), pricing, promotion, place, personnel, and presentation (store design and display) strategies to reach and serve consumers.

Like other marketers, retailers perform important functions that increase the value of products and services they sell to consumers. We now examine in more detail how retailers develop the retail mix.

## Product (Merchandise Assortment)

A typical grocery store carries 30,000 to 40,000 different items; a regional department store might carry as many as 200,000. Providing the right mix of merchandise and services that satisfies the needs of the target market is one of retailers' most fundamental activities. Offering assortments gives customers choice and helps attract new and existing customers: Loblaw has created many different store formats for different target customers. For example, Loblaw's Real Canadian Superstores are for customers who want high-quality products, a wide range of product assortments, and high levels of service, and are willing to pay a premium, but Loblaw's No Frills stores are for customers who want to pay much lower prices and don't mind narrower product assortments and less service.

Hudson's Bay added designer shoe lines to its mix when its analysis showed that footwear sales trends were rising, while clothing and accessory sales were falling.[22] It is now the top seller of women's shoes in Canada. To further boost sales, it will focus on shoes and other key areas including clothing, handbags, jewellery, and cosmetics.[23] Staples added

Many retailers have developed private-label brands to differentiate their merchandise.

crystalfoto/Shutterstock

more upscale headphones, such as Beats by Dre and Monster, which resulted in double-digit sales increases.[24] Likewise, the merchandise strategy at Chapters Indigo stores has moved away from books and gift items to home decor, electronics, and higher-end toys such as American Girl dolls. Not all changes are successful, however. HMV Canada shook up music retailing with the addition of headphones, books, gadgets, and clothing designed to attract teens and 20-somethings looking to make a fashion statement into its stores. And still, the chain was put into receivership, closing all its stores in 2017.[25]

Manufacturers don't like to store inventory because their factories and warehouses are typically not available to customers. Consumers don't want to store more than they need because it takes up too much space. Neither group likes to store inventory that isn't being used because doing so ties up money that could be used for something else. Retailers thus provide value to both manufacturers and customers by performing the storage function, though many retailers are beginning to push their suppliers to hold the inventory until they need it. (Recall our discussion of just-in-time inventory systems in Chapter 12.)

It is difficult for retailers to distinguish themselves from their competitors through the merchandise they carry because competitors can purchase and sell many of the same popular brands. So, many retailers have developed private-label brands (also called store brands), which are products developed and marketed by a retailer and available only from that retailer. For example, if you want House & Home bedding, you have to go to Hudson's Bay.

## Price

Price helps define the value of both the merchandise and the service, and the general price range of a particular store helps define its image. Although both Banana Republic and Old Navy are owned by The Gap, their images could not be more different. Banana Republic prices its merchandise to attract young professionals, whereas Old Navy aims to satisfy trendy, price-sensitive consumers. Thus, when a manufacturer considers which of these stores is most appropriate for its new line of scarves and accessories, it must keep customers' perceived images of these retailers' price–quality relationship in mind.

As we showed in Chapter 11, there is much more to pricing than simply adding a markup onto a product's cost. Manufacturers must consider at what price they will sell the product to retailers so that both the manufacturer and the retailer can make a reasonable profit. At the same time, both the manufacturer and the retailer are concerned about what the customer is willing to pay. Clothing retailers address this in part by displaying new arrivals at the front of the store where fashion forward customers browse. Price sensitive customers likely head straight to the sale racks at the back of the store.

Technology can shape customer expectations of price by enabling them to quickly and easily access information. Canadian Tire launched a mobile app that allows in-store shoppers to scan product bar codes to get price, availability, and product information, as well as ratings and reviews by other customers. Shoppers can also access the Canadian Tire weekly flyer to check out current sales and special pricing or to get alerts when items on their wish list go on sale.[26] The app also allows customers to shop using a mobile device and then pick up in-store.

Costco attracts people of all ages and income brackets as consumers shift to value retailers.

The Canadian Press/
Ted S. Warren/AP Photo

Retailers that provide great value, such as Costco, were once known largely as a destination for monthly stock-up trips. But today, they have penetrated the weekly shopping routine. Consumers of all ages, nearly all income groups, and practically all segments have undertaken the "shift to value." Consumers have fundamentally changed their reference points for both price and quality, such that they have been trained to expect significantly lower prices from many retailers.

Price must always be aligned with the other elements of the retail mix: product, promotion, place, personnel, and presentation. For instance, you would not expect to pay $20 for a chocolate bar sold in your local grocery store, but a limited-edition bar made of fine Belgian dark chocolate, packaged in a gold-plated keepsake box, and sold at Holt Renfrew might be a real steal at $20.

## Promotion

Retailers and manufacturers know that good promotion, both within their retail environments and in the media, can mean the difference between flat sales and a growing consumer base. Advertising in traditional media such as newspapers, magazines, and television continues to be important to get customers into the stores. Increasingly, electronic communications are being used for promotions. In the store, however, retailers use displays and signs, placed at the point of purchase or in strategic areas such as the ends of aisles (known as end caps), to inform customers and stimulate purchases of the featured products.

Technology is expanding the ways in which retailers can reach customers with their promotional message. For example, customers can access a retailer's website using a variety of devices, ranging from a computer to a mobile

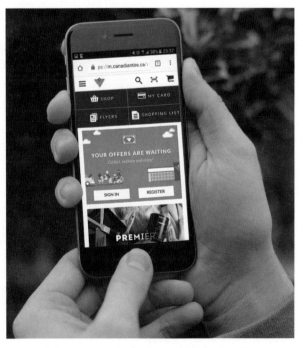

The Canadian Tire app lets customers easily shop from mobile devices.

Trademarks of Canadian Tire Corporation, Limited used under licence.

Retailers used augmented reality apps such as Pokémon Go to attract shoppers to their stores.

Artissăra/Shutterstock.com

**cooperative (co-op) advertising**
An agreement between a manufacturer and retailer in which the manufacturer agrees to defray some advertising costs.

device. However, the typical retailer's website is not designed to accommodate a mobile device's small screen and slower download speeds. As a result, companies such as Sephora have developed special sites for users to access through mobile devices. As noted earlier, Canadian Tire has created a specialized app to enable mobile device users to shop or obtain more merchandise information.

A coordinated effort between the manufacturer and retailer helps guarantee that the customer receives a cohesive message. The extent to which manufacturers work with their retailers to coordinate promotional activities can ensure that both the manufacturer and the retailer can maintain their consistent images. For example, Coach for Men might work with its most important retailers to develop advertising and point-of-sale signs. It may even help defray the costs of advertising by paying all or a portion of the advertising's production and media costs, an agreement called **cooperative (co-op) advertising**.

Store credit cards and gift cards are more subtle forms of promotion that also facilitate shopping. Retailers also might offer pricing promotions—such as coupons, rebates, in-store or online discounts, or perhaps buy-one-get-one-free offers—to attract consumers and stimulate sales. These promotions play a very important role in driving traffic to retail locations, increasing the average purchase size, and creating opportunities for repeat purchases. But retail promotions also are valuable to customers; they inform customers about what is new and available and how much it costs.

Augmented reality is being used by more and more retailers to attract customers to their stores. For example, both large and small retailers leveraged the Pokémon Go app when it first launched. Lowes Canada used augmented reality technology to allow customers using an iPhone to see 3D renderings of Maytag appliances. From the comfort of their homes, users were able to not only view refrigerators, washers, and dryers, but also open and close doors and get a feel for how the appliances worked.[27]

My Virtual Model overcomes the limitations associated with trying on clothing.

Used by permission of modelmydiet.com

## Presentation (Store Design and Display)

In addition to more traditional forms of promotion, many retailers are devoting more resources to their overall retail environment as a means to promote and showcase what the store has to offer. Their displays of merchandise, both in the store and in windows, have become an important form of promotion. For example, Shoppers Drug Mart has redesigned its cosmetics counters as Beauty Boutiques. Since many shopping activities can be rather mundane, those retailers that can distinguish themselves with unusual and exciting store atmospherics add value to the shopping experience. Tesla's stores are set up with interactive displays. Customers can configure their own vehicle using a touchscreen and then view their design on an 85-inch video wall when they have finished.[28]

Smart mirrors have been introduced by retailers such as Neiman Marcus and Nordstrom. The mirrors allow customers to take photos of themselves in an outfit and then view side-by-side images[29] for comparison to determine which outfit they like the best.

Retailers continue to improve their "shopability," by providing more convenient store layouts and shopping experiences that make the task faster, easier, or more interesting. The Body Shop has embraced a concept known as "entertailing" to provide stories behind products and a more interactive experience that encourages customers to stay in stores longer.[30] Apple Stores have used experiential retailing by giving customers something to touch, read, or play with, at their Genius Bars. At Sport Chek, technology is transforming the in-store experience with the launch of digital walls that allow browsers to learn more about its products. For example, by picking up two Nike shoes that are connected to a gaming controller, customers can compare features; get in-depth product information, such as sizes and colours available; and even learn about the performance of athletes who wear the shoes.[31] Customers can even use a video camera on the treadmill to record their stride and gait and then replay the video in slow motion to analyze leg inclination and foot angle.[32]  The digital signage is intended to inspire and enhance the customer service experience. In 2013, the strategy translated to sales that were running 150 percent higher than expected.[33]

Various theories have been developed to explain the structure and evolution of the retail industry.[34] The Wheel of Retailing (shown in Exhibit 13.3) offers one view of how new forms of retail outlets compete in the market. Generally, retailers enter with low prices, low margins, and low status. Over time, they add more and more service and other improvements and thus are able to raise prices, earn higher margins, and achieve higher status with consumers. For example, the first menu at McDonald's offered only hamburgers, french fries, and milkshakes for takeout. Today, McDonald's has a wide and varied menu, upscale coffee, indoor seating, Wi-Fi access,  play areas for children, and even table service in some locations.

In the Wheel of Retailing concept, as stores add services and improvements, expand the mix of merchandise carried, and upgrade their facilities, costs are generally added to

**EXHIBIT 13.3**    The Wheel of Retailing

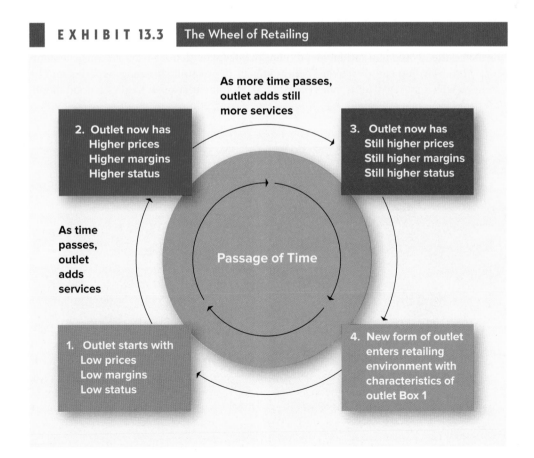

the day-to-day operations, which results in higher prices. This change opens up opportunities for new lean, mean entrants at the beginning of the wheel.

In some Canadian McDonald's outlets, tasteless plastic is being replaced by appealing colours and natural materials, fireplaces, flat-screen TVs, leather chairs, and modern lighting fixtures. Stores are being redesigned, featuring up to four different zones geared to the needs of different target markets; for example, a high-traffic zone for people on the go, a comfortable seating area where customers can linger, and an area specifically for families and large groups.[35] The retrofit is linked to McDonald's strategy to gain a large part of the specialty beverage market, which is dominated by retailers such as Starbucks and Second Cup. By introducing upscale coffee and comfortable seating, McDonald's can earn higher margins and gain higher status. These innovations have enabled McDonald's to continue to serve its existing loyal customers and reach out to new target segments while charging competitive prices—key factors for successful retailing. Thus, it is hardly surprising that McDonald's continues to dominate its industry and stave off competition from new entrants.

Even beer stores across Canada are sprucing up their outlets in an attempt to improve the customer experience. In British Columbia, signature stores now offer broader selection and better presentation of products. To refresh the store experience in Manitoba, the government has opened new express and mini-stores. You can browse product selection on wall-mounted tablets in Ontario stores that feature upbeat music and trained staff who suggest food pairings for your beer. Whenever a lease comes up for renewal, the Société des alcools du Québec invests heavily in improving the look of the stores. Although most store fronts in Nova Scotia were renovated years ago, the focus is now on the back area, in pursuit of a browsing experience that doesn't feel like being in a warehouse. And in Prince Edward Island, a rebranding effort has taken place to provide a new name, new colours, and new store layout and design.[36]

A variety of factors influence whether customers will actually buy once they are in the store; some of these are quite subtle. Consumers' perceptions of value and their subsequent patronage are heavily influenced by their perceptions of the store's "look and feel." Consider the difference between having coffee at Tim Hortons® versus Second Cup. In which outlet would you rather spend time socializing with your friends? Music, colour, scent, and crowding can also significantly impact the overall shopping experience. The extent to which stores offer a more pleasant shopping experience fosters a good mood,

McDonald's redesigned restaurant (right) in Scarborough, Ontario, is considerably more upscale compared to early restaurants (left).

(left): © James Leynse/CORBIS RF; (right): Rene Macura/ AP Photo/The Canadian Press

resulting in greater spending. As Sustainable Marketing 13.1 notes, some retailers are committing to publicly stated sustainability measures to help both their stores and their customers embrace greener practices.

## Personnel

Personal selling and customer service representatives are also part of the overall promotional package. Retailers must provide services that make it easier to buy and use

## Sustainable Marketing 13.1

### MEC Strives for the Smallest Possible Footprint[37]

Active outdoor enthusiasts recognize Mountain Equipment Co-Op (MEC) as this country's leading specialty retailer for clothing and gear. Founded over 40 years ago, the company operates as a member-owned co-op, providing quality products at fair prices. Reporting $366 million in sales in 2015, up 9 percent from the previous year, MEC has over 4.5 million members, 18 stores, and a robust ecommerce site (www.mec.ca). In 2007, MEC became the first major Canadian retailer to become involved with 1% for the Planet, an alliance of businesses in support of outdoor and environmental initiatives. Through the alliance, 1 percent of all purchases by MEC members help to preserve habitats and support community projects.

A deep rooted connection to nature makes sustainability an integral part of MEC's approach to doing business. With a goal to leave the world better place than they found it, the company's managers make no decisions before considering society and the environment. MEC embraces leading sustainability practices, setting an example it hopes will inspire other companies to follow suit. It believes that quality products have the smallest possible footprint, evidenced by its expanded assortment of Fair Trade Certified clothing from two to 32 styles. In an effort to minimize the environmental and health impacts of manufacturing, MEC works closely with Bluesign, an organization that sets best practice standards for the textile industry.

Collaboration with supply chain members is helping MEC to improve both social and environmental performance. For example, its Responsible Sourcing Program ensures MEC products are made in safe conditions in locations that implement fair labour practices. The company is one of only 23 companies globally to be accredited by the Fair Labor Association, an organization formed to protect the rights of workers. In conducting factory audits in 2015, it found 10 unacceptable violations and worked with manufacturers to resolve them. After repeated fruitless efforts to address two violations at one facility, MEC stopped doing business there. A toll-free hotline, Clear Voice Services, allows employees to report grievances and concerns.

MEC's Ottawa store was designed to comply with Canada's C2000 Green Building Standards and incorporates 75 percent of the materials in the site's existing building.
Used with permission of Mountain Equipment Co-Op (MEC)

MEC has set aggressive goals for reducing its carbon footprint, publicly committing to reducing emissions from energy use and diverting waste. It cut out unnecessary packaging, limits glue, and uses recyclable materials. Single-use shopping bags were eliminated in stores in 2008. Although it had produced a hard copy catalogue for years, it stopped doing so in 2011, saving 300,000 kilograms of paper annually. With its willingness to repair items, donate usable products, and take back or recycle items such as batteries and bike tires, MEC was able to divert 2.4 million pounds of waste in 2015.

Continuous improvements are made to green its building and stores, eight of which have been designed to LEED Gold Standards, and one to a LEED platinum model. Many green features have been incorporated, including the use of reclaimed materials, motion sensors to turn off lights in unoccupied areas, solar panels, rainwater collection on roofs, and the reduction of wastewater through composting toilets. If you visit a store, you can take a self-guided Green Building Tour to see other sustainable features at work.

products. As a part of the Dairy Farmers of Canada's "Cooking With Cheese" campaign, brand ambassadors were sent to stores armed with handheld scanners. In the stores, the ambassadors could scan items in shoppers' carts on the spot and then print out cheese-based recipes and dinner suggestions based on the ingredients.[38] Retail associates—whether in the store, on the phone, or over the Internet—provide customers with information about product characteristics and availability. They can also facilitate the sale of products or services that consumers perceive as complicated, risky, or expensive, such as an air conditioning unit or a diamond ring. Manufacturers can play an important role in getting retail sales and service associates prepared to sell their products. Estée Lauder, for example, could conduct seminars about how to use and sell a new line of cosmetics. In some retail firms, these salesperson and customer service functions are being augmented, or even replaced, by technology used through in-store kiosks, the Internet, or self-checkout lanes.

Traditionally, retailers treated all their customers the same. Today, the most successful retailers concentrate on providing more value to their best customers. The knowledge retailers gain from their store personnel, the Internet browsing and buying activities of customers, and the data they collect on customer shopping habits can be used in customer relationship management (CRM). Using this information, retailers may modify product, price, and/or promotion in an attempt to increase their **share of wallet**—the percentage of the customer's purchases made from that particular retailer. For instance, multi-channel retailers use consumer information collected from the customers' Internet browsing and buying behaviour to send personalized emails promoting specific products or services. Retailers may also offer special discounts to good customers to make them even more loyal.

**share of wallet**
The percentage of the customer's purchases made from a particular retailer.

## Place

Retailers already have realized that convenience is a key ingredient to success, and an important aspect of this success is convenient locations. As the old cliché claims, the three most important things in retailing are "location, location, location." Location is key for customers who shop on the basis of the store, as noted in Entrepreneurial Marketing 13.1. Great locations provide a competitive advantage that few rivals can duplicate. Although fashion retailer Zara spends almost nothing on advertising, it invests heavily in locating its shops in venues that offer beauty and historical appeal.[39] And once Starbucks saturates a market by opening in the best locations, it will be difficult for a new competitor to break into that same market—where would it put its stores?

In pursuit of better and better locations, retailers are experimenting with different options to reach their target markets. Canada's largest drugstore retailer, Shoppers Drug Mart, now has some stores that are open 24 hours a day so customers can pick up prescriptions and other items at any time. P&G took the store to consumers when it opened a virtual store in Toronto's Union Station. Partnering with Well.ca, the month-long initiative presented consumers with photos of products with QR codes that could be scanned, allowing them to order 120 different items and have them delivered to their homes at no cost.[40] It followed with another mobile exercise that launched mobile stores in 50 Toronto bus shelters offering P&G personal care, baby, and beauty items from Walmart. The shopping experience let consumers turn idle time waiting for the bus into productive time, ordering products on the go.[41]

To offer more convenience, some Shoppers Drug Mart stores are open 24 hours a day so customers can pick up prescriptions or other items at any time.

Jeff Whyte/Shutterstock.com

## Entrepreneurial Marketing 13.1

### Born of Overused Slang, Amazeballs Fly Off Shelves[42]

While browsing the Internet one day, Dan Fallak came across an article about the 20 most overused terms of 2013. Near the top of the list was "amazeballs." The word was used to describe something that was beyond amazing. And it gave Fallak an idea on how to monetize the word and build a brand around it. He brainstormed ideas that could work as products branded as Amazeballs and came up with round drink chillers.

Although he stumbled on the name, Fallak was not new to business. Based near Ottawa in Almonte, Ontario, he had already created a line of printed marble drink coasters and had cofounded Small Town Thinking, a consulting company to help small businesses generate ideas.

However, when it came to drink chillers, he wasn't first to market. Other companies had previously introduced square shaped "drink stones" made of granite. Like drink stones, Amazeballs keep drinks cold without watering them down. However, the combination of being made of stainless steel and filled with freezer gel means drinks

Amazeballs chill drinks faster, better, and for longer than other products, making them a hit at retail outlets.

Used with permission of Dan Fallak, founder, Amazeballs

chill faster, chill better, and stay cold longer. Being round is also an advantage as there is a larger surface area for chilling. Testing shows that Amazeballs chill twice as well as square drink stones.

Fallak approached Chapters Indigo through a friend who is a bar and drink accessory buyer for the store. With his background in advertising and design, he was able to mock up a logo and retail packaging. Being in the right place at the right time led to an order for 500 units for Father's Day 2014 since customers recognize the store as a convenient gift location. Amazeballs outperformed Chapters Indigo's strong product sales metric for a "strong product" by five times and resulted in a Christmas order. This success created interest from stores such as Urban Outfitters, Marshalls, and Winners. The product—which includes two Amazeballs, a freezer pouch, and stainless steel tongs—sells for $25 to $35 and is available in over 700 North American retail outlets as well as online at TheChive webstore.

Hoping to build a brand around Amazeballs, Fallak trademarked the name and is now working to expand Amaze products into a gift line. He has already introduced a second product, Amazerods, a stainless steel rod designed for beer or other bottles.

## MANAGING OMNICHANNEL OPTIONS

**LO4**

So far in this chapter, we have explored the most traditional method for a manufacturer to get merchandise to the ultimate consumer, namely, through retailers. There are, however, other options. A manufacturer can sell directly to consumers by using its own stores, kiosks, catalogues, or the Internet. For example, Canadian fast-food chain Pizza Pizza gives customers the choice of ordering in-store, by phone, on the company's website, and now through a free app for the iPhone, iPod Touch, iPad, and Android smartphones. The app lets customers order and pay for their pizza and then track the guaranteed delivery time.[43]

In this section, we explore the relative advantages of each of these options from both a manufacturer's and a retailer's perspective. We also consider the synergies inherent to providing products through multiple channels. As more consumers embrace a variety of channels available for browsing and purchasing, retailers must develop an **omnichannel** strategy to create a consistent experience across all channels. James Connell, vice-president of marketing and ecommerce for Roots, says that they "focus on providing a seamless multi-channel experience. We know a customer will interact five or six times [with us] before they make a purchase."[44]

**omnichannel**
A strategy that creates a consistent experience for consumers across all distribution channels.

## Benefit of Stores for Consumers

In this section, we explore the relative advantages of the most traditional retail channel, the brick-and-mortar store, from consumers' perspective. In the following section, we examine how kiosks, catalogues, and the Internet channel add value to retailers' ability to satisfy their customers' needs. Each channel—stores, kiosks, catalogues, and the Internet—offers its own unique benefits for selling to consumers (see Exhibit 13.4).

**Store Channel**   Traditional stores, or brick-and-mortar retailers as they often are called, offer several benefits to customers that they cannot get when they shop through catalogues or on the Internet. Lee Valley Tools started as a catalogue retailer. It opened its first store in 1982 and now has 18 retail outlets across Canada.

*Browsing.*   Shoppers often have only a general sense of what they want (e.g., a sweater, something for dinner, a gift) but don't know the specific item they want. They go to a store to see what is available before they decide what to buy. Although some consumers surf the web and look through catalogues for ideas, many still prefer browsing in stores. Some use both approaches, getting a sense of what's available through catalogues or the Internet, and then going to the store to try on apparel or view the actual product.

*Touching and Feeling Products.*   Perhaps the greatest benefit offered by stores is the opportunity for customers to use all five of their senses—touching, smelling, tasting, seeing, and hearing—when examining products.

*Personal Service.*   Sales associates have the capability to provide meaningful, personalized information. Sales people can be particularly helpful when purchasing a complicated product, such as consumer electronics, or something the customer doesn't know much about, such as a diamond ring.

*Cash and Credit Payment.*   Stores are nearly the only channel that accepts cash payments. Some customers prefer to pay with cash because it is easy, resolves the transaction immediately, and does not result in potential interest payments. Some customers prefer to use their credit or debit card in person rather than send payment information electronically.

*Entertainment and Social Interaction.*   In-store shopping can be a stimulating experience for some people, providing a break in their daily routine and enabling them to interact with friends.

*Instant Gratification.*   Stores have the advantage of allowing customers to get the merchandise immediately after they buy it.

*Risk Reduction.*   When customers purchase merchandise in physical stores, it reduces their perceived risk of buying and increases their confidence that any problems with the merchandise will be corrected.

**EXHIBIT 13.4**   **Benefits Provided by Different Channels**

| Stores | Kiosks | Catalogues | Internet |
|---|---|---|---|
| • Browsing<br>• Touching and feeling merchandise<br>• Personal service<br>• Cash and credit payment<br>• Entertainment and social interaction<br>• Instant gratification<br>• Risk reduction | • Broader selection than stores<br>• Access to items online that are out of stock in stores<br>• Access to wish lists and gift registries<br>• Access to loyalty program information | • Convenience<br>• Information<br>• Safety | • Deeper and broader selection<br>• More information<br>• Personalization<br>• Expanded market presence |

## Benefits of Internet and Omnichannel Retailing

In the previous section, we detailed the relative benefits of stores from the consumers' perspective. In this section, we examine how the Internet has improved retailers' ability to serve their customers and build a competitive advantage. More and more Canadians are embracing ecommerce. Forrester Research predicts that online retail sales in Canada will reach $39.9 billion by 2019, representing 10 percent of all Canadian retail sales.[45]

**Internet Channel**   First, the addition of an Internet channel has the potential to offer a greater selection of products. Second, an Internet channel enables retailers to provide customers with more personalized information about products and services. Third, it offers sellers the unique opportunity to collect information about consumer shopping behaviour—information that they can use to improve the shopping experience across all channels. Finally, the Internet channel allows sellers to enter new markets economically.

Although offering an electronic channel may draw away some sales from other channels, using it with other channels can result in consumers making more total purchases from the seller.

***Deeper and Broader Selection.***   One benefit of the Internet channel is the vast number of alternatives available to consumers without stores having to grow their aisles or increase their square footage. By shopping on the Internet, consumers can easily "visit" and select merchandise from a broader array of retailers. People living in London, Ontario, can shop electronically at Harrod's in London, England, in less time than it takes them to visit their local supermarket. Websites typically offer deeper assortments of merchandise (more colours, brands, and sizes) than are available in stores or catalogues. This expanded offering enables them to satisfy consumer demand for less popular styles, colours, or sizes and still keep their overall inventory costs low. Many retailers also offer a broader assortment (more categories) on their websites. Staples.com, for instance, offers soft drinks and cleaning supplies, which are not available in stores, so that its business customers will view it as a one-stop shop.

***More Information to Evaluate Merchandise.***   Using an Internet channel, firms can provide as much information as each customer wants and more information than he or she could get through store or catalogue channels. Customers can drill down through web pages until they have enough information to make a purchase decision. Unlike in catalogues, the information on an electronic channel database can be frequently updated and will always be available—24/7, 365 days per year. Furthermore, the cost of adding

Consumers who shop at omnichannel retailers—retailers that sell merchandise in more than one retail channel (such as a catalogue (right), the Internet (centre) or a Canadian store (left)—typically buy more than those who shop in only one retail channel.

Trademarks of Canadian Tire Corporation, Limited used under licence.

information to an Internet channel is likely to be far less than the cost of continually training sales associates.

The depth of information available on a website even can provide solutions to customer problems. Home Depot walks its online customers through the steps of installation and repair projects, thereby giving do-it-yourselfers confidence prior to tackling home improvement tasks. The directions include the level of difficulty and a list of the tools and materials needed to complete the project successfully.

***Personalization.***    The most significant potential benefit of the Internet channel is its ability to personalize promotions and services for each customer economically. Canadian consumers are increasingly embracing personalized offers received on their smartphones, with 82 percent saying they like to get detailed product information while they are in stores shopping.[46] Refer to Exhibit 13.5 for more details on personalizing the mobile experience for shoppers.

**EXHIBIT 13.5**    Keeping It Personal: Marketing Success in a Mobile World

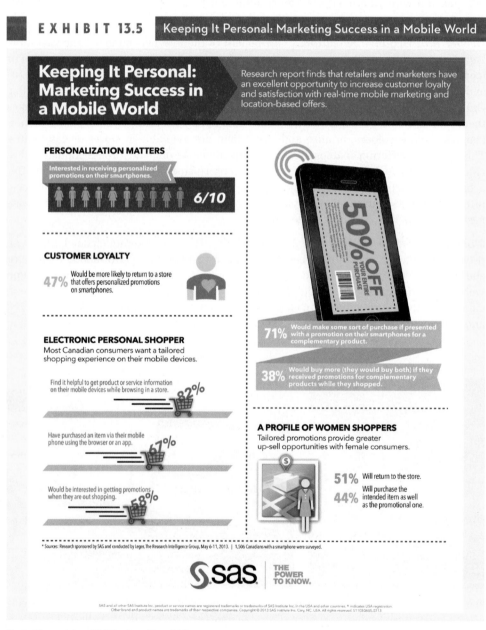

Used with permission of SAS Institute (Canada), Inc.

***Personalized Customer Service.*** Traditional Internet channel approaches for responding to customer questions—such as frequently asked questions (FAQ) pages and offering a toll-free number or email address to ask questions—often do not provide the timely information customers are seeking. To improve customer service from an electronic channel, many firms offer live, online chats. The online chat feature provides customers with the opportunity to click a button at any time and have an instant messaging email or voice conversation with a customer service representative. This technology also enables firms to send a proactive chat invitation to customers on the site. Virgin Airlines programs its chat windows to appear at the moment a customer chooses a flight, because its goal is to upsell buyers a more expensive fare.[47] Other online retailers use metrics such as the amount of time the visitor has spent on the site or number of repeat visits to determine when to invite customers to chat.

***Personalized Offering.*** The interactive nature of the Internet also provides an opportunity for retailers to personalize their offerings for each of their customers. Using cookies that provide identifying information, Amazon.ca enhances the shopping experience by serving up personalized homepages with information about books and other products of interest based on visitors' past purchases. Amazon.ca will also send interested customers customized email messages that notify them that their favourite author or recording artist has published a new book or released a new CD. Another personalized offering that online retailers are able to present to customers is recommendations of complementary merchandise. Just as a well trained salesperson would make recommendations to customers prior to checkout, an interactive web page can make suggestions to the shopper about items that he or she might like to see, such as what other customers who bought the same item also purchased.

Some omnichannel retailers are able to personalize promotions and Internet homepages on the basis of several attributes tied to the shopper's current or previous web sessions, such as the time of day, time zone as determined by a computer's Internet address, and assumed gender. However, some consumers worry about this ability to collect information about purchase histories, personal information, and search behaviour on the Internet. How will this information be used in the future? Will it be sold to other firms, or will the consumer receive unwanted promotional materials online or in the mail?

***Expanded Market Presence.*** With the Internet's low entry costs and constantly improving search engines and shopping bots, smaller niche sources for hard-to-find products, collectibles, and hobbies can expand their trade area—the geographical area that contains the potential customers of a particular retailer or shopping centre—from a few city blocks to the world. The Internet has facilitated market expansions by traditional retailers as well. Not only can a customer in Zurich shop online at CanadianTire.ca or Lee Valley Tools Ltd. (leevalley.com), but a Staples customer can buy a computer online and pick it up at the store. In addition to increasing sales by expanding the current customer base and attracting new customers, omnichannel retailers can achieve economies of scale by coordinating their buying and logistics activities across channels and consolidating their marketing information and activities. Generally, consumers who shop at omnichannel retailers typically buy more than those who shop in only one retail channel.

**Kiosk Channel** One of the greatest constraints facing store-based retailers is the size of their stores. The amount of merchandise that can be displayed and offered for sale in stores is limited. By blending stores with Internet-enabled kiosks, retailers can dramatically expand the assortment offered to their customers. Retailers using a kiosk channel may simply provide store associates with access to the company website so that they can more easily help customers find product information or place orders. Other retailers, such as Chapters, offer self-service kiosks that allow customers to check product selection and availability at their stores. Of course, today many consumers arrive in store armed with a mobile kiosk in the form of a smartphone capable of accessing product information and even comparing prices at other retailers via the Internet.

Another limitation that store-based retailers face is inconsistent execution. The availability and knowledge of sales associates can vary considerably across stores or even within a store at different times during the day. This inconsistency is most problematic for retailers selling new, complex merchandise. For example, consumer electronics retailers such as Best Buy find it difficult to communicate the features and benefits of the newest products to all of their sales associates. To address this problem, Best Buy installed kiosks designed to be used by sales associates and customers to obtain product information.

***Broader Selection.*** Customers with the ability to shop in a store and look up products at a kiosk generally get access to an expanded assortment of products than just those in stock in the store. For example, Staples carries roughly five times as many items online as in stores.

***Access to Items Online That Are Out of Stock in Store.*** Retailers using in-store kiosks can often save a sale if an item is out of stock or if their location does not carry a broad product assortment.

***Access to Wish Lists and Gift Registries.*** Customers buying gifts can check gift registries for wedding or baby shower gifts as well as wish lists for themselves or the gift recipient.

***Access to Loyalty Program Information.*** Being able to check the status of a loyalty program and determine whether points are available to be used is a benefit to consumers. It also allows retailers to overcome resource constraints by freeing up staff to provide sales assistance to other customers.

**Catalogue Channel** The catalogue channel provides some benefits to customers that are not available from the store or Internet channels. However, once a catalogue is printed, it cannot be updated with price changes and new merchandise. Therefore, retailers such as Lands' End use Internet sites to provide customers with real-time information about stock availability and price reductions on clearance merchandise. Like all nonstore formats, catalogues offer the convenience of looking at merchandise and placing an order 24/7. Catalogues have other advantages over other nonstore formats as follows.

***Convenience.*** The information in a catalogue is easily accessible for a long period of time. Consumers can refer to the information in a catalogue anytime by simply picking it up from the coffee table. The development of magalogs—catalogues with magazine-type editorial content—enhances consumers' desire to keep catalogues readily available. Williams–Sonoma produces a magalog featuring its gourmet cooking tools and foods for sale, offering inspirational stories along with kitchen tips and recipes.

***Information.*** Catalogues have information about the products and how they can be used. For example, the IKEA catalogue shows consumers how its products can be put together in a kitchen, office, or child's room. The catalogue was also integrated with an augmented reality app that let customers see how furniture would look in their homes.

***Safety.*** Security in malls and shopping areas is becoming an important concern for many shoppers, particularly the elderly. Nonstore retail formats offer the advantage of enabling customers to view merchandise and place orders from a safe environment— their homes.

## Effective Omnichannel Retailing

Consumers want a seamless experience when interacting with omnichannel retailers. They want to be recognized by a retailer, whether they interact with a sales associate, the retailer's website, or the retailer's call centre by telephone. Retailers also need to offer mobile services, as Social and Mobile Marketing 13.1 describes. Customers want to buy a product through the retailer's Internet or catalogue channels and pick it up or return it

## Social and Mobile Marketing 13.1

## Retailers Not Ready for Mobile[48]

A study by Accenture found that 44 percent of Canadians want to use their mobile devices to access retail services. Although real-time in-store promotions are highly desired, only 7 percent of retailers are able to do this. And while shoppers want to scan products with their mobile devices, scanning capabilities are provided by only 17 percent of retailers. Coupons are another bone of contention, as 28 percent of Canadians would like to be automatically credited for coupons but only 16 percent of retailers are able to deliver this function. Checking product availability, using a shopping list, and having access to an in-store product locator are among other desired features for which the majority of retailers receive a failing grade.

When it comes to the shopping experience, mobile devices have evolved from nice to have to mandatory. Slow-moving retailers are frustrating customers who would like to experience a seamless shopping experience across all channels.

Some retailers are trying to use Instagram to allow shoppers to browse and buy through mobile devices. However, although Instagram has changed its algorithm, it does not yet allow active links. Retailers like Michael Kors have been working to make products found in its posts easier to find and buy. It launched Insta-Kors, which mirrors its Instagram feed on its website. Posts are paired with links to make it easy to find items pictured. Customers who use InstaKors

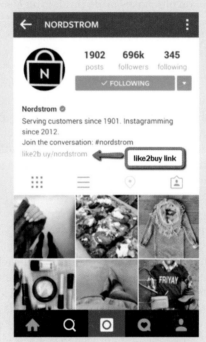

Big retailers such as Nordstrom use Like2Buy to make it easy for customers to buy from Instagram.

Source: Business2Community, "Instagram's Answer to Social Media Advertising: Like2Buy" by Andrew Jung. January 12, 2015.

can access special promotions and preview products before they are available in the online store.[49]

Roots has launched a "virtual showroom" on Instagram to feature its leather goods. The site provides photos of soon-to-be-released products and allows consumers to purchase them before the new items even hit stores. In addition, the showroom will act as a research tool, giving Roots insights on popular products before they are manufactured and letting the company order more to meet demand. However, while the Instagram showroom features photos of Roots products, the process is not seamless. Shoppers must open a link from the Instagram description before they can get to a page to order the product.[50]

Big brands such as Nordstrom and Forever21 get around these challenges by using a tool called Like-2Buy. Developed by Curalate, the tool makes buying on Instagram much smoother. Consumers who "Like" products can go directly to that company's Like2Buy page to purchase or add to a wish list. Like2Buy eliminates the requirement for consumers to open a new page looking for products. Customers on Nordstrom's Instagram feed would simply select a photo of a product and within two clicks be at a landing page where they could purchase it.[51]

While shoppers may be disappointed today, a recent American Express study indicates a brighter future. Retailers plan to invest in mobile and contactless payment options as well as create or update mobile apps.[52]

---

to a local store; find out if a product offered on the Internet channel is available at a local store; and, when unable to find a product in a store, determine if it is available for home delivery through the retailer's Internet channel.

However, providing this seamless experience for customers is not easy for retailers. Because each of the channels is somewhat different, a critical decision facing omnichannel retailers is the degree to which they should or are able to integrate the operations of the channels.[53] To determine how much integration is best, each retailer must address issues such as integrated CRM, brand image, pricing, and the supply chain.

Adding an electronic channel is particularly attractive to firms with strong brand names but limited locations and distribution. For example, retailers such as Harrod's, IKEA, and Harry Rosen are widely known for offering unique, high-quality merchandise, but they require customers to travel to England or major cities to buy many of the items they carry. Interestingly, most of these store-based retailers currently are omnichannel retailers through their successful catalogue and Internet offerings. Harry Rosen has annual sales of around $300 million. While its ecommerce sales make up only a small portion of overall revenues, president Larry Rosen feels they could increase to 10 percent over time.[54]

There are challenges and advantages in selling merchandise via the Internet. When you buy products from brick-and-mortar stores, some critical information might include "touch-and-feel" attributes, such as how a shirt fits, how the ice cream flavour tastes, or how the perfume smells. This information cannot be experienced via the Internet. As a result, etailers strive for "look-and-see" attributes, such as colour, style, and grams of carbohydrates. Fit can be predicted if the apparel has consistent sizing and the consumer has learned over time which size to buy from a particular brand. Because of the problems of providing touch-and-feel information, apparel retailers experience return rates of more than 20 percent on purchases made through an electronic channel but only 10 percent for purchases made in stores. Whereas some products, such as apparel, can be difficult for customers to purchase over the Internet because of their need to touch, feel, and try on these products, Amazon's offerings do well in the worldwide Internet marketplace.

Integrated CRM    Effective omnichannel operations require an integrated customer relationship management (CRM) system with a centralized customer data warehouse that houses a complete history of each customer's interaction with the retailer, regardless of whether the sale occurred in a store, on the Internet, or on the telephone.[55] This information storehouse allows retailers to efficiently handle complaints, expedite returns, target future promotions, and provide a seamless experience for customers when they interact with the retailer through multiple channels.

Brand Image    Retailers need to provide a consistent brand image across all channels. For example, Mountain Equipment Co-Op (MEC) reinforces its image of selling high-quality, environmentally friendly sports equipment in its stores, catalogues, and website. Each of these channels emphasizes function, not fashion, in the descriptions of MEC's products. Its position about taking care of the environment is communicated by carefully lighting its stores and using recycled polyester and organic, rather than pesticide-intensive, cotton in many of its clothes. A positive omnichannel experience yields results. According to Sandy Treagus, chief financial officer for Mountain Equipment Co-Op, "Our ecommerce presence has had a profound impact on our retail stores, and vice versa."[56]

Pricing    Pricing represents another difficult decision for an omnichannel retailer. Customers expect pricing consistency for the same SKU across channels (excluding shipping charges and sales tax). However, in some cases, retailers need to adjust their pricing strategy because of the competition they face in different channels. Retailers with stores in multiple markets often set different prices for the same merchandise to compete better with local stores. Customers generally are not aware of these price differences because they are only exposed to the prices in their local markets. However, omnichannel retailers may have difficulties sustaining these regional price differences when customers can easily check prices on the Internet.

Supply Chain    Omnichannel retailers struggle to provide an integrated shopping experience across all their channels because unique skills and resources are needed to manage each channel. For example, store-based retail chains operate and manage many stores, each requiring the management of inventory and people. With Internet and catalogue operations, inventory and telephone salespeople instead are typically centralized in one or two locations. Also, retail distribution centres (DCs) supporting a store channel are designed to ship many cartons of merchandise to stores. In contrast, the DCs supporting a catalogue and Internet channel are designed to ship a few items to individual customers. The difference in shipping orientation for the two types of operations requires a completely different type of distribution centre.

Due to these operational differences, many store-based retailers have a separate organization to manage their Internet and catalogue operations. But as the omnichannel operation matures, retailers tend to integrate all operations under one organization. Walmart initially had separate organizations for its Internet channel but subsequently integrated them with stores and catalogues.

## LEARNING OBJECTIVES REVIEW

**LO1**  **Outline the considerations associated with choosing retail partners**

Because manufacturers want their offerings available where, when, and in the form that customers prefer, they must consider whether customers expect to find their products at specific retailers. For example, customers probably do not expect, or want, to find a value-priced product at a luxury retailer. The manufacturer also must consider the basic channel structure in which it functions, along with the characteristics of the members of that channel. Finally, manufacturers need to determine the distribution intensity they prefer.

**LO2**  **Identify what types of retailers are available to distribute products**

Retailers generally fall into one of two categories: food retailers and general merchandise retailers. Each of the categories consists of various formats, including supermarkets, supercentres, warehouse clubs, convenience stores, department stores, discount stores, specialty retailers, drugstores, category specialists, extreme-value retailers, and off-price stores.

**LO3**  **Describe the components of a retail strategy building on the four Ps to create value for consumers**

To develop a coordinated strategy—which represents a key goal for an effective channel partnership between retailers and manufacturers—these functions need to consider the four Ps. Retailers provide customers with a choice of merchandise in the quantities they want to buy and services that facilitate the sale and use of those products. They offer convenient locations to shop and an atmosphere and presentation that enhance the shopping experience. Promotions, both in the store and outside, provide customers with information. Finally, price provides signals to the customer about the image of the store, its merchandise, and its services.

**LO4**  **Identify the benefits and challenges of omnichannel retailing**

The various types of retail channels—stores, kiosks, catalogues, and the Internet—offer their own benefits and limitations, including those related to availability, convenience, and safety, among others. If a retailer adopts an omnichannel strategy, it can exploit the benefits and mitigate the limitations of each channel and expand its overall market presence. Furthermore, an omnichannel strategy offers the chance to gain a greater share of customers' wallets and more insight into their buying behaviour. Of course, there are challenges as well. To function in multiple channels, retailers must organize their operations carefully to ensure an integrated customer experience. In particular, they have to have an integrated CRM system, and determine how to maintain a consistent brand image across the various channels, whether to charge the same or different prices, and how best to deliver merchandise to multiple channels.

## KEY TERMS

- big-box food retailer
- category killer
- category specialist
- conventional supermarket
- cooperative (co-op) advertising

- discount store
- drugstore
- extreme-value retailer
- general merchandise retailers
- off-price retailer
- omnichannel

- omnichannel strategy
- retail mix
- retailing
- services retailers
- share of wallet
- specialty stores

## CONCEPT REVIEW

1. Describe the factors that manufacturers must consider when choosing retail partners.

2. How would a manufacturer's strategy for choosing a retailer change depending on its overall market power and the consistency of the new product with existing offerings?

3. Discuss the types of retailers that operate in Canada and identify some of the issues facing each type.

4. Generally merchandise retailers are classified into several different groups such as discount stores, specialty stores, category killers, and so on. However, it seems that increasingly many of these retailers are looking quite similar. Why is this so, and what factors may explain this trend?

5. How do marketers use the four Ps to create value in retailing?

6. Does Reebok pursue an intensive, an exclusive, or a selective distribution intensity strategy? Would you suggest any changes to this strategy?

7. In this chapter, we discuss the fact that researchers have found that store image and atmospherics exert a huge impact on customers' shopping behaviour. What are the key elements of a store's atmospherics and image, and why do you think they affect consumers so strongly?

8. Explain how the Internet has helped reshape retail marketing strategies. What are some of the unique advantages of physical store retailing, website selling, and kiosks?

9. Discuss the advantages of multichannel retailing from the perspectives of both retailers and consumers.

10. Explain why it is important for retailers to develop effective retailing strategy and positioning. How do retailers develop such a strategy? (*Hint:* Look at the various store formats of Loblaw or any national grocery chain.)

## MARKETING APPLICATIONS

1. Assume you have been given some money to invest in a retailer's stock. What type of retailer would you choose? Provide a rationale for your answer.

2. Why don't traditional department stores have the same strong appeal to Canadian consumers that they once enjoyed during their height in the last half of the 20th century? Discuss which types of retailers are now competing with department stores.

3. What do retailers do to increase the value of products and services for consumers? Discuss the extent to which brick-and-mortar retailers are threatened by Internet-only retailers with regard to these factors.

4. Some argue that retailers can be eliminated from the distribution channel because they add only costs to the final product without creating any value-added services in the process. Do you agree with this perspective? Is it likely that consumers will make most purchases directly from manufacturers in the near future? Provide justification for your answers.

5. Assume that Adidas, the shoe manufacturer, has decided to sell expensive wristwatches for men and women. What factors should it consider when developing its strategy for choosing retail partners?

6. Identify three categories of products especially suited for sale on the Internet. Identify three categories that are not currently suitable for sale on the Internet. Justify your choices.

7. How do Staples.com and Officedepot.com provide value to their customers beyond the physical products that they sell? Identify some of the ways that the companies have overcome the inhibitors to successful Internet retailing.

8. Why have so many brick-and-mortar retailers adopted an omnichannel strategy?

9. You can purchase apparel at a discount store, specialty store, category specialist, off-price retailer, department store, or Internet-only store. From which of these types of stores do you shop? Explain why you prefer one type over another.

10. Search the Internet for a product you want to buy. Are there differences in the prices, shipping charges, or return policies among the different retailers offering the product? From which retailer would you buy? Explain the criteria you would use to make the decision.

## NET SAVVY

**1.** Companies such as Lee Valley Tools have expanded their offerings beyond their original channels to sell through multiple channels. Visit the company's website (http://www.leevalley.com) and determine in which channels it operates (Internet, stores, and/or catalogue). Discuss the advantages of using a multichannel strategy over a single channel strategy.

**2.** Select a familiar omnichannel retailer. Evaluate its website in terms of how well it provides value to its customers. Do you believe that offering multiple selling channels to customers enhances their shopping experience? How does it help the retailer? Explain your answer.

## CHAPTER CASE STUDY

### ALDO, A RETAILER WITH A CONSCIENCE AND "SOLE"

The philosophy of Canadian shoe retailer Aldo is to inspire and move forward. With over 2,300 points of sale in 100 countries, the company wants to be seen as a key player in the world of fashion, footwear, and accessories.[57] Aldo Bensadoun launched his business in Montreal by selling shoes in concessions located in Le Château stores. His first standalone store opened in 1978, followed by stores in the United States in 1993, and overseas two years later with its first franchise store in Israel.[58]

The son of a shoe merchant whose grandfather was a cobbler, Bensadoun was guided by a set of values that focused on compassion and ethics. His goal was to create a brand that had a conscience, one that cares. This commitment to society is evidenced through its Aldo Fights Aids campaign, an initiative started in 1985 when many retailers were reluctant to take a stand on the disease. Numerous other causes are supported, including War Child and the Cure Foundation.[59]

Canada's retail footwear industry is valued at $6.8 billion, however, the market is stalling with annual growth rates projected at only 3 percent. In Canada, fashion conscious men have propelled sales to $2.8 billion, up 10 percent. However, the all-important women's market has fallen by 0.9 percent to $3.4 billion.[60] Competition has dramatically increased—fewer shoppers are visiting physical stores; fashion and department stores such as Zara, H&M, and Hudson's Bay are stocking more shoes; and low-cost rivals are attracting price conscious consumers. Many clothing

Aldo Bensadoun founded his company with a desire to be seen as a brand that cares. Aldo Fights Aids is just one of many philanthropic initiatives the retailer supports.

(both): Used with permission of The ALDO Group Inc.

retailers have aggressively added to their footwear selection, increasing sales from 0.2 percent to 5 percent of projected revenues.[61]

Consumers expect Aldo to be in its own branded stores as well as other fashion retailers and online. That's why the company sells its products through Nordstrom, Hudson's Bay, Zappos, and Amazon.[62] Of course, selling via other outlets means fewer opportunities to interact with shoppers directly. To get better insights on what customers want, Aldo uses tools from Salesforce. Its Service Cloud tool lets customer service reps quickly access customer data and respond to their questions in real time. Through the Marketing Cloud tool, Aldo can join in social media conversations related to its brand.[63]

In 2014, Patrik Fisk took over as the company's CEO, launching international expansion plans and high-tech store changes projected to double its business in five years. Already recognized as an early adopter of ecommerce technology, Aldo has built on its digital prowess through consumer facing solutions. A suite of mobile apps let shoppers digitally interact with the brand. Customers can browse and access the collection by size, colour, or key silhouettes, along with user-friendly self-service tools which allow for try-on requests.[64] The Aldo Connected Store app allows customers to scan boots or bags for more product and style information.[65] The mobile app and virtual shelf features lifestyle content with fully styled imagery to inspire customers and help them visualize ways to style the collection into their own wardrobe. Apps are designed to enhance the shopping experience while providing Aldo with the opportunity to offer better service.

David Bensadoun, named CEO in 2017, continues to tweak the company's retail strategy involving redesigning its brick-and-mortar stores. Aldo is seen as being very savvy and recognizing trends faster than other retailers, which makes it an attractive tenant according to Cadillac Fairview, one of Canada's largest enclosed mall owners. Aldo is investing more than $500 million in store renovations, new systems, and staff education.[66] Digital screens and tablets are being added to stores. Prices will be raised 5–10 percent to help pay for "premiumized" stores that will scale back the number of shoes offered by 25 percent to focus more on global styles. Mobile will feature heavily in all of Aldo's stores, including its new "connected store" at the Westfield World Trade Center in New York. When app subscribers enter the store, alerts will be sent to sales staff with information about past purchases, items in their digital carts, and also an estimate of the person's lifetime value as an Aldo customer.[67]

Staff is being trained to bring the pair of shoes requested plus a second pair that matches consumers' specific needs, for example, a sandal that matches the style of a high-heeled pump.

Aldo has heavily invested in store renovations, new systems, and staff training, and has introduced apps that blend the online experience with that of shopping in a physical store.

Photo by Luciana Pampalone. Used with permission of The ALDO Group Inc.

And although mall traffic has been falling, in some cases as much as 10 percent, Aldo is not worried about fewer browsers in its stores. Most consumers do their research before arriving at a store, make targeted trips, are more focused when shopping, and arrive ready to purchase.[68]

The company uses social media to reach customers, too. A survey by Weddingbells found that 80 percent of Canadian brides indicated they would use Pinterest to plan their wedding. So when Aldo launched its bridal and special occasion collection, it created a contest on Pinterest called "Inspired by I Do." Contest participants created a Pinterest board of their dream wedding, pinning at least five Aldo products to it for a chance to win shoes and accessories for the whole wedding party.[69] The contest was promoted on other social media channels as well, generating 400 entries and over 2,000 Pinterest pins. Even after the contest ended, people continued to pin and re-pin items, extending the campaign's reach.

Aldo has come a long way in the past four decades. Today it is able to deliver new products in less than a year, sometimes in less than three months, to locations around the world, introducing new products in stores each month. The company has synced its in-store, online, and mobile platforms to create a consistent, personalized, and seamless omnichannel experience for shoppers. Built on a foundation of ethics and compassion, Aldo has successfully navigated choppy retail waters. And along the way, it has been recognized as a good corporate citizen, one that cares, and one with "sole."

## Questions

1. Assess the role of consumer expectations in Aldo's success as a footwear retailer.

2. How has Aldo used technology to differentiate it from other footwear retailers in a crowded, competitive marketplace?

3. CEO David Bensadoun developed a new retail strategy for Aldo to increase value for customers. Discuss how specific changes made to the four Ps and personnel will help the company to attract more customers online and in stores.

4. While other retailers focus on pricing, Aldo has invested in staff training and introducing global styles. Discuss how the company can increase sales and the level of customer service through non-traditional initiatives like this.

# CHAPTER 14

Women have balls. They're called ovaries, actually. And they're at risk. There is no reliable test for ovarian cancer. Yet it kills five Canadian women every day. Have the ladyballs to do something about it. Donate at ladyballs.org

Ovarian Cancer c

Used with permission of Ovarian Cancer Canada and Grey Canada ULC.

## LEARNING OBJECTIVES

**After studying this chapter you should be able to**

**LO1** Outline the process that firms use to communicate with consumers

**LO2** List the steps in planning an integrated marketing communications campaign

**LO3** Describe what appeals advertisers use to get customers' attention

**LO4** Identify how firms determine which media to use

**LO5** Summarize how firms measure integrated marketing communications success

**LO6** Explain the six tools of integrated marketing communications campaigns

# Integrated Marketing Communications

How do you raise the profile for a disease with single-digit awareness that claims five women every day yet has no reliable screening test and few advocates? If you are Ovarian Cancer Canada, you hire an ad agency to develop a provocative message to draw attention below the belt, aiming for the "lady-balls" in fact. Darlene Remlinger, president at Grey Canada, says that non-profit organizations typically use campaigns that tug at heartstrings. So a message that told women they had balls was a big switch from traditional fundraising efforts.[1]

The creative idea focused around a video of ballsy women showing fearlessness under pressure. For example, when a co-worker disagrees with a male boss's decision, a woman says "Look at the ladyballs on her." The campaign included testimonials from women living with ovarian cancer. One of those women, Lauren Richards, had stage 2 ovarian cancer. With no screening for the disease, it is often overlooked and underdiagnosed.

While still undergoing chemotherapy, Richards approached Ovarian Cancer Canada about getting involved. Karen Cinq Mars, vice-president of marketing at the organization, learned that Richards ran her own media consultancy, Pollin8. Formerly media CEO of the Starcom MediaVest Group, Richards helped propel #Ladyballs into a campaign that would win two Cannes Lion awards and two Cassie awards.[2]

Although Grey developed a breakthrough idea, Ovarian Cancer Canada had a limited media budget to get the creative message out. That's where Richards shone. She recommended working with the media to maximize exposure. This meant launching in December when advertising demand drops off for a few months.[3] In addition to reaching out to industry colleagues to secure millions of dollars in non-paid advertising, she involved her daughter, Erin Richards, owner of HYPE PR, to build national media coverage through leading outlets such as CBC.

The integrated marketing communications campaign included video spots designed for TV, online, and cinema, as well as print ads for newspapers and magazines, radio spots, social media, and out of home executions. It featured taglines such as "I have the ladyballs to talk about it. Do you?"[4] The campaign got results, leading to a nationwide increase in calls and a 118 percent increase in requests for By Your Side, a resource created for newly diagnosed women battling the disease. Donations were up too, with one caller pledging $100,000. Only two months after being launched, the campaign was credited with 60 million earned media impressions.[5]

The campaign achieved its goal, increased awareness, and raised funds to support the organization's mission. Karen Cinq Mars says that "Some love it, some hate it, but either way, people are talking about it,"[6] and that's what really matters. ∎

Throughout the last six chapters, we focused our attention on how firms create value by developing products and services and delivering them to consumers when and where they want to buy them. However, consumers are not likely to come flocking to new products and services unless they are aware of them. Marketers must consider how to communicate the value of a new product and/or service—or more specifically, the value proposition—to the target market. The chapter vignette about Ovarian Cancer Canada illustrates how a non-profit agency developed a communication strategy to increase the impact of its message. Let's begin by examining what integrated marketing communications is, how it has developed, and how it contributes to value creation.

**Integrated marketing communications (IMC)** represents promotion, the last of the four Ps. It encompasses a variety of communication disciplines—advertising, personal selling, sales promotion, public relations, direct marketing, and digital media—in combination to provide clarity, consistency, and maximum communicative impact.[7] Instead of separate marketing communication elements with no unified control, IMC programs regard each of the firm's marketing communications elements as part of a whole, each of which offers a different means to connect with the target audience. This integration of elements provides the firm with the best means to reach the target audience with the desired message, and it enhances the value story by offering a clear and consistent message.

**integrated marketing communications (IMC)** Represents the promotion dimension of the four Ps; encompasses a variety of communication disciplines—general advertising, personal selling, sales promotion, public relations, direct marketing, and digital media—in combination to provide clarity, consistency, and maximum communicative impact.

There are three components in any IMC strategy: the consumer or target market, the channels or vehicles through which the message is communicated, and the evaluation of the results of the communication. In the first section of this chapter, we focus on *consumers*, examining the communication process: how consumers receive communications, whether via media or other methods, and how the delivery of that communication affects a message's form and content. The second section identifies the steps involved in planning successful campaigns, from identifying a target audience to creating an actual ad and assessing its performance. Although we apply these steps specifically to advertising, the same process can be used when planning sales promotions, direct marketing, public relations, and digital media. We also consider how the level of complexity in IMC strategies leads marketers to design new ways to measure the *results* of IMC campaigns. Our last section examines the six distinct *tools* of IMC—advertising, personal selling, sales promotion, direct marketing, public relations, and digital media—and how each is used in an overall IMC strategy.

## **L01**  COMMUNICATING WITH CONSUMERS

As the number of communication media has increased, the task of understanding how best to reach target consumers has become far more complex. In this section, we examine a model that describes how communications go from the firm to the consumer, and the factors that affect the way the consumer perceives the message. Then we look at how marketing communications influence consumers, from making them aware that a product or service exists to moving them to buy.

### The Communication Process

Exhibit 14.1 illustrates the communication process. Let's first define each component and then discuss how they interact.

**sender**
The firm from which an IMC message originates; the sender must be clearly identified to the intended audience.

**deceptive advertising**
A representation, omission, act, or practice in an advertisement that is likely to mislead consumers acting reasonably under the circumstances.

**The Sender**   The message originates from the **sender**, who must be clearly identified to the intended audience. For instance, an organization such as Home Depot working with one of its vendors, Stanley Tools Company, can send a message that it is having a special "Father's Day sale."

In the quest for innovative ways to reach consumers, some marketers have been accused of **deceptive advertising**, which is a representation, omission, act, or practice in an advertisement that is likely to mislead consumers acting reasonably under the

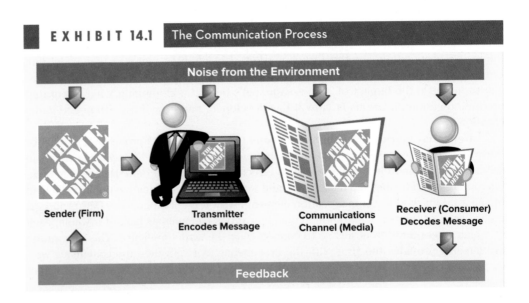

**EXHIBIT 14.1**    The Communication Process

Noise from the Environment

Sender (Firm) — Transmitter Encodes Message — Communications Channel (Media) — Receiver (Consumer) Decodes Message

Feedback

circumstances. For example, a Surrey, British Columbia, car dealer mailed a flyer in an envelope that looked like one from Canada Revenue Agency. The flyer told prospective car buyers that the "Canada Automotive Rebate Program" would expire on March 31 and promised to match 2015 tax refunds by up to $1,000. Angry customers soon learned that there was no such program. The car dealer was fined for advertising a nonexistent program and insinuating that refunds were available.

### The Transmitter

The sender works with the creative department, whether in-house or from a marketing (or advertising) agency, to develop marketing communications. Stanley likely develops advertising materials with its ad agency and provides the materials to Home Depot. Such an agent or intermediary is the **transmitter**.

### Encoding

**Encoding** means converting the sender's ideas into a message, which could be verbal, visual, or both. Home Depot may take out full-page ads in every major newspaper proclaiming, "Amazing Father's Day Deals at 25 Percent Off!" A TV commercial showing men examining and testing tools at Home Depot is another way to encode the message that "there are great deals to be had." As the old saying goes, a picture is worth a thousand words. But the most important facet of encoding is not what is sent but rather what is received. Home Depot shoppers must believe that the sale is substantial enough to warrant a trip to a store.

### The Communication Channel

The **communication channel** is the medium—print, broadcast, the Internet—that carries the message. Home Depot could transmit through TV, radio, and various print ads, and it realizes that the media chosen must be appropriate to connect itself (the sender) with its desired recipient. So Home Depot might advertise on channels such as HGTV and in magazines such as *Canadian Homes & Cottages*.

### The Receiver

The **receiver** is the person who reads, hears, or sees and processes the information contained in the message or advertisement. The sender, of course, hopes that the person receiving it will be the one for whom it was originally intended. For example, Home Depot wants its message received and decoded properly by people who are likely to shop in its stores. **Decoding** refers to the process by which the receiver interprets the sender's message.

### Noise

**Noise** is any interference that stems from competing messages, a lack of clarity in the message, or a flaw in the medium, and it poses a problem for all communication channels. Home Depot may choose to advertise in newspapers that its target market doesn't read, which means the rate at which the message is received by those to whom it has relevance has been slowed considerably. As we have already defined, encoding is what the sender intends to say, and decoding is what the receiver hears. If there is a difference between them, it is probably due to noise.

### Feedback Loop

The **feedback loop** allows the receiver to communicate with the sender and thereby informs the sender whether the message was received and decoded properly. Feedback can take many forms: a customer's purchase of the item, a complaint or compliment, the redemption of a coupon or rebate, a tweet about a product, and so on. If Home Depot observes an increase in store traffic and sales, its managers know that their intended audience received the message and understood that there were great Father's Day bargains to be found in the store.

## How Consumers Perceive Communication

The actual communication process is not as simple as the model in Exhibit 14.1 implies. Each receiver may interpret the sender's message differently, and senders often adjust

---

**transmitter**
An agent or intermediary with which the sender works to develop the marketing communications; for example, a firm's creative department or an advertising agency.

**encoding**
The process of converting the sender's ideas into a message, which could be verbal, visual, or both.

**communication channel**
The medium—print, broadcast, the Internet—that carries the message.

**receiver**
The person who reads, hears, or sees and processes the information contained in the message or advertisement.

**decoding**
The process by which the receiver interprets the sender's message.

**noise**
Any interference that stems from competing messages, a lack of clarity in the message, or a flaw in the medium; a problem for all communication channels.

**feedback loop**
Allows the receiver to communicate with the sender and thereby informs the sender whether the message was received and decoded properly.

Receivers decode messages differently. What does this Chipotle billboard mean to you?

Onsite Insite

Consumers will perceive this giant billboard differently depending on their level of knowledge and attitude toward the brand.

imago stock&people/Newscom

their message according to the medium used and the receivers' level of knowledge about the product or service. And in spite of marketers' best efforts to create clear messages, consumers may not always respond as expected.

**Receivers Decode Messages Differently** Each receiver decodes a message in his or her own way, which is not necessarily the way the sender intended. Different people shown the same message will often take radically different meanings from it. For example, what does the Chipotle billboard convey to you?

If you are a user of this brand, it may convey satisfaction. If you recently went on a diet and gave up your favourite foods, it may convey dismay or a sense of loss. If you have chosen to be a non-user, it may convey some disgust. If you are a recently terminated employee, it may convey anger. The sender has little, if any, control over what meaning any individual receiver will take from the message.

**Senders Adjust Messages According to the Medium and Receivers' Traits** Different media communicate in very different ways. So marketers make adjustments to their messages and media depending on whether they want to communicate with suppliers, shareholders, customers, or the general public.[8] Kellogg's would not, for instance, send the same message to its shareholders in a targeted email as it would to its consumers on Saturday morning TV.

Now that we've examined various aspects of the communication process, let's look at the steps in planning an IMC campaign that achieves the organization's strategic objectives.

# STEPS IN PLANNING AN IMC CAMPAIGN

**LO2**

Designing a successful IMC campaign requires a great deal of planning. Exhibit 14.2 shows some of the key steps in the planning process, each of which helps ensure that the intended message reaches the right audience and has the desired effect. As mentioned earlier, these steps can be used for all IMC tools. Let's examine each of these steps as they pertain to developing a campaign.

## 1. Identify Target Audience

The success of any campaign depends on how well the advertiser can identify its target audience. Firms conduct research to identify their target audience, and then use the information they gain to set the tone for the advertising program and help them select the media they will use to deliver the message to that audience. SoCIAL LITE Vodka, which you read about in Chapter 6, identified segments that include health-seeking individuals as the target audiences for its campaigns.

Who is the target audience for this ad: men or women?

Trademarks of Kimberly-Clark Worldwide, Inc. © KCWW Used with permission.

During this research, firms must keep in mind that their target audience may or may not be the same as current users of the product. For example, Adidas knows that FIFA fans likely are at least familiar with its offerings, even if they do not currently purchase sports gear from Adidas. Some advertisements feature the international football (soccer) stars Zinedine Zidane and Lionel Messi, to encourage FIFA fans to buy more of the brand's products.[9] But teenaged pop music fans might be less likely to

Adidas uses different ads to appeal to different target markets. Lionel Messi (left) appeals to soccer fans, while Selena Gomez (right) attracts teenaged pop music fans.

(left): Maxisport/Shutterstock.com; (right): WENN Ltd / Alamy Stock Photo

**EXHIBIT 14.2**   Steps in Planning an IMC Campaign

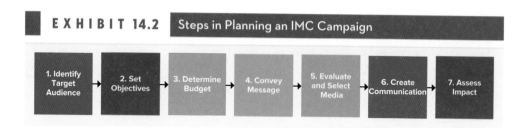

1. Identify Target Audience → 2. Set Objectives → 3. Determine Budget → 4. Convey Message → 5. Evaluate and Select Media → 6. Create Communication → 7. Assess Impact

pay attention to sporting goods. So Adidas also brought in Selena Gomez to put her name on its Neo line and appear in related advertising.[10]

Another example of marketing and advertising toward different segments (e.g., consumer vs. business users) is illustrated by Visa and MasterCard, which have different ads and offerings aimed at these segments. Some advertising messages also may be directed at portions of audiences who are not part of the marketer's target market but who participate in the purchase process. Many companies run ads for their products during Saturday morning children's viewing hours. These ads are designed to build brand awareness on the part of the children who, the companies hope, will influence their parents' purchases.

## 2. Set Objectives

Advertising objectives are derived from the overall objectives of the marketing program and clarify the specific goals that the ads are designed to accomplish. Firms need to understand the outcome they hope to achieve before they begin. Objectives, or goals, are crucial since they will later serve as the standard against which success or failure is measured. These objectives can be short-term, such as generating inquiries, increasing awareness, and prompting trial. Or they can be long-term in nature, such as increasing sales, market share, and customer loyalty. Increasing donations to support research efforts was the primary and long-term goal of Ovarian Cancer Canada's "Ladyballs" campaign but, in the short term, the non-profit needed to increase awareness of the disease. Thus, the campaign was designed to get consumers' attention through an edgy message delivered through TV, print, digital, and billboard advertisements. For SoCIAL LITE Vodka, campaign objectives revolved around driving trial among its health conscious target markets. Both short- and long-term goals should be explicitly defined and measured. We discuss how firms measure IMC success later in this chapter.

Exhibit 14.3 outlines some campaign goals for a variety of companies as well as the target markets, media used, and outcomes.

**EXHIBIT 14.3**    Sample Marketing Goals and Related Campaigns

| Company and Campaign | Goals | Target Market | Media Used | Outcome |
|---|---|---|---|---|
| ASICS **Sound Mind, Sound Body** | Branch out beyond serious runner market segment and target casual runners. | Even split males and females, aged 30–49 | Television and print ads, online advertising | 12% increase in market share |
| Columbia Sportswear Company **Greater Outdoors** | Showcase Columbia's technical innovation ability and overcome perceptions of inferior products. | 60% males, aged 20–59 | Print ads, mobile media, social media, videos, online advertising | 1% increase in sales, and +2 point brand awareness increase compared with previous year |
| GAP **Ready for Holiday Cheer** | Capture consumers' attention and get them to shop in the store during the holiday season. | Even split males and females, aged 20–39 | Print inserts, television ads, special website, social media, customizable videos | Kelly Awards Best Inset Winner; sales turned from a 12% decline in the previous year to a 1% increase |
| BMW **Diesel Reinvented** | Overcome the negative image of diesel that most consumers have. | Three segments: idea class, enthusiasts, and environmentally conscious | Print ads, videos | +1,463% year-to-year sales increase |

*Source:* The Association of Magazine Media, http://www.magazine.org/sound-mind-sound-body-2010; http://www.magazine.org/greater-outdoors-2010; http://www.magazine.org/ready-holiday-cheer-2010; http://www.magazine.org/insights-resources/magazine-advertising-case-studies/kelly-awards/inspiration-video-bmw-diesel

All marketing communications aim to achieve certain objectives: to inform, persuade, and remind customers. These objectives are examined in more depth in Chapter 15. Communication objectives also need to consider focus—for example, does the company hope to stimulate demand for a new product or service or to increase awareness for the company in general?

In Chapter 12, you learned about using push or pull marketing in determining distribution channel strategy. When setting objectives, the overarching strategy used is one of push versus pull. However, marketers also have to consider other factors, such as the nature of the market (consumer versus business), the nature of the product (simple versus technologically complex), and the stage in the product life cycle (PLC). Generally, when advertising to consumers, the objective is a pull strategy in which the goal is to get consumers to pull the product into the supply chain by demanding that retailers carry it. Push strategies also exist and are designed to increase demand by focusing on wholesalers, distributors, or salespeople, who push the product to consumers via distribution channels. These campaigns attempt to motivate the seller to highlight the product, rather than the products of competitors, and thereby push the product onto consumers.

Once the campaign's objectives are defined, the firm sets the advertising budget.

## 3. Determine Budget

Firms use a variety of methods to plan their IMC budgets (see Exhibit 14.4). Because all the methods of setting a promotional budget have both advantages and disadvantages, no one method should be used in isolation. Budgeting is not a simple process. It may take several rounds of negotiations among the company's managers, who are each competing for resources for their own areas of responsibility.

**EXHIBIT 14.4** | Budgeting Methods

| Method | Definition | Limitations |
|---|---|---|
| Objective and Task | The communication budget is set based on the cost of specific tasks required to achieve stated communication objectives. | • It can be difficult to identify the specific tasks that will achieve the objectives and, as a result, it is the most difficult method to use. |
| Competitive Parity | A method of determining a communications budget in which the firm's share of the communication expenses is in line with its market share. | • Prevents firms from exploiting the unique opportunities or problems they confront in a market.<br>• If all competitors use this method to set communication budgets, their market shares will stay approximately the same over time. |
| Percentage of Sales | A method of determining a communications budget that is based on a fixed percentage of forecasted sales. For example, a company with $2.5 million in projected sales that allocates 3.5% to advertising would have a budget of $87,500. | • Assumes the percentage used in the past, or by competitors, is still appropriate for the firm.<br>• Does not take into account new plans (e.g., to introduce a new line of products in the current year). |
| Affordable Budgeting | A method of determining a communications budget based on what is left over after other operating costs have been covered. That is, marketers forecast their sales and expenses, excluding communication, during the budgeting period. The difference between the forecast sales, minus expenses plus desired profit is applied to the communication budget (i.e., the budget is the money available after operating costs and profits). | • Assumes communication expenses do not stimulate sales and profit. |

**objective-and-task method**

An IMC budgeting method that determines the cost required to undertake specific tasks to accomplish communication objectives; process entails setting objectives, choosing media, and determining costs.

**competitive parity method**

A method of determining a communications budget in which the firm's share of the communication expenses is in line with its market share.

**percentage-of-sales method**

A method of determining a communications budget that is based on a fixed percentage of forecasted sales.

**affordable method**

A method of determining a communications budget based on what is left over after other operating costs have been covered.

The **objective-and-task method** determines the budget required to undertake specific tasks to accomplish communication objectives. For example, Netflix increased its advertising budget by 50 percent in the fourth quarter of 2015 to boost subscriptions.[11] To use this method, marketers first establish a set of communication objectives, and then determine which media best reach the target market and how much it will cost to run the number and types of communications necessary to achieve the objectives. This process—set objectives, choose media, and determine costs—must be repeated for each product or service. The sum of all the individual communication plan budgets becomes the firm's total marketing communications budget.

In addition to the objective-and-task method, three rule-of-thumb methods—**competitive parity method**, **percentage-of-sales method**, and **affordable method** of budgeting—can be used to set budgets.

These rule-of-thumb methods use prior sales and communication activities to determine the present communication budget. Although they are easy to implement, they obviously have various limitations, as noted in Exhibit 14.4. While small companies often use the affordable budgeting method, it generally results in underspending and thus may not accomplish the company's sales objectives. Large companies such as Coca-Cola and PepsiCo may use the competitive parity method. However, this method is setting a budget based on market share, which may result in PepsiCo being outspent. The percentage-of-sales method is popular as well, and standard percentages are sometimes used in some product categories, as shown in Exhibit 14.5. Since everyone needs to eat, the grocery industry needs to spend only a small percentage—around 1 percent—of its revenues on advertising, whereas the toy and game industry must spend about 11 percent. Although alcoholic drink makers spend around 13 percent of revenues on advertising,[12] SoCIAL LITE Vodka spent considerably less to launch its product, relying more heavily on publicity to get its message out.

**EXHIBIT 14.5**    Advertising Spending as a Percentage of Sales for Illustrative Product Categories

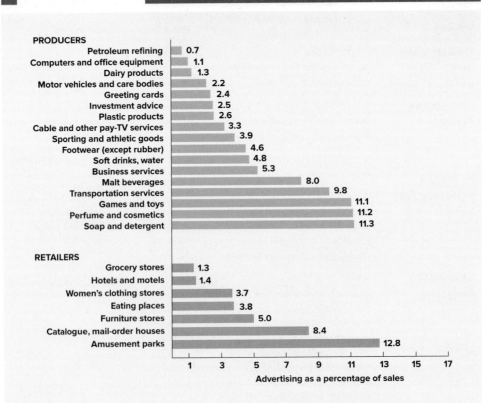

When selecting the various budgeting methods for marketing communications, firms must first consider the role that advertising plays in their attempt to meet their overall promotional objectives. Second, advertising expenditures vary over the course of the PLC, with considerably higher levels of spending during the introduction stage. Third, the nature of the market and the product influence the size of advertising budgets. For example, advertising for Starbucks is much lower than other outlets because of its high awareness and extensive use of PR. In the highly competitive consumer packaged goods industry, spending by firms such as P&G is around 11 percent of sales.[13] It all depends on the objectives of the overall IMC campaign.

The nature of the market also determines the amount of money spent on advertising. For instance, less money is spent on advertising in B2B marketing contexts than in B2C markets. Personal selling, as we discuss in Chapter 15, likely is more important in B2B markets.

## 4. Convey Message

**L03**

In this step, marketers determine what they want to convey about the product or service. First, the firm determines the key message it wants to communicate to the target audience. Second, the firm decides what appeal would most effectively convey the message. We present these decisions sequentially but, in reality, they must be considered simultaneously.

**The Message**   The message provides the target audience with reasons to respond in the desired way. A logical starting point for deciding on the advertising message is to tout the key benefits of the product or service. The message should communicate the product's problem-solving ability clearly and in a compelling fashion. In this context, advertisers must remember that products and services solve problems, whether real or perceived. That is, people are not looking for 1/4-inch drill bits; they are looking for 1/4-inch holes.[14] Because there are many ways to make a 1/4-inch hole, a firm such as Black and Decker must convey to consumers that its drill bit is the best way to get that hole. SoCIAL LITE Vodka focused on functional benefits and communicating the drink's great taste.

**unique selling proposition (USP)**
A strategy of differentiating a product by communicating its unique attributes; often becomes the common theme or slogan in the entire advertising campaign.

Another common strategy differentiates a product by establishing its unique benefits. This distinction forms the basis for the **unique selling proposition (USP)**, which is often the common theme or slogan in an advertising campaign. Briefly, a good USP communicates the unique attributes of the product and thereby becomes a snapshot of the entire campaign. Some of the most famous USPs include the following: Ford, "Built Tough"; Red Bull, "Gives You Wings"; Nike, "Just Do It."

The selling proposition communicated by the advertising must be not only *unique* to the brand, but also *meaningful* to the consumer; it furthermore must be *sustainable* over time, even with repetition.

**The Appeal**   According to early theories of rhetoric (the study of principles and rules of composition), an argument may use three main types of appeals: logos (logical), ethos (ethical), and pathos (emotional). Likewise, advertisers use different appeals to portray their product or service. Although advertising tends to combine the types of appeals into two broad categories (rational and emotional), moral appeals are sometimes considered as a third category.

The unique selling proposition establishes a product or firm's unique benefits in an advertising campaign. Ford's USP is "Built Tough."
Carlos Osorio/AP Photo

Marketers, especially those who work in non-profit organizations, often use this type of message. Since moral appeals can be rational or emotional, they are not addressed as a separate category.

***Rational Appeals.*** A **rational appeal** helps consumers make purchase decisions by offering factual information and strong arguments built around relevant issues that encourage consumers to evaluate the brand favourably on the basis of the key benefits it provides.[15] Rational appeals focus on consumers' sense of reasoning, logic, and learning. Kimberly-Clark, for example, relies heavily on rational appeals to sell Kleenex Anti-Viral Tissues. It is advertised as having a moisture-activated middle layer that is scientifically proven to kill cold and flu viruses. When moisture from a runny nose, cough, or sneeze comes in contact with Kleenex Anti-Viral Tissues' special middle layer, 99.9% of cold and flu viruses are trapped and killed within 15 minutes.[16]

This appeal is perfectly suited to this type of product. The source of its competitive advantage is a tangible feature of the product. By stressing the superior benefits of this product over regular facial tissue, the advertising copy directly delivers a rational persuasive message.

***Emotional Appeals.*** An **emotional appeal** aims to satisfy consumers' emotional desires rather than their utilitarian needs. The key to a successful emotional appeal is the use of emotion to create a bond between the consumer and the brand. For example, think about Coca-Cola's use of polar bears in its ads. The emotions most often invoked in advertising include fear appeal and humour appeal, but also safety, happiness, love (or sex), comfort, and nostalgia. Companies must pay attention to cultural influences because humour is not perceived the same way across different cultural groups and sexual appeals are taboo in some cultures.

Although the term *emotion* often conveys the image of tears, many other effective emotional appeals are used in advertising, ranging from sex appeal (e.g., Axe Body Spray), need for affiliation, need for guidance (e.g., Betty Crocker), and need for attention (e.g., cosmetics). People need a sense of self-esteem, so advertisements for Bowflex and Jenny Craig tend to feature celebrities or regular people talking about how much better they feel about themselves after they've used the exercise equipment, joined the program, and lost weight. Weight-loss ads also tend to play a bit on consumers' fears, showing "before and after" pictures as if the heavier version were a horror to behold.

**L04**

## 5. Evaluate and Select Media

The content of an advertisement is tied closely to the characteristics of the media that firms select to carry the message, and vice versa. **Media planning** refers to the process of evaluating and selecting the **media mix**—the combination of the media used and the

**rational appeal**
Helps consumers make purchase decisions by offering factual information and strong arguments built around relevant issues that encourage consumers to evaluate the brand favourably on the basis of the key benefits it provides.

**emotional appeal**
Aims to satisfy consumers' emotional desires rather than their utilitarian needs.

**media planning**
The process of evaluating and selecting the media mix that will deliver a clear, consistent, compelling message to the intended audience.

**media mix**
The combination of the media used and the frequency of advertising in each medium.

Coca-Cola uses emotional appeals with its polar bears to create a bond between the consumer and the brand.

© 2006–2012 The Coca-Cola Company

The emotional appeal of Rihanna's perfume is sex.

rune hellestad/Corbis via Getty Images

frequency of advertising in each medium—that will deliver a clear, consistent, compelling message to the intended audience.[17] For example, IKEA may determine that a heavy dose of television, radio, print, and billboards is appropriate for the back-to-school selling season between August and September each year. As a small company, SoCIAL LITE Vodka selectively used print and digital ads to make its target audiences aware of where its products could be purchased.

Because the **media buy** (the purchase of airtime or print pages) is generally the largest expense in the advertising budget, marketers must make their decisions carefully. TV advertising is by far the most expensive. Total ad spending in Canada is $12.4 billion per year. With the exception of online advertising, which has grown dramatically, advertising expenditures per medium have remained relatively constant over time: TV, 27.2 percent; newspapers, 18.6 percent; radio, 12.7 percent; magazines, 3.5 percent; and online, 37.1 percent. Other media, such as out-of-home advertising (e.g., billboards, bus wraps, posters) account for the remainder.[18] To characterize these various types of media, we again use a dichotomy: mass and niche media.

**Mass and Niche Media**    **Mass media** channels include national newspapers, magazines, radio, and television, and are ideal for reaching large numbers of anonymous audience members. **Niche media** channels are more focused and are generally used to reach narrower segments, often with unique demographic characteristics or interests. Cable TV, direct mail, and specialty magazines such as *Skateboarder* or *CosmoGirl* all provide examples of niche media. In some cases, niche media offer advertisers the opportunity to change and even personalize their messages, which is generally not an option with mass media. For example, magazine advertisers can print response cards with the name of the subscriber already on the card or change advertisements to reflect local differences, such as climate or preferences.

**Choosing the Right Medium**    For each class of media, each alternative has specific characteristics that make it suitable for meeting specific objectives (see Exhibit 14.6).

**media buy**
The purchase of airtime or print pages.

**mass media**
Channels, such as national newspapers, magazines, radio, and television, that are ideal for reaching large numbers of anonymous audience members.

**niche media**
Channels that are focused and generally used to reach narrow segments, often with unique demographic characteristics or interests.

**EXHIBIT 14.6    Types of Media Available for Advertising**

| Medium | Advantages | Disadvantages |
|---|---|---|
| **Television** | • Wide reach<br>• Incorporates sound and view | • High cost<br>• Multitude of channel and program options may increase awareness of competitors' products |
| **Radio** | • Relatively inexpensive<br>• Selectively targeted<br>• Wide reach | • No video, which limits presentation<br>• Consumers give less focused attention<br>• Exposure periods are short |
| **Magazines** | • Very targeted<br>• Subscribers pass along to others | • Relatively inflexible<br>• Long lead times |
| **Newspapers** | • Flexible<br>• Timely<br>• Can localize | • Expensive in some markets<br>• Ads have short lifespan |
| **Digital** | • Can be linked to detailed content<br>• Highly flexible and interactive<br>• Allows for specific targeting | • Becoming diluted<br>• Ad may be blocked by software prohibiting delivery |
| **Out-of-Home** | • Relatively inexpensive<br>• Offers opportunities for repeat exposure | • Not easily targeted<br>• Placement problems in some markets<br>• Exposure time is very short |
| **Direct Marketing** | • Highly targeted<br>• Allows for personalization | • Cost can vary depending on type of direct marketing used<br>• Direct mail is more expensive than newer media |

MINI Cooper uses out-of-home advertising and humour to effectively deliver messages to prospective customers.
© Horizons WWP/Alamy Stock Photo

For example, consumers use different media for different purposes, to which advertisers should match their messages. Television is used primarily for escapism and entertainment, so most TV advertising relies on a mix of visual and auditory techniques. Out-of-home advertising can also be effectively used to deliver a message. MINI Cooper developed an innovative method of advertising to its current customers in select cities through an interactive billboard. Owners received an RFID chip–embedded key fob. Every time they passed by the billboard, they received a customized message that displayed their name on the billboard.

Communication media also vary in their ability to reach the desired audience. For instance, radio is a good medium for products such as grocery purchases or fast food because many consumers decide what to purchase either on the way to the store or while in the store. Because many people listen to the radio in their cars, it becomes a highly effective means to reach consumers at a crucial point in their decision process. Each medium also varies in its reach and frequency. Advertisers can determine how effective their media mix has been in reaching their target audience by calculating the total gross rating points (GRP) (Reach × Frequency) of the advertising schedule, which we discuss later in this chapter.

The cost of each medium differs as well, with television being the most expensive. Many marketers are shifting their budgets to more digital media as a result. For example, Mondelēz, which owns the Oreo brand, has been steadily shifting its budget toward digital media based on research that indicates the ROI is higher. According to the Television Bureau of Canada, advertising expenditures in 2015 reached $12.81 billion, with a breakdown as follows: TV $3.37 billion; newspapers, $2.3 billion; digital, $4.6 billion; radio, $1.57 billion; magazines, $0.43 billion; and out-of-home $0.54 billion.[19]

**advertising schedule**
Specifies the timing and duration of advertising.

**continuous advertising schedule**
Runs steadily throughout the year and therefore is suited to products and services that are consumed continually at relatively steady rates and that require a steady level of persuasive or reminder advertising.

**Determining the Advertising Schedule** Another important decision for the media planner is the **advertising schedule**, which specifies the timing and duration of advertising. There are three types of schedules:

- A **continuous advertising schedule** runs steadily throughout the year and therefore is suited to products and services that are consumed continually at relatively steady rates and that require a steady level of persuasive or reminder advertising. For example, P&G advertises its Tide brand of laundry detergent continuously.

- A **flighting advertising schedule** refers to one implemented in spurts, with periods of heavy advertising followed by periods of no advertising. This pattern generally functions for products whose demand fluctuates, such as suntan lotion, which manufacturers may advertise heavily in the months leading up to and during the summer.

- A **pulsing advertising schedule** combines the continuous and flighting schedules by maintaining a base level of advertising but increasing advertising intensity during certain periods. For example, furniture retailer IKEA advertises throughout the year but boosts its advertising expenditures to promote school supplies in August.

## 6. Create Communication

After the marketer has decided on the message, type of ad, and appeal, its attention must shift to the actual creation of the advertisement. During this step, the message and appeal are translated creatively into words, pictures, colours, and/or music. Often, the execution style for the ad will dictate the type of medium used to deliver the message. For example, crash tests demonstrating the safety of cars often rely on the visual impact of the crash. This style of execution works only on television. Therefore, it is common for advertisers to make decisions about their message and appeal, the appropriate medium, and the best execution concurrently.

Automobile manufacturers and their dealers advertise by using many media vehicles, taking care that the media fit the message. To demonstrate an image, they may use television and magazines. To promote price, they can use newspapers and radio. To appeal to specific target markets, they can use some of the digital media vehicles described earlier. When using multiple media to deliver the same message, however, advertisers must maintain consistency across the execution styles—that is, integrated marketing—so the different executions deliver a consistent and compelling message to the target audience.

Although creativity plays a major role in the execution stage, advertisers must be careful not to let their creativity overshadow the message. Whatever the execution style, the advertisement must be able to attract the audience's attention, provide a reason for the audience to spend its time viewing the advertisement, and accomplish what it set out to do. In the end, the execution style must match the medium and objectives. An additional complication in Canada is the necessity to design some advertising messages in two official languages. And, as mentioned earlier, Canada's multicultural population means that companies must carefully consider cultural influences so as not to alienate groups through inappropriate messages.

Print advertising can be especially difficult because it is a static medium: it has no sound, no motion, and only one dimension. Instead, print relies on several key components that appear in most ads: the *headline*, or large type designed to draw attention and be read first; the *body copy*, which represents the main text portion of the ad; the *background* for the ad, usually a single colour; the *foreground*, which refers to everything that appears on top of the background, and the *branding*, which identifies the sponsor of the ad. The advertiser must convey its message by using compelling visuals and limited text.

**flighting advertising schedule**
Implemented in spurts, with periods of heavy advertising followed by periods of no advertising.

**pulsing advertising schedule**
Combines the continuous and flighting schedules by maintaining a base level of advertising but increasing advertising intensity during certain periods.

Grey Canada was the Grand Prix winner at the 2015 Cassies for its campaign for Moms Demand Action.

Used with permission of Grey Canada ULC

One particularly effective set of ads was developed by Grey Canada for the advocacy group Moms Demand Action for Gun Sense in America. The campaign's objectives were to put pressure on U.S. retailers that allowed their customers to bring guns into their stores. Ads were developed showing two people side by side, one of whom was holding an assault rifle, while the other person was holding a poodle or a Kinder Egg or was pictured with a skateboard. The Kinder Egg ad headline read, "One child is holding something that's been banned in America to protect them. Guess which one." The ads targeted grocery retailer Kroger, noting that it prohibits the sale of Kinder Eggs and does not allow skateboarding in its stores because skateboards are unsafe, but allows loaded guns.[20] The campaign was a 2015 Cassies Grand Prix winner.

**LO5**

**pretesting**

Assessments performed before an ad campaign is implemented to ensure that the various elements are working in an integrated fashion and doing what they are intended to do.

**tracking**

Includes monitoring key indicators, such as daily or weekly sales volume, while the advertisement is running to shed light on any problems with the message or the medium.

**post-testing**

The evaluation of an IMC campaign's impact after it has been implemented.

## 7. Assess Impact Using Marketing Metrics

The effectiveness of an advertising campaign must be assessed before, during, and after the campaign has run. Each step in the IMC process can be measured to determine how effective it has been at motivating consumers to move to the next step in the buying process. **Pretesting** refers to assessments performed before an ad campaign is implemented to ensure that the various elements are working in an integrated fashion and doing what they are intended to do.[21] **Tracking** includes monitoring key indicators, such as daily or weekly sales volume, while the advertisement is running to shed light on any problems with the message or the medium. **Post-testing** is the evaluation of the campaign's impact after it has been implemented. At this last stage, advertisers assess the sales and/or communication impact of the advertisement or campaign. The Ladyballs campaign resulted in a 118 percent annual increase in inquiries about ovarian cancer, an increase in donor calls of 22 calls per week, and a 220 percent increase in social engagement.[22]

Measuring sales impact can be especially challenging because of the many influences other than advertising on consumers' choices, purchase behaviour, and attitudes. These influences include the level of competitors' advertising, economic conditions in the target market, sociocultural changes, and even the weather, all of which can influence consumer purchasing behaviour. Advertisers must try to identify these influences and isolate those of the particular advertising campaign.

For frequently purchased consumer goods in the maturity stage of the PLC, such as cola, sales volume offers a good indicator of advertising effectiveness. Because their sales are relatively stable, and if we assume that the other elements of the marketing mix and the environment have not changed, we can attribute changes in sales volume to changes in advertising.

For other types of goods in other stages of the PLC, sales data offer but one of the many indicators that marketers need to examine to determine advertising effectiveness. For instance, SoCIAL LITE Vodka measured feedback from consumers (which was 90 plus percent positive), trial to purchase conversion metrics, and sales data that indicated 20 cases of its drinks were sold in a four-hour period.

In high-growth markets, sales growth alone can be misleading because the market as a whole is growing. In such a situation, marketers measure sales relative to those of competitors to determine their relative market share. Firms find creative ways to identify advertising effectiveness; for example, digital cable allows them to present a specific advertisement to certain neighbourhoods and then track sales by local or regional retailers. Some product categories experience so many influences that it is almost impossible to identify advertising's contribution to any individual consumer's choice to purchase a particular product. This is especially true for products such as cigarettes and alcohol or those with potentially negative health consequences, such as fast food or high-sugar breakfast cereals.

Because of the cumulative effect of marketing communications, it may take several exposures before consumers are moved to buy, so firms cannot expect too much too soon. They must invest in the marketing communications campaign with the idea that it may not reach its full potential for some time. One internal campaign to increase an

## Sustainable Marketing 14.1

## Sustainability Ingrained in Top Drawer Creative's DNA

When it comes to advertising agencies, sustainable practices are not generally what comes to mind. Yet Toronto-based Top Drawer Creative has woven sustainability into its DNA.[23] It has created a green office and pays employees to bike to work. The agency's tagline, "Practicing the art of influence," is applied to social good, not just developing marketing campaigns for clients such as Bullfrog Power, CAA, Callaway Golf, fitnessDepot, SAIL, and TSC Stores.

A multi-million-dollar agency with over 40 staff, Top Drawer has used sustainable building practices throughout its offices, including incorporating recycled and reclaimed materials wherever possible. Ultra-low wattage LED lighting is supplemented by lots of natural lighting. A green roof was added complete with a community garden that allows staff to grow fresh produce. Even its power is sustainable, as it's provided by Bullfrog Power.[24] And, as of 2016, Top Drawer became certified carbon neutral.

Food for client and employee events is sourced from local and organic companies. Even office equipment is sourced from ethical and sustainable vendors. The agency's efforts have not gone unnoticed.

It is the first full service ad agency in Canada to earn B-Corp certification for corporate social and environmental responsibility. Fewer than 110 companies in Canada and 900 companies globally have received this seal of approval. Top Drawer's CEO, Howard Chang, received the Clean50 Award for the agency's commitment to using entirely green energy, convincing many clients to convert media to digital from paper, and supporting

Top Drawer Creative offices use recycled and reclaimed materials wherever possible.

Used with permission of Top Drawer Creative

a host of social causes including health, nutrition, and fitness.[25]

The agency has been recognized for its corporate social responsibility efforts as well. For example, it donates 10 percent of staff billable hours to clients with social causes and supports numerous charities. Recently, it launched an Art of Influence online store selling artistic work imprinted on towels, pillows, mugs, posters, T-shirts, and greeting cards. The sales of the items—made by agency staff, family, and friends—support both the artist and two charities: Handicap International and Environmental Defense.[26]

While Chang acknowledges that individually these initiatives may not make a big difference, cumulatively they help to "move the needle."[27] And everyone benefits when companies make a commitment to sustainability.

---

advertising agency's environmental scorecard wasn't measured by conventional methods. Instead, as presented in Sustainable Marketing 14.1, success was measured by how good it made employees feel about the company.

**Traditional Media** When measuring IMC success, the firm should examine when and how often consumers have been exposed to various marketing communications. Specifically, firms use measures of *frequency* and *reach* to gauge consumers' *exposure* to marketing communications. For most products and situations, a single exposure to a communication is not enough to generate the desired response. Therefore, marketers measure the **frequency** of exposure—how often the target audience is exposed to a communication within a specified period of time. The other measure used to determine consumers' exposure to marketing communications is **reach**, which describes the percentage of the target population exposed to a specific marketing communication, such as an advertisement, at least once. Marketing communications managers usually state their media objectives in terms of **gross rating points (GRP)**, which represents reach multiplied by frequency (GRP = Reach × Frequency). This measure can be used for various media advertising—print, radio, or television.

GRP can be measured for print, radio, or television but, when comparing the calculations, they must refer to the same medium. Suppose that Unilever, the maker of Sunsilk,

**frequency**

Measure of how often the target audience is exposed to a communication within a specified period of time.

**reach**

Measure of consumers' exposure to marketing communications; the percentage of the target population exposed to a specific marketing communication, such as an advertisement, at least once.

**gross rating points (GRP)**

Measure used for various media advertising—print, radio, or television; GRP = Reach × Frequency.

places five advertisements in *Flare* magazine, which reaches 50 percent of the "fashion forward" target segment. The total GRP generated by these five magazine ads is 50 reach × 5 advertisements = 250 GRP. Now suppose that Sunsilk includes 15 TV ads as part of the same campaign, run during the program *Lost*, which has a rating of 9.2, meaning 9.2 percent of the population watches the show. The total GRP generated by these 15 advertisements is 138 (9.2 reach × 15 ads = 138 GRP). However, ads typically appear during more than one TV program, so the total GRP equals the sum of the GRPs generated by all of the programs.

Digital Media    Firms in Canada spend over $4.6 billion annually on online advertising, which includes paid search, display ads, email, and sponsorships.[28] Although GRP is an adequate measure for TV and radio ads, assessing the effectiveness of any digital communications efforts in an IMC campaign generally requires web tracking software to indicate how much time viewers spend on particular web pages and the number of pages they view. **Click-through tracking** measures how many times users click on banner advertising on websites. All these performance metrics can be easily measured and assessed by using tools such as Google Analytics. Facebook also helps companies see who has been visiting their fan pages, what these people are doing on the fan pages, and who is clicking on their ads. By keeping track of who is visiting their fan pages, marketers can get to know these visitors and better customize the material on these pages for them.

**click-through tracking**
Measures how many times users click on banner advertising on websites.

## Planning, Implementing, and Evaluating IMC Programs— An Illustration of Google Advertising

Imagine a hypothetical upscale sneaker store in New York City, called Transit, that is modelled after vintage New York City subway trains. Transit's target market is young, well educated, hip men and women aged 17–34 years. The owner's experience indicates the importance of personal selling for this market because they (1) make large purchases, and (2) seek considerable information before making a decision. Jay Oliver, the owner, spends part of his communication budget on training his sales associates. Oliver has realized that his communication budget is considerably less than that of other sneaker stores in the area. He has therefore decided to concentrate his limited budget on a specific segment and use digital media exclusively in his IMC program.

The IMC program Oliver has developed emphasizes his store's distinctive image and uses his website, social shopping, and some interesting community-building techniques. For instance, he has an extensive customer database as part of his CRM system from which he draws information for matching new merchandise with his customers' past purchase behaviours and little personal nuggets of information that sales associates have collected on the customers. He then emails specific customers information about new products that he believes they will be interested in. He also encourages customers to use blogs hosted on his website. Customers chat about the "hot" new sneakers, club events, and races. He does everything with a strong sense of style.

**search engine marketing (SEM)**
Uses tools such as Google AdWords to increase the visibility of websites in search engine results.

To reach new customers, he uses **search engine marketing (SEM)**. In particular, he uses Google AdWords, a search engine marketing tool that allows advertisers to show up in the Sponsored Links section of the search results page based on the keywords potential customers use (see the sponsored link section in the right-hand column of the Google screen grab).

Oliver must determine the best keywords to use for his sponsored link advertising program. Some potential customers might search using the keywords, "sneakers," "sneakers in New York City," "athletic shoes," or other such versions. Using Google AdWords, Oliver can assess the effectiveness of his advertising expenditures by measuring the reach, relevance, and return on investment for each of the keywords that potential customers used during their Internet searches.

Advertisers pay Google to show up in the Sponsored Link section in the right-hand column of this screen grab.

© Google Inc.

To estimate reach, Oliver uses the number of **impressions** (the number of times the ad appears in front of the user) and the **click-through rate (CTR)**. To calculate CTR, he takes the number of times a user clicks on an ad and divides it by the number of impressions. For example, if a sponsored link was delivered 100 times and 10 people clicked on it, then the number of impressions is 100, the number of clicks is 10, and the CTR would be 10 percent.

The relevance of the ad describes how useful an ad message is to the consumer doing the search. Google provides a measure of relevance through its AdWords system using a quality score. The quality score looks at a variety of factors to measure how relevant a keyword is to an ad's text and to a user's search query. In general, a high quality score means that a keyword will trigger ads in a higher position and at a lower cost per click.[29] In a search for "sneaker store," the Transit ad showed up fourth, suggesting high relevance.

Using the following formula, Oliver also can determine an ad's **return on investment (ROI)**:

$$ROI = \frac{\text{Sales revenue} - \text{Advertising cost}}{\text{Advertising cost}}$$

For the two keyword searches in Exhibit 14.7, Oliver finds how much the advertising cost him (Column 3), the sales produced as a result (Column 4), and the ROI (Column 6). For "sneaker store," the Transit website had a lot more clicks (110) than the clicks

**impressions**
The number of times an ad appears to a user.

**click-through rate (CTR)**
The number of times a user clicks on an ad divided by the number of impressions.

**return on investment (ROI)**
Used to measure the benefit of an investment, ROI is calculated by dividing the gain of an investment by its cost.

**EXHIBIT 14.7** ROI Assessment

| (1) Keyword | (2) Clicks | (3) Cost | (4) Sales | (5) Sales Revenue (Col. 4) − Cost (Col. 3) | (6) ROI = (Col. 5 ÷ Col. 3) × 100 |
|---|---|---|---|---|---|
| Sneaker store | 110 | $10/day | $35/day | $25 | 250% |
| New York City sneakers | 40 | $25/day | $40/day | $15 | 60% |

| EXHIBIT 14.8 | Program Effectiveness Results | | | |

| Communication Objective | Questions | Before Campaign | 6 Months After | One Year After |
| --- | --- | --- | --- | --- |
| Awareness (% mentioning store) | What stores sell sneakers? | 38% | 46% | 52% |
| Knowledge (% giving outstanding rating for sales assistance) | Which stores would you rate outstanding on the following characteristics? | 9 | 17 | 24 |
| Attitude (% first choice) | On your next shopping trip for sneakers, which store would you visit first? | 13 | 15 | 19 |
| Visit (% visited store) | Which of the following stores have you been to? | 8 | 15 | 19 |

received from "New York City sneakers" (40) (Column 2). Even though the sales were lower for the keywords "sneaker store" at \$35/day, versus \$40/day for the keywords "New York City sneakers," the ROI was much greater for the "sneaker store" keyword combination. In the future, Oliver should continue this keyword combination, in addition to producing others that are similar to it, in the hope that he will attain an even greater return on investment.

To evaluate his IMC program, Oliver compares the results of the program with his objectives (Exhibit 14.8). To measure his program's effectiveness, he conducted an inexpensive online survey using the questions in Exhibit 14.8, which shows the survey results for one year. The results show a steady increase in awareness, knowledge of the store, and choice of the store as a primary source of sneakers. This research provides evidence that the IMC program was conveying the intended message to the target audience.

As IMC programs become more sophisticated, measurement is not the only concern. Marketers need to worry about a host of legal and ethical issues, which we will examine in the next chapter. Now that we've examined the steps in planning integrated marketing communications, let's look at the specific tools used in creating IMC campaigns.

## LO6 INTEGRATED MARKETING COMMUNICATIONS TOOLS

For any communications campaign to succeed, the firm must deliver the right message to the right audience through the right media. Reaching the right audience is becoming more difficult, however, as the media environment grows more complicated. No single communication channel is better than another. The goal of IMC tools is to use them in such a way that the sum exceeds the total of the parts.

Advances in technology have led to a variety of new media options, such as satellite radio, wireless technology, pop-up and banner ads on websites, brand-sponsored websites, and text messaging, all of which vie for consumers' attention. Not so long ago, advertisers could reach the masses with media buys on three TV networks. Today, they have to buy on 74 stations to reach the same number of people. Print media have also grown and become more specialized. In Canada, there are currently 91 daily newspapers, 1,083 community newspapers, more than 1,300 consumer magazines, and 708 business publications.[30]

**EXHIBIT 14.9** Integrated Marketing Communications Tools

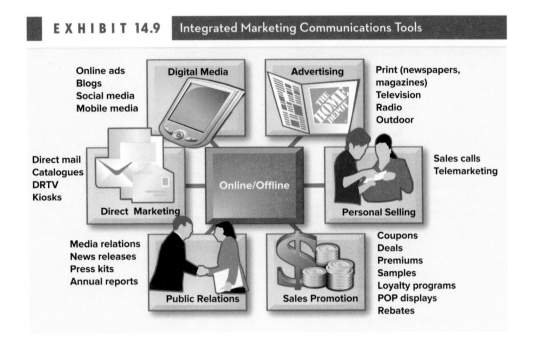

This proliferation of media has led many firms to shift their promotional dollars from advertising to direct marketing, website development, product placements, and other forms of promotion in search of the best way to deliver messages to their target audiences. Media fragmentation has also occurred on television. Networks are dedicated to certain types of sports (Outdoor Life Network, Golf Channel), to children (YTV), to ethnic minorities (APTN—Aboriginal Peoples Television Network), and to religions (CTS). Each of these channels allows IMC planners to target their desired audience narrowly.

We now examine the individual tools of IMC and the way each contributes to a successful IMC campaign (see Exhibit 14.9). Most of these tools work along a continuum from passive to interactive and can be used either offline or online. Some tools—advertising, personal selling, and sales promotion—appear in detail in the next chapter, and so we discuss them only briefly here.

## Advertising

Perhaps the most visible of the IMC components, **advertising** is a paid form of communication from an identifiable source, delivered through a communication channel, and designed to persuade the receiver to take some action, now or in the future. Traditionally, advertising has been passive and offline; however, these days advertising is increasingly placed online and is interactive. For instance, print ads in newspapers and magazines are offline, with customers simply viewing them (passive). In contrast, banner ads, web-based contests, or online coupons are all offered online and require customers to provide some information or take action (interactive). Basically, advertising can be either offline or online and either passive or interactive.

In Chapter 15, we discuss the purpose of advertising and its various types, but for now, we note that advertising is extremely effective for creating awareness of a product or service and generating interest. As mentioned in the chapter vignette, the #Ladyballs campaign made people more aware of ovarian cancer and convinced them to donate to the cause. However, advertising can also be used to remind consumers of existing brands. For example, McDonald's "I'm Lovin' It" ads helped revitalize interest in the company's products, driving both traffic and sales.

Advertising can entice consumers into a conversation with marketers. However, advertising must break through the clutter of other messages to reach its intended

**advertising**
A paid form of communication from an identifiable source, delivered through a communication channel, and designed to persuade the receiver to take some action, now or in the future.

## Entrepreneurial Marketing 14.1

### From Single Mom to Success Story

Advertising and sales promotion is all about persuasion. According to Arlene Dickinson, CEO of Venture Communications and author of *Persuasion*, in business and in life it's important to be honest and authentic and to understand that *"persuasion* doesn't involve tricks, coercion, or shading the truth."[31]

Born in South Africa, Dickinson immigrated to Canada when she was only three years old. She did well academically and finished high school early at age 16. Although her father wanted her to attend university, having grown up in a strict Mormon household Arlene's goal was to get married and have children. She married at 19 and had four children in quick succession. When the marriage fell apart, she worked at almost every job imaginable. Her sales experience led to an offer to join Venture Communications in 1988, working without pay for two years. Ten years later, she bought the company.

Since then, she has grown the business from a small local firm based in Calgary to one of the largest independent marketing firms in Canada.[32] Clients include organizations such as Cenovus and Toyota. An out-of-home campaign for Travel Alberta aimed to make the province the number-one choice for Ontario skiers. Tactics included station domination at Toronto's Union Station and resulted in traffic to the Travel Alberta website increasing by over 150 percent.[33]

Dickinson is also the CEO of Arlene Dickinson Enterprises (ADE) and YouInc.com, companies she launched

Arlene Dickinson grew Venture Communications into one of the largest independent marketing firms in Canada.

Kevin Van Paassen/The Globe and Mail/The Canadian Press

in late 2012 that work to invest in, serve, and support entrepreneurs. In her second book, *All In: You, Your Business, Your Life*, she shares insights into the cost of her success—sacrifices to relationships, vacations forgone—to deal with business issues.[34]

From single mom living in poverty to self-made millionaire, Dickinson is a Canadian success story. Although she has won numerous awards and been ranked as one of *PROFIT Magazine*'s Top 100 Women Entrepreneurs many years in a row, Dickinson is quick to admit that she's made mistakes. "Go out there and try. Don't be afraid to make mistakes. You never know what's around the corner if you just put yourself out there."[35] Looking back, she says one of her marketing blunders was passing up on the opportunity to work with a snowboard company. She thought snowboards were just a fad and wouldn't last. The experience taught her to pay attention to trends and to bear in mind that just because she didn't like something didn't mean others would feel the same.[36]

Today Dickinson is perhaps best known for her role as one of the venture capitalists on the CBC television series *Dragons' Den*, where she spent eight seasons, as well as her roles on *The Big Decision* and *Recipe to Riches*. Companies that pitch on the shows are often looking for just the kind of marketing expertise Arlene Dickinson brings to deals. After leaving *Dragons' Den*, she set up District Ventures Accelerator in Calgary to help early stage health care and food sector companies get mentoring and leadership assistance as well as access to investment funds. An entrepreneur at heart, Dickinson views the accelerator centre "like pouring water on the seed."[37]

audience. In the past decade, advertising's share of total promotional dollars has fallen as the budgets for other forms of sales promotion, especially direct marketing and public relations, have increased, resulting in a more balanced approach to the use of marketing communications elements. Entrepreneurial Marketing 14.1 examines a marketing firm run by an entrepreneur with a dragon legacy.

### Personal Selling

**personal selling**
The two-way flow of communication between a buyer and a seller that is designed to influence the buyer's purchase decision.

**Personal selling** is the two-way flow of communication between a buyer and a seller that is designed to influence the buyer's purchase decision. Personal selling can take place in various settings: face to face, video teleconferencing, on the telephone, or over the Internet. Although consumers don't often interact with professional salespeople, personal selling represents an important component of many IMC programs, especially in business-to-business (B2B) settings.

The cost of communicating directly with a potential customer is quite high compared with other forms of promotion, but it is simply the best and most efficient way to sell certain products and services. Customers can buy many products and services without the help of a salesperson, but salespeople simplify the buying process by providing information and services that save customers time and effort. In many cases, sales representatives add significant value, which makes the added expense of employing them worthwhile. Chapter 15 devotes more attention to personal selling.

## Sales Promotion

**Sales promotions** are special incentives or excitement-building programs that encourage the purchase of a product or service, such as coupons, rebates, contests, free samples, and point-of-purchase displays. While some sales promotions are offline (e.g., printed coupons or contest entries), others are online (e.g., ecoupons downloaded to a smartphone). Marketers typically design these incentives for use in conjunction with other advertising or personal selling programs. Many sales promotions, such as free samples or point-of-purchase displays, are designed to build short-term sales; though others, such as contests and sweepstakes, have become integral components of firms' CRM programs as means to build customer loyalty. We discuss such sales promotions in more detail in Chapter 15.

**sales promotions** Special incentives or excitement-building programs that encourage the purchase of a product or service, such as coupons, rebates, contests, free samples, and point-of-purchase displays.

## Direct Marketing

The component of IMC that has received the greatest increase in aggregate spending recently is **direct marketing**, or marketing that communicates directly with target customers to generate a response or transaction.[38] Unlike mass media, which communicate to a wide audience, direct marketing allows for personalization of the message, a key advantage. Direct marketing contains a variety of traditional and new forms of marketing communication initiatives, including offline forms such as direct mail, direct response TV commercials (infomercials), catalogues, and kiosks, as well as online technologies such as email, mobile, and podcasts. Digital technologies have had a profound effect on direct marketing initiatives. Email, for instance, can be directed to specific consumers to inform them about new merchandise and special promotions, confirm receipt of an order, and indicate when an order has been shipped. Currently available technologies also mean handheld devices can function as a payment medium: Just tap your smartphone, and the transaction occurs in much the same way it occurs with a credit card.

**direct marketing** Marketing that communicates directly with target customers to generate a response or transaction.

Direct marketing has four defining characteristics: it is targeted, motivates an action, is measurable, and can provide information for the development of a marketing database.[39] It is an information-driven process that enables marketers to narrowly target the appropriate audiences. For example, a company selling a health supplement can use direct marketing to reach only people who subscribe to health-related magazines in an effort to motivate them to take action, such as calling a toll-free number, visiting a website, or placing a mail order. The company can easily measure the response for each magazine by using uniquely assigned coded coupons, toll-free numbers, or Internet microsites. The use of response-generating direct marketing forms (such as direct mail, direct response television, or telemarketing) can provide meaningful results and allow the evaluation of a marketing campaign in a timely manner.[40]

Direct marketers now use mobile devices to reach potential customers.
© Maksym Yemelyanov | Dreamstime.com

Direct marketing offers benefits to both buyers and sellers. Companies that use direct marketing campaigns appreciate the ability to sell to a much wider target audience than could be reached with traditional marketing channels. In comparison to personal selling or mass media advertising, the cost of reaching consumers is much lower with direct marketing. As mentioned earlier, one of the defining characteristics of direct marketing is its measurability—campaigns can be closely monitored to track results. Measurability means marketers know who responds to their campaigns, allowing them to build rich databases that can be used to cross-sell, tailor offers, and create specific promotions geared to individual customers in future campaigns.

The increased use of customer databases has enabled marketers to identify and track consumers over time and across purchase situations, which has contributed to the rapid growth of direct marketing. Marketers have been able to build these databases thanks to consumers' increased use of credit and debit cards, store-specific credit and loyalty cards, and online shopping, all of which require the buyer to give the seller personal information that becomes part of its database. Because firms understand customers' purchases better when they possess such information, they can more easily focus their direct marketing efforts appropriately. Ethical Dilemma 14.1 describes how companies

## Ethical Dilemma 14.1

## Protecting Consumer Privacy

The digital age has allowed companies to more narrowly target consumers. Is this a good thing? Maybe. But what if, through data mining efforts based on web browsing activity, a retailer is able to determine that a woman is pregnant and send ads and coupons for baby-related products directly to her? The father of a U.S. teen who received such promotions was justifiably upset.[41] A Consumer Privacy Bill of Rights was passed to protect people from changes to how firms now use data collected from customers.

In Canada, consumers are protected against such infringements of privacy by the federal Personal Information Protection and Electronic Documents Act (PIPEDA). The Act has three fundamental objectives: transparency regarding how personal information will be used, that information will not be used for anything other than the stated purpose, and that only directly relevant information to the declared purpose should be collected.[42] These objectives are further broken down as 10 privacy principles shown below.

| | |
|---|---|
| **Accountability** | Organizations are responsible for personal information collected and must designate an individual to be accountable for compliance. |
| **Identifying Purposes** | Companies must identify the purposes for which personal information is collected at or before the time it is collected. |
| **Consent** | Individuals must consent to the collection, use, or disclosure of personal information. |
| **Limiting Collection** | Only information that is necessary for the stated purposes may be collected. |
| **Limiting Use, Disclosure, and Retention** | Organizations may not use or disclose personal information for purposes other than those for which it was collected, unless individual consent is given or as required by law. The information may only be retained for the time needed to fulfill its purpose. |
| **Accuracy** | Personal information must be as accurate, complete, and current as needed to satisfy collection purposes. |
| **Safeguards** | Security safeguards must be implemented appropriate to the sensitivity of the information. |
| **Openness** | Individuals must be informed about an organization's policies and practices regarding the management of personal information. |
| **Individual Access** | Individuals must be informed of the existence, use, and disclosure of personal information and have access to it on request. Individuals can challenge the accuracy and completeness of information to have it amended if appropriate. |
| **Challenging Compliance** | Individuals can voice concerns to the designated individual accountable for the organization's compliance.[43] |

PIPEDA aims to protect consumer privacy, however, violations still occur. For example, a man who searched for sleep apnea devices complained after he received ads for similar devices on other websites. The Office of the Privacy Commissioner of Canada investigated and found that Google had not complied with its privacy law.[44]

To allow consumers to get information and more easily opt out of targeted ads, the Digital Advertising Alliance of Canada (DAAC) has launched Ad Choices.[45] Ads that are presented to consumers based on their search behaviour are noted with a special icon, an "i" inside a blue triangle. Consumers will still receive ads, but those ads won't be targeted based on browsing history.

The federal government also passed the Canadian Anti-Spam Legislation (CASL) to help citizens deal with unwanted email and reduce harm from ecommerce threats. The legislation came into effect in July 2014 and requires companies that send electronic communication to ensure that they have consent from the recipient, that they clearly identify the sender of communications, and that they provide an unsubscribe mechanism.[46] Rogers Media paid a $200,000 fine after consumers complained about receiving emails with a non-working unsubscribe function.[47]

Are consumers' personal privacy rights being unjustly invaded by firms that provide them with targeted promotions based on their browsing habits? Or are the marketing firms engaged in these activities just providing them with helpful information that may make their buying decisions more efficient?

## EXHIBIT 14.10    Forms of Direct Marketing

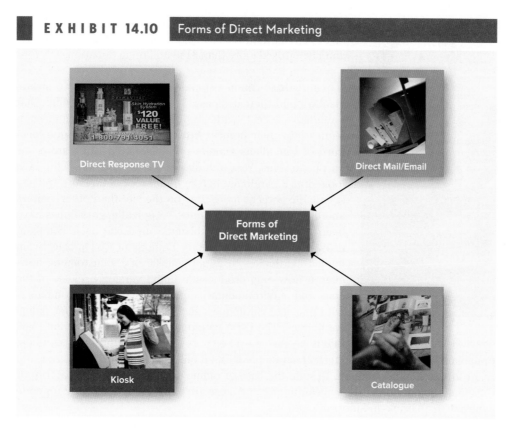

are targeting consumers with promotions based on their purchasing behaviour, which is sometimes seen as an infringement on their privacy.

As shown in Exhibit 14.10, direct marketing can take a number of forms, including direct mail/email, catalogues, direct response TV, and kiosks. We focus on the first four forms here.

**Direct Mail/Email**    We consider **direct mail/email** primarily as targeted forms of communication distributed to a prospective consumer's mailbox or inbox. Mailing lists are a critical component of direct mail. Choose the wrong list and your promotion will be perceived as "junk mail" since the information and offer will not be targeted to the appropriate audience. Canada Post research shows that Canadian households receive an average of 27 pieces of direct mail per week. In spite of such high volumes, addressed mail continues to be welcomed by Canadians. Recipients are twice as likely to notice and read direct mail than email, and 81 percent are likely to read it the day it is received.[48] Studies consistently report that consumers are more receptive to direct mail than email. Most of us receive far more email marketing messages, not all of which are welcome. (As noted in Ethical Dilemma 14.1, tough new anti-spam legislation, CASL, is in effect in Canada to protect residents from unwanted electronic communication.) And today, 45 percent of marketing emails are received and opened on mobile devices, making it critical for marketers to ensure their messages are optimized for mobile platforms.[49]

According to the Direct Marketing Association, direct mail generates $12 of revenue for every dollar invested. For direct mail to be effective, a good contact list is a must and a good offer is also needed to compel consumers to take immediate action. Good offers must be relevant both to consumers and to the product, and are important whether a company is promoting products to consumers or to businesses. But offers don't always involve selling a product. Registered charities rely on direct mail in their fundraising efforts. For example, the Heart and Stroke Foundation of Canada, which receives no operational funding from government sources, uses direct mail extensively to promote its

**direct mail/email**
A targeted form of communication distributed to a prospective customer's mailbox or inbox.

The IKEA catalogue is a key part of its IMC strategy and allows consumers to purchase a wide variety of products.

© Inter IKEA Systems B.V. 2017.

**direct response TV (DRTV)**

TV commercials or infomercials with a strong call to action.

cause. The Foundation's efforts have resulted in the recruitment of more than 125,000 volunteers and 13 million donors[50] and have raised more than $149 million in donations.[51]

**Catalogues**   Many companies use catalogues to strategically build their business. They represent a medium that Canadians accept, with 80 percent welcoming retail catalogues into their homes. After receiving a catalogue, one-third of Canadians make a purchase online, in a store,  or by phone. Plus, research shows that consumers who have looked at a catalogue before going to a company's website spend 109 percent more time on the site than other visitors and buy more expensive items.[52] Typically, catalogues have been mailed, which can become an issue as a company grows. At one time Mountain Equipment Co-Op selectively mailed catalogues to about 200,000 of its customers, however, it now only produces a digital version because of the cost and environmental impact. Today, most companies with physical catalogues, such as Staples, also offer online catalogues. The IKEA catalogue is so well known and liked that it has become a key part of the company's IMC strategy.

Canadian Tire replaced its physical catalogue with an online one, however has recently reintroduced a paper version. Despite the ease of online shopping, the vast majority of Canadians still prefer hard-copy catalogues and these are particularly important for companies with no brick-and-mortar locations.

**Direct Response TV**   **Direct response TV (DRTV)** refers to TV commercials or infomercials with a strong call to action, usually via toll-free number, return mail address, or website. Although many people may question the effectiveness of this form of direct marketing, DRTV and the Shopping Channel have historically been two of the most welcome forms of direct marketing among Canadians. DRTV  accounts for about 25 percent of all TV commercials, with the top purchases being exercise products, diet/health/weight merchandise, videos, and beauty products/cosmetics.[53]

Most DRTV ads have short 60- and 120-second formats or are much longer 30-minute infomercials. For many people, the term *infomercial* conjures up images of a late-night TV pitchman telling them how his product slices and dices better than anything on the market. Most infomercials appear to be selling products that seem too good to be true: fitness routines that promise to melt the pounds away, a miracle knife so sharp you'll never have to buy another, or rejuvenating face creams that magically erase wrinkles. Some products, such as the Food Saver vacuum sealing system, are sold only using DRTV and not in retail outlets.

DRTV is used for its power to drive results not only through infomercials, but also in shorter-format ads. SickKids Foundation launched a campaign to build brand awareness and attract new donors. A compelling, emotional message was developed that told the story of children who were being treated at SickKids Hospital. With a strong call to action, ads in this campaign have proven to be among the most powerful tools of touching hearts and minds and acquiring donors. Its Better Tomorrows "Life Unpaused" campaign increased donations by 370 percent.[54]

**Kiosks**   As discussed in Chapter 10, digital kiosks can be used to facilitate the way services companies deliver their services to customers; for example, allowing passengers at airports to quickly print prebooked tickets. However, kiosks can also be used to sell both services and products to end consumers. For example, after you print your ticket at an airport kiosk, you can get a 10-minute manicure at another kiosk while you wait for your flight. Some kiosks are temporary, such as the kiosks that are set up in malls primarily to sell gift items in the weeks leading up to Christmas. Others kiosks are permanent. For example, Dell's mall kiosks allow shoppers to talk to a Dell representative face-to-face and find the computer that's just right for them. Consumers can customize their PC, order it, and have it shipped directly to their homes. In Ontario, Virgin Mobile unveiled a network of mall kiosks, which it may use to sell other Virgin products and services in the future. Real estate companies such as Century 21 use kiosks in malls where thousands of potential buyers can connect with property listings. Kiosks from Hallmark allow customers to create their own personalized cards, and McDonald's kiosks let customers order personalized hamburgers and toppings. Disposable cameras and batteries are available at kiosks throughout the Rogers Centre in Toronto.[55] Business marketers use kiosks as well, particularly at trade shows to collect sales leads and to provide information on their products.

## Public Relations

**Public relations (PR)** is the organizational function that manages the firm's communications to achieve a variety of objectives, including building and maintaining a positive image, handling or heading off unfavourable stories or events, and maintaining positive relationships with the media. Like advertising, this tactic is relatively passive in that customers do not have to take any action to receive it. However, PR efforts span both offline and online media. PR activities support the other promotional efforts by the firm by generating "free" media attention and general goodwill. For example, Ovarian Cancer Canada's "Ladyballs" campaign was frequently in the news and discussed in numerous newspaper and magazine articles.

While it can be very difficult to convince the media to write about a company or its products and services, this media attention can be crucial to a company's success. As a relatively new company with a limited marketing budget, SoCIAL LITE Vodka relied heavily on PR to get awareness. It was successful in getting coverage on TV (*Breakfast Television, CityLine, The Social, Dragons' Den,* Food Network, Women's Network), in print (*National Post, The Toronto Star, The Globe & Mail, Marketing Magazine, Strategy Magazine*), and numerous online blogs related to entrepreneurs, fitness, fashion, lifestyle, and business. It doesn't hurt to have help from former *Dragons' Den* marketing expert Arlene Dickinson, who has appeared at launch parties and done media interviews.

In essence, PR is the free placement of a company's message in the media. In the past, many companies used PR primarily to communicate with the news media, hoping their messages would be picked up. Today, PR is more about connecting with consumers and interacting in the hopes of having a conversation.[56] Electric car maker Tesla spends minimally on advertising because it benefits from PR resulting from media coverage, bloggers, and word-of-mouth. Unilever's Dove Campaign for Real Beauty demonstrates the viral power of digital media to quickly spread a message and generate a wealth of valuable publicity. Its "Evolution" film generated over $150 million in unpaid media impressions. Its "Real Beauty Sketches" video was the most watched online ad ever, generating more than 163 million YouTube views.[57]

Car Heaven's support of Mothers Against Drunk Driving (MADD) Canada illustrates how using a combination of promotional and PR campaigns can enhance a firm's image while supporting a worthwhile cause.[58] The Car Heaven program gives car owners a way to conveniently dispose of old vehicles by towing them at no charge to a recycling facility. The proceeds from the scrap metal are donated to MADD Canada and donors receive charitable tax receipts.[59] The program creates a positive association between the brand and a social cause, in this case, prevention of drunk driving. This form of promotional campaign, called **cause-related marketing**, refers to commercial activity in which businesses and charities form a partnership to market an image, product, or service for their mutual benefit.[60]

Designers vie to have celebrities, especially those nominated for awards, wear their fashions on the red carpet. Their brands offer intangible benefits, not just

**public relations (PR)**
The organizational function that manages the firm's communications to achieve a variety of objectives, including building and maintaining a positive image, handling or heading off unfavourable stories or events, and maintaining positive relationships with the media.

**cause-related marketing**
Commercial activity in which businesses and charities form a partnership to market an image, product, or service for their mutual benefit; a type of promotional campaign.

Prada garnered positive public relations when Lupita Nyong'o wore its gown to the Academy Awards.

Jason LaVeris/Getty Images

**event sponsorship**
A popular PR tool; occurs when corporations support various activities (financially or otherwise), usually in the cultural or sports and entertainment sectors.

functional benefits. Events such as the Oscars, with its 35 million annual viewers, provide an unparalleled opportunity to showcase the emotional benefits of the brand and make others want to be a part of it. Thus, the celebrities whom designers pursue and offer their items to are those who will sell the most or provide the best iconic images. Lupita Nyong'o's great popularity during the recent awards season meant that she could wear Ralph Lauren to the Golden Globes, then switch to Prada for the Academy Awards, and garner press for both design firms.[61] The placement of designer apparel at media events benefits both the designer and the celebrity. And neither happens by accident. PR people on both sides help orchestrate the events to get the maximum benefit for both parties.

Good PR has always been an important success factor. Yet in recent years, the importance of PR has grown, as the cost of other forms of marketing communications has increased. At the same time, the influence of PR has become more powerful, as consumers have become increasingly skeptical of marketing claims made in other media.[62] In many instances, consumers view media coverage generated through PR as more credible and objective than any other aspects of an IMC program, because the firm does not "buy" the space in print media or time on radio or television.

For example, TOMS Shoes, a company founded by Blake Mycoskie, illustrates how a well orchestrated IMC effort, using a combination of promotional and PR campaigns, can enhance a firm's image while supporting a worthwhile cause.[63] Mycoskie took traditional Argentinean shoes, known as *alpargatas*, and began selling and marketing them to consumers outside the generally impoverished nation in which they originated. The company's website proclaims that Mycoskie's inspiration was simple. Noting the comfort of the shoes and the extreme poverty of Argentina, he promises that "With every pair you purchase, TOMS will give a pair of new shoes to a child in need." This message is found on his website and other press vehicles, including a mention as the "Good Guy of the Month" in *O, The Oprah Winfrey Magazine*. TOMS Shoes embraces cause-related marketing. The company is not just about making and selling shoes, but also partners with groups such as Insight Argentina, an organization offering volunteer activities in Argentina to help that area address its most pressing social issues.[64]

Another very popular PR tool is event sponsorship. **Event sponsorship** occurs when corporations support various activities (financially or otherwise), usually in the cultural or sports and entertainment sectors. For example, Subaru sponsors the Subaru Ironman Canada Triathlon, regarded as one of the best Ironman events in the world. The race helps Subaru promote its vehicles, which, like athletes, must possess both the versatility to excel in a variety of environments and the durability to outlast the competition. Red Bull is a frequent sponsor of various kinds of sports events, such as Red Bull Air Race and numerous extreme sports events (e.g., cliff diving).

Part of Red Bull's PR toolkit is its event sponsorship of a cliff diving event.

James Davies/Alamy Stock Photo

Firms often distribute a PR toolkit to communicate with various audiences. Some toolkit elements are designed to inform specific groups directly, whereas others are created to generate media attention and disseminate information. We depict the various elements of a PR toolkit in Exhibit 14.11.

| EXHIBIT 14.11 | Elements of a PR Toolkit |
|---|---|

| PR Element | Function |
|---|---|
| Publications: brochures, special-purpose single-issue publications such as books | Inform various constituencies about the activities of the organization and highlight specific areas of expertise |
| Video and audio: programs, public service announcements | Highlight the organization or support cause-related marketing efforts |
| Annual reports | Give required financial performance data and inform investors and others about the unique activities of the organization |
| Media relations: press kits, news releases, speeches, event sponsorships | Generate news coverage of the organization's activities or products/services |
| Digital media: websites, email campaigns | Websites can contain all the previously mentioned toolbox elements, while email directs PR efforts to specific target groups |

## Digital Media

The Internet has had a dramatic impact on how marketers communicate with their customers. **Digital media** tools range from simple website content to far more interactive features such as corporate blogs, online games, text messaging, social media, and mobile apps. (Chapter 16 explores social and mobile media in much more detail.) Unlike the other IMC tools discussed previously, these forms of digital media were designed only for the online world. Marketers are using them more and more often for the following reasons, among others: they can be targeted to specific customer segments, their impact can be easily and quickly measured in real time, modifications can be quickly made to increase their effectiveness, and customers can be engaged to forward the message to their social networks.

**digital media**
Tools ranging from simple website content to far more interactive features such as corporate blogs, online games, text messaging, social media, and mobile apps.

Websites   Firms have increased their emphasis on communicating with customers through their websites. They use them to build their brand image and educate customers about their products or services and where they can be purchased. Retailers and some manufacturers sell merchandise directly to consumers online. For example, in addition to selling merchandise, Office Depot's website has a Business Solutions Centre that provides advice and product knowledge, as well as a source of networks to other businesses. It includes forms that businesses would use to comply with Occupational Safety and Health Act (OSHA) requirements, to check job applicant records, to estimate cash flow, and to develop a sexual harassment policy; workshops for running a business; and local and national business news. By providing this information on its website, Office Depot reinforces its image as the essential source of products, services, and information for small businesses. Many firms, especially retailers, encourage customers to post reviews of products they have bought or used and even have visitors to their websites rate the quality of the reviews. Research has shown that these online product reviews increase customer loyalty and provide a competitive advantage for sites that offer them.[65]

Blogs   A **blog (weblog)** contains periodic posts on a common web page. A well received blog can communicate trends, promote special events, create positive word-of-mouth, connect customers by forming a community, increase sales, improve customer satisfaction because the company can respond directly to customers' comments, and develop a long-term relationship with the company. By its very nature, a blog is supposed to be transparent and contain authors' honest observations, which can help customers

**blog (weblog)**
A web page that contains periodic posts; corporate blogs are a new form of marketing communications.

determine their trust and loyalty levels. Nowadays, blogs are becoming more interactive as the communication between bloggers and customers has increased.

Social Media    Social media is media content distributed through social interactions. We introduce the topic here and expand our discussion in Chapter 16. Although there is a broad spectrum of online communities and social networking sites, the three most popular are YouTube, Facebook, and Twitter. In these online sites, consumers review, communicate about, and aggregate information about products, prices, and promotions. These social media also allow users to interact among themselves (e.g., form a community), as well as provide other like-minded consumers (i.e., members of their community) and marketers with their thoughts and evaluations about a firm's products or services. Social media help facilitate the consumer decision process (Chapter 4) by encouraging need recognition, information search, alternative evaluation, purchase, and postpurchase reviews.

Marketers can use social media to engage their customers in a proactive dialogue, as seen in many of the Social and Mobile Marketing boxes throughout this book. When it comes to social media, there is considerably more transparency and honesty than in most other forms of marketing communication. And, because members share so much personal information, marketers can tailor messages and applications to very specific and desirable target markets. For example, most universities and colleges use Facebook groups and student-made videos on YouTube (commissioned and paid for by the university) to recruit future students. And as seen in Social and Mobile Marketing 14.1, social media can sometimes get your picture on a cereal box.

## Social and Mobile Marketing 14.1

### General Mills Flips for Bautista

Toronto Blue Jays player José Bautista caused quite a stir with his iconic bat flip during baseball playoffs. Photos of the now famous bat flip were published around the world, adding to the publicity this act generated. After he continually posted selfies of himself with boxes of Cinnamon Toast Crunch and Golden Grahams, General Mills recognized an opportunity to make cereal lovers everywhere flip their spoons.

His love of General Mills' products did not come as a surprise. In the previous year, the slugger posted numerous Instagram photos showing him holding Cinnamon Toast Crunch and Golden Grahams cereal boxes, professing his love for the products. Bautista is active on social media, with 660,000 Instagram followers, 1.1 million Twitter followers, and 362,000 Facebook likes.[66] Long before the bat flip, General Mills actually sent him some of his favourite cereal as a way of thanking him.[67] However, when the company realized that Bautista shared its desire to give back to the community,[68] it knew it had found a new poster boy to promote its cereals.

While the company does feature amateur athletes on its cereal boxes during the Olympic Games, in Canada General Mills does not advertise using celebrities.[69] There had not been a formal relationship with the Blue Jays for over 15 years and it had not associated a pro baseball player with cereal since Roger Clemens.[70]

Toronto Blue Jays slugger José Bautista holds boxes of his favourite cereals, General Mills Cinnamon Toast Crunch and Golden Grahams Crunch.

Dave Abel/Toronto Sun; Golden Grahams and Cinnamon Toast Crunch package courtesy of General Mills.

Bautista, who is a well liked and popular player, says he loves many of the company's products and enjoys eating its cereals, especially after a game.[71] A grand slam partnership was formed between General Mills and Bautista to feature his image on cereal boxes for a limited time. In return for his involvement, the cereal giant agreed to donate $10,000 to each of three charities (the Bautista Family Education Fund, the Jays Care Foundation, and the Breakfast Clubs of Canada[72]), hitting the ball out of the park and scoring a home run for baseball and cereal fans alike.

## REAL MARKETER PROFILE

# Debra Goldblatt-Sadowski (rock-it promotions)

Used with permission of rock-it promotions

With a degree in creative writing from Concordia University, I dreamed of becoming a poet and playwright. Tomson Highway, one of my profs who is an internationally recognized playwright and novelist, told me I was a good writer but he didn't think I would be able to cut it. An artist himself, he told it straight and didn't sugar-coat things. After graduating, I tried my hand in sales—telemarketing and fundraising—and also did a short stint at a PR agency working as an assistant. Then I met a publicist. Hearing about what she did, I thought, "Isn't this neat!" I could write and represent artists from the business side of things.

When my mom got sick, I wanted to spend time with her. So, in January 2000, I started rock-it promotions out of my parents' spare bedroom with only a phone book, a fax machine, and tons of determination. Everything I learned about PR was through reading, networking, and gut instinct. Yet, in my very first year I made more money than I'd made in past jobs.

In 2005 I launched Tastemakers, a full-service product placement company specializing in celebrity gifting, at the Toronto International Film Festival (TIFF). Although there were "swag lounges" in the United States, no one was offering this service in Canada. Over a decade later, Tastemakers is well recognized at TIFF and other high-profile events. Although it is a separate endeavour from rock-it, the lounge works because of our close ties to PR and our marketing experience.

One of my favourite projects has been Toronto Fashion Week. We've been the Fashion Design Council of Canada's agency of record and have managed publicity for Fashion Week for over 20 seasons. Our job was to grow the event, building national and international awareness. We facilitate media requests, secure all advance media coverage, and manage media and industry accreditation for more than 300 guests. Our metrics have been through the roof with over 10 million media impressions.

We managed PR efforts for Adidas's VIP All-Star suite, the hub for the reveal of the 2016 All-Star jerseys/footwear, apparel gifting, and interview destination for Adidas athletes, including James Harden and Andrew Wiggins. In combination with other All-Star events we handled, including the launch of new gear such as YEEZY Boost 350 and Pure Boost X, Okayu generated over 264,232,057 media impressions.

I've had the good fortune to work with stars such as Sir Anthony Hopkins, Gerard Butler, Jane Seymour, Emily Blunt, Woody Harrelson, Scott Speedman, Morgan Freeman, and Sarah Polley. Sir Anthony Hopkins will always be one of my favourites. He is a true gentleman. Morgan Freeman was also lovely. He rubbed my belly when I was pregnant with my son and gave me his blessing on the name I chose.

My proudest career accomplishment is being awarded the W100 by *Profit* and *Chatelaine* magazine naming me one of Canada's top female entrepreneurs. Considering I didn't take a course in business and started my company out of my parents' spare bedroom, that was a major milestone.

If I had to give advice to students who wanted to work in the field, I'd tell them this is much more than a 9-to-5 job, so don't try to make it one. To be really successful in PR you have to read, watch, listen, and talk—all the time. It's terrible that today's students don't read. In this business you have to read everything—newspapers, magazines, trade publications. If you don't love reading, this isn't the right business for you because that's what clients want, is to be read. You have to get to know the media. You can't pitch stories to people you don't know. But make no mistake, you can generate all the impressions in the world, but if the client doesn't see the needle move, the company will move on to another agency.

Like him or not, Justin Bieber's vast social media platform reaches millions of followers worldwide, including 77 million fans on his Facebook page. In 2011, Bieber broke YouTube records by reaching 2 billion views.[73] Twitter helped build so much buzz that one New York concert had to be cancelled after 5,000 fans suddenly swarmed the venue in a flash mob. In 2011, with 14 million followers, Bieber's account represented 3 percent of the total traffic on Twitter. Today he has over 85 million Twitter followers and is the sixth most followed person on Instagram with 75.6 million fans, and is the first artist to reach 10 billion views on Vevo.[74]

**Mobile Apps** Mobile marketing is marketing through wireless handheld devices, such as cellular telephones. Smartphones have become far more than tools to place calls; they offer a kind of mobile computer with the ability to obtain sports scores, weather, music, videos, and text messages, as well as to purchase merchandise. Marketing success rests on integrating marketing communications with fun, useful apps that are consistent with these consumer attitudes toward mobile devices. In response, firms are steadily improving customers' potential experience with their mobile interface. Applications (apps) have become very popular. Apps are used for a variety of purposes, from games and advertising to business applications, or even to order a pizza and then track its delivery. Apple's App Store boasts the world's largest collection of mobile apps, with more than 2,000,000 applications, including a wide range of categories such as music, cooking, travelling, the great outdoors, learning tools for students, and business. CIBC was the first Canadian bank to introduce an iPhone banking app that allows customers to access their bank accounts. The Android Marketplace has experienced huge growth, making it one of the fastest-growing mobile application stores on the market today.

Technology will continue to improve, and other new means of communicating with consumers will undoubtedly be added to the IMC media mix.

# LEARNING OBJECTIVES REVIEW

**LO1** **Outline the process that firms use to communicate with consumers**

On the surface, marketing communications look simple: People become aware of a product or service, then grow interested, then desire it, and finally take an action such as purchasing it. But it isn't quite that simple. First, there is the cumulative effect of marketing communications, or messages a company has sent to consumers. Even ads from the past help influence consumers' actions in the future. Second, messages are encoded, and everyone interprets commercial messages differently, thus making it difficult for a marketer to be assured that a particular, clear signal is getting through. Third, to be effective, marketers must adjust their messages to fit the media, or communications channel, and the receiver's knowledge level. Lastly, consumers receive and decode the messages.

**LO2** **List the steps in planning an integrated marketing communications campaign**

Firms (1) identify their target market; (2) set objectives; (3) determine the budget; (4) convey the message; (5) evaluate and select the media; (6) create the communication; and (7) assess the impact of the ad.

**LO3** **Describe what appeals advertisers use to get customers' attention**

Advertising appeals are either rational or emotional. Rational appeals influence purchase decisions with factual information and strong arguments built on relevant key benefits that encourage consumers to evaluate the brand favourably. Emotional appeals indicate how the product satisfies emotional desires rather than utilitarian needs.

**LO4** **Identify how firms determine which media to use**

Firms can use mass media channels such as newspapers or television to reach large numbers of anonymous audience members. Niche media, such as cable TV, direct mail, and specialty magazines, are generally used to reach narrower segments with unique demographic characteristics or

interests. When choosing the media, firms must match their objectives to the media. Also, certain media are better at reaching a particular target audience than others.

**LO5** **Summarize how firms measure integrated marketing communications success**

Planning an IMC budget should encompass a combination of factors. The process could start by setting the overall IMC budget as a percentage of sales. Then, the firm might examine what other firms are spending on similar product categories. When it gets down to planning the budget for individual product categories or items, the firm should set its objectives for the campaign and allocate enough money to meet those objectives.

Marketers rely on a mix of traditional and nontraditional measures to determine IMC success. Because potential customers generally need to be exposed to IMC messages several times before they will buy, firms estimate the degree to which customers are exposed to a message by multiplying frequency (the number of times an audience is exposed to a message) by reach (the percentage of the target population exposed to a specific marketing communication). Measuring Internet IMC effectiveness requires different measures, such as click-through tracking, which measures how many times users click on banner advertising on websites.

**LO6** **Explain the six tools of integrated marketing communications campaigns**

The six tools of IMC campaigns are advertising, personal selling, sales promotions, direct marketing, public relations, and digital media. In the past, most of a firm's promotional budget was spent on advertising. Although advertising still demands a sizable portion, other media channels have taken up a substantial chunk of the total budget. While the cost of personal selling to reach potential customers directly is quite high, it remains the best and most efficient way to sell certain products and services. Sales promotions are incentives or programs that promote immediate purchase. Many drive sales in the short run, while others exist as part of a company's customer loyalty programs. Direct marketing expenditures are growing because the number of direct marketing media options has increased in recent years; direct mail, infomercials, alternative media such as catalogues, and other new communication technologies such as smartphones are all expanding. Public relations also has become increasingly important as other media forms become more expensive and as consumers grow more skeptical of commercial messages. Finally, digital media have spawned innovative new ways to promote products and services.

# KEY TERMS

- advertising
- advertising schedule
- affordable method
- blog (weblog)
- cause-related marketing
- click-through rate
- click-through tracking
- communication channel
- competitive parity method
- continuous advertising schedule
- deceptive advertising
- decoding
- direct mail/email
- direct marketing
- direct response TV (DRTV)
- digital media
- emotional appeal

- encoding
- event sponsorship
- feedback loop
- flighting advertising schedule
- frequency
- gross rating points (GRP)
- impressions
- integrated marketing communications (IMC)
- mass media
- media buy
- media mix
- media planning
- niche media
- noise
- objective-and-task method
- percentage-of-sales method

- personal selling
- post-testing
- pretesting
- public relations (PR)
- pulsing advertising schedule
- rational appeal
- reach
- receiver
- return on investment (ROI)
- sales promotions
- search engine marketing (SEM)
- sender
- tracking
- transmitter
- unique selling proposition (USP)

# CONCEPT REVIEW

1. Briefly describe the marketing communication process and identify the possible sources of noise at each stage of the process.

2. What is meant by *integrated marketing communications*?

3. Describe the IMC tools marketers use in campaigns.

4. Explain the differences between advertising and sales promotion.

5. Describe some of the elements in a PR toolkit. Why would a company include PR in its IMC mix?

6. Identify some of the key digital media that marketers use to communicate with their customers. How are these media changing the nature of the communication between the firm and its customers?

7. What are the steps involved in developing an IMC campaign? Briefly explain each step.

8. Describe why a company would use a pull strategy versus a push strategy in its marketing communications.

9. Briefly describe the two main appeals of advertising.

10. Explain the three different ways marketers measure the success of their marketing communications. What types of information does each method provide?

# MARKETING APPLICATIONS

1. The designer jean company Juicy Couture has embarked on a new IMC strategy. It has chosen to advertise on the NBC *Nightly News* and in *Time* magazine. The message is designed to announce new styles for the season and uses a 17-year-old woman as the model. Evaluate this strategy.

2. It's holiday time, and you've decided to purchase a jewellery item for a friend at Birks. Evaluate how the company's advertising, personal selling, public relations, and digital media might influence your purchase decision. How might the relative importance of each of these IMC tools be different if your parents were making the purchase?

3. Suppose a snack company introduces a new product called SumSeeds—sunflower seeds with energy boosters like caffeine, taurine, lysine, and ginseng. How would you

expect this product's IMC program to differ from that for regular sunflower seeds sold as snacks?

4. Bernard's, a local furniture company, targets its marketing at college and university students with apartments and households of young people purchasing their first furniture items. If you worked for Bernard's, what type of media would you use for your advertising campaign? Justify your answer.

5. Should Bernard's use continuous, pulsing, or flighting for its advertising schedule? Why?

6. Suppose you saw your instructor for this course being interviewed on TV about the impact of gift certificates on an upcoming holiday's sales. Is this interview part of your university's IMC program? If so, do you believe it benefits the university? How?

7. A retail store places an ad for yoga pants in the local newspaper. The sales of the featured pants increase significantly for the next two weeks; sales in the rest of the sportswear department go up as well. What do you think are the short- and long-term objectives of the ad? Justify your answer.

8. As an intern for Michelin tires, you have been asked to develop an IMC budget. The objective of the IMC strategy is to raise Michelin's market share by 5 percent in Canada in the next 18 months. Your manager explains, "It's real simple; just increase the budget 5 percent over last year's." Evaluate your manager's strategy.

9. McDonald's spends millions of dollars on advertising. Discuss how it can assess the impact of its advertising by using marketing metrics.

10. You heard a friend talking about GNC's healthy drinks and decided to visit its website. Assume that GNC used the services of behavioural advertising firm Tacoda to track how consumers move through its website and to create more targeted advertising. Would you view these efforts as an invasion of privacy? Do you believe this action constitutes an ethical IMC strategy? How will it affect your attitude toward GNC and the likelihood that you will purchase its products?

## NET SAVVY

1. View the website of Taxi (http://www.taxi.ca), a well known IMC consulting firm. The site contains a lot of information about what IMC is and how it can be used effectively by a wide variety of companies. Of particular interest is the Work section. Locate the Work link, view a video, and discuss the following: What were the goals of the IMC campaign? Which IMC components were used in that particular campaign? How do those components contribute to the success of the IMC campaign in achieving its stated goals?

2. The Canadian Marketing Association (CMA) is the primary source of information about direct marketing activities for both academics and practitioners. The website for the CMA (http://www.the-cma.org) contains information about direct marketing practices and self-regulation. How many different target markets does the CMA address on its home page? What services does the CMA provide for consumers? Why do you think it offers those services?

## CHAPTER CASE STUDY

### HOW INTEGRATED IS VOLVO'S IMC STRATEGY?

For consumers, Volvo means one thing—safety. For businesses that rely on the automotive manufacturer for their delivery trucks and large-capacity vehicles, it means something else—precision engineering. In turn, the company faces the challenge of communicating about its offers to a wide variety of audiences, promising different solutions to different needs while still maintaining a consistent positioning.

A long-running joke once held that a truthful advertising campaign for Volvo's cars would read, "We're boxy, but we're safe." That is, the company tended to ignore stylish designs or fashionable add-ons in its single-minded focus on making the safest automobiles on the road. The business-to-business (B2B) side of the company similarly designed and marketed itself as technically superior. In both consumer and business markets, Volvo made relatively straightforward promises of safety and effectiveness that, while not particularly exciting, seemed consistent.

However, consistency is not enough in the modern, cut-throat competition for automotive sales. In response, Volvo has undergone several renewed attempts at communicating and positioning itself as something exciting, mainly because it is so dependable.

For example, in B2B markets, Volvo began issuing a series of award-winning marketing films designed to demonstrate just how precise the engineering is on its trucks. Through recent innovations, Volvo's designers and engineers have enhanced the maneuverability, sensitivity, and driving precision of the big rigs that it sells worldwide. To reveal the sensitivity of Volvo Dynamic Steering on the FMX truck line, it filmed "The Hamster Stunt," in which a hamster named Charlie runs on a hamster track built into the steering wheel and thereby determines the direction of the massive semitrailer vehicle.[75]

In "The Technician," a live engineer who worked on designing the truck series agrees to be buried in dirt up to his neck. His head protrudes 275 millimeters (11 inches) out of the ground, which is enough for the truck, with its 300-mm (12-inch) clearance to the undercarriage, to literally drive over him.

The steadiness and ease of handling the trucks is a significant benefit, especially for long-haul truckers. Therefore, Volvo used two different films to highlight this promise: In "The Ballerina Stunt," a woman dressed in a tutu walks a tightrope strung between two moving trucks. Not to be outdone by a ballerina, the martial arts expert and actor Jean-Claude Van Damme holds himself in the splits between the windows of two trucks while they drive—in reverse in this case.[76] As Volvo has been quick to assure viewers, there are no special effects or computer graphics in any of these shots. At age 53, the action star really did do the splits, and the trucks truly were moving in reverse.

Each of the short films is available exclusively on YouTube, where they have attracted more than 100 million views. In addition, traditional news media reported widely on the campaign, especially after the spots started earning awards in marketing competitions such as the "best in show" winner of The One Show advertising event. Not only did people who viewed the films start following Volvo more readily on YouTube, Twitter, and Facebook, but they also left YouTube to visit Volvo's own branded site. According to the company's calculations, unique buyer visits to the Volvo truck website increased from around 175,000 to 300,000 per month in the aftermath of the campaign.[77]

But few regular consumers worry about whether their station wagons or sedans can hold Van Damme in a split stance. Instead, they want a strong, reliable car that offers some sense of luxury. Volvo is a relatively higher-priced brand, which means that it regards its main competitors as other luxury car brands, including Mercedes-Benz, Audi, BMW, and Lexus. Even as it competes with them, though, Volvo recognizes and seeks to build on its distinctiveness, in that it has never been primarily about "looking good."

Accordingly, its consumer marketing focuses on how the benefits of driving a Volvo are unique from those associated with driving other luxury brands. The theme is consistent across several marketing channels. For example, one comparative television spot shows a perfectly coiffed, stylish female driver of a Mercedes SUV checking her makeup in her rearview mirror. The shot pans to the car in the next lane—a Volvo, of course—in which the female driver also is checking her rearview mirror. But in this case, she is checking on and making funny faces at two children in the backseat, who giggle in response. The tagline—"Volvos aren't for everyone, and we kinda like it that way"—gives buyers and potential buyers a means to distinguish themselves from a stereotype of conspicuous consumption.[78]

The linked Facebook element of this same campaign features a small dog in a purse, with the tagline, "If your dog has a wardrobe, the Volvo S60 probably isn't for you." On billboards and outdoor media in the greater Los Angeles area, Volvo also promises that its S60 is "100% real. Can't say that about everything around here." Although this ad ran mainly in Southern California, Volvo also has moved to consolidate its communications globally, such as by working with a single global marketing firm and strongly encouraging collaboration between its U.S. and European in-house marketing teams.[79]

The campaigns are a little cheeky and funny, while also promising a distinct benefit to consumers who prefer not to appear ostentatious or flashy. To coincide with these advertising campaigns, Volvo also has introduced some new, updated, slightly sportier models. In these categories, it recognizes that it competes most directly with Audi, which similarly seeks a "new luxury" positioning, rather than the "old luxury" widely associated with BMW or Mercedes. In this head-to-head competition, Volvo made a daring promise: For any consumer who test drove both its S60 and the Audi A4, then purchased the A4, Volvo would pay the first month's car payment.[80]

Even as Volvo has undergone changes in ownership and some fluctuations in its share of both B2B and consumer markets, it has maintained a sense of uniqueness and distinction. Its goal in its marketing communications, across the board, is to make sure that identity—or "what the brand is all about"[81]—is clear to all its customers in all its markets and across all channels of communication.

### Questions

**1.** Which IMC components do Volvo's business and consumer advertising efforts use? How are they integrated?

**2.** How might Volvo measure the effectiveness of the campaign?

Volvo demonstrates precision engineering and enhanced maneuverability in its integrated campaigns.
Taina Sohlman/Shutterstock.com

# CHAPTER 15

## LEARNING OBJECTIVES

**After studying this chapter you should be able to**

**LO1** Describe advertising and three objectives of advertising

**LO2** Summarize the regulatory and ethical issues of concern to advertisers

**LO3** Explain how sales promotions supplement a firm's IMC strategy

**LO4** Describe personal selling and how it adds value for customers

**LO5** Identify the steps in the personal selling process

## RINK ON A ROOF. AS PROMISED.

Used with permission of Molson Coors Canada

# Advertising, Sales Promotions, and Personal Selling

Torontonians returning to work in the New Year were surprised to see an ice rink being built on a rooftop in the city's financial district. They speculated that its sponsor might be Molson, since the beer company had posted a teaser video alluding to this possibility a few months earlier. Four days into the New Year, the company posted a photo of the rink with the text, "Rink on a roof. As promised." Within 24 hours the photo had 15,000 Facebook likes and about 1,000 retweets on Twitter.[1]

The previous fall, Molson had asked fans to share stories noting what they would do for hockey on Facebook, Instagram, and Twitter. Called #AnythingForHockey, the contest offered a grand prize of a trip to Toronto and being featured in a Molson ad. The contest had over 3,000 entries from which four winners were chosen. Contestants showed their love of the game by getting married at centre ice in hockey gear, playing hockey on a frozen pond after a golf game, promising to do polar bear dips, or even shaving their heads.

What winners didn't know was that the rink they would be skating on in the ad would measure 100 feet by 45 feet and be 32 storeys high, bringing them and the game of hockey to new heights. It's not every day that you get to see the CN Tower from above while skating on an outdoor rink.

Molson looks for "ideas acting as currency" in its marketing campaigns. According to vice-president of marketing Christine Jackovcic, this is a better approach to advertising because consumers latch on to the ideas themselves rather than feeling they are being marketed to.[2] Still, the costs to build the rink were high. Imagine having to get a crane to airlift all the equipment (scaffolding, chiller systems, boards, glass, subfloor), hire a structural engineer to address the roof's weight restrictions, and work through six weeks of construction.

So much interest was generated by the rooftop rink that Molson ran a second social media contest for a chance to skate on the rink, this time with winners being chosen at random. Groups of 20 people were also able to buy 90-minute sessions on the ice for one week between January 29 and February 7. Only 15 sessions were available at a cost of $2,000 each,[3] which helped offset the $100,000 a week cost to keep the rink going.[4] Everyone was talking about it. The rink generated a wealth of publicity, earning a wide range of media coverage including by CBC, Sportsnet, and *Breakfast Television*,[5] with each mention raising Molson's profile with consumers.

In spite of the costs involved, Molson felt that it was a good investment. Marketing manager Duncan Fraser said, "We can't be a company or brand that just says we're irrationally obsessed for anything about hockey; we need to prove that we are too."[6] ∎

In the previous chapter, we discussed the tools of integrated marketing communications (IMC) and the steps involved in planning a campaign. While we briefly touched on all of these tools in Chapter 14, we now focus more attention on three elements in particular: advertising, sales promotions, and personal selling. We begin by introducing the AIDA model, which is the process, or mental stages, marketers try to move consumers through as they are making purchase decisions. As a consumer, you are exposed only to the end product—for example, a finished advertisement—yet many decisions must take place before you actually get to see an ad. We discuss some of these decisions, starting with determining the advertising objectives and the focus of advertisements. We consider some of the regulatory and ethical issues in advertising and those arising from the use of new forms of marketing communications. Then we move on to examine sales promotions and how they add value both as consumer promotions and in the trade channel. The chapter concludes with an examination of how companies use personal selling to influence the buyer's purchase.

## ADVERTISING

As we saw in Chapter 14, marketing communication is not a straightforward process. After being exposed to an advertisement, consumers go through several steps before actually buying or taking some other action. There is not always a direct link between a particular marketing communication and a consumer's purchase.

### The AIDA Model

To create effective advertising, marketers must understand how marketing communications work. Generally, marketing communications move consumers step-wise

**AIDA model**
A common model of the series of mental stages through which consumers move as a result of marketing communications: **A**ttention leads to **I**nterest, which leads to **D**esire, which leads to **A**ction.

through a series of mental stages, for which there are several models. The most common is the **AIDA model** (Exhibit 15.1),[7] which suggests that **A**ttention leads to **I**nterest, which leads to **D**esire, which leads to **A**ction. At each stage, the consumer makes judgments about whether to take the next step in the process. Customers actually have three types of responses, so the AIDA model is also known as the "think, feel, do" model. In making a purchase decision, consumers go through each of the AIDA steps to some degree, but the steps may not always follow the AIDA order. For instance, during an impulse purchase, consumers may "feel" and "do" before they "think."

**Attention**     Even the best marketing communication can be wasted if the sender doesn't gain the attention of the consumer first. Brand awareness refers to a potential customer's ability to recognize or recall that the brand name is a particular type of retailer or product/service. As such, brand awareness is the strength of the link between the brand name and the type of merchandise or service in the minds of customers. Coca-Cola already has excellent brand awareness and might not have to focus as much effort on this step when it wants to introduce a new flavour. In contrast, when Ovarian Cancer Canada wanted to raise its profile with potential donors, it needed an edgy message to get people to stop and consider its cause, as the opening vignette in Chapter 14 described.

There are a number of awareness metrics, from aided recall to top-of-mind awareness. **Aided recall** occurs when consumers recognize the brand when its name is presented to them. **Top-of-mind awareness**, the highest level of awareness, occurs when a brand has a prominent place in people's memories that triggers a response without them having to put any thought into it. For example, Harley-Davidson has top-of-mind awareness if a consumer responds "Harley" when asked about motorcycles. High top-of-mind awareness means that a particular brand will probably be carefully considered

**aided recall**
Occurs when consumers recognize the brand when its name is presented to them.

**top-of-mind awareness**
A prominent place in people's memories that triggers a response without them having to put any thought into it.

**EXHIBIT 15.1**     The AIDA Model

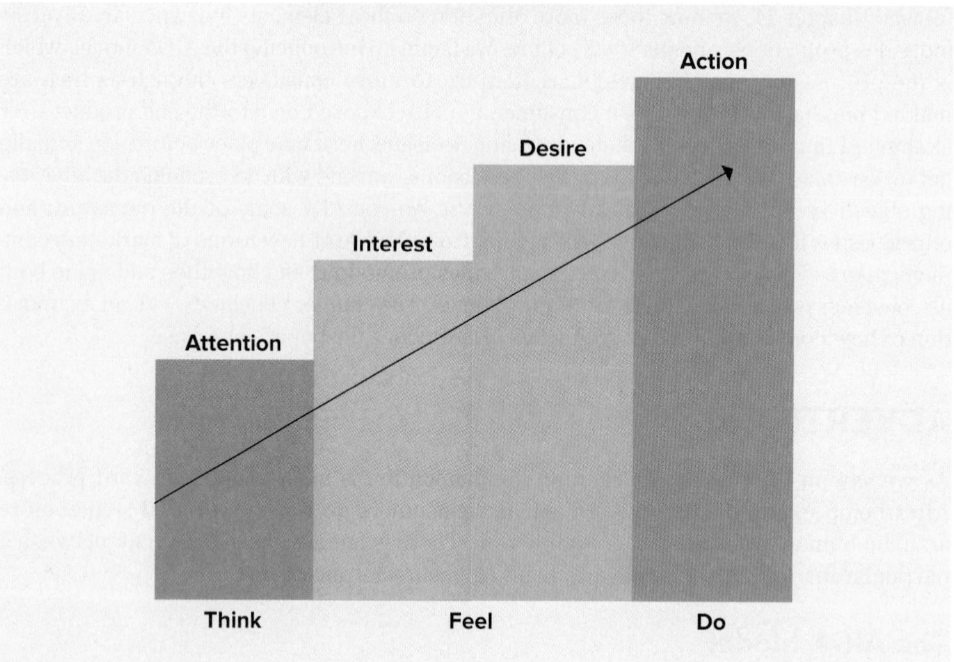

when customers decide to shop for that product or service. Manufacturers, retailers, and service providers build top-of-mind awareness by having memorable names; repeatedly exposing their name to customers through advertising, locations, and sponsorships; and using memorable symbols.

As an example of memorable symbols, imagine two smaller circles, sitting on opposite sides atop a larger circle. Did you think of Mickey Mouse ears and Disney? The company uses images to ensure that its name comes easily to the front of young consumers' minds. Whether they are individual acts like Austin Mahone, Lucy Hale, or Demi Lovato or groups such as R5 and Lemonade Mouth, Disney starts off its stars with Disney Channel shows, records them on the Disney-owned Hollywood Record label, plays the songs in heavy rotation on Radio Disney and Disney movie soundtracks, organizes concert tours with Disney-owned Buena Vista Concerts, and sells tie-in merchandise throughout Disney stores. Each of these marketing elements reminds the various segments of the target market about both the brand (e.g., "One Direction," "Forever In Your Mind") and their owner, Disney. With this multi-channel approach, Disney gets the same "product" into more markets than would be possible with a more conservative approach—further building top-of-mind awareness for both Disney and its stars.[8]

**Interest** Once the consumer is aware that the company or product exists, communication must work to increase his or her interest level. It isn't enough to let people know that the product exists; consumers must be persuaded that it is a product worth investigating. Marketers do so by ensuring that the ad's message includes attributes that are of interest to the target audience. Disney increases interest in an upcoming tour or record by including a mention, whether casual or not, in the stars' television shows. Because the primary target market for the tour is also probably watching the show, the message gets received by the correct recipient.

**Desire** After the firm has piqued the interest of its target market, the goal of subsequent messages should move the consumer from "I like it" to "I want it." If Lucy Hale appears on *Good Morning America* and talks about her upcoming album and how great it is going to be, the viewing audience is all the more likely to demand access—in this case, probably parents who hope to score points with their adolescent children by buying the latest single or reserving seats to an upcoming tour.

**Action** The ultimate goal of any marketing communication is to drive the receiver to action. If the message has caught consumers' attention and made them interested enough to consider the product as a means to satisfy a specific desire of theirs, they likely will act on that interest by making a purchase. Sustainable Marketing 15.1 discusses how the launch of Mother Parker's recyclable coffee pods got consumer attention and interest, then led to desire and action. And if young consumers watch the Disney Channel's show *Shake It Up* or visit Disney's Fashion Studio website to see what the stars are wearing, they might in turn beg their parents to make an actual purchase of Bella Thorne and Zendaya's most recent "Shake It Up" album.

When Zendaya (left) and Bella Thorne (right) appear on *Shake It Up*, demand for their albums increases.

© Jen Lowery/Splash News/Newscom

## Recyclable Coffee Pods Get Attention and Action

In 2000, single serve coffee-brewing machines were virtually unheard of. Invented for the corporate workplace, the machines were designed by Keurig for businesses as an alternative to the common break-room coffee pot that loses its freshness over the workday. In 2002, Keurig sold 10,000 commercial brewers.[9] Today, almost 27 percent of American households own a single-cup coffee-brewing machine.[10]

However, Keurig's leader status has been dwindling recently. A key reason for this is the lack of sustainability of its K-Cups. Unlike their competitors, K-Cups are not recyclable or compostable because the vast majority of recycling operations don't accept the pods. Recycling facilities need clean, separated materials to sort into clean streams in order to repurpose. These pods are mixed components of plastic, foil, and organic that are not easily separated. In fact, the K-Cups that ended up in landfills in 2011 would have encircled the globe more than six times, and in 2013, more than 10 times.[11]

Consumers love the convenience and variety offered by K-Cups, but hate that they are not recyclable. To meet this unmet need in the market and displace sales of Keurig's K-Cups, Mother Parker's introduced the RealCup—a recyclable K-Cup designed to be compatible with Keurig machines. With the RealCup, consumers must separate the filter from the K-Cup—the coffee grinds can be composted and the plastic cup recycled—leaving only the filter. This eliminates 95 percent of the waste from K-Cups.[12]

To advertise the new innovation, Mother Parker's rolled out its first video in June 2016, showing a series of cringeworthy things, including fingernails on a blackboard, brain freeze, and a kick to the groin, and among them, 9 billion non-recyclable K-Cups going into landfills. The first video has received more than 1.2 million views on YouTube and Facebook. It also drove viewers to the RealCup.com website, which saw traffic grow fivefold since the video launched.[13]

Keurig is planning to launch a recyclable K-Cup® capsule, but unfortunately the roll-out will take time and the full transition won't be complete until 2020.[14] Unfortunately for Keurig, Mother Parker's seems to have gained the first-mover advantage in the recyclable K-Cup space.

Toyota's "Prius Goes Plural" campaign promoted a new family-sized (Prius v) and urban version (Prius c) of its popular hybrid car.

Jeff Kowalsky/Bloomberg via Getty Images

**lagged effect**
A delayed response to a marketing communication campaign.

**The Lagged Effect**  Sometimes consumers don't act immediately after receiving a marketing communication because of the **lagged effect**—a delayed response to a marketing communication campaign. It generally takes multiple exposures to an ad before a consumer fully processes its message. In turn, measuring the effect of a current campaign becomes more difficult because of the possible lagged response to a previous one. For example, Toyota's "Prius Goes Plural" campaign promoted the addition of a family-sized (Prius v) and urban version (Prius c) of its popular hybrid car model. The campaign demanded consumer participation, by challenging the viewing public to come up with a plural form of the word "Prius" (e.g., Prii, Prien, Priuses), as touted in online banner and television ads, virtual polling booths, and videos. But the Prius v was not slated for release until six months after the campaign started, and the lag time for the Prius c was even longer. Toyota may never know for sure whether exposure to this campaign led consumers to check out or purchase the new vehicles.[15]

### L01  Advertising Objectives

As noted in Chapter 14, advertising is a paid form of communication from an identifiable source, delivered through a communication channel, and designed to persuade the receiver to take some action, now or in the future.[16] This definition provides some important distinctions between advertising and other forms of promotion, which we discussed in the previous chapter. First, unlike public relations, advertising is not free; someone has paid—with money, trade, or other means—to get the message shown. Second, advertising must be carried by some medium: television, radio, print, the Internet, T-shirts, sidewalks, and so on. Third, legally, the source of the message must be known or knowable. Fourth, advertising represents a persuasive form of communication, designed to get the consumer to take some action. That desired action can range from "Don't drink and drive" to "Buy Molson Canadian beer."

Some activities that are called advertising really are not, such as word-of-mouth advertising. Even political advertising technically is not advertising because it is not for commercial purposes and thus is not regulated in the same manner as true advertising.

Advertising encompasses an enormous industry and clearly is the most visible form of marketing communications—so much so that many people think of *marketing* and *advertising* as synonymous. Global advertising expenditures are projected to exceed $550 billion. It is not just a perception that advertising is everywhere; it *is* everywhere.[17]

Yet, how many of the advertisements that you were exposed to yesterday do you remember today? Probably not more than three or four. As you learned in Chapter 4, perception is a highly selective process. Consumers simply screen out messages that are not relevant to them. When you notice an advertisement, you may not react to it; or, even if you react to it, you may not remember it later. If you remember seeing it, you still may not remember the brand or sponsor of the advertisement. Worse yet (from the advertiser's point of view), you may remember it as an advertisement for another brand.

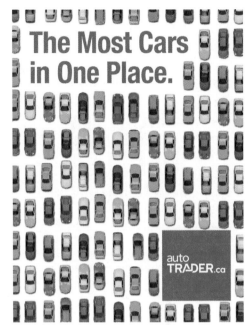

Informative advertising was used to change the brand perception for Autotrader.

Used with permission of autoTRADER.

To get you to remember their ad and the brand, advertisers must first get your attention. As we discussed in Chapter 14, the increasing number of communication channels and changes in consumers' media usage have made the job of advertisers far more difficult. As the chapter vignette demonstrated, advertisers attempt to use creativity and a mix of promotional elements that offer better opportunities to reach their target markets. As a consumer, you are exposed only to the end product: the finished advertisement. But a lot of work must take place before you actually get to see an ad.

As mentioned in Chapter 14, all advertising campaigns aim to achieve certain objectives: to inform, persuade, and remind customers. Another way of looking at advertising objectives is to examine an ad's focus. Is the ad designed to stimulate demand for a particular product or service, or is its focus, more broadly, the institution in general? Marketers use ads to stimulate demand for a product category or an entire industry, or for a specific brand, firm, or item. Let's look at the broad overall objectives of informing, persuading, and reminding.

**Informative Advertising** **Informative advertising** communicates to create and build brand awareness, with the ultimate goal of moving the consumer through the buying cycle to a purchase. Such advertising helps determine some important early stages of the product life cycle (PLC; see Chapter 8), particularly when consumers have little information about the specific product or type of product. Retailers often use informative advertising to tell their customers about an upcoming sales event or the arrival of new merchandise. Ovarian Cancer Canada used informative advertising to change the perception of the disease, as discussed in the chapter vignette from Chapter 14.

The Canadian National Institute for the Blind (CNIB) works with people who are blind or visually impaired to get rehabilitation support and help them lead more independent lives. Part of the registered charity's mandate includes public education efforts with the goal of eliminating avoidable sight loss. To help achieve this objective, it launched a

**informative advertising** Communication used to create and build brand awareness, with the ultimate goal of moving the consumer through the buying cycle to a purchase.

The Canadian National Institute for the Blind uses informative advertising to warn consumers of the damage the sun's UV rays could do to their eyes.

Used with permission of CNIB

**persuasive advertising**
Communication used to motivate consumers to take action.

campaign to inform consumers that the sun's UV rays are the leading cause of vision loss in Canada.[18] While many people love the sun, its rays are dangerous, increasing the risk of developing cataracts, macular degeneration, and other serious eye problems. The ad cites statistics to inform Canadians that one in two of them did not realize the need to wear sunglasses even in the shade and urges them to wear UV protective sunglasses even on cloudy days. The campaign is also promoted on social media, including on a Facebook page (cnib.ca/wearapair) that reflects a daily weather forecast for the city of your choice.

**Persuasive Advertising**   When a product has gained a certain level of brand awareness, firms use **persuasive advertising** to motivate consumers to take action. Persuasive advertising generally occurs in the growth and early maturity stages of the PLC, when competition is most intense, and attempts to accelerate the market's acceptance of the product. In later stages of the PLC, persuasive advertising may be used to reposition an established brand such as Axe by persuading consumers to change their existing perceptions of the advertised product. Firms such as Lancôme often use persuasive advertising to convince consumers to take action, switch brands,[19] try a new product, or even continue to buy the advertised product.

Kobo has grown from a Toronto start-up to a global company that sells books in 77 languages in over 190 countries.[20] To recognize people who are book lovers and to inspire others to embrace the joy of reading, Kobo launched two persuasive campaigns. The first, "Reader's Passion," focused on people who read on a daily basis as a way to stimulate their imaginations and grey cells. The second campaign, "The Gift of Reading," used an emotional appeal, tapping images of mothers

Lancôme used persuasive advertising to convince consumers to take action.

© Bill Aron/PhotoEdit, Inc.

Kobo's "The Gift of Reading" hopes to persuade consumers to give an ereader to someone who inspired them to read.

© Pixellover RM 2/Alamy Stock Photo

reading to young children. The second campaign, which was introduced just before Mother's Day, encouraged people to give an ereader to whoever had sparked their passion for reading. Until this point, Kobo had done very little advertising. However, research showed that the number of people who did not use an ereader was two to three times higher than those who did.[21] While partnerships with booksellers and publishers helped attract early adopters, to reach and persuade other consumers, a mass advertising push was needed. The multi-million dollar campaign represents a tripling of the previous advertising budget, which, coincidentally, mirrors Kobo's sales increases year over year.[22]

**Reminder Advertising**   Finally, **reminder advertising** is communication used to remind consumers of a product or to prompt repurchases, especially for products that have gained market acceptance and are in the maturity stage of their life cycle. For example, if you decide to buy tissues, do you carefully consider all the options, comparing their sizes, prices, and performance, or do you just grab the first thing you see on the shelf? When your grocery store places a display of Kleenex facial tissues on the end of the paper products aisle, it relies on your top-of-mind awareness of the Kleenex brand, which the manufacturer has achieved through advertising. That is, Kleenex tissue maintains a prominent place in people's memories and triggers their response, without their having to put any thought into it. The advertising and the end cap display thus prompt you, and many other consumers, to respond by buying a package, just the response Kleenex hoped to provoke.

Although most children grow up drinking milk, consumption drops during the teen years and into adulthood. In the past, many campaigns have focused on winning back these consumers. However, a new initiative by the Strategic Milk Alliance (members include the BC Dairy Association, Alberta Milk, SaskMilk, Dairy Farmers of Manitoba, and Dairy Farmers of Canada) hopes to attract new parents. Research provided two key insights. First, since milk is always located at the back corner of stores, it's easy to miss or forget. Second, focus groups conducted by DDB Canada found that consumers believe that some foods simply taste better when paired with milk.[23] To capitalize on these insights, point of sale signs were placed strategically in stores—for example, in the cookie aisle—to evoke childhood memories of eating milk and cookies. The message was, literally, if it tasted great then, it will still taste great now. Nostalgia was further developed in television, radio, print, and billboard ads. A contest, called "Milk Your Moments," encouraged consumers to share photos of themselves or of other family members depicting memorable childhood moments.[24]

**reminder advertising**
Communication used to remind consumers of a product or to prompt repurchases, especially for products that have gained market acceptance and are in the maturity stage of their life cycle.

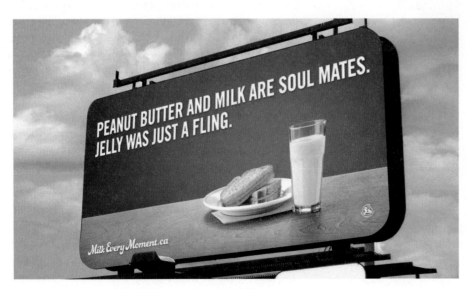

In-store signage and billboards were all part of a campaign to remind consumers to buy milk.
Used with permission of Strategic Milk Alliance

**product-focused advertisements**
Used to inform, persuade, or remind consumers about a specific product or service.

**institutional advertisements**
Used to inform, persuade, and remind consumers about issues related to places, politics, an industry, or a particular corporation.

**product placement**
Inclusion of a product in nontraditional situations, such as in a scene in a movie or TV program.

**Focus of Advertisements**  To help determine the focus for advertisements, many companies consider the stages in the AIDA model discussed earlier. Some companies will focus their efforts on attracting awareness, for example, in the case of a new product introduction. If consumers are already aware of a product or service, the company will need to build interest and then desire. Lastly, they need to ensure that consumers will be motivated to take action as a result of the company's advertising efforts.

The ad campaign's objectives determine the specific ad's focus. **Product-focused advertisements** are used to inform, persuade, or remind consumers about a specific product or service. For example, Coke ads are designed to generate sales for Coca-Cola. The focus of **institutional advertisements** is to inform, persuade, and remind consumers about issues related to places, politics, an industry, or a particular corporation. Some advertisements are designed to generate demand for the product category (e.g., the "All You Need Is Cheese" campaign) or an entire industry (e.g., the Strategic Milk Alliance), while others are designed to generate demand for a specific brand (e.g., Cracker Barrel cheese), firm (e.g., Kraft), or item.

Perhaps the best-known campaign to build demand for a product category is the long-running institutional campaign "Got Milk?" which encouraged milk consumption by appealing to consumers' needs to affiliate with the milk-mustached celebrities shown in the ads.[25] One campaign, as exemplified in the ad with Taylor Swift, promised that consuming milk will help people get more B vitamins and protein. Most ads highlight the beneficial properties of milk for building strong bones, which reflects an informative appeal, combined with a mild emotional fear appeal in its assertion that failing to drink milk can lead to medical problems.

**Swift Pick.**
On the road you need energy. That's why I drink milk. It has B vitamins and protein I need to help get me going. So I'm always ready for the next city, the next crowd, the next encore.

**got milk?**

whymilk.com/taylorswift

The "Got Milk?" institutional advertising campaign is used to encourage milk consumption, appealing to consumers by associating it with milk-mustached celebrities like Taylor Swift.
Used with permission of MilkPEP

**Product Placement**  When marketers use **product placement**, they include their product in nontraditional situations, such as in a scene in a movie or TV program. The first visible movie product placement was Hershey's Reese's Pieces in the film *ET*. The product actually became part of the storyline, offered the candy high levels of visibility, and resulted in a large increase in sales.[26] Although Hershey's did not pay to place Reese's Pieces in *ET*, other firms have been more than willing to shell out for product placements. Companies spend approximately $4.38 billion on product placements in television and movies annually (e.g., Mercedes in the film *Jurassic World*). Coca-Cola reportedly paid $10 million to gain product placements and advertising space on *American Idol*,[27] stepping away after 13 seasons.

The hard part is determining which movies will be successes. For Apple, the challenge is a little less stringent, because U.S. film directors seem to love its sleek white laptops, ear-budded iPods, and ubiquitous iPhones. More than one-third of all top-grossing films at the box office—129 of 374 movies—have included Apple-branded products in the past decade. Its products appeared in seven of 31 top films in 2015.[28] An analytics firm that estimates the dollar value of product placements has reported that Apple's five-minute screen time in *Mission: Impossible* alone was worth more than $23 million.[29] Apple claims it does not pay for product placement. Mercedes took the top spot for product placements in 2015 with nine of the top 31 films, including appearances in *50 Shades of Grey, Spectre, Furious 7, Spy,* and *Jurassic World.*[30]

Other companies have also been lucky enough not to pay for product placement. Whenever Sophie Gregoire Trudeau appears in public, the media reports on what she has been spotted wearing (e.g., Ava shoes from Zvelle, dresses from Canadian designers Jay Godfrey and Wayne Clark, a white coat made of baby alpaca hair from Sentaler, accessories from WANT Les Essentiels).[31] Toronto-based designer Lucian Matis said sales of his line went up 2,500 percent after Gregoire Trudeau was photographed in two of his dresses during a visit to the White House. Dubbed "the Sophie effect," the ensuing publicity has been a boon to Canadian designers. However, there are far more examples of paid placement, especially in music videos where product placement revenues exceed $20 million annually.[32] Lady Gaga, Jennifer Lopez, Britney Spears, Eminem, and numerous other artists have all promoted products through their videos.

**Public Service Announcements**   A special class of demand advertising is the **public service announcement (PSA)**, which focuses on public welfare and generally is sponsored by non-profit institutions, civic groups, religious organizations, trade associations, or political groups.[33] PSAs represent a form of **social marketing**, which is the application of marketing principles to a social issue to bring about attitudinal and behavioural change among the general public or a specific population segment. Because PSAs are a special class of advertising, under the Canadian Radio-television and Telecommunications Commission rules, broadcasters must devote a specific amount of free airtime to them. Some of the most successful PSA campaigns include wildfire prevention (Smokey the Bear), teen drug use (Partnership for a Drug Free Canada), Internet safety ("BeWebAware.ca"), and breast cancer screening (Breast Cancer Society of Canada).

Because they often are designed by top advertising agencies for non-profit clients, PSAs usually are quite creative and stylistically appealing. For example, what is your reaction to the Internet safety campaign "BeWebAware.ca" from the Media Awareness Network? The Ottawa-based non-profit organization is designed to educate parents about the risks and benefits of letting their kids surf in cyberspace. Supported by Microsoft Canada and Bell Canada, ads highlight eye-opening statistics—such as the fact that 25 percent of kids have been asked to meet in person with someone they've only encountered online—and encourage people to check out BeWebAware.ca, a website created to help parents get involved in monitoring their children's online activity. One print ad shows a middle-aged man at a computer, typing away in a kids' chat room. The accompanying copy reads, "To 12-year-old Lisa, he was simply 11-year-old Jenny."

**public service announcement (PSA)**
Advertising that focuses on public welfare and generally is sponsored by non-profit institutions, civic groups, religious organizations, trade associations, or political groups; a form of social marketing.

**social marketing**
The application of marketing principles to a social issue to bring about attitudinal and behavioural change among the general public or a specific population segment.

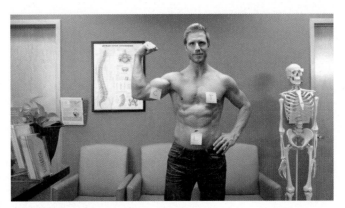

Public service advertising, for causes such as breast cancer awareness, focus on public welfare and generally are sponsored by non-profit institutions.

Used with permission of Rethink Breast Cancer

Regardless of whether the advertising campaign's objective is to inform, persuade, or remind, or to focus on a particular product or the institution in general, each campaign's objectives must be specific and measurable. For a brand awareness campaign, for example, the objective might be to increase brand awareness among the target market by 50 percent within six months. Another campaign's goal may be to persuade 10 percent of a competitor's customers to switch to the advertised brand.

## L02 REGULATORY AND ETHICAL ISSUES IN ADVERTISING

IMC brings together many diverse forms of communication under one umbrella. But, in Canada, each form of communication media traditionally has been regulated separately. For example, rather than ban cigarette advertising completely, the federal 1997 Tobacco Act imposed numerous restrictions, including a phased-in ban on tobacco sponsorship of events. However, an amendment to Bill C-32 has long since put an end to all print advertising.[34] Companies are allowed to advertise in places where only people over the age of 18 are permitted and in magazines where adults account for more than 85 percent of their readership.[35] We begin this section by detailing the various agencies that regulate the different forms and media for advertising. Then we discuss some controversies surrounding new forms of potential deception.

In Canada, the regulation of advertising involves a complex mix of formal laws and informal restrictions designed to protect consumers from deceptive practices. Many federal and provincial laws, as well as a wide range of self-regulatory agencies and agreements, affect advertising (see Exhibit 15.2). The primary federal agencies that regulate advertising activities are the Competition Bureau, the Canadian Radio-television and Telecommunications Commission (CRTC), the Food and Drugs Act, and Advertising Standards Canada. In addition to these agencies, marketers must adhere to other pieces of legislation such as the Consumer Packaging and Labelling Act and the Tobacco Act.

The Competition Bureau enforces the Competition Act, the most comprehensive legislation affecting the marketing activities of companies in Canada. The Competition Act maintains and encourages competition while protecting consumers from misleading and deceptive advertising practices. Rogers Communications promised "fewer dropped calls" when it launched its discount cellphone service, Chatr. The Competition Bureau

### EXHIBIT 15.2    Agencies That Regulate Advertising

| Agency/Legislation | General Purpose | Specific Jurisdiction |
|---|---|---|
| Competition Bureau Canada/ The Competition Act (1986) | Enforces federal laws that ensure businesses in Canada operate in a fair and equitable manner. | Enforces laws relating to misleading advertising and deceptive marketing practices. |
| Canadian Radio-television and Telecommunications Commission (CRTC; 1968) | Regulates and supervises all aspects of the Canadian broadcasting system, and regulates telecommunications common carriers and service providers that fall under federal jurisdiction. | Enforces restrictions on broadcasting material. Also administers codes that have an impact on specific categories of advertising; for example, the Code for Broadcast Advertising of Alcoholic Beverages. |
| Health Canada/Food and Drugs Act (1954) | Regulates food, drugs, cosmetics, and medical devices. | Establishes standards and requirements for the safety and sanitation of products. Regulates the labelling of food products pertaining to nutrition labelling, nutrient content, and health claims. |
| Advertising Standards Canada (ASC; 1957) | Monitors voluntary advertising industry codes. | Administers the Canadian Code of Advertising Standards, the Gender Portrayal Guidelines, and the Broadcast Code for Advertising to Children. |

charged Rogers with false advertising when the company failed to back up its claims and imposed a $10 million fine.[36] More recently the Competition Bureau accused Moose Knuckles, which makes high-end winter jackets, with deceptive marketing over its "Made in Canada" claims when it was discovered that its coats were primarily made in Vietnam and other Asian countries. Canadian law dictates that the "Made in Canada" claim can only be made if 51 percent of the cost of producing or manufacturing a product is incurred in Canada, or the product is labelled as "Made in Canada with imported parts."[37]

The CRTC controls the advertising industry and governs broadcast media and licensing. The CRTC must approve all TV and radio advertisements before they can be broadcast. The Food and Drugs Act prohibits the advertising or selling of unsafe or misbranded foods, cosmetics, and drugs. It also requires companies to adhere to regulations regarding health claims. Although used for many years in the United States, diet-related health claims for food products (related to risk reduction of heart disease, cancer, osteoporosis, and high blood pressure) have only recently been allowed in Canada. The Consumer Packaging and Labelling Act requires manufacturers, packagers, and distributors to disclose full information about their products. All prepackaged products must be labelled in both French and English and bear the quantity in metric and imperial for weight, volume, or other measures.

Many product categories fall under self-regulatory restrictions or guidelines. For example, Advertising Standards Canada (ASC) is a self-regulating body that monitors voluntary industry codes. Advertising to children is regulated primarily through self-regulatory mechanisms designed by ASC and its Broadcast Code for Advertising to Children. The exception is the province of Quebec, where all advertising to children under the age of 13 is prohibited under the Quebec Consumer Protection Act. Messages with no promotional or selling intent are protected by the Charter of Rights and Freedoms. As seen in Ethical Dilemma 15.1, product performance claims must be adequately tested and supported if they do not want to fall afoul of the Competition Bureau.

 **Ethical Dilemma 15.1**

## Making Safety Claims? Back Them Up or Back Off

Concussions are top-of-mind for anyone who plays high-impact sports. But as Reebok–CCM discovered, if you are going to make claims about the safety features of your product, you'd better make sure you can back them up. The company claimed that its Resistance hockey helmet could protect players from head injuries. However, after investigating, the Competition Bureau ruled that the testing done was "not adequate and proper" to make such claims.[38]

A study by the Department of Biomedical Engineering at Virginia Tech University concluded that little has changed in the past 50 years when it came to helmet safety standards.[39] In fact, it found that most hockey helmets fail to meet the safety evaluation its research proposed. An investigation by Canada's Competition Bureau showed that while companies are working to improve product safety, testing standards for hockey helmets revolve around protecting players from skull fractures and brain injuries, not concussions. It noted that, "The science behind concussions in sports is still in its infancy, and the role that any hockey helmet can play in protecting players from concussions remains unclear."[40]

Reebok–CCM advertised its helmet as carrying a "Rotational Energy Dampening System … to help better manage the rotational impacts" with a "liner engineered through cutting-edge science."[41] Although the company said it did not suggest that the helmet would protect those who wore it from a concussion, it did agree to modify or remove misleading claims. It also agreed to donate $475,000 worth of sports equipment and pay the Competition Bureau $30,000 to cover the cost of the investigation.

It's not the first time that the Competition Bureau has called an offside on such claims. A year earlier, it targeted Bauer Hockey Corp., which also agreed to stop advertising performance claims for its RE-AKT helmet.[42] Bauer agreed to stop making performance related claims it was unable to prove, and to donate $500,000 worth of equipment to a Canadian charity that aids youth participation in sports.[43]

Is this billboard ad an example of puffery or deception?

© Bill Aron/PhotoEdit, Inc.

**puffery**
The legal exaggeration of praise, stopping just short of deception, lavished on a product.

Recently, to make matters even more complicated for advertisers whose products sell in the United States, the offices of state attorneys general have begun to assert their authority to regulate advertising in their states. The European Union also has increased its regulation of advertising for EU member nations. Many of these state and European regulations are more restrictive than existing federal or self-regulatory requirements.

Another difference between advertising regulations in Canada and the European Union pertains to **puffery**, the legal exaggeration of praise, stopping just short of deception, lavished on a product. In Canada, consumers are viewed as rational and capable of evaluating advertising claims. Does a certain sneaker brand really make you run faster and jump higher? Does Papa John's pizza really have "better ingredients" that make "better pizza"? When Match.com claims that it leads to "better first dates," it's puffery because *better* is a subjective measure. But if it claims it produces "more second dates," it must be able to back up its numerical, quantitative assertion. In the European Union, however, puffery is considered deception. For instance, Kraft had no problem advertising its orange-flavoured drink Tang surrounded by oranges in North America. But in Germany, the ad was declared deceptive because there are no oranges in Tang. Advertisers must understand these differences to keep from violating EU advertising laws.

## LO3  SALES PROMOTION

Advertising rarely provides the only means to communicate with target customers. As we discussed in Chapter 14, a natural link appears between advertising and sales promotion. Sales promotions are special incentives or excitement-building programs that encourage consumers to purchase a particular product or service, typically used in conjunction with other advertising or personal selling programs. In the context of IMC campaigns, advertising generally creates attention, interest, and desire, while the value in sales promotions is in closing the deal. Many sales promotions, such as free samples or point-of-purchase (POP) displays, attempt to build short-term sales, whereas others, such as loyalty programs, contests, and sweepstakes, have become integral components of firms' long-term customer relationship management (CRM) programs, which they use to build customer loyalty. In this section, we examine the various tools firms use for their sales promotions and how those tools complement the advertiser's efforts to achieve its strategic objectives.

The tools of any sales promotion can be focused on either channel members, such as wholesalers or retailers, or end-user consumers. Just as we delineated for advertising, when sales promotions are targeted at channel members, the marketer is employing a push strategy; when it targets consumers themselves, it is using a pull strategy. Some sales promotion tools can be used with either a push or pull strategy. We now consider each of the tools and how they are used.

### Consumer Sales Promotions

Exhibit 15.3 displays the many different types of tools used in consumer sales promotions, along with their advantages and disadvantages. We will discuss how marketers

**EXHIBIT 15.3** Types of Consumer Sales Promotions

| Promotion | Objective | Advantages | Disadvantages |
|---|---|---|---|
| Coupons | Stimulate demand. | • Encourage retailer support.<br>• Allow for direct tracing of sales. | • Have low redemption rates.<br>• Have high cost. |
| Deals | Encourage trial. | • Reduce consumer risk.<br>• Retaliate against competitive action. | • May reduce perception of value. |
| Premiums | Build goodwill. | • Increase perception of value. | • Result in consumers who buy for the premium, not the product.<br>• Have to be carefully managed. |
| Contests | Increase consumer involvement. | • Generate excitement. | • Require creativity.<br>• Must be monitored. |
| Sweepstakes | Encourage higher consumption. | • Minimize brand switching among existing consumers. | • Sales often decline afterward. |
| Samples | Encourage trial. | • Offer direct involvement. | • Have high cost to the firm. |
| Loyalty Programs | Encourage repurchase. | • Create loyalty. | • Have high cost to the firm. |
| POP Displays | Increase brand trial. | • Provide high visibility.<br>• Provide in-store support. | • It is difficult to get a good location in the store.<br>• Can be costly to the firm. |
| Rebates | Stimulate demand. | • Increase value perception. | • Are easily copied by competitors.<br>• May just advance future sales. |

choose which tool to use based on their specific marketing objectives. Then, we examine some ways in which IMC programs make use of sales promotions.

Coupons   A coupon offers a discount on the price of specific items when they're purchased. Coupons are issued by manufacturers and retailers in newspapers, magazines, and free-standing inserts, on products, on shelves, at the cash register, over the Internet, and by mail to stimulate demand. They are commonly used in supermarkets, but other retailers, such as department stores and restaurants, also use coupons to pull customers away from the competition. Some retailers even accept coupons from competitors. More than 6.8 billion coupons are distributed every year in Canada, driving over $750 million in sales.[44] While redemption rates average around 2 percent, rates vary dramatically depending on how consumers obtain the coupon. A segment of the market, the diehard "coupon clippers," devote a great deal of time and effort to searching for, clipping, and redeeming coupons. Many coupon clippers have streamlined this process by using the Internet, which offers entire forums dedicated to coupon sharing and management (e.g., http://www.couponforum.com). Coupons carried in newspapers, magazines, in-store displays, and direct mail have very low redemption rates of only 1–2 percent, whereas those downloaded from the Internet experience a 56 percent redemption rate. The reason for this dramatic difference is that consumers seek out online coupons for specific items or stores, whereas many people who have no interest in purchasing the product receive traditional coupons. Entrepreneurial Marketing 15.1 discusses another alternative that lets consumers easily access coupons via a digital app.

Some coupons, whether printed from the Internet or sent to mobile phones, also contain information about the customer who uses them.[51] The bar code may identify the customer, his or her Internet address, Facebook page information, and even the search terms

## Entrepreneurial Marketing 15.1

### Flyers and Coupons to Flipp Over

Sifting through a stack of flyers has been part of the Canadian weekend ritual for decades. Through flyers, consumers have been informed of the latest and greatest products and promotions from laundry detergent to laptops, and they are where the weekly shopping trip often begins. For retailers, this medium has been a key component of their marketing mix and a way to drive traffic to stores. However, with digital technology reshaping so many customer–retailer interactions, it's no surprise that the traditional flyer practice is being turned on its head.

The days of flipping through flyers and clipping coupons may soon be behind us, with Flipp leading the way in this evolution. Flipp (formerly Wishabi) was founded in 2007 by four University of Waterloo alumni who were determined to disrupt the flyer industry to change the way people found deals and shopped.[45] Their company has seen exponential growth and has evolved into something much greater today. Flipp's CEO, Wehuns Tan, explains that Flipp gives retailers "the capability to create

Flipp allows users to browse through flyers in their area, digitally "clip" coupons, and redeem them in stores.

Used with permission of Flipp Corporation

better merchandising, marketing, personalization and consumer experiences."[46]

The Flipp app allows users to browse through flyers in their area, digitally "clip" coupons and redeem them in stores. It has also introduced functionalities that they hope will make Flipp the one-stop shop for everything a consumer needs to do on a weekly basis. It allows users to sync up their loyalty and rewards cards, keep track of shopping lists, and search for a specific store, item, or brand across all retailers. With millions and millions of downloads since its North American debut in 2013, Flipp has been converting print flyer enthusiasts into digital users.[47]

Flipp is helping retailers transform their marketing strategy by connecting them with their consumers.[48] It enables retailers to achieve incremental store trips, increase consumer engagement, and earn a higher ROI with reduced costs.[49] In addition, the entire Flipp platform offers in-depth analytics. They provide retailers with real-time metrics on sales and consumer engagement from both in-store and online channels, which give retailers valuable consumer insights.[50]

the customer used to find the coupon in the first place. These new breeds of coupons may look standard, but they offer up a startling amount of data, which promises benefits for advertisers who want to target their marketing more closely, as discussed in Social and Mobile Marketing 15.1.

**deal**

A type of short-term price reduction that can take several forms, such as a "featured price" (a price lower than the regular price); a "buy one, get one free" offer; or a certain percentage "more free" offer contained in larger packaging.

**Deals**  A **deal** refers generally to a type of short-term price reduction that can take several forms, such as a "featured price" (a price lower than the regular price); a "buy one, get one free" offer; or a percentage "more free" offer contained in larger packaging. Another form of a deal involves a special financing arrangement, such as reduced percentage interest rates or extended repayment terms. Deals encourage trial because they lower the risk for consumers by reducing the cost of the good, but they can also alter perceptions of value.

But deals can also alter perceptions of value—a short-term price reduction may signal a different price/quality relationship than would be ideal from the manufacturer's perspective. As Old Spice learned, offering too many deals can offset likely gains. Its popular "Old Spice Guy" campaign attracted consumer attention through funny television commercials and interactive online campaigns, and sales of Old Spice jumped. But the company offered so many "buy one, get one free" deals at the same time that the

## Social and Mobile Marketing 15.1

### Checkout 51 Helps Companies Target Offers[52]

Have you ever stopped to consider the power of a grocery store receipt? It contains a list of products purchased, how much was spent, the price paid for each item, and more—data critical to marketers for understanding shopping behaviour. The founders of Checkout 51 (CO51) came to this realization while brainstorming their next big venture in a Toronto-area café in 2011.

Using CO51 is simple: download the mobile app that showcases new coupon offers each week. When you make a qualifying purchase at any Canadian retailer, simply use your mobile phone to snap a picture of your receipt and upload it. Each time you redeem a coupon offered, your account balance grows until you request payout. You not only get real dollars refunded, but also don't have to fumble with clippings at the register or deal with the stares of impatient customers behind you. And having CO51 on your smartphone allows you to have the coupons in-store with you while you shop.

It's appealing for marketers too, because the app's digital nature gives them complete control. They can design a coupon offer for a budget of any level, and instantly end the offer as soon as the budget is spent. The app can also target groups of consumers based on demographics or previous purchasing behaviour. The summary report at the end of the offer can show marketers who was redeeming the offers, when, and where. This data is then used to gain insights about shopping behaviour or to target different users the next time. The app also virtually eliminates coupon fraud since the CO51 team can limit redemption by receipt submitted by mobile phone.

CO51 was formally launched in December 2012. The crew leveraged strong PR to encourage app downloads. Just two weeks after launch it was the number one lifestyle app in Canada. The team continued to drive the value proposition through extremely targeted Facebook and Google advertising and in-game ads. Less than one year later, over 500,000 Canadians were using it, making CO51 the leading mobile coupon app.

Enrollment numbers like this made it possible to attract major corporate interest from Kraft, Unilever, Kellogg's, VISA, and others, without a single outbound sales call. Creating true value for marketers and combining that with media agency partnerships and word-of-mouth promotion resulted in calls from nearly all major packaged-goods companies, which wanted to work with CO51.

Such rapid success caught the attention of investors, too. In 2013, the company raised over $9 million in capital, allowing an expansion into a desktop version of the tool to attract users beyond mobile, and also enable a platform launch into the United States, expanding the company's potential target audience. CO51 currently has 2 million Canadian and nearly 11 million U.S. subscribers.[53] The app is also available in French and Spanish.

With CO51, everyone is happy: consumers have a new and convenient way to save money, manufacturers can build a direct relationship with their shoppers and access valuable consumer data, and retailers can expedite register times and watch basket sizes grow.

---

potential profit impact of the great ads was essentially eliminated by the costs of the deals.[54]

**Premiums**  A **premium** offers an item for free or at a bargain price to reward some type of behaviour, such as buying, sampling, or testing. These rewards build goodwill among consumers, who often perceive high value in them. Premiums can be distributed in a variety of ways. They can be included in the product packaging, such as the toys inside cereal boxes; placed visibly on the package, such as a coupon for free milk on a box of Cheerios; handed out in the store; or delivered in the mail, such as the free perfume offers that Victoria's Secret mails to customers.

This sales promotion deal for Payless ShoeSource is a short-term promotion that encourages consumers to buy two pairs of shoes—one at the regular price and a second pair at 50 percent off.

Used with permission of Payless ShoeSource Worldwide, Inc.

**premium**
An item offered for free or at a bargain price to reward some type of behaviour, such as buying, sampling, or testing.

Furthermore, premiums can be very effective if they are consistent with the brand's message and image and highly desirable to the target market. Finding a premium that meets these criteria at a reasonable cost can be a serious challenge. At fast-food restaurants such as McDonald's and Burger King, for instance, the average order cost is around $5, while the average premium distributed costs less than 50 cents.

**contest**

A brand-sponsored competition that requires some form of skill or effort.

**Contests** A **contest** refers to a brand-sponsored competition that requires some form of skill or effort. In Canada, you cannot give a prize away by chance alone. There must also be a skill component, which is why skill-testing questions are used, making the game one of mixed chance and skill. The effort required by these contests often keeps participation lower than that for other forms of promotion. When Jason Priestley joked about a doughnut called "The Priestley" (strawberry-vanilla doughnut stuffed with a chocolate Timbit) in a cameo appearance on *How I Met Your Mother*, Tim Hortons® kept the publicity going strong by launching a contest. The winning entry in the "Duelling Donuts" contest was the Tortoise Torte, a concoction of chocolate, caramel, and pecans. It beat out 63,000 other entries and earned contestant Andrew Shepherd $10,000.[55]

Contests are often used to drive sales, draw attention to a company's initiatives, and even promote environmental causes. To be effective, contests must be advertised and enjoy high levels of retailer or dealer support. Sport Chek ran an online contest to drive up its membership database and increase store traffic. Shoppers received unique contest-entry PIN codes on their receipts. They got a discount coupon when they registered at GetIntoGear.ca. In the first week, 3,000 people registered for the contest and sent information about it to friends 1,000 times.[56] Cineplex ran a tournament for Call of Duty video game enthusiasts to shoot it out, and vie for $65,000 in cash and other contest prizes.[57]

**sweepstakes**

A form of sales promotion that offers prizes based on a chance drawing of entrants' names.

**Sweepstakes** A form of sales promotion that offers prizes based on a chance drawing of entrants' names, **sweepstakes** do not require the entrant to complete a task other than buying a ticket or completing a form. Often the key benefit of sweepstakes is that they encourage current consumers to consume more if the sweepstakes form appears inside the packaging or with the product. Unlike contests, sweepstakes winners are determined by a random draw. Reader's Digest Canada runs an annual national sweepstakes for which it invites both subscribers and others to enter.

**sampling**

Offers potential customers the opportunity to try a product or service before they make a buying decision.

**Samples** **Sampling** offers potential customers the opportunity to try a product or service before they make a buying decision. Distributing samples is one of the most costly sales promotion tools but also one of the most effective. Quick-service restaurants and grocery stores frequently use sampling. For instance, McDonald's offers free coffee a couple of times a year to attract customers to its outlets. Costco uses so many samples that customers can eat an entire meal while shopping. Sometimes trial-size samples come in the mail or are distributed in stores. SoCIAL LITE Vodka used heavy sampling at LCBO stores to gain awareness and trial of its products. Nespresso gives full size servings in stylish glass mugs, bringing a premium feel to its samples. Many companies use pop-up stores for sampling purposes. For instance, Campbell's opened a pop-up restaurant on Queen Street in Toronto to let customers sample dishes made with a variety of its soup products. The goal was to demonstrate how soup could be used as an ingredient. Product samples were also given out so consumers could recreate dishes such as Thai Chicken & Rice Khao Soi curry at home.[58]

SoCIAL LITE Vodka offered samples of its products at LCBO stores to raise awareness and trial.

Used with permission of SoCIAL LITE Vodka

**Loyalty Programs** As part of a sales promotion program, a **loyalty program** is specifically designed to retain customers by offering premiums or other incentives to customers who make multiple purchases over time. Such sales promotions are growing increasingly popular and are often tied to long-term CRM systems. In Canada, some of the most popular loyalty programs include Canadian Tire "Money," Aeroplan, Air Miles, and the Shoppers Drug Mart Optimum program.

**loyalty program**
Specifically designed to retain customers by offering premiums or other incentives to customers who make multiple purchases over time.

**Point-of-Purchase Displays** A **point-of-purchase (POP) display** is a merchandise display located at the point of purchase, such as at the checkout counter in a grocery store. Marketers spend almost as much on POP materials as they do on consumer magazine advertising, but the key to a successful POP is to make the display "pop out" in a crowded store. In addition, manufacturers must encourage retailers to feature and use the POP displays to maximize their investments. Lindt Canada launched an illustrated storybook app based on its iconic Gold Bunny just in time for Easter. "The Bell That Rang in Easter" told the story of a little girl and a bunny in a way that allowed families to discuss values such as giving, love, and friendship. For every story downloaded, Lindt donated $1 to The Children's Aid Foundation. To promote the story and sales of the Gold Bunny, a 1,400-square-foot point-of-purchase display featuring life-sized scenes from the book was used at Mississauga's Square One.[59]

**point-of-purchase (POP) display**
A merchandise display located at the point of purchase, such as at the checkout counter in a grocery store.

POP displays are merchandise displays located at the point of purchase, such as at the checkout counter in a grocery store.
RosaIreneBetancourt 5/Alamy Stock Photo

**Rebates** Rebates are a particular type of price reduction in which a portion of the purchase price is returned by the seller to the buyer. Many products, such as consumer electronics, now offer significant mail-in rebates that may lower the price of the item significantly. Firms offer such generous rebates because the likelihood that consumers will actually apply for the rebate is low, even though consumers indicate that rebate offers are a factor in their purchase decisions. The firms thus garner considerable value from rebates because they attract consumers with a minimal risk that the firm will have to pay off all the rebates offered.

Heavy rebate users, such as Best Buy, have changed their approach. As with any promotional tool, too much of a good thing can be a problem. Best Buy found that consumers were becoming increasingly annoyed by having to mail in the rebate forms and wait to receive their money. Many were requesting that the rebate be given at the time of purchase and wondering why this immediate reduction was not possible. In addition, a growing number of lawsuits claim rebate cheques were never sent to consumers and that rebate offers contain overly detailed clauses that cause consumers to have to submit and resubmit their claims. Best Buy has since put an end to mail-in rebates.[60]

## Trade Channel Sales Promotions

Although sales promotions are often associated with coupons, contests, and other consumer tactics, far more money is spent on trade channel sales promotions than on consumer sales promotions. Trade channel promotions help convince retailers and wholesalers to stock a new brand, give it eye-level shelf space, and promote it in their flyers and other advertisements. Many types of consumer sales promotions can be used for channel members, including discounts and allowances, cooperative advertising, and sales force training.

### Discounts and Allowances

Discounts and allowances are effective incentives used to maintain or increase inventory levels in the distribution channel. Manufacturers sometimes offer a case allowance, for example, a discount or dollar amount taken off each case ordered during a specific time period. Alternatively, retailers may receive a set quantity of products free, for example, one case at no charge with an order of 10 cases. A merchandise allowance may be offered in return for extra in-store support or for the retailer's featuring the product in some way. For instance, if a store agreed to run an ad with a coupon promoting a specific product, the merchandise allowance may provide a discounted case price for orders received during the promotional period.

### Cooperative Advertising

One of the important functions retailers perform is promoting products to consumers. Cooperative (co-op) advertising helps to compensate trade channel members for money they spend promoting products and encourages them to feature products more often. Generally, manufacturers will pay 50 percent of the cost of advertising up to an agreed-upon limit. This limit is usually determined based on the amount of business a retailer does with a manufacturer. To ensure high-quality advertisements are placed at the local level, some companies will provide a selection of final ads to choose from, ready to place in a variety of media or adapt as necessary.

### Sales Force Training

Because retailers have contact with end consumers and are ultimately responsible for selling the products they carry, manufacturers may offer to train the retailer's sales staff. This training gives a company's sales force more in-depth product knowledge, which enhances their confidence in the product and increases the likelihood of future sales. When VitalScience Corp. launched its Dermaglow skin care line, it trained cosmeticians at Shoppers Drug Mart, since they were the staff members who would most likely field questions about the new product. Other training activities might include providing manuals or brochures, sales meetings, or field visits. Manufacturers sometimes run contests to help motivate trade channel members to sell their products.

## Using Sales Promotion Tools

Marketers must be careful in their use of promotions, especially those that focus on lowering prices. Depending on the item, consumers may stock up when items are offered at a lower price, which simply shifts sales from the future to now and thereby leads to short-run benefits at the expense of long-term sales stability. For instance, using sales promotions such as coupons to stimulate sales of household cleaning supplies may cause consumers to stockpile the products and decrease demand for those products in the future. But a similar promotion used with a perishable product such as Danone yogurt should increase its demand at the expense of competitors like Yoplait.

The tools connected to sales promotions are as varied as the imaginations of the marketers who devise them, and new forms are constantly popping up. Take, for example, **pop-up stores**—such as the one Adidas launched in Toronto for All-Star Weekend. It featured sneakers from the new Tubular line along with NBA All-Star clothing and shoes, and gave consumers access to exclusive launches of Adidas Originals.[61] Pop-up stores only exist for a limited time and generally focus on a new product or a limited group of products offered by a retailer, manufacturer, or service provider. These temporary storefronts give consumers a chance to interact with the brand and build brand awareness, but are not designed primarily to sell products. Most companies hope that consumers who visit a pop-up will later buy from retailers that carry the products.

Retailers tend not to mind manufacturers' pop-up stores because most are designed to drive traffic to the retailers through give-aways of coupons and samples. Because pop-ups are short lived, they don't pose any long-term competition to retailers or cause channel conflict.

Many firms are also realizing the value of **cross-promoting**, when two or more firms join together to reach a specific target market. To achieve a successful cross-promotion,

**pop-up stores**
Temporary storefronts that exist for only a limited time and generally focus on a new product or a limited group of products offered by a retailer, manufacturer, or service provider; give consumers a chance to interact with the brand and build brand awareness.

**cross-promoting**
Efforts of two or more firms joining together to reach a specific target market.

the two products must appeal to the same target market and together create value for consumers. J. Crew has teamed up with several famous brands—including Timex, New Balance, Ray-Ban, and Speedo—to offer exclusive products in J. Crew stores and on its website.

The goal of any sales promotion is to create value for both the consumers and the firm. By understanding the needs of its customers, as well as how best to entice them to purchase or consume a particular product or service, a firm can develop promotional messages and events that are of interest to and achieve the desired response from those customers. Traditionally, the role of sales promotion has been to generate short-term results, whereas the goal of advertising was to generate long-term results. As this chapter demonstrates, though, both sales promotion and advertising can generate both long- and short-term effects. The effective combination of both types of activities leads to impressive results for the firm and the consumers.

## Evaluating Sales Promotions by Using Marketing Metrics

Many sales promotion opportunities undertaken by retailers are initiated by manufacturers. For example, Sharp might offer the following special promotion to Costco: During a one-week period, Costco can order 37-inch Sharp Aquos LCD HDTVs at $300 below the standard wholesale price. However, if Costco elects to buy these HDTVs at the discounted price, then it must feature them prominently on its web page for $1099.00 ($325 below the suggested retail price). In addition, Costco must agree to purchase enough of this particular model to have front-of-store displays in each of its stores.

Before Costco decides whether to accept such a trade promotion and promote the Sharp HDTV to its customers, it needs to assess the promotion's impact on its own profitability. Such a promotion may be effective for Sharp but not for Costco.

To evaluate a trade promotion, retailers consider

- the realized margin from the promotion
- the cost of the additional inventory carried because of buying more than the normal amount of the product
- the potential increase in sales from the promoted merchandise
- the long-term impact on sales of the promotion
- the potential loss suffered when customers switch to the promoted merchandise from more profitable TVs
- the additional sales made to customers attracted to the store by the promotion

When the HDTV's price is reduced to $1099.00, Costco will sell more Sharp HDTVs than it normally does. But Costco's margin on the HDTVs will be less because the required retail discount of $325 isn't offset by the normal wholesale discount of $300. In addition, Costco might suffer losses because the promotion encourages customers to buy these special HDTVs, which have a lower margin than Costco makes on its other HDTVs. In contrast, the promotion may attract customers who don't normally purchase electronics at Costco but who will visit to buy the Sharp HDTV at the discounted price. These customers might buy additional merchandise, providing a sales gain to the store that it wouldn't have realized if it hadn't promoted this item.

# PERSONAL SELLING                                                   L04

Almost everyone is engaged in some form of selling. On a personal level, you sell your ideas or opinions to your friends, family, employers, and professors. Even if you have no interest in personal selling as a career, a strong grounding in the topic will help you in numerous career choices. Consider, for instance, Tony D'Souza, a very successful labour attorney. He worked his way through university selling alpaca sweaters to fraternities across the country. Although he loved his part-time job, D'Souza decided to become an attorney. When asked whether he misses selling, he said, "I use my selling skills every day. I have to sell new clients on the idea that I'm the best attorney for the job. I have to sell my partners on my legal point of view. I even use selling skills when I'm talking to a judge or jury." In this chapter though, we take a straightforward business perspective on selling.

## The Scope and Nature of Personal Selling

Personal selling is the two-way flow of communication between a buyer (or buyers) and a seller that is designed to influence the buyer's purchase decision. Personal selling can take place in various situations: face to face, via video teleconferencing, on the telephone, or over the Internet. More than a million people are employed in sales positions in Canada, including those involved in B2B transactions—such as manufacturers' representatives selling to retailers or other businesses—and those completing B2C transactions—such as retail salespeople, real estate agents, and insurance agents. Salespeople are referred to in many ways: as sales representatives or reps; account executives; or agents. And, as Tony D'Souza found, most professions rely on personal selling to some degree.

Many salespeople now rely on virtual offices, which enable them to communicate via the Internet with colleagues and customers.

© Stanley Fellerman/Corbis

Salespeople don't always get the best coverage in popular media. In Arthur Miller's play *Death of a Salesman*, the main character, Willy Loman, leads a pathetic existence and suffers from the loneliness inherent in being a travelling salesman.[62] Unfortunately, this powerful Pulitzer Prize–winning piece of literature weighs heavily on our collective consciousness and often overshadows the millions of hard-working professional salespeople who have fulfilling and rewarding careers and who add value to their firm and provide value for their customers.

Professional selling can be a satisfying career for several reasons. First, many people love the lifestyle. Salespeople are typically out on their own. Although they occasionally work with their managers and other colleagues, salespeople are usually responsible for planning their own day. This flexibility translates into an easier balance between work and family than many office-bound jobs can offer. Many salespeople now rely on virtual offices, which enable them to communicate via the Internet with colleagues and customers. Because salespeople are evaluated primarily on the results they produce, as long as they meet and exceed their goals, they experience little day-to-day supervision.

Second, the variety of the job often attracts people to sales. Every day is different, bringing different clients and customers, often in a variety of places. Their issues and problems and the solutions to those problems all differ and require creativity.

Third, professional selling and sales management can be a very lucrative career. Sales is among the highest-paying careers for college and university graduates, and compensation often includes perks, such as the use of a company car and bonuses for high performance. A top performer can have a total compensation package of more than $150,000; even lower-level salespeople can make well over $50,000. Although the monetary compensation can be significant, the satisfaction of being involved in interesting, challenging, and creative work is rewarding in and of itself.

Professional selling can be a very lucrative career and is very visible to management.

© Alex Maloney/Corbis

Fourth, because salespeople are the front-line emissaries for their firm, they are very visible to management. Because it is fairly straightforward for management to identify top performers, those high-performing salespeople who aspire to management positions are in a good position to be promoted.

Although personal selling is an essential part of many firms' IMC strategy, it offers its own unique contribution to the four Ps. Because of the one-to-one nature of sales, a salesperson is in a unique position to customize a message for a specific buyer—a preplanned sales presentation or demonstration can be altered at any time as the need arises. In a personal selling situation, the salesperson can probe the buyer for his or her potential reservations about a product or service, educate the buyer when appropriate, and ask for the order at the appropriate time. Unlike other types of promotion, the sales presentation can be directed toward those customers with the highest potential. This highly directed approach to promotion is important because experts estimate that the average cost of a single B2B sales call is about $600.[63]

## The Value Added by Personal Selling

Why have salespeople in the supply chain? They are expensive and can be a challenge to manage. Some firms, such as retailers, have made the decision not to use a sales force and become, for the most part, almost completely self-service. Other firms have turned to the Internet and technology to lower the costs of personal selling. Those that use personal selling as part of their IMC program do so because it adds value to their product or service mix—that is, personal selling is worth more than it costs. Personal selling adds value by building relationships, educating and providing advice, and saving customers time and simplifying things for them.[64]

A good CRM system provides salespeople with the information they need to suggest specific items and services to individual customers.

© Photographerlondon/Dreamstime.com/GetStock.com

**Salespeople Build Relationships** As we discussed in Chapter 12, building strong distribution channel relationships is a critical success factor. Who in the organization is better equipped to manage this relationship than the salesperson, the firm's front-line representative? The most successful salespeople are those who build strong relationships with their customers—a rule that holds across all sorts of sales. That is, whether you are selling yourself as a job candidate, a product produced by your company, or a concept to a client, your sale is not successful if it leads to just a one-time transaction. Instead, good salespeople take a long-term perspective. Building on the strategic relationship concept introduced in Chapter 12, **relationship selling** is a sales philosophy and process that emphasizes a commitment to maintaining the relationship over the long term and investing in opportunities that are beneficial to all parties. Relationship salespeople work with their customers to find mutually beneficial solutions to their wants and needs.

Research has shown that a positive customer–salesperson relationship contributes to trust, increased customer loyalty, and the intent to continue the relationship with the salesperson.[65] To help build strong relationships, many firms undertake active CRM programs that identify and focus on building loyalty with the firm's most valued customers. Because the sales force interacts directly with customers, its members are in the best position to help a firm accomplish its CRM objectives.

CRM programs have several components. There is a customer database or data warehouse. Whether the salesperson is working for a retail store or managing a selling team for an aerospace contractor, he or she can record transaction information, customer contact information, customer preferences, and market segment information about the customer. Once the data has been analyzed and CRM programs developed, salespeople can help implement the programs. For instance, bankers use a "high-touch approach" in which they frequently call on their best customers or contact them by phone. A salesperson can contact customers when there are new products or changes to existing product lines. He or she can probe customers about what they liked or disliked about their recent

**relationship selling**

A sales philosophy and process that emphasizes a commitment to maintaining the relationship over the long term and investing in opportunities that are mutually beneficial to all parties.

transactions with the firm. Or the purpose of the call can be purely social. If done properly, customers will feel special and important when a salesperson calls just to see how things are going.

### Salespeople Educate and Provide Advice

Imagine how difficult it would be to buy a new suit, a diamond engagement ring, or a plasma TV without the help of a salesperson. Similarly, UPS wouldn't dream of investing in a new fleet of airplanes without the benefit of Boeing's selling team. Sure, it could be done, but customers see the value in and are willing to pay indirectly for the education and advice salespeople provide. Retail salespeople can provide valuable information about how a garment fits, new fashions, or directions for operating products. Boeing's sales team can provide UPS with technical information about the aircraft, as well as the economic justification for the purchase.

Five years ago, many observers thought that travel agents and other service providers would be replaced by more efficient Internet services, and the Internet has certainly changed the way many consumers make travel decisions. Thousands use sites such as Expedia.ca and Travelocity.ca or visit airlines, rail companies, hotels, and car rental firms online to make reservations directly. But when planning to visit an exotic locale or booking a complicated trip or cruise, or for those who don't feel comfortable buying online, travel agents add significant value. They can help with itineraries, give helpful tips, and even save the customer money.

### Salespeople Save Time and Simplify Buying

Time is money! Customers perceive value in time and labour savings. In many grocery and drugstore chains, salespeople employed by the vendor supplying merchandise straighten stock, set up displays, assess inventory levels, and write orders. In some cases, such as with baked goods or soft drinks, salespeople and truck drivers even bring in the merchandise and stock the shelves. These are all tasks that retail employees would otherwise have to do.

Sometimes, however, turning over too many tasks to suppliers' salespeople can cause problems. If they take over the inventory management function, for instance, they may buy a suboptimal quantity of competitors' products. They might also place competitor products in disadvantageous shelf positions. Salespeople can help facilitate a buying situation, but they shouldn't take it over.

## L05 THE PERSONAL SELLING PROCESS

Although selling may appear to be a rather straightforward process, successful salespeople follow several steps. Depending on the sales situation and the buyer's readiness to purchase, the salesperson may not use every step, and the time required for each step will vary depending on the situation. For instance, if a customer goes into The Bay already prepared to purchase some khaki pants, the selling process will be fairly quick. But if Dell is attempting to sell personal computers for the first time to a university, the process may take several months. With this in mind, let's examine each step of the selling process (see Exhibit 15.4).

### Step 1: Generate and Qualify Leads

**leads**
A list of potential customers.

**qualify**
The process of assessing the potential of sales leads.

The first step in the selling process is to generate a list of potential customers (**leads**) and assess their potential (**qualify**). Salespeople who already have an established relationship with a customer will skip this step, and it is not used extensively in retail settings. In B2B situations, however, it is important to work continually to find new and potentially profitable customers.

Salespeople can discover potential leads by talking to their current customers, doing research on the Internet, and networking at events such as industry conferences or chamber of commerce meetings. The Internet and sites like LinkedIn have been a boon for generating and qualifying leads. For instance, salespeople can gather information

**EXHIBIT 15.4**   The Personal Selling Process

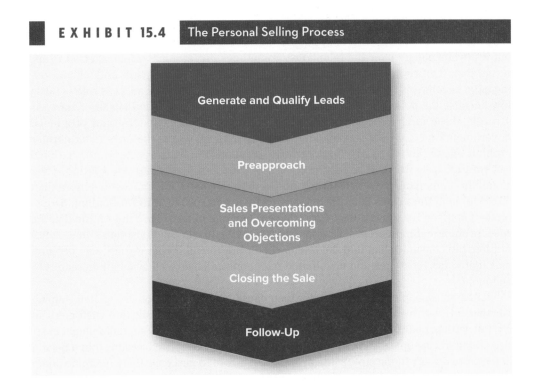

Generate and Qualify Leads

Preapproach

Sales Presentations and Overcoming Objections

Closing the Sale

Follow-Up

collected on the firm's website or Google a few keywords and instantly generate enough potential leads to keep them busy for weeks. Another excellent forum for finding leads is **trade shows**, which are major events attended by buyers who choose to be exposed to products and services offered by potential suppliers in an industry. Consumer electronics buyers always make sure that they attend the annual International Consumer Electronics Show (CES) in Las Vegas, the world's largest trade show for consumer technology. The most recent show was attended by 177,000 people, such as vendors, developers, and suppliers of consumer-technology hardware, content, technology delivery systems, and related products and services.[66] Vendor exhibits took up 2.47 million net square feet of exhibit space, showcasing the very latest products and services. Vendors often use CES to introduce new products, including the first camcorder (1981), high-definition television (HDTV, 1998), and Internet protocol television (IP TV, 2005). At the 2016 CES conference, more than 3,600 exhibitors showed off tens of thousands of new products.[67]

**trade shows**
Major events attended by buyers who choose to be exposed to products and services offered by potential suppliers in an industry.

A great place to generate leads is at a trade show.

George Doyle/Stockbyte/Getty Images

**Cold calls** are a method of prospecting in which salespeople telephone or go to see potential customers without appointments. **Telemarketing** is similar to a cold call, but it always occurs over the telephone. Sometimes professional telemarketing firms, rather than the firm's salespeople, make such calls. However, cold calls and telemarketing have become less popular than they were in the past. First, the success rate is fairly low because the potential customer's need has not been established ahead of time. As a result, these methods can be very expensive. Second, both federal and provincial governments have begun to regulate the activities of telemarketers. Federal rules prohibit telemarketing to consumers whose telephone numbers appear on the national Do-Not-Call List, which is maintained by the Canadian Marketing Association. Over 13 million Canadians have added their numbers to this list. CRTC has levied more than $3.6 million in fines since 2008. SiriusXM was fined $650,000 in 2016[68] for calling people on the list. Even for those consumers whose telephone numbers are not on the list, the rules prohibit calling before 8:00 a.m. or after 9:00 p.m. (in the consumer's time zone) or after the consumer has told the telemarketer not to call. Federal rules also prohibit unsolicited fax messages and unsolicited telephone calls, as well as email messages to cellphones.

After salespeople generate leads, they must qualify those leads by determining whether it is worthwhile to pursue them and attempt to turn the leads into customers. In a retail setting, qualifying potential can be a very dangerous and potentially illegal practice. Retail salespeople should never "judge a book by its cover" and assume that a person in the store doesn't fit the store's image or cannot afford to purchase there. Imagine going to an upscale jewellery store to purchase an engagement ring, only to be snubbed because you are dressed in your everyday, casual clothes. But in B2B settings, where the costs of preparing and making a presentation can be substantial, the seller must assess a lead's potential. Salespeople should consider, for instance, whether the potential customer's needs pertain to a product or a service. They should also assess whether the lead has the financial resources to pay for the product or service.

## Step 2: Preapproach and the Use of CRM Systems

The **preapproach** occurs prior to meeting the customer for the first time and extends the qualification of leads procedure described in Step 1. Although the salesperson has learned about the customer during the qualification stage, in this step, he or she must conduct additional research and develop plans for meeting with the customer. Suppose, for example, that a management consulting firm wants to sell a bank a new system for finding chequing account errors. The consulting firm's salesperson should first find out everything possible about the bank: How many cheques does it process? What system is the bank using now? What are the benefits of the consultant's proposed system compared with the competition? The answers to these questions provide the basis for establishing value for the customer. In the past, this customer information, if it was available at all, was typically included in a manual system that each individual salesperson kept, using a notebook or a series of cards. Today, salespeople often can access all this information immediately and conveniently from their firm's customer relationship management (CRM) system.

Retail salespeople should never "judge a book by its cover" and assume that a person in the store doesn't fit the store's image or cannot afford to purchase there.

Big Cheese Photo/SuperStock

Having done the additional research, the salesperson establishes goals for meeting with the customer; it is important that he or she know ahead of time exactly what should be accomplished. For instance, the consulting firm's salesperson can't expect to get a commitment from the bank that it will buy on the first visit. But a demonstration of the system and a short presentation about how the system would benefit the customer would be appropriate.

## Step 3: Sales Presentation and Overcoming Objections

**The Presentation**   Once all the background information has been obtained and the objectives for the meeting are set, the salesperson is ready for a person-to-person meeting. Let's continue with our bank example. During the first part of the meeting, the salesperson needs to get to know the customer, get his or her attention, and create interest in the presentation to follow. The beginning of the presentation may be the most important part of the entire selling process, because this is when the salesperson establishes exactly where the customer is in his or her buying process (see Exhibit 15.5). (For a refresher on the B2B buying process, see Chapter 5.) Suppose, for instance, the bank is in the first stage of the buying process, need recognition. It would not be prudent for the salesperson to discuss the pros and cons of different potential suppliers because doing so would assume that the customer already had reached Stage 4, proposal analysis and supplier selection. By asking a series of questions, however, the salesperson can assess the bank's need for the product or service and adapt or customize the presentation to match the customer's need and stage in the decision process.[69]

Asking questions is only half the battle; carefully listening to the answers is equally important. Some salespeople, particularly inexperienced ones, believe that to be in

**EXHIBIT 15.5**    Aligning the Personal Selling Process With the B2B Buying Process

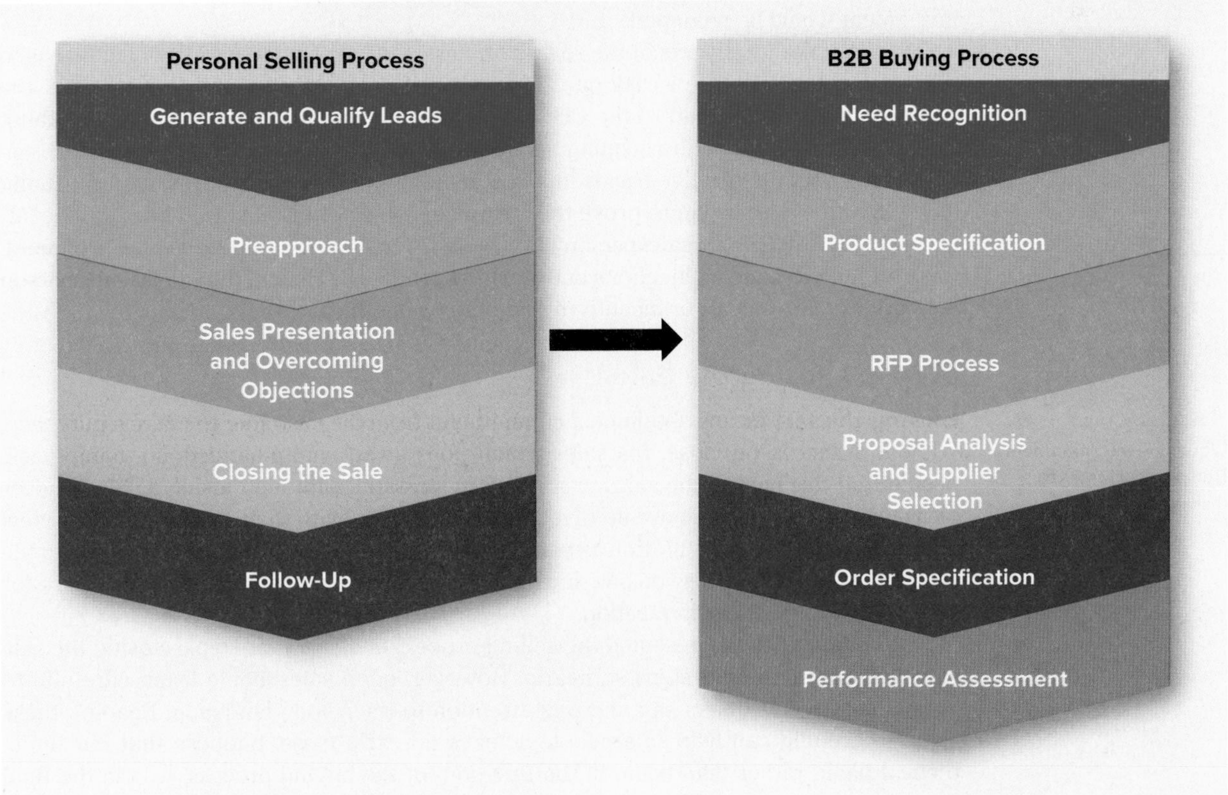

**Personal Selling Process**

- Generate and Qualify Leads
- Preapproach
- Sales Presentation and Overcoming Objections
- Closing the Sale
- Follow-Up

**B2B Buying Process**

- Need Recognition
- Product Specification
- RFP Process
- Proposal Analysis and Supplier Selection
- Order Specification
- Performance Assessment

control, they must do all the talking. Yet it is impossible to really understand where the customer stands without listening carefully. What if the COO says, "It seems kind of expensive"? If the salesperson isn't listening carefully, he or she won't pick up on the subtle nuances of what the customer is really thinking. In this case, it probably means that the COO doesn't see the value in the offering.

When the salesperson has a good feel for where the customer stands, he or she can apply that knowledge to help the customer solve the problem or satisfy the need. The salesperson might begin by explaining the features or characteristics of the system that will reduce chequing account errors. It may not be obvious, based solely on these features, however, that the system adds value beyond the bank's current practices. Using the answers to some of the questions the customer posed earlier in the meeting, the salesperson can clarify the product's advantages over current or past practices, as well as the overall benefits of adopting the new system. The salesperson might explain, for instance, that the bank can expect a 20 percent decrease in chequing account errors and that, based on the size of the bank and the number of cheques it processes per year, this improvement would represent $2 million in annual savings. Because the system costs $150,000 per year and will take only three weeks to integrate into the current system, it will add significant and almost immediate value.

Handling Objections    An integral part of the sales presentation is handling objections that the buyer might have about the product or service. Although objections can arise during any stage of the selling process, they are very likely to occur during the sales presentation. Customers may raise objections pertaining to a variety of issues, but they usually relate in some way to value, such as that the price is too high for the level of quality or service.

Good salespeople know the types of objections buyers are likely to raise. They may know, for instance, that their service is slower than competitors' or that their selection is limited. Although not all objections can be forestalled, effective salespeople can anticipate and handle some of them. For example, when the bank COO said the cheque service seemed expensive, the salesperson was ready with information about how quickly the investment would be recouped.

Similar to other aspects of the selling process, the best way to handle objections is to relax and listen, and then to ask questions to clarify any reservations. For example, the salesperson could respond to the COO's objection by asking, "How much do you think the bank is losing through chequing account errors?" Her answer might open up a conversation about the positive trends in a cost/benefit analysis. Such questions are usually more effective than trying to prove the customer's objection is not valid because the latter approach implies the salesperson isn't really listening and could lead to an argument. In an attempt to handle objections and start the process of closing the sale, a salesperson may offer creative deals or incentives that may be unethical.

## Step 4: Closing the Sale

**closing the sale**

Obtaining a commitment from the customer to make a purchase.

**Closing the sale** means obtaining a commitment from the customer to make a purchase. Without a successful close, the salesperson goes away empty-handed, so many salespeople find this part of the sales process very stressful. Although losing a sale is never pleasant, salespeople who are involved in a relationship with their customers must view any particular sales presentation as part of the progression toward ultimately making the sale. An unsuccessful close on one day may just be a means of laying the groundwork for a successful close the next meeting.

Although we have presented the selling process in a series of steps, closing the sale rarely follows the other steps so neatly. However, good salespeople listen carefully to what potential customers say and pay attention to their body language. Reading these signals carefully can help salespeople achieve an early close. Suppose that our hypothetical bank, rather than being in the first step of the buying process, was in the final step of negotiation and selection. An astute salesperson will pick up on these signals and ask for the sale.

## Step 5: Follow-Up

With relationship selling, the sale is never really over, even after it has been made. The attitudes customers develop after the sale become the basis for how they will purchase in the future. The follow-up therefore offers a prime opportunity for a salesperson to solidify the customer relationship through great service quality. Let's apply the five service quality dimensions we discussed in Chapter 10 to the follow-up:[70]

Good salespeople, particularly in difficult selling situations such as door-to-door sales, don't easily take no for an answer. They keep coming back until they get a yes.

© Royalty-Free/CORBIS

- *Reliability.* The salesperson and the supporting organization must deliver the right product or service on time.

- *Responsiveness.* The salesperson and support group must be ready to deal quickly with any issue, question, or problem that may arise.

- *Assurance.* Customers must be assured through adequate guarantees that their purchase will perform as expected.

- *Empathy.* The salesperson and support group must have a good understanding of the problems and issues faced by their customers. Otherwise, they cannot give them what they want.

- *Tangibles.* Because tangibles reflect the physical characteristics of the seller's business, such as its website, marketing communications, and delivery materials, their influence is more subtle than that of the other four service quality dimensions. That doesn't mean it is any less important. Retail customers are generally more pleased with a purchase if it is carefully wrapped in nice paper instead of being haphazardly thrown into a crumpled plastic bag. The tangibles offer a signal that the product is of high quality, even though the packaging has nothing to do with the product's actual performance.

When customers' expectations are not met, they often complain—about deliveries, the billing amount or process, the product's performance, or after-sale services such as installation or training. Effectively handling complaints is critical to the future of the relationship. As we noted in Chapter 10, the best way to handle complaints is to listen to the customer, provide a fair solution to the problem, and resolve the problem quickly.

The best way to nip a post-sale problem in the bud is to check with the customer right after he or she takes possession of the product or immediately after the service has been completed. This speed demonstrates responsiveness and empathy; it also shows the customer that the salesperson and the firm care about customer satisfaction. Finally, a post-sale follow-up call, email, or letter takes the salesperson back to the first step in the sales process for initiating a new order and sustaining the relationship.

Personal selling is an integral component of some firms' IMC strategy. Although it doesn't make sense for all firms, it is widely used in B2B markets, as well as in B2C markets in which the price of the merchandise is relatively high and customers need some one-to-one assistance before they can buy. Because of the relatively high expense of maintaining a personal selling force, it is important that salespeople be adequately trained, motivated, and compensated.

# LEARNING OBJECTIVES REVIEW

**LO1** **Describe advertising and three objectives of advertising**

Advertising is a paid form of communication from an identifiable source, delivered through a communication channel, that is designed to persuade consumers to take action. All advertising campaigns are designed to either inform, persuade, or remind customers. Ads can also be used to stimulate demand for a particular category or industry, or for a specific brand, firm, or item.

**LO2** **Summarize the regulatory and ethical issues of concern to advertisers**

Advertising is regulated by a plethora of federal and provincial agencies. The most important agencies are the Competition Bureau, which protects consumers against general deceptive advertising; the Canadian Radio-television and Telecommunications Commission, which has jurisdiction over radio, television, wire, satellite, and cable, and covers issues regarding the use of tobacco products; and Health Canada, whose Food and Drugs Act regulates food, drugs, cosmetics, and medical devices. Advertising Standards Canada maintains a strict broadcast code regarding advertising to children.

If a message is designed to promote or sell a product or service, it is generally considered to have an economic motivation, but if the message has no promotional or selling intent, it is fully protected by the Charter of Rights and Freedoms. The line becomes blurred, however, when normally noncommercial venues are used to sell something. Another practice that is causing a stir emerges when the sender of a commercial message is not clearly identified. Activities such as using bogus websites or certain stealth marketing programs, in which the identity of the sponsor of an activity or event is intentionally kept from prospective customers, can be considered deceptive promotional practices.

**LO3** **Explain how sales promotions supplement a firm's IMC strategy**

Sales promotions are special incentives or excitement-building programs that encourage purchase and include coupons, rebates, contests, free samples, and POP displays.

They either push sales through the channel, as is the case with contests directed toward retail salespeople, or pull sales through the channel, as coupons and rebates do. Sales promotions usually occur in conjunction with other elements of a firm's IMC strategy, such as price promotions or loyalty programs. Trade channel sales promotions include discounts and allowances, co-op advertising, and sales force training.

**LO4** **Describe personal selling and how it adds value for customers**

Personal selling is the two-way flow of communication between a buyer and a seller and can take place in a variety of situations. Although the cost of an average B2B sales call is considerable (about $400), many firms believe they couldn't do business without their sales force. Customers can buy many products and services without the help of a salesperson, but in many other cases, it is worth the extra cost built into the price of a product to be educated about the product or to get valuable advice. Salespeople can also simplify the buying process and therefore save the customer time and hassle.

**LO5** **Identify the steps in the personal selling process**

Although we discuss selling in terms of steps, it truly represents a process, and the time spent in each step varies according to the situation. In the first step, the salesperson generates a list of viable customers. During the second step, the preapproach, the salesperson gathers information about the customer and prepares for the presentation. The third step, the sales presentation, consists of a personal meeting between the salesperson and the customer. Through discussion and by asking questions, the salesperson learns where the customer is in the buying process and tailors the discussion around what the firm's product or service can do to meet that customer's needs. During the fourth step, closing the sale, the salesperson asks for the order. Finally, during the follow-up, the salesperson and support staff solidify a long-term relationship by making sure the customer is satisfied with the purchase and by addressing any complaints. The follow-up therefore sets the stage for the next purchase.

# KEY TERMS

- AIDA model
- aided recall
- closing the sale
- cold calls
- contest
- cross-promoting
- deal

- informative advertising
- institutional advertisements
- lagged effect
- leads
- loyalty program
- persuasive advertising
- point-of-purchase (POP) display

- pop-up stores
- preapproach
- premium
- product placement
- product-focused advertisements
- public service announcement (PSA)
- puffery

- qualify
- relationship selling
- reminder advertising

- sampling
- social marketing
- sweepstakes

- telemarketing
- top-of-mind awareness
- trade shows

## CONCEPT REVIEW

1. What is advertising?

2. What is the AIDA model? How does the AIDA model facilitate the planning and execution of marketing communications?

3. What are the three primary objectives of advertising?

4. List and explain some of the potential regulatory and ethical issues firms should consider when developing their marketing communications strategy.

5. What is sales promotion? What are the main objectives of sales promotion?

6. List six different kinds of consumer sales promotion tactics and discuss the advantages and disadvantages of each.

7. Describe the different kinds of sales promotions targeted to distribution channel members. Why are these trade channel promotions necessary? Are they ethical?

8. What is personal selling? Describe the steps in the personal selling process. Which stage do you consider to be the most important and why?

9. What is sales management? Why is sales management considered a complicated task?

10. What are the main considerations involved in recruiting, training, and compensating salespeople?

## MARKETING APPLICATIONS

1. Choose one of the ads featured in this book. What are the objectives of this ad? Does the ad have more than one objective? Explain your answer.

2. Using the steps in the AIDA model, explain why a potential consumer who views advertising by designer jean company Parasuco may not be ready to go out and purchase a new pair of jeans.

3. Suppose Lexus is introducing a new line of light trucks and has already created the advertising campaign. How would you assess the effectiveness of the campaign?

4. Suppose now Lexus is planning a sales promotion campaign to augment its advertising campaign for the new line of light trucks. Which sales promotion tools do you believe would be the most effective? Why?

5. How would the Lexus sales promotion differ if it was geared to a business organization with a fleet of company-owned trucks?

6. Choose an ad that you believe unreasonably overstates what the product or service can do. (If you can't think of a real ad, make one up.) Explain whether the ad is actually deceptive or just puffery. How would your answer change if you lived in France?

7. You are invited to your six-year-old niece's birthday party and bring her the new superhero doll being advertised on TV. She's thrilled when she unwraps the gift but is in tears a short time later because her new doll is broken. She explains that, on TV, the doll flies and does karate kicks, but when she tried to play with the doll this way, it broke. You decide to call the manufacturer, and a representative tells

you he is sorry your niece is so upset but that the ad clearly states the doll does not fly. The next time you see the televised ad, you notice very small print at the bottom of the screen that states the doll does not fly. You decide to write a letter to Advertising Standards Canada about this practice. What information should you include in your letter?

8. "Salespeople just make products cost more." Agree or disagree with this statement and discuss why you've taken that position.

9. Choose an industry or a specific company that you would like to work for as a salesperson. How would you generate and qualify leads?

10. You have taken a summer job in the windows and doors department of a large home improvement store. During sales training, you learn about the products, how best to address customers' needs, why the lifetime value of the customer concept is so important to a store like this, and how to sell customers the best product to fit their needs regardless of price point. One day your manager informs you that you are to recommend Smith Windows to every window customer. Smith Windows are more expensive than other brands and don't really provide superior benefit except in limited circumstances. The manager is insistent that you recommend Smith Windows. Not knowing what else to do, you recommend Smith Windows to customers who would have been better served by lower-cost windows. The manager rewards you with a sales award. Later, the manager tells you that he received an all-expenses-paid cruise for his family from Smith Windows. What, if anything, should you do with this information?

## NET SAVVY

**1.** Go to the website for the Canadian Children's Food & Beverage Advertising Initiative, one of the industry's self-regulatory bodies for children's advertising, at http://www.adstandards.com/en/childrensinitiative/default.htm. Click on "About the CAI" to learn more about the activities of CAI. Now look under the "Media Releases and Announcements" link. Choose one of the news releases and discuss what the main issue was in the case.

**2.** Go to https://www.smartsource.ca and identify five of the products featured. How effective are coupons for selling these products? Why? What are the benefits to the seller of using SmartSource.ca over other IMC options? How do you think SmartSource.ca makes money?

## CHAPTER CASE STUDY

### MAKING MASTERCARD PRICELESS

How do you pay for books, clothing, groceries, or travel? For many consumers, the answer is MasterCard, which has 192 million cards in circulation.[71] Yet, despite the credit card's popularity, it lags behind its major competitor, Visa, by nearly 125 million cards. It is also outstripped by American Express for both monthly and annual purchases and spending volume. Because MasterCard's primary function is to process transactions between each customer's bank and each merchant's bank, the company must appeal to two customer bases to build market share: the merchants who accept MasterCard for payment, and the purchasers who use the card. These audiences are closely related, which implies that a single campaign can target both, likely even for an extended period.

In 1997, MasterCard International and the advertising agency McCann Erickson Worldwide launched the emotion-based "Priceless" campaign, which celebrated life's most precious moments with the tagline, "There are some things money can't buy. For everything else, there's MasterCard."[72] The campaign was hugely successful, saving MasterCard from disaster, even in direct competition with the more widely accepted Visa card. Let's look at how MasterCard evolved to where it is today.

### Expanding Services to Meet Market Demand

In 1966, a group of California banks created a member-owned association called the Interbank Card Association. This association grew its services, changing its name to MasterCard in 1979 to reflect a commitment to international growth.[73] As it reached new markets across the globe, MasterCard also focused on technology innovation to help make economic transactions faster, more convenient, and more secure. The company acquired interest in the international credit card EuroCard (known today as Europay International), as well as Cirrus, a worldwide interbank network that links MasterCard, Maestro, and Diner's Club credit, debit, and prepaid cards to an international network of ATMs. The company also added fraud/risk management providers to its network of services.

Today MasterCard's technology platform can handle more than 160 million transactions every hour with a 99.9 percent reliability rate,[74] and the company has issued a contactless (or smart) card that communicates with terminals via radio waves. This payment method does not require a signature and can be a card or key fob that is tapped rather than swiped; it also appears as a smartphone app. To provide even more value to customers, the company has added sophisticated consulting and information services that help merchants gain insight into consumer spending, according to their transaction data and in-depth analyses.[75] These efforts have dovetailed with changes in consumer behaviour as shoppers have begun relying more on electronic payment options and less on paper-based currency. In 2006, the company transitioned to a new corporate governance and ownership structure and began trading on the New York Stock Exchange.

### "Priceless" Revisited

MasterCard began its "Priceless" campaign by identifying its target audience, which in this case was consumers. Hoping to persuade shoppers to keep their MasterCard at the top of their wallets, the campaign stressed the relationship between the card and experiences, as opposed to possessions. In early television ads, the narration linked the price of beauty parlour visits and new outfits to the "priceless" expression on an ex-boyfriend's face at a reunion, to create positive self-assessment feelings.[76] In another, the costs of tickets, refreshments, and souvenirs at a game were tied to the "priceless" opportunity for meaningful conversation between father and son, to invoke both happiness and love.[77] The "Priceless" campaign included various promotions and competitions, in addition to these television spots.

In 2004, "Priceless" print ads took a new tack, weaving well known retailers into the ads, together with MasterCard's theme. These retailers—which represented another of MasterCard's target audiences—received value from the prominent placement of their names and product images in the ads. Messaging moved from the general to the specific; an ad showing a teenaged rock band playing in a garage that might once have said, "Extra-long extension cord: $11; Moving them out of the living room: Priceless," was modified to indicate that the extension cord was from Radio Shack. The result was a form of symbiotic marketing in which well known brand names helped attract consumer attention to MasterCard ads, and each brand appeared to be endorsing the other.[78]

## Four Experiential Platforms: Priceless Cities, Priceless Surprises, Priceless Causes, and Priceless Specials

However, even the most successful campaigns can grow stale. As consumer values and needs changed and the marketplace evolved, MasterCard faced a new challenge: how to retain customer loyalty and brand identification while reinvigorating its advertising. The solution was four experiential platforms, designed to create priceless experiences, as opposed to simply celebrating priceless moments.

The evolution in the "Priceless" campaign started with "Priceless Cities," an expanded campaign launched in July 2011. This platform concentrates on the world's key cities, and MasterCard is spending hundreds of millions of dollars on experiences that are especially curated for members in 45 of those cities.[79] The campaign kicked off initially in New York, offering cardholders special experiences in major cities that can be shared with family and friends.[80] A few months later, the campaign made its debut in Toronto, where MasterCard piqued the interest of consumers by placing a huge vault in Maple Leaf Square. Messaging invited Torontonians to discover what was inside the vault and their city, and tweet about it using #unlockTO.[81] Designed to provide busy consumers with memorable opportunities in the realms of sports, music, entertainment, shopping, travel, arts, culture, and dining out, the campaign offers exclusive discounts and experiences for MasterCard holders. Promotions included $10 off the CN Tower EdgeWalk, $50 off Porter Airlines flights, and 20 percent off Ontario Science Centre admission.[82] The idea, says MasterCard's chief marketing officer, is to transform consumers' perception of the card from simply part of a priceless moment to being the force that enables such experiences.

At the 2014 GRAMMYS, with brand ambassador Justin Timberlake, MasterCard unveiled #PricelessSurprises—a brand platform built to deliver surprises, big and small, to members. By tweeting with #PricelessSurprises, or using their MasterCard, cardholders could be surprised with anything from headphones to once-in-a-lifetime experiences—like spending a day with Justin Timberlake.[83] Since the 2014 GRAMMY night, #PricelessSurprises has been incorporated into all social activities—connecting with consumers through the things they are passionate about. This platform has rapidly become one of MasterCard's most successful initiatives. Cardholders used #PricelessSurprises over 877,000 times.[84] According to MasterCard's chief marketing officer, Raja Rajamannar, in just over a year of running the campaign, MasterCard created more than a quarter of a million surprises and expanded the campaign into different regions around the world, leveraging music and sports stars and their 4,000 event sponsorships.[85]

"Priceless Causes," the third pillar of the "Priceless" campaign, creates opportunities for consumers to support philanthropic causes. For example, MasterCard collaborates yearly with Stand Up to Cancer (SU2C) in the United States, Canada, and Russia, and invites cardholders to give back through the simple act of dining out. When cardholders spend $10 or more when dining out or ordering in and choose to pay with their MasterCard, the company makes a 1-cent donation to SU2C.[86] MasterCard also hosts Priceless Tables across the country. For each Priceless Table purchased by MasterCard cardholders, MasterCard donates 100 percent of the ticket price to SU2C to support cancer research programs.[87] During its first five years running, MasterCard raised more than $30 million for Stand Up for Cancer in the United States, Russia, and Canada.[88]

Finally, the "Priceless Specials" campaign rewards cardholders with discounts, extras, and freebies such as the ability to jump the queue at exclusive restaurants in Brazil if they use their cards in-store.[89]

In a shaky economy, when most competitors focus on deals and discounts, the MasterCard campaign attracts attention by appealing to emotions rather than wallets and stressing unforgettable experiences rather than cost savings. The campaign forges an additional bond with card users, because it places MasterCard at the centre of these memorable social activities.

The ads run in more than 112 countries and air in more than 53 languages[90] and the overall campaign uses print, radio, transit, outdoor advertising, and television. It also includes digital platforms to drive home its message, including a new section of the MasterCard website created specifically for the campaign, as well as social media channels such as Facebook and Twitter.

Marketers must continuously evaluate their campaigns and update them to ensure they are effectively communicating with their customers. New channels like social marketing can change shopping behaviours, creating opportunities that must be considered as part of any marketing strategy. And so, MasterCard regularly tests the strength of its "Priceless" campaign.[91] Doing so has allowed it to move from simply observing priceless moments to actually enabling experiences that matter to consumers. MasterCard knows that even the best ideas need new infusions and innovations to keep appealing to their targets.

## Questions

1. Why was the original "Priceless" campaign such a success?

2. Why has MasterCard started to use "Priceless" more actively in its messaging?

# CHAPTER 16

© VCG/Getty Images

# Social and Mobile Marketing

Social media have revolutionized how companies communicate with, listen to, and learn from customers. The influence is far-reaching, whether firms are selling online or in stores, providing services or products, or dealing primarily with consumers or business customers. Modern listening and analysis tools allow firms to identify salient, pertinent trends and customer input through social media.

For example, Under Armour's carefully designed social media plan enables it to connect effectively with customers, control buzz, and respond to trends as they arise. Largely through its stellar social media use, applied in combination with and parallel to various other marketing tactics, Under Armour has overtaken Adidas and moved into second place in the sportswear market.[1]

Some elements of Under Armour's basic marketing strategy, such as leveraging the popularity and authenticity of famous athletic spokespersons, also constitute key aspects of its social media strategy.[2] Under Armour might have almost a million Twitter followers,[3] but the athletes it sponsors have far more. Stephen Curry, for example, has 8.6 million followers.[4] As part of the NBA phenom's partnership with Under Armour, in his Twitter profile and cover pictures, Curry sports Under Armour gear. In parallel, Under Armour's Twitter cover picture prominently features Curry.[5]

Curry's profile also includes Under Armour's current slogan, #IWILL.[6] The brand constantly seeks to develop and spread encouraging and inspiring taglines, including "I Will," in its marketing communication.[7] Its Facebook page contains little explicit advertising. Instead, the brand posts inspirational quotes, videos, and graphics in an attempt to engage customers with its product and brand.[8] In contrast, Nike, the top brand in the market, uses its Facebook page primarily to promote its latest products.[9] On YouTube, Under Armour offers easy access to some of its most famous commercials, including the "I Will What I Want" and "Rule Yourself" campaigns. The channel also includes a series of interviews with top athletes. Such inspirational approaches in turn inform the multiple, specific social media accounts that Under Armour develops for various target markets. For example, different Twitter accounts highlight Under Armour's links to basketball, baseball, football, and running.

Inspiring storylines and exciting brand images are clearly important, but success on social media also demands the ability to respond actively and promptly to customers' comments. In this sense, Under Armour again achieves notable advantages because it takes this aspect seriously. Designated Twitter handle @AskTeamUA connects customers directly with customer service representatives.[10] Customers expect responses from brands on Twitter, especially if they tweet a complaint.[11] Under Armour's ability to respond to both negative and positive feedback, often within an hour, is fundamental to the success of its social media presence.

When consumers search for Under Armour on popular search engines, they usually see a page of company-sponsored results. The brand has done the preliminary work, through search engine optimization and brand-building, to control most of the brand-related content people see online. Even if an uncontrolled story pops up (e.g., when Nike spokesperson LeBron James mockingly asked "Who's that?" in response to a reporter's question about Under Armour), the brand's own communications dominate the first page of results.[12] No company can prevent negative comments completely, but Under Armour has managed to ensure that most of them are hidden under a wave of positive, company-approved messages. ∎

## LO1  THE 4E FRAMEWORK FOR SOCIAL MEDIA

As we have seen throughout the book, social media has become an integral component of any integrated marketing communications strategy. The term *social media* refers to content distributed through online and mobile technologies to facilitate interpersonal interactions. These media utilize various firms that offer services or tools to help consumers and firms build connections. Through these connections, marketers and customers share information of all forms—from their thoughts about products or images to uploaded pictures, music, and videos.

The changes and advances in social, mobile, and online technologies have created a perfect storm, forcing firms to change how they communicate with their customers.

| **EXHIBIT 16.1** | The 4E Framework for Social Media |

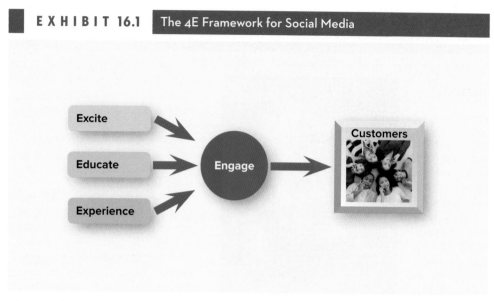

© Jose Luis Pelaez Inc/Blend Images LLC

Traditional ways to market their products—using brick-and-mortar stores, traditional mass media (e.g., print, television, radio), and other sales promotional vehicles (e.g., mail, telemarketing)—are no longer sufficient for many firms. The presence of social, mobile, and online marketing is steadily expanding relative to these more traditional forms of integrated marketing communication (IMC).

The changing role of traditional media, sales promotions, and retail, coupled with the new media of social, mobile, and online, has led to a different way of thinking about the objectives of marketing communications using the 4E framework (see Exhibit 16.1):

- Excite customers with relevant offers.

- Educate them about the offering.

- Help them Experience products, whether directly or indirectly.

- Give them an opportunity to Engage with their social network.

## Excite the Customer

Marketers use many kinds of social media–related offers to excite customers, including mobile applications and games to get customers excited about an idea, product, brand, or company. Firms actively use social networks like Facebook, Twitter, and Pinterest to communicate deals that are likely to excite consumers, such as a Groupon price promotion that is disseminated through the social networks of already interested consumers.

Social and Mobile Marketing 16.1 recounts how Jimmy Fallon got viewers more excited and engaged with his talk show by leveraging the power of social media.

To excite customers, an offer must be relevant to its targeted customer. Relevancy can be achieved by providing personalized offers, which are determined through insights and information obtained from customer relationship management and/or loyalty programs. To obtain these insights and information, the firm might use online analytic tools such as Google analytics or a listening system such as those provided by Salesforce.com through its Radian6 platform.

To drive awareness about serious developing world problems, non-profit Water Is Life launched a "Hashtag Killer" campaign in which it took aim at the #firstworldproblems

## Social and Mobile Marketing 16.1

# Late Night Laughs to Order[13]

Social media appear to have brought us full circle. In the early days of television, nearly all the advertisements were live. Then taping became the main method. But as recent technologies have made it easy for viewers to speed past or completely skip the advertising messages, some marketers are revisiting the idea of live advertising. This isn't the same old notion, though. By recombining an idea from broadcast media with new functionalities enabled by social media, marketers seek to ensure that viewers are not only interested in the new content but even might determine it.

A Lexus-sponsored program, "It's Your Move After Dark," ran on *Late Night With Jimmy Fallon* over the course of four weeks. During the first commercial break on each Thursday's show, a Lexus advertisement prominently displayed a hashtag. By linking to it, viewers could submit their ideas for commercials. Then in a later advertising break during the same show, an improvisational comedy troupe acted out the chosen ideas. The acting troupes—Fun Young Guys, Magnet Theater Touring Company, MB's Dream, and Stone Cold Fox—were all from New York, and well known for their comedy. In actuality, their performances took place under the Brooklyn Bridge, adding to the vibrancy and reality of the setting.

To appeal to the widest audience of Fallon fans possible, separate advertisements were chosen and enacted for the East and West Coast broadcasts. The submissions came through a wide variety of media channels, including Facebook, Twitter, and Tumblr. Such ready access,

Jimmy Fallon asked viewers to submit ideas for Lexus commercials via Twitter and see an improvised version later on the show.

© NBC, Lloyd Bishop/AP Images

real-time interactivity, and potential influence—together with the promise of funny, totally new advertising content and perhaps even a live, on-air goof—enticed Fallon's youthful, edgy audience to want to tune in to the commercials as much as they did to the show.

The advertisements are not the only way Fallon has relied on social media to connect with his audience, of course. He has over 42 million Twitter followers, and on a regular basis he challenges them to post the funniest, silliest, or craziest responses to topics he provides, such as "#howigwotfired," "#whydontthey makethat," and "#awkwarddate." The best contributions are highlighted on Fallon's Twitter feed but also might make it onto the network broadcast, as he reads out his favourite bits. That is, the consumers of his content also provide some of that content.

On the flip side, content from the traditional television channel constantly makes it onto social media sites. Excerpts from Fallon's shows are some of the most popular YouTube videos, including a skit in which President Barack Obama "slow jams" the news, a lip-sync battle with Seth Rogen, a sing-along with Carly Rae Jepsen and the Roots of "Call Me Maybe" using found materials as instruments, and of course, any skits featuring his pal Justin Timberlake.

When Fallon moved from *Late Night* to the *Tonight Show*, he promised that such tactics and antics would continue. Keeping his viewers excited and willing to contribute and engage with him makes his social media dominance likely to persist, regardless of what time he appears on people's televisions.

Water Is Life's "Hashtag Killer" campaign posted videos on YouTube of Haitians reading and responding to tweets to excite individuals to donate to its cause.

Courtesy WATERisLIFE

hashtag and Twitter meme. It began by creating a video on YouTube in which Haitians read tweets that had been tagged as #firstworldproblems. For example, a child sitting on a mound of dirt said, "I hate when my leather seats aren't heated." Amazingly, Haitians engaged with the campaign and offered consolation to people with tweets such as, "I'm sorry your leather seats weren't heated ... I hope your day gets better!" The campaign was a remarkable success—individuals donated over 1 million days of clean water.

In some cases location-based software and applications help bring the offer to the customers when they are in the process of making a purchase decision. For instance, Staples may provide a loyal customer with a relevant coupon based on previous purchases through his or her mobile phone, while he or she is in the store—a very relevant and, it is hoped, exciting experience.

## Educate the Customer

An imperative of well designed social media marketing offers is that they have a clear call to action: To draw customers through their computers, tablets, and mobile devices into online websites or traditional retail stores. When potential customers arrive at the websites or stores, the marketer has a golden opportunity to educate them about its value proposition and communicate the offered benefits. Some of this information may be new, but in some cases, education is all about reminding people about what they already know. Therefore, by engaging in appropriate education, marketers are expanding the overlap of the benefits that they provide with the benefits that customers require. In this sense, the second E of the 4E framework constitutes a method to develop a sustainable competitive advantage.

Staples excites its customers by giving them instant rewards through their mobile phones while they are in the store.

Courtesy Staples, Inc.

Several social media tools are critical in helping marketers educate their potential customers, such as blogs and blogging tools (e.g., WordPress and Twitter), HubSpot (all-in-one marketing software), and YouTube, as well as lesser-known options, such as Schedulicity.

## Experience the Product or Service

Although most of the top videos on YouTube are funny, silly, or otherwise entertaining, the site's most useful contribution may be the vivid information it provides about a firm's goods and services—how they work, how to use them, and where they can be obtained. YouTube and similar sites can come relatively close to simulating real experiences. Such benefits are very common for products that have long been sold online—so much so that we might forget that it used to be difficult to assess these products before buying them. But today, consumers can download a chapter of a new book onto their tablet before buying it. They can try out a software option for a month before buying it. They often view tutorials on everything from how to purchase caviar to what to look for in cowboy boots. Being able to experience a product before buying it has expanded the market significantly.

For other offerings, such as services, social media again offer experience-based information that was not previously available unless consumers bought and tried the product or service. Home Depot has long been a source for do-it-yourselfers (DIYers). But if eager customers forget what the salesclerk said about installing a newly purchased water heater, they can check the retailer's website (http://www.homedepot.com/c/diy _projects_and_ideas) to get detailed, in-depth instructions. They also will find a section that enables them to chat with other users who might have run into similar problems in their own installation projects.

Sephora has perfected the art of customer service in-store, online, and in social media. Customers know they can find beauty advice and makeovers in Sephora stores. But they

Sephora maintains its own YouTube channel with dedicated videos that encourage customers to experience specific product lines, such as the "Kat Von D playlist."

© Steve Jennings/Getty Images

can also visit Sephora.com for information. The advice section contains nearly 1 million conversations among Sephora customers, and to facilitate these conversational experiences, Sephora suggests a featured topic each week, asking contributors to indicate their favourite eyebrow products, for example. The how-to section contains video tutorials by customers who offer testimonials about their experiences, as well as by beauty professionals who describe how viewers can achieve similar experiences with their hair, nail, makeup, and skincare beauty tools.[14] For customers seeking an experience in other settings, Sephora also maintains its own YouTube channel featuring not only all the tutorial videos but also dedicated videos that encourage them to experience specific product lines, such as the "Kat Von D playlist."[15]

### Engage the Customer

In a sense, the first three Es set the stage for the last one: engaging the customer. With engagement comes action, the potential for a relationship, and possibly even loyalty and commitment. Through social media tools such as blogging and microblogging, customers actively engage with firms and their own social networks. Such engagement can be negative or positive. Positively engaged consumers tend to be more profitable consumers, purchasing 20–40 percent more than less engaged customers.[16]

But negative engagement has the potential to be even more damaging than positive engagement is beneficial. In the aftermath of Hurricane Sandy, for example, The Gap and American Apparel each sought to promote online sales. American Apparel sent out an email blast to customers on the East Coast, promising 20 percent off all online purchases, "in case you're bored during the storm." The Gap instead relied on Twitter, posting the notice, "Stay safe! We'll be doing lots of Gap.com shopping today. How about you?" In both cases, consumers reacted angrily and rapidly. On Twitter, thousands of them complained that the promotions exhibited "tackiness" and a lack of consideration for the very real threat facing people affected by the storm. The story also made it into mainstream media, prompting the retailers to issue apologies and explanations.[17] When McDonald's launched a Twitter campaign to highlight its supply chain, using the hashtag #McDstories, the vagueness of the hashtag allowed consumers to move the conversation in a very different direction, sharing horror stories about their negative experiences eating at the fast food chain.[18]

Next, let's look at the role of various social media tools in shaping the 4E framework for social media.

## L02    CATEGORIES OF SOCIAL MEDIA

Consider your own Facebook account. Are all your real-life friends your online friends too? Do you actually know all your Facebook friends? In all likelihood, you have online friends you've never met, and your circle of virtual friends may be larger than the number of people you see regularly or talk to personally. Accordingly, the audience for marketers is bigger on social media sites than through other, more traditional forms of media. Such a huge potential audience has captured the attention of marketers. Spending on social media continues to rise. Global spending on paid social advertising is projected to

**EXHIBIT 16.2**   Types of Social Media

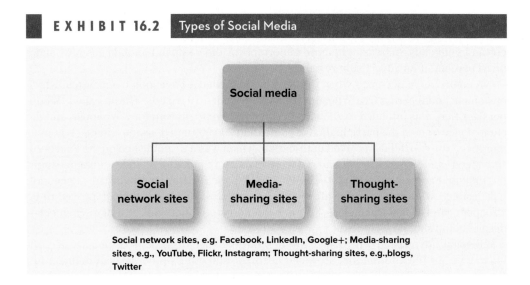

Social network sites, e.g. Facebook, LinkedIn, Google+; Media-sharing sites, e.g., YouTube, Flickr, Instagram; Thought-sharing sites, e.g.,blogs, Twitter

increase by 26.3 percent to almost $36 billion in 2017, while spending in the United States is expected to reach over $17 billion by 2019.[19]

Marketers rely on the three types of social media: social network sites, media-sharing sites, and thought-sharing sites (or blogs) (see Exhibit 16.2) to achieve three objectives. First, members promote themselves to gain more friends. Second, the sites promote themselves to get more members. Third, outside companies promote their products and services to appeal to the potential consumers that are active on the sites.

## Social Network Sites

Social network sites are an excellent way for marketers to create excitement, the first of the four Es. People can interact with friends (e.g., Facebook, Snapchat) or business acquaintances (e.g., LinkedIn). Although the amount of time people spend on such sites varies, research indicates that they are widely used, between one to four hours every day.

Facebook   On this well known social network platform, more than 1.6 billion active users give companies a forum for interacting with their fans. In Canada, over 21 million people log on to Facebook at least once a month and 14 million people check their account daily. Of these users, 18 million use a phone or tablet to access their accounts.[20] In fact, Canadians have higher daily Facebook usage at 71 percent than the global daily average.[21] This fact not only lets individual users connect with others but also gives marketers the ability to carefully target their audience.

Companies have access to the same features that regular users do, including a "wall" where they can post company updates, photos, and videos or participate in a discussion board. Through this form of free exposure, the company can post content and information regarding products, events, news, or promotions that might be exciting to customers. Only the followers of its page generally have access to such information, so the company can specifically target its fans. Successful companies on Facebook attempt to excite their customers regularly. When a fan indicates that he or she "likes" a certain post—for example, on the fan page for the discount clothing retailer Forever 21[22]—the message gets relayed to a news feed. Then every friend of that user sees what he or she likes, creating an exciting and huge multiplier effect.[23] Imagine the multiplier effect for Coca-Cola with over 98 million followers on its fan page!

In an attempt to extend the viral reach of posts, Facebook added the use of hashtags in late 2013. However, early studies show that hashtags actually reduce reach and engagement.[24] Trending topics were added in 2014 in an attempt to turn Facebook into more of a news discovery platform. Later Facebook added an "autoplay" feature on videos and video ads. Increasingly more important for the company, mobile ads now make up 84 percent of its advertising revenues.[25]

A controversy occurred when Burger King launched a Facebook campaign in which customers could earn a free Whopper if they defriended 10 friends. The so-called "Whopper Sacrifice" was intended to show what someone would give up for a Whopper, and the campaign attracted the participation of more than 200,000 active users. After a "Whopper Sacrifice," the ex-friends received notification, which was also published on the Facebook "mini-feed" and thus helped spread the word even more quickly. As the campaign caught on, though, Facebook disabled it. The Facebook page for Burger King read: "Facebook has disabled Whopper Sacrifice after your love for the Whopper sandwich proved to be stronger than 233,906 friendships." Burger King created a notable form of excitement— despite being shut down quickly.[26]

Display advertising with Facebook ads targets specific groups of people, according to their profile information, browsing histories, and other preferences. If online users reveal an interest in ski equipment or Burton snowboards, marketers can target both groups. Facebook offers a variation on more traditional forms of promotion, with the promise of more accurate targeting and segmentation. But being effective and relevant on Facebook is not simply a matter of shifting an offline ad into social network sites.

**Snapchat** Snapchat—the ephemeral picture-sharing and chat app—has reached 150 million daily users, surpassing Twitter in only four years of operation.[27] Snapchat has grown quickly, supported by its popularity among youth. On any given day, the app is used by 41 percent of consumers aged 18–34 in the United States.[28] Snapchat has made communicating into more of a game by letting people send selfies and short videos. It has allowed people to use filters to swap faces in a photo, transform themselves into puppies, and distort users' faces in silly ways.

Brands are just beginning to experiment with the marketing capabilities of Snapchat, using features like Discover, Live Stories advertisements, geofilters, and sponsored Lenses to engage with their target markets. For example, in celebration of Cinco de Mayo, Taco Bell launched a sponsored Lens that turned consumers' heads into giant taco shells, resulting in 224 million views in one day—a Snapchat record.[29] The average user engaged with Taco Bell's ad for 24 seconds before sharing it with friends. Taco Bell's marketing team has tracked the brand's Snapchat engagement, finding an average of 100,000 views per video with a completion rate of over 80 percent.[30]

Some brands are also creating Snapchat accounts and sharing content with their followers. Tiffany & Co. was the first luxury brand to do so. The jewellery brand has launched branded geofilters, which are live at all 93 of its stores across the United States, and is also investing in video ads as it builds its presence under the handle @Tiffanyofficial.[31] The goal is to attract Generation Y users (millennials born between 1977 and 1995) and Gen Z Snapchat users born in 1996 and after, who may not be Tiffany shoppers today but may aspire to be brand loyalists tomorrow.

LinkedIn is an excellent place to begin your search for a marketing job.

Courtesy of LinkedIn

**LinkedIn** A professional—instead of casual or friendship-based—site, LinkedIn allows users to share their professional lives. With more than 467 million users, it is a place where users can post their resumés, network with other professionals, and search for jobs.[32] It is not the place where you will see games such as Mafia Wars or FarmVille; instead, users post to question-and-answer forums, do job searches, and post personal intellectual property, such as presentations they have given.

The professional networking benefits of LinkedIn are particularly beneficial for small business owners. More than 12 million of LinkedIn's users are small business owners, making it an excellent resource for entrepreneurs to network with like-minded firms, identify the best vendors, or build brand reputation by participating in LinkedIn's professional association groups. With more than 7.2 million company pages on LinkedIn, it also offers a great place to prospect for new business customers, and keep an eye on and get key information about competitors.[33]

Google+   The company that defined search engines sought to compete in the social media realm with its launch of Google+. Although it has attracted hundreds of millions of users, most analysts suggest it is not an effective competitor to date. Even when users register, they do not engage closely with the site; Google+ accounted for a mere 2 percent of all social media shares.[34] In an apparent response to this lack of interest, Google recently sought to force closer engagement. For example, on YouTube, users must provide a Google+ account, as well as their real names, before they may post a comment. Rather than attracting more members, the move angered longtime active YouTube participants—so much so that more than 110,000 of them petitioned Google to rescind the requirement.[35] While many believe Google+ is no longer relevant, others feel it may be risky to ignore it completely since it offers functions other sites still do not.

## Media-Sharing Sites

The Internet has the ability to connect people more easily and in more ways than have ever been possible before. Media-sharing sites explicitly rely on this capability to enable users to share content they have generated, from videos on YouTube, Vimeo, and Vine to pictures on Flickr and Instagram. In terms of the 4E framework, companies use such sites to highlight how consumers can experience their goods or services, as well as to encourage consumers to engage with the firm, its other social media outlets, and other consumers.

Marketers are increasingly investing in online video. According to eMarketer research, by 2019 Canadian advertisers will spend 8.2 percent of their $6.04 billion digital ad spend on video.[36] Taulia uses video to increase qualified leads for its cloud invoicing and supplier financing offerings. Working with the world's leading video marketing platform, Vidyard in Kitchener, Ontario, Taulia discovered that "it's easier to get people to press play and watch a minute long video" than it is to convince them to download a white paper.[37] Knowing it would be difficult to make one video suited for everyone, Taulia creates separate videos to appeal to each audience it serves. By narrowcasting humorous videos that target the company's audience types and buying personas, it gets better sales results. Testing shows that 79 percent of its viewers watched one video in its entirety. That's a key point. According to Unruly, viewer enjoyment increases purchase intent by 97 percent.[38] Video helps leverage social capital to build brand identity and relationships.[39] And, according to a study done by Twitter, adding video boosts retweet rates by 28 percent.[40]

Because video and social media are a perfect match, Vidyard has a solution that meshes them. Most companies don't know what to do with all their videos, which can get lost in a black hole when hosted on YouTube or Vimeo.[41] Through a Vidyard app, users can put their entire video library on the HootSuite dashboard and add video to any social post directly from HootSuite. Measurement of video performance can track metrics such as number of views, click-through rates, attention spans, and shares on social media sites. Being able to see how much of the video was watched and when/if it was stopped helps to determine what content is striking a chord with viewers. And the inherent trackability shows marketers whether a video posted to Facebook is engaging consumers more effectively than on Twitter or other social media platforms.

While video is a natural fit for social media, companies can use it to enhance customer service, too. By monitoring social media, companies may see tweets from customers who can't figure out how to use a product. Companies could respond and include a video that helps customers better understand how the product functions.

**YouTube**    On this video-sharing social media platform, users upload, share, and view videos. This medium gives companies a chance to express themselves in a different way than they have in the past. YouTube videos also show up in Google searches, making YouTube an appealing vehicle for retailers.[42] The site's demographics indicate visitors are affluent, of the age range most appealing to retailers, and racially reflective of the wider population.[43]

YouTube also provides an effective medium for hosting contests and posting instructional videos. The Home Depot attracts more than 4,400 viewers with an array of videos detailing new products available in stores, as well as instructional do-it-yourself videos, like "How-to Tips for Mowing Your Lawn" or "How to Repair a Toilet."[44] These videos maintain the core identity of the Home Depot brand while also adding value for consumers, who learn useful ways to improve their homes. As a good example of IMC, Home Depot reinforces its brand image and makes itself more relevant to the consumer's life.

Companies can broadcast from their own channel, that is, a YouTube site that contains content relevant only to the company's own products.[45] For example, Home Shopping Network (HSN) offers consumers an interesting vehicle to utilize the 4E framework—excite, educate, experience, and engage—using a multi-channel strategy with its television channel as its central focus. As competition in this field has increased, HSN has added to its communication arsenal an ecommerce site, and Facebook, Instagram, Twitter, and Pinterest, which are all integrated across each platform and into the live TV segment. But perhaps the most powerful tool it has added is its dedicated YouTube channel, which it exploits to reach target shoppers in an exciting way that maximizes the value of its media content. Products promoted on HSN are available on YouTube almost immediately after they appear on television. Then HSN marketers can use the information gathered from YouTube to target direct mail campaigns. For example, HSN could send jewellery promotions to households that viewed the YouTube video clip for a necklace. Consumer responses are monitored 24/7 and measured against hourly sales goals.

One company went to great heights, perhaps straying into ethical grey areas, in the hopes of having people watch its videos and associate it with its brands, as discussed in Ethical Dilemma 16.1.

**Instagram**    More than 500 million people have downloaded the Instagram app and can take photos of themselves or their surroundings.[52] The app enables them to add fun filters, such as causing the picture to look as if it were taken by an old Polaroid camera. Then they can upload the artistic creation to various social networking sites, including Twitter, Tumblr, and Facebook.

The name of this app evokes the founders' idea of its use: a sort of modern-day, immediate telegram.[53] It was effective enough that it attracted the attention of some of the most famous names in media sharing, including Justin Bieber, Kim Kardashian, and Tony Hawk—which increased its popularity even more. Recognizing the value of a mobile option, Facebook purchased Instagram in 2012. For the first time, the social media giant promised not to absorb its purchase, but to allow Instagram to continue functioning much as it had been all along.[54]

Instagram later added video-sharing capabilities as well, though another app had beaten it to that punch. Vine, which was purchased by Twitter in 2012, lets users capture and share six-second videos. Advertisers already have embraced this option, finding that

## Ethical Dilemma 16.1

## Daredevil Stunts Not for the Faint of Heart

For most people, jumping from a plane with no parachute is something that only happens in nightmares. For others, it is a test of skill, preparation, and guts—and something Luke Aikins took on for the #StrideHeavenSent campaign.

On Saturday, July 30, 2016, 42-year-old professional skydiver Luke Aikins became the first person to safely land after skydiving without a parachute. He jumped out of an airplane at an altitude of 25,000 feet, landing on a net just above ground. This stunt was set in motion by Stride as part of its #StrideHeavenSent campaign, and perfectly embodied Stride Gum's brand image of "mad intense experiences" targeting teens.[46]

A dedicated Tumblr page at http://strideheavensent .tumblr.com/ was also set up, and Stride's spokescharacter, The Mouth, live-tweeted the event from the @StrideGum account using the hashtag #StrideHeavenSent. The brand also set up exclusive, behind-the-scenes interviews on Facebook Live and Aikins also posted about the stunt on his personal social media accounts.[47] The jump has generated more than 500 million impressions internationally and 700 press mentions.[48]

This stunt is one of the first projects in Mondelēz International's new content strategy, which includes a marketing deal with Fox to create content that cuts through advertising clutter and isn't ad-blocked.[49]

According to Laura Henderson, Mondelēz International's global head of content and media monetization, programs and partnerships like this one help marketers overcome consumers' tendency to avoid ads at all costs by creating content that people actually want to watch.[50] She says it represents the future of how brands will engage with audiences. Building quality, stand-alone entertainment that will earn attention is a key component of their new marketing strategy. Still, Mondelēz was criticized by consumers for making the live event pay-per-view. Even with the low fee of $1.99, comments on

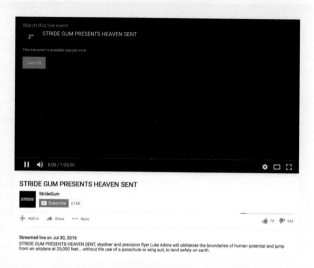

Some consumers were upset when Mondelēz made its #StrideHeavenSent video pay-per-view.

© Google

YouTube noted out that the company was asking people to pay to "watch an ad."

Aikins survived his skydive. But what if the daredevil stunt had failed? While Felix Baumgartner survived his Red Bull Stratos jump, Karl Wallenda plunged to his death during a high wire act between hotels in Puerto Rico. Evel Knievel crashed his rocket-powered motorcycle while trying to cross Utah's Snake River Canyon. And in a twilight wingsuit BASE jump from Taft Point in Yosemite National Park, Dean Potter and Graham Hunt both lost their lives.[51] Unlike Aikins, Wallenda and Knievel had no sponsors. Potter did have corporate sponsorship, however, Patagonia and Clif Bars withdrew it long before his fatal last jump, saying he took risks that made them uncomfortable.

Death defying stunts beg the question as to how far companies will go to get publicity for their products. Is it ethical to sponsor potentially fatal events to raise your brand's profile?

the short time limit appeals to consumers. People are ready to share a quick video, far more so than a longer commercial, which enhances the chances of a Vine marketing campaign going viral.[55]

**Flickr and Other Photo Sites**   Whereas YouTube allows users to share videos, Flickr, TwitPic, Photobucket, and Instagram allow them to share photos. They tend to be less popular as marketing tools, yet some innovative companies have found ways to engage with customers. The U.K. brand Innocent, known for selling pure 100 percent fruit smoothies, uses Flickr to communicate its quirky brand image. Its photo posting competitions, such as the Funny Shaped Fruit Competition (http://www.flickr.com/groups /funnyshapedfruit/), provide significant entertainment value. But it also uses Flickr for

Innocent uses Flickr to post photos for its Big Knit charity promotion.

© John Boud/Alamy Stock Photo

more serious purposes, such as to post photos related to its Big Knit charity promotion, which provides knitted hats and funding to help keep older residents of the United Kingdom warm during cold winter months.[56]

## Thought-Sharing Sites

Thought-sharing sites consist of different types of blogs: corporate, professional, personal, and micro. In terms of the 4E framework, blogs are particularly effective at educating and engaging users, and in many cases enhance their experience with the products and services being discussed.

Blogs   Once confined to a journal or diary in a person's room, the blog (shortened from "web log") on the Internet has allowed us to air our thoughts to the world through thought-sharing websites. For corporations, the comment section allows marketing managers to create a two-way dialogue directly with the end users. The wide availability of free blogging tools such as WordPress, Blogger, and TypePad, which enable non-technically oriented people to create their own blogs, has made blogging a very popular pastime. In 2016 there were 305.9 Tumblr blogs and 76.5 million Word Press blogs alone.[57]

Companies have responded to this interest and now have several ways to include blogging in their social media marketing strategy. Blogs provide firms with the opportunity to educate their customers about their offerings, and to engage them by responding to their communications, both positive and negative. The reach that marketers have to their customers from blogs can be categorized by the level of control they offer. Corporate blogs, which are created by the companies themselves, have the highest level of control, because to a large degree, they can control the content posted on them. Of course, blogs also allow customers to respond to posts, so the content can never be completely controlled, but marketing managers have a good opportunity to pepper their blogs with the messages they wish their customers to see. The best corporate blogs illustrate the importance of engaging customers around the core brand tenets without being overly concerned with a hard sell.

Starbucks (http://mystarbucksidea.force.com) uses its blog for new product development by generating new product and *experience* ideas from its customers. General Electric (http://www.gereports.com) *educates* customers through its blog by telling entertaining stories geared at getting customers to realize it sells more than just light bulbs.[58]

From a marketing perspective, professional blogs are those written by people who review and give recommendations on products and services. Marketers often offer free products or provide modest remuneration to top-rated professional bloggers, in the hopes of getting a good product review. Marketers have less control over professional bloggers than they do their own corporate blogs. But consumers seem to trust professional bloggers' reviews much more than corporate blogs and other more traditional media, like advertising. Such trust may be fleeting, however, as more consumers realize that professional bloggers are often compensated for positive reviews. "Mommy Blogs," a particularly popular type of professional blog, feature advice and product recommendations from one mother to many others.

Finally, personal blogs are written by people who receive no products or remuneration for their efforts. Thus, of the various types of blogs, marketers have the lowest level of control over this type. However, personal blogs are useful for monitoring what is going on in the marketplace and for responding to customer complaints or compliments.

**Microblogs** As the name implies, a microblog differs from a traditional blog in size—short sentences, short videos, or individual images. On the most popular micro-blogging site, Twitter, users are limited to 140-character messages. Twitter provides another option for companies to educate their customers by providing corporate and product information, and to engage them by providing a platform for two-way communications. Even companies that may have once resisted social media have realized that Twitter is an important communications channel. However, growth in new users has slowed and is projected to increase at only 2 percent by 2020. Growth is virtually stagnant in the 12–17 year range according to eMarketer.com.[59]

As much as Twitter can help build a firm's brand image though, it can also tarnish it instantly. Firms have to watch out for hacked Twitter accounts or ill-considered tweets. And Twitter can also act as an international, rapidly spread complaint forum. Companies also need to consider the frequency of their tweets since overcommunication

Justin Bieber has relied on social media to reach his target audience.

Debby Wong/Shutterstock.com

can have negative effects on a brand. A central problem for companies is ownership of relevant Twitter handles and responsibility for outgoing Twitter communication. If Twitter control is shared by a lot of people, the message usually gets muddled. But if only one or two people are in charge, the need to respond to the vast number of incoming tweets might become overwhelming. Different companies thus manage their Twitter strategies in various ways.

Whole Foods tries to develop a broader engagement with customers by interacting with its 4.83 million Twitter followers. It instituted a weekly Twitter chat, for an hour every Thursday, during which Whole Foods representatives discuss topics such as holiday menu planning and healthy eating. Many Whole Foods stores also have their own Twitter accounts to answer questions directly related to their stores.

In contrast, Best Buy hires an army of specialists to manage its Twitter accounts: not just the main account @Best Buy, but also @BestBuy_Deals, @GeekSquad, and @BestBuyNews. The specialists who work Best Buy's help desk also will answer questions through Twitter, at @Twelpforce. Users who tweet the help desk receive an almost instant response from one of Best Buy's 3,000 employees who have signed up to participate on

The use of social media by astronaut Chris Hadfield made him a celebrity in space.

the task force, which further helps showcase the broad spectrum of expertise available through Best Buy.[60]

For small companies with limited marketing budgets, the use of tweeted promotional messages is particularly appealing. A local bakery tweeted, "Two new scones: Lemon Blueberry and Chorizo Cheddar!" and received responses from 400 Twitter followers—a huge captive audience for a local entity.

Of course, some of the most famous Twitter users are celebrities, who have their own brands to manage and marketing goals to reach. Teen idol Justin Bieber and his management team have relied on Twitter and other social media to reach his target audience. Social media turned astronaut Chris Hadfield into a celebrity. Many Canadians got to know him through his regular Twitter posts and the photos he took from space while on a space exploration mission. He shared videos of creating meals in space, doing experiments with water, and even singing the David Bowie hit song "Space Oddity" while playing his guitar. Hadfield also hosted a live Google+ Hangout from space and took part in an "Ask Me Anything" on Reddit.[61]

**paid media**
Media such as TV, print, radio, or display ads used to reach mass markets.

**owned media**
Media controlled by the advertiser, such as its website, Facebook fan page, or YouTube channel.

**earned media**
Media that results from word-of-mouth, buzz, or publicity.

## Paid, Owned, Earned Media

Marketers know that they must use a combination of media when implementing their IMC plans. As shown in Exhibit 16.3, they use **paid media** such as TV, print, radio, or display ads to reach mass markets. Paid media is created and controlled by the advertiser. **Owned media**, such as a website, is also controlled by the advertiser. Other forms of owned media include a company's blog, YouTube channel, or Facebook fan page. While there are costs associated with these media, they are less expensive than paid media. Lastly, **earned media** comes as a result of word-of-mouth, buzz, or publicity. Customers, the public, or the press become the media channel. Brand mentions are given voluntarily by customers, the public, or the press, and so the company "earns" the visibility.

---

**EXHIBIT 16.3** | Paid, Owned, Earned Media

**PAID**

**Definition:** Use of paid advertising channels to deliver a brand's message and/or drive traffic to owned or controlled properties.

**Role:** Create awareness, drive traffic and jumpstart owned, earned, and shared and efforts.

**Tactics:** Engagement ads, display, ads, email, TV, print, radio, OOH experiential, paid influencer outreach.

**OWNED**

**Definition:** Media, content, assets and community platforms partially or wholly owned and controlled by the brand.

**Role:** Platform to house robust brand content and create long-term relationships /engagement with customers.

**Tactics:** Pre-existing social properties, social links on website, email database.

**EARNED**

**Definition:** Unique brand presence on established channels gained through editorial influence other than advertising.

**Role:** Expand reach and credibility of the brand's message in trusted channels.

**Tactics:** Word-of-mouth, influencer outreach, blogs, social engagement.

Used wtih permission of IAB Canada.

# UNDERSTANDING MOBILE APPLICATIONS                    `L03`

Although most consumers use computers, 76 percent of the time they spend on social media is via their mobile phones.[62] Of the more than 100 million people who have smartphones in North America, approximately half make purchases on them. In this huge market, consumers generally are younger and wealthier than others who own older-model mobile phones (or none at all). For example, more than 50 percent of mobile retail consumers earn at least $75,000 annually. Not surprisingly, mobile ad spending is growing fast. By 2018, mobile spending was projected to reach more than $2 billion, representing one out of every four digital advertising dollars spent.[63]

Even though 92 percent of apps downloaded are free, nearly 156 billion apps were downloaded in 2015 generating revenues of US$41.1 billion. Mobile app downloads are expected to grow to 210 billion by 2020,[64] demonstrating that mobile marketing is significant and growing. Although a large number of people in every age group own smartphones, the highest ownership is for young adults and teens. And while smartphone apps are called "mobile," they aren't always used by people "on the go"—people spend 68 percent of their time using smartphone apps from their home![65]

According to the *Harvard Business Review*, apps meet seven primary needs: to find "me time," socialize, shop, accomplish, prepare, discover, and self-express. We will briefly discuss each of these needs, as well as popular apps that have been developed to attract customers with these needs. Finally, we discuss the four types of pricing models for apps: ad-supported, freemium, paid apps, and paid apps with in-app purchases.

Need for "Me Time"   Although we need to organize, accomplish, and socialize, we also need to have time set aside just for us—to be unproductive. The most popular need is all about entertainment and relaxation. Not surprisingly, people spend the most time each month seeking fun—about 46 percent of their smartphone time—by watching TV and movies, playing games, and reading.[66] Common apps for watching videos include Netflix, YouTube, and Hulu. For reading, there's Kindle for adults and storybook apps like Nighty Night HD for children. The most popular game on the planet (as of 2017) is Candy Crush Saga. With more than 500 million downloads, it is a match-three game similar to Bejeweled in which players have to match coloured candies in sets of three to complete different level objectives.

Need to Socialize   Consumers want to stay connected with their friends, and apps can help people achieve this goal. The average person spends about 19 percent of their smartphone time interacting with friends (and the rest of the world).[67] Although we are all familiar with Twitter and Facebook, a number of specialized apps to interact through different mediums exist as well. The app Vine allows users to share mini-movies on Twitter; Skype allows people to place video calls; Tumblr and Pinterest focus on image sharing; and Snapchat sends pictures and videos that are automatically deleted a few seconds after opening. In China, the social networking app Weixin (pronounced way-SHEEN) allows users to send videos, photos, messages, web links, status updates, and news; it has been released as WeChat in the United States. Weixin has had a faster adoption rate than either Facebook or Twitter, with more than 300 million users in only three years.[68]

With more than 500,000,000 downloads, Candy Crush Saga clearly fulfills for many people an important need for unproductive "me time."

© Gabriel Bouys/AFP/Getty Images

Need to Shop   Customers demand to be able to shop when and where they want. Shopping apps allow consumers not only to make purchases from a smartphone 24/7, but also to do many other tasks such as comparing prices and creating grocery lists. The average person spends about 12 percent of his or her smartphone time shopping.[69]

MyFitnessPal fulfills the common need to accomplish weight loss.

Courtesy of MyFitnessPal, Inc.

When out shopping, smartphone users no longer have to go from store to store, or to stop at home to go online and compare prices. A process called *showrooming* enables customers to scan a product in a store and instantly compare the prices online to see whether a better deal is available. Using the showrooming Amazon app, if the Amazon price is better, the customer can buy the product online with a single click. The grocery app Out of Milk has brought social to grocery lists; users can create a grocery (or any other type) list and sync it automatically with everyone else's devices in the same household. Out of bread? No need to call and ask someone to pick it up next time he or she is at the store; just put it in the app and it will appear in the grocery list.

**Need to Accomplish**   Consumers live busy lives and look to mobile apps to help them manage their activities and goals. On average, people spend about 11 percent of their smartphone time using apps to accomplish something, including managing finances, increasing overall health, and enhancing productivity.[70] Consumers trying to get in shape and live a healthy lifestyle can download MyFitnessPal, as more than 50 million people worldwide have done. It allows users to create a profile and track their daily exercise, create a food diary to track calories, and track weight loss. The app also adds a social component by enabling people to post their success at, for instance, keeping below a target calorie level. Additionally, the app can interact with a number of products, including FitBit, Jawbone UP, and iHealth Wireless Scales. For people seeking instead to accomplish a financial goal or create a budget, the Mint.com app allows customers to see all of their account balances and transactions across banks and credit cards in one convenient place.

**Need to Prepare**   As our lives get busier and faster paced, the need to keep organized and make quick decisions continues to grow. Apps meet this need by helping us prepare and plan. Users spend about 7 percent of their smartphone time using apps like calendars, trip planners, and flight trackers.[71] Kayak, a free app on all major platforms, provides a convenient way for people to plan trips. Kayak allows users to find flights, hotels, and rental cars and compare prices across hundreds of travel sites to find the best deals. Once the trip is booked, travellers can get up-to-the-minute information on flight statuses, and if there is a problem with a flight, the app has the phone numbers for all major airlines. Cloud-based file storage apps like Dropbox and Google Drive allow customers to store files in the cloud and access them from any device. Finally, Business Calendar helps people plan their day with an interactive calendar that integrates multiple calendars (e.g., Google Calendar, Outlook Calendar) and allows users to link an event to people in their contact list and put a daily agenda widget on their smartphone home screen.

**Need to Discover**   Apps also help fulfill our need for information, to know what's going on around us, and to open our minds to new ideas. This need is met through news and weather apps, on which people spend about 4 percent of their smartphone time.[72] One of the most popular apps for news and information is Flipboard, a unique app that produces a full-screen magazine aggregating a number of news and entertainment sources based on user-defined topics such as top stories, entertainment, local news, and business news. The app also adds a social component by allowing the reader to send stories to friends or post on Facebook. Speaking of Facebook, in early 2014 Facebook launched Paper, an app designed to compete directly with Flipboard. However the app was closed down in 2016 after failing to attract large audiences.[73]

**Need to Self-Express**   Finally, individuals have diverse interests and tastes and, as a result, have a need for apps that are tailored to their hobbies and passions. Surprisingly, the average person spends only about 1 percent of his or her smartphone time engaging in personal interests.[74] For the beginning astronomer, Google's SkyMap allows users to hold their smartphones up to the sky and, using GPS and compass data, the app shows them what they are looking at. Want to know how to use a badger brush while shaving? How about finding people who love balloon animals as much as you? TapaTalk aggregates tens of thousands of interest groups into a single app, making it easy to connect aficionados of just about any interest or hobby.

As you can see, apps can meet several needs at once. Sharing an interesting story with friends via Flipboard can meet the needs of discovery and socialization. When a person looks at the latest 4K TVs sold on Amazon just for fun, she can be meeting three needs—me time, discovery, and shopping. Consider the person who purchases Chinese food via GrubHub's app on her ride home; she's not only shopping, but also avoiding making dinner to get some extra me time. With this information in mind, apps (and advertising within those apps) can be designed and targeted in ways that better apply the four Es.

Not only does Flipboard aggregate all of the news important to you in one place, but its unique format gives the app the look and feel of a printed magazine.

© Alliance Images/Alamy Stock Photo

## App Pricing Models

A key decision for firms producing apps is what to charge for them. There are four basic ways of generating revenue from apps—ad-supported apps, freemium apps, paid apps, and paid apps with in-app purchases.

Ad-supported apps are free to download, but place ads on the screen when using the program to generate revenue. Although there are many of these types of apps, the majority of app revenue is generated from the remaining three pricing models, discussed next.

Freemium apps are apps that are free to download but include in-app purchases. In-app purchases are when a game or app prompts or allows customers to make small "micropurchases" to enhance an app or game. Common examples include extra lives, bonus maps, in-game currency, a subscription, and unique character unlocks. In Candy Crush Saga, you get five lives to play in the game. When you lose a life, it takes 30 minutes in real-life time to get that life back. If you're playing a particularly hard level and lose all your lives in minutes, you'll have to wait two and a half hours to play again. This is where in-app purchases come in. For just $0.99, you can get all five lives back immediately so you can keep playing.[75] Candy Crush Saga is estimated to earn the developer between $623,000 and $850,000 *a day* in revenue from in-app purchases.[76]

The remaining two pricing models are paid apps and paid apps with in-app purchases. Paid apps charge the customer an up-front price to download the app ($0.99 is the most common), but offer full functionality once downloaded. Similar to the freemium model, paid apps with in-app purchases require the consumer to pay initially to download the app and then offer the ability to buy additional functionality.

Which is the best pricing model? Time will tell, but it appears that freemium apps may be the winner. Free apps with in-app purchases make up the vast majority of revenue from Apple's App Store in 8 of 10 app categories. According to Distimo, a research firm specializing in the mobile app market, 71 percent of apps in Apple's App Store implement a freemium pricing model, and 92 percent of revenues from Apple's App Store and 98 percent from Google's Play App Store come from freemium pricing.[77]

In terms of the 4E framework, mobile marketing is particularly useful for creating excitement with consumers at the time of sale. Several applications have been developed to better market goods and services to these attractive consumers, as seen in Entrepreneurial Marketing 16.1. We briefly discuss a few other types: price check apps, fashion apps, and location apps.

# Entrepreneurial Marketing 16.1

## PumpedUp on Social Media[78]

"A personal trainer in your pocket" is how PumpUp initially pitched its mobile fitness app to consumers. Based out of the Velocity garage in the Communitech Hub in Kitchener, Ontario, PumpUp was founded in May 2012 by Garrett Gottlieb and Phil Jacobson.

Garrett noticed he was plateauing in his fitness workouts and decided to build an algorithm that emulated the brain of a personal trainer, creating high-quality, personalized workout routines. He designed *PumpUp: Workout Coach* for his own use and also for coaching friends who were just starting to work out. His background in computer science at the University of Waterloo and co-op work terms with BlackBerry, TribeHR, and other start-ups were key to getting started. But he lacked business and marketing skills, precisely what Phil Jacobson brought to the partnership. Phil graduated with a business degree from Wilfrid Laurier University and did co-op work terms with Unilever, PepsiCo, and ConAgra Foods.

PumpUp's app solves a problem most people have with fitness—incorporating it into your life is hard. Additionally, many people don't really know what they're doing when it comes to working out and lack the motivation to stay active. A whopping 80 percent of gym memberships go unused. Designed to fit busy lives, *PumpUp: Workout Coach* makes it easy for beginners and intermediates to get a personalized workout routine for home, the gym, or on the go. Users enter basic information (age, weight, sex, and workout goals) as well as the amount of time they want to spend working out. The app removes the guesswork from working out, provides a low-cost, personal training experience, and isn't tied to an expensive gym or trainer.

Officially launched on the iTunes App Store in January 2013, the app uses a "freemium" business model with a free and a pro (paid) version. Although there are over 13,000 health and fitness apps on iTunes, *PumpUp: Workout Coach* quickly ranked among the top three free apps.[79] Looking for investors, Gottlieb and Jacobson pitched on CBC's *Dragons' Den*. They didn't end up taking any of the offers made, however, the exposure resulted in more than 8,000 app downloads. Today over 6 million people have downloaded the app.[80]

As a start-up, its marketing budget was small so the company used social media to spread the word. Today its primary social media channels are on Instagram,

The community aspect of the PumpUp app helps find fitness buddies to cheer users on and keep them motivated.

Used with permission of PumpUp

Snapchat, Twitter, and Facebook, but it also has a presence on YouTube, Pinterest, and Tumblr. Over 220,000 followers on Instagram share information about the app and brand with their networks. The company's blog regularly highlights success stories from PumpUp users. These stories are also shared on social media channels.

Social Media Sites

- **Website:** pumpup.com
- **App Page:** itunes.apple.com/app/id573070442
- **Instagram:** instagram.com/pumpup
- **Snapchat:** @pumpup
- **Blog:** http://blog.pumpup.com
- **Facebook:** facebook.com/pumpupfitness
- **Twitter:** twitter.com/pumpup

Designed to fit busy lives, the app makes it easy for beginners and intermediates to get a personalized workout routine for at home, at the gym, or on the go. Since it was introduced, PumpUp has changed its focus from being a workout app to building a global community with which to share and achieve your health goals. Jacobson and Gottlieb recognized that when people share their progress with others, they are four times more likely to achieve their goals.[81] The evolution in focus led to a new tagline, "Become the best version of you." Today you can connect with millions of like-minded people from over 150 countries, all interested in health and fitness.[82]

The community aspect of the app helps you to find fitness buddies to cheer you on and keep you motivated, as well as to find role models ranging from Olympic athletes to personal trainers to nutritionists who provide workout advice and tips.[83]

Prior to the 2016 Olympic Summer Games in Rio de Janeiro, PumpUp reached out to athletes to take over their Snapchat channel for one day during the games. Michelle Williams on the women's 4x100m freestyle relay led the takeover, along with team members Penny Oleksiak, Taylor Ruck, Sandrine Mainville, and Chantal van Landeghem. The result was an authentic, behind-the-scenes look at where the Canadians trained, the Olympic Village, and what it was like to be in Rio, adding a very human aspect to the takeover. And best of all, the takeover reached countless Snapchat users at absolutely no cost, helping the company keep users pumped up about the fitness community to which they belong.

In the past two decades, marketers have developed websites and other methods to communicate information about and to sell their goods and services. Their quest for new ways to improve, integrate, and enhance these outcomes has resulted in a confluence of social, mobile, and online marketing. Exhibit 16.4 is a brief summary of how these forces and their manifestations align with our 4E framework. It highlights how social network and mobile applications and the associated relevant offers are ideal for stimulating excitement in the offers. In particular, mobile location-based apps are exciting because they provide customers with highly relevant offers when they are in close proximity to the retailer or service provider, or they can even be used to provide competitive offers. Media-sharing sites (e.g., YouTube and Flickr) are excellent social media tools that provide customers with visual experiences of other customers or professionals who are using these goods and services. They also provide customers with an opportunity to engage with the firms as well as their own social network by posting their own experiences (i.e., uploading videos), as well as sharing their thoughts (blogs and Twitter posts). Finally, thought-sharing sites, like blogs, are excellent for providing customer education.

**EXHIBIT 16.4** Firms' Use of Social and Mobile Tools From the 4E Lens

| | Excite | Educate | Experience | Engage |
|---|---|---|---|---|
| **Social networks** | ◈ ◈ | | | |
| **Media-sharing sites** | | | ◈ ◈ | ◈ ◈ |
| **Thought-sharing sites** | | ◈ ◈ | ◈ | ◈ ◈ |
| **Mobile applications** | ◈ ◈ | | | ◈ |

## L04 ENGAGING CUSTOMERS USING SOCIAL MEDIA

Now that we have an understanding of the various social and mobile media that are at the firm's disposal, it is important to determine how firms should go about engaging customers through social and mobile media. The three-stage process is to listen to what customers have to say, analyze the information available through various touchpoints, and finally implement social media tactics to excite customers.

### Listen

From a market research point of view, companies can learn a lot about their customers by listening to (and monitoring) what they say on their social networks, blogs, review sites, etc. Customers appear willing to provide their opinions about just about anything including their interests and purchases—both their own and those of their friends. Writing blogs and providing opinions via polls about such diverse topics as Botox treatments, ASICS running shoes, or a particular play run by an NFL team during the playoffs all constitute new ways in which customers communicate with one another—and with marketers who are paying attention.

**sentiment analysis**
An analysis of online content to determine favourability or unfavourability.

Marketers can analyze the content found on sites like Facebook, Twitter, online blogs, and reviews to assess the favourableness or unfavourableness of the sentiments, using a technique known as **sentiment analysis**. Sentiment analysis allows marketers to analyze data from these sources to collect consumer comments about companies and their products. The data are then analyzed to distill customer attitudes and preferences, including reactions to specific products and IMC campaigns. Scouring millions of sites with sentiment analysis techniques provides new insights into what consumers really think. Companies plugged into such real-time information and insights can become more nimble, allowing for numerous quick changes, such as in a product roll-out, a new advertising campaign, or a reaction to customer complaints.

There are several companies that specialize in monitoring social media. For example, Salesforce.com's Radian6 tool offers sentiment analysis to help its clients such as Aldo, Bombardier, Algonquin College, Telus, and Vidyard engage with their customers.[84] Using sentiment analysis techniques, it processes a constant stream of online consumer opinion from blogs, Facebook, and other networking sites, including 400 million tweets a day. The Salesforce.com tools for managing consumer sentiment data allow companies to identify opinion trends that might warrant an online corporate response. For instance, Salesforce.com may identify negative consumer sentiment and then provide services to help its client respond. Reacting to attitudes uncovered in sentiment analysis allows companies to counteract negative opinions, maybe influence those perceptions, and perhaps win customer loyalty.[85]

Salesforce.com's Radian6 website analyzes customer sentiment for its customers, which enables them to identify opinion trends that might warrant an online corporate response.

Courtesy Salesforce Radian6.

As an example of how a firm like Salesforce.com can help its clients engage with customers, consider Ottawa-based Algonquin College. Changing demographics mean that the number of high school graduates is steadily declining. That creates fierce competition among colleges and universities. Algonquin rolled out a new student recruitment program using Salesforce.com that let it automate student lead capture through its website and social media channels. It was able to perform segmentation analysis, send targeted communication, and track the results. According to Elizabeth Babiak, social media community officer, Salesforce.com allowed the college "to track our prospective students throughout the entire recruitment lifecycle."[86] The effort was highly successful. Lead generation increased by 23 percent, and the time to send fulfillment materials was reduced by over 50 percent. Productivity for the student recruiter has tripled. "What used to take weeks or months now takes minutes," says Doug Wotherspoon, vice-president of international and strategic priorities.[87]

## Analyze

Fortunately, the companies that help facilitate listening also provide analytic tools to assess what customers are saying about the firm and its competitors. Three main categories of analysis are used for understanding data collected from social media.[88]

First, it is important to determine the amount of traffic using their sites, visiting their blogs, or tweeting about them. Measures used for this purpose include **hits** (i.e., total requests for a page), visits to a particular site or page, unique visitors to the site, and **page views** (i.e., the number of times any page gets viewed by any visitor).

Second, while knowing how many people are using a firm's social media is important, it is even more critical to learn who those visitors are, what they are doing, and what engages and excites them. To analyze these factors, social media marketers uses such metrics as the **bounce rate**, which refers to the percentage of times a visitor leaves the site almost immediately, such as after viewing only one page. Analyzing which pages are the most frequent entry and exit locations provides direction on how to make a website more effective. In addition, following visitors' **click paths** shows how users proceed through the information—not unlike how grocery stores try to track the way shoppers move through their aisles. A firm can use this information to provide users with an easier navigation experience through the site so they can more quickly find what they are looking for. The data analysis can also reveal **conversion rates**, a measure that indicates what percentage of visitors or potential customers act as the marketer hopes, whether by clicking, buying, or donating. Click paths and conversion rates can also reveal what users might have wanted, but not found, on the site.

Third, some companies want to analyze data that comes from other sites, such as measuring where people have come from to get to the company's site. Did they search through Google or Amazon? Did they receive a referral from a friend? Which keywords did they use to find the firm? Firms can use **keyword analysis** to determine what keywords people use to search on the Internet for their products and services. With this information, they can refine their websites by using keywords on their site that their customers also use. Then they can assess the ROI of the investment made by improving the site. This would be done by calculating the incremental profit increase divided by the investment on the site improvement. For social media, it is more challenging to determine ROI than for more traditional IMC applications, because the revenue generated by social media is often not directly related to the expenditure. So, instead of traditional ROI measures, firms often examine questions like: Does having more Twitter followers correlate with having higher sales? Do Facebook fans of the company buy more than nonfans?[89]

These analyses require well trained marketing managers, marketing analytic software, and perhaps some help from consulting specialists (e.g., IBM, SAS, PricewaterhouseCoopers). But almost everyone seems to be turning to Google Analytics these days, because it offers a sophisticated, in-depth form of analysis, all for free. Google Analytics not only tracks the elements that are shown in Exhibit 16.5, but also is highly customizable.[90]

**hits**
The total number of requests for a web page.

**page views**
The number of times any web pages are viewed by visitors.

**bounce rate**
The percentage of times a visitor leaves a site almost immediately.

**click paths**
Show how users navigate through a site.

**conversion rates**
The percentage of visitors to a site who click, buy, or donate.

**keyword analysis**
Determines which keywords visitors to a site use to find it.

| EXHIBIT 16.5 | Analytics | |
| --- | --- | --- |
| **Type of Analytic** | **How It's Used** | **Competitors Offering Similar Analytics** |
| Content | Understand what's popular and what's not on a firm's website, including page load times and site navigation. | Adobe Catlyst, Clickstreamr, IBM Digital Analytics, Mtracking, VisiStat |
| Social | Track effectiveness of social media programs, including information on social media referred conversion rates, and engagement metrics. | Facebook Insights, Twitter Web Analytics, Webtrends |
| Mobile | Track website access from mobile devices, track which ads direct people to a firm's app, understand what mobile platform performs best. | Bango, Flurry, Localytics, Medialets, Webtrends |
| Conversion | Moving beyond page views and visitor counts, conversion analytics measures sales, downloads, video plays, or any other action important to a firm. | Clicktale, KeyMetric, Latitude |
| Advertising | Track the effectiveness of social, mobile, search and display ads; divide ad effectiveness by device, platform, or type. | AOL Advertising, MediaMelon MediaCloud, Snoobi, PathMatics. |

Sources: Google Analytics Solutions, http://www.google.com/analytics/features/index.html.

## Do

Even the greatest analysis has little use if firms fail to implement what they have learned from analyzing their social and mobile media activity. That is, social media may be all about relationships, but ultimately, firms need to use their connections to increase their business.[91] They might launch a new Facebook campaign, actively blog, or provide mobile offers.

What do you do when consumers get tired of the flavours you offer? Instead of developing several new flavours and giving them to focus groups and test markets, Lay's took to the Internet. Its "Do Us a Flavour" campaign let customers suggest new flavour combinations online. People were able to vote for their favourite chip flavour. The person whose idea earned the most votes won $50,000 and 1 percent of the chip's future sales revenue. In 2015, the four finalist flavours included Cowboy BBQ Beans, Butter Chicken, Montreal Smoked Meat, and lastly, PEI Scalloped Potatoes, which later claimed the prize. After running the contest for four years, Lay's Canada introduced a twist in 2016. Instead of contestants suggesting their own chip ideas, they were asked to vote based on 12 chip flavours in three categories: iconic ingredients, home cooked classics, and street food.[92]

Deciding which tactics to employ and when is key. The social media marketer needs to act like an orchestra conductor, making sure that hundreds of "musicians," playing a variety of instruments, come together to create some beautiful music. A well developed marketing strategy involves a host of social and mobile tools, working in conjunction with the firm's traditional IMC tactics, to move the consumer up the purchase decision hierarchy from awareness to purchase to loyalty.

YouTube still earns more daily video views than Facebook does, and being second is not a position that Facebook enjoys. Accordingly, it has launched a new program entitled Anthology to facilitate the production of marketing videos for advertisers by well known content providers such as College Humor, Vice, Funny or Die, Vox Media, The Onion, Taste-made, and Oh My Disney. The resulting videos must be made available through Facebook. However, in addition to running the communications on Facebook, the advertiser also can run them on its own websites, insert them into traditional channels (e.g., television), or pay the content provider to run the videos on its site. Such links can benefit advertisers, which obtain high-quality marketing communications designed specifically for a social media platform. They also help content providers find new clients and outlets for their creativity.

To illustrate how firms might go about undertaking such campaigns, consider the steps involved in developing and implementing a Facebook marketing campaign.[93] These steps are not unlike the steps used in any integrated marketing communications (IMC) program. (See Chapters 14 and 15 for more details.) Assume a marketer was developing a Facebook marketing campaign for a new product.

1. *Identify strategy and goals.* The firm has to determine exactly what it hopes to promote and achieve through its campaign. Does it want to increase awareness of the product? Is it hoping more potential customers might visit and like its Facebook page? Is its focus mainly on increasing sales of the product? Depending on what the company aims to achieve, it might focus on developing a Facebook page, creating a Facebook app, or hosting a Facebook event.

2. *Identify target audience.* The next step is to determine whom the company is targeting. Facebook enables the firm to perform targeting that is based on location, language, education, gender, profession, age, relationship status, likes/dislikes, and friends or connections. The marketer's aim is to find a big enough audience to reach those who might adopt the product without being so big that the company ends up trying to appeal to someone way outside its target audience.

3. *Develop the campaign: experiment and engage.* Now that the firm knows whom it is targeting, the next step is to develop the communication, including the copy and images. Here again, the process is not very different from any other IMC campaign. There should be a call to action that is clear and compelling. Strong, eye-catching images and designs are important. And the campaign must appeal to the right customers. However, an aspect that is more critical with social media than other forms of IMC is that the images and messages need to be updated almost constantly. Because people expect changing content online, it would be inappropriate to run the same campaign for several months, as the firm might if it were advertising on television, for example.

4. *Develop the budget.* Budgeting is key. Facebook allows advertisers to set a daily budget: Once their costs (usually per click) reach a certain level, the ad disappears for the rest of the day. Of course, this option can be risky if the firm is getting great feedback and, suddenly, a compelling ad disappears. Therefore, similar to the campaign content, budgets demand nearly constant review. For example, if a competitor lowers its price significantly, it might be necessary to follow suit to avoid being excluded from customers' consideration sets.

5. *Monitor and change.* The final step is to review the success of the campaign and make changes as necessary. Facebook's Ad Manager offers various metrics and reports, such as number of clicks on ads, audience demographics, and ad performance for specific time periods.

## MANAGING YOUR PERSONAL BRAND IN A SOCIAL MEDIA WORLD

**L05**

The branding concepts examined in Chapter 9 apply in unique ways in the social media world, in which people engage in self-branding in new and exciting ways. Recall that brands attempt to build awareness, aim to develop loyalty, and exert an impact. If one applies these concepts to individual brand equity, one might think of individual brand management in some of the following ways.

Measures of individual social media effectiveness or equity use metrics such as:

- **social reach**, which refers to how many people a person influences (e.g., number of individuals in the person's social networks such as Facebook and LinkedIn)

**social reach**
The number of people a person influences.

**influence**
The extent to which a
person influences others.

**extended network**
The influence of a
person's extended
network.

- **influence**, which is the extent to which the person influences others (e.g., how much do the people in a person's network read that person's content)

- **extended network**, or the influence of the person's extended network, that is, the cumulative number of members (10,000 = 100 members each having 100 members of their own)

Several firms have developed metrics to assess a person's social impact (e.g., Klout, PeerIndex, Twitalyzer, and Kred). For example, Klout combines these three elements—social reach, influence, and extended network—to define a Klout score that can range from 0 to 100. The average score earned by regular people who aren't celebrities or heavily involved in social media, such as bloggers, is around 20. Justin Bieber is the only person ever to earn a perfect 100, however, his score has since dropped to 91. But a person does not have to be a star to earn a high Klout score.

Although Klout offers a good general view of social influence, various other options exist for more specific or detailed analyses, such as PeerIndex (http://www.peerindex .net), How Sociable (http://www.howsociable.com), or TwitterGrader (https://mokumax .com/).[94] Links shared through Twitter or Facebook also affect search rankings on search engines such as Google or Bing, such that greater influence increases the chances that people can find a more influential source of information or fashion.

In a sense, social media are like high school. In both places, people self-select into groups or cliques. Many people define their self-worth based on how many "friends" they can count. People's expressions and actions determine their reputation—whether negatively or positively. The environment can be either inclusive or exclusive—and sometimes both. Users seek out others, both as individuals and as groups. Wallflowers get ignored; fun, active, exciting contributors attract attention.

But remember, "No matter how brilliant and talented you are, you won't be sufficiently appreciated ... until the broader public recognizes you."[95] Thus, beyond creating an online presence, people with true influence also make use of networks of contacts they make in various realms, give presentations and speeches, publish books and articles as well as blogs, submit themselves for prestigious awards, and try to get on television or other national news outlets.

Even if a person's goal is not necessarily to become the premier expert on a particular topic, social influence can have significant effects on other elements of his or her life, such as hiring success.[96] Employers can check these social presence scores or impact factors, along with other sources of information, to assess how well connected, creative, and active a potential hire is. This source is particularly critical for the rapidly expanding field of social media jobs for marketers.

A student who graduates with a marketing degree likely has a good foundation for one of the following social media jobs:[97]

1.  Social media strategist. In this quite high paying social media job, people create social media marketing campaigns, then measure the results, using an effective strategic plan.

2.  Community manager. These positions are responsible for handling corporate forums and blogs, increasing traffic to the site, and broadening their company's community.

3.  Blogger. These highly sought jobs provide great flexibility and freedom. By posting articles on relevant websites, bloggers can earn $35–$75 hourly.

4.  Social media marketing specialist. These well paid professionals distribute promotional channels using a range of social media channels, which requires strong online marketing skills.

5.  Search engine marketing associate. Focusing on search engines, these online marketers rely on their knowledge of optimization techniques to increase the organic search rankings for a website.

6.  Online customer service representative. Customers like to provide feedback, often online, and the best service companies make sure that someone is on hand to respond.

## REAL MARKETER PROFILE

# Corey Sherwood
# (Shopper Futures)

In my career planning, I've always tried to balance what I love to do and what I'm good at. When I was a young kid, I loved to build things—it started with Lego, but I always took pride in anything that I created and showcasing it to others. Also from a young age, I was usually very good at convincing people—I would tend to get a desired outcome by putting myself in the shoes of the person listening and saying or doing what was needed to get what I wanted. At that time, it was usually to get a new video game from my parents, or selling chocolates door to door. The balance of my skill in convincing and passion of creating led me to marketing at the young age of 14 years old. I discovered what marketing/advertising was after watching the first season of *The Apprentice* and realized that was exactly what I wanted to do. I saw it as <u>creating</u> a proposition/campaign to <u>convince</u> people to purchase—seemed like a perfect fit for me.

Used with permission of Corey Sherwood

As I progressed through high school, I also picked up a passion for entrepreneurship and began my own start-up with a few of my friends with the mission to partner university mentors with high school students pursuing a post-secondary education. We created a social platform for students to get unbiased "inside scoop" as to what universities and colleges across the country were like. This project stayed true to my identity of loving to build things, and allowed me to offer a solution for many that I knew were struggling to find out what they wanted to do as a career. This allowed me to experience what it is like to build a brand from the ground up and create a strong perception of it in the minds of my target audience (high school students). After growing this social platform to thousands of students across the globe in just a short couple of years, I decided to pursue a university degree myself and continue my beloved study of marketing.

I attended Wilfrid Laurier University and completed my business administration degree. I was fortunate enough to be enrolled in the co-op program and completed various marketing internships that reassured me of my passion for this field of study and career. Upon graduating, I joined Mondelēz International (makers of Oreo, Cadbury, and Ritz, to name a few) where I had several brand management assignments. Mondelēz seemed like a great fit for me as they had newly separated from Kraft Foods and were looking to build an identity—definitely appealing to the entrepreneur

in me. I quickly learned that the great thing about this field is that every day is different—I would manage the P&L, build IMC plans, be a part of consumer research—marketing is a multi-faceted field that enables you to interact with people from various functions, while still having line of sight to the consumer.

After about two years with Mondelēz, I built a reputation of having strong ties in the start-up community and knowledge in digital marketing tech, which enabled me to co-lead a start-up incubator initiative called Shopper Futures. It connected our power brands, with top start-up innovators and grocery retailers to launch pilots in the retail environments within 90 days. As we searched for start-up talent, a key theme of technology emerged: beacons. We selected a couple of start-ups that were offering beacon and mobile integration that could trigger a message (in our case, a coupon offer) once in close proximity with a shopper's mobile phone. This technology unlocked a huge opportunity, which was to send the right message at the right time (at the point of sale). With the enforcement of CASL (anti-spam law legislation) in Canada, any execution of this kind needed to ensure that a user was opting to receive this message. So we had our participating retailers request and receive opt-ins via their CRM database of loyalty shoppers. The potential for beacon technology is tremendous—they are extremely small, are easy to install, and usually only require Wi-Fi Internet. You can install several beacons in a store with different messages, for example, one in each aisle delivering a message that is relevant to the category in the aisle (e.g., a cookies coupon offer in the snacks aisle).

I was later appointed into a media specialist role, where I now focus my time in advertising and building commercials, social media content, and strategic partnerships. I now get to work with agencies around the world to develop content for some of our most notable brands. In addition to every day being different, another great thing about marketing is that it drastically evolves over time—I've seen so much shifting in how we advertise to consumers in only three years of my career—the most obvious being the emergence of digital marketing and mobile. It definitely keeps things interesting!

If you can connect what characteristics about yourself would fit well into a role as a marketer, you will find yourself not only enjoying it, but also tapping into those qualities that will make you successful.

Regardless of the exact job title, social media jobs are increasing. They also offer good salaries and the promise of continued growth. Getting such jobs implies that candidates truly have influence, and these social media impact scores offer some idea about what personal branding really means.[98] First, influence by itself has little impact. Rather, a person needs to leverage his or her personal brand to induce some action, whether that entails convincing friends to support a cause the person likes or convincing a company to hire that person for an internship. Second, just as it does for a product or service brand, building a personal brand takes time, as well as consistent effort. It would be impossible to become really influential by exhibiting a flurry of activity for a couple of days, and then taking a month-long break. Third, there is a big difference between being active and being influential. Simply retweeting comments from other creators is insufficient to achieve true influence. To be influential, a personal brand must follow the four Es: You need to excite, educate, give experience, and engage your followers.

Moreover, just like any other marketing tactic, personal branding needs to take ethical considerations under advisement. For example, we might think carefully about the spread of metrics, especially amid reports about the ways they are being used, perhaps without people's knowledge. For example, at the Palms Casino Resort Hotel, clerks check the Klout scores of guests as they check in and then offer upgrades to those with the highest scores.[99] Is that great marketing, or an ethically questionable exploitation?

The importance of such scores also implies the potential for abuse. What if firms "game" the system, such that the only search engine results you see are those that have developed influence because the companies have paid legions of followers to tweet about their offering?[100] Are you really getting the best choices then?

On a more personal note, it has been pretty well established that embarrassing pictures on Facebook can be detrimental to your future career. But what about just basic posts and influence efforts? Despite the benefits of building your social influence, the more information is available about you online, the more information potential employers and others have. One study even suggests that human resource managers should assess social media sources to determine if a potential hire is agreeable (pleasant in interactions, or caustic in humour?), emotionally stable (did an interpersonal fight go viral?), or conscientious.[101] You may be held accountable for everything you do to enhance your social influence. So, think before you post, tweet, or blog: Is this something you want to answer for in the court of public opinion?

# LEARNING OBJECTIVES REVIEW

**LO1**  **Describe the 4E framework of social media marketing**

The 4E framework recognizes that marketers must *excite* customers with relevant offers; *educate* them about the offering; help them *experience* products, whether directly or indirectly; and give them an opportunity to *engage*.

**LO2**  **Understand the types of social media**

Users of social media employ them to promote themselves or their products and services. They do so through three main categories: social networking sites (e.g., Facebook, LinkedIn), media-sharing sites (e.g., YouTube), and thought-sharing sites (e.g., blogs, Twitter).

**LO3**  **Understand various motivations for using mobile applications and how they are priced**

As mobile users increase in number and diversity, the applications developed to appeal to them are spreading as well. Although there are well over a million apps, they meet seven basic customer motivations: for "me time," to socialize, to shop, to accomplish, to prepare, to discover, and to self-express. By meeting a multiple of these motivations, companies can attract a large number of customers. When choosing how to charge for apps, firms have four options: ad-supported, freemium, paid apps, and paid apps with in-app purchases.

**LO4** Recognize and understand the three components of a social media strategy

Firms engage with customers through social and mobile media using a three-step process. First, they listen to the customer using techniques like sentiment analysis. Second, they analyze the data collected in the first step using metrics like bounce rates, click paths, and conversion rates. Finally, they use this information to develop tactics to engage their customers.

**LO5** Understand the methods for marketing yourself using social media

To market themselves, people need to ensure that they reach a large number of people, that they influence those people, and that the network of people whom they influence is also influential. Several firms, such as Klout, have devised metrics to assess one's social network impact. Having a social network presence is becoming increasingly important in finding certain types of marketing jobs. But, on a cautionary note, it is important for people to carefully choose how they are portrayed in social media because once something is posted, it is there for all to see, including potential employers.

## KEY TERMS

- bounce rate
- click paths
- conversion rates
- earned media
- extended network

- gamification
- hits
- influence
- keyword analysis
- owned media

- page views
- paid media
- sentiment analysis
- social reach

## CONCEPT REVIEW

1. What are the four Es?

2. What social media elements work best for each of the four Es?

3. What is an example of a social network, a media-sharing site, a thought-sharing site, and a mobile application?

4. On which of the 4E dimensions do social networks, media-sharing sites, thought-sharing sites, and mobile applications excel?

5. What are the three steps in developing social media engagement strategies?

6. How do firms examine customer sentiments?

7. What are the steps in developing a social media campaign?

8. Why might it be important to develop a personal social media presence?

## MARKETING APPLICATIONS

1. Evaluate Under Armour's social media strategy using the 4E framework.

2. Using the components of the 4E framework, outline how an entrepreneur marketing low-sugar candy can augment or enhance his or her marketing mix efforts.

3. Suppose David's Tea introduced a new product called mint-enhanced tea—mint and lemon herbal tea. How should it go about creating excitement using various social and mobile media tools?

4. If you were marketing a new sneaker, what sorts of mobile applications might enhance your marketing efforts?

5. Assume you work for a large consumer packaged goods firm that has discovered that its latest line of snack foods is moving very slowly off store shelves. Recommend a strategy for listening to what consumers are saying on blogs, review sites, and the firm's website. Describe how

your strategy might provide insights into consumers' sentiments about the new product line.

6. If you were assessing the effectiveness of your social media marketing campaign, would sentiment analysis be helpful?

7. As an intern for Tim Hortons®, you have been asked to develop a social media campaign for a new glazed muffin. The objective of the campaign is to increase awareness and trial of the new line of muffins. How would you go about putting such a campaign together?

8. You were just hired by a company that wants to produce apps that help people become healthier by exercising, eating well, and reducing stress. Which customer motivations would you recommend the company focus on? Describe the app you would design, the customer motivations it meets, and why your app is the right design for your potential customers.

## NET SAVVY

1. Go to http://www.facebook.com/business and learn about how to build pages, ads, and sponsored stories, and take advantage of mobile applications. What are some of the steps that Facebook suggests a person consider when marketing using ads?

2. Go to Salesforce.com Radian6's website (http://www .salesforcemarketingcloud.com/products/social-media-listening/) and check out its top case studies. How do these case studies provide insights into how listening and analytic systems can help firms improve their social media marketing?

## CHAPTER CASE STUDY

### IMAGES, SALES, BRANDS: HOW RED BULL USES VARIOUS SOCIAL MEDIA TECHNIQUES TO ACHIEVE ALL ITS OBJECTIVES

It isn't as if the social media strategy adopted by Red Bull—the energy drink that "gives you wings"—is a trade secret. Granted, the private company has a policy that discourages employees from giving interviews. But its overall strategy is clear from its actions and their outcomes. The success it has accrued from this strategy therefore isn't a matter of doing things differently from anyone else; it's a function of doing them better.

To begin, Red Bull distinguishes its goals for leveraging social media contacts. Is it hoping for more brand exposure, or is it pursuing sales increases? Depending on its focus, it adopts distinct, appealing methods that are specific and unique to each social media platform. Then it implements these tactics consistently and comprehensively, to increase the chances that they will be widely shared and recognized.

### Social Media for Name Recognition

While Red Bull has a long history of posting incredible feats on its YouTube channel, one still stands out years later. Felix Baumgartner (purposefully) fell to Earth from 127,852 feet up, breaking all sorts of records. His jump was from the highest height ever achieved by a human. During the 4-minute, 20-second freefall, he also reached greater speeds—up to Mach 1.25, faster than the speed of sound—than anyone else ever has. The event was a breakthrough on various levels. Baumgartner's pressure suit was the first version to be able to protect the human body in space but still enable maneuverability. To address the threat of ebullism (i.e., when liquid in the body evaporates due to high altitudes, causing a person's blood to literally boil), Baumgartner and his team derived new medical techniques with widespread applications. His parachute also adopted a new "reefed" design to reduce drifting, with clear implications for airdrops of materials and supplies.[102]

In reporting on all these remarkable feats, Baumgartner's name was mentioned frequently—though not as frequently as the project that sponsored his jump and all the technology that went into supporting it: the Red Bull Stratos project. Every official mention of the event included the full name, such that Red Bull Stratos often appeared as a single term. It was not just the Stratos project. It was the Red Bull Stratos project.

And what a project it was, leading to the creation of not just scientific advances but also a remarkable video. That video, taken from the camera mounted on Baumgartner's helmet, features vast, picturesque views of Earth and the sense of plummeting. Red Bull immediately made it available for people to check out at their leisure. But the real target—the people whom Red Bull hoped would be most engaged by the video and the stunt in general—were extreme sports fanatics. These folks willingly put their bodies at risk on a regular basis to perform some cool stunt to cause their friends to marvel. For them, there may be no better stunt than having some guy fall from space.[103] In full awareness of this appeal, Red Bull made sure that the video was prominent on its YouTube channel. On the day of the jump itself, approximately 8 million streamed the video live and in real time. Also on that day, the number of subscribers to Red Bull's YouTube channel increased by a remarkable 87,801.[104]

On Twitter, recognizing that 140 characters was not nearly enough to communicate the awesomeness of the stunt, it simply used hashtags and links to connect followers to

Sponsored by Red Bull, Felix Baumgartner's jump reached speeds of Mach 1.25.

© Jay Nemeth/ZUMA Press/Newscom

the video, whether through YouTube or on a Red Bull site. Although Red Bull's main Twitter feed did not exhibit any notable differences, the dedicated Red Bull Stratos Twitter feed prompted more than 20,000 mentions in tweets by others on that day.

The Red Bull Stratos Facebook page featured several photos during and after the jump. Just one shot of a landed Baumgartner, still in his space suit and on his knees beside his reefed parachute, prompted more than 20,000 comments, more than 50,000 shares, and nearly half a million likes.[105]

The example of the Red Bull Stratos project and its attendant coverage through social media demonstrates several things Red Bull did well. It knew its audience and its own goals, and it understood how different channels could help it attain those goals. To ensure that it appealed to the target audience, it engaged them in an exciting, never-before-tried, daredevil experience. Moreover, it shared the scientific lessons learned through the project, to give those who wanted it an education.

But it also spent a lot of money to get Baumgartner to space and back down again. And that meant that it needed to translate some of the brand awareness it developed into sales. Luckily for Red Bull, its social media strategy also has room for that effort.

### Social Media for Performance

Red Bull does not just send athletes to space. It also sponsors them on the pitch, in the form of the New York Red Bulls MLS team, which plays in Red Bull Arena in Harrison, New Jersey. In one recent game, the team's star forward, Thierry Henry, scored yet another goal. Afterward, he leaned with his right arm up against the goal post and left hand on his hip. The pose, caught on camera, almost immediately became a Twitter meme as amateur photo editors placed him against a variety of backgrounds.[106]

The team was quick to move on this social media coup. It rapidly posted the photo to its website and encouraged fans to vote for it as their favourite shot of the season. Immediately above and below the encouragement to engage with the brand also appeared links that would allow fans to purchase tickets for a full season, half season, or individual games.[107]

Beyond these consumer-related uses of social and mobile media, Red Bull's international sales efforts depend on "SoLoMo" (referring to social, location, and mobile) software. Users who download the Red Bull app receive alerts on their smartphones about in-store promotions as soon as they arrive at the retail site. If they also attend Red Bull events, such as a flugtag or BMX race, selected patrons even might receive a special invitation to come backstage to meet some of the stars of the show.

Each of Red Bull's mobile sales representatives is equipped with her or his own tablet computer, loaded with mobile software. Thus, on visits to retail sites and vendors, the salespeople can provide the latest inventory information. They also present detailed analytics to show vendors how best to position their coolers of Red Bull products and how to line up the cans in the display case to encourage sales.[108]

### Combining the Uses of Social Media

When you are as good at engaging and exciting people through social media as Red Bull is, the next step might be to make social media your main focus. Although the privately held company has not publicized any such plans, commentators suggest that it appears poised to transform itself into a media company that just happens to sell energy drinks.[109] The extent and amount of content it creates, featuring extreme sports and even sports it has created (ever hear of ice racing?), is similar in quality to sports videos produced by well known networks. If Red Bull can convince networks to purchase its coverage of Shaun White on the half-pipe, it enters a new market. If Shaun White happens to be wearing a hat with the Red Bull logo, well then that's just an added bonus.

Such predictions actually resonate quite well with what Red Bull already does in social media. For example, though it maintains a plethora of Facebook pages and Twitter accounts for various events and locations, virtually none of them ever feature pictures of its drink product. Instead, they offer exciting in-sport shots or humorous images. Fans can—and do—comment, but Red Bull rarely responds. That may be because its primary goal is to establish an edgy, exciting image as a lifestyle brand, which it feels confident will translate into product sales.[110]

### Questions

1. What social and mobile media tools is Red Bull using?

2. Evaluate Red Bull's social media marketing strategy using the 4E framework.

3. How should Red Bull assess the effectiveness of these campaigns? Describe how it should respond to insights gained by this assessment.

# CHAPTER 17

## LEARNING OBJECTIVES

**After studying this chapter you should be able to**

**LO1** Explain the components of global market assessments

**LO2** Understand the marketing opportunities in BRIC countries

**LO3** Describe the various global market entry strategies

**LO4** List the similarities and differences between a domestic marketing strategy and a global marketing strategy

**LO5** Explain how ethical issues affect global marketing practices

Erica Simone Leeds RF

# Global Marketing

Reviewing the tumultuous history and modern operations of Coca-Cola in India is like taking a quick survey of global marketing issues. From early failures to notable impacts on local regulations to joint efforts to growth efforts, the story of how this global brand has sought to make its mark in this developing nation is instructive.

When Coke first moved into India in the 1970s, it confronted a critical cultural difference between its home base and this foreign market. India was officially closed to foreign investment at the time, which meant that, in order to enter, Coke would have to find an equal, Indian partner. Such a joint venture partnership would have required it to share its famously protected, secret formula for making its carbonated beverage. It was totally unwilling to do this and so, it left for more than 20 years.

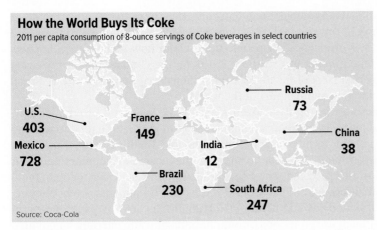

**How the World Buys Its Coke**

2011 per capita consumption of 8-ounce servings of Coke beverages in select countries

Russia **73**

U.S. **403**

France **149**

China **38**

Mexico **728**

India **12**

Brazil **230**

South Africa **247**

Source: Coca-Cola

Coke is a top global brand. However, its typical customer in India only buys 12 bottles per year, compared to 728 in Mexico, making India a country with enormous growth potential.

Source: Coca-Cola Company

But, as many developing nations have, India liberalized its economy, opening it to more foreign investments and offering more opportunities for foreign companies to enter. Accordingly, Coca-Cola came back in the mid-1990s,[1] a few years after its primary rival Pepsi had established a strong base there. To ensure its competitiveness and expand its coverage of the Indian consumer market, Coke bought four local soda brands from the Indian company Parle, so that it gained about 60 percent of the market, far outpacing Pepsi's 30 percent. Yet Coke itself is not the most popular carbonated drink. That distinction belongs to Thums Up, one of the Indian brands Coca-Cola purchased.[2]

Coke still faces critical problems in the Indian market. In particular, people just don't drink that much Coke. Whereas the average global consumer drinks 92 bottles of Coke each year, the average Indian consumer drinks only 12 of them (in Brazil, the average consumer drinks around 290 bottles each year).[3] But Coke believes it cannot just ignore this massive and growing consumer market, one of the few remaining parts of the world that offers such excellent growth opportunities.

Noting this potential, and in its efforts to "stay ahead of the curve," Coke planned to invest approximately $5 billion in India alone.[4] The investment was to increase its bottling capacity, build the brand, and expand its distribution. Brand building efforts are especially necessary, considering the water controversies that continue to plague Coca-Cola. Various groups have accused the company of using too much groundwater in its bottling operations, creating an ethical and societal backlash, protests, government fines, and even threats to demolish some of the most controversial plants. In fact, in 2016, Coca-Cola closed three plants in the state of Rajasthan where financially devastated farmers launched widespread protests due to the depleted watershed in the area.[5]

Plant closures have not deterred the beverage giant from launching new products such as Vio, a flavoured milk-based drink specially formulated to suit the tastes of Indian consumers.[6] The milk is sourced from local farmers and formulated with a blend of flavours including saffron, pistachio, and almond. Dairy is seen as an important growth pillar for Coca-Cola following close on the heels of investments in sparkling drinks, water, and juices as well as bottled tea and coffee.

However, with its investments in India and other developing nations, Coca-Cola is taking a very optimistic position: It plans to double its volumes sold and revenues by 2020. That's a pretty tall order for a fizzy drink that already ranks among the top global brands. ∎

Increasing globalization affects all companies—large, small, medium, and entrepreneurial—in Canada, and around the world. Many Canadian companies find themselves becoming part of the global supply chain. Competition is no longer local, provincial, or even national; it is global. Canadian companies have to compete with other global companies not only for raw materials, labour, knowledge, and other inputs, but also for markets for their products. Few people think about how globalization impacts their daily lives, but take a minute to read the labels on the clothing you are wearing right now. Chances are that most of the items, even if they carry Canadian or U.S. brand names, were manufactured in another part of the world.

**globalization**
Refers to the increased flow of goods, services, people, technology, capital, information, and ideas around the world; has economic, political, social, cultural, and environmental impacts.

In Canada, the market has evolved from a system of local and provincial marketplaces, to national markets, to geographically regional markets (e.g., Canada and the United States together), to international markets, and finally to global markets. According to the Government of Canada and the Business Development Bank of Canada, **globalization** refers to the increased flow of goods, services, people, technology, capital, information, and ideas around the world. Its impacts are economic, political, social, cultural, and environmental.[7] Global markets are the result of several fundamental changes, such as reductions or eliminations of trade barriers by country governments, the decreasing concerns of distance and time with regard to moving products and ideas across countries, the standardization of laws across borders, and globally integrated production processes. For instance, consider the Lululemon pants you own. It is possible that Lululemon Athletica buys its raw materials from a supplier in one country and its sewing machines and washers from a supplier in another country, while its workers come from a third country, and its marketers are placed in several countries around the world where its pants are sold (i.e., customers are spread across the globe).

Globalization has not only created economies of scale because of the global scale in which research, production, and marketing are performed, but also made it possible for many market niches that are not profitable at the provincial or national level to become profitable at the global level. Some companies may find the Canadian market too small for their products yet still be able to profitably serve market niches on a global scale. And many Canadian companies are part of the global supply chain, supplying inputs and raw materials rather than marketing finished products.

These fundamental changes have paved the way for marketing to flourish in other countries. The elimination of trade barriers and other governmental actions, for instance, allows goods and ideas to move quickly and efficiently around the world, which in turn facilitates the quick delivery of goods to better meet the needs of global consumers. As a consequence, consumers have easy access to global products and services. When we walk into a toy store, we expect to find Lego from Denmark. In the local sporting goods store, we anticipate finding running shoes made in China by the German firm Adidas. In the grocery store, we demand out-of-season produce like blueberries from Chile in January. Or consider how a $12 digital camera for your keychain, made in Taiwan, could be produced, transported halfway around the world, and sold for so little money at your local Walmart. These are the questions we will be examining in this chapter.

We begin by looking at how firms assess the potential of a given market, with particular attention to Brazil, Russia, India, and China (collectively known as "the BRIC countries"). We'll see how firms assess the potential of a given market, make decisions to go global, and choose markets in which to sell globally. Then we explore how to build the marketing mix for global products and consider some of the ethical issues of globalization.

## LO1   ASSESSING GLOBAL MARKETS

Because different countries, at their various stages of globalization, offer marketers a variety of opportunities, firms must assess the viability of a variety of international markets. This assessment is done through an environmental analysis similar to what is described in Chapter 3. As illustrated in Exhibit 17.1, four sets of factors are often used to assess a country's market: **P**olitical, **E**conomic, **S**ociocultural, and **T**echnology and

**EXHIBIT 17.1**    Components of a Country Market Assessment

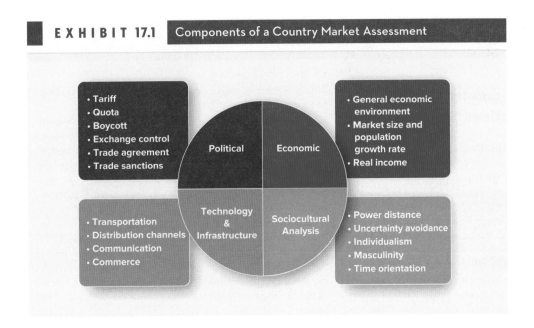

infrastructure factors. The acronym *PEST* is used as shorthand to refer to these factors. Analysis of these four factors offers marketers a more complete picture of a country's potential as a market for products and services. Although we describe each factor separately, it is important to note that marketers consider them together in order to obtain a complete picture of a country's marketing potential. In fact, marketers often have to make trade-offs between these factors when entering or doing business in a foreign market. For instance, Canadian oil and mining companies may enter markets where the economic opportunity is great but the political risks are higher.

## Analyzing the Political Environment

Governmental actions, as well as the actions of non-governmental political groups, can significantly influence firms' ability to sell goods and services, because they often result in laws or other regulations that either promote the growth of the global market or close off the country and inhibit growth. Some of the effects are difficult to predict in advance, as Ethical Dilemma 17.1 discusses.

Policies aimed at restricting trade and global marketing are called protectionist policies, and those that encourage global trade and marketing are referred to as trade liberalization policies. The White Spot restaurant chain, based in Vancouver, opened its first Asian location in Hong Kong. CEO Warren Earhart says that the company evaluates new markets on a country-by-country basis since countries have different rules that need to be considered. For example, Thailand and South Korea have protectionist policies regarding the importation of beef products.[9] In this section, we discuss various forms of protectionist and liberalization policies. These issues include trade sanctions such as tariffs, quotas, boycotts, exchange controls, and trade agreements (see Exhibit 17.2).

**EXHIBIT 17.2**    Government Actions

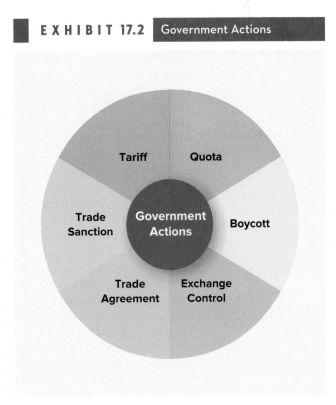

## Ethical Dilemma 17.1

### How Chinese Regulations Change Car-Buying Practices[8]

As the Scottish poet Robert Burns wrote, "The best laid schemes of mice and men/Go often awry." That is, we might have the best intentions to produce beneficial outcomes, but sometimes those plans have a way of leading to the opposite effect. It's a truth that consumer behaviour researchers and marketers know only too well.

Consider, for example, the case of China and its latest attempt to limit automobile induced air pollution. The expansion of China's middle class has created a vast new population of consumers who can now afford cars. The nation's roads—especially in urban centres such as Shanghai, Guangzhou, Guiyang, and Beijing—have become clogged with vehicles. Pollution levels also have reached critical proportions. And China has moved into the top spot in terms of consumer car purchases, with some estimates suggesting that Chinese consumers will buy 30 million vehicles annually by 2020.

In response to these concerns, Chinese government officials began testing a licensing regulation that requires people to enter a lottery for a limited number of car registration tags. Without the licence plate, drivers would face severe penalties. Officials hoped to halt the growth in this sector and thereby limit pollution and congestion on the roads. But the odds of winning the licence plate lottery were low, with odds of 9 percent in 2011 dropping to 2 percent one year later.

Consumers took the threat that the regulations would spread as a great reason to buy a new car immediately. If they might not be able to next year, they had better snag a car right now! In cities in which the regulations are already in place, the lucky licence lottery winners also bought bigger (i.e., more polluting), more expensive vehicles. As one consumer noted, "Would you want to put a 100,000 yuan plate on a 50,000 yuan car?" Because these consumers already are spending more than they might have planned, just to have the chance to enter the lottery for a licence, they feel more justified spending more on the car itself. The average price paid per car thus has leapt up approximately 88 percent in just two years.

To encourage the sale of new, energy-efficient vehicles, the government announced that buyers of electric cars would be able to access plates without having to go through the lottery process. These trends are great news for foreign luxury carmakers like Audi and Mercedes-Benz, whose sales in China have jumped. It is not so great for Chinese carmakers, which have long provided the lower-end, functional vehicles that China's population previously demanded. It also might not be great news for the environment, which was not at all what authorities planned when they implemented these regulations. The best-laid schemes, indeed.

---

**trade sanctions**
Penalties or restrictions imposed by one country over another country for importing and exporting of goods, services, and investments.

Trade Sanctions　**Trade sanctions** are penalties or restrictions imposed by one country over another country for importing and exporting goods, services, and investments. In 2016, Ukraine banned Russian food imports that included beef, chocolate, alcohol, and tobacco products. The action came about as a result of Russia closing its borders to many Ukrainian food products after its government implemented a free trade agreement with the European Union.[10] An embargo is a form of trade sanction that prohibits trading with a certain country or trading in specific goods (e.g., oil embargo) by other signatory countries.

**tariff (or duty)**
A tax levied on a good imported into a country.

Tariffs　A **tariff (or duty)** is a tax levied on a good imported into a country. In most cases, tariffs are intended to make imported goods more expensive and thus less competitive with domestic products, which in turn protects domestic industries from foreign competition. In other cases, tariffs might be imposed to penalize another country for trade practices that the home country views as unfair. For example, companies wishing to export dairy products to Canada face a whopping 240 percent tariff put in place to protect Canadian dairy farmers. In 2002, the United States imposed a 9.31 percent duty on Canadian softwood lumber exported to the United States because the U.S. softwood industry claimed that Canada was subsidizing Canadian softwood lumber and Canadian lumber producers were **dumping** (selling a good in a foreign market at a price that is lower than its domestic price or below its cost) low-cost softwood lumber on the U.S. market. The duty increased the prices of Canadian lumber sold in the United States by 27 percent, making it difficult for Canadian companies to compete with U.S. lumber producers.[11] In

**dumping**
The practice of selling a good in a foreign market at a price that is lower than its domestic price or below its cost.

2010, the Government of Canada made Canada a tariff-free zone for industrial manufacturers by eliminating all tariffs on machinery, equipment, and goods imported into Canada for further manufacturing. The elimination of tariffs along with $450 million in tax relief gives small and medium-sized manufacturers a competitive advantage.[12]

**quota**
Designates the maximum quantity of a product that may be brought into a country during a specified time period.

Quotas    A **quota** designates the maximum quantity of a product that may be brought into a country during a specified time period. Many Canadian quotas on foreign-made textiles were eliminated in 2005, which reduced the cost of imported apparel products sold in Canada. It opened the floodgates for garments made in Bangladesh. Some firms have chosen to pass the bulk of these savings on to consumers—in Walmart's case, 75 percent of them—whereas others, such as bebe, planned to share only 25 percent and keep the rest as profit.[13]

**boycott**
A group's refusal to deal commercially with some organization to protest against its policies.

Tariffs and quotas can impose a potentially devastating blow on a firm's ability to sell products in another country. Tariffs artificially raise prices and therefore lower demand, and quotas reduce the availability of imported merchandise. Conversely, tariffs and quotas benefit domestically made products because they reduce foreign competition. In the case of softwood lumber being exported from Canada to the U.S., tariffs and quotas benefit U.S. lumber producers and reduce competition from Canadian lumber producers. Unfortunately, U.S. consumers end up paying higher prices for U.S. softwood lumber rather than benefiting from cheaper Canadian lumber, and Canadian lumber producers lost huge market share.

**exchange control**
Refers to the regulation of a country's currency exchange rate.

**exchange rate**
The measure of how much one currency is worth in relation to another.

Boycott    A **boycott** pertains to a group's refusal to deal commercially with some organization to protest against its policies. Boycotts might be called by governments or non-governmental organizations, such as trade unions, or human rights or environmental groups. For example, the United States has only recently eased economic sanctions imposed against Cuba. Both the United States and Canada have imposed sanctions on Iran.

Exchange Control    **Exchange control** refers to the regulation of a country's currency **exchange rate**, the measure of how much one currency is worth in relation to another.[14] A designated agency in each country, often the central bank, sets the rules for currency exchange. In Canada, the Bank of Canada sets the rules for the currency exchange rates. The value of the Canadian dollar against the U.S. dollar has been a roller coaster over the past two decades. It increased significantly, from around C$0.60 for US$1.00 in 2001, to C$1.10 in November 2007. The exchange rate held steady at par until 2014 when it slipped to $0.90. Since then, it continued its slide to $0.69 in January 2016 before improving to $0.78. The fluctuating Canadian dollar has a twofold effect on the ability of Canadian firms to conduct global business. For Canadian firms that depend on U.S. imports of finished products, raw materials, or services, the cost of doing business has gone up dramatically with the low Canadian dollar. However, U.S. buyers find the costs of Canadian goods and services less expensive than they were before. This tends to have a positive impact on Canadian manufacturing exports to the United States, as Americans will find that

Many quotas on foreign-made textiles have been eliminated. Some firms chose to pass the bulk of these savings on to consumers—in Walmart's case, 75 percent of the savings—whereas other firms, such as bebe, planned to share only 25 percent of the savings and keep the rest as profit.

YellowMoon/Alamy Stock Photo

The increase in value of the Canadian dollar against the U.S. dollar has made Canadian exports to the United States less expensive, and imports from the United States more expensive.

Bank note image used with the permission of the Bank of Canada/Images de billet de banque utilisées avec la permission de la Banque du Canada

**trade agreement**

Intergovernmental agreement designed to manage and promote trade activities for specific regions.

**trading bloc**

Consists of those countries that have signed a particular trade agreement.

their dollar can buy them more in Canada while Canadians find that they can buy less in the United States with their Canadian dollars.

**Trade Agreements** Marketers must consider the trade agreements to which a particular country is a signatory or the trading bloc to which it belongs. A **trade agreement** is an intergovernmental agreement designed to manage and promote trade activities for a specific region, and a **trading bloc** consists of those countries that have signed the particular trade agreement.[15]

Some major trade agreements cover two-thirds of the world's international trade: the European Union (EU), the North American Free Trade Agreement (NAFTA), the Central America Free Trade Agreement (CAFTA), Mercosur, and the Association of Southeast Asian Nations (ASEAN).[16] These trade agreements are summarized in Exhibit 17.3. The European Union represents the highest level of integration across individual nations, whereas the other agreements vary in their integration levels. The United Kingdom had been an EU member until a 2016 BREXIT referendum saw British citizens vote in favour of leaving. A Trans-Pacific Partnership (TPP) trade deal was proposed in late 2015 between Australia, Brunei, Canada, Chile, Japan, Malaysia, Mexico, New Zealand, Peru, Singapore, the United States, and Vietnam. However, this latest free trade agreement has yet to be ratified.[17]

These trading blocs affect how Canadian firms can conduct business in the member countries. Some critics contend that such blocs confer an unfair advantage on their member nations because they offer favourable terms for trade, whereas others believe they stimulate economies by lowering trade barriers and allowing higher levels of foreign investment.

**EXHIBIT 17.3**  Trade Agreements

| Name | Countries |
| --- | --- |
| European Union | 29 member countries include: Austria, Belgium, Bulgaria, Croatia, Cyprus, Czech Republic, Denmark, Estonia, Finland, France, Germany, Greece, Hungary, Ireland, Italy, Latvia, Lithuania, Luxembourg, Malta, Netherlands, Poland, Portugal, Romania, Slovakia, Slovenia, Spain, Sweden, and the United Kingdom. There are six official candidate countries to join the EU: Macedonia, Serbia, Turkey, Iceland, Montenegro, and Albania. Bosnia and Herzegovina and Kosovo are also potential candidates. |
| NAFTA | Canada, Mexico, the United States |
| CAFTA | Costa Rica, the Dominican Republic, El Salvador, Guatemala, Honduras, Nicaragua, the United States |
| Mercosur | Full members: Argentina, Brazil, Paraguay, Uruguay, Venezuela |
| ASEAN | Brunei, Darussalam, Cambodia, Indonesia, Laos, Malaysia, Myanmar, Philippines, Singapore, Thailand, Vietnam |

**Political Risk Analysis** Before a company decides to engage in global marketing, it must conduct a political risk analysis—assessing the level of political, socioeconomic, and security risks of doing business with a country. Such analysis usually involves weighing the likelihood of certain events (such as change in government, violence, and the imposition of restrictive trade policies) taking place over a specific period of time. This type of analysis requires sophisticated expertise, which most companies do not possess. Thus, they rely on government agencies (e.g., Export Development Canada; Department of Foreign Affairs, Trade, and Development) and private companies that specialize in political risk analysis to provide information and guidance. Political risk analysis helps to reduce the risk of a company losing its investment or goods and the possibility of harm to its employees.

The European Union has resulted in lowering trade barriers and strengthening global relationships among member nations.

© Digital Vision/Getty Images

## Analyzing the Economic Environment Using Metrics

The greater the wealth of people in a country, generally, the better the opportunity a firm will have in that particular country. A firm conducting an economic analysis of a country's market must look at three major economic factors: general economic environment, market size and population growth, and real income (see Exhibit 17.4).

**Evaluating the General Economic Environment** Generally, healthy economies provide better opportunities for global marketing expansions. A firm can measure the relative health of a particular country's economy in several ways. Each way offers a slightly different view, and some may be more useful for some products and services than for others.

**EXHIBIT 17.4** Economic Analysis

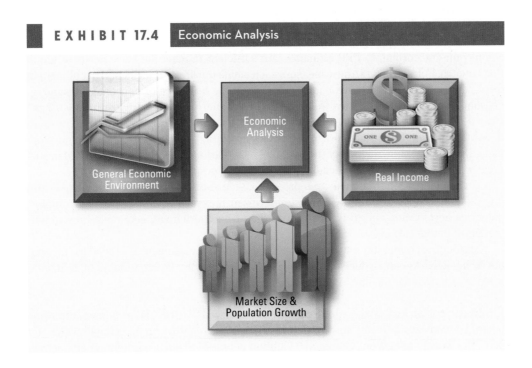

**trade deficit**
Results when a country imports more goods than it exports.

**trade surplus**
Results when a country exports more goods than it imports.

**gross domestic product (GDP)**
The market value of the goods and services produced by a country in a year; the most widely used standardized measure of output.

**purchasing power parity (PPP)**
A theory that states that if the exchange rates of two countries are in equilibrium, a product purchased in one will cost the same in the other, expressed in the same currency.

**human development index (HDI)**
A composite measure of three indicators of the quality of life in different countries: life expectancy at birth, educational attainment, and whether the average incomes are sufficient to meet the basic needs of life in that country.

To determine the market potential for its particular product or service, a firm should use as many measures as it can obtain. One measure is the relative level of imports and exports. Canada had enjoyed a trade surplus until 2009, when the trade balance shifted into a deficit as the cost of imports rose.[18] The United States has run trade deficits since 1976 due to high volumes of imported oil and consumer products.[19] A **trade deficit** means that the country imports more goods than it exports. Firms would prefer to manufacture in a country, such as Canada, that has a **trade surplus**, or a higher level of exports than imports, because it signals a greater opportunity to export products to more markets.

The most common way to gauge the size and market potential of an economy, and therefore the potential the country has for global marketing, is to use standardized measures of output. One of the most widely used measures is **gross domestic product (GDP)**, which is defined as the market value of the goods and services produced by a country in a year. So what does the size of a country's GDP have to do with global marketing? GDP growth means that production and consumption in the country is expanding, therefore, there are greater marketing opportunities for most goods and services. When GDP growth is slowing, it means that the economy is contracting, or that production and consumption are falling, and marketing opportunities for certain goods and services will decline.

Another frequently used measure of an overall economy is the **purchasing power parity (PPP)**, a theory that states that if the exchange rates of two countries are in equilibrium, a product purchased in one will cost the same in the other, expressed in the same currency.[20] A novel measure that employs PPP to assess the relative economic buying power among nations is *The Economist's* Big Mac Index, which suggests that exchange rates should adjust to equalize the cost of a basket of goods and services, wherever it is bought around the world. Using McDonald's Big Mac, the index shows that the cheapest burger is in Ukraine, where it costs $1.57, compared with an average Canadian price of $4.60. This difference implies that the Ukrainian hryvnia is undervalued by 68.8 percent: that is, the hryvnia is priced too low relative to the Canadian dollar. In this case, the undervalued hryvnia makes Ukraine's exports to Canada cheaper than they would otherwise be, thereby providing an unfair trade advantage to Ukraine. It also makes Canadian exports to Ukraine more expensive.

These various metrics help marketers understand the relative wealth of a particular country; however, as scholars have argued, they may not give a full picture of the economic health of a country because they are based solely on material output. As a corollary measure to those described previously, the United Nations has developed the **human development index (HDI)**, a composite measure of three indicators of the quality of life in different countries: life expectancy at birth; educational attainment; and whether the average incomes, according to PPP estimates, are sufficient to meet the basic needs of life in that country. For marketers, these measures determine the lifestyle elements that ultimately drive consumption (recall that Chapter 4 discussed the influence of consumer lifestyle on consumption). The HDI is scaled from 0 to 1: those countries that score lower than 0.5 are classified as nations with low human development, those that score 0.5 to 0.8 have medium development, and those that score above 0.8 are classified as having high human development. Exhibit 17.5 shows a map of the world with the various HDI scores. Higher HDI means greater consumption levels, especially of discretionary goods and services.

These macroeconomic measures provide a snapshot of a particular country at any one point in time. Because they are standardized measures, it is possible to compare countries across time and to identify those that are experiencing economic growth and increased globalization.

Although an understanding of the macroeconomic environment is crucial for managers facing a market entry decision, of equal importance is the understanding of economic metrics of individual income and household size.

## Evaluating Market Size and Population Growth Rate

Global population has been growing dramatically since the turn of the 20th century. It is estimated that by 2050, the world population will reach 9.7 billion people.[21] From a marketing perspective,

**EXHIBIT 17.5** Global Human Development Index Scores

| | |
|---|---|
| Very High Human Development | ■ |
| High Human Development | ■ |
| Medium Development | ■ |
| Low Human Development | ■ |

*Source:* United Nations Development Programme (2016), *The Human Development Report 2016: Human Development for Everyone.* http://hdr.undp.org/en/countries.

however, growth has not been equally dispersed. Less developed nations, by and large, are experiencing rapid population growth, while many developed countries are experiencing either zero or negative natural population growth. Population growth in many developed countries, such as Canada, is attributed to high levels of immigration. The countries with the highest purchasing power today may become less attractive in the future for many products and services because of stagnated growth. And the BRIC countries are likely to be the source of most market growth.

In response, consumer goods companies are paying close attention to the strong demand in BRIC nations. Procter & Gamble, which enjoys a strong advantage in the Chinese market, is expanding aggressively into India and Brazil. Oral care is highly competitive in Brazil, with Colgate enjoying a 50 percent share of the market[22] and P&G competing. In India, big-name Western firms are competing for sales of laundry products, with Unilever leading the way at a 38 percent share of the market.[23] In some cases, the companies will sell the same products in China and in North America; in other situations, they are creating new products to meet Chinese consumers' tastes. The "Minute Maid Pulpy Super Milky" combines fruit juice, milk powder, whey protein, and coconut bits.

Another aspect related to population and growth pertains to the distribution of the population within a particular region;

"Minute Maid Pulpy Super Milky" combines fruit juice, milk powder, whey protein, and coconut bits for the Chinese market.

Weng lei - Imaginechina via AP Images

To adjust for India's lower income, Cadbury International sells its Dairy Milk Shots for the equivalent of about four cents.

© Mike Hruby

namely, is the population located primarily in rural or urban areas? This distinction determines where and how products and services can be delivered. Long supply chains, in which goods pass through many hands, are necessary to reach rural populations and therefore add costs to products. India's 1.2 billion people live overwhelmingly in rural areas, though the population is moving toward urban areas to meet the demands of the growing industrial and service centres located in major cities such as Bangalore and New Delhi. This population shift, perhaps not surprisingly, is accompanied by rapid growth in the middle class.[24] In the capital of India, New Delhi, crowded streets traditionally were filled with horse-drawn carts, bicycles, scooters, and taxis. Yet the growing Indian middle class is demanding more products previously available only to the wealthy. Relatively careful banking policies and minimal dependence on exports have helped protect India from the global financial crisis. The business impacts of these combined trends of increasing urbanization, a growing middle class, a degree of protectionism by the central government, and a youthful populace make India an absolutely enormous market for consumer goods.

The prevalence of cellphones has grown with the emerging Indian middle class. Fifteen years ago, the country hosted only 5 million total telecom connections, and that number included land lines. Today, there are more than 1 billion.[25] The rapid growth rates of industries create significant opportunities for global companies to sell products. In the telecommunications industry, for example, sellers of accessories such as ringtones and new batteries are enjoying a greatly expanded market. In general, India's economy is expected to continue to outpace world growth.

**Evaluating Real Income** Firms can make adjustments to an existing product or change the price to meet the unique needs of a particular country's market. Such shifts are particularly common for low-priced consumer goods. In settings in which consumers earn very low wages, the market is known as the "bottom of the pyramid." That is, there is a large, impoverished population that still wants and needs consumer goods but cannot pay the prices that the fewer, wealthier consumers in developed nations can. So, for example, Procter & Gamble developed a single-use shampoo packet for consumers in less developed nations who cannot afford an entire bottle at one time. To increase consumption of Coca-Cola in rural India, the company lowered its price to the equivalent of about 10 cents per bottle; Cadbury International introduced the Dairy Milk Shots for the equivalent of about 4 cents.[26] Textbook publishers sell paperback versions of Canadian books for a fraction of the Canadian price to countries where students would not otherwise be able to afford a text. But pricing adjustments aren't only for inexpensive products. Fashion and jewellery manufacturers also make downward adjustments to their prices in countries where the incomes of their target markets cannot support higher prices. Nor is price the only factor that companies adjust to appeal to lower income markets. Haier sells washing machines that also have the capacity to wash vegetables to Chinese consumers who confront limited access to resources, such as water and electricity.[27]

For the Chinese market, Haier sells washing machines that can wash both clothes and vegetables.

Courtesy of Haier America

Speaking of affordability, who would believe that Africa is the fastest-growing market for cellphones, given the stereotypes of poverty in Africa? Today, 41 percent of people living in Sub-Saharan African have a mobile subscription, making this the fastest growing cellphone market in the world.[28] The explosive growth occurred when many African governments privatized their telephone monopolies and fierce competition resulted in decreased prices for airtime and handsets.

Even as multinationals battle for dominance in emerging economies, local marketers also are becoming increasingly price competitive in selling their wares. Local marketers already have strong familiarity with their markets, existing distribution channels, and good name recognition. These smaller firms can often exhibit greater flexibility in their pricing to hold on to market share. They also might be able to find a market niche that remained hidden to international firms. In Macau, for example, big international brands have built massive luxury casinos for the gambling public. But a local casino offers very low minimum buy-in amounts so that lower-income gamblers have a place to go.[29] The best outcome for everyone involved is not just a higher share of an existing market but rather the ongoing development of the market for everyone.[30]

## Analyzing Sociocultural Factors

Understanding another country's culture is crucial to the success of any global marketing initiative. Culture (or the set of values, guiding beliefs, understandings, and ways of doing things shared by members of a society) exists on two levels: visible artifacts (e.g., behaviour, dress, symbols, physical settings, ceremonies), and underlying values (thought processes, beliefs, and assumptions). Visible artifacts are easy to recognize, but businesses often find it more difficult to understand the underlying values of a culture and appropriately adapt their marketing strategies to them.[31]

For example, IKEA stores around the world are open seven days a week—except in France. French law prevents retailers from selling on Sundays, and when IKEA tried to challenge the law by keeping one of its stores open, it provoked a lawsuit from a French workers' union. Although IKEA would love to sell over the whole weekend, when it earns approximately one-quarter of its weekly revenues, neither the workers' unions nor French consumers are likely to change their ways any time soon; leaving Sunday as a day of relaxation constitutes a fundamental foundation of French culture.[32] For the Swiss, a similar prohibition against Sunday retailing may soon fall by the wayside, though. If stores remain closed, Switzerland will continue to lose tourism revenues, because most foreign visitors, who tend to visit on the weekend, are accustomed to shopping on Sundays. Opening retail stores on Sundays could mean increased consumption and wages for workers who work more hours, as well as employment for more people. But the loss of a day traditionally designated for family time and relaxation might be something the country cannot abide.[33] There may be no completely right answer to this dilemma, but global marketers clearly must be aware of the regulations and cultural norms of the countries they enter.

France is the only place on the globe where IKEA is not open on Sundays. Notice that times for "Dimanche," the French word for "Sunday," are absent from the store hours sign.

Philippe Huguen/Getty Images

Even global companies with many years of experience operating in a country occasionally end up offending their customers, which causes the companies huge embarrassment, lost sales, and financial losses. Several examples of these cultural gaffes are presented in this section for illustrative purposes.

One important cultural classification scheme that firms can use is Geert Hofstede's cultural dimensions concept, which sheds more light on these underlying values. Hofstede believes cultures differ on six dimensions:[34]

1. *Power distance.* Willingness to accept social inequality as natural.
2. *Uncertainty avoidance.* The extent to which the society relies on orderliness, consistency, structure, and formalized procedures to address situations that arise in daily life.

3. *Individualism.* Perceived obligation to and dependence on groups.

4. *Masculinity.* The extent to which dominant values are male oriented. A lower masculinity ranking indicates that men and women are treated equally in all aspects of society; a higher masculinity ranking suggests that men dominate in positions of power.[35]

5. *Time orientation.* Short- versus long-term orientation. A country that tends to have a long-term orientation values long-term commitments and is willing to accept a longer time horizon for, say, the success of a new product introduction.

6. *Indulgence.* The extent to which society allows for the gratification of fun and enjoyment needs or else suppresses and regulates such pursuits.[36]

To illustrate two of the six dimensions, consider the data and graph in Exhibit 17.6. Power distance is on the vertical axis and individualism is on the horizontal axis. Several Latin American countries cluster high on power distance but low on individualism; Canada, the United States, Australia, and the United Kingdom, in contrast, cluster high on individualism but low on power distance. Using this information, firms should expect that if they design a marketing campaign that stresses equality and individualism, it will be well accepted in the English-speaking countries, all other factors being equal. The same campaign, however, might not be as well received in Latin American countries.

China scores very high on its time orientation but low in individualism; India has medium to high levels on all six dimensions; and Russia posts notably high uncertainty avoidance and power distance scores. Hofstede is careful to warn that these scores are informative only in a comparative sense, but marketers clearly can use them to design strategies for the varied, promising, BRIC growth markets.[37]

Another means of classifying cultures distinguishes them according to the importance of verbal communication.[38] In Canada, the United States, and most European countries, business relationships are governed by what is said and written down, often through formal contracts. In countries such as China and South Korea, however, most relationships rely on nonverbal cues, so that the situation or context means much more than mere words. For instance, business relationships in China often are formalized by

**EXHIBIT 17.6**     Country Clusters

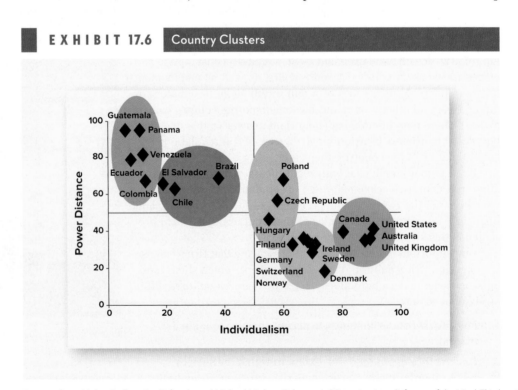

*Sources:* Geert Hofstede, Gert Jan Hofstede, and Michael Minkov, *Cultures and Organizations, Software of the Mind*, Third Revised Edition, McGraw-Hill 2010, ISBN: 0-07-166418-1. ©Geert Hofstede B.V. quoted with permission.

just a handshake, and trust and honour are often more important than legal arrangements.

Overall, culture affects every aspect of consumer behaviour: why people buy; who is in charge of buying decisions; and how, when, and where people shop. Essentially, understanding consumer behaviour is about understanding consumers' culture, particularly in global marketing. For example, in India, McDonald's sells its Maharajah Mac made from chicken instead of beef because the cow is sacred in Hindu culture. In Israel, McDonald's kosher restaurants use the blue and white colours of Israel's flag instead of the yellow and red of its Golden Arches.[39] Similarly, Coca-Cola developed a new drink, Vitango, to be sold in Africa, and P&G developed its Nutristar for Venezuelan consumers.[40] Both companies claim that their soft drinks have special health benefits for their customers in these markets. In North America, people often use their smartphones almost everywhere—in subways, lobbies, restaurants, ballparks, and hockey arenas, as well as while driving. However, in Japan, sending a message on your smartphone when in company—say, during a sit-down dinner or a child's little league baseball game—is considered taboo.[41]

The challenge for marketers is that culture is very subtle, and a failure to recognize the subtleties could lead to very embarrassing and costly mistakes. The following examples illustrate what happens when marketers have a poor understanding of the culture of their global markets.[42]

Business relationships in China often are formalized by just a handshake, and trust and honour are often more important than legal arrangements.

Polka Dot/JupiterImages

- A curling iron Clairol named "Mist Stick" was introduced in Germany, where "mist" is slang for manure.

- Coors' slogan "Turn It Loose," when translated to Spanish, referred to a colloquial term for diarrhea.

- Mercedes-Benz entered China originally as "Bensi" which translated as "rush to die."

- A web-ready personal computer from Panasonic was promoted using a Woody Woodpecker theme. Its slogan was "Touch Woody: The Internet Pecker."

- Colgate introduced a toothpaste in France called Cue, which was the name of a local porn magazine.

**infrastructure**
The basic facilities, services, and installations needed for a community or society to function, such as transportation and communications systems, water and power lines, and public institutions such as schools, post offices, and prisons.

## Analyzing Technology and Infrastructure Capabilities

The next component of any market assessment is a technology and infrastructure analysis. **Infrastructure** is defined as the basic facilities, services, and installations needed for a community or society to function, such as transportation and communications systems, water and power lines, and public institutions such as schools, post offices, and prisons. In Pakistan, companies struggled with an electricity crisis and daily blackouts for over a year. The energy shortage fuelled demand for solar power from companies such as Canadian Solar[43] in Guelph, Ontario. Canadian Solar currently has projects in 24 countries including Mexico, Japan, Vietnam, and China.

Marketers are especially concerned with four key elements of a country's infrastructure:

In Israel, McDonald's kosher restaurants use the blue and white colours of Israel's flag.

© Ronen Zvulun/Reuters/CORBIS

For a country to be a viable option for a new market entry, firms must assess its transportation, distribution channels, communications, and commerce.

Greg Baker/AP Photo/The Canadian Press

transportation, distribution channels, communications, and commerce. First, there must be a system to transport goods throughout the various markets and to consumers in geographically dispersed marketplaces. Second, distribution channels must exist to deliver products in a timely manner and at a reasonable cost. Third, communications systems, particularly media access, must be sufficiently developed to allow consumers to find information about the products and services available in the marketplace. Fourth, the commercial infrastructure consists of the legal, banking, and regulatory systems that allow markets to function. Marketers—especially those that are interested in offshoring research, production, and marketing—will be particularly interested in the technical sophistication of the workforce of the country. Generally, a more sophisticated workforce means that a higher proportion of product design, development, and marketing activities can be decentralized to the foreign country.

Sustainable Marketing 17.1 highlights how Canada's Bombardier, a world leader in the transportation industry, is implementing sustainable business practices across its global operations with great success.

## Sustainable Marketing 17.1

### Bombardier: Moving Forward Responsibly[44]

Canada's Bombardier is a global transportation company that operates in more than 60 countries on five continents. It is a world-leading manufacturer of innovative transportation solutions, from commercial aircraft and business jets to rail transportation equipment, systems, and services. Its revenues for the fiscal year 2013 were US$18.2 billion. Bombardier's 76,400 employees around the globe do everything from R&D to the design, manufacture, sales, and support stages for a broad range of world-class products in aerospace and rail transportation. Some high-profile projects include a fully automated people mover in the Beijing airport and high-altitude railcars for a railway to Lhasa, Tibet.

Bombardier has made sustainability an integral part of its global business strategy, implementing a wide range of initiatives across the entire global organization. According to Pierre Beaudoin, president and CEO of Bombardier, "Our ongoing investments attest to our belief that excellence in corporate social responsibility makes business sense in all economic cycles. That is why we made corporate social responsibility a key element of our new business strategy." The company also actively promotes the UN Global Compact's principles of social responsibility and has embedded these principles in its code of ethics and business conduct. To demonstrate its commitment and to measure and

communicate its progress, Bombardier has undertaken to produce an annual report card, Moving Forward Responsibly, detailing its many initiatives and accomplishments.

On the product innovation side, for example, Bombardier has developed the all-new CSeries commercial aircraft. When the CSeries took flight, it burned 20 percent less fuel and generated 20 percent less carbon dioxide emissions than other aircraft in its class. Similarly, the ZEFIRO portfolio features the world's most economical and eco-friendly high-speed trains. It includes ECO4 technologies, which can yield overall energy savings of up to 50 percent.

Between 2009 and 2013, Bombardier successfully achieved its goal of reducing its water consumption by 12.6 percent, energy consumption by 15 percent, and greenhouse gas emissions by 24.4 percent.[45] The progress made by Bombardier in the area of sustainability has earned it a spot on two prestigious Dow Jones sustainability indexes and, for the second time, on the Carbon Disclosure Project (CDP), the world standard for carbon disclosure methodology and process. The CDP named Bombardier one of the 10 Canadian Climate Disclosure Leaders.

In keeping with its theme of Moving Forward Responsibly, Bombardier has identified four areas in which it will make additional investments over the next few years: community investment, stakeholder engagement, employee volunteering, and corporate social responsibility reporting and communication.

## The Appeal of the BRIC Countries

**LO2**

Changes in technology, especially communications, have been a driving force for growth in global markets for decades. The telegraph, radio, television, computer, and Internet have increasingly connected distant parts of the world. Today, communication is instantaneous. Sounds and images from across the globe are delivered to TV sets, radios, and computers in real time, which enables receivers in all parts of the world to observe how others live, work, and play. Perhaps the greatest change facing the global community in recent years has been the growth and expansion of four countries that together have come to be known as the BRIC countries: Brazil, Russia, India, and China. Some commentators suggest adding South Africa, to make BRICS, because of that nation's remarkable transformation into a functioning democracy.[46] The inspiring changes to South Africa suggest its increasing promise as a market, but its relatively smaller size leads us to focus on the four BRIC nations, with seemingly the greatest potential for growth, here. Let's examine each in turn.

**Brazil**[47]   Long a regional powerhouse, Brazil's ability to weather and even thrive during the most recent economic storm has transformed it into a global contender. Brazil is the world's ninth largest economy,[48] but high inflation and political crises have prompted Brazil to project some significant economic declines in the near future.[49] Still, Brazil's impressive economic growth in the 21st century largely can be attributed to the expansion of its literate population and the imposition of social programs that have allowed more than half of the 201 million Brazilians to enter the middle class.[50] Even as the nation struggles with a recession, it continues to experiment with innovative financial approaches in an effort to ensure that the Brazilian economy rebounds.[51] This large South American democracy welcomes foreign investors.

Like other countries in which McDonald's thrives, Brazil has a strong and growing middle class.
Bloomberg/Getty Images

**Russia**[52]   Relations with Russia are a little more complicated than for Brazil. Since the fall of the former Soviet Union, Russia has undergone multiple up- and downturns in its economy. However, its overall growth prospects appear promising, especially as a consumer market. Long denied access to consumer goods, the well educated population exhibits strong demand for North American products and brands. In particular, the 84.4 million Russian Internet users are growing at a rate of approximately 14 percent annually and Russia is already Europe's largest Internet market. The country also is negotiating to enter the World Trade Organization (WTO) to improve trade relations with other countries. In 2015 it ranked as one of the top countries in terms of retail growth; even though economic and political issues challenge its retail growth prospects, the market simply is too big for most firms to disregard. Yet Russia still faces an aging population and low birthrate. If these trends persist, Russia's population could decline by one-third in the next half-century. At the same time, corruption is widespread, creating ethical dilemmas for firms trying to market their goods and services.

Relaxed Indian governmental restrictions now allow foreign retailers that carry their own brand, like Levi's, to own 100 percent of their Indian businesses.

Aijaz Rahi/AP Images

India[53] With more than 1.25 billion people, or approximately 15 percent of the world's population, together with expanding middle and upper classes, India is one of the world's fastest-growing markets. With a median age of 27.3 years, India has one of the youngest populations in the world. Its young inhabitants increasingly are adopting global attitudes while living in growing urban centres and shopping at large malls. The well educated modern generation is largely fluent in English, and the highly skilled workforce holds great attraction for firms that hope to expand using local talent, especially in technical fields.

India's retail environment is still dominated by millions of small stores, and lacks modern supply chain management facilities and systems.[54] Recent changes by the Indian government, however, have the potential to significantly modernize the retail landscape, as the description in the opening vignette suggested. For example, foreign retailers that carry multiple brands, like Walmart, are now allowed to own up to 51 percent of joint ventures in India, whereas previously these retailers were permitted only to enter into wholesale joint ventures. Also, retailers that carry only their own brand, like Reebok, can now own 100 percent of their Indian businesses.[55] India is also projected to become the fastest growing ecommerce market in the world, with ecommerce sales forecast to reach $55 billion in 2018.[56]

China[57]   For most of the 20th century, China experienced foreign occupation, civil unrest, major famine, and a strict one-party communist regime. However, since 1978, China's leadership, while maintaining communist political ideals, has embraced market-oriented economic development, which has led to startlingly rapid gains. For many Chinese, recent developments have dramatically improved their living standards and their levels of personal freedom. Increasing liberalization in the economy has prompted a large increase in China's Global Retail Development Index (GRDI). Even as growth in its gross domestic product (GDP) has slowed, China maintains a thriving retail market, likely to reach the $8 trillion mark soon and surpass the United States as the world's largest.[58]

Yet the country continues to suffer from drastically unequal economic distribution, which has led to a significant migrant workforce who subsist on part-time, low-paying jobs. These workers were hit hard by the global financial crisis, which reduced demand for Chinese exports for the first time in years. Furthermore, actual growth of the 1.3 billion-strong Chinese population slowed as a result of government population controls that limit each family to one child. Although China's median age is slightly younger than that in North America currently, at 36.8 years, the application of the one-child policy means that China is one of the most rapidly aging countries in the world. The central government has recently made changes to this policy, however, the effects of the original policy are likely to persist for generations to come.

Even as vast numbers of North American companies actively target the massive Chinese market or explore options for entering it, as Social and Mobile Marketing 17.1 highlights, some challenges remain.

## Social and Mobile Marketing 17.1

### The Growth of Social Networking— Brazil's Free Market Versus China's Restrictions[59]

In Brazil, Facebook already has 90 million members, making the South American nation the third-largest market, behind India and the United States. It also ranks among the top markets for YouTube, Google, and Twitter. Part of the explanation for this great growth is Brazil's status as one of the most rapidly developing economies in the world. As people gain economic security, they have more resources to spend on social networking gadgets, as well as more leisure time to play with them.

But it also has to do with the culture. Brazil is known for the open, friendly attitudes of its people. For these "hyper-social" consumers, new ways to connect with friends and loved ones represent an important form of need fulfillment. International companies can enter freely, function according to a relatively well established legal structure, and enjoy a pretty strong infrastructure as well.

In contrast, when companies confront the inherent openness of social networking with China's strict censorship rules, significant challenges arise. Successful entry by social and mobile marketers into China requires a particular blend of timing, skill, cultural understanding, and political savvy. These factors may not be quite in alignment for Facebook. The timing may be wrong because China's autocratic leaders have enforced greater controls on social networking and blogging recently. Nor do Facebook executives appear to have a full grasp of the political and cultural nuances of business in China, despite a good track record of respecting local cultural values, such as when it agreed to block content about Nazism in Germany or drawings of Muhammad in Pakistan. And even if Facebook were to navigate these challenges

CEO Mark Zuckerberg (centre) claims that Facebook will employ diplomacy in China, but censorship issues are highly complex.

Lao Chen/ChinaFotoPress/ZUMAPRESS.com/Newscom

safely, China has a strong, enduring preference for companies owned and run by its own people.

Censorship issues are highly complex. For instance, how would Facebook respond to retaliation against users who criticize the government? For Google, whose mission statement simply advises "Don't be evil," such questions became all too pertinent when hackers in China gained access to the email accounts of prominent human rights activists. When Western companies have cooperated with the Chinese government, some operations have led to the imprisonment of online activists.

In Brazil, the question is how many users the company can encourage to enjoy all the fun of Facebook. In China, a post on Facebook can lead to jail time. Thus, it becomes a question of basic human rights.

## CHOOSING A GLOBAL MARKET ENTRY STRATEGY          **LO3**

When a firm has concluded its assessment analysis of the most viable markets for its products and services, it must then conduct an internal assessment of its capabilities. As we discussed in Chapter 2, this analysis includes an assessment of the firm's access to capital, the current markets it serves, its manufacturing capacity, its proprietary assets, and the commitment of its management to the proposed strategy. These factors ultimately contribute to the success or failure of a market expansion strategy, whether at home or in a foreign market. After these internal market assessments, it is time for the firm to choose its entry strategy.

A firm can choose from many approaches when it decides to enter a new market. These approaches vary according to the level of risk the firm is willing to take. Many firms actually follow a progression in which they begin with less risky strategies to enter

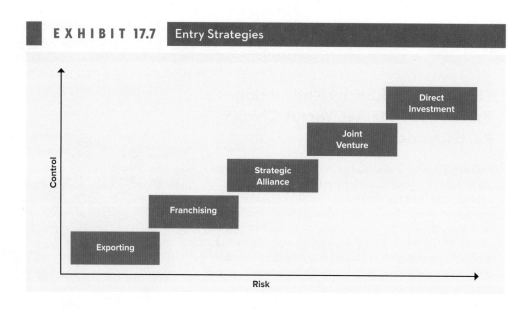

**EXHIBIT 17.7** Entry Strategies

their first foreign markets and move to increasingly risky strategies as they gain confidence in their abilities, as illustrated in Exhibit 17.7. Generally, profit potential increases with higher levels of risks. We examine these different approaches that marketers take when entering global markets, beginning with the least risky.

## Exporting

**exporting**
Producing goods in one country and selling them in another.

**Exporting** means producing goods in one country (exporting country) and selling them in another (host country). This entry strategy requires the least financial risk but also allows for only a limited return to the exporting firm. Global expansion often begins when a firm receives an order for its product or service from another country, in which case it faces little risk because it can demand payment before it ships the merchandise. By the same token, it is difficult to achieve economies of scale when everything has to be shipped internationally. The Swiss watchmaker Rolex sells relatively small numbers of expensive watches all over the world. Because its transportation costs are relatively small compared with the cost of the watches, the best way for it to service any market is to export from Switzerland. Exporting generally provides less employment for citizens of the host country than either joint venture or direct investment.

Exporting may take two forms: indirect or direct. Indirect exporting occurs when the exporting firm sells its goods in the host country through an intermediary. Ossetra Wondrous Earth in Newfoundland produces an organic skincare line that uses water from local icebergs. It has distributors in the United States, Greece, Hong Kong, and South Korea, ensuring the company is in compliance with international regulations.[60] This approach carries the least risk but probably returns the least profit for the exporting company. This approach is likely to be used when the company has limited contacts in the foreign country but wants to market to that country. Direct exporting is when the exporting company sells its products in the host country directly without the intermediaries. This approach carries more risk and offers greater returns to the exporting firm than indirect exporting. For example, Christie Digital, a firm based in Kitchener, Ontario, manufactures a variety of display technologies and solutions for cinemas, large audience environments, control rooms, business presentations, training facilities, 3D and virtual

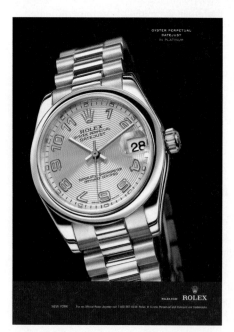

Rolex exports its watches to countries all over the world from its factory in Switzerland.

Courtesy of Rolex USA

reality, simulation, education, media, and government. Christie has installed more than 100,000 projection solutions in the United States, the United Kingdom, Japan, China, and many other countries around the world.[61] Similarly, IBM sells its intelligence tools and applications to businesses around the world by using its own sales force. Entrepreneurial Marketing 17.1 describes how Steeped Tea successfully entered the U.S. market using a direct sales model.

In Canada, the top five Canadian exporters account for 25 percent of Canada's exports, and the top 50 Canadian exporters account for 50 percent of Canada's exports. The remaining 45,210 exporters are responsible for the remaining 50 percent. Almost three-quarters (72.6 percent) of Canadian exporters had exports of less than $1 million. More than two-thirds of Canada's exports come from two sectors: energy and motor vehicles.[64]

# Entrepreneurial Marketing 17.1

## Get Ready to ParTea[62]

After water, tea is the most consumed beverage in the world. Tonia Jahshan fell in love with tea while on vacation with her husband. She shared her love of tea with friends at a party in her home, serving them a variety of loose-leaf blends and talking about tea's amazing health benefits. When people started asking her to hold parties in their homes, Steeped Tea was born. It didn't take long for her Hamilton, Ontario, business to become a veritable tempest in a teapot. Only 15 months after hosting her first event, she was doing 15 parties a month.

To help manage the rapid growth, Tonia got her husband, Hatem, involved in her business. With his chemistry degree, chemical engineering degree, and MBA, you might question his fit for the tea business. However, he had also owned three Subway franchises. Based on this experience, Hatem felt that franchising wasn't the best approach to expansion. Instead, they opted for a direct sales model based on commission. Six years later Tonia had 500 consultants in Canada selling the company's loose-leaf teas and tea accessories.

Consultants present Steeped Tea's products at parties and facilitate sales to consumers. Creativity is encouraged, with some consultants using themes, such as MarTEAni, to drive sales beyond the $500 party average. There are strict guidelines about what consultants can and cannot say. For example, they are not allowed to comment on health issues and must refer consumers to their doctors. All consultants have the option to upgrade the services they receive from Steeped Tea to set up their own personal site with an online shopping cart and the ability to send newsletters. A party management system lets consultants set up a website for hostesses to do evites and collect orders from people who can't attend the party.

Ranked number 27 on the PROFIT 500 list of Canada's fastest-growing companies, Tonia was ready to expand to the U.S. market. Knowing she would need

Steeped Tea's consultants work on a direct sales model in Canada and in the United States.

Used with permission of Steeped Tea

help, she pitched her story on CBC's *Dragons' Den*. With impressive annual sales of $1.3 million, she earned financial backing from David Chilton and Jim Treliving. David Chilton even got his daughter to sign up as a consultant to test the business model.[63] In the first month and a half, Steeped Tea signed up 60 U.S. consultants, most of them in northeast Michigan, Ohio, and New York State, but also in Florida, California, and Hawaii.

Hatem Jahshan says the beauty of direct sales is that it builds from word-of-mouth. He expects to have 3,000 consultants in the United States in two years. Growth can take off quickly and he says they need to be prepared. As orders grew, they needed to find new suppliers—they were completely buying out the supply of small companies. Today they source tea from all around the world, buying it in lots, six months in advance of when they need it. Even with such long lead times, it can be difficult to forecast demand or know if suppliers will run out.

Although they have just scratched the surface with U.S. sales, they have received calls to expand to the United Kingdom and Australia. One of the biggest challenges entering the U.S. market was getting FDA approval because tea is a food product. Since the United Kingdom has a whole different set of standards, Steeped Tea is not actively pursuing this option yet. For now, the company's focus is on steeping strong TEAms in North America.

## Franchising

Franchising is a contractual agreement between a firm (the franchisor) and another firm or individual (the franchisee). A franchising contract allows the franchisee to operate a business—a retail product or service firm or a B2B provider—using a name and format developed and supported by the franchisor. Many of the best-known retailers in Canada are also successful global franchisers, including McDonald's, Pizza Hut, Tim Hortons®, Domino's Pizza, KFC, and Holiday Inn, all of which have found that global franchising entails lower risks and requires less investment than does opening units owned wholly by the firm. Tim Hortons® has over 4,400 stores in Canada, the United States, and the Middle East, and recently announced it will head to the Philippines and Mexico.[65]

However, with franchising, firms have limited control over the market operations in the foreign country, potential profit is reduced because it must be split with the franchisee, and, once the franchise is established, there is always the threat that the franchisee will break away and operate as a competitor under a different name. White Spot, one of Canada's oldest restaurant chains, successfully used franchising to expand its operations into Asia. To protect its brand reputation, it provides experienced supervisors and "off the shelf" marketing programs to ensure consistency.[66] In Canada, more than 78 000 franchise operations employ over 1 million people and generate in excess of $68 billion in annual sales.[67]

## Strategic Alliance

**strategic alliance**
A collaborative relationship between independent firms, though the partnering firms do not create an equity partnership; that is, they do not invest in one another.

A **strategic alliance** is a collaborative relationship between independent firms, though the partnering firms do not create an equity partnership; that is, they do not invest in one another. For example, Star Alliance constitutes one of the most complex strategic alliances in the world, with 27 airline members representing different countries, some of which include Air Canada, Air China, Air New Zealand, All Nippon Airways (Japan), Asiana Airlines (South Korea), Austrian Airlines, Brussels Airlines (Belgium), EgyptAir, LOT (Poland), Lufthansa (Germany), Scandinavian Airlines (Denmark, Norway, and Sweden), Singapore Airlines, South African Airways, Swiss International Air Lines, TAP Portugal, Thai Airways International, Turkish Airlines, and United Airlines (United States).[68]

What began as a series of bilateral agreements among five airlines grew over time into Star Alliance, which now acts as a separate legal entity in which each member is a stakeholder but no member is an equity owner in the others. Star Alliance coordinates the members on projects of mutual interest, such as helping members in their individual brand-building efforts by creating value through their membership in the Alliance. This plan offers passengers benefits from individual airlines when they purchase from alliance partners. For instance, an Air Canada frequent-flier member could earn Aeroplan

KFC and Pizza Hut are successful global franchisors.

(left): © Yang zheng/AP Images; (right): © Zhou junxiang/AP Images

miles by flying EgyptAir. This coalition also allows seamless booking and other transactions across the Alliance membership.

## Joint Venture

A **joint venture** is formed when a firm entering a new market pools its resources with those of a local firm to form a new company in which ownership, control, and profits are shared. In addition to sharing the financial burden, the local partner offers the foreign entrant greater understanding of the market and access to resources such as vendors and real estate. Some countries require joint ownership of firms entering their domestic markets, as is the case with the new regulations affecting multi-line retailers entering India, though many of these restrictions have loosened as a result of WTO negotiations and ever-increasing globalization pressures.

Tesco—the U.K. supermarket, finance, telecom, and insurance superstar—entered China, which usually requires joint ownership from entering firms. Through a joint venture it purchased a 50 percent share in Ting Hsin—which owns and operates the 25-store hypermarket chain Hymall. More recently it combined 131 stores with China Resource Enterprise (CRE) to become the country's largest food retailer.[69] Bombardier signed a $3.4 billion contract with Russia for the sale of 100 Q400 NextGen airplanes. Until 2013, all of its airplanes had been assembled in Canada; however, the Q400s were to be assembled in Russia as part of the joint venture agreement. This plan was later put on hold due to the political situation in Russia.[70] Problems with joint ventures can arise if the political situation changes, if the partners disagree, if the government places restrictions on the firm's ability to move its profits out of the foreign country and back to its home country, or if the objectives, responsibilities, and benefits of the venture are not clearly defined from the outset. Conflicts could also arise if larger partners benefit more than smaller partners, which could threaten the venture. Differences in organizational cultures, management styles, and leadership, as well as disagreements about marketing and investment policies, could seriously affect the performance of the venture.

Two variants of joint ventures are contract manufacturing and management contracting. Contract manufacturing is when a foreign firm contracts with a local firm in the host market to manufacture the product. For example, NutraLab Canada is a contract manufacturer that has provided original equipment manufacture (OEM) and private label service for vitamin, natural health, and dietary supplement products for more than 15 years.[71] NutraLab Canada produces many of the pharmaceutical softgels, capsules, liquid, and tablets that we consume.

Management contracting occurs when the domestic firm provides management consulting and advice to a foreign firm. For example, many Canadian technology companies will supply their technology to firms and governments in developing countries with a specific agreement that only the Canadian supplier can maintain the technology or provide know-how regarding technology use and repair. Management contracting is a low-risk method of entering a country's market without setting up operations in the country. It also generates returns immediately upon execution of the agreement. Management contracting tends to be long-term since it extends over the life of the technology.

## Direct Investment

**Direct investment** requires a firm to maintain 100 percent ownership of its plants, operation facilities, and offices in a foreign country, often through the formation of wholly owned subsidiaries. This entry strategy requires the highest level of investment and exposes the firm to significant risks, including the loss of its operating and/or initial investments. For example, a dramatic economic downturn caused by a natural disaster or war, political instability, or changes in the country's laws can increase a foreign entrant's risk considerably. Many firms believe that in certain markets these potential risks are outweighed by the high potential returns; with this strategy, none of the potential profits

**joint venture**
Formed when a firm entering a new market pools its resources with those of a local firm to form a new company in which ownership, control, and profits are shared.

**direct investment**
When a firm maintains 100 percent ownership of its plants, operation facilities, and offices in a foreign country, often through the formation of wholly owned subsidiaries.

Lenovo actively promotes its products in Brazil.

Lenovo

must be shared with other firms. In addition to the high potential returns, direct investment offers the firm complete control over its operations in the foreign country.

Hundreds of Canadian mining, manufacturing, and technology companies have direct investments in several countries around the world. For example, Barrick Gold is the world's largest gold producer, with a portfolio of 25 operating mines, and advanced exploration and development projects in South America, North America, Africa, and Australia. Similarly, Bombardier has production and engineering sites in 28 countries including all the BRICs.[72]

Although we often tend to think of direct investment flowing from more to less developed economies, the dynamic international market means that sometimes it goes the other way. The computer maker Lenovo started in China but has since expanded. In addition to purchasing IBM's PC division and Motorola's handset business unit, it established parallel headquarters in both Beijing and North Carolina. When it entered Brazil, it quickly established separate manufacturing plants, to keep its costs low.[73]

As we noted, each of these entry strategies entails different levels of risk and rewards for the foreign entrant. But even after a firm has determined how much risk it is willing to take, and therefore how it will enter a new global market, it still must establish its marketing strategy, as we discuss in the next section.

## **L04** CHOOSING A GLOBAL MARKETING STRATEGY

Just like any other marketing strategy, a global marketing strategy includes two components: determining the target market(s) to pursue, and developing a marketing mix that will sustain a competitive advantage over time. In this section, we examine marketing strategy as it relates specifically to global markets.

### Target Market: Segmentation, Targeting, and Positioning

Global segmentation, targeting, and positioning (STP) is more complicated than domestic STP, as discussed in Chapter 6, for several reasons. First, firms considering a global expansion have much more difficulty understanding the cultural nuances of other countries. Second, subcultures within each country also must be considered. Third, consumers often view products and their role as consumers differently in different countries. A product or service often must be positioned differently in different markets.

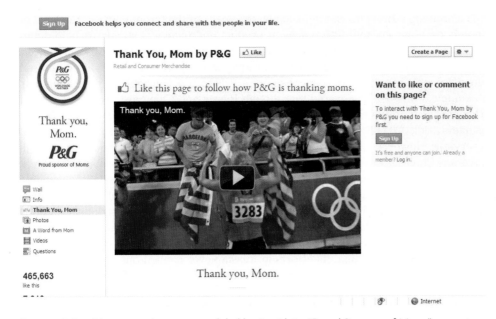

Procter & Gamble targeted moms on a global basis with its "Proud Sponsor of Moms" campaign, which ran during the 2016 Summer Olympics.

The Procter & Gamble Company

Clearly in Vancouver originally set up online operations to sell contact lenses to Canadian consumers. A decade later, it diversified by adding eyeglasses, a category with rapid growth that now accounts for 25 percent of its revenues. Based on data showing that the number of American consumers over 50 years old would increase by 19 percent in the next 10 years, it set up a new division, Coastal.com, to meet demand from boomers needing glasses. After only three years, sales to the United States made up 16 percent of the company's revenues.[74]

Segments and target markets can and should be defined by more than just geography. For example, when Yahoo determines its segmentation and positioning strategies, it relies on research into a segment familiar throughout the world: moms. By working with a global market research firm, Yahoo investigates how moms in Russia, Colombia, China, the United States, Mexico, India, the United Kingdom, Argentina, and France understand and use social media and other modern technologies. Looking on with great interest is the global product brand Procter & Gamble, which has run a global "Proud Sponsor of Moms" campaign during each recent iteration of the Olympic Games.[75]

When it identifies its positioning within the market, the firm then must decide how to implement its marketing strategies by using the marketing mix. Just as firms adjust their products and services to meet the needs of national target market(s), they must alter their marketing mix to serve the needs of global markets.

## The Global Marketing Mix

The PEST factors described earlier in this chapter, as well as consumers' psychological, social, and situational factors, influence how marketers configure the marketing mix and implement their marketing strategy. In this section, we explore the four Ps (product, place, promotion, price) from a global perspective.

### Global Product or Service Strategies    There are three potential global product strategies:

- Sell the same product or service in both the home country market and the host country.
- Sell a product or service similar to that sold in the home country but include minor adaptations.
- Sell totally new products or services.

Pringles sometimes changes flavours to reflect local tastes and demand, such as with these paprika-flavoured chips sold in Italy and Germany.

Whitebox Media/Mediablitzimages/Alamy Stock Photo

**glocalization**
When firms offer standardized products globally and change promotional campaigns geared to local markets.

The strategy a firm chooses depends on the needs of the target market. The level of economic development and differences in product and technical standards help determine the need for product adaptation. Cultural differences such as food preferences, language, and religion also play a role in product strategy planning. In varied cultural settings, bringing even the simplest consumer goods to new markets can be challenging. For example, Campbell discovered that though Russia and China are two of the largest markets for soup in the world, cooks in those countries have unique demands. Chinese consumers drink 320 billion bowls of soup each year, and Russian buyers consume 32 billion servings. However, Chinese cooks generally refuse to resort to canned soup; though the average Chinese consumer eats soup five times each week, he or she also takes great pride in preparing it personally with fresh ingredients. In contrast, Russian consumers, though they demand very high quality in their soups, had grown tired of spending hours preparing their homemade broths. To identify opportunities in these markets, Campbell sent teams of social anthropologists to study how Chinese and Russian cooks prepare and consume soup. When it faced further hurdles, it entered into a joint venture with the Swire soup company in China. Its efforts in Russia never panned out, forcing Campbell to withdraw after around four years. Even with extensive, devoted efforts by an industry giant, global marketing remains a challenge.[76]

Nestlé created 20 unique flavours of Kit Kat for Japanese consumers; in Japan, Kit Kat is one of the top confectionery brands. By creating flavours that reflect the local produce and tastes of different regions of Japan, Nestlé aims to promote its unique Kit Kat bars as regional souvenirs. Kit Kat varieties now range from yubari melon from Hokkaido Island, to green beans and cherries from Tohoku in northeastern Japan, to yuzu fruit and red potatoes from Kyushu/Okinawa region at the southernmost tip of the country. The Kanto region, including Tokyo, contributed the sweet potato, blueberry, and soy sauce flavours. Wasabi-flavoured white chocolate Kit Kat is also quite popular with Japanese consumers.[77]

The level of economic development also affects the global product strategy because it relates directly to consumer buying behaviour. Consumers in developed countries tend to demand more attributes in their products than do consumers in less developed countries. In Canada, Honda does not offer its line of "urban" motorcycles, available in Mexico, China, and India, because the product line resembles a motor scooter more than a motorcycle, which does not tend to appeal to consumers. Motorcycles sold in North America have more horsepower and bigger frames and come with an array of options that are not offered in other countries.

In a practice referred to as **glocalization**, some firms also standardize their products globally but use different promotional campaigns to sell them. The original Pringles potato chip product remains the same globally, as do the images and themes of the promotional campaign, with limited language adaptations for local markets, although English is used whenever possible. However, the company does change Pringles' flavours in different countries, including paprika-flavoured chips, which are sold in Italy and Germany.[78] McCain Foods, which markets frozen potato specialties in 100 countries, localizes its product by, for instance, calling french fries *chips* in the United Kingdom and developing local advertising for markets by region.[79]

Manufacturers are not the only ones that must adapt their offering. On the retail side, for example, Whole Foods is making shopping an experience in the United Kingdom to compete with the local organic supermarket chains. And as Sustainable Marketing 17.2 notes, General Mills has committed to sustainable sourcing of the key ingredients it uses in its products around the world.

Despite persistent differences across borders, marketers have found a growing convergence in tastes and preferences in many product categories. Starbucks is a good example of a company that has both influenced and exploited this global convergence in tastes. Even in China and Great Britain, traditional strongholds for tea marketers, coffee is quickly gaining ground as the beverage of choice. Increasingly, because of the Internet and other information technologies, there seems to be not only a convergence of taste

## Sustainable Marketing 17.2

### General Mills Commits to Sustainable Sourcing

Agriculture is among the greatest contributors to global warming, emitting more greenhouse gases than all our cars, trucks, trains, and airplanes combined.[80] Agriculture alone produces up to 35 percent of the world's greenhouse gas emissions and uses 70 percent of the water.[81]

With the global population expected to reach 9 billion people by 2050, food production is required to increase by 70 percent to feed the additional 2.3 billion mouths.[82] Today, the biggest players in the agriculture industry have the opportunity to have significant impact on the sustainability of these practices going into the future.

General Mills has taken a proactive approach to ensure that it operates a sustainable business. The company has announced a commitment to cut its emissions by 28 percent across the entire value chain by 2025.[83] To do this, General Mills continues to invest in energy efficiency and clean energy innovation at its manufacturing facilities, as well as to search for and make changes from farm to fork. Over the long term beyond 2025, General Mills aims to achieve sustainable emission levels in line with scientific consensus by 2050, which requires a reduction of 50–70 percent in absolute emissions across the value chain.[84]

Perhaps its most significant goal is its commitment to sustainably source 100 percent of its 10 priority ingredients by 2020.[85] These 10 ingredients—which include vanilla, cocoa, palm oil and sugarcane—represent over 41 percent of General Mills' annual raw material purchases and are ingredients the company believes can have the greatest impact from a sourcing standpoint. In order to reach this goal, General Mills tailors its approach to each ingredient and geography to improve the economic, environmental, and social sustainability of each ingredient's production.

For instance, to improve the sustainability of vanilla, General Mills invested in local communities in Madagascar—where more than 90 percent of the world's vanilla is produced and where the vanilla used in Häagen-Dazs ice cream is grown.[86] The biggest challenges come

### By 2020, General Mills commits to sourcing 100% of its...

 ... **oats** from growing regions that demonstrate continuous improvement against industry-based environmental metrics.

 ... **cocoa** through origin-direct investment, which will improve the incomes of smallholder farmers and the quality of ingredients.

 ... **U.S. wheat** from growing regions that demonstrate continuous improvement against the Field-to-Market framework* or comparable environmental metrics.

 ... **vanilla** through origin direct investment, which will improve the incomes of smallholder farmers and the quality of ingredients.

 ... **dry milled corn** from growing regions that demonstrate continuous improvement against the Field-to-Market framework or comparable environmental metrics.

 ... **palm oil** from responsible and sustainable sources in 2015.

 ... **sugar cane** from responsible and sustainable sources.

 ... directly sourced **fluid milk** from producing regions that demonstrate continuous improvement as measured by the Dairy Sustainability Framework (U.S.) or other comparable environmental metrics (globally).

 ... **fiber packaging** from recycled material or from virgin wood fiber regions that are known to not contribute to deforestation. Any high-risk regions will be independently verified.

 ... **U.S. beet sugar** from growing regions that demonstrate continuous improvement against the Field-To-Market framework or comparable environmental metrics.

*The Field-to-Market framework studies the environmental impact of crop production in different regions.

SOURCE: GENERAL MILLS, INC. | FOODBUSINESSNEWS.NET

General Mills commits to sustainably source 10 key ingredients, such as the vanilla used in its Häagen-Dazs ice cream.
Used with permission of General Mills

from the small family-operated farms that harvest vanilla beans, the food security of those communities, and the quality of ingredients they deliver.

Since the start of the initiative, General Mills has launched a program in the village of Belambo, located in Madagascar's Sava region, to train farming families about vanilla production practices.[87] Farmers who know how to cure the vanilla they grow significantly increase their earnings. To combat food insecurity in the area, the company also funded the construction of a storage warehouse in Belambo that makes rice available to local families year-round at lower prices, improving the reliability of their source of food.

By spearheading these initiatives, General Mills has become a role model in sustainability for other consumer packaged goods companies.

among youths but also the emergence of global homogeneous segments. That is, groups of consumers from around the world now share similar buying characteristics.

**Global Pricing Strategies**   Determining the selling price in the global marketplace is an extremely difficult task.[88] (Refer back to Chapter 11 for a refresher on pricing.) Many countries still have rules governing the competitive marketplace, including those that affect pricing. For example, in parts of Europe—including Belgium, Italy, Spain, Greece, and France—promotional sales are allowed only twice a year, in January and in June or July. In most European countries, retailers can't sell below cost, and they can't advertise reduced prices in advance of sales or discount items until they have been on shelves for more than a month. For firms such as Walmart and other discounters, these restrictions threaten their core competitive positioning as the lowest-cost provider in the market. In China, Singles' Day offers consumers deep discounts on a range of merchandise, as discussed in Entrepreneurial Marketing 17.2. Other issues, such as tariffs, quotas, antidumping laws, and currency exchange policies, can also affect pricing decisions.[89]

Competitive factors influence global pricing in the same way they do home country pricing, but because a firm's products or services may not have the same positioning in the global marketplace as they do in its home country, market prices must be adjusted to reflect the local pricing structure. Spain's fashion retailer Zara, for instance, is relatively inexpensive in the European Union but is priced about 50 percent higher in North America, putting it right in the middle of its moderately priced competition.[95] Since it is important for Zara to get its fashions to the consumers in a timely manner, it incurs additional transportation expenses, which it passes on to its North American customers. Finally,

## Entrepreneurial Marketing 17.2

### Deep Discounts Attract Online Purchasers

Ecommerce in China is just plain booming. Shoppers spread throughout China's vast landscape have limited access to traditional shopping sites but vastly increasing access to smartphones.[90] Thus they check with etailers such as Taobao and Alibaba to find virtually anything they want, then have it delivered to their doors.[91]

Some of the most successful sites are those that provide a wide range of options, all in one place. As long as they can procure the chosen items, consumers keep flocking to these sites. That service provision can be tough, though, especially on special occasions such as Singles' Day when deep discounts can be found. This recently created holiday falls on November 11 (the numerical form, 11/11, with its four 1s, signifies loneliness) and has sparked a retail revolution. *Fortune* magazine has called it "Black Friday on steroids." During the most recent Singles' Day, 402 million different shoppers visited one of Alibaba's linked sites to shop. That's more than one-third of China's total population. Consumers purchased $14.3 billion worth of goods, which far outpaced any previous one-day sales total, anywhere in the world. (In comparison, that same year, the biggest online shopping day in the United States, Cyber Monday, reached $1.35 billion.) Alibaba has succeeded in attracting 80 percent of China's online shoppers, 73 percent of whom made their purchases via a mobile phone.[92]

Executive chairman and Alibaba founder Jack Ma told the press he estimates that Singles' Day future growth will be over 50 percent per year.[93] That's impressive for any company, but even more so for a company that was founded in 1999 with Ma's wife and 17 friends in his

Alibaba's Singles Day in China far surpasses Cyber Monday sales in the United States.

REUTERS/Alamy Stock Photo

apartment.[94] The little start-up that grew now outstrips both Amazon and eBay in sales revenue.

Ma built Alibaba with a "service first, business second" approach. By placing the customer first, instead of following conventional wisdom that holds investors in the highest esteem, Ma earned the trust of Chinese consumers. In a country rife with counterfeit products, Alibaba implemented strict quality control measures and worked closely with suppliers to ensure that high standards were met. Ma implicitly knew that if customers weren't happy, they would not return to the site. As a result, Alibaba is able to attract consumers who buy everything from music and movie tickets to clothing and wine.

From having fewer than two dozen employees in 1999, Alibaba now is responsible for creating jobs for 10 million people and helping more than 10 million small businesses to survive.

as we discussed earlier in this chapter, currency fluctuations impact global pricing strategies. Yet, in spite of fierce competition and fluctuating currencies, the Chinese luxury car market is on track to become the largest in the world.[96]

## Global Distribution Strategies

Global distribution networks form complex value chains that involve intermediaries, exporters, importers, and different transportation systems. (Refer back to Chapter 12 for a refresher on distribution.) These additional intermediaries typically add cost and ultimately increase the final selling price of a product. As a result of these cost factors, constant pressure exists to shorten distribution channels wherever possible.

Dominated by BMW, Audi, Mercedes-Benz, and Buick, the Chinese luxury car market is projected to become the world's largest.

Courtesy of Leo Burnett Beijing

The number of firms the seller needs to deal with in order to get its merchandise to the consumer determines the complexity of a channel. In most developing countries, manufacturers must go through many different types of distribution channels to get their products to end users, who often lack adequate transportation to shop at central shopping areas or large malls. Therefore, these consumers shop near their homes at small, family-owned retail outlets. To reach these small retail outlets, most of which are located far from major rail stations or roads, marketers have devised a variety of creative solutions. Unilever's strategy in India is a prime example of how a global company can adopt its distribution network to fit local conditions. Unilever trained 45,000 Indian women to serve as distributors, who in turn extended Unilever's reach to 100,000 villages and their 3 million residents all across India. The program generates $250 million each year in villages that otherwise would be too costly to serve.[97]

## Global Communication Strategies

The major challenge in developing a global communication strategy (refer back to Chapter 14 for a refresher on IMC) is identifying the elements that need to be adapted to be effective in the global marketplace. For instance, literacy levels vary dramatically across the globe. Consider again the BRIC nations: In India, approximately 29 percent of the adult population is illiterate (and for Indian women, the illiteracy rate surpasses 50 percent), compared with 7.4 percent in Brazil, 3.6 percent in China, and less than half a percent in Russia.[98] And even though Japan has one of the world's most sophisticated digital-media markets, Nestlé took a low-tech route to promote its unique 20 flavours of Kit Kat, which are sold as souvenirs in railway stations, airports, and expressway service shop areas. Nestlé was struck by the discovery that Kit Kat sounds similar to the Japanese phrase *Kitto Katsu*, which means "surely win." The company realized the chocolate bar could be paired with the tradition of sending students good-luck wishes before they take tough higher-education entrance exams. So it partnered with Japan's postal service to create Kit Mail, a postcard-like product sold only at the post office that could be mailed to students as an edible good-luck charm. Nestlé decorates post offices with a cherry blossom theme that coincides with Japan's annual exam period. It also stocks a sales point in each post office, a move that became possible when Japan's postal service was privatized in 2007. Nestlé noted that, if post offices were

Nestlé's Kit Mail could be mailed to students as an edible good-luck charm.

Kyodo/Newscom

still government-owned, the company probably could not have done this: "The post office is a great distribution channel for Kit Kat, because there is no competition, unlike in convenience stores or supermarkets," said Mr. Kageyama, CEO of JWT Japan, Nestlé Japan's advertising agency.[99]

Media availability also varies widely; some countries offer only state-controlled media. Advertising regulations differ too. In an attempt at standardization, the European Union recently recommended common guidelines for its member countries regarding advertising to children, and launched a voluntary EU Pledge to "change food and beverage advertising to children under the age of 12 in the European Union."[100]

Differences in language, customs, and culture also complicate marketers' ability to communicate with customers in various countries. Language can be particularly vexing for advertisers. For example, in the United Kingdom and Australia, a thong is a sandal; whereas in Canada, it can also be an undergarment. To avoid the potential embarrassment that language confusion can cause, firms spend millions of dollars to develop brand names that have no pre-existing meaning in any known language, such as Accenture (a management consulting firm) or Avaya (a subsidiary of Lucent Technologies, formerly Bell Labs).

Within many countries, there are multiple variants on a language. Some firms choose names that sound similar to their English-language names, such as Nike, whose Chinese brand name is pronounced *nai ke*. Others focus on the meanings of the characters, such that Citibank is known as *hui qi yinhang*, which means "star-spangled banner bank." Still other firms, such as Mercedes-Benz, have adapted their names for each language: *peng zee* in Cantonese for Hong Kong, *peng chi* in Mandarin for Taiwan, and *ben chi* in Mandarin for mainland China. Naming is a constant challenge in China, especially to avoid the threat that a brand name evokes unwanted connotations, such as when Microsoft realized that the sound of its search engine name, Bing, meant "virus" in China—not the best image for an online company![101]

Even with all these differences, many products and services serve the same needs and wants globally with little or no adaptation in their form or message. Firms whose products have global appeal can run global advertising campaigns, and simply translate the wording in the ads and product labelling. Other products require a more localized approach because of cultural and religious differences. In a classic advertisement for Longines watches, a woman's bare arm and hand appear, with a watch on her wrist. The advertisement was considered too risqué for predominantly Muslim countries, where women's bare arms are never displayed in public. The company changed the advertisement to show a gloved arm and hand wearing the same watch.

Even among English speakers, there can be significant differences in the effectiveness of advertising campaigns. Take the popular "What Happens in Vegas Stays in Vegas" advertising campaign, which has been very successful and spawned numerous copycat slogans in the United States. Essentially, the U.S. mass market thought the provocative campaign pushed the envelope, but just far enough to be entertaining. However, when the Las Vegas tourism group extended its advertising to the United Kingdom, it found that the ad campaign was not nearly as effective. After conducting focus groups, the group found that British consumers did not find the advertisements edgy enough for their more irreverent British tastes. In response, the advertising agency began studying British slang and phrases to find ways to make the campaign even sexier and more provocative.[102]

Regulatory actions in the host country can also affect communication strategies. For example, the WTO has become involved in several cases that involve firms' rights to use certain names and affiliations for their products and promotions. Several products in the European Union have established worldwide brand recognition on the basis of where they are made. For instance, the European Union currently allows only ham made in Parma, Italy, to be called Parma ham and sparkling wine made in the Champagne region of France to be called Champagne.

# ETHICAL ISSUES IN GLOBAL MARKETING

`L05`

Although ethical issues abound domestically, an extra layer of complexity arises for global marketing. Firms that market globally must recognize that they are, in essence, visitors in another country and, as such, must be aware of the ethical concerns of their potential customers, both at home and abroad. In this section, we examine three areas of particular concern: environmental concerns, labour issues, and impact on host country culture.

## Environmental Concerns

People throughout the world are worried about the amount of waste being generated, especially in developed countries. Current **environmental concerns** include, but are not limited to, the excessive use of natural resources and energy, refuse from manufacturing processes, excess trash created by consumer goods packages, and hard-to-dispose-of products such as tires, cellphones, and computer monitors.

Many developed countries produce almost two tonnes of household and industrial waste per person per year![103] Although developing countries do not produce nearly the same level of waste, much of the waste in these areas is not properly disposed of.

**environmental concerns** Include, but are not limited to, the excessive use of natural resources and energy, refuse from manufacturing processes, excess trash created by consumer goods packages, and hard-to-dispose-of products such as tires, cellphones, and computer monitors.

## Global Labour Issues

**Global labour issues**, especially concerns about working conditions and wages paid to factory workers in developing countries, have become increasingly prominent. Many large U.S. firms (such as Nike, PepsiCo, and Walmart) have been questioned by various groups, including non-governmental organizations and human rights activists, about the degree to which workers the companies employ are paid less than a living wage or forced to work long hours in poor working conditions.

In this context, high prices offer no guarantee of a supply chain free of sweatshops. Apple has been questioned repeatedly about the working conditions in the manufacturing plants that produce iPods and iPhones. Even though iPod boxes proudly state that the music player was designed in California, the entire manufacturing process has been subcontracted to Taiwanese and Chinese manufacturers.[104] Because Apple does not own the plants in which its goods are produced, it must negotiate with factory owners to improve or ensure adequate working conditions and wages, while at the same time attempting to get the cheapest prices. Because Apple negotiates very hard on price, suppliers sometimes try to make money by paying labourers less, making them work long hours, or providing unsafe working conditions. Labour conditions for Chinese workers in "iPod city" recently became so deplorable that several high-profile strikes protested their working conditions, and many Chinese workers resorted to committing suicide.

**global labour issues** Include concerns about working conditions and wages paid to factory workers in developing countries.

**cultural imperialism** The belief that one's own culture is superior to that of other nations; can take the form of an active, formal policy or a more subtle general attitude.

## Impact on Host Country Culture

The final ethical issue involves **cultural imperialism**, or the belief that one's own culture is superior to that of other nations. Cultural imperialism can take the form of an active, formal policy or a more subtle general attitude.[105] Critics of U.S. firms entering foreign markets claim that U.S. products and services overwhelm the local culture, often replacing its foods, music, movies, and traditions with those of the West.

In Iran, for example, the ruling clerics have forbidden the celebration of Valentine's Day.[106] Despite strict Iranian laws regarding the interactions of men and women, especially unmarried men and women, Valentine's Day has become a popular holiday among the youth market. These Iranians were exposed to Valentine's Day through the Internet and satellite television, two information sources the government cannot control. Holiday-themed products arrive through underground distribution channels and are displayed in local shops. Risking legal action, florists, gift shops, and restaurants make special accommodations for the holiday. Many parents sponsor Valentine

Many developed countries produce almost two tonnes of household and industrial waste per person per year that requires proper disposal.

© Digital Vision/PunchStock

When Western firms enter foreign markets, they must be cognizant of the host country's culture.

Hi Brow Arabia/Alamy Stock Photo

parties with both men and women in attendance. Apparently, there is no stopping love. Half the Iranian population is younger than 25 years of age, and this youth market has embraced the holiday and continues to celebrate it in traditional Western ways.

For other Iranians though, this type of celebration represents a threat to Iran's culture. Many firms find themselves squarely in the middle of this cultural conflict. Various countries around the world encompass competing desires: the desire to modernize and participate in the global marketplace versus the desire to hold on to traditional cultural values and ways of life. There is no simple way to resolve these dilemmas. Firms that enter new markets simply must tread lightly to ensure that their business practices, products, and services do not create any unnecessary friction or offence in the host country.

# LEARNING OBJECTIVES REVIEW

**LO1**  **Explain the components of global market assessments**

First, firms must determine whether a proposed country has a political and legal environment that favours business. Second, firms must assess the general economic environment. For instance, countries with a trade surplus, strong domestic and national products, population growth, and income growth tend to be favourable prospects. Third, firms should be cognizant of the sociocultural differences between their home and host countries and adapt to those differences to ensure successful business relationships. Fourth, firms should assess a country's technology and infrastructure capabilities. To be successful in a particular country, the firm must have access to adequate transportation, distribution channels, and communications.

**LO2**  **Understand the marketing opportunities in BRIC countries**

Technology, particularly in the communication field, has facilitated the growth of global markets. Firms can communicate with their suppliers and customers instantaneously, easily take advantage of production efficiencies in other countries, and bring together parts and finished goods from all over the globe. Four countries that provide tremendous marketing opportunities are the BRIC nations—Brazil, Russia, India and China. These countries have large populations that are increasingly interested in the latest goods and services.

**LO3**  **Describe the various global market entry strategies**

Firms have several options for entering a new country, each with a different level of risk and control. Direct investment is the most risky but also has the potential to be the most lucrative. Firms that engage in a joint venture with other firms already operating in the host country share the risk and obtain knowledge about the market and how to do business there. A strategic alliance is similar to a joint venture, but the relationship is not as formal. A less risky method of entering a new market is franchising, in which, similar to domestic franchise agreements, the franchisor allows the franchisee to operate a business using its name and strategy in return for a fee. The least risky method of entering another country is exporting.

**LO4**  **List the similarities and differences between a domestic marketing strategy and a global marketing strategy**

The essence of a global marketing strategy is no different than that of a domestic strategy. The firm starts by identifying its target markets, chooses specific markets to pursue, and crafts a strategy to meet the needs of those markets. However, additional issues make global expansion more difficult. For instance, the company needs to ask the following questions: Should the product or service be altered to fit the new market better? Does the firm need to change the way it prices its products in different countries? What is the best way to get the product or service to the new customers?

How should the firm communicate its product or service offering in other countries?

| **L05** | **Explain how ethical issues affect global marketing practices** |

In particular, firms must be cognizant of the impact their businesses have on the environment. When producing merchandise or employing service personnel in another country, companies must be certain that the working conditions and wages are fair and adequate, even if the workers are employed by a third party. Finally, marketers must be sensitive to the impact their business has on the culture of the host country.

# KEY TERMS

- boycott
- cultural imperialism
- direct investment
- dumping
- environmental concerns
- exchange control
- exchange rate
- exporting
- global labour issues
- globalization
- glocalization
- gross domestic product (GDP)
- human development index (HDI)
- infrastructure
- joint venture
- purchasing power parity (PPP)
- quota
- strategic alliance
- tariff (or duty)
- trade agreement
- trade deficit
- trade sanctions
- trade surplus
- trading bloc

# CONCEPT REVIEW

1. What is globalization? What are the factors that facilitate globalization? Explain how globalization has influenced marketing in Canada.

2. List and describe the four components of market assessments firms must conduct to evaluate the viability of different global markets.

3. Which of the four components of market assessment do you think are often most difficult to assess? Why?

4. List the five types of strategies companies can use to enter global markets. Compare these strategies in terms of level of risk, expected return, and control.

5. Discuss the advantages and disadvantages of using a global product strategy (i.e., offering the same product both at home and in overseas markets).

6. What are the primary considerations marketers should use in deciding whether to customize the four Ps to specific markets?

7. What is political risk? Why is it important to assess political risk? How is political risk assessed? List two or three organizations in Canada that provide marketers with political risk assessments.

8. Protectionist policies restrict trade and global marketing, while trade agreements facilitate global marketing. Explain the reasons a country may want to impose protectionist policies in some industries and liberalize other industries.

9. Explain how measures such as GDP, PPP (e.g., the Big Mac Index), and HDI help marketers decide whether to enter a global market. What are the weaknesses of these measures?

10. Explain how useful Hofstede's five dimensions of culture are to our understanding of different cultures around the world. Where and how can marketers learn about the culture of a country to which they are interested in marketing?

# MARKETING APPLICATIONS

1. Of the four BRIC markets, explain why you think one country might be more welcoming to Lululemon than others.

2. Cervélo is a high-end Canadian bicycle manufacturer. Assume the company is considering entering the United Kingdom and Chinese markets. When doing its market assessment, what economic factors should Cervélo consider when making its decision? Which market do you expect will be more lucrative for Cervélo? Why?

3. Now consider the political, economic, and legal systems of China versus the United Kingdom. Explain why you think one country might be more hospitable to Cervélo than the other.

4. Colgate sells products in many countries throughout the world. How would you expect its market position to differ in those countries compared with that in Canada?

5. Global brands that gain status on a local level have the best of both worlds: local loyalty with all the advantages

of global connections. How do huge global companies such as McCain Foods and McDonald's achieve multi-local status?

**6.** What is cultural imperialism? Why would a recording company such as Def Jam Recordings need to be aware of and sensitive to this issue?

**7.** Provide an example of a potentially ethically troubling practice by a foreign firm doing business in Canada.

**8.** Many Canadian and United States–based firms are relocating their production facilities and services overseas (outsourcing or offshoring). Why do you believe they are doing so? Do the benefits outweigh the potential losses of Canadian and U.S. jobs? Why or why not?

**9.** Assume you work for a Canadian-based financial services firm that positions itself as having experts that personally manage the clients' accounts. The clients are unaware that most of the tax preparation work, the bookkeeping, and other record keeping is done by a company in India. The local office simply reviews the file and signs the cover letters. Yet, as your manager pointed out, there is still only one person who *manages* each account. After recent news stories about the practice of offshoring sensitive transactions such as tax preparation, clients have been commenting about how grateful they are to have a local firm. What, if anything, should you tell your clients about the firm's practice of offshoring?

**10.** Canadian companies such as Tim Hortons® and Lululemon have expanded their global presence through company-owned stores. In what instances might these companies consider using joint ventures as their global market entry strategy into new markets?

## NET SAVVY

**1.** For many small businesses, the idea of entering a foreign market is frightening. The Government of Canada and most provincial and territorial governments now offer assistance designed specifically for small business owners. Two such government departments are Foreign Affairs and International Trade Canada (DFAIT) and Industry Canada. Visit Industry Canada's Canada Business website at http://www.canada business.ca and examine the types of services it provides for Canadian businesses wishing to do business in a foreign country. Evaluate the usefulness of the information provided.

**2.** McCain Foods is a global brand but it alters its products and promotions to accommodate local tastes in each country. Go to http://www.mccain.ca and visit the Canadian website. Then go to http://www.mccain.com/about-us /contact-us and check out the websites for McCain in South America, the United States, and France. How are these websites different from the Canadian site? What products are different? What promotional elements are different?

## CHAPTER CASE STUDY

### THE GLOBALIZATION OF THE MOST UBIQUITOUS OF AMERICAN CUISINES—THE HAMBURGER

From the Maharaja Mac in India to the Prosperity Burger prepared especially for the Chinese New Year celebrations, McDonald's has built a global fast-food empire under its golden arches. Only 34 percent of McDonald's revenue now comes from sales in the United States, and most of its international growth has come from the surging economies of Russia, China, Brazil, and India.[107] A pioneer in overseas franchising, McDonald's has spared no effort in its attempts to penetrate foreign markets. In China, it plans to open 1,000 new outlets in the next five years.[108] In Brazil, it created Latin America's first environmentally certified fast-food restaurant. A vast market defined by stark cultural differences, India has required a more modest approach that would allow McDonald's to develop its real estate and supply infrastructure, train its local workforce and management at its famed Hamburger University, and adjust the menu for vegetarian customers.[109] The McAloo Tikki Burger has been a great success, and the company has started opening more McCafe storefronts.[110]

But McDonald's growth strategy relies on more than just added locations. In crowded cities, with real estate prices too high to build drive-through restaurants, the company has hired droves of motorbike drivers to bring Big Macs to customers. This nimble delivery approach is now a mainstay in cities from Beijing to Kuwait City. In addition, McDonald's keeps looking for new mobile innovations, such as mobile ordering or payment options, to keep up with consumer demand. It is testing a mobile app in some regions in the United States. already.[111]

Fast-food restaurants enjoy some segment-specific benefits as they pursue such international expansion. Unlike retail brands, such as Walmart or Carrefour, restaurants present fewer perceived competitive threats. Local eateries can exist side-by-side with a McDonald's, in a way that a mom-and-pop grocer cannot survive if an international hypermarket moves in next door.[112]

McDonald's France uses a French approximation of "I'm lovin' it."

William Ryall 2010

But even considering the massive growth in rapidly transitioning economies, Europe still generates the bulk of foreign sales for McDonald's. In France, for example, "MacDo" restaurants attract crowds that line up outside for a bite of lunch. But lunch might mean something a little different in this case: French McDonald's offer menus that feature Camembert cheese on the burgers, Heineken, and a McBaguette. Once, the secret to McDonald's success was "lockstep" consistency, the fact that a meal in Memphis tasted the same as it did in Moscow or Madrid. But the novelty of the American hamburger stand has worn off in the new millennium, and with it McDonald's ability to export American culture as its staple commodity. A cheeseburger, fries, and Coke don't inspire the same level of excitement when the café next door and the bistro down the block are also serving burgers. More and more, the key to McDonald's future appears to be found in the DNA of the places it inhabits. And with it, suddenly the fast-food giant that to many represents the globalization of taste suddenly finds itself in a very unlikely position: as a defender of local cuisine.[113]

The kosher burger has been a hit in Israel, and Indian consumers seem to appreciate the opening of McDonald's first vegetarian restaurant. However, most new growth comes from Russia, where the company has 245 locations and controls 70 percent of the booming fast-food business. Even as fast-food competitors face potential market saturation in the United States, Russian demand for quick burgers appears to be insatiable.[114] Driving this Russian appetite has been the growth of a newly affluent middle class, with money to spend to dine out. Infrastructure development in Russia also has been a boon as cities open malls with food courts, highways are constructed with drive-through locations, and specialty suppliers of frozen food and packaging have appeared.

McDonald's is successful in Israel because of its kosher offerings.

David Silverman/Getty Images

In the early years of Russian expansion, few private businesses existed to supply all the ingredients McDonald's needed to produce Big Macs and fries. The company solved the problem by building an enormous food processing plant outside Moscow. But it also worked to cultivate relationships with local Russian vendors and contractors to which it eventually could outsource its supply chain. Today, a grower who began selling cucumbers to McDonald's in 1990 has become the Pickle King of Russia, dominating the processed foods market.[115]

### Questions

1. Which sociocultural factors have informed McDonald's global expansion?

2. Describe some of the global distribution strategies that McDonald's uses or might consider using to spread throughout the world.

3. Define the likely global STP strategy for McDonald's. In what ways does it need to vary its STP? In which target markets can it rely on a consistent positioning? Which consumers should it target in each national market?

# CHAPTER 18

## LEARNING OBJECTIVES

**After studying this chapter you should be able to**

**LO1** Identify why marketers should be concerned about ethics

**LO2** Distinguish between ethics and social responsibility

**LO3** Describe consumerism and explain how it fosters ethical and socially responsible business practices

**LO4** Identify the four steps in ethical decision making

**LO5** Outline how ethics and social responsibility can be integrated into a firm's marketing strategy

# Ethics and Socially Responsible Marketing

Imagine if every time you played Angry Birds or some other silly, fun game on your mobile phone, personally identifying information—such as your location, the other apps loaded on your phone, your gender, your age, your political leanings, your sexual orientation, and your buying habits—got sent to a massive data repository, accessible to various marketers and government agencies. Or don't just imagine it. Read about it in documents leaked by Edward Snowden.[1] Such information gathering is really nothing new, of course. When people access the web through their computers, they create cookies, or snippets of data that enable marketers to discern where a shopper starts the search process, how he or she proceeds, and where the online encounter ends—as well as what the shopper buys, or doesn't. A long history of arguments—even before the computer era—debated the acceptability of wiretaps on telephones, whether traditional or mobile, and whether governments had the right to gather specific information (e.g., recordings) or only metadata (e.g., general information about the number called, when, and for how long).

These debates are complex, in-depth, and serious. They also are becoming increasingly important for marketers as the marketing environment expands to include advanced technology and brand-new methods for collecting data. On one side, the marketing industry has sought to find solutions and self-regulation that would calm customers, avoid the imposition of stronger regulations, and still enable marketing firms to gain access to valuable information about consumer behaviours. But those attempts appear to have stalled, because the online marketing industry simply has not been able to agree about how to police itself. On the other side, legislation introduced by the U.S. Senate attempts to police these activities, mandating the provision of a do-not-track option that would allow computer users to opt out, easily and quickly, from cookies being planted.[2] In Canada, the Canadian Anti-Spam Legislation (CASL) ensures that companies that collect personal data about consumers must do so with their knowledge and consent. However, there is no do-not-track provision to prevent companies from collecting information about online behaviour.[3]

As it turns out, cookies may not be the real problem soon. In the growing movement away from computer interfaces and toward mobile commerce, marketers can turn to cutting-edge technologies to locate customers through their smartphones and other devices, determine their collective behaviours, and target them with incredibly specific advertisements. For example, a new venture called Drawbridge (founded by a former employee of Google's mobile advertising division) maintains partnerships with various advertising platforms and publishers, which create notifications of every visit a user makes to a website or app. These notifications in turn enter data analyses that rely on statistical modelling to determine which person is using which devices and link them together—as well as determine whether multiple users rely on the same device. Thus when a person downloads an app through her phone, then later visits a site that appeared in that app, the software enables advertisers to connect those devices as belonging to a single user. In turn, information from both devices gets integrated. The next day, if this user visits a travel site through her computer, she might receive an advertisement for rental cars through her phone. However, if her spouse visits a gaming site instead, Drawbridge knows that it is a different user and personalizes the advertising accordingly.[4]

Many consumers reject such tactics and issue increasing demands for privacy protections. Online browsers, such as Apple's Safari and Mozilla's Firefox, have introduced or are working on cookie-blocking technology, which might just prompt marketers to seek new ways to get around the blocks. Instead, noting the increasing sophistication of the technologies, some mobile service providers are asking for users' permission to track them. For example, in the United States, Verizon promised coupons to consumers who agreed to let it share information about their mobile browsing behaviours with advertisers, and AT&T simply announced that it had begun selling aggregated consumer data to advertisers.

Denying that they are tracking users has proven unsuccessful, because it largely is not true. Just weeks after Microsoft initiated a publicity campaign that asserted that its consumers' privacy was its top priority, Snowden-related leaks showed that the U.S. National Security Administration had been tapping its records for half a decade.[5]

The scandal surrounding wiretapping by government agencies, especially in the United States and United Kingdom, adds another wrinkle to this discussion. An estimate by Forrester Research suggested that consumer fear and worry—sparked by the disclosure that spy agencies were collecting vast amounts of personal data from Internet and mobile service providers—would cost the cloud computing industry approximately $180 billion in lost revenues.[6]

The reason for marketers' insistence on using cookies and other tracking technologies, even in the face of customer discontent and legislative threats, is the outstanding value that the information collected can provide. Only by knowing how, when, and where people really browse online and through their mobile devices can marketers make sure that they target consumers accurately. These data also represent a major source of revenue for targeted advertising firms that sell consumer data to other advertisers, promising the most accurate information when it comes to selecting who will receive their marketing messages. But they also represent potentially serious intrusions into people's privacy. Thus marketers sit at the heart of modern, international discussions of the efficacy, ethicality, and effectiveness of technological snooping. ∎

Which is the more important corporate objective: making a profit, or obtaining and keeping customers?[7] Although firms cannot stay in business without earning a profit, using profit as the sole guiding light for corporate action can lead to short-term decisions that may in fact cause the firm to lose customers in the long run. The balancing act may turn out to be the quest to place the company on the firmest footing possible. This question leads into the primary ethical dilemma facing managers; that is, how to balance shareholder interests with the needs of society. In our opening example, consumers seek greater protections of their privacy, whereas marketers want access to more and better data about those individual consumers to be able to target them with appealing products, at the right time, in the right place, and at the right price—and thereby make more sales.

Other industries face similar ethical dilemmas and seek to find appropriate balances. In the past two decades most processed foods (e.g., cereals, salad dressings) have contained ingredients made from plants whose DNA has been manipulated in a laboratory. To weather frosts better and produce a greater yield of crops, tomatoes are spliced with salmon genes, for example. Such genetically modified organisms, or GMOs, appear in a majority of the foods that consumers eat daily, yet most people remain unaware of their presence because Health Canada does not require GMO food product labelling.[8] The ethical question for food manufacturers is whether they label their products as containing GMOs. On one hand, many consumers express a preference to know and worry about potential negative health effects (though no available scientific evidence has confirmed this threat). On the other hand, genetic modifications increase crop yields and lower production costs, and avoiding a GMO label could help companies sell more of their products. Most food manufacturers seem to be fighting GMO labelling. However, in 2014 General Mills decided to make some of its products, such as Cheerios, completely free of GMOs, and Whole Foods has committed to issuing labels on all GMO-containing foods it sells by 2018.[9]

As these examples show, sometimes the ethical dilemma has as much to do with defining our terms as with what the products contain. But even if the question seems to be one of terminology, if customers believe that they can no longer trust a company or that the company is not acting responsibly, they will no longer support it by purchasing its products or services or investing in its stock. For marketers, the firm's ability to build and maintain consumer trust by conducting ethical transactions must be of paramount importance.

In this chapter, we start by examining what marketing ethics is and why behaving ethically is so important to successful marketing. We then discuss how firms can create an ethical climate among employees and how individual behaviour can affect the ability of the firm to act ethically. Next, we discuss how consumers contribute to the corporate social responsibility (CSR) decisions that businesses make. To help you make ethical marketing decisions, we also provide a framework for ethical decision making and then examine some ethical issues within the context of the strategic marketing planning process (from Chapter 2). Finally, we present some scenarios that highlight typical ethical challenges marketing managers often must face.

# THE SCOPE OF MARKETING ETHICS

**Business ethics** refers to the moral or ethical dilemmas that might arise in a business setting. **Marketing ethics**, in contrast, examines those ethical problems that are specific to the domain of marketing.[10] Because the marketing profession often is singled out among business disciplines as the root cause of a host of ethical concerns (e.g., unethical advertising or the promotion of shoddy products), anyone involved in marketing activities must recognize the ethical implications of their actions. These can involve societal issues, such as the sale of products or services that may damage the environment; global issues, such as the use of sweatshops and child labour; and individual consumer issues, such as deceptive advertising and the marketing of dangerous products.

**business ethics**
Refers to the moral or ethical dilemmas that might arise in a business setting.

**marketing ethics**
Refers to those ethical problems that are specific to the domain of marketing.

# ETHICAL ISSUES ASSOCIATED WITH MARKETING DECISIONS

**LO1**

Unlike other business functions, such as accounting or finance, people in marketing interact directly with the public. Because they are so much in the public eye, it should not be surprising that marketing and sales professionals sometimes rank poorly in ratings of the most trusted professions. In a recent Gallup survey, most professions were rated much higher than marketing: advertising practitioners fared only slightly better than car salesmen and telemarketers (see Exhibit 18.1).[11] For marketers, who depend on the long-term trust of their customers, this low ranking is very disappointing.

Yet there is some good news. In a recent survey, it was found that almost three-quarters of Canadians pay attention to issues related to corporate ethics and social responsibility and believe that firms have a responsibility to actively engage in doing good for society.[12] Many consumers remain highly skeptical of business, however, and especially of marketing. But because the marketing function interacts with so many entities outside the firm on a regular basis, it has a tremendous opportunity to build the public's trust. As many marketing executives correctly believe, creating an ethical climate that establishes

| **E X H I B I T  18.1** | Attitudes About Ethical Standards of Various Professionals |
|---|---|
| **High Approval (>60%)** | **Low Approval (<15%)** |
| Nurses | Stockbrokers |
| Pharmacists | Advertising Practitioners |
| Medical Doctors | Car Salespeople |
| High School Teachers | Telemarketers |

*Source:* Adapted from Gallup Poll, "Attitudes About the Ethical Standards of Various Professions," December 7–11, 2016.

the health and well-being of consumers as the firm's number-one priority just makes good business sense.

## Creating an Ethical Climate in the Workplace

**ethical climate**

The set of values within a marketing firm, or in the marketing division of any firm, that guides decision making and behaviour.

The process of creating a strong **ethical climate** within a marketing firm (or in the marketing division of any firm) includes having a set of values that guides decision making and behaviour. In 1943, General Robert Wood Johnson of Johnson & Johnson (J&J) wrote and published the company's first "credo"—a one-page document outlining the firm's commitments and responsibilities to its various stakeholders.[13] The J&J Credo can be summarized as follows:

> We believe our first responsibility is to doctors, nurses, patients, mothers, fathers, and all others who use our products and services. We are responsible to our employees. We must respect their dignity and recognize their merit. Compensation must be fair and adequate and working conditions clean, orderly, and safe. We are responsible to the communities in which we live and work and to the world community as well. Our final responsibility is to our stockholders. When we operate according to these principles, the stockholders should realize a fair return.

Today, J&J continues to follow this credo in its daily business practices, as was evidenced by the infamous Tylenol recall. In the 1980s, seven people taking Tylenol died of cyanide poisoning. Without worrying initially about whether the poison got into the products during production or on the shelf, J&J immediately and voluntarily withdrew all Tylenol from the market until it could ensure its products' safety.

J&J responded to new limits on dosages of acetaminophen (the active ingredient in Tylenol) by reassuring consumers that they were safe—as long as they followed the dosage instructions on the packaging.[14] In advertising communications that touted Tylenol as "the safest brand of pain reliever you can choose," J&J also was careful to remind people that taking more than the recommended dosage could cause serious liver damage.

Everyone within the firm must share the same understanding of these values and how they translate into the business activities of the firm, and they must share a consistent language to discuss them. Once the values are understood, the firm must develop a set of explicit rules and implicit understandings that govern all the firm's transactions. Top management must commit to establishing an ethical climate, but employees throughout the firm also must be dedicated because the roots of ethical conflict often are the competing values of individuals. Each individual holds his or her own set of values, and sometimes those values result in conflicts between employees or even within them. For instance, a salesperson may feel pressure to make a sale because her family depends on her for support; but, at the same time, she may feel that the product she is selling is not appropriate for a particular customer. Once the rules are in place, there must be a system of controls that rewards appropriate behaviour—that is, behaviour consistent with the firm's values—and punishes inappropriate behaviour.

Like companies that develop and apply their own ethical codes, many professions, including marketing, have their own codes of ethics that firms and individuals in the profession agree to abide by. The generally accepted code in marketing, developed by the Canadian Marketing Association (CMA; see

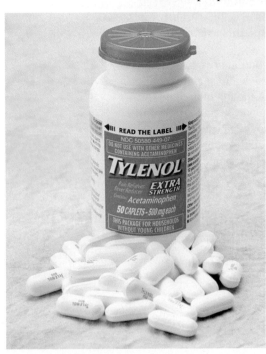

Johnson & Johnson, maker of Tylenol, continues to act in accordance with its 1943 "credo."

Exhibit 18.2), flows from general norms of conduct to specific values to which marketers should aspire. Each subarea within marketing—such as marketing research, advertising, pricing, and so forth—has its own code of ethics that deals with the specific issues that arise when conducting business in those areas.

Now we examine the role of the individuals within the firm and how they contribute to the firm's ethical climate.

 **EXHIBIT 18.2** Canadian Marketing Association's Code of Ethics

## ETHICAL NORMS AND VALUES FOR MARKETERS

### B. Purpose of CMA Code of Ethics and Standards of Practice
The CMA Code of Ethics and Standards of Practice (the "Code") is designed to establish and maintain standards for the conduct of marketing in Canada.

Marketers acknowledge that the establishment and maintenance of high standards of practice are a fundamental responsibility to the public, essential to winning and holding consumer confidence, and the foundation of a successful and independent marketing industry in Canada.

Members of the Canadian Marketing Association recognize an obligation—to the consumers and the businesses they serve, to the integrity of the discipline in which they operate and to each other—to practise to the highest standards of honesty, truth, accuracy, fairness and professionalism.

### E. Responsibility for Marketing Communications
Marketers are responsible for the content of their marketing communications and the practices of their suppliers and advertising agencies when in the course of executing marketing communications on their behalf. This responsibility extends to suppliers which are not CMA members.

### H. Overarching Ethical Principles
**H2 Truthfulness:** Marketing communications must be clear and truthful. Marketers must not knowingly make a representation to a consumer or business that is false or misleading.

### I. Universal Marketing Practices
These practices apply regardless of industry sector, sub-discipline or marketing medium employed.

### I1 Accuracy of Representation
I1.1 Marketers must not misrepresent a product, service or marketing program and must not mislead by statement or manner of demonstration or comparison.

### I2 Clarity
Marketing communications must be executed in a manner that is simple and easy to understand.

### I5 Disguise
I5.1 Marketers should identify themselves and must not engage in marketing communications in the guise of one purpose when the intent is a different purpose.

### J. Protection of Personal Privacy
All consumer marketers must abide by the *Personal Information Protection and Electronics Documents Act* (PIPEDA), and/or applicable provincial privacy laws and the following ten Privacy Principles from the National Standard of Canada and five additional requirements as outlined in this section.

### J5 Source of Personal Information
Marketers must provide consumers with the source of their personal information, upon request.

### L. Special Considerations in Marketing to Teenagers
### L2 Responsibility
Marketing to teenagers imposes special responsibilities on marketers. Marketers will use discretion and sensitivity in marketing to teenagers, to address the age, knowledge, sophistication and maturity of teenagers. Marketers should exercise caution that they do not take advantage of or exploit teenagers.

### P. Protection of the Environment
Marketers recognize and acknowledge a continuing responsibility to manage their businesses to minimize environmental impact.

### Q. Enforcement Procedures for the CMA Code of Ethics and Standards of Practice
Q1 Upon receipt of a consumer complaint regarding violation of this Code, whether regarding a member or a non-member, the Canadian Marketing Association will contact the organization and use the Association's internal mediation procedures to attempt to resolve the consumer complaint.

*Source:* Adapted from "Code of Ethics and Standards of Practice," Canadian Marketing Association, www.the-cma.org

## The Influence of Personal Ethics

Every firm is made up of individuals, each with his or her own needs and desires. Let's look at why people may make unethical decisions and how firms can establish a process for decision making that ensures individuals choose ethical alternatives instead.

**Why People Act Unethically**    Every individual is a product of his or her culture, upbringing, genes, and various other influences. In spite of these factors, however, people do continue to grow emotionally in their understanding of what is and is not ethical behaviour. For example, a six-year-old child might think nothing of bonking a brother on the head with a toy, but adults are expected to recognize that violence is an unethical means of interacting with others. All of us vary in the way we view various situations, depending on our own level of understanding about ethical dilemmas.

Consider product recalls of toys, for example. How can certain manufacturers engage in such egregious behaviour as using lead paint on toys or including magnets that can be swallowed in toys marketed toward young children? What makes people take actions that create so much harm? Are all the individuals who contributed to that behaviour just plain immoral? These questions have very complex answers.

As another example, imagine that a brand manager for a car company discovers, from conversations with a member of the development team, that the hot new energy-efficient hybrid model set to go into full production shortly has a potentially dangerous design flaw. The brand manager can (1) delay production and remedy the design flaw, which pushes production off schedule, delays revenue, and may result in layoffs and loss of a bonus, or (2) stay on schedule, put the flawed design into production, and hope it does not result in injuries to consumers and loss of revenue for the firm. This type of dilemma, and its competing outcomes, occurs nearly every day in thousands of different business environments.

When asked in a survey whether they had seen any unethical behaviour among their colleagues, chief marketing officers responded that they had observed employees participating in high-pressure, misleading, or deceptive sales tactics (45 percent); misrepresenting company earnings, sales, and/or revenues (35 percent); withholding or destroying information that could hurt company sales or image (32 percent); and conducting false or misleading advertising (31 percent).[15] Did all the marketers in these situations view their actions as unethical? In making marketing decisions, managers are often faced with the dilemma between doing what is beneficial for them and possibly the firm in the short run, and doing what is right and beneficial for the firm and society in the long run.

For instance, a manager might feel confident that earnings will increase in the next few months and therefore believe it benefits himself, his branch, and his employees to exaggerate current earnings just a little. Another manager might feel considerable pressure to increase sales in a retail store, so she brings in some new merchandise, marks it at an artificially high price, and then immediately puts it on sale. Consumers are deceived into thinking they are getting a good deal because they view the initial price as the "real" price. Each decision may have been justifiable at the time for the individual, but each decision would have potentially serious ethical and legal consequences for the company.

What is the "real" price? Did the manager bring the T-shirts in at an artificially high level and then immediately mark them down?

© Dennis MacDonald/PhotoEdit

To avoid such dire consequences, the short-term goals of each employee must be aligned with the long-term goals of the firm. In our hybrid car example, the brand manager's short-term drive to receive a bonus conflicted with the firm's long-term aim of providing consumers with safe, reliable cars. To align personal and corporate goals, firms need to have a strong ethical climate; explicit rules for governing a firm's transactions, including a code of ethics; and a system for rewarding and punishing behaviour. In the next section, we discuss this link between ethics and social responsibility by businesses.

## Corporate Social Responsibility

**LO2**

Although no single, established definition of the concept exists, the Government of Canada defines **corporate social responsibility (CSR)** as the voluntary activities undertaken by a company to operate in an economically, socially, and environmentally sustainable manner.[16] For a company to act in a socially responsible manner, the employees within the company must also maintain high ethical standards and recognize how their individual decisions lead to the collective actions of the firm. Firms with strong ethical climates tend to be more socially responsible.

**corporate social responsibility (CSR)** Refers to the voluntary activities undertaken by a company to operate in an economically, socially, and environmentally sustainable manner.

Today, companies are undertaking a wide range of corporate social responsibility initiatives, such as establishing corporate charitable foundations, supporting and associating with existing non-profit groups, supporting minority activities, and following responsible marketing, sales, and production practices. Social responsibility is even one of the key measures that *Fortune* magazine uses to create its list of the most admired companies. One of those companies is Cadillac Fairview, described in Sustainable Marketing 18.1.

## Sustainable Marketing 18.1

### Cadillac Fairview Takes the WE Pledge

The back-to-school season often starts with a trip to the mall to buy a cornucopia of new school supplies, a new wardrobe, and fresh kicks. Unfortunately, for many Canadian families, even the basic necessities can be a challenge to obtain. Cadillac Fairview has partnered with WE in an effort to inspire Canadian youth and remind young Canadians shopping for the start of the new school year of big-picture issues that affect local, national, and global communities.[17]

Cadillac Fairview is the owner of 72 properties in Canada, including the CF Toronto Eaton Centre.[18] In 2016, it forged a three-year partnership with WE, a movement that brings people together and gives them the tools to change the world locally and globally. This partnership is part of CF's youth-focused philanthropy platform aimed at inspiring and empowering today's youth, and represents an important part of CF's corporate social responsibility strategy and core values.[19] It supports several youth empowerment initiatives, events, and celebrations across CF's retail properties nationwide, giving young people an opportunity to get involved in communities where CF operates.

The "We Stand With WE" campaign launched in 2016 was the first of many joint efforts. The month preceding the start of the school year, CF shopping centres across the country displayed colourful interactive pledge-walls where participants were able to learn more about five causes: Education, Health, Hunger, Environment, and Shelter.[20] Visitors could take the WE Pledge, joining a movement of caring and compassionate people to show their commitment to improving the communities around them. Along with taking the WE Pledge, visitors were encouraged to take a selfie in front of the cause of their choice, and share their commitment to change on social media with the campaign hashtag #WhoWillYouBe. Participants who used the hashtag and tagged their local CF shopping centre received a limited edition enamel pin representing the cause they pledged to support.

As part of their partnership, WE also set up their first brick-and-mortar store at CF Toronto Eaton Centre to sell socially conscious goods from Me to We (the social enterprise division of WE). It marked the first time CF has donated long-term retail space to a charitable partner.[21] This multi-year partnership between two passionate organizations creates a national alliance committed to empowering young people.

Danone, which makes Activia yogurt products, is both ethical and socially responsible. It has a commitment to make healthy food and is involved in many activities and charities that help people.

Some economists and social commentators suggest that CSR is unnecessary, that the goal of any corporation in a capitalist economy is single and simple: Make money.[22] How does it benefit the company or its shareholders if a company worries about such unquantifiable issues as being a good citizen? But the fallout from the most recent global economic crisis seems to have pushed economists to repudiate this school of thought.

However, it is important to distinguish between ethical business practices and corporate social responsibility programs. Ideally, firms should implement programs that are socially responsible, *and* employees should act in an ethically responsible manner (see Exhibit 18.3, upper left quadrant). Danone yogurt, for example, has long supported internal research into healthy eating, which supports its ethical commitment to bring "health food to as many people as possible."[23] It is also socially responsible since it donates food and money to the hunger-relief charity Feeding America, encourages employees to volunteer in their communities, holds annual "Children's Day" outreach programs, and tries to reduce its environmental footprint.

Being socially responsible generally means going above and beyond the norms of corporate ethical behaviour. For example, a firm's employees may conduct their activities in an ethically acceptable manner but still not be considered socially responsible because their activities have little or no impact on anyone other than their closest stakeholders: their customers, employees, and shareholders (Exhibit 18.3, upper right quadrant). In this case, employees would not, for instance, be involved in volunteer activities to clean up a local park, coach the community's youth baseball league, or take part in any other socially responsible activities that improve the communities in which the company operates.

Likewise, some firms that are perceived as socially responsible can still take actions that are viewed as unethical (Exhibit 18.3, lower left quadrant). For instance, a firm might be considered socially responsible because it makes generous donations to

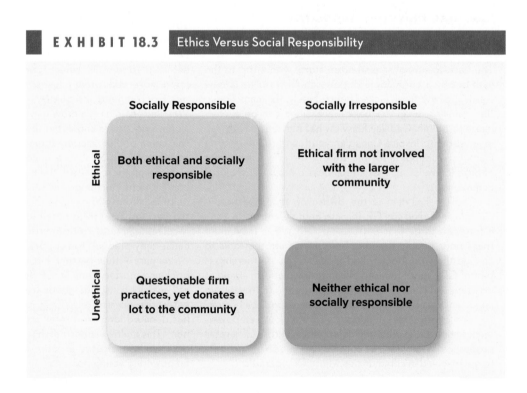

charities but is simultaneously involved in questionable sales practices. Walmart was recently ranked as the worst-paying company by the National Employment Law Project, but even as it was underpaying its employees, it was donating more than $1 billion in cash and in-kind items to charitable causes.[24] Ethically, how do we characterize a firm that obtains its profits through illicit actions but then donates a percentage of those profits to charity?

The worst situation, of course, is when firms behave both unethically *and* in a socially irresponsible manner (Exhibit 18.3, lower right quadrant). For example, Premier Fitness Club was fined $130,000 for nearly 40 violations of the Employment Standards Act (ESA 2000) in connection with wages owed to former employees, and paid a $200,000 settlement to the Competition Bureau for misleading advertising.[25] After facing numerous lawsuits from trade creditors, the company was forced into receivership. Both the Walmart and Premier Fitness examples go against the norms of socially acceptable business practices.

Walmart employees protest low wages.
© Jae C. hong/AP Images

Consumers and investors increasingly appear to want to purchase products and services from and invest in companies that act in socially responsible ways. According to the Conference Board of Canada, CSR is the business issue of the 21st century. The importance of CSR is underlined by the finding that a majority of Canadians have rewarded or punished companies for their corporate citizenship. About 74 percent of people polled by Ipsos reported that social responsibility was an important aspect of how they formed their purchase decisions. And 37 percent of employed respondents said it was very important that their "own employer is responsible to society and the environment."[26] Nielsen's Global Survey on Corporate Social Responsibility indicated that consumers were more willing to buy products and services from companies with programs that give back to society. This willingness to spend more increased to 66 percent of the 30,000 people polled in 60 countries.[27]

Pepsi recognizes that it makes good business sense to adopt the principles of sustainable development, which could provide short- and long-term returns for its shareholders, clients, and employees while preserving the environment for future generations. Its manufacturing plants in Colombia recycle 75 percent of the water they use. Instead of using water to purify Gatorade bottles, air is used. The company improved its water efficiency by 20 percent, cutting about 14 billion litres of water. A goal it set to provide safe water to 3 million people worldwide was met three years ahead of schedule.[28]

Companies earn both tangible and intangible benefits for acting in a socially desirable manner because it just makes good business sense to take actions that benefit society. Consider, for example, companies such as Tim Hortons® and HP Canada, which have established strong programs to support Canadian children. The Tim Horton Children's Foundation was established in 1974 to honour Tim Horton's love for children and his desire to help those less fortunate. To support this initiative, Tim Hortons® restaurant owners hold an annual Camp Day, donating coffee sales and collecting public donations. In 2016, more than $13.61 million was raised on Camp Day, which helped to send 19,000 children from low-income families to camp.[29]

Corporations such as Pepsi, Tim Hortons®, Sleep Country Canada, and many others increasingly include socially responsible programs when planning and defining their strategic initiatives. Unfortunately, being a socially responsible corporation does not ensure that all members of the firm or all subunits within it will act ethically; rather, it means only that the firm is committing time and resources to projects in the community that may not directly relate to generating profit.

Every year, coffee sold on Tim Hortons®' Camp Day® helps ensure that thousands of children are able to go to camp.

All Tim Hortons® trademarks referenced herein are owned by Tim Hortons®. Used with permission.

**L03** # CONSUMERISM, ETHICS, AND SOCIALLY RESPONSIBLE PRACTICES

Companies that do not pay sufficient attention to ethical conduct and strong corporate responsibility are often targeted by consumer groups and other advocacy groups, which generate negative publicity and sometimes even boycott their products. *Consumer Reports* and *Lemon Aid* are two key publications that are dedicated to informing and protecting consumers from harmful products and poor business practices by marketers. *Consumer Reports* states its mission as "We test, inform, and protect." **Consumerism**—a social movement aimed at protecting consumers from business practices that infringe upon their rights—and enhanced environmental awareness and activism are two key factors that have been driving the trend toward greater CSR in Canada. Today, most Canadian companies have CSR policies and projects that support their communities. Exhibit 18.4 provides several illustrations of the CSR programs undertaken by major firms.

Many companies have established CSR programs that enable consumers to safely dispose of the products they buy in order to minimize the harmful effects on the environment. For example, Mountain Equipment Co-Op offers a recycling program where customers can bring their worn-out polyester garments back to a store to be recycled into new items.[30] Similarly, personal computer vendors such as Dell and Hewlett-Packard collect used equipment for recycling. All HP laser cartridges come with instructions for returning the old cartridges. Cellphone manufacturers promote recycling of old phones and batteries, encouraging consumers to drop them off at collection depots across the country.

FedEx has implemented social responsibility initiatives in several ways,[31] including:

- *Charitable donations.* Through its "Delivering for Good" program, FedEx has donated more than 3.5 million pounds of delivery weight valued at $4.7 million for disaster relief efforts around the globe.
- *Diversity.* FedEx maintains formal groups to ensure it meets global diversity standards. For example, its Employment Pathways Program develops and

**consumerism**
A social movement aimed at protecting consumers from business practices that infringe upon their rights.

**EXHIBIT 18.4**  Examples of CSR Programs

| Company | Illustration of CSR Program |
|---|---|
| Amazon.com | Developed non-profit Simple Pay Donation system to help non-profits raise money easily |
| BMW | Light Up Hope and BMW's Children's Safety programs |
| Coca-Cola | Spent $102 million through The Coca-Cola Campaign focusing on water stewardship, healthy and active lifestyles, community recycling, and education |
| FedEx | Transported more than 67 planes' worth of aid to disaster victims |
| General Electric | Ecomagination campaign, GE Volunteers Foundation |
| Google | Google.org funds for pro-profit entrepreneurship in Africa, Google China Social Innovation Cup for College Students |
| McDonald's | 99 percent of fish come from MSC-fisheries, transitioning to sustainable food and packaging sources, Ronald McDonald House charities |
| Procter & Gamble | Live, Learn, and Thrive improves the lives of children worldwide |
| Starbucks | Develops ecologically friendly growing practices, LEED certified stores |

*Source:* Adapted from *Fortune*, "The World's Most Admired Companies," http://money.cnn.com/magazines/fortune/most-admired

promotes diversity programs within the company to create meaningful employment opportunities for underserved populations.

- *Fuel conservation.* FedEx surpassed its goal to boost vehicle fuel efficiency by 30 percent, five years ahead of schedule. It reduced overall mileage through route optimization, replaced older vehicles with new, efficient models, and introduced alternative fuel vehicles to its fleet.

- *Volunteerism.* Almost 16,000 employees participate in FedEx Cares Week, supporting charitable and community needs where they live and work.

Consumers increasingly want to purchase products and services from companies that act in socially responsible ways. Most large companies understand this and actively promote their efforts. Guelph-based The Co-operators, a cooperatively owned insurance company, has built a reputation for caring about its members' needs and the quality of life in their communities. Safety-related events such as car-seat inspection clinics and bike safety rodeos, anti–drinking and driving initiatives, and sponsorship of the Block Parent Program of Canada are funded by its Community Economic Development program. The Co-operators is designated as a Caring Company, donating 3.5 percent of pre-tax profits to initiatives that support Canadian communities.[32] Some companies have social responsibility woven into the very fabric of their business, as Entrepreneurial Marketing 18.1 demonstrates.

## Entrepreneurial Marketing 18.1

### Money Does Grow on Trees[33]

When Saskatchewan brothers Kalen and Derrick Elmsley and their friend David Luba realized that there was no option for consumers to buy clothing and give back to society, they decided to do something about it. Social responsibility and concern for the environment were foremost in their minds when they started tentree International, which makes T-shirts, tank tops, hats, and hoodies.

They came up with a unique approach to demonstrate that their company is socially responsible in a way that also gives customers the opportunity to contribute to sustainability. For every item it sells, the company plants 10 trees. It produces clothing in a responsible manner in Oregon, not offshore or in a developing country with low labour costs and a poor safety record. It was important for tentree to source a manufacturer close to home to avoid environmental issues related to shipping and oil consumption. Of course, local production increases the costs of the clothing. And it costs about $3 to plant 10 trees. As a result, the company's clothing sells for up to $6 more at retailers than comparable clothing.

In spite of this, Kalen Elmsley says it not been an issue—there has been no pushback from consumers on price. It helps that tentree's products are tagged with the message "Ten trees are planted for every item

For every T-shirt sold, tentree International plants 10 trees.

Used with permission of tentree International

purchased," which helps to attract an audience of socially and/or environmentally enlightened consumers. In Canada, trees are planted near Edenwold, about 30 minutes outside Regina. Through a partnership with WeForest, tentree can plant trees in 14 countries, including Ethiopia, Burkina Faso, India, Madagascar, Senegal, Tanzania, the Philippines, and Haiti. In the future, the WeForest arrangement will allow tentree's customers to visit its website to indicate the country in which they wish to have trees planted.

Although the trio had been operational for only three months when they appeared on CBC's *Dragons' Den*, they had already earned revenues of $120,000. While some of the Dragons were skeptical, Bruce Croxon and Arlene Dickinson were sold. Since tentree made the pitch, it has secured distribution at 300 retailers across Canada and is looking to expand in the United States, having successfully tested the waters for online sales.

tentree was formally recognized when it won the Saskatchewan Young Professional and Entrepreneurs Volta award. It was also showcased during Saskatchewan Fashion Week as a hot new design company.[34] More importantly, says Elmsley, its sustainability efforts resulted in planting over 400,000 trees in the company's first year of operation, contributing to the financial, social, and environmental bottom line. Today, almost 10 million trees have been planted.[35]

When companies embrace CSR, they appeal not only to their shareholders but also to their key stakeholders, including their own employees, consumers, the marketplace, and society at large. Let's consider each of these stakeholder categories to understand the meaning and effects of corporate social responsibility in the modern marketing arena, as well as how CSR ultimately can benefit the firm that undertakes it.

Employees    Perhaps the most basic corporate social responsibility to employees is to ensure a safe working environment, free of threats to their physical safety, health, or well-being. In some cases, though, this basic level of safety seems insufficient to achieve responsibility to workers. Insurance provider Aflac regards its pay-for-performance structure as a key element of its responsibility to its employees, with the notion that everyone—from call centre operators to the CEO—faces the same compensation standards. By ensuring equality of treatment and fairness in compensation, it earns a reputation as a good place to work and increases the number of people who apply for jobs there. These happy employees also should provide better service to customers, which in turn ensures better outcomes for the firm. Companies that do not treat employees well may face negative publicity and even legal action, as seen in Ethical Dilemma 18.1.

In addition to focusing on employees, more and more firms realize that happy employee families make happy and productive employees. Consequently, firms are focusing their efforts on outreach programs aimed at their employees' families.

Customers    Especially as changes in the marketing environment emerge, firms must consider the effects on the customers who currently patronize them and future customers whom they are targeting. Corporate social responsibility programs must take such shifts and trends into account and react to them quickly. A few of the trends that are receiving the most attention include respecting and protecting privacy in an electronic world. When infidelity dating site Ashley Madison was the victim of computer hacking, it shone a spotlight on "inadequate security safeguards and policies" and the deception caused by phony Trustmark icons on the company's site.

## Ethical Dilemma 18.1

### DavidsTea Scheduling Practices Deemed Unfair

For its customers, DavidsTea means relaxing with a warm cup of tea or enjoying an iced-tea pick-me-up during the day. For its employees, however, DavidsTea can be a source of stress and concern, according to recent allegations.

The retailer has come under fire over its alleged use of on-call scheduling practices. An employee assigned to on-call shifts must call an hour or two before the scheduled shift to check if his or her services are required. Using such scheduling can help retailers reduce wage costs by avoiding overstaffing during slow periods, while making sure they have enough employees working when stores are busy.[36] But according to New York

Attorney General Eric Schneiderman, on-call shifts are unfair because unpredictable work schedules make it difficult for employees to arrange reliable childcare or other pursuits while adding to stress and strain on family life.[37]

On-call scheduling may also violate state labour laws in the United States. For example, New York has enacted "call in pay" regulations that entitle workers to four hours of pay if a shift is cancelled.[38] In Canada, there is a provision for a minimum payment if an employee comes to work but then is not needed—in this situation, federal law states that employees must be paid a minimum call-out pay of three hours.[39]

Other retailers have eliminated the use of on-call shifts in their scheduling, including The Gap and Victoria's Secret,[40] while Hudson's Bay has made a conscious effort to avoid on-call scheduling and creates its employees' schedules weeks, if not months, in advance.[41]

Ashley Madison deceived would-be customers by using phony security icons on its website.
amer ghazzal/Alamy Stock Photo

Other efforts work to ensure the healthfulness of products, especially those aimed at children. Moreover, CSR often increases consumer awareness of the firm, which can lead to better brand equity and sales in the long run. ParticipACTION Canada has helped launch a variety of initiatives to help develop a healthier way of life through an active lifestyle, offering tools and programs for teenagers and corporations.[42] The goal of such programs is to increase consumer awareness of the need to make healthier, more active choices. These efforts ultimately benefit consumers too, who not only gain additional consumption choices but also suffer less risk of the dangers associated with inactivity.

**Marketplace**  When one firm in the industry leads the way toward CSR, its partners and competitors often have no choice but to follow—or run the risk of being left behind. To address issues such as global warming, water scarcity, and energy consumption, GE uses a program it calls *ecomagination,* which encompasses a business strategy comprising four commitments: invest in clean R&D, increase revenues from ecomagination products, reduce greenhouse gas emissions, and inform the public about these issues.[43] When confronted with such initiatives, other energy companies are forced to make a decision: continue as they have been doing, or adopt more responsible practices themselves. In either case, the initiating firm enjoys an advantage by gaining a reputation for being on the cutting edge of CSR efforts.

**Society**  Firms expend considerable time and energy engaging in activities aimed at improving the overall community and the physical environment. According to a McKinsey survey, it is increasingly important for company leaders to work with outside stakeholders[44] who have come to expect it. That is, in a broad sense, companies cannot ignore societal demands that they act responsibly. A firm that fails to do so causes damage to all the preceding stakeholders, as well as itself, putting 30 percent of corporate earnings at risk. Perhaps the most famous recent example is Volkswagen. After news broke about its emissions testing scandal, the company's stock price plummeted almost 35 percent in only two days.[45] Society quickly punished Volkswagen for its actions, resulting in damage to its corporate reputation, profits, and outlook for the future.

Are consumers doing their part to promote and support various CSR programs aimed at protecting the environment? When you buy a new digital camera or cellphone, do you first consider what will happen to your old one? What do you think? Should marketers take more responsibility for educating consumers on the downside of consumption, or is it up to consumers to take a proactive role?

## LO4  A FRAMEWORK FOR ETHICAL DECISION MAKING

We cannot expect every member of a firm to always act ethically. However, a framework for ethical decision making can help move people to work toward common ethical goals. Exhibit 18.5 outlines a simple framework for ethical decision making. Let's consider each of the steps.

**Step 1: Identify Issues**  The first step is to identify the issue. For illustrative purposes, we'll investigate the use (or misuse) of data collected from consumers by a marketing research firm. One of the issues that might arise is the way the data are collected. For instance, are the respondents told about the real purpose of the study? Another issue questions whether the results are going to be used in a way that might mislead or even harm the public.

**Step 2: Gather Information and Identify Stakeholders**  In this step, the firm focuses on gathering facts that are important to the ethical issue, including all relevant legal information. To get a complete picture, the firm must also identify and have discussions with the individuals and groups that have a stake in how the issue is resolved.

Stakeholders typically include the firm's current and retired employees, suppliers, the government, customer groups, shareholders, environmentalists, and members of the community in which the firm operates. Beyond these, many firms now also analyze the needs of the industry and the global community, as well as one-off stakeholders, such as future generations, and the natural environment itself.

**Step 3: Brainstorm and Evaluate Alternatives**  After the marketing firm has identified the stakeholders and their issues and gathered the available data, all parties relevant to the decision should come together to brainstorm any alternative courses of action. In our example, these might include halting the market research project, making responses anonymous, instituting training on the CMA's Code of Ethics for all research-ers, and so forth. Management then reviews and refines these alternatives, leading to the final step.

**Step 4: Choose a Course of Action**  The objective of this last step is to weigh the various alternatives and choose a course of action that generates the best solution for the stakeholders by using ethical practices. Management will rank the alternatives in order of preference, clearly establishing the advantages and disadvantages of each. It is

**EXHIBIT 18.5**  Ethical Decision-Making Framework

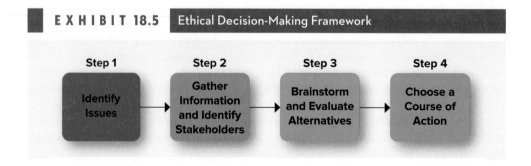

also crucial to investigate any potential legal issues associated with each alternative. Of course, any illegal activity should immediately be rejected.

To choose the appropriate course of action, marketing managers will evaluate each alternative by using a process something like the sample ethical decision-making metric in Exhibit 18.6. Marketers' task here is to ensure that they have applied all relevant decision-making criteria and to assess their level of confidence that the decision being made meets those stated criteria. A marketer who isn't confident about the decision should reexamine the other alternatives.

Using Exhibit 18.6, you can gauge your own ethical response. If your scores tend to be in the low numbers (1 and 2), then the situation is not an ethically troubling situation for you. If, in contrast, your scores tend to be in the high numbers (6 and 7), it is ethically troubling and you know it. If your scores are scattered or in the middle numbers, you need to step back and reflect on how you wish to proceed. At the end of the chapter, you will find a series of ethical scenarios designed to assist you in developing your skills at identifying ethical issues. Use Exhibit 18.6 to help you evaluate these scenarios.

In using such an ethical metric or framework, decision makers must consider the relevant ethical issues, evaluate the alternatives, and then choose a course of action that will help them avoid serious ethical lapses.

Next, let's illustrate how the ethical decision-making metric in Exhibit 18.6 can be used to make ethical business decisions.

Myra Jansen, the head cook at Confederation High School in Anytown, Canada, has had enough. Reports showing that children rarely eat enough vegetables have combined with studies that indicate school kids have a limited amount of time to eat their lunches. The combination has led to increasing obesity rates and troublesome reports about the long-term effects. Jansen has therefore decided that the tater-tots and hot dogs are out. Vegetables and healthy proteins are in.

## ■ EXHIBIT 18.6     Ethical Decision-Making Metric

| | | | | Decision | | | |
|---|---|---|---|---|---|---|---|
| | Yes | | | Maybe | | | No |
| **Test** | 1 | 2 | 3 | 4 | 5 | 6 | 7 |
| 1. **The Publicity Test**<br>Would I want to see this action that I'm about to take described on the front page of the local paper or in a national magazine? | | | | | | | |
| 2. **The Moral Mentor Test**<br>Would the person I admire the most engage in this activity? | | | | | | | |
| 3. **The Admired Observer Test**<br>Would I want the person I admire most to see me doing this? | | | | | | | |
| 4. **The Transparency Test**<br>Could I give a clear explanation for the action I'm contemplating, including an honest and transparent account of all my motives, that would satisfy a fair and dispassionate moral judge? | | | | | | | |
| 5. **The Person in the Mirror Test**<br>Will I be able to look at myself in the mirror and respect the person I see there? | | | | | | | |
| 6. **The Golden Rule Test**<br>Would I like to be on the receiving end of this action and all its potential consequences? | | | | | | | |

*Source:* Adapted from Tom Morris, *The Art of Achievement: Mastering the 7 Cs of Success in Business and in Life* (Kansas City, MO: Andrews McMeel Publishing, 2002); http://edbrenegar.typepad.com/leading_questions/2005/05/real_life_leade.html (accessed July 27, 2017).

The problem, of course, is getting the kids to eat raw vegetables, plant proteins, and lean meat. For many teenagers, recommending that they eat healthy food at lunch is akin to calling detention a play date. But Myra has a plan: She's going to reformulate various menu items using different ingredients, and just never tell the students. Thus the regular hot dogs will be replaced with turkey or soy dogs. The hash browns will contain more nutrient-dense sweet potatoes instead of the vitamin-deficient regular spuds they used to be made out of. She is convinced she can make such switches for most of the menu items, and none of the children need to know.

Most of the kitchen staff is on board with the idea and even have suggested other possible menu switches that would benefit the students by ensuring that they received a well balanced meal at school. When apprised of the idea, school board members got very excited and praised Myra for her innovative thinking. But the community liaison for the school, whose job it is to communicate with parents and other members of the community, is not so sure. Salim Gibran is nervous about how students will react when they learn that they have been deceived. He also has two small children of his own, one of whom has a severe wheat allergy. Thus the Gibrans are extremely cautious about eating out, always asking for a detailed, specific list of ingredients for anything they order.

Using his training in ethical decision making, Salim sits down to evaluate his alternatives, beginning with identifying possible options available to the school district, as well as the various stakeholders that might be impacted by the decision. He comes up with the following list:

1. Switch out the food without telling students.

2. Leave menus as they are.

3. Switch out the food ingredients but also tell students exactly what is in each item in the cafeteria.

To make a clear recommendation to the board about what would be the best ethical choice, Salim decides to evaluate each alternative using a series of questions similar to those in Exhibit 18.6.

Question 1: Would I want to see this action described on the front page of the local paper? The school board's reaction caused Salim to think that the larger community would appreciate the effort to improve students' health. Thus, option 1 appears best for these stakeholders, and possibly for society, which may reduce the prevalence of obesity among these students. However, he shudders to think about how angry students might be if they learned they had been tricked. They also likely are accustomed to their menu as it is and, therefore, they would prefer option 2.

Question 2: Would the person I admire most engage in this activity, and would I want him or her seeing me engage in this activity? For most of his life, Salim has held up Mahatma Gandhi as his ideal for how to act in the world. For Mahatma Gandhi, truth was an absolute concept, not something that could be changed depending on the situation. Therefore, Salim believes Mahatma Gandhi would strongly disapprove of option 1. However, Mahatma Gandhi also worried about the ethics of eating and took care to avoid food choices that had negative effects on society, so he might reject option 2 as well.

Question 3: Can I give a clear explanation for my action, including an honest account of my motives? In thinking about his children, Salim realizes that he is prioritizing their needs, more so than the needs of other children, such as those who struggle with weight issues. That is, he worries that his daughter might unknowingly be exposed to wheat in a school cafeteria, so he prefers option 3.

Question 4: Will I be able to look at myself in the mirror and respect what I see? By bringing up the ethics of this decision, even when it seems as if everyone else has agreed with it, Salim feels confident that he has taken the right first step. The option chosen is still important, but it is a group decision, and Salim thinks he is doing his part.

Question 5: Would I want to be on the receiving end of this action and its consequences? Salim struggles most with this question. He remembers the junk foods he chose when he was in college, and the 10 kilograms he put on as a result. He wishes now that his parents had given him rules to follow about what to eat at school. But he also remembers how rebellious he was and knows that he probably would not have followed those rules. And at the same time, he hates the idea that someone could give him food to eat with falsified ingredients.

On the basis of this exercise, Salim decides that he wants to recommend option 3 to the school board. When he does so, Myra Jansen protests loudly: "This is ridiculous! I know better what kids should be eating, and I know too that some community liaison has no idea what they are willing to eat. You've got to trick them to get them to eat right." Another school board member agrees, noting, "They're just kids. They don't necessarily have the same rights as adults, so we are allowed to decide what's best for them. And hiding the healthy ingredients to get the kids to eat healthy foods is what's best."

So what does the school board decide?

## INTEGRATING ETHICS INTO MARKETING STRATEGY   `LO5`

Ethical decision making is not a simple process, though it can get easier as decision makers within the firm become accustomed to thinking about the ethical implications of their actions from a strategic perspective. In this section, we examine how ethical decision making can be integrated into the strategic marketing planning process introduced in Chapter 2.

The questions vary at each stage of the strategic marketing planning process. For instance, in the planning stage, the firm will decide what level of commitment to its ethical policies and standards it is willing to declare publicly. In the implementation stage, the tone of the questions switches from "*Can we* serve the market with the firm's products or services in an ethically responsible manner?" to "*Should we* be engaging in particular marketing practices?" The key task in the control phase is to ensure that all potential ethical issues raised during the planning process have been addressed and that all employees of the firm have acted ethically. Let's take a closer look at how ethics can be integrated at each stage of the strategic marketing planning process.

Ben & Jerry's mission statement is known for reflecting its strong ethical climate.
TravnikovStudio/Shutterstock

General Mills switched to whole grains in all its breakfast cereal lines to improve dietary benefits.
© Mike Hruby

## Planning Phase

Marketers can introduce ethics at the beginning of the planning process simply by including ethical statements in the firm's mission statement. Many Canadian firms such as RBC, Sleep Country, and others have clearly articulated ethical and corporate social responsibility policies and programs, recognizing that profits and social responsibility go hand in hand. Some firms use mission statements that include ethical precepts for shaping the organization. The mission statements from organizations such as The Body Shop and Ben & Jerry's are known for reflecting strong ethical climates. The mission statement for natural skin care company Burt's Bees is to "create natural, Earth-friendly personal care products formulated to help you maximize your well-being and that of the world around you,"[46] reflecting not only what is good for its customers but what is good for society in general.

Even large firms such as General Mills provide a statement of values that defines the priorities of the organization and its commitment to promoting those values in all that the firm does. Every year, General Mills issues a Global Responsibility Report discussing how the firm has performed against its own standards of ethical conduct.[47]

## Implementation Phase

In the implementation phase of the marketing strategy, when firms are identifying potential markets and ways to deliver the four Ps to them, companies must consider several ethical issues. Sometimes a firm's choice of target market and how it pursues it can lead to charges of unethical behaviour. For instance, Molson Brewery launched a Facebook campaign targeted toward university and college students in which it asked them to post party pictures, which it would use to identify the "top party school." This effort not only encouraged underage drinking but also deeply irritated universities across Canada and the United States, which had little interest in being thus identified. Although these student groups might have been responsive to the firm's efforts, they did not represent an appropriate target market.

However, social media can be an effective means for students to make their communities aware of issues that matter to them, such as homelessness, as discussed in Social and Mobile Marketing 18.1.

The question of resource allocation in the implementation phase can be an ethical minefield, and perhaps no business is more susceptible to charges of unethical resource allocation than the pharmaceutical industry. For example, AIDS activists claim that pharmaceutical companies are not doing enough to develop affordable drugs for underdeveloped countries to treat AIDS among their poor citizens. Some public health officials also have sounded alarm bells about the lack of research into the next generation of antibiotics, at a time when bacteria continue to become increasingly resistant to existing drugs. Critics of the pharmaceutical industry can also point to the increasing number of "lifestyle" drugs, such as those for erectile dysfunction, obesity, male-pattern baldness, nail fungus, and such, as possible causes for the lack of new treatments for serious diseases, even though the pharmaceutical companies vehemently deny that they have been transferring assets from research on treatments for life-threatening illnesses to fund lifestyle drugs.

Sourcing decisions are another problem area for some firms, such as companies choosing to do business with factories in Bangladesh. Charges that they use sweatshop labour to produce their goods have been made against many well known companies. Locating production in an underdeveloped country can make economic

## Social and Mobile Marketing 18.1

### Putting the Face of Homelessness on Facebook[48]

While on a co-op work term in Toronto, Justin Chan regularly walked past people experiencing homelessness. He was concerned that too many of us are trained to ignore the homeless, and so he struck up a conversation with a man outside Union Station. As a business student at Wilfrid Laurier University in Waterloo, Chan recognized the power of social media to effect change. So he and his team set up a Facebook page called Homeless in Waterloo, to share the stories and photographs of people they met. They wanted to show their community that "people experiencing homelessness are real people with real stories, and not just someone they pass by on the street."

Chan and his team regularly hit the streets in Kitchener, Waterloo, and Cambridge armed with food to give the people they meet, a camera to take their photos, and a notepad to capture their stories. Along the way they met a 22-year-old musician who ended up in Kitchener with a broken guitar and nowhere to stay. More than 20 people reached out to help, fixed her guitar, and offered up a spare room. Chan is quick to note that the role of Homeless in Waterloo is

After Homeless in Waterloo reached out via its Facebook page, it was able to provide boxes of supplies and a brand new mattress to a community member in need.

Used with permission of Justin Chan

not necessarily to find accommodation. Rather it helps connect those who are willing to help in any way with those who could benefit from that assistance, whether it comes in the form of food, blankets, clothing, or perhaps job opportunities.

Through the power of social media, Chan is able to broadcast messages to people he would never otherwise be able to reach. Stories posted on the Facebook page can be easily shared, allowing even more people to be reached and take action if they are so moved. A 49-year-old man received an outpouring of support from the community after his story was profiled. He'd grown up with abusive parents, was orphaned at age 12, and was put in foster care. He feels ignored on the streets so was very happy to receive so much love from strangers who had their attitudes changed after reading his story. And that is Chan's goal—to reduce some of the stigma people dealing with homelessness face.

The Homeless in Waterloo Facebook page was set up in March 2016 and attracted over 6,000 Likes in only a few months. Chan says that the people he meets set the terms for any relationship. But even if they don't want their stories shared, the friendship doesn't end. He experiences a lot of joy in helping others. It gives him a warm feeling just making someone else smile.

sense, because it allows the company to take advantage of the lower production costs offered in poorer nations, but it also raises a host of ethical issues, the most prominent of which deals with responsibility. Who is responsible for ensuring that the workers in the factories that produce the goods are treated fairly and paid a living wage? Even the public faces of firms have been faulted for failing to take responsibility for the conditions in factories that produce products bearing their names. An Adidas brand ambassador, Selena Gomez, was accosted by an anti-sweatshop protester while she was attending a fashion show.[49] Environmental organizations have also joined the attack recently, noting that many overseas factories do not maintain the highest environmental standards.

Once the strategy is implemented, controls must be in place to be certain that the firm has actually done what it has set out to do. These activities take place in the next phase of the strategic marketing planning process.

## Control Phase

During the control phase of the strategic marketing planning process, managers must be evaluated on their actions from an ethical perspective. Systems must be in place to check whether each ethical issue raised in the planning process was actually successfully implemented. Systems used in the control phase must also react to change. The emergence of new technologies and new markets ensures that new ethical issues continually arise. In particular, people expect to be able to move normally in public spaces without their location being recorded for subsequent use.[50]

Many firms have emergency response plans in place just in case they ever encounter a situation similar to the Tylenol tampering case or an industrial accident at a manufacturing plant. Firms that respond in the first few hours of a crisis with an organized plan and compassion for those affected suffer fewer long-term negative effects on their reputation, credibility, and level of trust among consumers. The advent of social media has only increased the need to respond quickly.[51]

Ethics thus remains a crucial component of the strategic marketing planning process and should be incorporated into all the firm's decision making. At issue is the problem of policing potential violations of human rights and labour laws.

# UNDERSTANDING ETHICS BY USING SCENARIOS

In this section, we present a series of ethical scenarios designed to assist you in developing your skills at identifying ethical issues. There is no one right answer to the dilemmas below, just as there will be no "correct" answers to many of the ethical situations you will face throughout your career. Instead, these scenarios can help you develop your sensitivity toward ethical issues, as well as your ethical reasoning skills.

Exhibit 18.6 provides simple tests to assist you in evaluating these scenarios. By asking yourself these simple questions, you can gauge your own ethical response.

## Scenario 1: Retailers Lack Ethical Guidelines

Renata has been working at Peavy's Bridal for less than a year now. Her sales figures have never been competitive with those of her co-workers, and the sales manager has called her in for several meetings to discuss her inability to close the sale. Things look desperate; in the last meeting, the sales manager told her that if she did not meet her quota next month, the company would likely have to fire her.

In considering how she might improve her methods and sales, Renata turned to another salesperson, namely, the one with the most experience in the store. Marilyn has been with Peavy's for nearly 30 years, and she virtually always gets the sale. But how?

"Let me tell you something, sweetie," Marilyn tells her. "Every bride-to-be wants one thing: to look beautiful on her wedding day, so everyone gasps when they first see her. And hey, the husband is going to think she looks great. But let's be honest here—not everyone is all that beautiful. So you have to convince them that they look great in one, and only one, dress. And that dress had better be the most expensive one they try, or they won't believe you anyway! And then you have to show them how much better they look with a veil. And some shoes. And a tiara … you get the picture! I mean, they need all that stuff anyway, so why shouldn't we make them feel good while they're here and let them buy from us?"

Should she follow Marilyn's advice and save her job?

## Scenario 2: Giving Credit Where Credit Isn't Due

A catalogue retailer that carries home and children's items (such as children's furniture, clothing, and toys) was seeking a way to reach a new audience and stop the declining sales and revenue trends it was suffering. A market research firm hired by the cataloguer identified a new but potentially risky market: lower-income single parents. The new market seems attractive because of the large number of single parents, but most of these homes are severely constrained in terms of their monetary resources.

The research firm proposed that the cataloguer offer a generous credit policy that would allow consumers to purchase up to $500 worth of merchandise on credit without a credit check, provided they sign up for direct payment of their credit account from a chequing account. Because these are high-risk consumers, the credit accounts would carry extremely high interest rates. The research firm believes that even with losses, enough accounts will be paid off to make the venture extremely profitable for the catalogue retailer.

Should the cataloguer pursue this new strategy?

## Scenario 3: The Jeweller's Tarnished Image

Sparkle Gem Jewellers, a family-owned and -operated costume jewellery manufacturing business, traditionally sold its products only to wholesalers. Recently however, Sparkle Gem was approached by the charismatic Barb Stephens, who convinced the owners to begin selling through a network of distributors she had organized. The distributors recruited individuals to host "jewellery parties" in their homes. Sparkle Gem's owners, the Billing family, has been thrilled with the revenue generated by these home parties and started making plans for the expansion of the distributor network.

However, Mrs. Billing just received a letter from a jewellery party customer, who expressed sympathy for her loss. Mrs. Billing was concerned and contacted the letter writer, who told her that Barb Stephens had come to the jewellery party at her church and told the story of Sparkle Gem. According to Barb's story, Mrs. Billing was a young widow struggling to keep her business together after her husband died on a missionary trip. The writer had purchased $200 worth of jewellery at the party and told Mrs. Billing that she hoped it helped. Mrs. Billing was stunned. She and her very much alive husband had just celebrated their 50th wedding anniversary.

What should Mrs. Billing do now?

## Scenario 4: No Wonder It's So Good

Enjoy Cola is a new product produced by ABC Beverage and marketed with the slogan "Relax with Enjoy." Unlike other colas on the market, Enjoy does not contain caffeine and therefore is positioned as the perfect beverage to end the day or for a slow-paced weekend, and as a means to help consumers relax and unwind. The market response has been tremendous, and sales of Enjoy have been growing rapidly, especially among women.

ABC Beverage decided not to list on the ingredient label that Enjoy contains a small amount of alcohol because the government does not require it to do so unless the alcohol content is more than 1 percent.

Mia Rodriquez, the marketing director for Enjoy, only recently learned that Enjoy contains small amounts of alcohol and is troubled about ABC's failure to disclose this information on the ingredients list. If the alcohol content is less than 1 percent, the beverage is not an alcoholic beverage. But she worries about the impact of this omission on consumers who have alcohol sensitivities or those who shouldn't be consuming alcohol, such as pregnant women, recovering alcoholics, and children.

What should Mia do? What would you do in Mia's place?

## Scenario 5: Bright Baby's Bright Idea

Bartok Manufacturing produces a line of infant toys under the Bright Baby brand label. The Consumer Product Safety Commission (CPSC) recently issued a recall order for the Bright Baby car seat gym, a very popular product. According to the CPSC, the gym contains small parts that present a choking hazard. The CEO of Bartok Manufacturing, Bill Bartok, called an executive meeting to determine the firm's strategy in response to the recall.

Mike Henderson, Bartok's CFO, stated that the recall could cost as much as $1 million in lost revenue from the Bright Baby line. Noting that there had been no deaths or injuries from the product, just the *potential* for injury, Mike proposed that the remaining inventory of car seat gyms be sold in Mexico, where there are no rules such as the CPSC's. Sue Tyler, the marketing director for Bartok, recommended that the product be repackaged and sold in Mexico under a different brand name so that the Bright Baby name would not be associated with the product. Bill, though a bit leery of the plan, agreed to go along with it to avoid the monetary losses.

What would you have recommended to the CEO?

# LEARNING OBJECTIVES REVIEW

### LO1   Identify why marketers should be concerned about ethics

The most important reason to worry about making ethically correct decisions is that it is simply the right thing to do! Being a part of an ethically responsible firm should be important to every employee, but it is particularly important to marketers because they interact most directly with customers and suppliers, which offers them a multitude of opportunities to address ethically challenged issues. It is often challenging to make ethically correct decisions because they can conflict with other personal or corporate objectives.

### LO2   Distinguish between ethics and social responsibility

Individuals and firms can (and should) act ethically, but the outcome of their acts may not affect anyone other than the firm's immediate stakeholders, such as its employees, customers, and suppliers. To be socially responsible, a firm also must take actions that benefit the community in a larger sense, such as helping people who have been affected by a natural disaster such as a hurricane. Socially responsible firms try to conduct their business operations in such a way as to eliminate or minimize the negative impacts on the natural environment and vulnerable groups of consumers such as children, elderly people, and people with disabilities. They also inform consumers of potential harmful effects of their products, promote their products and services in a truthful and responsible way, and are quick to take corrective actions when deficiencies in their products and services are revealed.

### LO3   Describe consumerism and explain how it fosters ethical and socially responsible business practices

Consumers can pressure businesses to practise ethical and socially responsible behaviour in a variety of ways. They can protest poor practices, boycott companies' products

or services, and publicly call for higher ethical standards. In addition, consumers encourage companies to be socially responsible by supporting those companies that have strong ethical practices. Consumerism—a social movement aimed at protecting consumers from business practices that infringe upon their rights—has been a major force driving the trends of increased ethics and CSR. Unfortunately, many consumers are not making full use of the CSR programs established by corporations and governments to foster greater environmental responsibility. Marketers must also be aware that consumers have levelled ethical and social criticisms against marketing, especially when marketers breach the trust of consumers with inappropriate business practices.

### LO4   Identify the four steps in ethical decision making

First, firms can include ethics and social responsibility in their corporate mission. Second, they should institute policies and procedures to ensure that everyone working for the firm is acting in an ethically responsible manner. Third, firms can model their ethical policies after a well established code of ethics, such as the one provided by the Canadian Marketing Association. The ethical decision framework described in this chapter could be used as a template for developing policies and procedures. Fourth, when making ethically sensitive decisions, firms can utilize an ethical decision-making evaluation questionnaire, such as the one in Exhibit 18.6. Firms could also recognize and reward employees for making ethical decisions.

### LO5   Outline how ethics and social responsibility can be integrated into a firm's marketing strategy

Firms can ensure that ethics and social responsibility issues are an integral part of their planning processes. These considerations even could be integrated into the firm's mission statement, as long as top management commits to supporting a strong ethical climate within the organization. When considering their marketing strategy, firms should ask not only "*Can we* implement a certain policy?" but also "*Should* we do it?" Firms should hold their marketing mix—the four Ps—to the highest standard of social responsibility; that is, they must develop safe products, price their products fairly at all times, promote them truthfully, and distribute without undue discrimination. Finally, in the control phase, marketers must determine whether they truly have acted in an ethical and socially responsible manner. If not, they should quickly rectify the situation.

# KEY TERMS

- business ethics
- consumerism

- corporate social responsibility (CSR)
- ethical climate

- locational privacy
- marketing ethics

# CONCEPT REVIEW

1. Explain the meaning of ethics and corporate social responsibility in marketing. What are the main differences between ethics and social responsibility?

2. List four factors that determine whether an individual or firm will act ethically. List the different ways firms could demonstrate their commitment to corporate social responsibility.

3. Describe how firms can integrate ethics and corporate social responsibility into their marketing strategy.

4. Explain how the use of a sustainability scorecard could add value to a company in the eyes of its consumers.

5. Is it possible for companies that have a code of ethics to behave unethically? How might this happen?

6. What is consumerism? Name two organizations that you think are at the forefront of consumerism in Canada. How has consumerism helped foster ethical behaviour and good corporate social responsibility in Canadian companies?

7. Is it ever possible to eliminate or reduce the social and ethical criticisms of marketing? What actions might help in this regard?

8. Problems can arise when businesses from one culture (e.g., the United States) operate in another culture (e.g., China) that has vastly different ethical standards. Google can be seen as trying to impose its ethical standards on China and meddling in China's domestic politics. Do you agree with this perception? Should North American firms abide by the standards of foreign countries even though they may conflict with North American standards?

9. Many commentators suggest that socially responsible marketing is not simply a fad but can actually enhance the revenues and profitability of a firm. Explain how socially responsible marketing may contribute to improved revenues and profitability. Can you name one or two firms in Canada that explicitly make the claim that their corporate social responsibility efforts have resulted in increased revenues and profitability?

10. Many marketers have developed programs to help consumers dispose of their products after use in safe and environmentally responsible ways, either through recycling or by taking the used product to a retailer or depot. Yet tonnes of recyclable materials end up in landfills all across Canada. What factors do you think might explain the behaviours of consumers who do not dispose of their products in an environmentally friendly manner?

# MARKETING APPLICATIONS

1. Why are marketers likely to be faced with more ethical dilemmas than members of other functional areas of the firm, such as finance, accounting, or real estate?

2. Develop an argument for why a cosmetics firm should build and maintain an ethical climate.

3. An insurance company gives generously to charities and sponsors cancer awareness programs. It also makes it difficult for elderly consumers to make claims on policies that they have owned for years. Evaluate this company from an ethical and social responsibility perspective.

4. A clothing company gives generously to charities and sponsors donation drives to help lower-income teen girls get reasonably priced prom dresses. It also locates its manufacturing plants in countries with few labour laws, such that it does not know if children are working in its factories, and works to prevent union activity among its

employees. Evaluate this company from an ethical and social responsibility perspective.

5. Based on the evaluation you developed for Question 4, provide responses to the ethical decision-making metric from Exhibit 18.6. Provide a rationale for your score for each question.

6. A company that makes granola and other "healthful" snacks has the following mission statement: "Our goal is to profitably sell good-tasting, healthy products and to better society." Although its products are organic, they are also high in calories. The company gives a small portion of its profits to United Way. Evaluate the mission statement.

7. The granola company described in Question 6 is thinking about starting an advertising campaign directed at children that would air on Saturday morning television. Explain why you think it should or should not do so.

8. Discuss why marketers use Internet cookies and the potential ethical issues this practice creates.

9. A women's clothing retailer has been found guilty of misleading pricing practices. In spite of significant fines, its pricing practices remain unchanged. Explain how consumerism could force the company to act more ethically in the future.

10. Choose a company that you believe is particularly socially responsible that is not discussed in this chapter. How do you justify your choice? What counterarguments might someone make to suggest that your chosen company is not responsible? Consider all key stakeholders in developing both sides of the argument.

## NET SAVVY

1. Perhaps no subdiscipline of marketing receives more scrutiny regarding ethical compliance than direct marketing, a form of nonstore retailing in which customers are exposed to and purchase merchandise or services through an impersonal medium such as telephone, mail, or the Internet.[52] Ethical issues in direct marketing cover a broad spectrum because this means of selling is conducted through all forms of communication. The Canadian Marketing Association (CMA) takes ethics very seriously and has several programs to ensure that its member organizations comply with its Code of Ethics. Go to the CMA website (http://www.the-cma.org) and type the word *ethics* into the search box. Discuss the results of your search. How many different ways did you find that the CMA was involved in assisting consumers and the industry to create a more ethical marketplace?

2. An increasing number of firms are stating their strong commitment to corporate social responsibility initiatives. The Corporate Social Responsibility Newswire service keeps track of these various initiatives and posts stories on its website about what various corporations are doing. Go to http://www.csrwire.com and choose one story. Write a description of the corporation and the initiative.

## CHAPTER CASE STUDY

### IS THERE AN APP FOR GOOD PARENTING?

If you've gone to a mall or family restaurant recently, it's likely that you have seen children playing games or watching videos on tablets. Whereas it used to be difficult to get children to behave in stores or at a restaurant, parents are finding that a tablet or smartphone can be an effective babysitter. Manufacturers have picked up on this trend and offer several tablets designed specifically for kids: Samsung has the Galaxy Tab 3 Kids Edition, LeapFrog sells the LeapPad2 PowerLearning Tablet, nabi provides the nabi XD and nabi 2, and ClickN offers the KIDS 7 tablet, to name just a few.

Producing and selling technology for kids has proven a profitable business. But when is it too much technology? The American Academy of Pediatrics and the Mayo Clinic both urge parents not to allow children younger than two years of age to interact with any device with a screen (television, computer, tablet), out of concern that it will have negative effects on children's brain development, including the threats of language delays and damage to their social, emotional, and cognitive skills.[53] Furthermore, research has shown that increased "screen time" (defined as the number of hours children spend interacting with any device with an electronic screen) leads to increased risks of obesity, irregular sleep, behavioural problems, and impaired academic performance.

Despite such warnings, companies continue to produce technology products geared toward younger and younger children.[54] One such product is Fisher-Price's Newborn-to-Toddler Apptivity

Seat[55]—essentially a small chair for newborns, with a bar that hangs an iPad a few inches from the child's face. As might be expected, the introduction prompted a massive outcry from child advocacy groups, such as the Campaign for a Commercial-Free Childhood (CCFC), which filed complaints with the Federal Trade Commission about claims Fisher-Price has posted on its website, asserting that the chair in concert with a tablet actually helps babies' brain development.

Fisher-Price's response? It has added a "note to customers" on the product's web page. After suggesting that parents limit their children's screen time, it goes on to state, "We realize this type of technology in infant products isn't for everyone. That's why our Apptivity Seat is just one of more than a dozen baby seats we make, giving parents lots of choices with the options they prefer for their family's lifestyle."[56]

Nor is the company alone in its efforts. With the 2-in-1 iPotty, CTA Digital suggests that parents affix their tablet to their children's potty training seats. Then the children can play with an app or watch a video while learning how to use the potty—often a challenging task for both parents and their children. Since its introduction, the potty seat has been extremely popular, becoming one of the company's top-selling products.[57]

While parents may want devices that keep their children entertained, screen time at such a young age may be harmful to children's cognitive development.

© Minneapolis Star Tribune/ZUMAPRESS/Newscom

The offerings also do not stop at products. Mattel (the parent company of Fisher-Price) has developed a suite of iPad Apptivity apps, available for free to parents who buy the seat. The early development content shows high-contrast patterns, so babies' young eyes can follow them, and features soothing sounds of nature. For slightly older children, the app advances to introduce numbers and letters. Each visual presentation times out after 10 to 12 minutes.

On an even more advanced level, Netflix has expanded its line of self-produced content, beyond fan favourites such as *Arrested Development* or *Orange Is the New Black,* to include original series for children.[58] By appealing to young consumers, Netflix hopes to increase the loyalty of the entire household, reasoning that parents are unlikely to cancel their subscription if Netflix is the only place kids can get the latest episodes of some of their favourite shows.

For parents, innovative products for children can be a lifesaver: They keep kids entertained, help with potty training, and offer a convenient distraction. Moreover, many parents today already rely heavily on tablets and other screens for their own purposes, making it difficult for them to avoid screen time for their children. In this sense, companies are merely providing the products and services that parents, and their children, want.

## Questions

1. Who benefits from products designed to give children and babies more screen time? Who is harmed?

2. Who has a greater ethical responsibility in relation to children and screen time: companies or parents? Present arguments for both sides.

3. What does Fisher-Price's "note to parents" on its website suggest about its corporate ethics policy?

# glossary

**administered vertical marketing system** A supply chain system in which there is no common ownership and no contractual relationship, but the dominant channel member controls the channel relationship.

**advanced shipping notice** An electronic document that the supplier sends the retailer in advance of a shipment to tell the retailer exactly what to expect in the shipment.

**advertising** A paid form of communication from an identifiable source, delivered through a communication channel, and designed to persuade the receiver to take some action, now or in the future.

**advertising allowance** Tactic of offering a price reduction to channel members if they agree to feature the manufacturer's product in their advertising and promotional efforts.

**advertising schedule** Specifies the timing and duration of advertising.

**affective component** A component of attitude that reflects what a person feels about the issue at hand—his or her like or dislike of something.

**affordable method** A method of determining a communications budget based on what is left over after other operating costs have been covered.

**AIDA model** A common model of the series of mental stages through which consumers move as a result of marketing communications:Attention leads to Interest, which leads to Desire, which leads to Action.

**aided recall** Occurs when consumers recognize the brand when its name is presented to them.

**alpha testing** An attempt by the firm to determine whether a product will perform according to its design and whether it satisfies the need for which it was intended; occurs in the firm's R&D department.

**associated services (or augmented product)** The nonphysical attributes of the product, including product warranties, financing, product support, and after-sale service.

**attitude** A person's enduring evaluation of his or her feelings about and behavioural tendencies toward an object or idea; consists of three components: cognitive, affective, and behavioural.

**autocratic buying centre** A buying centre in which one person makes the decision alone, though there may be multiple participants.

**B2B (business-to-business)** The process of selling merchandise or services from one business to another.

**B2C (business-to-consumer)** The process in which businesses sell to consumers.

**baby boomers** Generational cohort of people born after World War II until 1965.

**bait and switch** A deceptive practice of luring customers into the store with a very low advertised price on an item (the bait), only to aggressively pressure them into purchasing a higher-priced item (the switch) by disparaging the low-priced item, comparing it unfavourably with the higher-priced model, or professing an inadequate supply of the lower-priced item.

**behavioural component** A component of attitude that comprises the actions a person takes with regard to the issue at hand.

**behavioural segmentation** Groups consumers based on the benefits they derive from products or services, their usage rate, their loyalty, and the occasion.

**benefit segmentation** Groups consumers based on the benefits they derive from products or services.

**beta testing** Having potential consumers examine a product prototype in a real-use setting to determine its functionality, performance, potential problems, and other issues specific to its use.

**big-box food retailer** Comes in three types: supercentre, hypermarket, and warehouse club; larger than a conventional supermarket; carries both food and nonfood items.

**big data** Refers to extremely large quantities of data that companies have access to but are unable to handle using conventional data management and data mining software.

**blog (weblog)** A web page that contains periodic posts; corporate blogs are a new form of marketing communications.

**bounce rate** The percentage of times a visitor leaves a site almost immediately.

**boycott** A group's refusal to deal commercially with some organization to protest against its policies.

**brand associations** The mental links that consumers make between a brand and its key product attributes; can involve a logo, slogan, or famous personality.

**brand awareness** Measures how many consumers in a market are familiar with the brand and what it stands for; created through repeated exposures of the various brand elements (brand name, logo, symbol, character, packaging, or slogan) in the firm's communications to consumers.

**brand dilution** Occurs when a brand extension adversely affects consumer perceptions about the attributes the core brand is believed to hold.

**brand equity** The set of assets and liabilities linked to a brand that add to or subtract from the value provided by the product or service.

**brand extension** The use of the same brand name for new products being introduced to the same or new markets.

**brand licensing** A contractual arrangement between firms, whereby one firm allows another to use its brand name, logo, symbols, or characters in exchange for a negotiated fee.

**brand loyalty** Occurs when a consumer buys the same brand's product or service repeatedly over time rather than buying from multiple suppliers within the same category.

**brand personality** Refers to a set of human characteristics associated with a brand, which has symbolic or self-expressive meanings for consumers.

**brand repositioning (rebranding)** A strategy in which marketers change a brand's focus to target new markets or realign the brand's core emphasis with changing market preferences.

**brands** The names, terms, designs, symbols, or any other features that identify one seller's good or service as distinct from those of other sellers.

**break-even point** The point at which the number of units sold generates just enough revenue to equal the total costs; at this point, profits are zero.

**business ethics** Refers to the moral or ethical dilemmas that might arise in a business setting.

**business-to-business (B2B) marketing** The process of buying and selling goods or services to be used in the production of other goods and services, for consumption by the buying organization, or for resale by wholesalers and retailers.

**buyer** The buying centre participant who handles the paperwork of the actual purchase.

**buying centre** The group of people typically responsible for the buying decisions in large organizations.

**C2C (consumer-to-consumer)** The process in which consumers sell to other consumers.

**cash discount** Tactic of offering a reduction in the invoice cost if the buyer pays the invoice prior to the end of the discount period.

**category killer** Offers an extensive assortment in a particular category, so overwhelming the category that other retailers have difficulty competing.

**category specialist** Offers a narrow variety but a deep assortment of merchandise.

**cause-related marketing** Commercial activity in which businesses and charities form a partnership to market an image, product, or service for their mutual benefit; a type of promotional campaign.

**channel conflict** Results when supply chain members are not in agreement about their goals, roles, or rewards.

**click paths** Show how users navigate through a site.

**click-through rate (CTR)** The number of times a user clicks on an ad divided by the number of impressions.

**click-through tracking** Measures how many times users click on banner advertising on websites.

**closing the sale** Obtaining a commitment from the customer to make a purchase.

**cobranding** The practice of marketing two or more brands together, on the same package or promotion.

**cognitive component** A component of attitude that reflects what a person believes to be true.

**cold calls** A method of prospecting in which salespeople telephone or go to see potential customers without appointments.

**communication channel** The medium—print, broadcast, the Internet—that carries the message.

**communication gap** Refers to the difference between the actual service provided to customers and the service that the firm's promotion program promises.

**compensatory decision rule** Is at work when the consumer is evaluating alternatives and trades off one characteristic against another, such that good characteristics compensate for bad ones.

**competitive intelligence (CI)** Used by firms to collect and synthesize information about their position with respect to their rivals; enables companies to anticipate changes in the marketplace rather than merely react to them.

**competitive parity** A firm's strategy of setting prices that are similar to those of major competitors.

**competitive parity method** A method of determining a communications budget in which the firm's share of the communication expenses is in line with its market share.

**competitor-based pricing method** An approach that attempts to reflect how the firm wants consumers to interpret its products relative to the competitors' offerings.

**competitor orientation** A company objective based on the premise that the firm should measure itself primarily against its competition.

**complementary products** Products whose demand curves are positively related, such that they rise or fall together; a percentage increase in demand for one results in a percentage increase in demand for the other.

**concentrated (or niche) targeting strategy** A marketing strategy of selecting a single, primary target market and focusing all energies on providing a product to fit that market's needs.

**concept testing** The process in which a concept statement that describes a product or a service is presented to potential buyers or users to obtain their reactions.

**concepts** Brief written descriptions of a product or service; its technology, working principles, and forms; and what customer needs it would satisfy.

**consensus buying centre** A buying centre in which all members of the team must reach a collective agreement that they can support a particular purchase.

**consultative buying centre** A buying centre in which one person makes the decision, but he or she solicits input from others before doing so.

**consumer decision rules** The set of criteria consumers use consciously or subconsciously to quickly and efficiently select from among several alternatives.

**consumer products** Products and services used by people for their personal use.

**consumerism** A social movement aimed at protecting consumers from business practices that infringe upon their rights.

**contest** A brand-sponsored competition that requires some form of skill or effort.

**continuous advertising schedule** Runs steadily throughout the year and therefore is suited to products and services that are consumed continually at relatively steady rates and that require a steady level of persuasive or reminder advertising.

**contractual vertical marketing system** A system in which independent firms at different levels of the supply chain join together through contracts to obtain economies of scale and coordination and to reduce conflict.

**contribution per unit** Equals the price less the variable cost per unit; variable used to determine the break-even point in units.

**control phase** The part of the strategic marketing planning process when managers evaluate the performance of the marketing strategy and take any necessary corrective actions.

**convenience goods/services** Products or services for which the consumer is not willing to spend any effort to evaluate prior to purchase.

**conventional supermarket** Offers groceries, meat, and produce with limited sales of nonfood items, such as health and beauty aids and general merchandise, in a self-service format.

**conversion rates** The percentage of visitors to a site who click, buy, or donate.

**cooperative (co-op) advertising** An agreement between a manufacturer and retailer in which the manufacturer agrees to defray some advertising costs.

**core customer value** The basic problem-solving benefits that consumers are seeking.

**corporate brand** The use of a firm's own corporate name to brand all of its product lines and products.

**corporate social responsibility (CSR)** Refers to the voluntary activities undertaken by a company to operate in an economically, socially, and environmentally sustainable manner.

**corporate vertical marketing system** A system in which the parent company has complete control and can dictate the priorities and objectives of the supply chain; it may own facilities such as manufacturing plants, warehouse facilities, retail outlets, and design studios.

**cost-based pricing method** Determines the final price to charge by starting with the cost, without recognizing the role that consumers or competitors' prices play in the marketplace.

**cost of ownership method** A value-based method for setting prices that determines the total cost of owning the product over its useful life.

**country culture** Easy-to-spot visible nuances that are particular to a country, such as dress, symbols, ceremonies, language, colours, and food preferences, and more subtle aspects, which are trickier to identify.

**coupon** Provides a stated discount to consumers on the final selling price of a specific item; the retailer handles the discount.

**cross-price elasticity** The percentage change in demand for Product A that occurs in response to a percentage change in price of Product B.

**cross-promoting** Efforts of two or more firms joining together to reach a specific target market.

**cross-shopping** The pattern of buying both premium and low-priced merchandise or patronizing both expensive, status-oriented retailers and price-oriented retailers.

**cultural imperialism** The belief that one's own culture is superior to that of other nations; can take the form of an active, formal policy or a more subtle general attitude.

**culture** The shared meanings, beliefs, morals, values, and customs of a group of people.

**cumulative quantity discount** Pricing tactic that offers a discount based on the amount purchased over a specified period and usually involves several transactions.

**customer excellence** Involves a focus on retaining loyal customers and excellent customer service.

**customer lifetime value (CLV)** The expected financial contribution from a particular customer to the firm's profits over the course of their relationship.

**customer orientation** Pricing orientation that explicitly invokes the concept of customer value and setting prices to match consumer expectations.

**customer relationship management (CRM)** A business philosophy and set of strategies, programs, and systems that focus on identifying and building loyalty among the firm's most valued customers.

**customer service** Specifically refers to human or mechanical activities firms undertake to help satisfy their customers' needs and wants.

**data** Raw numbers or other factual information of limited value.

**data mining** The use of statistical analysis tools to search for patterns in data or relationships among variables.

**deal** A type of short-term price reduction that can take several forms, such as a "featured price" (a price lower than the regular price); a "buy one, get one free" offer; or a certain percentage "more free" offer contained in larger packaging.

**deceptive advertising** A representation, omission, act, or practice in an advertisement that is likely to mislead consumers acting reasonably under the circumstances.

**decider** The buying centre participant who ultimately determines any part of or the entire buying decision—whether to buy, what to buy, how to buy, or where to buy.

**decision heuristics** Mental shortcuts that help consumers narrow down choices; examples include price, brand, and product presentation.

**decline stage** Stage of the product life cycle when sales decline and the product eventually exits the market.

**decoding** The process by which the receiver interprets the sender's message.

**delivery gap** The difference between the firm's service standards and the actual service it provides to customers.

**demand curve** Shows how many units of a product or service consumers will demand during a specific period at different prices.

**democratic buying centre** A buying centre in which the majority rules in making decisions.

**demographic segmentation** The grouping of consumers according to easily measured, objective characteristics such as age, gender, income, and education.

**demographics** Characteristics of human populations and segments, especially those used to identify consumer markets, such as age, gender, income, race, ethnicity, and education.

**derived demand** The linkage between consumers' demand for a company's output and its purchase of necessary inputs to manufacture or assemble that particular output.

**determinant attributes** Product or service features that are important to the buyer and on which competing brands or stores are perceived to differ.

**differentiated targeting strategy** A strategy through which a firm targets several market segments with a different offering for each.

**diffusion of innovation** The process by which the use of an innovation, whether a product or a service, spreads throughout a market group over time and over various categories of adopters.

**digital media** Tools ranging from simple website content to far more interactive features such as corporate blogs, online games, text messaging, social media, and mobile apps.

**direct investment** When a firm maintains 100 percent ownership of its plants, operation facilities, and offices in a foreign country, often through the formation of wholly owned subsidiaries.

**direct mail/email** A targeted form of communication distributed to a prospective customer's mailbox or inbox.

**direct marketing** Marketing that communicates directly with target customers to generate a response or transaction.

**direct response TV (DRTV)** TV commercials or infomercials with a strong call to action.

**discount store** Offers a broad variety of merchandise, limited service, and low prices.

**dispatcher** The person who coordinates deliveries to distribution centres.

**disruptive innovations** New product introductions that are simpler, less sophisticated, and usually less expensive than existing products or services.

**distribution centre** A facility for the receipt, storage, and redistribution of goods to company stores or customers; may be operated by retailers, manufacturers, or distribution specialists.

**distribution channel** The institutions that transfer the ownership of goods and move goods from the point of production to the point of consumption.

**distribution intensity** The number of channel members to use at each level of the supply chain.

**distributive fairness** Pertains to a customer's perception of the benefits he or she received compared with the costs (inconvenience or loss) that resulted from a service failure.

**diversification strategy** A growth strategy whereby a firm introduces a new product or service to a market segment that it does not currently serve.

**downsizing** Exiting markets, reducing product portfolios, or closing certain businesses or store or plant locations.

**drugstore** A specialty store that concentrates on health and personal grooming merchandise, though pharmaceuticals may represent more than 60 percent of its sales.

**dumping** The practice of selling a good in a foreign market at a price that is lower than its domestic price or below its cost.

**early adopters** The second group of consumers in the diffusion of innovation model, after innovators, to use a product or service innovation; generally don't like to take as much risk as innovators.

**early majority** A group of consumers in the diffusion of innovation model that represents approximately 34 percent of the population; members don't like to take much risk and therefore tend to wait until bugs are worked out.

**earned media** Media that results from word-of-mouth, buzz, or publicity.

**economic situation** Economic changes that affect the way consumers buy merchandise and spend money; see inflation, foreign currency fluctuations, interest rates, and recession.

**elastic** Refers to a market for a product or service that is price sensitive; that is, relatively small changes in price will generate fairly large changes in the quantity demanded.

**electronic data interchange (EDI)** The computer-to-computer exchange of business documents from a retailer to a vendor and back.

**emotional appeal** Aims to satisfy consumers' emotional desires rather than their utilitarian needs.

**empowerment** In the context of service delivery, means allowing employees to make decisions about how service is provided to customers.

**encoding** The process of converting the sender's ideas into a message, which could be verbal, visual, or both.

**environmental concerns** Include, but are not limited to, the excessive use of natural resources and energy, refuse from manufacturing processes, excess trash created by consumer goods packages, and hard-to-dispose-of products such as tires, cellphones, and computer monitors.

**esteem needs** Allow people to satisfy their inner desires.

**ethical climate** The set of values within a marketing firm, or in the marketing division of any firm, that guides decision making and behaviour.

**ethnography** An observational method that studies people in their daily lives and activities in their homes, work, and communities.

**evaluative criteria** Consist of a set of salient, or important, attributes about a particular product that are used to compare alternative products.

**event sponsorship** A popular PR tool; occurs when corporations support various activities (financially or otherwise), usually in the cultural or sports and entertainment sectors.

**everyday low pricing (EDLP)** A strategy companies use to emphasize the continuity of their retail prices at a level somewhere between the regular, nonsale price and the deep-discount sale prices their competitors may offer.

**evoked set** Comprises the alternative brands or stores that the consumer states would be considered when making a purchase decision.

**exchange** The trade of things of value between the buyer and the seller so that each is better off as a result.

**exchange control** Refers to the regulation of a country's currency exchange rate.

**exchange rate** The measure of how much one currency is worth in relation to another.

**exclusive distribution** Strategy of granting exclusive rights to sell to one or very few retail customers so no other customers can sell a particular brand.

**experience curve effect** Refers to the drop in unit cost as the accumulated volume sold increases; as sales continue to grow, the costs continue to drop, allowing even further reductions in the price.

**experimental research** A type of quantitative research that systematically manipulates one or more variables to determine which variable has a causal effect on another variable.

**exporting** Producing goods in one country and selling them in another.

**extended network** The influence of a person's extended network.

**extended problem solving** A purchase decision process during which the consumer devotes considerable time and effort to analyzing alternatives; often occurs when the consumer perceives that the purchase decision entails a great deal of risk.

**external locus of control** Refers to when consumers believe that fate or other external factors control all outcomes.

**external search for information** Occurs when the buyer seeks information outside his or her personal knowledge base to help make the buying decision.

**extreme-value retailer** A general merchandise discount store found in lower-income urban or rural areas.

**family brand** The use of a combination of the company brand name and individual brand name to distinguish a firm's products.

**feedback loop** Allows the receiver to communicate with the sender and thereby informs the sender whether the message was received and decoded properly.

**financial risk** Risk associated with a monetary outlay; includes the initial cost of the purchase, as well as the costs of using the item or service.

**first movers** Product pioneers that are the first to create a market or product category, making them readily recognizable to consumers and thus establishing a commanding and early market share lead.

**fixed costs** Those costs that remain essentially at the same level, regardless of any changes in the volume of production.

**flighting advertising schedule** Implemented in spurts, with periods of heavy advertising followed by periods of no advertising.

**focus group** A research technique in which a small group of persons (usually 8 to 12) comes together for an in-depth discussion about a particular topic, with the conversation guided by a trained moderator using an unstructured method of inquiry.

**foreign currency fluctuations** Changes in the value of a country's currency relative to the currency of another country; can influence consumer spending.

**franchising** A contractual agreement between a franchisor and a franchisee that allows the franchisee to operate a retail outlet, using a name and format developed and supported by the franchisor.

**frequency** Measure of how often the target audience is exposed to a communication within a specified period of time.

**functional needs** Pertain to the performance of a product or service.

**gamification** The process of using games or gamelike elements to encourage participation.

**gatekeeper** The buying centre participant who controls information or access to decision makers and influencers.

**general merchandise retailers** May be discount stores, specialty stores, category specialists, department stores, drugstores, off-price retailers, or extreme-value retailers; may sell through multiple channels, such as the Internet and catalogues.

**Generation X** Generational cohort of people born between 1966 and 1971.

**Generation Y/millennials** Generational cohort of people born between 1972 and 1992; the biggest cohort since the original postwar baby boom.

**Generation Z/digital natives** Generational cohort of people born after 1993.

**generational cohort** A group of people of the same generation who typically have similar purchase behaviours because they have shared experiences and are in the same stage of life.

**generic** A product sold without a brand name, typically in commodities markets.

**geodemographic segmentation** The grouping of consumers on the basis of a combination of geographic, demographic, and lifestyle characteristics.

**geographic pricing** The setting of different prices depending on a geographical division of the delivery areas.

**geographic segmentation** The grouping of consumers on the basis of where they live.

**global labour issues** Include concerns about working conditions and wages paid to factory workers in developing countries.

**globalization** Refers to the increased flow of goods, services, people, technology, capital, information, and ideas around the world; has economic, political, social, cultural, and environmental impacts.

**glocalization** When firms offer standardized products globally and change promotional campaigns geared to local markets.

**goods** Items that can be physically touched.

**green marketing** Involves a strategic effort by firms to supply customers with environmentally friendly merchandise.

**grey market** Employs irregular but not necessarily illegal methods; generally, it legally circumvents authorized channels of distribution to sell goods at prices lower than those intended by the manufacturer.

**gross domestic product (GDP)** The market value of the goods and services produced by a country in a year; the most widely used standardized measure of output.

**gross rating points (GRP)** Measure used for various media advertising—print, radio, or television; GRP = Reach × Frequency.

**growth stage** Stage of the product life cycle when the product gains acceptance, demand and sales increase, and competitors emerge in the product category.

**habitual decision making** A purchase decision process in which consumers engage with little conscious effort.

**high/low pricing** A pricing strategy that relies on the promotion of sales, during which prices are temporarily reduced to encourage purchases.

**hits** The total number of requests for a web page.

**horizontal price fixing** Occurs when competitors that produce and sell competing products collude, or work together, to control prices, effectively taking price out of the decision process for consumers.

**human development index (HDI)** A composite measure of three indicators of the quality of life in different countries: life expectancy at birth, educational attainment, and whether the average incomes are sufficient to meet the basic needs of life in that country.

**hypothesis** A statement or proposition predicting a particular relationship among multiple variables that can be tested through research.

**ideal point** The position at which a particular market segment's ideal product would lie on a perceptual map.

**ideas** Thoughts, opinions, philosophies, and intellectual concepts.

**implementation phase** Where marketing managers identify and evaluate different opportunities by engaging in a process known as segmentation, targeting, and positioning. They then develop and implement the marketing mix by using the four Ps.

**impressions** The number of times an ad appears to a user.

**improvement value** Represents an estimate of how much more (or less) consumers are willing to pay for a product relative to other comparable products.

**impulse buying** A buying decision made by customers on the spot when they see the merchandise.

**income effect** Refers to the change in the quantity of a product demanded by consumers because of a change in their income.

**inconsistent** A characteristic of a service: its quality may vary because it is provided by humans.

**in-depth interview** A research technique in which trained researchers ask questions, listen to and record the answers, and then pose additional questions to clarify or expand on a particular issue.

**individual brand** The use of individual brand names for each of a firm's products.

**inelastic** Refers to a market for a product or service that is price insensitive; that is, relatively small changes in price will not generate large changes in the quantity demanded.

**inflation** Refers to the persistent increase in the prices of goods and services.

**influence** The extent to which a person influences others.

**influencer** The buying centre participant whose views influence other members of the buying centre in making the final decision.

**information** Data that has been organized, analyzed, interpreted, and converted into a useful form for decision makers.

**informative advertising** Communication used to create and build brand awareness, with the ultimate goal of moving the consumer through the buying cycle to a purchase.

**infrastructure** The basic facilities, services, and installations needed for a community or society to function, such as transportation and communications systems, water and power lines, and public institutions such as schools, post offices, and prisons.

**initiator** The buying centre participant who first suggests buying the particular product or service.

**innovation** The process by which ideas are transformed into new products and services that will help firms grow.

**innovators** Those buyers who want to be the first to have the new product or service.

**inseparable** A characteristic of a service: it is produced and consumed at the same time—that is, service and consumption are inseparable.

**institutional advertisements** Used to inform, persuade, and remind consumers about issues related to places, politics, an industry, or a particular corporation.

**intangible** A characteristic of a service; it cannot be touched, tasted, or seen like a pure product can.

**integrated marketing communications (IMC)** Represents the promotion dimension of the four Ps; encompasses a variety of communication disciplines—general advertising, personal selling, sales promotion, public relations, direct marketing, and digital media—in combination to provide clarity, consistency, and maximum communicative impact.

**intensive distribution** A strategy designed to get products into as many outlets as possible.

**interest rates** Represent the cost of borrowing money.

**internal locus of control** Refers to when consumers believe they have some control over the outcomes of their actions, in which case they generally engage in more search activities.

**internal search for information** Occurs when the buyer examines his or her own memory and knowledge about the product or service, gathered through past experiences.

**introduction stage** Stage of the product life cycle when innovators start buying the product.

**inventory** A characteristic of a service: it is perishable and cannot be stored in inventory for future use.

**involvement** The consumer's degree of interest in or concern about the product or service.

**joint venture** Formed when a firm entering a new market pools its resources with those of a local firm to form a new company in which ownership, control, and profits are shared.

**just-in-time (JIT) inventory systems** Inventory management systems designed to deliver less merchandise on a more frequent basis than traditional inventory systems; the firm gets the merchandise "just in time" for it to be used in the manufacture of another product; also known as quick-response (QR) systems in retailing.

**keyword analysis** Determines which keywords visitors to a site use to find it.

**knowledge gap** Reflects the difference between customers' expectations and the firm's perception of those expectations.

**laggards** Consumers who like to avoid change and rely on traditional products until they are no longer available.

**lagged effect** A delayed response to a marketing communication campaign.

**late majority** The last group of buyers to enter a new product market.

**lead time** The amount of time between the recognition that an order needs to be placed and the arrival of the needed merchandise at the seller's store, ready for sale.

**lead users** Innovative product users who modify existing products according to their own ideas to suit their specific needs.

**leader pricing** Consumer pricing tactic that attempts to build store traffic by aggressively pricing and advertising a regularly purchased item, often priced at or just above the store's cost.

**leads** A list of potential customers.

**learning** Refers to a change in a person's thought process or behaviour that arises from experience and takes place throughout the consumer decision process.

**lifestyle** Refers to the way consumers spend their time and money.

**lifestyles** Lifestyles are how we live our lives to achieve goals.

**limited problem solving** Occurs during a purchase decision that calls for, at most, a moderate amount of effort and time.

**listing allowances** Fees paid to retailers simply to get new products into stores or to gain more or better shelf space for their products.

**locational excellence** Involves a focus on a good physical location and Internet presence.

**locational privacy** A person's ability to move about in public spaces with the expectation that the location will not be recorded for future use.

**logistics management** The integration of two or more activities for the purpose of planning, implementing, and controlling the efficient flow of raw materials, in-process inventory, and finished goods from the point of origin to the point of consumption.

**loss leader pricing** Loss leader pricing takes the tactic of leader pricing one step further by lowering the price below the store's cost.

**love (social) needs** Relate to our interactions with others.

**loyalty program** Specifically designed to retain customers by offering premiums or other incentives to customers who make multiple purchases over time.

**loyalty segmentation** Strategy of investing in retention and loyalty initiatives to retain the firm's most profitable customers.

**macroenvironmental factors** Aspects of the external environment—culture, demographics, social trends, technological advances, economic situation, and political/legal environment (CDSTEP)—that affect companies.

**manufacturer brands** Brands owned and managed by the manufacturer.

**manufacturer's suggested retail price (MSRP)** Manufacturers encourage retailers to sell their merchandise at a specific price.

**markdowns** Reductions retailers take on the initial selling price of the product or service.

**market development strategy** A growth strategy that employs the existing marketing offering to reach new market segments, whether domestic or international or segments not currently served by the firm.

**market growth rate** The annual rate of growth of the specific market in which the product competes.

**market penetration pricing** A pricing strategy of setting the initial price low for the introduction of the new product or service, with the objective of building sales, market share, and profits quickly.

**market penetration strategy** A growth strategy that employs the existing marketing mix and focuses the firm's efforts on existing customers.

**market positioning** Involves the process of defining the marketing mix variables so that target customers have a clear, distinct, desirable understanding of what the product does or represents in comparison with competing products.

**market segment** A group of consumers who respond similarly to a firm's marketing efforts.

**market segmentation** The process of dividing the market into distinct groups of customers—where each individual group has similar needs, wants, or characteristics—who therefore might appreciate products or services geared especially for them in similar ways.

**market** The groups of people who need or want a company's products or services and have the ability and willingness to buy them.

**marketing** A set of business practices designed to plan for and present an organization's products or services in ways that build effective customer relationships.

**marketing ethics** Refers to those ethical problems that are specific to the domain of marketing.

**marketing mix (four Ps)** Product, price, place, and promotion—the controllable set of activities that a firm uses to respond to the wants of its target markets.

**marketing plan** A written document composed of an analysis of the current marketing situation, opportunities and threats for the firm, marketing objectives and strategy specified in terms of the four Ps, action programs, and projected or pro forma income (and other financial) statements.

**marketing research** A set of techniques and principles for systematically collecting, recording, analyzing, and interpreting data that can aid decision makers involved in marketing goods, services, or ideas.

**marketing strategy** Identifies a firm's target market(s), a related marketing mix—the four Ps, and the bases upon which the firm plans to build a sustainable competitive advantage.

**mass customization** The practice of interacting on a one-to-one basis with many people to create custom-made products or services; providing one-to-one marketing to the masses.

**mass media** Channels, such as national newspapers, magazines, radio, and television, that are ideal for reaching large numbers of anonymous audience members.

**maturity stage** Stage of the product life cycle when industry sales reach their peak, so firms try to rejuvenate their products by adding new features or repositioning them.

**maximizing profits strategy** A mathematical model that captures all the factors required to explain and predict sales and profits, which should be able to identify the price at which its profits are maximized.

**media buy** The purchase of airtime or print pages.

**media mix** The combination of the media used and the frequency of advertising in each medium.

**media planning** The process of evaluating and selecting the media mix that will deliver a clear, consistent, compelling message to the intended audience.

**micromarketing (one-to-one)** An extreme form of segmentation that tailors a product or service to suit an individual customer's wants or needs.

**mission statement** A broad description of a firm's objectives and the scope of activities it plans to undertake; attempts to answer two main questions: What type of business is it? and What does it need to do to accomplish its goals and objectives?

**modified rebuy** Refers to when the buyer has purchased a similar product in the past but has decided to change some specifications, such as the desired price, quality level, customer service level, and options.

**monopolistic competition** Occurs when many firms sell closely related but not homogeneous products; these products may be viewed as substitutes but are not perfect substitutes.

**monopoly** Occurs when only one firm provides the product or service in a particular industry.

**motive** A need or want that is strong enough to cause the person to seek satisfaction.

**need** A basic necessity, such as food, clothing, shelter, and safety.

**need recognition** The beginning of the consumer decision process; occurs when consumers recognize they have an unsatisfied need and want to go from their needy state to a different, desired state.

**negative word-of-mouth** Occurs when consumers spread negative information about a product, service, or store to others.

**new buy** In a B2B setting, a purchase of a good or service for the first time; the buying decision is likely to be quite involved because the buyer or the buying organization does not have any experience with the item.

**niche media** Channels that are focused and generally used to reach narrow segments, often with unique demographic characteristics or interests.

**noise** Any interference that stems from competing messages, a lack of clarity in the message, or a flaw in the medium; a problem for all communication channels.

**noncompensatory decision rule** Is at work when consumers choose a product or service on the basis of a subset of its characteristics, regardless of the values of its other attributes.

**noncumulative quantity discount** Pricing tactic that offers a discount based on only the amount purchased in a single order.

**North American Industry Classification System (NAICS) codes** A classification scheme that categorizes all firms into a hierarchical set of six-digit codes.

**objective-and-task method** An IMC budgeting method that determines the cost required to undertake specific tasks to accomplish communication objectives; process entails setting objectives, choosing media, and determining costs.

**observation** A qualitative research method that entails examining purchase and consumption behaviours through personal or video camera scrutiny.

**occasion segmentation** Groups consumers based on when they purchase or consume a product or service.

**odd prices** Prices that end in odd numbers, usually 9, such as $3.99.

**off-price retailer** A type of retailer that offers an inconsistent assortment of merchandise at relatively low prices.

**oligopoly** Occurs when only a few firms dominate a market.

**omnichannel** A strategy that creates a consistent experience for consumers across all distribution channels.

**omnichannel strategy** Selling in more than one channel (e.g., store, catalogue, kiosk, and Internet).

**operational excellence** Involves a focus on efficient operations and excellent supply chain management.

**organizational culture** Reflects the set of values, traditions, and customs that guides a firm's employees' behaviour.

**owned media** Media controlled by the advertiser, such as its website, Facebook fan page, or YouTube channel.

**page views** The number of times any web pages are viewed by visitors.

**paid media** Media such as TV, print, radio, or display ads used to reach mass markets.

**panel data** A type of quantitative research that involves collecting information from a group of consumers (the panel) over time; data collected may be from a survey or a record of purchases.

**perceived value** The relationship between a product or service's benefits and its cost.

**percentage-of-sales method** A method of determining a communications budget that is based on a fixed percentage of forecasted sales.

**perception** The process by which people select, organize, and interpret information to form a meaningful picture of the world.

**perceptual map** Displays, in two or more dimensions, the position of products or brands in the consumer's mind.

**performance risk** Involves the perceived danger inherent in a poorly performing product or service.

**personal selling** The two-way flow of communication between a buyer and a seller that is designed to influence the buyer's purchase decision.

**persuasive advertising** Communication used to motivate consumers to take action.

**physiological needs** Relate to the basic biological necessities of life: food, drink, rest, and shelter.

**physiological risk** Risk associated with the fear of an actual harm should the product not perform properly.

**pioneers** New product introductions that establish a completely new market or radically change both the rules of competition and consumer preferences in a market; also called breakthroughs.

**planning phase** Where marketing executives and other top managers define the mission and objectives of the business, and evaluate the situation by assessing how various players, both inside and outside the organization, affect the firm's potential for success.

**point-of-purchase (POP) display** A merchandise display located at the point of purchase, such as at the checkout counter in a grocery store.

**political/legal environment** Comprises political parties, government organizations, and legislation and laws that promote or inhibit trade and marketing activities.

**pop-up stores** Temporary storefronts that exist for only a limited time and generally focus on a new product or a limited group of products offered by a retailer, manufacturer, or service provider; give consumers a chance to interact with the brand and build brand awareness.

**positioning** The mental picture that people have about a company and its products or services relative to competitors.

**positioning statement** Expresses how a company wants to be perceived by consumers.

**postpurchase dissonance** An internal conflict that arises from an inconsistency between two beliefs, or between beliefs and behaviour; buyer's remorse.

**post-testing** The evaluation of an IMC campaign's impact after it has been implemented.

**preapproach** In the personal selling process, occurs prior to meeting the customer for the first time and extends the qualification of leads procedure; in this step, the salesperson conducts additional research and develops plans for meeting with the customer.

**predatory pricing** A firm's practice of setting a very low price for one or more of its products with the intent of driving its competition out of business; illegal under the Competition Act.

**premarket tests** Conducted before a product or service is brought to market to determine how many customers will try and then continue to use it.

**premium** An item offered for free or at a bargain price to reward some type of behaviour, such as buying, sampling, or testing.

**prestige products or services** Those that consumers purchase for status rather than functionality.

**pretesting** Assessments performed before an ad campaign is implemented to ensure that the various elements are working in an integrated fashion and doing what they are intended to do.

**price** The overall sacrifice a consumer is willing to make—money, time, energy—to acquire a specific product or service.

**price bundling** Consumer pricing tactic of selling more than one product for a single, lower price than the items would cost sold separately; can be used to sell slow-moving items, to encourage customers to stock up so they won't purchase competing brands, to encourage trial of a new product, or to provide an incentive to purchase a less desirable product or service to obtain a more desirable one in the same bundle.

**price discrimination** The practice of selling the same product to different resellers (wholesalers, distributors, or retailers) or to the ultimate consumer at different prices; some, but not all, forms of price discrimination are illegal.

**price elasticity of demand** Measures how changes in a price affect the quantity of the product demanded; specifically, the ratio of the percentage change in quantity demanded to the percentage change in price.

**price fixing** The practice of colluding with other firms to control prices.

**price lining** Consumer market pricing tactic of establishing a price floor and a price ceiling for an entire line of similar products and then setting a few other price points in between to represent distinct differences in quality.

**price skimming** A strategy of selling a new product or service at a high price that innovators and early adopters are willing to pay to obtain it; after the high-price market segment becomes saturated and sales begin to slow down, the firm generally lowers the price to capture (or skim) the next most price-sensitive segment.

**price war** Occurs when two or more firms compete primarily by lowering their prices.

**pricing tactics** Short-term methods, in contrast to long-term pricing strategies, used to focus on company objectives, customers, costs, competition, or channel members; can be responses to competitive threats (e.g., lowering price temporarily to meet a competitor's price reduction) or broadly accepted methods of calculating a final price for the customer that is short-term in nature.

**primary data** Data collected to address the specific research needs/questions currently under investigation. Some primary data collection methods include focus groups, in-depth interviews, and surveys.

**private-label brands (store brands)** Brands developed and marketed by a retailer and available only from that retailer.

**procedural fairness** Refers to the customer's perception of the fairness of the process used to resolve complaints about service.

**product** Anything that is of value to a consumer and can be offered through a marketing exchange.

**product category** An assortment of items that the customer sees as reasonable substitutes for one another.

**product development** Entails a process of balancing various engineering, manufacturing, marketing, and economic considerations to develop a product.

**product development strategy** A growth strategy that offers a new product or service to a firm's current target market.

**product excellence** Involves a focus on achieving high-quality products and effective branding and positioning.

**product-focused advertisements** Used to inform, persuade, or remind consumers about a specific product or service.

**product life cycle** Defines the stages that new products move through as they enter, get established in, and ultimately leave the marketplace and thereby offers marketers a starting point for their strategy planning.

**product line** A group of products that consumers may use together or perceive as similar in some way.

**product line depth** The number of products within a product line.

**product lines** Groups of associated items, such as those that consumers use together or think of as part of a group of similar products.

**product mix** The complete set of all products offered by a firm.

**product mix breadth** The number of product lines, or variety, offered by the firm.

**product placement** Inclusion of a product in nontraditional situations, such as in a scene in a movie or TV program.

**profit orientation** A company objective that can be implemented by focusing on target profit pricing, maximizing profits, or target return pricing.

**projective technique** A type of qualitative research in which subjects are provided with a scenario and asked to express their thoughts and feelings about it.

**prototype** The first physical form or service description of a new product, still in rough or tentative form, that has the same properties as a new product but is produced through different manufacturing processes, sometimes even crafted individually.

**psychographics** This segmentation base delves into how consumers describe themselves; allows people to describe themselves by using those characteristics that help them choose how they occupy their time (behaviour) and what underlying psychological reasons determine those choices.

**psychological needs** Pertain to the personal gratification consumers associate with a product or service.

**psychological risk** Associated with the way people will feel if the product or service does not convey the right image.

**PSYTE clusters** The grouping of all neighbourhoods in Canada into 60 different lifestyles clusters.

**public relations (PR)** The organizational function that manages the firm's communications to achieve a variety of objectives, including building and maintaining a positive image, handling or heading off unfavourable stories or events, and maintaining positive relationships with the media.

**public service announcement (PSA)** Advertising that focuses on public welfare and generally is sponsored by non-profit institutions, civic groups, religious organizations, trade associations, or political groups; a form of social marketing.

**puffery** The legal exaggeration of praise, stopping just short of deception, lavished on a product.

**pull marketing strategy** Designed to get consumers to pull the product into the supply chain by demanding that retailers carry it.

**pulsing advertising schedule** Combines the continuous and flighting schedules by maintaining a base level of advertising but increasing advertising intensity during certain periods.

**purchasing power parity (PPP)** A theory that states that if the exchange rates of two countries are in equilibrium, a product purchased in one will cost the same in the other, expressed in the same currency.

**pure competition** Occurs when different companies sell commodity products that consumers perceive as substitutable; price usually is set according to the laws of supply and demand.

**push marketing strategy** Designed to increase demand by focusing on wholesalers, distributors, or salespeople, who push the product to consumers via distribution channels.

**qualify** The process of assessing the potential of sales leads.

**qualitative research** Attempts to begin to understand the phenomenon of interest; also provides initial information when the problem lacks any clear definition.

**quantitative research** Provides the information needed to confirm preliminary insights, which managers can use to pursue appropriate courses of action.

**quantity discount** Pricing tactic of offering a reduced price according to the amount purchased; the more the buyer purchases, the higher the discount and, of course, the greater the value.

**questionnaire** A form that features a set of questions designed to gather information from respondents and thereby accomplish the researchers' objectives; questions can be either unstructured or structured.

**quick-response (QR)** An inventory management system used in retailing; merchandise is received just in time for sale when the customer wants it.

**quota** Designates the maximum quantity of a product that may be brought into a country during a specified time period.

**radio frequency identification (RFID) tags** Tiny computer chips that automatically transmit to a special scanner all the information about a container's contents or individual products.

**rational appeal** Helps consumers make purchase decisions by offering factual information and strong arguments built around relevant issues that encourage consumers to evaluate the brand favourably on the basis of the key benefits it provides.

**reach** Measure of consumers' exposure to marketing communications; the percentage of the target population exposed to a specific marketing communication, such as an advertisement, at least once.

**rebate** A consumer discount in which a portion of the purchase price is returned to the buyer in cash; the manufacturer, not the retailer, issues the refund.

**receiver** The person who reads, hears, or sees and processes the information contained in the message or advertisement.

**recession** A period of economic downturn when the economic growth of the country is negative for at least two consecutive quarters.

**reference group** One or more persons an individual uses as a basis for comparison regarding beliefs, feelings, and behaviours.

**reference price** The price against which buyers compare the actual selling price of the product and that facilitates their evaluation process.

**relational orientation** A method of building a relationship with customers based on the philosophy that buyers and sellers should develop a long-term relationship.

**relationship selling** A sales philosophy and process that emphasizes a commitment to maintaining the relationship over the long term and investing in opportunities that are mutually beneficial to all parties.

**relative market share** A measure of the product's strength in a particular market, defined as the sales of the focal product divided by the sales achieved by the largest firm in the industry.

**reliability** The extent to which the same result is achieved when a study is repeated in identical situations.

**reminder advertising** Communication used to remind consumers of a product or to prompt repurchases, especially for products that have gained market acceptance and are in the maturity stage of their life cycle.

**request for proposals (RFP)** A process through which buying organizations invite alternative suppliers to bid on supplying their required components.

**resellers** Marketing intermediaries that resell manufactured products without significantly altering their form.

**retail mix** Product (merchandise assortment), pricing, promotion, place, personnel, and presentation (store design and display) strategies to reach and serve consumers.

**retailers** Sell products directly to consumers.

**retailing** The set of business activities that add value to products and services sold to consumers for their personal or family use; includes products bought at stores, through catalogues, and over the Internet, as well as services such as fast-food restaurants, airlines, and hotels.

**retrieval sets** Consist of those brands or stores that can be readily brought forth from memory.

**return on investment (ROI)** Used to measure the benefit of an investment, ROI is calculated by dividing the gain of an investment by its cost.

**reverse engineering** Involves taking apart a competitor's product, analyzing it, and creating an improved product that does not infringe on the competitor's patents, if any exist.

**ritual consumption** Refers to a pattern of behaviours tied to life events that affect what and how people consume.

**safety needs** Pertain to protection and physical well-being.

**sales orientation** A company objective based on the belief that increasing sales will help the firm more than will increasing profits.

**sales promotions** Special incentives or excitement-building programs that encourage the purchase of a product or service, such as coupons, rebates, contests, free samples, and point-of-purchase displays.

**sample** A segment or subset of the population that adequately represents the entire population of interest.

**sampling** Offers potential customers the opportunity to try a product or service before they make a buying decision.

**sampling** The process of picking a sample.

**scanner data** A type of quantitative research that uses data obtained from scanner readings of UPC codes at checkout counters.

**search engine marketing (SEM)** Uses tools such as Google AdWords to increase the visibility of websites in search engine results.

**seasonal discount** Pricing tactic of offering an additional reduction as an incentive to retailers to order merchandise in advance of the normal buying season.

**secondary data** Pieces of information that have been collected prior to the start of the focal project.

**selective distribution** Lies between the intensive and exclusive distribution strategies; uses a few selected customers in a territory.

**self-actualization** Occurs when you feel completely satisfied with your life and how you live.

**self-concept** The image a person has of himself or herself; a component of psychographics.

**self-values** Goals for life, not just the goals one wants to accomplish in a day; a component of psychographics that refers to overriding desires that drive how a person lives his or her life.

**sender** The firm from which an IMC message originates; the sender must be clearly identified to the intended audience.

**seniors** North America's fastest-growing generational cohort; people aged 65 and older.

**sentiment analysis** An analysis of online content to determine favourability or unfavourability.

**service** Any intangible offering that cannot be physically possessed.

**service gap** Results when a service fails to meet the expectations that customers have about how it should be delivered.

**service quality** Customers' perceptions of how well a service meets or exceeds their expectations.

**services** Intangible customer benefits that are produced by people or machines and cannot be separated from the producer.

**services retailers** Firms that primarily sell services rather than merchandise.

**share of wallet** The percentage of the customer's purchases made from a particular retailer.

**shopping goods/services** Products or services—such as apparel, fragrances, and appliances—for which consumers will spend time comparing alternatives.

**showrooming** Occurs when consumers visit a physical store to get information about a product but then buy online from another retailer that offers a lower price.

**simple random sampling** Uses a subset of a statistical population with each person having the equal probability to be selected

**situation analysis (SWOT)** The second step in a marketing plan; uses a SWOT analysis that assesses both the internal environment with regard to its **s**trengths and **w**eaknesses and the external environment in terms of its **o**pportunities and **t**hreats.

**situational factors** Factors affecting the consumer decision process; those that are specific to the purchase and shopping situation and temporal state that may override, or at least influence, psychological and social issues.

**size discount** The most common implementation of a quantity discount at the consumer level; the larger the quantity bought, the less the cost per unit (e.g., per gram).

**social marketing** The application of marketing principles to a social issue to bring about attitudinal and behavioural change among the general public or a specific population segment.

**social media** The use of digital tools to easily and quickly create and share content to foster dialogue, social relationships, and personal identities.

**social reach** The number of people a person influences.

**social risk** Involves the fears that consumers suffer when they worry that others might not regard their purchases positively.

**specialty goods/services** Products or services toward which the customer shows a strong preference and for which he or she will expend considerable effort to search for the best suppliers.

**specialty stores** Concentrate on a limited number of complementary merchandise categories in a relatively small store.

**standards gap** Pertains to the difference between the firm's perceptions of customers' expectations and the service standards it sets.

**stock keeping units (SKUs)** Individual items within each product category; the smallest unit available for inventory control.

**STP** The processes of segmentation, targeting, and positioning that firms use to identify and evaluate opportunities for increasing sales and profits.

**straight rebuy** Refers to when the buyer or buying organization simply buys additional units of products that had previously been purchased.

**strategic alliance** A collaborative relationship between independent firms, though the partnering firms do not create an equity partnership; that is, they do not invest in one another.

**strategic business unit (SBU)** A division of the company that can be managed somewhat independently from other divisions since it markets a specific set of products to a clearly defined group of customers.

**strategic relationship (partnering relationship)** A supply chain relationship that the members are committed to maintaining long-term, investing in opportunities that are mutually beneficial; requires mutual trust, open communication, common goals, and credible commitments.

**structured questions** Closed-ended questions for which a discrete set of response alternatives, or specific answers, is provided for respondents to evaluate.

**substitute products** Products for which changes in demand are negatively related—that is, a percentage increase in the quantity demanded for Product A results in a percentage decrease in the quantity demanded for Product B.

**substitution effect** Refers to consumers' ability to substitute other products for the focal brand, thus increasing the price elasticity of demand for the focal brand.

**supply chain** The group of firms and set of techniques and approaches firms use to make and deliver a given set of goods and services.

**supply chain management** Refers to a set of approaches and techniques firms employ to efficiently and effectively integrate their suppliers, manufacturers, warehouses, stores, and transportation intermediaries into a seamless value chain in which merchandise is produced and distributed in the right quantities, to the right locations, and at the right time.

**survey** A systematic means of collecting information from people using a questionnaire.

**sustainable competitive advantage** Something the firm can persistently do better than its competitors that is not easily copied and thus can be maintained over a long period of time.

**sweepstakes** A form of sales promotion that offers prizes based on a chance drawing of entrants' names.

**syndicated data** Data available for a fee from commercial research firms such as Symphony IRI Group, National Diary Panel, Nielsen, and Léger Marketing.

**target market** The customer segment or group to whom the firm is interested in selling its products and services.

**target marketing/targeting** The process of evaluating the attractiveness of various segments and then deciding which to pursue as a market.

**target profit pricing** A pricing strategy implemented by firms when they have a particular profit goal as their overriding concern; uses price to stimulate a certain level of sales at a certain profit per unit.

**target return pricing** A pricing strategy implemented by firms less concerned with the absolute level of profits and more interested in the rate at which their profits are generated relative to their investments; designed to produce a specific return on investment, usually expressed as a percentage of sales.

**tariff (or duty)** A tax levied on a good imported into a country.

**technological advances** Technological changes that have contributed to the improvement of the value of both products and services in the past few decades.

**telemarketing** A method of prospecting in which salespeople telephone potential customers.

**test marketing** Introduces a new product or service to a limited geographical area (usually a few cities) prior to a national launch.

**top-of-mind awareness** A prominent place in people's memories that triggers a response without them having to put any thought into it.

**total cost** The sum of the variable and fixed costs.

**tracking** Includes monitoring key indicators, such as daily or weekly sales volume, while the advertisement is running to shed light on any problems with the message or the medium.

**trade agreement** Intergovernmental agreement designed to manage and promote trade activities for specific regions.

**trade deficit** Results when a country imports more goods than it exports.

**trade sanctions** Penalties or restrictions imposed by one country over another country for importing and exporting of goods, services, and investments.

**trade shows** Major events attended by buyers who choose to be exposed to products and services offered by potential suppliers in an industry.

**trade surplus** Results when a country exports more goods than it imports.

**trading bloc** Consists of those countries that have signed a particular trade agreement.

**transmitter** An agent or intermediary with which the sender works to develop the marketing communications; for example, a firm's creative department or an advertising agency.

**tweens** Generational cohort of people who are not quite teenagers but are not young children either (ages 9 to 12); they're in beTWEEN.

**undifferentiated targeting strategy (mass marketing)** A marketing strategy a firm can use if the product or service is perceived to provide the same benefits to everyone, with no need to develop separate strategies for different groups.

**uniform delivered pricing** The shipper charges one rate, no matter where the buyer is located.

**unique selling proposition (USP)** A strategy of differentiating a product by communicating its unique attributes; often becomes the common theme or slogan in the entire advertising campaign.

**universal product code (UPC)** The black and white bar code found on most merchandise.

**universal sets** Consist of all possible choices for a product category.

**unstructured questions** Open-ended questions that allow respondents to answer in their own words.

**usage rate** How often a person uses the product or service: occasional, light, regular, or heavy users.

**user** The person who consumes or uses the product or service purchased by the buying centre.

**validity** The extent to which a study measures what it is supposed to measure.

**VALS** A psychological tool developed by Strategic Business Insights that classifies consumers into eight segments: Innovators, Thinkers, Believers, Achievers, Strivers, Experiencers, Makers, or Survivors.

**value** Reflects the relationship of benefits to costs, or what the consumer gets for what he or she gives.

**value-based pricing method** Focuses on the overall value of the product offering as perceived by consumers, who determine value by comparing the benefits they expect the product to deliver with the sacrifice they will need to make to acquire the product.

**value proposition** Communicates the customer benefits to be received from a product or service and the reason(s) for wanting to buy it.

**variable costs** Those costs, primarily labour and materials, that vary with production volume.

**vendor-managed inventory (VMI)** An approach in which the manufacturer is responsible for replenishing inventory to meet retailers' needs.

**vertical marketing system** A supply chain in which the members act as a unified system; there are three types: administrated, contractual, and corporate.

**vertical price fixing** Occurs when parties at different levels of the same marketing channel (e.g., manufacturers and retailers) collude to control the prices passed on to consumers.

**voice-of-customer (VOC) program** An ongoing marketing research system that collects customer insights and intelligence to influence and drive business decisions.

**want** The particular way in which a person chooses to satisfy a need, which is shaped by a person's knowledge, culture, and personality.

**wholesalers** Those firms engaged in buying, taking title to, often storing, and physically handling goods in large quantities, and then reselling the goods (usually in smaller quantities) to retailers or industrial or business users.

**zone of tolerance** The area between customers' expectations regarding their desired service and the minimum level of acceptable service—that is, the difference between what the customer really wants and what he or she will accept before going elsewhere.

# endnotes

## CHAPTER 1

1. "Shopper Innovation Awards: Tim Hortons®' New Level of Chill," *Strategy* Online, April 20, 2016, http://strategyonline .ca/2016/04/19/shopper-innovation-awards-tim-hortons-new -level-of-chill/ (accessed April 20, 2016).

2. Reputation Institute Canada, "Most Reputable Companies in Canada—2014," https://www.reputationinstitute.com /Resources/Registered/PDF-Resources/The-2014-Canada -RepTrak%C2%AE-Results-and-Report.aspx; Tim Hortons® Corporate, "Fresh Facts," http://www.timhortons.com/ca/en /corporate/fresh-facts.php#!open_flyout (accessed April 20, 2016).

3. Sylvain Charlebois, "Tim Hortons® Must Not Forget the Coffee Market It Shaped," *The Globe and Mail*, September 7, 2016, http://www.theglobeandmail.com/report-on-business/rob -commentary/tim-hortons-must-not-forget-the-coffee-market -it-shaped/article31726583/ (accessed September 8, 2016).

4. 2015 Tim Hortons® Annual Report on Form 10-K, https://www.sec .gov/Archives/edgar/data/1345111/000119312511047696/d10k.htm (accessed April 20, 2016).

5. Tim Hortons®, www.timhortons.com (accessed July 4, 2017).

6. Canada Newswire, "Tim Hortons® Announces Electric Vehicle Charging Station Pilot in Canada," http://www.newswire.ca/en /story/1113505/tim-hortons-announces-electric-vehicle-charging -station-pilot-in-canada (accessed May 17, 2013).

7. Alicia Androich, "TimsTV Coming Soon to More Restaurants," *Marketing Magazine*, January 9, 2014, http://www.marketingmag.ca /news/marketer-news/timstv-soon-coming-to-more-restaurants -97952 (accessed April 3, 2014).

8. Marina Strauss, "The $12,000 Espresso Machine: Tim Hortons® Brews Up New Plan in Coffee Wars," *The Globe and Mail*, December 12, 2016, http://www.theglobeandmail.com/report-on -business/tim-hortons-to-roll-out-new-premium-espresso -options/article33302351/ (accessed January 9, 2017).

9. The Canadian Marketing Association, https://www.the-cma.org /regulatory/code-of-ethics (accessed May 31, 2016). More discussion on marketing is provided by Stephen L. Vargo and Robert F. Lusch, "Evolving to a New Dominant Logic for Marketing," *Journal of Marketing* 68 (January 2004), pp. 1–17; and George S. Day, John Deighton, Das Narayandas, Evert Gummesson, Shelby D. Hunt, C.K. Prahalad, Roland T. Rust, and Steven M. Shugan, "Invited Commentaries on 'Evolving to a New Dominant Logic for Marketing,'" *Journal of Marketing* 68 (January 2004), pp. 18–27. Also see W. Stephen Brown et al., "Marketing Renaissance: Opportunities and Imperatives for Improving Marketing Thought, Practice, and Infrastructure," *Journal of Marketing*, 69, no. 4 (2005), pp. 1–25.

10. Mike Esterl, "Coke Tailors Its Soda Sizes," *The Wall Street Journal*, September 19, 2011, http://online.wsj.com/article /SB10001424053111903374004576578980270401662.html; Natalie Zmuda, "Diet Coke Blasts Past Pepsi," *Advertising Age*, March 17, 2011, http://adage.com/article/news/diet-coke-blasts-past-pepsi /149453; Natalie Zmuda, "Can Pepsi's Big Marketing Shake-Up Bring Back Fizz to Its Beverage Brands?" *Advertising Age*, June 20, 2011, http://adage.com/article/news/pepsi-s-marketing-reorg -bring-back-fizz-beverages/228292 (accessed June 16, 2014).

11. http://www.lexus.com/models/LSh/index.html (accessed June 16, 2014).

12. The idea of the four Ps was conceptualized by E. Jerome McCarthy, *Basic Marketing: A Managerial Approach* (Homewood, IL: Richard D. Irwin, 1960). Also see Walter van Waterschoot and Christophe Van den Bulte, "The 4P Classification of the Marketing Mix Revisited," *Journal of Marketing* 56 (October 1992), pp. 83–93.

13. Harpreet Singh, "Mondelēz Brings Back the Love," *Strategy Magazine*, April 20, 2016, http://strategyonline.ca/2016/04/20 /mondelez-brings-back-the-love; Andrew Adam Newman, "Snacks for Soccer Stars, and Their Fans," *The New York Times*, October 8, 2013; Warc, "Mondelēz in Twitter Tie-Up," Warc.com, September 13, 2013, http://www.warc.com; Angela Watercutter, "How Oreo Won the Marketing Super Bowl With a Timely Blackout Ad on Twitter," *Wired*, February 4, 2013, http://www .wired.com.

14. Tim Hortons®, "Sustainability and Responsibility 2014 Performance Highlights," 2014-performance-report Tim Hortons® sustainability.pdf; Jacquelyn Stevens and Marc McAree, "Greenwashing Environmental Claims Give Rise to Legal Liability," http://www.willmsshier.com/docs/default-source /articles/greenwashing-environmental-claims-sept-oct-2014.pdf; "How Companies Manage Sustainability: McKinsey Global Survey Results," http://www.mckinseyquarterly.com/How_companies _manage_sustainability_McKinsey_Global_Survey_results_2558; Rebecca Harris, "Greenwashing: Cleaning Up By Saving the World," http://www.marketingmag.ca/news/marketer-news /greenwashing-cleaning-up-by-saving-the-world-77259 (accessed April 19, 2016).

15. Websites such as http://www.whymilk.com and http://www .milkdelivers.org/campaign/index.cfm provide examples of this popular campaign.

16. George S. Day, "Aligning the Organization With the Market," *Marketing Science Institute* 5, no. 3 (2005), pp. 3–20.

17. Dhruv Grewal, Kent B. Monroe, and R. Krishnan, "The Effects of Price Comparison Advertising on Buyers' Perceptions of Acquisition Value and Transaction Value," *Journal of Marketing* 62 (April 1998), pp. 46–60; Kent B. Monroe, *Pricing: Making Profitable Decisions*, 3rd ed. (New York: McGraw-Hill, 2004).

18. Anne L. Roggeveen, Michael Tsiros, and Dhruv Grewal, "Understanding the Co-Creation Effect: When Does Collaborating With Customers Provide a Lift to Service Recovery?" *Journal of the Academy of Marketing Science* 40, no. 6 (2012), pp. 771–90; Sigurd Troye and Magne Supphellen, "Consumer Participation in Coproduction: 'I Made It Myself' Effects on Consumers' Sensory Perceptions and Evaluations of Outcome and Input Product," *Journal of Marketing* 76 (March 2012), pp. 33–46.

19. Anita Luo and V. Kumar, "Recovering Hidden Buyer–Seller Relationship States to Measure the Return on Marketing Investment in Business-to-Business Markets," *Journal of Marketing Research* 50, no. 1 (2013), pp. 143–60; V. Kumar and Denish Shah, "Can Marketing Lift Stock Prices?" *Sloan Management Review* 52, no. 4 (2011), pp. 24–26; V. Kumar et al., "Is Market Orientation a Source of Sustainable Competitive Advantage or Simply the Cost of Competing?" *Journal of Marketing* 75 (January 2011), pp. 16–30; Stephen A. Samaha, Robert W. Palmatier, and Rajiv P. Dant, "Poisoning Relationships: Perceived Unfairness in Channels of Distribution," *Journal of Marketing* 75 (May 2011), pp. 99–117.

20. Rajendra K. Srivastava, Tasadduq A. Shervani, and Liam Fahey, "Marketing, Business Processes, and Shareholder Value: An Embedded View of Marketing Activities and the Discipline of Marketing," *Journal of Marketing* 63 (special issue, 1999), pp. 168–179; R. Venkatesan and V. Kumar, "A Customer Lifetime Value Framework for Customer Selections and Resource Allocation Strategy," *Journal of Marketing* 68, no. 4 (October 2004), pp. 106–125; V. Kumar, G. Ramani, and T. Bohling, "Customer Lifetime Value Approaches and Best Practice Applications," *Journal of Interactive Marketing* 18, no. 3 (Summer 2004), pp. 60–72; and J. Thomas, W. Reinartz, and V. Kumar, "Getting the Most Out of All Your Customers," *Harvard Business Review* (July–August 2004), pp. 116–123.

21. http://thenextweb.com (accessed April 19, 2016).

22. Statista, "Statistics and Facts About Mobile Social Media," https://www.statista.com/topics/2478/mobile-social-networks/ (accessed February 9, 2017).

23. "World Internet Penetration Rates," Internet World Stats, http://www.internetworldstats.com (accessed April 19, 2016).

24. U.S. Travel Association, "Travel Facts and Statistics," http://www.ustravel.org.

25. Elizabeth Olson, "Restaurants Reach Out to Customers With Social Media," *The New York Times*, January 19, 2011.

26. Matthew Panzarino, "The Open Secret of iBeacon: Apple Could Have 250M Potential Units in the Wild by 2014," *TechCrunch*, December 7, 2013, http://techcrunch.com; Zach Miners, "Apple Tracks Shoppers in Its Stores With Nationwide iBeacon Rollout," *InfoWorld*, December 9, 2013, http://www.infoworld.com.

27. Hennes & Mauritz AB, http://www.hm.com (accessed May 22, 2011).

28. Zara, http://www.zara.com (accessed May 22, 2011).

29. Example based on Loblaw Company Limited Supply Chain Management, http://www-acad.sheridanc.on.ca/syst35412/patenime/intro.htm (accessed March 29, 2007).

30. WWF, "Companies We Work With," http://www.wwf.ca/about_us/howwework/business/companies_we_work_with/ (accessed April 19, 2016).

31. "Understanding the Power Behind Today's Leading Brands—2011 Harris Poll EquiTrend," http://www.harrisinteractive.com; Calvert, "Corporate Responsibility and Investor Confidence Survey," November 18, 2003: http://www.harrisinteractive.com. Also see the Trustees of Boston College, "The State of Corporate Citizenship in the United States: 2003," July 2003; Luisa Kroll and Allison Fass, "The World's Billionaires," http://www.forbes.com (accessed March 29, 2007).

32. http://dictionary.reference.com/search?q=Entrepreneurship (accessed May 16, 2005).

33. "Monumental Moments," http://www.timhortons.com/ca/en/about/index.html# (accessed May 22, 2013).

34. "Ron Joyce," http://www.timhortons.com/ca/en/about/bio_ronjoyce.html (accessed May 22, 2013).

35. Clare O'Connor, "Billionaire Founder Chip Wilson Out at Yoga Giant Lululemon," http://www.forbes.com/sites/clareoconnor/2012/01/09/billionaire-ceo-chip-wilson-out-at-yoga-giant-lululemon (accessed May 22, 2013).

36. "Financial Information," http://investor.lululemon.com/financials-keyratios.cfm (accessed January 9, 2017).

37. "Store Finder," http://www.lululemon.com/stores/#show-location-list (accessed May 22, 2013).

38. GreenStrike, "Who We Are," http://green-strike.com/home/who-we-are (accessed April 22, 2016); Terry Pender, "Entrepreneur Believes Mosquito Trap Will Slow Spread of Disease," *The Waterloo Region Record*, March 5, 2016, page D12.

39. Starbucks Investor Relations, "Financial Release, "March 23, 2016, http://investor.starbucks.com/phoenix.zhtml?c=99518&p=irol-newsArticle&ID=2150528 (accessed April 22, 2016).

40. Alexandra Wolfe, "Howard Schultz: What Next, Starbucks?" http://www.wsj.com/articles/SB10001424052702304213904579093583249134984 (accessed April 19, 2016).

41. Starbucks Investor Relations, "Investor Overview," http://investor.starbucks.com/phoenix.zhtml?c=99518&p=irol-irhome (accessed April 22, 2016).

42. "Starbucks Company Profile," http://www.starbucks.com/about-us/company-information/starbucks-company-profile (accessed April 22, 2016).

43. Julie Jargon, "Starbucks Tries Franchising to Perk Up Europe Business," *The Wall Street Journal*, November 29, 2013.

44. Susan Berfield, "Starbucks Starts Throwing a Very Big Tea Party," http://www.bloomberg.com/news/articles/2013-10-25/starbucks-starts-throwing-a-very-big-tea-party (accessed April 19, 2016).

45. Linda Nguyyen, "Starbucks Canada's Alcohol Sales Begin With Toronto Locations," *The Canadian Press*, April 1, 2016, http://www.huffingtonpost.ca/2016/04/01/starbucks-canada-alcohol_n_9594630.html (accessed April 22, 2016).

46. Stephanie Strom, "Starbucks Aims to Move Beyond Beans," http://www.nytimes.com/2013/10/09/business/a-juice-and-croissant-with-that-starbucks-latte.html?_r=0 (accessed April 19, 2016).

## CHAPTER 2

1. Austin Carr, "Nike: The Number 1 Most Innovative Company of 2013," *Fast Company*, February 11, 2013.

2. Don Blair, "Case Study: Nike CFO Don Blair Reveals Strategy for Profit Growth," *CFOGlobalHQ*, October 30, 2013, http://www.cfoglobalhq.com.

3. Nike, "Nike, Inc. Unveils ColorDry Technology and High-Tech Facility to Eliminate Water and Chemicals in Dyeing," December 2, 2013, http://nikeinc.com.

4. "Select Financials," *Nike FY2015 Annual Report*, http://s1.q4cdn.com/806093406/files/doc_financials/2015/ar/#select_financials (accessed April 26, 2016).

5. Trefis Team, "Why Nike Will Outpace the Sports Apparel Market's Growth," *Forbes.com*, May 13, 2013, http://www.forbes.com; *Nike News*, "Nike, Inc. Reports Fiscal 2016 Fourth Quarter and Full Year Results," June 28, 2016, http://news.nike.com/news/nike-inc-reports-fiscal-2016-fourth-quarter-and-full-year-results (accessed January 13, 2017).

6. Carr, "Nike: The Number 1 Most Innovative Company of 2013."

7. Michael Treacy and Fred Wiersema, *The Disciplines of Market Leaders* (Reading, MA: Addison Wesley, 1995).

8. V. Kumar et al., "Establishing Profitable Customer Loyalty for Multinational Companies in the Emerging Economies: A Conceptual Framework," *Journal of International Marketing 21* (March 2013), pp. 57–80; Yuping Liu-Thompkins and Leona Tam, "Not All Repeat Customers Are the Same: Designing Effective Cross-Selling Promotion on the Basis of Attitudinal Loyalty and Habit," *Journal of Marketing 77* (September 2013), pp. 21–36.

9. Melea Press and Eric J. Arnould, "How Does Organizational Identification Form? A Consumer Behavior Perspective," *Journal of Consumer Research 38* (December 2011), pp. 650–66.

10. Rosemarky McCracken, "Rewards Have Their Own Virtues," *National Post*, April 26, 2007: IS1.

11. Valarie A. Zeithaml, Mary Jo Bitner, and Dwayne D. Gremler, *Services Marketing: Integrating Customer Focus Across the Firm*, 5th ed. (Burr Ridge, IL: McGraw-Irwin, 2009).

12. Brooks Barnes, "At Disney Parks, a Bracelet Meant to Build Loyalty (and Sales)," *The New York Times*, January 7, 2013.

13. Carmine Gallo, "Customer Service the Disney Way," *Forbes*, April 14, 2011.

14. James R. Stock, Stefanie L. Boyer, and Tracy Harmon, "Research Opportunities in Supply Chain Management," *Journal of the Academy of Marketing Science*, 2010, 38, no. 1, pp. 32–41. Also see articles in a special issue edited by John T. Mentzer and Greg Gundlach, "Exploring the Relationship Between Marketing and Supply Chain Management: Introduction to the Special Issue," *Journal of the Academy of Marketing Science*, 2010, 38, no. 1, pp. 1–4.

15. "Best Canadian Brands 2014," *Interbrand*, http://interbrand.com/wp-content/uploads/2015/08/Interbrand-Best-Canadian-Brands-2014.pdf (accessed February 9, 2017).

16. WestJet Airlines, http://www.westjet.com (accessed April 23, 2011); http://www.newswire.ca/en/releases/archive/April2007/23/c8051.html (accessed June 16, 2014).

17. "Marketing Plan," *American Marketing Association Dictionary*, https://www.ama.org/resources/Pages/Dictionary.aspx (accessed February 9, 2017).

18. Donald Lehman and Russell Winer, *Analysis for Marketing Planning*, 7th ed. (Burr Ridge, IL: McGraw-Hill/Irwin, 2008).

19. Andrew Campbell, "Mission Statements," *Long Range Planning* 30 (1997), pp. 931–933.

20. Alfred Rappaport, *Creating Shareholder Value: The New Standard for Business Performance* (New York: Wiley, 1988); Robert C. Higgins and Roger A. Kerin, "Managing the Growth–Financial Policy Nexus in Marketing," *Journal of Marketing* 59, no. 3 (1983), pp. 19–47; and Roger Kerin, Vijay Mahajan, and P. Rajan Varadarajan, *Contemporary Perspectives on Strategic Market Planning* (Boston: Allyn & Bacon, 1991), Chapter 6.

21. Tim Hortons®, "About Us," http://www.timhortons.com/ca/en/about/faq.html (accessed April 23, 2011).

22. Matt Townsend, "As Nike Scoffs, Toning Shoes Gain Traction," *Bloomberg Business Week*, June 7–13, 2010, pp. 22–24.

23. Eric Siemers, "Nike Takes New Marketing Tack," *Portland Business Journal*, September 12, 2010, http://www.bizjournals.com/portland/stories/2010/09/13/story9.html (accessed June 16, 2014).

24. Nike 10-K report, July 20, 2010.

25. Russel Parsons, "Nike Beating Official Sponsor Adidas in World Cup Stakes," *Marketing Week*, June 24, 2010, p. 7.

26. Eric Siemans, "New Balance TV Spots Target Nike," *Portland Business Journal*, March 7, 2011, http://www.bizjournals.com/portland/blog/2011/03/new-balance-tv-spots-target-nike.html?page52 (accessed June 16, 2014).

27. Nike 10-K report, July 23, 2015, http://s1.q4cdn.com/806093406/files/doc_financials/2015/ar/docs/nike-2015-form-10K.pdf (accessed April 25, 2016).

28. http://www.hertz.com/rentacar/vehicleguide/index.jsp?targetPage5vehicleGuideHomeView.jsp&countryCode5UScategory5Car/Sedan.

29. http://www.leevalley.com (accessed April 30, 2007); "Conversations on Working and Well-Being: Working by the Golden Rule: Lee Valley Tools," http://www.vifamily.ca/library/social/lee_valley.html (accessed April 30, 2007); "Lee Valley Tools Case Study," http://www.nerac.com/research-victories/lee-valley-tools-case-study (accessed April 30, 2007); "A Visit to Lee Valley Tools: A Company Built on Innovation and Customer Service," http://www.woodcentral.com/shots/shot643.shtml (accessed June 16, 2014).

30. Annie Gasparro, "In the Low-Carb Age, Does Cereal Have a Future?" *The Wall Street Journal*, September 19, 2013.

31. Kirsten Acuna, "Google Says It Can Predict Which Films Will Be Huge Box Office Hits," *Business Insider*, June 6, 2013.

32. James Surowiecki, "After Rana Plaza," *The New Yorker*, May 20, 2013.

33. "Sustainability's Strategic Worth: McKinsey Global Survey Results," http://www.mckinsey.com/Insights/Sustainability/Sustainabilitys_strategic_worth_McKinsey_Global_Survey_results?cid=other-eml-alt-mip-mck-oth-1407 (accessed April 26, 2016).

34. http://www.loblaw.ca/en/abt_corprof.html (accessed April 30, 2007). ® President's Choice, PC Financial, PC are registered trademarks of Loblaws Inc., used with permission.

35. This discussion is adapted from Roger A. Kerin, Steven W. Hartley, and William Rudelius, *Marketing*, 10th ed. (Burr Ridge, IL: McGraw-Hill/Irwin, 2011).

36. Farris et al., *Marketing Metrics: 50+ Metrics Every Executive Should Master* (Upper Saddle River, NJ: Prentice Hall, 2006), p. 17.

37. Relative market share = Brand's market share ÷ Largest competitor's market share. If, on the one hand, there are only two products in a market, A and B, and product B has 90 percent market share, then A's relative market share is 10 ÷ 90 = 11.1 percent. If, on the other hand, B has only 50 percent market share, then A's relative market share is 10 ÷ 50 = 20 percent. Farris et al., *Marketing Metrics*, p. 19.

38. *Fortune*, "How Many iPhones Did Apple Sell Last Quarter?" http://fortune.com/2015/10/21/apple-iphone-q4-sales/ (accessed April 26, 2016).

39. Shane Dingman, "iPhone Sales Show First-Ever Decline", *The Globe and Mail*, April 26, 2016, http://www.theglobeandmail.com/report-on-business/rob-commentary/executive-insight/apple-iphone-sales-show-first-ever-decline-amid-challenging-quarter/article29766216/ (accessed April 26, 2016).

40. Kif Leswing, "Apple Shares Sink on First Annual Drop in Revenue Since 2001," *Business Insider*, October 25, 2016, http://www.businessinsider.com/apple-q4-2016-earnings-2016-10 (accessed January 13, 2017).

41. *Silconbeat*, "Apple Drops iPods From Earnings Report,"http://www.siliconbeat.com/2015/01/28/apple-drops-ipods-from-earnings-report/ (accessed April 26, 2016).

42. "Apple Reports Record Results," Apple, January 23, 2013, http://www.apple.com/pr/library/2013/01/23Apple-Reports-Record-Results.html (accessed June 16, 2014).

43. "Global Apple iPad Sales From Third Fiscal Quarter of 2010 to First Fiscal Quarter of 2016 (in Million Units)," (accessed April 26, 2016).

44. "Media Tablet Shipments Outpace Fourth Quarter Targets; Strong Demand for New iPad and Other Forthcoming Products Leads to Increase in 2012 Forecast, According to IDC," IDC, March 13, 2012, http://www.idc.com/getdoc.jsp?containerId=prUS23371312 (accessed May 24, 2013).

45. "Low Cost Products Drive Forecast Increases in Tablet Market, According to IDC," IDC, March 12, 2013, http://www.idc.com/getdoc.jsp?containerId=prUS24002213 (accessed May 24, 2013).

46. Joe Wilcox, "iPad Market Share Plunged 20 Percent in Q4 2010," BetaNews, February 2011, http://betanews.com; Mohit Agrawal, "Tablets OS Market Share," *Telecom Circle*, October 7, 2011, http://www.telecomcircle.com; Apple, "Apple Reports Fourth Quarter Results," October 28, 2011, http://www.apple.com.

47. Kerin, Mahajan, and Varadarajan, *Contemporary Perspectives on Strategic Market Planning*; see also Susan Mudambi, "A Topology of Strategic Choice in Marketing," *International Journal of Market & Distribution Management* (1994), pp. 22–25.

48. http://www.gamestop.com/xbox-360/movies-tv/yoostar-on-mtv/91616.

49. http://www.mtv.com/shows/teen_mom/season_3/series.jhtml.

50. http://www.viacom.com/ourbrands/globalreach/Pages/default.aspx.

51. http://www.stayteen.org; http://www.mtv.com/mobile.

52. http://www.mtv.com/shows/made/series.jhtml; Tim Arango, "Make Room, Cynics; MTV Wants to Do Some Good," *The New York Times*, April 18, 2009; Robert Seidman, "MTV Continues to Diversify Slate With New Scripted Comedies *The Hard Times of RJ Berger* and *Warren the Ape*," tvbythenumbers.com, January 15, 2010.

53. http://solutions.3m.com/wps/portal/3M/en_US/about-3M/information/about/businesses/.

54. Lawrence Delevigne, "What Private Equity Loves About the Booming Frozen Yogurt Trend," CNBC.com, October 13, 2013, http://www.cnbc.com/id/101103927.

55. Yogurty's, "About Us," http://www.yogurtys.com/about-us/ (accessed April 26, 2016).

56. Pinkberry, "Menu," http://www.pinkberry.com/our-story/ (accessed April 26, 2016).

57. Menchie's, "Vision," http://www.menchies.ca/frozen-yogurt-store-vision (accessed April 26, 2016).

58. TCBY, "Menu & Nutrition," http://tcbycanada.com/ (accessed April 26, 2016).

59. Canadian Dairy Information Centre, "Dairy Facts and Figures,"http://www.dairyinfo.gc.ca/index_e.php?s1=dff-fcil&s2=proc-trans&s3=kp-pc (accessed April 26, 2016).

60. Susan Krashinsky, "Frozen Yogurt's Next Heatwave Comes North," http://www.theglobeandmail.com/report-on-business/industry-news/marketing/frozen-yogurts-next-heat-wave-comes-north/article4572859 (accessed April 26, 2016).

## CHAPTER 3

1. Sidhartha Banerjee, "Montreal to Forge Ahead With Ban on Plastic Shopping Bags in 2018", www.theglobeandmail.com/news /national/montreal-to-forge-ahead-with-ban-on-plastic-shopping -bags-in-2018/article28834461/ (accessed April 28, 2016).

2. Peter F. Drucker, *The Essential Drucker* (New York: HarperCollins, 2001).

3. Maureen Morrison, "Pearle Vision Set to Unveil Brand Reboot," *Advertising Age*, April 22, 2013.

4. Linda Doell, "In Razor vs. Razor, Neither Gillette Nor Schick Gains Edge With Ad Watchdog," March 17, 2011, http://www .dailyfinance.com/2011/03/17/in-razor-vs-razor-neither-gillette -nor-schick-gains-edge-with.

5. Matt Fish, "Silicon Belly: The Value of Competitive Intelligence," November 10, 2003, http://lexis-nexis.com (accessed September 6, 2006).

6. Steve Mossop, "Companies Not Spending Enough on Business Intelligence Activities," http://www.ipsos-na.com/news /pressrelease.cfm?id=2874 (accessed June 30, 2014).

7. Sam Costello, "How Many iPhones Have Been Sold Worldwide?" *Lifewire*, March 9, 2017, https://www.lifewire.com/how-many -iphones-have-been-sold-1999500 (accessed June 26, 2017).

8. Seth Fiegerman, "Apple Vs. Samsung: Everything You Need to Know About the (Patent) Trial of the Century." *Business Insider*, n.p., July 30, 2012, http://www.businessinsider.com/apple-vs -samsung-everything-you-need-to-know-about-the-patent -trial-of-the-century-2012-7?op=1 (accessed June 30, 2014).

9. Ibid.

10. Nick Wingfield, "Jury Awards $1 Billion to Apple in Samsung Patent Case," *The New York Times*, n.p., August 24, 2012, http://www .nytimes.com/2012/08/25/technology/jury-reaches-decision-in -apple-samsung-patent-trial.html?_r=0 (accessed June 30, 2014).

11. Ian Sherr, "Apple Faces Product Ban After Samsung Victory," *The Globe and Mail*, June 5, 2013, p. B8.

12. http://www.nau.com (accessed April 29, 2010); Polly Labarre, "Leap of Faith," *Fast Company*, June 2007.

13. Michael Solomon, *Consumer Behavior: Buying, Having and Being* (Upper Saddle River, NJ: Prentice Hall, 2006).

14. Rob Gerlsbeck, "Research: A Distinct Shopping Society," http:// www.marketingmag.ca/magazine/current/quebec_rpt/article. jsp?content=20070625_69884_69884 (accessed June 25, 2007).

15. John Feto, "Name Games," *American Demographics*, February 15, 2003.

16. "Orthodox," *American Demographics*, May 2004, p. 35.

17. Bonnie Fuller, "Baby-Boomer Marketers Are Misreading Millennials' Media Behavior," *Advertising Age*, May 13, 2013; Chingching Chang, "Dual System Model Comparisons of Print Advertisements and e-Store Product Pages: The Influence of Dominant Pictures on Decision Making," working paper (under review at *Journal of Advertising*); CBCNews, "Millennials Have More Spending Power Than Parents But Also More Debt," May 16, 2014, http://www.cbc.ca/news/world/millennials-have-more -spending-power-than-parents-did-but-also-more-debt-1.2644833 (accessed May 3, 2014).

18. "Census Profile, 2016," Statistics Canada, August 25, 2017, http:// www12.statcan.gc.ca/census-recensement/2016/dp-pd/prof /details/page.cfm?Lang=E&Geo1=PR&Code1=01&Geo2=PR&Cod e2=01&Data=Count&SearchText=01&SearchType=Begins&Search- PR=01&B1=All&Custom=&TABID=3 (accessed Sept. 13, 2017).

19. Pamela Paul, "Getting Inside Gen Y," *American Demographics* 23, no. 9.

20. Noah Rubin Brier, "Move Over Prime-Time!" *American Demographics* (July/August 2004), pp. 14–20; John Hoeffel, "The Next Baby Boom," *American Demographics* (October 1995), pp. 22–31.

21. "Census Profile, 2016," Statistics Canada, August 25, 2017, http://www12.statcan.gc.ca/census-recensement/2016/dp-pd /prof/details/page.cfm?Lang=E&Geo1=PR&Code1=01&Geo2 =PR&Code2=01&Data=Count&SearchText=01&SearchType =Begins&SearchPR=01&B1=All&Custom=&TABID=3 (accessed Sept. 13, 2017).

22. Lesley Young, "Portrait of the New Family," http://www .marketingmag.ca/magazine/current/feature/article.jsp?con- tent=20040315_61585_61585 (accessed May 11, 2007).

23. Transparency Market Research, "Global Anti-Aging Market Boosted by Boomer Population Nearing Retirement; Market to Be Worth US$191.7 Billion in 2019," August 31, 2015, http://www .transparencymarketresearch.com/pressrelease/anti-aging -market.htm (accessed May 3, 2016).

24. Lauren R. Hartman, "Foods for Aging Baby Boomers," *Food Processing*, January 25, 2016, http://www.foodprocessing.com /articles/2016/foods-for-aging-baby-boomers/ (accessed May 3, 2016).

25. "Household income in Canada: Key results from the 2016 Census," Statistics Canada, September 13, 2017, http://www .statcan.gc.ca/daily-quotidien/170913/dq170913a-eng.htm ( accessed September 13, 2017).

26. http://www.statscan.ca

27. Dave Hodges and Mark Brown, "Are You in the Middle Class?" *Money Sense*, January 27, 2015, http://www.macleans.ca /economy/money-economy/are-you-in-the-middle-class/ (accessed May 3, 2016).

28. "The Daily—Survey of Household Spending, 2015," Statistics Canada, January 27, 2017, http://www.statcan.gc.ca/daily -quotidien/170127/dq170127a-eng.htm; "Shares of total expendi- ture of major spending categories y income quinitile, Canada, 2015," Statistics Canada, January 27, 2017, http://www.statcan .gc.ca/daily-quotidien/170127/t002a-eng.htm (accessed Sept. 13, 2017).

29. http://www.hammacher.com (accessed May 3, 2010).

30. "Education and Occupation of High-Income Canadians," *Statistics Canada*, December 23, 2015, https://www12.statcan .gc.ca/nhs-enm/2011/as-sa/99-014-x/99-014-x2011003_2-eng .cfm (accessed May 3, 2016).

31. "Table 7 Average Income by Highest Level of Education Attained, School/Work Status and Gender," *Statistics Canada*, January 30, 2013, http://www.statcan.gc.ca/pub/81-595-m/2009075/tbl /tbl7-eng.htm (accessed June 30, 2014).

32. "Median Earnings of Recent Immigrants and Canadian Born Earners, Both Sexes, Aged 25 to 54 With or Without University Degree, 2005, For Canada, Provinces and Territories—20% Sample Data," Statistics Canada, October 6, 2010, http://www12 .statcan.ca/census-recensement/200<?_anchored_object_"ro _u4c3cins8e4e"?><?_anchored_object_ "ro_u4c3cins8e4f"?>6 /dp-pd/hlt/97-563/T802-eng.cfm?Lang=E&T=802&GH=4&SC=13& SO=99&O=A (accessed June 30, 2014).

33. Bethany Clough, "Home-Improvement Store Empowers Female Customers With Do-It-Herself Tools," *Knight Ridder Tribune Business Service* March 20, 2005: 1; Fara Warner, "Yes, Women Spend (and Saw and Sand)," *The New York Times*, February 29, 2004: C1.

34. http://www.statscan.ca (accessed April 23, 2011).

35. Tavia Grant, "Women Still Earning Less Than Men Despite Gains in Education," *The Globe and Mail*, March 7, 2016, http://www .theglobeandmail.com/news/national/women-still-earning -less-money-than-men-despite-gains-in-education-study /article29044130/(accessed May 3, 2016).

36. http://www.theglobeandmail.com/servlet/story/RTGAM .20071205.wcensusmain1005/BNStory/census2006/home (accessed December 18, 2007).

37. "Ethnic Diversity and Immigration," *Statistics Canada*, November 27, 2015, http://www.statcan.gc.ca/pub/11-402-x/2011000/chap /imm/imm-eng.htm (accessed May 3, 2016).

38. "Tapping Into the Hot Chinese and South Asian Marketplace," *Ipsos Ideas*, http://www.ipsos-ideas.com/article.cfm?id=3391 (accessed June 30, 2014).

39. "Aboriginal Peoples in Canada: First Nations People, Métis and Inuit," Statistics Canada, May 7, 2013, http://www12.statcan.gc.ca/nhs-enm/2011/as-sa/99-011-x/99-011-x2011001-eng.cfm (accessed June 30, 2014); "Projections of the Aboriginal Population and Households in Canada, 2011 to 2036," Statistics Canada, September 17, 2015, http://www.statcan.gc.ca/daily-quotidien/150917/dq150917b-eng.htm (accessed January 16, 2017).

40. Chris Daniels, "Multicultural Marketing: The Visible Minority," *Marketing Magazine*, March 12, 2012, http://www.marketingmag.ca/brands/multicultural-marketing-the-visible-majority-48428 (accessed May 3, 2016).

41. Harris, "Skin Deep."

42. Raizel Robin, "How Grocers Are Aiming to Connect With Ethnic Consumers," *Canadian Grocer*, February 10, 2016, http://www.marketingmag.ca/consumer/how-grocers-are-aiming-to-connect-with-ethnic-consumers-167698 (accessed May 4, 2016).

43. "About Us," http://freshco.com/about-us/ (accessed May 4, 2016).

44. "How Sobey's Is Taking on Loblaws," http://www.theglobeandmail.com/report-on-business/rob-magazine/top-1000/how-sobeys-is-taking-on-loblaws/article1603663 (accessed June 30, 2014); Andy Holloway, "Getting Fresh," *Canadian Grocer* (June/July 2010), p. 23; "Sobeys Inc. Launches FreshCo. Discount Stores" (press release), http://www.sobeyscorporate.com/App_Themes/SobeysCorporate/media/en/Sobeys-Inc-Launches-FreshCo-Discount-Stores.pdf (accessed June 30, 2014).

45. James Cowan, "How FreshCo Is Connecting With South Asian Shoppers," *Canadian Business*, November 23, 2015, http://www.marketingmag.ca/consumer/how-freshco-is-connecting-with-south-asian-shoppers-162175 (accessed May 4, 2016).

46. Marianne Wilson, "Growing Power of Mobile," *Chain Store Age*, December 2010; Deena M. Amato-McCoy, "Focus on: The Mobile Channel," *Chain Store Age*, March 2011.

47. http://www.cbc.com (accessed April 24, 2011).

48. http://www.yourdictionary.com (accessed September 5, 2006).

49. http://www.bankofcanada.ca/en (accessed May 15, 2007).

50. "Key Interest Rate," *Bank of Canada* http://www.bankofcanada.ca/core-functions/monetary-policy/key-interest-rate (accessed May 4, 2016).

51. Drew Hasselback, "The 'Don Cherry' of Economic Statistics: Debt to Income Makes a Lot of Noise But Does It Really Matter?" *Financial Post*, March 31, 2017, http://business.financialpost.com/news/economy/the-don-cherry-of-economic-statistics-debt-to-income-makes-a-lot-of-noise-but-does-it-really-matter (accessed June 6, 2017); David Parkinson, "Canadian Household Debt Soars to Yet Another Record," *The Globe and Mail*, March 11, 2016, http://www.theglobeandmail.com/report-on-business/economy/canadians-debt-burden-still-growing-hits-record-in-fourth-quarter/article29172712/ (accessed May 4, 2016).

52. Lauren Krugel, "Nexen Pipeline Spill Investigation Taking Longer Than Expected," *Huffpost Alberta*, January 25, 2016, http://www.huffingtonpost.ca/2016/01/25/nexen-oil-spill-investigation-taking-longer-than-expected-documents-show_n_9066952.html (accessed May 4, 2016).

53. This section draws heavily from Jacquelyn A. Ottman, *Green Marketing: Opportunity for Innovation* (Chicago, IL: NTC Publishing, 1997), also available online at http://www.greenmarketing.com.

54. "Haagen-Dazs and General Mills to Help Smallholder Vanilla Farmers Increase Yields and Improve Sustainability Practices in Madagascar," press release, February 20, 2013, http://3blmedia.com/News/CSR/H%C3%A4agen-Dazs-and-General-Mills-Help-Smallholder-Vanilla-Farmers-Increase-Yields-and-Improve (accessed May 4, 2016); Elizabeth Crawford, "General Mills Nears Goal of 100% Sustainably Sourced Palm Oil," http://www.foodnavigator-usa.com/Manufacturers/General-Mills-nears-goal-of-100-sustainably-sourced-palm-oil (accessed May 4, 2016); Rhett A. Buter, "Amazon Deforestation Jumps in Brazil, but Remains Historically Low," *Mongaby*, November 27, 2015, https://news.mongabay.com/2015/11/amazon-deforestation-jumps-in-brazil/ (accessed May 4, 2016).

55. "How Is the Environment on This Day?" *The Globe and Mail*, June 5, 2013, p. A9.

56. *Dragons' Den*, "Episode 14," aired January 28, 2013. http://www.cbc.ca/dragonsden/2013/01/episode-14-3.html (accessed May 26, 2013); personal interview with Lisa von Sturmer in Vancouver, May 13, 2016.

57. "Our Story," http://www.growingcity.com/our-story (accessed May 24, 2016).

58. Sean Stanleigh, "Best Business Award Winners Compete for $20,000," *The Globe and Mail*, October 18, 2012, http://www.theglobeandmail.com/report-on-business/small-business/sb-tools/small-business-briefing/best-business-award-winners-compete-for-20000/article4621103 (accessed June 30, 2014).

59. Sheila Shayon, "Adidas x Parley Recycled Shoes Use Plastic Trash From the Ocean," *Brand Channel*, July 3, 2015, http://www.brandchannel.com/2015/07/03/adidas-recycled-shoes-070315 (accessed May 4, 2016); Adidas Group, "Adidas and Parley for the Oceans Stop the Industry's Waiting Game," December 8, 2015, http://www.adidas-group.com/en/media/news-archive/press-releases/2015/adidas-and-parley-oceans-stop-industrys-waiting-game/ (accessed May 4, 2016); 2015 *Sustainability Report*, http://www.adidas-group.com/media/filer_public/9c/f3/9cf3db44-b703-4cd0-98c5-28413f272aac/2015_sustainability_progress_report.pdf (accessed May 4, 2016); Alexandra Jardine, "Adidas Unveils Its First Sportswear Items Made From Recycled Plastic," *Creativity Online*, Nov. 4, 2016, http://creativity-online.com/work/adidas-parley-unveil/49816?utm_visit=41154 (accessed Jan. 17, 2017).

60. "Cleanshowing," *Marketing Magazine*, April 22, 2013, p. 40.

61. Paola Loriggio, "Ashley Madison Hack Not the Wake-up Call Some Expected, Experts Say," *The Globe and Mail*, December 16, 2015, http://www.theglobeandmail.com/technology/tech-news/ashley-madison-hack-not-the-wake-up-call-some-expected-experts-say/article27779319/(accessed May 4, 2016).

62. Phoenix Strategic Perspectives, "Final Report: 2014 Survey of Canadians on Privacy," December 2014, https://www.priv.gc.ca/information/por-rop/2015/por_2014_12_e.pdf (accessed May 4, 2016).

63. Martin Peers, "Buddy, Can You Spare Some Time?" *The Wall Street Journal*, January 26, 2004: B1, B3.

64. Ibid.

65. Statistics Canada, "Body Mass Index," http://www.statcan.gc.ca/tables-tableaux/sum-som/l01/cst01/health81b-eng.htm (accessed June 30, 2014).

66. Ibid.

67. "Yoga Statistics," http://www.statisticbrain.com/yoga-statistics (accessed June 30, 2014).

68. Serena Ng, "Seventh Generation Picks Up Bobble Brand," *The Wall Street Journal*, May 30, 2013, http://www.wsj.com/articles/SB10001424127887324682204578515512439788042 (accessed April 29, 2016).

69. "71% of Consumers Think Green When Purchasing," *Environmental Leader*, April 3, 2013; "Seventh Gen, Whole Foods Top Green Brands Ranking," *Environmental Leader*, June 10, 2011, http://www.environmentalleader.com.

70. "The Best Cleaning Products," *Real Simple*, http://www.realsimple.com.

71. Andrew Adam Newman, "Seventh Generation Highlights Its Chemical-Free Detergent," *The New York Times*, December 29, 2010, http://www.nytimes.com/2010/12/30/business/media

/30adco.html; "Seventh Generation Promotes Eco-Friendly Detergents Through Multichannel Marketing Initiative," December 30, 2010, http://www.ricg.com.

72. Press Releases, "Seventh Generation Introduces Energy Smart Laundry and Dishwasher Detergents", August 24, 2015, http://seventhgeneration.mwnewsroom.com/press-releases/seventh-generation-introduces-energy-smart-laundry-and-dishwasher-detergents-1213701 (accessed April 29, 2016).

73. Press Releases, "Bobble Introduces Presse by Bobble for Gourmet, Single Serve Coffee Without the Waste of Plastic Pods," April 10, 2015, http://seventhgeneration.mwnewsroom.com/press-releases/bobbler-introduces-presse-by-bobble-for-gourmet-single-serve-coffee-without-t-1187246 (accessed April 29, 2016).

74. "Seventh Generation Acquires bobble for Undisclosed Sum," press release, May 31, 2013, http://seventhgeneration.mwnewsroom.com/press-releases/seventh-generation-acquires-bobble-for-undisclosed-1022443.

75. Press Releases, "Seventh Generation Ranks Best Company on the Planet in 'The Better World Shopping Guide'," September 17, 2015, http://seventhgeneration.mwnewsroom.com/press-releases/seventh-generation-ranks-best-company-on-the-planet-in-the-better-world-shopping-1217829 (accessed April 29, 2016).

## CHAPTER 4

1. Naomi Tajitsu, "Toyota Lowers Global Sales Targets for New Model Prius Amid Low Petrol Prices," *Reuters*, December 9, 2015, http://uk.reuters.com/article/uk-autos-toyota-prius-idUKKB-N0TS0VK20151209 (accessed May 10, 2016).

2. Elon Musk, "The Mission of Tesla," https://www.teslamotors.com/en_CA/blog/mission-tesla (accessed May 10, 2016).

3. Michael McCarthy, "Tesla Generates Small Sales, Big Buzz Without Paid Ads," *Advertising Age*, June 10, 2013, http://adage.com/article/news/tesla-generates-small-sales-big-buzz-paid-ads/241994/ (accessed May 10, 2016).

4. Rebecca Harris, "Canadians Thinking Green for Next Car Purchase (Survey)," *Marketing Magazine*, April 26, 2016, http://www.marketingmag.ca/consumer/canadians-thinking-green-for-next-car-purchase-survey-173084 (accessed May 10, 2016).

5. For a detailed discussion of customer behaviour, see Michael R. Solomon, *Consumer Behavior: Buying, Having, and Being*, 11th ed. (Upper Saddle River, NJ: Pearson Prentice Hall, 2014).

6. Liz C. Wang et al., "Can a Retail Web Site Be Social?" *Journal of Marketing* 71, no. 3 (2007), pp. 143–57; Barry Babin, William Darden, and Mitch Griffin, "Work and/or Fun: Measuring Hedonic and Utilitarian Shopping Value," *Journal of Consumer Research* 20 (March 1994), pp. 644–56.

7. "Lana Marks Cleopatra Bag," *Lord Glamour*, February 8, 2014, http://www.lordglamour.com/; Lopa Mohanty, "10 Most Expensive Handbag Brands in the World," *Fashion Lady*, May 31, 2013, http://www.fashionlady.in/; "Celebrities," *Lana Marks*, http://www.lanamarks.com/.

8. Alistair Barr, "Was Expedia Targeted by 'Negative SEO' Campaign?" *USA Today*, January 22, 2014, http://www.usatoday.com; Joshua Steimle, "Expedia, Negative SEO, and Google Penalties," *Forbes*, January 31, 2014, http://www.forbes.com; Denis Pinsky, "Understanding Negative SEO and Your Saboteur Within," *Forbes*, February 11, 2014, http://www.forbes.com; "Expedia Shares Fall With Online Search Visibility," *Seattle Times*, January 21, 2014, http://www.seattletimes.com.

9. The term *determinance* was first coined by James Myers and Mark Alpert nearly three decades ago.

10. http://www.sawtoothsoftware.com.

11. Caroline Goukens, Siegfried Dewitte, and Luk Warlop, "Me, Myself, and My Choices: The Influence of Private Self-Awareness on Choice," *Journal of Marketing Research* 46, no. 5 (October 2009), pp. 682–92.

12. Paul S. Richardson, Alan S. Dick, and Arun K. Jain, "Extrinsic and Intrinsic Cue Effects on Perceptions of Store Brand Quality," *Journal of Marketing* 58 (October 1994), pp. 28–36; Rajneesh Suri and Kent B. Monroe, "The Effects of Time Constraints on Consumers' Judgments of Prices and Products," *Journal of Consumer Research* 30 (June 2003), pp. 92–104.

13. Merrie Brucks, Valerie A. Zeithaml, and Gillian Naylor, "Price and Brand Name as Indicators of Quality Dimensions for Consumer Durables," *Journal of the Academy of Marketing Science* 28, no. 3 (2000), pp. 359–374; Niraj Dawar and Philip Parker, "Marketing Universals: Consumers' Use of Brand Name, Price, Physical Appearance, and Retailer Reputation as Signals of Product Quality," *Journal of Marketing* 58 (April 1994), pp. 81–95; William B. Dodds, Kent B. Monroe, and Dhruv Grewal, "Effects of Price, Brand, and Store Information on Buyers' Product Evaluations," *Journal of Marketing Research* 28 (August 1991), pp. 307–319.

14. Mary Jo Bitner, "Servicescapes: The Impact of Physical Surroundings on Customers and Employees," *Journal of Marketing* 56 (April 1992), pp. 57–71; Dhruv Grewal and Julie Baker, "Do Retail Store Environmental Factors Affect Consumers' Price Acceptability? An Empirical Examination," *International Journal of Research in Marketing* 11 (1994), pp. 107–115; Eric R. Spangenberg, Ayn E. Crowley, and Pamela W. Henderson, "Improving the Store Environment: Do Olfactory Cues Affect Evaluations and Behaviors?" *Journal of Marketing* 60 (April 1996), pp. 67–80; Kirk L. Wakefield and Jeffrey G. Blodgett, "Customer Response to Intangible and Tangible Service Factors," *Psychology and Marketing* 16 (January 1999), pp. 51–68.

15. Ruby Roy Dholakia and Miao Zhao, "Retail Web Site Interactivity: How Does It Influence Customer Satisfaction and Behavioral Intentions?" *International Journal of Retail & Distribution Management*, 37, 2009, pp. 821–838.

16. Claire Cain Miller, "Closing the Deal at the Virtual Checkout Counter," *The New York Times*, October 12, 2009 (accessed December 13, 2009).

17. Ruby Roy Dholakia and Miao Zhao, "Retail Web Site Interactivity: How Does It Influence Customer Satisfaction and Behavioral Intentions?" *International Journal of Retail & Distribution Management* 37 (2009), pp. 821–838.

18. A.H. Maslow, *Motivation and Personality* (New York: Harper & Row, 1970).

19. "About Us," Cole + Parker, http://coleandparker.co/about (accessed April 10, 2014).

20. "About Us," Kiva, http://www.kiva.org/about (accessed April 10, 2014).

21. Telephone interview with Diana House, April 11, 2014.

22. Sue McGill, "Taking the Long View of Consumer Habits," *Strategy Magazine*, November 16, 2015, http://strategyonline.ca/2015/11/16/taking-the-long-view-of-consumer-habits/#ixzz3rgqauT6U; Inspiring Green Action, http://www.r3volved.com/ (accessed May 23, 2016); "About," Onyx+Green, http://www.onyxandgreen.com/; "Onyx+Green—A Canadian Company Making School and Office Supplies More Sustainable," http://greendeal.ca/onyxgreen-a-canadian-company-making-school-and-office-supplies-more-sustainable(accessed February 27, 2017).

23. Michael Levy and Barton A. Weitz, *Retailing Management*, 6th ed. (Burr Ridge IL: Irwin/McGraw-Hill, 2007), Chapter 4.

24. "2005 YTV Tween Report, Solutions Research Group, A Corus Entertainment Inc. Company," http://www.corusmedia.com/ytv/research/index.asp (accessed June 14, 2013).

25. Sandra Yin, "Kids; Hot Spots," *American Demographics* (December 1, 2003); Peter Francese, "Trend Ticker: Trouble in Store," *American Demographics* (December 1, 2003).

26. Rod Duclos, Echo Wen Wan, and Yuwei Jiang, "Show Me the Honey! Effects of Social Exclusion on Financial Risk-Taking," *Journal of Consumer Research, 40* (June 2013), pp. 122–35.

27. Carol Bryant, "The Truth About Paid Product Reviews and Disclosure," *Blog Paws*, September 5, 2013, http://www.blogpaws.com; see sites that recruit bloggers to do paid reviews: http://www.sponsoredreviews.com, http://www.payperpost.com, http://www.reviewme.com.

28. Rebecca Harris, "Skin Deep, Canada's Big Banks Have Taken Great Strides to Reach Newcomers to the Country. But, They Need to Look Beneath the Surface to Truly Connect to Multicultural Consumers," *Marketing Magazine* January 29, 2007.

29. Jonathan Paul, "Brita's First Ethnic Program Turns Red to Green," *Strategy Magazine*, March 13, 2012. http://strategyonline.ca/2012/03/13/britas-first-ethnic-program-turned-red-into-green (accessed June 12, 2013).

30. The concept of atmospherics was introduced by Philip Kotler, "Atmosphere as a Marketing Tool," *Journal of Retailing 49* (Winter 1973), pp. 48–64.

31. Anna S. Mattila and Jochen Wirtz, "Congruency of Scent and Music as a Driver of In-Store Evaluations and Behavior," *Journal of Retailing 77*, no. 2 (Summer 2001), pp. 273–289; Teresa A. Summers and Paulette R. Hebert, "Shedding Some Light on Store Atmospherics; Influence of Illumination on Consumer Behavior," *Journal of Business Research 54*, no. 2 (November 2001), pp. 145–150; for a review of this research, see Joseph A. Bellizzi and Robert E. Hite, "Environmental Color, Consumer Feelings, and Purchase Likelihood," *Psychology and Marketing 9*, no. 5 (September–October 1992), pp. 347–363; J. Duncan Herrington and Louis Capella, "Effects of Music in Service Environments: A Field Study," *Journal of Services Marketing 10*, no. 2 (1996), pp. 26–41; Richard F. Yalch and Eric R. Spangenberg, "The Effects of Music in a Retail Setting on Real and Perceived Shopping Times," *Journal of Business Research 49*, no. 2 (August 2000), pp. 139–148; Michael Hui, Laurette Dube, and Jean-Charles Chebat, "The Impact of Music on Consumers' Reactions to Waiting for Services," *Journal of Retailing 73*, no. 1 (1997), pp. 87–104; and Julie Baker, Dhruv Grewal, and Michael Levy, "An Experimental Approach to Making Retail Store Environmental Decisions," *Journal of Retailing 68* (Winter 1992), pp. 445–460; Maxine Wilkie, "Scent of a Market," *American Demographics* (August 1995), pp. 40–49; Spangenberg, Crowley, Henderson, "Improving the Store Environment"; Paula Fitzgerald Bone and Pam Scholder Ellen, "Scents in the Marketplace: Explaining a Fraction of Olfaction," *Journal of Retailing 75*, no. 2 (Summer 1999), pp. 243–263.

32. Tracy Turner, "New Hangout Supermarket," *Columbus Dispatch*, March 20, 2011 (accessed May 23, 2016).

33. Carmine Gallo, "Apple's Secret Employee Training Manual Reinvents Customer Service in Seven Ways," *Forbes*, August 30, 2012.

34. Julie Baker et al., "Wait Expectations, Store Atmosphere and Store Patronage Intentions," *Journal of Retailing 79*, no. 4 (2003), pp. 259–268.

35. Lauren Johnson, "Sephora Magnifies Mobile Ambitions via In-Store Signage, Updated App," *Mobile Commerce Daily*, August 23, 2013.

36. Jagdish Sheth, Banwari Mittal, and Bruce I. Newman, *Customer Behavior: Consumer Behavior and Beyond* (Fort Worth, TX: The Dryden Press, 1999); J. Paul Peter and Jerry C. Olson, *Consumer Behavior and Marketing Strategy* (McGraw-Hill/Irwin, 2007); Michael R. Solomon, *Consumer Behavior: Buying, Having, and Being* (Toronto: Prentice Hall, 2009).

37. Yuping Liu-Thompkins and Leona Tam, "Not All Repeat Customers Are the Same: Designing Effective Cross-Selling Promotion on the Basis of Attitudinal Loyalty and Habit," *Journal of Marketing 77* (September 2013), pp. 21–36; Karen M. Stilley, J. Jeffrey Inman, and Kirk L. Wakefield, "Planning to Make Unplanned Purchases? The Role of In-Store Slack in Budget Deviation," *Journal of Consumer Research 37*, no. 2 (2010), pp. 264–78; doi: 10.1086/651567.

38. Harmeet Singh, "Yours, Mine and Ours," *Strategy Magazine*, June 2016 issue, http://strategyonline.ca/2016/05/30/yours-mine-and-ours (accessed May 30, 2016).

39. Barrie McKenna, "Young, Educated Most Keen on Sharing Economy: Statscan," *The Globe and Mail*, March 1, 2017, P. B2.

40. Goldman Sachs, "Millennials Coming of Age," http://www.goldmansachs.com/our-thinking/pages/millennials/ (accessed May 26, 2016).

41. Terry O'Reilly, "The Sharing Economy," http://www.cbc.ca/radio/undertheinfluence/the-sharing-economy-1.2983680 (accessed May 26, 2016).

42. Josh Kolm, "Has the Sharing Economy Impacted Spending Habits?" *Strategy Magazine*, January 29, 2016, http://strategyonline.ca/2016/01/29/has-the-sharing-economy-impacted-spending-habits (accessed May 26, 2016).

43. Terry O'Reilly, "The Sharing Economy," http://www.cbc.ca/radio/undertheinfluence/the-sharing-economy-1.2983680 (accessed May 26, 2016).

44. Bradley Voytek, "Is There Any Reason to Take Uber Versus NYC Cabs?" *Forbes*, February 28, 2012, http://www.forbes.com/sites/quora/2012/02/28/is-there-any-reason-to-take-uber-versus-nyc-cabs/#2c3ad22d5183 (accessed May 26, 2016).

45. "What That Car Really Costs to Own," *Consumer Reports*, August 2012, http://www.consumerreports.org/cro/2012/12/what-that-car-really-costs-to-own/index.htm (accessed May 26, 2016).

46. Car2Go, "Mobility for a Reasonable Price," https://www.car2go.com/en/toronto/what-does-car2go-cost/#tid=cost (accessed May 26, 2016).

47. Josh Kolm, "Has the Sharing Economy Impacted Spending Habits?" *Strategy Magazine*, January 29, 2016, http://strategyonline.ca/2016/01/29/has-the-sharing-economy-impacted-spending-habits (accessed May 26, 2016).

## CHAPTER 5

1. Shopify, "About," https://www.shopify.ca/about (accessed February 14, 2017).

2. Shopify, "2015 Annual Report," https://investors.shopify.com/financial-reports/default.aspx (accessed May 28, 2016).

3. Shopify, "Investor FQs," https://investors.shopify.com/Resources/Investor-FAQs/default.aspx (accessed May 27, 2016).

4. Shopify Plus, "How Manitobah Mukluks Uses Shopify Plus for Brand Storytelling," https://www.shopify.com/enterprise/78237702-case-study-how-manitobah-mukluks-uses-shopify-plus-for-brand-storytelling (accessed May 28, 2016).

5. http://www.profitguide.com/microsite/profit500/2016/

6. Jeff Fraser, "Tech Player of the Year 2015: Shopify," *Marketing Magazine*, February 4, 2016, http://www.marketingmag.ca/tech/tech-player-of-the-year-2015-shopify-167247 (accessed May 28, 2016).

7. Nate Shivar, "Shopify Review: Pros & Cons of Using Shopify for eCommerce," May 10, 2016, https://www.shivarweb.com/2748/shopify-review-pros-cons-of-using-shopify-for-ecommerce/ (accessed May 28, 2016).

8. Shopify, "2015 Annual Report," https://investors.shopify.com/financial-reports/default.aspx (accessed May 28, 2016).

9. Ibid.

10. James Cowan, "Shopify COO Harvey Finkelstein on the Future of Digital Retail," *Canadian Business*, March 10, 2016, http://www.canadianbusiness.com/leadership/shopify-coo-harley-finkelstein/ (accessed May 28, 2016).

11. Jeff Fraser, "Tech Player of the Year 2015: Shopify," *Marketing Magazine*, February 4, 2016, http://www.marketingmag.ca/tech/tech-player-of-the-year-2015-shopify-167247 (accessed May 28, 2016).

12. James Cowan, "Shopify COO Harvey Finkelstein on the Future of Digital Retail," *Canadian Business*, March 10, 2016, http://www.canadianbusiness.com/leadership/shopify-coo-harley-finkelstein/ (accessed May 28, 2016).

13. Shopify, "Shopify Announces Shopify Capital," April 27, 2016, https://investors.shopify.com/Investor-News-Details/2016/Shopify-Announces-Shopify-Capital/default.aspx (accessed May 27, 2016).

14. SEC Filing, Form 20-F, "Shopify Inc. 2016 Annual Information Form," February 14, 2017, http://d18rn0p25nwr6d.cloudfront.net/CIK-0001594805/c6f2bbf3-8d32-46dc-a60e-cd8ef1146e5d.pdf; Shopify, "About," https://www.shopify.ca/about (accessed February 16, 2017).

15. Shane Dingman, "Shopify Slumps on First Quarter Sales," *The Globe and Mail*, May 4, 2016, http://www.theglobeandmail.com/technology/tech-news/shopify-results-top-expectations/article29851017/ (accessed May 28, 2016).

16. "About Magna," Magna, http://www.magna.com/about-magna (accessed February 9, 2017).

17. Martin Hofmann, Emily-Sue Sloane, and Elena Malykhina, "VW Revs Its B2B Engine," *Optimize*, March 2004, pp. 22–26, http://www.volkswagenag.com/vwag/vwcorp/content/en/brands_and_companies/automotive_and_financial.html.

18. http://www.vwgroupsupply.com/b2bpub/zusammenarbeit/kbp/daten_fakten.html (accessed June 17, 2013).

19. This Sustainable Marketing box was written with information gathered in a telephone interview with Joanne Secord of PaperNuts on June 18, 2013, and Tyler Pearson, CEO of PaperNuts, on May 31, 2016.

20. Packaging Association of Canada, "International Sustainable Packaging Executive to Lead PAC NEXT," September 23, 2012, http://www.sustainability-in-packaging.com/international-sustainable-packaging-executive-to-lead-pac-next.aspx (accessed July 1 2014).

21. Retail Council of Canada, "Canadian Retailer 2015 Media Package," http://www.retailcouncil.org/sites/default/files/documents/RET_2015_Media_Kit.pdf pdf (accessed May 28, 2016).

22. Statistics Canada, "Wholesale Trade," http://www.statcan.gc.ca/pub/63-008-x/63-008-x2015012-eng; http://www.statcan.gc.ca/daily-quotidien/170123/cg-a001-eng.htm (accessed January 24, 2017).

23. Imagine Canada, "Sector Impact," http://sectorsource.ca/research-and-impact/sector-impact (accessed May 28, 2016).

24. http://www.pwgsc.gc.ca (accessed April 24, 2011).

25. https://buyandsell.gc.ca and https://www.merx.com (accessed June 3, 2011).

26. "Canadian Public Tenders," MERX, http://www.merx.com (accessed February 9, 2017).

27. Murat Yukselir, "Tech From Above, Top Drone Markets by 2020," *The Globe and Mail*, May 19, 2016, p. B4; Joanna Pachner, "How Aeryon Labs Intends to Keep Its Industrial Drone Business Aloft," *Canadian Business*, December 3, 2015, http://www.canadianbusiness.com/innovation/aeryon-labs-industrial-drones/; Keenan Kusan, "Sudbury's Rise of the Drones," *The Sudbury Star*, April 12, 2016, http://www.thesudburystar.com/2016/04/12/sudburys-rise-of-the-drones; Aeryon Labs blog, "Ventus Geospatial Inc. Approved to Provide UAS Assistance in Fort McMurray Fire Response," May 10, 2016, https://www.aeryon.com/blog/ventus-geospatial-fort-mcmurray-fire; Aeryon Labs, "Local Drones Helping Survey Damage to Fort McMurray," May 12, 2016, https://www.aeryon.com/in-the-news/skyranger-fort-mcmurray; Government of Canada, "Company Profile – Canadian Company Capabilities, Aeryon Labs, Inc.," http://www.ic.gc.ca/app/ccc/srch/nvgt.do?prtl=1&estblmntNo=234567121891&profile=cmpltPrfl&profileId=501&app=sold&lang=eng (accessed January 24, 2017).

28. "Odyssey Identified as Buyers of 10 Bombardier CSeries Jets," *CBC News*, June 17, 2013, http://www.cbc.ca/news/business/story/2013/06/17/business-bombardier-cseries.html (accessed July 1, 2014).

29. "Bombardier Bank," http://www.canadianbusiness.com/article.jsp?content=20040329_59236_59236 (accessed April 24, 2011).

30. http://www.shepherd.ca (accessed May 21, 2007); http://www.shepherd.ca; "RoyNat Capital Entrepreneurial Profile," *Financial Post* May 7, 2007: FP12.

31. www.census.gov/epcd/naics02/SICNO2E.HTM#S48; http://www.census.gov/epcd/www/naics.html; http://www.census.gov/epcd/naics02/N2SIC51.HTM.

32. Michael Posner, "ROM Asks Caterers for Preferred-List Fee," *The Globe & Mail*, October 22, 2012, http://www.theglobeandmail.com/news/toronto/torontos-rom-to-ask-caterers-for-preferred-list-fee-of-10000/article4627477 (accessed July 1, 2014).

33. http://www.marketingpower.com/live/mg-dictionary-view435.php. These definitions are provided by http://www.marketing-power.com (the American Marketing Association's website). We have bolded our key terms.

34. Sean Silverthorne, "Business Ethics: Pay the Bribe?" CBS Money Watch, http://www.cbsnews.com; Stephen H. Unger, "Ethical Aspects of Bribing People in Other Countries," http://www1.cs.columbia.edu; Transparency International, "Bribe Payers Index 2011," http://bpi.transparency.org/; "International Back Scratching," *The Economist*, November 2, 2011, http://www.economist.com; Julia Kollewe, "GlaxoSmithKline's Boss's 2013 Bonus Doubled, Despite Scandal in China," *The Guardian*, February 27, 2014, http://www.thegudardian.com; Ernst and Young, "European Fraud Survey 2011: Recovery, Regulation and Integrity," http://www.ey.com.

35. E. J. Schultz, "GE Tells the Secret of Making Geeky Cool," *Advertising Age*, October 5, 2013, http://adage.com/article/special-report-ana-annual-meeting-2013/ge-making-geeky-cool/244603/ (accessed May 29, 2017).

36. Amber Bowerman, *The Economics of Donation*, http://www.avenuecalgary.com/articles/page/item/the-economics-of-donations (accessed April 25, 2011); Value Village, http://www.valuevillage.com/downloads/SaversValueVillagePressKits.pdf (accessed April 25, 2011).

37. Kimberly Maul, "More B-to-B Companies Find That Social Media Is an Essential Business Platform," PRweekus.com, June 2009; Ellis Booker, "B-to-B Marketers Apply Analytics to Social Media," *BtoB*, April 12, 2010; Elisabeth A. Sullivan, "A Long Slog," *Marketing News*, February 28, 2009.

38. http://www.tweetdeck.com (accessed July 20, 2010).

39. Daniel B. Honigman, "Make a Statement," *Marketing News* May 1, 2008.

40. http://www.hubspot.com; "Should Your Startup Be Hubspotting?" *TechCocktail*, May 6, 2013, http://www.tech.co; "2013 State of Inbound Marketing," HubSpot, May 2013, http://www.stateofinboundmarketing.com, "Shopify Uses HubSpot CRM to Transform High Volume Sales Organization," http://www.hubspot.com/customers/shopify (accessed May 24, 2016).

41. Fabiana Ferreira et al., "The Transition From Products to Solutions: External Business Model Fit and Dynamics," *Industrial Marketing Management* 42, no. 7 (2013), pp. 1093–1101; Mark W. Johnston and Greg W. Marshall, *Contemporary Selling: Building Relationships, Creating Value* (Routledge, 2013); Barton A. Weitz, Stephen B. Castleberry, and John F. Tanner, *Selling Building Partnerships*, 6th ed. (Burr Ridge, IL: McGraw-Hill/Irwin, 2005), p. 93.

42. Maggie Hira, "How Does a Fashion Buyer Spend a Workday?" http://www.ehow.com; U.S. Department of Labor, http://www.bls.gov.

43. Leslie Kaufman, "Stone Washed Blue Jeans (Minus the Wash)," *The New York Times*, November 1, 2011, http://www.nytimes.com.

44. "Raw Materials," http://www.levistrauss.com/sustainability/production/#intro (accessed May 24, 2016).

45. "Apparel Workers," http://www.levistrauss.com/sustainability/people/#apparel-workers (accessed May 24, 2016).

46. Thomas Schueneman, "The Better Cotton Initiative: Making Sustainable Cotton Mainstream," http://www.triplepundit.com/special/sustainable-fashion-2014/better-cotton-initiative-making-sustainable-cotton-mainstream/# March 5, 2014; "Water," http://www.levistrauss.com/sustainability/planet/ (accessed May 24, 2016).

47. "Water," http://www.levistrauss.com/sustainability/planet/ (accessed May 24, 2016).

48. Marc Gunther, "Levi Strauss Seeks to Slow Down Fast Fashion With Sustainable Practices," *The Guardian*, November 6, 2013, http://www.theguardian.com.

49. "Lifecycle Assessment," http://www.levistrauss.com/sustainability/planet/ (accessed May 24, 2016).

50. Ashley Lutz, "Levi's CEO Explains Why Jeans Should Never Go in the Washing Machine," *Business Insider*, http://www.businessinsider.com/levis-ceo-dont-wash-your-jeans-2014-7, July 15, 2014 (accessed May 24, 2016).

51. "LS&Co. Expands Clothing Recycling Initiative to All U.S. Stores," http://levistrauss.com/unzipped-blog/2015/07/clothing-recycling-us-expansion/ (accessed May 24, 2016).

## CHAPTER 6

1. Information in this opening vignette comes from personal Interviews with Neetu Godara, co-founder of SoCIAL LITE Vodka, in May and June of 2016.

2. "Thinking Outside the Cardboard Box," http://metronews.ca/news/165605/thinking-outside-the-cardboard-box; "Meet Doug Burgoyne, FrogBox Inc.," *Small Business BC*, http://smallbusinessbc.ca/success-story/meet-doug-burgoyne-frogbox-inc/ (accessed June 1, 2016).

3. "Meet Doug Burgoyne, Frogbox Inc.," *Small Business BC*, http://smallbusinessbc.ca/success-story/meet-doug-burgoyne-frogbox-inc/ (accessed June 1, 2016) .

4. Frogbox Blog, "1,000,000 Million Frogboxes Delivered," August 4, 2015, http://www.frogbox.com/blog/2015/08/1000000-frogboxes-delivered-and-were-feeling-golden/ (accessed June 1, 2016).

5. Chris Matyszczyk, "For Teens, Facebook Is 'Dead and Buried,'" CNET, December 27, 2013, http://news.cnet.com.

6. Michael R. Solomon, *Consumer Behavior: Buying, Having, and Being*, 10th ed. (Upper Saddle River, NJ: Prentice Hall, 2012).

7. Rosellina Ferraro, Amna Kirmani, and Ted Matherly, "Look at Me! Look at Me! Conspicuous Brand Usage, Self–Brand Connection, and Dilution," *Journal of Marketing Research* 50, no. 4 (2013), pp. 477–88; Keith Wilcox and Andrew T. Stephen, "Are Close Friends the Enemy? Online Social Networks, Self-Esteem, and Self-Control," *Journal of Consumer Research* 40, no. 1 (2013), pp. 90–103.

8. Eric Wilson, "Less Ab, More Flab," *The New York Times*, May 22, 2013.

9. Michael R. Solomon, *Consumer Behavior: Buying, Having, and Being*, 10th ed. (Upper Saddle River, NJ: Prentice Hall, 2012).

10. James M. Hagerty, "Harley, With Macho Intact, Tries to Court More Women," *The Wall Street Journal*, October 31, 2011, http://online.wsj.com/article/SB100014240529702045053045766552442175568/6.html#articleTabs%3Darticle (accessed July 1, 2014); Harley-Davidson, "Global Customer Focus," http://investor.harley-davidson.com/phoenix.zhtml?c=87981&p=irol-demographics.

11. VALS1, the original lifestyle survey, assessed general values and lifestyles. The VALS survey focuses more on values and lifestyles related to consumer behaviour and thus has more commercial applications. Another lifestyle segmentation system is Yankelovich's Monitor Mindbase (yankelovich.com).

12. "Segmentation and Targeting," http://www.kellogg.northwestern.edu; Carson J. Sandy, Samuel D. Gosling, and John Durant, "Predicting Consumer Behavior and Media Preferences: The Comparative Validity of Personality Traits and Demographic Variables," *Psychology & Marketing* 30, no. 11 (2013), pp. 937–49.

13. Kathleen Krhialla, "CRM Case Study: The Analytics That Power CRM at Royal Bank [of Canada]," http://www.teradata.com/library/pdf/towergroup_020701.pdf (accessed June 6, 2010).

14. V. Kumar, Ilaria Dalla Pozza, and Jaishankar Ganesh, "Revisiting the Satisfaction–Loyalty Relationship: Empirical Generalizations and Directions for Future Research," *Journal of Retailing* 89, no. 3 (2013), pp. 246–62; Irit Nitzan and Barak Libai, "Social Effects on Customer Retention," *Journal of Marketing* 75, no. 6 (November 2011), pp. 24–38.

15. Terry O'Reilly, "Persuasive Perks: The World of Loyalty Programs," *The Age of Persuasion*, http://www.cbc.ca/radio/popup/audio/listen.html?autoPlay=true&clipIds=&mediaIds=2689446465&contentarea=radio&subsection1=radio1&subsection2=factual&subsection3=under_the_influence&contenttype=audio (accessed May 26, 2016).

16. https://altitude.aircanada.com/status/program-privileges (accessed June 7, 2017).

17. "PSYTE Canada Advantage Cluster Descriptions," http://tetrad.com/pub/documents/psyteadv_clusters.pdf (accessed February 9, 2017).

18. "Prizm5," Environics Analytics, http://www.environicsanalytics.ca/prizm5 (accessed February 9, 2017).

19. Dhruv Grewal, "Marketing Is All About Creating Value: 8 Key Rules," in *Inside the Mind of Textbook Marketing* (Boston: Aspatore Inc., 2003), pp. 79–96.

20. www.lasenza.ca (accessed June 3, 2016).

21. "The Founder," http://www.chezcora.com/a/01-belle-histoire/1-3-fondatrice2.htm (accessed June 7, 2010).

22. Sabritir Ghosh, "Made to Order," *Report on [Small] Business* (September 2009), http://www.theglobeandmail.com/report-on-business/your-business/start/franchising/made-to-order/article1265158 (accessed July 1, 2014).

23. "The Founder," http://www.chezcora.com/en/about-cora#founder accessed June 3, 2016).

24. Ibid.

25. B. Joseph Pine, *Mass Customization: The New Frontier in Business Competition* (Cambridge, MA: Harvard Business School Publishing, 1999); James H. Gilmore and B. Joseph Pine, eds., *Markets of One: Creating Customer-Unique Value Through Mass Customization* (Cambridge, MA: Harvard Business School Publishing, 2000).

26. Kristin Laird, "High Wired Retail," *Marketing Magazine*, February 25, 2013, p. 14.

27. C. Page Moreau, Leff Bonney, and Kelly B Herd, "It's the Thought (and the Effort) That Counts: How Customizing for Others Differs From Customizing for Oneself," *Journal of Marketing* 75, no. 5 (September 2011), pp. 120–133.

28. "Frequently Asked Questions," http://www.gatorade.com/frequently_asked_questions/default.aspx (accessed February 9, 2017).

29. "7UP," http://www.drpeppersnapplegroup.com/brands/7up (accessed February 9, 2017).

30. Allen Adamson, "Pitch Your Luxury Offering as an 'Investment Brand,'" *Forbes*, May 4, 2010, http://www.forbes.com/2010/05/04/luxury-branding-platinum-brands-bmw-hermes-investment-branding-cmo-network-allen-adamson.html.

31. Jean Halliday, "Maloney Wants Volvo Viewed as Both Safe and Luxurious," *Advertising Age* 75, no. 12 (2004), p. 22.

32. "McDonald's Legal Cases," http://en.wikipedia.org/wiki/McDonald's_legal_cases (accessed December 18, 2007).

33. Crane et al., *Marketing* (6th Can. ed.) (Whitby, ON: McGraw-Hill Ryerson, 2006), p. 243.

34. Elizabeth A. Harris and Stephanie Strom, "Walmart to Sell Organic Food, Undercutting Big Brands," *The New York Times*, April 10, 2014, http://www.nytimes.com; Dan Charles, "Can Wal-Mart Really Make Organic Food Cheap for Everyone?" *NPR*,

April 19, 2014, http://www.wbur.org/npr/; Steven Overly, "Wal-Mart Plans to Bring Its Compete-on-Price Approach to Organic Food: Here's How," *The Washington Post*, April 10, 2014, http://www.washingtonpost.com (accessed June 3, 2016).

35. Carly Lewis, "The Source Continues Brand Repositioning With On the Go," *Marketing Magazine*, March 12, 2013, http://www.marketingmag.ca/news/marketer-news/the-source-continues-brand-repositioning-with-on-the-go-74015 (accessed July 1, 2014).

36. Stephen Brown, Robert V. Kozinets, and John F. Sherry Jr., "Teaching Old Brands New Tricks: Retro Branding and the Revival of Brand Meaning," *Journal of Marketing* 67, no. 2 (July 2003), p. 19.

37. David Carr, "Giving Viewers What They Want," *The New York Times*, February 24, 2013, http://www.nytimes.com.

38. Craig Smith, "By the Numbers: 70 Amazing Netflix Statistics and Facts," *DMR*, June 2, 2016, http://expandedramblings.com/index.php/netflix_statistics-facts/ (accessed June 3, 2016).

39. Brian Barrett, "Netflix's Grand, Daring, Maybe Crazy Plan to Conquer the World," *WIRED*, March 27, 2016, http://www.wired.com/2016/03/netflixs-grand-maybe-crazy-plan-conquer-world/ (accessed June 3, 2016).

40. Jordan Hieshetter, "House of Ads: The Advertising Strategy Behind Netflix's Top Show," March 21, 2016, http://blog.pathmatics.com/house-of-ads-the-advertising-strategy-behind-netflixs-top-show (accessed June 3, 2016).

41. Brian Barrett, "Netflix's Grand, Daring, Maybe Crazy Plan to Conquer the World," *WIRED*, March 27, 2016, http://www.wired.com/2016/03/netflixs-grand-maybe-crazy-plan-conquer-world/ (accessed June 3, 2016).

42. Neil Hughes, "Netflix Boasts 37% Share of Internet Traffic in North America, Compared With 3% for Apple's iTunes," *Appleinsider*, January 20, 2016, http://appleinsider.com/articles/16/01/20/netflix-boasts-37-share-of-internet-traffic-in-north-america-compared-with-3-for-apples-itunes (accessed June 3, 2016).

43. "Dreamworks Animation to Create Netflix's First Original Kids' Show," *Advertising Age*, February 12, 2013.

44. Brian Barrett, "Netflix's Grand, Daring, Maybe Crazy Plan to Conquer the World," *WIRED*, March 27, 2016, http://www.wired.com/2016/03/netflixs-grand-maybe-crazy-plan-conquer-world/ (accessed June 3, 2016).

## CHAPTER 7

1. In-Store Marketing Institute, "Shaping Retail: The Use of Virtual Store Simulations in Marketing Research and Beyond," http://kelley.iu.edu/cerr/files/09ismi_virtualretailing.pdf, p. 3.

2. Alliston Ackerman, "P&G Shapes the Store," *Consumer Goods Technology*, November 16, 2011, http://consumergoods.edgl.com/case-studies/P-G-Shapes-the-Store75556.

3. Accenture, "Accenture and Procter & Gamble Partner in Delivering Virtual Solutions BPO Services," http://www.accenture.com/SiteCollectionDocuments/PDF/Accenture_CGS_PG_Virtual_Solutions.pdf.

4. Michael Letchford, "Pioneering Virtual Stores With Procter and Gamble," *Insights in Retail*, http://www.insightsinretail.com/virtual-stores/pioneering-virtual-stores-with-procter-and-gamble (accessed July 2, 2014).

5. Michael Letchford, "Virtual Shelf–Next Generation Visual Merchandising?" *Insights in Retail*, http://www.insightsinretail.com/visual-merchandising-virtual-shelf/virtual-shelf-a-new-generation-of-visual-merchandising.

6. A. Parasuraman, Dhruv Grewal, and R. Krishnan, *Marketing Research* (Boston: Houghton Mifflin, 2004), p. 9.

7. Erhard K. Valentin, "Commentary: Marketing Research Pitfalls in Product Development," *Journal of Product & Brand Management* 3, no. 4–6 (1994), pp. 66–69.

8. Detailed illustrations of scales are provided in two books: Gordon C. Bruner, *Marketing Scales Handbook, Volume V: A Compilation of Multi-Item Measures* (Carbondale, IL: GCBII Productions, 2009); William O. Bearden and Richard G. Netemeyer, *Handbook of Marketing Scales: Multi-Item Measures for Marketing and Consumer Behavior Research* (Thousand Oaks, CA: Sage Publications, 1999). Sources for the scales used in the exhibit are Dhruv Grewal, Gopalkrishnan Iyer, Jerry Gotlieb, and Michael Levy, "Developing a Deeper Understanding of Post-Purchase Perceived Risk and Repeat Purchase Behavioral Intentions in a Service Setting," *Journal of the Academy of Marketing Science* 35, no. 2 (2007), pp. 250–258; Anthony Miyazaki, Dhruv Grewal, and Ronald C. Goodstein, "The Effect of Multiple Extrinsic Cues on Quality Perceptions: A Matter of Consistency," *Journal of Consumer Research* 32 (June 2005), pp. 146–153.

9. For a more thorough discussion of effective written reports, see Parasuraman, Grewal, and Krishnan, *Marketing Research*, Chapter 16.

10. Jeff Kelly, "Big Data: Hadoop, Business, Analytics, and Beyond," Wikibon, February 5, 2014, http://wikibon.org.

11. Rachel Wolfson, "Retailers Using Big Data: The Secret Behind Amazon and Nordstrom's Success," *Big Data News*, December 11, 2014, http://www.bigdatanews.com.

12. "How Amazon Is Leveraging Big Data," *BigData Startups*, http://www.bigdata-startups.com/BigData-startup/amazon-leveraging-big-data/.

13. Amazon, http://www.amazon.com.

14. Wolfson, "Retailers Using Big Data."

15. Quentin Hardy, "Big Data Picks Up the Pace," *The New York Times*, March 5, 2014, http://bits.blogs.nytimes.com.

16. Google, "Analytic Guide," http://www.google.com.

17. Google, "Puma Kicks Up Order Rate 7% With Insights From Google Analytics and Viget," *case study*, 2013.

18. Adapted from Crane, Kerin, Hartley, Berkowitz, and Rudelius, *Marketing*, 6th Canadian ed. (Whitby ON: McGraw-Hill Ryerson, 2007).

19. "Léger Analytics," Léger, http://www.leger360.com/en-ca/serviceglobalexperience (accessed February 9, 2017).

20. Edward G. Carmines and Richard A. Zeller, *Reliability and Validity Assessment (Quantitative Applications in the Social Sciences)* (London, UK: Sage University Press, 1979).

21. Carmines and Zeller, *Reliability and Validity Assessment*.

22. "In Retail Stores, Research Tool Uses Kinect to Track Shoppers' Behavior," *Retail*, December 29, 2011, http://www.springwise.com.

23. Jennifer Reingold, "Can P&G Make Money in a Place Where People Earn $2 Per Day?" *CNN Money*, January 6, 2011, http://features.blogs.fortune.cnn.com/2011/01/06/can-pg-make-money-in-places-where-people-earn-2-a-day (accessed July 2, 2014).

24. "The Truth About Cars," http://www.thetruthaboutcars.com (accessed February 9, 2017).

25. Facebook, "Polls for Facebook," http://fbpoll.co/pricing/ (accessed June 8, 2006).

26. George Slefo, "Twitter Turns 12,000 Users Into Quick-Research Panel for Marketers," *Advertising Age*, June 8, 2016, http://adage.com/article/digital/twitter-launches-insiders/304351 (accessed June 8, 2016).

27. "Client Story: Kraft," http://www.communispace.com/assets/pdf/C_Cli_casestudy_kraft_final.pdf.

28. Sarah Needleman, "For Companies, a Tweet in Time Can Avert PR Mess," *The Wall Street Journal*, August 3, 2009.

29. Adapted from Kieran Griffiths, "Social Media in Research: Pros and Cons," May 17, 2012, http://www.intersperience.com/blog/post/05/2012/Social-Media-in-Research--Pros-and-Cons (accessed July 2, 2014), Mike Moran, "Will Social Media Listening Replace Market Research," April 4, 2011, http://www.biznology.com/2011/04/will_social_media_listening_re (accessed July 2, 2014).

30. Rachael King, "Sentiment Analysis Gives Companies Insight Into Consumer Opinion," *Bloomberg BusinessWeek*, March 1, 2011, http://www.businessweek.com/technology/content/feb2011/tc20110228_366762.htm

31. "My Starbucks Idea," https://Twitter.com/MyStarbucksIdea (accessed January 30, 2017).

32. Sheila Shayon, "My Starbucks Idea Turns 5, Sparking a Latte Innovations," April 1, 2013, http://www.brandchannel.com/home/post/2013/04/01/My-Starbucks-Idea-Turns-5-040113.aspx (accessed January 30, 2017).

33. Christine Barone, "Coconut Milk Is Here!" February 17, 2015, (http://blogs.starbucks.com/blogs/customer/archive/2015/02/17/coconut-milk-is-here.aspx) (accessed June 8, 2016.)

34. http://mystarbucksidea.force.com/apex/ideaList?lsi=2 (accessed January 30, 2017).

35. "Campbell's Select Harvest Soups Top 2009 IRI New Product Pacesetters List: Second Time in Three Years That Campbell's Soups Top List," *MarketWatch*, March 23, 2010, http://www.marketwatch.com/story/campbells-select-harvest-soups-top-2009-iri-new-product-pacesetters-list-2010-03-23?reflink5MW_news_stmp.

36. http://www.campbellsoup.com/select.aspx.

37. http://www.e-focusgroups.com/online.html.

38. Allison Fass, "Collective Opinion," Forbes.com, November 11, 2005, http://www.forbes.com/forbes/2005/1128/076.html (accessed July 9, 2011).

39. Adapted from A. Parasuraman, D. Grewal, and R. Krishnan, *Marketing Research* (Boston: Houghton Mifflin, 2004), p. 64.

40. Dan Ralph, "Canadian Families Shunning Hockey, Survey Finds," *The Globe and Mail*, August 2, 2013, p. S4.

41. Rebecca Harris, "Canadians Thinking Green for Next Car Purchase (Survey)," *Marketing Magazine*, April 26, 2016, http://www.marketingmag.ca/consumer/canadians-thinking-green-for-next-car-purchase-survey-173084 (accessed June 8, 2016).

42. Clean Tech Canada, "Canadians Believe Hydrogen Fuel Cell Vehicles, Not Battery Electrics, the Way of the Future," August 11, 2015, http://www.canadianmanufacturing.com/sustainability/canadians-believe-hydrogen-fuel-cell-vehicles-not-battery-electrics-the-way-of-the-future-152695/ (accessed June 8, 2016).

43. Peter Cheney, "Study Shows Why Canadians Aren't Buying Green Cars," *The Globe and Mail*, May 9, 2016, http://www.theglobeandmail.com/globe-drive/adventure/red-line/study-shows-why-canadians-arent-buying-green-cars/article29936481/ (accessed June 6, 2016).

44. Adapted from A. Parasuraman, Dhruv Grewal, and R. Krishnan, *Marketing Research*, 2nd ed. (Boston, MA: Houghton Mifflin, 2007), Ch. 10.

45. Floyd J. Fowler, *Survey Research Methods* (Thousand Oaks, CA: Sage, 2009); Don A. Dillman, Glenn Phelps, Robert Tortora, Karen Swift, Julie Kohrell, Jodi Berck, and Benjamin L. Messer, "Response Rate and Measurement Differences in Mixed-Mode Surveys Using Mail, Telephone, Interactive Voice Response (IVR) and the Internet," *Social Science Research 38* (March 2009), pp. 1–18.

46. Chris Powell, "Shaw Establishes New Online Research Tool the Viewers Lounge," *Marketing Magazine*, February 12, 2014, http://www.marketingmag.ca/news/media-news/shaw-establishes-new-online-research-tool-the-viewers-lounge-100742 (accessed July 2, 2014).

47. https://pulse.asda.com (accessed April 15, 2010); Joel Warady, "Asda Takes the 'Pulse of the Nation,'" *Retail Wire* (July 16, 2009).

48. Facebook, "State Bicycle Co.: Building a Strong Customer Base," case study, https://www.facebook.com/business/success/state-bicycle (accessed June 8, 2016).

49. Facebook, "Grow Your Business Online," https://www.facebook.com/business/a/online-sales (accessed June 8, 2016).

50. Roger Dooley, "Neuromarketing: For Coke, It's the Real Thing," *Forbes*, March 7, 2013, http://www.forbes.com (accessed June 8, 2016).

51. Andrew Roberts, "In Some Stores, the Mannequins Are Watching You," *Bloomberg Businessweek*, December 6, 2012, http://www.businessweek.com; Amar Toor, "EyeSee Mannequin Silently Collects Customer Data for Overzealous Retailers," The Verge, November 20, 2012, http://www.theverge.com; Joanna Stern, "Department Store Mannequins Are Watching You. No, Really," ABC News, November 26, 2012, http://abcnews.go.com.

52. "Privacy Laws in Canada," Office of the Privacy Commissioner of Canada, https://www.priv.gc.ca/en/privacy-topics/privacy-laws-in-canada/ (accessed February 9, 2017).

53. Natasha Singer, "Face Recognition Makes the Leap From Sci-Fi," *The New York Times*, November 12, 2011.

54. Ilan Brat, "The Emotional Quotient of Soup Shopping," *The Wall Street Journal*, February 17, 2010, http://online.wsj.com (accessed June 8, 2016).

55. AutoTrader, "Fact Sheet," http://press.autotrader.com/press-kits?cat=3495 (accessed June 6, 2016).

56. Joe Richards, "How AutoTrader.com Uses Primary Research to Clarify the Car-Shopping Process," *Quirk's Marketing Research Review* (July 2011), p. 36, http://www.quirks.com/articles/2011/20110704.aspx (accessed June 6, 2016).

57. Bruce Giffin and Joe Richards, "The Role of the Internet in the New and Used Vehicle Purchase Process," *Polk View*, February 2011, http://www.industryrelations.autotrader.com (accessed June 6, 2016).

58. Josh Kolm, "What Are Car Buyers Looking For?" *Strategy Magazine*, May 13, 2016, http://strategyonline.ca/2016/05/13/what-are-car-buyers-looking-for (accessed June 6, 2016).

## CHAPTER 8

1. "LEGO History Timeline," http://aboutus.lego.com/en-us/lego-group/the_lego_history (accessed July 2, 2013).

2. "MyLegoNetwork," http://mln.lego.com/en-us/network/status.aspx?icmp5COUSCreateShareSL100MLN (accessed July 2, 2013).

3. Brad Wieners, "Lego Is for Girls," *BusinessWeek*, December 14, 2011.

4. Shari Roan, "A New Lego Line for Girls Is Offensive, Critics Say," *Los Angeles Times*, January 23, 2012, http://www.latimes.com/health/boostershots/la-heb-lego-girls-toy-protest-20120123,0,141471.story (accessed July 2, 2014).

5. "Lego Friends," http://friends.lego.com/en-us/Products/Default.aspx (accessed July 2, 2014).

6. Lego, "Lego Friends Doubled Expectations for Sales in 2012," http://www.lego.com/en-us/aboutus/news-room/2013/february/lego-friends-doubled-expectations-for-sales-in-2012 (accessed June 9, 2016).

7. Jonathan Ringer, "How Lego Became the Apple of Toys," *FastCompany* January 8, 2015, http://www.fastcompany.com/3040223/when-it-clicks-it-clicks (accessed June 9, 2016).

8. Lego, "More Children Than Ever Experienced LEGO® Play in 2015 as a Result of 19% Sales Growth," http://www.lego.com/en-us/aboutus/news-room/2016/march/2015-annual-result; Jena McGregor, "For Lego CEO, Rebuilding Was No Children's Game," *Waterloo Region Record*, December 13, 2016, http://www.therecord.com/news-story/7016449-for-lego-ceo-rebuilding-was-no-children-s-game/ (accessed February 7, 2017).

9. P&G, "Latest Sustainability Stories," http://us.pg.com/sustainability/latest_sustainability_stories/ (accessed June 13, 2016).

10. P&G, "2015 Sustainability Report Executive Summary," http://cdn.pg.com/-/media/PGCOMUS/Documents/PDF/Sustainability_PDF/sustainability_reports/2015SustainabilityReportExecutive-Summary.pdf?la=en-US&v=1-201512231810 (accessed June 13, 2016).

11. P&G, "Latest Sustainability Stories," http://us.pg.com/sustainability/latest_sustainability_stories/ (accessed June 13, 2016).

12. P&G, "Purclean Fact Sheet," http://cdn.pg.com/-/media/PGCOM/Documents/Innovations/PDF/6224PGInnovationFSTidePurCleancontact%20pdf.pdf?v=1-201603011053 (accessed June 13, 2016).

13. Dale Buss, "Tide Ups Pods and Boosts Purclean as Sustainable Laundry Brand," *Brand Channel*, http://www.brandchannel.com/2016/06/10/tide-purclean-061016/, June 10, 2016 (accessed June 13, 2016).

14. http://www.dove.com.

15. Koen Pauwels et al., "New Products, Sales Promotions, and Firm Value: The Case of the Automobile Industry," *Journal of Marketing* 68, no. 4 (October 2004), p. 142.

16. Elaine Watson, "What's the Size of the US Gluten-Free Prize? $490m, $5bn, or $10bn?" *Food Navigator USA*, February 17, 2014, http://www.foodnavigator-usa.com (accessed June 14, 2016).

17. http://www.bettycrocker.com/products/gluten-free-products; Keith O'Brien, "Should We All Go Gluten-Free?" *The New York Times*, November 25, 2011, http://www.nytimes.com (accessed June 14, 2016).

18. Kalpesh Kaushik Desai and Kevin Lane Keller, "The Effects of Ingredient Branding Strategies on Host Brand Extendibility," *Journal of Marketing* 66, no. 1 (January 2002), pp. 73–93.

19. Erik Kain, "'Madden NFL 25' Sales Down Over Last Year, First Week Still Tops 1M Units," *Forbes*, September 5, 2013, http://www.forbes.com (accessed June 14, 2016).

20. IDEO, "Safeway Supply Chain Innovation for Kraft Foods," http://www.ideo.com/work/safeway-supply-chain-innovation-for-kraft (accessed July 2, 2014).

21. http://www.marketingpower.com (accessed September 18, 2006).

22. Rajesh K. Chandy, Jaideep C. Prabhu, and Kersi D. Antia, "What Will the Future Bring? Dominance, Technology Expectations, and Radical Innovation," *Journal of Marketing* 67, no. 3 (July 2003), pp. 1–18; Harald J. van Heerde, Carl F. Mela, and Puneet Manchanda, "The Dynamic Effect of Innovation on Market Structure," *Journal of Marketing Research* 41, no. 2 (May 2004), pp. 166–183.

23. http://www.apple.com; Clayton M. Christensen and Michael E. Raynor, *The Innovator's Solution* (Boston: Harvard Business School Press, 2003).

24. Philip Kotler, *Marketing Management*, 11th ed. (Upper Saddle River, NJ: Prentice-Hall, 2003), pp. 330–331. Kotler's work was based on the following research: William T. Robinson and Claes Fornell, "Sources of Market Pioneer Advantages in Consumer Goods Industries," *Journal of Marketing Research* 22, no. 3 (August 1985), pp. 305–317; Glen L. Urban et al., "Market Share Rewards to Pioneering Brands: An Empirical Analysis and Strategic Implications," *Management Science* 32 (June 1986), pp. 645–659; and G.S. Carpenter and Kent Nakamoto, "Consumer Preference Formation and Pioneering Advantage," *Journal of Marketing Research* 26, no. 3 (August 1989), pp. 285–298.

25. Katie Marsal, "iPod Adoption Rate Faster Than Sony Walkman," www.appleinsider.com/articles/04/11/29/ipod_adoption_rate_faster_than_sony_walkman.html (accessed July 2, 2014).

26. Eliot Van Buskirk, "Apple iPad Reaches '1 Million Sold' Twice as Fast as iPhone," http://www.wired.com/epicenter/2010/05/apple-ipad-reaches-one-million-sold-twice-as-fast-as-iphone (accessed July 2, 2014).

27. http://www.quickmba.com (accessed September 16, 2006).

28. Ellen Byron, "The Cleanest House of All," *The Wall Street Journal*, March 20, 2013, http://online.wsj.com (accessed June 14, 2016).

29. Carol Matlack, "Electrolux's Holy Trinity for Hit Products," *Bloomberg Businessweek*, October 31, 2013, http://www.businessweek.com (accessed June 14, 2016).

30. Jeffrey A. Trachtenberg, "E-Book Readers Face Sticker Shock," *The Wall Street Journal*, December 15, 2011.

31. Gabriel Beltrone, *Adweek*, January 21, 2014, http://www.adweek.com (accessed June 14, 2016).

32. Matlack, "Electrolux's Holy Trinity for Hit Products."

33. Blendtec, "Will It Blend?" https://www.youtube.com/user/Blendtec (accessed June 14, 2016).

34. Subin Im and John P. Workman Jr., "Market Orientation, Creativity, and New Product Performance in High-Technology Firms," *Journal of Marketing* 68, no. 2 (April 2004), p. 114.

35. Dana Mattioli and Kris Maher, "At 3M, Innovation Comes in Tweaks and Snips," *The Wall Street Journal*, March 2, 2010.

36. Chuck Salter, "The 9 Passions of 3M's Mauro Porcini," *Fast Company*, October 2011, pp. 128–134.

37. Natalie Zmuda, "P&G, Levi's, GE Innovate by Thinking in Reverse," *Ad Age*, June 13, 2011, http://adage.com/article/global-news/p-g-levi-s-ge-innovate-thinking-reverse/228146 (accessed July 2, 2014); "Minute Maid Pulpy Joins Growing List of Billion Dollar Brands for the Coca-Cola Company," press release, February 1, 2011, http://www.thecoca-colacompany.com/dynamic/press_center/2011/02/pulpy-joins-roster-of-billion-dollar-brands.html.

38. Stefan Stremersch and Walter Van Dyck, "Marketing of the Life Sciences: A New Framework and Research Agenda for a Nascent Field," *Journal of Marketing* 73 (July 2009), pp. 4–30; Brady Huggett, John Hodgson, and Riku Lähteenmäki, "Public Biotech 2010—The Numbers," *Nature Biotechnology* 29 (2011), pp. 585–91, http://www.nature.com.

39. Jack Adams, "US Search Engine Market Share Figures Steady in February," *Clickthrough*, March 21, 2014, http://www.clickthrough-marketing.com; Steve Lohr, "Can Microsoft Make You 'Bing'?" *The New York Times*, July 30, 2011, http://www.nytimes.com; Dina Bass and Jack Clark, "How Microsoft Plans to Beat Google and Facebook to the Next Tech Breakthrough," *Bloomberg*, January 25, 2016, http://www.bloomberg.com/features/2016-microsoft-research/; *NetMarketShare*, "Desktop Search Engine Market Share," May 2016, https://www.netmarketshare.com/search-engine-market-share.aspx; *Statista*, "Share of Search Queries Handled by Leading U.S. Search Engine Providers as of April 2016," http://www.statista.com/statistics/267161/market-share-of-search-engines-in-the-united-states/ (accessed June 9, 2016).

40. Glen L. Urban and John R. Hauser, "'Listening In' to Find and Explore New Combinations of Customer Needs," *Journal of Marketing* 68, no. 2 (April 2004), p. 72; Steve Hoeffler, "Measuring Preferences for Really New Products," *Journal of Marketing Research* 40, no. 4 (November 2003), pp. 406–420.

41. Glen L. Urban and John R. Hauser, *Design and Marketing of New Products*, 2nd ed. (Upper Saddle River, NJ: Prentice Hall, 1993), pp. 120–121.

42. Jeff Bellairs, "Innovation and Collaboration Swiftly Launch Green Giant Snack Chips," *Taste of General Mills*, June 19, 2013, http://www.blog.generalmills.com (accessed June 14, 2016).

43. Josephy Flaherty, "How Home Depot Copied Apple to Build an Ingenious New Bucket," *Wired*, December 31, 2013, http://www.wired.com (accessed June 14, 2016).

44. http://www.betterproductdesign.net/tools/user/leaduser.htm (accessed November 12, 2004); Eric von Hippel, "Successful Industrial Products From Consumers' Ideas," *Journal of Marketing* 42, no. 1 (January 1978), pp. 39–49; Eric von Hippel, "Lead Users: A Source of Novel Product Concepts," *Management Science* 32 (1986), pp. 791–805; Eric von Hippel, *The Sources of Innovation* (New York: Oxford University Press, 1988); Glen L. Urban and Eric von Hippel, "Lead User Analysis for the Development of Industrial Products," *Management Science* 34 (May 1988), pp. 569–582.

45. Karl T. Ulrich and Steven D. Eppinger, *Product Design and Development*, 2nd ed. (Boston: Irwin-McGraw-Hill, 2000).

46. http://www.marketingpower.com (accessed September 18, 2006).

47. Ulrich and Eppinger, *Product Design and Development*, p. 166.

48. Ely Dahan and V. Srinivasan, "The Predictive Power of Internet-Based Product Concept Testing Using Visual Depiction and Animation," *Journal of Product Innovation Management* 17 (2000), pp. 99–109.

49. http://www.marketingpower.com (accessed September 18, 2006).

50. All information presented in Entrepreneurial Marketing 8.1 comes from personal interviews with Bryan Fedorak, co-founder of Bartesian.

51. Ulrich and Eppinger, *Product Design and Development*.

52. Frederic Lardinois, *Tech Crunch*, May 7, 2013, http://www.techcrunch.com (accessed June 14, 2016).

53. http://www2.acnielsen.com/products/crs_bases2.shtml (accessed September 20, 2006).

54. Kotler, *Marketing Management*.

55. Emily Wexler, "McDonald's Plans to Win," http://www.strategyonline.ca/articles/magazine/20090901/bizmcdonalds.html (accessed July 2, 2014).

56. Patricia Sellers, "P&G: Teaching an Old Dog New Tricks," *Fortune* (May 31, 2004), pp. 166–180.

57. "Tim Hortons® Tests Its First New Coffee Blend in 49 Years," *The Globe and Mail*, October 28, 2013, http://www.theglobeandmail.com/report-on-business/tim-hortons-targets-rivals-tests-new-dark-roast-coffee/article15114207 (accessed July 2, 2014).

58. Hollie Shaw, "Loblaw to Test New Health Store Concept, Take on Whole Foods as Grocery Battle Heats Up," July 11, 2013, http://business.financialpost.com/2013/07/11/loblaw-nutshell-live-life-well (accessed July 2, 2014).

59. Associated Press, "KFC Looks Upmarket With New Restaurant Format," http://www.marketingmag.ca/news/marketer-news/kfc-looks-upmarket-with-new-restaurant-format-83832 (accessed July 2, 2014).

60. Michael Cieply, "New Challenge for Filmmakers: Adding Dimension to 3-D Movies," *The New York Times*, August 11, 2013, http://www.nytimes.com (accessed June 14, 2016).

61. Product of the Year is the world's largest consumer-voted award for product innovation and publishes a list of best new products launched each year (http://productoftheyear.ca). The products listed were winners in the 2016 Product of the Year Awards, a competition judged by thousands of Canadian consumers coast to coast.

62. Product Development Management Association, *The PDMA Handbook of New Product Development*, 2nd ed., Kenneth K. Kahn, ed. (New York: John Wiley & Sons, 2004).

63. Ashwin W. Joshi and Sanjay Sharma, "Customer Knowledge Development: Antecedents and Impact on New Product Success," *Journal of Marketing* 68, no. 4 (October 2004), p. 47.

64. Katherine Bourzac, "Colorful Quantum Dot Displays Coming to Market," *Technology Review*, http://www.technologyreview.com/computing/25460/?a5f (accessed July 2, 2014).

65. Yuhong Wu, Sridhar Balasubramanian, and Vijay Mahajan, "When Is a Preannounced New Product Likely to Be Delayed?" *Journal of Marketing* 68, no. 2 (April 2004), p. 101.

66. "Ten of the Biggest Product Flops of All Time," *The Calgary Herald*, March 22, 2103, http://www.calgaryherald.com/business/biggest+product+flops+time/8148934/story.html (accessed July 2, 2014).

67. http://www.pdma.org (accessed September 15, 2006).

68. Amberly McAteer, "Will McDonald's Ditch the Salad," *The Globe and Mail*, May 30, 2013, http://www.theglobeandmail.com/life/the-hot-button/will-mcdonalds-ditch-the-salad/article12279474 (accessed July 2, 2014).

69. Earls, "About," https://earls.ca/about (accessed June 13, 2016).

70. Earls, "Conscious Sourcing," http://conscious-sourcing.earls.ca (accessed February 7, 2017).

71. Jamie Dirom, "Earls Backtracks on Move Away From Canadian beef, Vows to Put It Back on the Menu," *PostMedia*, May 4, 2016, http://business.financialpost.com/news/agriculture/earls-backtracks-on-move-away-from-canadian-beef-vows-to-put-it-back-on-the-menu (accessed June 13, 2016).

72. Theodore Levitt, *Marketing Imagination* (New York: The Free Press, 1986).

73. Donald R. Lehmann and Russell S. Winer, *Analysis for Marketing Planning*, 6th ed. (Boston: McGraw-Hill/Irwin, 2004).

74. Urban and Hauser, *Design and Marketing*.

75. http://www.organicearthday.org/DelMonteFoods.htm (accessed June 10, 2010); http://www.delmonte.com/Products (accessed June 10, 2010).

76. Miriam Jordan and Jonathan Karp, "Machines for the Masses; Whirlpool Aims Cheap Washer at Brazil, India and China; Making Do With Slower Spin," *The Wall Street Journal*, December 9, 2003: A19.

77. Dale Buss, "Tide Ups Pods and Boosts Purclean as Sustainable Laundry Brand," *Brand Channel*, June 10, 2016 (accessed June 15, 2016).

78. Claire Briney, "Wiping Up the Market," *Global Cosmetic Industry* 172, no. 4 (April 2004), pp. 40–43.

79. Kara Swisher, "Home Economics: The Hypoallergenic Car; Wave of Cleaning Products Caters to Finicky Drivers; Premoistened Auto Wipes," *The Wall Street Journal* (Eastern Edition; May 6, 2004): D1.

80. http://www.toiletwand.com (accessed September 20, 2006).

81. Natalie Zmuda and Jennifer Rooney, "Hallmark Breaks Out of Special Occasion Mold," *Advertising Age*, July 6, 2011, http://adage.com.

82. http://www40.statcan.ca/l01/cst01/arts28.htm (accessed June 12, 2007).

83. Josh O'Kane, "Vinyl Revival: Canadian Company Reinvents the Record Pressing Plant," *The Globe and Mail*, February 4, 2016, http://www.theglobeandmail.com/report-on-business/small-business/startups/canadian-firm-comes-to-the-rescue-of-vinyl-lovers-by-building-new-pressing-machines/article28507701/; Nielsen, "2016 Canada Music Year-End Report," January 10, 2017, http://www.nielsen.com/ca/en/insights/reports/2017/2016-music-canada-year-end-report.html (accessed February 7, 2017).

84. "Vinyl Lovers Spur New Boom for Old Medium," http://www.cbc.ca/consumer/story/2007/01/03/vinyl-boom.html (accessed June 12, 2007).

85. Josh O'Kane, "Vinyl Revival: Canadian Company Reinvents the Record Pressing Plant," *The Globe and Mail*, February 4, 2016, http://www.theglobeandmail.com/report-on-business/small-business/startups/canadian-firm-comes-to-the-rescue-of-vinyl-lovers-by-building-new-pressing-machines/article28507701/ (accessed June 15, 2016).

86. Kevin J. Clancy and Peter C. Krieg, "Product Life Cycle: A Dangerous Idea," *Brandweek*, March 1, 2004, p. 26; Nariman K. Dhalla and Sonia Yuseph, "Forget the Product Life-Cycle Concept," *Harvard Business Review* (January–February 1976), p. 102ff.

87. David Pogue, "Google Glass and the Future of Technology," *The New York Times*, September 13, 2012, http://pogue.blogs.nytimes.com (accessed June 15, 2016).

88. Google Glass, http://www.google.com/glass/start/how-to-get-one/w zmzHq

89. David Zax, "Google Glass's Unexpected Lessons in Product Launching," *Fast Company*, February 3, 2014, http://www.fastcompany.com (accessed June 15, 2016).

90. Ibid.

91. Claire Cain Miller, "Google Glass to Be Covered by Vision Care Insurer VSP," *The New York Times*, January 28, 2014, http://www.nytimes.com (accessed June 15, 2016).

92. Ben Sisario, "Google Glass Will Expand Its Features Into Music," *The New York Times*, November 12, 2013, http://www.nytimes.com (accessed June 15, 2016).

93. Tony Danova, "BI Intelligence Forecast: Google Glass Will Become a Mainstream Product and Sell Millions by 2016," *Business Insider*, December 31, 2013, http://www.businessinsider.com (accessed June 15, 2016).

94. Kevin C. Tofel, "Why Google Glass Costs $1500 Now and Will Likely Be Around $299 Later," *Gigaom*, August 8, 2013, http://gigaom.com; Liz Gannes, "Google Glass Could Be $3-Billion-a-Year Business, Says Analyst," *All Things Digital*, September 4, 2013, http://allthingsd.com (accessed June 15, 2016).

95. Google Glass, https://www.google.ca/glass/start/ (accessed June 15, 2016).

96. Ian Altman, "Why Google Glass Failed and Why Apple Watch Could Too," *Forbes*, April 28, 2015, http://www.forbes.com/sites/ianaltman/2015/04/28/why-google-glass-failed-and-why-apple-watch-could-too/2/#3bb9eddb5103 (accessed June 15, 2016).

97. Bob Doyle, "5 Reasons Why Google Glass Was a Miserable Failure," February 28, 2016, http://www.business2community.com/tech-gadgets/5-reasons-google-glass-miserable-failure-01462398#qygGm3uscVi3reMD.97 (accessed June 15, 2016).

98. Brooke Crothers, "The Google Glass Epic Fail: What Happened?" *Fox News*, http://bgr.com/2015/06/27/google-glass-epic-fail-what-happened/ (accessed June 15, 2016).

99. Amir Efrati and Geoffrey A. Fowler, "Google Glass Is Watching—Now What?" *The Wall Street Journal*, May 17, 2013, http://online.wsj.com (accessed June 15, 2016).

100. Nick Bilton, "Google Offers a Guide to Not Being a 'Creepy' Google Glass Owner," *The New York Times*, February 19, 2014, http://bits.blogs.nytimes.com (accessed June 15, 2016).

## CHAPTER 9

1. Josh O'Kane, "Canada Goose CEO's 'Aha' Moment: 'I realized the brand was real,'" *The Globe and Mail*, April 11, 2013, http://www.theglobeandmail.com/report-on-business/small-business/sb-growth/day-to-day/canada-goose-ceos-aha-moment-i-realized-the-brand-was-real/article10982951 (accessed July 18, 2014).

2. Greig Dyomd, "Guiding the Flock," *The Grid*, March 6, 2013, http://www.thegridto.com/life/fashion/guiding-the-flock (accessed July 18, 2014).

3. "Frequently Asked Questions," http://www.canada-goose.com/faq (accessed July 22, 2013).

4. "Cannes 2016: Canada Goose, Leo, Grey and Critical Mass Pick Up Lions," *Strategy Online*, June 21, 2016, http://strategyonline.ca/2016/06/21/cannes-2016-canada-goose-leo-grey-and-critical-mass-pick-up-lions (accessed June 21, 2016).

5. Sanjay Sanghoee, "Should Canada Goose, Maker of the $1,000-Plus Parka, Go Public?" *Fortune*, February 2, 2015, http://fortune.com/2015/02/02/should-canada-goose-maker-of-the-1000-plus-parka-go-public/; Kim Bhasin, "Can Canada Goose Come In From the Cold?" *Bloomberg*, June 7, 2016, http://www.bloomberg.com/news/articles/2016-06-06-can-canada-goose-come-in-from-the-cold (accessed August 4, 2016).

6. Francine Kopun, "Moose Knuckles CEO Confirms Not All Parkas Made in Canada," *The Toronto Star*, April 26, 2016, www.thestar.com/business/2016/04/27/moose-knuckles-rapped-over-made-in-canada-claims.html (accessed June 20, 2016).

7. Adrienne Pasquarelli, "Canada Goose Wants Shoppers to Know It's More Than Just Parkas," *Advertising Age*, April 20, 2016, http://adage.com/article/cmo-strategy/canada-goose-parkas/303629 (accessed June 20, 2016).

8. Kim Bhasin, "Can Canada Goose Come In From the Cold?" *Bloomberg*, June 6, 2016, http://www.bloomberg.com/news/articles/2016-06-06-can-canada-goose-come-in-from-the-cold? (accessed June 20, 2016).

9. Harmeet Singh, "Canada Goose Set to Open Flagships," *Strategy Online*, May 26, 2016, http://strategyonline.ca/2016/05/26/canada-goose-set-to-open-flagships (accessed June 20, 2016).

10. Harmeet Singh, "Canada Goose Gets Into Travel," *Strategy Online*, November 11, 2016, http://strategyonline.ca/2016/11/10/canada-goose-gets-into-travel (accessed February 8, 2017).

11. Jesse Silvertown, "Canada Goose: The South Korean Opportunity," *Richard Ivey School of Business*, February 6, 2012, http://www.asiapacific.ca/sites/default/files/canada_goose_9b11a036.pdf (accessed July 18, 2014).

12. Colgate, "Toothpastes," http://www.colgate.ca/en/ca/oc/products/toothpaste (accessed February 8, 2017).

13. Simon Pittman, "Revlon Switches CEO as Pressure Mounts Over Performance," Cosmeticsdesign.com, September 19, 2006.

14. Naoko Fujimura and Mike Firn, "Starbucks Says Via Sales May Pass $1 Billion Globally," http://www.businessweek.com/news/2010-04-13/starbucks-says-via-sales-may-pass-1-billion-globally-correct-.html (accessed May 30, 2010).

15. "Starbucks Introduces Starbucks® Natural Fusions Naturally Flavored Coffee in Grocery Stores Nationwide," http://news.starbucks.com/article_display.cfm?article_id=388 (accessed May 30, 2010).

16. "J&J to Buy Skin Care Business," *The Wall Street Journal*, December 18, 1998: 1.

17. http://scjohnson.com/products (accessed June 22, 2016).

18. Austin Carr, Fast Company, May 1, 2013, http://www.fastcompany.com/3008346/deep-inside-taco-bells-doritos-locos-taco (accessed June 22, 2016).

19. Ellen Byron, "Tide Turns 'Basic' for P&G in Slump," *The Wall Street Journal*, August 6, 2009; Barry Silverstein, "P&G Scrubs Out Tide Basic," *BrandChannel*, June 6, 2010, http://www.brandchannel.com.

20. Natalie Zmuda, "Under Armour Unveils Anthem to Kick Off Its Biggest Global Ad Push," *Advertising Age*, February 12, 2013, http://adage.com/article/see-the-spot/armour-unveils-biggest-global-advertising-campaign/239769/ (accessed June 22, 2016).

21. Kevin Lane Keller, *Strategic Brand Management: Building, Measuring, and Managing Brand Equity*, 4th ed. (Upper Saddle River, NJ: Prentice Hall, 2012); David A. Aaker, *Building Strong Brands* (New York: Simon & Schuster, 2012).

22. This discussion of the advantages of strong brands is adapted from Keller, *Strategic Brand Management*.

23. Kevin Lane Keller and Donald R. Lehmann, "Assessing Long-Term Brand Potential," *Journal of Brand Management* 17 (2009), pp. 6–17.

24. Grant Robertson, "Year of the Goose," *The Globe and Mail*, February 25, 2010, http://www.theglobeandmail.com/report-on-business/rob-magazine/year-of-the-goose/article4307839/?page=all (accessed July 18, 2014).

25. Mike O' Brien, "What Makes Ben & Jerry's So Good at Social?" *ClickZ*, June 7, 2016, https://www.clickz.com/2016/06/07/what-makes-ben-jerrys-so-good-at-social?; Meira Bernstein, "How Ben and Jerry's Celebrates Community and Creates Loyal Fans," *Global Strategy Group*, www.globalstrategygroup.com/2013/07/how-ben-and-jerrys-celebrates-community-and-creates-loyal-fans/; Tom Szaky, "Social Media an Invaluable Tool for Helping Conscious Consumers Live Even More Consciously," *Sustainable Brands*, http://www.sustainablebrands.com/news_and_views/behavior_change/tom_szaky/social_media_invaluable_tool_helping_conscious_consumers_li (accessed June 22, 2016).

26. Hollie Shaw, "Canada Goose's Made-in-Canada Marketing Strategy Translates Into Success," *Financial Post*, May 18, 2012. http://business.financialpost.com/2012/05/18/canada-gooses-made-in-canada-marketing-strategy-translates-into-success (accessed July 18, 2014).

27. Rob Walker, "How RadioShack Plans to Rescue Itself From Irrelevance," *Yahoo Tech*, February 12, 2014, https://www.yahoo

.com/tech/how-radioshack-plans-to-rescue-itself-from -irrelevance-76424164006.html (accessed June 22, 2016).

28. *Interbrand*, "Anatomy of Growth," http://interbrand.com/best -brands/best-global-brands/2016 (accessed February 8, 2017).

29. Harmeet Singh, "Brand Finance Reveals This Year's Most Valuable Brands," February 6, 2017, *Strategy Online*, http:// strategyonline.ca/2017/02/06/canadas-most-valuable-brands (accessed February 7, 2017).

30. David Aaker, *Brand Portfolio Strategy: Creating Relevance, Differentiation, Energy, Leverage, and Clarity* (New York: Free Press, 2004); David A. Aaker, *Managing Brand Equity* (New York: Free Press, 1991).

31. "Best Global Brands 2015," http://interbrand.com/best-brands /best-global-brands/2015/ranking/ (accessed June 22, 2016).

32. Tiffany Hsu, "Coca-Cola Anti-Obesity Promises Include No Advertising to Kids," *Los Angeles Times*, May 8, 2013, http://articles .latimes.com; Mike Esterl and Paul Ziobro, "Coke to Limit Ads to Kids, Push Diet Drinks," *The Wall Street Journal*, http://online.wsj .com; Henriette Jacobsen, "Denmark Scraps Its Infamous Fat Tax After Only One Year," *EurActiv.com*, February 21, 2016, http://www .euractiv.com/section/agriculture-food/news/denmark-scraps -its-infamous-fat-tax-after-only-one-year/; Ivana Kottasova, "UK to Charge Soda Tax on Sugary Drinks," *CNN Money*, April 4, 2016, http://money.cnn.com/2016/03/16/news/sugar-levy-uk-budget/; "Philadelphia Becomes First Major US City With a Soda Tax," *The Guardian*, June 16, 2016, https://www.theguardian.com/us-news /2016/jun/16/philadelphia-passes-soda-tax-first-city-sugar; Patrick Luciani, "Soda Tax Would Leave Canadians Poorer, but No Healthier," *The Financial Post*, May 11, 2016, http://business.finan-cialpost.com/fp-comment/patrick-luciani-soda-tax-would-leave -canadians-poorer-but-no-healthier (accessed June 21, 2016); Harmeet Singh, "Canadians Concerned About Sugar's Impact on Health," *StrategyOnline*, February 15, 2017, http://strategyonline .ca/2017/02/15/canadians-concerned-about-sugars-impact-on -health (accessed February 15, 2017).

33. David A. Aaker, "Measuring Brand Equity Across Products and Markets," *California Management Review* 38 (Spring 1996), pp. 102–120.

34. "List of generic and genericized trademarks," https://en.wikipedia .org/wiki/List_of_generic_and_genericized_trademarks (accessed February 8, 2017).

35. Katherine Rosman, "Grumpy Cat Has an Agent, and Now a Movie Deal," *The Wall Street Journal*, May 31, 2013, http://www.wsj.com /articles/SB10001424127887324412604578513352795950958 (accessed June 22, 2016).

36. Jennifer L. Aaker, "Dimensions of Brand Personality," *Journal of Marketing Research* 34, no. 3 (August 1997), pp. 347–356.

37. Kevin Lane Keller, "Conceptualizing, Measuring, and Managing Customer-Based Brand Equity," *Journal of Marketing* 57, no. 1 (January 1993), pp. 1–22.

38. Robert Klara, "For Some Retail Brands, Lifetime Guarantees Never Went Out of Fashion," *Adweek*, March 17, 2014, http:// www.adweek.com/news/advertising-branding/some-retail -brands-lifetime-guarantees-never-went-out-fashion-156314 (ac-cessed June 22, 2016).

39. Mai Nguyen, "'Crave More' Attempts to Make PC a Lifestyle Brand," *Marketing Magazine*, September 18, 2014, http://www .marketingmag.ca/advertising/crave-more-attempts-to-make -pc-a-lifestyle-brand-124926 (accessed June 21, 2016).

40. PC The Decadent Chocolate Chip Cookie, http://www .presidentschoice.ca/en_CA/products/productlisting/pc_the _decadent_chocolate_chip_cookie.html (accessed June 22, 2016).

41. *Canada Newswire*, "For Over 30 Years, Loblaw's No Name Products Have Shown Canadians They Don't Have to Trade Quality for Price," January 13, 2016, http://www.newswire.ca /news-releases/for-over-30-years-loblaws-no-namer-products -have-shown-canadians-they-dont-have-to-trade-quality-for -price-536984231.html (accessed June 16, 2016).

42. *P&G*, "All Brands," http://www.pg.com (accessed February 9, 2017).

43. Eve Lazarus, "New Beer Goes With Flies and a Croak," http:// www.marketingmag.ca/magazine/marketingdaily/article.jsp?con-tent=20060914_102950_5424 (accessed June 7, 2007).

44. For recent research on brand extensions, see Subramanian Balachander and Sanjoy Ghose, "Reciprocal Spillover Effects: A Strategic Benefit of Brand Extensions," *Journal of Marketing* 67, no. 1 (January 2003), pp. 4–13; Kalpesh Kaushik Desai and Kevin Lane Keller, "The Effects of Ingredient Branding Strategies on Host Brand Extendibility," *Journal of Marketing* 66, no. 1 (January 2002), pp. 73–93; Tom Meyvis and Chris Janiszewski, "When Are Broader Brands Stronger Brands? An Accessibility Perspective on the Success of Brand Extensions," *Journal of Consumer Research* 31, no. 2 (September 2004), pp. 346–357.

45. David Aaker, *Aaker on Branding: 20 Principles That Drive Success* (Morgan James, 2014); Aaker, *Building Strong Brands*.

46. Braun, "Shop All Products," http://ca.braun.com/en-ca/products (accessed June 22, 2016).

47. http://www.neutrogena.com; Vanitha Swaminathan, Richard J. Fox, and Srinivas K. Reddy, "The Impact of Brand Extension Introduction on Choice," *Journal of Marketing* 65, no. 3 (2001), pp. 1–15.

48. Frito-Lay, "Snacks," http://www.fritolay.com/snacks (accessed February 8, 2017).

49. Rosellina Ferraro, Amna Kirmani, and Ted Matherly, "Look at Me! Look at Me! Conspicuous Brand Usage, Self-Brand Connection, and Dilution," *Journal of Marketing Research* 50, no. 4 (August 2013), pp. 477–88; Sanjay Sood and Kevin Lane Keller, "The Effects of Brand Name Structure on Brand Extension Evaluations and Parent Brand Dilution," *Journal of Marketing Research* 49, no. 3 (June 2012), pp. 373–82.

50. Ferraro et al., "Look at Me!"; Sharon Ng, "Cultural Orientation and Brand Dilution: Impact of Motivation Level and Extension Typicality," *Journal of Marketing Research* 47, no. 1 (February 2010), pp. 186–98.

51. Susan Spiggle, Hang T. Nguyen, and Mary Caravella. "More Than Fit: Brand Extension Authenticity," *Journal of Marketing Research* 49, no. 6 (2012), pp. 967–83; Franziska Völckner et al., "The Role of Parent Brand Quality for Service Brand Extension Success," *Journal of Service Research* 13, no. 4 (2010), pp. 379–96.

52. Mario Marsicano, "Cheetos Lip Balm & More Bizarre Brand Extensions," *The Wall Street Journal*, July 15, 2009.

53. Marriott, "Explore Our Brands," http://www.marriott.com /marriott-brands.mi (accessed February 8, 2017).

54. Kristen Laird, "Joe Fresh Begins Relationship With Barbie," http://www.marketingmag.ca/english/news/marketer/article .jsp?content=20101103_164846_9592 (accessed April 27, 2011).

55. David Friend, "Tim Hortons® Pulling Cold Stone Creamery Ice Cream From Canadian Stores," *The Canadian Press*, February 20, 2014, http://www.ctvnews.ca/business/tim-hortons-pulling -cold-stone-creamery-ice-cream-from-canadian-stores-1.1695303 (accessed June 22, 2016).

56. Aaker, *Building Strong Brands*.

57. Keller, *Strategic Brand Management*.

58. "NASCAR Launches New Stock Car Racing Series in Canada and National Title Sponsorship Agreement With Canadian Tire," http://www.newswire.ca/en/releases/archive/September2006/12 /c5003.html; Jeff Appone, "Canadian Tire Ending Partnership With Canadian NASCAR Series," *The Globe and Mail*, February 17, 2015, http://www.theglobeandmail.com/globe-drive/news /motorsports/canadian-tire-looking-to-end-partnership-with -canadian-nascar-series/article23023894/ (accessed February 9, 2017).

59. Keller, *Strategic Brand Management*.

60. This Entrepreneurial Marketing box was written with information gathered in a telephone interview with Elysia Vandenhurk Secord of Three Farmers; The Greater Saskatoon Chamber of Commerce, "Celebrate Success! Announces 2016 Award Recipients," May 19, 2016, http://celebrate-success.ca/images /EmbargoedMediaRelease_2016CelebrateSuccessAwards _May192016.pdf (accessed June 22, 2016).

61. Jamie Matsusow, "The Estée Lauder Companies—Beauty Company of the Year: Excellence in Packaging," *BeautyPackaging*, January 27, 2014, http://www.beautypackaging.com/issues/2014-01/view _features/the-estee-lauder-companies-beauty-company-of-the -year-excellence-in-packaging (accessed February 9, 2017).

62. "Microsoft, Waste Management, The Coca-Cola Company and More at Sustainability in Packaging 2014," *Sustainability in Packaging*, January 6, 2014, http://www.smitherspira.com /news/2014/january/companies-at-sustainability-in-packaging -2014 (accessed June 23, 2016).

63. Sheila Shayon, "Unilever Makes Progress on Sustainable Living Plan," *Brand Channel*, November 24, 2015, http://www .brandchannel.com/2015/11/24/unilever-sustainability-112415; Sheila Shayon, "Unilever Urges Consumers to Rethink Recycling and Fight 'Bottle Bias'," *Brand Channel*, April 20, 2016, http:// www.brandchannel.com/2016/04/20/unilever-recycling-042016; Unilever, "Our Sustainability Journey: How Far Have We Come?" May 12, 2016, https://www.unilever.com/sustainable-living /sustainable-living-news/news/Our-sustainability-journey-how -far-have-we-come.html (accessed June 23, 2016).

64. Kate Little, "Chobani Yogurt Is Latest Victim in Shrinking Grocery Case," *CNBC*, January 4, 2014, http://www.cnbc .com/2014/01/04/chobani-yogurt-is-latest-victim-in-shrinking -grocery-case.html (accessed June 23, 2016).

65. Susan Berfield, "Brand Oprah Has Some Marketing Lessons," *Bloomberg Businessweek*, May 19, 2011, http://www.bloomberg .com/news/articles/2011-05-19/brand-oprah-has-some-marketing -lessons (accessed June 23, 2016).

66. Ibid.

67. Luisa Kroll and Kerry Dolan, "The World's Billionaires," *Forbes*, March 1, 2016, https://www.forbes.com/billionaires/; "America's Richest Self-Made Women," *Forbes*, https://www.forbes.com /self-made-women/list/ (accessed February 9, 2017).

68. Sara Krulwich, "Oprah Winfrey," *The New York Times*, May 25, 2011, http://topics.nytimes.com.

69. "The Dr. Oz Show," *Oprah Radio*, June 3, 2011, http://www.oprah .com; "The Dr. Laura Berman Show," *Oprah Radio*, June 1, 2011, http://www.oprah.com.

70. "eCirc for Consumer Magazines," *Alliance for Audited Media*, http://abcas3.auditedmedia.com/ecirc/magtitlesearch.asp (accessed June 23, 2016).

71. Alessandra Stanley, "Among the Lectures, a Bit of Shtick," *The New York Times*, October 14, 2011, http://www.nytimes.com /2011/10/15/arts/television/the-rosie-show-and-oprahs-lifeclass -on-own.html (accessed June 23, 2016).

72. Oprah's Lifeclass, Oprah.com, http://www.oprah.com (accessed June 23, 2016).

73. Tierney Sneed, "'Lindsay' Just as Much About Oprah's Recovery as Lindsay Lohan's," *U.S. News & World Report*, March 5, 2014, http://www.usnews.com/news/articles/2014/03/05/lindsay-just -as-much-about-oprahs-recovery-as-lindsay-lohans (accessed June 23, 2016).

## CHAPTER 10

1. This opening vignette was written with information gathered in a telephone interview with Heather Murphy, co-founder, GoTire, on Friday June 21, 2013.

2. "Why GoTire?" http://www.gotirefranchise.com (accessed June 29, 2016).

3. Bruce Davis, "GoTire Evaluating Options for U.S. Launch," July 22, 2015, http://www.tirebusiness.com/article/20150722 /NEWS/150729960/go-tire-evaluating-options-for-u-s-launch (accessed June 29, 2016).

4. "Service Sector Key to Canada's Economic Growth, Bank of Canada Governor Says," *The Canadian Press*, November 28, 2016, http://www.cbc.ca/news/business/stephen-poloz-service -sector-bank-governor-canada-1.3871928 (accessed March 1, 2017).

5. Calgary Poop Troop, "Common Questions," http:// calgarypooptroop.com/questions; *Poop Patrol*, "FAQ," http://www.poop-patrol.com/faq.html; (http://www.cbc.ca/news /canada/nova-scotia/halifax-dog-poop-cleaning-companies -taking-care-of-business-1.3048401; Scoopy Doo, "How Does It Work?"http://www.scoopydoo.ca/how-does-it-work.html; Scoopy Doo, "The Poop Patrol," http://scoopydoodoo.com/about-us/ (accessed July 1, 2016).

6. Valarie A. Zeithaml, A. Parasuraman, and Leonard L. Berry, *Delivering Quality Service: Balancing Customer Perceptions and Expectations* (New York: The Free Press, 1990).

7. "MyFinanceTracker From RBC a First for Canada," http://www .clickweekly.com/articles/June1_2010/RBC.htm (accessed June 29, 2016).

8. Konrad Yakabuski, "The Greatest Canadian Company on Earth," *Report on Business Magazine* (September 2007), p. 57.

9. Choice Hotels, "Special Guest Policies," http://www.choicehotels .com.

10. Andrew Adam Newman, "A Gym for People Who Don't Like Gyms," *The New York Times*, January 2, 2013, http://www.nytimes .com.

11. Rebecca Harris, "Confident Customers," http://www .marketingmag.ca/magazine/current/in_context/article .jsp?content=20060410_76174_76174 (accessed June 17, 2007).

12. Megan Griffith-Greene, "Self-Checkouts: Who Really Benefits From the Technology?" *CBC News*, January 28, 2016, http:// www.cbc.ca/news/business/marketplace-are-you-being- served-1.3422736 (accessed June 29, 2016).

13. Cineplex, "2016 First Quarter," March 31, 2016, http://irfiles .cineplex.com/reportsandfilings/annuallyquarterlyreports/2016 /CineplexQ1Report2016-FINAL.pdf (accessed June 29, 2016).

14. Karen Pulla, "Top Five Fitness Trends for 2016: YMCA Simcoe/ Muskoka," *The Barrie Examiner*, February 14, 2016, http://www .thebarrieexaminer.com/2016/02/14/top-five-fitness-trends -for-2016-ymca-simcoemuskoka (accessed June 29, 2016).

15. Andrew Willis, "Sports Fan Munchies Fatten Cineplex's Bottom Line," http://www.theglobeandmail.com/servlet/story/LAC .20070104.RCINEPLEX04/TPStory/Entertainment; "Air Canada Centre Tickets," http://aircanadacentre.ticketoffices.com (accessed March 1, 2017).

16. Velofix, "About Us," http://www.velofix.com/; " Velofix Announces 50th Franchise Sold," June 8, 2016, http://www.velofix.com/velofix -announces-50th-franchise-sold/; Bob Vrbanac, "Shifting Into High Gear," *The Waterloo Chronicle*, May 11, 2016, http://www .waterloochronicle.ca/news-story/6548796-shifting-into-high-gear/; BDC, "Franchising Accelerates Growth for Bike Repair Firm," https:// www.bdc.ca/en/articles-tools/business-strategy-planning/manage -growth/pages/one-company-growth-story.aspx; Mary Teresa Bitti, "How a $300,000 *Dragons' Den* Deal Is Setting Velofix on the Road to Growth," *The Financial Post*, November 30, 2014, http://business .financialpost.com/entrepreneur/deal-with-dragon-sets-mobile -repair-shop-on-road-to-growth-2 (accessed June 29, 2016).

17. The discussion of the service gap model and its implications draws heavily from Michael Levy and Barton A. Weitz, *Retailing Management*, 6th ed. (Burr Ridge, IL: Irwin/McGraw-Hill 2007) and also is based on Deon Nel and Leyland Pitt, "Service Quality in a Retail Environment: Closing the Gaps," *Journal of General Management* 18 (Spring 1993), pp. 37–57; Zeithaml, Parasuraman, and Berry, *Delivering Quality Customer Service*; Valerie Zeithaml, Leonard Berry, and A. Parasuraman, "Communication and

Control Processes in the Delivery of Service Quality," *Journal of Marketing* 52, no. 2 (April 1988), pp. 35–48.

18. Velitchka D. Kaltcheva, Robert D. Winsor, and A. Parasuraman, "Do Customer Relationships Mitigate or Amplify Failure Responses?" *Journal of Business Research* 66, no. 4 (2013), pp. 525–32; Ruth N. Bolton, Anders Gustafsson, Janet McColl-Kennedy, Nancy J. Sirianni, and K. Tse David, "Small Details That Make Big Differences: A Radical Approach to Consumption Experience as a Firm's Differentiating Strategy," *Journal of Service Management* 25, no. 2 (2014), pp. 253–74; Lance A. Bettencourt, Stephen W. Brown, and Nancy J. Sirianni, "The Secret to True Service Innovation," *Business Horizons* 56, no. 1 (2013), pp. 13–22.

19. Zeithaml et al., *Services Marketing*.

20. Rebecca Harris, "Marketing 2.0," http://www.marketingmag.ca /brands/marketing-2-0-19444 (accessed June 29, 2016).

21. Michael Hinshaw, "The Real Value in Voice of the Customer: The Customer Experience," *CMO*, March 29, 2016, http://www.cmo .com/opinion/articles/2016/3/29/the-real-value-in-voice-of-the -customer-the-customer-experience.html (accessed June 29, 2016).

22. Janelle Barlow, "A Complaint Is a Gift, Using Customer Feedback as a Strategic Tool," http://www.tmius.com/ (accessed June 29, 2016).

23. "Customer Commitment," Delta, www.delta.com; "Delta Customers to Benefit From New Employee Training, Technology, Seasonal Hiring," *Delta News Hub*, http://news.delta.com/delta -customers-benefit-new-employee-training-technology-seasonal -hiring; Lauren Colby, "Delta Beefs Up Diversity Training for Crews Amid Tension," January 17, 2017, https://www.bloomberg .com/news/articles/2017-01-17/delta-adds-diversity-training-for -flight-crews-as-tensions-rise (accessed March 1, 2017).

24. Vanessa Lu, "WestJet's CEO May Be Big Boss, but Emphasizes Team Attitude," *The Star*, May 28, 2012, https://www.thestar .com/business/2012/05/28/westjets_ceo_may_be_big_boss_but _emphasizes_team_attitude.html (accessed March 1, 2017).

25. WestJet, "2015 Annual Report," www.westjet.com/pdf /investorMedia/financialReports/WestJet2015AR.pdf (accessed June 29, 2016).

26. Joe Castaldo, "Just Be Nice: Providing Good Customer Service," http://www.canadianbusiness.com/managing/strategy/article .jsp?content=20061009_81513_81513 (accessed June 17, 2007).

27. "On-Time Performance," *WestJet*, https://www.westjet.com/ en-ca/about-us/media-investor-relations/on-time-performance (accessed March 1, 2017).

28. *Skytrax*, "The World's Best Low-Cost Airlines in 2015," http:// www.worldairlineawards.com/Awards/worlds_best_lowcost _airlines.html (accessed June 29, 2016).

29. Steven W. Rayburn, "Improving Service Employee Work Affect: The Transformative Potential of Work Design," *Journal of Services Marketing* 28, no. 1 (2014), pp. 71–81; Zhu et al., "Fix It or Leave It?"; Ying Hong, Hui Liao, Jia Hu, and Kaifeng Jiang, "Missing Link in the Service Profit Chain: A Meta-Analytic Review of the Antecedents, Consequences, and Moderators of Service Climate," *Journal of Applied Psychology* 98, no. 2 (2013), p. 237.

30. Blake Morgan, "Happy Employees Equals Happy Customers," March 4, 2015, *Forbes*, http://www.forbes.com/sites/blakemorgan /2015/03/04/happy-employees-equals-happy-customers /#15f553a75147 (accessed June 30, 2016).

31. "Canada's Best Employers 2015: How The Keg Keeps Its Sizzle," *Canadian Business*, November 10, 2014, http://www .canadianbusiness.com/lists-and-rankings/best-jobs/2015 -best-employers-keg-restaurants/ (accessed June 29, 2016).

32. "About Travelocity," Travelocity, https://www.travelocity.ca /p/about (accessed March 1, 2017).

33. *J.D. Power*, "Travelocity.com Ranks Highest in Overall Satisfaction Among Online Travel Agencies," April 30, 2014, http://www

.jdpower.com/press-releases/2014-online-travel-agency -satisfaction-report (accessed June 30, 2016).

34. Wency Leung, "Why Remote Workouts Are the Next Big Thing," *The Globe and Mail*, April 8, 2013, http://www.theglobeandmail .com/life/health-and-fitness/why-remote-workouts-are-the-next -big-thing/article10823458 (accessed July 18, 2014).

35. Kirsten Acuna, "Google Says It Can Predict Which Films Will Be Huge Box Office Hits," *Business Insider*, June 6, 2013.

36. Brodie Thomas, "McDonald's Rolls Out Touchscreen Order Kiosks in Calgary," *Calgary Metro*, November 26, 2015, http:// www.metronews.ca/news/calgary/2015/11/26/mcdonalds -rolls-out-touchscreen-order-kiosks-in-calgary.html (accessed June 30, 2016).

37. David Streitfeld, "Faking It to Make It: A Beautiful Try," *The New York Times*, January 27, 2012, http://bits.blogs.nytimes .com/2012/01/27/faking-it-to-make-it-a-beautiful-try/?scp520& sq5customer%20service&st5cse; "Yelp, Google and UrbanSpoon Targets for Fake Reviews," *CBC News*, November 7, 2014, http:// www.cbc.ca/news/business/yelp-google-and-urbanspoon -targets-for-fake-reviews-1.2826154; Ben Rubin Fox, "Amazon Continues Crackdown on Alleged Fake Reviews," *Cnet*, April 25, 2016, http://www.cnet.com/news/amazon-continues-crack-down -on-alleged-fake-reviews-site/; "How Yelp Is Weeding Out Fake Reviews," *CBS News*, May 3, 2016, http://www.cbsnews.com /news/yelp-behind-the-scenes-consumer-protections-eliminate -fake-reviews/ (accessed June 29, 2016).

38. Zhu et al., "Fix It or Leave It?"; María Leticia Santos-Vijande, Ana María Díaz-Martín, Leticia Suárez-Álvarez, and Ana Belén del Río-Lanza, "An Integrated Service Recovery System (ISRS): Influence on Knowledge-Intensive Business Services Performance," *European Journal of Marketing* 47, no. 5/6 (2013), pp. 934–63.

39. Christian Grönroos and Päivi Voima, "Critical Service Logic: Making Sense of Value Creation and Co-creation," *Journal of the Academy of Marketing Science* 41, no. 2 (2013), pp. 133–50; Anne L. Roggeveen, Michael Tsiros, and Dhruv Grewal, "Understanding the Co-Creation Effect: When Does Collaborating With Customers Provide a Lift to Service Recovery?" *Journal of the Academy of Marketing Science* 40, no. 6 (2012), pp. 771–90.

40. "About Us," http://www.zipcar.com/about (accessed March 28, 2017).

41. "Zipcar Media Kit Backgrounder," http://zipcar.mediaroom.com /media-kit (accessed July 29, 2013).

42. April Kilcrease, "A Conversation With Zipcar's CEO Scott Griffith," *GigaOM*, December 5, 2011, http://gigaom.com /cleantech/a-conversation-with-zipcars-ceo-scott-griffith (accessed July 18, 2014).

43. "Zipcar Overview," http://www.zipcar.com/press/overview (accessed March 28, 2017).

44. United States Securities and Exchange Commission, "Zipcar S-1 Filing," June 1, 2010, http://sec.gov/Archives/edgar/data/1131457 /000095013010001923/ds1.htm (accessed July 18, 2014).

45. Kilcrease, op. cit.

46. "Rates and Plans," http://www.zipcar.ca/check-rates/toronto (accessed June 30, 2016).

47. United States Securities and Exchange Commission, op. cit.

48. "Zipcar Canada Inc." *Livegreen Toronto*, http://www.livegreencard .ca/business/96 (accessed July 18, 2014).

49. Navigant, "Global Carsharing Services Revenue Is Expected to Reach $6.5 Billion in 2024," https://www.navigantresearch.com /newsroom/global-carsharing-services-revenue-is-expected-to -reach-6-5-billion-in-2024 (accessed June 30, 2016).

50. Robin Walters, "Zipcar Buys U.K. Car Sharing Company Streetcar for $50 Million," *TechCrunch*, April 21, 2010, https://techcrunch. com/2010/04/21/zipcar-streetcar/; "Zipcar Invests in Barcelona-Based Avancar," *PR Newswire*, December 18, 2011, http://www .prnewswire.com/news-releases/zipcar-invests-in-barcelona -based-avancar-79609022.html (accessed March 28, 2017).

51. http://www.zipcar.com.

52. Courtney Rubin, "How Will the IPO Market Treat Zipcar?" Inc. com, June 2, 2010, http://www.inc.com/news/articles/2010/06/zipcar-files-for-ipo.html (accessed July 18, 2014).

53. Guy Dixon, "Avis Overcomes Reservations With Purchase of Zipcar," *The Globe and Mail*, January 2, 2013, http://www.theglobeandmail.com/globe-investor/avis-overcomes-reservations-with-purchase-of-zipcar/article6841893 (accessed July 18, 2014).

54. "With Zipcar You Always Have a Window Seat," *Zipcar*, https://www.zipcar.ca/airports; Greg Keenan, "Zipcar Coming to Toronto's Pearson Airport," *The Globe and Mail*, May 2, 2013, http://www.theglobeandmail.com/report-on-business/zipcar-coming-to-torontos-pearson-airport/article11684468 (accessed March 28, 2017).

## CHAPTER 11

1. Serena Ng, "At P&G, New Tide Comes In, Old Price Goes Up," *The Wall Street Journal*, February 10, 2014, http://www.wsj.com/articles/SB10001424052702304450904579368852980301572 (accessed July 3, 2016).

2. Dale Buss, "P&G Looks to Wring More Value Out of Tide Brand With Lower-Priced Detergent," *BrandChannel*, September 4, 2013, http://brandchannel.com/2013/09/04/pg-looks-to-wring-more-value-out-of-tide-brand-with-lower-priced-detergent/ (accessed July 3, 2016).

3. Ng, "At P&G, New Tide Comes In."

4. P&G, "Tide," http://www.tide.com/en-CA/product/tide-simply-clean-fresh.jspx (accessed July 3, 2016).

5. Mae Anderson, "Procter & Gamble to Introduce Lower-Priced Tide Called 'Tide Simply Clean and Fresh' in 2014," *Canadian Business*, http://www.canadianbusiness.com/business-news/procter-gamble-to-introduce-lower-priced-tide-called-tide-simply-clean-and-fresh-in-2014/ (accessed July 3, 2016).

6. R. Suri and M. V. Thakor, "'Made in Country' Versus 'Made in County': Effects of Local Manufacturing Origins on Price Perceptions," *Psychology & Marketing* 30, no. 2 (2013), pp. 121–32; R. Suri, K. B. Monroe, and U. Koc, "Math Anxiety and Its Effects on Consumers' Preference for Price Promotion Formats," *Journal of the Academy of Marketing Science* 41, no. 3 (2013), pp. 271–82; Kent B. Monroe, *Pricing: Making Profitable Decisions*, 3rd ed. (New York: McGraw-Hill, 2003); Dhruv Grewal, Kent B. Monroe, and R. Krishnan, "The Effects of Price Comparison Advertising on Buyers' Perceptions of Acquisition Value and Transaction Value," *Journal of Marketing* 62 (April 1998), pp. 46–60.

7. "Rising Prices Greatest Factor in Grocery Purchase Decisions," *Nielsen*, August 21, 2012, http://www.nielsen.com/us/en/insights/news/2012/global-survey-says-rising-prices-greatest-factor-in-grocery-purchase-decisions.html; "Price Is Most Important Factor for Consumers, Whatever They May Say About Ethics," *Trade Extensions*, July 30, 2014, http://www.tradeextensions.com/news/2014/7/30/price-is-most-important-factor-for-consumers-whatever-they-may-say-about-ethics (accessed March 2, 2017).

8. Crentsil Kofi Agyekum, Huang Haifeng, and Amma Agyeiwaa, "Consumer Perception of Product Quality," *Scientific & Academic Publishing*, March 3, 2015, http://article.sapub.org/10.5923.j.m2economics.20150302.01.html (accessed March 2, 2017).

9. Dhruv Grewal et al., "Evolving Pricing Practices: The Role of New Business Models," *Journal of Product & Brand Management* 20, no. 7 (2011), pp. 510–13; Bang-Ning Hwang et al., "An Effective Pricing Framework in a Competitive Industry: Management Processes and Implementation Guidelines," *Journal of Revenue and Pricing Management* (November 2009); Robert J. Dolan, "Note on Marketing Strategy," *Harvard Business School Background Note* (November 2000), pp. 1–17.

10. Ethan Smith and Yukari Iwatani Kane, "Apple Changes Tune on Music Pricing," *The Wall Street Journal*, January 7, 2009, http://online.wsj.com/news/articles/SB123126062001057765 (accessed July 21, 2014).

11. Taylor Martin, "How to Share Spotify Premium With Your Family," *Cnet*, June 6, 2016, http://www.cnet.com/how-to/how-to-share-spotify-premium-with-your-family/ (accessed July 4, 2016).

12. Rick Stella and Brandon Widder, "Spotify vs. Apple Music: Who Wins the Ultimate Streaming Showdown?" *Digital Trends*, March 7, 2016, http://www.digitaltrends.com/music/apple-music-vs-spotify/ (accessed July 4, 2016).

13. "We Did It Again! Paradigm Wins *Inside Track*'s Best Price/Value Award," May 14, 2012, http://paradigmspeakers.blogspot.ca/2012/05/we-did-it-again-paradigm-wins-inside.html; "Paradigm: A Sensory Experience," https://www.paradigm.com/downloads/catalogs/Sensory_Experience_Catalog_Print_version.pdf (accessed July 3, 2016).

14. Clare O'Connor, "Two 24-Year-Old Women Raise $1.7M for Tech to Streamline Construction Projects," April 22, 2016, http://nytlive.nytimes.com/womenintheworld/2016/04/22/meet-the-24-year-old-women-streamlining-the-construction-industry/ (accessed July 4, 2016).

15. Peter Nowak, "How BridgIt's App Keeps Big Construction Projects on Time and Budget," *Canadian Business*, July 15, 2015, http://www.canadianbusiness.com/innovation/waterloo-startups-2015-bridgit/ (accessed July 4, 2016).

16. Lauren Lake, Keynote Speech at WIMin Ideathon, University of Waterloo, March 5, 2016.

17. Deidre Kelly, "Graduates' App for Tracking Construction Defects Takes Off," *The Globe and Mail*, December 24, 2014, http://www.theglobeandmail.com/report-on-business/small-business/sb-growth/the-challenge/graduates-app-for-tracking-construction-defects-takes-off/article22164725/; Andrea Bellemare and Danielle Kappele, "Kitchener Construction Tech Firm Bridgit Raises $2.2 Million in Seed Funding," *CBC News*, http://www.cbc.ca/news/canada/kitchener-waterloo/kitchener-construction-tech-firm-bridgit-raises-2-2-million-in-seed-funding-1.3544552 (accessed July 4, 2016).

18. Clare O'Connor, "Two 24-Year-Old Women Raise $1.7M For Tech To Streamline Construction Projects," April 22, 2016, http://nytlive.nytimes.com/womenintheworld/2016/04/22/meet-the-24-year-old-women-streamlining-the-construction-industry/ (accessed July 4, 2016).

19. Monroe, *Pricing: Making Profitable Decisions*.

20. Richard Blackwell and David Parkinson, "Why Tourism Is a Bright Spot," *The Globe and Mail*, February 13, 2016, p. B6.

21. "Dictionary," *American Marketing Association*, https://www.ama.org/resources/Pages/Dictionary.aspx?dLetter=C&dLetter=C (accessed March 2, 2017).

22. Barbara Shecter, "Canadian Banks Got Slightly Better Deal on Apple Pay: Source," *The Financial Post*, May 10, 2016, http://business.financialpost.com/news/fp-street/canadian-banks-got-slightly-better-deal-on-apple-pay-source (accessed July 4, 2016).

23. David Berman, "The Price of Apple Pay: A Hard Bargain for Canada's Banks," *The Globe and Mail*, May 10, 2016, http://www.theglobeandmail.com/report-on-business/big-banks-pay-a-steep-price-to-bring-apple-pay-to-canada/article29961276/ (accessed July 4, 2016).

24. Shane Dingman, "Five Things to Know About Using Apple Pay in Canada," *The Globe and Mail*, May 10, 2016, http://www.theglobeandmail.com/technology/tech-news/five-things-to-know-about-using-apple-pay-in-canada/article29953516/; Apple Pay, http://www.apple.com/ca/apple-pay/ (accessed July 4, 2016).

25. A.R. Rao, M.E. Bergen, and S. Davis, "How to Fight a Price War," *Harvard Business Review* 78 (March–April 2000), pp. 107–116; Luis Cabral, "We're Number 1: Price Wars for Market Leadership," July 2013, http://econ.msu.edu/seminars/docs/pwarsMay2013.pdf (accessed March 2, 2017).

26. Rao, Bergen, and S. Davis, "How to Fight a Price War."

27. *Merriam-Webster's Dictionary of Law*, https://www.merriam -webster.com/dictionary/gray%20market, (accessed March 2, 2017).

28. Marina Strauss, "McDonald's Canada Opens First Cafe to Take on Tim Hortons®, Starbucks," *The Globe and Mail*, December 9, 2015, http://www.theglobeandmail.com/report-on-business /mcdonalds-canada-opens-first-mccafe-standalone-in-toronto /article27653086/; Brenda Bouw, "McDonald's Gets Social Over Coffee Grams," *Marketing Magazine*, February 29, 2016, http:// www.marketingmag.ca/consumer/mcdonalds-gets-social-over -coffee-grams-169176 (accessed March 2, 2017).

29. Marina Strauss, "Sears Canada to Adjust Prices Daily in Bid to Return to Profit," *The Globe and Mail*, June 9, 2016, p. B3.

30. Mason Wright, "Online Sources Gain, but CD Still Reigns," *The Globe and Mail*, August 6, 2012: R3.

31. "Walmart Launches Major Initiative to Make Food Healthier and Healthier Food More Affordable," http://walmartstores .com/pressroom/news/10514.aspx; Stephanie Rosenbloom, "At Walmart, Labeling to Reflect Green Intent," *The New York Times*, July 16, 2009; Stephanie Rosenbloom, "Wal-Mart to Toughen Standards," *The New York Times*, October 22, 2008; Adam Aston, "Walmart: Making Its Suppliers Go Green," *BusinessWeek*, May 18, 2009; Anne D'Innocenzio, "Walmart Goes Eco as Shoppers Seek Green Items," *The Associated Press*, November 5, 2016, https://www.pressreader.com/canada/waterloo-region-rec ord/20161105/282132111007688 (accessed March 2, 2017).

32. Sustainable Plant Staff, "Walmart's 2012 Sustainability Report Talks Softly About Suppliers," *Sustainable Plant*, April 19, 2012, http://www.sustainableplant.com/2012/04/walmart-s-2012 -sustainability-report-talks-softly-about-suppliers; Walmart "2016 Global Responsibility Report," http://corporate.walmart .com/2016grr/enhancing-sustainability/moving-toward-a-zero -waste-future (accessed March 2, 2017).

33. Stephanie Rosenbloom, "Wal-Mart to Toughen Standards," *The New York Times*, October 22, 2008, http://www.nytimes .com/2008/10/22/business/22walmart.html?_r=0 (accessed June 23, 2017).

34. Simon Houpt and Steve Ladurantaye, "Kids: Not Coming Soon to a Theatre Near You," *The Globe and Mail*, October 16, 2012, p. B1; Cineplex Odeon, 2016 Annual Report, Management's Discussion & Analysis, http://irfiles.cineplex.com/reportsandfil- ings/annuallyquarterlyreports/2017/CGX_MDA_2016_FINAL.pdf (accessed March 2, 2017).

35. Thomas T. Nagle, John E. Hogan, and Joseph Zale, *The Strategy and Tactics of Pricing: A Guide to Growing More Profitability*, 5th ed. (Upper Saddle River, NJ: Pearson, 2010).

36. Michael Levy, Barton A. Weitz, and Dhruv Grewal, *Retailing Management*, 9th ed. (Burr Ridge, IL: Irwin/McGraw-Hill, 2014).

37. Abhijit Biswas et al., "Consumer Evaluations of Sale Prices: Role of the Subtraction Principle," *Journal of Marketing 77*, no. 4 (2013), pp. 49–66.

38. This section draws from Levy and Weitz, *Retailing Management*.

39. Nailya Ordabayeva and Pierre Chandon, "Predicting and Managing Consumers' Package Size Impressions," *Journal of Marketing 77*, no. 5 (2013), pp. 123–37; Xiaoyan Deng and Raji Srinivasan, "When Do Transparent Packages Increase (or Decrease) Food Consumption?" *Journal of Marketing 77*, no. 4 (2013), pp. 104–17; Sha Yang and Priya Raghubir, "Can Bottles Speak Volumes? The Effect of Package Shape on How Much to Buy," *Journal of Retailing 81*, no. 4 (2005), pp. 269–81.

40. "Competition Bureau Investigates HBC, Sears for Deceptive Mattress Marketing," *CBC News*, http://www.cbc.ca/news /business/competition-bureau-investigates-hbc-sears-for -deceptive-mattress-marketing-1.2967460; Solomon Israel, "Hudson's Bay Co. Misled Consumers on Mattress Prices, Says Competition Bureau," *CBC News*, http://www.cbc.ca/news /business/competition-bureau-hudsons-bay-mattress-1.3994068 (accessed March 2, 2017).

41. Comeptition Bureau, "Price-Related Representations," http:// www.competitionbureau.gc.ca/eic/site/cb-bc.nsf/eng/00522 .html#false (accessed July 3, 2016).

42. Steve Lohr, "Drafting Antitrust Case, F.T.C. Raises Pressure on Google," *The New York Times*, October 12, 2012, http://www .nytimes.com; Claire Cain Miller, "Europeans Reach Deal With Google on Searches," *The New York Times*, April 14, 2013, http://www.nytimes.com.

43. Ryan McQueeney, "Google's Antitrust Case in Europe, Explained," August 28, 2015, http://www.nasdaq.com/article /googles-antitrust-case-in-europe-explained-cm514694 (accessed July 3, 2016).

44. Joe Schneider, "Victory Is Sweet in BC Price-Fixing Case," *The Globe and Mail*, April 13, 2010: B13.

45. Jeff Gray, "Chocolate Fix: Three Charged in Alleged Pricing Scheme," *The Globe and Mail*, June 6, 2013, http://m. theglobeandmail.com/report-on-business/industry-news /the-law-page/chocolate-bar-executives-accused-of -price-fixing-in-canada/article12380660 (accessed July 18, 2014).

46. "Chocolate Companies to Pay $23.2M in Price-Fixing Class Action," *Canadian Press*, September 16, 2013, http://www .ctvnews.ca/business/chocolate-companies-to-pay-23-2m-in -price-fixing-class-action-1.1457685 (accessed July 3, 2016).

47. Tom Bawden, "Bloody Nose for OFT in Row Over Tobacco Price- Fixing," *The Independent (London)*,December 13, 2011, http:// www.independent.co.uk; "The Marlboro Cartel," http://www .smokingate.com.

48. "Chocolate Companies to Pay $23.2M in Price-Fixing Class Action," *Canadian Press*, September 16, 2013, http://www .ctvnews.ca/business/chocolate-companies-to-pay-23-2m-in -price-fixing-class-action-1.1457685 (accessed July 3, 2016).

49. Jeff Gray, "Chocolate Bar Price-Fixing Case Against Mars Dropped by Prosecutors," *The Globe and Mail*, September 10, 2015, http://www.theglobeandmail.com/report-on-business /industry-news/the-law-page/chocolate-price-fixing-charges -dropped-against-mars-others/article26308396/ (accessed July 3, 2016).

50. This case was written by Jeanne L. Munger (University of Southern Maine) in conjunction with the textbook authors Dhruv Grewal and Michael Levy, as a basis for class discussion rather than to illustrate effective or ineffective marketing practices.

51. Planet Fitness, "Planet Fitness Continues Successful Growth With Puerto Rico Expansion," November 9, 2013, http://www .planetfitness.com/news/planet-fitness-continues-successful -growth-puerto-rico-expansion (accessed July 3, 2016).

52. Planet Fitness, "Welcome to Planet Fitness," http://www .planetfitness.com/ (accessed July 3, 2016).

53. Andrew Adam Newman, "A Gym for People Who Don't Like Gyms," *The New York Times*, January 3, 2013 (accessed July 3, 2016).

54. Judith Ohikuare, "The Secret of Planet Fitness's Success," *Inc.*, February 2013, http://www.inc.com/magazine/201302/ju- dith-ohikuare/the-secret-of-planet-fitnesss-success.html (accessed July 3, 2016).

55. "Planet Fitness Continues Successful Growth."

56. Beth Kowitt, "The Southwest Airlines of the Gym Business," *Fortune*, November 21, 2013, http://fortune.com/2013/11/21/the -southwest-airlines-of-the-gym-business/ (accessed July 3, 2016).

57. Newman, "A Gym for People."

58. Mallory Schlossberg, "The Fastest-Growing Gym in America has $10 Memberships and Gives Out Free Pizza, Bagels, and Candy," *Business Insider*, December 12, 2015, http://www.businessinsider .com/planet-fitnesss-business-profile-2015-10 (accessed July 4, 2016).

59. Kowitt, "The Southwest Airlines."

## CHAPTER 12

1. Greg Besinger, "Amazon Wants to Ship Your Package Before You Buy It," *The Wall Street Journal*, January 17, 2014, http://blogs.wsj.com/digits/2014/01/17/amazon-wants-to-ship-your-package-before-you-buy-it/ (accessed July 5, 2016).

2. Based on Barton A. Weitz, "PenAgain Sells to Walmart," in Michael Levy and Barton A. Weitz, *Retailing Management*, 8th ed. (Burr Ridge, IL: McGraw-Hill/Irwin, 2012), pp. 564–565; http://www.Penagain.com; Gwendolyn Bounds, "The Long Road to Walmart," *The Wall Street Journal*, September 19, 2005, p. R1: Gwendolyn Bounds, "One Mount to Make It," *The Wall Street Journal*, May 30, 2006, p. B1.

3. This Entrepreneurial Marketing box was written with information gathered in a telephone interview with AWAKE Chocolate co-founder Matt Schnarr.

4. American Marketing Association Dictionary, https://www.ama.org/resources/Pages/Dictionary.aspx?dLetter=D (accessed March 9, 2017).

5. American Marketing Association Dictionary, https://www.ama.org/resources/Pages/Dictionary.aspx?dLetter=L. Definition from the Council of Logistics Management. (accessed March 9, 2017).

6. American Marketing Association Dictionary, https://www.ama.org/resources/Pages/Dictionary.aspx?dLetter=D (accessed March 9, 2017).

7. American Marketing Association Dictionary, https://www.ama.org/resources/Pages/Dictionary.aspx?dLetter=C (accessed March 9, 2017).

8. Canadian Franchise Association, "Franchising Fast Facts," http://www.cfa.ca/wp-content/uploads/2016/06/CFA_AR2016_FranchisingFastFacts.pdf (accessed July 5, 2016).

9. "Business With a Safety Net," *Sponsor Content: Franchises in the Globe and Mail*, February 17, 2017, p. F1.

10. Rachel Sam, "Warby Parker: No Blind Spots for the Company That's Revolutionizing Eyewear," *Harvard Business School Open Knowledge*, December 7, 2015, https://rctom.hbs.org/submission/warby-parker-no-blind-spots-for-the-company-thats-revolutionizing-eyewear/ (accessed July 6, 2016).

11. Steve Proulx, "Pascal Benaksas, ÖOM Ethikwear: Les Valeurs Avant l'Argent," *Canoe.ca*, November 7, 2014, http://fr.canoe.ca/argent/asurveiller/madeinquebec/archives/2014/07/20140711-113009.html (accessed April 4, 2017).

12. "Where It's Made," *Encircled*, https://www.encircled.ca/pages/ethically-made-clothing (accessed April 4, 2017).

13. "About Us," ÖOM, http://www.oom.ca/en/about-us/montreal-fashion.html (accessed April 4, 2017.

14. comScore, "2012 Digital Advertising Highlights," http://iabcanada.com/files/comScore_Various-Categories-Canada-IAB-Report_Feb-26-20131.pdf (accessed July 18, 2014).

15. "About Us, Eco-Responsible Fashion," ÖOM, http://www.oom.ca/en/about-us/eco-responsible-fashion.html (accessed April 4, 2017).

16. "About Us, Social Commitment," ÖOM, http://www.oom.ca/en/about-us/social-commitment.html (accessed April 4, 2017).

17. Donna Davis and Susan Golicic, "Gaining Comparative Advantage in Supply Chain Relationships: The Mediating Role of Market-Oriented IT Competence," *Journal of the Academy of Marketing Science* 38, no. 1 (2010), pp. 56–70; Beth Davis-Sramek, Richard Germain, and Karthik Iyer, "Supply Chain Technology: The Role of Environment in Predicting Performance," *Journal of the Academy of Marketing Science* 38, no. 1 (2010), pp. 42–55; Erin Anderson and Barton Weitz, "The Use of Pledges to Build and Sustain Commitment in Distribution Channels," *Journal of Marketing Research 29* (February 1992), pp. 18–34.

18. Kyle Stock and Venessa Wong, "Chipotle: The Definitive Oral History," http://www.bloomberg.com/graphics/2015-chipotle-oral-history/ (accessed June 3, 2016).

19. Ibid.

20. *Millennial Marketing*, "Millennial Target: Chipotle Has Fresh Appeal," http://www.millennialmarketing.com/2009/09/millennial-target-chipotle-has-fresh-appeal/ (accessed June 3, 2016).

21. *Fundable*, "Chipotle Startup Story," https://www.fundable.com/learn/startup-stories/chipotle (accessed June 3, 2016).

22. Chipotle, "2015 Annual Report," http://ir.chipotle.com/phoenix.zhtml?c=194775&p=irol-reportsAnnual (accessed June 3, 2016).

23. Sarah Whitten, "CDC Declares Chipotle-Linked *E. coli* Outbreak Over," http://www.cnbc.com/2016/02/01/cdc-declares-chipotle-linked-e-coli-outbreak-over.html (accessed June 3, 2016).

24. Ibid.

25. Susan Berfield, "Inside Chipotle's Contamination Crisis," http://www.bloomberg.com/features/2015-chipotle-food-safety-crisis/ (accessed June 3, 2016).

26. *Bloomberg*, "Chipotle Sales Plunged 36% in January," http://www.bloomberg.com/news/videos/2016-02-03/chipotle-sales-plunged-36-in-january (accessed June 3, 2016).

27. *Chipotle*, "Chipotle Commits to Become Industry Leader in Food Safety," http://ir.chipotle.com/phoenix.zhtml?c=194775&p=irol-newsArticle&ID=2120228 (accessed July 6, 2016).

28. Mark Miller, "Burritos With Benefits: Chipotle Seeks Growth With Limited Loyalty Program," http://www.brandchannel.com/2016/06/28/chipotle-chiptopia-loyalty-program-062816/ (accessed July 6, 2016).

29. *Independent Equity Research Corp.*, "Coastal Contacts Inc. Update Report" (eResearch coastal contacts.pdf), http://eresearch.ca/profile.asp?companyID=437 (accessed June 24, 2010).

30. Sabrina Maddeaux, "Vision Quest," *The Globe and Mail*, June 25, 2016, p. 5.

31. Mary Biti, "Clearly a Winning Strategy," http://investors.coastalcontacts.com/mediacoverage.asp?ticker=T.COA&report=show&id=6151&lang=EN&title=null (accessed June 24, 2010).

32. Eve Lazarus, "Trevor Linden Plays With Clearly Contacts," http://www.marketingmag.ca/english/news/marketer/article.jsp?content=20100528_164119_13472 (accessed June 24, 2010).

33. Jennifer Horn, "Clearly Contacts Opens First Brick-and-Mortar Store," *Strategy Magazine*, February 14, 2013, http://strategyonline.ca/2013/02/14/clearlycontacts-ca-opens-first-brick-and-mortar-store/#ixzz2b0dipjvJ (accessed July 18, 2014).

34. Biti, "Clearly a Winning Strategy."

35. Clearly Facebook page, https://www.facebook.com/Clearly.ca (accessed July 6, 2016).

36. Sabrina Maddeaux, "Vision Quest," *The Globe and Mail*, June 25, 2016, p. 5.

37. "The Timeline," http://investors.coastalcontacts.com/custommessage.asp?ticker=t.coa&message=fifth&title=null (accessed August 8, 2013).

38. Jennifer Horn, "ClearlyContacts."

39. Sabrina Maddeaux, "Vision Quest," *The Globe and Mail*, June 25, 2016, p. 5.

40. Shirley Lichti, "Listing Fees Can Decide a Food Product's Fate," http://www.marketingmagic.ca/listing-fees-can-decide-a-products-fate.html (accessed March 9, 2017).

41. Eve Lazarus, "Martin's Puts New Apple Snack on Ontario Shelves," *Marketing Magazine*, July 2, 2013, http://www.marketingmag.ca/news/marketer-news/martins-puts-new-apple-snack-on-ontario-shelves-82737 (accessed July 18, 2014).

42. Frances Barrick, "Fruit Farm Bites Into New Market With Apple Chips," *The Record*, August 1, 2013, http://www.therecord.com/news-story/3915759-fruit-farm-bites-into-new-market-with-apple-chips (accessed August 7, 2013).

43. "Martin's Family Fruit Farm Apple Chips Now Available at Starbucks," *570NEWS*, January 13, 2015, http://www.570news.com/2015/01/13/martins-family-fruit-farm-apple-chips-now-available-at-starbucks/ (July 5, 2016).

44. Dale Buss, "Nespresso Sticks With Distribution Model Despite Increased Competition," *Brand Channel*, May 22, 2013, http://www.brandchannel.com/home/post/2013/05/22/Nespresso-Growth-052213.aspx (accessed July 18, 2014).

45. G. P. Kiesmüller and R. A. C. M. Broekmeulen, "The Benefit of VMI Strategies in a Stochastic Multi-Product Serial Two Echelon System," *Computers and Operations Research* 37, no. 2 (2010), pp. 406–16; Dong-Ping Song and John Dinwoodie, "Quantifying the Effectiveness of VMI and Integrated Inventory Management in a Supply Chain With Uncertain Lead-Times and Uncertain Demands," *Production Planning & Control* 19, no. 6 (2008), pp. 590–600; S. P. Nachiappan, A. Gunasekaran, and N. Jawahar, "Knowledge Management System for Operating Parameters in Two-Echelon VMI Supply Chains," *International Journal of Production Research* 45, no. 11 (2007), pp. 2479–505; Andres Angulo, Heather Nachtmann, and Matthew A. Waller, "Supply Chain Information Sharing in a Vendor Managed Inventory Partnership," *Journal of Business Logistics* 25 (2004), pp. 101–20.

46. This section draws from Levy and Weitz, *Retailing Management*, Chapter 10.

47. "David Chilton," *Speakers' Spotlight*, http://www.speakers.ca/speakers/david-chilton (accessed July 18, 2014).

48. "David Chilton," *The Lavin Daily*, http://www.thelavinagency.com/blog-finance-speaker-david-chilton-on-failure.html (accessed July 18, 2014).

49. Shirley Lichti, "Listing Fees Can Decide a Food Product's Fate," *The Record*, December 17, 2003, http://www.marketingmagic.ca/articles/ListingFees.htm (accessed July 18, 2014).

50. Vertica Bhardwaj and Ann Fairhurst, "Fast Fashion: Response to Changes in the Fashion Industry," *International Review of Retail, Distribution and Consumer Research* 20 (February 2010), pp. 165–73; Felipe Caro, Jérémie Gallien, Miguel Díaz Miranda, Javier García Torralbo, Jose Manuel Corrediora Corras, Marcos Montes Vazques, José Antonio Ramos Calamonte, and Juan Correa, "Zara Uses Operations Research to Reengineer Its Global Distribution Process," *Interfaces* 40 (2010), pp. 71–84; Carmen Lopez and Ying Fan, "Case Study: Internationalisation of the Spanish Fashion Brand Zara," *Journal of Fashion Marketing and Management* 13, no. 2 (2009), pp. 279–96; Mark Mulligan, "Spanish Professor Who Uncovers the Detail in Retail; Constant Contact With Corporate Life Is a Valuable Teaching Tool," *Financial Times*, August 18, 2008, p. 12; "Combining Art With Science, Zara Competes With 'Fast Fashion'," *SupplyChainBrain*, February 7, 2008.

51. Zeynep Ton, Elena Corsi, and Vincent Dessain, "Zara: Managing Stores for Fast Fashion," *Harvard Business School*, March 2011.

## CHAPTER 13

1. The details that follow were provided by Teresa Cugliari at Canadian Tire Corporation on February 3, 2017.

2. Details provided by Teresa Cugliari at Canadian Tire Corporation on February 3, 2017.

3. Russ Martin, "The 10 Most Reputable Brands in Canada," *Marketing Magazine*, May 10, 2016, http://www.marketingmag.ca/brands/the-10-most-reputable-brands-in-canada-174142 (accessed March 10, 2017).

4. "Canadian Tire Corporation, Limited," http://www.referenceforbusiness.com/history/Ca-Ch/Canadian-Tire-Corporation-Limited.html (accessed July 28, 2016).

5. "Canadian Tire Corporation, Limited."

6. Josh Kolm, "Canadian Tire Navigates a Reinvention," *Strategy Online*, July 8, 2015, http://strategyonline.ca/2015/07/08/canadian-tire-navigates-a-reinvention (accessed March 12, 2017).

7. Canadian Tire, "Awards & Recognition," http://corp.canadiantire.ca/EN/ABOUTUS/Pages/AwardsRecognition.aspx (accessed July 28, 2016).

8. Marina Strauss, "Canadian Tire's Innovative Digital Move Raises Sales," *The Globe and Mail*, May 12, 2016, http://www.theglobeandmail.com/report-on-business/canadian-tire-goes-back-to-the-future-with-innovative-new-print-catalogue/article29999871/ (accessed July 28, 2016).

9. Ibid.

10. National Retail Federation, "2017 Top 250 Global Powers of Retailing," January 16, 2017, https://nrf.com/news/2017-top-250-global-powers-of-retailing (accessed March 11, 2017).

11. Statistics Canada, "Table 1-1 Retail Sales by NAICS and by Region, Seasonally Adjusted (Current Periods)—Sales," http://www.statcan.gc.ca/pub/63-005-x/2015012/t032-eng.htm March 18, 2016; Josh O'Kane, "Swelling Household Debt Likely to Slow Consumer Spending: Conference Board," *The Globe and Mail*, February 23, 2017, http://www.theglobeandmail.com/report-on-business/economy/swelling-household-debt-likely-to-slow-consumer-spending-conference-board/article34116856/ (accessed March 11, 2017).

12. http://www.retailcouncil.org/news/media/profile/print/default.asp; Ed Strapagiel, "2016: A Recovery Year for Canadian Retail Sales," February 23, 2017, http://strapagiel.com/retail-sales-analysis-Canada.html (accessed March 11, 2017).

13. This chapter draws heavily from Michael Levy, Barton A. Weitz, and Dhruv Grewal, *Retailing Management*, 9th ed. (Burr Ridge, IL: McGraw-Hill/Irwin, 2015).

14. Pete's Fine Foods, http://petes.ca/; Patricia Brooks, "Pete's COO Wins Major Award," October 26, 2015, http://thechronicleherald.ca/business/1318922-pete's-coo-wins-major-award; Rai-Lee Garnder, Dietitans' Network Nova Scotia, http://www.dietitiansns.com/halifax-metro (accessed March 11, 2017).

15. Holt Renfrew, "About hr2," http://www.holtrenfrew.com/en/holt/twocolumn/footer/hr2/about-hr2; Marina Strauss, "Fashion Chains Eye Closings as Retailers Feel Pinch," February 28, 2017, *The Globe and Mail*, http://www.theglobeandmail.com/report-on-business/fashion-chains-eye-store-closings-as-retailers-feel-pinch/article34154092/ (accessed March 11, 2017).

16. Jeromy Lloyd, "Hudson's Bay Opens First Outlet Store Near Toronto," *Marketing Magazine*, August 1, 2013, http://www.marketingmag.ca/news/marketer-news/hudsons-bay-opens-first-outlet-store-near-toronto-85013; Amanda Phuong, "What's Happening to All the Hudson's Bay Outlets?" January 11, 2016, http://www.styledemocracy.com/whats-happening-to-all-the-hudsons-bay-outlets/ (accessed July 30, 2016).

17. Melissa Mancini, "Bargains at Winners Not Always What They Appear," *CBC News*, January 8, 2016, http://www.cbc.ca/news/business/winners-compare-at-prices-1.3393883.

18. Ibid.

19. Marketplace Blog, January 8, 2016, http://www.cbc.ca/marketplace/blog/company-response-winners (accessed July 29, 2016).

20. Ibid.

21. "TJ Maxx Sued Over 'Compare At' Prices," *ABC News*, July 23, 2015, http://abcnews.go.com/Business/tj-maxx-sued-compare-prices/story?id=32636566 (accessed July 29, 2016).

22. Marina Strauss, "The Bay Steps Up Its Game With a Focus on Shoes," *The Globe and Mail*, June 5, 2010: B3.

23. Marina Strauss, "New-Look Hudson's Bay Pushes Retail Growth Plan," *The Globe and Mail*, April 8, 2013, http://www.theglobeandmail.com/report-on-business/new-look-hudsons-bay-pushes-retail-growth-plan/article10836382 (accessed March 12, 2017).

24. Marina Strauss, "In Store Aisles, Dr. Dre Meets Big Data," *The Globe and Mail*, March 5, 2013, http://www.theglobeandmail.com/technology/business-technology/in-store-aisles-dr-dre-meets-big-data/article9302024 (accessed March 12, 2017).

25. Marina Strauss, "HMV Moves Beyond Music," *The Globe and Mail*, June 14, 2010: B1; *Canadian Press*, "Struggling HMV Canada Goes Into Receivership, Set to Close Stores," January 27, 2017, *CBC News*, http://www.cbc.ca/news/business/struggling-hmv-canada-goes-into-receivership-set-to-close-stores-1.3956302 (accessed March 12, 2017).

26. Canadian Tire, "The Canadian Tire App," http://www.canadiantire.ca/en/mobile.html (accessed July 30, 2016).

27. Megan Hynes, "Augmenting the Shopping Experience Reality," *Strategy Magazine*, July 16, 2012, http://strategyonline.ca/2012/07/16/augmenting-the-shopping-experience-reality (accessed July 30, 2016).

28. Nurun, "Building a Better Shopping Experience," http://www.nurun.com/en/our-thinking/future-of-retail/building-a-better-shopping-experience/ (accessed July 25, 2016).

29. Aimee Picchi, "How 'Smart Mirrors' Are Boosting Clothing Sales," *MoneyWatch*, May 13, 2015, http://www.cbsnews.com/news/how-smart-mirrors-are-boosting-clothing-sales/ (accessed July 25, 2016).

30. Leane Delap, "At the Body Shop, It's an Experience With the World," *The Globe and Mail*, May 28, 2012, http://www.theglobeandmail.com/report-on-business/industry-news/property-report/at-the-body-shop-its-an-experience-with-the-world/article4217870 (accessed March 12, 2017).

31. Marjo Johne, "Sport Chek Sprints Into Digital," *The Globe and Mail*, May 24, 2013, http://www.theglobeandmail.com/technology/tech-news/sport-chek-sprints-into-digital/article12098883 (accessed March 12, 2017).

32. Christopher Reynolds, "Sport Chek Blends Physical and Digital With New Square One Store," *The Star*, November 19, 2015, https://www.thestar.com/business/2015/11/19/sport-chek-blends-physical-and-digital-with-new-square-one-store.html (accessed July 25, 2016).

33. Ibid.

34. Michael Levy, Barton A. Weitz, and Dhruv Grewal, *Retailing Management*, 9th ed. (Burr Ridge, IL: McGraw-Hill/Irwin, 2015).

35. Paul Brent, "McLatte Anyone?" *Marketing Magazine*, December 10, 2007: 10; *Canadian Press*, "McDonald's Earmarks $1-Billion for Canadian Renovations," September 7, 2011, http://www.theglobeandmail.com/globe-investor/mcdonalds-earmarks-1-billion-for-canadian-renovations/article593454/ (accessed March 12, 2017).

36. Susan Krashinsky, "Beer Spruces Up in Battle for Market Share," *The Globe and Mail*, May 18, 2013, http://www.theglobeandmail.com/report-on-business/industry-news/marketing/beer-spruces-up-in-battle-for-market-share/article12000094 (accessed March 12, 2017).

37. MEC, "Sustainability by Design," https://www.mec.ca/en/explore/sustainability-innovation/; MEC, "2015 Annual Report," http://meccms.wpengine.com/wp-content/uploads/2016/05/2015-MEC-Annual-Report.pdf; MEC, "Our Environmental Commitment," https://www.mec.ca/en/explore/our-environmental-commitment/ (accessed July 29, 2016).

38. "Shelf Help: A Guide to Shopper Marketing," *Strategy Magazine* (July 2010), p. S56.

39. Rupal Parekh, "How Zara Ballooned Into a Multi-Billion Dollar Brand Without Advertising," *Advertising Age*, August 19, 2013, http://adage.com/article/cmo-strategy/zara-grew-a-multi-billion-dollar-brand-sans-ads/243730 (accessed August 20, 2013).

40. Matt Semansky, "Well.ca Opens Virtual Store in Toronto," *Marketing Magazine*, April 12, 2012, http://www.marketingmag.ca/news/marketer-news/well-ca-opens-virtual-store-in-toronto-49725 (accessed July 18, 2014).

41. Alicia Androich, "Walmart Canada and P&G Launch Bus Shelter Mobile Store," *Marketing Magazine*, June 5, 2013, http://www.marketingmag.ca/news/marketer-news/walmart-canada-and-pg-launch-bus-shelter-mobile-store-80530 (accessed July 18, 2014).

42. Rebecca Harris, "Amazeballs Creator Heads to *Dragons' Den*," *Marketing Magazine*, March 15, 2016, http://www.marketingmag.ca/brands/amazeballs-creator-heads-to-dragons-den-170193; Kelly McCarthy, "Almonte Entrepreneur Unveils Amazeballs Drink Chiller," *Inside Ottawa Valley*, July 29, 2015, http://www.insideottawavalley.com/news-story/5766414-almonte-entrepreneur-unveils-amazeballs-drink-chiller/; "They're Amazeballs," https://www.indiegogo.com/projects/amazeballs--3#/; Dan Fallak, "How I Monetized the Word Amazeballs," July 7, 2015, https://medium.com/@danfallak/how-i-monetized-the-word-amazeballs-a0b8a9e470b0#.o0z908e0y (accessed July 31, 2016).

43. Amit Shilton, "Convenience Is Key for Pizza Pizza's New App," *The Globe and Mail*, April 5, 2011: B9; Pizza Pizza, "Pizza Pizza's Mobile Family," http://www.pizzapizza.ca/Mobile/ (accessed March 12, 2017).

44. "Demystifying the Online Shopper, 10 Myths of Multi-Channel Retailing," PricewaterhouseCoopers, http://www.pwc.com/ca/multichannelshopping (accessed July 31, 2016).

45. Forester, "Canadian Online Retail Forecast, 2014 To 2019," October 14, 2014, https://www.forrester.com/report/Canadian+Online+Retail+Forecast+2014+To+2019/-/E-RES115497 (accessed July 25, 2016).

46. Jeff Fraser, "Infographic: Canadians Want In-Store Mobile Offers, But Only If They're Relevant," *Marketing Magazine*, July 19, 2013, http://www.marketingmag.ca/news/marketer-news/infographic-canadians-want-in-store-mobile-offers-but-only-if-theyre-relevant-84006; Accenture Consulting, "Retail Customers Are Shouting—Are You Adapting?" February 1, 2016, https://www.accenture.com/t20160201T094645_w_/us-en/_acnmedia/PDF-7/Accenture-Adaptive-Retail-Research-Executive-Summary-V2.pdf%20-%20zoom=50 (accessed March 12, 2017).

47. Sherice Jacobs, "3 Ways Live Chat Software Can Improve Your Conversion Rates," *The Daily Egg*, July 23, 2013, http://blog.crazyegg.com (accessed July 31, 2016).

48. Accenture Consulting, "Retail Customers Are Shouting—Are You Adapting?" February 1, 2016, https://www.accenture.com/t20160201T094645_w_/us-en/_acnmedia/PDF-7/Accenture-Adaptive-Retail-Research-Executive-Summary-V2.pdf%20-%20zoom=50; Rebecca Harris, "Retailers Failing to Deliver on Mobile Services (Study)," *Marketing Magazine*, February 16, 2016, http://www.marketingmag.ca/media/retailers-failing-to-deliver-on-mobile-services-study-168125 (accessed July 31, 2016).

49. "Michael Kors Is Turning Instagram Into a Customer-Loyalty Vehicle," *Glossy*, http://www.glossy.co/instagram-effect/beyond-social-shopping-retailers-are-building-social-loyalty-programs (accessed July 31, 2016).

50. Rebecca Harris, "Roots Launches Virtual Showroom," *Marketing Magazine*, July 12, 2016, http://www.marketingmag.ca/brands/roots-launches-virtual-showroom-179185 (accessed July 31, 2016).

51. Andrew Jung, "Instagram's Answer to Social Media Advertising: Like2Buy," *B2C*, January 12, 2015, http://www.business2community.com/instagram/instagrams-answer-social-media-advertising-like2buy-01122471#OJUPZRFkMsDt6bf6.99 (accessed July 31, 2016).

52. Rebecca Harris, "American Express Data Shows Where Retailers Are Investing," *Marketing Magazine*, May 31, 2016, http://www.marketingmag.ca/consumer/american-express-data-shows-where-retailers-are-investing-175605 (accessed July 31, 2016).

53. Christian Homburg, Josef Vollmayr, and Alexander Hahn, "Firm Value Creation Through Major Channel Expansions: Evidence From an Event Study in the United States, Germany, and China," *Journal of Marketing*, 2014, http://dx.doi.org/10.1509/jm.12.0179.

54. Marina Strauss. "New Boxes on the Block," *The Globe and Mail*, August 3, 2013: B7; Hollie Shaw, "Online Sales Complement Brick-and-Mortar Retail, Harry Rosen CEO Says," *Financial Post*, August 1, 2013, http://business.financialpost.com/news/retail-marketing/online-sales-complement-brick-and-mortar-retail-harry-rosen-ceo-says (accessed July 31, 2016).

55. Hongshuang (Alice) Li and P. K. Kannan, "Attributing Conversions in a Multichannel Online Marketing Environment: An Empirical Model and a Field Experiment," *Journal of Marketing Research* 51 (February 2014), pp. 40–56.

56. "Demystifying the Online Shopper."

57. Rebecca Harris, "Aldo Ups Its Fashion Game for Fall," July 26, 2016, *Marketing Magazine*, http://www.marketingmag.ca/brands/aldo-ups-its-fashion-game-for-fall-180123 (accessed August 1, 2016).

58. Marina Strauss, "Aldo's Reboot," *The Globe and Mail*, March 14, 2016, http://www.theglobeandmail.com/report-on-business/aldos-reboot-a-shoe-giants-bold-next-steps/article29191757/ (accessed August 1, 2016).

59. Aldo Group, "Aldo Fights Aids," http://www.aldofightsaids.com/#thestory; Aldo, "Who We Are," http://www.aldogroup.com/about-us.html (accessed August 1, 2016).

60. "Aldo's Reboot."

61. Susan Krashinsky, "Aldo Seizes 'Put Up or Shut Up' Moment for Shoes," *The Globe and Mail*, February 27, 2014, http://www.theglobeandmail.com/report-on-business/industry-news/marketing/aldo-seizes-put-up-or-shut-up-moment-for-shoes/article17139623/ (accessed August 1, 2016).

62. "Aldo's Reboot."

63. Salesforce, "Aldo Steps Into the Future of Retail With Salesforce," http://www.salesforce.com/ca/customers/stories/aldo.jsp (accessed August 1, 2016).

64. Jennie Bell, "5 Things You Should Know About Aldo Group," *Footwear News*, August 10, 2015, http://footwearnews.com/2015/business/retail/aldo-group-shoes-stores-growth-initiatives-50729/; Bryan Pearson, "We Have A Bot For That: How Aldo, Frank + Oak Put The Shopper Experience In Context," *Forbes*, May 25, 2016, http://www.forbes.com/sites/bryanpearson/2016/05/25/we-have-a-bot-for-that-how-aldo-frank-oak-put-the-shopper-experience-in-context/#1838280b72ea (accessed August 1, 2016), and with direct input from the marketing department at ALDO Group (May 3, 2017).

65. Aldo, "Timeline," http://www.aldogroup.com/timeline.html (accessed August 1, 2016).

66. "Aldo's Reboot."

67. Russ Martin, "How Aldo Is Merging Retail Tech With Brick and Mortar," *Marketing Magazine*, October 11, 2016, http://www.marketingmag.ca/brands/how-aldo-is-merging-retail-tech-with-brick-and-mortar-184286 (accessed March 12, 2017).

68. Ibid.

69. Rebecca Harris, "How Aldo Got Engaged With Brides," *Marketing Magazine*, July 12, 2016, http://www.marketingmag.ca/brands/how-aldo-got-engaged-with-brides-179210 (accessed August 1, 2016).

## CHAPTER 14

1. Chris Powell, "Lauren Richards Puts Her 'Ladyballs' on the Line," *Marketing Magazine*, February 26, 2016, http://www.marketingmag.ca/media/lauren-richards-puts-her-ladyballs-on-the-line-169069 (accessed August 2, 2016).

2. David Brown, "Cannes 2016: Ladyballs Wins PRS Lion," *Marketing Magazine*, June 21, 2016, http://www.marketingmag.ca/cannes/cannes-2016-ladyballs-wins-pr-lion-177512 (accessed August 2, 2016).

3. "Lauren Richards Puts Her 'Ladyballs' on the Line."

4. Sonya Fatah, "Grabbing Life by the Lady Balls," *Strategy Online*, December 1, 2015, http://strategyonline.ca/2015/12/01/shes-got-some-lady-balls-2/ (accessed August 2, 2016).

5. Russ Martin, "Cannes 2016: 'Ladyballs' Wins Silver, Shortlisted in Glass," *Marketing Magazine*, June 19, 2016, http://www.marketingmag.ca/cannes/cannes-2016-ladyballs-wins-silver-shortlisted-in-glass-177036 (accessed August 2, 2016).

6. Patricia Kozicka, "'Got Ladyballs?' Ovarian Cancer Campaign a Bit Too 'Ballsy' for Some," *Global News*, January 6, 2016, http://globalnews.ca/news/2437188/got-ladyballs-ovarian-cancer-campaign-a-bit-too-ballsy-for-some/ (accessed August 2, 2016).

7. Terence Shimp and J. Craig Andrews, *Advertising Promotion and Other Aspects of Integrated Marketing Communications* (Boston: Cengage Learning, 2013).

8. Ibid.

9. Brendan Greeley, "World Cup Shootout: Can Nike Beat Adidas at Soccer?" *Bloomberg Businessweek*, May 15, 2014, http://www.businessweek.com.

10. Adidas, "Neo," http://www.adidas.com/us/content/selenagomez.

11. Tim Peterson, "Netflix's Subscriber Numbers Beat Estimates as It Spends More on Marketing," *Advertising Age*, January 20, 2015, http://adage.com/article/digital/netflix-s-marketing-costs-grow-subscriber-numbers/296670/ (accessed August 3, 2016).

12. Schonfeld and Associates, Inc., "2015 Ad-to-Sales Ratios," http://www.outburstadvertising.com/resources/adtosales.pdf (accessed August 4, 2016).

13. P&G, "Financial Highlights," 2016 Annual Report and Proxy, http://www.pginvestor.com/Financial-Highlights/Index?KeyGenPage=209707; Statista, "Advertising Expenditure of Procter & Gamble Worldwide From 2011 to 2016 (in Million U.S. Dollars)," https://www.statista.com/statistics/262022/advertising-expenditure-of-procter-und-gamble-worldwide/ (accessed June 28, 2017).

14. Theodore Levitt, *The Marketing Imagination* (New York: The Free Press, 1986).

15. George E. Belch and Michael A. Belch, *Advertising and Promotion: An Integrated Marketing Communications Perspective*, 10th ed. (New York: McGraw-Hill Education, 2015).

16. Kleenex, "Kleenex Anti-Viral Tissues," https://www.kleenex.com/en-ca/products/facialtissues/antiviral (accessed August 3, 2016).

17. AMA Dictionary, http://www.marketingpower.com/_layouts/Dictionary.aspx?dLetter=M (accessed March 13, 2017).

18. The Television Bureau of Canada, "Canadian Net Advertising Volume (NAV)"; the most recent information TVB has is for 2014: http://www.tvb.ca/pages/nav; "Net Advertising Volume," Think TV, http://thinktv.ca/wp-content/uploads/2016/11/thinktv_Net-Advertising-Revenue_2006-to-2015.pdf (accessed March 13, 2017).

19. "Net Advertising Volume," Think TV, http://thinktv.ca/wp-content/uploads/2016/11/thinktv_Net-Advertising-Revenue_2006-to-2015.pdf (accessed March 13, 2017).

20. Susan Krashinsky, "Award-Winning Ads Showcase Canadian Agencies' High-Profile Work," *The Globe and Mail*, February 18, 2016, http://www.theglobeandmail.com/report-on-business/industry-news/marketing/cassies-award-winners-showcase-ad-appeal-both-personal-and-political/article28805764/ (accessed August 2, 2016).

21. AMA Dictionary, https://www.ama.org/resources/Pages/Dictionary.aspx?dLetter=P (accessed March 13, 2017).

22. "Taking Cancer by the Ladyballs," *Strategy Magazine*, March/April 2017, http://strategyonline.ca/2017/02/22/cassies-gold-taking-cancer-by-the-ladyballs/ (accessed April 17, 2017).

23. Top Drawer, "Sustainability," http://www.topdrawercreative.com/who_sustainability.php#green-building (accessed August 3, 2016).

24. Howard Chang, "Corporate Social Responsibility—Marketing Hype or Real Change?" October 27, 2011, http://www.topdrawercreative.com/blog/corporate-social-responsibility-marketing-hype-or-real-change/ (accessed August 3, 2016).

25. Michelle Dipardo, "Top Drawer Creative Sets Up Shop for a Good Cause," *Marketing Magazine*, January 7, 2015, http://www.marketingmag.ca/advertising/top-drawer-creative-sets-up-shop-for-a-good-cause-134241 (accessed August 3, 2016).

26. Ibid.

27. "Sustainability."

28. IAB Canada, "2015 Actual + 2016 Estimated Canadian Internet Advertising Revenue Survey DETAILED REPORT," September 12, 2016, http://iabcanada.com/research/annual-internet-advertising-revenue-reports/ (accessed March 13, 2017).

29. Publishing 2.0, "Google AdWords: A Brief History of Online Advertising Innovation," http://publishing2.com/2008/05/27

/google-adwords-a-brief-history-of-online-advertising-innovation (accessed March 13, 2017).

30. Canadian Media Directors' Council, "Media Digest," 2015 2016," http://www.cmdcdigest.mozaicreader.com/2015-2016 (accessed March 13, 2017).

31. Arlene Dickinson, *Persuasion* (Harper Collins Publishers, 2011), p. 12.

32. Sarah Hamspon, "Arlene Dickinson Proves 'Emotion' Doesn't Have to Be a Dirty Word," *The Globe and Mail*, September 26, 2011, http://www.theglobeandmail.com/life/relationships /arlene-dickinson-proves-emotion-doesnt-have-to-be-a-dirty -word/article1361388 (accessed August 5, 2016).

33. "We'll Move Mountains for You," Venture Communications, http://www.openminds.ca (accessed August 1, 2013).

34. Carmel Kilkenny, "Arlene Dickinson Honoured With Doctorate at John Molson School of Business," http://www.rcinet.ca /en/2016/06/08/arlene-dickinson-honoured-with-doctorate -at-john-molson-school-of-business/ (accessed August 5, 2016).

35. "*Persuasion* Book Launch for Arlene Dickinson (Sept. 2011)," http://youinc.com/video/persuasion-book-launch-for-arlene -dickinson-sept-2011 (accessed August 6, 2013).

36. "Arlene Dickinson: What Was Your Worst Marketing Blunder and What Did You Learn from It?" *Financial Post*, July 29, 2013, http:// business.financialpost.com/2013/07/29/arlene-dickinson-what -was-your-worst-marketing-blunder-and-what-did-you-learn-from -it (accessed August 5, 2016).

37. Peter Kuitenbrouwer, "Life After the Den: Arlene Dickinson Heads Home to Calgary With a Dragon's Legacy," *Financial Post*, May 15, 2015, http://business.financialpost.com/entrepreneur/ life-after-the-den-arlene-dickinson-heads-home-to-calgary-with -a-dragons-legacy (accessed August 4, 2016).

38. http://online.wsj.com/article/SB10001424052748703481004 574646904234860412.html; George E. Belch and Michael A. Belch, *Advertising and Promotion: An Integrated Marketing Communications Perspective* (New York: McGraw-Hill, 2015).

39. Ruth Stevens, "Crash Course in Direct Marketing," http://www. marketingprofs.com/premium/seminar_detail.asp?adref=sems- rch&semid=104 (accessed August 14, 2014).

40. Canadian Media Directors' Council, "Media Digest."

41. Kashmir Hill, "How Target Figured Out a Teen Girl Was Pregnant Before Her Father Did," *Forbes*, February 16, 2012, http://www .forbes.com/sites/kashmirhill/2012/02/16/how-target-figured-out -a-teen-girl-was-pregnant-before-her-father-did/2/#1c06695c71cc (accessed August 3, 2016).

42. Yves Faguy, "Privacy in the Age of Big Data," *National*, November 11, 2014, http://www.nationalmagazine.ca/Articles/November -2014-Web/Privacy-in-the-age-of-Big-Data.aspx (accessed August 3, 2016).

43. Office of the Privacy Commissioner of Canada, "Legal informa- tion Related to PIPEDA," https://www.priv.gc.ca/leg_c/p_principle _e.asp (accessed August 3, 2016).

44. Susan Krashinsky, "Google Broke Canada's Privacy Laws With Targeted Health Ads, Watchdog Says," January 15, 2014, http:// www.theglobeandmail.com/technology/tech-news/google -broke-canadas-privacy-laws-with-targeted-ads-regulator-says /article16343346/ (accessed August 3, 2016).

45. Susan Krashinsky, "Advertisers to Open Up on Web-Usage Data Collection, Targeted Advertising," *The Globe and Mail*, September 17, 2013, http://www.theglobeandmail.com/report-on-business /industry-news/marketing/advertisers-to-open-up-on-web-use -data-collection-targeted-advertising/article14390838/#dashboard /follows/ (accessed August 3, 2016).

46. CRTC, "Frequently Asked Questions About Canada's Anti-Spam Legislation," http://crtc.gc.ca/eng/com500/faq500.htm (ac- cessed August 5, 2016).

47. "Rogers to Pay $200,000 Fine Under CRTC's Anti Spam Law," *Canadian Press*, November 23, 2015, http://www.marketingmag .ca/media/rogers-to-pay-200000-fine-under-crtcs-anti-spam -law-162131 (accessed August 8, 2016).

48. Canada Post, "Breaking Through the Noise," https://www .canadapost.ca/assets/pdf/blogs/CPC_BreakThruNoise _EN_150626.pdf (accessed August 2, 2016).

49. Russ Martin, "5 Tips for Mobile E-Mail Marketing," *Marketing Magazine*, June 30, 2013, http://www.marketingmag.ca/news /media-news/5-tips-for-mobile-e-mail-marketing-84815 (accessed August 14, 2014).

50. Heart & Stroke Foundation of Canada, "What We Do," http:// www.heartandstroke.ca/what-we-do/our-impact/our-story (accessed March 13, 2017).

51. Heart & Stroke Foundation of Canada, "Consolidated Financial Statements August 31, 2015," http://www.heartandstroke.ca/-/media /pdf-files/canada/financial-statements/heart-and-stroke-foundation -canada-2015-financialstatement.ashx (accessed March 13, 2017).

52. Canada Post, "Small Is Beautiful, if You Want to Break Through the Holiday Marketing Clutter," October 16, 2015, https://www .canadapost.ca/web/en/blogs/business/details.page?article =2015/10/16/mini-catalogues_brea&cattype=business&cat =directmail (accessed August 2, 2016).

53. "Direct Response Television," http://www.direct-response -television.com (accessed June 26, 2007).

54. "Unpausing SickKids' Lives," *Strategy Magazine*, November/ December 2016, http://strategyonline.ca/2016/11/03/strategy -awards-2016-shortlists-part-three/ (accessed March 13, 2017).

55. "About Rogers Centre—Venue Policies," http://www.rogerscentre .com/inaround/visitors_policies.jsp (accessed March 13, 2017).

56. Emily Wexler, "Marketer Survey 2012," *Strategy Magazine*, December 7, 2012, http://strategyonline.ca/2012/12/07/2012-mar- keter-survey (accessed August 14, 2014).

57. "Real Beauty Shines Through: Dove Wins Titanium Grand Prix 163 Million Views on YouTube," *Google Think Insights*, http:// www.thinkwithgoogle.com/case-studies/dove-real-beauty -sketches.html (accessed August 14, 2014).

58. MADD, "Car Heaven," http://madd.ca/pages/car-heaven/ (accessed August 4, 2016).

59. MADD Canada, "Cause Related Marketing," http://www.madd .ca/madd2/en/giving/giving_cause_related_programs.html (accessed March 13, 2017).

60. Jackie Huba, "A Just Cause Creating Emotional Connections With Customers," http://www.inc.com.

61. Blue Carreon, "The 2014 Oscars Best Dressed List," *Forbes*, March 2, 2014, http://www.forbes.com/sites/bluecarreon/2014/03 /02/the-2014-oscars-best-dressed-list/#69d8462936ed (accessed August 4, 2016).

62. Diego Rinallo and Suman Basuroy, "Does Advertising Spending Influence Media Coverage of the Advertiser?" *Journal of Marketing* 73 (November 2009), pp. 33–46; Carl Obermiller and Eric R. Spangenberg, "On the Origin and Distinctness of Skepticism Toward Advertising," *Marketing Letters* 11, no. 4 (2000), p. 311.

63. "Improving Lives," TOMS Shoes, http://www.toms.com/improving -lives (accessed March 13, 2017).

64. "Insight Argentina," One World 365, http://www.oneworld365 .org/company/insight-argentina (accessed March 13, 2017).

65. Yubo Chen, Scott Fay, and Qi Wang, "The Role of Marketing in Social Media: How Online Consumer Reviews Evolve," *Journal of Interactive Marketing* 25, no. 2 (May 2011), pp. 85–94.

66. Instagram, "joeybats19" https://www.instagram.com/joey- bats19/?hl=en; Facebook, "José Bautista," https://www.facebook .com/JoeyBats19/; Twitter, "José Bautista @joeybats," https:// twitter.com/joeybats19?lang=en (accessed August 5, 2016).

67. Canada Newswire, "Spoon Flip! José Bautista Coming to Cinnamon Toast Crunch and Golden Grahams Crunch Cereal

Boxes," May 2, 2016, http://www.newswire.ca/news-releases /spoon-flip-jose-bautista-coming-to-cinnamon-toast-crunch-and -golden-grahams-crunch-cereal-boxes-577832961.html (accessed August 5, 2016).

68. Rita Demontis, "Jays' Bautista Teams Up With Cereal Giant to Help Kids," *Toronto Sun*, May 2, 2016, http://www.torontosun .com/2016/05/02/jays-bautista-teams-up-with-cereal-giant-to -help-kids (accessed August 5, 2016).

69. Susan Krashinsky, "Can José Bautista Flip Consumers Back on to Cereal?" *The Globe and Mail*, May 2, 2016, http://www .theglobeandmail.com/report-on-business/industry-news /marketing/can-jose-bautista-flip-consumers-back-on-to -cereal/article29827597/ (accessed August 5, 2016).

70. Ibid.

71. "Spoon Flip! José Bautista Coming to Cinnamon Toast Crunch and Golden Grahams Crunch Cereal Boxes."

72. "Can José Bautista Flip Consumers Back on to Cereal?"

73. The Hollywood Reporter, "Justin Bieber Becomes First Artist to Top 2 Billion YouTube Views (Video)," November 2, 2011, http:// www.hollywoodreporter.com/news/justin-bieber-mistletoe-video -lady-gaga-256887 (accessed August 2, 2016).

74. "Justin Bieber," https://twitter.com/justinbieber; https://www .instagram.com/justinbieber; Gil Kaufman, "Justin Bieber Is the First Artist to Crack 10 Billion Views on Vevo," March 24, 2016, http://www.billboard.com/articles/news/7272496/justin-bieber -10-billion-views-vevo (accessed August 2, 2016).

75. Nathan Velayudhan, "Volvo Trucks Videos—From Hamsters to Van Damme," *Auto Express*, November 18, 2013, http://www .autoexpress.co.uk (accessed August 5, 2016).

76. Ibid.

77. Ibid.

78. Dale Buss, "Unapologetically, Volvo Aims Its New Campaign at True Believers," *Forbes*, April 15, 2013, http://www.forbes.com (accessed August 5, 2016).

79. Alexandra Bruell, "Volvo Consolidates Global Media With Mindshare," *Advertising Age*, February 24, 2014, http://adage .com (accessed August 5, 2016).

80. Ibid.

81. Ibid.

## CHAPTER 15

1. Russ Martin, "Look at This: Molson Makes Good on Its Promise," *Marketing Magazine*, January 6, 2016, http://www.marketingmag .ca/brands/look-at-this-molson-makes-good-on-its-promise-164913 (accessed August 9, 2016).

2. Josh Kolm, "Meet the New Brewmaster?" *Strategy Magazine*, April/May 2016, http://strategyonline.ca/2016/04/18/meet-the -new-brewmaster (accessed August 9, 2016).

3. Josh Kolm, "What's Next for Molson's Rooftop Rink?" *Strategy Online*, January 19, 2016, http://strategyonline.ca/2016/01/19 /whats-next-for-molsons-rooftop-rink/ (accessed August 9, 2016).

4. Josh Kolm, "Molson Canadian's Latest Grand Hockey Gesture," *Strategy Online*, January 8, 2016, http://strategyonline.ca/2016 /01/08/molson-canadians-latest-grand-hockey-gesture/ (accessed August 9, 2016).

5. Russ Martin, "How Molson Pulled Off Its Rooftop Rink," *Marketing Magazine*, January 19, 2016, http://www.marketingmag .ca/brands/how-molson-pulled-off-its-rooftop-rink-166089 (accessed August 9, 2016).

6. Dan Rosen, "Molson Canadian Builds Rooftop Rink in Toronto," NHL.com, January 18, 2016, https://www.nhl.com/news /molson-canadian-builds-rooftop-rink-in-toronto/c-798365 (accessed August 9, 2016).

7. E.K. Strong, *The Psychology of Selling* (New York: McGraw-Hill, 1925).

8. Belinda Luscombe, "How Disney Builds Stars," *Time*, November 2, 2009; Disney, "Disney Music Group," http://waltdisneystudios .com/corp/unit/72 (accessed August 10, 2016).

9. Daniel McGinn, "The Buzz Machine," *The Boston Globe*, May 11, 2015, https://www.bostonglobe.com/2015/05/11/keurig /LM4WD6w2xEg1Wgvsqmwt7O/story.html (accessed August 10, 2016).

10. Luiz Ann Javier and Marvin G. Perez, "Coffee Farmers Are Hurt by Single-Serving Pods Revolution in U.S.," *Bloomberg*, April 15, 2015, http://www.bloomberg.com/news/articles/2015-04-15 /the-coffee-revolution-is-just-too-efficient-for-hurting-farmers (accessed August 10, 2016).

11. Robert Ferdman, "The World's Growing Love Affair With the Most Wasteful Form of Coffee There Is," *Quartz*, March 30, 2014, http://qz.com/193138/the-worlds-growing-love-affair-with -the-most-wasteful-form-of-coffee-there-is/ (accessed August 10, 2016).

12. "The Truth About Single-Serve Coffee Will Make You Cringe," *RealCup*, June 6, 2016, http://realcup.com/en-ca/truth-single -serve-coffee-will-make-cringe/ (accessed August 11, 2016).

13. Mark Burgess, "Something to Make You Cringe (Because You Like It)," *Strategy*, June 28, 2016, http://strategyonline. ca/2016/06/28/something-to-make-you-cringe-because-you -like-it/ (accessed August 10, 2016).

14. "The First Recyclable K-Cup Pod Is Here," *Keurig Green Mountain*, June 7, 2016, http://www.keuriggreenmountain.com /en/OurStories/SustainabilityStories/FirstRecyclableKCupPod .aspx (accessed August 11, 2016).

15. http://popsop.com/wp-content/uploads/toyota_prius_plural_02 .jpg; http://www.youtube.com/watch?v5nUor4gdFoyg&feature- 5player_embedded#!; http://www.saatchi.com/news/archive /prius_goes_plural_through_new_integrated_campaign.

16. Jef I. Richards and Catherine M. Curran, "Oracles on 'Advertising': Searching for a Definition," *Journal of Advertising* 31, no. 2 (Summer 2002), pp. 63–77.

17. eMarketer.com, "Worldwide Ad Spending: eMarketer's Updated Estimates and Forecast for 2015–2020," October 27, 2016, https://www.emarketer.com/Report/Worldwide-Ad-Spending -eMarketers-Updated-Estimates-Forecast-20152020/2001916 (accessed March 14, 2017).

18. CNIB, "Protect Your Eyes. Wear a Pair," https://cni053.3he.ca /pdfs/CNI053_Plaintext_IG_Eng.pdf (accessed August 27, 2013).

19. Tulin Erdem, Michael Keane, and Baohong Sun, "The Impact of Advertising on Consumer Price Sensitivity in Experience Goods Markets," *Quantitative Marketing and Economics* 6 (June 2008), pp. 139–76; Xiaojing Yang and Robert E. Smith, "Beyond Attention Effects: Modeling the Persuasive and Emotional Effects of Advertising Creativity," *Marketing Science* 28 (September/ October 2009), pp. 935–49; Matthew Shum, "Does Advertising Overcome Brand Loyalty? Evidence From the Breakfast Cereal Market," *Journal of Economics and Management Strategy* 13, no. 2 (2004), pp. 77–85.

20. Susan Krashinsky, "Kobo Targets Mother in Biggest Ad Campaign Ever," *The Globe and Mail*, May 1, 2013, http://www.theglobeandmail .com/report-on-business/industry-news/marketing/kobo-targets -mothers-in-biggest-ad-campaign-to-date/article11669886; Kobo, "Our Company," https://www.kobo.com/aboutus?style=onestore& store=CA&language=en-CA&utm_source=rim&_store=ca-en (accessed August 10, 2016).

21. Ibid.

22. Ibid.

23. Megan Haynes, "The Strategic Milk Alliance Milks Every Store Moment," *Strategy Magazine*, July 15, 2013, http://strategyonline .ca/2013/07/15/the-strategic-milk-alliance-milks-every-store -moment (accessed August 25, 2014).

24. "Canadians Reminded to 'Milk Every Moment' in Strategic Milk Alliance Campaign via DDB Canada," June 13, 2013, http://www.campaignbrief.us/2013/06/canadians-reminded-to-milk-eve.html (accessed August 25, 2014).

25. "Got Milk," http://www.gotmilk.com/fun/decade/year_1993.html (accessed March 14, 2017).

26. "The Power of Product Placement," October 28, 2015, http://brandsandfilms.com/2015/10/the-power-of-product-placement/ (accessed March 14, 2017).

27. Jeanine Poggi and E. J. Schultz, "How Coca-Cola's *American Idol* Deal Transformed TV Advertising," *Advertising Age*, December 14, 2014, http://adage.com/article/media/coke-s-american-idol-deal-transformed-tv-advertising/296309/ (August 10, 2016).

28. Abe Sauer, "Announcing the 2016 Brandcameo Product Placement Awards," *Brand Channel*, February 24, 2016, http://brandchannel.com/2016/02/24/2016-brandcameo-product-placement-awards-022416/ (accessed August 10, 2016).

29. Ibid.

30. Abe Sauer, "Announcing the 2016 Brandcameo Product Placement Awards," *Brand Channel*, February 24, 2016, http://brandchannel.com/2016/02/24/2016-brandcameo-product-placement-awards-022416/ (accessed August 10, 2016).

31. Laura Hensley, "'The Sophie Effect': Gregoire Trudeau Putting Canada's Fashion Industry on the Map," *The National Post*, May 27, 2016, http://news.nationalpost.com/arts/weekend-post/the-sophie-effect-how-canadas-first-lady-is-helping-the-local-fashion-industry-blossom; Deidre Kelly, "The Sophie Grégoire Trudeau Coat: A Canadian Fashion Success Story," *The Globe and Mail*, July 14, 2016, http://www.theglobeandmail.com/report-on-business/economy/growth/the-sophie-gregoire-trudeau-coat-a-canadian-fashion-success-story/article30900639/ (accessed August 10, 2016).

32. Abe Sauer, "Avril Lavigne May Have Just Pulled Off the Greatest (and Worst) Product Placement of All Time," *Brand Channel*, August 20, 2013, http://www.brandchannel.com/home/post/2013/08/20/Avril-Lavigne-Product-Placement-Rock-N-Roll-082013.aspx (accessed August 15, 2014).

33. TVB, "Public Service Announcements," http://www.tvb.ca/pages/TCEPSA.htm (accessed August 10, 2016).

34. Matt Semansky, "Print Advertising Window Closing for Tobacco Companies," *Marketing Magazine*, June 24, 2009, http://www.tvb.ca/pages/TCEPSA.htm (accessed August 10, 2016).

35. Grant Robertson, "Tobacco Ban Stays, But Expect Ad Blitz Anyway," http://www.theglobeandmail.com/news/national/tobacco-ban-stays-but-expect-ad-blitz-anyway/article1088391/ (accessed March 14, 2017).

36. Jeff Gray, "Chatr Ads Misleading, Court Told," *The Globe and Mail*, May 14, 2013, p. B3.

37. Pete Evans, "Moose Knuckles Coat Maker Accused of Faking 'Made in Canada' Claims," *CBC News*, April 27, 2016, http://www.cbc.ca/news/business/moose-knuckles-1.3555250 (accessed August 10, 2016).

38. Chris Powell, "Reebok-CCM Ordered to Back Off Helmet Safety Claims," *Marketing Magazine*, January 8, 2016, http://www.marketingmag.ca/brands/reebok-ccm-ordered-to-back-off-helmet-safety-claims-165150 (accessed August 10, 2016).

39. Ibid.

40. Competition Bureau, "Reebok-CCM Ceases Certain Resistance Hockey Helmet Performance Claims," December 21, 2015, http://www.competitionbureau.gc.ca/eic/site/cb-bc.nsf/eng/04015.html (accessed August 10, 2016).

41. Susan Krashinsky, "Reebok-CCM to Cease Helmet Safety Claims After Competition Bureau Probe," *The Globe and Mail*, December 21, 2015, http://www.theglobeandmail.com/report-on-business/industry-news/the-law-page/reebok-reaches-agreement-with-competition-bureau-over-helmet-safety-claims/article27893245/ (accessed August 10, 2016).

42. "Reebok-CCM Ordered to Back Off Helmet Safety Claims."

43. Competition Bureau, "Bauer Ceases Certain RE-AKT Hockey Helmet Performance Claims," November 13, 2014, http://www.competitionbureau.gc.ca/eic/site/cb-bc.nsf/eng/03839.html (accessed August 11, 2016).

44. CDCA, "Coupon Redemption in Canada; Some Interesting Data," http://www.canadiandealsassociation.com/coupon-redemption-in-canada-some-interesting-data/ (accessed August 11, 2016).

45. Dana Ciak, "Interview With Wishabi," *University of Waterloo*, https://uwaterloo.ca/alumni/interview-wishabi (accessed August 9, 2016).

46. Murad Hemmadi, "Flipp CEO Wehuns Tan on the Personalized Future of Coupons," *Canadian Business*, July 11, 2016, http://www.canadianbusiness.com/innovation/change-agent/flipp-ceo-wehuns-tan-on-the-personalized-future-of-coupons/ (accessed August 9, 2016).

47. Shane Dingman, "Digital Flyer Company Flipp Raises $61-million," *The Globe and Mail*, April 14, 2016, http://www.theglobeandmail.com/technology/digital-flyer-company-flipp-raises-61-million/article29637850/ (accessed August 8, 2016).

48. Ibid.

49. "Toronto's Flipp Lands $61 Million Investment From General Atlantic," *Techvibes*, https://techvibes.com/2016/04/14/flipp-2016-04-14 (accessed August 8, 2016).

50. "Flipp and General Atlantic Announce Strategic Partnership," *Canadian Newswire*, April 14, 2016, http://www.newswire.ca/news-releases/flipp-and-general-atlantic-announce-strategic-partnership-575688471.html (accessed August 8, 2016).

51. Stephanie Clifford, "Web Coupons Know Lots About You, and They Tell," *The New York Times*, April 16, 2010.

52. This box is based on information taken from a personal telephone interview by Stacey Biggar with Pema Hegan, September 21, 2013.

53. Current subscribers provided by Dai Williams, Content Strategist + Community Lead, Checkout 51, March 2, 2017; Rob Engen, "Flipp vs. Checkout 51: Grocery App Comparison," *boomer and echo*, March 31, 2016, http://boomerandecho.com/flipp-vs-checkout-51-grocery-app-comparison/; Jennifer Horn, "Checkout51 Grows Staff, User Base," *Strategy Online*, http://strategyonline.ca/2014/04/16/checkout51-grows-staff-user-base (accessed August 11, 2016).

54. Jack Neff, "Old Spice Is Killing It on YouTube Again, But Sales Are Down Double-Digits," *AdAge*, August 4, 2011, http://adage.com/article/the-viral-video-chart/spice-killing-youtube-sales/229080.

55. The Canadian Press, "Tortoise Torte Finishes the Race First," *The Guelph Mercury*, August 20, 2013, http://www.guelphmercury.com/whatson-story/4038979-tortoise-torte-finishes-the-race-first (accessed March 16, 2017).

56. Annette Bourdeau, "Sport Chek, Contiki and Subaru Rally for Data," http://www.strategymag.com/articles/magazine/20070601/sportchek.html (accessed August 11, 2016).

57. Andrew Willis, "Cineplex Goes Big With Call of Duty Contest," *The Globe and Mail*, January 11, 2017, http://www.theglobeandmail.com/report-on-business/video-gaming-goes-big-league-with-cineplexs-call-of-duty-tournament/article33561747/ (accessed March 16, 2017).

58. Chris Powell, "Campbell's Opens Pop-Up Restaurant in Toronto," *Canadian Grocer*, February 2, 2016, http://www.canadiangrocer.com/top-stories/campbells-opens-pop-up-restaurant-in-toronto-61553 (accessed August 11, 2016).

59. Danny Kucharsky, "Lindt Brings Its Iconic Gold Bunny to Life," *Marketing Magazine*, March 17, 2016, http://www.marketingmag.ca/media/lindt-brings-its-iconic-gold-bunny-to-life-170350 (accessed August 11, 2016).

60. Dana Flavelle, "Best Buy Puts Stop to Mail-In Rebates," *The Toronto Star*, March 31, 2007, https://www.thestar.com/business

/2007/03/31/best_buy_puts_stop_to_mailin_rebates.html (accessed March 16, 2017).

61. Rebecca Harris, "Adidas Kicks Off All-Star Weekend With a Pop-Up Shop," *Marketing Magazine*, February 11, 2016, http://www.marketingmag.ca/brands/adidas-kicks-off-all-star-weekend-with-a-pop-up-shop-167944 (accessed August 11, 2016).

62. This section draws from Mark W. Johnston and Greg W. Marshall, *Relationship Selling*, 3rd ed. (Burr Ridge, IL: Irwin/McGraw-Hill, 2009) and Mark W. Johnston and Greg W. Marshall, *Relationship Selling and Sales Management*, 2nd ed. (Burr Ridge, IL: Irwin/McGraw-Hill, 2007).

63. 4DSales, "The Cost of a Sales Call," October 22, 2012, http://4dsales.com/the-cost-of-a-sales-call/ (accessed August 11, 2016).

64. Bill Stinnett, *Think Like Your Customer*, 1st ed. (Burr Ridge, IL: McGraw-Hill, 2004).

65. Michael Beverland, "Contextual Influences and the Adoption and Practice of Relationship Selling in a Business-to-Business Setting: An Exploratory Study," *Journal of Personal Selling and Sales Management* (Summer 2001), p. 207.

66. CES, "CES by the Numbers," https://www.ces.tech/Why-CES/CES-by-the-Numbers (accessed August 11, 2016).

67. CES, "CES Implements New Bag Restrictions, Enhanced Security Measures for CES 2016," https://www.ces.tech/News/Press-Releases/CES-Press-Release.aspx?NodeID=108c88bf-5d38-4f2c-a172-e6fd6d0ffa8a (accessed August 11, 2016).

68. Government of Canada, "Six Companies Pay $1.23 Million for Making Telemarketing Calls to Canadians," June 29, 2016, http://news.gc.ca/web/article-en.do?nid=1091989 (accessed August 11, 2016).

69. Barton A. Weitz, Harish Sujan, and Mita Sujan, "Knowledge, Motivation, and Adaptive Behavior: A Framework for Improving Selling Effectiveness," *Journal of Marketing* (October 1986), pp. 174–191.

70. Al Jury, "The Golden Ratio of Virtual Meetings to Face-to-Face," June 19, 2011, http://virtualteamsblog.com/2011/the-golden-ratio-of-virtual-meetings-to-face-to-face.

71. Card Hub, "Market Share by Credit Card Network," http://www.cardhub.com/edu/market-share-by-credit-card-network (accessed August 15, 2014).

72. YouTube.com, "1998—Commercial—Mastercard—Class Reunion—Priceless," http://www.youtube.com/watch?v=3dcxQ2dvqmc (accessed August 15, 2014).

73. MasterCard, "About Us," http://www.mastercard.com/corporate/ourcompany/about-us.html (accessed August 26, 2013).

74. MasterCard 2012 Annual Report, p. 8, http://investorrelations.mastercardintl.com/phoenix.zhtml?c=148835&p=irol-reportsannual (accessed August 26, 2013).

75. MasterCard Advisors, "Information Services," http://www.mastercardadvisors.com/information-services.html (accessed August 26, 2013).

76. YouTube.com, "1998—Commercial."

77. YouTube.com, "MasterCard Priceless Baseball (Commercial, 1997)," http://www.youtube.com/watch?v=Q_6stXKGuHo (accessed August 15, 2014).

78. Stuart Elliott, "MasterCard Revamps Print Ads," *The New York Times*, August 11, 2004.

79. Dale Buss, "'Priceless' Evolution: 5 Questions With MasterCard CMO Raja Rajamannar," *Brand Channel*, January 4, 2016, http://www.brandchannel.com/2016/01/04/5-questions-mastercard-010416/ (accessed August 11, 2016).

80. Stuart Elliott, "MasterCard Brings 'Priceless' to a Pricey Place," *The New York Times*, July 7, 2011; http://www.creditcardeducation.com/news/mastercard-offers-priceless-city-experiences.html.

81. MasterCard, "Torontonians Know Their City Is Unique, But Now It's Priceless!" November 7, 2011, http://newsroom.mastercard.com/canada/press-releases/torontonians-know-their-city-is-unique-but-now-its-priceless (accessed August 15, 2014).

82. MasterCard, "Priceless Toronto," https://www.priceless.com/toronto/Home (accessed August 15, 2014).

83. Shorty Awards, "Priceless Surprises," http://shortyawards.com/7th/pricelesssurprises (accessed August 11, 2016).

84. Ibid.

85. Mike Fletcher, "MasterCard Brings Priceless Campaign Into Digital Age," *M&M Global*, September 30, 2015, http://mandmglobal.com/mastercard-brings-priceless-campaign-into-the-digital-age/ (accessed August 11, 2016).

86. MasterCard Press Releases, "Dine Out With MasterCard and Support a Priceless Cause: Fighting Cancer," http://newsroom.mastercard.com/canada/press-releases/dine-out-with-mastercard-and-support-a-priceless-cause-fighting-cancer/ (accessed August 11, 2016).

87. Priceless Causes, "Dine Out With Your MasterCard and Help Raise Money for Stand Up to Cancer," https://www.priceless.com/standup (accessed August 11, 2016).

88. "MasterCard Brings Priceless Campaign Into Digital Age."

89. Ibid.

90. MasterCard 2015 Annual Report, p. 11, http://www.ezodproxy.com/mastercard/2016/ar/HTML1/mastercard-ar2015_0017.htm (accessed August 11, 2016).

91. Mark Burgess, "Staying Priceless," *Strategy Magazine*, April/May 2016, pp. 44–48.

## CHAPTER 16

1. Sarah Germano, "Under Armour Overtakes Adidas in U.S. Sportswear Market," *The Wall Street Journal*, January 8, 2015.

2. Ibid.

3. @UnderArmour, https://twitter.com/UnderArmour (accessed March 20, 2017).

4. @StephenCurry30, https://twitter.com/StephenCurry30 (accessed March 20, 2017).

5. @UnderArmour, https://twitter.com/UnderArmour (accessed March 20, 2017).

6. @StephenCurry30, https://twitter.com/StephenCurry30 (accessed March 20, 2017).

7. Yuyu Chen, "How Does Under Armour Differentiate Itself From Nike Via Digital Marketing?" *ClickZ*, October 30, 2015, https://www.clickz.com/clickz/news/2432655/how-does-under-armour-differentiate-itself-from-nike-via-digital-marketing (accessed March 21, 2017).

8. https://www.facebook.com/Underarmour/; Artemiss Berry, "How Under Armour and Warby Parker Win With Social Media," *National Retail Federation*, February 29, 2015, https://nrf.com/news/how-under-armour-and-warby-parker-win-social-media (accessed March 21, 2017).

9. Chen, "How Does Under Armour Differentiate Itself."

10. https://twitter.com/AskTeamUA/with_replies.

11. Pamela Vaughan, "72% of People Who Complain on Twitter Expect a Response Within an Hour," *HubSpot*, July 23, 2014, https://blog.hubspot.com/marketing/twitter-response-time-data (accessed March 21, 2017).

12. https://www.google.com/#q=under+armour.

13. Stuart Elliot, "Live Commercials Coming to 'Late Night,'" *The New York Times*, September 18, 2013; Jeanine Poggi, "Lexus to Air Live Ads, Fueled by Social Suggestions, During NBC's 'Late Night,'" *Advertising Age*, September 18, 2013; Chris Perry, "How Social Media Propelled Fallon's *Tonight Show* Takeover," *Forbes*, April 6, 2013; Twitter, "Jimmy Fallon," https://twitter.com/jimmyfallon; *YouTube*, "The Tonight Show Starring Jimmy Fallon," https://www.youtube.com/user/latenight (accessed August 12, 2016).

14. www.sephora.com.

15. https://www.youtube.com/user/sephora (accessed March 22, 2017).

16. Chris Barry, Rob Markey, Eric Almquist, and Chris Brahm (2011), "Putting Social Media to Work," Bain & Co.

17. Tim Nudd, "American Apparel, Gap Blasted for Hurricane Sandy Ad Fails," *Adweek*, October 30, 2012.

18. Seth Fendley, "7 Hilarious Twitter Brand Hashtag Fails," *HubSpot*, March 12, 2015, https://blog.hubspot.com/marketing/hilarious -twitter-brand-hashtag-fails (accessed March 22, 2107).

19. Evan LePage, "All the Social Media Advertising Stats You Need to Know," *HootSuite*, https://blog.hootsuite.com/social-media -advertising-stats/ (accessed March 20, 2017).

20. Ian Hardy, "Facebook Canada Head Jordan Banks Says the Social Network Is 'Just Getting Started'," *mobile syrup*, April 29, 2016, http://mobilesyrup.com/2016/04/29/facebook-canada-head -jordan-banks-says-the-social-network-is-just-getting-started/ (accessed August 13, 2016).

21. "Most Internet Users in Canada Dedicated to Using Facebook Daily," eMarketer.com, June 22, 2016, http://www.emarketer.com /Article/Most-Internet-Users-Canada-Dedicated-Using-Facebook -Daily/1014121 (accessed August 13, 2016).

22. Forever 21 Facebook Fan Page, http://www.facebook.com/#!/ Forever21?ref5ts.

23. Ibid.

24. FedEx Express Canada Facebook page, "Zoo Passes Contest," https://www.facebook.com/FedExCanada/app_134425496630143 (accessed August 15, 2014).

25. Susan Krashinsky, "Facebook Ups Efforts to Protect Ad Space," *The Globe and Mail*, August 10, 2016, page B3.

26. Andrew LaVallee, "Burger King Cancels Facebook Ad Campaign," *The Wall Street Journal*, January 15, 2009.

27. Sarah Frier, "Snapchat Passes Twitter in Daily Usage," *Bloomberg*, June 2, 2016, http://www.bloomberg.com/news/articles/2016-06 -02/snapchat-passes-twitter-in-daily-usage (accessed August 13, 2016).

28. Christopher Heine, "Snapchat Launches a Colossal Expansion of Its Advertising, Ushering in a New Era for the App," *AdWeek*, June 13, 2016, http://www.adweek.com/news/technology /snapchat-launches-colossal-expansion-its-advertising -ushering-new-era-app-171924 (accessed August 13, 2016).

29. Ibid.

30. Ibid.

31. "#LoveNotLike: Tiffany Becomes First Luxury Brand on Snapchat," *Brandchannel*, August 1, 2016, http://www.brandchannel.com/2016 /08/01/tiffany-snapchat-080116/ (accessed August 14, 2016).

32. Russ Martin, "Social Scanner: The State of Community Management," *Marketing Magazine*, April 23, 2014, http://www .marketingmag.ca/news/media-news/social-scanner-the-state-of -community-management-108361; "About Us," LinkedIn, https:// press.linkedin.com/about-linkedin (accessed March 20, 2017).

33. Alex Ryne, "Our Journey to 100K: How We Built an Always-On Content Strategy," *LinkedIn*, May 17, 2016, https://business. linkedin.com/marketing-solutions/blog/best-practices--con- tent-marketing/2016/our-journey-to-100k--how-we-built-an -always-on-content-strategy (accessed August 13, 2016).

34. Joe Hindy, "The Latest Social Share Numbers Are In and Google+ Isn't Doing So Well," AndroidAuthority.com, July 19, 2013, http:// www.androidauthority.com.

35. Violet Blue, "Forced Google Plus Integration on YouTube Backfires, Petition Hits 112,000," ZDNet.com, November 14, 2013, http://www.zdnet.com.

36. "Canada's Ad Market Continues Inexorable Shift to Digital," *eMarketer*, December 23, 2015, http://www.emarketer

.com/Article/Canadas-Ad-Market-Continues-Inexorable-Shift -Digital/1013379 (accessed August 14, 2016).

37. "Vidyard Customer Case Study: Taulia, How Taulia Uses Video to Be the Most Remarkable Supplier Financing Provider," http:// www.vidyard.com/resources (accessed August 15, 2014).

38. Ibid.

39. Jennifer Pepper, "Jill Rowley: Leveraging Video for Social Selling," *Thought Leadership*, http://www.vidyard.com/blog /jill-rowley-video-for-social-selling (accessed August 15, 2014).

40. Jessica Lee, "Twitter Reveals Which Tweets Get the Most Engagement," http://searchenginewatch.com/article/2335279 /Twitter-Reveals-Which-Tweets-Get-the-Most-Engagement -Study (accessed August 15, 2014).

41. Candace So, "Vidyard Adds HootSuite Hookup to Its Video Marketing Integration Powers," August 15, 2013, http://www .itbusiness.ca/news/vidyard-adds-hootsuite-hookup-to-its -video-marketing-integration-powers/41928 (accessed August 15, 2014).

42. M.P. Mueller, "Small Businesses That Understand Social Media," *The New York Times*, July 11, 2011, http://boss.blogs.nytimes .com/2011/07/11/small-businesses-that-understand-social-media.

43. Ibid.

44. David H. Freedman, "Debating the Merits of Facebook and Google+," *The New York Times*, February 7, 2012, http://boss. blogs.nytimes.com/2012/02/07/debating-the-merits-of-facebook- and-google.

45. Ross Blum, "Where Have All the Customers Gone?" p. 8.

46. Jeff Beer, "Jumping Out of a Plane Without a Parachute on Live TV Is One Helluva Gum Ad," *Fast Company & Inc*, July 29, 2016, http://www.fastcocreate.com/3062307/jumping-out-of-a-plane -without-a-parachute-on-live-tv-is-one-helluva-gum-ad (accessed August 13, 2016).

47. Diana Bradley, "How Gum Brand Stride Got Behind Luke Aikins' Record-Setting Parachute-less Jump," *PR Week*, August 1, 2016, http://www.prweek.com/article/1404245/gum-brand-stride -behind-luke-aikins-record-setting-parachute-less -jump#H7L1kKesDx9Jplzh.99 (accessed August 13, 2016).

48. Ibid.

49. Nathalie Tadena, "MondelēzMakes Moves to Look More Like a Media Company," *The Wall Street Journal*, May 31, 2016, http:// www.wsj.com/articles/mondelez-makes-moves-to-look-more-like -a-media-company-1464692402 (accessed August 13, 2016).

50. "How Gum Brand Stride Got Behind Luke Aikins' Record-Setting Parachute-less Jump."

51. "Daredevil Survives 25,000-Foot Jump Without Chute Over Simi Valley," *The Associated Press*, July 30, 2016, http://www.vcstar .com/news/local/simi-valley/sky-diver-prepares-for-simi-valley -free-fall-38bc558f-3861-5f8c-e053-0100007f02a8-388755401 .html (accessed August 13, 2016).

52. Craig Smith, "By The Numbers: 190+ Interesting Instagram Statistics (June 2016)," *DMR*, July 14 2016, http://expandedramblings.com /index.php/important-instagram-stats/ (accessed August 14, 2016).

53. Somini Sengupta, Nicole Perlroth, and Jenna Wortham, "Behind Instagram's Success, Networking the Old Way," *The New York Times*, April 13, 2012, http://www.nytimes.com/2012/04/14/technology /instagram-founders-were-helped-by-bay-area-connections .html?pagewanted=all&_r=2& (accessed August 14, 2016).

54. Shayndi Raice and Spencer E. Ante, "Insta-Rich: $1 Billion for Instagram," *The Wall Street Journal*, April 10, 2012, http://online .wsj.com/article/SB1000142405270230381540457733384037738167 0.html (accessed August 14, 2016).

55. Finlo Rohrer, "Vine: Six Things People Have Learned About Six- Second Video in a Week," *BBC News Magazine*, January 31, 2013, http://www.bbc.co.uk/news/magazine-21267741 (accessed August 14, 2016).

56. "What's the Big Knit?" http://thebigknit.co.uk/about (accessed August 16, 2014).

57. "Cumulative Total of Tumblr Blogs Between May 2011 and July 2016 (in millions)," *Statista*, http://www.statista.com/statistics/256235/total-cumulative-number-of-tumblr-blogs/; "Word Press Statistics," DMR, http://expandedramblings.com/index.php/wordpress-statistics/ (accessed August 14, 2016).

58. Mark W. Schaefer, "The 10 Best Corporate Blogs in the World," BusinessGrow.com, January 1, 2011, http://www.businessesgrow.com/2011/01/05/the-10-best-corporate-blogs-in-the-world.

59. "Twitter's Share of US Social Network Users Is Dropping," eMarketer.com, August 15, 2016, www.emarketer.com/Article/Twitters-Share-of-US-Social-Network-Users-Dropping/1014343?ecid=NL1003 (accessed August 15, 2016).

60. Marketing Charts Staff, "Majority of Top Brands Tweeting At Least 30 Times Per Week," August 19, 2013, http://www.marketingcharts.com/wp/interactive/majority-of-top-brands-tweeting-at-least-30-times-per-week-35991 (accessed August 14, 2016).

61. Allan Woods, "Chris Hadfield: The Superstar Astronaut Taking Social Media by Storm," *The Guardian*, February 22, 2013, http://www.theguardian.com/science/2013/feb/22/chris-hadfield-canada-superstar-astronaut (accessed August 15, 2014).

62. Dave Bolton, "Smartphones Are Now the Dominant Driver of Social Media," *arc*, July 16, 2015, https://arc.applause.com/2015/07/16/social-media-consumption-on-smartphones-2015/ (accessed August 14, 2016).

63. Mira Shenker, "Mobile Ad Spending Outpacing Digital: Report," *Marketing Magazine*, March 24, 2014, http://www.marketingmag.ca/news/marketer-news/mobile-ad-spending-outpacing-digital-report-105047 (accessed August 14, 2016).

64. "Worldwide Mobile App Revenues in 2015, 2015 and 2020 (in Billion U.S. Dollars)," *Statista*, http://www.statista.com/statistics/269025/worldwide-mobile-app-revenue-forecast/; "Mobile App Revenue Outlook Remains Healthy Despite Slowing Download Volumes and Smartphone Growth, According to IDC," *IDC*, May 9, 2016, https://www.idc.com/getdoc.jsp?containerId=prUS41240816 (accessed August 14, 2016).

65. "Seven Shades of Mobile," *AOL, BBDO, and InsightsNow! Report*, November 12, 2012, http://www.behaviorlens.com.

66. "Vision Statement: How People Really Use Mobile," *Harvard Business Review*, January–February 2013, https://hbr.org/2013/01/how-people-really-use-mobile (accessed August 14, 2016).

67. Ibid.

68. David Barboza, "A Popular Chinese Social Networking App Blazes Its Own Path," *The New York Times*, January 20, 2014.

69. "Vision Statement: How People Really Use Mobile."

70. Ibid.

71. Ibid.

72. Ibid.

73. Casey Newton, "Facebook Is Shutting Down Its Paper Newsreading App on July 29," *The Verge*, June 30, 2016, http://www.theverge.com/2016/6/30/12062124/facebook-paper-shutdown (accessed August 14, 2016).

74. "Vision Statement: How People Really Use Mobile."

75. Ashley Feinberg, "I Just Spent $236 on Candy Crush, Help," *Gizmodo*, August 7, 2013, http://www.gizmodo.com.

76. Stuart Dredge, "Candy Crush Saga: '70% of People on the Last Level Haven't Paid Anything,'" *The Guardian*, September 10, 2013, http://www.theguardian.com; "Candy Crush Saga Most Popular Game App on the Planet," *Metro*, January 30, 2014, http://www.metro.co.uk.

77. Josh Wolonick, "Here's How Big the In-App Purchases Market Is for Apple and Google," *Minyanville*, January 16, 2014, http://www.minyanville.com.

78. This Entrepreneurial Marketing box was written with information gathered in personal interviews with Phil Jacobson of PumpUp between April and July 2013, and August 2016.

79. "PumpUp: Workout Coach," https://itunes.apple.com/app/id573070442 (accessed March 20, 2017).

80. "PumpUp—Health & Fitness Community," *iTunes*, https://itunes.apple.com/ca/app/pumpup-health-fitness-community/id573070442?mt=8 (accessed August 15, 2016).

81. "Case Study: PumpUp", *Freycinet Ventures*, http://freycinetventures.com/case-studies/pumpup/ (accessed August 29, 2016).

82. Jessica Galang, "PumpUp App Aims to Be the Gym Buddy You've Always Wanted," *Techvibes*, April 10, 2015, https://techvibes.com/2015/04/10/pumpup-2015-04-10 (accessed August 14, 2016).

83. "PumpUp—Health & Fitness Community," *iTunes*, https://itunes.apple.com/ca/app/pumpup-health-fitness-community/id573070442?mt=8 (accessed August 15, 2016).

84. "Marketing Cloud," Salesforce.com, https://www.salesforce.com/ca/marketing-cloud/overview/ (accessed August 14, 2016).

85. Ibid.

86. "Algonquin College," Salesforce.com, https://www.salesforce.com/ca/customers/stories/algonquin.jsp (accessed August 14, 2016).

87. Ibid.

88. Laura S. Quinn and Kyle Andrei, "A Few Good Web Analytics Tools," May 19, 2011, http://www.techsoup.org/learningcenter/internet/page6760.cfm.

89. Christina Warren, "How to Measure Social Media ROI," October 27, 2009, http://mashable.com/2009/10/27/social-media-roi/.

90. "iNoobs: What Is Google Analytics?" http://inspiredm.com; http://www.google.com/analytics/features/index.html; http://www.advanced-web-metrics.com; Kevin Ryan, "What Can the Average Marketer Learn From Google Creative Lab?" *Advertising Age*, April 19, 2013.

91. Amy Porterfield, "3 Steps to an Effective Social Media Strategy," *Social Media Examiner*, March 1, 2012, http://www.socialmediaexaminer.com/3-steps-to-an-effective-social-media-strategy.

92. "Lay's Do Us a Flavour Campaign Returns, With a New Spin," *Food Canada*, February 25, 2016, http://www.foodincanada.com/food-in-canada/lays-contest-returns-with-a-new-spin-133339/ (accessed August 14, 2016).

93. Andy Shaw, "How to Create a Facebook Ad Campaign," *Social Media Tips*, September 23, 2011, http://exploringsocialmedia.com/how-to-create-a-facebook-ad-campaign.

94. Lauren Jung, "What Is the Best Alternative to Klout?" January 3, 2016, http://www.quora.com/What-is-the-best-alternative-to-Klout (accessed March 20, 2017).

95. Landman, "Are You a V.I.P.? Check Your Klout Score," *The New York Times*, November 18, 2011.

96. "Social Media Career Advice From Leading Marketers," http://www.onwardsearch.com/Social-Media-Career-Advice; Griffith, op. cit.

97. James Tomerson, "Looking for Job Opportunities in Social Media?" http://www.jobdiagnosis.com/myblog/social-media-jobs.htm.

98. "The Klout Score," http://klout.com/understand/score.

99. Seth Stevenson, "What Your Klout Score Really Means," *Wired*, April 24, 2012, http://www.wired.com/epicenter/2012/04/ff_klout.

100. Schaefer, op. cit.

101. Kashmir Hill, "Facebook Can Tell You If a Person Is Worth Hiring," *Forbes*, March 5, 2012, http://www.forbes.com/sites/kashmirhill/2012/03/05/facebook-can-tell-you-if-a-person-is-worth-hiring/?partner5yahoo.

102. Red Bull Stratos, "Scientific Data Review," http://www.redbullstratos.com (accessed August 14, 2016).

103. Rick Mulready, "The Secret to Red Bull's Media Success Is There Is No Secret," November 6, 2013, http://rickmulready.com (accessed August 14, 2016).

104. SocialBakers, "Red Bull Stratos on Social Media," http://www.socialbakers.com (accessed August 14, 2016).

105. Ibid.

106. Jack Bell, "Red Bulls' Henry Strikes a Pose, and Starts a Trend," *The New York Times*, September 21, 2013.

107. New York Red Bulls, MLS, http://www.newyorkredbulls.com/ (accessed August 14, 2016).

108. Clint Boulton, "Red Bull Eyes 'SoLoMo' Software to Grow Business," *The Wall Street Journal*, April 30, 2012.

109. Wall Street Journal Live, "Lunch Break: Interview With John Jurgensen," December 20, 2013, http://online.wsj.com.

110. David Moth, "How Red Bull Uses Facebook, Twitter, Pinterest, and Google+," eConsultancy.com, February 21, 2013, https://econsultancy.com/blog/62178-how-red-bull-uses-facebook-twitter-pinterest-and-google/ (accessed August 14, 2016).

## CHAPTER 17

1. Coca-Cola India, "Company History," http://www.coca-colaindia.com (accessed March 25, 2017).

2. Ratna Bhushan, "Coca-Cola Plans Aggressive Ad Campaign in 2014 to Be India's Favourite Soft Drink," *Economic Times*, January 1, 2014, http://economictimes.indiatimes.com/industry/services/advertising/coca-cola-plans-aggressive-ad-campaign-in-2014-to-be-indias-favourite-soft-drink/articleshow/28202832.cms (accessed August 16, 2016).

3. Nikhil Gulati and Rumman Ahmed, "India Has 1.2 Billion People, but Not Enough Drink Coke," *The Wall Street Journal*, July 13, 2012, http://www.wsj.com/articles/SB10001424052702304870304577490092413939410 (accessed August 16, 2016).

4. Ibid.

5. "Coca-Cola Shuts Down Three Bottling Plants in India Amid Severe Water Shortages," *FRSN*, March 11, 2016, https://fsrn.org/2016/03/coca-cola-shuts-down-three-bottling-plants-in-india-amid-severe-water-shortages/ (accessed August 16, 2016).

6. "Coca-Cola India Launches Ready-to-Drink Flavoured Milk Offering—VIO in Bangalore," Coca-Cola India, February 4, 2016, http://www.coca-colaindia.com/coca-cola-india-launches-ready-drink-flavoured-milk-offering-vio-bangalore/ (accessed August 16, 2016).

7. Business Development Bank of Canada, http://www.bdc.ca (accessed March 25, 2017).

8. Rose Yu and Colum Murphy, "In China, Air Pollution Rules Spur Big Car Purchases," *The Wall Street Journal*, August 7, 2013, http://www.wsj.com/articles/SB10001424127887323342060457865147107799 3746; Jun Yang, Ying Liu, Ping Qin, and Antung A. Liu, "A Review of Beijing's Vehicle Lottery," Environment for Development, January 2014, http://www.rff.org/files/sharepoint/WorkImages/Download/EfD-DP-14-01.pdf; "E-vehicles: No Lottery for License Plates!" Scout Real Estate, September 30, 2015, http://www.beijingrelocation.com/blog/e-vehicles-no-lottery-for-license-plates/ (accessed August 16, 2016).

9. http://www.whitespot.com (accessed April 25, 2011); Patrick Brethour, "Burgers Go From Burnaby to Bangkok" (interview with Warren Erhart, president of White Spot Restaurants), www.theglobeandmail.com/report-on-business/your-business/start/franchising/burgers-go-from-burnaby-to-bangkok/article1336289 (accessed March 25, 2017).

10. Roland Oliphant, "Ukraine Bans Russian Foods as Trade War Escalates," *The Telegraph*, January 3, 2016, http://www.telegraph.co.uk/news/worldnews/europe/ukraine/12078921/Ukraine-bans-Russian-foods-as-trade-war-escalates.html (accessed August 16, 2016).

11. Global Affairs Canada, http://www.international.gc.ca/eicb/softwood/menu-en.asp (accessed May 26, 2007).

12. "Canada Eliminates All Tariffs on Machinery, Equipment and Inputs Used in Industrial Mfg," *Manufacturing and Automation*, April 20, 2015, http://www.automationmag.com/industry-news/news/5148-canada-eliminates-all-tariffs-on-machinery-equipment-and-inputs-used-in-industrial-mfg (accessed August 16, 2016).

13. http://www.bloomberg.com/apps/news?pid=10000103&sid=ajtp-C2UYVKwk&refer=us.

14. Wikipedia, "Exchange Rate," http://en.wikipedia.org/wiki/Exchange_rate.

15. "Trade Agreements," Office of the United States Trade Representative, https://ustr.gov/trade-agreements (accessed March 25, 2017).

16. http://www.unescap.org/tid/mtg/postcancun_rterta.pps#1.

17. Bill Curry, "The ABCs of TPP," *The Globe and Mail*, January 25, 2016, http://www.theglobeandmail.com/report-on-business/international-business/what-is-tpp-understanding-the-new-pacific-tradedeal/article26648948/ (accessed August 18, 2016).

18. "Canada Balance of Trade," *Trading Economics*, http://www.tradingeconomics.com/canada/balance-of-trade (accessed August 18, 2016).

19. "US Balance of Trade," *Trading Economics*, http://www.tradingeconomics.com/united-states/balance-of-trade (accessed August 18, 2016).

20. http://siteresources.worldbank.org/DATASTATISTICS/Resources/GNIPC.pdf; Arthur O'Sullivan, Steven Sheffrin, and Steve Perez, *Macroeconomics: Principles and Tools*, 8th ed. (Upper Saddle River, NJ: Prentice Hall, 2013).

21. "World Population Clock," http://www.worldometers.info/world-population/ (accessed August 18, 2016).

22. "Oral Care in Brazil," *Euromonitor International*, June 2016, http://www.euromonitor.com/oral-care-in-brazil/report (accessed August 18, 2016).

23. "Laundry Care in India," *Euromonitor International*, March 2016, http://www.euromonitor.com/laundry-care-in-india/report (accessed August 18, 2016).

24. "The Rise of India's Middle New Class," *The Times of India*, July 25, 2016, http://timesofindia.indiatimes.com/india/The-rise-of-Indias-new-middle-class/articleshow/53377389.cms (accessed March 25, 2017).

25. "India," *The CIA World Factbook*, https://www.cia.gov/library/publications/the-world-factbook/geos/in.html (accessed August 18, 2016).

26. Sonya Misquitta, "Cadbury Redefines Cheap Luxury—Marketing to India's Poor, Candy Maker Sells Small Bites for Pennies," *The Wall Street Journal*, p. B4, June 8, 2009, http://online.wsj.com/article/SB124440401582092071.html (accessed August 15, 2014).

27. Melissa Ip, "Bottom of the Pyramid—a Decade of Observations," *Social Enterprise Buzz*, January 21, 2013, http://www.socialenterprisebuzz.com/2013/01/21/bottom-of-the-pyramid-a-decade-of-observation/ (accessed August 18, 2016).

28. Morgan Winsor, "Mobile Phones in Africa: Subscriber Growth to Slow Sharply as Companies Struggle to Reach Rural Populations and Offer Faster, Cheaper Services," *International Business Times*, October 15, 2015, http://www.ibtimes.com/mobile-phones-africa-subscriber-growth-slow-sharply-companies-struggle-reach-rural-2140044 (accessed August 18, 2016).

29. Kate O'Keeffe, "The Cheapest, Richest Casino in Macau," *The Wall Street Journal*, February 5, 2014.

30. Jack Neff, "Emerging-Market Growth War Pits Global Brand Giants Against Scrappy Local Rivals," *Ad Age*, June 13, 2011, http://adage.com/article/global-news/global-brand-giants-battle-scrappy-local-rivals/228142.

31. Philip R. Cateora, Mary C. Gilly, and John L. Graham, *International Marketing*, 17th ed. (New York: McGraw-Hill, 2015); Danielle Medina Walker and Thomas Walker, *Doing Business Internationally: The Guide to Cross-Cultural Success*, 2nd ed. (Princeton, NJ: Trade Management Corporation, 2003).

32. Karin Bosteels, "Ikea France Convicted for Illegal Sunday Openings," *Retail Detail*, September 7, 2014, https://www.retaildetail.eu/en/news/wonen/ikea-france-convicted-illegal-sunday-openings (accessed March 25, 2017).

33. Urs Geiser, "Sunday Shopping to Lure More Tourists," *Swiss Info*, February 18, 2015, http://www.swissinfo.ch/eng/consumer-boost_sunday-shopping-to-lure-more-tourists/41280070 (accessed March 25, 2017).

34. For a website dedicated to Hofstede's research, see http://www.geert-hofstede.com/. For research specific to Canada, see https://geert-hofstede.com/canada.html.

35. http://www.geert-hofstede.com (accessed September 10, 2006).

36. Note that the time orientation and indulgence dimensions are relatively more recent additions to the categorization. See Geert Hofstede, "Dimensions of National Cultures," http://geerthofstede.com/culture-geert-hofstede-gert-jan-hofstede/6d-model-of-national-culture/ (accessed March 25, 2017).

37. The Hofstede Centre, http://geert-hofstede.com/countries.html (accessed August 18, 2016).

38. James W. Carey, *Communication as Culture*, rev. ed. (New York: Routledge, 2009).

39. World Jewish Congress, "McDonald's Changes Logo in Israel to Show That Its Food Is Kosher," March 13, 2006, http://www.worldjewishcongress.org/en/news/mcdonalds-changes-logo-in-israel-to-show-that-its-food-is-kosher (accessed March 25, 2017).

40. Betsy McKay, "Procter & Gamble, Coca-Cola Formulate Vitamin Drinks for Developing Countries," *The Wall Street Journal*, https://www.wsj.com/articles/SB1006818282554536760 (accessed March 25, 2017).

41. "Japanese Mobile Phone Culture: Learning the Ins and Outs," *Sakura Mobile*, June 5, 2015, https://www.sakuramobile.jp/japan-travel-guide/japanese-mobile-phone-culture-learning-the-ins-and-outs/ (accessed August 18, 2016).

42. Geoffrey James, "20 Epic Fails in Global Branding," *Inc.*, October 29, 2014, http://www.inc.com/geoffrey-james/the-20-worst-brand-translations-of-all-time.html (accessed August 18, 2016).

43. Affan Chowdhry, "Pakistanis Turn to Canadian Solar Power," *The Globe and Mail*, July 15, 2013, http://www.theglobeandmail.com/news/world/pakistanis-turn-to-canadian-solar-power/article13239061 (accessed August 15, 2014).

44. About Us, http://www.bombardier.com/en/about-us.html (accessed March 25, 2017).

45. Bombardier, "Shaping the Future of Mobility, Responsibly," http://csr.bombardier.com/pdf/en/EDL_Bombardier_ENGLISH-mapL.pdf (accessed August 15, 2014).

46. *The Economist*, "Why Is South Africa Included in the BRICS?" March 29, 2013, http://www.economist.com/blogs/economist-explains/.

47. "Brazil," U.S. Department of State, July 29, 2015, http://www.state.gov/r/pa/ei/bgn/35640.htm (accessed August 18, 2016).

48. Prableen Bajpai, "The World's Top 10 Economies," *Investopedia*, February 8, 2017, http://www.investopedia.com/articles/investing/022415/worlds-top-10-economies.asp (accessed March 25, 2017).

49. "Brazil Economic Outlook," *FocusEconomics*, January 19, 2016, http://www.focus-economics.com/countries/brazil; "Brazil Economic Growth," *FocusEconomics*, January 19, 2016.

50. Asher Levine, "Brazil's 'New Middle Class' Struggles as Economy Plunges," Reuters, October 12, 2015, http://www.reuters.com/article/us-brazil-economy-fearsidUSKCN0S61QF20151012.

51. "Brazil Economic Outlook," *FocusEconomics*, January 19, 2016, http://www.focus-economics.com/countries/brazil; "Brazil Economic Growth," *FocusEconomics*, January 19, 2016.

52. "Russia," U.S. Department of State, March 28, 2014, http://www.state.gov/r/pa/ei/bgn/3183.htm (accessed August 18, 2016).

53. "India," U.S. Department of State, http://www.state.gov/p/sca/ci/in (accessed August 18, 2016).

54. Megha Bahree, "India Unlocks Door for Global Retailers, *The Wall Street Journal*, November 25, 2011.

55. "Retail Industry in India," India Brand Equity Foundation, March 2017, http://www.ibef.org/industry/retail-india.aspx (accessed March 25, 2017).

56. Ibid.

57. "China," U.S. Department of State, January 21 2015, http://www.state.gov/r/pa/ei/bgn/18902.htm (accessed August 18, 2016).

58. Marianne Wilson, "China Is Top Emerging Retail Market," *The New York Times*, June 1, 2015.

59. Jason Kincaid, "Mark Zuckerberg on Facebook's Strategy for China (and His Wardrobe)," *Tech Crunch*, October 16, 2010, https://techcrunch.com/2010/10/16/mark-zuckerberg-on-facebooks-strategy-for-china-and-his-wardrobe/; Loretta Chao, "Brazil: The Social Media Capital of the Universe," *The Wall Street Journal*, February 4, 2013, http://www.wsj.com/articles/SB10001424127887323301104578257950857891898; Normandy Madden, " What Will Facebook Find If It Ventures Into China?" *Advertising Age Global*, June 13, 2011, http://adage.com/article/global-news/facebook-find-ventures-china/228068/; Chloe Albanesius, "Human Rights Group Slams Facebook Over China Strategy," PCMag.com, June 3, 2011, http://www.pcmag.com/article2/0,2817,2386380,00.asp; "Leading Countries Based on Number of Facebook Users as of May 2016 (in millions)," *Statista*, http://www.statista.com/statistics/268136/top-15-countries-based-on-number-of-facebook-users/ (accessed August 16, 2016).

60. Lisa Evans, "Skin-Care Company Finds Canada Is Just the Tip of the Iceberg," *The Globe and Mail*, October 25, 2012, http://www.theglobeandmail.com/report-on-business/economy/canada-competes/skin-care-company-finds-canada-is-just-the-tip-of-the-iceberg/article4638073 (accessed August 15, 2014).

61. "About Christie," Christie, https://www.christiedigital.com/en-us/about-christie (accessed August 18, 2016).

62. This Entrepreneurial Marketing box was written with information gathered in a telephone interview with Hatem Jahshan, CEO, Steeped Tea, June 21, 2013.

63. Telephone interview with David Chilton, July 16, 2013.

64. "Canada's State of Trade: Trade and Investment Update—2015," Global Affairs Canada, http://www.international.gc.ca/economist-economiste/performance/state-point/state_2015_point/index.aspx?lang=eng (accessed August 18, 2016).

65. Harmeet Singh, "Tim Hortons® Heads to Southeast Asia," *Strategy Online*, July 28, 2016, http://strategyonline.ca/2016/07/28/tim-hortons-heads-to-southeast-asia; Jeromy Lloyd, "Tim Hortons Is Heading to Mexico," *Strategy Online*, January 27, 2017, http://strategyonline.ca/2017/01/27/tim-hortons-is-heading-to-mexico (accessed March 25, 2017).

66. http://www.whitespot.com (accessed April 25, 2011); Patrick Brethour, "Burgers Go From Burnaby to Bangkok" (interview with Warren Erhart, president of White Spot Restaurants), http://www.theglobeandmail.com/report-on-business/your-business/start/franchising/burgers-go-from-burnaby-to-bangkok/article1336289 (accessed August 15, 2014).

67. Canadian Franchise Association, "Fast Franchise Facts," http://www.cfa.ca/wp-content/uploads/2016/06/CFA_AR2016_FranchisingFastFacts.pdf (accessed August 18, 2016).

68. "Member Airlines," Star Alliance, http://www.staralliance.com/en/member-airlines (accessed August 18, 2016).

69. "Tesco Signs Deal For China Joint Venture," Sky News, July 5, 2016, http://news.sky.com/story/tesco-signs-deal-for-china-joint-venture-10403284 (accessed August 18, 2016).

70. Bertrand Marcotte, "Bombardier's $3.4-Billion Russian Gambit," *The Globe and Mail*, August 28, 2013, http://www.theglobeandmail.com/report-on-business/international-business/bombardier-deals-with-russia-could-total-34-billion/article13994479; Vanessa Lu, "Bombardier Puts Q400 Plant in Russia on Hold," *The Star*, October 30, 2014 (accessed August 18, 2016).

71. "Our Company," Nutralab, http://www.nutralab.ca (accessed August 18, 2016).

72. "Worldwide Presence," Bombardier, http://www.bombardier.com /content/bombardiercom/en/worldwide-presence.html (accessed August 18, 2016).

73. Juro Osawa and Lorraine Luk, "How Lenovo Built a Tech Giant," *The Wall Street Journal*, January 30, 2014, http://online.wsj.com; Juro Osawa and Yun-Hee Kim, "PC Firm Lenovo Hunts for Brazil Acquisitions," *The Wall Street Journal*, May 28, 2012, http://online .wsj.com (accessed August 18, 2016).

74. Brent Jang, "Setting Their Sights on U.S. Boomers," *The Globe and Mail*, February 14, 2013, https://secure .globeadvisor.com/servlet/ArticleNews/story/gam/20130214 /RBCOASTALEYEGLASSESJANGATL (accessed August 15, 2014).

75. "Thank You Mom," P&G, https://www.pgeveryday.com/tag/thank -you-mom (accessed August 18, 2016).

76. Julie Jargon, "Campbell Soup to Exit Russia," *The Wall Street Journal*, June 29, 2011, http://online.wsj.com/article/SB10001424 052702304447804576414202460491210.html (accessed August 20, 2014).

77. Normandy Madden, "Soy-Sauce-Flavored Kit Kats? In Japan, They're No. 1," http://adage.com/globalnews/article?article _id=142461 (accessed March 25, 2017).

78. http://www.pringles.it.

79. "McCain Around the World," http://www.mccain.com/around -the-world (accessed March 25, 2017).

80. Jonathan Foley, "Feed the World," *National Geographic*, http:// www.nationalgeographic.com/foodfeatures/feeding-9-billion/ (accessed August 19, 2016).

81. Andrew Winston, "How General Mills and Kellogg Are Tackling Greenhouse Gas Emissions," *Harvard Business Review*, June 2, 2016, https://hbr.org/2016/06/how-general-mills-and-kellogg -are-tackling-greenhouse-gas-emissions (access August 19, 2016).

82. Food and Agriculture Organization of the United Nations, "2050: A Third More Mouths to Feed," http://www.fao.org/news/story /en/item/35571/icode/ (accessed August 19, 2016).

83. Shannon Heine, "General Mills Makes New Commitment on Climate Change," *Taste of General Mills*, August 31, 2015, http:// blog.generalmills.com/2015/08/general-mills-makes-new -commitment-on-climate-change/ (accessed August 19, 2016).

84. John Church, "Inside the General Mills Roadmap to a Sustainable Food Future," *The Guardian*, October 23, 2015, https://www .theguardian.com/sustainable-business/2015/oct/23/general -mills-sustainable-supply-chain-un-climate-conference-paris (accessed August 19, 2016).

85. General Mills, "Sustainable Sourcing," https://www.generalmills. com/en/Responsibility/Sustainable-sourcing (accessed August 19, 2016).

86. General Mills, "Vanilla," https://www.generalmills.com/en /Responsibility/Sustainable-sourcing/Ingredients/Vanilla -new (accessed August 19, 2016).

87. Ibid.

88. Silvia Fabiana et al., eds., *Pricing Decisions in the Euro Era: How Firms Set Prices and Why* (Oxford: Oxford University Press, 2007); Cateora et al., *International Marketing*.

89. Ibid.; Amanda J. Broderick, Gordon E. Greenley, and Rene Dentiste Mueller, "The Behavioural Homogeneity Evaluation Framework: Multi-Level Evaluations of Consumer Involvement in International Segmentation," *Journal of International Business Studies 38* (2007), pp. 746–63; Terry Clark, Masaaki Kotabe, and Dan Rajaratnam, "Exchange Rate Pass-Through and International Pricing Strategy: A Conceptual Framework and Research Propositions," *Journal of International Business Studies 30*, no. 2 (1999), pp. 249–68.

90. Christina Larson, "How to Reach China's Avid Shoppers," *Bloomberg Businessweek*, February 13, 2014, http://www .bloomberg.com/news/articles/2014-02-13/how-to-reach -china-s-avid-online-shoppers (accessed August 16, 2016).

91. Christina Larson, "The Secret of Taobao's Success," *Bloomberg Businessweek*, February 18, 2014, http://www.bloomberg.com /news/articles/2014-02-18/the-secret-of-taobaos-success/ (accessed August 16, 2016).

92. "China's Alibaba Breaks Singles Day Record as Sales Surge," BBC News, November 11, 2015, http://www.bbc.com/news /business-34773940 (accessed August 16, 2016).

93. Paul Carsten, "Alibaba's Singles' Day Sales Surge 60 Percent to $14.3 Billion," Reuters, November 11, 2015, http://www.reuters .com/article/us-alibaba-singles-day-idUSKCN0SZ34J20151111 (accessed August 16, 2016).

94. Sissi Wang, "Jack Ma's Philosophy for Building a Company That 'Lasts Forever'," *Financial Post*, October 20, 2014, http://business.financialpost.com/executive/c-suite/jack -mas-philosophy-for-building-a-company-that-lasts-forever (accessed August 16, 2016).

95. "Zara: Worldwide Pricing Strategy Revealed by Study," Fashion Network, June 26, 2015, http://us.fashionnetwork .com/news/Zara-worldwide-pricing-strategy-revealed -by-study,544318.html#.V7ZtevkrJaQ (accessed August 18, 2016).

96. Andrew Jacobs and Adam Century, "In China, Car Brands Evoke an Unexpected Set of Stereotypes," *The New York Times*, November 14, 2011, http://www.nytimes.com/2011/11/15/business /global/in-china-car-brands-evoke-an-unexpected-set-of -stereotypes.html?pagewanted5all.

97. "India: Creating Rural Entrepreneurs," http://www.unilever .com (accessed August 16, 2016).

98. Central Intelligence Agency, *The World Factbook*, https://www .cia.gov/library/publications/the-world-factbook/fields/2103.html (accessed August 18, 2016).

99. Madden, "Soy-Sauce-Flavored Kit Kats?"

100. "About the EU Pledge," http://www.eu-pledge.eu/content/about -eu-pledge (accessed August 18, 2016).

101. Michael Wines, "Picking Brand Names in Asia Is a Business Itself," *Ad Age*, November 11, 2011, http://www.nytimes.com/interactive /2011/11/12/world/asia/12brands-english-chinese-pdf.html?ref5asia; *Brand Channel*, http://www.brandchannel.com.

102. Joan Voight, "How to Customize Your U.S. Branding Effort to Work Around the World," *Adweek*, September 3, 2008.

103. Paul Muggeridge, "Which Countries Produce the Most Waste?" *World Economic Forum*, August 20, 2015, https://www.weforum .org/agenda/2015/08/which-countries-produce-the-most-waste/ (accessed March 25, 2017).

104. Bruce Einhorn, "Apple's Chinese Supply Lines," *BusinessWeek*, January 8, 2008; "Responsible Supplier Management," http:// www.apple.com/supplierresponsibility; Shai Oster, "Behind the Scenes at Apple's Controversial China iPhone Factory," *Chicago Tribune*, April 26, 2016, http://www.chicagotribune.com/business /ct-behind-the-scenes-apple-china-iphone-factory-20160426 -story.html (accessed March 25, 2017).

105. Theresa Weynand Tobin, "Cultural Imperialism," Encyclopedia Britannica, June 29, 2016, https://www.britannica.com/topic /cultural-imperialism (accessed March 25, 2017).

106. "Valentine's Day Is Now a Crime in Iran," *New York Post*, February 13, 2016, http://nypost.com/2016/02/13/iran-rules -decadent-valentines-day-celebrations-a-crime/ (accessed March 25, 2017).

107. "Form 10-K," United States Securities and Exchange Commission, http://www.aboutmcdonalds.com/content/dam /AboutMcDonalds/Investors%202/2015%20Annual%20Report .pdf (accessed August 17, 2016).

108. Claire Zillman, "McDonald's Wants to Open More Than 1,000 New Restaurants in China," *Fortune*, March 31, 2016, http://fortune.com/2016/03/31/mcdonalds-restaurants-china/ (accessed August 17, 2016).

109. "McDonald's Best Practices," http://www.aboutmcdonalds.com/mcd/sustainability/signature_programs/best_practices.html; Annie Gasparro, "Yum Splits India Into Separate Division," *The Wall Street Journal*, November 23, 2011, http://www.wsj.com/articles/SB10001424052970204443404577054332348348586 (accessed August 16, 2016).

110. Neha Thirani Bagri, "A Growing Taste for U.S. Fast Food in India," *The New York Times*, January 8, 2014, http://india.blogs.nytimes.com/2014/01/08/a-growing-taste-for-u-s-fast-food-in-india/ (accessed August 17, 2016).

111. Nat Rudarakanchana, "McDonald's (MCD) Going Mobile, Expanding in China and Three Other Takeaways From Last Scheduled Consumer Presentation of Uninspiring 2013," *International Business Times*, September 11, 2013, http://www.ibtimes.com; "Now Testing: Mobile Ordering On the McDonald's App," *Forbes*, March 30, 2016, http://www.forbes.com/sites/greatspeculations/2016/03/30/now-testing-mobile-ordering-on-the-mcdonalds-app/#7082c03b2c17 (accessed August 16, 2016).

112. Bagri, "A Growing Taste for U.S. Fast Food in India."

113. Matt Goulding, "Why the French Secretly Love the Golden Arches," *Slate*, August 2013, http://www.slate.com/articles/news_and_politics/roads/2013/08/mcdonald_s_global_expansion_the_american_fast_food_chain_has_become_an_unexpected.html (accessed August 17, 2016).

114. "McDonald's Sees Strong Revenue"; Ravi Krishnani, "McDonald's in Russia: Defeated Communism With a 'Happy' Meal," *Business Today*, http://www.businesstoday-eg.com; McDonald's Europe Virtual Press Office, press brief, http://www.mcdpressoffice.eu.

115. Andrew E. Kramer, "Russia's Evolution, Seen Through Golden Arches," *The New York Times*, February 2, 2010, http://www.nytimes.com/2010/02/02/business/global/02mcdonalds.html (accessed August 16, 2016).

## CHAPTER 18

1. James Glanz, Jeff Larson, and Andrew W. Lehren, "Spy Agencies Tap Data Streaming From Phone Apps," *The New York Times*, January 27, 2014.

2. John Bussey, "Taming the Spies of Web Advertising," *The Wall Street Journal*, August 8, 2013.

3. Janet Lo, "A 'Do Not Track List' for Canada?" Government of Canada, November 10, 2015, http://www.ic.gc.ca/app/oca/crd/dcmnt.do?id=3240&lang=eng; Dan Misener, "Do Not Track Me Online, Please," CBC News, March 22, 2011, http://www.cbc.ca/news/technology/do-not-track-me-online-please-1.980357 (accessed August 22, 2016).

4. Claire Cain Miller and Somini Sengupta, "Selling Secrets of Phone Users to Advertisers," *The New York Times*, October 5, 2013; "Cross-Device Creative Capabilities," *Drawbridge*, https://drawbridge.com/c/platform (accessed August 22, 2016).

5. Simon Dumenco, "Microsoft: 'Your Privacy Is Our Priority.' NSA: 'LOL!'" *Advertising Age*, June 7, 2013.

6. Matt Appuzo and Nicole Perlroth, "U.S. Relaxes Some Data Disclosure Rules," *The New York Times*, January 27, 2014.

7. Theodore Levitt, *Marketing Imagination* (Detroit, MI: The Free Press, 1983).

8. Lois Abraham, "Canada Won't Be Following U.S. in Labelling GMO Food Products," *The Star*, March 30, 2016, https://www.thestar.com/business/2016/03/30/canada-wont-be-following-us-in-labelling-gmo-food-products.html (August 23, 2016).

9. Laura Parker, "The GMO Labeling Battle Is Heating Up—Here's Why," *National Geographic*, January 11, 2014; Stefanie Strom, "Major Grocer to Label Foods With Gene-Modified Content,"

*The New York Times*, March 8, 2013; "Our Commitment to GMO Transparency," Whole Foods, http://www.wholefoodsmarket.com/our-commitment-gmo-transparency (accessed March 26, 2017).

10. For a detailed discussion on ethical and societal issues, see *An Introduction to Business Ethics*, 5th edition, by Joseph Desjardins (McGraw-Hill Education), or *Business Ethics: Decision Making for Personal Integrity & Social Responsibility* by Laura Hartman, Joseph Desardins, and Chris MacDonald (McGraw-Hill Education).

11. Gallup, "Honesty/Ethics in Professions," http://www.gallup.com/poll/1654/honesty-ethics-professions.aspx (accessed August 23, 2016).

12. Rebecca Harris, "Consumers Expect Brands to Do Social Good," *Marketing Magazine*, February 2, 2016, http://www.marketingmag.ca/consumer/consumers-expect-brands-to-do-social-good-study-167090 (accessed August 23, 2016).

13. Johnson & Johnson, "Our Credo Values," http://www.jnj.com/about-jnj/jnj-credo (accessed March 26, 2017).

14. Vanessa O'Connell and Shirley Wang, "J&J Acts Fast on Tylenol," *The Wall Street Journal*, July 9, 2009.

15. BSR (a global non-profit organization that works with a network of more than 250 member companies and other partners to build a just and sustainable world) http://www.bsr.org (accessed March 25, 2017). http://www.cmomagazine.com. This survey was conducted in 2006; more recent reports suggest that 49 percent of respondents to a 2009 survey reported having seen ethical misconduct overall. See Ethics Resource Center, "2009 National Business Ethics Survey," http://www.ethics.org.

16. Global Affairs Canada, "Corporate Social Responsibility," http://www.international.gc.ca/trade-agreements-accords-commerciaux/topics-domaines/other-autre/csr-rse.aspx?lang=eng (accessed August 23, 2016).

17. Sonya Fatah, "Cadillac Fairview Pledges to Do Good," *Strategy Online*, August 15, 2016, http://strategyonline.ca/2016/08/15/teens-malls-and-we-join-to-paint-a-bigger-picture/ (accessed August 20, 2016).

18. Cadillac Fairview, "About Cadillac Fairview," https://www.cadillacfairview.com/en_CA/about-us.html (accessed August 20, 2016).

19. Cadillac Fairview, "Cadillac Fairview Invests in Future Community Leaders," June 8, 2016, https://www.cadillacfairview.com/en_CA/news/Cadillac-Fairview-Invests-in-Future-Community-Leaders.html (accessed August 20, 2016).

20. Cadillac Fairview, "Cadillac Fairview Launches National 'Back to School' Campaign at Retail Properties," August 9, 2016, https://www.cadillacfairview.com/en_CA/news/Cadillac_Fairview_launches_national_back_to_school_campaign_at_retail_properties.html (accessed August 21, 2016).

21. Rebecca Harris, "CF Launches Back-to-School Campaign With a Social Cause," *Marketing*, August 9, 2016, http://www.marketingmag.ca/brands/cf-launches-back-to-school-campaign-with-a-social-cause-180925 (accessed August 21, 2016).

22. The most famous proponent of this view was Milton Friedman. See, for example, *Capitalism and Freedom* (Chicago: University of Chicago Press, 2002) or *Free to Choose: A Personal Statement* (Orlando, FL: Harcourt, 1990).

23. "Our Heritage," Danone, http://www.danone.com/en/for-all/our-mission-in-action/our-heritage/ (accessed March 26, 2017).

24. Rick Ungar, "Walmart Store Holding Thanksgiving Charity Food Drive—for Its Own Employees!" *Forbes*, November 18, 2013, http://foundation.walmart.com (accessed March 26, 2017).

25. "Premier Fitness Fined $130,000 Over Failure to Pay Employees on Time," *Hamilton Spectator*, January 24, 2012, http://www.thespec.com/news-story/2231374-premier-fitness-fined-130-000-over-failure-to-pay-employees-on-time/ (accessed August 23, 2016).

26. Ipsos, "Four in Ten (37%) Employees Rate Corporate Social Responsibility 'Very Important' When It Comes to Their Employer; Three in Ten (29%) Say So Regarding Purchase Decisions," June 25, 2013, http://www.ipsos-na.com/news-polls/pressrelease.aspx?id=6167 (accessed August 23, 2016).

27. Nielsen, "The Sustainability Imperative," October 2015, http://www.nielsen.com/content/dam/nielsenglobal/dk/docs/global-sustainability-report-oct-2015.pdf (accessed August 23, 2016).

28. Julie Smythe, "Canada's Top 50 Socially Responsible Corporations: 2015," *Macleans*, June 8, 2015, http://www.macleans.ca/economy/business/canadas-top-50-most-socially-responsible-companies/ (accessed August 23, 2016).

29. Tim Hortons®, "Tim Hortons® Camp Day Brews $12.6 Million to Make 19,000 Kids' Futures Brighter," June 7, 2016, https://www.timhortons.com/ca/en/corporate/news-release.php?id=10122 (accessed August 23, 2016).

30. "Our Environmental Commitment," Mountain Equipment Co-Op, https://www.mec.ca/en/explore/our-environmental-commitment/ (accessed August 23, 2016).

31. FedEx, "FedEx Cares," http://about.van.fedex.com/social-responsibility/fedex-cares/ (accessed August 23, 2016).

32. "The Cooperators Foundation," The Cooperators, http://www.cooperators.ca/en/about-us/foundation.aspx (accessed August 23, 2016).

33. This Entrepreneurial Marketing box was written with information gathered in a telephone interview with Kalen Elmsley of Ten Tree Apparel on June 26, 2013.

34. Raquel Fletcher, "Ten Tree Sees the Forest and the Trees," *Degrees*, Fall/Winter 2012, http://www.uregina.ca/business/assets/about-us/news/2012/Degrees-Ten-Tree-Winter2012.pdf (accessed August 15, 2014).

35. Ten Tree Apparel, http://www.tentree.com/ca/ (accessed August 23, 2016).

36. The Globe and Mail, "DavidsTea Under Scrutiny in U.S. Over Alleged Use of 'On-Call' Shifts," April 13, 2016, http://www.theglobeandmail.com/report-on-business/davidstea-under-scrutiny-in-us-over-alleged-use-of-on-call-shifts/article29620646/ (accessed August 16, 2016).

37. "DavidsTea's Hiring Practices Come Under Fire," April 15, 2016, *Marketing Magazine*, http://www.marketingmag.ca/brands/davidsteas-hiring-practices-come-under-fire-172442 (accessed August 16, 2016).

38. Jennifer Wells, "DavidsTea Leaves a Sour Taste Amid 'On-Call' Shifts: Wells," *The Toronto Star*, April 15, 2016, https://www.thestar.com/business/2016/04/15/with-on-call-letter-another-bump-for-davids-tea-wells.html (accessed August 18, 2016).

39. Seres Lu, "On-Call Scheduling Under Increasing Scrutiny in Canada," *The Globe and Mail*, September 6, 2015, http://www.theglobeandmail.com/report-on-business/on-call-scheduling-under-increasing-scrutiny-in-canada/article26240704/ (accessed August 18, 2016).

40. Seres Lu, "On-Call Scheduling Under Increasing Scrutiny in Canada," *The Globe and Mail*, September 6, 2015, http://www.theglobeandmail.com/report-on-business/on-call-scheduling-under-increasing-scrutiny-in-canada/article26240704/ (accessed August 18, 2016).

41. David Friend, "Canada's 'On-Call' Workers Face Stress, Financial Turmoil: Time to End the Practice?" *The Huffington Post*, September 3, 2015, http://www.huffingtonpost.ca/2015/09/03/waiting-for-work-canadian-retail-workers-face-volatility-of-on-call-shifts_n_8082668.html (accessed August 18, 2016).

42. ParticipACTION Canada, "Our Strategic Goals," http://www.participaction.com/about/our-vision (accessed August 23, 2016).

43. Mike Hower, "GE Renews Ecomagination Initiative, Commits $25B to CleanTech R&D by 2020 ," March 4, 2014, http://www.sustainablebrands.com/news_and_views/cleantech/mike_hower/ge_renews_ecomagination_initiative_commits_25_b_clean_tech_rd_20 (accessed August 23, 2016).

44. McKinsey, "How to Reinvent the External-Affairs Function," July 2016, http://www.mckinsey.com/business-functions/strategy-and-corporate-finance/our-insights/how-to-reinvent-the-external-affairs-function (accessed August 23, 2016).

45. John Browne, "Here's a Better Way for Companies to Tackle Big Social Problems," *Harvard Business Review*, March 30, 2016, https://hbr.org/2016/03/heres-a-better-way-for-companies-to-tackle-big-social-problems (accessed August 23, 2016).

46. "Our Mission and Vision," Burt's Bees, https://www.burtsbees.ca/c/root-our-mission-and-vision-burt-s-bees.html (accessed August 24, 2016).

47. "Responsibility," General Mills, https://www.generalmills.com/en/Responsibility/Overview (accessed August 24, 2016).

48. Laurie Snell, "Putting Faces to Homelessness," *The Kitchener Post*, April 6, 2016, http://www.kitchenerpost.ca/news-story/6442434-putting-faces-to-homelessness/; Ryan Flanagan, "Homeless in Waterloo: Sharing Stories of an Overlooked Population," CTV Kitchener, June 24, 2016, http://kitchener.ctvnews.ca/homeless-in-waterloo-sharing-stories-of-an-overlooked-population-1.2960747; Homeless in Waterloo, Facebook page, August 12, 2016, https://www.facebook.com/HomelessInWaterloo/?fref=ts (accessed August 24, 2016).

49. Justin Ravitz, "Selena Gomez Ambushed at Fashion Show by Anti-Sweatshop Protester," *US Weekly*, February 7, 2013, http://www.usmagazine.com/celebrity-style/news/selena-gomez-ambushed-at-fashion-show-by-anti-sweatshop-protester-201372 (accessed August 23, 2016).

50. Andrew J. Blumberg and Peter Eckerdsly, "On Locational Privacy, and How to Avoid Losing It Forever," Electronic Frontier Foundation White Paper, August 2009, http://www.eff.org (accessed August 24, 2016).

51. W. Timothy Coombs, "Crisis Management Communications," Institute for Public Relations, September 23, 2014, http://www.instituteforpr.org/crisis-management-communications/ (accessed March 26, 2017).

52. Carolyn Hotchkiss, "Business Ethics: One Slide Cases," Babson College, Wellesley, Massachusetts, 2004; http://www.usatoday.com/news/nation/2004-03-23-tshirts_x.htm (accessed August 25, 2006); http://www.marketingpower.com/live/mg-dictionary.php?SearchFor=direct+marketing&Searched=1 (accessed August 5, 2005).

53. "Screen Time and Children—How to Guide Your Child," Mayo Clinic, http://www.mayoclinic.org/children-and-tv/art-20047952 (accessed March 26, 2017).

54. Cecilia Kang, "Infant iPad Seats Raise Concerns About Screen Time for Babies," *The Washington Post*, December 10, 2013.

55. "Fisher-Price iPad Apptivity Seat, Newborn-to-Toddler," Amazon.ca, https://www.amazon.ca/Fisher-Price-Ipad-Apptivity-Seat-Newborn-to-Toddler/dp/B00EL4NI5U (accessed August 24, 2016).

56. John Brownlee, "Fisher-Price Releases a Bouncy Seat For Baby's First iPad, And Parents Freak Out," Co.Design, December 12, 2013, http://www.fastcodesign.com/3023334/design-crime/fisher-price-releases-a-bouncy-seat-for-babys-first-ipad-and-parents-freak-out (accessed August 24, 2016).

57. Kang, "Infant iPad Seats Raise Concerns About Screen Time for Babies."

58. "Netflix Original Children's Series," Netflix, https://www.whats-on-netflix.com/originals/children/ (accessed March 26, 2017).

## APPENDIX

1. V. Kumar, A. Petersen, and R.P. Leone, "How Valuable Is the Word of Mouth?"*Harvard Business Review* (October 2007), pp. 139–146; V. Kumar and Morris George, "Measuring and Maximizing Customer Equity: A Critical Analysis,"*Journal of the Academy of Marketing Science* 35, no. 2 (June 2007), pp. 157–171; V. Kumar, Denish Shah, and Rajkumar Venkatesan, "Managing

Retailer Profitability: One Customer at a Time!"*Journal of Retailing* 82, no. 4 (October 2006), pp. 277-294; V. Kumar, "Profitable Relationships,"*Marketing Research: A Magazine of Management and Applications* 18, no. 3 (Fall 2006), pp. 41-46; V. Kumar, "Customer Lifetime Value: A Databased Approach,"*Journal of Relationship Marketing* 5, no. 2/3 (2006), pp. 7-35; Sunil Gupta et al., "Modeling Customer Lifetime Value,"*Journal of Service Research* 9 (November 2006), pp. 139-155; V. Kumar, R. Venkatesan, and Werner Reinartz, "Knowing What to Sell, When and to Whom,"*Harvard Business Review* (March 2006), pp. 131-137; Werner Reinartz, J. Thomas, and V. Kumar, "Balancing Acquisition and Retention Resources to Maximize Profitability,"*Journal of Marketing* 69 (January 2005), pp. 63-79; R. Venkatesan and V. Kumar, "A Customer Lifetime Value Framework for Customer Selection and Resource Allocation Strategy,"*Journal of Marketing* 68 (October 2004), pp. 106-125; V. Kumar and J. Andrew Petersen, "Maximizing ROI or Profitability: Is One Better Than the Other,"*Marketing Research: A Magazine of Management and Applications* 16, no. 3 (Fall 2004), pp. 28-34; V. Kumar, G. Ramani, and T. Bohling, "Customer Lifetime Value Approaches and Best Practice Applications,"*Journal of Interactive Marketing* 18, no. 3 (Summer 2004), pp. 60-72; J. Thomas, Werner Reinartz, and V. Kumar, "Getting the Most out of All Your Customers,"*Harvard Business Review* (July-August 2004), pp. 116-123; Werner Reinartz and V. Kumar, "The Impact of Customer Relationship Characteristics on Profitable Lifetime Duration,"*Journal of Marketing* 67 (January 2003), pp. 77-99; Werner Reinartz and V. Kumar, "The Mismanagement of Customer Loyalty,"*Harvard Business Review* (July 2002), pp. 86-97; W. Reinartz and V. Kumar, "On the Profitability of Long Lifetime Customers: An Empirical Investigation and Implications for Marketing,"*Journal of Marketing* 64 (October 2000), pp. 17-32.

2. We have made some minor adjustments to the formula suggested by Gupta et al., "Modeling Customer Lifetime Value."

3. Sunil Gupta and Donald R. Lehmann, *Managing Customers as Investments* (Philadelphia, PA: Wharton School Publishing, 2005); Gupta et al., "Modeling Customer Lifetime Value."

# name index

# company index

# subject index